D1564840

Handbook of Computer Vision and Applications

Volume 2
Signal Processing and Pattern Recognition

Handbook of Computer Vision and Applications

Volume 2
Signal Processing and Pattern Recognition

Editors

Bernd Jähne

Interdisciplinary Center for Scientific Computing
University of Heidelberg, Heidelberg, Germany
and
Scripps Institution of Oceanography
University of California, San Diego

Horst Haußecker
Peter Geißler

Interdisciplinary Center for Scientific Computing
University of Heidelberg, Heidelberg, Germany

ACADEMIC PRESS

San Diego London Boston
New York Sydney Tokyo Toronto

This book is printed on acid-free paper. ♾
Copyright © 1999 by Academic Press.

All rights reserved.
No part of this publication may be reproduced or transmitted in any form or by any means, electronic or mechanical, including photocopy, recording, or any information storage and retrieval system, without permission in writing from the publisher.

The appearance of code at the bottom of the first page of a chapter in this book indicates the Publisher's consent that copies of the chapter may be made for personal or internal use of specific clients. This consent is given on the condition, however, that the copier pay the stated per-copy fee through the Copyright Clearance Center, Inc. (222 Rosewood Drive, Danvers, Massachusetts 01923), for copying beyond that permitted by Sections 107 or 108 of the U.S. Copyright Law. This consent does not extend to other kinds of copying, such as copying for general distribution, for advertising or promotional purposes, for creating new collective works, or for resale. Copy fees for pre-1999 chapters are as shown on the title pages; if no fee code appears on the title page, the copy fee is the same as for current chapters. ISBN 0-12-379770-5/$30.00

ACADEMIC PRESS
A Division of Harcourt Brace & Company
525 B Street, Suite 1900, San Diego, CA 92101-4495
http://www.apnet.com

ACADEMIC PRESS
24-28 Oval Road, London NW1 7DX, UK
http://www.hbuk.co.uk/ap/

Library of Congress Cataloging-In-Publication Data
Handbook of computer vision and applications / edited by Bernd Jähne, Horst Haussecker, Peter Geissler.
p. cm.
Includes bibliographical references and indexes.
Contents: v. 1. Sensors and imaging — v. 2. Signal processing and pattern recognition — v. 3. Systems and applications.
ISBN 0-12-379770-5 (set). — ISBN 0-12-379771-3 (v. 1)
ISBN 0-12-379772-1 (v. 2). — ISBN 0-12-379773-X (v. 3)
1. Computer vision — Handbooks, manuals. etc. I. Jähne, Bernd 1953- . II. Haussecker, Horst, 1968- . III. Geissler, Peter, 1966- .
TA1634.H36 1999
006.3′7 — dc21 98-42541
CIP

Printed in the United States of America
99 00 01 02 03 DS 9 8 7 6 5 4 3 2 1

Contents

II Elementary Spatial Processing

III Feature Estimation

Preface

What this handbook is about

This handbook offers a fresh approach to computer vision. The whole vision process from image formation to measuring, recognition, or reacting is regarded as an integral process. Computer vision is understood as the host of techniques to acquire, process, analyze, and understand complex higher-dimensional data from our environment for scientific and technical exploration.

In this sense the handbook takes into account the interdisciplinary nature of computer vision with its links to virtually all natural sciences and attempts to bridge two important gaps. The first is between modern physical sciences and the many novel techniques to acquire images. The second is between basic research and applications. When a reader with a background in one of the fields related to computer vision feels he has learned something from one of the many other facets of computer vision, the handbook will have fulfilled its purpose.

The handbook comprises three volumes. The first volume, *Sensors and Imaging*, covers image formation and acquisition. The second volume, *Signal Processing and Pattern Recognition*, focuses on processing of the spatial and spatiotemporal signal acquired by imaging sensors. The third volume, *Systems and Applications*, describes how computer vision is integrated into systems and applications.

Prerequisites

It is assumed that the reader is familiar with elementary mathematical concepts commonly used in computer vision and in many other areas of natural sciences and technical disciplines. This includes the basics of set theory, matrix algebra, differential and integral equations, complex numbers, Fourier transform, probability, random variables, and graphing. Wherever possible, mathematical topics are described intuitively. In this respect it is very helpful that complex mathematical relations can often be visualized intuitively by images. For a more formal treatment of the corresponding subject including proofs, suitable references are given.

How to use this handbook

The handbook has been designed to cover the different needs of its readership. First, it is suitable for *sequential reading*. In this way the reader gets an up-to-date account of the state of computer vision. It is presented in a way that makes it accessible for readers with different backgrounds. Second, the reader can look up specific topics of interest. The individual chapters are written in a self-consistent way with extensive cross-referencing to other chapters of the handbook and external references. The CD that accompanies each volume of the handbook contains the complete text of the handbook in the Adobe Acrobat portable document file format (PDF). This format can be read on all major platforms. Free Acrobat reader version 3.01 for all major computing platforms is included on the CDs. The texts are hyperlinked in multiple ways. Thus the reader can collect the information of interest with ease. Third, the reader can delve more deeply into a subject with the material on the CDs. They contain additional reference material, interactive software components, code examples, image material, and references to sources on the Internet. For more details see the readme file on the CDs.

Acknowledgments

Writing a handbook on computer vision with this breadth of topics is a major undertaking that can succeed only in a coordinated effort that involves many co-workers. Thus the editors would like to thank first all contributors who were willing to participate in this effort. Their cooperation with the constrained time schedule made it possible that the three-volume handbook could be published in such a short period following the call for contributions in December 1997. The editors are deeply grateful for the dedicated and professional work of the staff at AEON Verlag & Studio who did most of the editorial work. We also express our sincere thanks to Academic Press for the opportunity to write this handbook and for all professional advice.

Last but not least, we encourage the reader to send us any hints on errors, omissions, typing errors, or any other shortcomings of the handbook. Actual information about the handbook can be found at the editors homepage `http://klimt.iwr.uni-heidelberg.de`.

Heidelberg, Germany and La Jolla, California, December 1998
Bernd Jähne, Horst Haußecker, Peter Geißler

Contributors

Etienne Bertin received the PhD degree in mathematics from Université Joseph Fourier in 1994. From 1990 to 1995 he worked on various topics in image analysis and computational geometry. Since 1995, he has been an assistant professor at the Université Pierre Mendès France in the Laboratoire de statistique et d'analyses de données; he works on stochastic geometry.

Dr. Etienne Bertin
Laboratoire de Statistique et d'analyse de donnés
Université Pierre Mendès, Grenoble, France
bertin@labsad.upmf-grenoble.fr

Anke Meyer-Bäse received her M. S. and the PhD in electrical engineering from the Darmstadt Institute of Technology in 1990 and 1995, respectively. From 1995 to 1996 she was a postdoctoral fellow with the Federal Institute of Neurobiology, Magdeburg, Germany. Since 1996 she was a visiting assistant professor with the Dept. of Electrical Engineering, University of Florida, Gainesville, USA. She received the Max-Kade award in Neuroengineering in 1996 and the Lise-Meitner prize in 1997. Her research interests include neural networks, image processing, biomedicine, speech recognition, and theory of nonlinear systems.

Dr. Anke Meyer-Bäse, Dept. of Electrical Engineering and Computer Science,
University of Florida, 454 New Engineering Building 33, Center Drive
PO Box 116130, Gainesville, FL 32611-6130, U.S., anke@alpha.ee.ufl.edu

Tobias Dierig graduated in 1997 from the University of Heidelberg with a master degree in physics and is now pursuing his PhD at the Interdisciplinary Center for Scientific Computing at Heidelberg university. He is concerned mainly with depth from focus algorithms, image fusion, and industrial applications of computer vision within the OpenEye project.

Tobias Dierig, Forschungsgruppe Bildverarbeitung, IWR
Universität Heidelberg, Im Neuenheimer Feld 368
D-69120 Heidelberg, Germany
Tobias.Dierig@iwr.uni-heidelberg.de
http://klimt.iwr.uni-heidelberg.de/~tdierig

Roland Eils studied mathematics and computer science in Aachen, where he received his diploma in 1990. After a two year stay in Indonesia for language studies he joint the Graduiertenkolleg "Modeling and Scientific Computing in Mathematics and Sciences" at the Interdisciplinary Center for Scientific Computing (IWR), University of Heidelberg, where he received his doctoral degree in 1995. Since 1996 he has been leading the biocomputing group, Structures in Molecular Biology. His research interests include computer vision, in particular computational geometry, and application of image processing techniques in science and biotechnology.

Dr. Roland Eils, Biocomputing-Gruppe, IWR, Universität Heidelberg
Im Neuenheimer Feld 368, D-69120 Heidelberg, Germany
eils@iwr.uni-heidelberg.de
http://www.iwr.uni-heidelberg.de/iwr/bioinf

Peter Geißler studied physics in Heidelberg. He received his diploma and doctoral degree from Heidelberg University in 1994 and 1998, respectively. His research interests include computer vision, especially depth-from-focus, adaptive filtering, and flow visualization as well as the application of image processing in physical sciences and oceanography.

Dr. Peter Geißler
Forschungsgruppe Bildverarbeitung, IWR
Universität Heidelberg, Im Neuenheimer Feld 368
D-69120 Heidelberg, Germany
Peter.Geissler@iwr.uni-heidelberg.de
http://klimt.iwr.uni-heidelberg.de

Georgy Gimel'farb received his PhD degree from the Ukrainian Academy of Sciences in 1969 and his Doctor of Science (the habilitation) degree from the Higher Certifying Commission of the USSR in 1991. In 1962, he began working in the Pattern Recognition, Robotics, and Image Recognition Departments of the Institute of Cybernetics (Ukraine). In 1994–1997 he was an invited researcher in Hungary, the USA, Germany, and France. Since 1997, he has been a senior lecturer in computer vision and digital TV at the University of Auckland, New Zealand. His research interests include analysis of multiband space and aerial images, computational stereo, and image texture analysis.

Dr. Georgy Gimel'farb, Centre for Image Technology and Robotics,
Department of Computer Science, Tamaki Campus
The University of Auckland, Private Bag 92019, Auckland 1, New Zealand
g.gimelfarb@auckland.ac.nz, http://www.tcs.auckland.ac.nz/~georgy

Horst Haußecker studied physics in Heidelberg. He received his diploma in physics and his doctoral degree from Heidelberg University in 1994 and 1996, respectively. He was visiting scientist at the Scripps Institution of Oceanography in 1994. Currently he is conducting research in the image processing research group at the Interdisciplinary Center for Scientific Computing (IWR), where he also lectures on optical flow computation. His research interests include computer vision, especially image sequence analysis, infrared thermography, and fuzzy-image processing, as well as the application of image processing in physical sciences and oceanography.

Dr. Horst Haußecker, Forschungsgruppe Bildverarbeitung, IWR
Universität Heidelberg, Im Neuenheimer Feld 368, D-69120 Heidelberg
Horst.Haussecker@iwr.uni-heidelberg.de
http://klimt.iwr.uni-heidelberg.de

Jürgen Hesser is assistant professor at the Lehrstuhl für Informatik V, University of Mannheim, Germany. He heads the groups on computer graphics, bioinformatics, and optimization. His research interests are real-time volume rendering, computer architectures, computational chemistry, and evolutionary algorithms. In addition, he is co-founder of Volume Graphics GmbH, Heidelberg. Hesser received his PhD and his diploma in physics at the University of Heidelberg, Germany.

Jürgen Hesser, Lehrstuhl für Informatik V
Universität Mannheim
B6, 26, D-68131 Mannheim, Germany
jhesser@rumms.uni-mannheim.de,

Joachim Hornegger graduated in 1992 and received his PhD degree in computer science in 1996 from the Universität Erlangen-Nürnberg, Germany, for his work on statistical object recognition. Joachim Hornegger was research and teaching associate at Universität Erlangen-Nürnberg, a visiting scientist at the Technion, Israel, and at the Massachusetts Institute of Technology, U.S. He is currently a research scholar and teaching associate at Stanford University, U.S. Joachim Hornegger is the author of 30 technical papers in computer vision and speech processing and three books. His research interests include 3-D computer vision, 3-D object recognition, and statistical methods applied to image analysis problems.

Dr. Joachim Hornegger, Stanford University, Robotics Laboratory
Gates Building 1A, Stanford, CA 94305-9010, U.S.
jh@robotics.stanford.edu, http://www.robotics.stanford.edu/~jh

Bernd Jähne studied physics in Saarbrücken and Heidelberg. He received his diploma, doctoral degree, and habilitation degree from Heidelberg University in 1977, 1980, and 1985, respectively, and a habilitation degree in applied computer science from the University of Hamburg-Harburg in 1992. Since 1988 he has been a Marine Research Physicist at Scripps Institution of Oceanography, University of California, and, since 1994, he has been professor of physics at the Interdisciplinary Center of Scientific Computing. He leads the research group on image processing. His research interests include computer vision, especially filter design and image sequence analysis, the application of image processing techniques in science and industry, and small-scale air-sea interaction processes.

Prof. Dr. Bernd Jähne, Forschungsgruppe Bildverarbeitung, IWR
Universität Heidelberg, Im Neuenheimer Feld 368, D-69120 Heidelberg
Bernd.Jaehne@iwr.uni-heidelberg.de
http://klimt.iwr.uni-heidelberg.de

Reinhard Klette studied mathematics at Halle University, received his master degree and doctor of natural science degree in mathematics at Jena University, became a docent in computer science, and was a professor of computer vision at Berlin Technical University. Since June 1996 he has been professor of information technology in the Department of Computer Science at the University of Auckland. His research interests include theoretical and applied topics in image processing, pattern recognition, image analysis, and image understanding. He has published books about image processing and shape reconstruction and was chairman of several international conferences and workshops on computer vision. Recently, his research interests have been directed at 3-D biomedical image analysis with digital geometry and computational geometry as major subjects.

Prof. Dr. Reinhard Klette, Centre for Image Technology and Robotics,
Computer Science Department, Tamaki Campus
The Auckland University, Private Bag 92019, Auckland, New Zealand
r.klette@auckland.ac.nz, http://citr.auckland.ac.nz/~rklette

Christoph Klauck received his diploma in computer science and mathematics from the University of Kaiserslautern, Germany, in 1990. From 1990 to 1994 he worked as research scientist at the German Research Center for Artificial Intelligence Inc. (DFKI GmbH) at Kaiserslautern. In 1994 he finished his dissertation in computer science. Since then he has been involved in the IRIS project at the University of Bremen (Artificial Intelligence Group). His primary research interests include graph grammars and rewriting systems in general, knowledge representation, and ontologies.

Prof. Dr. Christoph Klauck, Dep. of Electrical Eng. and Computer Science
University of Hamburg (FH), Berliner Tor 3, D-20099 Hamburg, Germany
cklauck@t-online.de, http://fbi010.informatik.fh-hamburg.de/~klauck

Stefan Körkel is member of the research groups for numerics and optimization of Prof. Bock and Prof. Reinelt at the Interdisciplinary Center for Scientific Computing at the University of Heidelberg, Germany. He studied mathematics in Heidelberg. Currently he is pursuing his PhD in nonlinear and mixed integer optimization methods. His research interests include filter optimization as well as nonlinear optimum experimental design.

Stefan Körkel
Interdisciplinary Center for Scientific Computing
Im Neuenheimer Feld 368, 69120 Heidelberg
Stefan.Koerkel@IWR.Uni-Heidelberg.de
http://www.iwr.uni-heidelberg.de/~Stefan.Koerkel/

Ryszard Kozera received his M.Sc. degree in pure mathematics in 1985 from Warsaw University, Poland, his PhD degree in computer science in 1991 from Flinders University, Australia, and finally his PhD degree in mathematics in 1992 from Warsaw University, Poland. He is currently employed as a senior lecturer at the University of Western Australia. Between July 1995 and February 1997, Dr. Kozera was at the Technical University of Berlin and at Warsaw University as an Alexander von Humboldt Foundation research fellow. His current research interests include applied mathematics with special emphasis on partial differential equations, computer vision, and numerical analysis.

Dr. Ryszard Kozera, Department of Computer Science, The University of Western Australia, Nedlands, WA 6907, Australia, ryszard@cs.uwa.edu.au
http://www.cs.uwa.edu.au/people/info/ryszard.html

Tony Lindeberg received his M.Sc. degree in engineering physics and applied mathematics from KTH (Royal Institute of Technology), Stockholm, Sweden in 1987, and his PhD degree in computing science in 1991. He is currently an associate professor at the Department of Numerical Analysis and Computing Science at KTH. His main research interests are in computer vision and relate to multiscale representations, focus-of-attention, and shape. He has contributed to the foundations of continuous and discrete scale-space theory, as well as to the application of these theories to computer vision problems. Specifically, he has developed principles for automatic scale selection, methodologies for extracting salient image structures, and theories for multiscale shape estimation. He is author of the book "Scale-Space Theory in Computer Vision."

Tony Lindeberg, Department of Numerical Analysis and Computing Science
KTH, S-100 44 Stockholm, Sweden.
tony@nada.kth.se, http://www.nada.kth.se/~tony

Steffen Lindek studied physics at the RWTH Aachen, Germany, the EPF Lausanne, Switzerland, and the University of Heidelberg, Germany. He did his diploma and PhD theses in the Light Microscopy Group at the European Molecular Biology Laboratory (EMBL), Heidelberg, Germany, developing high-resolution light-microscopy techniques. Since December 1996 he has been a postdoctoral fellow with the BioImage project at EMBL. He currently works on the design and implementation of the image database, and he is responsible for the administration of EMBL's contribution to the project.

Dr. Steffen Lindek, European Molecular Biology Laboratory (EMBL)
Postfach 10 22 09, D-69120 Heidelberg, Germany
lindek@EMBL-Heidelberg.de

Hanspeter A. Mallot studied biology and mathematics at the University of Mainz where he also received his doctoral degree in 1986. He was a postdoctoral fellow at the Massachusetts Institute of Technology in 1986/87 and held research positions at Mainz University and the Ruhr-Universität-Bochum. In 1993, he joined the Max-Planck-Institut für biologische Kybernetik in Tübingen. In 1996/97, he was a fellow at the Institute of Advanced Studies in Berlin. His research interests include the perception of shape and space in humans and machines, cognitive maps, as well as neural network models of the cerebral cortex.

Dr. Hanspeter A. Mallot, Max-Planck-Institut für biologische Kybernetik
Spemannstr. 38, 72076 Tübingen, Germany
Hanspeter.Mallot@tuebingen.mpg.de
http://www.kyb.tuebingen.mpg.de/bu/

Heinrich Niemann obtained the degree of Dipl.-Ing. in electrical engineering and Dr.-Ing. at Technical University Hannover in 1966 and 1969, respectively. From 1967 to 1972 he was with Fraunhofer Institut für Informationsverarbeitung in Technik und Biologie, Karlsruhe. Since 1975 he has been professor of computer science at the University of Erlangen-Nürnberg and since 1988 he has also served as head of the research group, Knowledge Processing, at the Bavarian Research Institute for Knowledge-Based Systems (FORWISS). His fields of research are speech and image understanding and the application of artificial intelligence techniques in these fields. He is the author or co-author of 6 books and approximately 250 journal and conference contributions.

Prof. Dr.-Ing. H. Niemann, Lehrstuhl für Mustererkennung (Informatik 5)
Universität Erlangen-Nürnberg, Martensstraße 3, 91058 Erlangen, Germany
niemann@informatik.uni-erlangen.de
http://www5.informatik.uni-erlangen.de

Dietrich Paulus received a bachelor degree in computer science at the University of Western Ontario, London, Canada (1983). He graduated (1987) and received his PhD degree (1991) from the University of Erlangen-Nürnberg, Germany. He is currently a senior researcher (Akademischer Rat) in the field of image pattern recognition and teaches courses in computer vision and applied programming for image processing. Together with J. Hornegger, he has recently written a book on pattern recognition and image processing in C++.

Dr. Dietrich Paulus, Lehrstuhl für Mustererkennung
Universität Erlangen-Nürnberg, Martensstr. 3, 91058 Erlangen, Germany
paulus@informatik.uni-erlangen.de
http://www5.informatik.uni-erlangen.de

Christoph Poliwoda is PhD student at the Lehrstuhl für Informatik V, University of Mannheim, and leader of the development section of Volume Graphics GmbH. His research interests are real-time volume and polygon raytracing, 3-D image processing, 3-D segmentation, computer architectures and parallel computing. Poliwoda received his diploma in physics at the University of Heidelberg, Germany.

Christoph Poliwoda
Lehrstuhl für Informatik V
Universität Mannheim
B6, 26, D-68131 Mannheim, Germany
poliwoda@mp-sun1.informatik.uni-mannheim.de

Nicholas J. Salmon received the master of engineering degree from the Department of Electrical and Electronic Engineering at Bath University, England, in 1990. Then he worked as a software development engineer for Marconi Radar Systems Ltd., England, helping to create a vastly parallel signal-processing machine for radar applications. Since 1992 he has worked as software engineer in the Light Microscopy Group at the European Molecular Biology Laboratory, Germany, where he is concerned with creating innovative software systems for the control of confocal microscopes, and image processing.

Nicholas J. Salmon, Light Microscopy Group,
European Molecular Biology Laboratory (EMBL)
Postfach 10 22 09, D-69120 Heidelberg, Germany
salmon@EMBL-Heidelberg.de,

Kurt Sätzler studied physics at the University of Heidelberg, where he received his diploma in 1995. Since then he has been working as a PhD student at the Max-Planck-Institute of Medical Research in Heidelberg. His research interests are mainly computational geometry applied to problems in biomedicine, architecture and computer graphics, image processing and tilted view microscopy.

Kurt Sätzler, IWR, Universität Heidelberg
Im Neuenheimer Feld 368, D-69120 Heidelberg
or
Max-Planck-Institute for Medical Research, Department of Cell Physiology
Jahnstr. 29, D-69120 Heidelberg, Germany
Kurt.Saetzler@iwr.uni-heidelberg.de

Hanno Scharr studied physics at the University of Heidelberg, Germany and did his diploma thesis on texture analysis at the Interdisciplinary Center for Scientific Computing in Heidelberg. Currently, he is pursuing his PhD on motion estimation. His research interests include filter optimization and motion estimation in discrete time series of n-D images.

Hanno Scharr
Interdisciplinary Center for Scientific Computing
Im Neuenheimer Feld 368, 69120 Heidelberg, Germany
Hanno.Scharr@iwr.uni-heidelberg.de
http://klimt.iwr.uni-heidelberg.de/~hscharr/

Karsten Schlüns studied computer science in Berlin. He received his diploma and doctoral degree from the Technical University of Berlin in 1991 and 1996. From 1991 to 1996 he was research assistant in the Computer Vision Group, Technical University of Berlin, and from 1997 to 1998 he was a postdoctoral research fellow in computing and information technology, University of Auckland. Since 1998 he has been a scientist in the image processing group at the Institute of Pathology, University Hospital Charité in Berlin. His research interests include pattern recognition and computer vision, especially three-dimensional shape recovery, performance analysis of reconstruction algorithms, and teaching of computer vision.

Dr. Karsten Schlüns, Institute of Pathology,
University Hospital Charité, Schumannstr. 20/21, D-10098 Berlin, Germany
Karsten.Schluens@charite.de, http://amba.charite.de/~ksch

Christoph Schnörr received the master degree in electrical engineering in 1987, the doctoral degree in computer science in 1991, both from the University of Karlsruhe (TH), and the habilitation degree in Computer Science in 1998 from the University of Hamburg, Germany. From 1987–1992, he worked at the Fraunhofer Institute for Information and Data Processing (IITB) in Karlsruhe in the field of image sequence analysis. In 1992 he joined the Cognitive Systems group, Department of Computer Science, University of Hamburg, where he became an assistant professor in 1995. He received an award for his work on image segmentation from the German Association for Pattern Recognition (DAGM) in 1996. Since October 1998, he has been a full professor at the University of Mannheim, Germany, where he heads the Computer Vision, Graphics, and Pattern Recognition Group. His research interests include pattern recognition, machine vision, and related aspects of computer graphics, machine learning, and applied mathematics.

Prof. Dr. Christoph Schnörr, University of Mannheim
Dept. of Math. & Computer Science, D-68131 Mannheim, Germany
schnoerr@ti.uni-mannheim.de, http://www.ti.uni-mannheim.de

Eero Simoncelli started his higher education with a bachelor's degree in physics from Harvard University, went to Cambridge University on a fellowship to study mathematics for a year and a half, and then returned to the USA to pursue a doctorate in Electrical Engineering and Computer Science at MIT. He received his PhD in 1993, and joined the faculty of the Computer and Information Science Department at the University of Pennsylvania that same year. In September of 1996, he joined the faculty of the Center for Neural Science and the Courant Institute of Mathematical Sciences at New York University. He received an NSF Faculty Early Career Development (CAREER) grant in September 1996, for teaching and research in "Visual Information Processing", and a Sloan Research Fellowship in February 1998.

Dr. Eero Simoncelli, 4 Washington Place, RM 809, New York, NY 10003-6603
eero.simoncelli@nyu.edu, http://www.cns.nyu.edu/~eero

Pierre Soille received the engineering degree from the Université catholique de Louvain, Belgium, in 1988. He gained the doctorate degree in 1992 at the same university and in collaboration with the Centre de Morphologie Mathématique of the Ecole des Mines de Paris. He then pursued research on image analysis at the CSIRO Mathematical and Information Sciences Division, Sydney, the Centre de Morphologie Mathématique of the Ecole des Mines de Paris, and the Abteilung Mustererkennung of the Fraunhofer-Institut IPK, Berlin. During the period 1995-1998 he was lecturer and research scientist at the Ecole des Mines d'Alès and EERIE, Nîmes, France. Now he is a senior research scientist at the Silsoe Research Institute, England. He worked on many ap-

plied projects, taught tutorials during international conferences, co-organized the second International Symposium on Mathematical Morphology, wrote and edited three books, and contributed to over 50 scientific publications.
Prof. Pierre Soille, Silsoe Research Institute, Wrest Park
Silsoe, Bedfordshire, MK45 4HS, United Kingdom
Pierre.Soille@bbsrc.ac.uk, http://www.bbsrc.ac.uk

Hagen Spies graduated in January 1998 from the University of Heidelberg with a master degree in physics. He also received an MS in computing and information technology from the University of Dundee, Scotland in 1995. In 1998/1999 he spent one year as a visiting scientist at the University of Western Ontario, Canada. Currently he works as a researcher at the Interdisciplinary Center for Scientific Computing at the University of Heidelberg. His interests concern the measurement of optical and range flow and their use in scientific applications.
Hagen Spies, Forschungsgruppe Bildverarbeitung, IWR
Universität Heidelberg, Im Neuenheimer Feld 368
D-69120 Heidelberg, Germany, Hagen.Spies@iwr.uni-heidelberg.de
http://klimt.iwr.uni-heidelberg.de/~hspies

E. H. K. Stelzer studied physics in Frankfurt am Main and in Heidelberg, Germany. During his Diploma thesis at the Max-Planck-Institut für Biophysik he worked on the physical chemistry of phospholipid vesicles, which he characterized by photon correlation spectroscopy. Since 1983 he has worked at the European Molecular Biology Laboratory (EMBL). He has contributed extensively to the development of confocal fluorescence microscopy and its application in life sciences. His group works on the development and application of high-resolution techniques in light microscopy, video microscopy, confocal microscopy, optical tweezers, single particle analysis, and the documentation of relevant parameters with biological data.
Prof. Dr. E. H. K. Stelzer, Light Microscopy Group,
European Molecular Biology Laboratory (EMBL), Postfach 10 22 09
D-69120 Heidelberg, Germany, stelzer@EMBL-Heidelberg.de,

Hamid R. Tizhoosh received the M.S. degree in electrical engineering from University of Technology, Aachen, Germany, in 1995. From 1993 to 1996, he worked at Management of Intelligent Technologies Ltd. (MIT GmbH), Aachen, Germany, in the area of industrial image processing. He is currently a PhD candidate, Dept. of Technical Computer Science of Otto-von-Guericke-University, Magdeburg, Germany. His research encompasses fuzzy logic and computer vision. His recent research efforts include medical and fuzzy image processing. He is currently involved in the European Union project INFOCUS, and is researching enhancement of medical images in radiation therapy.
H. R. Tizhoosh, University of Magdeburg (IPE)

P.O. Box 4120, D-39016 Magdeburg, Germany
tizhoosh@ipe.et.uni-magdeburg.de
http://pmt05.et.uni-magdeburg.de/~hamid/

Thomas Wagner received a diploma degree in physics in 1991 from the University of Erlangen, Germany. In 1995, he finished his PhD in computer science with an applied image processing topic at the Fraunhofer Institute for Integrated Circuits in Erlangen. Since 1992, Dr. Wagner has been working on industrial image processing problems at the Fraunhofer Institute, from 1994 to 1997 as group manager of the intelligent systems group. Projects in his research team belong to the fields of object recognition, surface inspection, and access control. In 1996, he received the "Hans-Zehetmair-Habilitationsförderpreis." He is now working on automatic solutions for the design of industrial image processing systems.

Dr.-Ing. Thomas Wagner, Fraunhofer Institut für Intregrierte Schaltungen
Am Weichselgarten 3, D-91058 Erlangen, Germany
wag@iis.fhg.de, http://www.iis.fhg.de

Joachim Weickert obtained a M.Sc. in industrial mathematics in 1991 and a PhD in mathematics in 1996, both from Kaiserslautern University, Germany. After receiving the PhD degree, he worked as post-doctoral researcher at the Image Sciences Institute of Utrecht University, The Netherlands. In April 1997 he joined the computer vision group of the Department of Computer Science at Copenhagen University. His current research interests include all aspects of partial differential equations and scale-space theory in image analysis. He was awarded the Wacker Memorial Prize and authored the book "Anisotropic Diffusion in Image Processing."

Dr. Joachim Weickert, Department of Computer Science, University of Copenhagen, Universitetsparken 1, DK-2100 Copenhagen, Denmark
joachim@diku.dk, http://www.diku.dk/users/joachim/

Dieter Willersinn received his diploma in electrical engineering from Technical University Darmstadt in 1988. From 1988 to 1992 he was with Vitronic Image Processing Systems in Wiesbaden, working on industrial applications of robot vision and quality control. He then took a research position at the Technical University in Vienna, Austria, from which he received his PhD degree in 1995. In 1995, he joined the Fraunhofer Institute for Information and Data Processing (IITB) in Karlsruhe, where he initially worked on obstacle detection for driver assistance applications. Since 1997, Dr. Willersinn has been the head of the group, Assessment of Computer Vision Systems, Department for Recognition and Diagnosis Systems.

Dr. Dieter Willersinn, Fraunhofer Institut IITB, Fraunhoferstr. 1
D-76131 Karlsruhe, Germany, wil@iitb.fhg.de

1 Introduction

Bernd Jähne

Interdisziplinäres Zentrum für Wissenschaftliches Rechnen (IWR)
Universität Heidelberg, Germany

The second volume of the *Handbook on Computer Vision and Applications* deals with signal processing and pattern recognition. The signals processed in computer vision originate from the *radiance* of an object that is collected by an optical system (Volume 1, Chapter 5). The *irradiance* received by a single photosensor or a 2-D array of photosensors through the optical system is converted into an electrical signal and finally into arrays of digital numbers (Volume 2, Chapter 2). The whole chain of image formation from the illumination and interaction of radiation with the object of interest up to the arrays of digital numbers stored in the computer is the topic of Volume 1 of this handbook (subtitled *Sensors and Imaging*).

This volume deals with the processing of the signals generated by imaging sensors and this introduction covers four general topics. Section 1.1 discusses in which aspects the processing of higher-dimensional signals differs from the processing of 1-D time series. We also elaborate on the task of signal processing for computer vision. Pattern recognition (Section 1.2) plays a central role in computer vision because it uses the features extracted by lowlevel signal processing to classify and recognize objects.

Given the vast amount of data generated by imaging sensors the question of the computational complexity and of efficient algorithms is of utmost importance (Section 1.3). Finally, the performance evaluation of computer vision algorithms (Section 1.4) is a subject that has been neglected in the past. Consequently, a vast number of algorithms exist for which the performance characteristics are not sufficiently known.

Handbook of Computer Vision and Applications
Volume 2
Signal Processing and Pattern Recognition

Copyright © 1999 by Academic Press
All rights of reproduction in any form reserved.
ISBN 0-12-379772-1/$30.00

This constitutes a major obstacle for progress of applications using computer vision techniques.

1.1 Signal processing for computer vision

One-dimensional *linear signal processing* and *system theory* is a standard topic in electrical engineering and is covered by many standard textbooks, for example, [1, 2]. There is a clear trend that the classical signal processing community is moving into multidimensional signals, as indicated, for example, by the new annual international IEEE conference on image processing (ICIP). This can also be seen from some recently published handbooks on this subject. The digital signal processing handbook by Madisetti and Williams [3] includes several chapters that deal with image processing. Likewise the transforms and applications handbook by Poularikas [4] is not restricted to one-dimensional transforms.

There are, however, only a few monographs that treat signal processing specifically for computer vision and image processing. The monograph of Lim [5] deals with 2-D signal and image processing and tries to transfer the classical techniques for the analysis of time series to 2-D spatial data. Granlund and Knutsson [6] were the first to publish a monograph on signal processing for computer vision and elaborate on a number of novel ideas such as tensorial image processing and normalized convolution that did not have their origin in classical signal processing.

Time series are 1-D, signals in computer vision are of higher dimension. They are not restricted to digital images, that is, 2-D spatial signals (Chapter 2). *Volumetric sampling*, *image sequences* and *hyperspectral imaging* all result in 3-D signals, a combination of any of these techniques in even higher-dimensional signals.

How much more complex does signal processing become with increasing dimension? First, there is the explosion in the number of data points. Already a medium resolution volumetric image with 512^3 voxels requires 128 MB if one voxel carries just one byte. Storage of even higher-dimensional data at comparable resolution is thus beyond the capabilities of today's computers. Moreover, many applications require the handling of a huge number of images. This is also why appropriate databases including images are of importance. An example is discussed in Chapter 29.

Higher dimensional signals pose another problem. While we do not have difficulty in grasping 2-D data, it is already significantly more demanding to visualize 3-D data because the human visual system is built only to see surfaces in 3-D but not volumetric 3-D data. The more dimensions are processed, the more important it is that *computer graph-*

ics and *computer vision* come closer together. This is why this volume includes a contribution on *visualization* of volume data (Chapter 28).

The elementary framework for lowlevel signal processing for computer vision is worked out in part II of this volume. Of central importance are neighborhood operations (Chapter 5). Chapter 6 focuses on the design of filters optimized for a certain purpose. Other subjects of elementary spatial processing include fast algorithms for local averaging (Chapter 7), accurate and fast interpolation (Chapter 8), and image warping (Chapter 9) for subpixel-accurate signal processing.

The basic goal of signal processing in computer vision is the extraction of "suitable *features*" for subsequent processing to recognize and classify objects. But what is a suitable feature? This is still less well defined than in other applications of signal processing. Certainly a mathematically well-defined description of local structure as discussed in Chapter 10 is an important basis. The selection of the proper *scale* for image processing has recently come into the focus of attention (Chapter 11). As signals processed in computer vision come from dynamical 3-D scenes, important features also include *motion* (Chapters 13 and 14) and various techniques to infer the depth in scenes including *stereo* (Chapters 17 and 18), shape from shading and photometric stereo (Chapter 19), and depth from focus (Chapter 20).

There is little doubt that *nonlinear* techniques are crucial for feature extraction in computer vision. However, compared to linear filter techniques, these techniques are still in their infancy. There is also no single nonlinear technique but there are a host of such techniques often specifically adapted to a certain purpose [7]. In this volume, a rather general class of nonlinear filters by combination of linear convolution and nonlinear point operations (Chapter 10), and nonlinear diffusion filtering (Chapter 15) are discussed.

1.2 Pattern recognition for computer vision

In principle, *pattern classification* is nothing complex. Take some appropriate features and partition the feature space into classes. Why is it then so difficult for a computer vision system to recognize objects? The basic trouble is related to the fact that the dimensionality of the input space is so large. In principle, it would be possible to use the image itself as the input for a classification task, but no real-world classification technique—be it statistical, neuronal, or fuzzy—would be able to handle such high-dimensional feature spaces. Therefore, the need arises to extract features and to use them for classification.

Unfortunately, techniques for feature selection have widely been neglected in computer vision. They have not been developed to the same degree of sophistication as classification where it is meanwhile well understood that the different techniques, especially statistical and neural techniques, can been considered under a unified view [8].

Thus part IV of this volume focuses in part on some more advanced feature-extraction techniques. An important role in this aspect is played by morphological operators (Chapter 21) because they manipulate the shape of objects in images. Fuzzy image processing (Chapter 22) contributes a tool to handle vague data and information.

The remainder of part IV focuses on another major area in computer vision. Object recognition can be performed only if it is possible to represent the knowledge in an appropriate way. In simple cases the knowledge can just be rested in simple models. Probabilistic modeling in computer vision is discussed in Chapter 26. In more complex cases this is not sufficient. The graph theoretical concepts presented in Chapter 24 are one of the bases for knowledge-based interpretation of images as presented in Chapter 27.

1.3 Computational complexity and fast algorithms

The processing of huge amounts of data in computer vision becomes a serious challenge if the number of computations increases more than linear with the number of data points, $M = N^D$ (D is the dimension of the signal). Already an algorithm that is of order $O(M^2)$ may be prohibitively slow. Thus it is an important goal to achieve $O(M)$ or at least $O(M \operatorname{ld} M)$ performance of all pixel-based algorithms in computer vision. Much effort has been devoted to the design of fast algorithms, that is, performance of a given task with a given computer system in a minimum amount of time. This does not mean merely minimizing the number of computations. Often it is equally or even more important to minimize the number of memory accesses.

Point operations are of linear order and take cM operations. Thus they do not pose a problem. *Neighborhood operations* are still of linear order in the number of pixels but the constant c may become quite large, especially for signals with high dimensions. This is why there is already a need to develop fast neighborhood operations. Brute force implementations of global transforms such as the Fourier transform require cM^2 operations and can thus only be used at all if fast algorithms are available. Such algorithms are discussed in Section 3.4. Many other algorithms in computer vision, such as correlation, correspondence analysis, and graph search algorithms are also of polynomial order, some of them even of exponential order.

A general breakthrough in the performance of more complex algorithms in computer vision was the introduction of *multiresolutional data structures* that are discussed in Chapters 4 and 14. All chapters about elementary techniques for processing of spatial data (Chapters 5–10) also deal with efficient algorithms.

1.4 Performance evaluation of algorithms

A systematic evaluation of the algorithms for computer vision has been widely neglected. For a newcomer to computer vision with an engineering background or a general education in natural sciences this is a strange experience. It appears to him as if one would present results of measurements without giving error bars or even thinking about possible *statistical* and *systematic errors*.

What is the cause of this situation? On the one side, it is certainly true that some problems in computer vision are very hard and that it is even harder to perform a sophisticated error analysis. On the other hand, the computer vision community has ignored the fact to a large extent that any algorithm is only as good as its objective and solid evaluation and verification.

Fortunately, this misconception has been recognized in the meantime and there are serious efforts underway to establish generally accepted rules for the *performance analysis of computer vision algorithms*. We give here just a brief summary and refer for details to Haralick et al. [9] and for a practical example to Volume 3, Chapter 7. The three major criteria for the performance of computer vision algorithms are:

Successful solution of task. Any practitioner gives this a top priority. But also the designer of an algorithm should define precisely for which task it is suitable and what the limits are.

Accuracy. This includes an analysis of the statistical and systematic errors under carefully defined conditions (such as given *signal-to-noise ratio* (SNR), etc.).

Speed. Again this is an important criterion for the applicability of an algorithm.

There are different ways to evaluate algorithms according to the forementioned criteria. Ideally this should include three classes of studies:

Analytical studies. This is the mathematically most rigorous way to verify algorithms, check error propagation, and predict catastrophic failures.

Performance tests with computer generated images. These tests are useful as they can be carried out under carefully controlled conditions.

Performance tests with real-world images. This is the final test for practical applications.

Much of the material presented in this volume is written in the spirit of a careful and mathematically well-founded analysis of the methods that are described although the performance evaluation techniques are certainly more advanced in some areas than in others.

1.5 References

[1] Oppenheim, A. V. and Schafer, R. W., (1989). *Discrete-time Signal Processing. Prentice-Hall Signal Processing Series.* Englewood Cliffs, NJ: Prentice-Hall.

[2] Proakis, J. G. and Manolakis, D. G., (1992). *Digital Signal Processing. Principles, Algorithms, and Applications.* New York: McMillan.

[3] Madisetti, V. K. and Williams, D. B. (eds.), (1997). *The Digital Signal Processing Handbook.* Boca Raton, FL: CRC Press.

[4] Poularikas, A. D. (ed.), (1996). *The Transforms and Applications Handbook.* Boca Raton, FL: CRC Press.

[5] Lim, J. S., (1990). *Two-dimensional Signal and Image Processing.* Englewood Cliffs, NJ: Prentice-Hall.

[6] Granlund, G. H. and Knutsson, H., (1995). *Signal Processing for Computer Vision.* Norwell, MA: Kluwer Academic Publishers.

[7] Pitas, I. and Venetsanopoulos, A. N., (1990). *Nonlinear Digital Filters. Principles and Applications.* Norwell, MA: Kluwer Academic Publishers.

[8] Schürmann, J., (1996). *Pattern Classification, a Unified View of Statistical and Neural Approaches.* New York: John Wiley & Sons.

[9] Haralick, R. M., Klette, R., Stiehl, H.-S., and Viergever, M. (eds.), (1999). *Evaluation and Validation of Computer Vision Algorithms.* Boston: Kluwer.

Part I

Signal Representation

2 Continuous and Digital Signals

Bernd Jähne

Interdisziplinäres Zentrum für Wissenschaftliches Rechnen (IWR)
Universität Heidelberg, Germany

Handbook of Computer Vision and Applications
Volume 2
Signal Processing and Pattern Recognition

Copyright © 1999 by Academic Press
All rights of reproduction in any form reserved.
ISBN 0-12-379772-1/$30.00

2.1 Introduction

Images are signals with two spatial dimensions. This chapter deals with signals of arbitrary dimensions. This generalization is very useful because computer vision is not restricted solely to 2-D signals. On the one hand, higher-dimensional signals are encountered. Dynamic scenes require the analysis of image sequences; the exploration of 3-D space requires the acquisition of volumetric images. Scientific exploration of complex phenomena is significantly enhanced if images not only of a single parameter but of many parameters are acquired. On the other hand, signals of lower dimensionality are also of importance when a computer vision system is integrated into a larger system and image data are fused with time series from point measuring sensors.

Thus this chapter deals with continuous (Section 2.2) and discrete (Section 2.3) representations of signals with arbitrary dimensions. While the continuous representation is very useful for a solid mathematical foundation of signal processing, real-world sensors deliver and digital computers handle only discrete data. Given the two representations, the relation between them is of major importance. Section 2.4 discusses the spatial and temporal *sampling* on signals while Section 2.5 treats *quantization*, the conversion of a continuous signal into digital numbers.

2.2 Continuous signals

2.2.1 Types of signals

An important characteristic of a signal is its *dimension*. A zero-dimensional signal results from the measurement of a single quantity at a single point in space and time. Such a single value can also be averaged over a certain time period and area. There are several ways to extend a zero-dimensional signal into a 1-D signal (Table 2.1). A *time series* records the temporal course of a signal in time, while a *profile* does the same in a spatial direction or along a certain path.

A 1-D signal is also obtained if certain experimental parameters of the measurement are continuously changed and the measured parameter is recorded as a function of some control parameters. With respect to optics, the most obvious parameter is the wavelength of the electromagnetic radiation received by a radiation detector. When radiation is recorded as a function of the *wavelength*, a *spectrum* is obtained. The wavelength is only one of the many parameters that could be considered. Others could be temperature, pressure, humidity, concentration of a chemical species, and any other properties that may influence the measured quantity.

Table 2.1: *Some types of signals g depending on D parameters*

D	Type of signal	Function
0	Measurement at a single point in space and time	g
1	Time series	$g(t)$
1	Profile	$g(x)$
1	Spectrum	$g(\lambda)$
2	Image	$g(x, y)$
2	Time series of profiles	$g(x, t)$
2	Time series of spectra	$g(\lambda, t)$
3	Volumetric image	$g(x, y, z)$
3	Image sequence	$g(x, y, t)$
3	Hyperspectral image	$g(x, y, \lambda)$
4	Volumetric image sequence	$g(x, y, z, t)$
4	Hyperspectral image sequence	$g(x, y, \lambda, t)$
5	Hyperspectral volumetric image sequence	$g(x, y, z, \lambda, t)$

With this general approach to multidimensional signal processing, it is obvious that an image is only one of the many possibilities of a 2-D signal. Other 2-D signals are, for example, time series of profiles or spectra. With increasing dimension, more types of signals are possible as summarized in Table 2.1. A 5-D signal is constituted by a *hyperspectral* volumetric image sequence.

2.2.2 Unified description

Mathematically all these different types of multidimensional signals can be described in a unified way as continuous scalar functions of multiple parameters or generalized coordinates q_d as

$$g(\boldsymbol{q}) = g(q_1, q_2, \ldots, q_D) \quad \text{with} \quad \boldsymbol{q} = [q_1, q_2, \ldots, q_D]^T \tag{2.1}$$

that can be summarized in a D-dimensional *parameter vector* or generalized coordinate vector $\boldsymbol{q}$. An element of the vector can be a spatial direction, the time, or any other parameter.

As the signal g represents physical quantities, we can generally assume some properties that make the mathematical handling of the signals much easier.

Continuity. Real signals do not show any abrupt changes or discontinuities. Mathematically this means that signals can generally be regarded as arbitrarily often differentiable.

Finite range. The physical nature of both the signal and the imaging sensor ensures that a signal is limited to a finite range. Some signals are restricted to positive values.

Finite energy. Normally a signal corresponds to the amplitude or the energy of a physical process (see also Volume 1, Chapter 2). As the energy of any physical system is limited, any signal must be square integrable:

$$\int_{-\infty}^{\infty} |g(\boldsymbol{q})|^2 \, \mathrm{d}^D q < \infty \tag{2.2}$$

With these general properties of physical signals, it is obvious that the continuous representation provides a powerful mathematical approach. The properties imply, for example, that the Fourier transform (Section 3.2) of the signals exist.

Depending on the underlying physical process the observed signal can be regarded as a stochastic signal. More often, however, a signal is a mixture of a deterministic and a stochastic signal. In the simplest case, the measured signal of a deterministic process g_d is corrupted by additive *zero-mean homogeneous noise*. This leads to the simple signal model

$$g(\boldsymbol{q}) = g_d(\boldsymbol{q}) + n \tag{2.3}$$

where n has the *variance* $\sigma_n^2 = \langle n^2 \rangle$. In most practical situations, the noise is not homogeneous but rather depends on the level of the signal. Thus in a more general way

$$g(\boldsymbol{q}) = g_d(\boldsymbol{q}) + n(g) \quad \text{with} \quad \langle n(g) \rangle = 0, \left\langle n^2(g) \right\rangle = \sigma_n^2(g) \tag{2.4}$$

A detailed treatment of noise in various types of imaging sensors can be found in Volume 1, Sections 7.5, 9.3.1, and 10.2.3.

2.2.3 Multichannel signals

So far, only scalar signals have been considered. If more than one signal is taken simultaneously, a *multichannel signal* is obtained. In some cases, for example, taking time series at different spatial positions, the multichannel signal can be considered as just a sampled version of a higher-dimensional signal. In other cases, the individual signals cannot be regarded as samples. This is the case when they are parameters with different units and/or meaning.

A multichannel signal provides a vector at each point and is therefore sometimes denoted as a *vectorial signal* and written as

$$\boldsymbol{g}(\boldsymbol{q}) = [q_1(\boldsymbol{q}), q_2(\boldsymbol{q}), \ldots, q_D(\boldsymbol{q})]^T \tag{2.5}$$

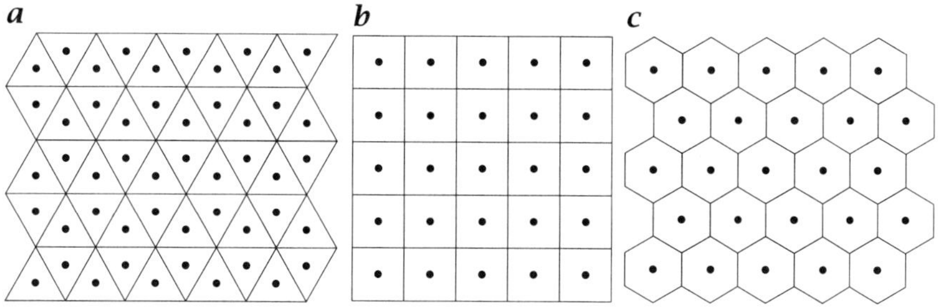

Figure 2.1: *Representation of 2-D digital images by meshes of regular polygons:* ***a*** *triangles;* ***b*** *squares;* ***c*** *hexagons.*

Table 2.2: *Properties of tessellations of the 2-D space with regular triangular, square, and hexagonal meshes; N_e: number of neighbors with common edge; N_c: number of neighbors with common edge and/or corner; l: basis length l of regular polygon; d: distance d to nearest neighbor; and A: area of cell*

	Triangular	Square	Hexagonal
N_e	3	4	6
N_c	12	8	6
l	$l = \sqrt{3}d = \sqrt{\sqrt{16/3}A}$	$l = d = \sqrt{A}$	$l = \frac{1}{3}\sqrt{3}d = \sqrt{\sqrt{4/27}A}$
d	$d = \frac{1}{3}\sqrt{3}l = \sqrt{\sqrt{16/27}A}$	$d = l = \sqrt{A}$	$d = \sqrt{3}l = \sqrt{\sqrt{4/3}A}$
A	$A = \frac{3}{4}\sqrt{3}d^2 = \frac{1}{4}\sqrt{3}l^2$	$A = d^2 = l^2$	$A = \frac{1}{2}\sqrt{3}d^2 = \frac{3}{2}\sqrt{3}l^2$

A multichannel signal is not necessarily a vectorial signal. Depending on the mathematical relation between its components, it could also be a higher-order signal, for example, a *tensorial signal*. Such types of multichannel images are encountered when complex features are extracted from images. One example is the tensorial description of local structure discussed in Chapter 10.

2.3 Discrete signals

2.3.1 Regular two-dimensional lattices

Computers cannot handle continuous signals but only arrays of digital numbers. Thus it is required to represent signals as D-dimensional arrays of points. We first consider images as 2-D arrays of points. A point on the 2-D grid is called a *pixel* or *pel*. Both words are abbreviations of *picture element*. A pixel represents the irradiance at the corresponding grid position. There are two ways to derive 2-D lattices from continuous signals.

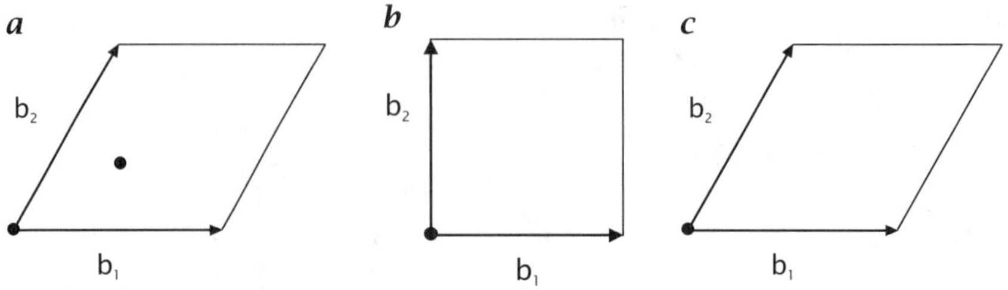

Figure 2.2: *Elementary cells of regular grids for 2-D digital images:* ***a*** *triangle grid,* ***b*** *square grid,* **c** *hexagonal grid.*

First, the continuous 2-D space can be partitioned into space-filling cells. For symmetry reasons, only *regular polygons* are considered. Then there are only three possible *tesselations* with regular polygons: triangles, squares, and hexagons as illustrated in Fig. 2.1 (see also Table 2.2). All other regular polygons do not lead to a space-filling geometrical arrangement. There are either overlaps or gaps. From the mesh of regular polygons a 2-D array of points is then formed by the symmetry centers of the polygons. In case of the square mesh, these points lie again on a square grid. For the hexagonal mesh, the symmetry centers of the hexagons form a triangular grid. In contrast, the symmetry centers of the triangular grid form a more complex pattern, where two triangular meshes are interleaved. The second mesh is offset by a third of the base length l of the triangular mesh.

A second approach to regular lattices starts with a *primitive cell*. A primitive cell in 2-D is spanned by two not necessarily orthogonal base vectors $\boldsymbol{b}_1$ and $\boldsymbol{b}_2$. Thus, the primitive cell is always a parallelogram except for square and rectangular lattices (Fig. 2.2). Only in the latter case are the base vectors $\boldsymbol{b}_1$ and $\boldsymbol{b}_2$ orthogonal. Translating the primitive cell by multiples of the base vectors of the primitive cell then forms the lattice. Such a *translation vector* or *lattice vector* $\boldsymbol{r}$ is therefore given by

$$\boldsymbol{r} = n_1\boldsymbol{b}_1 + n_2\boldsymbol{b}_2 \quad n_1, n_2 \in \mathbb{Z} \tag{2.6}$$

The primitive cells of the square and hexagonal lattices (Fig. 2.2b and c) contains only one grid located at the origin of the primitive cell. This is not possible for a triangular grid, as the lattice points are not arranged in *regular* distances along two directions (Fig. 2.1a). Thus, the construction of the triangular lattice requires a primitive cell with two grid points. One grid point is located at the origin of the cell, the other is offset by a third of the length of each base vector (Fig. 2.2a)

The construction scheme to generate the elementary cells of regular shape from the lattice points is illustrated in Fig. 2.3. From one lattice point straight lines are drawn to all other lattice points starting with

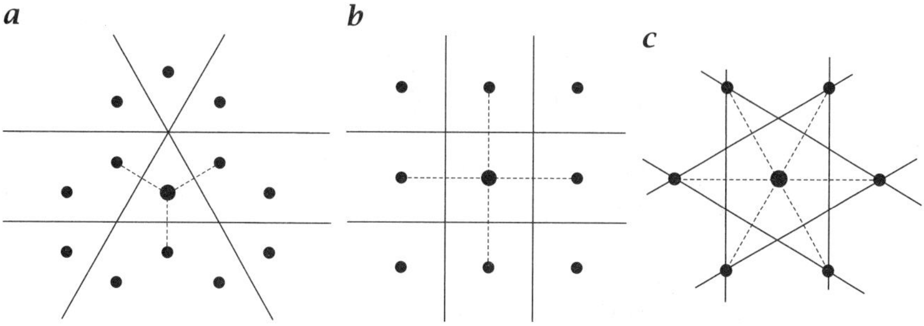

Figure 2.3: *Construction of the cells of a regular lattice from the lattice points:* ***a*** *triangle lattice;* ***b*** *square lattice; and* ***c*** *hexagonal lattice.*

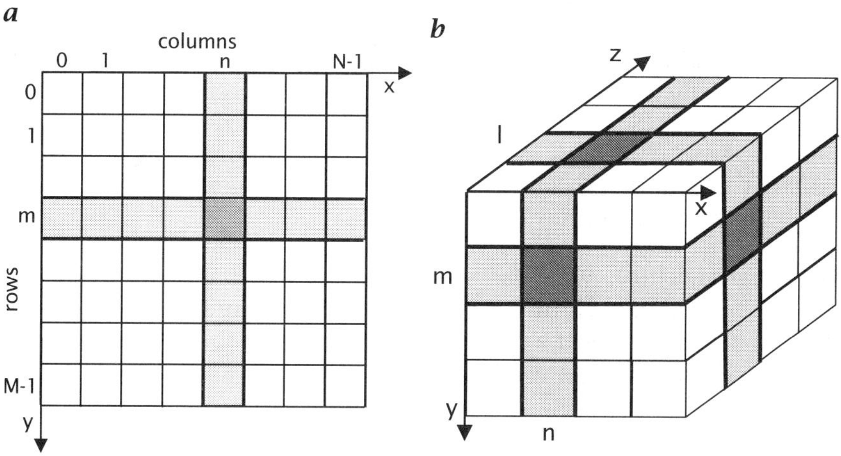

Figure 2.4: *Representation of digital images by orthogonal lattices:* ***a*** *square lattice for a 2-D image; and* ***b*** *cubic lattice for a volumetric or 3-D image.*

the nearest neighbors (dashed lines). Then the smallest cell formed by the lines perpendicular to these lines and dividing them into two halves results in the primitive cell. For all three lattices, only the nearest neighbors must be considered for this construction scheme.

The mathematics behind the formation of regular lattices in two dimensions is the 2-D analog to 3-D lattices used to describe crystals in solid state physics and mineralogy. The primitive cell constructed from the lattice points is, for example, known in solid state physics as the *Wigner-Seitz cell*.

Although there is a choice of three lattices with regular polygons—and many more if irregular polygons are considered—almost exclusively square or rectangular lattices are used for 2-D digital images.

The position of the pixel is given in the common notation for matrices. The first index, m, denotes the position of the row, the second, n, the position of the column (Fig. 2.4a). M gives the number of rows, N the number of columns. In accordance with the matrix notation, the vertical axis (y axis) runs from top to bottom and not vice versa as is common in graphs. The horizontal axis (x axis) runs as usual from left to right.

2.3.2 Regular higher-dimensional lattices

The considerations in the previous section can be extended to higher dimensions. In 3-D space, lattices are identical to those used in solid-state physics to describe crystalline solids. In higher dimensions, we have serious difficulty in grasping the structure of discrete lattices because we can visualize only projections onto 2-D space. Given the fact that already 2-D discrete images are almost exclusively represented by rectangular lattices (Section 2.3.1), we may ask what we lose if we consider only hypercubic lattices in higher dimensions. Surprisingly, it turns out that this lattice has such significant advantages that it is hardly necessary to consider any other lattice.

Orthogonal lattice. The base vectors of the hypercubic primitive cell are orthogonal to each other. As discussed in Chapter 6, this is a significant advantage for the design of filters. If separable filters are used, they can easily be extended to arbitrary dimensions.

Valid for all dimensions. The hypercubic lattice is the most general solution for digital data as it is the only geometry that exists in arbitrary dimensions. In practice this means that it is generally quite easy to extend image processing algorithms to higher dimensions. We will see this, for example, with the discrete Fourier transform in Section 3.3, with multigrid data structures in Chapter 4, with averaging in Chapter 7, and with the analysis of local structure in Chapter 10.

Only lattice with regular polyhedron. While in 2-D, three lattices with regular polyhedrons exist (Section 2.3.1), the cubic lattice is the only lattice with a regular polyhedron (the hexahedron) in 3-D. None of the other four regular polyhedra (tetrahedron, octahedron, dodecahedron, and icosahedron) is space filling.

These significant advantages of the hypercubic lattice are not outweighed by the single disadvantage that the neighborhood relations, discussed in Section 2.3.5, are more complex on these lattices than, for example, the 2-D hexagonal lattice.

In 3-D or *volumetric images* the elementary cell is known as a *voxel*, an abbreviation of *volume element*. On a rectangular grid, each voxel represents the mean gray value of a cuboid. The position of a voxel is given by three indices. The first, l, denotes the depth, m the row, and n the column (Fig. 2.4b). In higher dimensions, the elementary cell is denoted as a *hyperpixel*.

2.3.3 Irregular lattices

Irregular lattices are attractive because they can be adapted to the contents of images. Small cells are only required where the image contains fine details and can be much larger in other regions. In this way, a compact representation of an image seems to be feasable. It is also not difficult to generate an irregular lattice. The general principle for the construction of a mesh from an array of points (Section 2.3.1) can easily be extended to irregularly spaced points. It is known as Delaunay triangulation and results in the dual Voronoi and Delaunay graphs (Chapters 24 and 25).

Processing of image data, however, becomes much more difficult on irregular grids. Some types of operations, such as all classical filter operations, do not even make much sense on irregular grids. In contrast, it poses no difficulty to apply morphological operations to irregular lattices (Chapter 21).

Because of the difficulty in processing digital images on irregular lattices, these data structure are hardly ever used to represent raw images. In order to adapt low-level image processing operations to different scales and to provide an efficient storage scheme for raw data multigrid data structures, for example, pyramids have proved to be much more effective (Chapter 4). In contrast, irregular lattices play an important role in generating and representing segmented images (Chapter 25).

2.3.4 Metric in digital images

Based on the discussion in the previous two sections, we will focus in the following on hypercubic or orthogonal lattices and discuss in this section the metric of discrete images. This constitutes the base for all length, size, volume, and distance measurements in digital images. It is useful to generalize the *lattice vector* introduced in Eq. (2.6) that represents all points of a D-dimensional digital image and can be written as

$$\boldsymbol{r_n} = [n_1\Delta x_1, n_2\Delta x_2, \ldots, n_D\Delta x_D]^T \tag{2.7}$$

In the preceding equation, the lattice constants Δx_d need not be equal in all directions. For the special cases of 2-D images, 3-D volumetric images, and 4-D spatiotemporal images the lattice vectors are

$$\boldsymbol{r}_{m,n} = \begin{bmatrix} n\Delta x \\ m\Delta y \end{bmatrix}, \boldsymbol{r}_{l,m,n} = \begin{bmatrix} n\Delta x \\ m\Delta y \\ l\Delta z \end{bmatrix}, \boldsymbol{r}_{k,l,m,n} = \begin{bmatrix} n\Delta x \\ m\Delta y \\ l\Delta z \\ k\Delta t \end{bmatrix} \quad (2.8)$$

To measure distances, the *Euclidean distance* can be computed on an orthogonal lattice by

$$d_e(\boldsymbol{x}, \boldsymbol{x}') = \|\boldsymbol{x} - \boldsymbol{x}'\| = \left[\sum_{d=1}^{D} (n_d - n'_d)^2 \Delta x_d^2 \right]^{1/2} \quad (2.9)$$

On a square lattice, that is, a lattice with the same grid constant in all directions, the Euclidean distance can be computed more efficiently by

$$d_e(\boldsymbol{x}, \boldsymbol{x}') = \|\boldsymbol{x} - \boldsymbol{x}'\| = \left[\sum_{d=1}^{D} (n_d - n'_d)^2 \right]^{1/2} \Delta x \quad (2.10)$$

The Euclidean distance on discrete lattices is somewhat awkward. Although it is a discrete quantity, its values are not integers. Moreover, it cannot be computed very efficiently.

Therefore, two other metrics are sometimes considered in image processing. The *city block distance*

$$d_b(\boldsymbol{x}, \boldsymbol{x}') = \sum_{d=1}^{D} |n_d - n'_d| \quad (2.11)$$

simply adds up the magnitude of the component differences of two lattice vectors and not the squares as with the Euclidean distance in Eq. (2.10). Geometrically, the city block distance gives the length of a path between the two lattice vectors if we can only walk in directions parallel to axes. The *chessboard distance* is defined as the maximum of the absolute difference between two components of the corresponding lattice vectors:

$$d_c(\boldsymbol{x}, \boldsymbol{x}') = \max_{d=1,\ldots,D} |n_d - n'_d| \quad (2.12)$$

These two metrics have gained some importance for morphological operations (Section 21.2.5). Despite their simplicity they are not of much use as soon as lengths and distances are to be measured. The Euclidean distance is the only metric on digital images that preserves the *isotropy* of the continuous space. With the city block and chessboard distance, distances in the direction of the diagonals are longer and shorter than the Euclidean distance, respectively.

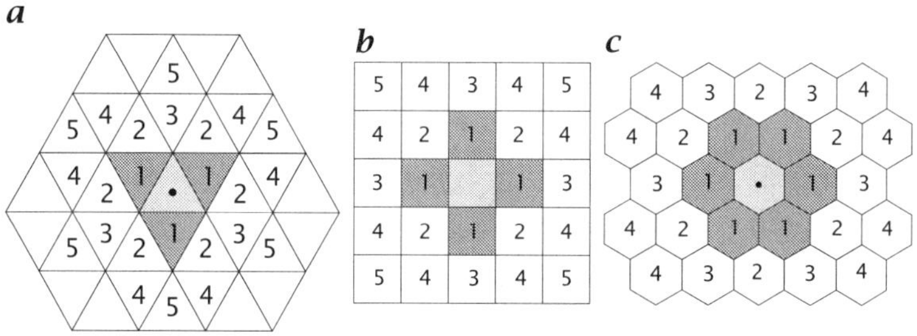

*Figure 2.5: Classification of the cells according to the distance from a given cell for the **a** triangular, **b** square, and **c** hexagonal lattices. The central cell is shaded in light gray, the nearest neighbors in darker gray. The numbers give the ranking in distance from the central cell.*

2.3.5 Neighborhood relations

The term *neighborhood* has no meaning for a continuous signal. How far two points are from each other is simply measured by an adequate metric such as the Euclidean distance function and this distance can take any value. With the cells of a discrete signal, however, a ranking of the distance between cells is possible. The set of cells with the smallest distance to a given cell are called the nearest neighbors. The triangular, square, and hexagonal lattices have three, four, and six nearest neighbors, respectively (Fig. 2.5). The figure indicates also the ranking in distance from the central cell.

Directly related to the question of neighbors is the term *adjacency*. A *digital object* is defined as a *connected region*. This means that we can reach any cell in the region from any other by walking from one neighboring cell to the next. Such a walk is called a *path*.

On a square lattice there are two possible ways to define neighboring cells (Fig. 2.5b). We can regard pixels as neighbors either when they have a joint edge or when they have at least one joint corner. Thus a pixel has four or eight neighbors and we speak of a *4-neighborhood* or an *8-neighborhood*. The definition of the 8-neighborhood is somewhat awkward, as there are neighboring cells with different distances.

The triangular lattice shows an equivalent ambivalence with the 3- and 12-neighborhoods with cells that have either only a joint edge or at least a joint corner with the central cell (Fig. 2.5a). In the 12-neighborhood there are three different types of neighboring cells, each with a different distance (Fig. 2.5a).

Only the hexagonal lattice gives a unique definition of neighbors. Each cell has six neighboring cells at the same distance joining one edge and two corners with the central cell.

A closer look shows that unfortunately both types of neighborhood definitions are required on triangular and square grids for a proper

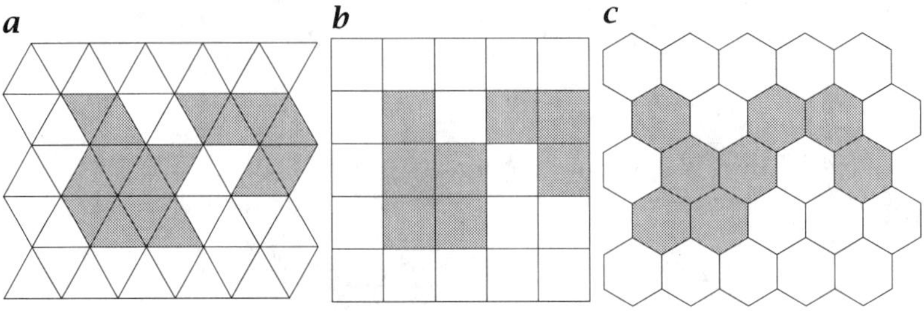

Figure 2.6: *Digital objects on **a** triangular, **b** square, and **c** hexagonal lattice. **a** and **b** show either two objects or one object (connected regions) depending on the neighborhood definition.*

definition of connected regions. A region or an object is called connected when we can reach any pixel in the region by walking from one neighboring pixel to the next. The black object shown in Fig. 2.6b is one object in the 8-neighborhood, but constitutes two objects in the 4-neighborhood. The white background, however, shows the same property. Thus we have either two connected regions in the 8-neighborhood crossing each other or four separated regions in the 4-neighborhood. This inconsistency between objects and background can be overcome if we declare the objects as 4-neighboring and the background as 8-neighboring, or vice versa.

These complications occur also on a triangular lattice (Fig. 2.6b) but not on a hexagonal lattice (Fig. 2.6c). The photosensors on the retina in the human eye, however, have a more hexagonal shape, see Wandell [1, Fig. 3.4, p. 49].

2.3.6 Errors in object position and geometry

The tessellation of space in discrete images limits the accuracy of the estimation of the position of an object and thus all other geometrical quantities such as distance, area, circumference, and orientation of lines. It is obvious that the accuracy of the position of a single point is only in the order of the lattice constant. The interesting question is, however, how this error propagates into position errors for larger objects and other relations. This question is of significant importance because of the relatively low spatial resolution of images as compared to other measuring instruments. Without much effort many physical quantities such as frequency, voltage, and distance can be measured with an accuracy better than 1 ppm, that is, 1 in 1,000,000, while images have a spatial resolution in the order of 1 in 1000 due to the limited number of pixels. Thus only highly accurate position estimates in the order of 1/100 of the pixel size result in an accuracy of about 1 in 100,000.

The discussion of position errors in this section will be limited to orthogonal lattices. These lattices have the significant advantage that the errors in the different directions can be discussed independently. Thus the following discussion is not only valid for 2-D images but any type of multidimensional signals and we must consider only one component.

In order to estimate the accuracy of the position estimate of a single point it is assumed that all positions are equally probable. This means a constant probability density function in the interval Δx. Then the variance σ_x^2 introduced by the position discretization is given by Papoulis [2, p. 106]

$$\sigma_x^2 = \frac{1}{\Delta x} \int_{x_n - \Delta x/2}^{x_n + \Delta x/2} (x - x_n)^2 \, \mathrm{d}x = \frac{(\Delta x)^2}{12} \tag{2.13}$$

Thus the standard deviation σ_x is about $1/\sqrt{12} \approx 0.3$ times the lattice constant Δx. The maximum error is, of course, $0.5\Delta x$.

All other errors for geometrical measurements of segmented objects can be related to this basic position error by statistical error propagation. We will illustrate this with a simple example computing the area and center of gravity of an object. For the sake of simplicity, we start with the unrealistic assumption that any cell that contains even the smallest fraction of the object is regarded as a cell of the object. We further assume that this segmentation is exact, that is, the signal itself does not contain noise and separates without errors from the background. In this way we separate all other errors from the errors introduced by the discrete lattice.

The area of the object is simply given as the product of the number N of cells and the area A_c of a cell. This simple estimate is, however, biased towards a larger area because the cells at the border of the object are only partly covered by the object. In the mean, half of the border cells are covered. Hence an unbiased estimate of the area is given by

$$A = A_c(N - 0.5N_b) \tag{2.14}$$

where N_b is the number of border cells. With this equation, the variance of the estimate can be determined. Only the statistical error in the area of the border cells must be considered. According to the laws of error propagation with independent random variables, the variance of the area estimate σ_A^2 is given by

$$\sigma_A^2 = 0.25 A_c^2 N_b \sigma_x^2 \tag{2.15}$$

If we assume a compact object, for example, a square, with a length of D pixels, it has D^2 pixels and $4D$ border pixels. Using $\sigma_x \approx 0.3$

(Eq. (2.13)), the absolute and relative standard deviation of the area estimate are given by

$$\sigma_A \approx 0.3 A_c \sqrt{D} \quad \text{and} \quad \frac{\sigma_A}{A} \approx \frac{0.3}{D^{3/2}} \quad \text{if } D \gg 1 \tag{2.16}$$

Thus the standard deviation of the area error for an object with a length of 10 pixels is just about the area of the pixel and the relative error is about 1%. Equations (2.14) and (2.15) are also valid for volumetric images if the area of the elementary cell is replaced by the volume of the cell. Only the number of border cells is now different. If we again assume a compact object, for example, a cube, with a length of D, we now have D^3 cells in the object and $6D^2$ border cells. Then the absolute and relative standard deviations are approximately given by

$$\sigma_V \approx 0.45 V_c D \quad \text{and} \quad \frac{\sigma_V}{V} \approx \frac{0.45}{D^2} \quad \text{if } D \gg 1 \tag{2.17}$$

Now the standard deviation of the volume for an object with a diameter of 10 pixels is about 5 times the volume of the cells but the relative error is about 0.5%. Note that the absolute/relative error for volume measurements in/decreases faster with the size of the object than for area measurements.

The computations for the error of the center of gravity are quite similar. With the same assumptions about the segmentation process, an unbiased estimate of the center of gravity is given by

$$\boldsymbol{x}_g = \frac{1}{N} \left(\sum_{n=1}^{N-N_b} \boldsymbol{x}_n + \frac{1}{2} \sum_{n'=1}^{N_b} \boldsymbol{x}_{n'} \right) \tag{2.18}$$

Again the border pixels are counted only half. As the first part of the estimate with the nonborder pixels is exact, errors are caused only by the variation in the area of the border pixels. Therefore the variance of the estimate for each component of the center of gravity is given by

$$\sigma_g^2 = \frac{N_b}{4N^2} \sigma^2 \tag{2.19}$$

where σ is again the variance in the position of the fractional cells at the border of the object. Thus the standard deviation of the center of gravity for a compact object with the diameter of D pixels is

$$\sigma_g \approx \frac{0.3}{D^{3/2}} \quad \text{if } D \gg 1 \tag{2.20}$$

Thus the standard deviation for the center of gravity of an object with 10 pixel diameter is only about 0.01 pixel. For a volumetric object with a diameter of D pixel, the standard deviation becomes

$$\sigma_{gv} \approx \frac{0.45}{D^2} \quad \text{if } D \gg 1 \tag{2.21}$$

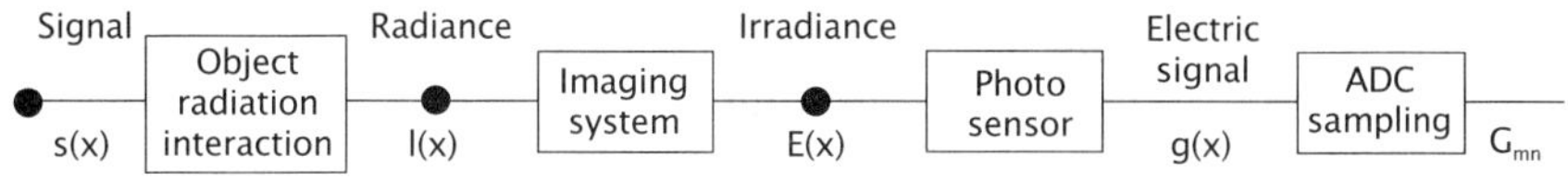

Figure 2.7: *Steps from a continuous to a discrete signal.*

This result clearly shows that the position of objects and all related geometrical quantities such as the distances can be performed even with binary images (segmented objects) well into the range of 1/100 pixel. It is interesting that the relative errors for the area and volume estimates of Eqs. (2.16) and (2.17) are equal to the standard deviation of the center of gravity Eqs. (2.20) and (2.21). Note that only the *statistical error* has been discussed. A bias in the segmentation might easily result in much higher systematic errors.

2.4 Relation between continuous and discrete signals

A continuous function $g(\boldsymbol{q})$ is a useful mathematical description of a signal as discussed in Section 2.2. Real-world signals, however, can only be represented and processed as discrete or digital signals. Therefore a detailed knowledge of the relation between these two types of signals is required. It is not only necessary to understand the whole chain of the image formation process from a continuous spatial radiance distribution to a digital image but also to perform subpixel-accurate image interpolation (Chapter 8) and warping of images (Chapter 9) as it is, for example, required for multiscale image operations (Chapter 14).

The chain of processes that lead from the "true" signal to the digital signal include all the steps of the image formation process as illustrated in Fig. 2.7. First the signal of interest, $s(\boldsymbol{x})$, such as reflectivity, temperature, etc. of an object is somehow related to the radiance $L(\boldsymbol{x})$ emitted by the object in a generally not linear function (Volume 1, Chapter 3). In some cases this relation is linear (e.g., reflectivity), in others it is highly nonlinear (e.g., temperature). Often other parameters that are not controlled or not even known, influence the signal as well. As an example, the radiance of an object is the product of its reflectivity and the irradiance. Moreover, the radiance of the beam from the object to the camera may be attenuated by absorption or scattering of radiation (Volume 1, Section 3.4.1). Thus the radiance of the object may vary with many other unknown parameters until it finally reaches the radiation collecting system (optics).

The optical system generates an irradiance $E(\boldsymbol{x})$ at the image plane that is proportional to the object radiance (Volume 1, Chapter 5). There is, however, not a point-to-point correspondence. Because of the limited resolution of the optical systems due to physical limitation (e.g., diffraction) or imperfections of the optical systems (various aberrations, Volume 1, Section 4.5). This blurring of the signal is known as the *point spread function* (*PSF*) of the optical system and described in the Fourier domain by the *optical transfer function*. The nonzero area of the individual sensor elements of the sensor array (or the scanning mechanism) results in a further spatial and temporal blurring of the irradiance at the image plane.

The conversion to electrical signal U adds noise and possibly further nonlinearities to the signal $g(\boldsymbol{x},t)$ that is finally measured. In a last step, the analog electrical signal is converted by an *analog-to-digital converter* (*ADC*) into digital numbers. The basic relation between continuous and digital signals is established by the sampling theorem. It describes the effects of spatial and temporal sampling on continuous signals and thus also tells us how to reconstruct a continuous signal from its samples. The discretization of the amplitudes of the signal (*quantization*) is discussed in Section 2.5.

The image formation process itself thus includes two essential steps. First, the whole image formation process blurs the signal. Second, the continuous signal at the image plane is sampled. Although both processes often happen together, they can be separated for an easier mathematical treatment.

2.4.1 Image formation

If we denote the undistorted original signal projected onto the image plane by $g'(\boldsymbol{x},t)$ then the signal $g(\boldsymbol{x},t)$ modified by the image formation process is given by

$$g(\boldsymbol{x},t) = \int_{-\infty}^{\infty} g'(\boldsymbol{x}',t')h(\boldsymbol{x},\boldsymbol{x}',t,t')\,\mathrm{d}^2x'\,\mathrm{d}t' \tag{2.22}$$

The function h is the PSF. The signal $g'(\boldsymbol{x},t)$ can be considered as the image that would be obtained by a perfect system, that is, an optical system whose PSF is a δ-distribution. Equation (2.22) says that the signal at the point $[\boldsymbol{x},t]^T$ in space and time is composed of the radiance of a whole range of points $[\boldsymbol{x}',t']^T$ nearby which linearly add up weighted with the signal h at $[\boldsymbol{x}',t']^T$. The integral can significantly be simplified if the point spread function is the same at all points (*homogeneous system* or *shift-invariant system*). Then the point spread function h depends only on the distance of $[\boldsymbol{x}',t']^T$ to $[\boldsymbol{x},t]^T$ and the integral in Eq. (2.22) reduces to the *convolution* integral

$$g(\boldsymbol{x},t) = \int_{-\infty}^{\infty} g'(\boldsymbol{x}',t')h(\boldsymbol{x}-\boldsymbol{x}',t-t')\,\mathrm{d}^2x'\,\mathrm{d}t' = (g' * h)(\boldsymbol{x},t) \tag{2.23}$$

For most optical systems the PSF is not strictly shift-invariant because the degree of blurring is increasing with the distance from the optical axis (Volume 1, Chapter 4). However, as long as the variation is continuous and does not change significantly over the width of the PSF, the convolution integral in Eq. (2.23) still describes the image formation correctly. The PSF and the system transfer function just become weakly dependent on $\boldsymbol{x}$.

2.4.2 Sampling theorem

Sampling means that all information is lost except at the grid points. Mathematically, this constitutes a multiplication of the continuous function with a function that is zero everywhere except for the grid points. This operation can be performed by multiplying the image function $g(\boldsymbol{x})$ with the sum of δ distributions located at all lattice vectors $\boldsymbol{r}_{m,n}$ Eq. (2.7). This function is called the two-dimensional δ comb, or "nail-board function." Then sampling can be expressed as

$$g_s(\boldsymbol{x}) = g(\boldsymbol{x}) \sum_{m=-\infty}^{m=\infty} \sum_{n=-\infty}^{n=\infty} \delta(\boldsymbol{x} - \boldsymbol{r}_{m,n}) \tag{2.24}$$

This equation is only valid as long as the elementary cell of the lattice contains only one point. This is the case for the square and hexagonal grids (Fig. 2.2b and c). The elementary cell of the triangular grid, however, includes two points (Fig. 2.2a). Thus for general regular lattices, p points per elementary cell must be considered. In this case, a sum of P δ combs must be considered, each shifted by the offsets $\boldsymbol{s}_p$ of the points of the elementary cells:

$$g_s(\boldsymbol{x}) = g(\boldsymbol{x}) \sum_{p=1}^{P} \sum_{m=-\infty}^{\infty} \sum_{n=-\infty}^{\infty} \delta(\boldsymbol{x} - \boldsymbol{r}_{m,n} - \boldsymbol{s}_p) \tag{2.25}$$

It is easy to extent this equation for sampling into higher-dimensional spaces and into the time domain:

$$g_s(\boldsymbol{x}) = g(\boldsymbol{x}) \sum_{p} \sum_{\boldsymbol{n}} \delta(\boldsymbol{x} - \boldsymbol{r}_{\boldsymbol{n}} - \boldsymbol{s}_p) \tag{2.26}$$

In this equation, the summation ranges have been omitted. One of the coordinates of the D-dimensional space and thus the vector $\boldsymbol{x}$ and the lattice vector $\boldsymbol{r}_{\boldsymbol{n}}$

$$\boldsymbol{r}_{\boldsymbol{n}} = [n_1 \boldsymbol{b}_1, n_2 \boldsymbol{b}_2, \ldots, n_D \boldsymbol{b}_D]^T \quad \text{with} \quad n_d \in \mathbb{Z} \tag{2.27}$$

is the time coordinate. The set of fundamental translation vectors $\{\boldsymbol{b}_1, \boldsymbol{b}_2, \ldots, \boldsymbol{b}_D\}$ form a not necessarily orthogonal base spanning the D-dimensional space.

The sampling theorem directly results from the Fourier transform of Eq. (2.26). In this equation the continuous signal $g(\boldsymbol{x})$ is multiplied by the sum of delta distributions. According to the convolution theorem of the Fourier transform (Section 3.2), this results in a convolution of the Fourier transforms of the signal and the sum of delta combs in Fourier space. The Fourier transform of a delta comb is again a delta comb (see Table 3.3). As the convolution of a signal with a delta distribution simply replicates the function value at the zero point of the delta functions, the Fourier transform of the sampled signal is simply a sum of shifted copies of the Fourier transform of the signal:

$$\hat{g}_s(\boldsymbol{k}, \nu) = \sum_p \sum_v \hat{g}(\boldsymbol{k} - \hat{\boldsymbol{r}}_v) \exp\left(-2\pi \mathrm{i} \boldsymbol{k}^T \boldsymbol{s}_p\right) \tag{2.28}$$

The phase factor $\exp(-2\pi \mathrm{i}\boldsymbol{k}^T\boldsymbol{s}_p)$ results from the shift of the points in the elementary cell by $\boldsymbol{s}_p$ according to the shift theorem of the Fourier transform (see Table 3.2). The vectors $\hat{\boldsymbol{r}}_v$

$$\hat{\boldsymbol{r}}_v = v_1\hat{\boldsymbol{b}}_1 + v_2\hat{\boldsymbol{b}}_2 + \ldots + v_D\hat{\boldsymbol{b}}_D \quad \text{with} \quad v_d \in \mathbb{Z} \tag{2.29}$$

are the points of the so-called *reciprocal lattice*. The fundamental translation vectors in the space and Fourier domain are related to each other by

$$\boldsymbol{b}_d\hat{\boldsymbol{b}}_{d'} = \delta_{d-d'} \tag{2.30}$$

This basically means that the fundamental translation vector in the Fourier domain is perpendicular to all translation vectors in the spatial domain except for the corresponding one. Furthermore the distances are reciprocally related to each other. In 3-D space, the fundamental translations of the reciprocial lattice can therefore be computed by

$$\hat{\boldsymbol{b}}_d = \frac{\boldsymbol{b}_{d+1} \times \boldsymbol{b}_{d+2}}{\boldsymbol{b}_1(\boldsymbol{b}_2 \times \boldsymbol{b}_3)} \tag{2.31}$$

The indices in the preceding equation are computed modulo 3, $\boldsymbol{b}_1(\boldsymbol{b}_2 \times \boldsymbol{b}_3)$ is the volume of the primitive elementary cell in the spatial domain. All these equations are familiar to solid state physicists or cristallographers [3]. Mathematicians know the lattice in the Fourier domain as the *dual base* or *reciprocal base* of a vector space spanned by a non-orthogonal base. For an orthogonal base, all vectors of the dual base show into the same direction as the corresponding vectors and the magnitude is given by $\left|\hat{\boldsymbol{b}}_d\right| = 1/\left|\boldsymbol{b}_d\right|$. Then often the length of the base vectors is denoted by Δx_d, and the length of the reciprocal vectors by $\Delta k_d = 1/\Delta x_d$. Thus an orthonormal base is dual to itself.

For further illustration, Fig. 2.8 shows the lattices in both domains for a triangular, square, and hexagonal grid. The figure also includes the primitive cell known as the *Wigner-Seitz cell* (Section 2.3.1 and

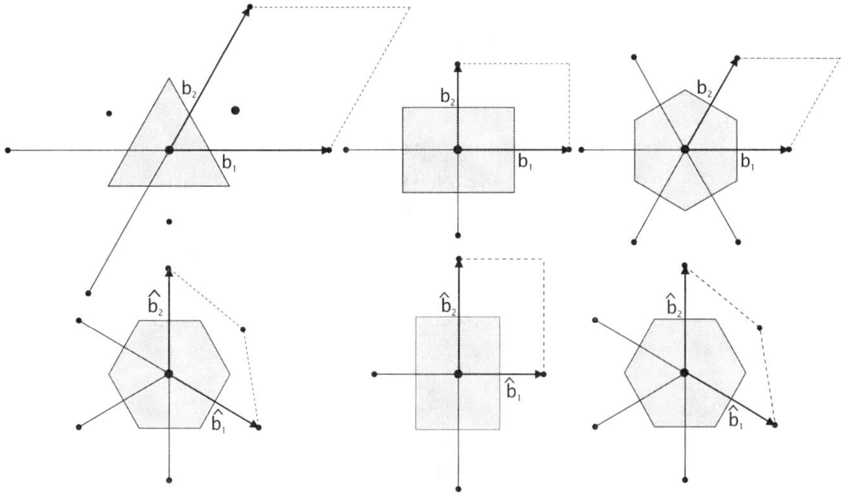

Figure 2.8: *Lattices with the fundamental translation vectors and primitive cell in the spatial and Fourier domain for a triangular (left), square (middle), and hexagonal (right) 2-D lattice.*

Fig. 2.3) and first *Brillouin zone* in the spatial and Fourier domain, respectively.

Now we can formulate the condition where we get no distortion of the signal by sampling, known as the *sampling theorem*. If the image spectrum $\hat{g}(\boldsymbol{k})$ contains such high wave numbers that parts of it overlap with the periodically repeated copies, we cannot distinguish whether the spectral amplitudes come from the original spectrum at the center or from one of the copies. In other words, a low wave number can be an alias of a high wave number and pretend an incorrect amplitude of the corresponding wave number. In order to obtain no distortions, we must avoid overlapping. A safe condition to avoid overlapping is as follows: the spectrum must be zero outside of the primitive cell of the reciprocal lattice, that is, the first Brillouin zone.

On a rectangular grid, this results in the simple condition that the maximum wave number (or frequency) at which the image spectrum is not equal to zero must be restricted to less than half of the grid constants of the reciprocal grid. Therefore the sampling theorem states:

Theorem 2.1 (Sampling Theorem) *If the spectrum $\hat{g}(\boldsymbol{k})$ of a continuous function $g(\boldsymbol{x})$ is* band-limited, *that is,*

$$\hat{g}(\boldsymbol{k}) = 0 \;\; \forall \, |k_d| \geq \Delta k_d/2 \tag{2.32}$$

then it can be reconstructed exactly from samples with a distance

$$\Delta x_d = 1/\Delta k_d \tag{2.33}$$

In other words, we will obtain a periodic structure correctly only if we take at least two samples per wavelength (or period). The maximum wave number that can be sampled without errors is called the *Nyquist* or *limiting* wave number (or frequency). In the following, we will often use dimensionless wave numbers (frequencies), which are scaled to the limiting wave number (frequency). We denote this scaling with a tilde:

$$\tilde{k}_d = \frac{k_d}{\Delta k_d/2} = 2k_d\Delta x_d \quad \text{and} \quad \tilde{\nu} = \frac{\nu}{\Delta \nu/2} = 2\nu\Delta T \tag{2.34}$$

In this scaling all the components of the wave number $\tilde{k}_d$ fall into the interval $]-1, 1[$.

2.4.3 Aliasing

If the conditions of the sampling theorem are not met, it is not only impossible to reconstruct the original signal exactly but also distortions are introduced into the signal. This effect is known in signal theory as *aliasing* or in imaging as the *Moiré effect*.

The basic problem with aliasing is that the band limitation introduced by the blurring of the image formation and the nonzero area of the sensor is generally not sufficient to avoid aliasing. This is illustrated in the following example with an "ideal" sensor.

Example 2.1: Standard sampling

An "ideal" imaging sensor will have a nonblurring optics (the PSF is the delta distribution) and a sensor array that has a 100% fill factor, that is, the sensor elements show a constant sensitivity over the whole area without gaps in-between. The PSF of such an imaging sensor is a box function with the width Δx of the sensor elements and the transfer function (TF) is a sinc function (see Table 3.4):

$$\begin{array}{ll} \text{PSF} & \dfrac{1}{\Delta x_1}\Pi(x_1/\Delta x_1)\dfrac{1}{\Delta x_2}\Pi(x_2/\Delta x_2) \\ \text{TF} & \dfrac{\sin(\pi k_1 \Delta x_1)}{\pi k_1 \Delta x_1}\dfrac{\sin(\pi k_2 \Delta x_2)}{\pi k_2 \Delta x_2} \end{array} \tag{2.35}$$

The sinc function has its first zero crossings when the argument is $\pm\pi$. This is when $k_d = \pm\Delta x_d$ or at twice the Nyquist wave number, see Eq. (2.34). At the Nyquist wave number the value of the transfer function is still $1/\sqrt{2}$. Thus standard sampling is not sufficient to avoid aliasing. The only safe way to avoid aliasing is to ensure that the imaged objects do not contain wave numbers and frequencies beyond the Nyquist limit.

2.4.4 Reconstruction from samples

The sampling theorem ensures the conditions under which we can reconstruct a continuous function from sampled points, but we still do not know how to perform the reconstruction of the continuous image from its samples, that is, the inverse operation to sampling.

Reconstruction is performed by a suitable *interpolation* of the sampled points. Again we use the most general case: a nonorthogonal primitive cell with P points. Generally, the interpolated points $g_r(\boldsymbol{x})$ are calculated from the values sampled at $\boldsymbol{r_n}+\boldsymbol{s}_p$ weighted with suitable factors that depend on the distance from the interpolated point:

$$g_r(\boldsymbol{x}) = \sum_p \sum_{\boldsymbol{n}} g_s(\boldsymbol{r_n} + \boldsymbol{s}_p) h(\boldsymbol{x} - \boldsymbol{r_n} - \boldsymbol{s}_p) \qquad (2.36)$$

Using the integral property of the δ distributions, we can substitute the sampled points on the right side by the continuous values and then interchange summation and integration:

$$\begin{aligned} g_r(\boldsymbol{x}) &= \sum_p \sum_{\boldsymbol{n}} \int_{-\infty}^{\infty} g(\boldsymbol{x}') h(\boldsymbol{x} - \boldsymbol{x}') \delta(\boldsymbol{r_n} + \boldsymbol{s}_p - \boldsymbol{x}') \, \mathrm{d}^D x' \\ &= \int_{-\infty}^{\infty} h(\boldsymbol{x} - \boldsymbol{x}') \sum_p \sum_{\boldsymbol{n}} \delta(\boldsymbol{r_n} + \boldsymbol{s}_p - \boldsymbol{x}') g(\boldsymbol{x}') \, \mathrm{d}^D x' \end{aligned}$$

The latter integral is a convolution of the weighting function h with a function that is the sum of the product of the image function g with shifted δ combs. In Fourier space, convolution is replaced by complex multiplication and vice versa. If we further consider the shift theorem and that the Fourier transform of a δ comb is again a δ comb, we finally obtain

$$\hat{g}_r(\boldsymbol{k}) = \hat{h}(\boldsymbol{k}) \sum_p \sum_{\boldsymbol{v}} \hat{g}(\boldsymbol{k} - \hat{\boldsymbol{r}}_{\boldsymbol{v}}) \exp\left(-2\pi \mathrm{i} \boldsymbol{k}^T \boldsymbol{s}_p\right) \qquad (2.37)$$

The interpolated function can only be equal to the original image if the periodically repeated image spectra are not overlapping. This is nothing new; it is exactly what the sampling theorem states. The interpolated image function is only equal to the original image function if the weighting function is one within the first Brillouin zone and zero outside, eliminating all replicated spectra and leaving the original band-limited spectrum unchanged. On a D-dimensional orthogonal lattice Eq. (2.37) becomes

$$\hat{g}_r(\boldsymbol{k}) = \hat{g}(\boldsymbol{k}) \prod_{d=1}^{D} \Pi(k_d \Delta x_d) \qquad (2.38)$$

and the ideal interpolation function h is the sinc function

$$h(\boldsymbol{x}) = \prod_{d=1}^{D} \frac{\sin(\pi x_d / \Delta x_d)}{\pi x_d / \Delta x_d} \qquad (2.39)$$

Unfortunately, this function decreases only with $1/x$ towards zero. Therefore, a correct interpolation requires a large image area; mathematically, it must be infinitely large. This condition can be weakened if we "overfill" the sampling theorem, that is, ensure that $\hat{g}(\boldsymbol{k})$ is already zero before we reach the Nyquist limit. According to Eq. (2.37), we can then choose $\hat{h}(\boldsymbol{k})$ arbitrarily in the region where $\hat{g}$ vanishes. We can use this freedom to construct an interpolation function that decreases more quickly in the spatial domain, that is, has a minimum-length interpolation mask. We can also start from a given interpolation formula. Then the deviation of its Fourier transform from a box function tells us to what extent structures will be distorted as a function of the wave number. Suitable interpolation functions will be discussed in detail in Chapter 8.

2.5 Quantization

After spatial and/or temporal sampling of a signal, the values of a signal are still continuous. As digital computers can only handle digital numbers, the continuous range of the electrical signal of the sensors must be mapped onto a limited number Q of discrete gray values:

$$[0, \infty[\xrightarrow{Q} \{g_0, g_1, \ldots, g_{Q-1}\} = G \tag{2.40}$$

This process is called *quantization*. The number of quantization levels can be chosen on the basis of two different criteria. The first criterion is based on our visual system. It should not be possible to recognize the quantization levels by our visual system. In this way, we perceive the illusion of an image with a continuous luminance.

The second criterion is application-oriented. The number of quantization levels is chosen such that the required resolution in gray values is achieved. For some applications where only the object must be distinguished from the background, for example, optical character recognition, a binary image with only two quantization levels might be sufficient. For other applications, where it is required to distinguish faint changes in the image irradiance, an 8-bit digitalization is much too coarse.

2.5.1 Equidistant quantization

Generally, image data are quantized in Q equidistant intervals Δg. Then all values between $g_q - \Delta g/2$ and $g_q + \Delta g/2$ are mapped onto the quantization level q with the value g_q:

$$q = \text{floor}\left(\frac{g - g_0}{\Delta g} + \frac{1}{2}\right) \quad \text{and} \quad g_q = g_0 + q\Delta g \tag{2.41}$$

If we assume a constant probability for all gray values, the *quantization error* can be computed immediately in the same way as the position error in Section 2.3.6, Eq. (2.13):

$$\sigma_q^2 = \frac{1}{\Delta g} \int\limits_{g_q-\Delta g/2}^{g_q+\Delta g/2} (g - g_q)^2 \, dg = \frac{1}{12}(\Delta g)^2 \qquad (2.42)$$

If g is below the lowest lower threshold, $g_0 - \Delta g/2$, or beyond the highest upper threshold, $g_{Q-1} + \Delta g/2$ as signal underflow or overflow occurs.

Normally, gray scale images are quantized into 256 gray values. Then each pixel occupies 8 bits or one byte. This pixel size is well adapted to the architecture of standard computers that can address memory bytewise. Furthermore, the resolution is good enough to give us the illusion of a continuous change in the gray values, because the relative intensity resolution of our visual system is no better than about 2%.

For demanding tasks, 8-bit quantization is not sufficient. Nowadays, high-end cameras achieve even at video rates resolutions of up to 12 bits. With so-called slow-scan cameras that read the charges out of the CCD sensor significantly slower than video rates, quantization with up to 16 bits is possible.

2.5.2 Unsigned or signed representation

Normally we think of image data as a positive quantity. Consequently, it appears natural to represent it by unsigned numbers ranging in an 8-bit representation, for example, from 0 to 255. This representation causes problems, however, as soon as we perform arithmetic operations with images. Subtracting two images is a simple example that can produce negative numbers. As negative gray values cannot be represented, they wrap around and appear as large positive values. The number −1, for example, results in the positive value 255 given that −1 modulo 256 = 255. Thus we are confronted with the problem of two different representations of gray values, as unsigned and signed 8-bit numbers. Correspondingly, we must have several versions of each algorithm, one for unsigned gray values, one for signed values, and others for mixed cases.

One solution to this problem is to handle gray values *always* as signed numbers. Unsigned numbers can be converted into signed numbers by subtracting the maximum positive number corresponding to the most significant bit of the signed representation. In an 8-bit representation, we can subtract 128 to get a signed representation. For an

n-bit representation we can write

$$q' = (q - 2^{n-1}) \mod 2^n, \quad 0 \le q < 2^n \tag{2.43}$$

Then the *mean* gray value intensity of $2^{(n-1)}$ becomes the gray value zero and gray values lower than this mean value become negative. Essentially, in this representation we regard gray values as deviations from a mean value.

This operation converts unsigned gray values to signed gray values, which can be stored and processed as such. Only for display must we convert the gray values again to unsigned values by the inverse point operation

$$q = (q' + 2^{n-1}) \mod 2^n, \quad -2^{n-1} \le q' < 2^{n-1} \tag{2.44}$$

which is the same operation as in Eq. (2.43) because all calculations are performed modulo 2^n.

2.5.3 Nonequidistant quantization

One of the significant disadvantages of linear quantization is the very low dynamical range. This is the reason why the quality of a digitized image, especially of a scene with high luminance contrast, appears inferior compared to what we see directly. In a digital image taken from such a scene with a linear image sensor, either the bright parts are overexposed or the dark parts are underexposed.

In contrast, the human visual system shows rather a logarithmic than a linear response. This means that we perceive relative luminance differences equally well. In a wide range of luminance values, we can resolve relative differences of about 2%. This threshold value depends on a number of factors, especially the spatial frequency (wavelength) of the pattern used for the experiment. At a certain wavelength the luminance resolution is optimal.

The characteristics of a machine vision sensor are quite different. The relative resolution for a linear sensor is generally given by

$$r_E = \frac{\Delta E}{E} = \frac{\Delta g}{g} \tag{2.45}$$

A dynamic range with respect to a minimum relative resolution r_{min} can then be defined as the ratio of the maximum irradiance for the maximum gray value and the minimum irradiance at which the minimum required resolution is obtained. Then for a linear sensor the dynamical range is

$$d_E = \frac{E_{\text{max}}}{E_{\text{min}}} = \frac{Q\Delta g}{\Delta g / r_{\text{min}}} = Q r_{\text{min}} \tag{2.46}$$

Although the *relative* resolution is far better than 2 % in the bright parts of the image, it is poor in the dark parts. At a gray value of 10, the luminance resolution is only 10 %. If we require a minimum resolution of 5 %, the dynamical range of an 8-bit sensor is just about 13. This means that the resolution is better than 5 % for a radiance range of only a little more than one decade.

As Eq. (2.46) shows, the relative resolution of a sensor can be increased by increasing the number of quantization levels. A better way, however, is to use a nonlinear relation between the irradiance E received by the sensor element and the resulting signal g. Two types of nonlinear relations are common, an exponential relation and a logarithmic relation.

The first relates the irradiance with an exponential law to the gray value:

$$g = cE^{\gamma} \tag{2.47}$$

The exponent γ is denoted the *gamma value*. Using $\Delta E = (1/\gamma) g \Delta g$, the relative irradiance resolution is given by

$$r = \frac{\Delta E}{E} = \frac{1}{\gamma}\frac{\Delta g}{g} \tag{2.48}$$

and the dynamical range is

$$d_E = \frac{E_{\mathrm{max}}}{E_{\mathrm{min}}} = \left(\frac{g_{\mathrm{max}}}{g_{\mathrm{min}}}\right)^{1/\gamma} = (\gamma Q r_{\mathrm{min}})^{1/\gamma} \tag{2.49}$$

Typically, $\gamma = 0.4$ is used. While a low γ factor lowers the maximal relative resolution (Eq. (2.48)), the dynamical range is considerably extended. With an 8-bit sensor the maximum relative resolution is now about 1 % and the dynamical range with a minimum resolution of 5 % is now 59.

In contrast, a sensor with a logarithmic response

$$g = c \ln E \tag{2.50}$$

shows a constant relative resolution:

$$r = \frac{\Delta E}{E} = \frac{1}{c}\Delta g \tag{2.51}$$

Consequently, the whole gray scale shows the same relative resolution:

$$d_E = \exp(Qr) \tag{2.52}$$

This means that an 8-bit sensor with a constant relative resolution $r = 5\,\%$ covers a dynamical range of about 346,000 or 5.5 decades. A detailed discussion on CMOS sensors with logarithmic response can be found in Volume 1, Chapter 8.

2.6 References

[1] Wandell, B. A., (1995). *Foundations of Vision.* Sunderland, MA: Sinauer Associates.

[2] Papoulis, A., (1991). *Probability, Random Variables, and Stochastic Processes.* New York: McGraw-Hill.

[3] Kittel, C., (1971). *Introduction to Solid State Physics.* New York: Wiley.

3 Spatial and Fourier Domain

Bernd Jähne

Interdisziplinäres Zentrum für Wissenschaftliches Rechnen (IWR)
Universität Heidelberg, Germany

3.1 Vector spaces and unitary transforms

3.1.1 Introduction

An $N \times M$ digital image has NM individual pixels that can take arbitrary values. Thus it has NM degrees of freedom. Without mentioning it explicitly, we thought of an image as being composed of individual

Handbook of Computer Vision and Applications
Volume 2
Signal Processing and Pattern Recognition

Copyright © 1999 by Academic Press
All rights of reproduction in any form reserved.
ISBN 0-12-379772-1/$30.00

pixels. Thus, we can compose each image of *basis images* ${}^{m,n}\boldsymbol{P}$ where just one pixel has a value of one while all other pixels are zero:

$$ {}^{m,n}P_{m',n'} = \delta_{m-m'}\delta_{n-n'} = \begin{cases} 1 & \text{if} \quad m = m' \wedge n = n' \\ 0 & \text{otherwise} \end{cases} \tag{3.1} $$

Any arbitrary image can then be composed of all basis images in Eq. (3.1) by

$$ \boldsymbol{G} = \sum_{m=0}^{M-1}\sum_{n=0}^{N-1} G_{m,n}\, {}^{m,n}\boldsymbol{P} \tag{3.2} $$

where $G_{m,n}$ denotes the gray value at the position $[m, n]$. The *inner product* (also known as *scalar product*) of two "vectors" in this space can be defined similarly to the scalar product for vectors and is given by

$$ (\boldsymbol{G}, \boldsymbol{H}) = \sum_{m=0}^{M-1}\sum_{n=0}^{N-1} G_{m,n}H_{m,n} \tag{3.3} $$

where the parenthesis notation $(\cdot, \cdot)$ is used for the inner product in order to distinguish it from matrix multiplication. The basis images ${}^{m,n}\boldsymbol{P}$ form an *orthonormal base* for an $N \times M$-dimensional vector space. From Eq. (3.3), we can immediately derive the *orthonormality relation* for the basis images ${}^{m,n}\boldsymbol{P}$:

$$ \sum_{m=0}^{M-1}\sum_{n=0}^{N-1} {}^{m',n'}P_{m,n}\, {}^{m'',n''}P_{m,n} = \delta_{m'-m''}\delta_{n'-n''} \tag{3.4} $$

This says that the inner product between two base images is zero if two different basis images are taken. The scalar product of a basis image with itself is one. The MN basis images thus span an $M \times N$-dimensional vector space $\mathbb{R}^{N\times M}$ over the set of real numbers.

An $M \times N$ image represents a point in the $M \times N$ vector space. If we change the coordinate system, the image remains the same but its coordinates change. This means that we just observe the same piece of information from a different point of view. All these representations are equivalent to each other and each gives a complete representation of the image. A coordinate transformation leads us from one representation to the other and back again. An important property of such a transform is that the *length* or (*magnitude*) of a vector

$$ \|\boldsymbol{G}\|_2 = (\boldsymbol{G}, \boldsymbol{G})^{1/2} \tag{3.5} $$

is not changed and that orthogonal vectors remain orthogonal. Both requirements are met if the coordinate transform preserves the inner product. A transform with this property is known as a *unitary transform*.

Physicists will be reminded of the theoretical foundations of *quantum mechanics*, which are formulated in an inner product vector space of infinite dimension, the *Hilbert space*.

3.1.2 Basic properties of unitary transforms

The two most important properties of a unitary transform are [1]:

Theorem 3.1 (Unitary transform) *Let V be a finite-dimensional inner product vector space. Let $\boldsymbol{U}$ be a one-one linear transformation of V onto itself. Then*

1. *$\boldsymbol{U}$ preserves the inner product, that is, $(\boldsymbol{G},\boldsymbol{H}) = (\boldsymbol{U}\boldsymbol{G},\boldsymbol{U}\boldsymbol{H})$, $\forall \boldsymbol{G},\boldsymbol{H} \in V$.*
2. *The inverse of $\boldsymbol{U}$, $\boldsymbol{U}^{-1}$, is the adjoin $\boldsymbol{U}^{*^T}$ of $\boldsymbol{U} : \boldsymbol{U}\boldsymbol{U}^{*^T} = \boldsymbol{I}$.*

Rotation in $\mathbb{R}^2$ or $\mathbb{R}^3$ is an example of a transform where the preservation of the length of vectors is obvious.

The product of two unitary transforms $\boldsymbol{U}_1\boldsymbol{U}_2$ is unitary. Because the identity operator $\boldsymbol{I}$ is unitary, as is the inverse of a unitary operator, the set of all unitary transforms on an inner product space is a *group* under the operation of composition. In practice, this means that we can compose/decompose complex unitary transforms of/into simpler or elementary transforms.

3.1.3 Significance of the Fourier transform (FT)

A number of unitary transforms have gained importance for digital signal processing including the cosine, sine, Hartley, slant, Haar, and Walsh transforms [2, 3, 4]. But none of these transforms matches in importance with the *Fourier transform*.

The uniqueness of the Fourier transform is related to a property expressed by the *shift theorem*. If a signal is shifted in space, its Fourier transform does not change in amplitude but only in phase, that is, it is multiplied with a complex phase factor. Mathematically this means that all base functions of the Fourier transform are *eigenvectors* of the *shift operator* $S(s)$:

$$S(s)\exp(-2\pi ikx) = \exp(-2\pi iks)\exp(-2\pi ikx) \tag{3.6}$$

The phase factor $\exp(-2\pi iks)$ is the *eigenvalue* and the complex exponentials $\exp(-2\pi ikx)$ are the base functions of the Fourier transform spanning the infinite-dimensional vector space of the square integrable complex-valued functions over $\mathbb{R}$. For all other transforms, various base functions are mixed with each other if one base function is shifted. Therefore the base functions of all these transforms are not an eigenvector of the shift operator.

The base functions of the Fourier space are the eigenfunctions of *all linear shift-invariant operators* or *convolution* operators. If an operator is shift-invariant, the result is the same at whichever point in space it is applied. Therefore a periodic function such as the complex exponential is not changed in period and does not become an aperiodic function. If a convolution operator is applied to a periodic signal, only its phase and amplitude change, which can be expressed by a complex factor. This complex factor is the (wave number dependent) eigenvalue or transfer function of the convolution operator.

At this point, it is also obvious why the Fourier transform is complex valued. For a real periodic function, that is, a pure sine or cosine function, it is not possible to formulate a shift theorem, as both functions are required to express a shift. The complex exponential $\exp(\mathrm{i}kx) = \cos kx + \mathrm{i}\sin kx$ contains both functions and a shift by a distance s can simply be expressed by the complex phase factor $\exp(\mathrm{i}ks)$.

Each base function and thus each point in the Fourier domain contains two pieces of information: the *amplitude* and the *phase*, that is, relative position, of a periodic structure. Given this composition, we ask whether the phase or the amplitude contains the more significant information on the structure in the image, or whether both are of equal importance.

In order to answer this question, we perform a simple experiment. Figure 3.1 shows two images of a street close to Heidelberg University taken at different times. Both images are Fourier transformed and then the phase and amplitude are interchanged as illustrated in Fig. 3.1c, d. The result of this interchange is surprising. It is the phase that determines the content of an image. Both images look somewhat patchy but the significant information is preserved.

From this experiment, we can conclude that the phase of the Fourier transform carries essential information about the image structure. The amplitude alone implies only *that* such a periodic structure is contained in the image but not *where*.

3.1.4 Dynamical range and resolution of the FT

While in most cases it is sufficient to represent an image with rather few quantization levels, for example, 256 values or one byte per pixel, the Fourier transform of an image needs a much larger dynamical range. Typically, we observe a strong decrease of the Fourier components with the magnitude of the wave number, so that a dynamical range of at least 3–4 decades is required. Consequently, at least 16-bit integers or 32-bit floating-point numbers are necessary to represent an image in the Fourier domain without significant rounding errors.

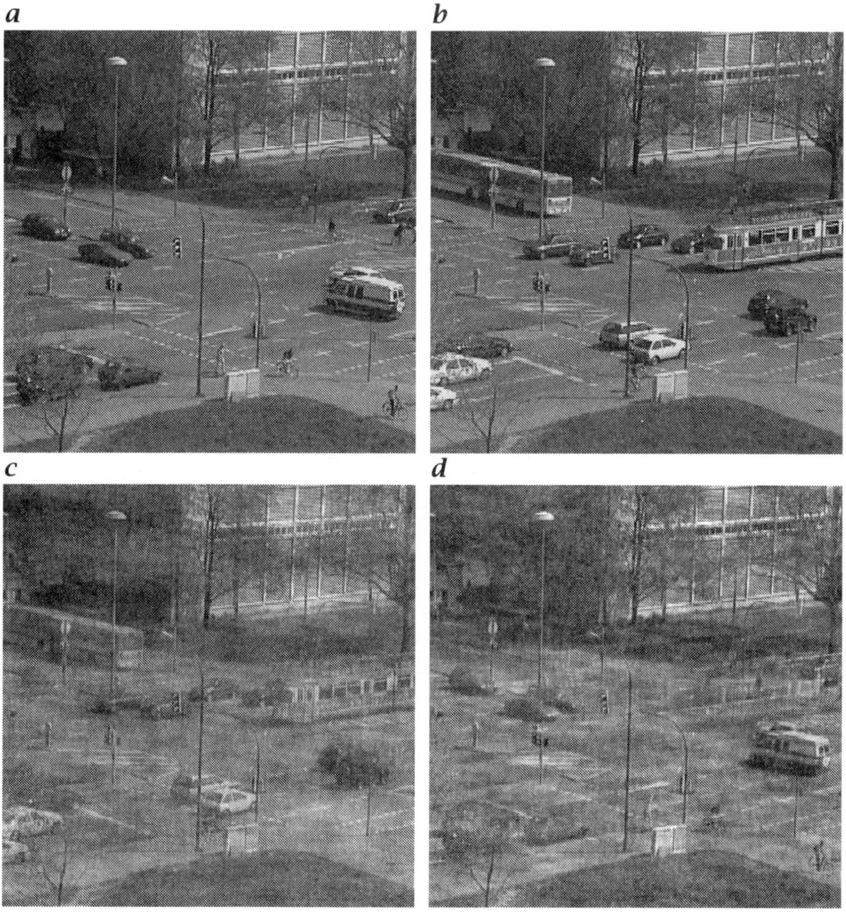

Figure 3.1: *Importance of phase and amplitude in Fourier space for the image content: **a**, **b** two images of a traffic scene taken at different times; **c** composite image using the phase from image **b** and the amplitude from image **a**; **d** composite image using the phase from image **a** and the amplitude from image **b**.*

The reason for this behavior is not the insignificance of high wave numbers in images. If we simply omitted them, we would blur the image. The decrease is caused by the fact that the *relative* resolution is increasing with the wave number. With the discrete Fourier transform (see Section 3.3), the Fourier transform contains only wave numbers that fit exactly integer times into the image:

$$k_{vp} = \frac{v}{d_p} \qquad (3.7)$$

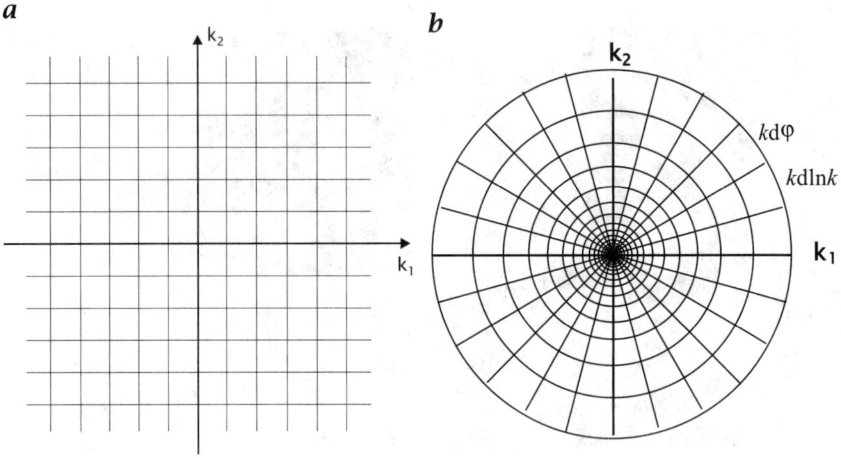

Figure 3.2: Tessellation of the 2-D Fourier domain into: ***a*** *Cartesian; and* ***b*** *logarithmic-polar lattices.*

where $\boldsymbol{d} = [d_1, \ldots, d_D]^T$ is the size of the D-dimensional signal. Therefore the absolute wave number resolution $\Delta k = 1/\Delta x$ is constant, equivalent to a Cartesian tessellation of the Fourier space (Fig. 3.2a). Thus the smallest wave number ($v = 1$) has a wavelength of the size of the image, the next coarse wave number a wavelength of half the size of the image. This is a very low resolution for large wavelengths. The smaller the wavelength, the better the resolution.

This ever increasing *relative resolution* is not natural. We can, for example, easily see the difference of 10 cm in 1 m, but not in 1 km. It is more natural to think of relative resolutions, because we are better able to distinguish relative distance differences than absolute ones. If we apply this concept to the Fourier domain, it seems to be more natural to tessellate the Fourier domain in intervals increasing with the wave number, a *log-polar coordinate system*, as illustrated in Fig. 3.2b. Such a lattice partitions the space into angular and ln$k$ intervals. Thus, the cell area is proportional to k^2. In order to preserve the norm, or—physically spoken—the energy, of the signal in this representation, the increase in the area of the cells proportional to k^2 must be considered:

$$\int_{-\infty}^{\infty} |\hat{g}(\boldsymbol{k})|^2 \, dk_1 \, dk_2 = \int_{-\infty}^{\infty} k^2 |\hat{g}(\boldsymbol{k})|^2 \, d\ln k \, d\varphi \tag{3.8}$$

Thus, the *power spectrum* $|\hat{g}(\boldsymbol{k})|^2$ in the log-polar representation is multiplied by k^2 and falls off much less steep than in the Cartesian representation. The representation in a log-polar coordinate system allows a much better evaluation of the directions of the spatial structures and of the smaller scales. Moreover a change in scale or orientation just causes a shift of the signal in the log-polar representation. Therefore it has gained importance in representation object for shape analysis (Volume 3, Chapter 8).

3.2 Continuous Fourier transform (FT)

In this section, we give a brief survey of the continuous Fourier transform and we point out the properties that are most important for signal processing. Extensive and excellent reviews of the Fourier transform are given by Bracewell [5], Poularikas [4, Chapter 2] or Madisetti and Williams [6, Chapter 1]

3.2.1 One-dimensional FT

Definition 3.1 (1-D FT) *If* $g(x) : \mathbb{R} \mapsto \mathbb{C}$ *is a square integrable function, that is,*

$$\int_{-\infty}^{\infty} |g(x)| \, \mathrm{d}x < \infty \tag{3.9}$$

then the Fourier transform *of* $g(x)$, $\hat{g}(k)$ *is given by*

$$\hat{g}(k) = \int_{-\infty}^{\infty} g(x) \exp(-2\pi \mathrm{i} kx) \, \mathrm{d}x \tag{3.10}$$

The Fourier transform maps the vector space of absolutely integrable functions onto itself. The inverse Fourier transform *of* $\hat{g}(k)$ *results in the original function* $g(x)$*:*

$$g(x) = \int_{-\infty}^{\infty} \hat{g}(k) \exp(2\pi \mathrm{i} kx) \, \mathrm{d}k \tag{3.11}$$

It is convenient to use an operator notation for the Fourier transform. With this notation, the Fourier transform and its inverse are simply written as

$$\hat{g}(k) = \mathcal{F} g(x) \quad \text{and} \quad g(x) = \mathcal{F}^{-1} \hat{g}(k) \tag{3.12}$$

A function and its transform, a *Fourier transform pair* is simply denoted by $g(x) \Longleftrightarrow \hat{g}(k)$.

In Eqs. (3.10) and (3.11) a definition of the wave number *without* the factor 2π is used, $k = 1/\lambda$, in contrast to the notation often used in

***Table 3.1:** Comparison of the continuous Fourier transform (FT), the Fourier series (FS), the infinite discrete Fourier transform (IDFT), and the discrete Fourier transform (DFT) in one dimension*

Type	Forward transform	Backward transform
FT: $\mathbb{R} \Longleftrightarrow \mathbb{R}$	$\int\limits_{-\infty}^{\infty} g(x) \exp(-2\pi \mathrm{i} kx) \, \mathrm{d}x$	$\int\limits_{-\infty}^{\infty} \hat{g}(k) \exp(2\pi \mathrm{i} kx) \, \mathrm{d}k$
FS: $[0, \Delta x] \Longleftrightarrow \mathbb{Z}$	$\frac{1}{\Delta x} \int\limits_{0}^{\Delta x} g(x) \exp\left(-2\pi \mathrm{i} \frac{vx}{\Delta x}\right) \mathrm{d}x$	$\sum\limits_{v=-\infty}^{\infty} \hat{g}_v \exp\left(2\pi \mathrm{i} \frac{vx}{\Delta x}\right)$
IDFT: $\mathbb{Z} \Longleftrightarrow [0, 1/\Delta x]$	$\sum\limits_{n=-\infty}^{\infty} g_n \exp(-2\pi \mathrm{i} n \Delta x k)$	$\Delta x \int\limits_{0}^{1/\Delta x} \hat{g}(k) \exp(2\pi \mathrm{i} n \Delta x k) \, \mathrm{d}k$
DFT: $\mathbb{N}_N \Longleftrightarrow \mathbb{N}_N$	$\frac{1}{N} \sum\limits_{n=0}^{N-1} g_n \exp\left(-2\pi \mathrm{i} \frac{vn}{N}\right)$	$\sum\limits_{v=0}^{N-1} \hat{g}_v \exp\left(2\pi \mathrm{i} \frac{vn}{N}\right)$

physics with $k' = 2\pi/\lambda$. For signal processing, the first notion is more useful, because k directly gives the number of periods per unit length.

With the notation that includes the factor 2π in the wave number, two forms of the Fourier transform are common, the asymmetric form

$$
\begin{aligned}
\hat{g}(k') &= \int\limits_{-\infty}^{\infty} g(x) \exp(-\mathrm{i} k' x) \, \mathrm{d}x \\
g(x) &= \frac{1}{2\pi} \int\limits_{-\infty}^{\infty} \hat{g}(k) \exp(\mathrm{i} k' x) \, \mathrm{d}k
\end{aligned}
\tag{3.13}
$$

and the symmetric form

$$
\begin{aligned}
\hat{g}(k') &= \frac{1}{\sqrt{2\pi}} \int\limits_{-\infty}^{\infty} g(x) \exp(-\mathrm{i} k' x) \, \mathrm{d}x \\
g(x) &= \frac{1}{\sqrt{2\pi}} \int\limits_{-\infty}^{\infty} \hat{g}(k') \exp(\mathrm{i} k' x) \, \mathrm{d}k'
\end{aligned}
\tag{3.14}
$$

As the definition of the Fourier transform takes the simplest form in Eqs. (3.10) and (3.11), most other relations and equations also become simpler than with the definitions in Eqs. (3.13) and (3.14). In addition, the relation of the continuous Fourier transform with the discrete Fourier transform (Section 3.3) and the Fourier series (Table 3.1) becomes more straightforward.

Because all three versions of the Fourier transform are in common use, it is likely to get wrong factors in Fourier transform pairs. The rules for conversion of Fourier transform pairs between the three versions can directly be inferred from the definitions and are summarized here:

$$\begin{array}{lrcl} k \text{ without } 2\pi, \text{ Eq. (3.10)} & g(x) & \Longleftrightarrow & \hat{g}(k) \\ k' \text{ with } 2\pi, \text{ Eq. (3.13)} & g(x) & \Longleftrightarrow & \hat{g}(k'/2\pi) \\ k' \text{ with } 2\pi, \text{ Eq. (3.14)} & g(x/\sqrt{(}2\pi)) & \Longleftrightarrow & \hat{g}(k'/\sqrt{(}2\pi)) \end{array} \tag{3.15}$$

3.2.2 Multidimensional FT

The Fourier transform can easily be extended to multidimensional signals.

Definition 3.2 (Multidimensional FT) *If $g(\boldsymbol{x}) : \mathbb{R}^D \mapsto \mathbb{C}$ is a square integrable function, that is,*

$$\int_{-\infty}^{\infty} |g(\boldsymbol{x})| \, \mathrm{d}^D x < \infty \tag{3.16}$$

then the Fourier transform *of $g(\boldsymbol{x})$, $\hat{g}(\boldsymbol{k})$ is given by*

$$\hat{g}(\boldsymbol{k}) = \int_{-\infty}^{\infty} g(\boldsymbol{x}) \exp\left(-2\pi \mathrm{i} \boldsymbol{k}^T \boldsymbol{x}\right) \, \mathrm{d}^D x \tag{3.17}$$

and the inverse Fourier transform *by*

$$g(\boldsymbol{x}) = \int_{-\infty}^{\infty} \hat{g}(\boldsymbol{k}) \exp\left(2\pi \mathrm{i} \boldsymbol{k}^T \boldsymbol{x}\right) \, \mathrm{d}^D k \tag{3.18}$$

The scalar product in the exponent of the kernel $\boldsymbol{x}^T \boldsymbol{k}$ makes the kernel of the Fourier transform separable, that is, it can be written as

$$\exp\left(-2\pi \mathrm{i} \boldsymbol{k}^T \boldsymbol{x}\right) = \prod_{d=1}^{D} \exp(-\mathrm{i} k_d x_d) \tag{3.19}$$

3.2.3 Basic properties

For reference, the basic properties of the Fourier transform are summarized in Table 3.2. An excellent review of the Fourier transform and its applications are given by [5]. Here we will point out some of the properties of the FT that are most significant for multidimensional signal processing.

Table 3.2: *Summary of the properties of the continuous D-dimensional Fourier transform. $g(\boldsymbol{x})$ and $h(\boldsymbol{x})$ are complex-valued functions, the Fourier transforms of which, $\hat{g}(\boldsymbol{k})$ and $\hat{h}(\boldsymbol{k})$, do exist; s is a real and a and b are complex constants; $\mathbf{A}$ and $\boldsymbol{U}$ are $D \times D$ matrices, $\boldsymbol{U}$ is unitary ($\boldsymbol{U}^{-1} = \boldsymbol{U}^T$, see Section 3.1.2).*

Property	Spatial domain	Fourier domain
Linearity	$ag(\boldsymbol{x}) + bh(\boldsymbol{x})$	$a\hat{g}(\boldsymbol{k}) + b\hat{h}(\boldsymbol{k})$
Similarity	$g(s\boldsymbol{x})$	$\hat{g}(\boldsymbol{k}/s)/\lvert s\rvert$
Similarity	$g(\mathbf{A}\boldsymbol{x})$	$\hat{g}\left((\mathbf{A}^{-1})^T\mathbf{k}\right)/\lvert\mathbf{A}\rvert$
Rotation	$g(\boldsymbol{U}\boldsymbol{x})$	$\hat{g}(\boldsymbol{U}\boldsymbol{k})$
Separability	$\prod_{d=1}^{D} g(x_d)$	$\prod_{d=1}^{D} \hat{g}(k_d)$
Shift in x space	$g(\boldsymbol{x} - \boldsymbol{x}_0)$	$\exp(-2\pi \mathrm{i}\boldsymbol{k}\boldsymbol{x}_0)\hat{g}(\boldsymbol{k})$
Shift in k space	$\exp(2\pi \mathrm{i}\boldsymbol{k}_0\boldsymbol{x})g(\boldsymbol{x})$	$\hat{g}(\boldsymbol{k} - \boldsymbol{k}_0)$
Differentiation in x space	$\dfrac{\partial g(\boldsymbol{x})}{\partial x_p}$	$2\pi \mathrm{i}k_p\hat{g}(\boldsymbol{k})$
Differentiation in k space	$-2\pi \mathrm{i}x_p g(\boldsymbol{x})$	$\dfrac{\partial \hat{g}(\boldsymbol{k})}{\partial k_p}$
Definite integral	$\int_{-\infty}^{\infty} g(\boldsymbol{x}')\,\mathrm{d}^D x'$	$\hat{g}(\mathbf{0})$
Moments	$\int_{-\infty}^{\infty} x_p^m x_q^n g(\boldsymbol{x})\,\mathrm{d}^D x$	$\left(\dfrac{1}{-2\pi\mathrm{i}}\right)^{m+n}\left(\dfrac{\partial^m \hat{g}(\boldsymbol{k})}{\partial k_p^m}\dfrac{\partial^n \hat{g}(\boldsymbol{k})}{\partial k_q^n}\right)\Bigg\rvert_{\mathbf{0}}$
Convolution	$\int_{-\infty}^{\infty} h(\boldsymbol{x}')g(\boldsymbol{x} - \boldsymbol{x}')\,\mathrm{d}^D x'$	$\hat{h}(\boldsymbol{k})\hat{g}(\boldsymbol{k})$
Multiplication	$h(\boldsymbol{x})g(\boldsymbol{x})$	$\int_{-\infty}^{\infty} \hat{h}(\boldsymbol{k}')\hat{g}(\boldsymbol{k} - \boldsymbol{k}')\,\mathrm{d}^D k'$
Finite difference	$g(\boldsymbol{x} + V\boldsymbol{x}_0) - g(\boldsymbol{x} - V\boldsymbol{x}_0)$	$2\mathrm{i}\sin(2\pi\boldsymbol{x}_0\boldsymbol{k})$
Modulation	$\cos(2\pi\boldsymbol{k}_0\boldsymbol{x})g(\boldsymbol{x})$	$(\hat{g}(\boldsymbol{k} - \boldsymbol{k}_0) + \hat{g}(\boldsymbol{k} + \boldsymbol{k}_0))/2$
Spatial correlation	$\int_{-\infty}^{\infty} g(\boldsymbol{x}')h(\boldsymbol{x}' + \boldsymbol{x})\,\mathrm{d}^D x'$	$\hat{g}(\boldsymbol{k})\hat{h}^*(\boldsymbol{k})$
Inner product	$\int_{-\infty}^{\infty} g(\boldsymbol{x})h^*(\boldsymbol{x})\,\mathrm{d}^D x$	$\int_{-\infty}^{\infty} \hat{g}(\boldsymbol{k})\hat{h}^*(\boldsymbol{k})\,\mathrm{d}^D k$

Symmetries. Four types of symmetries are important for the Fourier transform:

$$\begin{array}{ll} \text{even} & g(-\boldsymbol{x}) = g(\boldsymbol{x}), \\ \text{odd} & g(-\boldsymbol{x}) = -g(\boldsymbol{x}), \\ \text{Hermitian} & g(-\boldsymbol{x}) = g^*(\boldsymbol{x}), \\ \text{anti-Hermitian} & g(-\boldsymbol{x}) = -g^*(\boldsymbol{x}) \end{array} \tag{3.20}$$

Any function $g(\boldsymbol{x})$ can be split into its even and odd parts by

$${}^e g(\boldsymbol{x}) = \frac{g(\boldsymbol{x}) + g(-\boldsymbol{x})}{2} \quad \text{and} \quad {}^o g(\boldsymbol{x}) = \frac{g(\boldsymbol{x}) - g(-\boldsymbol{x})}{2} \tag{3.21}$$

With this partition, the Fourier transform can be parted into a cosine and a sine transform:

$$\hat{g}(\boldsymbol{k}) = 2\int_0^\infty {}^e g(\boldsymbol{x}) \cos(2\pi \boldsymbol{k}^T \boldsymbol{x})\, \mathrm{d}^D x + 2\mathrm{i}\int_0^\infty {}^o g(\boldsymbol{x}) \sin(2\pi \boldsymbol{k}^T \boldsymbol{x})\, \mathrm{d}^D x \tag{3.22}$$

It follows that if a function is even or odd, its transform is also even or odd. The full symmetry results are:

$$\begin{array}{lcl} \text{real} & \Longleftrightarrow & \text{Hermitian} \\ \text{real and even} & \Longleftrightarrow & \text{real and even} \\ \text{real and odd} & \Longleftrightarrow & \text{imaginary and odd} \\ \text{imaginary} & \Longleftrightarrow & \text{anti-Hermitian} \\ \text{imaginary and even} & \Longleftrightarrow & \text{imaginary and even} \\ \text{imaginary and odd} & \Longleftrightarrow & \text{real and odd} \\ \text{Hermitian} & \Longleftrightarrow & \text{real} \\ \text{anti-Hermitian} & \Longleftrightarrow & \text{imaginary} \\ \text{even} & \Longleftrightarrow & \text{even} \\ \text{odd} & \Longleftrightarrow & \text{odd} \end{array} \tag{3.23}$$

Separability. As the kernel of the Fourier transform (Eq. (3.19)) is separable, the transform of a separable function is also separable:

$$\prod_{d=1}^{D} g(x_d) \Longleftrightarrow \prod_{d=1}^{D} \hat{g}(k_d) \tag{3.24}$$

This property is essential to compute transforms of multidimensional functions efficiently from 1-D transforms because many of them are separable.

Convolution. Convolution is one of the most important operations for signal processing. It is defined by

$$(h * g)(\boldsymbol{x}) = \int_{-\infty}^{\infty} g(\boldsymbol{x}')h(\boldsymbol{x} - \boldsymbol{x}')\, \mathrm{d}^D x' \tag{3.25}$$

In signal processing, the function $h(\mathbf{x})$ is normally zero except for a small area around zero and is often denoted as the *convolution mask*. Thus, the convolution with $h(\mathbf{x})$ results in a new function $g'(\mathbf{x})$ whose values are a kind of weighted average of $g(\mathbf{x})$ in a small neighborhood around $\mathbf{x}$. It changes the signal in a defined way, that is, makes it smoother etc. Therefore it is also called a *filter operation*. The *convolution theorem* states:

Theorem 3.2 (Convolution) *If $g(\mathbf{x})$ has the Fourier transform $\hat{g}(\mathbf{k})$ and $h(\mathbf{x})$ has the Fourier transform $\hat{h}(\mathbf{k})$ and if the convolution integral (Eq. (3.25)) exists, then it has the Fourier transform $\hat{h}(\mathbf{k})\hat{g}(\mathbf{k})$.*

Thus, convolution of two functions means multiplication of their transforms. Likewise convolution of two functions in the Fourier domain means multiplication in the space domain. The simplicity of convolution in the Fourier space stems from the fact that the base functions of the Fourier domain, the complex exponentials $\exp\left(2\pi \mathrm{i}\mathbf{k}^T\mathbf{x}\right)$, are joint eigenfunctions of all convolution operators. This means that these functions are not changed by a convolution operator except for the multiplication by a factor.

From the convolution theorem, the following properties are immediately evident. Convolution is

$$\begin{array}{ll} \text{commutative} & h * g = g * h, \\ \text{associative} & h_1 * (h_2 * g) = (h_1 * h_2) * g, \\ \text{distributive over addition} & (h_1 + h_2) * g = h_1 * g + h_2 * g \end{array} \qquad (3.26)$$

In order to grasp the importance of these properties of convolution, we note that two operations that do not look so at first glance, are also convolution operations: the shift operation and all derivative operators. This can immediately be seen from the shift and derivative theorems (Table 3.2 and [5, Chapters 5 and 6]).

In both cases the Fourier transform is just multiplied by a complex factor. The convolution mask for a shift operation S is a shifted δ distribution:

$$S(\mathbf{s})g(\mathbf{x}) = \delta(\mathbf{x} - \mathbf{s}) * g(\mathbf{x}) \qquad (3.27)$$

The transform of the first derivative operator in x_1 direction is $2\pi \mathrm{i}k_1$. The corresponding inverse Fourier transform of $2\pi \mathrm{i}k_1$, that is, the convolution mask, is no longer an ordinary function ($2\pi \mathrm{i}k_1$ is not absolutely integrable) but the derivative of the δ distribution:

$$2\pi \mathrm{i}k_1 \quad \Longleftrightarrow \quad \delta'(x) = \frac{\mathrm{d}\delta(x)}{\mathrm{d}x} = \lim_{a \to 0} \frac{\mathrm{d}}{\mathrm{d}x}\left(\frac{\exp(-\pi x^2/a^2)}{a}\right) \qquad (3.28)$$

Of course, the derivation of the δ distribution exists—as all properties of distributions—only in the sense as a limit of a sequence of functions as shown in the preceding equation.

With the knowledge of derivative and shift operators being convolution operators, we can use the properties summarized in Eq. (3.26) to draw some important conclusions. As any convolution operator commutes with the shift operator, convolution is a shiftinvariant operation. Furthermore, we can first differentiate a signal and then perform a convolution operation or vice versa and obtain the same result.

The properties in Eq. (3.26) are essential for an effective computation of convolution operations as discussed in Section 5.6. As we already discussed qualitatively in Section 3.1.3, the convolution operation is a linear shiftinvariant operator. As the base functions of the Fourier domain are the common eigenvectors of all linear and shiftinvariant operators, the convolution simplifies to a complex multiplication of the transforms.

Central-limit theorem. The central-limit theorem is mostly known for its importance in the theory of probability [7]. It also plays, however, an important role for signal processing as it is a rigorous statement of the tendency that cascaded convolution tends to approach Gaussian form ($\propto \exp(-ax^2)$). Because the Fourier transform of the Gaussian is also a Gaussian (Table 3.3), this means that *both* the Fourier transform (the transfer function) and the mask of a convolution approach Gaussian shape. Thus the central-limit theorem is central to the unique role of the Gaussian function for signal processing. The sufficient conditions under which the central limit theorem is valid can be formulated in different ways. We use here the conditions from [7] and express the theorem with respect to convolution.

Theorem 3.3 (Central-limit theorem) *Given N functions $h_n(x)$ with zero mean $\int_{-\infty}^{\infty} h_n(x)\,\mathrm{d}x$ and the variance $\sigma_n^2 = \int_{-\infty}^{\infty} x^2 h_n(x)\,\mathrm{d}x$ with $z = x/\sigma$, $\sigma^2 = \sum_{n=1}^{N} \sigma_n^2$ then*

$$h = \lim_{N\to\infty} h_1 * h_2 * \ldots * h_N \propto \exp(-z^2/2) \tag{3.29}$$

provided that

$$\lim_{N\to\infty} \sum_{n=1}^{N} \sigma_n^2 \to \infty \tag{3.30}$$

and there exists a number $\alpha > 2$ and a finite constant c such that

$$\int_{-\infty}^{\infty} x^\alpha h_n(x)\,\mathrm{d}x < c < \infty \quad \forall n \tag{3.31}$$

The theorem is of much practical importance because—especially if h is smooth—the Gaussian shape is approximated sufficiently accurate already for values of n as low as 5.

Smoothness and compactness. The smoother a function is, the more compact is its Fourier transform. This general rule can be formulated more quantitatively if we express the smoothness by the number of derivatives that are continuous and the compactness by the asymptotic behavior for large values of k. Then we can state: If a function $g(x)$ and its first $n-1$ derivatives are continuous, its Fourier transform decreases at least as rapidly as $|k|^{-(n+1)}$ for large k, that is, $\lim_{|k|\to\infty} |k|^n g(k) = 0$.

As simple examples we can take the box and triangle functions (see next section and Table 3.4). The box function is discontinuous ($n = 0$), its Fourier transform, the sinc function decays with $|k|^{-1}$. In contrast, the triangle function is continuous, but its first derivative is discontinuous. Therefore its Fourier transform, the sinc^2 function decays steeper with $|k|^{-2}$. In order to include also impulsive functions (δ distributions) in this relation, we note that the derivative of a discontinous function becomes impulsive. Therefore, we can state: If the nth derivative of a function becomes impulsive, the function's Fourier transform decays with $|k|^{-n}$.

The relation between smoothness and compactness is an extension of reciprocity between the spatial and Fourier domain. What is strongly localized in one domain is widely extended in the other and vice versa.

Uncertainty relation. This general law of reciprocity finds another quantitative expression in the classical *uncertainty relation* or the *bandwidth-duration product*. This theorem relates the mean square width of a function and its Fourier transform. The mean square width $(\Delta x)^2$ is defined as

$$(\Delta x)^2 = \frac{\int\limits_{-\infty}^{\infty} x^2 \left|g(x)\right|^2}{\int\limits_{-\infty}^{\infty} \left|g(x)\right|^2} - \left(\frac{\int\limits_{-\infty}^{\infty} x \left|g(x)\right|^2}{\int\limits_{-\infty}^{\infty} \left|g(x)\right|^2}\right)^2 \tag{3.32}$$

It is essentially the variance of $\left|g(x)\right|^2$, a measure of the width of the distribution of the "energy" of the signal. The uncertainty relation states:

Theorem 3.4 (Uncertainty relation) *The product of the variance of* $\left|g(x)\right|^2$, $(\Delta x)^2$, *and of the variance of* $\left|\hat{g}(k)\right|^2$, $(\Delta k)^2$, *cannot be smaller*

Table 3.3: *Functions and distributions that are invariant under the Fourier transform; the table contains 1-D and multidimensional functions with the dimension D*

Space domain	Fourier domain
Gauss, $\exp\left(-\pi \boldsymbol{x}^T \boldsymbol{x}\right)$	Gauss, $\exp\left(-\pi \boldsymbol{k}^T \boldsymbol{k}\right)$
$\operatorname{sech}(\pi x) = \dfrac{1}{\exp(\pi x) + \exp(-\pi x)}$	$\operatorname{sech}(\pi k) = \dfrac{1}{\exp(\pi k) + \exp(-\pi k)}$
Pole, $\lvert\boldsymbol{x}\rvert^{-D/2}$	Pole, $\lvert\boldsymbol{k}\rvert^{-D/2}$
δ comb, $\text{III}(x/\Delta x) = \sum\limits_{n=-\infty}^{\infty} \delta(x - n\Delta x)$	δ comb, $\text{III}(k\Delta x) = \sum\limits_{v=-\infty}^{\infty} \delta(k - v/\Delta x)$

than $1/4\pi$*:*

$$\Delta x \Delta k \geq \frac{1}{4\pi} \tag{3.33}$$

The relations between compactness and smoothness and the uncertainty relation give some basic guidance for the design of linear filter (convolution) operators (Chapter 6).

3.2.4 Important transform pairs

In this section we summarize the most important *Fourier transform pairs* for signal processing. These pairs together with the basic properties of the Fourier transform discussed in the previous section are also very helpful to compute the Fourier transforms of even complex functions.

It is well known that the Fourier transform of a Gaussian function is again a Gaussian function with reciprocal variance:

$$\exp\left(\frac{-\pi x^2}{a^2}\right) \quad \Longleftrightarrow \quad \exp\left(\frac{-\pi k^2}{a^{-2}}\right) \tag{3.34}$$

But it is less well known that there are other functions that are invariant under the Fourier transform (Table 3.3). Each of these functions has a special meaning for the Fourier transform. The δ-comb function III is the basis for the sampling theorem and establishes the relation between the lattice in the spatial domain and the *reciprocal* lattice in the Fourier domain. The functions with a pole at the origin, $|x|^{D/2}$ in a D-dimensional space, are the limiting signal form for which the integral over the square of the function diverges (physically spoken, the total energy of a signal just becomes infinite).

Table 3.4: *Important transform pairs for the continuous Fourier transform; 2-D and 3-D functions are marked by † and ‡, respectively; for pictorial of Fourier transform pairs, see [4, 5]*

Space domain	Fourier domain
$\delta(x)$	1
Derivative of delta, $\delta'(x)$	$2\pi\mathrm{i}k$
$\cos(2\pi k_0 x)$	$\mathrm{II}(k/k_0) = \frac{1}{2}\left(\delta(k-k_0)+\delta(k+k_0)\right)$
$\sin(2\pi k_0 x)$	$\mathrm{I_I}(k/k_0) = \frac{\mathrm{i}}{2}\left(\delta(k-k_0)-\delta(k+k_0)\right)$
Box $\Pi(x) = \begin{cases} 1 & \lvert x\rvert < 1/2 \\ 0 & \lvert x\rvert \ge 1/2 \end{cases}$	$\mathrm{sinc}(k) = \dfrac{\sin(\pi k)}{\pi k}$
Triangle, $\Lambda(x) = \begin{cases} 1-\lvert x\rvert & \lvert x\rvert < 1 \\ 0 & \lvert x\rvert \ge 1 \end{cases}$	$\mathrm{sinc}^2(k) = \dfrac{\sin^2(\pi k)}{\pi^2 k^2}$
Disk†, $\Pi\left(\dfrac{\lvert\boldsymbol{x}\rvert}{2}\right)$	Bessel, $\dfrac{J_1(2\pi\lvert\boldsymbol{k}\rvert)}{\lvert\boldsymbol{k}\rvert}$
Ball‡, $\Pi\left(\dfrac{\lvert\boldsymbol{x}\rvert}{2}\right)$	$\dfrac{\sin(2\pi k) - 2\pi k\cos(2\pi k)}{2\pi^2 k^3}$
Half circle, $\left(1-k^2\right)^{1/2}\Pi\left(\frac{k}{2}\right)$	Bessel, $\dfrac{J_1(2\pi x)}{2x}$
$\exp(-\lvert x\rvert)$	Lorentzian, $\dfrac{2}{1+(2\pi k)^2}$
$\mathrm{sgn}(x) = \begin{cases} 1 & x \ge 0 \\ -1 & x < 0 \end{cases}$	$\dfrac{-\mathrm{i}}{\pi k}$
Unit step, $U(x) = \begin{cases} 1 & x \ge 0 \\ 0 & x < 0 \end{cases}$	$\dfrac{1}{2}\delta(k) - \dfrac{\mathrm{i}}{2\pi k}$
Relaxation, $\exp(-\lvert x\rvert)U(x)$	$\dfrac{1}{1+2\pi\mathrm{i}k}$
$\tanh(\pi x) = \dfrac{\exp(\pi x)-\exp(-\pi x)}{\exp(\pi x)+\exp(-\pi x)}$	cosech, $\dfrac{-2\mathrm{i}}{\exp(2\pi k)-\exp(-2\pi k)}$

Table 3.4 summarizes the most important other Fourier transform pairs. It includes a number of special functions that are often used in signal processing. The table contains various impulse forms, among others the Gaussian (in Table 3.3), the *box function* Π, the *triangle function* Λ, and the *Lorentzian function*. In the table important transition functions such as the Heaviside *unit step function*, U, the *sign function*, sgn, and the *hyperbolic tangent*, tanh, function are also defined.

3.3 The discrete Fourier transform (DFT)

3.3.1 One-dimensional DFT

Definition 3.3 (1-D DFT) *If* $\boldsymbol{g}$ *is an* N*-dimensional complex-valued vector,*

$$\boldsymbol{g} = [g_0, g_1, \ldots, g_{N-1}]^T \tag{3.35}$$

then the discrete Fourier transform of $\boldsymbol{g}$, $\hat{\boldsymbol{g}}$ *is defined as*

$$\hat{g}_v = \frac{1}{\sqrt{N}} \sum_{n=0}^{N-1} g_n \exp\left(-\frac{2\pi \mathrm{i} n v}{N}\right), \quad 0 \le v < N \tag{3.36}$$

The DFT maps the vector space of N-dimensional complex-valued vectors onto itself. The index v denotes how often the wavelength of the corresponding discrete exponential $\exp(-2\pi \mathrm{i} n v/N)$ with the amplitude $\hat{g}_v$ fits into the interval $[0, N]$.

The back transformation is given by

$$g_n = \frac{1}{\sqrt{N}} \sum_{v=0}^{N-1} \hat{g}_v \exp\left(\frac{2\pi \mathrm{i} n v}{N}\right), \quad 0 \le n < N \tag{3.37}$$

We can consider the DFT as the inner product of the vector $\boldsymbol{g}$ with a set of M orthonormal basis vectors, the *kernel* of the DFT:

$$\boldsymbol{b}_v = \frac{1}{\sqrt{N}} \left[1, W_N^v, W_N^{2v}, \ldots, W_N^{(N-1)v}\right]^T \text{ with } W_N = \exp\left(\frac{2\pi \mathrm{i}}{N}\right) \tag{3.38}$$

Using the base vectors $\boldsymbol{b}_v$, the DFT reduces to

$$\hat{g}_v = \boldsymbol{b}^{*T} \boldsymbol{g} \quad \text{or} \quad \hat{\boldsymbol{g}} = \boldsymbol{F}\boldsymbol{g} \quad \text{with} \quad \boldsymbol{F} = \begin{bmatrix} \boldsymbol{b}_0^{*T} \\ \boldsymbol{b}_1^{*T} \\ \ldots \\ \boldsymbol{b}_{N-1}^{*T} \end{bmatrix} \tag{3.39}$$

This means that the coefficient $\hat{g}_v$ in the Fourier space is obtained by projecting the vector $\boldsymbol{g}$ onto the basis vector $\boldsymbol{b}_v$. The N basis vectors $\boldsymbol{b}_v$ form an *orthonormal base* of the vector space:

$$\boldsymbol{b}_v^{*T} \boldsymbol{b}_v' = \delta_{v-v'} = \begin{cases} 1 & \text{if} \quad v = v' \\ 0 & \text{otherwise} \end{cases} \tag{3.40}$$

The real and imaginary parts of the basis vectors are sampled sine and cosine functions of different wavelengths (Fig. 3.3) with a characteristic periodicity:

$$\exp\left(\frac{2\pi \mathrm{i} n + pN}{N}\right) = \exp\left(\frac{2\pi \mathrm{i} n}{N}\right), \quad \forall p \in \mathbb{Z} \tag{3.41}$$

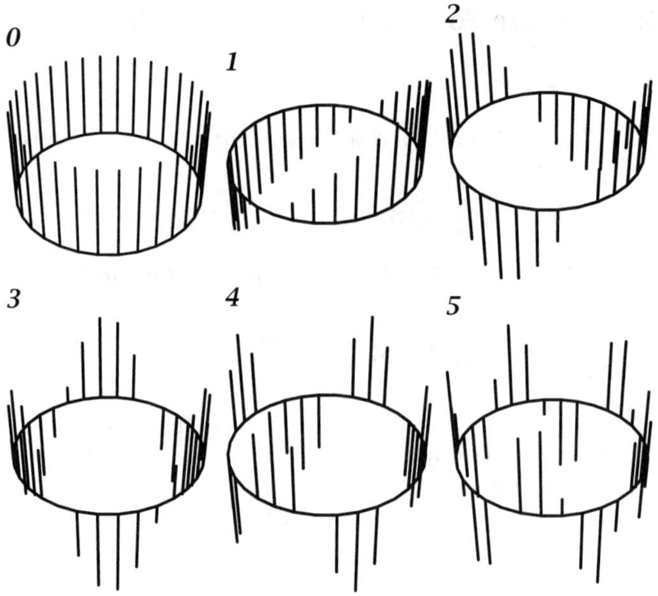

Figure 3.3: *The first six basis functions (cosine part) of the DFT for N = 32 in a cyclic representation on the unit circle.*

The basis vector $\boldsymbol{b}_0$ is a constant real vector.

With this relation and Eqs. (3.36) and (3.37) the DFT and the inverse DFT extend the vectors $\hat{\boldsymbol{g}}$ and $\boldsymbol{g}$, respectively, periodically over the whole space:

$$\begin{array}{lll} \text{Fourier domain} & \hat{g}_{v+pN} = \hat{g}_v, & \forall p \in \mathbb{Z} \\ \text{space domain} & g_{n+pN} = g_n & \forall p \in \mathbb{Z} \end{array} \tag{3.42}$$

This periodicity of the DFT gives rise to an interesting geometric interpretation. According to Eq. (3.42) the border points g_{M-1} and $g_M = g_0$ are neighboring points. Thus it is natural to draw the points of the vector not on a finite line but on a unit circle, or *Fourier ring* (Fig. 3.3).

With the double periodicity of the DFT, it does not matter which range of N indices we chose. The most natural choice of wave numbers is $v \in [-N/2, N/2-1]$, N even. With this index range the 1-D DFT and its inverse are defined as

$$\hat{g}_v = \frac{1}{\sqrt{N}} \sum_{n=0}^{N-1} g_n W_N^{-nv} \Longleftrightarrow g_n = \frac{1}{\sqrt{N}} \sum_{v=-N/2}^{N/2-1} \hat{g}_v W_N^{nv} \tag{3.43}$$

Then the wave numbers are restricted to values that meet the sampling theorem (Section 2.4.2), that is, are sampled at least two times per period. Note that the exponentials $\boldsymbol{b}_{N-v} = \boldsymbol{b}_{-v} = \boldsymbol{b}_v^*$ according to Eqs. (3.38) and (3.41).

As in the continuous case further variants for the definition of the DFT exist that differ by the factors applied to the forward and backward transform. Here again a symmetric definition was chosen that has the benefit that the base vectors become unit vectors. Other variants use the factor $1/N$ either with the forward or backward transform and not, as we did $1/\sqrt{N}$ with both transforms. The definition with the factor $1/N$ has the advantage that the zero coefficient of the DFT, $\hat{g}_0 = (1/N)\sum_{n=0}^{N-1} g_n$, directly gives the mean value of the sequence. The various definitions in use are problematic because they cause a lot of confusion with factors in DFT pairs and DFT theorems.

3.3.2 Multidimensional DFT

As with the continuous FT (Section 3.2.2), it is easy to extend the DFT to higher dimensions. In order to simplify the equations, we use the abbreviation for the complex exponentials already used in Eq. (3.38)

$$W_N = \exp\left(\frac{2\pi i}{N}\right) \quad \text{with} \quad W_N^{n+pN} = W_N^n,\ W_N^{-n} = W_N^{*n} \tag{3.44}$$

In two dimensions the DFT operates on $M \times N$ matrices.

Definition 3.4 (2-D DFT) *The 2-D DFT:* $\mathbb{C}^{M\times N} \mapsto \mathbb{C}^{M\times N}$ *is defined as*

$$\hat{G}_{u,v} = \frac{1}{\sqrt{MN}} \sum_{m=0}^{M-1} \left(\sum_{n=0}^{N-1} G_{m,n} W_N^{-nv} \right) W_M^{-mu} \tag{3.45}$$

and the inverse DFT as

$$G_{mn} = \frac{1}{\sqrt{MN}} \sum_{u=0}^{M-1}\sum_{v=0}^{N-1} \hat{G}_{u,v} W_M^{mu} W_N^{nv} \tag{3.46}$$

As in the 1-D case, the DFT expands a matrix into a set of NM orthonormal basis matrices $\boldsymbol{B}_{u,v}$, which span the $N \times M$-dimensional vector space over the field of complex numbers:

$$\boldsymbol{B}_{u,v} = \frac{1}{\sqrt{MN}} W_N^{-nv} W_M^{-mu} = \frac{1}{\sqrt{MN}} \boldsymbol{b}_u \boldsymbol{b}_v^T \tag{3.47}$$

In this equation, the basis matrices are expressed as an *outer product* of the column and the row vector that form the basis vectors of the 1-D DFT. Thus as in the continuous case, the kernel of the multidimensional DFTs are *separable*.

As in the 1-D case (Section 3.3.1), the definition of the 2-D DFT implies a periodic extension in both domains beyond the original matrices into the whole 2-D space.

3.3.3 Basic properties

The theorems of the 2-D DFT are summarized in Table 3.5. They are very similar to the corresponding theorems of the continuous Fourier transform, which are listed in Table 3.2 for a D-dimensional FT. As in Section 3.2.3, we discuss some properties that are of importance for signal processing in more detail.

Symmetry. The DFT shows the same symmetries as the FT (Eq. (3.20)). In the definition for even and odd functions $g(-\boldsymbol{x}) = \pm g(\boldsymbol{x})$ only the continuous functions must be replaced by the corresponding vectors $g_{-n} = \pm g_n$ or matrices $G_{-m,-n} = \pm G_{m,n}$. Note that because of the periodicity of the DFT, these symmetry relations can also be written as

$$G_{-m,-n} = \pm G_{m,n} \equiv G_{M-m,N-n} = \pm G_{m,n} \tag{3.48}$$

for even (+ sign) and odd (– sign) functions. This is equivalent to shifting the symmetry center from the origin to the point $[M/2, N/2]^T$.

The study of symmetries is important for practical purposes. Careful consideration of symmetry allows storage space to be saved and algorithms to speed up. Such a case is real-valued images. Real-valued images can be stored in half of the space as complex-valued images. From the symmetry relations Eq. (3.23) we can conclude that real-valued functions exhibit a Hermitian DFT:

$$G_{mn} = G^*_{mn} \quad \Longleftrightarrow \quad \hat{G}_{M-u,N-v} = \hat{G}^*_{uv} \tag{3.49}$$

The complex-valued DFT of real-valued matrices is, therefore, completely determined by the values in one half-space. The other half-space is obtained by mirroring at the symmetry center $(M/2, N/2)$. Consequently, we need the same amount of storage space for the DFT of a real image as for the image itself, as only half of the complex spectrum needs to be stored.

In two and higher dimensions, matters are slightly more complex. The spectrum of a real-valued image is determined completely by the values in one half-space, but there are many ways to select the half-space. This means that all except for one component of the wave number can be negative, but that we cannot distinguish between $\boldsymbol{k}$ and $-\boldsymbol{k}$, that is, between wave numbers that differ only in sign. Therefore we can again represent the Fourier transform of real-valued images in a half-space where only one component of the wave number includes negative values. For proper representation of the spectra with zero values of this component in the middle of the image, it is necessary to interchange the upper (positive) and lower (negative) parts of the image as illustrated in Fig. 3.4.

For real-valued image sequences, again we need only a half-space to represent the spectrum. Physically, it makes the most sense to choose

***Table 3.5:** Summary of the properties of the 2-D DFT; **G** and **H** are complex-valued M × N matrices, **Ĝ** and **Ĥ** their Fourier transforms, and a and b complex-valued constants; for proofs see Poularikas [4], Cooley and Tukey [8]*

Property	Space domain	Wave number domain
Mean	$\frac{1}{MN}\sum_{m=0}^{M-1}\sum_{n=0}^{N-1} G_{mn}$	$\hat{G}_{0,0}/\sqrt{MN}$
Linearity	$a\boldsymbol{G} + b\boldsymbol{H}$	$a\hat{\boldsymbol{G}} + b\hat{\boldsymbol{H}}$
Shifting	$G_{m-m',n-n'}$	$W_M^{-m'u} W_N^{-n'v} \hat{G}_{uv}$
Modulation	$W_M^{u'm} W_N^{v'n} G_{m,n}$	$\hat{G}_{u-u',v-v'}$
Finite differences	$(G_{m+1,n} - G_{m-1,n})/2$ $(G_{m,n+1} - G_{m,n-1})/2$	$\mathrm{i}\sin(2\pi u/M)\hat{G}_{uv}$ $\mathrm{i}\sin(2\pi v/N)\hat{G}_{uv}$
Spatial stretching	$G_{Pm,Qn}$	$\hat{G}_{uv}/(\sqrt{PQ})$
Frequency stretching	$G_{m,n}/(\sqrt{PQ})$	$\hat{G}_{Pu,Qv}$
Spatial sampling	$G_{m/P,n/Q}$	$\frac{1}{\sqrt{PQ}}\sum_{p=0}^{P-1}\sum_{q=0}^{Q-1}\hat{G}_{u+pM/P,v+qN/Q}$
Frequency sampling	$\frac{1}{\sqrt{PQ}}\sum_{p=0}^{P-1}\sum_{q=0}^{Q-1} G_{m+pM/P,n+qN/Q}$	$\hat{G}_{pu,qv}$
Convolution	$\sum_{m'=0}^{M-1}\sum_{n'=0}^{N-1} H_{m'n'} G_{m-m',n-n'}$	$\sqrt{MN}\hat{H}_{uv}\hat{G}_{uv}$
Multiplication	$\sqrt{MN} G_{mn} H_{mn}$	$\sum_{u'=0}^{M-1}\sum_{v'=0}^{N-1} H_{u'v'} G_{u-u',v-v'}$
Spatial correlation	$\sum_{m'=0}^{M-1}\sum_{n'=0}^{N-1} H_{m'n'} G_{m+m',n+n'}$	$\sqrt{N}\hat{H}_{uv}\hat{G}^*_{uv}$
Inner product	$\sum_{m=0}^{M-1}\sum_{n=0}^{N-1} G_{mn} H^*_{mn}$	$\sum_{u=0}^{M-1}\sum_{v=0}^{N-1} \hat{G}_{uv}\hat{H}^*_{uv}$
Norm	$\sum_{m=0}^{M-1}\sum_{n=0}^{N-1} \lvert G_{mn}\rvert^2$	$\sum_{u=0}^{M-1}\sum_{v=0}^{N-1} \lvert\hat{G}_{uv}\rvert^2$

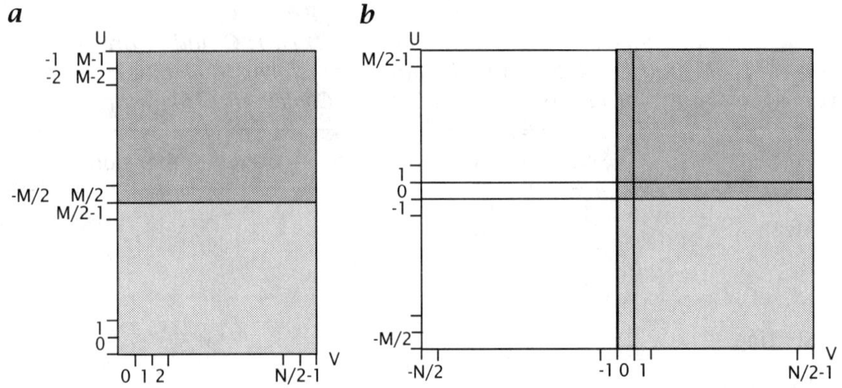

Figure 3.4: ***a*** *Half-space as computed by an in-place Fourier transform algorithm; the wave number zero is in the upper left corner.* ***b*** *FT with the missing half appended and remapped so that the wave number zero is in the center.*

the half-space that contains positive frequencies. In contrast to a single image, we obtain the full wave number space. Now we can identify the spatially identical wave numbers $\boldsymbol{k}$ and $-\boldsymbol{k}$ as structures propagating in opposite directions.

Convolution. One- and two-dimensional discrete convolution are defined by

$$g'_n = \sum_{n'=0}^{N-1} h_{n'} g_{n-n'}, \quad G'_{m,n} = \sum_{m'=0}^{M-1} \sum_{n'=0}^{N-1} H_{m'n'} G_{m-m',n-n'} \tag{3.50}$$

The *convolution theorem* states:

Theorem 3.5 (Discrete convolution) *If* $\boldsymbol{g}$ *(*$\boldsymbol{G}$*) has the Fourier transform* $\hat{\boldsymbol{g}}$ *(*$\hat{\boldsymbol{G}}$*) and* $\boldsymbol{h}$ *(*$\boldsymbol{H}$*) has the Fourier transform* $\hat{\boldsymbol{h}}$ *(*$\hat{\boldsymbol{H}}$*), then* $\boldsymbol{h} * \boldsymbol{g}$ *(*$\boldsymbol{H} * \boldsymbol{G}$*) has the Fourier transform* $\sqrt{N}\hat{\boldsymbol{h}}\hat{\boldsymbol{g}}$ *(*$\sqrt{MN}\hat{\boldsymbol{H}}\hat{\boldsymbol{G}}$*).*

Thus, also in the discrete case convolution of two functions means multiplication of their transforms. This is true because the *shift theorem* is still valid, which ensures that the eigenfunctions of all convolution operators are the basis functions $\boldsymbol{b}_v$ of the Fourier transform.

Convolution for arbitrary dimensional signals is also

$$\begin{array}{ll} \text{commutative} & \boldsymbol{h} * \boldsymbol{g} = \boldsymbol{g} * \boldsymbol{h}, \\ \text{associative} & \boldsymbol{h}_1 * (\boldsymbol{h}_2 * \boldsymbol{g}) = (\boldsymbol{h}_1 * \boldsymbol{h}_2) * \boldsymbol{g}, \\ \text{distributive over addition} & (\boldsymbol{h}_1 + \boldsymbol{h}_2) * \boldsymbol{g} = \boldsymbol{h}_1 * \boldsymbol{g} + \boldsymbol{h}_2 * \boldsymbol{g} \end{array} \tag{3.51}$$

These equations show only the 1-D case.

3.4 Fast Fourier transform algorithms (FFT)

Without an effective algorithm to calculate the discrete Fourier transform, it would not be possible to apply the FT to images and other higher-dimensional signals. Computed directly after Eq. (3.45), the FT is prohibitively expensive. Not counting the calculations of the cosine and sine functions in the kernel, which can be precalculated and stored in a lookup table, the FT of an $N \times N$ image needs in total N^4 complex multiplications and $N^2(N^2 - 1)$ complex additions. Thus it is an operation of $O(N^4)$ and the urgent need arises to minimize the number of computations by finding a suitable fast algorithm. Indeed, the fast Fourier transform (FFT) algorithm first published by Cooley and Tukey [8] is the classical example of a fast algorithm. The strategies discussed in the following for various types of FFTs are also helpful for other fast algorithms.

3.4.1 One-dimensional FFT algorithms

Divide-and-conquer strategy. First we consider fast algorithms for the 1-D DFT, commonly abbreviated as *FFT* algorithms for *fast Fourier transform*. We assume that the dimension of the vector is a power of two, $N = 2^l$. Because the direct solution according to Eq. (3.36) is $O(N^2)$, it seems useful to use the divide-and-conquer strategy. If we can split the transformation into two parts with vectors the size of $N/2$, we reduce the number of operations from N^2 to $2(N/2)^2 = N^2/2$. This procedure can be applied recursively $\mathrm{ld}\, N$ times, until we obtain a vector of size 1, whose DFT is trivial because nothing at all has to be done. Of course, this procedure works only if the partitioning is possible and the number of additional operations to put the split transforms together is not of a higher order than $O(N)$.

The result of the recursive partitioning is puzzling. We do not have to perform a DFT at all. The whole algorithm to compute the DFT has been shifted over to the recursive composition stages. If these compositions are of the order $O(N)$, the computation of the DFT totals to $O(N\, \mathrm{ld}\, N)$ because $\mathrm{ld}\, N$ compositions have to be performed. In comparison to the direct solution of the order $O(N^2)$, this is a tremendous saving in the number of operations. For $N = 2^{10}(1024)$, the number is reduced by a factor of about 100. In the following we detail the radix-2 decimation in time FFT algorithm. The name of this algorithm comes from the partition into two parts in the spatial (time) domain. We will first show that the decomposition is possible, that it implies a reordering of the elements of the vector (bitreversal), and then discuss the central operation of the composition stage, the butterfly operation.

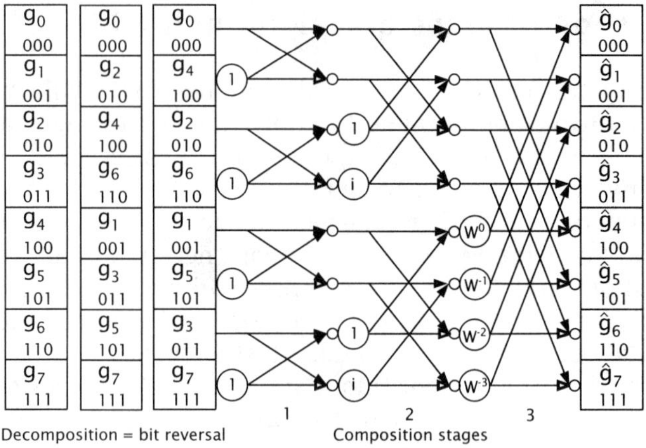

Figure 3.5: *Signal flow diagram of the radix-2 decimation-in-time Fourier transform algorithm for N = 8; for further explanation, see text.*

Decomposition. We separate the vector into two vectors by choosing the even and odd elements separately:

$$\begin{aligned} \hat{g}_v &= \sum_{n=0}^{N-1} g_n W_N^{-nv} = \sum_{n=0}^{N/2-1} g_{2n} W_N^{-2nv} + \sum_{n=0}^{N/2-1} g_{2n+1} W_N^{-(2n+1)v} \\ &= \sum_{n=0}^{N/2-1} g_{2n} W_{N/2}^{-nv} + W_N^{-v} \sum_{n=0}^{N/2-1} g_{2n+1} W_{N/2}^{-nv} \end{aligned} \tag{3.52}$$

where we used the identity $W_N^2 = W_{N/2}$ (see Eq. (3.44)). Both sums constitute a DFT with $N' = N/2$. The second sum is multiplied by a phase factor that depends only on the wave number v. This phase factor results from the shift theorem, as the odd elements are shifted one place to the left. The operations necessary to combine the partial Fourier transforms are just one complex multiplication and addition, that is, $O(N^1)$. Thus a fast Fourier transform algorithm is possible with the divide-and-conquer strategy.

Bitreversal. The left half of the diagram in Fig. 3.5 shows the decimation steps. The first column contains the original vector, the second the result of the first decomposition step into two vectors. The vectors with the even and odd elements are put in the lower and upper halves, respectively. This decomposition is continued until we obtain vectors with one element.

As a result of the recursive decomposition, the elements of the vectors are arranged in a new order. Except for the rearrangement of the vector elements, no computations are required. We can easily understand the new ordering scheme if we represent the indices of the vector by dual numbers. In the first decomposition step we reorder the elements according to the least significant bit, first the even elements (least significant bit is zero), then the odd elements (least significant bit is one). With each further decomposition step, the bit that governs sorting is shifted one place to the left. In the end, we obtain a sorting in which the ordering of the bits is reversed. The element with the index $1 = 001_2$, for example, will be at the position $4 = 100_2$, and vice versa. Consequently, the chain of decomposition steps can be performed with one operation by interchanging the elements at the normal and bit-reversed positions. This reordering is known as *bit reversal.*

Butterfly operation. In the second step of the FFT algorithm, we have to compose the decomposed vectors again according to Eq. (3.52). In order to see how the composition of the N values works, we study the values for v from 0 to $N/2-1$ and $N/2$ to $N-1$ separately. The partial transformations over the even and odd sampling points are abbreviated by ${}^e\hat{g}_v$ and ${}^o\hat{g}_v$, respectively. For the first part, we can just take the partitioning as expressed in Eq. (3.52). For the second part, $v' = v + N/2$, only the phase factor changes its sign:

$$W_N^{-(v+N/2)} = W_N^{-v} W_N^{-(N/2)} = -W_N^{-v}$$

Making use of this symmetry we can write

$$\left.\begin{array}{rcl} \hat{g}_v & = & {}^e\hat{g}_v + W_N^{-v}\,{}^o\hat{g}_v \\ \hat{g}_{v+N/2} & = & {}^e\hat{g}_v - W_N^{-v}\,{}^o\hat{g}_v \end{array}\right\} \quad 0 \le v < N/2 \tag{3.53}$$

The Fourier transforms for the indices v and $v + N/2$ differ only by the sign of the second term. Thus for the composition of *two* terms we need only *one* complex multiplication.

In the first composition step, we compose vectors with just two elements. Thus we need only the phase factor for $v = 0$, which is equal to one. Consequently, the first composition step has a very simple form:

$$\begin{array}{rcl} \hat{g}_0 & = & {}^e\hat{g}_0 + {}^o\hat{g}_0 \\ \hat{g}_{0+N/2} = \hat{g}_1 & = & {}^o\hat{g}_0 - {}^o\hat{g}_0 \end{array} \tag{3.54}$$

This is an inplace operation because $\hat{g}_0$ and $\hat{g}_1$ take the place of ${}^e\hat{g}_0$ and ${}^o\hat{g}_0$, respectively. Further steps on the right side of the signal flow diagram in Fig. 3.5 show the stepwise composition to vectors of double the size. The composition to the 2-D vectors is given by Eq. (3.54). The operations are pictured by vertices and nodes. The nodes represent storage stages or arithmetic units. Large open circles denote a

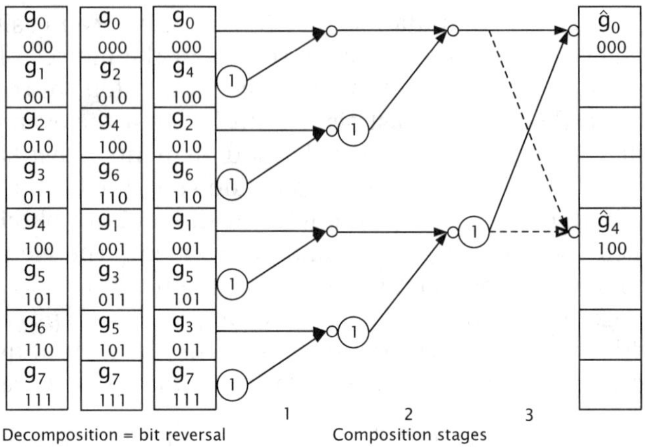

Figure 3.6: *Signal flow path for the calculation of $\hat{g}_0$ and $\hat{g}_4$ with the decimation-in-time FFT algorithm for an 8-dimensional vector.*

multiplication by the factor written into the circle. Small open circles are adder stages. The figures from all incoming vertices are added up; those with an open arrowhead are subtracted.

The elementary operation of the FFT algorithm involves only two nodes. The lower node is multiplied with a phase factor. The sum and difference of the two values are then transferred to the upper and lower node, respectively. Because of the crossover of the signal paths, this operation is denoted as a *butterfly operation.*

We gain further insight into the FFT algorithm if we trace back the calculation of a single element. Figure 3.6 shows the signal paths for $\hat{g}_0$ and $\hat{g}_4$. For each level we go back the number of knots contributing to the calculation doubles. In the last stage all elements are involved. The signal path for $\hat{g}_0$ and $\hat{g}_4$ are identical but for the last stage, thus nicely demonstrating the efficiency of the FFT algorithm.

All phase factors in the signal path for $\hat{g}_0$ are one. As expected from Eq. (3.36), $\hat{g}_0$ contains the sum of all the elements of the vector $\boldsymbol{g}$,

$$\hat{g}_0 = [(g_0 + g_4) + (g_2 + g_6)] + [(g_1 + g_5) + (g_3 + g_7)]$$

while for $\hat{g}_4$ the addition is replaced by a subtraction:

$$\hat{g}_4 = [(g_0 + g_4) + (g_2 + g_6)] - [(g_1 + g_5) + (g_3 + g_7)]$$

Computational costs. After this detailed discussion of the algorithm, we can now estimate the necessary number of operations. At each stage of the composition, $N/2$ complex multiplications and N complex additions are carried out. In total we need $N/2\,\mathrm{ld}N$ complex multiplications and $N\,\mathrm{ld}N$ complex additions. A more extensive analysis shows that we can save even more multiplications. In the first two composition steps only trivial multiplications by 1 or i occur (compare Fig. 3.6). For further steps the number of trivial multiplications decreases by a factor of two. If our algorithm could avoid all the trivial multiplications, the number of multiplications would be reduced to $(N/2)(\mathrm{ld}\,N - 3)$.

Using the FFT algorithm, the discrete Fourier transform can no longer be regarded as a computationally expensive operation, as only a few operations are necessary per element of the vector. For a vector with 512 elements, only 3 complex multiplications and 8 complex additions, corresponding to 12 real multiplications and 24 real additions, need to be computed per pixel.

Radix-4 FFT. The radix-2 algorithm discussed in the preceding is only one of the many divide-and-conquer strategies to speed up Fourier transform. It belongs to the class of *Cooley-Tukey algorithms* [9]. Instead of parting the vector into two pieces, we could have chosen any other partition, say P Q-dimensional vectors, if $N = PQ$.

An often-used partition is the *radix-4 FFT algorithm* decomposing the vector into four components:

$$\begin{aligned}\hat{g}_v &= \sum_{n=0}^{N/4-1} g_{4n} W_N^{-4nv} + W_N^{-v} \sum_{n=0}^{N/4-1} g_{4n+1} W_N^{-4nv} \\ &+ W_N^{-2v} \sum_{n=0}^{N/4-1} g_{4n+2} W_N^{-4nv} + W_N^{-3v} \sum_{n=0}^{N/4-1} g_{4n+3} W_N^{-4nv}\end{aligned}$$

For simpler equations, we will use similar abbreviations as for the radix-2 algorithm and denote the partial transformations by ${}^0\hat{g}, \cdots, {}^3\hat{g}$. Making use of the symmetry of W_N^v, the transformations into quarters of each of the vectors is given by

$$\begin{aligned}\hat{g}_v &= {}^0\hat{g}_v + W_N^{-v}\,{}^1\hat{g}_v + W_N^{-2v}\,{}^2\hat{g}_v + W_N^{-3v}\,{}^3\hat{g}_v \\ \hat{g}_{v+N/4} &= {}^0\hat{g}_v - \mathrm{i}W_N^{-v}\,{}^1\hat{g}_v - W_N^{-2v}\,{}^2\hat{g}_u + \mathrm{i}W_N^{-3v}\,{}^3\hat{g}_v \\ \hat{g}_{v+N/2} &= {}^0\hat{g}_v - W_N^{-v}\,{}^1\hat{g}_v + W_N^{-2v}\,{}^2\hat{g}_v - W_N^{-3v}\,{}^3\hat{g}_v \\ \hat{g}_{v+3N/4} &= {}^0\hat{g}_v + \mathrm{i}W_N^{-v}\,{}^1\hat{g}_v - W_N^{-2v}\,{}^2\hat{g}_v - \mathrm{i}W_N^{-3v}\,{}^3\hat{g}_v\end{aligned}$$

or, in matrix notation,

$$\begin{bmatrix}\hat{g}_v \\ \hat{g}_{v+N/4} \\ \hat{g}_{v+N/2} \\ \hat{g}_{v+3N/4}\end{bmatrix} = \begin{bmatrix}1 & 1 & 1 & 1 \\ 1 & -\mathrm{i} & -1 & \mathrm{i} \\ 1 & -1 & 1 & -1 \\ 1 & \mathrm{i} & -1 & -\mathrm{i}\end{bmatrix}\begin{bmatrix}{}^0\hat{g}_v \\ W_N^{-v}\,{}^1\hat{g}_v \\ W_N^{-2v}\,{}^2\hat{g}_v \\ W_N^{-3v}\,{}^3\hat{g}_v\end{bmatrix}$$

To compose 4-tuple elements of the vector, 12 complex additions and 3 complex multiplications are needed. We can reduce the number of additions further by decomposing the matrix into two simpler matrices:

$$\begin{bmatrix} \hat{g}_v \\ \hat{g}_{v+N/4} \\ \hat{g}_{v+N/2} \\ \hat{g}_{v+3N/4} \end{bmatrix} = \begin{bmatrix} 1 & 0 & 1 & 0 \\ 0 & 1 & 0 & -\mathrm{i} \\ 1 & 0 & -1 & 0 \\ 0 & 1 & 0 & \mathrm{i} \end{bmatrix} \begin{bmatrix} 1 & 0 & 1 & 0 \\ 1 & 0 & -1 & 0 \\ 0 & 1 & 0 & 1 \\ 0 & 1 & 0 & -1 \end{bmatrix} \begin{bmatrix} {}^0\hat{g}_v \\ W_N^{-v}\,{}^1\hat{g}_v \\ W_N^{-2v}\,{}^2\hat{g}_v \\ W_N^{-3v}\,{}^3\hat{g}_v \end{bmatrix}$$

The first matrix multiplication yields intermediate results that can be used for several operations in the second stage. In this way, we save four additions. We can apply this decomposition recursively $\log_4 N$ times. As for the radix-2 algorithm, only trivial multiplications in the first composition step are needed. At all other stages, multiplications occur for 3/4 of the points. In total, $3/4N(\log_4 N - 1) = 3/8N(\mathrm{ld}N - 2)$ complex multiplications and $2N\log_4 N = N\mathrm{ld}N$ complex additions are necessary for the radix-4 algorithm. While the number of additions remains equal, 25 % fewer multiplications are required than for the radix-2 algorithm.

Decimation-in-frequency FFT. The *decimation-in-frequency FFT* applys a different partition strategy known as a Sande-Tukey algorithm. This time, we break the N-dimensional input vector into $N/2$ first and $N/2$ second components. This partition breaks the output vector into its even and odd components:

$$\hat{g}_v = \sum_{n=0}^{N/2-1} g_n W_N^{-nv} + (-1)^v \sum_{n=N/2}^{N-1} g_n W_N^{-nv} \tag{3.55}$$

The two partial sums are not yet a DFT because the kernel is still wrong. However, they become correct DFTs if we compute the even and odd elements of the Fourier transform separately. Then

$$\begin{aligned} \hat{g}_{2v} &= \sum_{n=0}^{N/2-1} (g_n + g_{n+N/2}) W_{N/2}^{-nv} \\ \hat{g}_{2v+1} &= \sum_{n=0}^{N/2-1} W_N^{-n} (g_n - g_{n+N/2}) W_{N/2}^{-nv} \end{aligned} \tag{3.56}$$

The basic composition step of the DIF algorithms therefore is slightly different from Eq. (3.53):

$$\begin{aligned} {}^e g_n &= (g_n + g_{n+N/2}) \\ {}^o g_n &= W_N^{-n} (g_n - g_{n+N/2}) \end{aligned} \tag{3.57}$$

yet the same number of operations are required as for the decimation-in-time (DIT) butterfly.

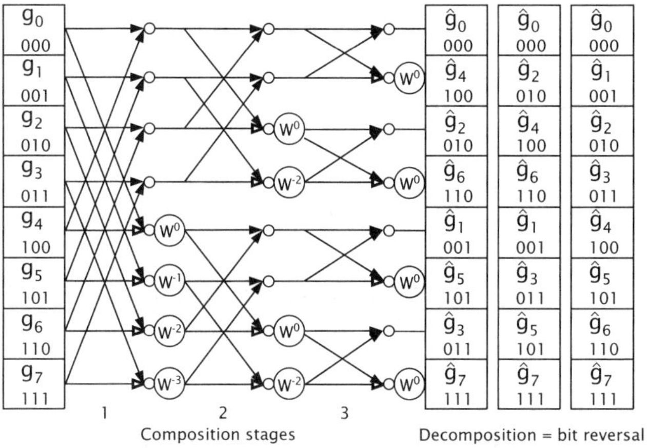

Figure 3.7: *Signal flow diagram of the radix-2 decimation-in-frequency FFT algorithm for $N = 8$.*

A recursive application of this partition results in a bit reversal of the elements in the output vector, but not the input vector. As an example, the signal flow graph for $N = 8$ is shown in Fig. 3.7. A comparison with the decimation-in-time flow graph (Fig. 3.5) shows that all steps are performed in reverse order. Even the elementary butterfly operations of the decimation-in-frequency algorithm are the inverse of the butterfly operation in the decimation-in-time algorithm.

3.4.2 Multidimensional FFT algorithms

Generally, there are two possible ways to develop fast algorithms for multidimensional discrete Fourier transforms. First, we can decompose the multidimensional DFT into 1-D DFTs and use fast algorithms for them. Second, we can generalize the approaches of the 1-D FFT for higher dimensions. In this section, we show examples for both possible ways.

Decomposition into 1-D transforms. A 2-D DFT can be broken up in two 1-D DFTs because of the separability of the kernel. In the 2-D case of Eq. (3.45), we obtain

$$\hat{G}_{u,v} = \frac{1}{MN} \sum_{m=0}^{M-1} \left[\sum_{n=0}^{N-1} G_{m,n} W_N^{-nv} \right] W_M^{-mu} \qquad (3.58)$$

The inner summation forms M 1-D DFTs of the rows, the outer N 1-D DFTs of the columns, that is, the 2-D FFT is computed as M row transformations followed by N column transformations:

$$\text{Row transform} \qquad \tilde{G}_{m,v} = \frac{1}{N}\sum_{n=0}^{N-1} G_{m,n} W_N^{-nv}$$

$$\text{Column transform} \quad \hat{G}_{u,v} = \frac{1}{M}\sum_{m=0}^{M-1} \tilde{G}_{m,v} W_M^{-mu}$$

In an analogous way, a D-dimensional DFT can be composed of D 1-D DFTs.

Multidimensional decomposition. A decomposition is also directly possible in multidimensional spaces. We will demonstrate such algorithms with the simple case of a 2-D radix-2 decimation-in-time algorithm.

We decompose an $M \times N$ matrix into four submatrices by taking only every second pixel in every second line. This decomposition yields

$$\begin{bmatrix} \hat{G}_{u,v} \\ \hat{G}_{u,v+N/2} \\ \hat{G}_{u+M/2,v} \\ \hat{G}_{u+M/2,v+N/2} \end{bmatrix} = \begin{bmatrix} 1 & 1 & 1 & 1 \\ 1 & -1 & 1 & -1 \\ 1 & 1 & -1 & -1 \\ 1 & -1 & -1 & 1 \end{bmatrix} \begin{bmatrix} {}^{0,0}\hat{G}_{u,v} \\ W_N^{-v}\ {}^{0,1}\hat{G}_{u,v} \\ W_M^{-u}\ {}^{1,0}\hat{G}_{u,v} \\ W_M^{-u} W_N^{-v}\ {}^{1,1}\hat{G}_{u,v} \end{bmatrix}$$

The superscripts in front of $\hat{G}$ denote the corresponding partial transformation. The 2-D radix-2 algorithm is very similar to the 1-D radix-4 algorithm. In a similar manner as for the 1-D radix-4 algorithm, we can reduce the number of additions from 12 to 8 by factorizing the matrix:

$$\begin{bmatrix} 1 & 1 & 1 & 1 \\ 1 & -1 & 1 & -1 \\ 1 & 1 & -1 & -1 \\ 1 & -1 & -1 & 1 \end{bmatrix} = \begin{bmatrix} 1 & 0 & 1 & 0 \\ 0 & 1 & 0 & 1 \\ 1 & 0 & -1 & 0 \\ 0 & 1 & 0 & -1 \end{bmatrix} \begin{bmatrix} 1 & 1 & 0 & 0 \\ 1 & -1 & 0 & 0 \\ 0 & 0 & 1 & 1 \\ 0 & 0 & 1 & -1 \end{bmatrix}$$

The 2-D radix-2 algorithm for an $N \times N$ matrix requires $(3/4N^2)\,\mathrm{ld}\,N$ complex multiplications, 25 % fewer than the separation into two 1-D radix-2 FFTs. However, the multidimensional decomposition has the disadvantage that the memory access pattern is more complex than for the 1-D Fourier transform. With the partition into a 1-D transform, the access to memory becomes local, yielding a higher cache hit rate than with the distributed access of the multidimensional decomposition.

3.4.3 Fourier transform of real images

So far, we have discussed only the Fourier transform of complex-valued signals. The same algorithms can also be used for real-valued signals.

Then they are less efficient, however, as the Fourier transform of a real-valued signal is Hermitian (Section 3.2.3) and thus only half of the Fourier coefficients are independent. This corresponds to the fact that also half of the signal, namely the imaginary part, is zero.

It is obvious that another factor two in computational speed can be gained for the DFT of real data. Three common strategies [2] that are used to map real vectors onto complex vectors are discussed in what follows.

Mapping of two real vectors onto one complex vector. The easiest way to do so is to compute two real 1-D sequences at once. This concept can easily be applied to the DFT of images, as many 1-D DFTs must be computed. Thus, we can put the first row $\boldsymbol{x}$ into the real part and the second row $\boldsymbol{y}$ into the imaginary part and yield the complex vector $\boldsymbol{z} = \boldsymbol{x} + \mathrm{i}\boldsymbol{y}$. From the symmetry properties discussed in Section 3.2.3, we infer that the transforms of the real and imaginary parts map in Fourier space to the Hermitian and anti-Hermitian parts, respectively. Thus the Fourier transforms of the two real M-dimensional vectors are given by

$$\begin{aligned} \hat{x}_v &= 1/2(\hat{z}_v + \hat{z}_{N-v}) \\ \hat{y}_v &= 1/2(\hat{z}_v - \hat{z}_{N-v}) \end{aligned} \tag{3.59}$$

Mapping of a $2N$ real vector onto an N complex vector. With this mapping strategy we just map a real vector $\boldsymbol{x}$ of the length $2N$ onto a complex vector $\boldsymbol{z}$ of length N in such a way that the even elements come into the real part and the odd values into the imaginary part. Thus we have the following DFT:

$$\hat{G}_v = \sum_{n=0}^{N-1} (x_{2n} + \mathrm{i}x_{2n+1}) W_N^{nv} \tag{3.60}$$

The vector with the even and odd elements results in a Hermitian and anti-Hermitian Fourier transform, respectively. Thus the first N coefficients of the partial DFTs are given according to Eq. (3.59) as

$$\begin{aligned} {}^e\hat{x}_v &= 1/2(\hat{g}_v + \hat{g}_{N-v}) \\ {}^o\hat{x}_v &= 1/2(\hat{g}_v - \hat{g}_{N-v}) \end{aligned} \tag{3.61}$$

From the radix-2 decimation in time FFT algorithm Eq. (3.52), we know how two such partial DFTs can be combined:

$$\hat{x}_v = {}^e\hat{x}_v + W_N^{-v}\,{}^o\hat{x}_v \tag{3.62}$$

FFT via fast Hardley transform. It has often been argued [5] that a real-valued variant of the Fourier transform, the *Hardley transform*, that uses the sum of a cosine and sine function as a kernel can compute the Fourier transform of a real vector faster than the Fourier transform itself. This is correct if the real vector is just put into the real part of a complex-valued vector and an FFT algorithm is used. A fast Hardley transform has, however, no performance advantage when one of the preceding strategies is applied that doubles the speed of computing the Fourier transform of a real-valued vector.

3.5 References

[1] Hoffman, K. and Kunze, R., (1971). *Linear Algebra,* 2nd edition. Englewood Cliffs, NJ: Prentice-Hall.

[2] Besslich, P. W. and Lu, T., (1990). *Diskrete Orthogonaltransformation. Algorithmen und Flußgraphen für die Signalverarbeitung.* Berlin: Springer.

[3] Jaroslavskij, J. P., (1985). *Einführung in die digitale Bildverarbeitung.* Berlin: VEB Deutscher Verlag der Wissenschaften.

[4] Poularikas, A. D. (ed.), (1995). *The Transforms and Applications Handbook.* Boca Raton, FL: CRC Press.

[5] Bracewell, R., (1986). *The Fourier Transform and its Applications,* 2nd edition, revised. New York: McGraw-Hill.

[6] Madisetti, V. K. and Williams, D. B. (eds.), (1997). *The Digital Signal Processing Handbook.* Boca Raton, FL: CRC Press.

[7] Papoulis, A., (1991). *Probability, Random Variables, and Stochastic Processes.* New York: McGraw-Hill.

[8] Cooley, J. W. and Tukey, J. W., (1965). An algorithm for the machine calculation of complex Fourier series. *Math. Comp.,* **19**:297–301.

[9] Blahut, R., (1985). *Fast Algorithms for Digital Signal Processing.* Reading, MA: Addison-Wesley.

4 Multiresolutional Signal Representation

Bernd Jähne

Interdisziplinäres Zentrum für Wissenschaftliches Rechnen (IWR)
Universität Heidelberg, Germany

4.1 Scale in signal processing

In Chapter 3 the representation of images in the spatial and wave-number domain were discussed. If an image is represented in the *spatial domain*, we do not have any information at all about the wave numbers contained at a point in the image. We know the position with an accuracy of the lattice constant Δx, but the local wave number at this position may be anywhere in the range of the possible wave numbers from $-1/(2\Delta x)$ to $1/(2\Delta x)$ (Fig. 4.1).

Handbook of Computer Vision and Applications
Volume 2
Signal Processing and Pattern Recognition

Copyright © 1999 by Academic Press
All rights of reproduction in any form reserved.
ISBN 0-12-379772-1/$30.00

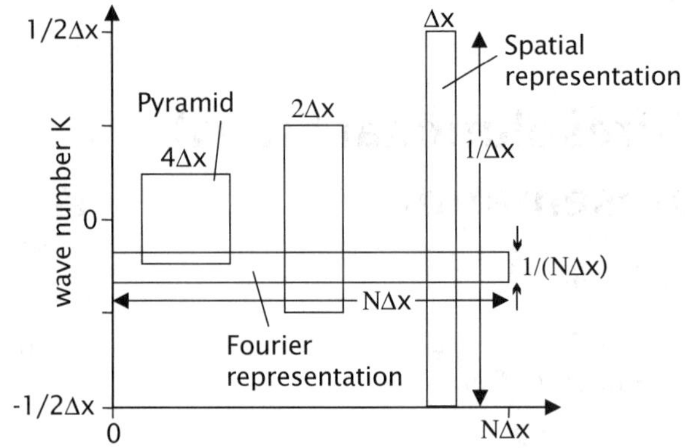

Figure 4.1: *Illustration of the interdependence of resolution in the spatial and wave-number domain in one dimension. Representations in the space domain, the wave-number domain, and the space/wave-number domain (2 planes of pyramid with half and quarter resolution) are shown.*

In the *wave-number domain* we have the reverse case. Each pixel in this domain represents one wave number with the highest wave-number resolution possible for the given image size, which is $-1/(N\Delta x)$ for an image with N pixels in each coordinate. But any positional information is lost, as one point in the wave-number space represents a periodic structure that is spread over the whole image (Fig. 4.1). Thus, the position uncertainty is the linear dimension of the image $N\Delta x$.

In this section we will revisit both representations under the perspective of how to generate a multiscale representation of an image.

The foregoing discussion shows that the representations of an image in either the spatial or wave-number domain constitute two opposite extremes. Although the understanding of both domains is essential for any type of signal processing, the representation in either of these domains is inadequate to analyze objects in images.

In the wave-number representation the spatial structures from various independent objects are mixed up because the extracted periodic structures cover the whole image. In the spatial representation we have no information about the spatial structures contained in an object, we just know the local pixel gray values.

What we thus really need is a type of joint representation that allows for a separation into different wave-number ranges (scales) but still preserves as much spatial resolution as possible. Such a representation is called a multiscale or *multiresolution representation*.

The limits of the joint spatial/wave-number resolution are given by the *uncertainty relation* discussed in Section 3.2.3. It states that the

Table 4.1: *Wave number and spatial resolutions of representations of images in various domains*

Domain / Resolution	Spatial resolution	Wave number resolution	Product
Spatial domain	Δx	$1/\Delta x$	1
Wave-number domain	$N\Delta x$	$1/(N\Delta x)$	1
Multiscale domain	$p\Delta x$	$1/(p\Delta x)$	1

product of the resolutions in the spatial and wave-number domain cannot be beyond a certain threshold. This is exactly what we observed already in the spatial and wave-number domains. However, besides these two domains any other combination of resolutions that meets the uncertainty relation can be chosen. Thus the resolution in wave numbers, that is, the distinction of various scales in an image, can be set to any value with a corresponding spatial resolution (Fig. 4.1, Table 4.1). As the uncertainty relation gives only the lower limit of the joint resolution, it is important to devise efficient data structures that approach this limit.

In the last two decades a number of various concepts have been developed for multiresolution signal processing. Some trace back to the early roots of signal processing. This includes various techniques to filter signals for certain scale ranges such as the windowed Fourier transform, Gabor filters, polar separable quadrature filters, and filters steerable in scale (Section 4.2).

Some of these techniques are directly suitable to compute a *local wave number* that reflects the dominant scale in a local neighborhood. Multigrid image structures in the form of pyramids are another early and efficient multiresolution [1]. More recent developments are the *scale space* (Section 4.2) and *wavelets* [2, 3].

Although all of these techniques seem to be quite different at first glance, this it not the case. They have much in common; they merely look at the question of multiresolutional signal representation from a different point of view. Thus an important issue in this chapter is to work out the relations between the various approaches.

An early account on multiresolution imaging was given by Rosenfeld [4]. The standard work on linear scale space theory is by Lindeberg [5] (see also Chapter 11) and nonlinear scale space theory is treated by Weickert [6] (see also Chapter 15).

4.2 Scale filters

4.2.1 Windowed Fourier transform

One way to a multiresolutional signal representation starts with the Fourier transform. If the Fourier transform is applied only to a section of the image and this section is moved around through the whole image, then a joint spatial/wave-number resolution is achieved. The spatial resolution is given by the size of the window and due to the uncertainty relation (Section 3.2.3) the wave-number resolution is reduced by the ratio of the image size to the window size. The window function $w(\boldsymbol{x})$ must not be a box function. Generally, a useful window function has a maximum at the origin, is even and isotropic, and decreases monotonically with increasing distance from the origin. This approach to a joint space/wave-number representation is the *windowed Fourier transform*. It is defined by

$$\hat{g}(\boldsymbol{x}, \boldsymbol{k}_0) = \int_{-\infty}^{\infty} g(\boldsymbol{x}')w(\boldsymbol{x}' - \boldsymbol{x}) \exp(-2\pi \mathrm{i} \boldsymbol{k}_0 \boldsymbol{x}') \, \mathrm{d}x'^2 \tag{4.1}$$

The integral in Eq. (4.1) almost looks like a convolution integral (Section 3.2.3). To convert it into a convolution integral we make use of the fact that the window function is even ($w(-\boldsymbol{k}) = w(\boldsymbol{k})$) and rearrange the second part of Eq. (4.1):

$$\begin{aligned} & w(\boldsymbol{x}' - \boldsymbol{x}) \exp(-2\pi \mathrm{i} \boldsymbol{k}_0 \boldsymbol{x}') = \\ & w(\boldsymbol{x} - \boldsymbol{x}') \exp(2\pi \mathrm{i} \boldsymbol{k}_0 (\boldsymbol{x} - \boldsymbol{x}')) \exp(-2\pi \mathrm{i} \boldsymbol{k}_0 \boldsymbol{x}) \end{aligned}$$

Then we can write Eq. (4.1) as a convolution:

$$\hat{g}(\boldsymbol{x}, \boldsymbol{k}_0) = [g(\boldsymbol{x}) * w(\boldsymbol{x}) \exp(2\pi \mathrm{i} \boldsymbol{k}_0 \boldsymbol{x})] \; \exp(-2\pi \mathrm{i} \boldsymbol{k}_0 \boldsymbol{x}) \tag{4.2}$$

This means that the local Fourier transform corresponds to a convolution with the complex convolution kernel $w(\boldsymbol{x}) \exp(2\pi \mathrm{i} \boldsymbol{k}_0 \boldsymbol{x})$ except for a phase factor $\exp(-2\pi \mathrm{i} \boldsymbol{k}_0 \boldsymbol{x})$. Using the *shift theorem* (Table 3.2), the transfer function of the convolution kernel can be computed to be

$$w(\boldsymbol{x}) \exp(2\pi \mathrm{i} \boldsymbol{k}_0 \boldsymbol{x}) \Longleftrightarrow \hat{w}(\boldsymbol{k} - \boldsymbol{k}_0) \tag{4.3}$$

This means that the convolution kernel is a *bandpass filter* with a peak wave number of $\boldsymbol{k}_0$. The width of the bandpass is inversely proportional to the width of the window function. In this way, the spatial and wave-number resolutions are interrelated to each other. As an example, we take a Gaussian window function

$$w(\boldsymbol{x}) = \frac{1}{\sigma^D} \exp\left(-\pi \frac{|\boldsymbol{x}|^2}{\sigma^2}\right) \Longleftrightarrow \hat{w}(\boldsymbol{k}) = \exp\left(-\pi \frac{|\boldsymbol{k}|^2}{\sigma^{-2}}\right) \tag{4.4}$$

The Gaussian window function reaches the theoretical limit set by the uncertainty relation and is thus an optimal choice; a better wave-number resolution cannot be achieved with a given spatial resolution.

The windowed Fourier transform Eq. (4.1) delivers a complex filter response. This has the advantage that both the phase and the amplitude of a bandpass filtered signal are retrieved.

4.2.2 Gabor filter

Definition. A *Gabor filter* is a bandpass filter that selects a certain wavelength range around the center wavelength $\boldsymbol{k}_0$ using the Gaussian function. The Gabor filter is very similar to the windowed Fourier transform if the latter is used with a Gaussian window function. The transfer function of the Gabor filter is real but asymmetric and defined as

$$\hat{G}(\boldsymbol{k}) = \exp\left(-\pi|\boldsymbol{k} - \boldsymbol{k}_0)|^2\sigma_x^2\right) \tag{4.5}$$

From this equation it is obvious that a Gabor filter is only a useful bandpass filter if it does not include the origin, that is, it is $\hat{G}(\boldsymbol{0}) = 0$. This condition is met in good approximation if $|\boldsymbol{k}_0|\sigma_x > 3$.

The filter mask (point spread function) of these filters can be computed easily with the shift theorem (Table 3.2):

$$G(\boldsymbol{x}) = \frac{1}{\sigma^D}\exp(2\pi i\boldsymbol{k}_0\boldsymbol{x})\exp\left(-\frac{\pi|\boldsymbol{x}|^2}{\sigma_x^2}\right) \tag{4.6}$$

The complex filter mask can be split into an even real and an odd imaginary part:

$$\begin{aligned} G_+(\boldsymbol{x}) &= \frac{1}{\sigma^D}\cos(\boldsymbol{k}_0\boldsymbol{x})\exp\left(-\frac{\pi|\boldsymbol{x}|^2}{\sigma_x^2}\right) \\ G_-(\boldsymbol{x}) &= \frac{1}{\sigma^D}\sin(\boldsymbol{k}_0\boldsymbol{x})\exp\left(-\frac{\pi|\boldsymbol{x}|^2}{\sigma_x^2}\right) \end{aligned} \tag{4.7}$$

Quadrature filters and analytic signals. Gabor filters are examples of quadrature filters. This general class of filters generates a special type of signal known as the *analytic signal* from a real-valued signal.

It is the easiest way to introduce the quadrature filter with the complex form of its transfer function. Essentially, the transfer function of a D-dimensional quadrature filter is zero for one-half space of the Fourier domain parted by the hyperplane $\boldsymbol{k}^T\bar{\boldsymbol{n}} = 0$:

$$\hat{q}(\boldsymbol{k}) = \begin{cases} 2h(\boldsymbol{k}) & \boldsymbol{k}^T\bar{\boldsymbol{n}} > 0 \\ 0 & \text{otherwise} \end{cases} \tag{4.8}$$

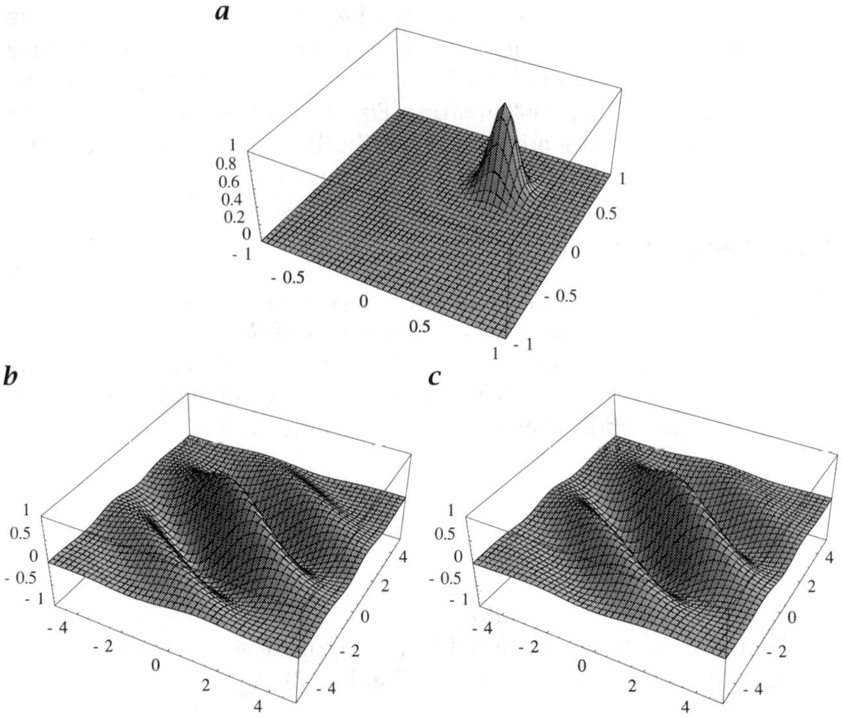

Figure 4.2: *__a__ Transfer function (Eq. (4.5)); __b__ even; and __c__ odd part of the filter mask (Eq. (4.7)) of a Gabor filter.*

where $h(\boldsymbol{k})$ is a real-valued function. Equation (4.8) can be separated into an even and odd function:

$$\begin{aligned} \hat{q}_+(\boldsymbol{k}) &= (\hat{q}(\boldsymbol{k}) + \hat{q}(-\boldsymbol{k}))/2 \\ \hat{q}_-(\boldsymbol{k}) &= (\hat{q}(\boldsymbol{k}) - \hat{q}(-\boldsymbol{k}))/2 \end{aligned} \tag{4.9}$$

The relation between the even and odd part of the signal response can be described by the *Hilbert transform*:

$$\hat{q}_-(\boldsymbol{k}) = \mathrm{i}\,\mathrm{sgn}(\boldsymbol{k}^T\bar{\boldsymbol{n}})\hat{q}_+(\boldsymbol{k}) \Longleftrightarrow q_-(\boldsymbol{x}) = \frac{\mathrm{i}}{\pi}\int_{-\infty}^{\infty} \frac{q_+(\boldsymbol{x}')}{(\boldsymbol{x}'-\boldsymbol{x})^T\bar{\boldsymbol{n}}}\,\mathrm{d}^D\boldsymbol{x}' \tag{4.10}$$

The even and odd part of a quadrature filter can be combined into a complex-valued signal by

$$q_A = q_+ - \mathrm{i}q_- \tag{4.11}$$

From Eq. (4.10) we can then see that this combination is consistent with the definition of the transfer function of the quadrature filter in Eq. (4.8).

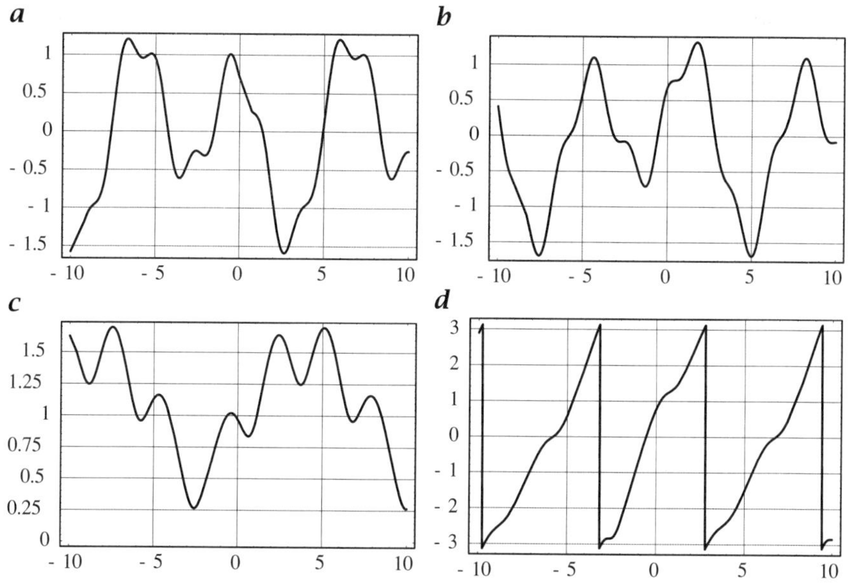

Figure 4.3: *Representation of a filtered 1-D signal as an analytic signal: Signal filtered with* ***a*** *the even and* ***b*** *the odd part of a quadrature filter;* ***c*** *amplitude; and* ***d*** *phase signal.*

The basic characteristic of the analytic filter is that its even and odd part have the *same* magnitude of the transfer function but that one is even and real and the other is odd and imaginary. Thus the filter responses of the even and odd part are shifted in phase by 90°. Thus the even part is cosine-like and the odd part is sine-like—as can be seen from the Gabor filter (Fig. 4.2b and c)—and they are shifted in phase by 90° (Fig. 4.3).

Although the transfer function of the analytic filter is real, it results in a complex signal because it is asymmetric. For a real signal no information is lost by suppressing the negative wave numbers. They can be reconstructed as the Fourier transform of a real signal is Hermitian (Section 3.2.3).

The analytic signal can be regarded as just another representation of a real signal with two important properties. The magnitude of the analytic signal gives the *local amplitude* (Fig. 4.3c)

$$|q_A|^2 = q_+^2 + q_-^2 \tag{4.12}$$

and the argument the *local phase* (Fig. 4.3d)

$$\arg(\mathcal{A}) = \arctan\left(\frac{-\mathcal{H}}{\mathcal{I}}\right) \tag{4.13}$$

While the concept of the analytic signal works with any type of 1-D signal, it must be used with much more care in higher-dimensional signals. These problems are related to the fact that an analytical signal cannot be defined for all wave numbers that lie on the hyperplane defined by $\boldsymbol{k}^T\bar{\boldsymbol{n}} = 0$ partitioning the Fourier domain in two half spaces. For these wave numbers the odd part of the quadrature filter is zero. Thus it is not possible to compute the local amplitude nor the local phase of the signal. This problem can only be avoided if the transfer function of the quadrature filter is zero at the hyperplane. For a phase definition in two-dimensions that does not show these restrictions, see Volume 3, Chapter 10.

4.2.3 Local wave number

The key to determining the local wave number is the *phase* of the signal. As an introduction we discuss a simple example and consider the 1-D periodic signal $g(x) = g_0 \cos(kx)$. The argument of the cosine function is known as the phase $\phi(x) = kx$ of the periodic signal. This is a linear function of the position and the wave number. Thus, we obtain the wave number of the periodic signal by computing the first-order spatial derivative of the phase signal

$$\frac{\partial \phi(x)}{\partial x} = k \tag{4.14}$$

These simple considerations emphasize the significant role of the phase in signal processing.

Local wave number from phase gradients. In order to determine the local wave number, we need to compute just the first spatial derivative of the phase signal. This derivative has to be applied in the same direction as the Hilbert or quadrature filter has been applied. The phase is given by

$$\phi(\boldsymbol{x}) = \arctan\left(\frac{-g_+(\boldsymbol{x})}{g_-(\boldsymbol{x})}\right) \tag{4.15}$$

Direct computation of the partial derivatives from Eq. (4.15) is not advisable, however, because of the inherent discontinuities in the phase signal. A phase computed with the inverse tangent restricts the phase to the main interval $[-\pi, \pi[$ and thus inevitably leads to a wrapping of the phase signal from π to $-\pi$ with the corresponding discontinuities.

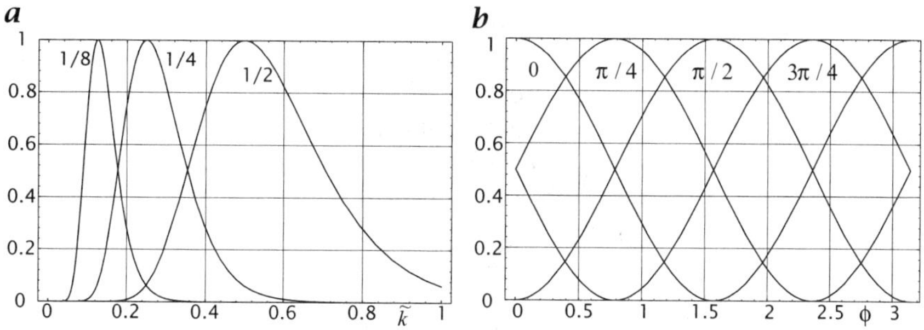

Figure 4.4: ***a** Radial and **b** angular part of quadrature filter according to Eq. (4.17) with $l = 2$ and $B = 2$ in different directions and with different peak wave numbers.*

As pointed out by Fleet [7], this problem can be avoided by computing the phase gradient directly from the gradients of $q_+(\boldsymbol{x})$ and $q_-(\boldsymbol{x})$:

$$\begin{aligned} k_p &= \frac{\partial \phi(\boldsymbol{x})}{\partial x_p} \\ &= \frac{\partial}{\partial x_p} \arctan(-q_+(\boldsymbol{x})/q_-(\boldsymbol{x})) \\ &= \frac{1}{q_+^2(\boldsymbol{x}) + q_-^2(\boldsymbol{x})} \left(\frac{\partial q_+(\boldsymbol{x})}{\partial x_p} q_-(\boldsymbol{x}) - \frac{\partial q_-(\boldsymbol{x})}{\partial x_p} q_+(\boldsymbol{x}) \right) \end{aligned} \tag{4.16}$$

This formulation of the phase gradient also eliminates the need for using trigonometric functions to compute the phase signal and is, therefore, significantly faster.

Local wave number from filter ratios. With *polar separable* quadrature filters ($\hat{r}(k)\hat{d}(\phi)$) as introduced by Knutsson [8] another scheme for computation of the local scale is possible. These classes of filters are defined by

$$\begin{aligned} \hat{r}(k) &= \exp\left[-\frac{(\ln k - \ln k_0)^2}{(B/2)^2 \ln 2} \right] \\ \hat{d}(\phi) &= \begin{cases} \cos^{2l}(\phi - \phi_k) & |\phi - \phi_k| < \pi/2 \\ 0 & \text{otherwise} \end{cases} \end{aligned} \tag{4.17}$$

In this equation, the complex notation for quadrature filters is used as introduced at the beginning of this section. The filter is directed into the angle ϕ_k.

The filter is continuous, as the cosine function is zero in the partition plane for the two half spaces ($|\phi - \phi_k| = \pi/2$). The constant k_0 denotes the peak wave number. The constant B determines the half-width of the wave number in number of octaves and l the angular resolution of the filter. In a logarithmic wave number scale, the filter has the shape of a Gaussian function. Therefore the radial part has a *lognormal* shape. Figure 4.4 shows the radial and angular part of the transfer function.

The *lognormal* form of the radial part of the quadrature filter sets is the key for a direct estimate of the *local wave number* of a narrow-band signal. According to Eq. (4.17), we can write the radial part of the transfer function as

$$\hat{r}_l(k) = \exp\left[-\frac{(\ln k - \ln k_l)^2}{2\sigma^2 \ln 2}\right] \tag{4.18}$$

We examine the ratio of the output of two different radial center frequencies k_1 and k_2 and obtain:

$$\begin{aligned}
\frac{\hat{r}_2}{\hat{r}_1} &= \exp\left[-\frac{(\ln k - \ln k_2)^2 - (\ln k - \ln k_1)^2}{2\sigma^2 \ln 2}\right] \\
&= \exp\left[\frac{2(\ln k_2 - \ln k_1)\ln k + \ln^2 k_2 - \ln^2 k_1}{2\sigma^2 \ln 2}\right] \\
&= \exp\left[\frac{(\ln k_2 - \ln k_1)[\ln k - 1/2(\ln k_2 + \ln k_1)]}{\sigma^2 \ln 2}\right] \\
&= \exp\left[\frac{\ln(k/\sqrt{k_2 k_1})\ln(k_2/k_1)}{\sigma^2 \ln 2}\right] \\
&= \left(\frac{k}{\sqrt{k_1 k_2}}\right)^{\ln(k_2/k_1)/(\sigma^2 \ln 2)}
\end{aligned}$$

Generally, the ratio of two different radial filters is directly related to the local wave number. The relation becomes particularly simple if the exponent in the last expression is one. This is the case, for example, if the wave number ratio of the two filters is two ($k_2/k_1 = 2$ and $\sigma = 1$). Then

$$\frac{\hat{r}_2}{\hat{r}_1} = \frac{k}{\sqrt{k_1 k_2}} \tag{4.19}$$

4.3 Scale space and diffusion

As we have seen with the example of the windowed Fourier transform in the previous section, the introduction of a characteristic *scale* adds a new coordinate to the representation of image data. Besides the spatial resolution, we have a new parameter that characterizes the current resolution level of the image data. The scale parameter is denoted by ξ[1].

[1]In Chapter 11 t is used for the scale parameter. Here we are using ξ in order to avoid confusion with the time coordinate t for scale spaces of image sequences.

A data structure that consists of a sequence of images with different resolutions is known as a *scale space*; we write $g(\boldsymbol{x}, \xi)$ to indicate the scale space of the image $g(\boldsymbol{x})$. Such a sequence of images can be generated by repeated convolution with an appropriate smoothing filter kernel.

This section is thought as a brief introduction into scale spaces. For an authoritative monograph on scale spaces, see Lindeberg [5].

4.3.1 General properties of a scale space

In this section, we discuss some general conditions that must be met by a filter kernel generating a scale space. We will discuss two basic requirements. First, new details must not be added with increasing scale parameter. From the perspective of information theory, we may say that the information content in the signal should continuously decrease with the scale parameter.

The second property is related to the general principle of *scale invariance*. This basically means that we can start smoothing the signal at any scale parameter in the scale space and still obtain the same scale space.

Minimum-maximum principle. The information-decreasing property of the scale space with ξ can be formulated mathematically in different ways. We express it here with the *minimum-maximum principle*, which states that local extrema must not be enhanced. This means that the gray value at a local maximum or minimum must not increase or decrease, respectively. For the physical process of diffusion this is an intuitive property. For example, in a heat transfer problem, a hot spot must not become hotter or a cool spot cooler.

Semi-group property. The second important property of the scale space is related to the *scale invariance* principle. We want to start the generating process at any scale parameter and still obtain the same scale space. More quantitatively, we can formulate this property as

$$\mathcal{B}(\xi_2)\mathcal{B}(\xi_1) = \mathcal{B}(\xi_1 + \xi_2) \tag{4.20}$$

This means that the smoothing of the scale space at the scale ξ_1 by an operator with the scale ξ_2 is equivalent to the application of the scale space operator with the scale $\xi_1 + \xi_2$ to the original image. Alternatively, we can state that the representation at the coarser level ξ_2 can be computed from the representation at the finer level ξ_1 by applying

$$\mathcal{B}(\xi_2) = \mathcal{B}(\xi_2 - \xi_1)\mathcal{B}(\xi_1) \quad \text{with} \quad \xi_2 > \xi_1 \tag{4.21}$$

In mathematics the properties Eqs. (4.20) and (4.21) are referred to as the *semi-group property*.

Conversely, we can ask what scale space generating kernels exist that meet both the minimum-maximum principle and the semi-group property. The answer to this question may be surprising. As shown by Lindeberg [5, Chapter 2], the Gaussian kernel is the *only* convolution kernel that meets both criteria and is in addition isotropic and homogeneous. From yet another perspective this feature puts the Gaussian convolution kernel into a unique position for signal processing. With respect to the Fourier transform we have already discussed that the Gaussian function is one of the few functions with a shape that is invariant under the Fourier transform (Section 3.2.4, Table 3.3) and optimal in the sense of the uncertainty relation (Section 3.2.3). In Section 7.4 we will see in addition that the Gaussian function is the only function that is separable and isotropic.

4.3.2 Linear scale spaces

Generation by a diffusion process. The generation of a scale space requires a process that can blur images to a controllable degree. Diffusion is a transport process that tends to level out concentration differences. In physics, diffusion processes govern the transport of heat, matter, and momentum [9] leading to an ever-increasing equalization of spatial concentration differences. If we identify the time with the scale parameter ξ, the diffusion process thus establishes a scale space.

To apply a diffusion process to an image, we regard the gray value g as the concentration of a scalar property. The elementary law of diffusion states that the flux density $\boldsymbol{j}$ is directed against the concentration gradient ∇g and proportional to it:

$$\boldsymbol{j} = -D\nabla g \tag{4.22}$$

where the constant D is known as the *diffusion coefficient*. Using the continuity equation

$$\frac{\partial g}{\partial t} + \nabla \boldsymbol{j} = 0 \tag{4.23}$$

the diffusion equation is

$$\frac{\partial g}{\partial t} = \nabla(D\nabla g) \tag{4.24}$$

For the case of a homogeneous diffusion process (D does not depend on the position), the equation reduces to

$$\frac{\partial g}{\partial t} = D\Delta g \quad \text{where} \quad \Delta = \sum_{d=1}^{D} \frac{\partial^2}{\partial x_d^2} \tag{4.25}$$

It is easy to show that the general solution to this equation is equivalent to a convolution with a smoothing mask. To this end, we perform a spatial Fourier transform that results in

$$\frac{\partial \hat{g}(\boldsymbol{k})}{\partial t} = -4\pi^2 D |\boldsymbol{k}|^2 \hat{g}(\boldsymbol{k}) \tag{4.26}$$

reducing the equation to a linear first-order differential equation with the general solution

$$\hat{g}(\boldsymbol{k}, t) = \exp(-4\pi^2 D t |\boldsymbol{k}|^2) \hat{g}(\boldsymbol{k}, 0) \tag{4.27}$$

where $\hat{g}(\boldsymbol{k}, 0)$ is the Fourier transformed image at time zero.

Multiplication of the image in Fourier space with the Gaussian function in Eq. (4.27) is equivalent to a convolution with the same function but of reciprocal width. Using

$$\exp\left(-\pi a\, |\boldsymbol{k}|^2\right) \Longleftrightarrow \frac{1}{a^{d/2}} \exp\left(-\frac{|\boldsymbol{x}|^2}{a/\pi}\right) \tag{4.28}$$

we obtain with $a = 4\pi D t$ for a d-dimensional space

$$g(\boldsymbol{x}, t) = \frac{1}{(2\pi)^{d/2} \sigma^d(t)} \exp\left(-\frac{|\boldsymbol{x}|^2}{2\sigma^2(t)}\right) * g(\boldsymbol{x}, 0) \tag{4.29}$$

with

$$\sigma(t) = \sqrt{2Dt} \tag{4.30}$$

Now we can replace the physical time coordinate by the scale parameter ξ with

$$\xi = 2Dt = \sigma^2 \tag{4.31}$$

and finally obtain

$$g(\boldsymbol{x}, \xi) = \frac{1}{(2\pi\xi)^{d/2}} \exp\left(-\frac{|\boldsymbol{x}|^2}{2\xi}\right) * g(\boldsymbol{x}, 0) \tag{4.32}$$

We have written all equations in such a way that they can be used for signals of any dimension. Thus, Eqs. (4.27) and (4.29) can also be applied to scale spaces of image sequences. The scale parameter is *not* identical to the time although we used a physical diffusion process that proceeds with time to derive it. If we compute a scale space representation of an image sequence, it is useful to scale the time coordinate with a characteristic velocity u_0 so that it has the same dimension as the spatial coordinates: $t' = u_0 t$. For digital signals (Section 2.3), of course, no such scaling is required. It is automatically fixed by the spatial and temporal sampling intervals: $u_0 = \Delta x / \Delta t$.

Figure 4.5: Scale space of a 2-D image: ***a*** *original image;* ***b, c,*** *and* ***d*** *at scale parameters σ 1, 2, and 4, respectively.*

As an illustration, Fig. 4.5 shows some individual images of the scale space of a 2-D image at values of ξ as indicated. This example nicely demonstrates a general property of scale spaces. With increasing scale parameter ξ, the signals become increasingly blurred, more and more details are lost. This feature can be most easily seen by the transfer function of the scale space representation in Eq. (4.27). The transfer function is always positive and monotonically decreasing with the increasing scale parameter ξ for all wave numbers. This means that no structure is amplified. All structures are attenuated with increasing ξ, and smaller structures always faster than coarser structures. In the limit of $\xi \to \infty$ the scale space converges to a constant image with the mean gray value. A certain feature exists only over a certain scale range. We can observe that edges and lines disappear and two objects merge into one.

Accelerated scale spaces. Despite the mathematical beauty of scale space generation with a Gaussian convolution kernel, this approach has one significant disadvantage. The standard deviation of the smoothing increases only with the square root of the scale parameter ξ (see

Eq. (4.31)). While smoothing goes fast for fine scales, it becomes increasingly slower for larger scales.

There is a simple cure for this problem. We need a diffusion process where the diffusion constant increases with time. We first discuss a diffusion coefficient that increases linearly with time. This approach results in the differential equation

$$\frac{\partial g}{\partial t} = D_0 t \Delta g \tag{4.33}$$

A spatial Fourier transform results in

$$\frac{\partial \hat{g}(\boldsymbol{k})}{\partial t} = -4\pi^2 D_0 t |\boldsymbol{k}|^2 \hat{g}(\boldsymbol{k}) \tag{4.34}$$

This equation has the general solution

$$\hat{g}(\boldsymbol{k}, t) = \exp(-2\pi^2 D_0 t^2 |\boldsymbol{k}|^2) \hat{g}(\boldsymbol{k}, 0) \tag{4.35}$$

which is equivalent to a convolution in the spatial domain as in Eq. (4.31) with $\xi = \sigma^2 = D_0 t^2$. Now the standard deviation for the smoothing is proportional to time for a diffusion process with a diffusion coefficient that increases linearly in time. As the scale parameter ξ is proportional to the time squared, we denote this scale space as the *quadratic scale space*. This modified scale space still meets the minimum-maximum principle and the semi-group property.

For even more accelerated smoothing, we can construct a *logarithmic scale space*, that is, a scale space where the scale parameter increases logarithmically with time. We use a diffusion coefficient that increases exponentially in time:

$$\frac{\partial g}{\partial t} = D_0 \exp(t/\tau) \Delta g \tag{4.36}$$

A spatial Fourier transform results in

$$\frac{\partial \hat{g}(\boldsymbol{k})}{\partial t} = -4\pi^2 D_0 \exp(t/\tau) |\boldsymbol{k}|^2 \hat{g}(\boldsymbol{k}) \tag{4.37}$$

The general solution of this equation in the Fourier domain is

$$\hat{g}(\boldsymbol{k}, t) = \exp(-4\pi^2 D_0 (\exp(t/\tau)/\tau) |\boldsymbol{k}|^2) \hat{g}(\boldsymbol{k}, 0) \tag{4.38}$$

Again,the transfer function and thus the convolution kernel have the same form as in Eqs. (4.27) and (4.35), now with the scale parameter

$$\xi_l = \sigma^2 = \frac{2D_0}{\tau} \exp(t/\tau) \tag{4.39}$$

This means that the logarithm of the scale parameter ξ is now proportional to the limiting scales still contained in the scale space. Essentially, we can think of the quadratic and logarithmic scale spaces as a coordinate transform of the scale parameter which efficiently compresses the scale space coordinate:

$$\xi_q \propto \sqrt{\xi}, \qquad \xi_l \propto \ln(\xi) \tag{4.40}$$

4.3.3 Differential scale spaces

The interest in a *differential scale space* stems from the fact that we want to select optimum scales for processing of features in images. In a differential scale space, the change of the image with scale is emphasized. We use the transfer function of the scale space kernel Eq. (4.27), which is also valid for quadratic and logarithmic scale spaces. The general solution for the scale space can be written in the Fourier space as

$$\hat{g}(\boldsymbol{k},\xi) = \exp(-2\pi^2 \left|\boldsymbol{k}\right|^2 \xi)\hat{g}(\boldsymbol{k},0) \tag{4.41}$$

Differentiating this signal with respect to the scale parameter ξ yields

$$\begin{aligned} \frac{\partial \hat{g}(\boldsymbol{k},\xi)}{\partial \xi} &= -2\pi^2 \left|\boldsymbol{k}\right|^2 \exp(-2\pi^2 \left|\boldsymbol{k}\right|^2 \xi)\hat{g}(\boldsymbol{k},0) \\ &= -2\pi^2 \left|\boldsymbol{k}\right|^2 \hat{g}(\boldsymbol{k},\xi) \end{aligned} \tag{4.42}$$

The multiplication with $-4\pi^2|\boldsymbol{k}|^2$ is equivalent to a second-order spatial derivative (Table 3.2), the *Laplacian operator*. Thus we can write in the spatial domain

$$\frac{\partial g(\boldsymbol{x},\xi)}{\partial \xi} = \frac{1}{2}\Delta g(\boldsymbol{x},\xi) \tag{4.43}$$

Equations (4.42) and (4.43) constitute a basic property of the differential scale space. The differential scale space is equivalent to a second-order spatial derivation with the Laplacian operator and thus leads to an isotropic *bandpass decomposition* of the image. This is, of course, not surprising as the diffusion equation in Eq. (4.25) relates just the first-order temporal derivative with the second-order spatial derivative. The transfer function at the scale ξ is

$$-2\pi^2 \left|\boldsymbol{k}\right|^2 \exp(-2\pi^2 \xi \left|\boldsymbol{k}\right|^2) \tag{4.44}$$

For small wave numbers, the transfer function is proportional to $-|\boldsymbol{k}|^2$. It reaches a maximum at

$$k_{\max} = \frac{1}{\sqrt{2\pi^2 \xi}} \tag{4.45}$$

and then decays exponentially.

4.3.4 Discrete scale spaces

The construction of a *discrete scale space* requires a discretization of the diffusion equation and *not* of the convolution kernel [5]. We start with a discretization of the 1-D diffusion equation

$$\frac{\partial g(x,\xi)}{\partial \xi} = \frac{\partial^2 g(x,\xi)}{\partial x^2} \tag{4.46}$$

The derivatives are replaced by discrete differences in the following way:

$$\begin{aligned} \frac{\partial g(x,\xi)}{\partial \xi} &\approx \frac{g(x,\xi+\Delta\xi) - g(x,\xi)}{\Delta\xi} \\ \frac{\partial^2 g(x,\xi)}{\partial x^2} &\approx \frac{g(x+\Delta x,\xi) - 2g(x,\xi) + g(x-\Delta x,\xi)}{\Delta x^2} \end{aligned} \tag{4.47}$$

This leads to the following iteration scheme for computing a discrete scale space:

$$g(x,\xi+\Delta\xi) = \Delta\xi g(x+\Delta x,\xi) + (1-2\Delta\xi)g(x,\xi) + \Delta\xi g(x-\Delta x,\xi) \tag{4.48}$$

or written with discrete coordinates

$$g_{n,\xi+1} = \Delta\xi g_{n+1,\xi} + (1-2\Delta\xi)g_{n,\xi} + \Delta\xi g_{n-1,\xi} \tag{4.49}$$

Lindeberg [5] shows that this iteration results in a discrete scale space that meets the minimum-maximum principle and the semi-group property if and only if

$$\Delta\xi \le \frac{1}{4} \tag{4.50}$$

The limit case of $\Delta\xi = 1/4$ leads to the especially simple iteration

$$g_{n,\xi+1} = 1/4 g_{n+1,\xi} + 1/2 g_{n,\xi} + 1/4 g_{n-1,\xi} \tag{4.51}$$

Each step of the scale space computation is given by a spatial smoothing of the signal with the binomial mask $\boldsymbol{B}^2 = [1/4\ 1/2\ 1/4]$ (Section 7.4). We can also formulate the general scale space generating operator in Eq. (4.49) using the convolution operator $\mathcal{B}$. Written in the operator notation introduced in Section 5.2.3, the operator for one iteration step to generate the discrete scale space is

$$(1-\epsilon)\mathcal{I} + \epsilon\mathcal{B}^2 \quad \text{with} \quad \epsilon \le 1 \tag{4.52}$$

where $\mathcal{I}$ denotes the identy operator.

This expression is significant, as it can be extended directly to higher dimensions by replacing $\mathcal{B}^2$ with a correspondingly higher-dimensional smoothing operator. The convolution mask $\boldsymbol{B}^2$ is the simplest mask in the class of smoothing binomial filters. These filters will be discussed in Section 7.4. A detailed discussion of discrete linear scale spaces is given by Lindeberg [5, Chapters 3 and 4].

4.4 Multigrid representations

4.4.1 Basics

The scale space discussed in Section 4.3 has one significant disadvantage. The use of the additional scale parameter adds a new dimension to the images and thus leads to an explosion of the data storage requirements and, in turn, the computational overhead for generating the scale space and for analyzing it. Thus, it is not surprising that before the evolution of the scale space more efficient multiscale storage schemes, especially pyramids, found widespread application in image processing. With data structures of this type, the resolution of the images decreases in such an extent as the scale increases. In this way an optimum balance between spatial and wave number resolution is achieved in the sense of the *uncertainty relation* (Section 3.2.3). Data structures of this type are known as *multiresolution representations* [4].

The basic idea is quite simple. While the representation of fine scales requires the full resolution, coarser scales can be represented at lower resolution. This leads to a scale space with smaller and smaller images as the scale parameter increases. In the following two sections we will discuss the *Gaussian pyramid* (Section 4.4.2) and the *Laplacian pyramid* (Section 4.4.3) as efficient discrete implementations of discrete scale spaces. In addition, while the Gaussian pyramid constitutes a standard scale space, the Laplacian pyramid is a discrete version of a differential scale space (Section 4.3.3).

4.4.2 Gaussian pyramid

When *subsampling* an image, for example, by taking every second pixel in every second line it is important to consider the *sampling theorem* (Section 2.4.2). Before subsampling, the image must be smoothed to an extent that no aliasing occurs in the subsampled image. Consequently, for subsampling by a factor two, we must ensure that all structures, which are sampled less than four times per wavelength, are suppressed by an appropriate smoothing filter. This means that size reduction must go hand-in-hand with appropriate smoothing.

Generally, the requirement for the smoothing filter can be formulated as

$$\hat{B}(\tilde{\boldsymbol{k}}) = 0 \quad \forall \tilde{k}_d \geq \frac{1}{r_d} \tag{4.53}$$

where r_d is the subsampling rate in the direction of the dth coordinate.

The combined smoothing and size reduction can be expressed in a single operator by using the following notation to compute the $q+1$th level of the Gaussian pyramid from the qth level:

$$\boldsymbol{G}^{(q+1)} = \mathcal{B}_{\downarrow 2}\boldsymbol{G}^{(q)} \tag{4.54}$$

The number behind the $\downarrow$ in the index denotes the subsampling rate. Level 0 of the pyramid is the original image: $\boldsymbol{G}^{(0)} = \boldsymbol{G}$.

If we repeat the smoothing and subsampling operations iteratively, we obtain a series of images, which is called the *Gaussian pyramid*. From level to level, the resolution decreases by a factor of two; the size of the images decreases correspondingly. Consequently, we can think of the series of images as being arranged in the form of a pyramid.

The pyramid does not require much storage space. Generally, if we consider the formation of a pyramid from a D-dimensional image with a subsampling factor of two and N pixels in each coordinate direction, the total number of pixels is given by

$$N^D\left(1 + \frac{1}{2^D} + \frac{1}{2^{2D}} + \ldots\right) < N^D\frac{2^D}{2^D - 1} \tag{4.55}$$

For a 2-D image, the whole pyramid needs just 1/3 more space than the original image, for a 3-D image only 1/7 more. Likewise, the computation of the pyramid is equally effective. The *same* smoothing filter is applied to each level of the pyramid. Thus the computation of the *whole* pyramid needs only 4/3 and 8/7 times more operations than for the first level of a 2-D and 3-D image, respectively.

The pyramid brings large scales into the range of local neighborhood operations with small kernels. Moreover, these operations are performed efficiently. Once the pyramid has been computed, we can perform neighborhood operations on large scales in the upper levels of the pyramid—because of the smaller image sizes—much more efficiently than for finer scales.

The Gaussian pyramid constitutes a series of low-pass filtered images in which the cut-off wave numbers decrease by a factor of two (an octave) from level to level. Thus the Gaussian pyramid resembles a logarithmic scale space. Only a few levels of the pyramid are necessary to span a wide range of wave numbers. If we stop the pyramid at an 8×8 image, we can usefully compute only a seven-level pyramid from a 512×512 image.

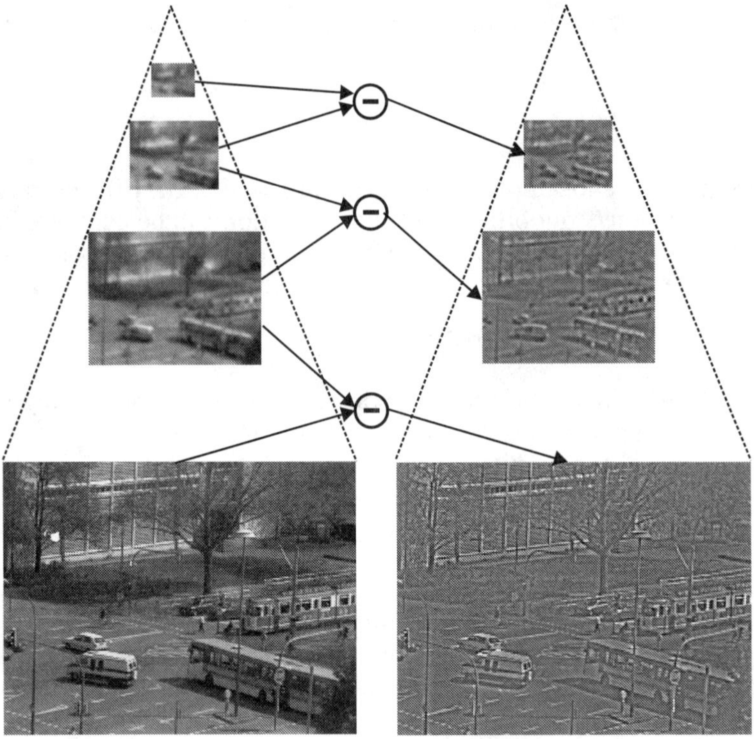

Figure 4.6: Construction of the Laplacian pyramid (right column) from the Gaussian pyramid (left column) by subtracting two consecutive planes of the Gaussian pyramid.

4.4.3 Laplacian pyramid

From the Gaussian pyramid, another pyramid type can be derived, the *Laplacian pyramid*. This type of pyramid is the discrete counterpart to the *differential scale space* discussed in Section 4.3.3 and leads to a sequence of bandpass filtered images. In contrast to the Fourier transform, the Laplacian pyramid leads only to a coarse wave number decomposition without a directional decomposition. All wave numbers, independently of their direction, within the range of about an octave (factor of two) are contained in one level of the pyramid.

Because of the coarse wave number resolution, we can preserve a good spatial resolution. Each level of the pyramid contains only matching scales, which are sampled a few times (two to six) per wavelength. In this way, the Laplacian pyramid is an efficient data structure well adapted to the limits of the product of wave number and spatial resolution set by the *uncertainty relation* (Section 3.2.3).

The differentiation in scale direction in the continuous scale space is approximated by subtracting two levels of the Gaussian pyramid in the discrete scale space. In order to do so, first the image at the coarser level must be expanded. This operation is performed by an *expansion operator* $\mathcal{E}_{\uparrow 2}$. As with the reducing smoothing operator, the degree of expansion is denoted by the figure after the $\uparrow$ in the index.

The expansion is significantly more difficult than the size reduction because the missing information must be interpolated. For a size increase of two in all directions, first every second pixel in each row must be interpolated and then every second row. Interpolation is discussed in detail in Chapter 8. With the introduced notation, the generation of the pth level of the Laplacian pyramid can be written as:

$$\mathcal{L}^{(p)} = \boldsymbol{G}^{(p)} - \mathcal{E}_{\uparrow 2}\boldsymbol{G}^{(p+1)} \tag{4.56}$$

The Laplacian pyramid is an effective scheme for a *bandpass decomposition* of an image. The center wave number is halved from level to level. The last image of the Laplacian pyramid is a low-pass-filtered image containing only the coarsest structures.

The Laplacian pyramid has the significant advantage that the original image can be reconstructed quickly from the sequence of images in the Laplacian pyramid by recursively expanding the images and summing them up. In a Laplacian pyramid with $p + 1$ levels, the level p (counting starts with zero!) is the coarsest level of the Gaussian pyramid. Then the level $p - 1$ of the Gaussian pyramid can be reconstructed by

$$\boldsymbol{G}^{(p-1)} = \mathcal{L}^{(p-1)} + \mathcal{E}_{\uparrow 2}\boldsymbol{G}^{p} \tag{4.57}$$

Note that this is just the inversion of the construction scheme for the Laplacian pyramid. This means that even if the interpolation algorithms required to expand the image contain errors, they affect only the Laplacian pyramid and not the reconstruction of the Gaussian pyramid from the Laplacian pyramid, because the same algorithm is used. The recursion in Eq. (4.57) is repeated with lower levels until level 0, that is, the original image, is reached again. As illustrated in Fig. 4.6, finer and finer details become visible during the reconstruction process.

The Gaussian and Laplacian pyramids are examples of multigrid data structures, which were introduced into digital image processing in the early 1980s and since then have led to a tremendous increase in speed of image processing algorithms. A new research area, *multiresolutional image processing*, was established by Rosenfeld [4].

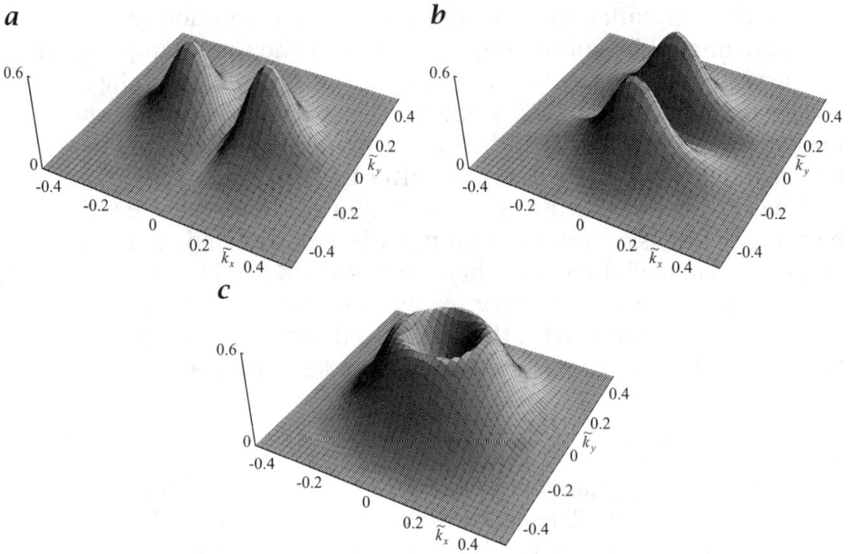

Figure 4.7: *Pseudo 3-D plots of the directio-pyramidal decomposition according to Eq. (4.60):* ***a*** *directional bandpass filter in x direction;* ***b*** *directional bandpass filter in y direction;* ***c*** *isotropic bandpass filter, sum of* ***a*** *and* ***b****.*

4.4.4 Directio-pyramidal decomposition

The Laplacian pyramid decomposes an image in logarithmic wave number intervals one octave (factor 2) distant. A useful extension is the additional decomposition into different directions. Such a decomposition is known as *directio-pyramidal decomposition* [10]. This decomposition should have the same properties as the Laplacian pyramid: the addition of all partial images should give the original. This implies that each level of the Laplacian pyramid must be decomposed into several directional components. An efficient scheme for decomposition into two directional components is as follows. The smoothing is performed by separable smoothing filters followed by a subsampling operator $\mathcal{R}_{\downarrow 2}$, taking only each second pixel in each second line,

$$\boldsymbol{G}^{(1)} = \mathcal{R}_{\downarrow 2}\mathcal{B}_x\mathcal{B}_y\boldsymbol{G}^{(0)} \tag{4.58}$$

The first level of the Laplacian pyramid then is

$$\mathcal{L} = \boldsymbol{G}^{(0)} - \mathcal{E}_{\uparrow 2}\boldsymbol{G}^{(1)} \tag{4.59}$$

Then, the two directional components are given by

$$\begin{aligned} \mathcal{L}_1 &= 1/2(\mathcal{L} - (\mathcal{B}_x - \mathcal{B}_y)\boldsymbol{G}^{(0)}) \\ \mathcal{L}_2 &= 1/2(\mathcal{L} + (\mathcal{B}_x - \mathcal{B}_y)\boldsymbol{G}^{(0)}) \end{aligned} \tag{4.60}$$

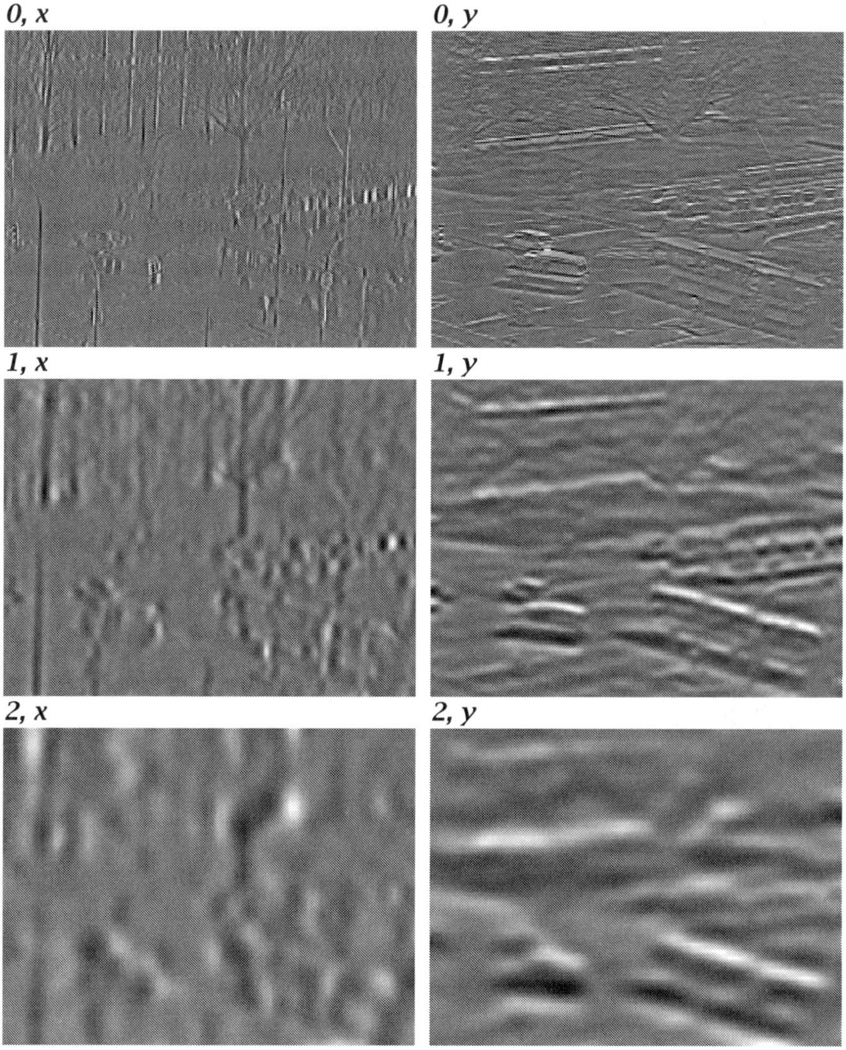

Figure 4.8: *Directio-pyramidal decomposition as indicated of the image shown in Fig. 4.6. Shown are the first three planes blown up to original size.*

From Eq. (4.60) it is evident that the two directional components $\mathcal{L}_1$ and $\mathcal{L}_2$ add up to the isotropic Laplacian pyramid $\mathcal{L}$. The scheme requires minimal additional computations as compared to the computation of the isotropic Laplacian pyramid. Only one more convolution (of $\boldsymbol{G}^{(0)}$ with B_y) and three more additions are required. The first three planes of the directio-pyramidal decomposition are shown in Fig. 4.8.

4.5 References

[1] Burt, P. J., (1984). The pyramid as a structure for efficient computation. In *Multiresolution Image Processing and Analysis*, A. Rosenfeld, ed., Vol. 12 of *Springer Series in Information Sciences*, pp. 6–35. New York: Springer.

[2] Meyer, Y., (1993). *Wavelets: Algorithms & Applications.* Philadelphia: SIAM.

[3] Kaiser, G., (1994). *A Friendly Guide to Wavelets.* Boston, MA: Birkhäuser.

[4] Rosenfeld, A. (ed.), (1984). *Multiresolution Image Processing and Analysis.* New York: Springer.

[5] Lindeberg, T., (1994). *Scale-space Theory in Computer Vision.* Boston: Kluwer Academic Publishers.

[6] Weickert, J., (1998). *Anisotropic Diffusion in Image Processing.* Stuttgart: Teubner-Verlag.

[7] Fleet, D. J., (1990). *Measurement of Image Velocity.* Diss., University of Toronto.

[8] Knutsson, H., (1982). *Filtering and Reconstruction in Image Processing.* Diss., Linköping Univ.

[9] Crank, J., (1975). *The Mathematics of Diffusion.* 2nd edition. New York: Oxford University Press.

[10] Jähne, B., (1987). Image sequence analysis of complex physical objects: nonlinear small scale water surface waves. In *Proceedings ICCV'87, London*, pp. 191–200, IEEE. Washington, DC: IEEE Computer Society Press.

Part II

Elementary Spatial Processing

5 Neighborhood Operators

Bernd Jähne

Interdisziplinäres Zentrum für Wissenschaftliches Rechnen (IWR)
Universität Heidelberg, Germany

Handbook of Computer Vision and Applications
Volume 2
Signal Processing and Pattern Recognition

Copyright © 1999 by Academic Press
All rights of reproduction in any form reserved.
ISBN 0-12-379772-1/$30.00

5.1 Introduction

The extraction of features from multidimensional signals requires the analysis of at least a local neighborhood. It is obvious that any processing of individual pixels, so-called *point operations*, will be of no use for this task. Such operations are just "cosmetics," changing the visual impression of the image but not extracting any useful information. By analysis of the local neighborhood a rich set of features can already be extracted. We can distinguish areas of constant gray values from those that contain an edge, a texture, or just noise.

Thus this chapter gives an important theoretical basis for lowlevel signal processing. We first discuss some basics, provide a general definition of neighborhood operators and introduce a useful operator notation (Section 5.2.3). The main part of the chapter is devoted to a detailed discussion of the various classes of neighborhood operators: linear shift-invariant operators or convolution operators (Section 5.3), and various classes of nonlinear operators (Section 5.5). In this respect we will also discuss the principal limitations of linear operators in Section 5.5.1. The last section of the chapter (Section 5.6) focuses on more practical questions. Can we establish some general rules as to how to compute neighborhood operators in an efficient way? How do we handle neighborhood operators at the borders of images?

5.2 Basics

5.2.1 Definition of neighborhood operators

A neighborhood operator takes the gray values of the neighborhood around a point, performs some operations with them, and writes the result back on the pixel. This operation is repeated for all points of the signal. Therefore, we can write a neighborhood operation with a multidimensional continuous signal $g(\boldsymbol{x})$ as

$$g'(\boldsymbol{x}) = N(\{g(\boldsymbol{x}')\}, \forall(\boldsymbol{x} - \boldsymbol{x}') \in M) \tag{5.1}$$

where M is an area, called *mask*, *region of support*, or *structure element*. The size and shape of M determines the neighborhood operation by specifying the input values of g in the area M shifted with its origin to the point $\boldsymbol{x}$. The neighborhood operation N itself is not specified here. It can be of any type; its result determines the value of the output g' at $\boldsymbol{x}$. For symmetry reasons the mask is often symmetric and has its center of gravity in the origin.

For digital signals a general neighborhood operation can be expressed as

$$G'_{m,n} = N(G_{m'-m,n'-n}\}, \forall\, [m, n]^T \in M) \tag{5.2}$$

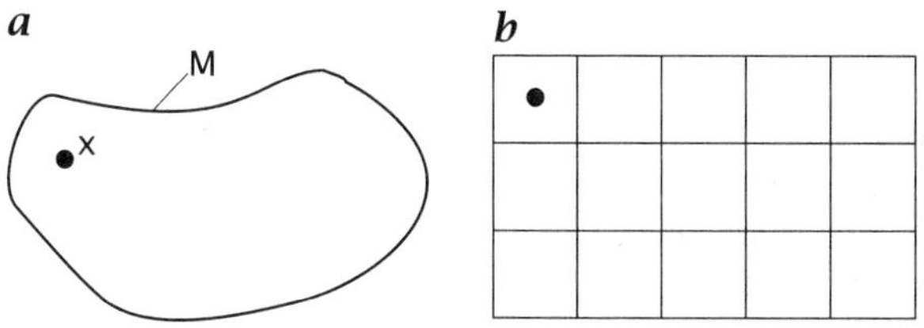

Figure 5.1: *Mask or structure element with **a** continuous; and **b** digital 2-D signals on a square lattice. The point that receives the result is marked.*

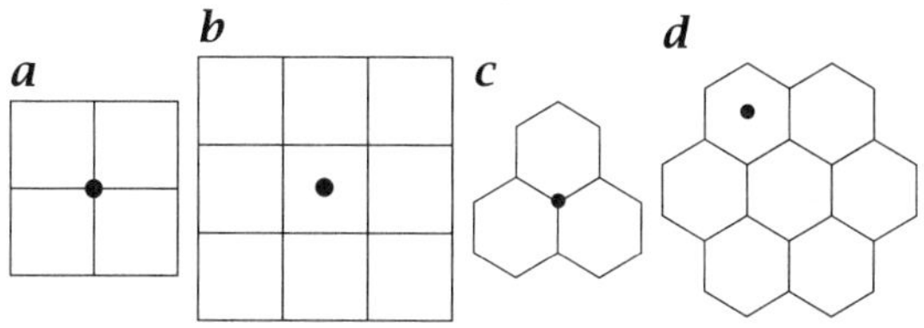

Figure 5.2: *Various types of symmetric masks on 2-D lattices: **a** 2×2 mask; and **b** 3×3 mask on a square lattice. **c** and **d** nearest-neighborhood mask on a hexagonal lattice.*

or by equivalent expressions for dimensions other than two.

Although these equations do not specify in any way the type of neighborhood operation that is performed, they still reveal the common structure of all neighborhood operations. Thus very general strategies can be developed to compute them efficiently as discussed in Section 5.6.

5.2.2 Shape and symmetry of neighborhoods

As we have seen, any type of neighborhood operator is first determined by the size of the mask. With continuous signals, the mask may take any shape. With digital data on orthogonal lattices, the mask is normally of rectangular shape. In any case, we must also specify the point relative to the mask which receives the result of the operation (Fig. 5.1).

With regard to symmetry, the most natural choice is to place the result of the operation at the pixel in the center of the mask. While this is straightforward for continuous masks, it requires more thought for digital signals. Natural choices for masks on an orthogonal lattice are rectangles. Basically there are two types of symmetric masks: masks with an even or odd size of pixels in each direction. For odd-sized masks, the symmetry center coincides with the central pixel and, thus, seems to be a good choice (Fig. 5.2b). The smallest size of odd-sized masks includes only the directly neighboring pixels. In one, two, and three dimensions, the mask includes 3, 9, and 27 pixels, respectively.

In contrast, even-sized masks seem not to be suitable for neighborhood operations because there is no pixel that lies in the center of the mask. With a trick, we can apply them nevertheless, and they turn out to be useful for certain types of neighborhood operations. The result of the neighborhood operation is simply written back to pixels that lie in between the original pixels (Fig. 5.2a). Thus, the resulting image is shifted by half the pixel distance into every direction and the receiving central pixel lies directly in the center of the neighborhoods. In effect, the resulting image has one pixel less in every direction. It is very important to be aware of this shift by half the pixel distance. Therefore, image features computed by even-sized masks should never be combined with original gray values because this would lead to considerable errors. Also, a mask must either be even-sided or odd-sized in *all* directions for multidimensional digital signals. Otherwise, the output lattices do not coincide.

On a hexagonal lattice (Section 2.3.1), two types of masks exist. For one type the output lattice coincides with the input lattice, for the other the output lattice lies in the center of the triangle spanned by three lattice points of the input lattice (Fig. 5.2c and d). The smallest masks have 7 and 3 pixels, respectively.

The number of pixels contained in the masks increases considerably with their size. If R is the linear size of a mask in D dimensions, the mask has R^D elements. The higher the dimension the faster the number of elements with the size of the mask increases. Even small neighborhoods include hundreds or thousands of elements. Therefore, it will be a challenging task for higher-dimensional signal processing to develop efficient schemes to compute a neighborhood operation with as few computations as possible. Otherwise, it would not be possible to use them at all.

The challenge for efficient computation schemes is to decrease the number of computations from $O(R^D)$ to a lower order. This means that the number of computations is no longer proportional to R^D but rather to a lower order of the size R of the mask. The ultimate goal is to achieve computation schemes that increase only linearly with the size of the mask ($O(R^1)$) or, even better, do not depend at all on the size of the mask ($O(R^0)$).

5.2.3 Operator notation

In this section, we introduce an *operator notation* for signal processing operations. It helps us to make complex composite neighbor operations easily comprehensible. All operators will be written in calligraphic letters, as $\mathcal{B}, \mathcal{D}, \mathcal{H}, \mathcal{S}$. We write

$$G' = \mathcal{H} G \tag{5.3}$$

for an operator $\mathcal{H}$ which transforms the image $\boldsymbol{G}$ into the image $\boldsymbol{G}'$. Note that this notation can be used for any type of signal. It can be used for continuous as well as digital signals and for signals of any dimension.

Consecutive application is denoted by writing the operators one after the other. The right-most operator is applied first. Consecutive application of the same operator is expressed by an exponent

$$\underbrace{\mathcal{H}\mathcal{H}\ldots\mathcal{H}}_{\text{p times}} = \mathcal{H}^p \tag{5.4}$$

If the operator acts on a single image, the operand, which stands to the right in the equations, will be omitted. In this way we can write operator equations without targets. Furthermore, we will use braces in the usual way to control the order of execution.

The operator notation leads to a *representation-independent notation* of signal processing operations. A linear shift-invariant operator (see Section 3.2.3) performs a convolution operation in the spatial domain and a complex multiplication in the Fourier domain. With the operator notation, we can write the basic properties of the linear shift-invariant operator (Eq. (3.26)) in an easily comprehensible way and without specifying a target as

$$\begin{array}{ll} \text{commutativity} & \mathcal{H}_1\mathcal{H}_2 = \mathcal{H}_2\mathcal{H}_1 \\ \text{associativity} & \mathcal{H}_1(\mathcal{H}_2\mathcal{H}_3) = (\mathcal{H}_1\mathcal{H}_2)\mathcal{H}_3 \\ \text{distributivity over addition} & (\mathcal{H}_1 + \mathcal{H}_2)\mathcal{H}_3 = \mathcal{H}_1\mathcal{H}_2 + \mathcal{H}_2\mathcal{H}_3 \end{array} \tag{5.5}$$

As can be seen from these equations, other operations such as addition can also be used in the operator notation. Care must be taken with any *nonlinear* operator. As soon as nonlinear operators are involved, the order in which the operators are executed must strictly be given. We stick with the notation that operators are executed from the left to the right, provided that braces are not used to change the order of execution.

The point operation of pixelwise multiplication in the spatial domain is a simple example for a nonlinear operator. As this operator occurs frequently, it is denoted by a special symbol, a centered dot $(\cdot)$. A special symbol is required in order to distinguish it from successive application of operators. The operator expression $\mathcal{B}(\mathcal{D} \cdot \mathcal{D})$, for instance, means: apply the operator $\mathcal{D}$ to the signal, square the result pixel-wise, and then apply the operator $\mathcal{B}$. Without parentheses the expression $\mathcal{B}\mathcal{D} \cdot \mathcal{D}$ would mean: apply the operator $\mathcal{D}$ to the image and apply the operator $\mathcal{B}\mathcal{D}$ to the image and then multiply the results point by point. This notation thus gives precedence to the point-wise multiplication over consecutive operator execution. As a placeholder for an object onto which an operator is acting, we will use the symbol ":".

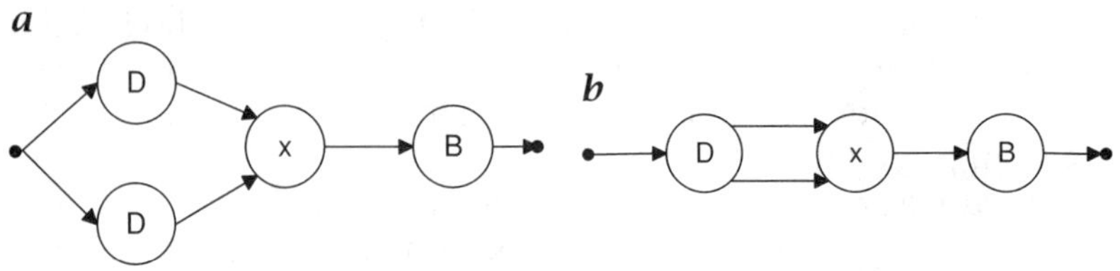

Figure 5.3: *Signal flow graphs of the operator combination $\mathcal{B}(\mathcal{D} \cdot \mathcal{D})$:* ***a*** *direct implementation;* ***b*** *optimized implementation.*

In this notation, the forementioned operator combination is written as $\mathcal{B}(\mathcal{D} : \cdot \mathcal{D} :)$.

The operator notation can also easily be mapped onto a signal flow graph. This is shown in Fig. 5.3 for the operator combination discussed in the preceding. Each operator is a node in this directed graph and represented by a circle. The operator to be performed is indicated in the circle. The flow of data is indicated by the directed vertices of the graph. Such graphs are very useful to investigate the optimal arrangement of processing units in a network. It is, for instance, evident that a single processing unit for the operator $\mathcal{D}$ is sufficient, provided that the output of this unit can feed both inputs of the multiplier.

5.3 Linear shift-invariant filters

5.3.1 Linearity

Linear operators are defined by the *principle of superposition*. If a and b are two complex-valued scalars, and $\mathcal{H}$ is an operator that maps an image onto another image of the same dimension, then the operator is linear if and only if

$$\mathcal{H}(a : +b :) = a\mathcal{H} : +b\mathcal{H} : \tag{5.6}$$

We can generalize Eq. (5.6) to the superposition of many inputs

$$\mathcal{H}\left(\sum_k a_k :\right) = \sum_k a_k \mathcal{H} : \tag{5.7}$$

The superposition property makes linear operators very useful. We can decompose a complex image into simpler components for which we can easily derive the response of the operator and then compose the resulting response from that of the components.

It is especially useful to decompose an image into its individual pixels as it has been discussed in Section 3.1.1.

5.3.2 Shift invariance and convolution

Another important property of an operator is shift invariance or homogeneity. It means that the response of the operator does not explicitly depend on the position. If we shift a signal, the output image is the same but for the shift applied. We can formulate this property more elegantly with a *shift operator* $\mathcal{S}$. For 2-D images, for example, the shift operator is defined as

$$^{mn}\mathcal{S}G_{m'n'} = G_{m'-m,n'-n} \tag{5.8}$$

An operator is then *shift-invariant* if and only if it commutes with the shift operator, that is,

$$\mathcal{H}\mathcal{S} = \mathcal{S}\mathcal{H} \tag{5.9}$$

Note that the shift operator $\mathcal{S}$ itself is a shift-invariant operator. An operator that is both linear and shift invariant is known as a *linear shift-invariant operator* or short *LSI* operator. This important class of operators is also known as *linear time-invariant* or *LTI* operators for time series.

It can be proven [1] that a linear shift-invariant operator must *necessarily* be a convolution operation in the space domain. There is *no* other operator type that is both linear and shift invariant. Thus, linear shift-invariant neighborhood operators share all the useful features of convolution that were discussed in Section 3.2.3. They are commutative, associative, and distribute over addition (see also Eq. (5.5)). These properties are very useful for an efficient design of filter operations (Chapter 6).

5.3.3 Point spread function

As just discussed in the previous section, an LSI filter can be represented in the space domain as a convolution operation. In two dimensions the image $\boldsymbol{G}$ is convolved with another image $\boldsymbol{H}$ that represents the LSI operator:

$$G'_{mn} = \sum_{m'=0}^{M-1}\sum_{n'=0}^{N-1} H_{m',n'}G_{m-m',n-n'} \tag{5.10}$$

Since for a neighborhood operation $\boldsymbol{H}$ is zero except for a small neighborhood this operation can also be written as

$$G'_{mn} = \sum_{m'=-R}^{R}\sum_{n'=-R}^{R} H_{-m',-n'}G_{m+m',n+n'} \tag{5.11}$$

In this equation it is assumed that coefficients of $\boldsymbol{H}$ are nonzero only in a (2R+1) × (2R+1) window. Both representations are equivalent if we consider the periodicity in the space domain (Section 3.3.1). The latter representation is much more practical and gives a better comprehension of the operator. For example, the following M × N matrix and 3 × 3 filter mask are equivalent:

$$\begin{bmatrix} 0\bullet & -1 & 0 & \ldots & 0 & 1 \\ 1 & 0 & 0 & \ldots & 0 & 2 \\ 0 & 0 & 0 & \ldots & 0 & 0 \\ \vdots & \vdots & \vdots & & \vdots & \vdots \\ 0 & 0 & 0 & \ldots & 0 & 0 \\ -1 & -2 & 0 & \ldots & 0 & 0 \end{bmatrix} \equiv \begin{bmatrix} 0 & -1 & -2 \\ 1 & 0\bullet & -1 \\ 2 & 1 & 0 \end{bmatrix} \tag{5.12}$$

For a D dimensional signal, the convolution sum can be written with a simplified vector indexing also used in Section 2.4.4:

$$G'_{\boldsymbol{n}} = \sum_{\boldsymbol{n}'=-\boldsymbol{R}}^{\boldsymbol{R}} H_{-\boldsymbol{n}'} G_{\boldsymbol{n}+\boldsymbol{n}'} \tag{5.13}$$

with $\boldsymbol{n} = [n_1, n_2, \ldots, n_D]$, $\boldsymbol{R} = [R_1, R_2, \ldots, R_D]$, where $G_{\boldsymbol{n}}$ is an element of a D-dimensional signal $G_{n_1,n_2,\ldots,n_D}$. The notation for the sums in this equation is an abbreviation for

$$\sum_{\boldsymbol{n}'=-\boldsymbol{R}}^{\boldsymbol{R}} = \sum_{n'_1=-R_1}^{R_1} \sum_{n'_2=-R_2}^{R_2} \ldots \sum_{n'_D=-R_D}^{R_D} \tag{5.14}$$

The vectorial indexing introduced here allows writing most of the relations for arbitary dimensional signals in a simple way. Moreover, it can also be used for skewed coordinate systems if $\boldsymbol{n}$ are regarded as the indices of the corresponding *lattice vectors* (see Eq. (2.27), Section 2.4.2).

The filter mask is identical to another quantity known as the *point spread function*, which gives the response of the filter to a point image:

$$P'_{\boldsymbol{n}} = \sum_{\boldsymbol{n}'=-\boldsymbol{R}}^{\boldsymbol{R}} H_{\boldsymbol{n}'} P_{\boldsymbol{n}-\boldsymbol{n}'} = H_{\boldsymbol{n}} \tag{5.15}$$

where

$$P_{\boldsymbol{n}} = \begin{cases} 1 & \boldsymbol{n} = \boldsymbol{0} \\ 0 & \text{otherwise} \end{cases} \tag{5.16}$$

The central importance of the point spread function is based on the fact that the convolution operation is linear. If we know the response to a point image, we can compute the response to any image, as any image can be composed of point images as discussed in Section 3.1.1. With respect to the analysis of time series, the point spread function is known as the *impulse response*, with respect to the solution of partial differential equations as the *Green's function* [2].

5.3.4 Transfer function

The Fourier transform of the convolution mask is known as the *transfer function* of a linear filter. The transfer function has an important practical meaning. For each wave number, it gives the factor by which a periodic structure is multiplied using the filter operation. This factor is generally a complex number. Thus, a periodic structure experiences not only a change in the amplitude but also a phase shift:

$$\begin{aligned} \hat{G}'_{\boldsymbol{v}} = \hat{H}_{\boldsymbol{v}}\hat{G}_{\boldsymbol{v}} &= r_H \exp(\mathrm{i}\varphi_H)\, r_G \exp(\mathrm{i}\varphi_G) \\ &= r_H r_G \exp[\mathrm{i}(\varphi_H + \varphi_G)] \end{aligned} \tag{5.17}$$

where the complex numbers are represented by their magnitude and phase as complex exponentials.

Using the wave number normalized to the Nyquist limit (Eq. (2.34) in Section 2.4.2), the transfer function is given by

$$\hat{h}(\tilde{k}) = \sum_{n'=-R}^{R} h_{n'} \exp(-\pi \mathrm{i} n' \tilde{k}) \tag{5.18}$$

for a 1-D signal and by

$$\hat{h}(\tilde{\boldsymbol{k}}) = \sum_{\boldsymbol{n}'=-\boldsymbol{R}}^{\boldsymbol{R}} H_{\boldsymbol{n}'} \exp(-\pi \mathrm{i} \boldsymbol{n}'^T \tilde{\boldsymbol{k}}) \tag{5.19}$$

for a multidimensional signal. For a nonorthogonal, that is, skewed lattice, the vectorial index $\boldsymbol{n}'$ has to be replaced by the reciprocal lattice vector (Eq. (2.29)), and Eq. (5.19) becomes

$$\hat{h}(\boldsymbol{k}) = \sum_{\boldsymbol{v}=-\boldsymbol{R}}^{\boldsymbol{R}} H_{\boldsymbol{r}} \exp(-2\pi \mathrm{i} \hat{\boldsymbol{r}}_{\boldsymbol{v}}^T \boldsymbol{k}) \tag{5.20}$$

5.3.5 Symmetries

Symmetries play a central rule for linear shift-invariant filters in the processing of higher-dimensional signal processing. This is because of the simplified transfer function of symmetric masks. According to Section 3.2.3, filters of even and odd symmetry have a real and purely imaginary transfer function, respectively. The symmetry of a filter is most generally expressed by:

$$H_{\boldsymbol{R}-\boldsymbol{r}} = \pm H_{\boldsymbol{r}} \tag{5.21}$$

This is a necessary and sufficient condition for a real or imaginary transfer function. Filters normally meet a stronger symmetry condition for each direction d:

$$H_{r_1,\ldots,R_d-r_d,\ldots,r_D} = \pm H_{r_1,\ldots,r_d,\ldots,r_D} \tag{5.22}$$

For separable symmetric filters, the symmetry conditions can be expressed for each 1-D component separately:

$$h_{R_d-r_d} = \pm h_{r_d} \tag{5.23}$$

As the transfer functions of the 1-D components of separable filters are combined multiplicatively, an even and odd number of odd components results in an even and odd filter according to Eq. (5.21) and thus into a real and imaginary transfer function, respectively.

Because of the significance of separable filters (Section 5.6.1), we focus on the symmetry of 1-D filters. Besides odd and even symmetry, it is necessary to distinguish filters with an even and odd number of coefficients.

The situation is straightforward for filters with an odd number of coefficients. Then the central coefficient is the center of symmetry and the result of a filter operation is written to the position of this central coefficient. This symmetry is implicitly considered in Eqs. (5.13) and (5.18) where the central coefficient has the index 0. With this indexing of the filter coefficients, the convolution sum and transfer function of even 1-D filters with $2R+1$ coefficients—also known as *type I FIR filter* [3]—can be expressed as

$$g'_n = h_0 g_n + \sum_{n'=1}^{R} h'_n (g_{n+n'} + g_{n-n'}), \quad \hat{h}(\tilde{k}) = h_0 + \sum_{n'=1}^{R} 2h_{n'} \cos(n'\pi\tilde{k}) \tag{5.24}$$

and for odd filters with $2R+1$ coefficients or *type III FIR filters* as

$$g'_n = \sum_{n'=1}^{R} h'_n (g_{n-n'} - g_{n+n'}), \quad \hat{h}(\tilde{k}) = \mathrm{i} \sum_{n'=1}^{R} 2h_{n'} \sin(n'\pi\tilde{k}) \tag{5.25}$$

For filters with an even number of coefficients, there is no central pixel. The symmetry center rather lies in-between two pixels. This means that the results of a filter operation with such a filter are to be placed on a grid that is shifted by half a pixel distance. Because of this shift between the output pixel and the input pixels, the transfer function of an even filter with $2R$ coefficients *type II FIR filter* is

$$\hat{h}(\tilde{k}) = h_0 + \sum_{n'=1}^{R} 2h_{n'} \cos((n' - 1/2)\pi\tilde{k}) \tag{5.26}$$

The transfer function of an odd filter with $2R$ coefficients or *type IV FIR filter* is

$$\hat{h}(\tilde{k}) = \mathrm{i} \sum_{n'=1}^{R} 2h_{n'} \sin((n' - 1/2)\pi\tilde{k}) \tag{5.27}$$

The equations for symmetric filters for two and more dimensions are significantly more complex and are discussed in Jähne [4].

5.3.6 LSI operators as least squares estimators

LSI operators compute a new value at each point in a signal from a linear combination of neighboring points. Likewise, a least squares estimator computes the estimate of a quantity from a linear combination of the input values. Thus it appears that a close relationship should exist between LSI operators and least squares estimators.

We assume that we want to fit a certain function with linear parameters a_p

$$f(\boldsymbol{x}) = \sum_{p=0}^{P-1} a_p f_p(\boldsymbol{x}) \tag{5.28}$$

to the local spatial gray value variation $g(\boldsymbol{x})$. For 2-D digital signals, the continuous functions $f_p(\boldsymbol{x})$ have to be replaced by matrices $\boldsymbol{F}_p$. All of the following equations are also valid for digital signals but it is more convenient to stick with the continuous case. In the least squares sense, the following error measure $e^2(\boldsymbol{x})$ should be minimized:

$$e^2(\boldsymbol{x}) = \int_{-\infty}^{\infty} w(\boldsymbol{x}') \left(\sum_{p=0}^{P-1} a_p(\boldsymbol{x}) f_p(\boldsymbol{x}') - g(\boldsymbol{x} + \boldsymbol{x}') \right)^2 \mathrm{d}^D x' \tag{5.29}$$

In this integral the window function $w(\boldsymbol{x}')$ has been introduced to limit the fit to a local neighborhood around the point $\boldsymbol{x}$. Therefore, the fit coefficients $a_p(\boldsymbol{x})$ depend on the position. Normally, the window function is an isotropic even function with a maximum at the origin monotonically decreasing with increasing distance from the origin. We further assume that the window function is normalized, that is,

$$\int_{-\infty}^{\infty} w(\boldsymbol{x}') \, \mathrm{d}^D x' = 1 \tag{5.30}$$

For the sake of simpler equations, the following abbreviations will be used in this section:

$$\begin{aligned} \langle f_p g_{\boldsymbol{x}} \rangle &= \int_{-\infty}^{\infty} w(\boldsymbol{x}') f_p(\boldsymbol{x}') g(\boldsymbol{x} + \boldsymbol{x}')\, \mathrm{d}^D x' \\ \langle f_p f_q \rangle &= \int_{-\infty}^{\infty} w(\boldsymbol{x}') f_p(\boldsymbol{x}') f_q(\boldsymbol{x}')\, \mathrm{d}^D x' \end{aligned} \tag{5.31}$$

Setting all derivatives of Eq. (5.29) with respect to the parameters $a_p(\boldsymbol{x})$ zero, the following linear equation system is obtained as the standard least squares solution of the minimization problem

$$\boldsymbol{a}(\boldsymbol{x}) = \boldsymbol{M}^{-1} \boldsymbol{d}(\boldsymbol{x}) \tag{5.32}$$

with

$$M_{p,q} = \langle f_p f_q \rangle\,,\ \boldsymbol{a} = [a_0(\boldsymbol{x}), a_1(\boldsymbol{x}), \ldots, a_{P-1}(\boldsymbol{x})]^T\ d_p = \langle f_p g_{\boldsymbol{x}} \rangle$$

The solution of Eq. (5.32) becomes most simple if the functions $f_p(\boldsymbol{x})$ are orthogonal to each other, that is, $\langle f_p f_q \rangle = \langle f_p^2 \rangle \delta_{p-q}$. Then the matrix $\boldsymbol{M}$ is diagonal and

$$a_p(\boldsymbol{x}) = \langle f_p g_{\boldsymbol{x}} \rangle \Big/ \left\langle f_p^2 \right\rangle \tag{5.33}$$

This expression can also be written as convolution integral by using Eq. (5.31) and substituting $\boldsymbol{x}'$ by $-\boldsymbol{x}'$:

$$a_p(\boldsymbol{x}) = \int_{-\infty}^{\infty} w(\boldsymbol{x}') f_p(-\boldsymbol{x}') g(\boldsymbol{x} - \boldsymbol{x}')\, \mathrm{d}^D x' \tag{5.34}$$

This means that the fit coefficient for each point is computed by convolving the windowed and mirrored orthonormal function with the signal.

Example 5.1: Plane fit

As a simple example we discuss the local plane fit, that is, the local approximation of the gray scale variation by a plane. The fit function is

$$f(\boldsymbol{x}) = a_0 + a_1 x_1 + a_2 x_2, \quad f_0 = 1, f_1 = x_1, f_2 = x_2 \tag{5.35}$$

It is easy to verify that these three functions are orthogonal to each other. Therefore

$$
\begin{aligned}
a_0 &= \int_{-\infty}^{\infty} w(\boldsymbol{x}')g(\boldsymbol{x}-\boldsymbol{x}')\,\mathrm{d}^D x' \\
a_1 &= -\int_{-\infty}^{\infty} w(\boldsymbol{x}')x_1' g(\boldsymbol{x}-\boldsymbol{x}')\,\mathrm{d}^D x' \Bigg/ \int_{-\infty}^{\infty} w(\boldsymbol{x}')x_1'^2\,\mathrm{d}^D x' \\
a_2 &= -\int_{-\infty}^{\infty} w(\boldsymbol{x}')x_2' g(\boldsymbol{x}-\boldsymbol{x}')\,\mathrm{d}^D x' \Bigg/ \int_{-\infty}^{\infty} w(\boldsymbol{x}')x_2'^2\,\mathrm{d}^D x'
\end{aligned}
\tag{5.36}
$$

As a special case for 2-D digital signals we take a binomial 3×3 window and obtain

$$
\begin{aligned}
\boldsymbol{W} &= \frac{1}{16}\begin{bmatrix} 1 & 2 & 1 \\ 2 & 4 & 2 \\ 1 & 2 & 1 \end{bmatrix}, \quad \boldsymbol{F}_0 = \begin{bmatrix} 1 & 1 & 1 \\ 1 & 1 & 1 \\ 1 & 1 & 1 \end{bmatrix} \\
\boldsymbol{F}_1 &= 2\begin{bmatrix} -1 & -1 & -1 \\ 0 & 0 & 0 \\ 1 & 1 & 1 \end{bmatrix}, \quad \boldsymbol{F}_2 = 2\begin{bmatrix} -1 & 0 & 1 \\ -1 & 0 & 1 \\ -1 & 0 & 1 \end{bmatrix}
\end{aligned}
\tag{5.37}
$$

The three matrices $\boldsymbol{F}_0$, $\boldsymbol{F}_1$, and $\boldsymbol{F}_2$ are already normalized, that is,

$$
\sum_{m=0}^{M-1}\sum_{n=0}^{N-1} W_{m,n}((F_p)_{m,n})^2 = 1 \tag{5.38}
$$

so that the division in Eq. (5.36) is not required. Then the convolution masks to obtain the fit coefficients a_0, a_1, and a_2 are

$$
\frac{1}{16}\begin{bmatrix} 1 & 2 & 1 \\ 2 & 4 & 2 \\ 1 & 2 & 1 \end{bmatrix}, \frac{1}{8}\begin{bmatrix} 1 & 2 & 1 \\ 0 & 0 & 0 \\ -1 & -2 & -1 \end{bmatrix}, \frac{1}{8}\begin{bmatrix} 1 & 0 & -1 \\ 2 & 0 & -2 \\ 1 & 0 & -1 \end{bmatrix} \tag{5.39}
$$

and we end up with the well-known binomial smoothing mask and the Sobel operator for the estimate of the mean and slopes of a local plane fit, respectively.

Thus, the close relationship between LSI operators and least squares fits is helpful to see what kind of properties an LSI operator is filtering out from a signal.

The case with nonorthogonal fit functions is slightly more complex. As the matrix $\boldsymbol{M}$ (Eq. (5.32)) depends only on the fit functions and the chosen window and not on the signal $g(\boldsymbol{x})$, the matrix $\boldsymbol{M}$ can be inverted once for a given fit. Then the fit coefficients are given as a linear combination of the results from the convolutions with all P fit functions:

$$
a_p(\boldsymbol{x}) = \sum_{p'=0}^{P-1} M_{p,p'}^{-1} \int_{-\infty}^{\infty} w(\boldsymbol{x}')f_{p'}(-\boldsymbol{x}')g(\boldsymbol{x}-\boldsymbol{x}')\,\mathrm{d}^D x' \tag{5.40}
$$

5.4 Recursive filters

5.4.1 Definition

Recursive filters are a special form of the linear convolution filters. This type of filter includes results from previous convolutions at neighboring pixels into the convolution sum. In this way, the filter gets directional. Recursive filters can most easily be understood if we apply them first to a 1-D discrete signal, a *time series*. Then we can write

$$g'_n = -\sum_{n''=1}^{S} a_{n''} g'_{n-n''} + \sum_{n'=-R}^{R} h_{n'} g_{n-n'} \tag{5.41}$$

While the neighborhood of the nonrecursive part (coefficients h) is symmetric around the central point, the recursive part is asymmetric, using only previously computed values. A filter that contains only such a recursive part is called a *causal filter*. If we put the recursive part on the left side of the equation, we observe that the recursive filter is equivalent to the following difference equation, also known as an *ARMA*(S,R) process (*autoregressive-moving average process*):

$$\sum_{n''=0}^{S} a_{n''} g'_{n-n''} = \sum_{n'=-R}^{R} h_{n'} g_{n-n'} \quad \text{with} \quad a_0 = 1 \tag{5.42}$$

5.4.2 Transfer function and z-transform

The transfer function of such a filter with a recursive and a nonrecursive part can be computed by applying the *discrete-space Fourier transform* (Section 3.1.1, Table 3.1) to Eq. (5.42). In the Fourier space the convolution of $\boldsymbol{g}'$ with $\boldsymbol{a}$ and of $\boldsymbol{g}$ with $\boldsymbol{h}$ is replaced by a multiplication of the corresponding Fourier transforms:

$$\hat{g}'(k) \sum_{n''=0}^{S} a_{n''} \exp(-2\pi \mathrm{i} n'' k) = \hat{g}(k) \sum_{n'=-R}^{R} h_{n'} \exp(-2\pi \mathrm{i} n' k) \tag{5.43}$$

Thus the transfer function is

$$\hat{h}(k) = \frac{\hat{g}'(k)}{\hat{g}(k)} = \frac{\sum\limits_{n'=-R}^{R} h_{n'} \exp(-2\pi \mathrm{i} n' k)}{\sum\limits_{n''=0}^{S} a_{n''} \exp(-2\pi \mathrm{i} n'' k)} \tag{5.44}$$

The nature of the transfer function of a recursive filter becomes more evident if we consider that both the numerator and the denominator can have zeros. Thus the nonrecursive part of the transfer function may cause zeros and the recursive part poles.

A deeper analysis of the zeros and thus the structure of the transfer function is not possible in the form as Eq. (5.44) is written. It requires an extension similar to the extension from real numbers to complex numbers that was necessary to introduce the Fourier transform (Section 3.1.3). We observe that the expressions for both the numerator and the denominator are polynomials in the *complex exponential* $\exp(2\pi i k)$. The complex exponential has a magnitude of one and thus covers the unit circle in the complex plane. It covers the whole complex plane if we add a radius r to the expression: $z = r\exp(2\pi i k)$.

With this extension, the expressions become polynomials in z. As such we can apply the fundamental law of algebra that any *complex polynomial* of degree n can be factorized in n factors containing the roots or zeros of the polynomial. Thus we can write a new expression in z, which becomes the transfer function for $z = \exp(2\pi i k)$:

$$\hat{h}(z) = \frac{\prod\limits_{n'=-R}^{R} (1 - c_{n'} z^{-1})}{\prod\limits_{n''=0}^{S} (1 - d_{n''} z^{-1})} \tag{5.45}$$

Each of the factors $c_{n'}$ and $d_{n''}$ is a zero of the according polynomial ($z = c_{n'}$ or $z = d_{n''}$).

The inclusion of the factor r in the extended transfer function results in an extension of the Fourier transform, the *z-transform* that is defined as

$$\hat{g}(z) = \sum_{n=-\infty}^{\infty} g_n z^{-n} \tag{5.46}$$

The z-transform of the series g_n can be regarded as the Fourier transform of the series $g_n r^{-n}$ [5]. The z-transform is the key mathematical tool to understand recursive filters. Detailed accounts of the z-transform are given by Oppenheim and Schafer [3] and Poularikas [6]; the 2-D z-transform is discussed by Lim [5].

The factorization of the z-transform of the filter in Eq. (5.45)—and in turn of the transfer function—is an essential property. Multiplication of the individual factors of the transfer function means that we can decompose any filter into elementary filters containing only one factor because multiplication of transfer functions is equivalent to cascaded convolution in the spatial domain (Section 3.2.3). The basic filters that are equivalent to a single factor in Eq. (5.45) will be discussed further in Section 5.4.6.

Recursive filters can also be defined in higher dimensions with the same type of equations as in Eq. (5.42); also the transfer function and z-transform of higher dimensional recursive filters can be written in the very same way as in Eq. (5.44). However, it is generally *not* possible to factorize the z-transform as in Eq. (5.45) [5]. From Eq. (5.45) we can immediately conclude that it will be possible to factorize a *separable* recursive filter because then the higher dimensional polynomials can be factorized into 1-D polynomials. Given these inherent difficulties of higher-dimensional recursive filters we will restrict the further discussion on 1-D recursive filters that can be extended by cascaded convolution into higher-dimensional filters.

5.4.3 Infinite and unstable response

The *impulse response* or *point spread function* of a recursive filter is no longer identical to the filter coefficients as for nonrecursive filters (Section 5.3.3). It must rather be computed as the inverse Fourier transform of the transfer function. The impulse response of nonrecursive filters has only a finite number of nonzero samples. A filter with this property is called a *finite-duration impulse response* or *FIR* filter. In contrast, recursive filters have an *infinite-duration impulse response* (*IIR*).

The *stability* of the filter response is not an issue for nonrecursive filters but of central importance for recursive filters. A filter is said to be *stable* if and only if *each* bound input sequence generates a bound output sequence. In terms of the impulse response this means that a filter is stable if and only if the impulse response is absolutely summable [3]. For 1-D filters the analysis of the stability is straightforward because the conditions are well established by same basic algebraic theorems. A filter is stable and causal if and only if all poles and zeros of the z-transform $\hat{h}(z)$ (Eq. (5.45)) are inside the unit circle [3].

5.4.4 Relation between recursive and nonrecursive filters

Any stable recursive filter can be replaced by a nonrecursive filter, in general with an infinite-sized mask. Its mask is given by the point spread function of the recursive filter. In practice, the masks cannot be infinite and also need not be infinite. This is due to the fact that the envelope of the impulse response of any recursive filter decays exponentially (Section 5.4.6).

Another observation is of importance. From Eq. (5.44) we see that the transfer function of a recursive filter is the ratio of its nonrecursive and recursive part. This means that a purely recursive and a nonrecursive filter with the same coefficients are inverse filters to each other. This general relation is a good base to construct inverse filters from nonrecursive filters.

5.4.5 Zero-phase recursive filtering

The causal 1-D recursive filters are of not much use for processing of higher-dimensional spatial data. While a filter that uses only previous data is natural and useful for real-time processing of time series, it makes not much sense for spatial data. There is no "before" and "after" in spatial data. Even worse, the spatial shift (delay) associated with recursive filters is not acceptable because it causes phase shifts and thus objects to be shifted depending on the filters applied.

With a single recursive filter it is impossible to construct a zero-phase filter. Thus it is required to combine multiple recursive filters. The combination should either result in a zero-phase filter suitable for smoothing operations or a derivative filter that shifts the phase by 90°. Thus the transfer function should either be purely real or purely imaginary (Section 3.2.3).

We start with a 1-D causal recursive filter that has the transfer function

$$^{+}\hat{h}(\tilde{k}) = a(\tilde{k}) + \mathrm{i}b(\tilde{k}) \tag{5.47}$$

The superscript + denotes that the filter runs in positive coordinate direction. The transfer function of the same filter but running in the opposite direction has a similar transfer function. We replace $\tilde{k}$ by $-\tilde{k}$ and note that $a(-\tilde{k}) = a(+\tilde{k})$ and $b(-\tilde{k}) = -b(\tilde{k}))$ because the transfer function of a real PSF is Hermitian (Section 3.2.3) and thus obtain

$$^{-}\hat{h}(\tilde{k}) = a(\tilde{k}) - \mathrm{i}b(\tilde{k}) \tag{5.48}$$

Thus, only the sign of the imaginary part of the transfer function changes when the filter direction is reversed.

We now have three possibilities to combine the two transfer functions (Eqs. (5.47) and (5.48)) either into a purely real or imaginary transfer function:

$$\begin{array}{ll} \text{Addition} & {}^{e}\hat{h}(\tilde{k}) = \frac{1}{2}\left({}^{+}\hat{h}(\tilde{k}) + {}^{-}\hat{h}(\tilde{k})\right) = a(\tilde{k}) \\ \text{Subtraction} & {}^{o}\hat{h}(\tilde{k}) = \frac{1}{2}\left({}^{+}\hat{h}(\tilde{k}) - {}^{-}\hat{h}(\tilde{k})\right) = \mathrm{i}b(\tilde{k}) \\ \text{Multiplication} & \hat{h}(\tilde{k}) = {}^{+}\hat{h}(\tilde{k})\,{}^{-}\hat{h}(\tilde{k}) = a^2(\tilde{k}) + b^2(\tilde{k}) \end{array} \tag{5.49}$$

Addition and multiplication (consecutive application) of the left and right running filter yields filters of even symmetry, while subtraction results in a filter of odd symmetry. This way to cascade recursive filters gives them the same properties as zero- or $\pi/2$-phase shift nonrecursive filters with the additional advantage that they can easily be tuned, and extended point spread functions can be realized with only a few filter coefficients.

5.4.6 Basic recursive filters

In Section 5.4.2 we found that the factorization of the generalized recursive filter is a key to analyze its transfer function and stability properties (Eq. (5.45)). The individual factors contain the poles and zeros. From each factor, we can compute the impulse response so that the resulting impulse response of the whole filter is given by a cascaded convolution of all components.

As the factors are all of the form

$$f_n(\tilde{k}) = 1 - c_n \exp(-2\pi i \tilde{k}) \tag{5.50}$$

the analysis becomes quite easy. Still we can distinguish two basic types of partial factors. They result from the fact that the impulse response of the filter must be real. Therefore the transfer function must be Hermitian, that is, $f^*(-k) = f(k)$. This can only be the case when either the zero c_n is real or a pair of factors exists with complex-conjugate zeros. This condition gives rise of two basic types of recursive filters, the relaxation filter and the resonance filter that are discussed in detail in what follows. As these filters are only useful for image processing if they are applied both in forward and backward direction, we discuss also the resulting symmetric transfer function and point spread function.

Relaxation filter. The transfer function of the relaxation filter running in forward or backward direction is

$$^{\pm}\hat{r}(\tilde{k}) = \frac{1-\alpha}{1-\alpha\exp(\mp\pi i\tilde{k})} \quad \text{with} \quad \alpha \in \mathbb{R} \tag{5.51}$$

In this equation, the wave number has been replaced by the wave number normalized with the Nyquist limit (see Section 2.4.2, Eq. (2.34)). It also has been normalized so that $\hat{r}(0) = 1$. Comparing Eqs. (5.42) and (5.43) it is evident that the transfer function Eq. (5.51) belongs to the simple recursive filter

$$g'_n = \alpha g'_{n\mp 1} + (1-\alpha) g_n = g_n + \alpha(g'_{n\mp 1} - g_n) \tag{5.52}$$

with the point spread function

$$^{\pm}r_{\pm n} = \begin{cases} (1-\alpha)\alpha^n & n \geq 0 \\ 0 & \text{else} \end{cases} \tag{5.53}$$

This filter takes the fraction α from the previously calculated value and the fraction $1-\alpha$ from the current pixel.

The transfer function Eq. (5.51) is complex and can be divided into its real and imaginary parts as

$$^{\pm}\hat{r}(\tilde{k}) = \frac{1-\alpha}{1-2\alpha\cos\pi\tilde{k}+\alpha^2}\left[(1-\alpha\cos\pi\tilde{k}) \mp i\alpha\sin\pi\tilde{k}\right] \tag{5.54}$$

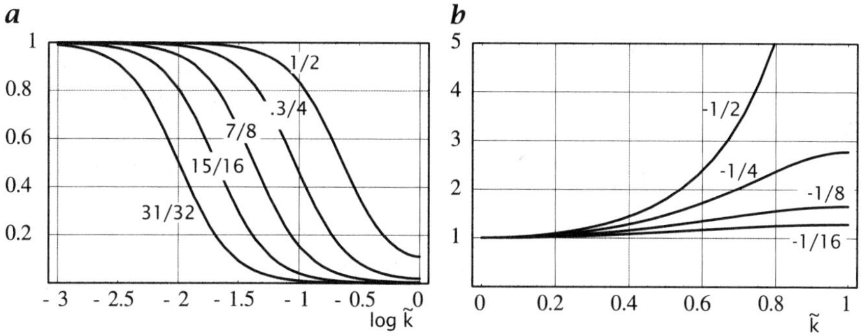

***Figure 5.4:** Transfer function of the relaxation filter $g'_n = \alpha g'_{n\mp1} + (1-\alpha)g_n$ applied first in forward and then in backward direction for **a** positive; and **b** negative values of α as indicated.*

From this transfer function, we can compute the multiplicative ($\hat{r}$) application of the filters by running it successively in positive and negative direction, see Eq. (5.49):

$$\hat{r}(\tilde{k}) = \frac{(1-\alpha)^2}{1-2\alpha\cos\pi\tilde{k}+\alpha^2} = \frac{1}{1+\beta-\beta\cos\pi\tilde{k}} \tag{5.55}$$

with

$$\beta = \frac{2\alpha}{(1-\alpha)^2} \quad \text{and} \quad \alpha = \frac{1+\beta-\sqrt{1+2\beta}}{\beta}$$

From Eq. (5.53) we can conclude that the relaxation filter is stable if $|\alpha| < 1$, which corresponds to $\beta \in]-1/2, \infty[$. As already noted, the transfer function is one for small wave numbers. A Taylor series in $\tilde{k}$ results in

$$\hat{r}(\tilde{k}) \approx= 1 - \frac{\alpha}{(1-\alpha)^2}(\pi\tilde{k})^2 + \frac{\alpha((1+10\alpha+\alpha^2)}{12(1-\alpha^2)^2}(\pi\tilde{k})^4 \tag{5.56}$$

If α is positive, the filter is a low-pass filter (Fig. 5.4a). It can be tuned by adjusting α. If α is approaching 1, the averaging distance becomes infinite. For negative α, the filter enhances high wave numbers (Fig. 5.4b).

This filter is the discrete analog to the first-order differential equation $\dot{y} + \tau y = 0$ describing a relaxation process with the relaxation time $\tau = -\Delta t / \ln \alpha$ [4].

Resonance filter. The transfer function of a filter with a pair of complex-conjugate zeros running in forward or backward direction is

$$\begin{aligned} {}^{\pm}\hat{s}(\tilde{k}) &= \frac{1}{1-r\exp(\mathrm{i}\pi\tilde{k}_0)\exp(\mp\mathrm{i}\pi\tilde{k})} \cdot \frac{1}{1-r\exp(-\mathrm{i}\pi\tilde{k}_0)\exp(\mp\mathrm{i}\pi\tilde{k})} \\ &= \frac{1}{1-2r\cos(\pi\tilde{k}_0)\exp(\mp\mathrm{i}\pi\tilde{k})+r^2\exp(\mp2\mathrm{i}\pi\tilde{k})} \end{aligned} \tag{5.57}$$

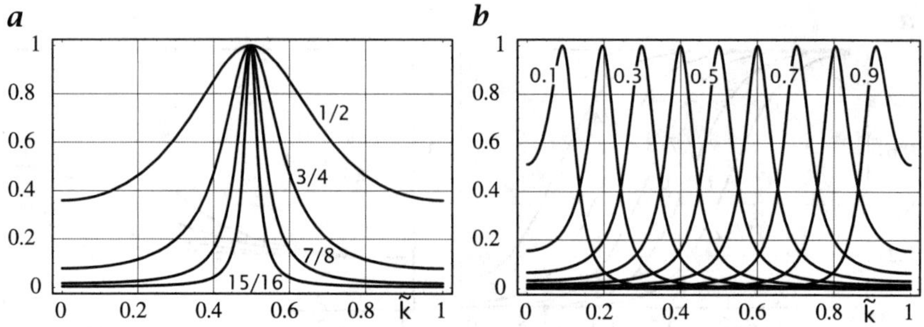

Figure 5.5: *Transfer function of the zero-phase recursive resonance filter for* ***a*** $\tilde{k}_0 = 1/2$ *and values of* r *as indicated; and* ***b*** $r = 7/8$ *and values of* $\tilde{k}_0$ *as indicated.*

The second row of the equation shows that this is the transfer function of the recursive filter

$$g'_n = g_n + 2r\cos(\pi\tilde{k}_0)g'_{n\mp1} - r^2 g'_{n\mp2} \tag{5.58}$$

The impulse response of this filter is [3]

$$h_{\pm n} = \begin{cases} \dfrac{r^n}{\sin\pi\tilde{k}_0}\sin[(n+1)\pi\tilde{k}_0] & n \geq 0 \\ 0 & n < 0 \end{cases} \tag{5.59}$$

If we run the filter back and forth, the resulting transfer function is

$$\hat{s}(\tilde{k}) = \frac{1}{\left(1-2r\cos[\pi(\tilde{k}-\tilde{k}_0)]+r^2\right)\left(1-2r\cos[\pi(\tilde{k}+\tilde{k}_0)]+r^2\right)} \tag{5.60}$$

From this equation, it is evident that this filter is a bandpass filter with a center wave number of $\tilde{k}_0$. The parameter r is related to the width of the bandpass. If $r = 1$, the transfer function has two *poles* at $\tilde{k} = \pm\tilde{k}_0$. If $r > 1$, the filter is unstable; even the slightest excitement will cause infinite amplitudes of the oscillation. The filter is only stable for $r \leq 1$.

The response of this filter can be normalized to obtain a bandpass filter with a unit response at the center wave number. The transfer function of this normalized filter is

$$\hat{s}(\tilde{k}) = \frac{(1-r^2)^2\sin^2(\pi\tilde{k}_0)}{(1+r^2)^2+2r^2\cos(2\pi\tilde{k}_0)-4r(1+r^2)\cos(\pi\tilde{k}_0)\cos(\pi\tilde{k})+2r^2\cos(2\pi\tilde{k})} \tag{5.61}$$

The denominator in Eq. (5.61) is still the same as in Eq. (5.60); it has only been expanded in terms with $\cos(n\pi\tilde{k}_0)$. The corresponding recursive filter coefficients are:

$$g'_n = (1-r^2)\sin(\pi\tilde{k}_0)g_n + 2r\cos(\pi\tilde{k}_0)g'_{n\mp1} - r^2 g'_{n\mp2} \tag{5.62}$$

Figure 5.5 shows the transfer function of this filter for values of $\tilde{k}_0$ and r as indicated.

For symmetry reasons, the factors become most simple for a resonance wave number of $\tilde{k}_0 = 1/2$. Then the recursive filter is

$$g'_n = (1 - r^2)g_n - r^2 g'_{n\mp 2} = g_n - r^2(g_n + g'_{n\mp 2}) \tag{5.63}$$

with the transfer function

$$\hat{s}(\tilde{k}) = \frac{(1 - r^2)^2}{1 + r^4 + 2r^2 \cos(2\pi\tilde{k})} \tag{5.64}$$

The maximum response of this filter at $\tilde{k} = 1/2$ is one and the minimum response at $\tilde{k} = 0$ and $\tilde{k} = 1$ is $((1 - r^2)/(1 + r^2))^2$.

This resonance filter is the discrete analog to a linear system governed by the second-order differential equation $\ddot{y} + 2\tau\dot{y} + \omega_0^2 y = 0$, the damped harmonic oscillator. The circular eigenfrequency ω_0 and the time constant τ of a real-world oscillator are related to the parameters of the discrete oscillator, r and $\tilde{k}_0$ by [4]

$$r = \exp(-\Delta t/\tau) \quad \text{and} \quad \tilde{k}_0 = \omega_0 \Delta t/\pi \tag{5.65}$$

5.5 Classes of nonlinear filters

5.5.1 Limitations of linear filters

In the previous sections, the theory of linear shift-invariant filters was discussed in detail. Although the theory of these filters is well established and they can be applied, they still have some severe limitations. Basically, linear filters cannot distinguish between a useful feature and noise. This property can be best demonstrated with a simple example. We assume a simple signal model with additive noise:

$$g'(\boldsymbol{x}) = g(\boldsymbol{x}) + n(\boldsymbol{x}) \Longleftrightarrow \hat{g}'(\boldsymbol{k}) = \hat{g}(\boldsymbol{k}) + \hat{n}(\boldsymbol{k}) \tag{5.66}$$

The signal to noise ratio (SNR) is defined by $|\hat{g}(\boldsymbol{k})| \,/\, |\hat{n}(\boldsymbol{k})|$. If we now apply a linear filter with the transfer function $\hat{h}(\boldsymbol{k})$ to this signal, the filtered signal is

$$\hat{h}(\boldsymbol{k})\hat{g}'(\boldsymbol{k}) = \hat{h}(\boldsymbol{k})(\hat{g}(\boldsymbol{k}) + \hat{n}(\boldsymbol{k})) = \hat{h}(\boldsymbol{k})\hat{g}(\boldsymbol{k}) + \hat{h}(\boldsymbol{k})\hat{n}(\boldsymbol{k}) \tag{5.67}$$

It is immediately evident that the noise and the signal are damped by the same factor. Consequently, the SNR does not increase at all by linear filtering, it just stays the same.

From the preceding considerations, it is obvious that more complex approaches are required than linear filtering. Common to all these approaches is that in one or the other way the filters are made dependent on the context or are tailored for specific types of signals. Often a control strategy is an important part of such filters that controls which filter or in which way a filter has to be applied at a certain point in the image. Here, we will outline only the general classes for nonlinear filters. Pitas and Venetsanopoulos [7] give a detailed survey on this topic.

5.5.2 Rank-value filters

Rank-value filters are based on a quite different concept than linear-shift invariant operators. These operators consider all pixels in the neighborhood. It is implicitly assumed that each pixel, distorted or noisy, carries still useful and correct information. Thus, convolution operators are not equipped to handle situations where the value at a pixel carries incorrect information. This situation arises, for instance, when an individual sensor element in a CCD array is defective or a transmission error occurred.

To handle such cases, operations are required that apply selection mechanisms and do not use all pixels in the neighborhood to compute the output of the operator. The simplest class of operators of this type are rank-value filters. While the convolution operators may be characterized by "weighting and accumulating," rank-value filters may be characterized by "comparing and selecting."

For this we take all the gray values of the pixels which lie within the filter mask and sort them by ascending gray value. This sorting is common to all rank-value filters. They only differ by the position in the list from which the gray value is picked out and written back to the center pixel. The filter operation that selects the medium value is called the *median filter*. The median filter is an excellent example for a filter that is adapted to a certain type of signal. It is ideally suited for removing a single pixel that has a completely incorrect gray value because of a transmission or data error. It is less well suited, for example, to reduce white noise.

Other known rank-value filters are the *minimum filter* and the *maximum filter*. As the names say, these filters select out of a local neighborhood, either the minimum or the maximum gray value forming the base for gray scale *morphological filters* (Chapter 21).

As rank-value filters do not perform arithmetic operations but select pixels, we will never run into rounding problems. These filters map a discrete set of gray values onto itself. The theory of rank-value filters has still not been developed to the same extent as of convolution filters. As they are nonlinear filters, it is much more difficult to understand their general properties. Rank-value filters are discussed in detail by Pitas and Venetsanopoulos [7].

5.5.3 Pixels with certainty measures

Linear filters as discussed in Section 5.3 treat each pixel equally. Implicitly, it is assumed that the information they are carrying is of equal significance. While this seems to be a reasonable first approximation, it is certain that it cannot be generally true. During image acquisition, the sensor area may contain bad sensor elements that lead to erroneous gray values at certain positions in the image. Furthermore, the sensitivity and noise level may vary from sensor element to sensor element. In addition, transmission errors may occur so that individual pixels may carry wrong information. Thus we may attach in one way or the other a certainty measurement to each picture element.

Once a certainty measurement has been attached to a pixel, it is obvious that the normal convolution operators are no longer a good choice. Instead, the certainty has to be considered when performing any kind of operation with it. A pixel with suspicious information should only get a low weighting factor in the convolution sum. This kind of approach leads us to what is known as *normalized convolution* [8, 9].

This approach seems to be very natural for a scientist or engineer. He is used to qualifying any measurement with an error. A measurement without a careful error estimate is of no value. The standard deviation of a measured value is required for the further analysis of any quantity that is related to the measurement. Normalized convolution applies this common principle to image processing.

The power of this approach is related to the fact that we have quite different possibilities to define the certainty measurement. It need not only be related to a direct measurement error of a single pixel. If we are, for example, interested in computing an estimate of the mean gray value in an object, we can take the following approach. We devise a kind of certainty measurement that analyzes neighborhoods and attaches low weighting factors where we may suspect an edge so that these pixels do not contribute much to the mean gray value or feature of the object.

In a similar way, we can, for instance, also check how likely the gray value of a certain pixel is if we suspect some distortion by transmission errors or defective pixels. If the certainty measurement of a certain pixel is below a critical threshold, we replace it by a value interpolated from the surrounding pixels.

5.5.4 Adaptive and steerable filters

Adaptive filters can be regarded as a linear filter operation that is made dependent on the neighborhood. Adaptive filtering can best be explained by a classical application, the suppression of noise without significant blurring of image features.

The basic idea of adaptive filtering is that in certain neighborhoods we could very well apply a smoothing operation. If, for instance, the neighborhood is flat, we can assume that we are within an object with constant features and thus apply an isotropic smoothing operation to this pixel to reduce the noise level. If an edge has been detected in the neighborhood, we could still apply some smoothing, namely along the edge. In this way, some noise is still removed but the edge is not blurred. With this approach, we need a set of filters for various unidirectional and directional smoothing operations and choose the most appropriate smoothing filter for each pixel according to the local structure around it. Because of the many filters involved, adaptive filtering may be a very computational-intensive approach. This is the case if either the coefficients of the filter to be applied have to be computed for every single pixel or if a large set of filters is used in parallel and after all filters are computed it is decided at every pixel which filtered image is chosen for the output image.

With the discovery of steerable filters [10], however, adaptive filtering techniques have become attractive and computationally much more efficient.

5.5.5 Nonlinear combinations of filters

Normalized convolution and adaptive filtering have one strategy in common. Both use combinations of linear filters and nonlinear point operations such as point-wise multiplication and division of images. The combination of linear filter operations with nonlinear point operations makes the whole operation nonlinear.

The combination of these two kinds of elementary operations is a very powerful instrument for image processing. Operators containing combinations of linear filter operators and point operators are very attractive as they can be composed of very simple and elementary operations that are very well understood and for which analytic expressions are available. Thus, these operations in contrast to many others can be the subject of a detailed mathematical analysis. Many advanced signal and image processing techniques are of that type. This includes operators to compute local structure in images and various operations for texture analysis.

5.6 Efficient neighborhood operations

The computational costs for neighborhood operations in higher-dimensional signals can be very high. If we assume that the number of operations is proportional to the size of the mask and size of the image, a neighborhood operation is an operation of the order $O((NR)^D)$ in a D-dimensional image, where R and N are the linear dimension of the mask and the image, respectively. With respect to a single point a neighborhood operation is of the order $O(R^D)$.

This means that the number of operations for neighborhood operations is exploding with the dimension of a signal. A neighborhood with $R = 5$ contains just 25 pixels in a 2-D image, while it has already 125 pixels in a 3-D image and 625 pixels in a 4-D image. For efficient neighborhood operations it is thus of utmost importance to reduce the order with efficient algorithms. The goal is to arrive at an algorithm of linear order, $O(R)$, or ultimately at an algorithm that does not depend at all on the size of the mask, that is, $O(R^0)$.

In the rest of this chapter, we will discuss three classes of optimization strategies:

- general strategies that are valid for all classes of neighborhood operations;
- operator class specific strategies; and
- operator specific optimizations.

The most preferable technique is, of course, the first one as it is most generic and accelerates all classes of neighborhood operations. Optimizing a specific operator is the least preferable strategy as it is highly specific and does not benefit any other operators. It may still be a valid choice for frequently used operators that have high computational cost.

In the following, we first discuss efficient algorithms for convolution in higher dimensional signals (Section 5.6.1). Strategies for efficient computation of morphological neighborhood operators are discussed in Chapter 21. Then we focus on general strategies to speed up all types of efficient neighborhood operators (Section 5.6.2). This is possible as the speed of an algorithm does not depend only on the number of arithmetic operations but also on efficient memory access techniques. This issue becomes increasingly important because the speed of memory access tends to lag more and more behind the computing power of modern microcomputer architectures, especially with multimedia instruction sets (Volume 3, Chapter 3).

5.6.1 Minimizing computational effort

For the optimization of neighborhood operations for higher dimensional signals, similar remarks are valid as for filter design (Section 6.2). Many of the classical techniques [11, 12] that have been developed with 1-D filtering of time series are simply not optimally suited for higher-dimensional signals. Thus the classical techniques are not reviewed here. We rather focus on the aspects for higher-dimensional signals.

Without doubt, a filter should have as few non-zero coefficients as possible for fast processing. Thus the minimization of the computational effort is a design problem in the first place. How can I devise a filter for a certain purpose that meets creation criteria concerning accuracy etc. with as few coefficients as possible? This topic is treated in Chapter 6. Here we will discuss the principles of general techniques to speed up convolution operations. Examples of the usage of these techniques are discussed in Chapters 6–8 and Chapter 10.

Symmetric masks. The effects of symmetries on the point spread function and transfer function are discussed in Section 5.3.5. Symmetries in filter masks reduce the number of multiplications. For each symmetry axis we can save one multiplication for a pair of pixels by writing

$$h_r g_{n-r} + h_{-r} g_{n+r} = h_r(g_{n-r} \pm g_{n+r}) \quad \text{if} \quad h_{-r} = \pm h_r \tag{5.68}$$

The number of additions/subtractions remains the same. If a D-dimensional filter mask is symmetric in all directions, the number of multiplications is thus reduced by a factor of 2^D. Although this constitutes a significant reduction in the number of multiplications, the number of additions still remains the same. Even if we saved all multiplications, the number of arithmetic operations would be just halved. This also means that the order of the convolution has not changed and is still $O(R^D)$ for a D-dimensional filter of the size R. While the reduction of multiplications was significant for early computer architectures where multiplication was significantly slower than addition (Volume 3, Section 3.2) this is no longer of importance for standard microprocessors because addition and multiplication operations are equally fast. It is still, however, an important issue for configurable hardware such as *field-programmable gate arrays* (*FPGA*, Volume 3, Chapter 2).

Equal coefficients. Without regard to symmetries, the number of multiplications can also be reduced by simply checking the filter masks for equal coefficients and adding all those pixels before they are multiplied with the common factor. We demonstrate this technique with two well-known filter masks:

$$\boldsymbol{S}_X = \begin{bmatrix} 1 & 0 & -1 \\ 2 & 0 & -2 \\ 1 & 0 & -1 \end{bmatrix}, \quad \boldsymbol{B}^4 = \begin{bmatrix} 1 & 4 & 6 & 4 & 1 \\ 4 & 16 & 24 & 16 & 4 \\ 6 & 24 & 36 & 24 & 6 \\ 4 & 16 & 24 & 16 & 4 \\ 1 & 4 & 6 & 4 & 1 \end{bmatrix} \tag{5.69}$$

In the first mask, one mask of the *Sobel operator*, there are only two different multiplication factors (1 and 2) for 9 coefficients. The 5×5

binomial operator has only six different factors (1, 4, 6, 16, 24, and 36) for 25 coefficients. In both cases substantial savings in the number of multiplications are achieved. However, as with the technique to make use of the symmetries of the filter mask, no additions/subtractions are saved and the order of the operation does not change.

Separable filters. Separable filters are one of the most efficient strategies to reduce the order of a D-dimensional convolution operation. A D-dimensional filter of the length R with $O(R^D)$ operations can be replaced by D 1-D convolution operations of order $O(R)$. Thus separable filters reduce the convolution operation from an order $O(R^D)$ operation to an operation of linear order $O(DR)$. The savings in the number of operations increase with the dimension of the signal. While for a 5×5 filter operation the number of operations can only be reduced from 25 multiplications and 24 additions to 10 multiplications and 8 additions, for a $5 \times 5 \times 5$ filter 125 multiplications and 124 additions are reduced to 15 multiplications and 12 additions.

Thus whenever possible, it is advisable to use separable neighborhood operations. This approach has the significant additional advantage that filters can be designed for arbitrary-dimensional signals.

Selection of optimal scale. Another simple but often not considered technique is to use multigrid image presentations such as pyramids (Section 4.4) and to select the right scale for the operation to be performed. Imagine that an operation with a rather large filter kernel could be performed on a representation of the image with only half the size. Then the number of pixels is reduced by a factor of 2^D and the number of operations per pixel by another factor of two if we assume that the filter operation is of linear order. In total the number of operations is reduced by a factor of 2^{D+1}. For a 2-D image this means an 8-fold speed-up and for a volumetric image a 16-fold speed-up.

5.6.2 Efficient storage schemes

In-place computation of nonrecursive neighborhood operations needs intermediate storage because the operation requires the access to pixels that are already overwritten with the result of previous neighborhood operations. Of course, it would be the easiest way to store the whole image with which a neighborhood operation should be performed. Sometimes this approach is useful, for instance when it is required to filter an image with different filters or when the original image must be preserved anyway. Often, however, not enough storage area is available to allow for such a simplistic approach. Thus we discuss in the following two efficient storage schemes for neighborhood operations.

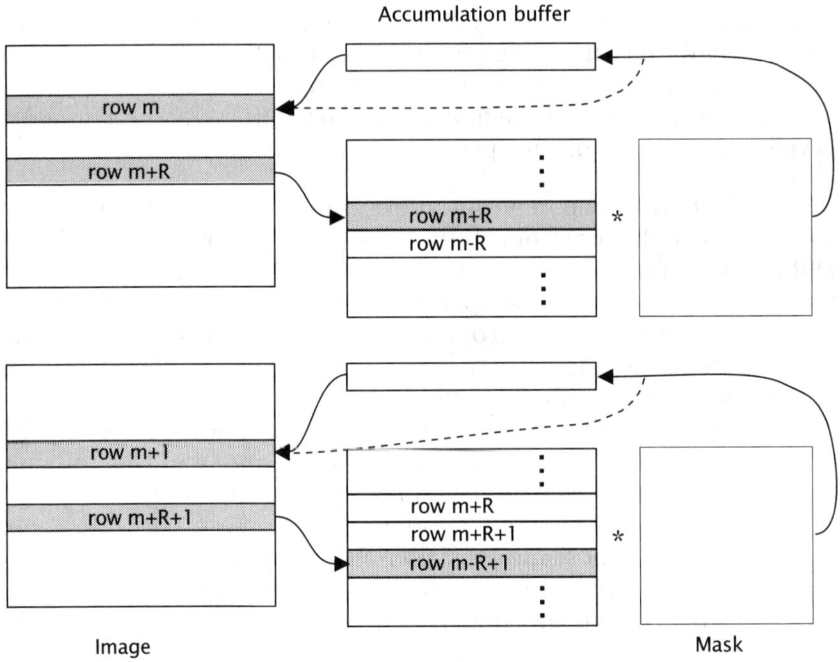

Figure 5.6: *In-place computation of the convolution with a (2R+1)$\times$(2R+1) mask using $2R+1$ line buffers and an accumulation buffer.* ***a*** *and* ***b*** *show the computation of rows m and $m+1$, respectively.*

Cyclic buffers. Any neighborhood operation with a 2-D mask on a 2-D signal requires four loops in total. Two loops scan through the 2-D mask accumulating the results for a single pixel. Two further loops are required to move the mask through the image rows and image columns. If the mask moves row by row through the image, it is obvious that an intermediate storage area with a minimum number of lines corresponding to the height of the mask is required. If the mask moves to the next row, it is not required to rewrite all lines. The uppermost line in the buffer can be discarded because it is no longer required and can be overwritten by the lowest row required now.

Figure 5.6 explains the details of how the buffers are arranged for the example of a neighborhood operation with a mask that has $2R+1$ rows. To compute the convolution for row m, row $m+R$ is read into one of the line buffers. The five line buffers then contain the rows $m-R$ through $m+R$. Thus, all rows are available to compute the neighborhood operation with a (2R+1)$\times$(2R+1) mask for row m.

When the computation proceeds to row $m+1$, row $m+R+1$ is loaded into one of the line buffers replacing row $m-R$ that is no longer required. The $2R+1$ line buffers now contain the rows $m-R+1$ through

$m + R + 1$. Generally, the line buffer number into which a row is written is given by the row number R modulo the number of line buffers, that is, $m \bmod (2R + 1)$.

As a whole row is available, further optimizations are possible. The neighborhood operation can be vectorized. The accumulation of the results can be performed with all pixels in a row for one coefficient of the mask after the other in parallel.

It is often advantageous to use an extra accumulation buffer to accumulate the intermediate results. This is, for instance, required when the intermediate results of the convolution sum must be stored with higher precision than the input data. For 8-bit, that is, 1-byte images, it is required to perform the accumulation with at least 16-bit accuracy. After the results with all filter coefficients are accumulated, the buffer is copied back to row m in the image with appropriate scaling.

The procedure described so far for neighborhood operations is also very effective from the point of memory caching. Note that many computations (for a 5×5 mask at least 25 operations per pixel) are performed, fetching data from the 5 line buffers and storing data into one accumulator buffer. These 6 buffers easily fit into the primary cache of modern CPUs if the image rows are not too long. Proceeding to the next row needs only the replacement of one of these buffers. Thus, most of the data simply remains in the cache and for all computations that are performed with one pixel it must be loaded only one time into the primary cache.

Separable neighborhood operations. For separable masks, a simpler approach could be devised as illustrated in Fig. 5.7. The convolution is now a two-step approach. First, the horizontal convolution with a 1-D mask takes place. Row m is read into a line buffer. Again, a vectorized neighborhood operation is now possible with the whole line with the 1-D mask. If higher-precision arithmetic is required for the accumulation of the results, an accumulation buffer is needed again. If not, the accumulation could directly take place in row m of the image. After the horizontal operation, the vertical operation takes place in the same way. The only difference is that now column by column is read into the buffer (Fig. 5.7).

This procedure for separable neighborhood operations can easily be extended to higher-dimensional images. For each dimension, a line in the corresponding direction is copied to the buffer, where the convolution takes place and then copied back into the image at the same place. This procedure has the significant advantage that the operations in different directions require only different copy operations but that the same 1-D neighborhood operation can be used for *all* directions. It has the disadvantage, though, that more data copying is required. For the processing of D-dimensional signals, each pixel is copied D times

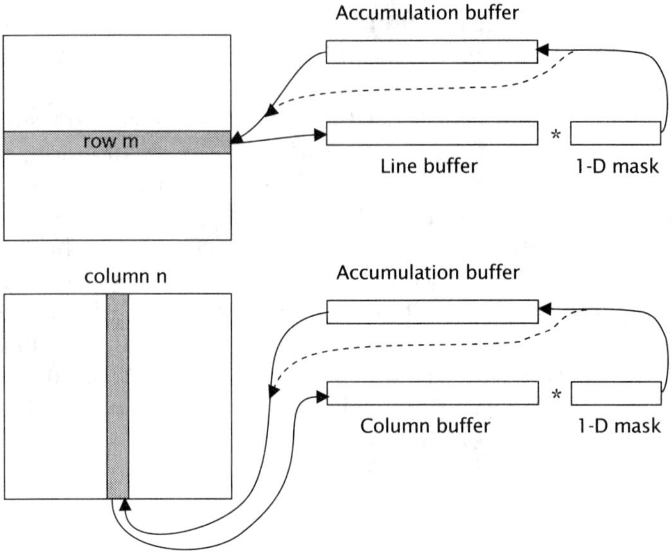

Figure 5.7: In-place computation of a separable neighborhood operation.

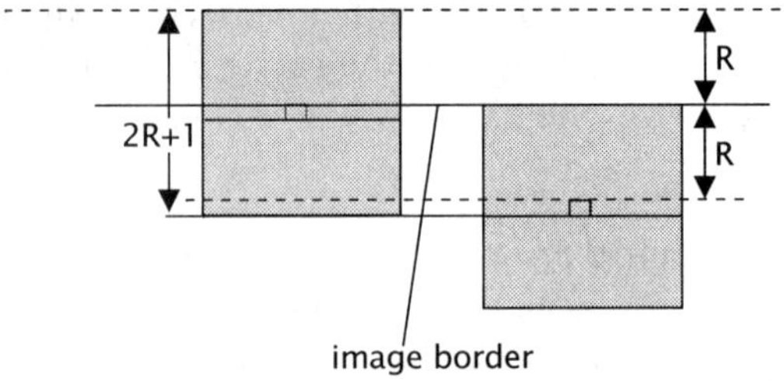

Figure 5.8: Neighborhood operations at the image border. A (2R+1)× (2R+1) mask is shown in two positions: with the center at the edge of the image sticking R pixel over the edge of the image and with the edge of the mask at the edge of the image.

from the main memory. If the neighborhood operation is performed in one step using cyclic row buffers and if all row buffers fit into the primary cache of the processor, it must be copied only once from the main memory.

5.6.3 Neighborhood operators at borders

If a neighborhood operation is performed with a (2R+1) × (2R+1) mask, a band of R rows and columns is required around the image in order to perform the convolution up to the pixels at the image edges (Fig. 5.8). The figure also shows that a band with R pixels at the edge of the image will be influenced by the way the off-image pixels are chosen. Three different strategies are available to extend the image.

Periodic extension. This is the theoretically correct method, as the Fourier transform expects that the image is periodically repeated through the whole space (Section 3.3). If a filter operation is performed in the Fourier domain by directly multiplying the Fourier transformed image with the transfer function of the filter, this periodic extension is automatically implied. This mode to perform the convolution is also referred to as *cyclic convolution*.

Zero extension. As we do not know how the images continue outside of the sector that is available, we do not know what kind of values we can expect. Therefore, it seems to be wise to accept our lack of knowledge and to extend the image just by zeros. This procedure, of course, has the disadvantage that the image border is seen as a sharp edge, which will be determined by any edge detector. Smoothing operators behave more graciously with this extension technique. The image just becomes darker at the borders and the mean gray value of the image is preserved.

Extrapolating extension. This technique takes the pixels close to the border of the image and tries to extrapolate the gray values beyond the borders of the image in an appropriate way. The easiest technique is just to set the required pixels outside of the image to the border pixel in the corresponding row or column. A more sophisticated extrapolation technique might use linear extrapolation. Extrapolation techniques avoid that edge detectors detect an edge at the border of the image and that the image gets darker due to smoothing operations at the edges. The extrapolation technique is, however, also far from being perfect, as we actually cannot know how the picture is extending beyond its border. In effect, we give too much weight to the border pixels. This also means that the mean gray value of the image is slightly altered.

It is obvious that any of these techniques is a compromise, none is ideal. Each of the techniques introduces errors into a band of a width of R pixels when a convolution operation is performed with a $(2R+1) \times (2R+1)$ mask. There is only one safe way to avoid errors. Make sure that the objects of interest are not too close to the border of the image, that is, within the R wide bands at the edges of the images. The border becomes, of course, wider when several convolution operations are cascaded.

5.7 References

[1] Jähne, B., (1997). *Digital Image Processing—Concepts, Algorithms, and Scientific Applications,* 4th edition. New York: Springer.

[2] Zachmanoglou, E. C. and Thoe, D. W., (1986). *Introduction to Partial Differential Equations with Applications.* New York: Dover Publications.

[3] Oppenheim, A. V. and Schafer, R. W., (1989). *Discrete-time Signal Processing. Prentice-Hall Signal Processing Series.* Englewood Cliffs, NJ: Prentice-Hall.

[4] Jähne, B., (1997). *Handbook of Digital Image Processing for Scientific Applications.* Boca Raton, FL: CRC Press.

[5] Lim, J. S., (1990). *Two-dimensional Signal and Image Processing.* Englewood Cliffs, NJ: Prentice-Hall.

[6] Poularikas, A. D. (ed.), (1996). *The Transforms and Applications Handbook.* Boca Raton, FL: CRC Press.

[7] Pitas, I. and Venetsanopoulos, A. N., (1990). *Nonlinear Digital Filters. Principles and Applications.* Norwell, MA: Kluwer Academic Publishers.

[8] Granlund, G. H. and Knutsson, H., (1995). *Signal Processing for Computer Vision.* Norwell, MA: Kluwer Academic Publishers.

[9] Knutsson, H. and Westin, C.-F., (1993). Normalized and differential convolution. In *Proceedings CVPR'93, New York City, NY,* pp. 515–523, IEEE. Washington, DC: IEEE Computer Society Press.

[10] Freeman, W. T. and Adelson, E. H., (1991). The design and use of steerable filters. *IEEE Transactions on Pattern Analysis and Machine Intelligence,* **13**: 891–906.

[11] Blahut, R., (1985). *Fast Algorithms for Digital Signal Processing.* Reading, MA: Addison-Wesley.

[12] Selesnick, I. W. and Burrus, C. S., (1997). Fast convolution and filtering. In *The Digital Signal Processing Handbook,* V. K. Madisetti and D. B. Williams, eds.,. Boca Raton, FL: CRC Press.

6 Principles of Filter Design

Bernd Jähne, Hanno Scharr, and Stefan Körkel

Interdisziplinäres Zentrum für Wissenschaftliches Rechnen (IWR)
Universität Heidelberg, Germany

6.1 Introduction

Filter design is a well-established area both in continuous-time and discrete-time signal processing and subject of standard textbooks [1, 2]. This is not the case, however, for multidimensional signal processing for three reasons:

- Filter design of higher-dimensional signals poses difficult mathematical problems [3, Chapter 2].
- While design criteria for the analysis of 1-D signals (time series) are quite clear, this is less certain for higher-dimensional signals including images.

Handbook of Computer Vision and Applications
Volume 2
Signal Processing and Pattern Recognition

Copyright © 1999 by Academic Press
All rights of reproduction in any form reserved.
ISBN 0-12-379772-1/$30.00

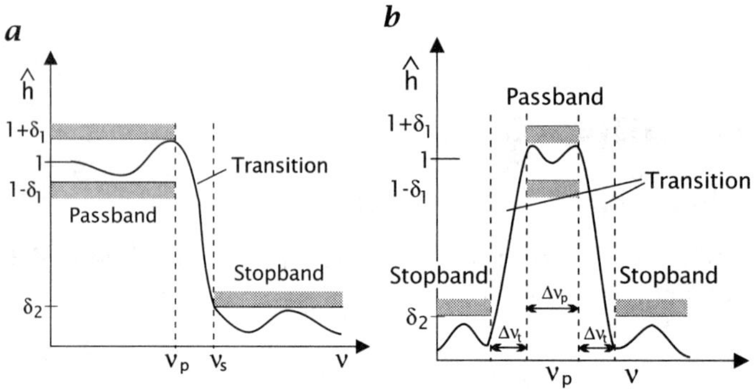

*Figure 6.1: Design criteria for 1-D filters: **a** low-pass; and **b** bandpass.*

- The higher the dimension of the signal, the more dominant becomes the question to design efficient filters, that is, filters that can be computed with a minimum number of operations.

Consequently, this chapter starts with a discussion of filter design criteria in Section 6.2. Then two filter design techniques are discussed: windowing (Section 6.3) and filter cascading (Section 6.4). In the final sections, filter design is formulated as an optimization problem (Section 6.5) and applied to the design of steerable filters and filter families (Section 6.6).

6.2 Filter design criteria

6.2.1 Classical design criteria in signal processing

Filter design is a well-established area both in continuous-time and discrete-time signal processing. Well-defined basic classes of filters can be distinguished. A *low-pass filter* suppresses all frequencies above a certain threshold. Conversely, a *high-pass filter* passes only frequencies above a certain threshold. Finally, a *bandpass filter* transfers frequencies only in a specified frequency range while a *bandstop filter* suppresses all frequencies in a specified band.

With these basic types of filters, the ideal transfer function takes only the values one and zero. Thus the design is centered around the idea of a *passband* and a *stopband* (Fig. 6.1). In the passband, the real transfer function should be one within a tolerance δ_1. Additional constraints may specify the tolerable degree of ripples. In contrast, in the stopband the frequencies should be suppressed as much as possible, with a maximum amplitude of δ_2. Finally, the width of the transition region $\nu_s - \nu_p$ determines how fast the filter changes from the passband to the stopband.

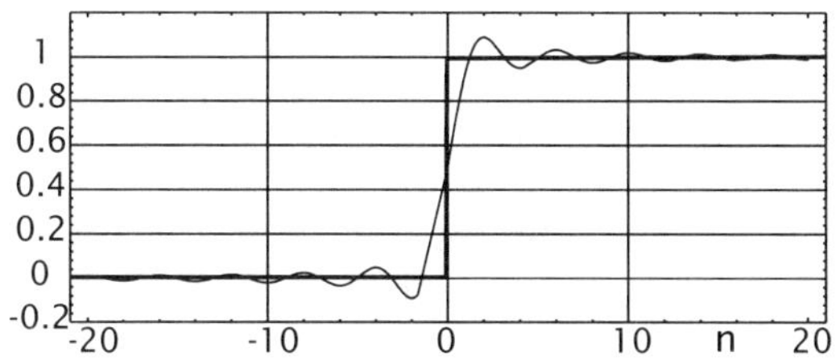

Figure 6.2: *Disadvantage of classical 1-D filtering for computer vision: convolution of a step edge with an ideal low-pass filter causes overshoots.*

An ideal filter, that is, a filter with a flat passband and stopband and a zero width transition region, can only be realized by a mask with an infinite number of coefficients. This general rule is caused by the reciprocity between the Fourier and space domains (Section 3.2.3). A discontinuity as shown for the ideal low-pass filter in Fig. 6.1a causes the envelope of the filter coefficients to decrease not faster than with $1/x$ from the center coefficient. From the uncertainty relation (Section 3.2.3), we can conclude that the narrower the selected wave-number range of a filter is, the larger its filter mask is.

Discrete-time signal processing is dominated by *causal recursive filters* (Section 5.4). This type of filters is more efficient than finite impulse response filters, that is, less filter coefficients are required to meet the same design criteria.

Filter design of 1-D filters according to the criteria discussed here is treated extensively in standard textbooks of signal processing. Good examples are, for example, [1, Chapter 7] and [2, Chapter 8].

6.2.2 Filter design criteria for computer vision

These design criteria for 1-D signals can, in principle, be applied for higher-dimensional signals including images. Depending on the application, the shape of the passband and/or stopband could be either circular (hyperspherical) for isotropic filters or rectangular (hypercubic) for separable filters. However, it is not advisable to use filters designed for the analysis of time series blindly in computer vision.

We demonstrate the disadvantages of these criteria applied to images with an ideal low-pass filter. Figure 6.2 shows that filtering of a step edge with an ideal low-pass filter leads to undesirable overshooting effects including negative gray values. A causal recursive filter—commonly used for time series—causes the edge to shift by a distance proportional to the relaxation length of the filter.

Because both of these effects are undesirable for computer vision, different design criteria have to be applied for filters to be used for computer vision. It is essential to establish such criteria *before* any design techniques are considered.

The purpose of filtering for computer vision is feature extraction. One of the most general features are gray value changes as they mark the edges of objects. Thus the general design criteria for filters to be used for image processing include the following rules:

No overshooting at step edges. This requirement implies monotonic transfer functions.

No shift of the center of gravity of an object or of edges of an object. This condition implies that filters have either an even or odd mask in all directions and leads to the four types of FIR filters discussed in Section 5.3.5.

Isotropy. In order not to bias any directions in images, smoothing filters, edge detectors, and other filters should generally be isotropic.

Separability. Separable filters are preferable because they can generally be computed much more efficiently than equivalent nonseparable filters (Section 5.6.1). This requirement is even more important for higher-dimensional images.

6.3 Windowing techniques

Most ideal filters contain discontinuities in their transfer functions. This includes not only the classical low-pass, high-pass, bandpass, and bandstop filters (Fig. 6.1) but also most key filters for low-level higher-dimensional signal processing. The ideal *derivative filter* $i\pi\tilde{k}$ has a hidden discontinuity. It appears right at $\tilde{k} = \pm 1$ where the value jumps from π to $-\pi$; the periodic extension of the ideal derivative filter leads to the sawtooth function. The transfer function of the ideal *interpolation filter* mask, the sinc function, is a box function, which is also discontinuous (Section 2.4.4). Finally, the transfer function of the *Hilbert filter*, the sgn function, has a discontinuity at $\tilde{k} = 0$ (Section 4.2.2).

The direct consequence of these discontinuities is that the corresponding nonrecursive filter masks, which are the inverse Fourier transforms of the transfer functions, are infinite. Although recursive filters have an infinite impulse response they do not help to solve this problem. The impulse response of IIR filters always decays exponentially, while discontinuities in the value (C^0) or the slope (C^1) of the transfer function cause the envelope of the filter coefficients only to decay with x^{-1} or x^{-2}, respectively.

The basic principle of filter design techniques by windowing is as follows:

1. Start with ideal transfer functions and compute the corresponding filter coefficients.

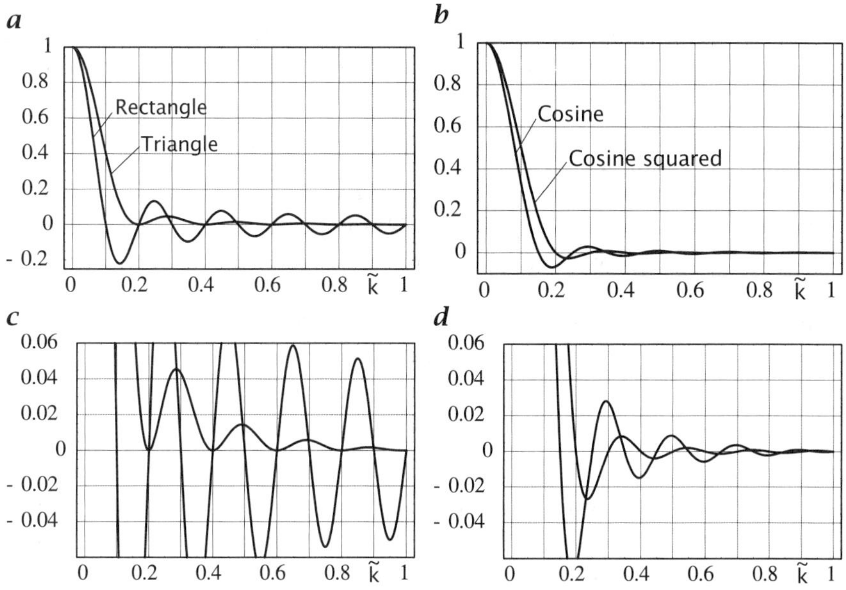

Figure 6.3: *Transfer functions of some classical window functions (here 20 pixels wide):* ***a*** *rectangle and triangle (Barlett) window;* ***b*** *cosine (Hanning) and cosine squared window;* ***c*** *and* ***d*** *show an expanded version of* ***a*** *and* ***b****, respectively.*

2. Apply a window function of finite size to the filter coefficients. The multiplication of the filter coefficients with the window function results in a filter mask with a limited number of coefficients.
3. Check the resulting transfer function by convolving the transfer function of the window with the ideal transfer function and compute critical design parameters. Optimize the window function until the desired criteria are met.

One of the big advantages of the windowing technique for filter design is that it is very easy to predict the deviations from the ideal behavior. As we multiply the filter mask with the window function, the transfer function—according to the convolution theory (Section 3.2.3)—is convolved by the Fourier transform of the window function. Convolution in Fourier space will have no effects where the transfer function is flat or linear-increasing and thus will only change the transfer functions near the discontinuities. Essentially, the discontinuity is blurred by the windowing of the filter mask. The scaling property of the Fourier transform (Section 3.2.3) says that the larger the blurring is the smaller the window is. The exact way in which the discontinuity changes depends on the shape of the window.

Table 6.1: Some commonly used 1-D window functions with a width of R pixels and their properties. The last column gives the width of the transition range. (For a definition of the sinc *function and other functions, see Table 3.4.)*

Name	Form	Transfer function	$\Delta\tilde{k}$
Rectangular	$\Pi(x/R)$	$R\,\mathrm{sinc}(R\tilde{k}/2)$	$1/R$
Triangular	$\Lambda(2x/R)$	$(R/2)\,\mathrm{sinc}^2(\tilde{k}/4)$	$2/R$
Cosine	$\cos(2\pi x/R)\Pi(x/R)$	$(R/(\pi\sqrt{2})(\mathrm{sinc}(R\tilde{k}/2+1/2)+\mathrm{sinc}(R\tilde{k}/2-1/2))$	$\pi/(2R)$
Cosine squared	$\cos^2(2\pi x/R)\Pi(x/R)$	$(1/R)(\mathrm{sinc}(R\tilde{k}/2+1)+2\,\mathrm{sinc}(R\tilde{k}/2)+\mathrm{sinc}(R\tilde{k}/2-1))$	$2/R$

Figure 6.3 shows the transfer functions of several common window functions. All transfer functions show unwanted oscillations. The rectangular window gives the sharpest transition but shows also the strongest oscillations decaying only with k^{-1}. The oscillations are much less for the cosine (Hanning) and cosine squared window (Fig. 6.3b) but still not completely removed. The triangle window (Bartlett window) has the advantage that its transfer function is nonnegative, resulting in a monotonous low-pass filter.

The Gaussian window is, in principle, infinite. However, it decays very rapidly so that it is not a practical problem. Its big advantage is that the shape of the window and its transfer functions are identical. Moreover, as the Gaussian window is strictly positive in both domains, there are no oscillations at all in the transition region of a transfer function nor any overshooting at step edges in the space domain. For discrete filters, the Gaussian function is well approximated by the binomial distribution.

These are some general properties of window functions for filter design:

- The integral over the transfer function of the window function is one:

$$\int_{-1}^{1} \hat{w}(\tilde{k})\,\mathrm{d}\tilde{k} = 1 \Longleftrightarrow w(0) = 1 \tag{6.1}$$

- The integral over the window function is equal to its transfer function at $\tilde{k} = 0$:

$$\int_{-\infty}^{\infty} w(x)\,\mathrm{d}x = \hat{w}(0) \tag{6.2}$$

- The steepness of the transition for a filter with a discontinuity is equal to $\hat{w}(0)$. This simple relation can be obtained by computing

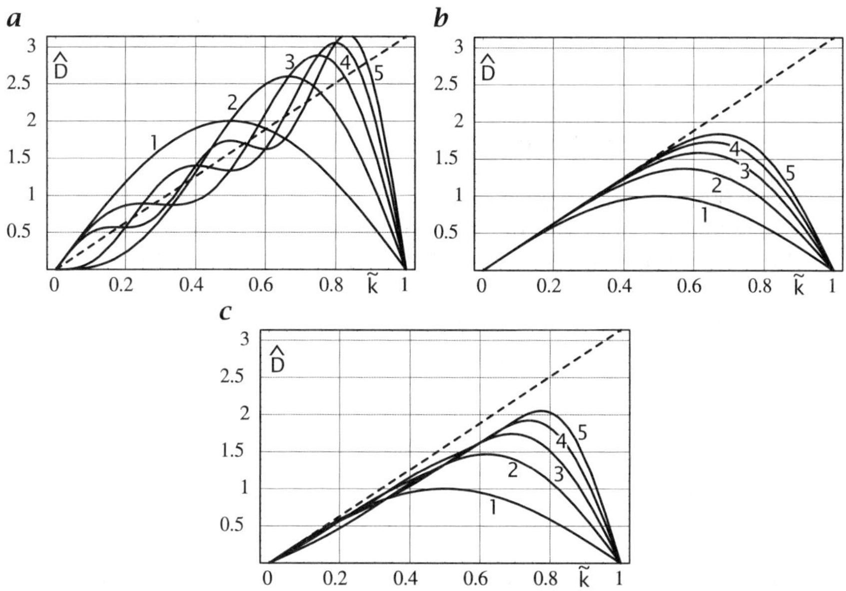

*Figure 6.4: Window technique applied to the design of a $2R+1$ first-order derivative filter for $R = 1$ to 5. Imaginary part of the transfer function for **a** rectangle; **b** binomial; and **c** triangular window. The dashed line is the ideal transfer function, $\mathrm{i}\pi\tilde{k}$.*

the derivative of the convolution between the transfer function of the filter and the window function and using a shifted unit step at $\tilde{k}_0$ for $\hat{h}$:

$$\begin{aligned} \frac{\mathrm{d}}{\mathrm{d}\tilde{k}}(\hat{h} * \hat{w})|_{\tilde{k}_0} &= -\int_{-\infty}^{\infty} u(\tilde{k}' - \tilde{k}_0)\frac{\mathrm{d}\hat{w}(\tilde{k}_0 - \tilde{k}')}{\mathrm{d}\tilde{k}'}\,\mathrm{d}\tilde{k}' \\ &= -\int_{\tilde{k}_0}^{\infty} \frac{\mathrm{d}\hat{w}(\tilde{k}_0 - \tilde{k}')}{\mathrm{d}\tilde{k}'}\,\mathrm{d}\tilde{k}' = \hat{w}(0) \end{aligned} \tag{6.3}$$

Thus the transition region is about $1/\hat{w}(0)$ wide.

Example 6.1: First-order derivative filter

The transfer function of an ideal derivative filter is purely imaginary and proportional to the wave number:

$$\hat{D} = \mathrm{i}\pi\tilde{k}, \quad |\tilde{k}| \le 1 \tag{6.4}$$

An expansion of this transfer function into a Fourier series results in

$$\hat{D}(\tilde{k}) = 2\mathrm{i}\left(\sin(\pi\tilde{k}) - \frac{\sin(2\pi\tilde{k})}{2} + \frac{\sin(3\pi\tilde{k})}{3} - \ldots\right) \tag{6.5}$$

corresponding to the following odd filter mask with the coefficients

$$h_r = -h_{-r} = \frac{(-1)^r}{r} \quad r \in [1, R] \tag{6.6}$$

The usage of the rectangular window would be equivalent to keeping only a number of elements in the Fourier series. As Fig. 6.4a shows, the oscillations are still large and the slope of the transfer function at low wave numbers flips with the order of the series between 0 and twice the correct value. Thus, the resulting truncated filter is not useful at all.

Much better results can be gained by using a binomial window function.

Window	Resulting mask	
1/4[1 2 1]	1/2[1 0 -1]	
1/16[1 4 6 4 1]	1/12[-1 8 0 -8 1]	(6.7)
1/64[1 6 15 20 15 6 1]	1/60[1 -9 45 0 -45 9 -1]	

These approximations show no oscillations; the deviation from the ideal response increases monotonically (Fig. 6.4b). The convergence, however, is quite slow. Even a filter with 11 coefficients ($R = 5$) shows significant deviations from the ideal transfer functions for wave numbers $\tilde{k} > 0.6$.

A triangular window results in other deficits (Fig. 6.4c). Although the transfer function is close to the ideal transfer function for much higher wave numbers, the slope of the transfer function is generally too low.

Example 6.1 indicates some general weaknesses of the windowing technique for filter design. While it is quite useful for filters with flat responses and discontinuities such as ideal low-pass filters in balancing overshooting and ripples vs steepness of the transitions, it does not obviously lead to optimal solutions. It is not clear in which way the filters are improved by the different windows.

6.4 Filter cascading

Cascading of simple filters is a valuable approach to filter design, especially for higher-dimensional signals. Complex filters can be built by applying simple 1-D filters repeatedly in all directions of the signal. This approach has a number of significant advantages.

Known properties. The properties of the simple filters are well known. The transfer function can be expressed analytically in simple equations. As cascading of filters simply means the multiplication of the transfer functions, the resulting transfer functions for even complex filters can be computed easily and analyzed analytically.

Arbitrary signal dimension. If filters can be composed of 1-D filters, that is, they are separable, then filter cascading works not only in two dimensions but also in *any* higher dimension. This greatly simplifies and generalizes the filter design process.

Efficient computation. In most cases, filters designed in this way are computed efficiently. This means that the filter cascading approach not only leads to filters that can be analyzed analytically but that can simultaneously be computed very efficiently.

Inclusion of recursive 1-D filters. In Section 5.4.2 the inherent difficulty of the design of higher-dimensional recursive filters is pointed out. Thus it appears advantageous to combine the elementary recursive relaxation and resonance filters (Section 5.4.6) with nonrecursive filters. Examples of such filter combinations are shown in Section 6.5.5.

6.5 Filter design as an optimization problem

The filter design techniques discussed in the previous sections provide useful ways but it is not really known whether the solutions are optimal. In other words, it is much better to treat filter design in a rigorous way as an optimization problem. This means that we seek an optimal solution in a sense that the filter deviates as little as possible from an ideal filter under given constraints. In order to perform such an approach, it is necessary to define a number of quantities carefully:

Parameterized ansatz. The number of coefficients and their values are the parameters to be varied for an optimal filter. This leads to a parameterized *ansatz function* for a specific design criterion of the filter, for example, its transfer function. For optimal results it is, however, of importance to reduce the number of parameters by incorporating given symmetries and other constraints into the ansatz function.

Reference function. The reference function describes the ideal design criterion of the filter, for example, the transfer function of the ideal filter (Section 6.5.2). Often better results can be gained, however, if functions related to the transfer function are used as a reference function.

Error functional. The deviation of the ansatz function from the reference function is measured by a suitable error functional (Section 6.5.3). Into this error functional often a specific weighting of wave numbers is included. In this way it is possible to optimize a filter for a certain wave number range.

Optimization strategies. While the solution is trivial for a linear optimization problem with the Euclidean norm, it can be much harder for nonlinear approaches, other error norms, and optimization for fixed-point filter coefficients. The strategies to solve the various types of optimization problems in filter design are summarized in Section 6.5.4.

Some examples that illustrate these rigorous optimization techniques for filter design are discussed in Section 6.5.5 in this chapter.

6.5.1 Parameterized ansatz

As discussed in Section 5.3.4 the transfer function of a filter can be expressed directly as a function of the filter coefficients. The transfer function of a 1-D filter with $R + 1$ coefficients can generally be written as

$$\hat{h}(\tilde{k}) = \sum_{r=0}^{R} h_r \exp(-\pi \mathrm{i}(r - R/2)\tilde{k}) \tag{6.8}$$

This equation corresponds to Eq. (5.18) except that the numbering of the filter coefficients has been rearranged and the correct shift in the exponential term has been considered when the output for filters with even number of coefficients (R odd) is written to a lattice shifted by half a pixel distance.

As all filters that are used in image processing are of odd or even symmetry, their transfer functions reduce to linear combinations of either sine or cosine functions as expressed in Section 5.3.5 by Eqs. (5.24) to (5.27).

If there are additional constraints for a filter to be designed, it is the best approach to include these directly into the ansatz function. In this way it is ensured that the constraints are met. Furthermore, each constraint reduces the number of parameters.

Example 6.2: First-order derivative filter

A *first-order derivative filter* of odd symmetry has a purely imaginary transfer function. Therefore the transfer function for a filter with $2R + 1$ coefficients is

$$\hat{D}(\tilde{k}) = 2\mathrm{i} \sum_{r=1}^{R} d_r \sin(\pi r \tilde{k}) \tag{6.9}$$

Often it is useful for a derivative filter to force the transfer function for low wave numbers to the correct behavior. At the wave-number origin, the slope of $\hat{D}(\tilde{k})$ has to be 1, so we obtain the constraint

$$1 = 2 \sum_{r=1}^{R} d_r r \tag{6.10}$$

This constraint is used to set the value of the first coefficient d_1 to

$$d_1 = 1/2 - \sum_{r=2}^{R} d_r r \tag{6.11}$$

If we introduce this equation into Eq. (6.9), we obtain a new constrained ansatz function with only $R - 1$ parameters:

$$\hat{D}(\tilde{k}) = \mathrm{i}\sin(\pi\tilde{k}) + 2\mathrm{i}\sum_{r=2}^{R} d_r(\sin(\pi r\tilde{k}) - r\sin(\pi\tilde{k})) \tag{6.12}$$

If a recursive filter is included into the first-order derivative filter, the ansatz function becomes nonlinear in the filter coefficients for the recursive part of the filter. The simplest case is the inclusion of the relaxation filter running back and forth as discussed in Section 5.4.6, Eq. (5.55). This filter adds one more parameter d_0 and the ansatz function becomes

$$\hat{D}(\tilde{k}) = \frac{(1-d_0)^2\left(\mathrm{i}\sin(\pi\tilde{k}) + 2\mathrm{i}\sum_{r=2}^{R} d_r(\sin(\pi r\tilde{k}) - r\sin(\pi\tilde{k}))\right)}{1 + d_0^2 - 2d_0\cos(\pi\tilde{k})} \tag{6.13}$$

Example 6.3: Smoothing filter

A normalized even smoothing filter with a $2R + 1$ mask

$$[b_R, \ldots, b_1, b_0, b_1, \ldots, b_R] \tag{6.14}$$

meets the constraint that the sum of all coefficients is equal to one. This can be forced by

$$b_0 = 1 - 2\sum_{r=1}^{R} b_r \tag{6.15}$$

The resulting transfer function $\hat{B}$ can then be written as

$$\hat{B}(\tilde{k}) = 1 + 2\sum_{r=1}^{R} b_r(\cos(r\pi\tilde{k}) - 1) \tag{6.16}$$

Example 6.4: Hilbert filter

A *Hilbert filter* (Section 4.2.2) is also of odd symmetry. Thus it has the same ansatz function as a first-order derivative filter in Eq. (6.9). The constraint applied in Eq. (6.12), however, makes no sense for a Hilbert filter. It may be useful to add the constraint that the Hilbert filter is symmetrical around $\tilde{k} = 0.5$. This additional symmetry constraint forces all filter coefficients with even r in Eq. (6.9) to zero. Thus the ansatz function for such a symmetric Hilbert filter is

$$\hat{D}(\tilde{k}) = 2\mathrm{i}\sum_{r=1}^{R} d_{2r-1}\sin(\pi(2r-1)\tilde{k}) \tag{6.17}$$

As with the first-order derivative filter, a recursive part can be included into the design of a Hilbert filter. As the correction that is performed by such a recursive filter must also be symmetric around $\tilde{k} = 0.5$ ($\hat{H}(1-\tilde{k}) = \hat{H}(\tilde{k})$) and enhance lower and higher wave numbers, the following ansatz function is useful:

$$\hat{H}(\tilde{k}) = \frac{(1+d_0)^2}{1+d_0^2-2d_0\cos(2\pi\tilde{k})} 2\mathrm{i}\sum_{r=1}^{R} d_{2r-1}\sin(\pi(2r-1)\tilde{k}) \tag{6.18}$$

The recursive filter is a mirrored *relaxation filter* (Section 5.4.6) with double step width.

6.5.2 Reference function

At first glance, it appears that not much has to be said about the reference function because often it is simply the ideal transfer function. This is, however, not always the best choice. As an example, we discuss the reference function for a first-order derivative filter in multidimensional signals.

Example 6.5: First-order derivative filter

The transfer function of an ideal first-order derivative filter in the direction d is

$$\hat{D}_d(\tilde{\boldsymbol{k}}) = \mathrm{i}\pi\tilde{k}_d \tag{6.19}$$

This is not always the best choice as a reference function as it is often required that only the gradient direction, for example, for motion determination in spatiotemporal images (Chapter 13), must be correct. The direction of the gradient can be expressed by the angles of polar coordinates in a natural way. The angles ϕ_i occurring in D-dimensional polar coordinates for the gradient direction are

$$\begin{array}{lclcl} \phi_1 & = & \arctan\left(\tilde{k}_2/\tilde{k}_1\right) & \in &]-\pi,\pi] \\ \phi_d & = & \arctan\left(\tilde{k}_{d+1}\Big/\left(\sum_{d'=1}^{d}\tilde{k}_{d'}^2\right)^{1/2}\right) & \in & [-\pi/2,\pi/2] \end{array} \tag{6.20}$$

as the ideal transfer function of the derivative is $\hat{D}_0(\tilde{k}) = \mathrm{i}\pi\tilde{k}$. Figure 6.5 explains the square root term in the denominator of the preceding formula for higher dimensions. Thus this set of angles is now the reference function and has to be compared with the angles of the gradient computed by the filter.

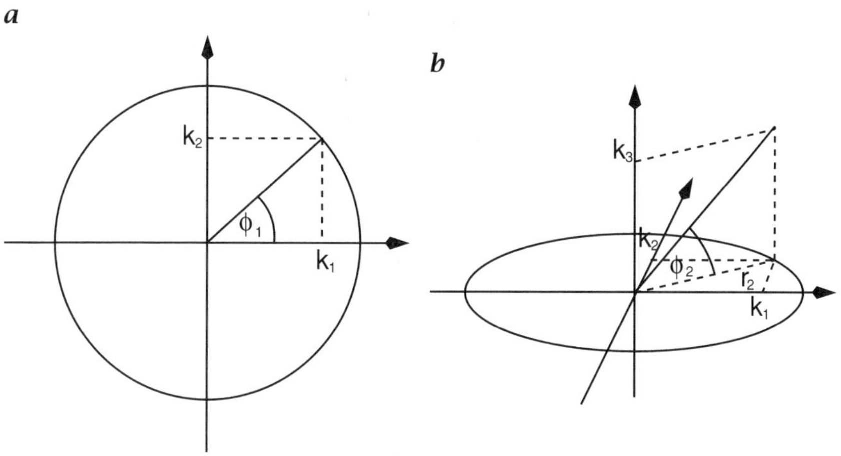

Figure 6.5: *Definition of the angles in D-dimensional polar coordinates:* ***a*** *2 dimensions,* $\phi_1 = \arctan(k_2/k_1)$*; and* ***b*** *3 dimensions,* $r_2 = (k_1^2 + k_2^2)^{1/2}$ *and* $\phi_2 = \arctan(k_3/r_2)$.

This different reference function gives additional degrees of freedom in defining the ansatz function. As only the ratio of the transfer functions of the components of the gradient occurs in the angle computation

$$\frac{\tilde{k}_p}{\tilde{k}_q} = \frac{\hat{D}_p(\tilde{\boldsymbol{k}})}{\hat{D}_q(\tilde{\boldsymbol{k}})} \tag{6.21}$$

the transfer functions can be multiplied by an arbitrary function $\hat{B}(\tilde{\boldsymbol{k}})$. Choosing $\hat{B}(\tilde{\boldsymbol{k}})$ suitably we get a regularized version of a first-order derivative filter

$$\hat{D}_d(\tilde{\boldsymbol{k}}) = \mathrm{i}\pi \hat{B}(\tilde{\boldsymbol{k}})\tilde{k}_d \tag{6.22}$$

Approaches like the one just discussed do not fix the transfer function but rather a nonlinear functional of it. Thus the optimization problem becomes nonlinear even if the ansatz function is linear in the filter coefficients.

6.5.3 Error functional

In order to compare the ansatz function $a(\tilde{k}, \boldsymbol{h})$, where $\boldsymbol{h}$ is the vector with the parameters, and the reference function $t(\tilde{k})$, a suitable measure for the difference between these two functions is required. An error functional $e(\boldsymbol{h})$ computes the norm of the difference between the two functions by

$$e(\boldsymbol{h}) = \left\| w(\tilde{k}) \left(t(\tilde{k}) - a(\tilde{k}, \boldsymbol{h}) \right) \right\| \Big/ \left\| w(\tilde{k}) \right\| \tag{6.23}$$

In this error functional, the ansatz and reference functions are compared directly. A weighting function $w(\tilde{k})$ is introduced in order to optimize the filter for a certain distribution of wave numbers. This is the error given in all figures and tables (Tables 6.2–6.8) in this chapter. Common norms are L_1 (sum of absolute values), L_2 (square root of the sum of squares),

$$e^2(\boldsymbol{h}) = \int\limits_0^1 w^2(\tilde{k}) \left(t(\tilde{k}) - a(\tilde{k}, \boldsymbol{h})\right)^2 \mathrm{d}\tilde{k} \Bigg/ \int\limits_0^1 w^2(\tilde{k})\,\mathrm{d}\tilde{k} \tag{6.24}$$

and L_∞ (maximum absolute value):

$$e(\boldsymbol{h}) = \max_{\tilde{k}=0,\dots,1} w(\tilde{k}) \left|t(\tilde{k}) - a(\tilde{k}, \boldsymbol{h})\right| \Bigg/ \max_{\tilde{k}=0,\dots,1} w(\tilde{k}) \tag{6.25}$$

Minimizing one of the first two norms provides the lowest expected mean error, the last one gives the best worst case estimation for an unknown data set or image content.

For multidimensional filters, the evaluation of Eq. (6.23) is extended over the corresponding k space. Often an isotropic weighting function is used. However, this is not required. As a multidimensional signal may have a nonisotropic power spectrum, the weighting function does not need to be isotropic as well.

6.5.4 Solution strategies

Generally, the optimization problem is of the form

$$\min_{\boldsymbol{h}} \left\| w(\tilde{\boldsymbol{k}}) \left(t(\tilde{\boldsymbol{k}})) - a(\tilde{\boldsymbol{k}}, \boldsymbol{h})\right) \right\| = \min_{\boldsymbol{h}} \left\| d(\tilde{\boldsymbol{k}}, \boldsymbol{h}) \right\| \tag{6.26}$$

This error functional is evaluated over the entire wave-number space. To this end it is required to approximate the continuous k space by discrete samples using a Cartesian lattice. We assume that space is sampled at J wave numbers $\tilde{\boldsymbol{k}}_j$.

In the following, we briefly describe which solution methods have been chosen to solve the various types of optimization problems that arise for different error norms and for real and fixed-point filter coefficients.

Euclidean norm. For the *Euclidean norm* (L_2) the minimum of the following expression has to be found:

$$\min_{\boldsymbol{h}} \sum_{j=1}^{J} d^2(\tilde{\boldsymbol{k}}_j, \boldsymbol{h}) \tag{6.27}$$

This optimization problem is (generally) a nonlinear regression problem. Problems of this type can be solved by a generalized Gauss-Newton-method, for example, [4, Section 6.1] .

Maximum norm. Using the *maximum norm* (L_∞), the Eq. (6.26) is not differentiable. Therefore we reformulate the problem using an additional variable δ

$$\delta := \max_{j=1,\ldots,J} \left| d(\tilde{\boldsymbol{k}}_j, \boldsymbol{h}) \right| \tag{6.28}$$

and write the maximum of the absolute value in Eq. (6.28) as inequality constraints

$$-\delta \leq d(\tilde{\boldsymbol{k}}_j, \boldsymbol{h}) \leq \delta \qquad \forall j = 1, \ldots, J$$

We obtain the following inequality constrained (generally) nonlinear optimization problem

$$\min_{\delta, \boldsymbol{h}} \delta, \text{ subject to } -\delta \leq d(\tilde{\boldsymbol{k}}_j, \boldsymbol{h}) \leq \delta \qquad \forall j = 1, \ldots, J \tag{6.29}$$

Such problems can be solved by a successive quadratic programming (SQP) method, for example, [5, Chapter 6] or [4, Section 12.4].

Fixed-point optimization. Using the methods described here, we get real numbers for the optimal filter coefficients. Because of recent hardware developments (like Intel's MMX or Sun's VIS) that improve integer arithmetic performance in computational calculations, it is also desirable to optimize filters with integer or rational filter coefficients.

Therefore we formulate the forementioned optimization problems as nonlinear integer problem, more precisely, we discretize the coefficient variable space

$$h_r = \alpha_r / 2^M, \quad r = 1, \ldots, R, \; \alpha_r \in \mathbb{Z}$$

with M chosen suitably. We optimize over the integer variables α_r instead of h_r. Problems of this type are known to be NP-hard [6, Section I.5]. In our case we use the branch and bound method [7, Chapter 5.3, Section 6.2] combined with the methods as described here for the solution of relaxed problems and some rounding heuristics to find integer feasible solutions.

6.5.5 Examples

In this section, some examples illustrate the various optimization techniques discussed in the previous sections.

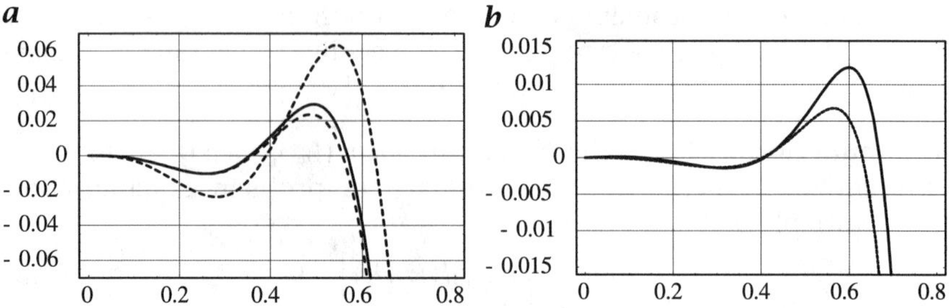

Figure 6.6: *Error in transfer function of optimized 1-D first-order derivative filters. Shown is the absolute deviation from the ideal transfer function* $\mathrm{i}\pi\tilde{k}$ *for* ***a*** *nonrecursive filter according to Eq. (6.12) with two free parameters (solid line floating-point solution, narrow-dashed line [28 -9 2]/32 integer coefficients, and wide-dashed line [108 -31 6]/128 integer coefficients); and* ***b*** *recursive filter according to Eq. (6.33) with two free parameters.*

Table 6.2: *Filter coefficients of first-order derivative filters optimized according to Eq. (6.12) with* $2R+1$ *coefficients. The second column contains the filter coefficients* $d_1, \ldots, d_R$ *and the lower part of the table the coefficients for fixed-point arithmetic with varying computational accuracy. Boldface filters are an optimal choice with minimal filter coefficients and still an acceptable error as compared to the floating-point solution.*

R	Filter coefficients	Error
1	0.5	1.5×10^{-1}
2	0.758, -0.129	3.6×10^{-2}
3	0.848, -0.246, 0.0480	1.3×10^{-2}
4	0.896, -0.315, 0.107, -0.0215	5.6×10^{-3}
5	0.924, -0.360, 0.152, -0.0533, 0.0109	2.8×10^{-3}
6	0.942, -0.391, 0.187, -0.0827, 0.0293, -0.00601	1.6×10^{-3}
2	**[6, -1]/8**	3.60×10^{-2}
2	[12, -2]/16	3.60×10^{-2}
2	[24, -4]/32	3.60×10^{-2}
2	[48, -8]/64	3.60×10^{-2}
2	[96, -16]/128	3.60×10^{-2}
2	[194, -33]/256	3.57×10^{-2}
3	[6, -1, 0]/8	3.6×10^{-2}
3	[12, -2, 0]/16	3.6×10^{-2}
3	**[28, -9, 2]/32**	1.6×10^{-2}
3	[55, -16, 3]/64	1.5×10^{-2}
3	**[108, -31, 6]/128**	1.3×10^{-2}
3	[216, -62, 12]/256	1.3×10^{-2}

Example 6.6: Optimal 1-D first-order derivative filter

The classical approaches to optimized 1-D derivative filters are well described in standard textbooks [8, 9]. For the optimization of a 1-D first-order derivative filter, the transfer function of the ideal derivative filter (Eq. (6.19)) is directly taken as the reference function.

Finite impulse response ansatz function. In this case, we take the ansatz function Eq. (6.12) with the additional constraint that we force the slope of the transfer function for small wave numbers to be $\mathrm{i}\pi\tilde{k}$. Equation (6.12) is valid for filters with an odd number of coefficients $(2R+1)$ with the mask

$$D = [d_R, \ldots, d_1, 0, -d_1, \ldots, -d_R] \tag{6.30}$$

For even-length filters the mask is

$$D = [d_R, \ldots, d_1, -d_1, \ldots, -d_R] \tag{6.31}$$

and the ansatz function is slightly different from Eq. (6.12):

$$\hat{D}(\tilde{k}) = \mathrm{i}\sin(\pi\tilde{k}/2) + 2\mathrm{i}\sum_{r=2}^{R} d_r(\sin(\pi(r-1/2)\tilde{k}) - (r-1/2)\sin(\pi\tilde{k})) \tag{6.32}$$

Infinite impulse response ansatz function. The ansatz function in Eq. (6.13) can be taken for optimization of filters with real filter coefficients for floating-point arithmetic. In integer arithmetic we directly include the coefficent $\alpha_1/2^M$ of the recursive relaxation filter:

$$\begin{aligned} \hat{D}(\tilde{k}) &= \mathrm{i}\frac{(1-\alpha_1/2^M)^2}{1+\alpha_1^2/2^{2M} - 2(\alpha_1/2^M)\cos(\pi\tilde{k})} \\ &\quad \left(\sin(\pi\tilde{k}) + 2\sum_{r=2}^{R}\alpha_r/2^M(\sin(\pi r\tilde{k}) - r\sin(\pi\tilde{k}))\right) \end{aligned} \tag{6.33}$$

The filter coefficients shown in Tables 6.2 and 6.3 and the corresponding transfer functions depicted in Fig. 6.6 are computed using the L_2 norm combined with the weighting function $w(\tilde{k}) = \cos^4(\pi\tilde{k}/2)$.

Example 6.7: Optimal Hilbert filter

As an example for the influence of the weighting function we use the 1-D Hilbert filter. As it is separable in n-D, the solution is valid for higher dimensions, too.

Reference function. We choose the transfer function $\hat{H}_r$ of the ideal Hilbert filter as reference function:

$$\hat{H}_r(\tilde{k}) = \mathrm{i}\,\mathrm{sgn}(k)$$

Ansatz function. For weighting functions with a symmetry of around $\tilde{k} = 0.5$ we use the ansatz function Eq. (6.17). If the weighting function does not have this symmetry, the optimal filter will not have it

Table 6.3: *Filter coefficients of first-order derivative filters optimized according to Eq. (6.33) with $2R + 1$ coefficients; the second column contains the filter coefficients $d_0, d_1, \ldots, d_R$, where d_0 is the filter coefficient for the recursive relaxation filter part, and the lower part of the table the coefficients for fixed-point arithmetic (note the loss of coefficients for small denominators shown for $R = 5$).*

R	Filter coefficients	Error
1	-3.13, 0.5	1.1×10^{-2}
2	-0.483, 0.442, 0.0292	2.1×10^{-3}
3	-0.583, 0.415, 0.0487, -0.00427	6.4×10^{-4}
4	-0.650, 0.402, 0.0596, -0.00851, 0.00112	2.4×10^{-4}
5	0.698, 0.394, 0.0662, -0.0115, 0.00249, -0.000400	1.1×10^{-4}
1	[801, 128]/256	1.1×10^{-2}
2	[-120, 114, 7]/256	2.3×10^{-3}
3	[-146, 107, 12, -1]/256	6.8×10^{-4}
4	[-146, 107, 12, -1, 0]/256	6.8×10^{-4}
5	[-146, 107, 12, -1, 0, 0]/256	6.8×10^{-4}
5	[-651, 414, 59, -8, 1, 0]/1024	2.8×10^{-4}
5	[-1495, 799, 142, -26, 6, -1]/2048	2.0×10^{-2}

either. In that case we choose a filter mask $[h_R \cdots h_1 \; 0 \; -h_1 \cdots -h_R]$, as the 1-D Hilbert filter shall be imaginary and antisymmetric. The corresponding transfer function $\hat{H}$ is

$$\hat{H}(\tilde{k}, \boldsymbol{h}) = 2\,\mathrm{i} \sum_{r=1}^{R} h_r \sin(r\pi\tilde{k}) \tag{6.34}$$

The filter coefficients are computed in L_2 norm combined with a weighting function $\cos^4(\pi/2\,\tilde{k})$ and given in Table 6.4. The slow convergence of the error indicates that the ansatz function with the weighting function $\cos^4(\pi/2\,\tilde{k})$ was not chosen properly. It puts the most weight at the discontinuity of the Hilbert filter at $\tilde{(k)} = 0$ (the discontinuities at $\tilde{(k)} = \pm 1$ are suppressed), which cannot be well approximated with a series of sinusoidal functions.

The weighting function $\sin^2(\pi\tilde{k})$, which emphasizes wave numbers around $\tilde{k} = 0.5$ and a Hilbert filter that is even with respect to $\tilde{k} = 0.5$, gives much better results (Table 6.5).

***Table 6.4:** Filter coefficients of Hilbert filters optimized according to Eq. (6.34) with $2R+1$ coefficients and weighting function $\cos^4(\pi/2\,\tilde{k})$; the second column contains the filter coefficients $d_1, \ldots, d_R$ in floating point arithmetic.*

R	Filter coefficients	Error
1	0.776	5.31×10^{-1}
2	0.274, 0.439	4.53×10^{-1}
3	0.922, -0.391, 0.467	3.89×10^{-1}
4	0.228, 0.651, 0.426, 0.409	3.54×10^{-1}
5	1.038, -0.671, 0.937, -0.560, 0.394	3.26×10^{-1}

***Table 6.5:** Filter coefficients of Hilbert filters optimized according to Eq. (6.17) with $4R-1$ coefficients and weighting function $\sin^2(\pi\,\tilde{k})$; The corresponding filter coefficients are given; the second column contains the filter coefficients $d_1, \ldots, d_R$ in floating point arithmetic and the lower part of the table the coefficients for fixed-point arithmetic.*

R	Filter coefficients	Error
1	0.543	1.3×10^{-1}
2	0.599, 0.111	4.4×10^{-2}
3	0.616, 0.154, 0.0431	2.1×10^{-2}
4	0.624, 0.175, 0.0698, 0.0214	1.2×10^{-2}
5	0.627, 0.186, 0.0861, 0.0384, 0.0122	7.5×10^{-3}
1	[139]/256	1.3×10^{-1}
2	[153, 28]/256	4.4×10^{-2}
3	[158, 40, 11]/256	2.1×10^{-2}
4	[160, 46, 19, 6]/256	1.2×10^{-2}
5	[161, 48, 22, 10, 3]/256	8.0×10^{-3}

6.6 Design of steerable filters and filter families

Steerable filters are well described in the literature [for example, 10, 11, 12, 13, 14, 15]. Because of existing detailed mathematical treatments [see, for example, 16, 17], only a short introduction to steerability shall be given here. As angular steerability is the most common case, it is used as an explanatory example, but steerability in any other domain works in the same way.

Steerable filters are a special case of filter families, fulfilling the sampling theorem (see Section 2.4) exactly in a specific domain. Therefore, the interpolation of the filter responses to a continuous response is exactly possible.

Example 6.8: Angular steerability

The question to answer is: Wanting to compute the exact answer of an anisotropic filter at any angle α only by linear combination of its answers at n given angles, which shape must it have? Or: Which properties has a signal to fulfill to be reconstructable to a continuous periodic signal (the answer of the filter at α) only by knowing n samples of the signal?

As we learned from Section 2.4 the signal has to be bandlimited. Further, the first Brillouin zone of the (discrete) Fourier domain of this signal must contain only n nonzero values. This implies that we have to smooth the signal by a suitable convolution first to obtain a signal we are able to reconstruct by n samples. Then we can sample the signal at least n points.

Having this in mind, the shape of an angular steerable filter is clear. Its angular part is the kernel of the smoothing convolution, its radial part is arbitrary.

6.6.1 Gradient computation

The smallest nontrivial set of steerable filters contains two filters in a 1-D domain like the one given by the angle α in 2-D polar coordinates. The signal $s(\alpha)$ we are able to reconstruct with only two samples is

$$s(\alpha) = \cos(\alpha - \alpha_0)$$

The smoothing kernel $k(\alpha)$ therefore is

$$k(\alpha) = \cos(\alpha)$$

This gives us the most common pair of steerable filters $\mathcal{D}$

$$\begin{aligned} \hat{D}_x(r,\phi) &= \quad f(r)\,k(\phi) &&= \quad f(r)\cos(\phi) \\ \hat{D}_y(r,\phi) &= \quad f(r)\,k(\phi - \pi/2) &&= \quad f(r)\sin(\phi), \end{aligned}$$

where $f(r)$ is the arbitrary radial component of the transfer function $\hat{D}$. These filters are derivative filters and α_0 is the direction of the gradient. With $\boldsymbol{D}$ denoting the result of a convolution of the image with the operator $\mathcal{D}$, the direction is computed by

$$\alpha_0 = \arctan(\frac{\boldsymbol{D}_y}{\boldsymbol{D}_x}) \tag{6.35}$$

as we can see by the reconstruction, that is, the interpolation of the signal $s(\alpha)$

$$s(\alpha) = \boldsymbol{D}_x \cos(\alpha) + \boldsymbol{D}_y \sin(\alpha) \tag{6.36}$$

Please note the difference between the angle α of the interpolating functions and the parameters r and ϕ used in the integration to obtain the filter values. The maximum of the signal is computed by building its derivative and solving for its zero crossing:

$$\begin{aligned} s'(\alpha_0) &= -\boldsymbol{D}_x \sin(\alpha_0) + \boldsymbol{D}_y \cos(\alpha_0) \stackrel{!}{=} 0 \\ \Leftrightarrow \alpha_0 &= \arctan(\frac{\boldsymbol{D}_y}{\boldsymbol{D}_x}) \end{aligned}$$

Similar results can be received for higher dimensions (compare Section 6.5.2).

6.6.2 Steerable one-dimensional higher-order derivatives

Using Eq. (6.36) for the exact computation of a steerable derivative, we get steerable higher order 1-D derivatives $\boldsymbol{D}_\alpha^n$ by

$$\boldsymbol{D}_\alpha^n = (\boldsymbol{D}_x \cos(\alpha) + \boldsymbol{D}_y \sin(\alpha))^n$$

for example, for the case $n = 2$ we obtain

$$\begin{aligned} \boldsymbol{D}_\alpha^2 &= (\boldsymbol{D}_x \cos(\alpha) + \boldsymbol{D}_y \sin(\alpha))^2 \\ &= \boldsymbol{D}_x^2 \cos^2(\alpha) + 2\,\boldsymbol{D}_x\boldsymbol{D}_y \cos(\alpha)\sin(\alpha) + \boldsymbol{D}_y^2 \sin^2(\alpha) \end{aligned}$$

where the successive application of the derivative filters can be replaced by the filter family $\mathcal{D}_{xx} := \mathcal{D}_x^2$, $\mathcal{D}_{xy} := \mathcal{D}_x\mathcal{D}_y$, $\mathcal{D}_{yy} := \mathcal{D}_y^2$. As in the preceding, the direction of maximal D_α^2 can be found in the zero crossing of its derivative. The angle α_0 of this direction is

$$\alpha_0 = \frac{1}{2}\arctan(\frac{2\,\boldsymbol{D}_{xy}}{\boldsymbol{D}_{yy} - \boldsymbol{D}_{xx}}) \tag{6.37}$$

6.6.3 Optimization of filter families

Having any property of a filter family formulated in Fourier space, we can optimize the whole family with the method already described here (see Section 6.5). Examples for these properties are Eqs. (6.35) and (6.37). Given the spatial support and the symmetries of the filters, these equations yield both a reference function and an ansatz function.

Example 6.9: Gradient—Cartesian lattice

As we have already seen in Section 6.6.1, optimizing the direction of the gradient is equivalent to an optimization of a steerable filter pair. As before, the characteristic design criterion is formulated in the reference function.

Reference function. We use the direction ϕ of the gradient as reference. For the 2-D case it is

$$\phi_{0,0}(\tilde{\boldsymbol{k}}) = \arctan(\frac{\tilde{k}_y}{\tilde{k}_x})$$

in 3-D

$$\phi_{0,0}(\tilde{\boldsymbol{k}}) = \arctan(\frac{\tilde{k}_y}{\tilde{k}_x}), \qquad \phi_{1,0}(\tilde{\boldsymbol{k}}) = \arctan(\frac{\tilde{k}_z}{\sqrt{\tilde{k}_x^2 + \tilde{k}_y^2}})$$

(compare Example 6.5).

Ansatz function. In an n-D isotropic domain a separable derivative filter with the same support length in every coordinate direction can be composed of a 1-D derivative filter D^1 and the same smoothing filter B for any other direction. In 2-D the filters D are

$$D_x = D_x^1 * B_y\,, \qquad D_y = D_y^1 * B_x$$

In 3-D the filters D are

$$D_x = D_x^1 * B_y * B_z\,, \qquad D_y = D_y^1 * B_x * B_z\,, \qquad D_z = D_z^1 * B_x * B_y$$

The transfer function of the smoothing filter and the derivative are given in Eq. (6.16) and Eqs. (6.12) and (6.32) respectively. The ansatz function $\phi(\tilde{\boldsymbol{k}}, \boldsymbol{d})$ in 2-D is

$$\phi_0(\tilde{\boldsymbol{k}}, \boldsymbol{d}) = \arctan(\frac{\hat{D}_y}{\hat{D}_x})$$

in 3-D

$$\phi_0(\tilde{\boldsymbol{k}}, \boldsymbol{d}) = \arctan(\frac{\hat{D}_y}{\hat{D}_x}), \qquad \phi_1(\tilde{\boldsymbol{k}}, \boldsymbol{d}) = \arctan(\frac{\hat{D}_z}{\sqrt{\hat{D}_x^2 + \hat{D}_y^2}})$$

Please note that the application of a filter to an image in Fourier space is a multiplication. Therefore the image data in the fraction cancel out.

Error. The error function $d(\tilde{\boldsymbol{k}}, \boldsymbol{d})$ is computed straightforward. In 2-D it is

$$d(\tilde{\boldsymbol{k}}, \boldsymbol{d}) = \phi_0(\tilde{\boldsymbol{k}}, \boldsymbol{d}) - \phi_{0,0}(\tilde{\boldsymbol{k}}) \tag{6.38}$$

and in 3-D

$$d(\tilde{\boldsymbol{k}}, \boldsymbol{d}) = \sqrt{(\phi_0(\tilde{\boldsymbol{k}}, \boldsymbol{d}) - \phi_{0,0}(\tilde{\boldsymbol{k}}))^2 + (\phi_1(\tilde{\boldsymbol{k}}, \boldsymbol{d}) - \phi_{1,0}(\tilde{\boldsymbol{k}}))^2} \tag{6.39}$$

Results. The filters in Table 6.6 are optimized in L_2 norm combined with a weighting function $\Pi_i \cos^4(\pi/2\,\tilde{k}_i)$. Some plots for the magnitude of the angle error in degree for the direction of the biggest error (22.5°) can be found in Fig. 6.7.

Table 6.6: *Filter coefficients for derivative filters optimized according to either Eq. (6.38) or Eq. (6.39). The first and second columns contain the filter parts. The first part of the table lists well-known approaches, followed by optimal filters in floating point and fixed-point arithmetic. The last part summarizes the results of a study on varying the denominator for fixed-point arithmetic.*

Derivative (odd mask)	Smoothing (even mask)	Error $[10^{-4}]$	Name
[1, 0]/2	none	400	3 tab
[1, 2, 0]/6	none	1700	5 tab.a
[-1, 8, 0]/12	none	150	5 tab.b
[1]	[1]/2	180	2×2
[1, 0]/2	[1, 2]/4	190	Sobel
[-1, 8, 0]/12	[1, 4, 6]/16	800	5×5 Gauß
[-0.262, 1.525, 0]	none	93	5-tab.opt
[1, 0]/2	[46.84 162.32]/256	22	3×3-opt
[77.68, 139.48]/256	[16.44, 111.56]/256	3.4	4×4-opt
[21.27, 85.46, 0]/256	[5.91, 61.77, 120.64]/256	0.67	5 ×5-opt
[21.38, 85.24, 0]/256	[5.96, 61.81, 120.46]/256	1.1	5×5×5-opt
[-67, 390 0]/256	none	92	5-tab.int
[1, 0]/2	[47, 162]/256	22	3×3-int
[76, 142]/256	[16, 112]/256	3.9	4×4-int
[24, 80, 0]/256	[7, 63, 116]/256	1.9	5×5-int
[1, 0]/2	[1, 2]/4	190	3×3-int
[1, 0]/2	[1, 6]/8	150	3×3-int
[1, 0]/2	[3, 10]/16	26	3×3-int
[1, 0]/2	[6, 20]/32	26	3 ×3-int
[1, 0]/2	[12, 40]/64	26	3×3-int
[1, 0]/2	[23, 82]/128	25	3×3-int
[1, 0]/2	[47, 162]/256	23.16	3×3-int
[1, 0]/2	[46.84, 162.32]/256	23.11	3×3-opt

Example 6.10: Gradient filters on a hexagonal grid

On a hexagonal grid only the ansatz function differs from the Cartesian case; reference function and error are the same. As in the Cartesian case there are two ways to get an ansatz function: a direct one simply using the fact that we want to compute the derivative; and a steerable one respecting the fact that we want to compute a direction.

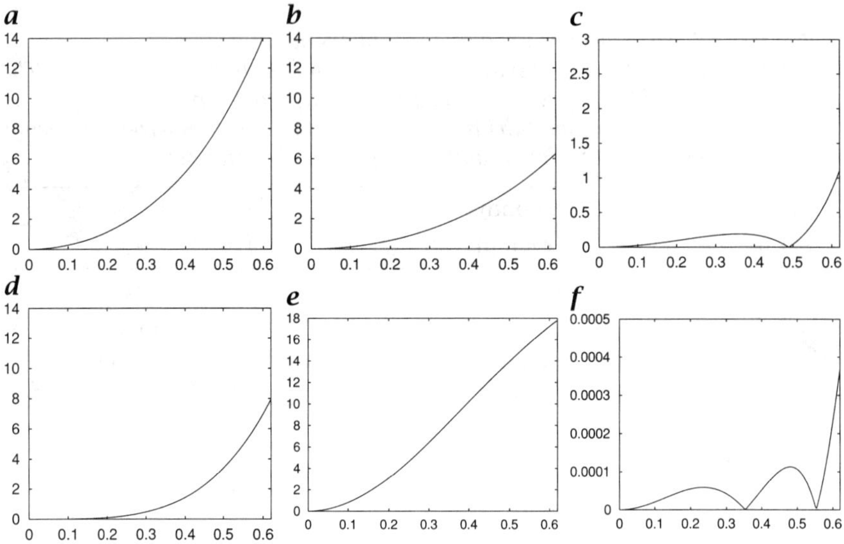

Figure 6.7: Magnitude of the angle error in degree for the direction of the largest error (22.5°). Upper line: 3×3*-filters (**a** symmetric difference, **b** Sobel, **c** optimized). Lower line:* 5×5*-filters (**d** [-1 8 0 -8 1]/16, **e** derivative of Gauss, **f** optimized; refer to results in Example 6.9 and Table 6.6). Please note the different scales of the* y *axes.*

Direct ansatz. A direct ansatz for the derivative filters is

$$D_x = \frac{1}{2}\begin{bmatrix} & d & & -d & \\ 1-d & & 0 & & -(1-d) \\ & d & & -d & \end{bmatrix} \tag{6.40}$$

$$D_y = \frac{1}{2\sqrt{3}}\begin{bmatrix} & -1 & & -1 & \\ 0 & & 0 & & 0 \\ & 1 & & 1 & \end{bmatrix} \tag{6.41}$$

with the transfer functions

$$\begin{aligned} \hat{D}_x &= (1-d)\sin(\pi\tilde{k}_x) + 2\,d\cos(\frac{\sqrt{3}\pi}{2}\tilde{k}_y)\sin(\frac{\pi}{2}\tilde{k}_x) \\ \hat{D}_y &= \frac{2}{\sqrt{3}}\sin(\frac{\sqrt{3}\pi}{2}\tilde{k}_y)\cos(\frac{\pi}{2}\tilde{k}_x) \end{aligned}$$

For this size of filters there are no more degrees of freedom, considering the symmetries and the claim $\hat{D}(\tilde{\boldsymbol{k}} = 0) = \mathrm{i}$. With these filters the reference function and error can be computed in the same way as in the 2-D case on a Cartesian grid.

Steerability ansatz. Gradient computation can be understood as computation of the maximum of the response D_ϕ of a set of steerable

Table 6.7: *Filter coefficients of a first-order derivative filter optimized for hexagonal lattices. The first column contains the filter coefficient in floating point and fixed-point arithmetic.*

Filter coefficient d	Error
85.31/256	1.28×10^{-5}
85/256	1.59×10^{-5}

directional derivative filters. They are of the same form as D_x in Eq. (6.40) for all three equivalent directions. The ansatz then is

$$D_\phi = D_1 \cos(\phi) + D_2 \cos(\phi + \frac{\pi}{3}) + D_3 \cos(\phi + \frac{2\pi}{3})$$

For the maximum at ϕ_0, we get

$$0 = D'_\phi \Leftrightarrow 0 = D_1 \sin(\phi_0) + D_2 \sin(\phi_0 + \frac{\pi}{3}) + D_3 \sin(\phi_0 + \frac{2\pi}{3})$$
$$\Leftrightarrow 0 = (D_1 + \frac{1}{2} D_2 - \frac{1}{2} D_3) \sin(\phi_0) + (\frac{\sqrt{3}}{2} D_2 + \frac{\sqrt{3}}{2} D_3) \cos(\phi_0)$$

The sum of filters $(\frac{\sqrt{3}}{2} D_2 + \frac{\sqrt{3}}{2} D_3)$ yields exactly $3\, D_y/2$ of Eq. (6.41), $(D_1 + D_2/2 - D_3/2)$ is equal to $3\, D_x/2$ of Eq. (6.40) for an adequate choice of the parameter d. This implies, as in the Cartesian case, that the steerable ansatz and the derivative ansatz lead to an identical optimization.

Results. For comparability, the results that follow are obtained with the same norm and weighting function as Example 6.9. Table 6.7 shows that the error of this filter with a single(!) parameter is about a factor 5 smaller than for the 5×5-opt filter on a Cartesian lattice providing 3 free parameters for optimization (see Fig. 10.2).

Example 6.11: Steerable 1-D second-order derivative

According to Section 6.6.2 we demonstrate how to optimize a filter family designed to compute the maximum direction of a 1-D second-order derivative.

Reference function. We use the direction ϕ_0 of maximal second-order 1-D derivative as reference. Referring to Eq. (6.37) it is

$$\phi_0(\tilde{\boldsymbol{k}}) = \frac{1}{2} \arctan(\frac{2\, \tilde{k}_x \tilde{k}_y}{\tilde{k}_y^2 - \tilde{k}_x^2})$$

Ansatz function. As in the preceding (see Example 6.9), separable filters can be composed by 1-D derivative filters D^1 and 1-D smoothing filters B. As in Section 6.6.2 we need

$$D_{xx} = D_x^1 * D_x^1 * B_x * B_y$$
$$D_{yy} = D_y^1 * D_y^1 * B_x * B_y$$
$$D_{xy} = D_x^1 * D_y^1 * B_x * B_y$$

Table 6.8: *Filter coefficients d_i of the optimized second-order steerable derivative filter basis according to Eq. (6.42); the first column contains the filter coefficients; the first part of the table lists well-known approaches, followed by the optimal filters in floating point arithmetic.*

Filter coefficients	Error
1/12, 0, 0, -1/6	4.69×10^{-2}
1/12, 4/16, 1/16, -1/6	3.72×10^{-2}
0.208, 0.113, -0.137, 0.128	2.54×10^{-4}

where the symbols for the filters do not always denote the same filter but the same filter behavior. For example, a 5×5 filter family is

$$\begin{aligned} D_{xx} &= [1\ -1]_x * [1\ -1]_x * [d_0\ (1-2\,d_0)\ d_0]_x * \\ &\quad [d_2\ d_1\ (1-2(d_1+d_2))\ d_1\ d_2]_y\,, \\ D_{yy} &= [1\ -1]_y * [1\ -1]_y * [d_0\ (1-2\,d_0)\ d_0]_y * \\ &\quad [d_2\ d_1\ (1-2(d_1+d_2))\ d_1\ d_2]_x\,, \\ D_{xy} &= \tfrac{1}{4}[d_3\ (1-2d_3)\ 0\ -(1-2d_3)\ -d_3]_x * \\ &\quad [d_3\ (1-2d_3)\ 0\ -(1-2d_3)\ -d_3]_y \end{aligned} \tag{6.42}$$

For this filter family all symmetries and degrees of freedom $\boldsymbol{d}$ are already considered. Standard parameter choices are

$$d_0 = 1/12, \quad d_1 = d_2 = 0, \quad d_3 = -1/6$$

and

$$d_0 = 1/12, \quad d_1 = 4/16, \quad d_2 = 1/16, \quad d_3 = -1/6$$

where the occurring derivative filters are optimized for small $\tilde{k}$ and there is either no or Gaussian smoothing in cross direction.

The ansatz function ϕ is

$$\phi(\tilde{\boldsymbol{k}}, \boldsymbol{d}) = \frac{1}{2}\arctan\left(\frac{2\,\hat{D}_{xy}}{\hat{D}_{yy} - \hat{D}_{xx}}\right)$$

The transfer function of the smoothing filters B and the derivatives d are given in Eq. (6.16) and Eqs. (6.12) and (6.32), respectively.

Results. For the example filter family of Eq. (6.42) the parameters $\boldsymbol{d}$ are given in Table 6.8. All results are computed in L_2 norm combined with the weighting function $\Pi_i \cos(\pi/2\,\tilde{k}_i)^4$.

6.7 References

[1] Oppenheim, (1975). *Digital signal processing.* Englewood Cliffs, NJ: Pentice-Hall.

[2] Proakis, J. G. and Manolakis, D. G., (1992). *Digital Signal Processing. Principles, Algorithms, and Applications.* New York: McMillan.

[3] Lim, J. S., (1990). *Two-dimensional Signal and Image Processing.* Englewood Cliffs, NJ: Prentice-Hall.

[4] Fletcher, R., (1987). *Practical Methods of Optimization,* 2 edition. New York: Wiley.

[5] Gill, P., Murray, W., and Wright, M., (1981). *Practical Optimization.* London: Academic Press.

[6] Nemhauser, G. and Wolsey, L., (1988). *Integer and Combinatorial Optimization.* New York: J. Wiley.

[7] Floudas, C., (1995). *Nonlinear and Mixed-Integer Optimization.* Oxford: Oxford University Press.

[8] Oppenheim, A. V. and Schafer, R. W., (1989). *Discrete-Time Signal Processing.* Englewood Cliffs, NJ: Prentice Hall.

[9] Proakis, J. G. and Manolakis, D. G., (1992). *Digital Signal Processing, Principles, Algorithms, and Applications.* New York: Macmillan.

[10] Karasaridis, A. and Simoncelli, E. P., (1996). A filter design technique for steerable pyramid image transforms. In *ICASSP,* Vol. IV, pp. 2389–2392. Atlanta, GA: IEEE Sig. Proc. Society.

[11] Manduchi, R. and Perona, P., (1995). Pyramidal implementation of deformable kernels. In *Proc. International Conference on Image Processing,* pp. 378–381. Washington: IEEE.

[12] Perona, P., (1991). *Deformable kernels for early vision.* Technical Report MIT-LIDS-P-2039, California Institute of Technology 116-81, Pasadena. CA 91126, USA.

[13] Perona, P., (1992). Steerable-scalable kernels for edge detection and junction analysis. *Image and Vision Comp.,* **10**:663–672.

[14] Simoncelli, E. and Farid, H., (1996). Steerable Wedge Filters for Local Orientation Analysis. *IEEE Trans Image Proc,* **5**(9):1377–1382.

[15] Simoncelli, E. P., Freeman, W. T., Adelson, E. H., and Heeger, D. J., (1992). Shiftable multiscale transforms. *IEEE Trans. Information Theory,* **38**:587–607.

[16] Manduchi, R., Perona, P., and Shy, D., (1997). *Efficient implementation of deformable filter banks.* Technical Report CNS-TR-97-04, California Institute of Technology 116-81, Pasadena. CA 91126, USA.

[17] Freeman, W. T. and Adelson, E. H., (1991). The design and use of steerable filters. *IEEE Trans. Patt. Anal. Mach. Intell.,* **13**:891–906.

7 Local Averaging

Bernd Jähne

Interdisziplinäres Zentrum für Wissenschaftliches Rechnen (IWR)
Universität Heidelberg, Germany

7.1 Introduction

Averaging is an elementary neighborhood operation for multidimensional signal processing. Averaging results in better feature estimates by including more data points. It is also an essential tool to regularize otherwise ill-defined quantities such as derivatives (Chapters 13 and 15). Convolution provides the framework for all elementary averaging filters. In this chapter averaging filters are considered for continuous signals and for discrete signals on square, rectangular and hexagonal

Handbook of Computer Vision and Applications
Volume 2
Signal Processing and Pattern Recognition

Copyright © 1999 by Academic Press
All rights of reproduction in any form reserved.
ISBN 0-12-379772-1/$30.00

lattices. The discussion is not restricted to 2-D signals. Whenever it is possible, the equations and filters are given for signals with arbitrary dimension.

The common properties and characteristics of all averaging filters are discussed in Section 7.2. On lattices two types of averaging filters are possible [1, Sect. 5.7.3]. Type I filters generate an output on the same lattice. On a rectangular grid such filters are of odd length in all directions. Type II filters generate an output on a grid with lattice points in-between the original lattice points (intermediate lattice). On a rectangular grid such filters are of even length in all directions. In this chapter two elementary averaging filters for digital multidimensional signals are discussed, box filters (Section 7.3) and binomial filters (Section 7.4). Then we will deal with techniques to cascade these elementary filters to large-scale averaging filters in Section 7.5. Filters with weighted signals (normalized convolution) in Section 7.6.

7.2 Basic features

7.2.1 General properties of transfer functions

Any averaging filter operator must preserve the mean value. This condition says that the transfer function for zero wave number is 1 or, equivalently, that the sum of all coefficients of the mask is 1:

$$\hat{h}(\mathbf{0}) = 1 \Longleftrightarrow \int_{-\infty}^{\infty} h(\boldsymbol{x})\,\mathrm{d}^D x = 1 \quad \text{or} \quad \sum_{\boldsymbol{n}\in\text{mask}} H_{\boldsymbol{n}} = 1 \tag{7.1}$$

Intuitively, we expect that any smoothing operator attenuates smaller scales more strongly than coarser scales. More specifically, a smoothing operator should not completely annul a certain scale while smaller scales still remain in the image. Mathematically speaking, this means that the transfer function decreases monotonically with the wave number. Then for any direction, represented by a unit vector $\bar{\boldsymbol{r}}$

$$\hat{h}(k_2\bar{\boldsymbol{r}}) \le \hat{h}(k_1\bar{\boldsymbol{r}}) \quad \text{if} \quad k_2 > k_1 \tag{7.2}$$

We may impose the more stringent condition that the transfer function approaches zero in all directions,

$$\lim_{k\to\infty} \hat{h}(k\bar{\boldsymbol{r}}) = 0 \tag{7.3}$$

On a discrete lattice the wave numbers are limited by the *Nyquist* condition, that is, the wave number must lay within the first Brillouin zone (Section 2.4.2). Then it makes sense to demand that the transfer function of an averaging filter is zero at the border of the Brillouin zone.

On a rectangular lattice this means

$$\hat{h}(\boldsymbol{k}) = 0 \quad \text{if} \quad \boldsymbol{k}\hat{\boldsymbol{b}}_d = |\hat{\boldsymbol{b}}_d|/2 \tag{7.4}$$

where $\hat{\boldsymbol{b}}_d$ is any of the D-basis vectors of the reciprocal lattice (Section 2.4.2). Together with the monotonicity condition and the preservation of the mean value, this means that the transfer function decreases monotonically from one to zero for each averaging operator.

For a 1-D filter we can easily use Eq. (5.24) to relate the condition in Eq. (7.4) to a condition for the coefficients of type I filters:

$$\hat{h}(1) = 0 \Longleftrightarrow h_0 + 2\sum_{r \text{ even}} h_r = 2\sum_{r \text{ odd}} h_r \tag{7.5}$$

One-dimensional type II filters are, according to Eq. (5.24), always zero for $\tilde{k} = 1$.

7.2.2 Symmetry and isotropy

Even filters in continuous space. With respect to object detection, the most important feature of an averaging operator is that it must not shift the object position. Any shift introduced by a preprocessing operator would cause errors in the estimates of the position and possibly other geometric features of an object. In order not to cause a spatial shift, a filter must not induce any phase shift in the Fourier space. A filter with this property is known as a *zero-phase filter*. This implies that the transfer function is real and this is equivalent with an *even symmetry* of the filter mask (Section 3.2.3):

$$h(-\boldsymbol{x}) = h(\boldsymbol{x}) \Longleftrightarrow \hat{h}(\boldsymbol{k}) \quad \text{real} \tag{7.6}$$

Averaging filters normally meet a stronger symmetry condition in the sense that each axis is a symmetry axis. Then Eq. (7.6) is valid for each component of $\boldsymbol{x}$:

$$h([x_1, \ldots, -x_d, \ldots, x_D]^T) = h([x_1, \ldots, x_d, \ldots, x_D]^T) \tag{7.7}$$

Even filters on 1-D lattices. For digital signals we distinguish filters with odd and even numbers of coefficients in *all* directions (Section 5.3.5). For both cases, we can write the symmetry condition for a filter with $R_d + 1$ coefficients in the direction d as

$$H_{r_0, r_1, \ldots, R_d - r_d, \ldots, r_D} = H_{r_0, r_1, \ldots, r_d, \ldots, r_D} \quad \forall d \in [1, D] \tag{7.8}$$

when we count the coefficients in each direction from left to right from 0 to R_d. This is not the usual counting but it is convenient as only one equation is required to express the evenness for filters with even and odd numbers of coefficients. For a 1-D filter the symmetry conditions reduce to

$$H_{R-r} = H_r \tag{7.9}$$

The symmetry relations significantly ease the computation of the transfer functions because for real transfer functions only the cosine term of the complex exponential from the Fourier transform remains in the equations (Sections 3.2 and 5.3.5). The transfer function for 1-D even masks with either $2R + 1$ (type I filter) or $2R$ coefficients (type II filter) is

$$\begin{aligned} {}^{I}\hat{h}(\tilde{k}) &= h_0 + 2\sum_{r=1}^{R} h_r \cos(r\pi\tilde{k}) \\ {}^{II}\hat{h}(\tilde{k}) &= 2\sum_{r=1}^{R} h_r \cos((r-1/2)\pi\tilde{k}) \end{aligned} \tag{7.10}$$

Note that in these equations only pairs of coefficients are counted from 1 to R. The central coefficient of a filter with an odd number of coefficients has the index zero. As discussed in Section 5.3.5, filters with an odd number of coefficients output the filter results to the same lattice while filters with an even number of coefficients output the filter result to the intermediate lattice.

Even filters on higher-dimensional lattices. On higher-dimensional lattices things become more complex. We assume that each axis is a symmetry axis according to the symmetry condition in Eq. (7.7). This condition implies that for type I filters with $2R + 1$ coefficients all coefficients on the symmetry axes must be treated separately because they are symmetric counterparts. Thus already the equation for the transfer function of a 2-D filter with even symmetry in both directions is quite complex:

$$\begin{aligned} {}^{I}\hat{H}(\tilde{\boldsymbol{k}}) &= H_{00} \\ &+ 2\sum_{n=1}^{R} H_{0n}\cos(n\pi\tilde{k}_1) + 2\sum_{m=1}^{R} H_{n0}\cos(n\pi\tilde{k}_2) \\ &+ 4\sum_{m=1}^{R}\sum_{n=1}^{R} H_{mn}\cos(n\pi\tilde{k}_1)\cos(m\pi\tilde{k}_2) \end{aligned} \tag{7.11}$$

For a type II filter with $2R$ coefficients, no coefficients are placed on the symmetry axes. With an even number of coefficients, the transfer function of a 1-D symmetric mask is given by

$${}^{II}\hat{H}(\tilde{\boldsymbol{k}}) = 4\sum_{n=1}^{R}\sum_{m=1}^{R} H_{mn}\cos((n-1/2)\pi\tilde{k}_1)\cos((m-1/2)\pi\tilde{k}_2) \tag{7.12}$$

A further discussion of the properties of symmetric filters up to three dimensions can be found in Jähne [2].

Isotropic filters. In most applications, the averaging should be the same in all directions in order not to prefer any direction. Thus, both the filter mask and the transfer function should be isotropic. Consequently, the filter mask depends only on the magnitude of the distance from the center pixel and the transfer function on the magnitude of the wave number:

$$H(\boldsymbol{x}) = H(|\boldsymbol{x}|) \Longleftrightarrow \hat{H}(\tilde{\boldsymbol{k}}) = \hat{H}(|\tilde{\boldsymbol{k}}|) \tag{7.13}$$

This condition can also be met easily in discrete space. It means that the coefficients at lattice points with an equal distance from the center point are the same. However, the big difference now is that a filter whose coefficients meet this condition has not necessarily an isotropic transfer function. The deviations from the isotropy are stronger the smaller the filter mask is. We will discuss the deviations from isotropy in detail for specific filters.

7.2.3 Separable averaging filters

The importance of separable filters for higher-dimensional signals is related to the fact that they can be computed much faster than nonseparable filters (Section 5.6.1). The symmetry conditions for separable averaging filters are also quite simple because only the symmetry condition Eq. (7.9) must be considered. Likewise, the equations for the transfer functions of separable filters are quite simple. If we apply the same 1-D filter in all directions, the resulting transfer function of a D-dimensional filter is given after Eq. (7.10) by

$$\begin{aligned} {}^{I}\hat{h}(\tilde{\boldsymbol{k}}) &= \prod_{d=1}^{D}\left(h_0 + 2\sum_{r=1}^{R} h_r \cos(r\pi\tilde{k}_d)\right) \\ {}^{II}\hat{h}(\tilde{\boldsymbol{k}}) &= \prod_{d=1}^{D}\left(2\sum_{r=1}^{R} h_r \cos((r-1/2)\pi\tilde{k}_d)\right) \end{aligned} \tag{7.14}$$

With respect to isotropy, there exists only a single separable filter that is also isotropic, the Gaussian function

$$\begin{aligned} \frac{1}{a^D}\exp(-\pi\boldsymbol{x}^T\boldsymbol{x}/a^2) &= \frac{1}{a^D}\prod_{d=1}^{D}\exp(-\pi x_d^2/a^2) \Longleftrightarrow \\ \exp(-\pi a^2\tilde{\boldsymbol{k}}^T\tilde{\boldsymbol{k}}/4) &= \prod_{d=1}^{D}\exp(-\pi a^2\tilde{k}_d^2/4) \end{aligned} \tag{7.15}$$

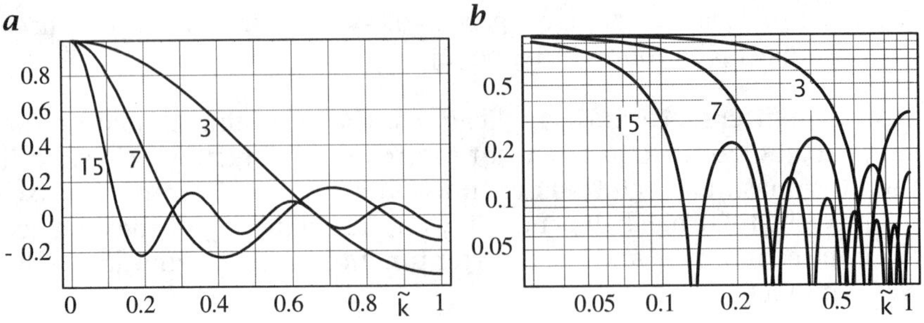

***Figure 7.1:** Transfer functions of type I box filters with 3, 7, and 15 coefficients in **a** a linear plot; and **b** a log-log plot of the absolute value.*

This feature shows the central importance of the Gaussian function for signal processing from yet another perspective.

To a good approximation, the Gaussian function can be replaced on orthogonal discrete lattices by the binomial distribution. The coefficients of a 1-D binomal filter with $R + 1$ coefficients and its transfer function are given by

$$B^R = \frac{1}{2^R}\left[b_0 = 1, \ldots, b_r = \binom{R}{r}, \ldots, b_{R+1} = 1\right] \Longleftrightarrow \hat{B}^R(\tilde{k}) = \cos^R(\pi\tilde{k}/2) \tag{7.16}$$

With the comments on the isotropy of discrete filters in mind (Section 7.2.2), it is necessary to study the deviation of the transfer function of binomial filters from an isotropic filter.

7.3 Box filters

The simplest method is to average pixels within the filter mask and to divide the sum by the number of pixels. Such a simple filter is called a *box filter*. It is also known under the name *running mean*. In this section, type I (Section 7.3.1) and type II (Section 7.3.2) box filters and box filters on hexagonal lattices (Section 7.3.3) are discussed.

7.3.1 Type I box filters

The simplest type I 1-D box filter is

$$^3\boldsymbol{R} = \frac{1}{3}[1, 1, 1] \Longleftrightarrow {}^3\hat{R}(\tilde{k}) = \frac{1}{3} + \frac{2}{3}\cos(\pi\tilde{k}) \tag{7.17}$$

The factor 1/3 scales the result of the convolution sum in order to preserve the mean value (see Eq. (7.1) in Section 7.2.1). Generally, a type I 1-D box filter with $2R + 1$ coefficients has the transfer function

$$
\begin{aligned}
{}^{I}\hat{R}(\tilde{k}) &= \frac{1}{2R+1} + \frac{2}{2R+1}\sum_{r=1}^{R}\cos(\pi r\tilde{k}) \\
&= \frac{1}{2R+1}\frac{\cos(\pi R\tilde{k}) - \cos(\pi(R+1)\tilde{k})}{1-\cos(\pi\tilde{k})}
\end{aligned}
\tag{7.18}
$$

For small wave numbers the transfer function can be approximated by

$$
{}^{I}\hat{R}(\tilde{k}) \approx 1 - \frac{R(R+1)}{6}(\pi\tilde{k})^2 + \frac{R(R+1)(3R^2+3R-1)}{360}(\pi\tilde{k})^4 \tag{7.19}
$$

Figure 7.1 shows that the box filter is a poor averaging filter. The transfer function is not monotonical and the envelope of the transfer function is only decreasing with k^{-1} (compare Section 3.2.3). The highest wave number is not completely suppressed even with large filter masks. The box filter also shows significant oscillations in the transfer function. The filter ${}^{2R+1}\mathcal{R}$ completely eliminates the wave numbers $\tilde{k} = 2r/(2R+1)$ for $1 \le r \le R$. In certain wave-number ranges, the transfer function becomes negative. This corresponds to a 180° phase shift and thus a contrast inversion.

Despite all their disadvantages, box filters have one significant advantage. They can be computed very fast with only one addition, subtraction, and multiplication independent of the size of the filter, that is, $O(R^0)$. Equation (7.18) indicates that the box filter can also be understood as a filter operation with a recursive part according to the following relation:

$$
g'_n = g'_{n-1} + \frac{1}{2R+1}(g_{n+R} - g_{n-R-1}) \tag{7.20}
$$

This recursion can easily be understood by comparing the computations for the convolution at neighboring pixels. When the box mask is moved one position to the right, it contains the same weighting factor for all pixels except for the last and the first pixel. Thus, we can simply take the result of the previous convolution, (g'_{n-1}), subtract the first pixel that just moved out of the mask, (g_{n-R-1}), and add the gray value at the pixel that just came into the mask, (g_{n+R}). In this way, the computation of a box filter does not depend on its size.

Higher-dimensional box filters can simply be computed by cascading 1-D box filters running in all directions, as the box filter is separable. Thus the resulting transfer function for a D-dimensional filter is

$$
{}^{2R+1}\hat{R}(\tilde{k}) = \frac{1}{(2R+1)^D}\prod_{d=1}^{D}\frac{\cos(\pi R\tilde{k}_d) - \cos(\pi(R+1)\tilde{k}_d)}{1-\cos(\pi\tilde{k}_d)} \tag{7.21}
$$

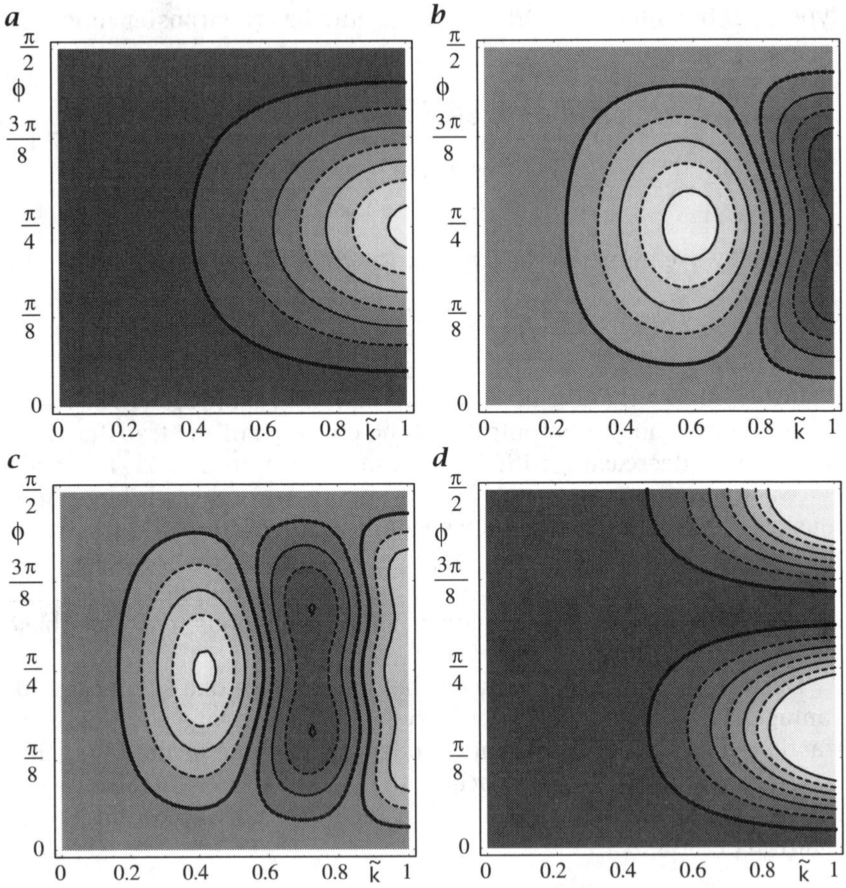

*Figure 7.2: Absolute deviation of the 2-D transfer functions of type I 2-D box filters from the transfer function along the x axis (1-D transfer function shown in Fig. 7.1) for a **a** 3× 3, **b** 5× 5, **c** 7× 7, and **d** a $^3\hat{R}(\tilde{k})$ filter running in 0°, 60°, and 120° on a hexagonal grid. The distance of the contour lines is 0.05 in **a** - **c** and 0.01 in **d**. The area between the thick contour lines marks the range around zero.*

For a 2-D filter, we can approximate the transfer function for small wave numbers and express the result in cylinder coordinates by using $k_1 = k\cos\phi$ and $k_2 = k\sin\phi$ and obtain

$$\begin{aligned} {}^I\hat{R}(\tilde{\boldsymbol{k}}) &\approx 1 - \frac{R(R+1)}{6}(\pi\tilde{k})^2 + \frac{R(R+1)(14R^2+14R-1)}{1440}(\pi\tilde{k})^4 \\ &- \frac{R(R+1)(2R^2+2R+1)}{1440}\cos(4\phi)(\pi\tilde{k})^4 \end{aligned} \tag{7.22}$$

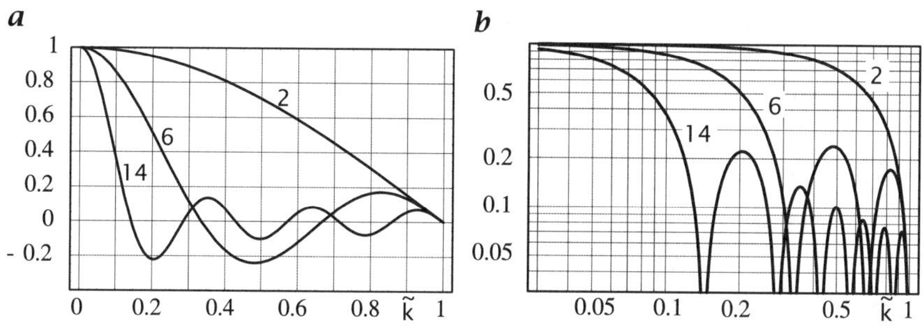

***Figure 7.3:** Transfer functions of type II box filters with 2, 6, and 14 coefficients in **a** a linear plot; and **b** a log-log plot of the absolute value.*

This equation indicates that—although the term with $\tilde{k}^2$ is isotropic—the term with $\tilde{k}^4$ is significantly anisotropic. The anisotropy does not improve for larger filter masks because the isotropic and anisotropic terms in $\tilde{k}^4$ grow with the same power in R.

A useful measure for the anisotropy is the deviation of the 2-D filter response from the response in the direction of the x_1 axis:

$$\Delta\hat{R}(\tilde{\boldsymbol{k}}) = \hat{R}(\tilde{\boldsymbol{k}}) - \hat{R}(\tilde{k}_1) \tag{7.23}$$

For an isotropic filter, this deviation is zero. Again in an approximation for small wave numbers we obtain by Taylor expansion

$$\Delta^I\hat{R}(\tilde{\boldsymbol{k}}) \approx \frac{2R^4 + 4R^3 + 3R^2 + R}{720}\sin^2(2\phi)(\pi\tilde{k})^4 \tag{7.24}$$

The anisotropy for various box filters is shown in Fig. 7.2a–c. Clearly, the anisotropy does not become weaker for larger box filters. The deviations are significant and easily reach 0.25. This figure means that the attenuation for a certain wave number varies up to 0.25 with the direction of the wave number.

7.3.2 Type II box filters

Type II box filters have an even number of coefficients in every direction. Generally, a type II 1-D box filter with $2R$ coefficients has the transfer function

$$\begin{aligned} {}^{II}\hat{R}(\tilde{k}) &= \frac{1}{R}\sum_{r=1}^{R}\cos(\pi(r-1/2)\tilde{k}) \\ &= \frac{1}{2R}\frac{\cos(\pi(R-1/2)\tilde{k}) - \cos(\pi(R+1/2)\tilde{k})}{1-\cos(\pi\tilde{k})} \end{aligned} \tag{7.25}$$

For small wave numbers the transfer function can be approximated by

$$^{II}\hat{R}(\tilde{k}) \approx 1 - \frac{4R^2-1}{24}(\pi\tilde{k})^2 + \frac{48R^4-40R^2+7}{5760}(\pi\tilde{k})^4 \quad (7.26)$$

Figure 7.3 also shows that type II box filter are poor averaging filters. Their only advantage over type I box filters is that as a result of the even number of coefficients the transfer function at the highest wave number is always zero.

Higher-dimensional type II box filters are formed in the same way as type I filters in Eq. (7.21). Thus we investigate here only the anisotropy of type II filters in comparison to type I filters. The transfer function of a 2-D filter can be approximated for small wave numbers in cylinder coordinates by

$$\begin{aligned} ^{II}\hat{R}(\tilde{\boldsymbol{k}}) &\approx 1 - \frac{4R^2-1}{24}(\pi\tilde{k})^2 + \frac{(4R^2-1)(28R^2-13)}{11520}(\pi\tilde{k})^4 \\ &- \frac{(4R^2-1)(4R^2+1)}{11520}\cos(4\phi)(\pi\tilde{k})^4 \end{aligned} \quad (7.27)$$

and the anisotropy according to Eq. (7.23) is given by

$$\Delta^{II}\hat{R}(\tilde{\boldsymbol{k}}) \approx \frac{16R^4-1}{5760}\sin^2(2\phi)(\pi\tilde{k})^4 \quad (7.28)$$

A comparison with Eq. (7.24) shows—not surprisingly—that the anisotropy of type I and type II filters is essentially the same.

7.3.3 Box filters on hexagonal lattices

On a *hexagonal lattice* (Section 2.3.1) a separable filter is running not in two but in three directions: 0°, 60°, and 120° with respect to the x axis. Thus the transfer function of a separable filter is composed of three factors:

$$\begin{aligned} ^{h}\hat{R}(\tilde{k}) = &\frac{1}{(2R+1)^3} \cdot \frac{\cos(\pi R\tilde{k}_1) - \cos(\pi(R+1)\tilde{k}_1)}{1-\cos(\pi\tilde{k}_1)} \\ &\frac{\cos(\pi R(\sqrt{3}\tilde{k}_2+\tilde{k}_1)/2) - \cos(\pi(R+1)(\sqrt{3}\tilde{k}_2+\tilde{k}_1)/2)}{1-\cos(\pi(\sqrt{3}\tilde{k}_2+\tilde{k}_1)/2)} \\ &\frac{\cos(\pi R(\sqrt{3}\tilde{k}_2-\tilde{k}_1)/2) - \cos(\pi(R+1)(\sqrt{3}\tilde{k}_2-\tilde{k}_1)/2)}{1-\cos(\pi(\sqrt{3}\tilde{k}_2-\tilde{k}_1)/2)} \end{aligned} \quad (7.29)$$

As for the box filters on a rectangular lattice (Eqs. (7.24) and (7.28)), we compute the anisotropy of the filter using Eq. (7.23) in the approximation for small wave numbers. The result is

$$\Delta^{h}\hat{R}(\tilde{k}) \approx \frac{3R+15R^2+40R^3+60R^4+48R^5+16R^6}{241920}\sin^2(3\phi)(\pi\tilde{k})^6 \quad (7.30)$$

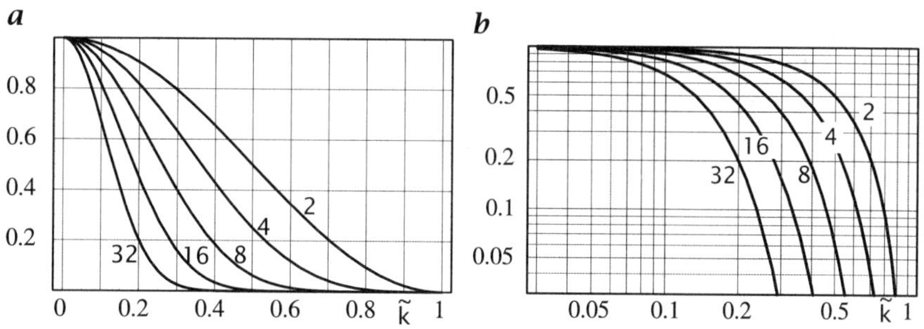

Figure 7.4: *Transfer functions of binomial filters $\mathcal{B}^R$ in **a** a linear plot and **b** a log-log plot of the absolute value with values of R as indicated.*

This equation indicates that the effects of anisotropy are significantly lower on hexagonal grids. In contrast to the box filters on a square grid, there is only an anisotropic term with $\tilde{k}^6$ and not already with $\tilde{k}^4$. From Fig. 7.2a and d we can conclude that the anisotropy is about a factor of 5 lower for a ${}^3\mathcal{R}$ filter on a hexagonal lattice than on a square lattice.

7.4 Binomial filters

7.4.1 General properties

In Section 7.2.3 we concluded that only the Gaussian function meets the most desirable features of an averaging filter: separability and isotropy. In this section we will investigate to which extent the binomial filter, which is a discrete approximation to the Gaussian filter, still meets these criteria. The coefficients of the one-dimensional binomial filter can be generated by repeatedly convolving the simple 1/2 [1 1] mask:

$$\boldsymbol{B}^R = \underbrace{1/2\,[1\ 1] * \ldots * 1/2\,[1\ 1]}_{R \text{ times}} \tag{7.31}$$

This cascaded convolution is equivalent to the scheme in *Pascal's triangle*. The transfer function of the elementary $\boldsymbol{B} = 1/2\,[1\ 1]$ filter is

$$\hat{\boldsymbol{B}} = \cos(\pi\tilde{k}/2) \tag{7.32}$$

There is no need to distinguish type I and type II binomial filters in the equations because they can be generated by cascaded convolution as in Eq. (7.31). Therefore, the transfer function of the $\boldsymbol{B}^R$ binomial filter is

$$\hat{\boldsymbol{B}}^R = \cos^R(\pi\tilde{k}/2) \tag{7.33}$$

The most important features of binomial averaging filters are:

Monotonic transfer function. The transfer function decreases monotonically from 1 to 0 (Fig. 7.4).

Spatial variance. The coefficients of the binomial filter quickly approach with increasing mask size a sampled normal distribution. The spatial variance is

$$\sigma_x^2 = R/4 \tag{7.34}$$

A binomial filter effectively averages over a width of $2\sigma_x$. In contrast to the box filters, the effective averaging width increases only with the square root of the filter length.

Variance. Also the transfer function of the binomial filter quickly approaches the Gaussian function with increasing mask size (Fig. 7.4a). It is instructive to compare the Taylor expansion of the Gaussian function for small wave numbers with those of the transfer functions of binomial filters:

$$\begin{aligned} \exp(-\tilde{k}^2/(2\sigma_{\tilde{k}}^2)) &\approx 1 - \frac{1}{2\sigma_k^2}\tilde{k}^2 + \frac{1}{8\sigma_k^4}\tilde{k}^4 \\ \hat{\boldsymbol{B}}^R(\tilde{k}) &\approx 1 - \frac{R\pi^2}{8}\tilde{k}^2 + \left(\frac{R^2\pi^4}{128} - \frac{R\pi^4}{192}\right)\tilde{k}^4 \end{aligned} \tag{7.35}$$

For large R both expansions are the same with

$$\sigma_k = \frac{2}{\sqrt{R}\pi} \tag{7.36}$$

7.4.2 Binomial filters on square lattices

Higher-dimensional binomial filters can be composed from 1-D binomial filters in all directions:

$$\mathcal{B}^R = \prod_{d=1}^{D} \mathcal{B}_d^R \tag{7.37}$$

Thus the transfer function of the multidimensional binomial filter $\mathcal{B}^R$ with $(R+1)^D$ coefficients is given by

$$\hat{B}^R = \prod_{d=1}^{D} \cos^R(\pi\tilde{k}_d/2) \tag{7.38}$$

The isotropy of binomial filters can be studied by expanding Eq. (7.38) in a Taylor series using cylindrical coordinates $\tilde{\boldsymbol{k}} = [\tilde{k}, \phi]^T$:

$$\hat{B}^R \approx 1 - \frac{R}{8}(\pi\tilde{k})^2 + \frac{2R^2 - R}{256}(\pi\tilde{k})^4 - \frac{R\cos 4\phi}{768}(\pi\tilde{k})^4 \tag{7.39}$$

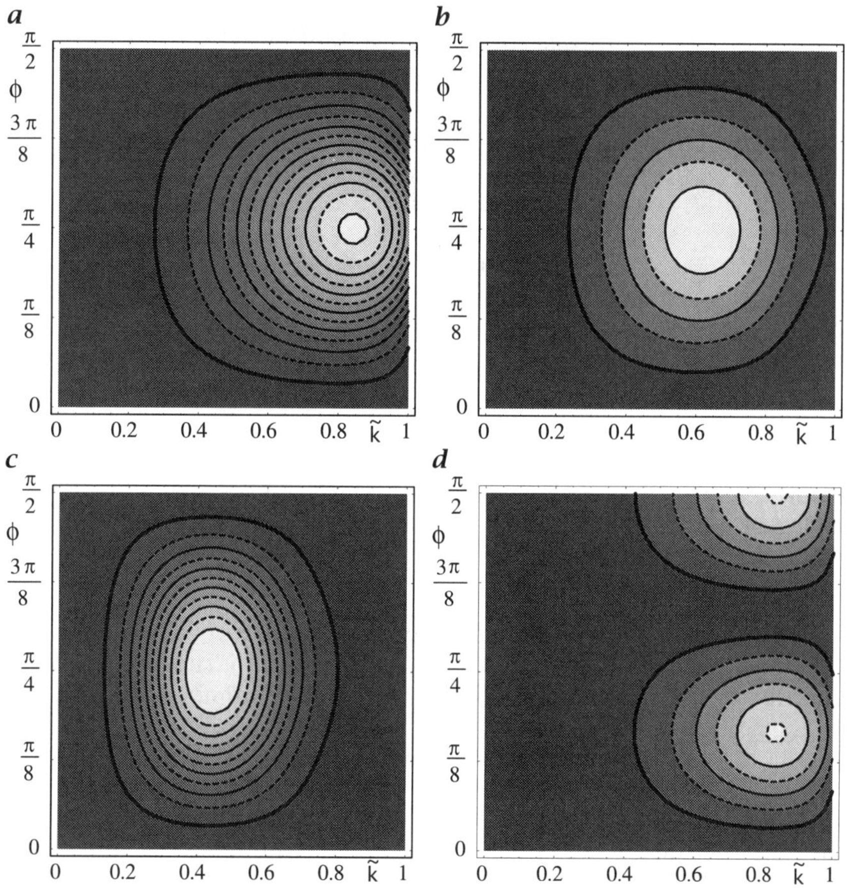

Figure 7.5: *Absolute deviation of the 2-D transfer functions of binomial filters from the transfer function along the x axis (1-D transfer function shown in Fig. 7.4) for a **a** 3× 3 ($\mathcal{B}^2$), **b** 5× 5 ($\mathcal{B}^4$), **c** 9× 9 ($\mathcal{B}^8$), and **d** a $\mathcal{B}^2(\tilde{k})$ filter running in 0°, 60°, and 120° on a hexagonal grid. The distance of the contour lines is 0.005 in **a** and **b** and 0.001 in **c** and **d**. The area between the thick contour lines marks the range around zero.*

Only the second-order term is isotropic. In contrast, the fourth-order term contains an anisotropic part, which increases the transfer function in the direction of the diagonals. A larger filter (larger R) is less anisotropic as the isotropic term with $\tilde{k}^4$ increases quadratically with R while the anisotropic term with $\tilde{k}^4 \cos 4\theta$ increases only linearly with R. The anisotropy deviation according to Eq. (7.23) is given by

$$\Delta \hat{B}^R \approx \frac{R}{384} \sin^2(2\phi)(\pi\tilde{k})^4 + \frac{5R^2 - 4R}{15360} \sin^2(2\phi)(\pi\tilde{k})^6 \tag{7.40}$$

and shown in Fig. 7.5.

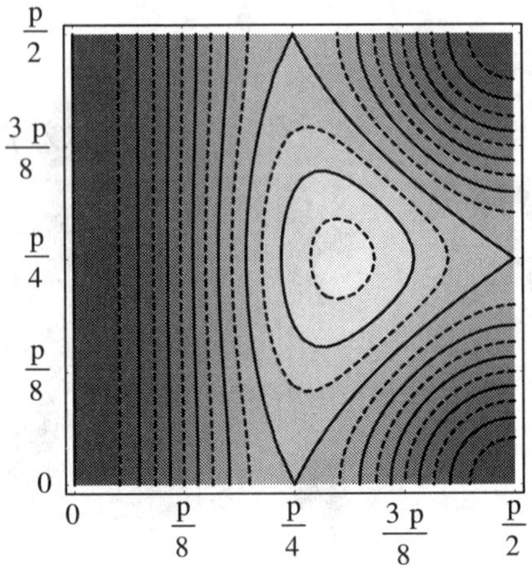

Figure 7.6: *Anisotropy with respect to the response of the axes for a 3-D binomial filter for small wave numbers. Shown is the factor of the term with* $(\pi\tilde{k})^4$ *as a function of the angles* ϕ *and* θ.

For a 3-D binomial filter, we can use the same procedures to analyze the anisotropy. It is only required to replace cylindrical by spherical coordinates. Then the anisotropy for small wave numbers is given by

$$\Delta\hat{B}^R \approx \frac{R}{384}\left(\sin^2(2\phi)\sin^4\theta + \sin^2(2\theta)\right)(\pi\tilde{k})^4 \qquad (7.41)$$

Figure 7.6 shows that the anisotropy is the same in the directions of the diagonals in the xy, xz, and yz planes. A maximum in the anisotropy that is slightly higher than in the direction of the area diagonals is reached in the direction of the space diagonal.

7.4.3 Binomial filters on hexagonal lattices

On a hexagonal lattice a separable binomial filter is running in three directions instead of two directions on a square lattice. Thus the masks

$$\frac{1}{4}\begin{bmatrix} 1 & 1 \\ 1 & 1 \end{bmatrix} \quad \text{and} \quad \frac{1}{16}\begin{bmatrix} 1 & 2 & 1 \\ 2 & 4 & 2 \\ 1 & 2 & 1 \end{bmatrix}$$

on a square lattice correspond to the masks

$$\frac{1}{8}\begin{bmatrix} & 1 & & 1 & \\ 1 & & 2 & & 1 \\ & 1 & & 1 & \end{bmatrix} \quad \text{and} \quad \frac{1}{64}\begin{bmatrix} & & 1 & & 2 & & 1 & & \\ & 2 & & 6 & & 6 & & 2 & \\ 1 & & 6 & & 10 & & 6 & & 1 \\ & 2 & & 6 & & 6 & & 2 & \\ & & 1 & & 2 & & 1 & & \end{bmatrix}$$

on a hexagonal lattice.

The anisotropy deviation according to Eq. (7.23) is given by

$$\Delta^h \hat{B}^R \approx \frac{R}{15360} \sin^2(3\phi)(\pi\tilde{k})^6 \tag{7.42}$$

for small wave numbers. Figure 7.5d shows that the anisotropy for $\mathcal{B}^2$ is already about 10 times lower than for the same filter on a square grid. The maximum anisotropy is well below 0.01 even for this small filter.

7.4.4 Efficient computation

We close our consideration of binomial filters with some remarks on fast algorithms. A direct computation of a $\mathcal{B}^R$ operator with $(R+1)^D$ filter coefficients requires $(R+1)^D$ multiplications and $(R+1)^D - 1$ additions. If we decompose the binomial mask into elementary smoothing masks $\boldsymbol{B} = 1/2\,[1\ 1]$ and apply this mask in all directions R times each, we only need DR additions. All multiplications can be handled much more efficiently as shift operations. For example, the computation of a 9×9 ($9 \times 9 \times 9$) binomial filter requires only 16 (24) additions and some shift operations compared to 81 (729) multiplications and 80 (728) additions needed for the direct approach.

7.5 Cascaded averaging

The approaches discussed so far for local averaging are no solution if the averaging should cover large neighborhoods for the following reasons: First, binomial filters are not suitable for large-scale averaging—despite their efficient implementation by cascaded convolution with $\mathcal{B}$—because the averaging distance increases only with the square root of the mask size (see Eq. (7.34) in Section 7.4.1). Secondly, box filters and recursive filters are, in principle, suitable for large-scale averaging because the number of operations does not increase with the size of the point spread function (operation of the order $O(R^0)$). However, both types of filters have a nonideal transfer function. The transfer function of the box filter is not monotonically decreasing with the wave number (Section 7.3) and both filters show too large deviations from an isotropic response. In this section, two techniques are discussed for large-scale averaging that overcome these deficits and limitations, multistep averaging (Section 7.5.1) and multigrid averaging (Section 7.5.2).

7.5.1 Multistep averaging

The problem of slow large-scale averaging originates from the small distance between the pixels averaged by small masks. In order to overcome this problem, we may use the same elementary averaging process

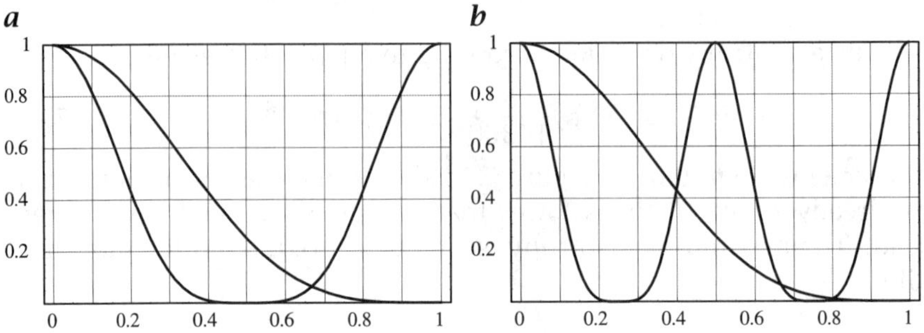

Figure 7.7: *Transfer functions of the binomial filter* $\mathcal{B}^4$ *(*$\boldsymbol{B} = 1/16[1\,4\,6\,4\,1]$*) and the same filter stretched by* ***a*** *a factor of two,* $\mathcal{B}_2^4$ *(*$\boldsymbol{B}_2 = 1/16[1\,0\,4\,0\,6\,0\,4\,0\,1]$*), and* ***b*** *a factor of four,* $\mathcal{B}_4^4$*.*

but with more distant pixels. As the box, binomial and recursive averaging filters are separable and thus are applied as cascaded filter operations running one after the other in all coordinate directions through a multidimensional signal, it is sufficient to discuss increasing the step width for 1-D filter operations. A 1-D convolution with a mask that operates only with every S-th pixel can be written as a stretched mask

$$(h_S)_n = \begin{cases} h_{n'} & n = Sn' \\ 0 & \text{else} \end{cases} \iff \hat{h}_S(\tilde{k}) = \hat{h}(\tilde{k}/S) \qquad (7.43)$$

Because of the reciprocity between the spatial and Fourier domains the stretching of the filter mask by a factor S results in a corresponding shrinking of the transfer function. This shrinking goes—because of the periodicity of the transfer function of discrete samples—along with an S-fold replication of the transfer function as illustrated in Fig. 7.7.

An averaging filter that is used with a larger step width is no longer a good averaging filter for the whole wave-number range but only for wave numbers up to $\tilde{k} = 1/S$. Used individually, these filters are thus not of much help. But we can use them in cascade in such a way that previous smoothing has already removed all wave numbers beyond $\tilde{k} = 1/S$. This is the basic principle for the design of cascaded filters.

For practical design there are two degrees of freedom. First, we can select the basic filter that is used repeatedly with different step widths. Here, box, binomial and relaxation filters are investigated. Second, we can choose the way in which the step width is increased. We will consider both a linear and an exponential increase in the step width. Generally, a cascaded filter operation consists of the following chain of P operations with the filter operation $\mathcal{B}$:

$$\underbrace{\mathcal{B}_{a_P} \ldots \mathcal{B}_{a_p} \ldots \mathcal{B}_{a_2}\mathcal{B}_{a_1}}_{P \text{ times}} \qquad (7.44)$$

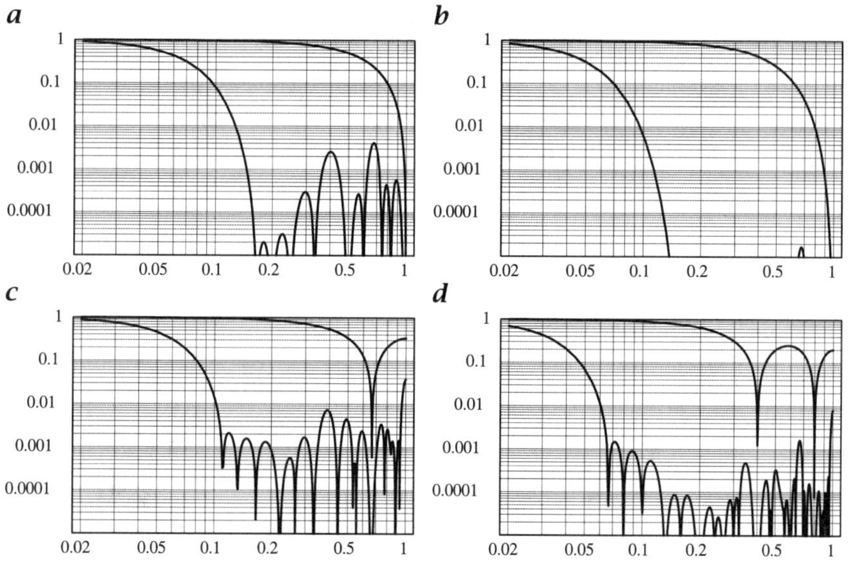

Figure 7.8: *Transfer functions of cascaded filtering with linear increase in step width with* **a** $\mathcal{B}^2$, **b** $\mathcal{B}^4$, **c** ${}^3\mathcal{R}$, *and* **d** ${}^5\mathcal{R}$. *Shown are the transfer functions of the original filters and of the cascaded filtering up to the six-fold step size with a resulting averaging width* $\sqrt{91} \approx 9.54$ *times larger than the original filter.*

where a_p consists of a sequence of step widths. Whereas in each step the same operator $\mathcal{B}$ with the spatial variance σ^2 is used and only the step width is changed, the resulting step width can be computed by

$$\sigma_c^2 = \sigma^2 \sum_{p=1}^{P} a_p^2 \tag{7.45}$$

From this equation it is also obvious that efficient filter cascading requires an increasing step width. If we keep the step width constant, the averaging width given by σ_c increases only with $\sqrt{P}$ and not linearly with P.

Linearly increasing step width. In the simplest case, the step width is increased linearly, that is, $a_p = p$. This results in the following sequence of P step widths: $1, 2, 3, 4, \ldots, P$. According to Eq. (7.45), the resulting series of variances is

$$\sigma_c^2 = \sigma^2 \sum_{p=1}^{P} p^2 = \frac{P(P+1)(2P+1)}{6} \sigma^2 \tag{7.46}$$

For large P, $\sigma_c = P^{3/2}\sigma/\sqrt{3}$. Thus the averaging width increases even stronger than linear with the number of steps. With only six steps, the

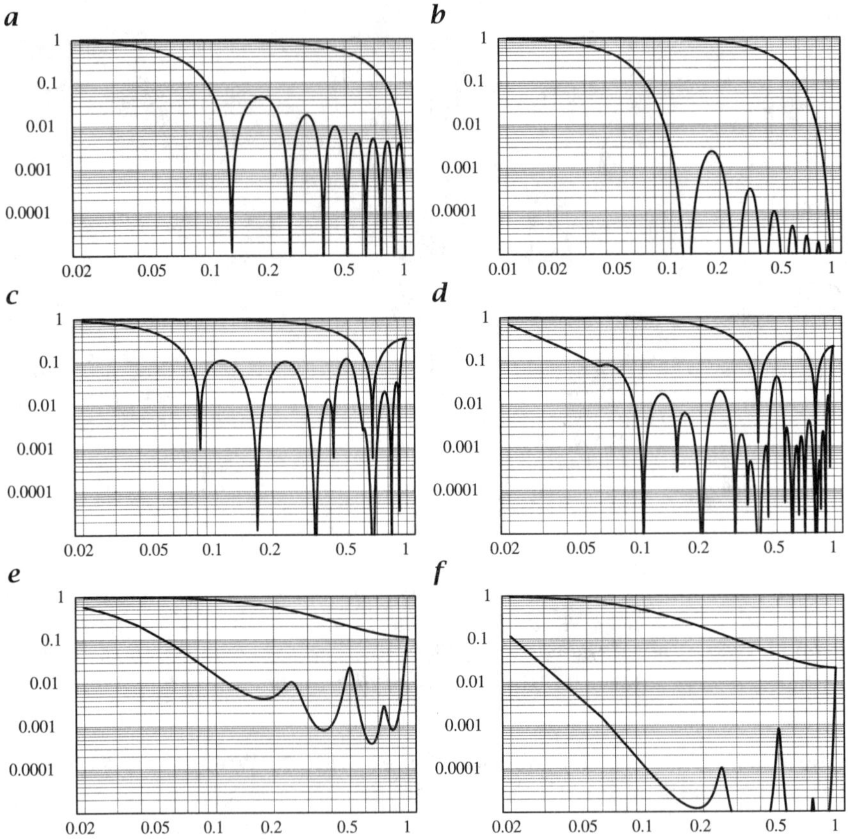

Figure 7.9: *Transfer functions of cascaded filtering with exponential increase in step width with **a** $\mathcal{B}^2$, **b** $\mathcal{B}^4$, **c** ${}^3\mathcal{R}$, **d** ${}^5\mathcal{R}$, **e** and **f** relaxation filter according to Eq. (5.55) with $\alpha = 1/2$ and $\alpha = 3/4$, respectively. Shown are the transfer functions of the original filters and of four cascaded filters (up to step size 8) with a resulting averaging width $\sqrt{85} \approx 9.22$ times larger than the original filter.*

resulting averaging width is $\sqrt{91} \approx 9.54$ times larger than that of the original filter (Fig. 7.8). To achieve this averaging width, the same filter would have to be applied 91 times.

The quality of the cascaded filtering, that is, the degree of deviation from a monotonic transfer function is determined by the basic filter. Figure 7.8 shows the transfer functions for a number of different filters in a double-logarithmic plot. Only the binomial filter $\mathcal{B}^4$ shows negligible secondary peaks well beyond 10^{-4}. The other filters in Fig. 7.8 have significantly more pronounced secondary peaks in the 10^{-4} to 10^{-2} range.

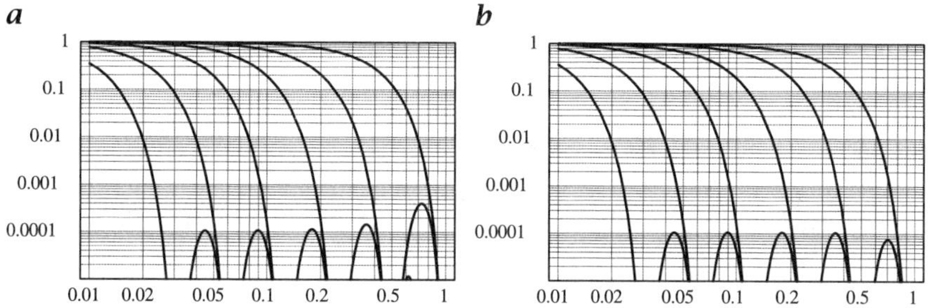

***Figure 7.10:** **a** Sequence of transfer functions of cascaded filtering with exponential increase in step width using the $\mathcal{B}^6$ binomial filter. **b** Shows the same sequence except that the first filter with step width 1 is $\mathcal{B}^8$.*

Exponentially increasing step width. A linear increase in the step width is still too slow to achieve averaging over very large scales. It is also disadvantageous that the increase in the averaging width is of the odd order $P^{3/2}$. This means that filtering does not increase the width of the averaging linearly. The increase is slightly stronger.

Both difficulties are overcome with an exponential increase in the step width. The easiest way is to increase the step width by a factor of two from filtering to filtering. The resulting mask has the standard deviation

$$\sigma_c^2 = \sigma^2 \sum_{p=1}^{P} 2^{2p-2} = \frac{2^{2P}-1}{3}\sigma^2 \qquad (7.47)$$

Thus the standard deviation grows exponentially to $\approx (2^P/\sqrt{3})\sigma$ with only P filtering steps. In other words, the number of computations increases only logarithmically with the averaging width.

As for the linear increase of the step width, the basic filter determines the quality of the resulting transfer function of the cascaded filtering. Figure 7.9 shows that only the binomial filter $\mathcal{B}^4$ results in an acceptable transfer function of the cascaded filtering. All other filters show too high secondary peaks.

Figure 7.10a shows a sequence of transfer functions for the cascading of the binomial filter $\mathcal{B}^6$. It can be observed that the filters are not of exactly the same shape but that the secondary peak is higher for the first steps and only gradually levels off to a constant value. This effect is caused by the constant term in Eq. (7.47). It can be compensated if the first filter ($p = 1$) does not have variance σ^2 but has variance $4/3\sigma^2$. Indeed, if a $\mathcal{B}^8$ filter is used instead of the $\mathcal{B}^6$ filter in the first step, the filters in the different steps of the filter cascade are much more similar (Figure 7.10b).

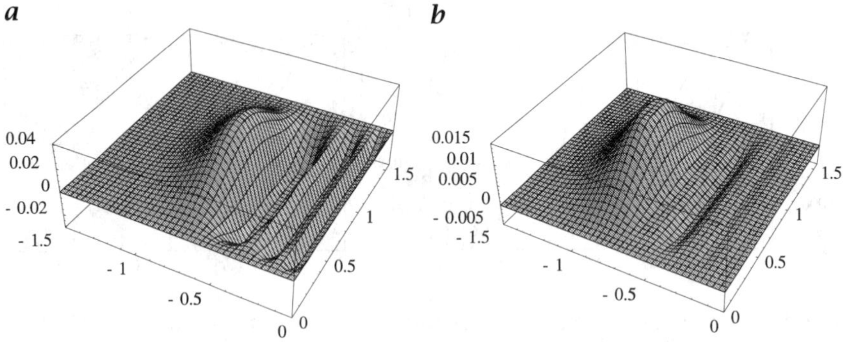

Figure 7.11: *Anisotropy of cascaded filtering with exponential increase of the step width in a log-polar plot. Shown is the deviation from the transfer function in the direction of the x axis for* ***a*** $\mathcal{B}_4^2\,\mathcal{B}_2^2\,\mathcal{B}_1^2$ *and* ***b*** $\mathcal{B}_4^4\,\mathcal{B}_2^4\,\mathcal{B}_1^4$.

For higher-dimensional signals the isotropy of the averaging is of significance. As we already know that all filters except for the binomial filters are significantly anisotropic, only binomial filters are discussed. While the $\mathcal{B}^2$ filter still shows a pronounced anisotropy of several percent (Fig. 7.11a), the anisotropy is already just slightly more than 0.01 for a $\mathcal{B}^4$ filter (Fig. 7.11b).

7.5.2 Multigrid averaging

Multistep cascaded averaging can be further enhanced by converting it into a multiresolution technique. The idea of multigrid smoothing is very simple. If a larger-step mask is involved, this operation can be applied on a correspondingly coarser grid. This means that the last operation before using the larger-step mask needs to compute the convolution only at the grid points used by the following coarser grid operator. This sampling procedure is denoted by a special syntax in the operator index. $\mathcal{O}_{\downarrow 2}$ means: Apply the operator in all directions and advance the mask two pixels in all directions. Thus, the output of the filter operator has only half as many pixels in every direction as the input.

Multigrid smoothing makes the number of computations essentially independent of the standard deviation of the smoothing mask. We again consider a sequence of 1-D averaging filters:

$$\underbrace{\mathcal{B}_{\downarrow 2}\cdots\mathcal{B}_{\downarrow 2}\mathcal{B}_{\downarrow 2}}_{P\text{ times}}$$

The standard deviation of the filter cascade is the same as for the multistep approach with exponential increase of the step width (Eq. (7.47)).

Also, as long as the sampling condition is met, that is, $\hat{B^p}(\tilde{k}) = 0$ $\forall \tilde{k} \geq 1/2$, the transfer functions of the filters are the same as for the multistep filters.

If $\mathcal{B}_{\downarrow 2}$ takes q operations, the operator sequence takes

$$q \sum_{p=1}^{P} \frac{1}{2^{p-1}} = 2q\left(1 - \frac{1}{2^{P-1}}\right) < 2q \tag{7.48}$$

Thus, smoothing to any degree takes no more than twice as many operations as smoothing at the first step.

7.6 Weighted averaging

Image data, just like any other experimental data, may be characterized by individual errors that have to be considered in any further processing. As an introduction, we first discuss the averaging of a set of N data g_n with standard deviations σ_n. From elementary statistics, it is known that appropriate averaging requires the weighting of each data point g_n with the inverse of the variance $w_n = 1/\sigma_n^2$. Then, an estimate of the mean value is given by

$$\langle g \rangle = \sum_{n=1}^{N} g_n/\sigma_n^2 \bigg/ \sum_{n=1}^{N} 1/\sigma_n^2 \tag{7.49}$$

while the standard deviation of the mean is

$$\sigma_{\langle g \rangle}^2 = 1 \bigg/ \sum_{n=1}^{N} 1/\sigma_n^2 \tag{7.50}$$

The application of *weighted averaging* to image processing is known as *normalized convolution* [3]. The averaging is now extended to a local neighborhood. Each pixel enters the convolution sum with a weighting factor associated with it. Thus, normalized convolution requires two signals. One is the image $\boldsymbol{G}$ to be processed, the other an image $\boldsymbol{W}$ with the weighting factors.

By analogy to Eqs. (7.49) and (7.50), normalized convolution with the mask $\boldsymbol{H}$ is defined as

$$\boldsymbol{G}' = \frac{\boldsymbol{H} * (\boldsymbol{W} \cdot \boldsymbol{G})}{\boldsymbol{H} * \boldsymbol{W}} \tag{7.51}$$

A normalized convolution with the mask $\boldsymbol{H}$ essentially transforms the image $\boldsymbol{G}$ and the weighting image $\boldsymbol{W}$ into a new image $\boldsymbol{G}'$ and a new weighting image $\boldsymbol{W}' = \boldsymbol{H} * \boldsymbol{W}$, which can undergo further processing.

Normalized convolution is just adequate consideration of pixels with spatially variable statistical errors. "Standard" convolution can be regarded as a special case of normalized convolution. Then all pixels are assigned the same weighting factor and it is not required to use a weighting image, because the factor remains a constant.

The flexibility of normalized convolution is given by the choice of the weighting image. The weighting image is not necessarily associated with an error. It can be used to select and/or amplify pixels with certain features. In this way, normalized convolution becomes a versatile nonlinear operator. The application of normalized convolution is discussed in a number of contributions in Volume 3 of this handbook: Sections 30.3.4, 32.4.4, 33.4.3, and 37.4.2.

7.7 References

[1] Oppenheim, A. V. and Schafer, R. W., (1989). *Discrete-time Signal Processing. Prentice-Hall Signal Processing Series.* Englewood Cliffs, NJ: Prentice-Hall.

[2] Jähne, B., (1997). *Handbook of Digital Image Processing for Scientific Applications.* Boca Raton, FL: CRC Press.

[3] Granlund, G. H. and Knutsson, H., (1995). *Signal Processing for Computer Vision.* Norwell, MA: Kluwer Academic Publishers.

8 Interpolation

Bernd Jähne

Interdisziplinäres Zentrum für Wissenschaftliches Rechnen (IWR)
Universität Heidelberg, Germany

8.1 Introduction

Interpolation of digital signals is required for a wide range of signal processing tasks whenever any operation shifts the digital points of the output signal so that they no longer coincide with the grid points of the input signal. This occurs, among others, with the following operations:

Geometric operations. For many applications, the geometrical distortions introduced by optical systems (Volume 1, Chapter 4) are not acceptable and must be corrected. For satellite images, it is often required to recompute the image data to a different projective mapping.

Signal registration. If data are taken with different sensors, these sensors will almost never be in perfect spatial alignment. Thus it is required to map them onto common spatial coordinates for further joint processing.

Handbook of Computer Vision and Applications
Volume 2
Signal Processing and Pattern Recognition

Copyright © 1999 by Academic Press
All rights of reproduction in any form reserved.
ISBN 0-12-379772-1/$30.00

Multiresolution signal processing. For multigrid data structures, such as pyramids (Section 4.4), signals are represented at different resolution levels. On such data structures it is necessary to interpolate missing points from coarser levels to be able to process them at a finer level.

Coarse-to-fine strategies. Coarse-to-fine strategies are an often used concept on multigrid data structures if the processing involves images that are shifted to each other either because of a different sensor (image registration), a different perspective (stereo images) or motion of objects (Chapter 13). In all these cases it is required to warp the images with the determined displacement vector field before processing at the next finer resolution (Chapter 14).

Test image generation. In order to evaluate algorithms, it is important to apply them to known signals. For image sequence processing, for example, it is useful to simulate displacement vector fields by warping images correspondingly.

For a long time there was little effort put into interpolation algorithms for computer vision. Thus most of the available procedures have been invented for computer graphics in the framework of *photorealistic rendering*. An excellent survey in this respect is provided by Wolberg [1]. Only with increasing demand for subpixel-accurate computer vision algorithms have the researchers became aware of the importance of accurate interpolation algorithms. The demands are quite high. As a rule of thumb, interpolation should neither change the amplitude of a signal by more than 1 % nor shift any signal by more than 0.01.

8.2 Basics

8.2.1 Interpolation as convolution

The basis of interpolation is the sampling theorem (Section 2.4.2). This theorem states that the digital signal *completely* represents the continuous signal provided the sampling conditions are met. This basic fact suggests the following general framework for interpolation:

Reconstruction of continuous signal. From the sampled signal a continuous or a higher-resolution representation is reconstructed.

Filtering. Before a resampling can be performed, it is necessary to check whether a prefiltering of the data is required. Whenever the data is to be resampled with a coarser resolution, aliasing could occur because the sampling condition is no longer met (Section 2.4.3).

Resampling. This step finally forms the new digital signal.

Of course, a certain procedure for interpolation can perform two or even all of these steps in a single operation. However, it is still helpful for a better understanding of the procedure to separate it into these steps.

Although these procedures sound simple and straightforward, they are not. The problem is related to the fact that the reconstruction of the continuous signal from the sampled signal in practice is quite involved and can be performed only approximately. Thus, we need to balance the computational effort with the residual error for a given interpolation task.

Generally, a continuous multidimensional signal is interpolated from values at all points of a lattice by (Section 2.4.4)

$$g_r(\boldsymbol{x}) = \sum_{p=1}^{P} \sum_{\boldsymbol{n}} g_s(\boldsymbol{r}_n + \boldsymbol{s}_p) h(\boldsymbol{x} - (\boldsymbol{r}_n + \boldsymbol{s}_p)) \qquad (8.1)$$

In this equation $\boldsymbol{r}_n$ are the translation vectors of the lattice and $\boldsymbol{s}_p$ the offsets of the P points in the *primitive cell* of the lattice. If a continuous signal is required but only the value at a shifted point $\boldsymbol{p}$ (Eq. (8.1)) reduces to

$$g_r(\boldsymbol{p}) = \sum_{p=1}^{P} \sum_{\boldsymbol{n}} g_s(\boldsymbol{r}_n + \boldsymbol{s}_p) h(\boldsymbol{p} - (\boldsymbol{r}_n + \boldsymbol{s}_p)) \qquad (8.2)$$

This equation reveals that interpolation is nothing else but a generalized convolution operation of the points on a discrete lattice with sampled values from the interpolation kernel. The only difference is that the result of the operation is not written back to the same lattice but to a shifted lattice. Thus an interpolation operation can be described by a transfer function. According to the discussion of the *sampling theorem* in Sections 2.4.2 and 2.4.4, the ideal interpolation function has a transfer function that is constantly one within the first Brillouin zone and zero outside.

8.2.2 Interpolation on orthogonal lattices

For the rest of this chapter, we will restrict all considerations to orthogonal lattices because interpolation of multidimensional signals is much easier to handle on these grids. On an orthogonal lattice with only one point per primitive cell ($P = 1$), the interpolation in Eq. (8.1) reduces to

$$g_r(\tilde{\boldsymbol{x}}) = \sum_{\boldsymbol{n}} g_s(\boldsymbol{n}) h(\tilde{\boldsymbol{x}} - \boldsymbol{n}) \qquad (8.3)$$

In this equation all vectors in the spatial domain are expressed in units of the lattice constants: $\tilde{x}_d = x_d / \Delta x_d$. Thus, the components of the translation vector $\boldsymbol{r}$ are integers and are replaced by $\boldsymbol{n} = [n_1, \ldots, n_D]^T$,

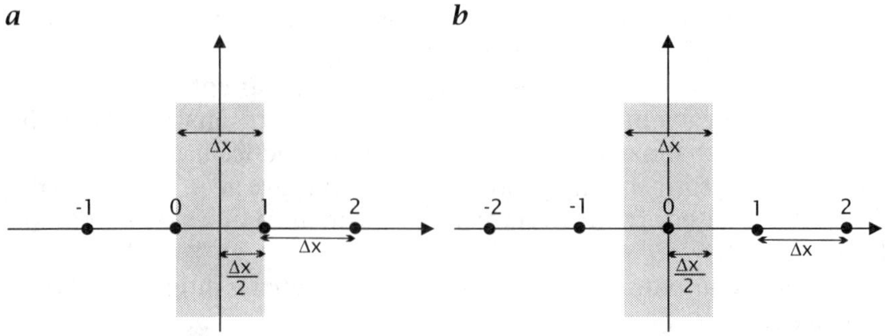

Figure 8.1: *Interpolation interval for interpolation masks with* ***a*** *an even and* ***b*** *an odd number of coefficients .*

the vectorial index that counts the translations vectors on a D-dimensional lattice.

The ideal transfer function for interpolation of a D-dimensional signal is then a D-dimensional box function

$$\hat{g}_r(\tilde{\boldsymbol{k}}) = \hat{g}(\tilde{\boldsymbol{k}}) \prod_{d=1}^{D} \Pi(2\tilde{\boldsymbol{k}}) \tag{8.4}$$

where $\tilde{\boldsymbol{k}}$ is the wave number normalized to the Nyquist limit according to Eq. (2.34). It follows that the ideal interpolation function h is the Fourier transform of the box function, the sinc function

$$h(\tilde{\boldsymbol{x}}) = \prod_{d=1}^{D} \frac{\sin(\pi \tilde{x}_d)}{\pi \tilde{x}_d} = \prod_{d=1}^{D} \operatorname{sinc}(\tilde{x}_d) \tag{8.5}$$

This ideal interpolation mask cannot be used in practice as it is infinite. Thus an optimal approximation must be found that minimizes the deviations from the ideal transfer function.

8.2.3 General properties of interpolation kernels

In this section some general properties of interpolation are summarized that are useful for the design of optimal interpolation masks.

Symmetries. An interpolation mask can have an even or odd number of coefficients. Because of symmetry reasons, the interpolation interval of these two types of interpolation masks is different. For a mask with an even number of coefficients (Fig. 8.1a), the symmetry center lies between the two central points of the interpolation mask. Because any interpolation mask has an interpolation interval of one distance between two points of the mask, the interpolation interval is limited to the interval between the two central points of the mask. For points outside of this range, the mask is shifted a corresponding number of points on the lattice, so that the point to be interpolated lies again within this central interval.

For a mask with an odd number of coefficients (Fig. 8.1b), the symmetry center coincides with the central point. Thus the interpolation interval is now half the distance between points on the lattice on both sides of the central point. The symmetry conditions for these two types of interpolation filters are analogous to type I and type II averaging filters discussed in Sections 5.3.5 and 7.3.

Interpolation condition. There are some general constraints that must be met by any interpolation filter. They result from the simple fact that the interpolated values in Eq. (8.3) at the lattice points $\boldsymbol{n}$ should reproduce the lattice points and not depend on any other lattice points. From this condition, we can infer the *interpolation condition*:

$$h(\boldsymbol{n}) = \begin{cases} 1 & \boldsymbol{n} = \boldsymbol{0} \\ 0 & \text{otherwise} \end{cases} \tag{8.6}$$

Therefore any interpolation mask must have zero crossings at all grid points except the zero point where it is one. The ideal interpolation mask in Eq. (8.5) meets this interpolation condition.

More generally, we can state that any discrete interpolation mask sampled from the continuous interpolation kernel should meet the following condition:

$$^{\tilde{x}}H_{\boldsymbol{n}} = \sum_{\boldsymbol{n}} h(\boldsymbol{n} + \tilde{\boldsymbol{x}}) = 1 \quad \Longleftrightarrow \quad ^{\tilde{x}}\hat{H}_0 = 1 \tag{8.7}$$

This generalized condition says nothing else but that a constant signal ($\tilde{\boldsymbol{k}} = \boldsymbol{0}$) is not changed by an interpolation operation.

Separability. The ideal interpolation function in Eq. (8.5) is separable. Therefore, interpolation can as easily be formulated for higher-dimensional images. We can expect that all solutions to the interpolation problem will also be separable. Consequently, we need only discuss the 1-D interpolation problem

$$g_r(\tilde{x}) = \sum_{n=-R}^{R} g_n h(\tilde{x} - n) \tag{8.8}$$

where n and R take half-integer values for interpolation masks with an even number of coefficients and integer values for interpolation masks with an odd number of coefficients; x is given here in units of the lattice

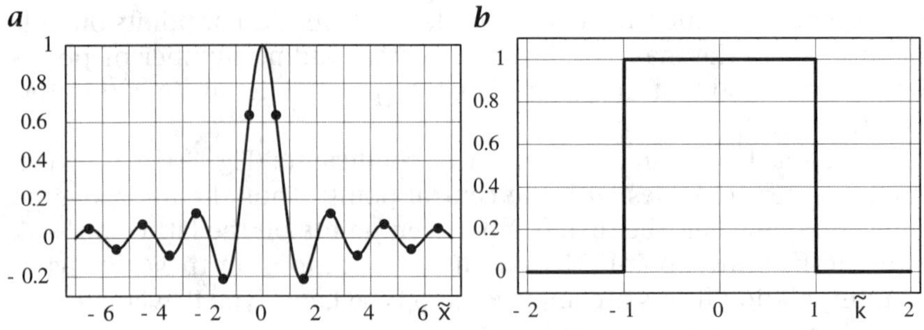

***Figure 8.2:** **a** Ideal 1-D interpolation mask and **b** its transfer function. The values for the coefficients of the discrete mask to interpolate intermediate lattice points ($\tilde{x} = 1/2$) are marked by dots.*

constant $\tilde{x} = x/\Delta x$. The 1-D ideal interpolation mask $\mathrm{sinc}(\tilde{x})$ and its transfer function $\Pi(2\tilde{k})$ are illustrated in Fig. 8.2.

Once a good interpolation mask is found for 1-D interpolation, we also have a solution for the D-dimensional interpolation problem.

An important special case is the interpolation to intermediate lattice points halfway between the existing lattice points. This scheme doubles the resolution and image size in all directions in which it is applied. The coefficients of the corresponding interpolation mask are the values of the $\mathrm{sinc}(\tilde{x})$ function sampled at all half-integer values:

$$h = \left[\frac{(-1)^{r-1} 2}{(2r-1)\pi} \quad \cdots \quad -\frac{2}{3\pi} \quad \frac{2}{\pi} \quad \frac{2}{\pi} \quad -\frac{2}{3\pi} \quad \cdots \quad \frac{(-1)^{r-1} 2}{(2r-1)\pi} \right] \tag{8.9}$$

The coefficients are of alternating sign.

Interpolation error analysis. The fact that interpolation is a convolution operation and thus can be described by a transfer function in Fourier space Eq. (8.5) gives us a tool to rate the errors associated with an interpolation technique. The box-type transfer function for the ideal interpolation function simply means that all wave numbers within the range of possible wave numbers $|k_d| \leq \Delta x_d/\pi$ experience neither a phase shift nor amplitude damping. Also, no wave number beyond the allowed interval is present in the interpolated signal, because the transfer function is zero there.

8.3 Interpolation in Fourier space

Interpolation reduces to a simple operation in the Fourier domain. The transfer function of an ideal interpolation kernel is a box function that is zero outside the wave numbers that can be represented (see

Eq. (8.5)). This basic fact suggests the following interpolation procedure in Fourier space:

1. *Enlargement of the Fourier transform of the signal.* If the discrete Fourier transform of an M^D multidimensional signal is increased to an M'^D array, the array in the spatial domain is also increased to the same size. Because of the reciprocity of the Fourier transform, the image *size* remains unchanged. Only the spacing between pixels in the spatial domain is decreased, resulting in a higher spatial resolution:

$$M\Delta k_d \to M'\Delta k_d \quad \Longleftrightarrow \quad \Delta x = \frac{2\pi}{M\Delta k} \to \Delta x' = \frac{2\pi}{M'\Delta k} \tag{8.10}$$

   The padded area in the Fourier space is filled with zeroes.

2. *Inverse Fourier transform.* All that needs to be done is the computation of an inverse Fourier transform to obtain a higher resolution signal.

The Fourier transform can also be used to shift a signal by any distance without changing the signal resolution. Then the following three-step procedure must be applied.

1. *Forward Fourier transform.*
2. *Multiplication with a phase factor.* According to the *shift theorem* (Table 3.5), a shift in the spatial domain by a distance x_s corresponds to the multiplication of the Fourier transform by the following phase factor:

$$g(\boldsymbol{x}) \to g(\boldsymbol{x} - \boldsymbol{s}) \quad \Longleftrightarrow \quad \hat{G}_{\boldsymbol{u}} \to \exp(-2\pi \mathrm{i}\boldsymbol{u}\boldsymbol{s})\hat{G}_{\boldsymbol{u}} \tag{8.11}$$

   where the vectorial shift $\boldsymbol{s}$ is given in units of the lattice constants Δx_d.

3. *Inverse Fourier transform.*

Theoretically, these simple procedures result in perfectly interpolated signals. A closer look, however, reveals that these techniques have some serious drawbacks.

First, the Fourier transform of a finite image implies a cyclic repetition of the image both in the spatial and Fourier domain. Thus, the convolution performed by the Fourier transform is also cyclic. This means that at the right or left edge of the image, convolution continues with the image at the opposite side. Because the real world is not periodic and interpolation masks are large, this may lead to significant distortions of the interpolation even at quite large distances from the edges of the image.

Second, the Fourier transform can be computed efficiently only for a specified number of values for M'. Best known are the fast radix-2

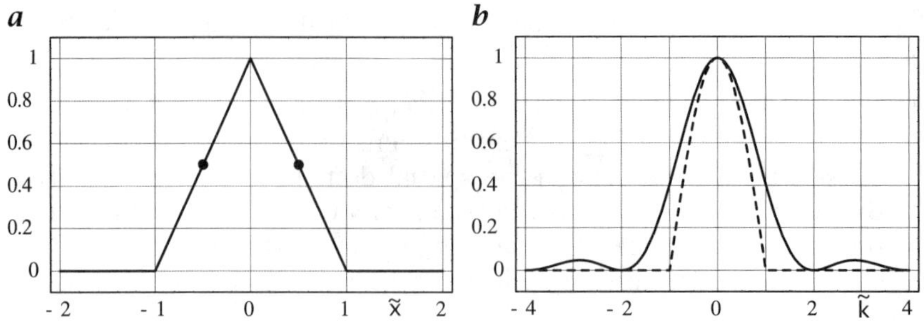

***Figure 8.3:** **a** 1-D linear interpolation: **a** continuous interpolation mask and **b** its transfer function. The values for the coefficients of the discrete mask to interpolate intermediate lattice points ($\tilde{x} = 1/2$) are marked by dots.*

algorithms that can be applied only to images of the size $M' = 2^{N'}$ (Section 3.4.1). Therefore, the Fourier transform-based interpolation is limited to scaling factors of powers of two.

Third, the Fourier transform is a global transform. Thus it can be applied only to a global scaling of the signal by an integer factor.

8.4 Polynomial interpolation

8.4.1 Linear interpolation

Linear interpolation is the classic approach to interpolation. The interpolated points lie on pieces of straight lines connecting neighboring grid points. In order to simplify the expressions in the following, we use normalized spatial coordinates $\tilde{x} = x/\Delta x$. We locate the two grid points at $-1/2$ and $1/2$. This yields the interpolation equation

$$g(\tilde{x}) = \frac{g_{1/2} + g_{-1/2}}{2} + (g_{1/2} - g_{-1/2})\,\tilde{x} \quad \text{for} \quad |\tilde{x}| \le 1/2 \tag{8.12}$$

By comparison of Eq. (8.12) with Eq. (8.8), we can conclude that the continuous interpolation mask for linear interpolation is the triangle function

$$h_1(\tilde{x}) = \Lambda(\tilde{x}) = \begin{cases} 1 - |\tilde{x}| & |\tilde{x}| \le 1 \\ 0 & \text{otherwise} \end{cases} \tag{8.13}$$

The transfer function of the interpolation mask for linear interpolation, the triangle function $h_1(x)$ Eq. (8.13), is the squared sinc function (Table 3.4)

$$\hat{h}_1(\tilde{k}) = \frac{\sin^2(\pi\tilde{k}/2)}{(\pi\tilde{k}/2)^2} = \operatorname{sinc}^2(\tilde{k}/2). \tag{8.14}$$

A comparison with the ideal transfer function for interpolation Eq. (8.4), see also Fig. 8.2b, shows that two distortions are introduced by linear interpolation:

1. While low wave numbers (and especially the mean value $\tilde{k} = 0$) are interpolated correctly, high wave numbers are reduced in amplitude, resulting in some degree of smoothing. At $\tilde{k} = 1$, the transfer function is reduced to about 40%: $\hat{h}_1(1) = (2/\pi)^2 \approx 0.4$.
2. As $\hat{h}_1(\tilde{k})$ is not zero at wave numbers $\tilde{k} > 1$, some spurious high wave numbers are introduced. If the continuously interpolated image is resampled, this yields moderate aliasing. The first sidelobe has an amplitude of $(2/3\pi)^2 \approx 0.045$.

If we interpolate only the intermediate grid points at $\tilde{x} = 0$, the continuous interpolation function Eq. (8.13) reduces to a discrete convolution mask with values at $\tilde{x} = [\ldots\ -3/2\ \ -1/2\ 1/2\ 3/2\ \ldots]$. As Eq. (8.13) is zero for $|\tilde{x}| \geq 1$, we obtain the simple interpolation mask $H = 1/2[1\ 1]$ with the transfer function

$$\hat{H}_1(\tilde{k}) = \cos \pi\tilde{k}/2 \tag{8.15}$$

The transfer function is real, so no phase shifts occur. The significant amplitude damping at higher wave numbers, however, shows that structures with high wave numbers are not correctly interpolated.

Phase shifts do occur at all other values except for the intermediate grid points at $\tilde{x} = 0$. We investigate the phase shift and amplitude attenuation of linear interpolation at arbitrary fractional integer shifts $\epsilon \in [-1/2, 1/2]$. This results in the following mask and transfer function for linear interpolation:

$$[(1/2-\epsilon)\ (1/2+\epsilon)] \quad \Longleftrightarrow \quad \hat{h}_1(\epsilon,\tilde{k}) = \cos \pi\tilde{k}/2 + 2\mathrm{i}\epsilon \sin \pi\tilde{k}/2 \tag{8.16}$$

The mask contains a symmetric part $[1/2\ 1/2]$ and an antisymmetric part $[-\epsilon\ \epsilon]$. In order to estimate the error in the phase shift, it is useful to compensate for the linear phase shift $\Delta\varphi = \epsilon\pi\tilde{k}$ caused by the displacement ϵ. Then we obtain

$$\hat{h}_1(\epsilon,\tilde{k}) = (\cos \pi\tilde{k}/2 + 2\mathrm{i}\epsilon \sin \pi\tilde{k}/2)\exp(-\mathrm{i}\epsilon\pi\tilde{k}) \tag{8.17}$$

A Taylor expansion in $\tilde{k}$ helps to reveal the amplitude response

$$\left|\hat{h}_1(\epsilon,\tilde{k})\right| = \left(\cos^2 \pi\tilde{k}/2 + 4\epsilon^2 \sin^2 \pi\tilde{k}/2\right)^{1/2} \approx 1 - \frac{1-4\epsilon^2}{8}(\pi\tilde{k})^2 \tag{8.18}$$

and phase error $\Delta\varphi$

$$\Delta\varphi \approx \frac{\epsilon(1-4\epsilon^2)}{12}(\pi\tilde{k})^3 \tag{8.19}$$

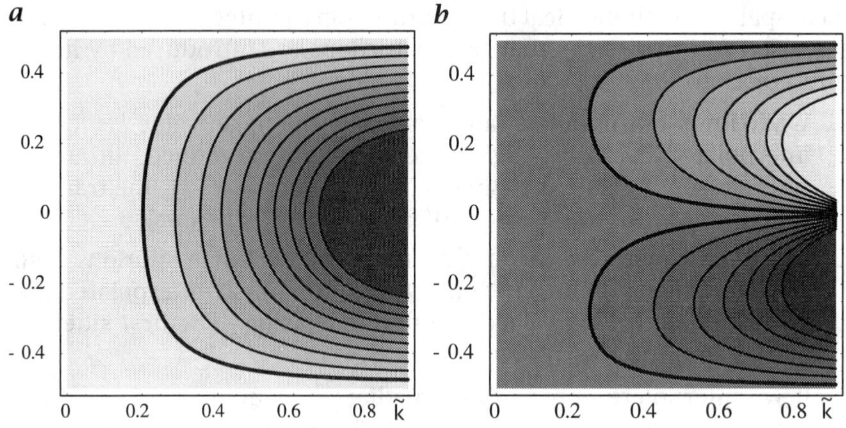

Figure 8.4: *Error maps for linear interpolation:* ***a*** *amplitude error (distance of contour lines 0.05); and* ***b*** *phase error expressed as a position shift $\Delta x = \Delta\varphi\lambda/(2\pi)$ (distance of contour lines 0.02; thick contour lines border the range around zero).*

of the transfer function.

Figure 8.4 shows error maps of the amplitude and phase error of linear interpolation. The amplitude error is significant. While structures with $\tilde{k} = 0.2$ are attenuated by 5%, structures with half the Nyquist limit ($\tilde{k} = 0.5$) are already attenuated by 30%. Moreover, the phase error is significant (Fig. 8.4b). The transfer function is real only for $\epsilon = 0$ and $\epsilon = 1/2$. But at all other fractional shifts, a nonzero phase shift remains. In Fig. 8.4b the phase shift $\Delta\varphi$ is expressed as the position shift Δx of the corresponding periodic structure, that is, $\Delta x = \Delta\varphi\lambda/(2\pi) = \Delta\varphi/(\pi\tilde{k})$. For wave numbers of $\tilde{k} = 0.5$, the maximum displacement is about 0.05. This is a significant relative error of 20% given the fact that the displacement ϵ is only 0.25 for the maximum phase error.

8.4.2 Higher-order polynomial interpolation

Given the significant limitations of linear interpolation as discussed in Section 8.4.1, we ask whether higher-order interpolation schemes perform better. The basic principle of linear interpolation was that a straight line was drawn to pass through two neighboring points. In the same way, we can use a polynomial of degree P with $P+1$ unknown coefficients a_p to pass through $P+1$ points:

$$g_r(\tilde{x}) = \sum_{p=0}^{P} a_p \tilde{x}^p \qquad (8.20)$$

For symmetry reasons, the lattice points are placed at the positions

$$\tilde{k}_p = \frac{2p - P}{2} \tag{8.21}$$

For an even number of points (P is odd), the lattice points are located at half-integer values.

From the interpolation condition at the grid points $g_r(\tilde{k}_p) = g_p$, we obtain a linear equation system with $P+1$ equations and $P+1$ unknowns a_P of the following form when P is odd:

$$\begin{bmatrix} g_0 \\ \vdots \\ g_{(P-1)/2} \\ g_{(P+1)/2} \\ \vdots \\ g_P \end{bmatrix} = \begin{bmatrix} 1 & -P/2 & P^2/4 & -P^3/8 & \cdots \\ \vdots & & & & \\ 1 & -1/2 & 1/4 & -1/8 & \cdots \\ 1 & 1/2 & 1/4 & 1/8 & \cdots \\ \vdots & & & & \\ 1 & P/2 & P^2/4 & P^3/8 & \cdots \end{bmatrix} \begin{bmatrix} a_0 \\ \vdots \\ a_{(P-1)/2} \\ a_{(P+1)/2} \\ \vdots \\ a_P \end{bmatrix} \tag{8.22}$$

or written as a matrix equation:

$$\boldsymbol{g} = \boldsymbol{Ma} \quad \text{with} \quad M_{pq} = \left(\frac{2q - P}{2}\right)^p, \; p, q \in [0, P] \tag{8.23}$$

For a cubic polynomial ($P = 3$), the solution of the equations system is

$$\begin{bmatrix} a_0 \\ a_1 \\ a_2 \\ a_3 \end{bmatrix} = \frac{1}{48} \begin{bmatrix} -3 & 27 & 27 & -3 \\ 2 & -54 & 54 & -2 \\ 12 & -12 & -12 & 12 \\ -8 & 24 & -24 & 8 \end{bmatrix} \begin{bmatrix} g_0 \\ g_1 \\ g_2 \\ g_3 \end{bmatrix} \tag{8.24}$$

Using Eqs. (8.20) and (8.24) we can express the interpolated values for the position ϵ in the interval $[-1/2, 1/2]$ as

$$\begin{aligned} g(\epsilon) &= \frac{9 - 4\epsilon^2}{16}(g_1 + g_2) - \frac{1 - 4\epsilon^2}{16}(g_0 + g_3) \\ &+ \frac{\epsilon(9 - 4\epsilon^2)}{8}(g_2 - g_1) - \frac{\epsilon(1 - 4\epsilon^2)}{24}(g_3 - g_0) \end{aligned} \tag{8.25}$$

Thus the interpolation mask is

$$\left[\frac{-\alpha}{16} + \frac{\epsilon\alpha}{24}, \frac{8 + \alpha}{16} + \frac{\epsilon(8 + \alpha)}{8}, \frac{8 + \alpha}{16} - \frac{\epsilon(8 + \alpha)}{8}, \frac{-\alpha}{16} - \frac{\epsilon\alpha}{24}\right] \tag{8.26}$$

with $\alpha = 1 - 4\epsilon^2$. For $\epsilon = 0$ ($\alpha = 1$), the mask reduces to

$$\frac{1}{16}[-1 \; 9 \; 9 \; -1] \tag{8.27}$$

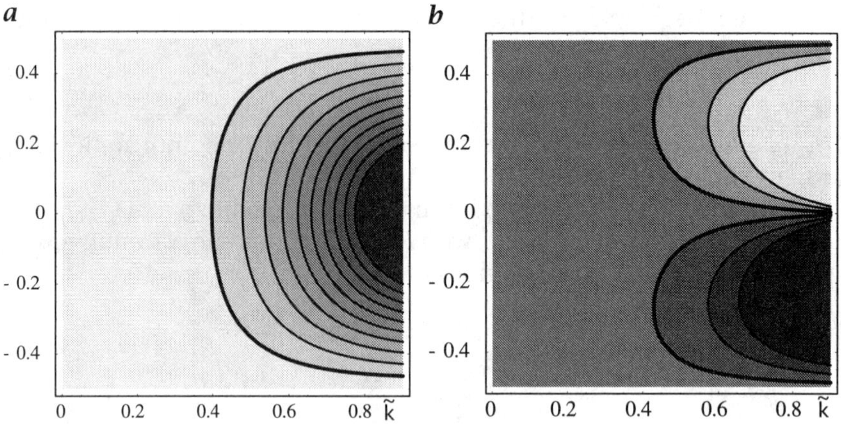

Figure 8.5: *Error maps for cubic interpolation:* ***a*** *amplitude error (distance of contour lines 0.05); and* ***b*** *phase error expressed as a position shift* $\Delta x = \Delta\varphi\lambda/(2\pi)$ *(distance of contour lines 0.02; thick contour lines border the range around zero), compare Fig. 8.4.*

From Eq. (8.26), we can also infer the transfer function and obtain

$$\begin{aligned}\hat{h}_3(\tilde{k}) &= \frac{8+\alpha}{8}\cos(\pi\tilde{k}/2) + \mathrm{i}\frac{\epsilon(8+\alpha)}{4}\sin(\pi\tilde{k}/2)\\ &- \frac{\alpha}{8}\cos(\pi 3\tilde{k}/2) - \mathrm{i}\frac{\epsilon\alpha}{12}\sin(\pi 3\tilde{k}/2)\end{aligned} \tag{8.28}$$

which reduces for small wave numbers to

$$\hat{h}_3(\tilde{k}) \approx 1 - \frac{9-40\epsilon^2+16\epsilon^4}{384}(\pi\tilde{k})^4 + \mathrm{i}\frac{9-40\epsilon^2+16\epsilon^4}{480}(\pi\tilde{k})^5 \tag{8.29}$$

Thus the amplitude attenuation goes only with $\tilde{k}^4$ and the error in the phase shift only with $\tilde{k}^5$ (compare Eqs. (8.18) and (8.19) for linear interpolation).

Figure 8.5 shows that the errors in amplitude and phase shift are significantly lower than for linear interpolation. However, for wave numbers higher than 0.5, the errors are still too high for many applications.

It is not very helpful to go to higher-order polynomial interpolation. With increasing degree P of the interpolating polynomial, the transfer function approaches the ideal transfer function better but convergence is too slow (Fig. 8.6). Less than 1% amplitude error is given only for a polynomial of degree 7 for $\tilde{k} < 0.45$. Thus the extra effort of higher-order polynomial interpolation does not pay off.

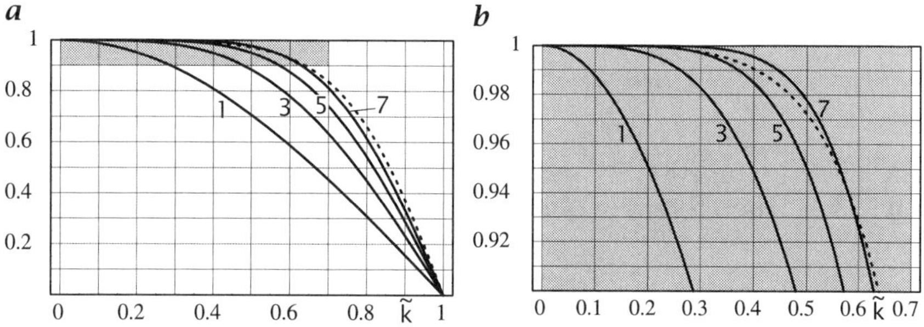

Figure 8.6: *Transfer function of polynomial interpolation filters to interpolate the value between two grid points (ϵ = 0). The degree of the polynomial (1 = linear, 3 = cubic, etc.) is marked in the graph. The dashed line marks the transfer function for cubic B-spline interpolation (Section 8.5):* ***a*** *Full range;* ***b*** *sector as marked in* ***a****.*

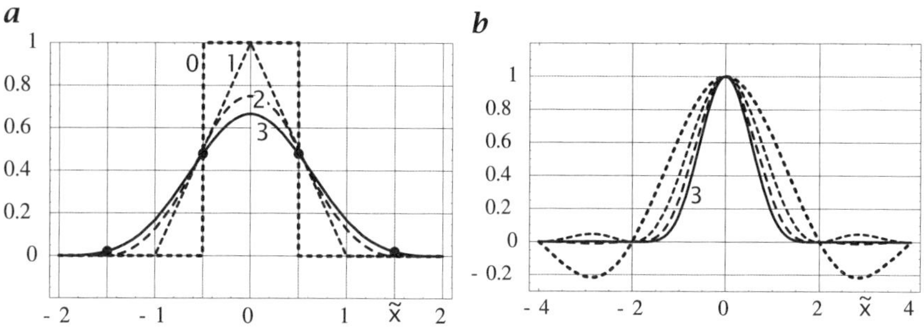

Figure 8.7: ***a*** *B-spline interpolation kernels of order 0 (nearest neighbor), 1 (linear interpolation), 2 (quadratic B-spline), and 3 (cubic B-spline);* ***b*** *corresponding transfer functions.*

8.5 Spline-based interpolation

Besides the still limited accuracy, polynomial interpolation has another significant disadvantage. The interpolated curve is not continuous at the grid points already in its first derivative. This is due to the fact that for each interval between grid points another polynomial is taken. Thus, only the interpolated function is continuous at the grid points but not the derivatives.

Splines avoid this disadvantage by additional constraints for the continuity of derivatives at the grid points. From the many classes of splines, we will here discuss only one class, *B-splines*, and introduce *cubic B-spline interpolation*. From the background of signal processing, the easiest access to B-splines is their convolution property. The kernel of a P-order B-spline curve is generated by convolving the box function

P times with itself (Fig. 8.7a):

$$\beta_P(\tilde{x}) = \underbrace{\Pi(\tilde{x}) * \ldots * \Pi(\tilde{x})}_{(P+1)\ \text{times}} \tag{8.30}$$

The transfer function of the box function is the sinc function (see Table 3.4). Therefore, the transfer function of the P-order B-spline is

$$\hat{\beta}_P(\hat{k}) = \left(\frac{\sin \pi\tilde{k}/2}{(\pi\tilde{k}/2)}\right)^{P+1} \tag{8.31}$$

Figure 8.7b shows that the B-spline function does not make a suitable interpolation function. The transfer function decreases too early, indicating that B-spline interpolation performs too much averaging. Moreover, the B-spline kernel does not meet the interpolation condition Eq. (8.6) for $P > 1$. Thus, B-splines can be used only for interpolation if the discrete grid points are first transformed in such a way that a following convolution with the B-spline kernel restores the original values at the grid points.

This transformation, known as the B-spline transformation, is constructed from the following condition:

$$g_p(x) = \sum_n c_n \beta_P(x - x_n) \quad \text{with} \quad g_p(x_n) = g(x_n) \tag{8.32}$$

If centered around a grid point, the cubic B-spline interpolation kernel is unequal to zero for only three grid points. The coefficients $\beta_3(-1) = \beta_{-1}, \beta_3(0) = \beta_0$, and $\beta_3(1) = \beta_1$ are 1/6, 2/3, and 1/6. The convolution of this kernel with the unknown B-spline transform values c_n should result in the original values g_n at the grid points. Therefore,

$$\boldsymbol{g} = \boldsymbol{c} * \boldsymbol{\beta}_3 \quad \text{or} \quad g_n = \sum_{n'=-1}^{1} c_{n+n'} \beta_{n'} \tag{8.33}$$

Equation (8.32) constitutes the sparse linear equation system

$$\begin{bmatrix} g_0 \\ g_1 \\ \vdots \\ g_{N-1} \end{bmatrix} = \frac{1}{6} \begin{bmatrix} 4 & 1 & 0 & \ddots & 0 & 1 \\ 1 & 4 & 1 & 0 & \ddots & 0 \\ 0 & 1 & 4 & 1 & 0 & \ddots \\ \ddots & & & & \ddots & \ddots \\ \ddots & \ddots & 1 & 4 & 1 & 0 \\ 0 & \ddots & 0 & 1 & 4 & 1 \\ 1 & 0 & \ddots & 0 & 1 & 4 \end{bmatrix} \begin{bmatrix} c_0 \\ c_1 \\ \vdots \\ c_{N-1} \end{bmatrix} \tag{8.34}$$

using cyclic boundary conditions. The determination of the B-spline transformation thus requires the solution of a linear equation system with N unknowns. The special form of the equation system as a convolution operation, however, allows for a more efficient solution. In Fourier space, Eq. (8.33) reduces to

$$\hat{\boldsymbol{g}} = \hat{\boldsymbol{\beta}}_3 \hat{\boldsymbol{c}} \tag{8.35}$$

The transfer function of $\boldsymbol{\beta}_3$ is $\hat{\beta}_3(\tilde{k}) = 2/3 + 1/3\cos(\pi\tilde{k})$. As this function has no zeroes, we can compute $\boldsymbol{c}$ by inverse filtering, that is, convoluting $\boldsymbol{g}$ with a mask that has the transfer function

$$\hat{\beta}_3^{-1}(\tilde{k}) = \hat{\beta}_T(\tilde{k}) = \frac{1}{2/3 + 1/3\cos(\pi\tilde{k})} \tag{8.36}$$

This is the transfer function of a recursive relaxation filter (Section 5.4.6) that is applied first in the forward and then in the backward direction with the following recursion [2]:

$$\begin{aligned} g'_n &= g_n - (2-\sqrt{3})(g'_{n-1} - g_n) \\ c'_n &= g'_n - (2-\sqrt{3})(c_{n+1} - g'_n) \end{aligned} \tag{8.37}$$

The entire operation takes only two multiplications and four additions.

The B-spline interpolation is applied after the B-spline transformation. In the continuous cubic case this yields the effective transfer function using Eqs. (8.31) and (8.36),

$$\hat{\beta}_I(\tilde{k}) = \frac{\sin^4(\pi\tilde{k}/2)/(\pi\tilde{k}/2)^4}{(2/3 + 1/3\cos(\pi\tilde{k}))} \tag{8.38}$$

Essentially, the B-spline transformation performs an amplification of high wave numbers (at $\tilde{k} = 1$ by a factor 3), which compensates the smoothing of the B-spline interpolation to a large extent.

We investigate this compensation at both the grid points and the intermediate points. From the equation of the cubic B-spline interpolating kernel (Eq. (8.30); see also Fig. 8.7a) the interpolation coefficients for the grid points and intermediate grid points are

$$1/6\,[1\;4\;1] \quad \text{and} \quad 1/48\,[1\;23\;23\;1] \tag{8.39}$$

respectively. Therefore, the transfer functions are

$$2/3 + 1/3\cos(\pi\tilde{k}) \quad \text{and} \quad 23/24\cos(\pi\tilde{k}/2) + 1/24\cos(3\pi\tilde{k}/2) \tag{8.40}$$

respectively. At the grid points, the transfer functions compensate exactly—as expected—the application of the B-spline transformation Eq. (8.36). Thus, the interpolation curve goes through the values at the

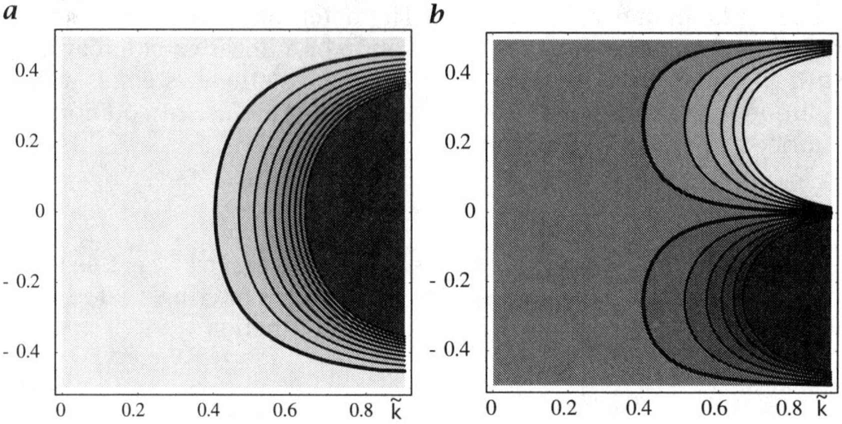

Figure 8.8: *Error maps for cubic B-spline interpolation:* ***a*** *amplitude error (distance of contour lines 0.01, five times more sensitive than in Figs. 8.4 and 8.5); and* ***b*** *phase error expressed as a position shift $\Delta x = \Delta\varphi\lambda/(2\pi)$ (distance of contour lines 0.005, four times more sensitive than in Figs. 8.4 and 8.5; thick contour lines border the range around zero).*

grid points. At the intermediate points the effective transfer function for the cubic B-spline interpolation is then

$$\hat{\beta}_I(1/2, \tilde{k}) = \frac{23/24\cos(\pi\tilde{k}/2) + 1/24\cos(3\pi\tilde{k}/2)}{2/3 + 1/3\cos\pi\tilde{k}} \tag{8.41}$$

The amplitude attenuation and the phase shifts expressed as a position shift in pixel distances are shown in Fig. 8.8. The shift and amplitude damping is zero at the grid points -1/2 and 1/2. While the amplitude damping is maximal for the intermediate point, the position shift is also zero at the intermediate point due to symmetry reasons. The interpolation errors are still too high for algorithms that ought to be accurate in the 1/100 pixel range. If no better interpolation technique can be applied, this means that the maximum wave number should be lower than 0.5. Then, the maximum shift is lower than 0.01 and the amplitude damping is less than 3 %.

8.6 Optimized interpolation

Filter design for interpolation—like any filter design problem—can be treated in a mathematically more rigorous way as an optimization problem, as discussed in Section 6.5. The general idea is to vary the filter coefficients in such a way that the derivation from a *target function* reaches a minimum. For a general discussion of this technique, we refer to Section 6.5.

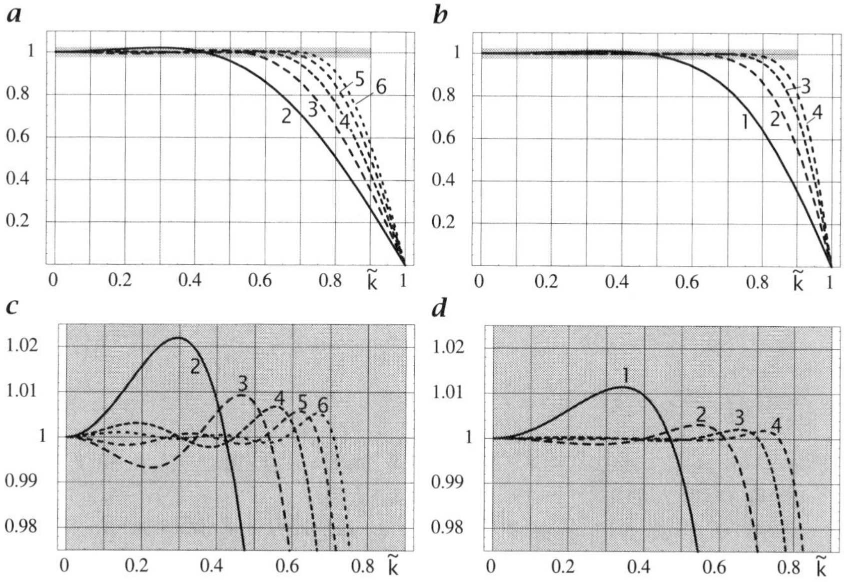

Figure 8.9: *Transfer function of interpolation kernels optimized with the weighted least squares technique of* ***a*** *Eq. (8.42) with R = 2 to 6 and* ***b*** *Eq. (8.43) with R = 1 to 4 (solid line).* ***c*** *and* ***d*** *show a narrow sector of the plots in* ***a*** *and* ***b*** *for a better estimation of small deviations from ideal values.*

The target function for an interpolation filter is the box function Eq. (8.4) as depicted in Fig. 8.2b. The ansatz functions for an interpolation filter include the following constraints. First, the transfer function is real. Thus only cos terms must be considered. Secondly, the mean value should be preserved by the interpolation function. This implies the condition $\hat{h}(0) = 1$. With these two conditions, the *ansatz function* for a nonrecursive filter technique is

$$\hat{h}(\tilde{k}) = \cos\left(\frac{1}{2}\pi\tilde{k}\right) + \sum_{r=2}^{R} h_r \left[\cos\left(\frac{2r-3}{2}\pi\tilde{k}\right) - \cos\left(\frac{1}{2}\pi\tilde{k}\right)\right] \quad (8.42)$$

The filters (Fig. 8.9a, c) are significantly better than those obtained by polynomial and cubic B-spline interpolation (Fig. 8.6). Even better interpolation masks can be obtained by using a combination of nonrecursive and recursive filters, as with the cubic B-spline interpolation (compare also Example 6.2 in Section 6.5.1):

$$\hat{h}(\tilde{k}) = \frac{\cos\left(1/2\,\pi\tilde{k}\right) + \sum_{r=2}^{R} h_r \left[\cos\left((2r-3)/2\,\pi\tilde{k}\right) - \cos\left(1/2\,\pi\tilde{k}\right)\right]}{1 - \alpha + \alpha\cos\left(\pi\tilde{k}\right)} \tag{8.43}$$

Figure 8.9b, d shows the transfer functions for $R = 1$ to 4. A more detailed discussion of interpolation filters including tables with optimized filters can be found in Jähne [3].

8.7 References

[1] Wolberg, G., (1990). *Digital Image Warping.* Los Alamitos, CA: IEEE Computer Society Press.

[2] Unser, M., Aldroubi, A., and Eden, M., (1991). Fast B-spline transforms for continuous image representation and interpolation. *IEEE Trans. PAMI,* **13**: 277–285.

[3] Jähne, B., (1997). *Handbook of Digital Image Processing for Scientific Applications.* Boca Raton, FL: CRC Press.

9 Image Warping

Bernd Jähne

Interdisziplinäres Zentrum für Wissenschaftliches Rechnen (IWR)
Universität Heidelberg, Germany

9.1 Introduction

Generally, the need for image warping arises from the fact that we want to relate the pixel coordinates to the world coordinates, to measure the position, size, distance, and other geometric parameters of the imaged objects, and to compare objects in different images. A perfect imaging system performs a *perspective transform* of the world coordinates to the pixel coordinates. Often it is possible to approximate the perspective transform by the simpler *affine transform*. Scaling and rotation of images are required if objects of different size and orientation are to be prepared for pixelwise comparison.

For precise geometric measurements, it is required to correct for the residual geometric distortion introduced by even well-corrected optical systems. Modern imaging solid-state sensors are geometrically very precise and stable. Therefore, a position accuracy of better than 1/100

Handbook of Computer Vision and Applications
Volume 2
Signal Processing and Pattern Recognition

Copyright © 1999 by Academic Press
All rights of reproduction in any form reserved.
ISBN 0-12-379772-1/$30.00

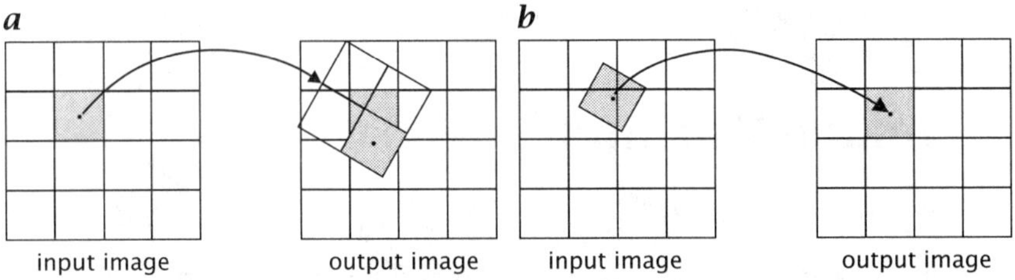

Figure 9.1: *Illustration of:* ***a*** *forward mapping; and* ***b*** *inverse mapping for spatial transformation of images. With forward mapping, the value at an output pixel must be accumulated from all input pixels that overlap it. With inverse mapping, the value of the output pixel must be interpolated from a neighborhood in the input image.*

pixel distance is feasible. To maintain this accuracy, all geometric transformations applied to digital images must preserve this high position accuracy. This demand goes far beyond the fact that no distortions are visible in the transformed images as it is required for computer graphics applications.

Image warping is a widely neglected subject in computer vision. Thus it is not surprising that many of the available techniques have been developed within the frame of computer graphics applications, especially for the mapping of textures onto objects. Image warping is treated in detail in a monograph by Wolberg [1] and also studied in Gomes and Velho [2]. This chapter covers the basics of geometric transforms (Section 9.3) and discusses fast algorithms for scaling, rotation and affine transforms of images (Section 9.4). All of these algorithms can be used with various techniques of subpixel accurate interpolation. This subject is treated in Chapter 8.

9.2 Forward and inverse mapping

A geometric transform defines the relationship between the points in two images. This relation can be expressed in two ways. Either the coordinates of the output image $\boldsymbol{x}'$ can be specified as a function of the coordinates of the input image $\boldsymbol{x}$ or vice versa:

$$\begin{aligned} \boldsymbol{x}' &= M(\boldsymbol{x}) && \text{forward mapping} \\ \boldsymbol{x} &= M^{-1}(\boldsymbol{x}'), && \text{inverse mapping} \end{aligned} \tag{9.1}$$

where M specifies the mapping function and M^{-1} its inverse. The two expressions in Eq. (9.1) give rise to two principal ways of spatial transformations: *forward mapping* and *inverse mapping*.

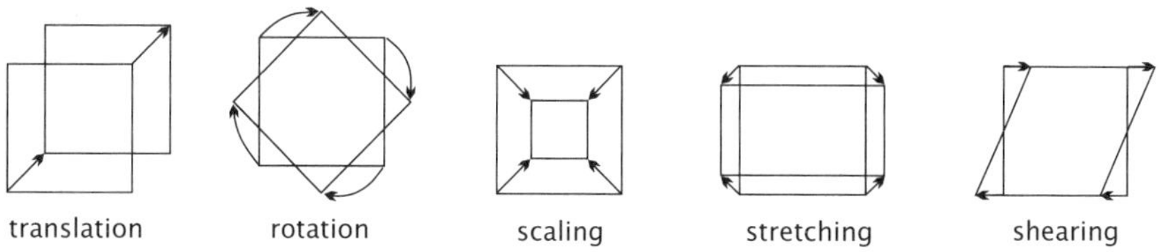

Figure 9.2: *Elementary geometric transforms for a planar surface element: translation; rotation; scaling; stretching; and shearing.*

With *forward mapping*, a pixel of the input image is mapped onto the output image (Fig. 9.1a). Generally, the pixel of the input image lies in between the pixels of the output image. With forward mapping, it is not appropriate to write the value of the input pixel just to the nearest pixel in the output image (point-to-point mapping). Then, it may happen that a value is never written to some of the pixels of the output image (holes) while others receive a value more than once (overlap). Thus, an appropriate technique must be found to distribute the value of the input pixel to several output pixels. The easiest procedure is to regard pixels as squares and to take the fraction of the area of the input pixel that covers the output pixel as the weighting factor. Each output pixel accumulates the corresponding fractions of the input pixels, which—if the mapping is continuous—add up to cover the whole output pixel.

With *inverse mapping*, the output pixels are mapped back onto the input image (Fig. 9.1b). It is obvious that this scheme avoids any holes and overlaps in the output image because all pixels are scanned sequentially. The interpolation problem occurs now in the input image. The coordinate of the output image does in general not hit a pixel in the input image but lies in between the pixels. Thus, its correct value must be interpolated from the surrounding pixels in the input image.

9.3 Basic geometric transforms

9.3.1 Affine transform

An *affine transform* is a linear coordinate transformation that includes the elementary transformations translation, rotation, scaling, stretching, and shearing (Fig. 9.2) and can be expressed by vector addition and matrix multiplication

$$\begin{bmatrix} x' \\ y' \end{bmatrix} = \begin{bmatrix} a_{11} & a_{12} \\ a_{21} & a_{22} \end{bmatrix} \begin{bmatrix} x \\ y \end{bmatrix} + \begin{bmatrix} t_x \\ t_y \end{bmatrix} \qquad (9.2)$$

With homogeneous coordinates [3, 4], the affine transform is written with a single matrix multiplication as

$$\begin{bmatrix} x' \\ y' \\ 1 \end{bmatrix} = \begin{bmatrix} a_{11} & a_{12} & t_x \\ a_{21} & a_{22} & t_y \\ 0 & 0 & 1 \end{bmatrix} \begin{bmatrix} x \\ y \\ 1 \end{bmatrix} \tag{9.3}$$

An affine transform has six degrees of freedom: two for translation (t_x, t_y) and one each for rotation, scaling, stretching, and shearing (a_{11}, a_{12}, a_{21}, and a_{22}). The affine transform maps a triangle into a triangle and a rectangle into a parallelogram. Therefore, it is also referred to as *three-point mapping*. Thus, it is obvious that the use of the affine transform is restricted. More general distortions such as the mapping of a rectangle into an arbitrary quadrilateral are not affine transforms.

9.3.2 Perspective transform

Perspective projection is the basis of geometric optical imaging as discussed in Volume 1, Chapter 4. The affine transform corresponds to parallel projection and can only be used as a model for optical imaging in the limit of a small field of view. The general *perspective transform* is most conveniently written with homogeneous coordinates as

$$\begin{bmatrix} w'x' \\ w'y' \\ w' \end{bmatrix} = \begin{bmatrix} a_{11} & a_{12} & a_{13} \\ a_{21} & a_{22} & a_{23} \\ a_{31} & a_{32} & 1 \end{bmatrix} \begin{bmatrix} wx \\ wy \\ w \end{bmatrix} \quad \text{or} \quad X' = PX \tag{9.4}$$

The two additional coefficients a_{31} and a_{32} in comparison to the affine transform Eq. (9.3) describe the perspective projection.

Written in standard coordinates, the perspective transform according to Eq. (9.4) reads as

$$\begin{aligned} x' &= \frac{a_{11}x + a_{12}y + a_{13}}{a_{31}x + a_{32}y + 1} \\ y' &= \frac{a_{21}x + a_{22}y + a_{23}}{a_{31}x + a_{32}y + 1} \end{aligned} \tag{9.5}$$

In contrast to the affine transform, the perspective transform is nonlinear. However, it is reduced to a linear transform by using homogeneous coordinates. A perspective transform maps lines into lines but only lines parallel to the projection plane remain parallel. A rectangle is mapped into an arbitrary quadrilateral. Therefore, the perspective transform is also referred to as *four-point mapping*.

9.3.3 Transforms defined by point correspondences

Generally, the coefficients of a transform, as described in the previous section, are not known. Instead we have a set of corresponding points between the object and image space and need to infer the coefficients of a transform from this set. Thus *point correspondences* give a general way to define a geometrical transform that need not necessarily be an affine or perspective transform. Once point correspondences are established, we have a list of corresponding points and need a suitable interpolation scheme to define the correspondences between all points in the two images by either a forward or backward mapping.

The simplest way to do this is to generate a mesh of triangles from the points and to perform a piecewise-affine transform triangle by triangle. This approach is a kind of generalization of linear interpolation (Section 8.4.1). In this section we thus discuss how the parameters for affine and perspective transforms can be computed from point correspondences.

For an affine transform, we need three noncollinear points (to map a triangle into a triangle). With these three points, Eq. (9.3) results in the following linear equation system:

$$\begin{bmatrix} x_1' & x_2' & x_3' \\ y_1' & y_2' & y_3' \\ 1 & 1 & 1 \end{bmatrix} = \begin{bmatrix} a_{11} & a_{12} & t_x \\ a_{21} & a_{22} & t_y \\ 0 & 0 & 1 \end{bmatrix} \begin{bmatrix} x_1 & x_2 & x_3 \\ y_1 & y_2 & y_3 \\ 1 & 1 & 1 \end{bmatrix} \tag{9.6}$$

or

$$\boldsymbol{P}' = \boldsymbol{A}\boldsymbol{P} \tag{9.7}$$

from which $\boldsymbol{A}$ can be computed as

$$\boldsymbol{A} = \boldsymbol{P}'\boldsymbol{P}^{-1} \tag{9.8}$$

The inverse of the matrix $\boldsymbol{P}$ exists when the three points $\boldsymbol{x}_1$, $\boldsymbol{x}_2$, $\boldsymbol{x}_3$ are linearly independent. This means geometrically that they must not lie on one line.

With more than three corresponding points, the parameters of the affine transform can be solved by the following equation system in a least squares sense:

$$\begin{aligned} \boldsymbol{A} &= \boldsymbol{P}'\boldsymbol{P}^T(\boldsymbol{P}\boldsymbol{P}^T)^{-1} \quad \text{with} \\ \boldsymbol{P}'\boldsymbol{P}^T &= \begin{bmatrix} \sum x_n' x_n & \sum x_n' y_n & \sum x_n' \\ \sum y_n' x_n & \sum y_n' y_n & \sum y_n' \\ \sum x_n & \sum y_n & N \end{bmatrix} \\ \boldsymbol{P}\boldsymbol{P}^T &= \begin{bmatrix} \sum x_n^2 & \sum x_n y_n & \sum x_n \\ \sum x_n y_n & \sum y_n^2 & \sum y_n \\ \sum x_n & \sum y_n & N \end{bmatrix} \end{aligned} \tag{9.9}$$

The inverse of an affine transform is itself affine. The transformation matrix of the inverse transform is given by the inverse A^{-1}.

The determination of the coefficients for the perspective projection is slightly more complex. Given four or more corresponding points, the coefficients of the perspective transform can be determined. To that end, we rewrite Eq. (9.5) as

$$\begin{aligned} x' &= a_{11}x + a_{12}y + a_{13} - a_{31}xx' - a_{32}yx' \\ y' &= a_{21}x + a_{22}y + a_{23} - a_{31}xy' - a_{32}yy' \end{aligned} \tag{9.10}$$

For N points, this leads to a linear equation system with $2N$ equations and 8 unknowns of the form

$$\begin{bmatrix} x'_1 \\ y'_1 \\ x'_2 \\ y'_2 \\ \vdots \\ x'_N \\ y'_N \end{bmatrix} = \begin{bmatrix} x_1 & y_1 & 1 & 0 & 0 & 0 & -x_1x'_1 & -y_1x'_1 \\ 0 & 0 & 0 & x_1 & y_1 & 1 & -x_1y'_1 & -y_1y'_1 \\ x_2 & y_2 & 1 & 0 & 0 & 0 & -x_2x'_2 & -y_2x'_2 \\ 0 & 0 & 0 & x_2 & y_2 & 1 & -x_2y'_2 & -y_2y'_2 \\ & & & & \vdots & & & \\ x_N & x_N & 1 & 0 & 0 & 0 & -x_Nx'_N & -y_Nx'_N \\ 0 & 0 & 0 & x_N & y_N & 1 & -x_Ny'_N & -y_Ny'_N \end{bmatrix} \begin{bmatrix} a_{11} \\ a_{12} \\ a_{13} \\ a_{21} \\ a_{22} \\ a_{23} \\ a_{31} \\ a_{32} \end{bmatrix}$$

or

$$\boldsymbol{d} = \boldsymbol{M}\boldsymbol{a}. \tag{9.11}$$

This can be solved as a least squares problem by

$$\boldsymbol{a} = (\boldsymbol{M}^T\boldsymbol{M})^{-1}\boldsymbol{M}^T\boldsymbol{d} \tag{9.12}$$

9.3.4 Transforms defined by displacement vector fields

Classical tasks in computer vision such as motion analysis (Chapter 13), stereo analysis (Chapter 18), and image registration give rise to the definition of geometric transforms by a *displacement vector field* (DVF) $\boldsymbol{s}$. With this approach for each pixel a displacement vector is given that establishes the spatial correspondence between two images.

Basically, there are three ways to define a displacement vector field. In the asymmetric formulation, the DVF is directly associated with the first of the two images and gives the displacement of the corresponding structure in the second image. Thus the location $\boldsymbol{x}'$ in the second image can be computed by

$$\boldsymbol{x}' = \boldsymbol{x} + \boldsymbol{s}(\boldsymbol{x}) \tag{9.13}$$

This definition allows for a forward mapping of the first image to the second or for a backward mapping of the second image to the first (compare Section 9.2). It is not possible, however, to perform a forward mapping of the second image to the first or a backward mapping of the first to the second image. Such an operation would require a DVF at all locations in the second image of the form

$$\boldsymbol{x} = \boldsymbol{x}' - \boldsymbol{s}(\boldsymbol{x}') \tag{9.14}$$

that is different from Eq. (9.13) as soon as the DVF is sufficiently inhomogeneous.

Finally, a symmetric definition of the DVF is possible. In this case the DVF is given for a virtual reference image halfway between the two images. The corresponding positions in the two images are then given by the following pair of equations:

$$\boldsymbol{x} = \boldsymbol{x}_r + \boldsymbol{s}(\boldsymbol{x}_r)/2 \quad \text{and} \quad \boldsymbol{x}' = \boldsymbol{x}_r - \boldsymbol{s}(\boldsymbol{x}_r)/2 \tag{9.15}$$

This formulation allows for backward mappings of the two images to the reference image. It is important to be aware of this difference in the definition of DVFs. If a DVF is not used according to its definition subtle errors occur where it is inhomogeneous and it is hard to distinguish these errors from those by imperfections in the algorithms that compute stereo or motion displacements.

The DVF approach to image warping makes it also easy to quantify the quality of the displacement vectors (DV). By adding a suitable weighting factor, the certainty of the DVs can be specified. The weight can become negative for areas where no corresponding points exist, that is, in regions with occlusions.

9.4 Fast algorithms for geometric transforms

With the extensive discussion on interpolation in Chapter 8 we are well equipped to devise fast algorithms for the different geometric transforms. Basically there are two common tricks to speed up the computation of geometric transforms.

First, many computations are required to compute the interpolation coefficients for fractional shifts. For each shift, different interpolation coefficients are required. Thus we must devise the transforms in such a way that we need only constant shifts for a certain pass of the transform. If this is not possible, it might still be valid to compute the interpolation coefficients for different fractional shifts in advance and to reuse them later.

Second, interpolation is a separable procedure (Section 8.2.3). Taking advantage of this basic fact considerably reduces the number of operations. In most cases it is possible to devide the transforms in a series of 1-D transforms that operate only in one coordinate direction.

9.4.1 Scaling

Scaling is a common geometric transform that is mostly used for interactive image inspection. Another important application is multigrid image data structures such as pyramids.

From the algorithmic point of view, magnification and diminishing must be distinguished. In the case of magnification, we can directly apply an appropriate interpolation algorithm. In the case of diminishing, however, it is required to presmooth to such an extent that no *aliasing* occurs (Section 2.4.3). According to the sampling theorem (Section 2.4.2), all fine structures must be removed that are sampled less than two times at the resolution of the scaled image.

The algorithms for scaling are rather simple because scaling in the different directions can be performed one after the other. In the following, we discuss scaling of a 2-D image using inverse mapping. In the first step, we scale the N points of a row to N' points in the scaled image. The coordinates of the scaled image mapped back to the original image size are given by

$$x'_{n'} = \frac{N-1}{N'-1}n' \quad \text{with} \quad 0 \le n' < N' \tag{9.16}$$

Note that the first and last points of the original image at 0 and $N'-1$ are mapped onto the first and last point of the scaled image: $x'_0 = 0$, $x'_{N'-1} = N-1$. All points in between in general do not meet a grid point on the original grid and thus must be interpolated. The horizontal scaling can significantly be sped up because the position of the points and thus the interpolation coefficients are the same for *all* rows. Thus we can compute all interpolation coefficients in advance, store them in a list, and then use them to interpolate all rows. We illustrate the approach with linear interpolation. In this case, we only need to use two neighboring points for the interpolation. Thus, it is sufficient to store the index of the point, given by $n = \text{floor}(x_{n'})$ (where the function floor computes the largest integer lower than or equal to $x_{n'}$), and the fractional shift $f_{n'} = x_{n'} - \text{floor}(x_{n'})$. Then we can interpolate the gray value at the n'th point in the scaled row from

$$g'_{n'} = g_n + f_{n'}(g_{n+1} - g_n) \tag{9.17}$$

Thus 1-D linear interpolation is reduced to 3 arithmetic operations per pixel. The computation of n and $f_{n'}$ must be performed only once for all rows.

In a very similar way, we can proceed for the interpolation in the other directions. The only difference is that we can now apply the same interpolation factor to all pixels of a row. If we denote rows n and rows n' in the original and scaled image with $\boldsymbol{g}_n$ and $\boldsymbol{g}'_{n'}$, respectively, we

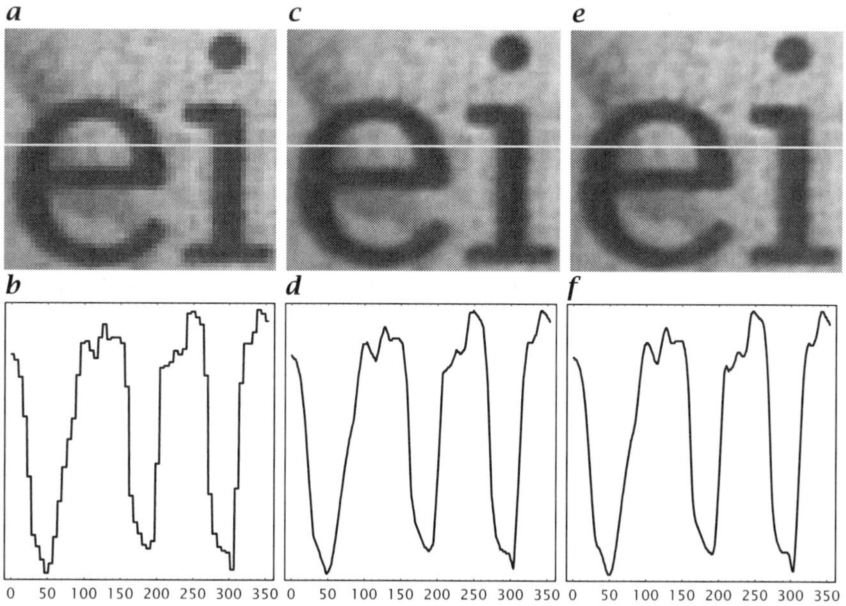

Figure 9.3: *A 51×59 sector of an image with the letters "ei" scaled to a size of 306×354 using:* ***a*** *pixel replication;* ***b*** *linear interpolation; and* ***c*** *cubic interpolation. The diagrams below each image show a row profile through the center of the corresponding images at the position marked by a white line.*

can rewrite Eq. (9.17) as the following vector equation:

$$\boldsymbol{g}'_{n'} = \boldsymbol{g}_n + f_{n'}(\boldsymbol{g}_{n+1} - \boldsymbol{g}_n) \qquad (9.18)$$

For higher-order interpolation nothing changes with the general computing scheme. Instead of Eqs. (9.17) and (9.18), we just have to take more complex equations to interpolate the gray value in the scaled image from more than two pixels of the original image. This also implies that more interpolation coefficients need to be precomputed before we apply the horizontal scaling. It is also straightforward to extend this approach to higher-dimensional signals.

Figure 9.3 compares scaling with zero-order (pixel replication), linear and cubic interpolation. A small sector is blown up by a scale factor of 6. Simple pixel replication leads to a pixelation of the image resulting in jagged edges. Linear interpolation gives smooth edges but some visual disturbance remains. The piecewise-linear interpolation between the pixels results in discontinuities in the slope as can be best seen in the profile (Fig. 9.3d) through the center row of Fig. 9.3c. The best results are obtained with cubic interpolation.

9.4.2 Translation

Translation is the simplest of all geometric transformations and does not require much consideration. The shift is the same for all pixels. Thus, we need only one set of interpolation coefficients that is applied to each pixel. As for scaling, we perform first the horizontal shift and then the vertical shift. Note that interpolation algorithms applied in this way have the same computational structure as a convolution operator. Therefore, we can use the same efficient storage scheme for the horizontally shifted or scaled rows as in Section 5.6 for neighborhood operators.

9.4.3 Rotation

With *rotation* it is less obvious how it can be decomposed into a sequence of one-dimensional geometrical transforms. Indeed, there are several possibilities. Interestingly, these algorithms have not been invented in the context of image processing but for computer graphics.

Catmull and Smith [5] suggested the following 2-pass shear-scale transform:

$$\boldsymbol{R} = \begin{bmatrix} \cos\theta & \sin\theta \\ -\sin\theta & \cos\theta \end{bmatrix} = \begin{bmatrix} 1 & 0 \\ -\tan\theta & 1/\cos\theta \end{bmatrix} \begin{bmatrix} \cos\theta & \sin\theta \\ 0 & 1 \end{bmatrix} \tag{9.19}$$

The first matrix performs a horizontal shear/scale operation, and the second, a vertical shear/scale operation. Written in components, the first transform is

$$\begin{aligned} x' &= x\cos\theta + y\sin\theta \\ y' &= y \end{aligned} \tag{9.20}$$

The image is shifted horizontally by the offset $y\sin\theta$ and is diminished by the factor of $x\cos\theta$. Thus Eq. (9.20) constitutes a combined shear-scale transform in horizontal direction only (Fig. 9.4).

Likewise, the second transform

$$\begin{aligned} x'' &= x' \\ y'' &= y'/\cos\theta - x'\tan\theta \end{aligned} \tag{9.21}$$

performs a combined shear-scale transform in vertical direction only. This time, the image is enlarged in vertical direction by the factor of $1/\cos\theta$.

This usage of scaling operations for image rotation has two disadvantages. First, the scale operations require extra computations since the image need not only be shifted but also scaled. Second, although the size of an image does not change during a rotation, the first scaling reduces the size of the image in horizontal direction and thus could

Figure 9.4: *Fast image rotation by a two-step shearing/scaling first in horizontal and then in vertical direction.*

cause aliasing. If a smoothing is applied to avoid aliasing, resolution is lost. Fortunately, the problem is not too serious because any rotation algorithm must only be applied for angles $|\theta| < 45°$. For larger rotation angles, first a corresponding transposition and/or mirror operation can be applied to obtain a rotation by a multiple of 90°. Then the residual rotation angle is always smaller than 45°.

Figure 9.5: *Fast image rotation by decomposition into three 1-D shear transforms only: first in horizontal, then in vertical, and again in horizontal direction.*

With a 3-pass transform [6, 7], rotation can be decomposed into three 1-D shear transforms avoiding scaling (Fig. 9.5):

$$
\begin{aligned}
\boldsymbol{R} &= \begin{bmatrix} \cos\theta & \sin\theta \\ -\sin\theta & \cos\theta \end{bmatrix} \\
&= \begin{bmatrix} 1 & \tan(\theta/2) \\ 0 & 1 \end{bmatrix} \begin{bmatrix} 1 & 0 \\ -\sin\theta & 1 \end{bmatrix} \begin{bmatrix} 1 & \tan(\theta/2) \\ 0 & 1 \end{bmatrix}
\end{aligned} \tag{9.22}
$$

9.4.4 Affine and perspective transforms

A 2-D *affine transform* adds three more degrees of freedom to a simple transform that includes only rotation and translation. These are two degrees of freedom for scaling in x and y direction, and one degree of freedom for shearing. Together with the degree of freedom for rotation, we have (without the translation) four degrees of freedom that can generally be described by a 2×2 matrix as discussed in Section 9.3.1:

$$
\boldsymbol{A} = \begin{bmatrix} a_{11} & a_{12} \\ a_{21} & a_{22} \end{bmatrix} \tag{9.23}
$$

One way to perform an affine transform efficiently is to decompose it into a rotation, shear, and scaling transform:

$$
\boldsymbol{A} = \begin{bmatrix} a_{11} & a_{12} \\ a_{21} & a_{22} \end{bmatrix} = \begin{bmatrix} s_x & 0 \\ 0 & s_y \end{bmatrix} \begin{bmatrix} 1 & s \\ 0 & 1 \end{bmatrix} \begin{bmatrix} \cos\theta & \sin\theta \\ -\sin\theta & \cos\theta \end{bmatrix} \tag{9.24}
$$

The parameters s_x, s_y, s, and θ can be computed from the matrix coefficients by

$$
\begin{aligned}
s_x &= \sqrt{a_{11}^2 + a_{21}^2} & s_y &= \frac{\det(\boldsymbol{A})}{s_x} \\
s &= \frac{a_{11}a_{12} + a_{21}a_{22}}{\det(\boldsymbol{A})} & \tan\theta &= -\frac{a_{21}}{a_{11}}
\end{aligned} \tag{9.25}
$$

where $\det(\boldsymbol{A})$ is the determinant of the matrix $\boldsymbol{A}$. The shear transform and the rotation can be computed simultaneously by the 3-pass shear transform discussed in Section 9.4.3 with the following modification to Eq. (9.22):

$$
\begin{aligned}
\boldsymbol{R} &= \begin{bmatrix} 1 & s \\ 0 & 1 \end{bmatrix} \begin{bmatrix} \cos\theta & \sin\theta \\ -\sin\theta & \cos\theta \end{bmatrix} \\
&= \begin{bmatrix} 1 & s + \tan(\theta/2) \\ 0 & 1 \end{bmatrix} \begin{bmatrix} 1 & 0 \\ -\sin\theta & 1 \end{bmatrix} \begin{bmatrix} 1 & \tan(\theta/2) \\ 0 & 1 \end{bmatrix}
\end{aligned} \tag{9.26}
$$

Thus the affine transform can be computed with a 3-pass shear transform Eq. (9.26) followed by a scaling transform as discussed in Section 9.4.1. Fast algorithms for perspective and more general transforms are treated in detail in Wolberg [1].

9.5 References

[1] Wolberg, G., (1990). *Digital image warping.* Los Alamitos, CA: IEEE Computer Society Press.

[2] Gomes, J. and Velho, L., (1997). *Image Processing for Computer Graphics.* New York: Springer.

[3] Foley, J. D., van Dam, A., Feiner, S. K., and Hughes, J. F., (1990). *Computer Graphics, Principles and Practice.* Reading, MA: Addison Wesley.

[4] Watt, A., (1990). *Fundamentals of three-dimensional computer graphics.* Workingham, England: Addison-Wesley.

[5] Catmull, E. and Smith, A. R., (1980). 3-D transformations of images in scanline order. *Computer Graphics (SIGGRAPH '80 Proceedings),* **14**:279–285.

[6] Paeth, A. W., (1986). A fast algorithm for general raster rotation. In *Graphics Interface '86,* pp. 77–81.

[7] Tanaka, A., Kameyama, M., Kazama, S., and Watanabe, O., (1986). A rotation method for raster image using skew transformation. In *Proc. IEEE Conf. Computer Vision and Pattern Recognition (CVPR'86),* pp. 272–277. IEE, IEEE Computer Society Press.

Part III

Feature Estimation

10 Local Structure

Bernd Jähne

Interdisziplinäres Zentrum für Wissenschaftliches Rechnen (IWR)
Universität Heidelberg, Germany

Handbook of Computer Vision and Applications
Volume 2
Signal Processing and Pattern Recognition

Copyright © 1999 by Academic Press
All rights of reproduction in any form reserved.
ISBN 0-12-379772-1/$30.00

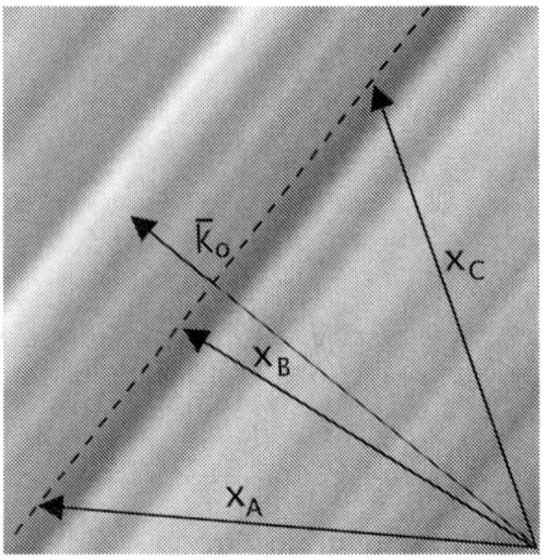

Figure 10.1: Illustration of a linear symmetric or simple neighborhood. The gray values depend only on a coordinate given by a unit vector $\bar{\boldsymbol{r}}$.

10.1 Introduction

The analysis of the structure in small neighborhoods is a key element in higher-dimensional signal processing. Changes in the gray values reveal either the edge of an object or the type of texture.

10.2 Properties of simple neighborhoods

10.2.1 Representation in the spatial domain

The mathematical description of a local neighborhood by continuous functions has two significant advantages. First, it is much easier to formulate the concepts and to study their properties analytically. As long as the corresponding discrete image satisfies the sampling theorem, all the results derived from continuous functions remain valid because the sampled image is an exact representation of the continuous gray-value function. Second, we can now distinguish between errors inherent to the chosen approach and those that are only introduced by the discretization.

A simple local neighborhood is characterized by the fact that the gray value only changes in one direction. In all other directions it is constant. Because the gray values are constant along lines and form oriented structures this property of a neighborhood is denoted as *local orientation* [1] or *linear symmetry* [2]. Only more recently, the term *simple neighborhood* has been coined by Granlund and Knutsson [3].

If we orient the coordinate system along the principal directions, the gray values become a 1-D function of only one coordinate. Generally, we will denote the direction of local orientation with a unit vector

$\bar{\boldsymbol{r}}$ perpendicular to the lines of constant gray values. Then, a simple neighborhood is mathematically represented by

$$g(\boldsymbol{x}) = g(\boldsymbol{x}^T\bar{\boldsymbol{r}}) \tag{10.1}$$

Equation Eq. (10.1) is also valid for image data with more than two dimensions. The projection of the vector $\boldsymbol{x}$ onto the unit vector $\bar{\boldsymbol{r}}$ makes the gray values depend only on a scalar quantity, the coordinate in the direction of $\bar{\boldsymbol{r}}$ (Fig. 10.1). The essential relation now is that the gradient is parallel to the direction $\bar{\boldsymbol{r}}$ into which the gray values change:

$$\nabla g(\boldsymbol{x}^T\bar{\boldsymbol{r}}) = \begin{bmatrix} \dfrac{\partial g(\boldsymbol{x}^T\bar{\boldsymbol{r}})}{\partial x_1} \\ \cdots \\ \dfrac{\partial g(\boldsymbol{x}^T\bar{\boldsymbol{r}})}{\partial x_W} \end{bmatrix} = \begin{bmatrix} \bar{r}_1 g'(\boldsymbol{x}^T\bar{\boldsymbol{r}}) \\ \cdots \\ \bar{r}_D g'(\boldsymbol{x}^T\bar{\boldsymbol{r}}) \end{bmatrix} = \bar{\boldsymbol{r}} g'(\boldsymbol{x}^T\bar{\boldsymbol{r}}) \tag{10.2}$$

The term g' denotes the derivative of g with respect to the scalar variable $\boldsymbol{x}^T\bar{\boldsymbol{r}}$. In the hyperplane perpendicular to the gradient, the values remain locally constant.

10.2.2 Representation in the Fourier domain

A simple neighborhood has a special form in Fourier space. Let us first assume that the whole image is described by Eq. (10.1), that is, $\bar{\boldsymbol{r}}$ does not depend on the position. Then, from the very fact that a simple neighborhood is constant in all directions except $\bar{\boldsymbol{r}}$, we infer that the Fourier transform must be confined to a line. The direction of the line is given by $\bar{\boldsymbol{r}}$:

$$g(\boldsymbol{x}^T\bar{\boldsymbol{r}}) \quad \Longleftrightarrow \quad \hat{g}(k)\delta(\boldsymbol{k} - \bar{\boldsymbol{r}}(\boldsymbol{k}^T\bar{\boldsymbol{r}})) \tag{10.3}$$

where k denotes the coordinate in the Fourier domain in the direction of $\bar{\boldsymbol{r}}$. The argument in the δ function is only zero when $\boldsymbol{k}$ is parallel to $\bar{\boldsymbol{r}}$.

In a second step, a window function $w(\boldsymbol{x} - \boldsymbol{x}_0)$ is used to restrict the area to a local neighborhood around a point $\boldsymbol{x}_0$. Thus $g(\boldsymbol{x}^T\bar{\boldsymbol{r}})$ in Eq. (10.3) is multiplied by the window function $w(\boldsymbol{x} - \boldsymbol{x}_0)$ in the spatial domain. The size and shape of the neighborhood is determined by the window function. Multiplication in the space domain corresponds to a convolution in the Fourier domain (Section 3.2.3). Thus,

$$w(\boldsymbol{x} - \boldsymbol{x}_0)g(\boldsymbol{x}^T\bar{\boldsymbol{r}}) \quad \Longleftrightarrow \quad \hat{w}(\boldsymbol{k}) * \hat{g}(k)\delta(\boldsymbol{k} - \bar{\boldsymbol{r}}(\boldsymbol{k}^T\bar{\boldsymbol{r}})) \tag{10.4}$$

where $\hat{w}(\boldsymbol{k})$ is the Fourier transform of the window function.

The limitation to a local neighborhood thus blurs the line in Fourier space to a "sausage-like" shape. Because of the reciprocity of scales between the two domains, its thickness is inversely proportional to the size of the window. From this elementary relation, we can already conclude qualitatively that the accuracy of the orientation estimate is directly related to the ratio of the window size to the wavelength of the smallest structures in the window.

10.2.3 Direction versus orientation

For an appropriate representation of simple neighborhoods, it is first important to distinguish *orientation* from *direction*. The direction is defined over the full angle range of 2π (360°). Two vectors that point in opposite directions, that is, differ by 180°, are different. The gradient vector, for example, always points into the direction into which the gray values are increasing. With respect to a bright object on a dark background, this means that the gradient at the edge is pointing towards the object. In contrast, to describe the direction of a local neighborhood, an angle range of 360° makes no sense. We cannot distinguish between patterns that are rotated by 180°. If a pattern is rotated by 180°, it still has the same direction. Thus, the direction of a simple neighborhood is different from the direction of a gradient. While for the edge of an object gradients pointing in opposite directions are conflicting and inconsistent, for the direction of a simple neighborhood this is consistent information.

In order to distinguish the two types of "directions," we will speak of *orientation* in all cases where an angle range of only 180° is required. Orientation is still, of course, a *cyclic* quantity. Increasing the orientation beyond 180° flips it back to 0°. Therefore, an appropriate representation of orientation requires an angle doubling.

In his pioneering paper on a general picture processing operator Granlund [1] introduced a vectorial representation of the local orientation. The magnitude of the *orientation vector* is set to the certainty with which the orientation could be determined and its direction to the doubled orientation angle. This vector representation of orientation has two significant advantages.

First, it is more suitable for further processing than a separate representation of the orientation by two scalar quantities. Take, for example, averaging. Vectors are summed up by chaining them together, and the resulting sum vector is the vector from the starting point of the first vector to the end point of the last vector. The weight of an individual vector in the vector sum is given by its length. In this way, the certainty of the orientation measurement is adequately taken into account. In a region with homogeneous orientation the vectors line up to a large vector, that is, give a certain orientation estimate. However, in a region with randomly distributed orientation the resulting vector remains small, indicating that no significant local orientation is present.

Second, it is difficult to display orientation as a gray-scale image. While orientation is a cyclic quantity, the gray-scale representation shows an unnatural jump between the smallest angle and the largest one. This jump dominates the appearance of the orientation images and thus does not give a good impression of the orientation distribution. The orientation vector can be well represented, however, as a color image. It appears natural to map the certainty measure onto the luminance and the orientation angle as the hue of the color. Our attention is then drawn to the bright parts in the images where we can distinguish the colors well. The darker a color is, the more difficult it becomes to distinguish the different colors visually. In this way, our visual impression coincides with the orientation information in the image.

10.3 Edge detection by first-order derivatives

Detection of edges is one of the most important tasks of low-level multi-dimensional signal processing. An edge marks the border of an object that is characterized by a different feature (gray value, color, or any other property) than the background. In the context of simple neighborhoods, an edge is a special type of simple neighborhood with a sharp transition. Low-level edge detection thus means to detect the strength of such a transition and the direction of the edge.

First-order derivative filters are one way for low-level edge detection. A first-order derivative operator corresponds to a multiplication by $2\pi i k_d$ in the wave-number space (Section 3.2.3). Thus, a first-order derivative operator in the direction d is represented by the following operations in the space and wave-number domain:

$$\frac{\partial}{\partial x_d} \Longleftrightarrow 2\pi i k_d \tag{10.5}$$

where $\tilde{k}$ is the dimensionless wave number normalized to the Nyquist limit Eq. (2.34). One-dimensional first-order derivative operators are not sufficient for edge detection in higher-dimensional signals because they predominantly detect edges that are perpendicular to the direction of the operator. As shown with Eq. (10.2) in Section 10.2.1, the *gradient vector*

$$\nabla g = \left[\frac{\partial g}{\partial x_1}, \frac{\partial g}{\partial x_2}, \ldots, \frac{\partial g}{\partial x_D}\right]^T \tag{10.6}$$

is parallel to the direction in which the gray-values change. Thus it is a good low-level measure for edges. In the operator notation introduced in Section 5.2.3, the gradient can be written as a vector operator. In 2-D and 3-D space this is

$$\mathcal{D} = \begin{bmatrix} \mathcal{D}_x \\ \mathcal{D}_y \end{bmatrix} \quad \text{or} \quad \mathcal{D} = \begin{bmatrix} \mathcal{D}_x \\ \mathcal{D}_y \\ \mathcal{D}_z \end{bmatrix} \tag{10.7}$$

The magnitude of the gradient vector

$$|\nabla g| = \left(\sum_{d=1}^{D} \left(\frac{\partial g}{\partial x_d} \right)^2 \right)^{1/2} \tag{10.8}$$

is rotation-invariant and a measure for the edge strength. Because of the rotation invariance, this measure is isotropic. The computation of the magnitude of the gradient can be expressed in operator notation as

$$|\mathcal{D}| = \left[\sum_{d=1}^{D} \mathcal{D}_d \cdot \mathcal{D}_d \right]^{1/2} \tag{10.9}$$

The principal problem with all types of edge detectors is that a derivative operator can only be approximated on a discrete grid. This is the basic reason why there is such a wide variety of solutions for edge detectors available. After the discussion of the general properties of first-order derivative operators in Section 10.3.1, a survey of various common edge detectors will be given.

10.3.1 General properties

Zero shift. With respect to object detection, the most important feature of a derivative convolution operator is that it must not shift the object position. For a first-order derivative filter, a real transfer function makes no sense, because extreme values should be mapped onto zero crossings and the steepest slopes to extreme values. This mapping implies a 90° phase shift, a purely imaginary transfer function and an antisymmetric or odd filter mask. According to the classification of *linear shift-invariant* (LSI) filters established in Section 5.3.5, first-order derivative filters are either type III or type IV filters. Thus the simplified equations Eqs. (5.25) and (5.27) can be used to compute the transfer function.

Suppression of mean value. A derivative filter of any order must not show response to constant values or an offset in a signal. This condition implies that the sum of the coefficients must be zero and that the transfer function is zero for a zero wave number:

$$\sum_{\boldsymbol{n}} H_{\boldsymbol{n}} = 0 \Longleftrightarrow \hat{H}(\mathbf{0}) = 0 \tag{10.10}$$

Nonselective derivation. Intuitively, we expect that any derivative operator amplifies smaller scales more strongly than coarser scales, as the transfer function of a first-order derivative operator goes with k. However, this condition is a too restrictive. Imagine that we first apply a smoothing operator to an image before we apply a derivative operator. Then the resulting transfer function would not increase monotonically with the wave number but decrease for higher wave numbers. We would, however, still recognize the joint operation as a derivation because the mean gray value is suppressed and the operator is only sensitive to spatial gray-value changes.

Thus a more general condition is required. Here we suggest

$$\hat{H}(\tilde{\boldsymbol{k}}) = \mathrm{i}\pi \tilde{k}_d \hat{B}(|\tilde{\boldsymbol{k}}|) \quad \text{with} \quad \hat{B}(0) = 1 \text{ and } \nabla \hat{B} = \mathbf{0} \qquad (10.11)$$

This condition ensures that the transfer function is still zero for the wave number zero and increases in proportion to $\tilde{k}_d$ for small wave numbers. One can regard Eq. (10.11) as a first-order derivative filter regularized by an isotropic smoothing filter.

Isotropy. For good edge detection, it is important that the response of the operator does not depend on the direction of the edge. If this is the case, we speak of an isotropic edge detector. The isotropy of an edge detector can best be analyzed by its transfer function. Equation (10.11), which we derived from the condition of nonselective derivation, gives a general form for an isotropic first-order derivative operator.

10.3.2 First-order difference operators

This is the simplest of all approaches to compute a gradient vector. For the first partial derivative in the x direction, one of the following approximations may be used:

$$\begin{aligned}
\frac{\partial g(\boldsymbol{x})}{\partial x_d} &\approx \frac{g(\boldsymbol{x}) - g(\boldsymbol{x} - \Delta x_d \bar{\boldsymbol{e}}_d)}{\Delta x_d} && \text{backward} \\
&\approx \frac{g(\boldsymbol{x} + \Delta x_d \bar{\boldsymbol{e}}_d) - g(\boldsymbol{x})}{\Delta x_d} && \text{forward} \qquad (10.12) \\
&\approx \frac{g(\boldsymbol{x} + \Delta x_d \bar{\boldsymbol{e}}_d) - g(\boldsymbol{x} - \Delta x_d \bar{\boldsymbol{e}}_d)}{2\Delta x_d} && \text{symmetric}
\end{aligned}$$

where $\bar{\boldsymbol{e}}_d$ is a unit vector in the direction d. These approximations correspond to the filter masks

$$^{-}\boldsymbol{D}_d = [1_{\bullet}\ -1],\ ^{+}\boldsymbol{D}_d = [1\ -1_{\bullet}],\ \boldsymbol{D}_{2d} = 1/2\ [1\ 0\ -1] \qquad (10.13)$$

The subscript • denotes the pixel of the asymmetric masks to which the result is written. The symmetric difference operator results in a type III operator (odd number of coefficients, odd symmetry, see Section 5.3.5). The forward and backward difference operators are asymmetric and thus not of much use in signal processing. They can be transformed in a type IV LSI operator if the result is not stored at the position of the right or left pixel but at a position halfway between the two pixels. This corresponds to a shift of the grid by half a pixel distance. The transfer function for the backward difference is then

$$^{-}\hat{D}_d = \exp(\mathrm{i}\pi\tilde{k}_d/2)\left[1 - \exp(-\mathrm{i}\pi\tilde{k}_d)\right] = \mathrm{i}\sin(\pi\tilde{k}_d/2) \tag{10.14}$$

where the first term results from the shift by half a lattice point.

According to Eq. (5.25), the transfer function of the symmetric difference operator is given by

$$\hat{D}_{2d} = \mathrm{i}\sin(\pi\tilde{k}_d) \tag{10.15}$$

This operator can also be computed from

$$\boldsymbol{D}_{2d} = {}^{-}\boldsymbol{D}_d\boldsymbol{B}_d = [1_\bullet \ -1] * 1/2\ [1\ 1_\bullet] = 1/2\,[1\ 0\ -1]$$

Unfortunately, these simple difference filters are only poor approximations for an edge detector. From Eq. (10.15), we infer that the magnitude and direction of the gradient ϕ' are given by

$$|\nabla g| = \left[\sin^2(\pi\tilde{k}\cos\phi) + \sin^2(\pi\tilde{k}\sin\phi)\right]^{1/2} \tag{10.16}$$

and

$$\phi' = \arctan\frac{\sin(\pi\tilde{k}\sin\phi)}{\sin(\pi\tilde{k}\cos\phi)} \tag{10.17}$$

when the wave number is written in polar coordinates (k, ϕ). The magnitude of the gradient decreases quickly from the correct value. A Taylor expansion of Eq. (10.16) in $\tilde{k}$ yields for the anisotropy in the magnitude

$$\Delta|\nabla g| = |\nabla g(\phi)| - |\nabla g(0)| \approx \frac{(\pi\tilde{k})^3}{12}\sin^2(2\phi) \tag{10.18}$$

The resulting errors are shown in Fig. 10.2 as a function of the magnitude of the wave number and the angle to the x axis. The decrease is also anisotropic; it is slower in the diagonal direction. The errors in the direction of the gradient are also large (Fig. 10.2b). While in the direction of the axes and diagonals the error is zero, in the directions

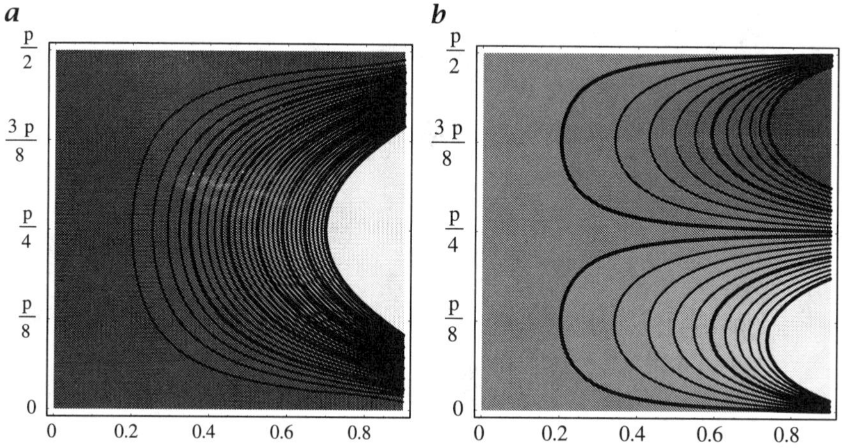

Figure 10.2: *Anisotropy of the* ***a*** *magnitude and* ***b*** *error in the direction of the gradient based on the symmetrical gradient operator* $[\mathcal{D}_{2x}, \mathcal{D}_{2y}]^T$*. The parameters are the magnitude of the wave number (0 to 0.9) and the angle to the x axis (0 to* $\pi/2$*). Distance of contour lines:* ***a*** *0.02 (thick lines 0.1);* ***b*** *2°.*

in-between it reaches values of about ± 10° already at $\tilde{k} = 0.5$. A Taylor expansion of Eq. (10.17) in $\tilde{k}$ gives in the approximation of small $\tilde{k}$ the angle error

$$\Delta\phi \approx \frac{(\pi\tilde{k})^2}{24}\sin 4\phi \tag{10.19}$$

From this equation, we see that the angle error is zero for $\phi = n\pi/4$ with $n \in \mathbb{Z}$, that is, for $\phi = 0°, 45°\ 90°, \ldots$.

10.3.3 Roberts operator

The *Roberts operator* uses the smallest possible difference filters to compute the gradients that have a common center point

$$\boldsymbol{D}_{x-y} = \begin{bmatrix} 1 & 0 \\ 0 & -1 \end{bmatrix} \quad \text{and} \quad \boldsymbol{D}_{x+y} = \begin{bmatrix} 0 & 1 \\ -1 & 0 \end{bmatrix} \tag{10.20}$$

The filters $\boldsymbol{D}_x = [1\ -1]$ and $\boldsymbol{D}_y = [1\ -1]^T$ are not suitable to form a gradient operator because $\boldsymbol{D}_x$ and $\boldsymbol{D}_y$ shift the convolution result by half a grid constant in the x and y directions, respectively. The difference filters in diagonal direction result in a gradient vector that is rotated by 45°. The errors in the magnitude and direction obtained with the Roberts operator are shown in Fig. 10.3. The improvement is only marginal as compared to the gradient computation based on the simple difference operator $\boldsymbol{D}_2 = 1/2\,[1\ 0\ -1]$ (Fig. 10.2).

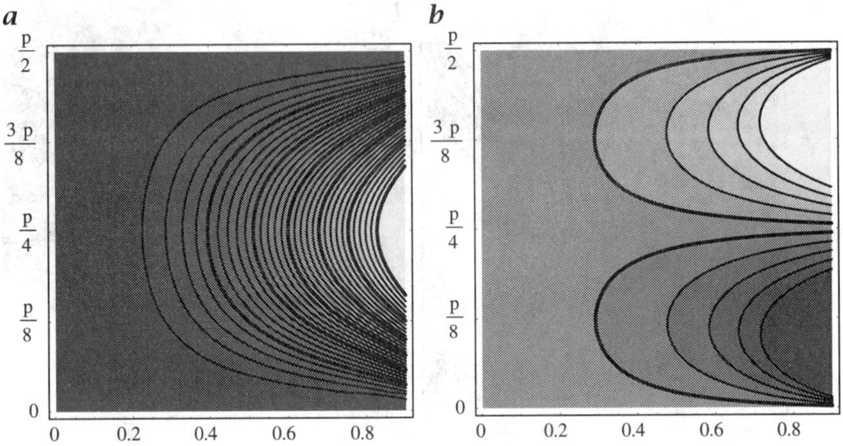

Figure 10.3: *Anisotropy of the* **a** *magnitude and* **b** *error in the direction of the gradient based on the Roberts edge detector Eq. (10.20). Distance of contour lines as in Fig. 10.2.*

10.3.4 Regularized difference operators

It is a common practice to regularize derivative operators by presmoothing the signal (see, e. g., Chapter 15). We will investigate here to what extent the direction and isotropy of the gradient is improved.

One type of regularized derivative filter is the derivate of a Gaussian. On a discrete lattice this operator is best approximated by the derivative of a binomial mask (Section 7.4) as

$$^{(B,R)}\mathcal{D}_d = \mathcal{D}_{2d}\mathcal{B}^R \tag{10.21}$$

with the transfer function

$$^{(B,R)}\hat{D}_d(\tilde{k}) = \mathrm{i}\sin(\pi\tilde{k}_d)\prod_{d=1}^{D}\cos^R(\pi\tilde{k}_d/2) \tag{10.22}$$

for even R. This approach leads to nonsquare masks and results in some improvement of the isotropy of the gradient magnitude. However, the error in the direction of the gradient is the same as for the symmetric difference operator since the smoothing terms in Eq. (10.22) cancel out in Eq. (10.17).

Slightly better are Sobel-type difference operators

$$^{R}\mathcal{S}_d = \mathcal{D}_{2d}\mathcal{B}_d^{R-1}\prod_{d'\neq d}\mathcal{B}_{d'}^{R} \tag{10.23}$$

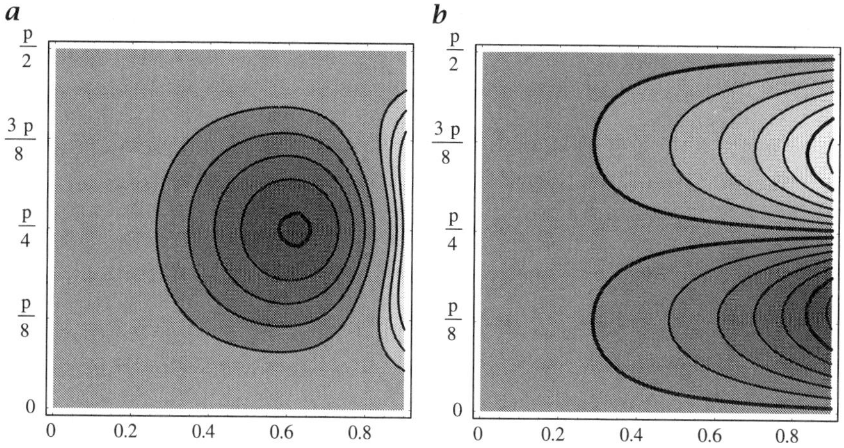

Figure 10.4: *Anisotropy of the* ***a*** *magnitude and* ***b*** *error in the direction of the gradient based on the Sobel operator Eq. (10.26). Distance of contour lines as in Fig. 10.2.*

with the transfer function

$$ {}^{R}\hat{S}_d(\tilde{k}) = \mathrm{i}\tan(\pi\tilde{k}_d/2)\prod_{d=1}^{D}\cos^R(\pi\tilde{k}_d/2) \qquad (10.24)$$

that lead to square masks by reducing the smoothing in the direction of the derivation. The smallest operator of this type ($R = 1$) has in two dimensions the masks

$$ {}^{1}\boldsymbol{S}_x = \frac{1}{2}\begin{bmatrix} 1 & -1 \\ 1 & -1 \end{bmatrix}, \quad {}^{1}\boldsymbol{S}_y = \frac{1}{2}\begin{bmatrix} 1 & 1 \\ -1 & -1 \end{bmatrix} \qquad (10.25)$$

The best-known example of this class of filters is the *Sobel operator*

$$ {}^{2}\boldsymbol{S}_x = \boldsymbol{D}_x\boldsymbol{B}_x\boldsymbol{B}_y^2 = \frac{1}{8}\begin{bmatrix} 1 & 0 & -1 \\ 2 & 0 & -2 \\ 1 & 0 & -1 \end{bmatrix}, \quad {}^{2}\boldsymbol{S}_y = \frac{1}{8}\begin{bmatrix} 1 & 2 & 1 \\ 0 & 0 & 0 \\ -1 & -2 & -1 \end{bmatrix} \qquad (10.26)$$

The errors in the magnitude and direction of the gradient based on Eq. (10.24) are given by

$$ \Delta|\nabla g| \approx -\frac{(\pi\tilde{k})^3}{24}\sin^2(2\phi) \qquad (10.27)$$

and

$$ \Delta\phi = \arctan\frac{\tan(\pi(\tilde{k}_d/2)\sin\phi)}{\tan(\pi(\tilde{k}_d/2)\cos\phi)} - \phi \approx -\frac{(\pi\tilde{k}_d)^2}{48}\sin 4\phi \qquad (10.28)$$

and shown in Fig. 10.4. The results are remarkable in two respects. First, the error in the direction does not depend at all on the degree of smoothing as for the derivatives of Gaussians and is only about two times lower than for the simple symmetric difference operator. Second, Fig. 10.4b shows that the anisotropy of the magnitude of the gradient is surprisingly low as compared to the symmetric difference filter in Fig. 10.2b. This could not be expected from the Taylor expansion because the term with $\tilde{k}^2$ is only a factor of two lower than for the symmetric difference operator in Eq. (10.19). Thus the extrapolation of the transfer functions from small wave numbers to high wave numbers is not valid. The example of the Sobel operator shows that oscillating higher-order terms may cancel each other and lead to much better results as could be expected from a Taylor expansion.

10.3.5 Spline-based difference operators

The cubic B-spline transform discussed in Section 8.5 for interpolation yields a continuous representation of a discrete image that is continuous in its first and second derivative

$$g_3(x_d) = \sum_n c_n \beta_3(x_d - n) \qquad (10.29)$$

where $\beta_3(x_d)$ is the cubic B-spline function. From such an analytical continuous representation, the spatial derivative can be computed directly as

$$\frac{\partial g_3(x_d)}{\partial x_d} = \sum_n c_n \frac{\partial \beta_3(x_d - n)}{\partial x_d} \qquad (10.30)$$

For a discrete derivative filter, we only need the derivatives at the grid points. From Fig. 8.7a it can be seen that the cubic B-spline function covers at most five grid points. The maximum of the spline function occurs at the central grid point. Therefore, the derivative at this point is zero. It is also zero at the two outer grid points. Thus, the derivative is only unequal to zero at the direct left and right neighbors of the central point. Consequently, the derivative at the grid point n reduces to

$$\left.\frac{\partial g_3(x_d)}{\partial x_d}\right|_n = (c_{n+1} - c_{n-1})/2 \qquad (10.31)$$

It follows that the computation of the first-order derivative based on the cubic B-spline transformation is indeed an efficient solution. We apply first the cubic B-spline transform in the direction of the derivative to be computed (Section 8.5) and then the $\mathcal{D}_{2x}$ operator. The transfer

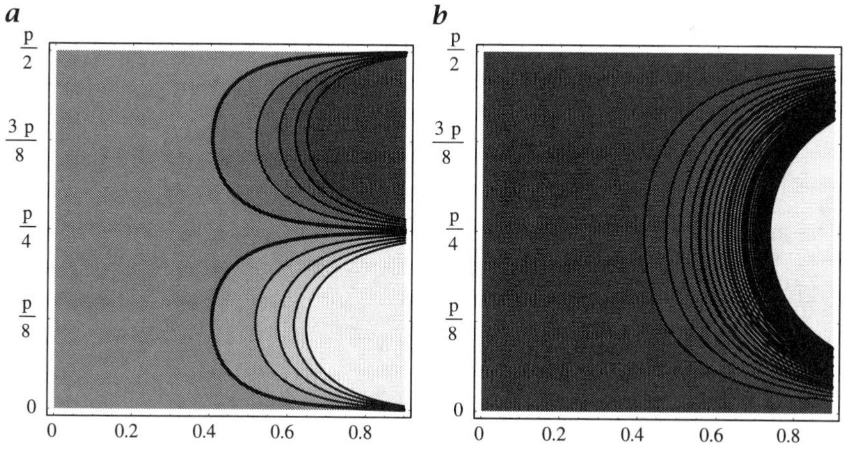

Figure 10.5: *Anisotropy of the* ***a*** *magnitude and* ***b*** *error in the direction of the gradient based on the cubic B-spline derivative operator according to Eq. (10.32). Distance of contour lines:* ***a*** *0.02 (thick lines 0.1);* ***b*** *0.5°.*

function of this filter is given by

$$
{}^{\text{B-spline}}\hat{\boldsymbol{D}}_d = \mathrm{i}\frac{\sin(\pi\tilde{k}_d)}{2/3 + 1/3\cos(\pi\tilde{k}_d)} \approx \mathrm{i}\pi\tilde{k}_d - \mathrm{i}\frac{\pi^5\tilde{k}_d^5}{180} \tag{10.32}
$$

The errors in the magnitude and direction of a gradient vector based on the B-spline derivative filter are shown in Fig. 10.5. They are considerably less than for the simple difference filters (Fig. 10.2). This can be seen more quantitatively from Taylor expansions for the relative error in the magnitude of the gradient

$$
\Delta|\nabla g| \approx -\frac{(\pi\tilde{k}_d)^5}{240}\sin^2(2\phi) \tag{10.33}
$$

and for the angle error

$$
\Delta\phi \approx \frac{(\pi\tilde{k}_d)^4}{720}\sin 4\phi \tag{10.34}
$$

The error terms are now contained only in terms with $\tilde{k}^4$ and $\tilde{k}^5$.

10.3.6 Least squares optimized gradient

The disadvantage of all approaches discussed in the previous sections is that they give no clear indication whether the achieved solution is good and whether any better exists. As discussed in detail in Section 6.5 the filter design problem can be treated in a rigorous mathematical way as an optimization problem. While these techniques do not only allow

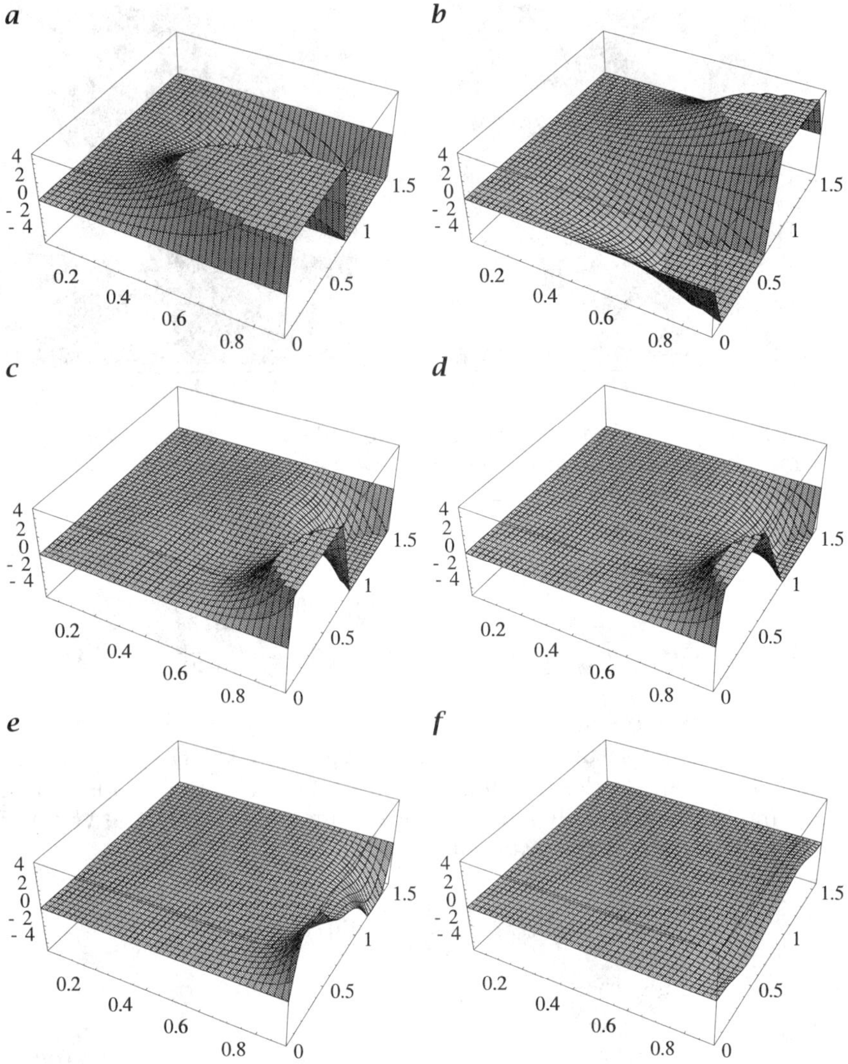

Figure 10.6: *Pseudo 3-D plot of the error map (in degree) in the gradient direction based on:* ***a*** *the symmetric difference operator;* ***b*** *the Sobel operator;* ***c*** *an optimized 1-D derivative filter with 7 coefficients;* ***d*** *an optimized* 3×3 *Sobel-type derivative operator;* ***e*** *an optimized 1-D derivative filter with 5 coefficients and a recursive relaxation filter for corrections; and* ***f*** *an optimized* 5×5 *Sobel-type derivative operator. All optimized filters were computed with a* $\cos^4(\pi\tilde{k}/2)$ *weighting function. The filter coefficients and the mean square error for the optimized filters are given in Table 10.1. Parameters are the magnitude of the wave number (0 to 0.9) and the angle to the* x *axis (0 to* $\pi/2$*).*

Table 10.1: *Gradient operators optimized for minimum error in the direction of the gradient. The mean square error is given in units of 10^{-4} rad. The lst column gives the number of operations per pixel (M = multiplication, A = addition/subtraction). For details see Chapter 6*

Name	Filter coefficients	Error	No. Ops.
$\mathcal{D}_1$	[1 0 -1]/2	400	1M, 1A
Sobel	$[1\ 0\ \text{-}1] * [1\ 2\ 1]^T/8$	190	2M, 3A
opt. 7-tap	[6 -31 108 0 -108 31 -6]/128	160?	3M, 3A
opt. 5-tap + relax	[7 114 0 -114 -7]/256, $\alpha = -15/32$	23	4M, 6A
opt. Sobel	$[1\ 0\ \text{-}1] * [3\ 10\ 3]^T/32$	26	2M, 3A
opt. 5×5	$[3\ 10\ 0\ \text{-}10\ \text{-}3]/32 * [7\ 63\ 116\ 63\ 7]^T/256$	1.9	4M, 5A

the design of optimal filters, it can also be decided precisely in respect to which criterion the solution is optimal.

Here, we will review some of the results obtained in Section 6.5 for gradient operators that have been optimized for a minimum error in the direction of the gradient. Figure 10.6 shows error maps of the gradients angle error as a function of the wave number and direction for six filters. Two of them, the *difference operator* and the *Sobel operator*, are standard solutions taken for comparison. The four other filters include two 1-D derivative operators and two Sobel-type filters with cross smoothing. The coefficients of the filters are summarized in Table 10.1.

All optimized filters are by far superior to the standard approaches. The mean square error in the direction of the gradient is at least one order of magnitude lower. The clear winner for a combination of accuracy and computational efficiency is the optimized 3×3 Sobel-type operator that requires per filter 2 multiplications and 3 additions only. For ultimate accuracy, the 5×5 Sobel-type operator is the best choice. This filter requires about two times more operations: 4 multiplications and 5 additions.

10.4 Edge detection by zero crossings

10.4.1 General properties

First-order derivative operators detect edges by maxima in the magnitude of the gradient. Alternatively, edges can be detected as zero crossings of second-order derivative operators. This technique is attractive since only *linear* operators are required to perform an isotropic detection of edges by zero crossings. In contrast, the magnitude of the gradient is only obtained after squaring and adding first-order derivative operators in all directions.

For an isotropic zero-crossing detector, only all second-order partial derivatives must be added up. The resulting operator is called the *Laplace operator* and denoted by Δ

$$\Delta = \sum_{d=1}^{D} \frac{\partial^2}{\partial x_w^2} \quad \Longleftrightarrow \quad -\sum_{d=1}^{D} 4\pi^2 k_d^2 = -4\pi^2 \left|\boldsymbol{k}\right|^2 \tag{10.35}$$

From this equation it is immediately evident that the Laplace operator is an isotropic operator.

A second-order derivative filter detects curvature. Extremes in function values should thus coincide with extremes in curvature. Consequently, a second-order derivative filter should be of even symmetry similar to a smoothing filter and all the properties for filters of even symmetry discussed in Sections 5.3.5 and 7.2 should also apply to second-order derivative filters. In addition, the sum of the coefficients must be zero as for first-order derivative filters:

$$\sum_{\boldsymbol{n}} H_{\boldsymbol{n}} = 0 \quad \Longleftrightarrow \quad \hat{H}(\mathbf{0}) = 0 \tag{10.36}$$

Also, a second-order derivative filter should not respond to a constant slope. This condition implies no further constraints as it is equivalent to the conditions that the sum of the coefficients is zero and that the filter is of even symmetry.

10.4.2 Laplace of Gaussian and difference of Gaussian filters

The standard implementations for the Laplace operator are well known and described in many textbooks (see, e.g., [4]). Thus, we will discuss here only the question of an optimal implementation of the Laplacian operator. Because of a transfer function proportional to $\tilde{k}^2$ (Eq. (10.35)), Laplace filters tend to enhance the noise level in images considerably. Thus, a better edge detector may be found by first smoothing the image and then applying the Laplacian filter. This leads to a kind of regularized edge detection and to two classes of filters known as *Laplace of Gaussian* or LoG filters and *difference of Gaussian* or DoG filters. While these filters reduce the noise level it is not clear to which extent they improve or even optimize the isotropy of the Laplace operator.

In the discrete case, a LoG filter is approximated by first smoothing the image with a binomial mask and then applying the discrete Laplace filter. Thus we have the operator combination $\mathcal{L}\mathcal{B}^R$ with the transfer function

$$\hat{\mathrm{LoG}} = \hat{L}\hat{B}^R = -4\sum_{d=1}^{D} \sin^2(\pi\tilde{k}_d/2)\prod_{d=1}^{D} \cos^R(\pi\tilde{k}_d/2) \tag{10.37}$$

For $R = 0$ this is the transfer function of the Laplace operator. In this equation, we used the standard implementation of the Laplace operator, which has in two dimensions the mask

$$\boldsymbol{L} = \begin{bmatrix} 0 & 1 & 0 \\ 1 & -4 & 1 \\ 0 & 1 & 0 \end{bmatrix} \quad (10.38)$$

and the transfer function

$$\hat{L} = \sin^2(\pi \tilde{k}_1/2) + \sin^2(\pi \tilde{k}_2/2) \quad (10.39)$$

For small wave numbers, the 2-D transfer function in Eq. (10.37) can be approximated in polar coordinates by

$$\hat{\mathrm{LoG}}(\tilde{k}, \phi) \approx -(\pi \tilde{k})^2 + \left[\frac{1}{16} + \frac{R}{8} + \frac{1}{48}\cos(4\phi)\right](\pi \tilde{k})^4 \quad (10.40)$$

The multidimensional *difference of Gaussian* type of Laplace filter, or *DoG* filter, is defined as

$$\mathrm{DoG} = 4(\mathcal{B}^2 - \mathcal{I})\mathcal{B}^R = 4(\mathcal{B}^{R+2} - \mathcal{B}^R) \quad (10.41)$$

and has the transfer function

$$\hat{\mathrm{DoG}}(\tilde{\boldsymbol{k}}) = 4\prod_{d=1}^{D} \cos^{R+2}(\pi \tilde{k}_d/2) - 4\prod_{d=1}^{D} \cos^{R}(\pi \tilde{k}_d/2) \quad (10.42)$$

For small wave numbers it can be approximated by

$$\hat{\mathrm{DoG}}(\tilde{k}, \phi) \approx -(\pi \tilde{k})^2 + \left[\frac{3}{32} + \frac{R}{8} - \frac{1}{96}\cos(4\phi)\right](\pi \tilde{k})^4 \quad (10.43)$$

The transfer function of the LoG and DoG filters are quite similar. Both have a significant anisotropic term. Increased smoothing (larger R) does not help to decrease the anisotropy. It is obvious that the DoG filter is significantly more isotropic but neither of them is really optimal with respect to a minimal anisotropy. That second-order derivative operators with better isotropy are possible is immediately evident by comparing Eqs. (10.40) and (10.43). The anisotropic $\cos 4\phi$ terms have different signs. Thus they can easily be compensated by a mix of LoG and DoG operators of the form 2/3DoG + 1/3LoG, which corresponds to the operator $(8/3\mathcal{B}^2 - 8/3\mathcal{I} - 1/3\mathcal{L})\mathcal{B}^p$.

This *ad hoc* solution is certainly not the best. Examples of optimized second-order differential operators are discussed in Section 6.6.

10.5 Edges in multichannel images

In multichannel images, it is significantly more difficult to analyze edges than to perform averaging, which simply can be performed channel by channel. The problem is that the different channels may contain conflicting information about edges. In channel A, the gradient can point to a different direction than in channel B. Thus a simple addition of the gradients in all channels

$$\sum_{p=1}^{P} \nabla g_p(\boldsymbol{x}) \tag{10.44}$$

is of no use. It may happen that the sum of the gradients over all channels is zero although the gradients themselves are not zero. Then we would be unable to distinguish this case from constant areas in all channels.

A more suitable measure of the total edge strength is the sum of the squared magnitudes of gradients in all channels

$$\sum_{p=1}^{P} |\nabla g_p|^2 = \sum_{p=1}^{P} \sum_{d=1}^{D} \left(\frac{\partial g_p}{\partial x_d}\right)^2 \tag{10.45}$$

While this expression gives a useful estimate of the overall edge strength, it still does not solve the problem of conflicting edge directions. An analysis of how edges are distributed in a D-dimensional multichannel image with P channels is possible with the following symmetric $\mathrm{D} \times \mathrm{D}$ matrix $\boldsymbol{S}$ (where D is the dimension of the image):

$$\boldsymbol{S} = \boldsymbol{J}^T \boldsymbol{J} \tag{10.46}$$

where $\boldsymbol{J}$ is known as the *Jacobian matrix*. This $\mathrm{P} \times \mathrm{D}$ matrix is defined as

$$\boldsymbol{J} = \begin{bmatrix} \dfrac{\partial g_1}{\partial x_1} & \dfrac{\partial g_1}{\partial x_2} & \cdots & \dfrac{\partial g_1}{\partial x_D} \\ \dfrac{\partial g_2}{\partial x_1} & \dfrac{\partial g_2}{\partial x_2} & \cdots & \dfrac{\partial g_2}{\partial x_D} \\ \vdots & & \ddots & \vdots \\ \dfrac{\partial g_P}{\partial x_1} & \dfrac{\partial g_P}{\partial x_2} & \cdots & \dfrac{\partial g_P}{\partial x_D} \end{bmatrix} \tag{10.47}$$

Thus the elements of the matrix $\boldsymbol{S}$ are

$$S_{kl} = \sum_{p=1}^{P} \frac{\partial g_p}{\partial x_k} \frac{\partial g_p}{\partial x_l} \qquad (10.48)$$

Since $\boldsymbol{S}$ is a symmetric matrix, we can diagonalize it by a suitable coordinate transform. Then, the diagonals contain terms of the form

$$\sum_{p=1}^{P} \left(\frac{\partial g_p}{\partial x'_d} \right)^2 \qquad (10.49)$$

In the case of an ideal edge, only one of the diagonal terms of the matrix will be nonzero. This is the direction perpendicular to the discontinuity. In all other directions it will be zero. Thus, $\boldsymbol{S}$ is a matrix of rank one in this case.

By contrast, if the edges in the different channels point randomly in all directions, all diagonal terms will be nonzero and equal. In this way, it is possible to distinguish random changes by noise from coherent edges. The trace of the matrix $\boldsymbol{S}$

$$\mathrm{trace}(\boldsymbol{S}) = \sum_{d=1}^{D} S_{dd} = \sum_{d=1}^{D} \sum_{p=1}^{P} \left(\frac{\partial g_p}{\partial x_d} \right)^2 \qquad (10.50)$$

gives a measure of the edge strength which we have already defined in Eq. (10.45). It is independent of the orientation of the edge since the trace of a symmetric matrix is invariant to a rotation of the coordinate system.

In conclusion, the matrix $\boldsymbol{S}$ is the key for edge detection in multichannel signals. Note that an arbitrary number of channels can be processed and that the number of computations increases only linearly with the number of channels. The analysis is, however, of order $O(D^2)$ in the dimension of the signal.

10.6 First-order tensor representation

10.6.1 Introduction

The vectorial representation discussed in Section 10.2.3 is incomplete. Although it is suitable for representing the orientation of simple neighborhoods, it cannot distinguish between neighborhoods with constant values and isotropic orientation distribution (e. g., uncorrelated noise). Both cases result in an orientation vector with zero magnitude.

Therefore, it is obvious that an adequate representation of gray-value changes in a local neighborhood must be more complex. Such a representation should be able to determine a unique orientation and to distinguish constant neighborhoods from neighborhoods without local orientation.

In their paper on analyzing oriented patterns, Kass and Witkin [5] started with the idea of using *directional derivative* filters by differentiating a *difference of Gaussian* (*DoG*, Section 10.4.2) filter (written in operator notation)

$$\mathcal{R}(\Theta) = [\cos\Theta \;\; \sin\Theta] \begin{bmatrix} \mathcal{D}_x(\mathcal{B}_1 - \mathcal{B}_2) \\ \mathcal{D}_y(\mathcal{B}_1 - \mathcal{B}_2) \end{bmatrix} = [\cos\Theta \;\; \sin\Theta] \begin{bmatrix} \mathcal{R}_x \\ \mathcal{R}_y \end{bmatrix}$$

where $\mathcal{B}_1$ and $\mathcal{B}_2$ denote two Gaussian smoothing masks with different variances. The direction in which this directional derivative is maximal in a mean square sense gives the orientation normal to lines of constant gray values. This approach results in the following expression for the variance of the directional derivative:

$$\mathcal{V}(\Theta) = \mathcal{B}(\mathcal{R}(\Theta) \cdot \mathcal{R}(\Theta)) \tag{10.51}$$

The directional derivative is squared and then smoothed by a binomial filter. This equation can also be interpreted as the inertia of an object as a function of the angle. The corresponding inertia tensor has the form

$$\begin{bmatrix} \mathcal{B}(\mathcal{R}_y \cdot \mathcal{R}_y) & -\mathcal{B}(\mathcal{R}_x \cdot \mathcal{R}_y) \\ -\mathcal{B}(\mathcal{R}_x \cdot \mathcal{R}_y) & \mathcal{B}(\mathcal{R}_x \cdot \mathcal{R}_x) \end{bmatrix} \tag{10.52}$$

Tensorial descriptions of local structure in images were also discussed by Bigün and Granlund [2] and Knutsson [6]. Without being aware of the work of these authors, Rao and Schunck [7] and Rao [8] proposed a moment tensor for the description and classification of oriented textures.

In the reminder of this chapter, several variants of tensorial description of local structure in multidimensional signals are discussed. The treatment here is more general in the sense that it is not restricted to 2-D single-channel images but that higher-dimensional and multichannel signals are considered as well.

10.6.2 The structure tensor

A suitable representation can be introduced by a optimization strategy to determine the orientation of a *simple neighborhood* in a slightly more general way as performed by Kass and Witkin [5] (Section 10.6.1). The optimum orientation is defined as the orientation that shows the least deviations from the directions of the gradient. A suitable measure for the deviation must treat gradients pointing in opposite directions equally. The squared scalar product between the gradient vector and the unit vector representing the local orientation $\bar{\boldsymbol{r}}$ meets this criterion

$$(\nabla g^T \bar{\boldsymbol{r}})^2 = |\nabla g|^2 \cos^2\left(\angle(\nabla g, \bar{\boldsymbol{r}})\right) \tag{10.53}$$

This quantity is proportional to the cosine squared of the angle between the gradient vector and the orientation vector and is thus maximal when ∇g and $\bar{\boldsymbol{r}}$ are parallel or antiparallel, and zero if they are perpendicular to each other. Therefore, the following integral is maximized in a D-dimensional local neighborhood:

$$\int w(\boldsymbol{x} - \boldsymbol{x}') \left(\nabla g(\boldsymbol{x}')^T \bar{\boldsymbol{r}}\right)^2 \mathrm{d}^D x' \tag{10.54}$$

where the window function w determines the size and shape of the neighborhood around a point $\boldsymbol{x}$ in which the orientation is averaged. The maximization problem must be solved for each point $\boldsymbol{x}$. Equation Eq. (10.54) can be rewritten in the following way:

$$\bar{\boldsymbol{r}}^T \boldsymbol{J} \bar{\boldsymbol{r}} \to \max \tag{10.55}$$

with

$$\boldsymbol{J} = \int_{-\infty}^{\infty} w(\boldsymbol{x} - \boldsymbol{x}') \left(\nabla g(\boldsymbol{x}') \nabla g(\boldsymbol{x}')^T\right) \mathrm{d}^D x'$$

The components of this symmetric $D \times D$ tensor are

$$J_{pq}(\boldsymbol{x}) = \int_{-\infty}^{\infty} w(\boldsymbol{x} - \boldsymbol{x}') \left(\frac{\partial g(\boldsymbol{x}')}{\partial x'_p} \frac{\partial g(\boldsymbol{x}')}{\partial x'_q}\right) \mathrm{d}^D x' \tag{10.56}$$

At this point it is easy to extend the tensor for multichannel signals. It is only needed to sum the tensor components for all channels. The weighting function might be different for each channel in order to consider the significance and spatial resolution of a certain channel. With all this, Eq. (10.56) extends to

$$J_{r,s}(\boldsymbol{x}) = \sum_{p=1}^{P} \int_{-\infty}^{\infty} w_p(\boldsymbol{x} - \boldsymbol{x}') \left(\frac{\partial g_p(\boldsymbol{x}')}{\partial x'_r} \frac{\partial g_p(\boldsymbol{x}')}{\partial x'_s}\right) \mathrm{d}^D x' \tag{10.57}$$

These equations indicate that a tensor is an adequate first-order representation of a local neighborhood. The term first-order has a double meaning. First, only first-order derivatives are involved. Second, only simple neighborhoods can be described in the sense that we can analyze in which direction(s) the gray values change. More complex structures such as structures with multiple orientations cannot be distinguished.

The complexity of Eqs. (10.55) and (10.56) somewhat obscures their simple meaning. The tensor is symmetric. By a rotation of the coordinate system, it can be brought into a diagonal form. Then, Eq. (10.55) reduces to

$$J = [\bar{r}'_1, \bar{r}'_2, \ldots, \bar{r}'_D] \begin{bmatrix} J_{1'1'} & 0 & \ldots & 0 \\ 0 & J_{2'2'} & \ldots & 0 \\ \vdots & \vdots & \ddots & \vdots \\ 0 & \ldots & \ldots & J_{D'D'} \end{bmatrix} \begin{bmatrix} \bar{r}'_1 \\ \bar{r}'_2 \\ \ldots \\ \bar{r}'_D \end{bmatrix} \rightarrow \max$$

or

$$J = \sum_{d'=1}^{D} J_{d'd'} (\bar{r}'_{d'})^2$$

Without loss of generality, we assume that $J_{1'1'} \geq J_{d'd'}\ \forall d' \neq 1$. Then, it is obvious that the unit vector $\bar{\boldsymbol{r}}' = [1\ 0\ \ldots\ 0]^T$ maximizes the foregoing expression. The maximum value is $J_{1'1'}$. In conclusion, this approach not only yields a tensor representation for the local neighborhood but also shows the way to determine the orientation. Essentially, we have to solve an *eigenvalue problem*. The eigenvalues λ_d and eigenvectors $\boldsymbol{k}_d$ of a D × D matrix are defined by

$$\boldsymbol{J}\boldsymbol{k}_d = \lambda_d \boldsymbol{k}_d \tag{10.58}$$

An eigenvector $\boldsymbol{k}_d$ of $\boldsymbol{J}$ is thus a vector that is not turned in direction by multiplication with the matrix $\boldsymbol{J}$, but is only multiplied by a scalar factor, the eigenvalue λ_w. This implies that the structure tensor becomes diagonal in a coordinate system that is spanned by the eigenvectors. For our further discussion it is important to keep in mind that the eigenvalues are all real and nonnegative and form an orthogonal basis [9, 10, 11].

10.6.3 Classification of local neighborhoods

The power of the tensor representation becomes apparent if we classify the eigenvalues of the structure tensor. The classifying criterion is the number of eigenvalues that are zero. If an eigenvalue is zero, this means that the gray values in the direction of the corresponding eigenvector do not change. The number of zero eigenvalues is also closely related to the rank of a matrix. The *rank* of a matrix is defined as the dimension of the subspace for which $\boldsymbol{J}\boldsymbol{k} \neq \boldsymbol{0}$. The space for which $\boldsymbol{J}\boldsymbol{k} = \boldsymbol{0}$ is denoted as the *null space*. The dimension of the null space is the dimension of the matrix minus the rank of the matrix and equal to the number of zero eigenvalues. We will perform an analysis of the eigenvalues for two and three dimensions. In two dimensions, we can distinguish the following cases:

$\lambda_1 = \lambda_2 = 0$, *rank 0 tensor.* Both eigenvalues are zero. The mean square magnitude of the gradient $(\lambda_1 + \lambda_2)$ is zero. The local neighborhood has constant values. It belongs to an object with a homogeneous feature;

$\lambda_1 > 0, \lambda_2 = 0$, *rank 1 tensor.* One eigenvalue is zero. The values do not change in the direction of the corresponding eigenvector. The local neighborhood is a simple neighborhood with ideal orientation. This could either be the *edge* of an object or an *oriented texture*;

$\lambda_1 > 0, \lambda_2 > 0$, *rank 2 tensor.* Both eigenvalues are unequal to zero. The gray values change in all directions as at the *corner* of an object or a texture with a distributed orientation. In the special case of $\lambda_1 = \lambda_2$, we speak of an isotropic gray-value structure since it changes equally in all directions.

The classification of the eigenvalues in three dimensions is similar to the 2-D case:

$\lambda_1 = \lambda_2 = \lambda_3 = 0$, *rank 0 tensor.* The gray values do not change in any direction; constant neighborhood.

$\lambda_1 > 0, \lambda_2 = \lambda_3 = 0$, *rank 1 tensor.* The gray values change only in one direction. This direction is given by the eigenvector to the nonzero eigenvalue. The neighborhood includes a boundary between two objects (*surface*) or a *layered texture.* In a space-time image, this means a constant motion of a spatially oriented pattern ("planar wave");

$\lambda_1 > 0, \lambda_2 > 0, \lambda_3 = 0$, *rank 2 tensor.* The gray values change in two directions and are constant in a third. The eigenvector to the zero eigenvalue gives the direction of the constant gray values. This happens at the edge of a three-dimensional object in a volumetric image, or if a pattern with distributed spatial orientation moves with constant speed; and

$\lambda_1 > 0, \lambda_2 > 0, \lambda_3 > 0$, *rank 3 tensor.* The gray values change in all three directions as at the corner of an object or a region with isotropic noise.

In practice, it will not be checked whether the eigenvalues are zero but below a critical threshold that is determined by the noise level in the image.

10.6.4 The inertia tensor

In this section, we discuss an alternative approach to describe the local structure in images. As a starting point, we consider an ideally oriented gray-value structure. As discussed in Section 10.2.2, the Fourier transform of such a structure reduces to a δ line in the direction of $\bar{\boldsymbol{r}}$. Thus it seems promising to determine local orientation in the Fourier domain because all we have to compute is the orientation of the line on which the spectral densities are nonzero. Bigün and Granlund [2] devised the following procedure:

- Use a window function to select a small local neighborhood from an image;
- Fourier transform the windowed image. The smaller the selected window, the more blurred the spectrum will be (*uncertainty relation*, see Section 3.2.3). This means that even with an ideal local orientation we will obtain a rather band-shaped distribution of the spectral energy; and
- Determine local orientation by fitting a straight line to the spectral density distribution. This yields the angle of the local orientation from the slope of the line.

The critical step of this procedure is fitting a straight line to the spectral densities in the Fourier domain. We cannot solve this problem exactly because it is generally *overdetermined*. When fitting a straight line, we minimize the sum of the squares of the distances of the data points to the line. This technique is known as the *total least squares* approach

$$\int_{-\infty}^{\infty} d^2(\boldsymbol{k},\bar{\boldsymbol{r}})|\hat{g}(\boldsymbol{k})|^2 \,\mathrm{d}^D k \rightarrow \min \tag{10.59}$$

The distance function is abbreviated using $d(\boldsymbol{k},\bar{\boldsymbol{r}})$. The integral runs over the whole wave number space; the wave numbers are weighted with the spectral density $|\hat{g}(\boldsymbol{k})|^2$. Equation (10.59) is not restricted to two dimensions, but is generally valid for *local orientation* or *linear symmetry* in a D-dimensional space. The distance vector $\boldsymbol{d}$ is given by

$$\boldsymbol{d} = \boldsymbol{k} - (\boldsymbol{k}^T\bar{\boldsymbol{r}})\bar{\boldsymbol{r}} \tag{10.60}$$

The square of the distance is then given by

$$|\boldsymbol{d}|^2 = |\boldsymbol{k} - (\boldsymbol{k}^T\bar{\boldsymbol{r}})\bar{\boldsymbol{r}}|^2 = |\boldsymbol{k}|^2 - (\boldsymbol{k}^T\bar{\boldsymbol{r}})^2 \tag{10.61}$$

In order to express the distance more clearly as a function of the vector $\bar{\boldsymbol{n}}$, we rewrite it in the following manner

$$|\boldsymbol{d}|^2 = \bar{\boldsymbol{r}}^T(\boldsymbol{I}(\boldsymbol{k}^T\boldsymbol{k}) - (\boldsymbol{k}\boldsymbol{k}^T))\bar{\boldsymbol{r}} \tag{10.62}$$

where $\boldsymbol{I}$ is the unit diagonal matrix. Substituting this expression into Eq. (10.59) we obtain

$$\bar{\boldsymbol{r}}^T\boldsymbol{J}'\bar{\boldsymbol{r}} \rightarrow \min \tag{10.63}$$

where $\boldsymbol{J}'$ is a symmetric tensor with the diagonal elements

$$J'_{r,r} = \sum_{r \neq s} \int_{-\infty}^{\infty} k_s^2 |\hat{g}(\boldsymbol{k})|^2 \, \mathrm{d}^D k \tag{10.64}$$

and the off-diagonal elements

$$J'_{r,s} = -\int_{-\infty}^{\infty} k_r k_s |\hat{g}(\boldsymbol{k})|^2 \, \mathrm{d}^D k, \quad r \neq s \tag{10.65}$$

The tensor $\boldsymbol{J}'$ is analogous to a well-known physical quantity, the *inertia tensor*. If we replace the wave number coordinates by space coordinates and the spectral density $|\hat{g}(\boldsymbol{k})|^2$ by the specific density ρ, Eqs. (10.59) and (10.63) constitute the equation to compute the inertia of a rotary body rotating around the $\bar{\boldsymbol{r}}$ axis.

With this analogy, we can reformulate the problem of determining local orientation. We must find the axis about which the rotary body, formed from the spectral density in Fourier space, rotates with minimum inertia. This body might have different shapes. We can relate its shape to the different solutions we get for the eigenvalues of the inertia tensor and thus for the solution of the local orientation problem in 2-D:

Ideal local orientation. The rotary body is a line. For a rotation around this line, the inertia vanishes. Consequently, the eigenvector to the eigenvalue zero coincides with the direction of the line. The other eigenvector is orthogonal to the line, and the corresponding eigenvalue is unequal to zero and gives the rotation axis for maximum inertia;

Isotropic gray value. In this case, the rotary body is a kind of flat isotropic disk. A preferred direction does not exist. Both eigenvalues are equal and the inertia is the same for rotations around all axes. We cannot find a minimum; and

Constant gray values. The rotary body degenerates to a point at the origin of the wave number space. The inertia is zero for rotation around any axis. Therefore both eigenvalues vanish.

We derived the inertia tensor approach in the Fourier domain. Now we will show how to compute the coefficients of the inertia tensor in the spatial domain. The integrals in Eqs. (10.64) and (10.65) contain terms of the form

$$k_q^2 |\hat{g}(\boldsymbol{k})|^2 = |\mathrm{i} k_q \hat{g}(\boldsymbol{k})|^2$$

and

$$k_p k_q |\hat{g}(\boldsymbol{k})|^2 = \mathrm{i} k_p \hat{g}(\boldsymbol{k}) [\mathrm{i} k_q \hat{g}(\boldsymbol{k})]^*$$

Integrals over these terms are *inner* or *scalar products* of the functions $ik_p\hat{g}(\boldsymbol{k})$. Since the inner product is preserved under the Fourier transform (Table 3.2), we can compute the corresponding integrals in the spatial domain as well. Multiplication of $\hat{g}(\boldsymbol{k})$ with ik_p in the wave number domain corresponds to the first spatial derivative in the direction of x_p in the space domain

$$\begin{aligned} J'_{pp}(\boldsymbol{x}) &= \sum_{q \neq p} \int_{-\infty}^{\infty} w(\boldsymbol{x}-\boldsymbol{x}') \left(\frac{\partial g}{\partial x_q}\right)^2 \mathrm{d}^D x' \\ J'_{pq}(\boldsymbol{x}) &= -\int_{-\infty}^{\infty} w(\boldsymbol{x}-\boldsymbol{x}') \frac{\partial g}{\partial x_p}\frac{\partial g}{\partial x_q} \mathrm{d}^D x' \end{aligned} \tag{10.66}$$

In Eq. (10.66), we already included the weighting with the window function w to select a local neighborhood.

The structure tensor discussed in Section 10.6.2, Eq. (10.56) and the inertia tensor are closely related

$$\boldsymbol{J}' = \mathrm{trace}(\boldsymbol{J})\boldsymbol{I} - \boldsymbol{J} \tag{10.67}$$

From this relationship it is evident that both matrices have the same set of eigenvectors. The eigenvalues λ_p are related by

$$\lambda_p = \sum_{q=1}^{n} \lambda_q - \lambda'_p, \quad \lambda'_p = \sum_{q=1}^{n} \lambda'_q - \lambda_p \tag{10.68}$$

Consequently, we can perform the eigenvalue analysis with any of the two matrices. For the inertia tensor, the direction of local orientation is given by the minimum eigenvalue, but for the structure tensor it is given by the maximum eigenvalue.

10.6.5 Computation of the structure tensor

The structure (Section 10.6.2) or inertia (Section 10.6.4) tensors can be computed straightforwardly as a combination of *linear convolution* and *nonlinear point operations*. The partial derivatives in Eqs. (10.56) and (10.66) are approximated by discrete derivative operators. The integration weighted with the window function is replaced by a convolution with a smoothing filter that has the shape of the window function. If we denote the discrete partial derivative operator with respect to the coordinate p by the operator $\mathcal{D}_p$ and the (isotropic) smoothing operator by $\mathcal{B}$, the local structure of a gray-value image can be computed with the structure tensor operator

$$\mathcal{J}_{pq} = \mathcal{B}(\mathcal{D}_p \cdot \mathcal{D}_q) \tag{10.69}$$

The equation is written in the operator notation introduced in Section 5.2.3. Pixelwise multiplication is denoted by a centered dot $\cdot$ to distinguish it from successive application of convolution operators. Equation (10.69) expresses in words that the $\mathcal{J}_{pq}$ component of the tensor is computed by convolving the image independently with $\mathcal{D}_p$ and $\mathcal{D}_q$, multiplying the two images pixelwise, and smoothing the resulting image with $\mathcal{B}$. For the inertia tensor method, a similar tensor operator can be formulated

$$\mathcal{J}'_{pp} = \sum_{q \neq p} \mathcal{B}(\mathcal{D}_q \cdot \mathcal{D}_q), \quad \mathcal{J}'_{pq} = -\mathcal{B}(\mathcal{D}_p \cdot \mathcal{D}_q) \tag{10.70}$$

These operators are valid in images of any dimension $D \geq 2$. In a D-dimensional image, the structure tensor has $D(D+1)/2$ independent components, hence 3 in 2-D and 6 in 3-D images. These components are best stored in a multichannel image with $D(D+1)/2$ channels.

The smoothing operations consume the largest number of operations. Therefore, a fast implementation must, in the first place, apply a fast smoothing algorithm. A fast algorithm can be established based on the general observation that higher-order features always show a lower resolution than the features from which they are computed. This means that the structure tensor can be stored on a coarser grid and thus in a smaller image. It is convenient and appropriate to reduce the scale by a factor of two by storing only every second pixel in every second row.

These procedures lead us in a natural way to multigrid data structures that are discussed in detail in Chapter 4.4. Multistep averaging is discussed in detail in Section 7.5.1.

Storing higher-order features on coarser scales has another significant advantage. Any subsequent processing is sped up simply by the fact that many fewer pixels have to be processed. A linear scale reduction by a factor of two results in a reduction in the number of pixels and the number of computations by a factor of 4 in two and 8 in three dimensions.

The accuracy of the orientation angle strongly depends on the implementation of the derivative filters. It is critical to use a derivative filter that has been optimized for a minimum error in the direction of the gradient. Such filters are discussed in Section 10.3.6.

10.6.6 Orientation vector

With the simple convolution and point operations discussed in the previous section, we computed the components of the structure tensor. In this section, we solve the eigenvalue problem to determine the orientation vector. In two dimensions, we can readily solve the eigenvalue problem. The orientation angle can be determined by rotating the inertia tensor into the principal axes coordinate system. As shown, for example, by Jähne [4], the orientation angle is given by

$$\tan 2\phi = \frac{2J_{12}}{J_{22} - J_{11}} \tag{10.71}$$

Without defining any prerequisites, we have obtained the anticipated angle doubling for orientation as discussed in Section 10.2.3 at the beginning of this chapter. Since $\tan 2\phi$ is gained from a quotient, we can regard the dividend as the y and the divisor as the x component of a vector and can form the *orientation vector* $\boldsymbol{o}$, as introduced by Granlund [1]

$$\boldsymbol{o} = \begin{bmatrix} J_{22} - J_{11} \\ 2J_{12} \end{bmatrix} \tag{10.72}$$

The argument of this vector gives the orientation angle and the magnitude a certainty measure for local orientation.

The result of Eq. (10.72) is remarkable in that the computation of the components of the orientation vector from the components of the orientation tensor requires just one subtraction and one multiplication by two. As these components of the orientation vector are all we need for further processing steps, we do not need the orientation angle or the magnitude of the vector. Thus, the solution of the eigenvalue problem in two dimensions is trivial.

10.6.7 Coherency

The orientation vector reduces local structure to local orientation. From three independent components of the symmetric tensor still only two are used. When we fail to observe an orientated structure in a neighborhood, we do not know whether any gray-value variations or distributed orientations are encountered. This information is included in the not yet used component of the tensor $J_{11}+J_{22}$, which gives the mean square magnitude of the gradient. Consequently, a well-equipped structure operator needs to include also the third component. A suitable linear combination is

$$\boldsymbol{s} = \begin{bmatrix} J_{11} + J_{22} \\ J_{11} - J_{22} \\ 2J_{12} \end{bmatrix} \tag{10.73}$$

This structure operator contains the two components of the orientation vector and, as an additional component, the mean square magnitude of the gradient, which is a rotation-invariant parameter. Comparing the latter with the magnitude of the orientation vector, a constant gray-value area and an isotropic gray-value structure without preferred orientation can be distinguished. In the first case, both squared quantities are zero; in the second, only the magnitude of the orientation vector. In the case of a perfectly oriented pattern, both quantities are equal. Thus their ratio seems to be a good *coherency measure* c_c for local orientation

$$c_c = \frac{(J_{22} - J_{11})^2 + 4J_{12}^2}{(J_{11} + J_{22})^2} = \left(\frac{\lambda_1 - \lambda_2}{\lambda_1 + \lambda_2}\right)^2 \tag{10.74}$$

The coherency c_c ranges from 0 to 1. For ideal local orientation ($\lambda_2 = 0, \lambda_1 > 0$) it is one, for an isotropic gray-value structure ($\lambda_1 = \lambda_2 > 0$) it is zero.

10.6.8 Color coding of the two-dimensional structure tensor

In Section 10.2.3 we discussed a color representation of the orientation vector. The question is whether it is also possible to represent the structure tensor adequately as a color image. A symmetric 2-D tensor has three independent pieces of information (Eq. (10.73)), which fit well to the three degrees of freedom available to represent color, for example, luminance, hue, and saturation.

A color represention of the structure tensor requires only two slight modifications as compared to the color representation for the orientation vector. First, instead of the length of the orientation vector, the squared magnitude of the gradient is mapped onto the intensity. Second, the coherency measure Eq. (10.74) is used as the saturation. In the color representation for the orientation vector, the saturation is always one. The angle of the orientation vector is still represented as the hue.

In practice, a slight modification of this color representation is useful. The squared magnitude of the gradient shows variations too large to be displayed in the narrow dynamic range of a display screen with only 256 luminance levels. Therefore, a suitable normalization is required. The basic idea of this normalization is to compare the squared magnitude of the gradient with the noise level. Once the gradient is well above the noise level it is regarded as a significant piece of information. This train of thoughts suggests the following normalization for the intensity I

$$I = \frac{J_{11} + J_{22}}{(J_{11} + J_{22}) + \gamma\sigma_n^2} \tag{10.75}$$

where σ_n is an estimate of the standard deviation of the noise level. This normalization provides a rapid transition of the luminance from one, when the magnitude of the gradient is larger than σ_n, to zero when the gradient is smaller than σ_n. The factor γ is used to optimize the display.

10.7 References

[1] Granlund, G. H., (1978). In search of a general picture processing operator. *Comp. Graph. Imag. Process.*, **8**:155–173.

[2] Bigün, J. and Granlund, G. H., (1987). Optimal orientation detection of linear symmetry. In *Proceedings ICCV'87, London 1987*, pp. 433–438, IEEE. Washington, DC: IEEE Computer Society Press.

[3] Granlund, G. H. and Knutsson, H., (1995). *Signal Processing for Computer Vision.* Norwell, MA: Kluwer Academic Publishers.

[4] Jähne, B., (1997). *Digital Image Processing—Concepts, Algorithms, and Scientific Applications,* 4th edition. New York: Springer.

[5] Kass, M. and Witkin, A., (1987). Analysing oriented patterns. *Comp. Vis. Graph. Im. Process.*, **37**:362–385.

[6] Knutsson, H., (1989). Representing local structure using tensors. In *The 6th Scandinavian Conference on Image Analysis, Oulu, Finland, June 19-22, 1989.*

[7] Rao, A. R. and Schunck, B. G., (1989). Computing oriented texture fields. In *Proceedings CVPR '89, San Diego, CA*, pp. 61–68, IEEE. Washington, DC: IEEE Computer Society Press.

[8] Rao, A. R., (1990). *A Taxonomy for Texture Description and Identification.* New York: Springer.

[9] Golub, G. H. and van Loan, C. F., (1989). *Matrix Computations. Johns Hopkins Series in the Mathematical Sciences, No. 3.* Baltimore: The Johns Hopkins University Press.

[10] Hoffman, K. and Kunze, R., (1971). *Linear Algebra,* 2nd edition. Englewood Cliffs, NJ: Prentice-Hall.

[11] Press, W. H., Flannery, B. P., Teukolsky, S. A., and Vetterling, W. T., (1992). *Numeral Recipes in C: the Art of Scientific Computing.* New York: Cambridge University Press.

11 Principles for Automatic Scale Selection

Tony Lindeberg

Computational Vision and Active Perception Laboratory (CVAP)
KTH (Royal Institute of Technology), Stockholm, Sweden

Handbook of Computer Vision and Applications
Volume 2
Signal Processing and Pattern Recognition

All figures copyright © 1999 by Tony Lindeberg
Copyright © 1999 by Academic Press
All rights of reproduction in any form reserved.
ISBN 0-12-379772-1/$30.00

11.1 Introduction

An inherent property of objects in the world is that they only exist as meaningful entities over certain ranges of scale. If one aims at describing the structure of unknown real-world signals, then a multiscale representation of data is of crucial importance. Whereas conventional scale-space theory provides a well-founded framework for dealing with image structures at different scales, this theory does not directly address the problem of how to *select* appropriate scales for further analysis.

This chapter outlines a systematic methodology for formulating mechanisms for automatic scale selection in the domains of feature detection and image matching.

11.2 Multiscale differential image geometry

A natural and powerful framework for representing image data at the earliest stages of visual processing is by computing differential geometric image descriptors at multiple scales [1, 2]. This section summarizes essential components of this *scale-space theory* [3], which also constitutes the vocabulary for expressing the scale selection mechanisms.

11.2.1 Scale-space representation

Given any continuous signal $g\colon \mathbb{R}^D \to \mathbb{R}$, its linear *scale-space representation* $L\colon \mathbb{R}^D \times \mathbb{R}_+ \to \mathbb{R}$ is defined as the solution to the *diffusion equation*

$$\partial_t L = \frac{1}{2}\nabla^2 L = \frac{1}{2}\sum_{d=1}^{D} \partial_{x_d x_d} L \tag{11.1}$$

with initial condition $L(\boldsymbol{x};0) = g(\boldsymbol{x})$. Equivalently, this family can be defined by convolution with *Gaussian kernels* $h(\boldsymbol{x};t)$ of various width t

$$L(\boldsymbol{x};t) = h(\boldsymbol{x};t) * g(\boldsymbol{x}) \tag{11.2}$$

where $h\colon \mathbb{R}^D \times \mathbb{R}_+ \to \mathbb{R}$ is given by

$$h(\boldsymbol{x},t) = \frac{1}{(2\pi t)^{D/2}} \exp\left(-\frac{x_1^2 + \ldots + x_D^2}{2t}\right) \tag{11.3}$$

and $\boldsymbol{x} = [x_1, \ldots, x_D]^T$. There are several results [3, 4, 5, 6, 7, 8, 9, 10, 11, 12, 13, 14, 15, 16, 17, 18, 19] stating that within the class of linear transformations the Gaussian kernel is the unique kernel for generating a scale-space. The conditions that specify the uniqueness are essentially linearity and shift invariance combined with different ways of formalizing the notion that new structures should not be created in the transformation from a finer to a coarser scale (see also [18, 20, 21, 22, 23] for reviews).

11.2.2 Gaussian and directional derivative operators

From the scale-space representation, we can at any level of scale define *scale-space derivatives* by

$$L_{x^\alpha}(\boldsymbol{x};t) = (\partial_{x^\alpha} L)(\boldsymbol{x};t) = \partial_{x^\alpha}(h(\boldsymbol{x};t) * g(\boldsymbol{x})) \tag{11.4}$$

where $\alpha = [\alpha_1, \ldots, \alpha_D]^T$ and $\partial_{x^\alpha} L = L_{{x_1}^{\alpha_1} \ldots {x_D}^{\alpha_D}}$ constitute multiindex notation for the derivative operator ∂_{x^α}. Because differentiation commutes with convolution, the scale-space derivatives can be written

$$L_{x^\alpha}(\boldsymbol{x};t) = (\partial_{x^\alpha} h(\cdot;\ t)) * g(\boldsymbol{x}) \tag{11.5}$$

and correspond to convolving the original image g with Gaussian derivative kernels $\partial_{x^\alpha} h$. Figure 11.1 shows a few examples of such *Gaussian derivative operators.*

The Gaussian derivatives provide a compact way to characterize the local image structure around a certain image point at any scale. With access to Gaussian derivative responses of all orders at one image point $\boldsymbol{x}_0$, we can for any $\boldsymbol{x}$ in a neighborhood of $\boldsymbol{x}_0$ reconstruct the original scale-space representation by a local Taylor expansion. With θ_α denoting the Taylor coefficient of order α, this reconstruction can be written

$$L(\boldsymbol{x};t) = \sum_{\alpha} \theta_\alpha L_{x^\alpha}(\boldsymbol{x}_0;\ t)\,(\boldsymbol{x} - \boldsymbol{x}_0)^\alpha \tag{11.6}$$

Truncating this representation to derivatives up to order N, results in a so-called *N-jet representation* [11].

The Gaussian derivatives according to Eq. (11.4) correspond to partial derivatives along the Cartesian coordinate directions. Using the well-known expression for the nth-order directional derivative $\partial_{\bar{\beta}}^n$ of a function L in any direction β

$$\partial_{\bar{\beta}}^n L = (\cos\beta\, \partial_x + \sin\beta\, \partial_y)^n L \tag{11.7}$$

we can express a *directional derivative* in any direction $(\cos\beta, \sin\beta)$ as a linear combination of the Cartesian Gaussian derivatives. (This property is sometimes referred to as "steerability" [24, 25].) For orders up to three, the explicit expressions are

$$\begin{aligned}
\partial_{\bar{\beta}} L &= L_x \cos\beta + L_y \sin\beta \\
\partial_{\bar{\beta}}^2 L &= L_{xx} \cos^2\beta + 2L_{xy} \cos\beta \sin\beta + L_{yy} \sin^2\beta \\
\partial_{\bar{\beta}}^3 L &= L_{xxx} \cos^3\beta + 3L_{xxy} \cos^2\beta \sin\beta \\
&+ 3L_{xyy} \cos\beta \sin^2\beta + L_{yyy} \sin^3\beta
\end{aligned} \tag{11.8}$$

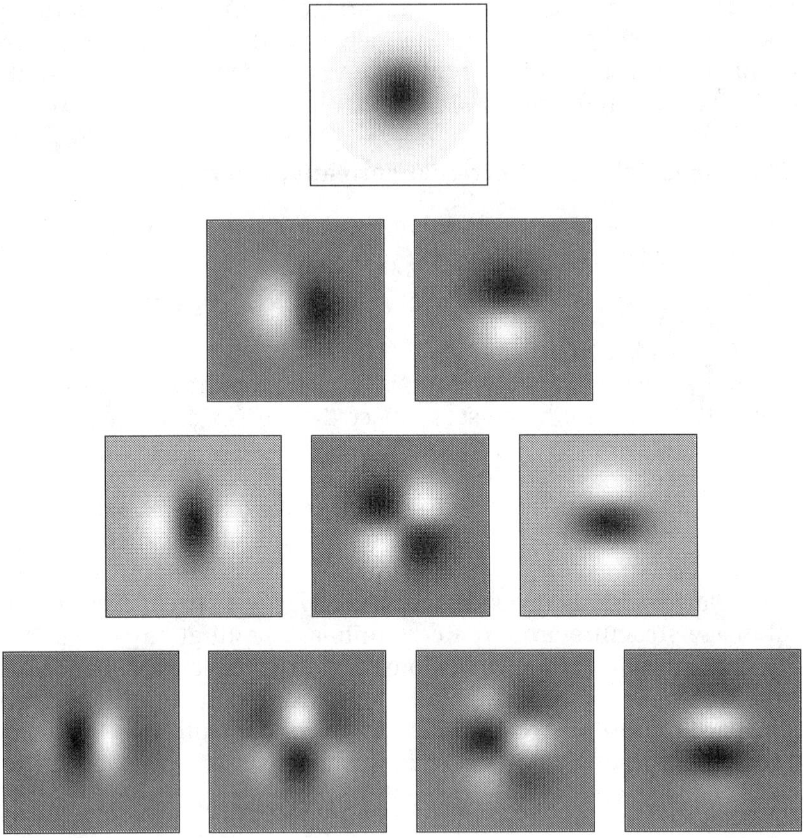

Figure 11.1: *Gaussian derivative kernels up to order three in the 2-D case.*

Figure 11.2 shows an example of computing first- and second-order directional derivatives in this way, based on the Gaussian derivative operators in Fig. 11.1.

More generally, and with reference to Eq. (11.6), it is worth noting that the Gaussian derivatives at any scale (including the zero-order derivative) serve as a complete linear basis, implying that any linear filter can be expressed as a (possibly infinite) linear combination of Gaussian derivatives.

11.2.3 Differential invariants

A problem with image descriptors as defined from Eqs. (11.4) and (11.7) is that they depend upon the orientation of the coordinate system. A simple way to define image descriptors that are invariant to rotations in

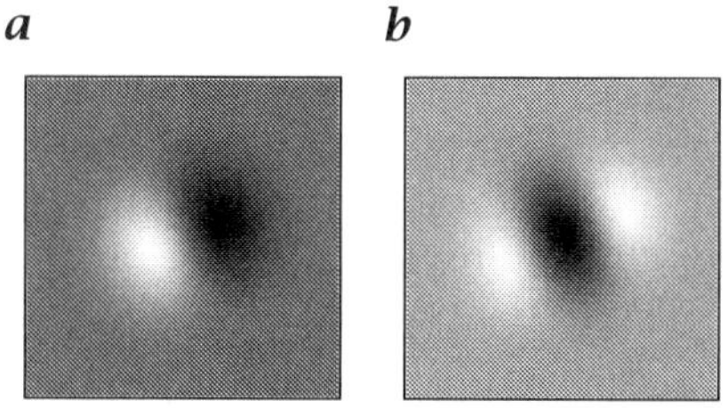

Figure 11.2: ***a*** *First- and* ***b*** *second-order directional derivative approximation kernels in the 22.5 degree direction computed as a linear combination of the Gaussian derivative operators.*

the image plane is by considering directional derivatives in a preferred coordinate system aligned to the local image structure.

One such choice of preferred directions is to introduce a local orthonormal coordinate system (u, v) at any point P_0, with the v-axis parallel to the gradient direction at P_0, and the u-axis perpendicular, that is, $e_v = (\cos\varphi, \sin\varphi)^T$ and $e_u = (\sin\varphi, -\cos\varphi)^T$, where

$$e_v|_{P_0} = \begin{pmatrix} \cos\varphi \\ \sin\varphi \end{pmatrix} = \frac{1}{\sqrt{L_x^2 + L_y^2}} \begin{pmatrix} L_x \\ L_y \end{pmatrix}\Bigg|_{P_0} \tag{11.9}$$

In terms of Cartesian coordinates, the corresponding local directional derivative operators can then be written

$$\partial_u = \sin\varphi\,\partial_x - \cos\varphi\,\partial_y, \quad \partial_v = \cos\varphi\,\partial_x + \sin\varphi\,\partial_y \tag{11.10}$$

and for the lowest orders of differentiation we have

$$\begin{aligned}
&L_u = 0, \quad L_v = \sqrt{L_x^2 + L_y^2} \\
L_v^2 L_{uu} &= L_{xx}L_y^2 - 2L_{xy}L_xL_y + L_{yy}L_x^2 \\
L_v^2 L_{uv} &= L_xL_y(L_{xx} - L_{yy}) - (L_x^2 - L_y^2)L_{xy} \\
L_v^2 L_{vv} &= L_x^2 L_{xx} + 2L_xL_yL_{xy} + L_y^2 L_{yy} \\
L_v^3 L_{uuu} &= L_y(L_y^2 L_{xxx} + 3L_x^2 L_{xyy}) \\
&\quad -L_x(L_x^2 L_{yyy} + 3L_y^2 L_{xxy}) \\
L_v^3 L_{uuv} &= L_x(L_y^2 L_{xxx} + (L_x^2 - 2L_y^2)L_{xyy}) \\
&\quad +L_y(L_x^2 L_{yyy} + (L_y^2 - 2L_x^2)L_{xxy}) \\
L_v^3 L_{uvv} &= L_y(L_x^2 L_{xxx} + (L_y^2 - 2L_x^2)L_{xyy}) \\
&\quad +L_x((2L_y^2 - L_x^2)L_{xxy} - L_y^2 L_{yyy})
\end{aligned} \tag{11.11}$$

By definition, these differential definition are invariant under rotations of the image plane, and this (u, v)-coordinate system is characterized by the first-order directional derivatives L_u being zero.

Another natural choice of a preferred coordinate system is to align a local (p, q)-coordinate system to the eigenvectors of the Hessian matrix. To express directional derivatives in such coordinates, characterized by the mixed second-order derivative L_{pq} being zero, we can rotate the coordinate system by an angle ψ defined by

$$\begin{aligned} \cos\psi\,|_{(x_0,y_0)} &= \left.\sqrt{\frac{1}{2}\left(1+\frac{L_{xx}-L_{yy}}{\sqrt{(L_{xx}-L_{yy})^2+4L_{xy}^2}}\right)}\,\right|_{(x_0,y_0)} \\ \sin\psi\,|_{(x_0,y_0)} &= (\operatorname{sgn} L_{xy}) \left.\sqrt{\frac{1}{2}\left(1-\frac{L_{xx}-L_{yy}}{\sqrt{(L_{xx}-L_{yy})^2+4L_{xy}^2}}\right)}\,\right|_{(x_0,y_0)} \end{aligned} \tag{11.12}$$

and define unit vectors in the p- and q-directions by $e_p = (\sin\psi, -\cos\psi)$ and $e_q = (\cos\psi, \sin\psi)$ with associated directional derivative operators

$$\partial_p = \sin\psi\,\partial_x - \cos\psi\,\partial_y, \qquad \partial_q = \cos\psi\,\partial_x + \sin\psi\,\partial_y \tag{11.13}$$

Then, it is straightforward to verify that this definition implies that

$$\begin{aligned} L_{pq} = \partial_p\partial_q L &= (\cos\psi\,\partial_x + \sin\psi\,\partial_y)\,(\sin\psi\,\partial_x - \cos\psi\,\partial_y)L \\ &= \cos\psi\,\sin\psi\,(L_{xx} - L_{yy}) - (\cos^2\psi - \sin^2\psi)\,L_{xy} = 0 \end{aligned} \tag{11.14}$$

A more general class of (nonlinear) differential invariants will be considered in Section 11.3.2.

11.2.4 Windowed spectral moment descriptors

The differential invariants defined so far depend upon the *local* differential geometry at any given *image point*. One way of defining *regional* image descriptors, which reflect the intensity distribution over *image patches*, is by considering windowed spectral moment descriptors (see also [3, 26, 27]). Using Plancherel's relation

$$\int_{\omega\in\mathbb{R}^2} \hat{f}_1(\omega)\,\hat{f}_2^*(\omega)\,d\omega = (2\pi)^2 \int_{x\in\mathbb{R}^2} f_1(x)\,f_2^*(x)\,dx \tag{11.15}$$

where $\hat{h}_i(\omega)$ denotes the Fourier transform of $h_i(x)$ (with $\omega = 2\pi k$ as variable in the frequency domain) and by letting $f_1 = L_{x^\alpha}$ and $f_2 = L_{x^\beta}$, we have

$$\int_{\omega\in\mathbb{R}^2} (i\omega)^{|\alpha|+|\beta|}\,|\hat{L}|^2(\omega)\,d\omega = (2\pi)^2 \int_{x\in\mathbb{R}^2} L_{x^\alpha}(x)\,L_{x^\beta}(x)\,dx \tag{11.16}$$

Let us next introduce a Gaussian window function $h(\cdot;\,s)$, depending on an *integration scale parameter* s, in addition to the *local scale parameter* t of the ordinary scale-space representation. Then, we can define the following *windowed spectral moments*:

$$\begin{aligned}
\mu_{20}(x;\, t, s) &= \int_{\xi \in \mathbb{R}^2} L_x^2(\xi;\, t)\, h(x-\xi;\, s)\, \mathrm{d}\xi, \\
\mu_{11}(x;\, t, s) &= \int_{\xi \in \mathbb{R}^2} L_x(\xi;\, t)\, L_y(\xi;\, t)\, h(x-\xi;\, s)\, \mathrm{d}\xi, \\
\mu_{02}(x;\, t, s) &= \int_{\xi \in \mathbb{R}^2} L_y^2(\xi;\, t)\, h(x-\xi;\, s)\, \mathrm{d}\xi
\end{aligned} \tag{11.17}$$

and higher-order spectral moment descriptors can be defined in an analogous fashion.

11.2.5 The scale-space framework for a visual front-end

The image descriptors defined in Section 11.2.2 to Section 11.2.4 provide a useful basis for expressing a large number of early visual operations, including image representation, feature detection, stereo matching, optic flow and shape estimation. There is also a close connection to biological vision. Neurophysiological studies by Young [28, 29] have shown that there are receptive fields in the mammalian retina and visual cortex, which can be well modeled by Gaussian derivatives up to order four. In these respects, the scale-space representation with its associated Gaussian derivative operators can be seen as a canonical idealized model of a visual front-end.

When computing these descriptors at multiple scales, however, as is necessary to capture the complex multiscale nature of our world, one can expect these descriptors to accurately reflect interesting image structures at certain scales, while the responses may be less useful at other scales. To simplify the interpretation tasks of later processing stages, a key problem of a visual front-end (in addition to making image structures more explicit by computing differential image descriptors at multiple scales) is to provide hypothesis about how to select locally appropriate scales for describing the data set.

11.2.6 The need for automatic scale selection

To illustrate the need for an explicit mechanism for automatic scale selection, let us first consider the problem of detecting edges. The left column in Fig. 11.3 shows the result of applying a standard edge detector (described in Section 11.4.1) to an image, which have been smoothed by convolution with Gaussian kernels of different widths.

As can be seen, different types of edge structures give rise to edge curves at different scales. For example, the shadow of the arm only appears as a connected edge curve at coarse scales. If such coarse scales are used at the finger tip, however, the shape distortions due to scale-space smoothing will be substantial. Hence, to extract this edge with

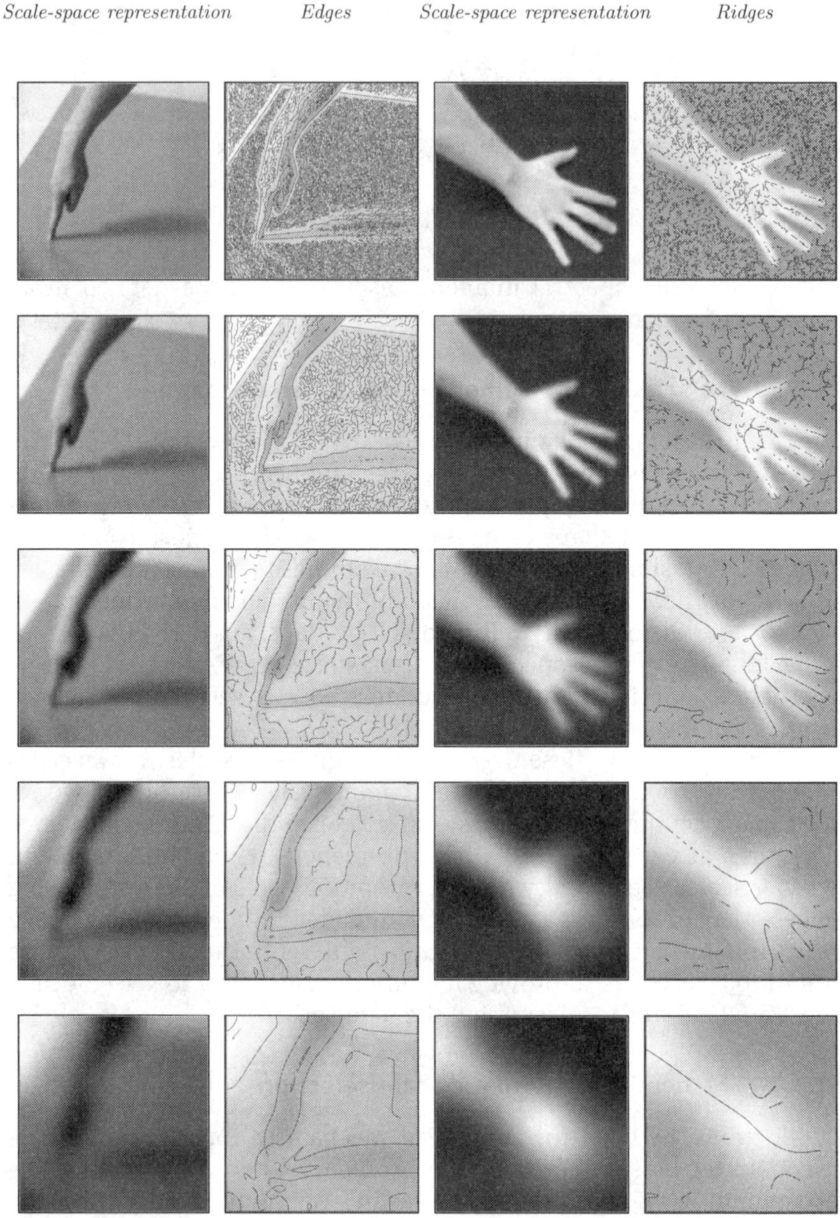

Figure 11.3: *Edges and ridges computed at different scales in scale-space (scale levels* $t = 1.0, 4.0, 16.0, 64.0$ *and* 256.0 *from top to bottom) using a differential geometric edge detector and ridge detector, respectively. (Image size:* 256×256 *pixels.)*

a reasonable trade-off between detection and localization properties, the only reasonable choice is to *allow the scale levels to vary along the edge.*

The right column in Fig. 11.3 shows corresponding results for a ridge detector (described in Section 11.4.2). Different types of ridge structures give rise to qualitatively different types of ridge curves depending on the scale level. The fingers respond at $t \approx 16$, whereas the arm as a whole is extracted as a long ridge curve at $t \approx 256$.

For these reasons, and because the choice of scale levels crucially affects the performance of any feature detector, and different scale levels will, in general, be required in different parts of the image, it is essential to *complement feature detectors by explicit mechanisms that automatically adapt the scale levels to the local image structure.*

11.3 A general scale-selection principle

A powerful approach to perform local and adaptive scale selection is by detecting local extrema over scales of normalized differential entities. This chapter presents a general theory by first introducing the notion of normalized derivatives, and then showing how local extrema over scales of normalized differential entities reflect the characteristic size of corresponding image structures.

11.3.1 Normalized derivatives and intuitive idea for scale selection

A well-known property of the scale-space representation is that the amplitude of spatial derivatives

$$L_{x^\alpha}(\cdot;\, t) = \partial_{x^\alpha} L(\cdot;\, t) = \partial_{x_1^{\alpha_1}} \ldots \partial_{x_D^{\alpha_D}} L(\cdot;\, t)$$

in general *decrease with scale,* that is, if a signal is subject to scale-space smoothing, then the numerical values of spatial derivatives computed from the smoothed data can be expected to decrease. This is a direct consequence of the *nonenhancement property of local extrema,* which means that the value at a local maximum cannot increase, and the value at a local minimum cannot decrease [3, 4]. In other words, the amplitude of the variations in a signal will always decrease with scale.

As a simple example of this, consider a sinusoidal input signal of some given angular frequency $\omega_0 = 2\pi k_0$; for simplicity, in one dimension

$$g(x) = \sin \omega_0 x \qquad (11.18)$$

It is straightforward to show that the solution of the diffusion equation is given by

$$L(x;\ t) = e^{-\omega_0^2 t/2} \sin \omega_0 x \tag{11.19}$$

Thus, the amplitude of the scale-space representation L_{max} as well as the amplitude of the mth-order smoothed derivative $L_{x^m,max}$ decrease exponentially with scale

$$L_{max}(t) = e^{-\omega_0^2 t/2}, \quad L_{x^m,max}(t) = \omega_0^m \, e^{-\omega_0^2 t/2}$$

Let us next introduce a γ-*normalized derivative operator* defined by

$$\partial_{\xi,\gamma-\text{norm}} = t^{\gamma/2} \, \partial_x \tag{11.20}$$

that corresponds to the change of variables

$$\xi = \frac{x}{t^{\gamma/2}} \tag{11.21}$$

For the sinusoidal signal, the amplitude of an mth-order normalized derivative as function of scale is given by

$$L_{\xi^m,max}(t) = t^{m\gamma/2} \, \omega_0^m \, e^{-\omega_0^2 t/2} \tag{11.22}$$

that is, it first increases and then decreases. Moreover, it assumes a unique maximum at $t_{max,L_{\xi^m}} = \frac{\gamma m}{\omega_0^2}$. If we define a scale parameter σ of dimension length by $\sigma = \sqrt{t}$ and introduce the wavelength λ_0 of the signal by $\lambda_0 = 2\pi/\omega_0$, we can see that the scale at which the amplitude of the γ-normalized derivative assumes its maximum over scales is *proportional* to the wavelength λ_0 of the signal

$$\sigma_{max,L_{\xi^m}} = \frac{\sqrt{\gamma m}}{2\pi} \lambda_0 \tag{11.23}$$

The maximum value over scales is

$$L_{\xi^m,max}(t_{max,L_{\xi^m}}) = \frac{(\gamma m)^{\gamma m/2}}{e^{\gamma m/2}} \, \omega_0^{(1-\gamma)m} \tag{11.24}$$

In the case when $\gamma = 1$, this maximum value is *independent* of the frequency of the signal (see Fig. 11.4), and the situation is highly symmetric, that is, given any scale t_0, the maximally amplified frequency is given by $\omega_{max} = \sqrt{m/t_0}$, and for any ω_0 the scale with maximum amplification is $t_{max} = m/\omega_0^2$. In other words, for normalized derivatives with $\gamma = 1$ it holds that sinusoidal signals are treated in a similar (scale-invariant) way independent of their frequency (see Fig. 11.4).

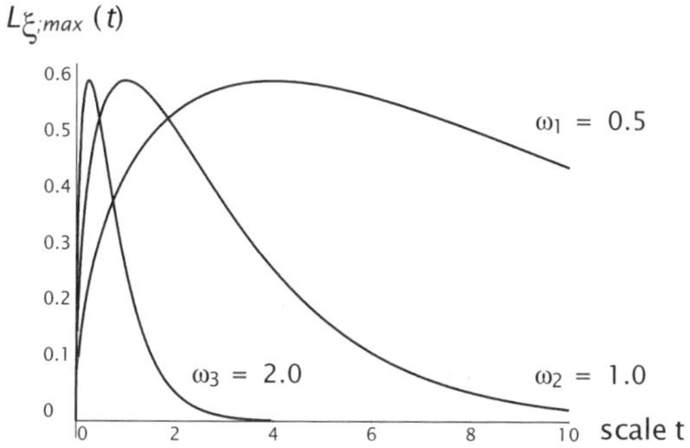

Figure 11.4: *The amplitude of first-order normalized derivatives as function of scale for sinusoidal input signals of different frequency ($\omega_1 = 0.5$, $\omega_2 = 1.0$ and $\omega_3 = 2.0$).*

11.3.2 A general principle for automatic scale selection

The example shows that the scale at which a normalized derivative assumes its maximum over scales is for a sinusoidal signal proportional to the wavelength of the signal. In this respect, maxima over scales of normalized derivatives reflect the scales over which spatial variations take place in the signal. This property is, however, not restricted to sine wave patterns or to image measurements in terms of linear derivative operators of a certain order. On the contrary, it applies to a large class of image descriptors that can be formulated as multiscale differential invariants expressed in terms of Gaussian derivatives. In [3], the following scale selection principle was proposed:

> *In the absence of other evidence, assume that a scale level, at which some (possibly nonlinear) combination of normalized derivatives assumes a local maximum over scales, can be treated as reflecting a characteristic length of a corresponding structure in the data.*

11.3.3 Properties of the scale-selection principle

A basic justification for the forementioned statement can be obtained from the fact that for a large class of (possibly nonlinear) combinations of normalized derivatives it holds that maxima over scales exhibit desirable behavior under rescalings of the intensity pattern. If the input image is rescaled by a constant scaling factor s, then the scale at which the maximum is assumed will be multiplied by the same factor (if measured in units of $\sigma = \sqrt{t}$). This is a fundamental requirement on a scale selection mechanism, as it guarantees that image operations commute with size variations.

Scaling properties. For two signals g and g' related by

$$g(x) = g'(sx) \tag{11.25}$$

the corresponding normalized derivatives defined from the scale-space representations L and L' on the two domains are related according to

$$\partial_{\xi^m} L(x;\ t) = s^{m(1-\gamma)}\, \partial_{\xi'^m} L'(x';\ t') \tag{11.26}$$

and when $\gamma = 1$, the normalized derivatives are equal at corresponding points $(x;\ t)$ and $(x';\ t') = (sx;\ s^2 t)$.

When $\gamma \neq 1$, a weaker scale-invariance properties holds. Let us consider a homogeneous polynomial differential invariant $\mathcal{D}L$ of the form

$$\mathcal{D}L = \sum_{i=1}^{I} c_i \prod_{j=1}^{J} L_{x^{\alpha_{ij}}} \quad \text{with} \quad \sum_{j=1}^{J} |\alpha_{ij}| = M \tag{11.27}$$

The sum of the orders of differentiation in the last term does not depend on the index i of that term. Then, normalized differential expressions in the two domains are related by

$$\mathcal{D}_{\gamma-\text{norm}} L = s^{M(1-\gamma)}\, \mathcal{D}'_{\gamma-\text{norm}} L' \tag{11.28}$$

that is, magnitude measures scale according to a power law. Local maxima over scales are, however, still preserved

$$\partial_t \left(\mathcal{D}_{\gamma-\text{norm}} L\right) = 0 \qquad \Leftrightarrow \qquad \partial_{t'} \left(\mathcal{D}'_{\gamma-\text{norm}} L'\right) = 0 \tag{11.29}$$

that gives sufficient scale invariance to support the scale selection methodology. More generally, it can be shown that the notion of γ-normalized derivatives arises *by necessity*, given natural requirements of a scale-selection mechanism [30].

11.3.4 Interpretation of normalized derivatives

L_p-norms. For a D-dimensional signal, it can be shown that the variation over scales of the L_p-norm of an mth-order normalized Gaussian derivative kernel is given by

$$\|h_{\xi^m}(\cdot;\ t)\|_p = \sqrt{t}^{\,m(\gamma-1)+D(1/p-1)}\, \|h_{\xi^m}(\cdot;\ t)\|_p \tag{11.30}$$

In other words, the L_p-norm of the mth-order Gaussian derivative kernel is constant over scales if and only if

$$p = \frac{1}{1 + \frac{m}{D}(1-\gamma)} \tag{11.31}$$

Hence, the γ-normalized derivative concept be interpreted as an L_p-normalization of the Gaussian derivative kernels over scales for a specific value of p, which depends upon γ, the dimension as well as the order m of differentiation. The perfectly scale-invariant case $\gamma = 1$ gives $p = 1$ for all orders m and corresponds to L_1-normalization of the Gaussian derivative kernels.

Power spectra. For a signal $g\colon \mathbb{R}^2 \to \mathbb{R}$ having a power spectrum of the form

$$S_g(\omega_1, \omega_2) = (\hat{f}\hat{f}^*)(\omega_1, \omega_2) = |\omega|^{-2\alpha} = (\omega_1^2 + \omega_2^2)^{-\alpha} \tag{11.32}$$

it can be shown that the variation over scales of the following energy measure:

$$P_{L(\cdot;\, t)} = \int_{x \in \mathbb{R}^2} |\nabla L(x;\, t)|^2 \,\mathrm{d}x \tag{11.33}$$

is given by

$$P_{\mathrm{norm}}(\cdot;\, t) = t^{\gamma} P_{L(\cdot;\, t)} \sim t^{\alpha+\gamma-2} \tag{11.34}$$

This expression is independent of scale if and only if $\alpha = 2 - \gamma$. In other words, in the 2-D case the normalized derivative model is *neutral* with respect to power spectra of the form $S_g(\omega) = |\omega|^{-2(2-\gamma)}$ (and natural images often have power spectra of this form [31]).

11.4 Feature detection with automatic scale selection

This section shows how the general principle for automatic scale selection described in Section 11.3.2 can be integrated with various types of feature detectors.

11.4.1 Edge detection

At any scale in scale-space, let us define an edge point as a point at which the second directional derivative L_{vv} in the v-direction is zero, and the third directional derivative L_{vvv} is negative

$$\begin{cases} L_{vv} = 0, \\ L_{vvv} < 0 \end{cases} \tag{11.35}$$

The edges in Fig. 11.3 have been computed according to this definition [3, 32, 33, 34].

In view of the scale-selection principle, a natural extension of this notion of *nonmaximum suppression* is by defining a *scale-space edge* a curve on this *edge surface*, such that some measure of edge strength $\mathcal{E}_{\gamma\text{-norm}}L$ assumes locally maxima with respect to scale on this curve

$$\begin{cases} \partial_t(\mathcal{E}_{\gamma\text{-norm}}L(x,y;\ t)) = 0, \\ \partial_{tt}(\mathcal{E}_{\gamma\text{-norm}}L(x,y;\ t)) < 0, \\ L_{vv}(x,y;\ t) = 0, \\ L_{vvv}(x,y;\ t) < 0 \end{cases} \tag{11.36}$$

Based on the γ-parameterized normalized derivative concept, we shall here consider the following two edge strength measures:

$$\mathcal{G}_{\gamma\text{-norm}}L = t^{\gamma}L_v^2 \quad \text{and} \quad \mathcal{T}_{\gamma\text{-norm}}L = -t^{3\gamma}L_v^3 L_{vvv} \tag{11.37}$$

Qualitative properties. For a *diffuse step edge*, defined as the primitive function of a 1-D Gaussian

$$f_{t_0}(x,y) = \int_{x'=-\infty}^{x} h(x';\ t_0)\,dx'$$

each of these edge strength measures assumes a unique maximum over scales at $t_{\mathcal{G}_{\gamma\text{-norm}}} = t_{\mathcal{T}_{\gamma\text{-norm}}} = (\gamma/(1-\gamma))t_0$. Requiring this maximum to occur at t_0 gives $\gamma = 1/2$.

For a local model of an *edge bifurcation*, expressed as

$$L(x;\ t) = \tfrac{1}{4}x^4 + \tfrac{3}{2}x^2(t-t_b) + \tfrac{3}{4}(t-t_b)^2 \tag{11.38}$$

with edges at $x_1(t) = (t_b - t)^{1/2}$ when $t \le t_b$, we have

$$(\mathcal{G}_{\gamma\text{-norm}}L)(x_1(t);\ t) = 4\,t^{\gamma}\,(t_b - t)^3 \tag{11.39}$$

and the selected scales are

$$t_{\mathcal{G}_{\gamma\text{-norm}}} = \frac{\gamma}{3+\gamma}\,t_b \quad \text{and} \quad t_{\mathcal{T}_{\gamma\text{-norm}}} = \frac{3\gamma}{5+3\gamma}\,t_b \tag{11.40}$$

In other words, the scale selection method has the qualitative property of *reflecting the degree of diffuseness of the edge.* Moreover, as the edge strength decreases rapidly at a bifurcation, the selected scales will tend away from bifurcation scales.

Results of edge detection. Let us now apply the integrated edge detection scheme to different real-world images. In brief, edges are extracted as follows [35]: The differential descriptors in the edge definition, (11.36) are rewritten in terms of partial derivatives in Cartesian coordinates and are computed at a number of scales in scale-space. Then, a polygon approximation is constructed of the intersections of the two zero-crossing surfaces of L_{vv} and $\partial_t(\mathcal{E}_{\gamma\text{-norm}})$ that satisfy the sign conditions $L_{vvv} < 0$ and $\partial_t(\mathcal{E}_{\gamma\text{-norm}}) < 0$. Finally, a significance

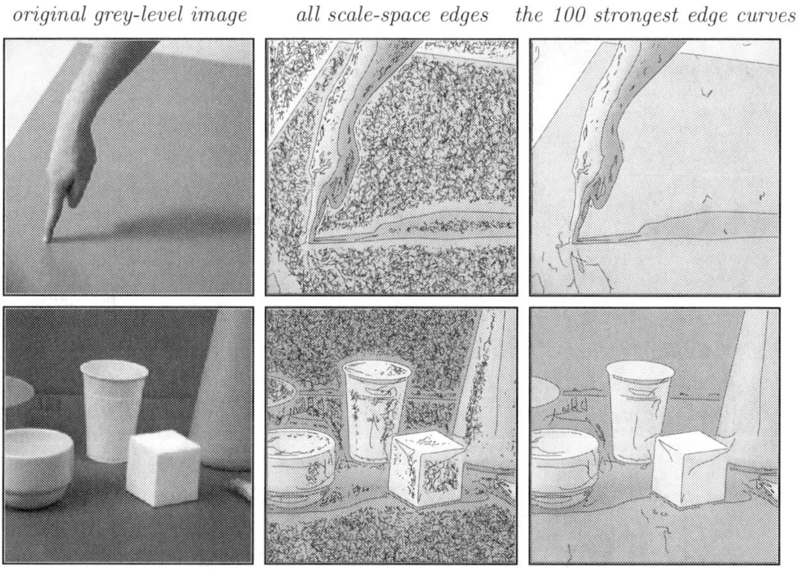

Figure 11.5: The result of edge detection with automatic scale selection based on local maxima over scales of the first-order edge strength measure $\mathcal{G}_{\gamma-norm}L$ with $\gamma = 1/2$. The middle column shows all the scale-space edges, whereas the right column shows the 100 edge curves having the highest significance values. Image size: 256 × 256 pixels.

measure is computed for each edge by integrating the normalized edge strength measure along the curve

$$H(\Gamma) = \int_{(x;\,t)\in\Gamma} \sqrt{(\mathcal{G}_{\gamma-\mathrm{norm}}L)(x;\,t)}\,\mathrm{d}s \qquad (11.41)$$

$$T(\Gamma) = \int_{(x;\,t)\in\Gamma} \sqrt[4]{(\mathcal{T}_{\gamma-\mathrm{norm}}L)(x;\,t)}\,\mathrm{d}s \qquad (11.42)$$

Figure 11.5 shows the result of applying this scheme to two real-world images. As can be seen, the sharp edges due to object boundaries are extracted as well as the diffuse edges due to illumination effects (the occlusion shadows on the arm and the cylinder, the cast shadow on the table, as well as the reflection on the table). (Recall from Fig. 11.3 that for this image it is impossible to capture the entire shadow edge at one scale without introducing severe shape distortions at the finger tip.)

Figure 11.6 illustrates the ranking on significance obtained from the integrated edge strength along the curve. Whereas there are inherent limitations in using such an entity as the *only* measure of saliency, note that this measure captures essential information.

Figure 11.7 gives a 3-D illustration of how the selected scale levels vary along the edges. The scale-space edges have been drawn as 3-D curves in scale-space, overlaid on a low-contrast copy of the original

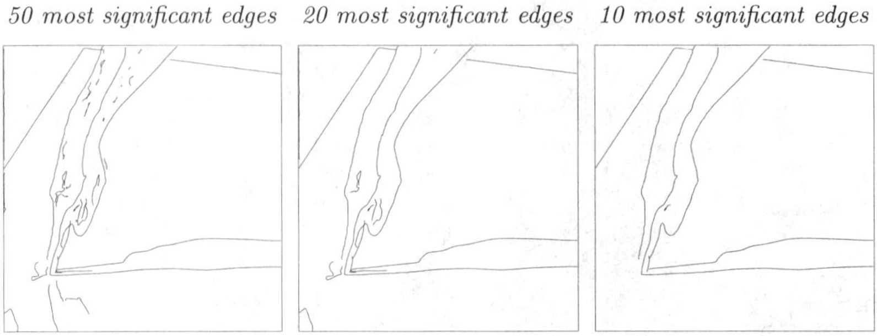

Figure 11.6: *Illustration of the ranking on saliency obtained from the integrated γ-normalized gradient magnitude along the scale-space edges. Here, the 50, 20, and 10 most significant edges, respectively, have been selected from the arm image.*

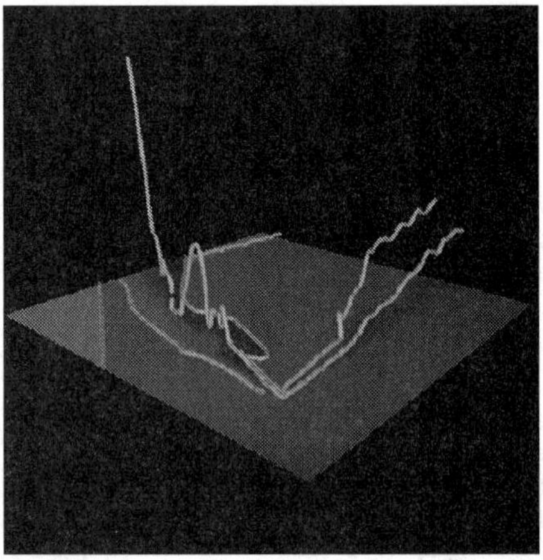

Figure 11.7: *Three-dimensional view of the 10 most significant scale-space edges extracted from the arm image. From the vertical dimension representing the selected scale measured in dimension length (in units of $\sqrt{t}$), it can be seen how coarse scales are selected for the diffuse edge structures (due to illumination effects) and that finer scales are selected for the sharp edge structures (the object boundaries).*

gray-level image in such a way that the height over the image plane represents the selected scale. Observe that coarse scales are selected for the diffuse edge structures due to illumination effects and that finer scales are selected for the sharp edge structures due to object boundaries.

Figure 11.8 shows the result of applying edge detection with scale selection based on local maxima over scales of $\mathcal{T}_{\gamma-\mathrm{norm}}L$ to an image containing a large amount of fine-scale information. At first glance,

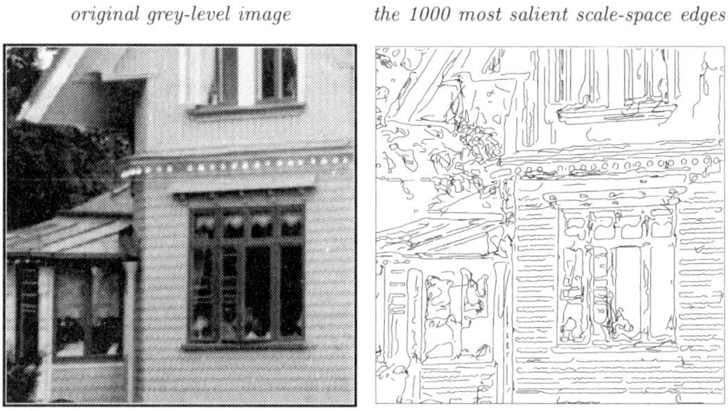

Figure 11.8: The 1000 strongest scale-space edges extracted using scale selection based on local maxima over scales of $\mathcal{T}_{\gamma-norm}L$ (with $\gamma = 1/2$). (Image size: 256×256 pixels.)

these results may appear very similar to the result of traditional edge detection at a fixed (very fine) scale. A more detailed study, however, reveals that a number of shadow edges are extracted, which would be impossible to detect at the same scale as the dominant fine-scale information. In this context, it should be noted that the fine-scale edge detection in this case is not the result of any manual setting of tuning parameters. It is a direct *consequence* of the scale-space edge concept, and is the result of applying the same mechanism as extracts coarse scale levels for diffuse image structures.

Summary. To conclude, for both these measures of edge strength, this scale selection scheme has the desirable property of adapting the scale levels to the local image structure such that *the selected scales reflect the degree of diffuseness of the edge.*

11.4.2 Ridge detection

By a slight reformulation, ridge detection algorithms can be expressed in a similar way. If we follow a differential geometric approach, and define a bright (dark) ridge point as a point for which the brightness assumes a maximum (minimum) in the main eigendirection of the Hessian matrix [20, 36, 37, 38], then in the (p, q)-system this definition can be stated as

$$\begin{cases} L_p = 0, \\ L_{pp} < 0, \\ |L_{pp}| \geq |L_{qq}| \end{cases} \quad \text{or} \quad \begin{cases} L_q = 0, \\ L_{qq} < 0, \\ |L_{qq}| \geq |L_{pp}| \end{cases}$$

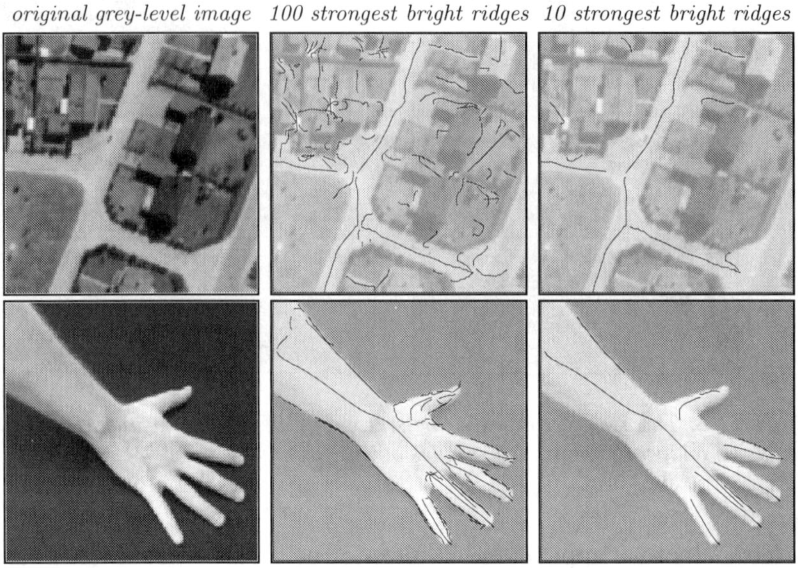

Figure 11.9: *The 100 and 10 strongest bright ridges, respectively, extracted using scale selection based on local maxima over scales of $\mathcal{A}_{\gamma-norm}$ (with $\gamma = 3/4$). Image size: 128×128 pixels in the top row, and 140×140 pixels in the bottom row.*

In the (u, v)-system, this condition can for nondegenerate L equivalently be written

$$L_{uv} = 0 \quad \text{and} \quad L_{uu}^2 - L_{vv}^2 > 0 \tag{11.43}$$

where the sign of L_{uu} determines the polarity; $L_{uu} < 0$ corresponds to bright ridges, and $L_{uu} > 0$ to dark ridges. Figure 11.3 shows the results of applying this ridge detector at different scales.

In analogy with Section 11.4.1, let us next sweep out a *ridge surface* in scale-space by applying this ridge definition at all scales. Then, given a measure $\mathcal{R}_{\gamma\text{-norm}}L$ of normalized ridge strength, define a *scale-space ridge* as a curve on this surface along which the ridge strength measure assumes local maxima with respect to scale

$$\begin{cases} \partial_t(\mathcal{R}_{\text{norm}}L(x, y;\, t)) = 0 \\ \partial_{tt}(\mathcal{R}_{\text{norm}}L(x, y;\, t)) < 0 \end{cases} \quad \text{and} \quad \begin{cases} L_p(x, y;\, t) = 0 \\ L_{pp}(x, y;\, t) < 0 \end{cases} \tag{11.44}$$

Here, we consider the following ridge strength measures:

$$\begin{aligned} \mathcal{N}_{\gamma\text{-norm}}L &= t^{4\gamma}(L_{pp}^2 - L_{qq}^2)^2 \\ &= t^{4\gamma}(L_{xx} + L_{yy})^2((L_{xx} - L_{yy})^2 + 4L_{xy}^2) \end{aligned} \tag{11.45}$$

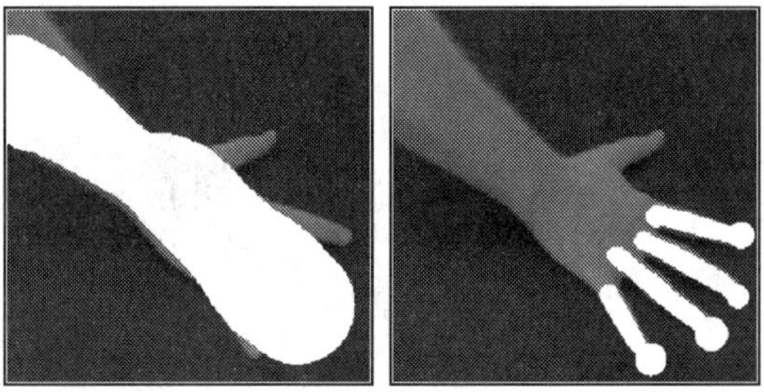

Figure 11.10: *Alternative illustration of the five strongest scale-space ridges extracted from the image of the arm in Fig. 11.9. Each ridge is backprojected onto a dark copy of the original image as the union of a set of circles centered on the ridge curve with the radius proportional to the selected scale at that point.*

Qualitative properties. For a Gaussian ridge defined by $g(x,y) = h(x;\ t_0)$, it can be shown that the selected scale will then be $t_{\mathcal{R}_{\gamma\text{-norm}}} = \frac{2\gamma}{3-2\gamma}\, t_0$. Requiring this scale to be $t_{\mathcal{R}_{\gamma\text{-norm}}} = t_0$, gives $\gamma = \frac{3}{4}$.

Results of ridge detection. Figure 11.9 shows the result of applying such a ridge detector to two images and selecting the 100 and 10 strongest bright ridges, respectively, by integrating a measure of normalized ridge strength along each curve. For the arm image, observe how a coarse-scale descriptor is extracted for the arm as a whole, whereas the individual fingers give rise to ridge curves at finer scales (see also Fig. 11.10).

11.4.3 Blob detection

The Laplacian operator $\nabla^2 L = L_{xx} + L_{yy}$ is a commonly used entity for blob detection, because it gives a strong response at the center of blob-like image structures [39, 40, 41]. To formulate a blob detector with automatic scale selection, we can consider the points in scale-space at which the the square of the normalized Laplacian

$$\nabla^2_{\text{norm}} L = t(L_{xx} + L_{yy}) \tag{11.46}$$

assumes maxima with respect to space and scale. Such points are referred to as *scale-space extrema* of $(\nabla^2_{\text{norm}} L)^2$.

Qualitative properties. For a Gaussian blob defined by

$$g(x,y) = h(x,y;\ t_0) = \frac{1}{2\pi t_0} e^{-(x^2+y^2)/2t_0} \tag{11.47}$$

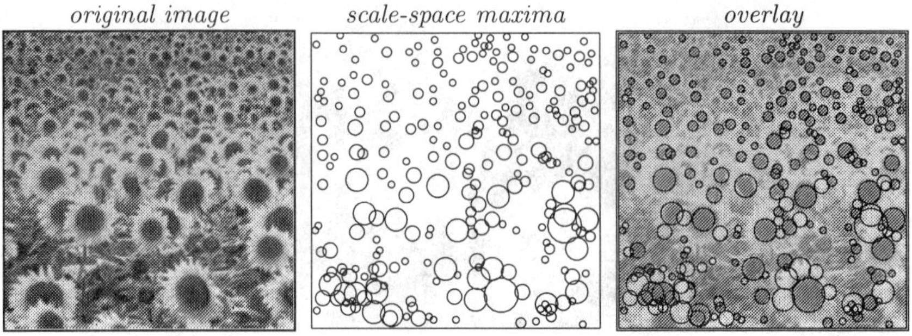

Figure 11.11: *Blob detection by detection of scale-space maxima of the normalized Laplacian operator:* ***a*** *original image;* ***b*** *circles representing the 250 scale-space maxima of* $(\nabla_{\text{norm}} L)^2$ *having the strongest normalized response;* ***c*** *circles overlaid on image.*

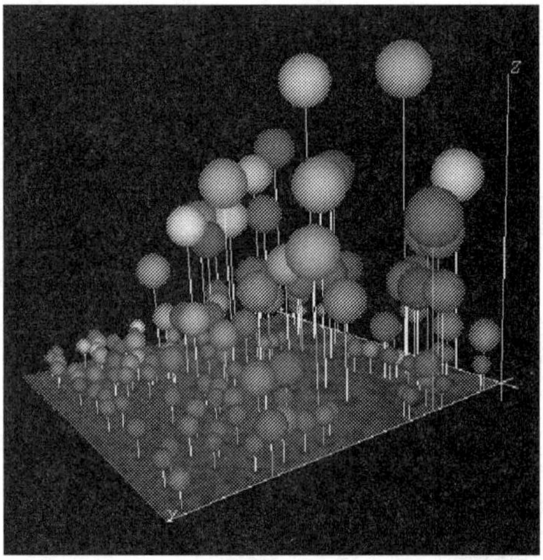

Figure 11.12: *Three-dimensional view of the 150 strongest scale-space maxima of the square of the normalized Laplacian of the Gaussian computed from the sunflower image.*

it can be shown that the selected scale at the center of the blob is given by

$$\partial_t (\nabla^2_{\text{norm}} L)(0, 0;\, t) = 0 \quad \Longleftrightarrow \quad t_{\nabla^2 L} = t_0. \tag{11.48}$$

Hence, the selected scale directly reflects the width t_0 of the Gaussian blob.

Results of blob detection. Figures 11.11 and 11.12 show the result of applying this blob detector to an image of a sunflower field. In Fig. 11.11, each blob feature detected as a scale-space maximum is illustrated by a circle, with its radius proportional to the selected scale.

Figure 11.12 shows a 3-D illustration of the same data set, by marking the scale-space extrema by spheres in scale-space. Observe how the size variations in the image are captured by this structurally very simple operation.

11.4.4 Corner detection

A commonly used technique for detecting junction candidates in gray-level images is to detect extrema in the curvature of level curves multiplied by the gradient magnitude raised to some power [42, 43]. A special choice is to multiply the level curve curvature by the gradient magnitude raised to the power of three. This leads to the differential invariant $\tilde{\kappa} = L_v^2 L_{uu}$, with the corresponding normalized expression

$$\tilde{\kappa}_{\mathrm{norm}} = t^{2\gamma} L_v^2 L_{uu} \tag{11.49}$$

Qualitative properties. For a *diffuse L-junction*

$$g(x_1, x_2) = \Phi(x_1;\ t_0)\,\Phi(x_2;\ t_0) \tag{11.50}$$

modeled as the product of two diffuse step edges

$$\Phi(x_i;\ t_0) = \int_{x'=-\infty}^{x_i} h(x';\ t_0)\,\mathrm{d}x' \tag{11.51}$$

it can be shown that variation of $\tilde{\kappa}_{\mathrm{norm}}$ at the origin is given by

$$|\tilde{\kappa}_{\mathrm{norm}}(0, 0;\ t)| = \frac{t^{2\gamma}}{8\pi^2 (t_0 + t)^2} \tag{11.52}$$

When $\gamma = 1$, this entity *increases monotonically* with scale, whereas for $\gamma \in]0, 1[$, $\tilde{\kappa}_{\mathrm{norm}}(0, 0;\ t)$ assumes a unique maximum over scales at $t_{\tilde{\kappa}} = \frac{\gamma}{1-\gamma} t_0$. On the other hand, for a *nonuniform Gaussian blob* $L(x_1, x_2;\ t) = h(x_1;\ t_1 + t)\,h(x_2;\ t_2 + t)$, the normalized response always *decreases* with scale at sufficiently coarse scales.

This analysis indicates that when $\gamma = 1$, $\tilde{\kappa}^2_{\mathrm{norm}}$ can be expected to increase with scales when a single corner model of infinite extent constitutes a reasonable approximation, whereas $\tilde{\kappa}^2_{\mathrm{norm}}$ can be expected to decrease with scales when so much smoothing is applied that the overall shape of the object is substantially distorted.

Hence, selecting scale levels (and spatial points) where $\tilde{\kappa}^2_{\mathrm{norm}}$ assumes maxima over scales can be expected to give rise to scale levels in the intermediate scale range (where a finite extent junction model constitutes a reasonable approximation) and the selected scale levels thus reflect over how large a region a corner model is valid. In practice, a slightly smaller value of $\gamma = 7/8$ is used.

Figure 11.13: Three-dimensional view of scale-space maxima of $\tilde{\kappa}^2_{\text{norm}}$ computed for a large scale corner with superimposed corner structures at finer scales.

Results of corner detection. Figure 11.13 shows the result of detecting scale-space extrema from an image with corner structures at multiple scales. Observe that a coarse scale response is obtained for the large-scale corner structure as a whole, whereas the superimposed corner structures of smaller size give rise to scale-space maxima at finer scales. (More results on real images will be shown in Section 11.5.)

11.4.5 Local frequency estimation

To extend the forementioned application of the scale selection methodology from the detection of sparse image features to the computation of dense image descriptors, a natural starting point is to consider the theory of quadrature filter pairs defined (from a Hilbert transform) in such a way as to be phase-independent for any sine wave. To approximate such operators within the Gaussian derivative framework, we can define a corresponding quasi-quadrature measure in the 1-D case by [11, 44]

$$\mathcal{P}L = L_\xi^2 + C L_{\xi\xi}^2 = t L_x^2 + C t^2 L_{xx}^2 \tag{11.53}$$

where a good choice of the parameter C is $C = e/4$. Note that, in order to achieve scale invariance, it is necessary to use normalized derivatives with $\gamma = 1$ in the (inhomogeneous) linear combination of Gaussian derivatives of different order. The γ-normalized derivative concept, however, leaves a degree of freedom, which can be parameterized by

$$\mathcal{P}L = t^{-\Gamma}(t L_x^2 + C t^2 L_{xx}^2) \tag{11.54}$$

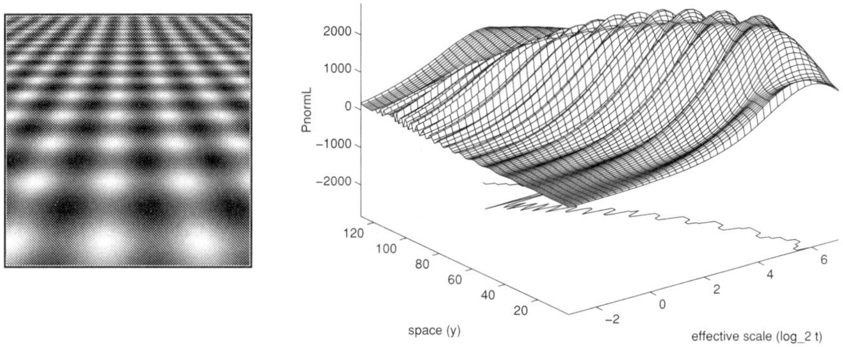

Figure 11.14: *Dense scale selection by maximizing the quasi-quadrature measure Eq. (11.55) over scales: (left) original gray-level image; (right) the variations over scales of the quasi-quadrature measure $\mathcal{P}L$ computed along a vertical cross section through the center of the image. The result is visualized as a surface plot showing the variations over scale of the quasi-quadrature measure as well as the position of the first local maximum over scales.*

To extend this entity to 2-D signals, we can consider

$$\mathcal{P}L = t^{-\Gamma}\left(t(L_x^2 + L_y^2) + C\,t^2\,(L_{xx}^2 + 2L_{xy}^2 + L_{yy}^2)\right) \tag{11.55}$$

$$\mathcal{R}L = t^{-\Gamma}\left(t\,(L_x^2 + L_y^2) + C\,t^2\,((L_{xx} - L_{yy})^2 + 4\,L_{xy}^2)\right) \tag{11.56}$$

Both these differential expressions are invariant under rotations and reduce to the form of Eq. (11.54) for a 1-D signal. The second-order differential expression in Eq. (11.55)

$$\mathcal{S}_{\gamma-norm}L = t^{2\gamma}\,(L_{xx}^2 + 2L_{xy}^2 + L_{yy}^2) \tag{11.57}$$

however, is a natural measure of the total amount of second-order information in the signal, whereas the second-order differential expression in (Eq. (11.56))

$$\mathcal{A}_{\gamma-\mathrm{norm}}L = t^{2\gamma}\,(L_{pp} - L_{qq})^2 = t^{2\gamma}\,((L_{xx} - L_{yy})^2 + 4\,L_{xy}^2) \tag{11.58}$$

is more specific to elongated structures (e.g., ridges). The specific choice of $\Gamma = 1/2$ means that Eq. (11.56) and can be interpreted as a linear combination of the edge strength measure Eq. (11.37) with $\gamma = 1/2$ and the ridge strength measure (Eq. (11.58)) with $\gamma = 3/4$.

Qualitative properties. These differential expressions inherit similar scale selection properties for sine waves as those described in Section 11.3.1; see [30, 44] for an analysis.

Results of frequency estimation. Figure 11.14 shows an example result of estimating local frequencies in this way, by detecting local maxima over scale of $\mathcal{P}L$ along a vertical cross section in an image of a periodic pattern. Observe how the selected scale levels capture the variations in frequency caused by the perspective effects.

11.5 Feature localization with automatic scale selection

The scale-selection techniques presented so far are useful in the stage of detecting image features. The role of the scale-selection mechanism is to estimate the approximate size of the image structures to which the feature detector responds. When computing features at coarse scales in scale-space, however, the shape distortions can be significant, and in many cases it is desirable to complement feature-detection modules by an explicit *feature-localization* stage.

The goal of this section is to show how the mechanism for automatic scale selection can be formulated in this context by minimizing measures of inconsistency over scales.

11.5.1 Corner localization

Given an approximate estimate x_0 of the location and the size s of a corner (computed according to Section 11.4.4), an improved estimate of the corner position can be computed as follows [3, 45]: Consider at every point $x' \in \mathbb{R}^2$ in a neighborhood of x_0, the line $l_{x'}$ perpendicular to the gradient vector $(\nabla L)(x') = (L_{x_1}, L_{x_2})^T(x')$ at that point

$$D_{x'}(x) = ((\nabla L)(x'))^T(x - x') = 0 \tag{11.59}$$

Then, minimize the perpendicular distance to all lines $l_{x'}$ in a neighborhood of x_0, weighted by the gradient magnitude, that is, determine the point $x \in \mathbb{R}^2$ that minimizes

$$\min_{x \in \mathbb{R}^2} \int_{x' \in \mathbb{R}^2} (D_{x'}(x))^2 \, w_{x_0}(x'; s) \, dx' \tag{11.60}$$

for a Gaussian window function $w_{x_0}(\cdot;\, s)\colon \mathbb{R}^2 \to \mathbb{R}$ with integration scale s set from the detection scale $t_{tilde\kappa}$ of the corner and centered at the candidate junction x_0. After expansion, this minimization problem can be expressed as a standard least squares problem

$$\min_{x \in \mathbb{R}^2} x^T A x - 2x^T b + c \quad \Longleftrightarrow \quad Ax = b \tag{11.61}$$

where $x = (x_1, x_2)^T$, and A, b, and c are determined by the local statistics of the gradient directions $\nabla L(\cdot;\, t)$ at scale t in a neighborhood of

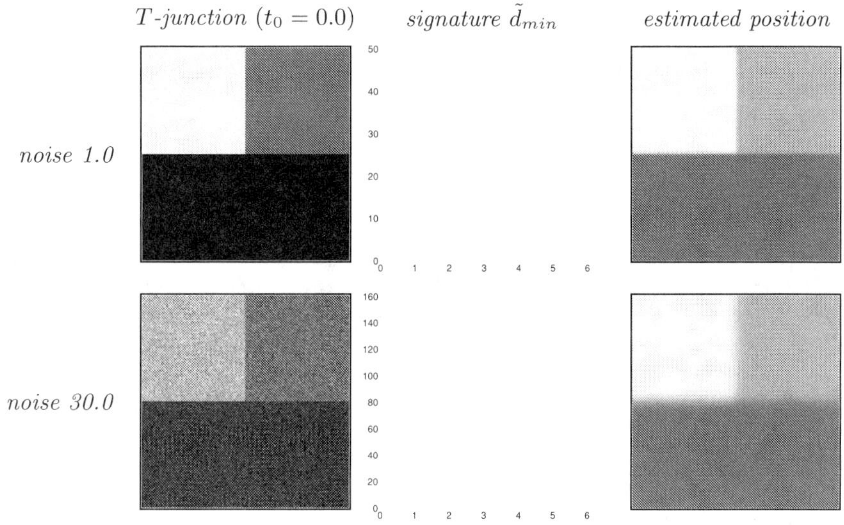

Figure 11.15: *Corner localization by minimizing the normalized residuals over scales for two corner structures. A basic property of the scale-selection mechanism is that an increase in the noise level implies that the minimum over scales is assumed at a coarser scale.*

x_0 (compare with Eq. (11.17))

$$A(x;\, t, s) = \int_{x' \in \mathbb{R}^2} (\nabla L)(x')\, (\nabla L)^T(x')\, w_{x_0}(x';\, s)\, \mathrm{d}x' \tag{11.62}$$

$$b(x;\, t, s) = \int_{x' \in \mathbb{R}^2} (\nabla L)(x')\, (\nabla L)^T(x')\, x'\, w_{x_0}(x';\, s)\, \mathrm{d}x' \tag{11.63}$$

$$c(x;\, t, s) = \int_{x' \in \mathbb{R}^2} x'^T\, (\nabla L)(x')\, (\nabla L)^T(x')\, x' w_{x_0}(x';\, s)\, \mathrm{d}x' \tag{11.64}$$

11.5.2 Scale-selection principle for feature localization

To express a scale-selection mechanism for this corner localizer, let us extend the minimization problem (Eq. (11.61)) from a single scale to optimization over multiple scales [46]

$$\min_{t \in \mathbb{R}_+} \min_{x \in \mathbb{R}^2} \frac{x^T A x - 2\, x^T b + c}{\mathrm{norm}(t)} = \min_{t \in \mathbb{R}_+} \min_{x \in \mathbb{R}^2} \frac{c - b^T A^{-1} b}{\mathrm{trace}\, A} \tag{11.65}$$

and introduce a normalization factor $\mathrm{norm}(t)$ to relate minimizations at different scales. The particular choice of $\mathrm{norm}(t) = \mathrm{trace}\, A$ implies that the *normalized residual*

$$\tilde{r} = \min_{x \in \mathbb{R}^2} \frac{\int_{x' \in \mathbb{R}^2} \left| ((\nabla L)(x'))^T (x - x') \right|^2 w_{x_0}(x';\, s)\, \mathrm{d}x'}{\int_{x' \in \mathbb{R}^2} \left| (\nabla L)(x') \right|^2 w_{x_0}(x';\, s)\, \mathrm{d}x'} \tag{11.66}$$

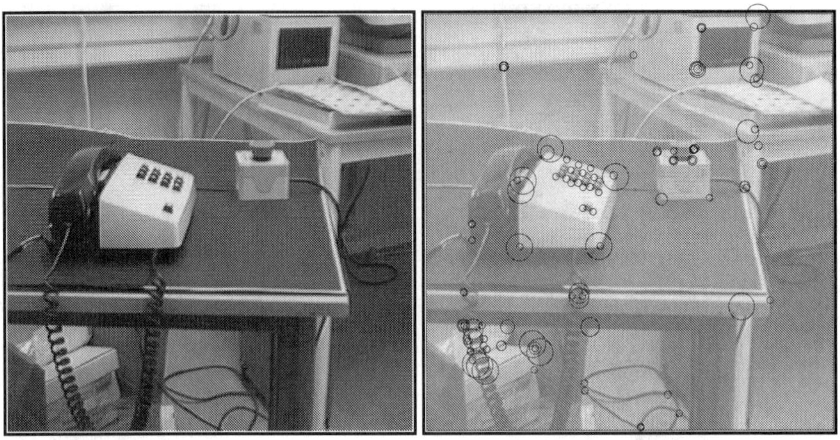

Figure 11.16: *Results of composed two-stage junction detection followed by junction localization. (left) Original gray-level image. (right) The 100 strongest junction responses ranked according to the scale-space maxima of* $\tilde{\kappa}^2_{\mathrm{norm}}$ *and illustrated by circles with their radii proportional to the detection scales of the junction responses.*

has dimension $[\text{length}]^2$ that can be interpreted as a weighted estimate of the localization error. Specifically, scale selection according to Eq. (11.65), by minimizing the normalized residual $\tilde{r}$ of Eq. (11.66) over scales, corresponds to selecting the scale that minimizes the estimated inaccuracy in the localization estimate.

Qualitative effects. Figure 11.15 shows the result of performing corner localization in this way, by minimizing the normalized residual $\tilde{r}$ over scales for two corner structures. Observe how an increase in the noise level implies that the minimum over scales is assumed at a coarser scale.

Results of corner localization. Figure 11.16 shows the result of integrating this corner localization module with the corner detector in Section 11.4.4. The resulting two-stage corner automatically adapts its detection scales and localization scales to size variations and noise variations in the image structures. In addition, the region of interest associated with each corner is useful for purposes such as matching.

Edge localization. In Lindeberg [3, 30] it is outlined how minimization over scales of a similar normalized residual applies to the problem of edge localization.

11.6 Stereo matching with automatic scale selection

This section shows how a scale selection mechanism can be formulated for a differential stereo matching scheme expressed within the Gaussian derivative framework. With appropriate modifications, similar ideas apply to the problem of flow estimation.

11.6.1 Least squares differential stereo matching

Let us assume that the flow field between the scale-space representations L and R of two images can be approximated by a constant flow field v over the support region of a window function w. Following [47, 48, 49, 50, 51] and several others, consider the discrete form of the *motion constraint equation* [52]

$$(\nabla L)(\xi)^T(\Delta\xi) + (L(\xi) - R(\xi)) = \mathcal{O}(|\Delta\xi|^2) \tag{11.67}$$

and integrate the square of this relation using w as window function. After expansion (and dropping the arguments) this gives the least-squares problem

$$\min_{v\in\mathbb{R}^2} v^T A v + 2b^T v + c \tag{11.68}$$

where A, b, and c are defined by

$$A = \int_{\xi\in\mathbb{R}^2} (\nabla L)(\nabla L)^T\, w\; d\xi$$

$$b = \int_{\xi\in\mathbb{R}^2} (R - L)\,(\nabla L)\, w\; d\xi, \quad c = \int_{\xi\in\mathbb{R}^2} (R - L)^2\, w\; d\xi \tag{11.69}$$

If we interpret $R - L$ as a discrete approximation to a temporal derivative, these image descriptors fall within the class of windowed spectral moments in Eq. (11.17). Assuming that A according to Eq. (11.69) is nondegenerate, the explicit solution of the flow estimate is

$$v = -A^{-1}b \tag{11.70}$$

11.6.2 Scale-selection principle for estimating image deformations

When implementing this scheme in practice, it is natural to express it within a coarse-to-fine multiscale framework. When performing image matching from coarse to fine scales, however, it is not obvious what should be the finest scales. If we attempt to match image features beyond a certain resolution, we could expect the errors in the deformation estimates to increase rather than to decrease.

In analogy with Section 11.5.2, a natural way to formulate a scale-selection mechanism for the differential stereo matching scheme is by

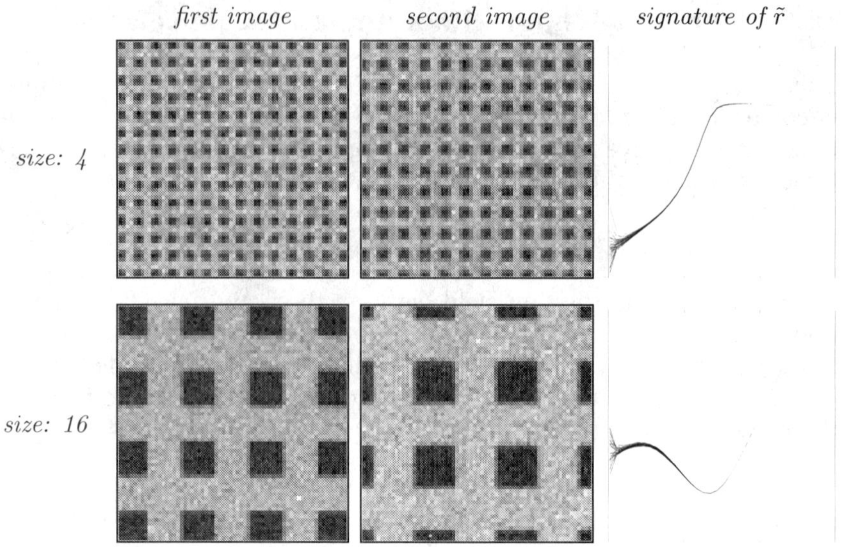

Figure 11.17: *Scale-space signatures of the normalized residual $\tilde{r}$ for synthetic expanding patterns with structures at different scales. Notice that with increasing size of the texture elements, the minimum over scales in the normalized residual is assumed at coarser scales.*

extending the least squares estimation (Eq. (11.68)) to the two-parameter least squares problem

$$\min_{t \in \mathbb{R}_+} \min_{v \in \mathbb{R}^2} \frac{v^T A v + 2b^T v + c}{\text{norm}(t)} \tag{11.71}$$

where the normalization factor $\text{norm}(t)$ determines how the information at different scales should be compared. Again, we choose $\text{norm}(t) = \text{trace}\, A$, while one could also conceive other normalization approaches, such as the minimum eigenvalue of A.

The resulting *normalized residual* is of dimension $[\text{length}]^2$ and constitutes a first-order approximation of the following error measure:

$$\begin{aligned} \mathcal{E}_{\nabla L} &= \frac{\int_{\xi \in \mathbb{R}^2} |(\nabla L)^T (v - \Delta\xi)|^2 \, w(\xi) \, \mathrm{d}\xi}{\int_{\xi \in \mathbb{R}^2} |\nabla L|^2 \, w(\xi) \, \mathrm{d}\xi} \\ &= \frac{\int_{\xi \in \mathbb{R}^2} (v - \Delta\xi)^T (\nabla L)(\nabla L)^T (v - \Delta\xi) \, w(\xi) \, \mathrm{d}\xi}{\int_{\xi \in \mathbb{R}^2} (\nabla L)^T (\nabla L) \, w(\xi) \, \mathrm{d}\xi} \end{aligned} \tag{11.72}$$

where v is the regional flow estimate and $\Delta\xi$ a pointwise flow estimate that satisfies Eq. (11.67). In other words, $\mathcal{E}_{\nabla L}$ can be seen as a measure of the internal consistency of the estimated flow field, weighted by the gradient magnitude.

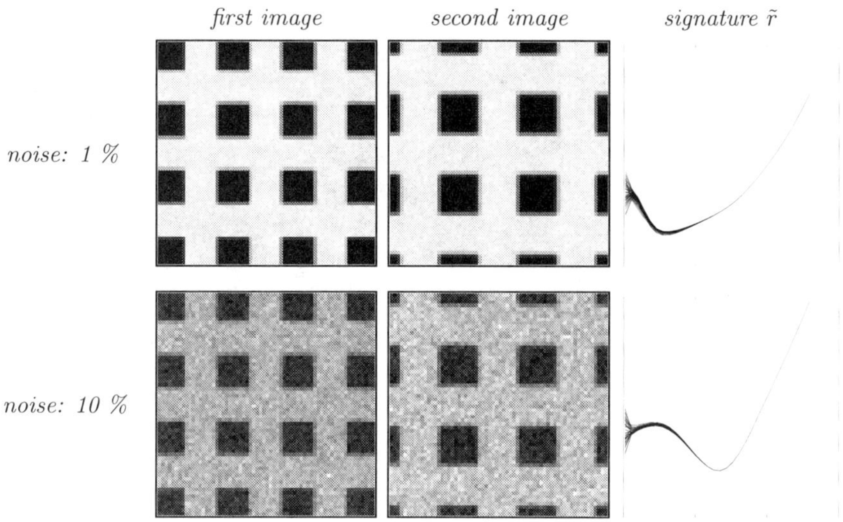

Figure 11.18: *Scale-space signatures of the normalized residual $\tilde{r}$ for a synthetic expanding pattern with different amounts of added white Gaussian noise. Observe that with increasing noise level, the minimum over scales in the normalized residual is assumed at coarser scales.*

11.6.3 Properties of matching with automatic scale selection

Selection of coarser scales for larger-sized image structures. Figure 11.17 shows two synthetic image patterns that have been subject to a uniform expansion. The underlying patterns are identical except for the size of the texture elements that differs by a factor of four, and 10 % white Gaussian noise added to each image independently after the deformation. Observe for the small-sized pattern in the first row the minima over scales in $\tilde{r}$ are assumed at the finest scales, while when the size of the image structures is increased in the second row, the minimum over scales is assumed at coarser scales. This behavior agrees with the intuitive notion that coarser scales should be selected for patterns containing larger-sized image structures.

Selection of coarser scales with increasing noise level. In Fig. 11.18 the image pattern is the same, whereas the noise level is varied. Observe that with an increasing amount of interfering fine scale structures, the minimum in $\tilde{r}$ over scales is assumed at coarser scales. This behavior agrees with the intuitive notion that a larger amount of smoothing is required for noisy data than otherwise similar data with less noise.

Selection of finer scales near discontinuities in the deformation field. Figure 11.19 shows the behavior of the scale selection method

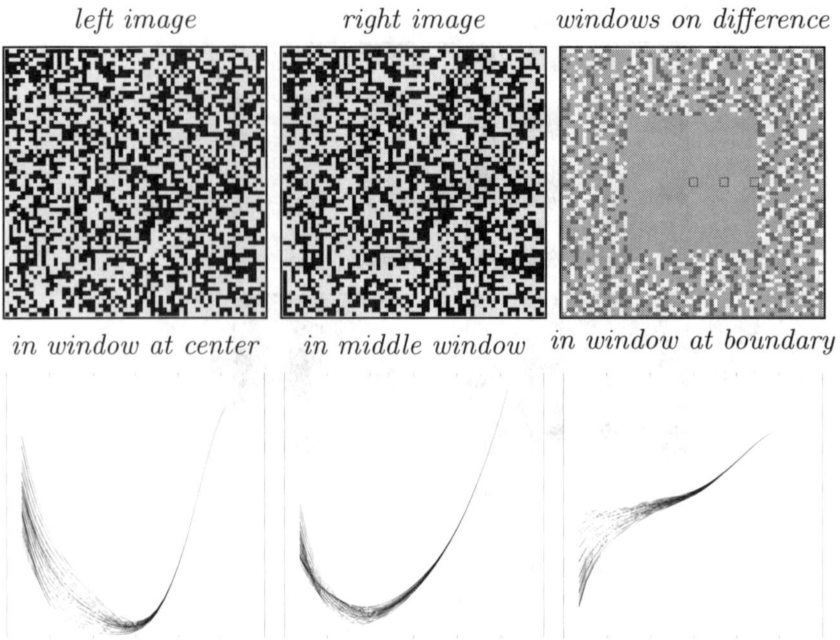

Figure 11.19: *The qualitative behavior of the scale selection method at a discontinuity in the deformation field. The bottom row shows scale-space signatures of the normalized residual computed in three windows at different distances to the discontinuity (with their positions indicated in the upper right image by three squares overlaid on the pointwise difference between the left and the right image). Observe that with decreasing distance to the discontinuity, the minimum over scales is assumed at finer scales.*

in the neighborhood of a discontinuity in the flow field. For a “wedding-cake type” random dot stereo pair to which 1% white Gaussian noise has been added, the results are shown of accumulating the scale-space signature of the normalized residual in three windows with different distance to the discontinuity. These windows have been uniformly spaced from the image center to one of the discontinuities in the disparity field as shown in Fig. 11.19c.

Observe that with decreasing distance to the discontinuity, the minimum over scales is assumed at finer scales. This qualitative behavior agrees with the intuitive notion that smaller windows for matching should be selected for image structures near a discontinuity in the disparity field than when matching otherwise similar image structures in a region where the disparity varies smoothly.

Notably, this rapid decrease of the selected scale levels could also provide a clue for detecting flow field discontinuities and signaling possible occlusions.

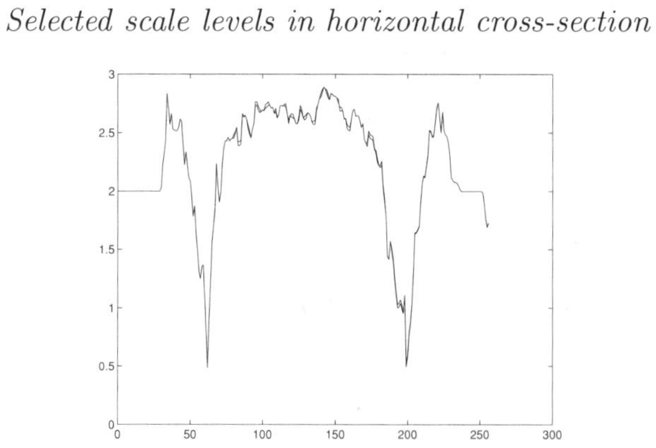

Figure 11.20: *Selected scale levels along a central horizontal cross section through the wedding-cake type random dot stereo pair in Fig. 11.19. Observe that distinct minima are obtained at the two discontinuities in the disparity field.*

11.7 Summary and conclusions

The scale-space framework provides a canonical way to model early visual operations in terms of linear and nonlinear combinations of Gaussian derivatives of different order, orientation and scale. This chapter has shown how scale-space descriptors can be complemented by mechanisms for automatic scale selection

For feature detectors expressed in terms of Gaussian derivatives, hypotheses about interesting scale levels can be generated from scales at which normalized measures of feature strength assume local maxima with respect to scale. The notion of γ-normalized derivatives arises by necessity given the requirement that the scale selection mechanism should commute with rescalings of the image pattern. Specific examples have been shown of how feature detection algorithms with automatic scale selection can be formulated for the problems of edge detection, blob detection, junction detection, ridge detection and frequency estimation. A general property of this scheme is that the selected scale levels reflect the size of the image structures.

When estimating image deformations, such as in image matching and optic flow computations, scale levels with associated deformation estimates can be selected from the scales at which normalized measures of uncertainty assume local minima with respect to scales. It has been illustrated how an integrated scale selection and flow estimation algorithm has the qualitative properties of leading to the selection of coarser scales for larger-sized image structures and increasing noise level, whereas it leads to the selection of finer scales in the neighborhood of flow-field discontinuities.

The material in this chapter is based on [3, chapter 13], [30], [35] and [50]; see also [53] for a complementary work. Applications of these scale selection principles to various problems in computer vision have been presented in [44, 54, 55, 56, 57, 58, 59]. For related works see [33, 36, 60, 61, 62, 63, 64, 65, 66, 67, 68, 69, 70].

11.8 References

[1] Koenderink, J. J., (1990). *Solid Shape.* Cambridge, Massachusetts: MIT Press.

[2] Koenderink, J. J., Kaeppers, A., and van Doorn, A. J., (1992). Local Operations: The Embodiment of Geometry. In *Artificial and Biological Vision Systems*, G. Orban and H.-H. Nagel, eds., pp. 1–23.

[3] Lindeberg, T., (1994). *Scale-Space Theory in Computer Vision.* The Kluwer International Series in Engineering and Computer Science. Dordrecht, Netherlands: Kluwer Academic Publishers.

[4] Babaud, J., Witkin, A. P., Baudin, M., and Duda, R. O., (1986). Uniqueness of the Gaussian Kernel for Scale-Space Filtering. *IEEE Trans. Pattern Analysis and Machine Intell.*, **8**(1):26–33.

[5] Florack, L. M. J., (1993). *The Syntactical Structure of Scalar Images.* , Dept. Med. Phys. Physics, Univ. Utrecht, NL-3508 Utrecht, Netherlands.

[6] Florack, L. M. J., (1997). *Image Structure.* Series in Mathematical Imaging and Vision. Dordrecht, Netherlands: Kluwer Academic Publishers.

[7] Florack, L. M. J., ter Haar Romeny, B. M., Koenderink, J. J., and Viergever, M. A., (1992). Scale and the Differential Structure of Images. *Image and Vision Computing*, **10**(6):376–388.

[8] Florack, L. M. J., ter Haar Romeny, B. M., Koenderink, J. J., and Viergever, M. A., (1993). Cartesian Differential Invariants in Scale-Space. *J. of Mathematical Imaging and Vision*, **3**(4):327–348.

[9] Hummel, R. A. and Moniot, R., (1989). Reconstructions from zero-crossings in scale-space. *IEEE Trans. Acoustics, Speech and Signal Processing*, **37**(12):2111–2130.

[10] Koenderink, J. J., (1984). The structure of images. *Biological Cybernetics*, **50**:363–370.

[11] Koenderink, J. J. and van Doorn, A. J., (1987). Representation of Local Geometry in the Visual System. *Biological Cybernetics*, **55**:367–375.

[12] Koenderink, J. J. and van Doorn, A. J., (1990). Receptive Field Families. *Biological Cybernetics*, **63**:291–298.

[13] Koenderink, J. J. and van Doorn, A. J., (1992). Generic neighborhood operators. *IEEE Trans. Pattern Analysis and Machine Intell.*, **14**(6):597–605.

[14] Lindeberg, T., (1990). Scale-Space for Discrete Signals. *IEEE Trans. Pattern Analysis and Machine Intell.*, **12**(3):234–254.

[15] Lindeberg, T., (1994). *On the Axiomatic Foundations of Linear Scale-Space: Combining Semi-Group Structure with Causality vs. Scale Invariance.* Technical Report ISRN KTH/NA/P--94/20--SE, Dept. of Numerical

Analysis and Computing Science, KTH, Stockholm, Sweden. Extended version to appear in J. Sporring and M. Nielsen and L. Florack and P. Johansen (eds.) Gaussian Scale-Space Theory: Proc. PhD School on Scale-Space Theory, Copenhagen, Denmark, Kluwer Academic Publishers, May 1996.

[16] Lindeberg, T., (1997). Linear spatio-temporal scale-space. In *Scale-Space Theory in Computer Vision: Proc. First Int. Conf. Scale-Space'97*, B. M. ter Haar Romeny, L. M. J. Florack, J. J. Koenderink, and M. A. Viergever, eds., Vol. 1252 of *Lecture Notes in Computer Science*, pp. 113–127. Utrecht, The Netherlands: Springer Verlag, New York.

[17] Pauwels, E. J., Fiddelaers, P., Moons, T., and van Gool, L. J., (1995). An extended class of scale-invariant and recursive scale-space filters. *IEEE Trans. Pattern Analysis and Machine Intell.*, **17**(7):691–701.

[18] Sporring, J., Nielsen, M., Florack, L., and Johansen, P. (eds.), (1996). *Gaussian Scale-Space Theory: Proc. PhD School on Scale-Space Theory.* Series in Mathematical Imaging and Vision. Copenhagen, Denmark: Kluwer Academic Publishers.

[19] Yuille, A. L. and Poggio, T. A., (1986). Scaling Theorems for Zero-Crossings. *IEEE Trans. Pattern Analysis and Machine Intell.*, **8**:15–25.

[20] Lindeberg, T., (1994). Scale-Space Theory: A Basic Tool for Analysing Structures at Different Scales. *Journal of Applied Statistics*, **21**(2):225–270. Supplement *Advances in Applied Statistics: Statistics and Images: 2*.

[21] Lindeberg, T., (1996). Scale-space theory: A framework for handling image structures at multiple scales. In *Proc. CERN School of Computing*, pp. 27–38. Egmond aan Zee, The Netherlands. Tech. Rep. CERN 96-08.

[22] Lindeberg, T. and ter Haar Romeny, B., (1994). Linear Scale-Space I: Basic Theory. In *Geometry-Driven Diffusion in Computer Vision*, B. ter Haar Romeny, ed., Series in Mathematical Imaging and Vision, pp. 1–41. Dordrecht, Netherlands: Kluwer Academic Publishers.

[23] Lindeberg, T. and ter Haar Romeny, B., (1994). Linear Scale-Space II: Early visual operations. In *Geometry-Driven Diffusion in Computer Vision*, B. ter Haar Romeny, ed., Series in Mathematical Imaging and Vision, pp. 43–77. Dordrecht, Netherlands: Kluwer Academic Publishers.

[24] Freeman, W. T. and Adelson, E. H., (1990). Steerable filters for early vision, image analysis and wavelet decomposition. In *Proc. 3rd Int. Conf. on Computer Vision*. Osaka, Japan: IEEE Computer Society Press.

[25] Perona, P., (1992). Steerable-Scalable Kernels for Edge Detection and Junction Analysis. In *Proc. 2nd European Conf. on Computer Vision*, pp. 3–18. Santa Margherita Ligure, Italy.

[26] Bigün, J., Granlund, G. H., and Wiklund, J., (1991). Multidimensional orientation estimation with applications to texture analysis and optical flow. *IEEE Trans. Pattern Analysis and Machine Intell.*, **13**(8):775–790.

[27] Rao, A. R. and Schunk, B. G., (1991). Computing oriented texture fields. *CVGIP: Graphical Models and Image Processing*, **53**(2):157–185.

[28] Young, R. A., (1985). *The Gaussian Derivative Theory of Spatial Vision: Analysis of Cortical Cell Receptive Field Line-Weighting Profiles.* Techni-

cal Report GMR-4920, Computer Science Department, General Motors Research Lab., Warren, Michigan.

[29] Young, R. A., (1987). The Gaussian derivative model for spatial vision: I. Retinal mechanisms. *Spatial Vision*, **2**:273–293.

[30] Lindeberg, T., (1996). *Feature detection with automatic scale selection.* Technical Report ISRN KTH/NA/P--96/18--SE, Dept. of Numerical Analysis and Computing Science, KTH, Stockholm, Sweden. Extended version in *Int. J. of Computer Vision*, vol 30, number 2, 1998. (In press).

[31] Field, D. J., (1987). Relations between the statistics of natural images and the response properties of cortical cells. *J. of the Optical Society of America*, **4**:2379–2394.

[32] Canny, J., (1986). A Computational Approach to Edge Detection. *IEEE Trans. Pattern Analysis and Machine Intell.*, **8**(6):679–698.

[33] Korn, A. F., (1988). Toward a Symbolic Representation of Intensity Changes in Images. *IEEE Trans. Pattern Analysis and Machine Intell.*, **10** (5):610–625.

[34] Lindeberg, T., (1993). Discrete Derivative Approximations with Scale-Space Properties: A Basis for Low-Level Feature Extraction. *J. of Mathematical Imaging and Vision*, **3**(4):349–376.

[35] Lindeberg, T., (1996). *Edge Detection and Ridge Detection with Automatic Scale Selection.* Technical Report ISRN KTH/NA/P--96/06--SE, Dept. of Numerical Analysis and Computing Science, KTH, Stockholm, Sweden. Also in Proc. IEEE Comp. Soc. Conf. on Computer Vision and Pattern Recognition, 1996. Extended version in *Int. J. of Computer Vision*, vol 30, number 2, 1998. (In press).

[36] Eberly, D., Gardner, R., Morse, B., Pizer, S., and Scharlach, C., (1994). Ridges for Image Analysis. *J. of Mathematical Imaging and Vision*, **4**(4): 353–373.

[37] Haralick, R. M., (1983). Ridges and valleys in digital images. *Computer Vision, Graphics, and Image Processing*, **22**:28–38.

[38] Koenderink, J. J. and van Doorn, A. J., (1994). Two-plus-one-dimensional differential geometry. *Pattern Recognition Letters*, **15**(5):439–444.

[39] Blostein, D. and Ahuja, N., (1989). Shape from texture: integrating texture element extraction and surface estimation. *IEEE Trans. Pattern Analysis and Machine Intell.*, **11**(12):1233–1251.

[40] Marr, D., (1982). *Vision.* W.H. Freeman, New York.

[41] Voorhees, H. and Poggio, T., (1987). Detecting Textons and Texture Boundaries in Natural Images. In *Proc. 1st Int. Conf. on Computer Vision.* London, England.

[42] Kitchen, L. and Rosenfeld, A., (1982). Gray-Level Corner Detection. *Pattern Recognition Letters*, **1**(2):95–102.

[43] Koenderink, J. J. and Richards, W., (1988). Two-Dimensional Curvature Operators. *J. of the Optical Society of America*, **5**:**7**:1136–1141.

[44] Lindeberg, T., (1997). On Automatic Selection of Temporal Scales in Time-Casual Scale-Space. In *Proc. AFPAC'97: Algebraic Frames for the Perception-Action Cycle*, G. Sommer and J. J. Koenderink, eds., Vol. 1315

of *Lecture Notes in Computer Science*, pp. 94–113. Kiel, Germany: Springer Verlag, Berlin.

[45] Förstner, W. A. and Gülch, E., (1987). A Fast Operator for Detection and Precise Location of Distinct Points, Corners and Centers of Circular Features. In *Proc. Intercommission Workshop of the Int. Soc. for Photogrammetry and Remote Sensing*. Interlaken, Switzerland.

[46] Lindeberg, T., (1994). Junction detection with automatic selection of detection scales and localization scales. In *Proc. 1st International Conference on Image Processing*, Vol. I, pp. 924–928. Austin, Texas: IEEE Computer Society Press.

[47] Bergen, J. R., Anandan, P., Hanna, K. J., and Hingorani, R., (1992). Hierarchical Model-Based Motion Estimation. In *Proc. 2nd European Conf. on Computer Vision*, G. Sandini, ed., Vol. 588 of *Lecture Notes in Computer Science*, pp. 237–252. Santa Margherita Ligure, Italy: Springer-Verlag.

[48] Förstner, W. A., (1993). Image Matching. In *Computer and Robot Vision*, R. M. Haralick and L. G. Shapiro, eds., Vol. II, pp. 289–378. Addison-Wesley.

[49] Lindeberg, T., (1995). Direct Estimation of Affine Deformations of Brightness Patterns Using Visual Front-End Operators with Automatic Scale Selection. In *Proc. 5th International Conference on Computer Vision*, pp. 134–141. Cambridge, MA.

[50] Lindeberg, T., (1996). *A Scale Selection Principle for Estimating Image Deformations.* Technical Report ISRN KTH/NA/P--96/16--SE, Dept. of Numerical Analysis and Computing Science, KTH, Stockholm, Sweden. Image and Vision Computing (In press).

[51] Lukas, B. D. and Kanade, T., (1981). An iterative image registration technique with an application to stereo vision. In *Image Understanding Workshop.*

[52] Horn, B. K. P. and Schunck, B. G., (1981). Determining Optical Flow. *J. of Artificial Intelligence*, **17**:185–204.

[53] Lindeberg, T., (1993). Detecting salient blob-like image structures and their scales with a scale-space primal sketch: A method for focus-of-attention. *Int. J. of Computer Vision*, **11**(3):283–318.

[54] Lindeberg, T. and Gårding, J., (1997). Shape-adapted smoothing in estimation of 3-D depth cues from affine distortions of local 2-D structure. *Image and Vision Computing*, **15**:415–434.

[55] Gårding, J. and Lindeberg, T., (1996). Direct computation of shape cues using scale-adapted spatial derivative operators. *Int. J. of Computer Vision*, **17**(2):163–191.

[56] Lindeberg, T. and Li, M., (1997). Segmentation and classification of edges using minimum description length approximation and complementary junction cues. *Computer Vision and Image Understanding*, **67**(1):88–98.

[57] Bretzner, L. and Lindeberg, T., (1998). Feature tracking with automatic selection of spatial scales. *Computer Vision and Image Understanding*, **71**(3):385–392. (To appear).

[58] Almansa, A. and Lindeberg, T., (1996). Fingerprint enhancement by shape adaptation of scale-space operators with automatic scale selection. in preparation.

[59] Wiltschi, K., Pinz, A., and Lindeberg, T., (1997). Classification of Carbide Distributions using Scale Selection and Directional Distributions. In *Proc. 4th International Conference on Image Processing*, Vol. II, pp. 122–125, IEEE. Santa Barbara, California.

[60] Mallat, S. G. and Zhong, S., (1992). Characterization of Signals from Multi-Scale Edges. *IEEE Trans. Pattern Analysis and Machine Intell.*, **14**(7):710–723.

[61] Mallat, S. G. and Hwang, W. L., (1992). Singularity Detection and Processing with Wavelets. *IEEE Trans. Information Theory*, **38**(2):617–643.

[62] Zhang, W. and Bergholm, F., (1993). An Extension of Marr's Signature Based Edge Classification and Other Methods for Determination of Diffuseness and Height of Edges, as Well as Line Width. In *Proc. 4th Int. Conf. on Computer Vision*, H.-H. N. et. al., ed., pp. 183–191. Berlin, Germany: IEEE Computer Society Press.

[63] Pizer, S. M., Burbeck, C. A., Coggins, J. M., Fritsch, D. S., and Morse, B. S., (1994). Object shape before boundary shape: Scale-space medial axis. *J. of Mathematical Imaging and Vision*, **4**:303–313.

[64] Koller, T. M., Gerig, G., Szèkely, G., and Dettwiler, D., (1995). Multiscale Detection of Curvilinear Structures in 2-D and 3-D Image Data. In *Proc. 5th International Conference on Computer Vision*, pp. 864–869. Cambridge, MA.

[65] Jägersand, M., (1995). Saliency Maps and Attention Selection in Scale and Spatial Coordinates: An Information Theoretic Approach. In *Proc. 5th International Conference on Computer Vision*, pp. 195–202. Cambridge, MA.

[66] Kanade, T. and Okutomi, M., (1994). A Stereo Matching Algorithm with an Adaptive Window: Theory and Experiment. *IEEE Trans. Pattern Analysis and Machine Intell.*, **16**(9):920–932.

[67] Battiti, R., Amaldi, E., and Koch, C., (1990). Computing Optical Flow Across Multiple Scales: An Adaptive Coarse-to-Fine Strategy. *Int. J. of Computer Vision*, **6**(2):133–145.

[68] Niessen, W. and Maas, R., (1996). Optic Flow and Stereo. In *Gaussian Scale-Space Theory: Proc. PhD School on Scale-Space Theory*, J. Sporring, M. Nielsen, L. Florack, and P. Johansen, eds. Copenhagen, Denmark: Kluwer Academic Publishers.

[69] Elder, J. H. and Zucker, S. W., (1996). Local scale control for edge detection and blur estimation. In *Proc. 4th European Conference on Computer Vision*, Vol. 1064 of *Lecture Notes in Computer Science*. Cambridge, UK: Springer Verlag, Berlin.

[70] Yacoob, Y. and Davis, L. S., (1997). Estimating Image Motion Using Temporal Multi-Scale Models of Flow and Acceleration. In *Motion-Based Recognition*, M. Shah and R. Jain, eds. Kluwer Academic Publishers.

12 Texture Analysis

Thomas Wagner

Fraunhofer Institute for Integrated Circuits, Erlangen, Germany

Handbook of Computer Vision and Applications
Volume 2
Signal Processing and Pattern Recognition

Copyright © 1999 by Academic Press
All rights of reproduction in any form reserved.
ISBN 0-12-379772-1/$30.00

12.1 Importance of texture

12.1.1 Definition and background

Among other object properties such as color, shape, or motion, *texture* is one of the most prominent image attributes in both human and automatic image analysis.

There are a number of different definitions for texture [1]. What all definitions have in common is the fact that they describe texture as an attribute of an image window. This attribute represents both

- spatially deterministic aspects of the gray levels (Fig. 12.1a);
- spatially stochastic aspects of the gray levels (Fig. 12.1b); and
- spatial aspects of color distribution.

In automatic image analysis, those attributes are represented by textural features, which are real numbers calculated from the image windows with the help of functions such as those described below. The number of potential textural features is large. Because some of them are to a certain extent invariant with respect to change in illumination, distortions, or scaling, they can also make an important contribution to both object segmentation and object recognition tasks.

The human visual system can also distinguish between different types of texture. From our daily experience, we know that we are capable of distinguishing between regular textures that differ in their orientation, scale, phase, color, etc. For stochastic textures, differences in the mean gray values or the variance will be noticed. Experiments on the human visual perception of texture have already been performed by Julesz [2]. A broad overview of this topic is given in Pratt [1].

Nevertheless, the way the human brain analyzes texture has not yet been fully understood. Though there are cell complexes that detect color, shape, or orientations, similar representations of textural attributes in the brain have not yet been found. Some artificial textural features may be based on biological models, but no biological representation of the large variety of complex artificial textural features is known. In that sense, texture analysis is a very complex problem for the human visual system, which might partially be performed on a higher level in the brain.

12.1.2 Texture analysis in machine vision

Texture analysis is also a demanding task for artificial machine vision systems. The computation of textural features such as those described in the following requires significantly more time and memory than the extraction of simple geometric or color-based features. A rough esti-

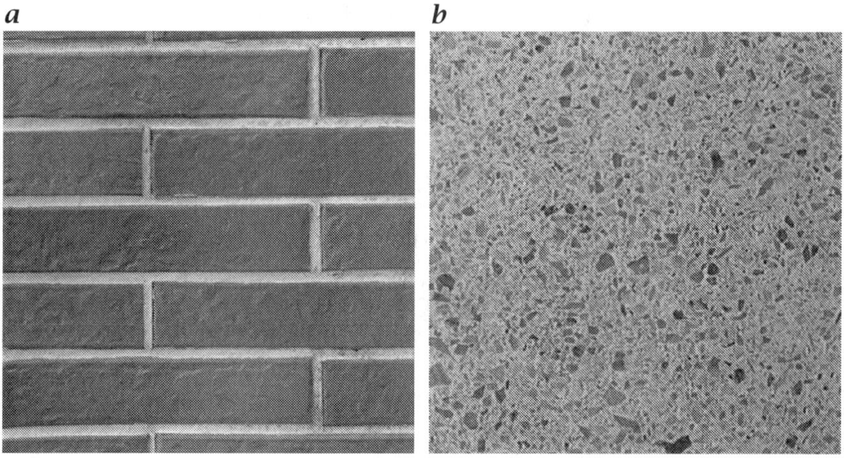

Figure 12.1: ***a*** *Determinstic texture: a brick wall;* ***b*** *stochastic texture: a tiled floor.*

mate is an average of 100 to 1000 operations per pixel for any textural feature.

The demand for vast computing power can be either satisfied by relying on special image processing hardware or by using clusters of standard computer processing units (CPUs). A number of comparisons between these hardware concepts suggests that for many practical applications of complex texture analysis the benefit of special hardware is less than a factor of 2 in terms of speed [3] (see also Volume 3, Section 3.2). At the same time, special hardware usually causes time delays during the development process, and considerable costs when porting solutions to a new (and quicker) hardware platform. For these reasons, in the author's opinion one can observe a clear shift towards standard hardware solutions in industrial texture analysis applications. Nevertheless, this position is controversial (see also Volume 3, Chapters 2 and 3 and Chapter 11).

In any case, a large variety of technical applications benefit from texture analysis:

- *Surface inspection* is essential for industrial quality control of wood, fabrics, or metal surfaces;
- In *object recognition*, textural features can complement other object attributes such as color or shape; and
- Finally, *object segmentation* profits from invariance properties of textural features with respect to rotation, illumination, or scaling.

The literature reports a number of different methods for texture analysis. In Section 12.2, some of the most prominent feature sets are introduced. This section will give the reader an idea of the basic concept of each feature set. Furthermore, it will allow the reader to implement those feature sets. For further reading, especially on details of the theoretical background, links to the corresponding original publications are given.

The list of textural feature sets given below is in no way complete, but tries to give an overview of the variety of different models. The author appreciates feedback on other important feature sets to be included.

Section 12.3 compares the performance of the different textural feature sets. For this task, benchmark sets from different fields of texture analysis are defined. Some of the sets are included on the attached CD rom (.) The performance comparison covers the aspects of speed and error rate in the recognition mode. Though this comparison is in no way exhaustive, it might indicate how to proceed in order to find adequate textural feature sets for a given problem.

Section 12.4 briefly shows that a quantitative evaluation of feature performance can serve as a basis for automatic design of texture analysis systems. As a method of reducing both development costs and time to market for image processing products, automatic design concepts have recently attracted increasing attention.

12.2 Feature sets for texture analysis

There are numerous broader theoretical reviews on texture analysis algorithms [4, 5]. Some papers compare the actual performance of feature sets, quite often on the basis of the Brodatz database (see [6] for an electronic version) or the Vistex [7] image set. There are also web sites containing benchmarks on some groups of textural features, such as the Meastex benchmark [8].

In this chapter, we compare the performance of 318 textural features from 18 feature sets. Because a benchmark can only be done on a common data basis, we define 7 data sets as a basis for benchmarking experiments. The available data sets can be used for further comparisons.

Table 12.1 gives an overview of the different feature sets, which are described in some more detail in this section. More details on the implementation can be found in the given references. The intention of the descriptions below is to provide the reader with a quick overview of the methods and to describe the parameter configurations we have used for our tests.

Table 12.1: Overview of feature sets for texture analysis, with number of features per set and theoretical principle

	No.	Principle
Haralick	14	gray-level co-occurrence matrix
Unser	32	sum and difference histograms
Galloway	20	gray-level run lengths
Laine	21	wavelet packet signatures
Local	14	direct functions of gray values
Fractal (1)	10	fractal box dimension
Fractal (2)	47	fractal dimension from blankets
Laws	14	Laws' convolution matrices
Fourier coeff.	33	energy in ring-shaped regions of Fourier space
Chen	16	geometric properties from binary image planes
Sun *et al.*	5	modified Haralick approach
Pikaz *et al.*	31	pyramid decomposition
Gabor	12	Gabor wavelets
Markov	7	Markov random fields
Dapeng	13	gray-level difference co-occurrence
Amadasun	5	neighboring difference histogram
Mao *et al.*	6	autoregressive models
Amelung	18	histogram and gradient features
Total:	**318**	**No. of feature sets: 18**

12.2.1 Haralick's gray-level co-occurrence features

The feature set of Haralick et al. [10] is probably one of the most famous methods of texture analysis. It is based on the calculation of the *co-occurrence matrix*, a *second-order statistics* of the gray levels in the image window. The co-occurrence matrix $P_{d,\alpha}^{Har}(g,g')$ counts the number of pixel pairs (m,n) and (m',n') in an image that have intensity values of g and g' and that are separated by a pixel distance d in a relative direction α.

In many cases, only eight neighbors and the corresponding four directions $\alpha = 0°, 45°, 90°$ and $135°$ are taken into consideration. With the definitions $L_x = \{1,2,\ldots,N\}$ and $L_y = \{1,2,\ldots,M\}$, this leads to

Table 12.2: *Abbreviations for Haralick's co-occurrence-based method for texture analysis (G is the number of gray levels in image)*

$$p_x(g) = \sum_{g'=1}^{G} p(g,g') \qquad p_y(g') = \sum_{g=1}^{G} p(g,g')$$

$$p_{x+y}(g'') = \sum_{\substack{g=1\\g+g'=g''}}^{G} \sum_{g'=1}^{G} p(g,g'), \qquad g'' = 2,3\ldots 2G$$

$$p_{x-y}(g'') = \sum_{\substack{g=1\\|g-g'|=g''}}^{G} \sum_{g'=1}^{G} p(g,g'), \qquad g'' = 0,1\ldots G-1$$

$$\mu_x = \sum_{g=1}^{G} g p_x(g), \qquad \mu_y = \sum_{g=1}^{G} g p_y(g)$$

$$\sigma_x = \sqrt{\sum_{g=1}^{G} p_x(g)(g-\mu_x)^2}, \qquad \sigma_y = \sqrt{\sum_{g=1}^{G} p_y(g)(g-\mu_y)^2}$$

$$HXY = -\sum_{g=1}^{G}\sum_{g'=1}^{G} p(g,g') \log\{p(g,g')\}$$

$$HXY1 = -\sum_{g=1}^{G}\sum_{g'=1}^{G} p(g,g') \log\{p_x(g)p_y(g')\}$$

$$HXY2 = -\sum_{g=1}^{G}\sum_{g'=1}^{G} p_x(g)p_y(g') \log\{p_x(g)p_y(g')\}$$

$$HX = -\sum_{g=1}^{G} p_x(g) \log p_x(g)$$

$$HY = -\sum_{g=1}^{G} p_y(g) \log p_y(g)$$

$$Q(g,g') = \sum_{g''=0}^{G} \frac{p(g,g'')p(g',g'')}{p_x(g)p_y(g')}$$

G: number of gray levels in the image

the following definitions for the respective co-occurrence matrices:

$$\begin{aligned} P_{d,0^\circ}^{\mathrm{Har}}(g,g') &= \operatorname{card}\{((m,n),(m',n')) \in (L_y \times L_x) \times (L_y \times L_x) | \\ &\quad m-m'=0, |n-n'|=d, G_{m,n}=g, G_{m',n'}=g'\} \\ P_{d,45^\circ}^{\mathrm{Har}}(g,g') &= \operatorname{card}\{((m,n),(m',n')) \in (L_y \times L_x) \times (L_y \times L_x) | \\ &\qquad (m-m'=d, n-n'=-d) \quad \text{or} \\ &\qquad (m-m'=-d, n-n'=d), \\ &\qquad G_{m,n}=g, G_{m',n'}=g'\} \end{aligned} \tag{12.1}$$

Table 12.3: *Features in Haralick's co-occurrence-based method for texture analysis.*

Feature	Definition
Angular second momentum	$F^{Har}_{ASM} = \sum_{g=1}^{G}\sum_{g'=1}^{G}(p(g,g'))^2$
Contrast	$F^{Har}_{Con} = \sum_{g=0}^{G-1} g^2 \left(\sum_{g=1}^{G}\sum_{\substack{g'=1 \\ \lvert g'-g''=g\rvert}}^{G} p(g',g'') \right)$
Correlation	$F^{Har}_{Cor} = \frac{1}{\sigma_x\sigma_y}\left(\sum_{g=1}^{G}\sum_{g'=1}^{G}(gg')p(g,g') - \mu_x\mu_y\right)$
Sum of squares: variance	$F^{Har}_{SSV} = \sum_{g=1}^{G}\sum_{g'=1}^{G}(g-\mu)^2 p(g,g')$
Inverse difference moment	$F^{Har}_{IDM} = \sum_{g=1}^{G}\sum_{g'=1}^{G}\frac{1}{1+(g-g')^2}p(g,g')$
Sum average	$F^{Har}_{SAv} = \sum_{g=2}^{2G} g\, p_{x+y}(g)$
Sum variance[1]	$F^{Har}_{SVa} = \sum_{g=2}^{2G}(g - F^{Har}_{SAv})^2 p_{x+y}(g)$
Sum entropy[2]	$F^{Har}_{SEn} = -\sum_{g=2}^{2G} p_{x+y}(g)\log\{p_{x+y}(g)\}$
Entropy	$F^{Har}_{Ent} = -\sum_{g=1}^{G}\sum_{g'=1}^{G} p(g,g')\log\{p(g,g')\}$
Difference variance	$F^{Har}_{DVa} = \sum_{g=0}^{G-1}(p_{x-y}(g)(g - \sum_{g'=0}^{G-1} g' p_{x-y}(g'))^2)$
Difference entropy	$F^{Har}_{DEn} = -\sum_{g=0}^{G-1} p_{x-y}(g)\log\{p_{x-y}(g)\}$
Information measures of correlation[3]	$F^{Har}_{IC1} = \frac{HXY-HXY1}{\max\{HX,HY\}}$
	$F^{Har}_{IC2} = (1-\exp[-2.0\lvert HXY2 - HXY\rvert])^{1/2}$
Max. correlation coefficient[4]	$F^{Har}_{MCC} = (\text{second largest eigenvalue of Q})^{1/2}$

[1]In the original paper of Haralick, this feature depends on F^{Har}_{SEn} instead of F^{Har}_{SAv}, but we assume this to be a typographic error.

[2]For all Haralick features, expressions containing a $\log(0)$ term are simply suppressed and do not contribute to the respective feature.

[3]In the original paper of Haralick, there are no absolute values. We have added them to avoid negative numbers in the argument of the square root function.

[4]If the second largest eigenvalue is negative, the feature is set to 0. The calculation of the eigenvalue has been performed with a routine from Press [9].

$P^{\text{Har}}_{d,90^\circ}(g,g')$ and $P^{\text{Har}}_{d,135^\circ}(g,g')$ have equivalent definitions. In the preceding equations, the card operator denotes the number of elements in a set.

For the actual evaluation, different methods of processing the co-occurrence matrices are known. In our case, the four co-occurrence matrices for the different directions and distance $d = 1$ are averaged:

$$P^{\text{Har}}_{\Sigma} = \frac{1}{4}\left(P^{\text{Har}}_{1,0^\circ} + P^{\text{Har}}_{1,45^\circ} + P^{\text{Har}}_{1,90^\circ} + P^{\text{Har}}_{1,135^\circ}\right) \tag{12.2}$$

A normalized co-occurrence matrix is calculated from

$$p^{\text{Har}}(g,g') = \frac{1}{N_{\text{pixpair}}} P^{\text{Har}}_{\Sigma}(g,g') \tag{12.3}$$

with N_{pixpair} as the total number of pixel pairs in the image

$$N_{\text{pixpair}} = \sum_{g=1}^{G}\sum_{g'=1}^{G} P^{\text{Har}}_{\Sigma}(g,g') \tag{12.4}$$

In order to reduce the size of the co-occurrence matrices and to speed up calculations, we have reduced the intensity resolution of the input image down to 128 gray levels. The letter G represents the number of distinct gray levels in the image after gray-level reduction. Additional definitions are listed in Table 12.2.

Fourteen features are calculated from the normalized co-occurrence matrix $p^{\text{Har}}(g,g')$ (see Table 12.3).

12.2.2 Unser's sum and difference histograms

In order to reduce the computation time necessary to calculate the co-occurrence matrix, Unser has suggested a method to estimate its coefficients using a first-order statistic on the image window [11]. He suggests *sum and difference histograms* on the gray levels.

Two image windows with centers at $G_{m,n}$ and $G_{m',n'}$ are displaced by a distance $\boldsymbol{d} = (d_1, d_2)$

$$G_{m',n'} = G_{m+d_1,n+d_2} \tag{12.5}$$

With the definition for the sum $s_{m,n}$ and the difference $d_{m,n}$ of the respective gray levels

$$s_{m,n} = G_{m,n} + G_{m+d_1,n+d_2} \quad \text{and} \quad d_{m,n} = G_{m,n} - G_{m+d_1,n+d_2} \tag{12.6}$$

the sum and difference histograms h_s and h_d are defined as follows:

$$\begin{aligned} h_s(i;d_1,d_2) &= h_s(i) = \text{card}\{G_{m,n} | s_{m,n} = i\} \\ h_d(j;d_1,d_2) &= h_d(j) = \text{card}\{G_{m,n} | d_{m,n} = j\} \end{aligned} \tag{12.7}$$

Table 12.4: *Unser's sum and difference histogram features.*

Feature	Definition
Mean	$F^{\text{Uns}}_{\text{Mea}} = \sum_{i=0}^{G-1} i\hat{P}(i)$
Angular Second Momentum	$F^{\text{Uns}}_{\text{ASM}} = \sum_{i=0}^{G-1} (\hat{P}(i))^2$
Contrast	$F^{\text{Uns}}_{\text{Con}} = \sum_{i=0}^{G-1} (i-\mu)^2\hat{P}(i)$
Entropy	$F^{\text{Uns}}_{\text{Ent}} = \sum_{i=0}^{G-1} -\hat{P}(i) log\hat{P}(i)$

The number of total counts is

$$N_{tot} = \text{card}\{\boldsymbol{G}\} = \sum_i h_s(i) = \sum_j h_d(j) \tag{12.8}$$

The histograms get normalized by

$$\begin{aligned} \hat{P}_s(i) &= \frac{h_s(i)}{N_{tot}}, \quad (i = 2, \ldots 2G), \\ \hat{P}_d(j) &= \frac{h_d(j)}{N_{tot}}, \quad (j = -G+1, \ldots G-1) \end{aligned} \tag{12.9}$$

with G being the number of gray levels in the image. Typically, a reduced gray-level resolution (e. g., 32) is used.

For both histograms $\hat{P}_s(i)$ and $\hat{P}_d(j)$, global features can be calculated according to Table 12.4. Doing this for all of the four possible nearest displacements in the directions 0°, 45°, 90° and 135°, this leads to a total of 32 Unser features.

12.2.3 Galloway's run-length-based features

Galloway has proposed a *run-length*-based technique, which calculates characteristic textural features from gray-level run lengths in different image directions [12].

The basis of the calculation of the features is a run-length matrix that is defined as

$$P^{Gal}_{\phi}(g, r) = (a_{g,r}) \tag{12.10}$$

where $a_{g,r}$ is the number of occurrences of a connected pixel interval of run length r in the direction ϕ with all pixel values of the interval being equal to the gray-level value g.

Table 12.5: Definitions and features of Galloway's run-length-based method for texture analysis.

Abbreviations	
N_{pix}: number of pixels in image window	
G: number of gray levels in image	
R: maximal run length in image	
$N = \sum_{g=1}^{G} \sum_{r=1}^{R} P_{\phi}^{Gal}(g,r)$	
Feature	**Definition**
Short run emphasis	$F_{\text{SRE}, \phi}^{\text{Gal}} = \frac{1}{N} \sum_{g=1}^{G} \sum_{r=1}^{R} \frac{P_{\phi}^{Gal}(g,r)}{l^2}$
Long run emphasis	$F_{\text{LRE}, \phi}^{\text{Gal}} = \frac{1}{N} \sum_{g=1}^{G} \sum_{r=1}^{R} l^2 \cdot P_{\phi}^{Gal}(g,r)$
Gray-level distribution	$F_{\text{GLD}, \phi}^{\text{Gal}} = \frac{1}{N} \sum_{g=1}^{G} \left(\sum_{r=1}^{R} P_{\phi}^{Gal}(g,r) \right)^2$
Run-length distribution	$F_{\text{RLD}, \phi}^{\text{Gal}} = \frac{1}{N} \sum_{r=1}^{R} \left(\sum_{g=1}^{G} P_{\phi}^{Gal}(g,r) \right)^2$
Run percentage	$F_{\text{RPe}, \phi}^{\text{Gal}} = \frac{1}{N_{pix}} \sum_{g=1}^{G} \sum_{r=1}^{R} r P_{\phi}^{Gal}(g,r)$

Usually, four run-length matrices for the directions $\phi = 0°, 45°, 90°$, and $135°$ are calculated. In order to get sufficiently high run-length values, a reduction of the gray values of an image is performed, in our case down to 16 values.

Table 12.5 shows the features derived from the four run-length matrices. Because they are calculated for each of the four run-length matrices, a total of 20 features is derived.

12.2.4 Chen's geometric features from binary image sequences

Chen [13] decomposes a gray-level image into a sequence of binary images and calculates a total of 16 features from geometric properties of the resulting blob regions.

From the original image, a series of binary images $\boldsymbol{G}^{bin,t}$ is constructed by help of thresholds $t \in 1, \ldots G - 1$ as follows:

$$G_{m,n}^{bin,t} = \begin{cases} 1 \text{ for } G_{m,n} \geq t \\ 0 \text{ else} \end{cases} \tag{12.11}$$

The features below are derived for each connected region I in the image, with a 4-neighborhood relation as the basis of connectivity. With the

Table 12.6: *Definitions and features of Chen's binarization-based method for texture analysis.*

Abbreviations	
Number of connected areas	$NOC_0(t)$: Number of connected black areas in binary image generated with threshold t. $NOC_1(t)$: Number of connected white areas in binary image generated with threshold t.
Average irregularity	$IRGL_b(t) = \dfrac{\sum_{I \in G^{bin,t}} [NOP_b(t,I) IRGL_b(t,I)]}{\sum_{I \in G^{bin,t}} NOP_b(t,I)}; b \in \{0,1\}$
Feature	**Definition**
For each $g(t) \in \{IRGL_0(t), IRGL_1(t), NOC_0(t), NOC_1(t)\}$ calculate	
Maximum	$F^{\mathrm{Che}}_{\mathrm{Max}} = \max_{1 \le t \le G-1} g(t)$
Average	$F^{\mathrm{Che}}_{\mathrm{Ave}} = \dfrac{1}{G-1} \sum_{t=1}^{G-1} g(t)$
Mean	$F^{\mathrm{Che}}_{\mathrm{Mea}} = \sum_{t=1}^{G-1} t g(t) \Big/ \sum_{t=1}^{G-1} g(t)$
Standard deviation	$F^{\mathrm{Che}}_{\mathrm{StD}} = \sqrt{\dfrac{1}{\sum_{t=1}^{G-1} g(t)} \sum_{t=1}^{G-1} (t - F^{\mathrm{Che}}_{\mathrm{Mea}})^2 g(t)}$

definitions

$$\overline{x} = \sum_{i \in I} x_i \Big/ |I|, \quad \overline{y} = \sum_{i \in I} y_i \Big/ |I| \tag{12.12}$$

and $|I|$ as the number of pixels in the area I, a center of gravity $(\overline{x}, \overline{y})$ is calculated for each connected region I. The index i runs over all pixels in a connected area I. For all connected areas I in f_t^{bin}, a measure of irregularity is defined as

$$IRGL_b(t, I) = \frac{1 + \sqrt{\pi} \max_{i \in I} \sqrt{(x_i - \overline{x})^2 + (y_i - \overline{y})^2}}{\sqrt{|I|}} - 1 \tag{12.13}$$

The parameter b denotes connected black areas $b = 0$ and white areas for $b = 1$. The forementioned definitions serve, together with further definitions of the parameters "number of connected areas" and "average irregularity," as a basis of textural features derived from the sequence of binary images. Those features are listed in Table 12.6. In our experiments, binary images are calculated with the 15 thresholds $t = 16, 32, 48, \ldots, 240$.

12.2.5 Laine's textural energy from Daubechies wavelets

Laine uses a *wavelet decomposition* with *Daubechies wavelets* and takes the energies in the different filter bands as features [14]. Details on implementation including a 2-D implementation and the Daubechies coefficients DAUB4 used here can be found in [9, Chapter 13.10].

Being interested in the application of wavelets it is sufficient to know that, similar to a Fourier transformation, a wavelet transform represents a transformation to different orthogonal basis functions. While for the Fourier Transform these basic functions are sine and cosine functions, so called wavelets are used for the wavelet transform.

For the wavelet transform of a 1-D signal the transformation can be expressed by use of a transformation matrix acting on the column vector of the signal.

For the following discussion we concentrate on the transformation coefficients of the DAUB4 wavelet transform used here, which is characterized by the four coefficients $c_0, \ldots, c_3$. The numerical values of the DAUB4 coefficients are

$$\begin{aligned} c_0 &= 0.4829629131445341, & c_1 &= 0.8365163037378079 \\ c_2 &= 0.2241438680420134, & c_3 &= -0.1294095225512604 \end{aligned} \qquad (12.14)$$

In the case of a DAUB4 wavelet transform the transformation matrix for a onedimensional signal with 8 components is

$$W = \begin{bmatrix} c_0 & c_1 & c_2 & c_3 & 0 & 0 & 0 & 0 \\ c_3 & -c_2 & c_1 & -c_0 & 0 & 0 & 0 & 0 \\ 0 & 0 & c_0 & c_1 & c_2 & c_3 & 0 & 0 \\ 0 & 0 & c_3 & -c_2 & c_1 & -c_0 & 0 & 0 \\ 0 & 0 & 0 & 0 & c_0 & c_1 & c_2 & c_3 \\ 0 & 0 & 0 & 0 & c_3 & -c_2 & c_1 & -c_0 \\ c_2 & c_3 & 0 & 0 & 0 & 0 & c_0 & c_1 \\ c_1 & -c_0 & 0 & 0 & 0 & 0 & c_3 & -c_2 \end{bmatrix} \qquad (12.15)$$

This transformation matrix can be interpreted as two different rotations in the space of basic functions, which are interwoven. One rotation operates on the even rows the other one on the odd rows. From a practical point of view the filter coefficients in the odd rows can be seen as a blurring filter while the coefficients in even rows perform a sharpening.

After applying the transformation matrix once a permutation of the resulting vector entries has to take place in order to "separate" the

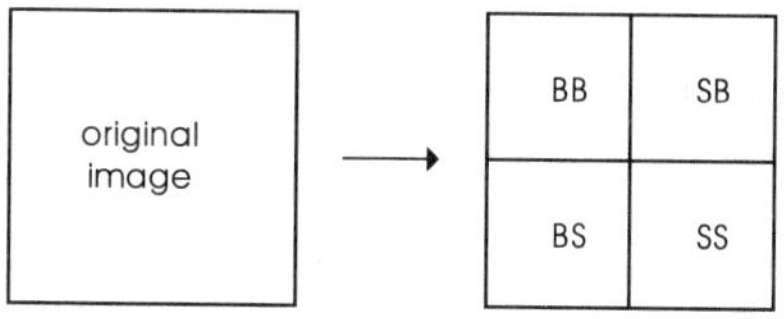

Figure 12.2: *Schematic figure of a wavelet transformation: An image is split into four subimages of equal size.*

two filter outputs from each other. As each rotation uses only half the number of rows a rescaling of a factor of two takes place but two outputs (in the vector below with 4 components each) are generated.

$$\begin{bmatrix} x_1 \\ x_2 \\ x_3 \\ x_4 \\ x_5 \\ x_6 \\ x_7 \\ x_8 \end{bmatrix} \xrightarrow{\text{transformation}} \begin{bmatrix} s_1 \\ d_1 \\ s_2 \\ d_2 \\ s_3 \\ d_3 \\ s_4 \\ d_4 \end{bmatrix} \xrightarrow{\text{permutation}} \begin{bmatrix} s_1 \\ s_2 \\ s_3 \\ s_4 \\ d_1 \\ d_2 \\ d_3 \\ d_4 \end{bmatrix} \qquad (12.16)$$

In order to apply a wavelet transform to a 2-D image one has to transform and reorder the rows and the columns of the image sequentially. As in Fourier transforms the order of operation is not important. Each transformation step generates four different subimages from one original image (Fig. 12.2). The letters, for example, in the top right subimage indicate the first transformation (e. g., on the rows) has been a sharpening while the second one (on the columns) was a blurring.

While many wavelet transforms do a multiresolution analysis by successively transforming only the top left subimage of each decomposition step, Laine has decided to do the decomposition for all four subimages successively.

For extracting textural features $\boldsymbol{F}^{\text{Lai}}$ an energy value is calculated for each subimage in a decomposition sequence by summing over the squares of all pixel values in the subimage. With three resolution steps in the wavelet decomposition 21 features can be calculated. One coefficient stems from the original image, four from the first decomposition level, and further 16 from the second level.

12.2.6 Local textural features

Local texture features are calculated directly from the original image window [15]. The feature set contains statistical features and gradient features. In the case of the first feature (gray level of central pixel),

Table 12.7: Local textural features. For definition of the Sobel and Kirsch operators see Table 12.8 and Table 12.9

Feature	Definition
Gray level of central pixel	$F^{\text{Loc}}_{\text{GLP}} = G$
Average of gray levels in window	$F^{\text{Loc}}_{\text{Ave}} = \text{mean}_U\, G$
Median	$F^{\text{Loc}}_{\text{Med}} = \text{median} G$
Standard deviation of gray levels	$F^{\text{Loc}}_{\text{Std}} = \text{mean}_U \left(G_{m',n'} - F^{\text{Loc}}_{\text{Ave}}\right)^2$
Difference of maximum and minimum gray level	$F^{\text{Loc}}_{\text{DMM}} = \max_U G - \min_U G$
Difference between average gray level in small and large window	$F^{\text{Loc}}_{\text{DSL}} = \text{mean}_{U_s} G - \text{mean}\, G$
Sobel feature	$F^{\text{Loc}}_{\text{Sob}} = \lvert S_x G\rvert + \lvert S_y G\rvert$
Kirsch feature	$F^{\text{Loc}}_{\text{Kir}} = \max\limits_{i \in \{0,\ldots,7\}} (\mathcal{K}_i G)$
Derivative in x-direction	$F^{\text{Loc}}_{\text{DXD}} = \text{mean}_{U_r} G - \text{mean}_{U_l} G$
Derivative in y-direction	$F^{\text{Loc}}_{\text{DYD}} = \text{mean}_{U_t} G - \text{mean}_{U_b} G$
Diagonal derivatives	$F^{\text{Loc}}_{\text{DD1}} = \text{mean}_{U_{tr}} G - \text{mean}_{U_{bl}} G$
	$F^{\text{Loc}}_{\text{DD2}} = \text{mean}_{U_{tl}} G - \text{mean}_{U_{br}} G$
Combined features	$F^{\text{Loc}}_{\text{CF1}} = \lvert G - F^{\text{Loc}}_{\text{Ave}}\rvert$
	$F^{\text{Loc}}_{\text{CF2}} = \lvert G - F^{\text{Loc}}_{\text{Std}}\rvert$

for a 64×64-image and indices running from 0 to 63, the gray level is taken at positions (32,32). Some features code derivatives in x, y, and diagonal directions by subtracting average gray levels in subwindows next to the central pixel. For this purpose the following subwindows are defined:

$$
\begin{aligned}
U_s &= \{G_{m,n} \mid \frac{M}{4} \le m < \frac{3M}{4} \wedge \frac{N}{4} \le n < \frac{3N}{4}\} \\
U_r &= \{G_{m,n} \mid \frac{M}{4} \le m < \frac{3M}{4} \wedge \frac{N}{2} \le n < N\} \\
U_{tl} &= \{G_{m,n} \mid 0 \le m < \frac{M}{2} \wedge 0 \le n < \frac{N}{2}\} && (12.17) \\
& && (12.18)
\end{aligned}
$$

U_l, U_t, and U_b are defined in a similar way as U_r while U_{tr}, U_{bl}, and U_{br} are similar to U_{tl}.

Feature $F^{\text{Loc}}_{\text{DXD}}$ with the derivative in x direction, for example, subtracts mean gray levels in windows to the right and to the left of the central pixel. Derivatives in y and in the diagonal directions are calculated in the same way.

Table 12.8: *Definitions of Kirsch matrices*

$$K_0 = \begin{bmatrix} 5 & 5 & 5 \\ -3 & 0 & -3 \\ -3 & -3 & -3 \end{bmatrix} \quad K_1 = \begin{bmatrix} 5 & 5 & -3 \\ 5 & 0 & -3 \\ -3 & -3 & -3 \end{bmatrix} \quad K_2 = \begin{bmatrix} 5 & -3 & -3 \\ 5 & 0 & -3 \\ 5 & -3 & -3 \end{bmatrix}$$

$$K_3 = \begin{bmatrix} -3 & -3 & -3 \\ 5 & 0 & -3 \\ 5 & 5 & -3 \end{bmatrix} \quad K_4 = \begin{bmatrix} -3 & -3 & -3 \\ -3 & 0 & -3 \\ 5 & 5 & 5 \end{bmatrix} \quad K_5 = \begin{bmatrix} -3 & -3 & -3 \\ -3 & 0 & 5 \\ -3 & 5 & 5 \end{bmatrix}$$

$$K_6 = \begin{bmatrix} -3 & -3 & 5 \\ -3 & 0 & 5 \\ -3 & -3 & 5 \end{bmatrix} \quad K_7 = \begin{bmatrix} -3 & 5 & 5 \\ -3 & 0 & 5 \\ -3 & -3 & -3 \end{bmatrix}$$

Table 12.9: *Definitions of Sobel operators*

$$S_x = \begin{bmatrix} -1 & -2 & -1 \\ 0 & 0 & 0 \\ 1 & 2 & 1 \end{bmatrix} \qquad S_y = \begin{bmatrix} -1 & 0 & 1 \\ -2 & 0 & 2 \\ -1 & 0 & 1 \end{bmatrix}$$

Local features of the input image are shown in Table 12.7. For an image with G gray levels, median($\boldsymbol{G}$) is defined as

$$\text{median}(\boldsymbol{G}) = \min_g \{\text{card}\{(m', n') | G_{m',n'} \leq g\} \geq \frac{MN}{2}\} \tag{12.19}$$

The *Kirsch matrices* used for feature $\boldsymbol{F}^{\text{Loc}}_{\text{Kir}}$ are shown in Table 12.8, and the *Sobel operators* (essential for calculating feature $\boldsymbol{F}^{\text{Loc}}_{\text{Sob}}$) are shown in Table 12.9. The Sobel operator is discussed in detail in Section 10.3.4.

12.2.7 Fractal features

A number of different fractal features are in use. In Roß et al. [16], fractal box dimensions are calculated on a set of binary images. These images are generated from the original image with the help of thresholds calculated from the maximal gradient value in the image.

From the original image $\boldsymbol{G}$, a gradient image $\boldsymbol{G}'$ is generated with the help of a Sobel operator (see Table 12.9):

$$\boldsymbol{D} = \begin{bmatrix} \boldsymbol{G}_x \\ \boldsymbol{G}_y \end{bmatrix} = \begin{bmatrix} S_x \boldsymbol{G} \\ S_y \boldsymbol{G} \end{bmatrix} \tag{12.20}$$

An absolute value[1] is calculated from the gradient image by

$$|\boldsymbol{D}| = \sqrt{\boldsymbol{G}_X \cdot \boldsymbol{G}_X + \boldsymbol{G}_Y \cdot \boldsymbol{G}_Y} \tag{12.21}$$

Binarization is accomplished with a threshold t such that

$$\boldsymbol{G}^{bin,t}_{m,n} = \begin{cases} 1 & \text{if } |D_{m,n}| > t \\ 0 & \text{else} \end{cases} \tag{12.22}$$

A fractal box dimension is calculated by covering the binary image with a lattice of grid size r and calculating the number of squares $N_g(\boldsymbol{G}^{bin,t}, r)$ containing pixels with value 1. From that, a fractal dimension D is calculated by means of linear regression[2] from a double-logarithmic plot of the equation

$$N_g(\boldsymbol{G}^{bin,t}, r) = \frac{1}{r^D} \tag{12.23}$$

The authors of the original paper have spent some effort in adapting the levels t for binarization to their data sample. Because our benchmark tends to follow a more general approach, we have chosen the 10 values $t_i = 25i$, $i \in 1, 2, \dots 10$. The 10 resulting feature values are taken as the feature set "Fractal (1)."

Another fractal feature set named "Fractal (2)" is defined in Peleg et al. [17]. Peleg's basic idea was to determine a fractal surface area by covering the surface with "blankets."

When covering a surface with a blanket of thickness 2ϵ, the area of the surface is calculated from dividing the blanket volume by 2ϵ. The covering blanket has an upper surface u_ϵ and a lower surface b_ϵ. With the image gray levels $G_{m,n}$ and initial conditions

$$u_0(m,n) = b_0(m,n) = G_{m,n} \tag{12.24}$$

a sequence of blanket surfaces for different thicknesses ϵ is defined as follows:

$$\begin{aligned} u_\epsilon(m,n) &= \max\left\{u_{\epsilon-1}(m,n) + 1, \max_{|(m,n)-(m',n')|\le 1} u_{\epsilon-1}(m',n')\right\} \\ b_\epsilon(m,n) &= \min\left\{b_{\epsilon-1}(m,n) - 1, \min_{|(m,n)-(m',n')|\le 1} b_{\epsilon-1}(m',n')\right\} \end{aligned}$$

---

[1]In our implementation, the argument of the square root is clipped to 255, and the result of the square root is converted to an integer value.

[2]In the regression all data points with $N_g = 0$ are suppressed; on a 64×64 pixel image, N_g is calculated for grid sizes $r = 2^i, i \in \{1, 2, \dots, 5\}$. For the implementation of the linear regression, see [9].

For calculation of the blanket position in step ϵ, this recursive definition uses the gray values of the four neighbors in step $\epsilon - 1$. With the definitions

$$v_\epsilon = \sum_{m,n} (u_\epsilon(m,n) - b_\epsilon(m,n)) \tag{12.25}$$

for the volume v_ϵ of the blanket and

$$A(\epsilon) = \frac{(v_\epsilon - v_{\epsilon-1})}{2} \tag{12.26}$$

for the surface area $A(\epsilon)$ corresponding to a blanket radius ϵ, a fractal dimension D is defined by

$$A(\epsilon) = F\epsilon^{2-D} \tag{12.27}$$

Slopes S_ϵ are calculated from best fit lines through the three points

$$\begin{array}{l} (\log(\epsilon - 1), \log(A(\epsilon - 1))), \\ (\log(\epsilon), \log(A(\epsilon))), \\ (\log(\epsilon + 1), \log(A(\epsilon + 1))) \end{array} \tag{12.28}$$

In our experiments, we use the slopes $S(\epsilon)$ as textural features. From 49 area values $A(\epsilon)$, $\epsilon = 1, \ldots 49$, 47 slopes $S(\epsilon)$ can be extracted.

12.2.8 Laws filter masks for textural energy

Laws has suggested a set convolution masks for feature extraction [18]. There are five 1-D filter masks with the labels "level," "edge," "spot," "wave," and "ripple" (Table 12.10). From them, 25 2-D filter masks can be constructed, for example,

$$\boldsymbol{F}_{le} = \boldsymbol{l}_5 \boldsymbol{e}_5^T = \begin{bmatrix} 1 \\ 4 \\ 6 \\ 4 \\ 1 \end{bmatrix} [-1, -2, 0, 2, 1] = \begin{bmatrix} -1 & -2 & 0 & 2 & 1 \\ -4 & -8 & 0 & 8 & 4 \\ -6 & -12 & 0 & 12 & 6 \\ -4 & -8 & 0 & 8 & 4 \\ -1 & -2 & 0 & 2 & 1 \end{bmatrix} \tag{12.29}$$

The 14 Laws features are calculated from

$$\boldsymbol{F}^{\text{Law}}_{\text{xy}} = \frac{g_{xy} + g_{yx}}{g_{ll}} \tag{12.30}$$

where

$$g_{xy} = \sum_m \sum_n |(\boldsymbol{x}_5 \boldsymbol{y}_5^T) * \boldsymbol{G}|, \text{ with } \boldsymbol{x}_5, \boldsymbol{y}_5 \in \{\boldsymbol{l}_5, \boldsymbol{e}_5, \boldsymbol{s}_5, \boldsymbol{w}_5, \boldsymbol{r}_5\} \tag{12.31}$$

Ten features are calculated from nondiagonal elements ($x \neq y$), while another four stem from diagonal elements, and the fifth diagonal element g_{ll} is used for normalization.

Table 12.10: Definitions of 1-D Laws matrices

Laws matrices
$\boldsymbol{l}_5 = \begin{bmatrix} 1 \\ 4 \\ 6 \\ 4 \\ 1 \end{bmatrix}$ $\boldsymbol{e}_5 = \begin{bmatrix} -1 \\ -2 \\ 0 \\ 2 \\ 1 \end{bmatrix}$ $\boldsymbol{s}_5 = \begin{bmatrix} -1 \\ 0 \\ 2 \\ 0 \\ -1 \end{bmatrix}$ $\boldsymbol{w}_5 = \begin{bmatrix} -1 \\ 2 \\ 0 \\ -2 \\ 1 \end{bmatrix}$ $\boldsymbol{r}_5 = \begin{bmatrix} 1 \\ -4 \\ 6 \\ -4 \\ 1 \end{bmatrix}$

12.2.9 Fourier features

In [16], energy values calculated from different regions in the power spectrum of the images Fourier transform are taken as textural features. A total of thirty-three Fourier coefficients are extracted for the description of textures.

The discrete Fourier transform $\hat{\boldsymbol{G}}$ of a two-dimensional real image $\boldsymbol{G}$ is defined as

$$\hat{G}_{u,v} = \frac{1}{MN} \sum_{m=0}^{M-1} \sum_{n=0}^{N-1} G_{m,n} \exp\left(-\frac{2\pi imu}{M}\right) \exp\left(-\frac{2\pi inv}{N}\right) \tag{12.32}$$

The resulting power spectrum $|\hat{\boldsymbol{G}}|$ is symmetrical (Section 3.3.3), therefore only the area $\{[u,v] | u \in \{-M/2+1, \ldots, M/2\} \wedge v \in \{0, \ldots, N/2\}$ will be the basis of the calculations below.

If the image is quadratic, that is, $M = N$, radial features can be defined as

$$c_{r_1,r_2} = \sum\sum_{r_1^2 \le u^2+v^2 \le r_2^2} |\hat{G}_{u,v}|^2 \tag{12.33}$$

The seven radial features $\boldsymbol{F}^{\text{Fou}}_{\text{ra0}} \ldots \boldsymbol{F}^{\text{Fou}}_{\text{ra6}}$ are calculated from

$$\boldsymbol{F}^{\text{Fou}}_{\text{ra}i} = c_{r_i,r_{i+1}}, \qquad i \in 0, \ldots 6, r_i = \frac{i}{7}\frac{N}{2} \tag{12.34}$$

An eighth radial feature $\boldsymbol{F}^{\text{Fou}}_{\text{ra7}}$ is defined as the sum over the coefficients in the "corners" of the Fourier domain, not included within the largest circle. Summing over the coefficients in the respective circle segments leads to energy values a_{θ_1,θ_2}

$$a_{\theta_1,\theta_2} = \sum\sum_{\theta_1 \le tan^{-1}\frac{v}{u} \le \theta_2} |\hat{G}_{u,v}|^2 \tag{12.35}$$

They are the basis of the 10 directional features $\boldsymbol{F}^{\text{Fou}}_{\text{di0}} \ldots \boldsymbol{F}^{\text{Fou}}_{\text{di9}}$ defined by

$$\boldsymbol{F}^{\text{Fou}}_{\text{di}i} = a_{\theta_i,\theta_{i+1}}, \qquad \theta_i = \frac{i\pi}{10} (i = 0, \ldots 9) \tag{12.36}$$

Finally, 10 horizontal and 5 vertical features are defined as

$$\boldsymbol{F}^{\text{Fou}}_{\text{hoi}} = \sum_{u=i\frac{1}{10}M+(-\frac{M}{2}+1)}^{(i-1)\frac{1}{10}M+(-\frac{M}{2}+1)} \sum_{v=0}^{\frac{N}{2}} |\hat{G}_{u,v}|^2, \qquad i \in \{0,\ldots,9\} \tag{12.37}$$

and

$$\boldsymbol{F}^{\text{Fou}}_{\text{vei}} = \sum_{u=-\frac{M}{2}+1}^{\frac{M}{2}} \sum_{v=i\frac{1}{5}\frac{N}{2}}^{(i+1)\frac{1}{5}\frac{N}{2}} |\hat{G}_{u,v}|^2, \qquad i \in \{0,\ldots,4\} \tag{12.38}$$

12.2.10 A modified gray-level co-occurrence approach

Sun and Wee [19] define five features from a modified Haralick approach. They calculated statistics in an 8-neighborhood and are therefore less dependent on image rotations.

The matrix $P_N(g, s, a, d)$ lists the number of pixels s in a neighborhood N of an image point $G_{m,n}$, for which the gray-level difference $|G_{m,n} - G_{m',n'}|$ is lower or equal to a given threshold d. The neighborhood is defined by a distance threshold ρ

$$\begin{aligned} P^{Sun}_{N,a,d}(g,s) &= \text{card}\{(m,n)|G_{m,n} = g \wedge \\ &\wedge \text{card}[(m',n')|\rho((m,n),(m',n')) \le a \\ &\wedge |G_{m,n} - G_{m',n'}| \le d] = s\} \end{aligned} \tag{12.39}$$

In our implementation, the parameter values $a = 0$ and $d = 1$ are used. From the matrix $P^{Sun}_{N,a,d}(g,s)$, five features are defined, which are shown in Table 12.11.

12.2.11 Texture analysis from pyramid decomposition

Pikaz and Averbuch [20] calculate textural features from a sequence of graphs $\{N_s(t)\}$, where $N_s(t)$ denotes the number of 4-connected structures of at least size s, and t denotes a threshold used to binarize the image. They suggest an optimized implementation that computes the sequence of graphs in almost linear time complexity in terms of number of pixels in the image.

In this paper, we follow the suggestion of the Pikaz and Averbuch to use $\{N_2(t)\}$ to characterize a texture. As thresholds $t(i)$ we choose

$$t(i) = i\frac{G-1}{N_t-1}, \qquad i \in \{0,1,\ldots,N_t-2\} \tag{12.40}$$

with G as the number of gray levels, and N_t the number of thresholds to be determined. In our implementation, N_t is defined as 32, which leads to a total of 31 features.

Table 12.11: Features from the modified Haralick approach by Sun and Wee

Abbreviations	
	$N = \sum_{g=1}^{G} \sum_{s=0}^{8} P^{\text{Sun}}_{N,1,d}(g,s)$
Feature	**Definition**
Small number emphasis	$F^{\text{Sun}}_{\text{SNE}} = \frac{1}{N} \sum_{g=1}^{G} \sum_{s=0}^{8} \frac{P^{\text{Sun}}_{N,1,d}(g,s)}{s^2}$
Large number emphasis	$F^{\text{Sun}}_{\text{LNE}} = \frac{1}{N} \sum_{g=1}^{G} \sum_{s=0}^{8} s^2 \cdot P^{\text{Sun}}_{N,1,d}(g,s)$
Number distribution	$F^{\text{Sun}}_{\text{NDi}} = \frac{1}{N} \sum_{s=0}^{8} \left(\sum_{g=1}^{G} P^{\text{Sun}}_{N,1,d}(g,s) \right)^2$
Angular second moment	$F^{\text{Sun}}_{\text{ASM}} = \frac{1}{N^2} \sum_{g=1}^{G} \sum_{s=0}^{8} P^{\text{Sun}}_{N,1,d}(g,s)^2$
Entropy	$F^{\text{Sun}}_{\text{Ent}} = \frac{-1}{ld(\frac{1}{8 \cdot G})} \sum_{g=1}^{G} \sum_{s=0}^{8} P^{\text{Sun}}_{N,1,d}(g,s) \cdot \text{ld}(\frac{P^{\text{Sun}}_{N,1,d}(g,s)}{N})$

12.2.12 Gabor wavelets

Fogel and Sagi [21] and many others suggest the use of so-called *Gabor wavelets* or *Gabor filters* for feature extraction. Gabor wavelets are defined in Section 4.2.2. They can be used to extract a certain wavelength and orientation from an image with a specified bandwidth. Because the Gabor filter is a *quadrature filter* (Section 4.2), the "energy" of the signal in the filter band can be determined by computing the square magnitude of the complex filter response. Here values for the wavelength λ and the orientation θ are $\lambda \in \{2, 4, 8\}$ and $\theta \in \{0°, 45°, 90°, 135°\}$, which leads to a total of 12 features.

12.2.13 Markov random field approach

In Kashyap et al. [22], a *Markov random field* approach is chosen to extract seven different textural features. Markov random fields model a texture by expressing all gray values of an image as a function of the gray values in a neighborhood η of each pixel. Each pixel $G_{m',n'}$ in this neighborhood is characterized by its distance $\boldsymbol{d} = (d_1, d_2)$ from the central pixel $G_{m,n}$:

$$G_{m',n'} = G_{m+d_1,n+d_2} \tag{12.41}$$

For each image, one set of global model parameters $\{\theta_{\boldsymbol{d}}\}$ is determined, which is characteristic of a special type of texture. This global set of parameters model the neighborhoods of all pixels in an image. As the fit will not be perfect, there is a remaining error ϵ

$$G_{m,n} = \sum_{\text{all } G_{m',n'} \in \eta} \theta_d G_{m',n'} + \epsilon_{m,n} \tag{12.42}$$

Figure 2.5b in Chapter 2 shows the neighboring pixels of a central pixel x. They are ordered with respect to their distance. In our current implementations, all neighbors 1, 2 and 3 are included in the model. However, one single model parameter represents a pair of point-symmetric neighbors at a time, which are averaged. In our case, 12 neighboring pixels help to fit six model parameters. The seventh parameter is the standard deviation that describes the error in the least squares fit. The fit is performed with a routine from Press [9].

12.2.14 Co-occurrence with average neighborhood

Dapeng and Zhongrong [23] construct a modified *co-occurrence matrix* $P^{Dap}(g, d)$. It represents the co-occurrence between gray levels g in the central pixel and a gray-level difference d. The gray-level difference d is the difference between the central gray level g and the average gray level of the eight neighboring pixels.

From this modified co-occurrence matrix, Dapeng extracts the 13 features shown in Table 12.12.

12.2.15 Co-occurrence histogram

Amadasun and King [24] use an approach similar to that of Dapeng, but do not construct a 2-D co-occurrence matrix. Instead, they average the differences for each gray-level value of the central pixel and construct features from this histogram distribution

$$P_T^{Ama}(i) = \sum_{m} \sum_{\substack{n \\ G_{m,n}=i}} |G_{m,n} - \overline{A}_{m,n}| \tag{12.43}$$

where $\overline{A}_{m,n}$ is the average of the gray levels of the eight neighboring pixels of pixel (m, n). From the histogram $P_T^{Ama}(i)$ and the conventional gray-tone histogram $P_H^{Ama}(i)$, Amadasun calculates the textural features presented in Table 12.13.

12.2.16 Autoregressive models

Mao and Jain [25] use multiresolution simultaneous *autoregressive models* for texture classification. The basic idea of a simultaneous autoregressive (SAR) model is to express a gray level of a pixel as a function of the gray levels in its neighborhood. The related model parameters for

Table 12.12: *Features from the Dapeng approach*

Abbreviations	
	$N = \sum_{g=1}^{G} \sum_{d=1}^{\mathrm{Dif}} P^{\mathrm{Dap}}(g,d)$
Feature	**Definition**
Gray-level average	$\boldsymbol{F}^{\mathrm{Dap}}_{\mathrm{GLA}} = \frac{1}{N} \sum_{g=1}^{G} g \cdot \sum_{d=1}^{\mathrm{Dif}} P^{\mathrm{Dap}}(g,d)$
Gray-level variance	$\boldsymbol{F}^{\mathrm{Dap}}_{\mathrm{GLV}} = \sqrt{\frac{1}{N} \sum_{g=1}^{G} (g - \boldsymbol{F}^{\mathrm{Dap}}_{\mathrm{GLA}})^2 \cdot \sum_{d=1}^{\mathrm{Dif}} P^{\mathrm{Dap}}(g,d)}$
Difference average	$\boldsymbol{F}^{\mathrm{Dap}}_{\mathrm{DAv}} = \frac{1}{N} \sum_{d=1}^{\mathrm{Dif}} d \cdot \sum_{g=1}^{G} P^{\mathrm{Dap}}(g,d)$
Difference variance	$\boldsymbol{F}^{\mathrm{Dap}}_{\mathrm{DVa}} = \sqrt{\frac{1}{N} \sum_{d=1}^{\mathrm{Dif}} (d - \boldsymbol{F}^{\mathrm{Dap}}_{\mathrm{DAv}})^2 \cdot \sum_{g=1}^{G} P^{\mathrm{Dap}}(g,d)}$
Small difference emphasis	$\boldsymbol{F}^{\mathrm{Dap}}_{\mathrm{SDE}} = \frac{1}{N} \sum_{g=1}^{G} \sum_{d=1}^{\mathrm{Dif}} \frac{P^{\mathrm{Dap}}(g,d)}{d^2}$
Large difference emphasis	$\boldsymbol{F}^{\mathrm{Dap}}_{\mathrm{LDE}} = \frac{1}{N} \sum_{g=1}^{G} \sum_{d=1}^{\mathrm{Dif}} d^2 \cdot P^{\mathrm{Dap}}(g,d)$
Gray-level distribution	$\boldsymbol{F}^{\mathrm{Dap}}_{\mathrm{GLD}} = \frac{1}{N} \sum_{g=1}^{G} \left(\sum_{d=1}^{\mathrm{Dif}} P^{\mathrm{Dap}}(g,d) \right)^2$
Difference distribution	$\boldsymbol{F}^{\mathrm{Dap}}_{\mathrm{DiD}} = \frac{1}{N} \sum_{d=1}^{Dif} \left(\sum_{g=1}^{G} P^{\mathrm{Dap}}(g,d) \right)^2$
Angular second moment	$\boldsymbol{F}^{\mathrm{Dap}}_{\mathrm{ASM}} = \frac{1}{N^2} \sum_{g=1}^{G} \sum_{d=1}^{\mathrm{Dif}} P^{\mathrm{Dap}}(g,d)^2$
Entropy	$\boldsymbol{F}^{\mathrm{Dap}}_{\mathrm{Ent}} = \frac{-1}{\mathrm{ld}(\frac{1}{G\,\mathrm{Dif}})} \sum_{g=1}^{G} \sum_{d=1}^{\mathrm{Dif}} P^{\mathrm{Dap}}(g,d)\ \mathrm{ld}(\frac{P^{\mathrm{Dap}}(g,d)}{N})$
Contrast	$\boldsymbol{F}^{\mathrm{Dap}}_{\mathrm{Con}} = \frac{1}{N} \sum_{g=1}^{G} \sum_{d=1}^{\mathrm{Dif}} (g-d)^2 P^{\mathrm{Dap}}(g,d)$
Inverse difference moment	$\boldsymbol{F}^{\mathrm{Dap}}_{\mathrm{IDM}} = \frac{1}{N} \sum_{g=1}^{G} \sum_{d=1}^{\mathrm{Dif}} \frac{1}{1+(g-d)^2} P^{\mathrm{Dap}}(g,d)$
Covariance	$\boldsymbol{F}^{\mathrm{Dap}}_{\mathrm{Cov}} = \frac{1}{N} \frac{1}{\boldsymbol{F}^{\mathrm{Dap}}_{\mathrm{GLV}} \boldsymbol{F}^{\mathrm{Dap}}_{\mathrm{DVa}}} \sum_{g=1}^{G} \sum_{d=1}^{\mathrm{Dif}} (g - \boldsymbol{F}^{\mathrm{Dap}}_{\mathrm{GLA}})(d - \boldsymbol{F}^{\mathrm{Dap}}_{\mathrm{DAv}}) P^{\mathrm{Dap}}(g,d)$

one image are calculated using a least squares technique and are used as textural features. This approach is similar to the Markov random fields described in Section 12.2.13.

However, a special neighborhood is used for rotation-invariant SAR models. In a rotation-invariant SAR model (RISAR), each central pixel value is a function of N_c average gray levels of N_c concentric circles.

Table 12.13: *Features from the Amadasun approach.*

Abbreviations	
N_{pix}: number of pixels in image window	
N_l: number of gray-level values actually occurring in image window with $P_H(i) \neq 0, P_H(j) \neq 0$.	
Feature	**Definition**
Coarseness	$F^{\text{Ama}}_{\text{Coa}} = \left(\sum_{l=0}^{N_l-1} P_T^{\text{Ama}}(l) P_H^{\text{Ama}}(l) \right)^{-1}$
Contrast	$F^{\text{Ama}}_{\text{Con}} = \frac{\sum_{l=0}^{N_l-1} \sum_{l'=0}^{N_l-1} (l-l')^2 \cdot P_H^{\text{Ama}}(l) \cdot P_H^{\text{Ama}}(l')}{N_l \cdot (N_l - 1)} \frac{\sum_{l=0}^{N_l-1} P_T^{\text{Ama}}(l)}{N_{pix}}$
Busyness	$F^{\text{Ama}}_{\text{Bus}} = \frac{\sum_{l=0}^{N_l-1} P_T^{\text{Ama}}(g) P_H^{\text{Ama}}(g)}{\sum_{l=0}^{N_l-1} \sum_{l'=0}^{N_l-1} \lvert P_T^{\text{Ama}}(l) P_H^{\text{Ama}}(l) - P_T^{\text{Ama}}(l') P_H^{\text{Ama}}(l') \rvert}$
Complexity	$F^{\text{Ama}}_{\text{Com}} = \sum_{l=0}^{N_l-1} \sum_{l'=0}^{N_l-1} \frac{\lvert l-l' \rvert (P_T^{\text{Ama}}(l) P_H^{\text{Ama}}(l) + P_T^{\text{Ama}}(l') P_H^{\text{Ama}}(l'))}{N_{pix}^2 (P_H^{\text{Ama}}(l) + P_H^{\text{Ama}}(l'))}$
Texture strength	$F^{\text{Ama}}_{\text{Str}} = \frac{\sum_{l=0}^{N_l-1} \sum_{l'=0}^{N_l-1} (l-l')^2 \cdot (P_H^{\text{Ama}}(l) + P_H^{\text{Ama}}(l'))}{\sum_{l=0}^{N_l-1} P_T^{\text{Ama}}(l)}$

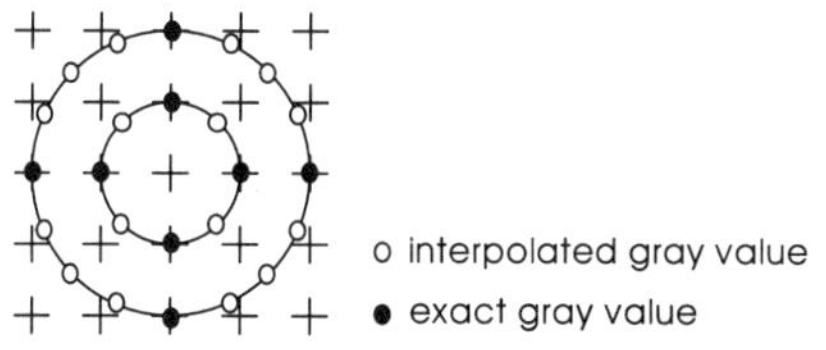

Figure 12.3: *Neighborhoods in a RISAR approach: The central pixel is modeled as a function of average gray levels on concentric circles.*

In case the pixels are not exactly located on the circle, the gray values are determined by a bilinear interpolation from the corresponding four neighboring values (see Fig. 12.3). It is sensible to calculate and store the weights only once with which each grid pixel contributes to the average gray value of a circle.

A model for all gray values $G_{m,n}$ in an image is established using

$$G_{m,n} = \mu + \sum_{i=1}^{N_c} \theta_i x_i^{m,n} + \epsilon_{m,n} \tag{12.44}$$

Table 12.14: Features from the Amelung approach

Abbreviations	
Number of pixels in image window: $N_{pix} = \sum_{g=1}^{G} P_H(g)$	
Feature	**Definition**
Average	$F^{\text{Ame}}_{\text{Ave}} = \frac{1}{N_{pix}} \sum_{g=1}^{Gw} P_H(g) \cdot g$
Variance	$F^{\text{Ame}}_{\text{Var}} = \frac{1}{N_{pix}} \sum_{g=1}^{Gw} P_H(g) \cdot (g - F^{\text{Ame}}_{\text{Ave}})^2$
3rd moment	$F^{\text{Ame}}_{\text{3Mo}} = \frac{1}{N_{pix}} \sum_{g=1}^{Gw} P_H(g) \cdot (g - F^{\text{Ame}}_{\text{Ave}})^3$
4th moment	$F^{\text{Ame}}_{\text{4Mo}} = \frac{1}{N_{pix}} \sum_{g=1}^{Gw} P_H(g) \cdot (g - F^{\text{Ame}}_{\text{Ave}})^4$
Angular second moment	$F^{\text{Ame}}_{\text{ASM}} = \frac{1}{N_{pix}^2} \sum_{g=1}^{Gw} P_H(g)^2$
Entropy	$F^{\text{Ame}}_{\text{End}} = \frac{-1}{\log(\frac{1}{G})} \sum_{g=1}^{Gw} P_H(g) \cdot \log(\frac{P_H(g)}{N_{pix}})$

to determine the parameters $\theta_1, \ldots, \theta_{N_c}, \mu, \sigma$ from the image, with σ being the standard deviation of ϵ and N_c being the number of circles used per pixel. In our implementation, we have used four circles, which leads to a total of six features.

A multiresolution SAR model calculates a sequence of image resolutions, for example, by means of a *Gaussian pyramid*, and determines model parameters for each image resolution. The collection of all model parameters is used as a feature vector.

12.2.17 Statistical features

Amelung [26] has constructed a system called AST to evaluate a number of different statistical features from seven feature sets. The rest of his features are already part of the foregoing discussion, therefore only features extracted from gray level and *gradient histograms* are combined in the features set discussed here.

Amelung's features are shown in Table 12.14. For the histogram $P_H(g)$ i the formulas of Table 12.14, three different histograms (gray level histogram, histogram of absolute value and of direction of gradient) are used. A Sobel filter generates the gradient image.

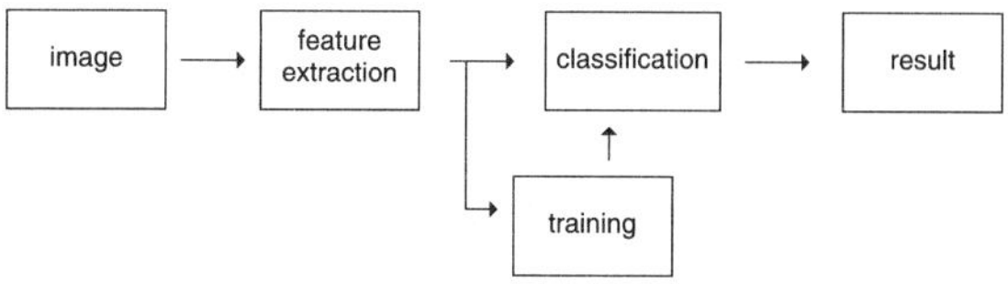

Figure 12.4: *Typical setup of a texture classification experiment—features are extracted from image windows and put into a classifier.*

12.3 Assessment of textural features

12.3.1 Setup and criteria

Assessment of textural features compares different types of feature sets on the basis of their performance in practical texture recognition tasks. The need for basic ideas on *performance characterization* of algorithms is discussed in Volume 3, Chapter 7.

The basis of our experiments is a typical classification setup as shown in Fig. 12.4. Textural features are extracted from an image window and forwarded to a classifier, which distinguishes between different texture types in a sample set. Each image window in the sample set contains only one texture type; therefore only one set of features is calculated for each image window[3]. Criteria for the *assessment of texture features* were the *recognition rate* on a verification sample set and the *computation time* of each feature set. We mention only that there are further criteria for assessment such as suitability for hardware implementation of a feature set, etc. All data samples are divided into a training sample set for the teach-in process of the classifier and a verification sample on which the recognition rate given in the following is calculated. For each textural feature and each data set, the feature values are normalized to zero average and a standard deviation of 1. This guarantees that features with extreme values do not dominate the classification result. A 1-nearest-neighborhood-algorithm with a L_2 distance measure is used for classification.

[3]In many practical applications, it is necessary to distinguish between different types of texture in one image. In that case, texture analysis is not primarily a means for texture classification, but for segmentation. In order to achieve sufficiently high segmentation accuracy for segmentation problems, one will have to extract textural features from overlapping instead of nonoverlapping image windows. As a consequence, processing time will be considerably larger. Additionally, there is a trade-off between the need of large windows sizes necessary for the computation of some textural features, on the one hand, and a demand for small windows in order to avoid a loss in spatial resolution during the segmentation process, on the other hand.
Nevertheless, texture segmentation problems are a very difficult basis for a benchmark, because the exact location of the border lines between different types of texture within one image is usually ambiguous.

Table 12.15: *Data sets for benchmarking*

	Data sets						
	Brodatz	Tumor	Tilda	Print	Slab	Vistex	Hon
Abbreviation	BRO_64	TUM_64	TIL_64	PRI_64	SLA_64	VIS_64	HON_64
Classes	13	2	6	26	11	15	6
Patterns per class							
Training	64	72	1600	16	12	32	24
Testing	64	72	1600	8	12	32	24
Verification	128	71	1600	16	12	64	24
Window size	64×64	368×280	64×64	64×64	64×64	64×64	64×64
Bits per pixel	8	8	8	8	8	8	8

The calculation time is defined as time for calculating the floating point vector of textural features from a 64×64 pixel image window. The actual implementation was done on a Pentium 200 MHz PC without MMX under Linux, Kernel Version 2.0.22 using the GNU g++ compiler, version 2.7.2.1. The calculation time was measured by averaging over a data set with Brodatz images containing 65 image windows. A comparison with other platforms can be performed on the basis of CPU benchmarks. A simple linpack benchmark that can be performed per internet using a java applet [27] has given a performance of 11.4 MFlops for our computer.

12.3.2 Data sets for benchmarking

An overview of the underlying data sets is given in Table 12.15. The number of classes in each data set is given as well as the patterns available per class. Note that all the data set have been divided into three subsets each for training, testing, and verification. All the recognition results given below were determined on the verification samples.

In order to allow the reader to benchmark his own textural feature sets with the features given in this paper, we have included most of the data sets in `/images/12` on the CD-ROM. A general description of the data sets is given in `/images/12/readme.txt`.

The testing sets are not used for any experiments in this paper, but are included to serve as intermediate performance check when automatically determining optimal feature subsets. While this will be one focus of our future work, we have decided immediately to keep one division of our data sets fixed. This will allow us to directly compare the performance of the feature sets from the literature given in this pa-

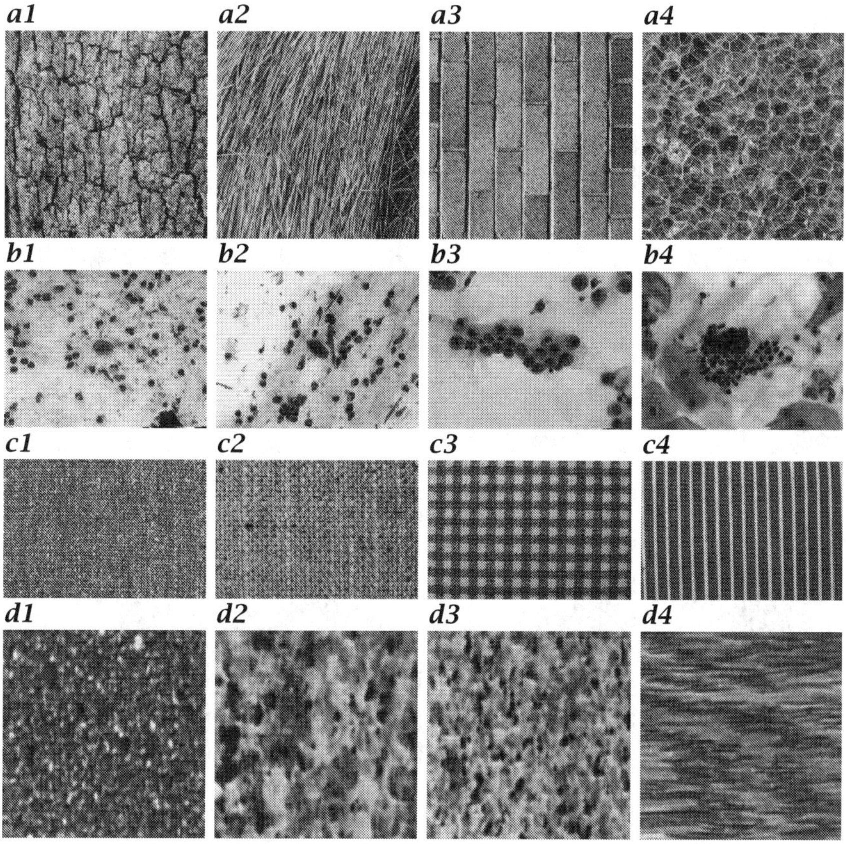

Figure 12.5: Sample images from the different benchmark sets: BRO (a1-a4): Brodatz set with natural textures; TUM (b1-b4): cell images with and without tumors; TIL (c1-c4): fabrics from the TILDA database; PRI (d1-d4): prints of artificial textures.

per with the performance of automatically generated feature subsets in future experiments.

Sample images from each data sets are shown in Figs. 12.5 and 12.6. References for obtaining the images are given with the descriptions below. Because the preparation of the data is critical for the actual recognition results, we can provide detailed information on this aspect on request. In a first step, the original images are cut into nonoverlapping 64×64 pixel image windows. In a second step, the subimages are separated into a training, a testing, and a verification sample. The actual composition of the three samples is documented in descriptor files, which list the subimage file names belonging to the different classes and samples. The data sets cover different aspects from scientific and

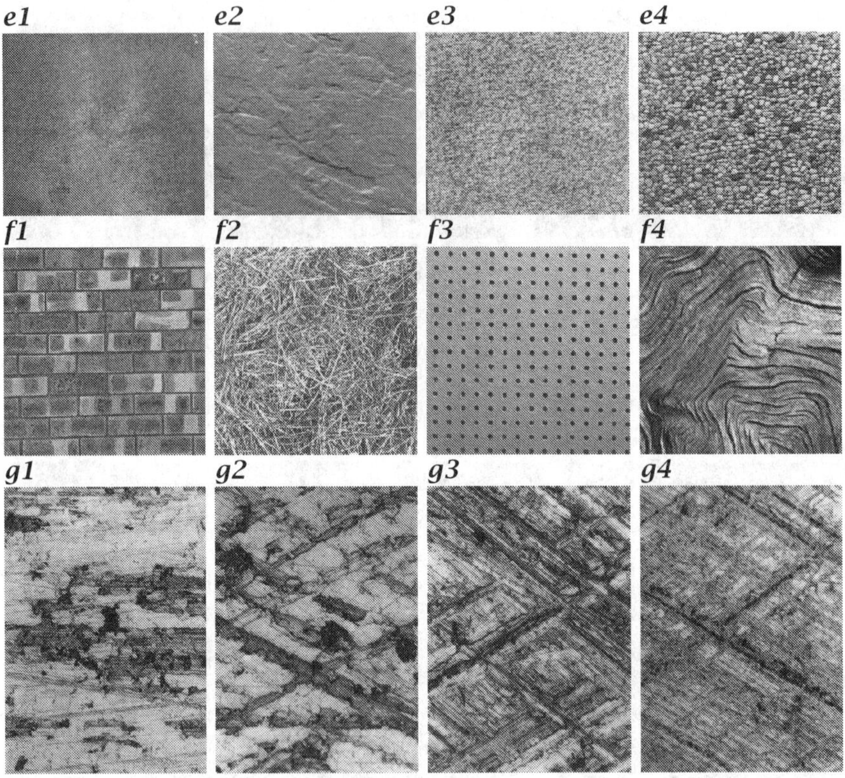

Figure 12.6: *Sample images from the different benchmark sets (II): SLA (e1-e4): slabs of different type; VIS (f1-f4): natural images from the Vistex database; HON (g1-g4): metal surfaces.*

applied texture analysis. Some of them are established as benchmark samples, others are quite new, but are both large and relevant.

The Brodatz sample (`/images/12/bro`) is a widespread benchmark sample for the comparison of textural features. It consists of a collection of natural textures. Our experiments are based on the electronic version from Weber [6], which consists of 13 different classes.

In the tumor data sample (`/images/12/tum`), cell images from human sputum are used for visual cancer diagnosis.This data set is the only one where the textural features are calculated on the complete image without extracting subimages. The reason for this is that each image contains regions of both diseased and healthy cells, and the exact assignment is not known. For those feature extraction methods which require quadratic input, the tumor images have been stretched to a quadratic size of 256×256 pixel by means of bilinear interpolation. Because the number of samples for the two classes was not equal in this data set, the number of patterns per class given in Table 12.15 is the minimum number for both classes.

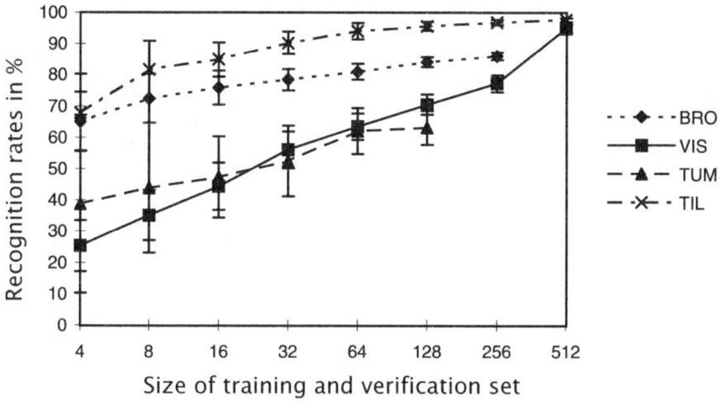

Figure 12.7: *Recognition rates as a function of data set size for different data sets. The error bars resemble the standard deviation calculated with randomly chosen data sets.*

Images of different fabrics are collected in the TILDA sample, which can be obtained from Schulz-Mirbach [28] (`http://www.informatik.uni-freiburg.de/~lmb/research/dfg-texture/tilda/indexE.html`. The data have been collected within the German research program "Automatische Sichtprüfung" (automatic visual inspection) of the "Deutsche Forschungsgemeinschaft" (DFG).

The print sample (`/images/12/pri`) consists of a collection of 26 different textures from paper prints with imitations of natural wooden surfaces. Such papers are used for coating chipboards, for example, for use in kitchens. The slab sample (`/images/12/sla`) gives a collection of 11 different surface types of slabs. The Vistex benchmark sample (`http://vismod.www.media.mit.edu/vismod/imagery/VisionTexture/vistex.html`) is avaliable in [7] and contains a collection of 15 different types of natural textures. The Hon sample (`/images/12/hon`) contains images of metal surfaces. It also stems from the research program "Automatische Sichtprüfung" and is described in [29].

12.3.3 Experiments and results

We first wanted to determine the sensitivity of the recognition rates with respect to the actual composition of the data set. For this reason, we have calculated standard deviations of the recognition rates for different data set sizes n using the Galloway feature set. The size n is the total number of image samples in the training set; the verification set is of the same size.

The results are shown in Fig. 12.7. The error bars given resemble the standard deviation σ, which was calculated on the basis of recognition results from 120 randomly chosen data subset selections. As expected, the recognition rates increase with growing training set sizes, while the standard deviation decreases. For reliable results, a sample set size of at least a few hundred images is a prerequisite. Table 12.16 gives the details of the benchmarking experiments with the different textural feature sets on the seven data sets. The table lists the recognition results and the feature extraction time on a 64×64 pixel image windows.

Table 12.16: *Benchmark results: Recognition rates and feature extraction time. The maximum recognition rate in each column is printed in boldface*

Feature Sets vs Data sets	Time in s	Brodatz	Tumor	Tilda	Print	Slabs	Vistex	Hon
Haralick	*0.536*	82.9	71.3	98.9	83.4	81.8	79.5	47.2
Unser	*0.050*	92.6	71.3	**99.9**	**91.6**	**87.1**	81.4	56.9
Galloway	*0.020*	84.7	65.5	99.1	83.7	83.3	70.4	**57.6**
Laine	*0.045*	92.4	78.4	97.9	82.9	79.5	75.6	50.7
Local features	*0.011*	61.1	68.4	94.6	63.5	51.5	47.1	22.2
Fractal (1)	*0.041*	62.6	70.8	97.8	54.8	64.4	54.5	37.5
Fractal (2)	*0.435*	66.5	66.1	96.8	64.4	67.4	48.5	29.2
Laws	*0.423*	89.7	67.3	99.6	89.9	84.1	79.8	44.4
Fourier coeff.	*0.024*	92.7	78.4	98.9	86.8	83.3	80.1	49.3
Chen	*1.507*	**93.1**	**83.0**	99.7	84.4	80.3	**84.5**	45.1
Sun & Wee	*0.061*	63.9	57.9	92.3	74.3	71.2	58.4	40.3
Pikaz & Averbuch	*0.028*	79.4	81.3	98.6	84.4	78.0	74.4	45.1
Gabor	*0.679*	92.2	76.6	**99.9**	86.8	84.1	75.4	54.2
Markov	*0.087*	83.1	77.8	88.8	78.6	62.9	69.6	54.2
Dapeng	*0.021*	85.8	73.1	94.8	72.6	73.5	74.6	32.6
Amadasun	*0.036*	83.4	69.0	98.9	79.6	79.5	65.6	52.8
Mao & Jain	*0.051*	86.3	67.3	94.6	83.4	68.9	73.0	52.1
Amelung	*0.082*	**93.0**	75.4	99.7	82.5	**87.1**	82.1	47.9

Though the exact extraction time may vary depending on the actual implementation, it is nevertheless remarkable that the computation times vary over more than two orders of magnitude. The differences between the recognition results of feature sets are not that drastic, though sufficiently high enough to justify a closer look at different feature sets when actually implementing practical applications.

Some feature sets such as the local features perform significantly worse than average. This result could be expected, as the underlying mathematics of those features is significantly less complex than the rest. On the other hand, they are easy to compute and therefore are potential candidates for applications with hard time restrictions. Obviously the average recognition rates depend on the data set. The commonly used Brodatz set seems to be less challenging for classification tasks than average textural data sets. It is necessary to condense the data from the different experiments. Therefore, we have calculated a performance rank for each data set. This rank was determined from the relative performance of each feature set with respect to the others, simply by ordering the feature sets with respect to their recognition

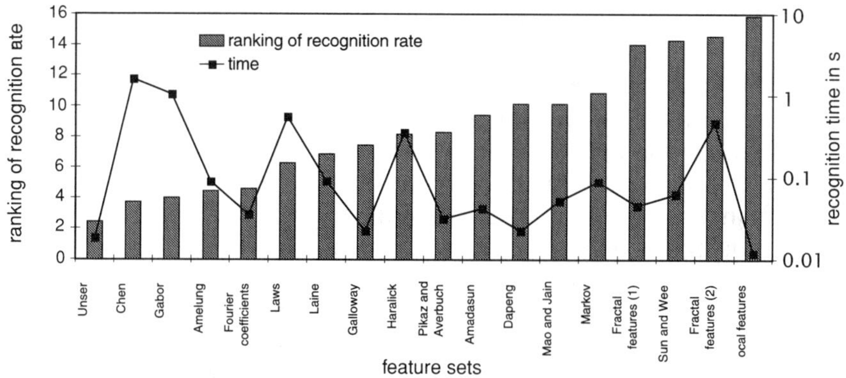

Figure 12.8: *Summary of texture benchmark results: Average performance ranking of the recognition rates and feature extraction time for different feature sets. In both cases, low numbers are the better results.*

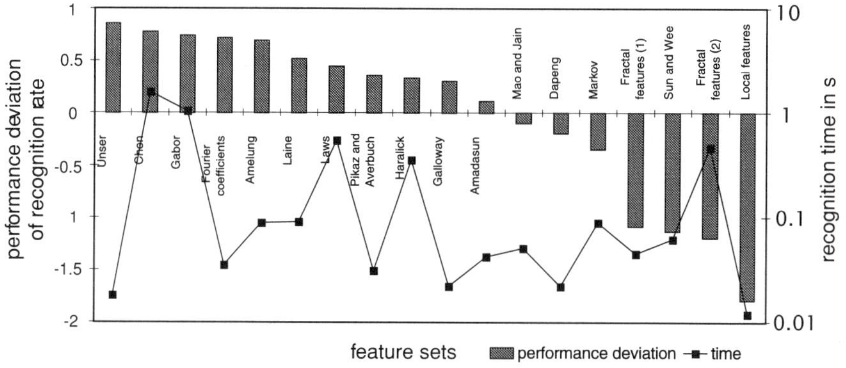

Figure 12.9: *Summary of texture benchmark results: The performance deviation expresses the deviation of the recognition rate of one feature set from the average rate of all feature sets in multiples of the standard deviation. Positive deviations resemble an above average performance. Again, feature extraction times are given for better comparison.*

rate on the respective data set. The best feature set gets rank 1, the second best rank 2, etc. To combine the results of all data sets, average ranks over the different data sets are calculated for each feature set.

In Fig. 12.8, a condensed version of the results is presented. It shows both the average performance rank and (on a logarithmic scale) the feature extraction time. Though this is only a rough measure, it can give a first clue for selecting an optimal feature set with respect to both calculation efforts and recognition efficiency.

A different and more quantitative way to extract relevant information from Table 12.16 is the following: From the recognition results of all feature sets for one data set, a mean value and a standard deviation of the performance are calculated. From that, the difference of each recognition result from the mean is expressed as a multiple of the standard deviation for that data sample, which gives a quantitative ranking of the performance of the different feature sets on one data sample. We call this measure “performance deviation.” Summing the performance deviation over all different data sets, one gets a characteristic that is more quantitative than the forementioned ranking method. The results are shown in Fig. 12.9.

It is obvious that the best results for a given data set will be obtained by combining optimal features from all different data sets. While both the methods for and the answers to this question lie beyond the scope of this paper, we will briefly summarize the main aspects of this approach in the next section. Note that the application of the feature selection technique to the area of object recognition has been demonstrated in Volume 3, Chapter 13.

12.4 Automatic design of texture analysis systems

Further work will focus on the implications from benchmarking textural features for the design of image processing systems. In order to lower costs and efforts for the construction of image processing solutions, it is, for a given problem or data set, desirable to have an automated design process for the image processing solution.

In the best case, an automatic optimization selects optimal subsets of textural features on the basis of a given data set. First experiments on that topic compare the performance of different selection strategies for textural features [30]. On state of the art computer hardware platforms, such selection processes can be performed within hours and are therefore already capable of supporting the design process for practical solutions by suggesting suboptimal feature subsets.

In order to further extend the idea of an automatic image processing system design, features themselves can be generated automatically, for example, by means of genetic programming. Such experiments are still in a more basic research stage. Unfortunately, huge amounts of computing power are necessary to perform such experiments because the evaluation of any newly created feature requires an evaluation on all images of a data set as well as training and classification of this configuration. This takes at least several seconds. Further experiments will extend the benchmarking approach in combination with automatic design considerations to other fields of application, such as object recognition, especially for data sets with a large number of classes. For first results on automatic feature selection for object recognition, the reader is referred to Volume 3, Chapter 13.

Acknowledgments

Nowadays, applied image processing is very much team-based. The results described in this contribution have been collected over many years. Thanks go to all members of the Intelligent System Group at the Fraunhofer Institute for Integrated Circuits, especially to (in alphabetic order) Christian Küblbeck, Peter Plankensteiner, Steffen Steinhoff, Peter Stransky, and Roland Weigelt. This work was partially supported by the Bavarian "Hans-Zehetmair-Habilitationsförderpreis."

12.5 References

[1] Pratt, W. K., (1991). *Digital Image Processing.* New York: John Wiley and Sons.

[2] Julesz, B., (1962). Visual pattern discrimination. *IRE Transactions on Information Theory*, **IT-8**:84–92.

[3] Schneider, B., (1995). *Schnelle Merkmalsextraktion auf der Basis pyramidaler Bilddatenstrukturen für die Oberflächeninspektion.* München, Wien: Carl Hanser Verlag.

[4] Haralick, R. M. and Shapiro, L. G., (1992). *Computer and Robot Vision*, chapter 9, pp. 453–507. Reading, MA: Addison-Wesley.

[5] Reed, T. R. and Buf, J. M. H. D., (1993). A review of recent texture segmentation and feature extraction techniques. *CVGIP: Image Understanding*, **57**(3):359–372.

[6] Weber, A., (1992). *The USC-SIPI Image Database Vers. 3.* Technical Report, University of Southern California.

[7] MIT, (1997). *VisTex Image database.* Technical Report, MIT Media Lab at http://vismod.www.media.mit.edu/vismod/imagery/VisionTexture/.

[8] Smith, G. and Burns, I., (1997). *MeasTex Image Texture Database.* Technical Report, Cooperative Research Center for Sensor Signal and Information Processing, Queensland, Australia `http://www.cssip.elec.uq.edu.au/~guy/meastex/meastex.html`.

[9] Press, W. H., (1992). *Numerical recipes in C.* Cambridge: Cambridge University Press.

[10] Haralick, M., Shanmugam, K., and Dinstein, I., (1973). Textural features for image classification. *IEEE Transactions on Systems, Man and Cybernetics*, **SMC-3**(6):610–621.

[11] Unser, M., (1986). Sum and difference histograms for texture analysis. *IEEE Trans. Pattern Analysis and Machine Intelligence*, **8**:118–125.

[12] Galloway, M. M., (1975). Texture analysis using gray level run lengths. *Computer Graphics and Image Processing*, **4**:172–179.

[13] Chen, Y., Nixon, M., and Thomas, D., (1995). Statistical geometrical features for texture classification. *Pattern Recognition*, **28**(4):537–552.

[14] Laine, A. and Fun, J., (1993). Texture classification by wavelet packet signatures. *IEEE Ttransactions on Pattern Analysis and Machine Intelligence*, **15**(11):1186–1191.

[15] Schramm, U., (1994). *Automatische Oberflächenprüfung mit neuronalen Netzen.* Stuttgart: IRB-Verlag.

[16] Roß, T., Handels, H., Busche, H., Kreusch, J., Wolff, H. H., and Pöppl, S. J., (1995). Automatische Klassifikation hochaufgelöster Oberflächenprofile von Hauttumoren mit neuronalen Netzen. In *Mustererkennung 1995,* G. Sagerer, S. Posch, and F. Kummert, eds. Berlin: Springer-Verlag.

[17] Peleg, S., Naor, J., Hartley, R., and Avnir, D., (1984). Multiple resolution texture analysis and classification. *IEEE Transactions on Pattern Analysis and Machine Intelligence,* **PAMI-6**(4):518–523.

[18] Laws, K. I., (1980). *Textured Image Segmentation.* PhD thesis, Faculty of the Graduate School, University of Southern California.

[19] Sun, C. and Wee, W. G., (1983). Neighboring gray level dependence matrix for texture classification. *Computer Vision, Graphics, and Image Processing,* **23**:341–352.

[20] Pikaz, A. and Averbuch, A., (1997). An efficient topological characterization of Gray-Level textures, using a multiresolution representation. *Graphical Models and Image Processing,* **59**(1):1–17.

[21] Fogel, I. and Sagi, D., (1989). Gabor filters as texture discriminator. *Biological Cybernetics,* **61**:103–113.

[22] Kashyap, R. L., Chellappa, R., and Khotanzad, A., (1982). Texture classification using features derived from random field models. *Pattern Recognition Letters,* **1**:43–50.

[23] Dapeng, Z. and Zhongrong, L., (1986). Digital image texture analysis using gray level and energy cooccurrence. In *Applications of Artificial Intelligence IV,* Vol. 657, pp. 152–156. Bellingham, WA: SPIE. Vol. 657.

[24] Amadasun, M. and King, R., (1989). Textural features corresponding to textural properties. *IEEE Trans. Systems, Man, and Cybernetics,* **19**(5): 1264–1276.

[25] Mao, J. and Jain, A. K., (1992). Texture classification and segmentation using multiresolution simultaneous autoregressive models. *Pattern Recognition,* **25**(2):173–188.

[26] Amelung, J., (1995). *Automatische Bildverarbeitung für die Qualitätssicherung.* Dissertation, Technische Hochschule Darmstadt, Darmstädter Dissertationen D17.

[27] Dongarra, J., (1997). *Linpack Benchmark in Java.* Technical Report, http://www.netlib.org/benchmark/linpackjava/.

[28] Schulz-Mirbach, H., (1996). *Ein Referenzdatensatz zur Evaluierung von Sichtprüfungsverfahren für Textiloberflächen.* Technical Report, TU Hamburg-Harburg, Technische Informatik I.

[29] Goetze GmbH, (1993). AE goetze honing guide - rating criteria for the honing of cylinder running surfaces. Technical report, AE Goetze GmbH, Burscheid, Germany.

[30] Küblbeck, C. and Wagner, T., (1996). Automatic configuration of systems for surface inspection. In *Proceedings of Machine Vision Application in Industrial Inspection (SPIE),* Vol. 3029, pp. 128–138. Bellingham, Washington: SPIE.

13 Motion

Horst Haußecker and Hagen Spies

Interdisziplinäres Zentrum für Wissenschaftliches Rechnen (IWR)
Universität Heidelberg, Germany

Handbook of Computer Vision and Applications
Volume 2
Signal Processing and Pattern Recognition

Copyright © 1999 by Academic Press
All rights of reproduction in any form reserved.
ISBN 0-12-379772-1/$30.00

13.1 Introduction

Motion is a powerful feature of image sequences, revealing the dynamics of scenes by relating spatial image features to temporal changes. The task of motion analysis remains a challenging and fundamental problem of computer vision. From sequences of 2-D images, the only accessible motion parameter is the *optical flow* $\boldsymbol{f}$, an approximation of the 2-D *motion field* $\boldsymbol{u}$, on the image sensor [1]. The motion field is given as the projection of the 3-D motion of points in the scene onto the image sensor. The estimated optical flow field can be used as input for a variety of subsequent processing steps including motion detection, motion compensation, motion-based data compression, 3-D scene reconstruction, autonomous navigation and the analysis of dynamical processes in scientific applications.

The difficulties in motion estimation are manifold and originate in the inherent differences between the optical flow and the real motion field. As only the apparent motion in the sequence can be extracted, further *a priori* assumptions on brightness changes, object properties, and the relation between relative 3-D scene motion and the projection onto the 2-D image sensor are necessary for quantitative scene analysis. Horn [2] gives an optimistic view of the possibility of 3-D reconstruction from motion fields. He shows that the motion field can almost always be unambiguously related to translational and rotational velocities of rigid surfaces. However, the motion field itself is often inaccessible. This can be nicely demonstrated by a simple example illustrated in Fig. 13.1. Consider a rigid sphere with homogeneous surface reflectance, spinning around an axis through the center of the sphere. If the surface is not textured and the illumination stays constant, the apparent optical flow field would equal zero over the entire sphere. If a directional light source moves around the same sphere the apparent illumination changes would be falsely attributed to motion of the sphere surface. This rather academic problem shows that even very simple experimental setups under perfect conditions can render motion estimation impossible. This and other examples are given by Horn [3]. Problems frequently encountered in real-world sequences include transparent overlay of multiple motions, occlusions, illumination changes, nonrigid motion, stop-and-shoot motion, low signal-to-noise (SNR) levels, aperture problem and correspondence problem—to mention only some of them. For this reason, Verri and Poggio [4] conclude that the true motion field is hardly ever accessible and suggest that only qualitative properties of the motion field should be computed [5].

These problems, however, are not always present and are usually not spread over the entire image area. Thus, there exist many applications where motion analysis becomes feasible. At the same time, they pose a constraint on optical flow computation that is often disre-

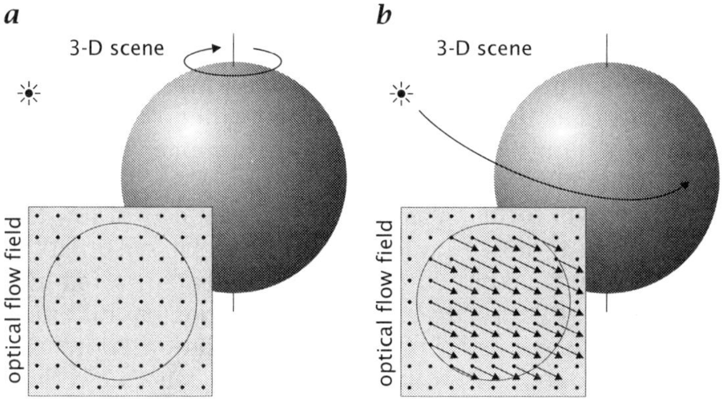

Figure 13.1: *Physical vs visual correspondence:* ***a*** *a spinning sphere with fixed illumination leads to zero optical flow;* ***b*** *a moving illumination source causes an apparent optical flow field without motion of the sphere.*

garded: errors have to be detected and quantified! This is especially important for quantitative scientific measurement tasks. In contrast to the more qualitative requirements of standard computer vision applications, such as motion detection or collision avoidance, quantitative measurements of dynamic processes require precise and dense optical flow fields in order to reduce the propagation of errors into subsequent processing steps. In addition to the optical flow field, measures of confidence have to be provided to discard erroneous data points and quantify measurement precision.

Despite all of the problems, the importance of motion estimation has continuously challenged investigations. There has been a recent revival of interest in low-level motion estimation in the literature [6, 7, 8, 9]. An excellent overview of optical flow techniques by Barron et al. [6] revisits existing techniques. Motion analysis seems to gain increasing interest with a trend towards a quantitative performance analysis of optical flow techniques. This trend might be accredited to the rapidly increasing performance of computer hardware in both speed and memory. More and more complicated and computationally costly techniques have become applicable that were beyond the range of feasibility only 10 yr ago. Rather than being restricted to only two consecutive images, an extension of computer vision into the temporal domain has led to new techniques with increasing performance.

Quantitative motion estimation requires the entirety of quantitative visualization, geometric and radiometric calibration, and a quantitative error analysis of the entire chain of computer vision algorithms. The final results are only as precise as the least precise part of the system. Quantitative visualization of object properties is up to the special requirements of applications. An overview of illumination and visualization techniques is given in Volume 1 of this handbook. Without doubt, camera calibration is an important step towards quantitative image analysis and has been extensively investigated by the photogrammetric society. Volume 1, Chapter 17 gives a summary of existing techniques for radiometric and geometric calibration.

This chapter will focus on the algorithmic aspects of low-level motion estimation in terms of performance and error sensitivity of individual parts, given a calibrated image, eventually corrupted by sensor noise. We will start with a discussion on the principal differences between optical flow-based techniques and correlation approaches and outline the appearance of motion in image sequences (Section 13.2). In Section 13.3 optical flow-based techniques will be detailed including differential and tensor based techniques. Sections 13.4 and 13.5 deal with quadrature filter-based and correlation-based techniques, respectively. In Section 13.6 we try to introduce different attempts to improve accuracy and overcome intrinsic problems of motion estimation by an appropriate model of the underlying motion field. As already mentioned, the detection and quantification of problems and errors is a crucial factor for motion analysis. Section 13.7 will give a unified perspective of existing quality measures. We will conclude in Section 13.8 with a comparative analysis of the different techniques applied to a variety of test sequences, both common examples as well as specially developed sequences with and without ground truth information.

13.2 Basics: flow and correspondence

13.2.1 Optical flow

Moving patterns cause temporal variations of the image brightness. The relationship between brightness changes and the optical flow field $\boldsymbol{f}$ constitutes the basis for a variety of approaches, such as differential, spatiotemporal energy-based, tensor-based, and phase-based techniques. Analyzing the relationship between the temporal variations of image intensity or the spatiotemporal frequency distribution in the Fourier domain serves as an attempt to estimate the optical flow field. This section introduces the fundamental relation between motion and brightness variations and its representation in image sequences and Fourier domain. All optical flow-based, as well as quadrature filter-based techniques rely inherently on the coherence of motion. Therefore, a basic prerequisite relating the scale of patterns to the frame rate of image acquisition is given by the temporal sampling theorem, detailed at the end of this section.

Brightness change constraint. A common assumption on optical flow is that the image brightness $g(\boldsymbol{x}, t)$ at a point $\boldsymbol{x} = [x, y]^T$ at time t should only change because of motion. Thus, the total time derivative,

$$\frac{\mathrm{d}g}{\mathrm{d}t} = \frac{\partial g}{\partial x}\frac{\mathrm{d}x}{\mathrm{d}t} + \frac{\partial g}{\partial y}\frac{\mathrm{d}y}{\mathrm{d}t} + \frac{\partial g}{\partial t} \tag{13.1}$$

needs to equal zero. With the definitions $f_1 = \mathrm{d}x/\mathrm{d}t$ and $f_2 = \mathrm{d}y/\mathrm{d}t$, this directly yields the well-known *motion constraint equation* or *brightness change constraint equation*, BCCE [10]:

$$(\nabla g)^T \boldsymbol{f} + g_t = 0 \tag{13.2}$$

where $\boldsymbol{f} = [f_1, f_2]^T$ is the optical flow, ∇g defines the spatial gradient, and g_t denotes the partial time derivative $\partial g/\partial t$.

This relation poses a single local constraint on the optical flow at a certain point in the image. It is, however, ill-posed as Eq. (13.2) constitutes only one equation of two unknowns. This problem is commonly referred to as the *aperture problem* of motion estimation, illustrated in Fig. 13.2a. All vectors along the *constraint line* defined by Eq. (13.2) are likely to be the real optical flow $\boldsymbol{f}$. Without further assumptions only the flow $\boldsymbol{f}_\perp$,

$$\boldsymbol{f}_\perp(\boldsymbol{x}, t) = -\frac{g_t(\boldsymbol{x}, t)}{\|\nabla g(\boldsymbol{x}, t)\|}\boldsymbol{n}, \quad \boldsymbol{n} = \frac{\nabla g(\boldsymbol{x}, t)}{\|\nabla g(\boldsymbol{x}, t)\|} \tag{13.3}$$

perpendicular to the constraint line can be estimated. This vector is referred to as *normal flow* as it points normal to lines of constant image brightness, parallel to the spatial gradient.

Although Eq. (13.2) is formulated for a single point in the image, any discrete realization of the spatial and temporal derivatives requires some neighborhood of the image point to be considered. From this fact, the question arises, should the search for $\boldsymbol{f}$ be extended to a neighborhood of finite size instead of focusing on a single point? If the spatial gradient changes within this region, additional constraints can be used to find the 2-D optical flow $\boldsymbol{f}$. This is the common representation of the aperture problem as illustrated in Fig. 13.2b and c. If the spatial structure within an aperture of finite size shows directional variations, the optical flow $\boldsymbol{f}$ can be estimated unambiguously (Fig. 13.2b). In this case the constraint lines of several points within the neighborhood have a joint intersection. If, on the other hand, all gradient vectors within the aperture are pointing into the same direction, all constraint lines fall together and the aperture problem persists (Fig. 13.2c). A variety of approaches have been proposed that directly use Eq. (13.2) by trying to minimize an objective function pooling constraints over a small finite area. They can be subdivided into differential techniques, using both local and global constraints and tensor-based techniques (Section 13.3).

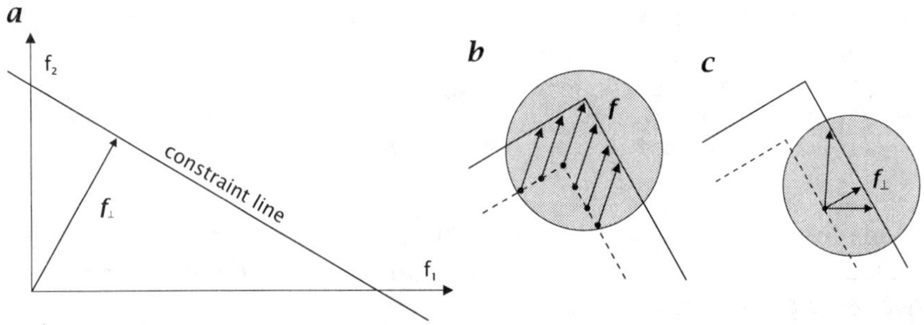

*Figure 13.2: Illustration of the aperture problem: **a** constraint line defined by Eq. (13.2). The normal optical flow vector $\boldsymbol{f}_{\perp}$ is pointing perpendicular to the line and parallel to the local gradient $\nabla g(\boldsymbol{x}, t)$; **b** no aperture problem for local neighborhoods with spatially distributed structures (moving corner); **c** within a local neighborhood all gradients are parallel (moving edge). The optical flow cannot be determined unambiguously.*

In order to overcome the aperture problem, the size of the region of interest has to be enlarged, as with the growing size of the local neighborhood the chances for distributed spatial structure increase. At the same time it becomes more likely that the region extends over motion boundaries. These two competing obstacles of optical flow computation are referred to as the *generalized aperture problem* [11]. Recent approaches to overcome this problem use robust statistics to avoid averaging independent optical flow fields [12] (Section 13.6.2).

Optical flow in spatiotemporal images. In the previous section we derived the brightness change constraint equation Eq. (13.2), relating temporal and spatial derivatives of the image brightness to the optical flow. Another basic relation can be found if we do not restrict the analysis to two consecutive images but rather assume the brightness pattern $g(\boldsymbol{x}, t)$ to be extended in both space and time, forming a 3-D *spatiotemporal image*.

The displacement of brightness patterns within consecutive images of a sequence yields inclined structures with respect to the temporal axis of spatiotemporal images. Figure 13.3 shows examples of spatiotemporal images for synthetic test patterns moving with constant velocity.

Let $\boldsymbol{r} = [r_1, r_2, r_3]^T = a\,[\delta_x, \delta_y, \delta_t]^T$ be the vector pointing into the direction of constant brightness within the 3-D $\boldsymbol{x}t$-domain. With δ_x and δ_y we denote infinitesimal shifts of the brightness pattern within the infinitesimal time step δ_t. The (arbitrary) scaling factor a will be set to 1 in the remainder of this chapter, as only the fractions, r_1/r_3 and r_2/r_3 are relating $\boldsymbol{r}$ to the optical flow $\boldsymbol{f}$. The relation between the orientation angles, the spatiotemporal vector $\boldsymbol{r}$, and the optical flow

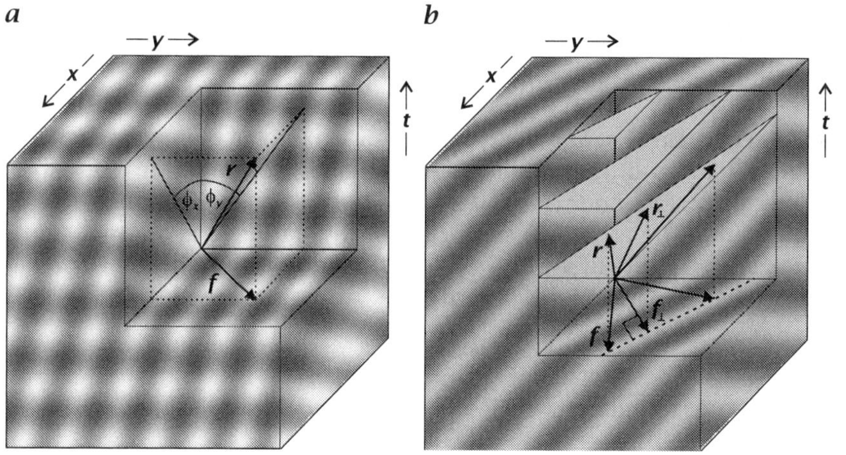

***Figure 13.3:** Illustration of the spatiotemporal brightness distribution of moving patterns: **a** moving sinusoidal plaid pattern (no aperture problem); **b** moving planar wave pattern (aperture problem). The upper right portions of the 3-D **x**t-cubes have been cut off, revealing the internal structure of the spatiotemporal images.*

can be derived from Fig. 13.3a to be

$$\boldsymbol{f} = \left[\frac{r_1}{r_3}, \frac{r_2}{r_3}\right]^T = -\left[\tan\phi_x, \tan\phi_y\right]^T \tag{13.4}$$

where ϕ_x and ϕ_y denote the angles between the t-axis and the projection of the vector $\boldsymbol{r}$ onto the xt- and yt-plane, respectively. Thus, optical flow computation reduces to an *orientation analysis* in spatiotemporal images, that is, an estimate of the 3-D vector $\boldsymbol{r}$.

The direction $\boldsymbol{r}$ of constant brightness at a certain point within a spatiotemporal image is pointing perpendicular to the spatiotemporal gradient vector $\nabla_{xt} g = \left[g_x, g_y, g_t\right]^T$. Using the relation Eq. (13.4), the brightness change constraint Eq. (13.2) can be formulated as:

$$\left[g_x, g_y, g_t\right] \begin{bmatrix} f_1 \\ f_2 \\ 1 \end{bmatrix} = r_3^{-1} \left(\nabla_{xt} g\right)^T \boldsymbol{r} = 0 \tag{13.5}$$

As soon as an aperture persists within a local spatial neighborhood the direction $\boldsymbol{r}$ of smallest brightness changes is no longer unambiguous and the local spatiotemporal neighborhood consists of layered structures instead of lines. This can be observed in Fig. 13.3b, which shows the spatiotemporal structure of a moving planar wave pattern. Without further constraints only the normal flow $\boldsymbol{f}_\perp$ can be computed.

It is important to note that Eqs. (13.2) and (13.5) are mathematically equivalent and no constraint is added by extending the formulation of the brightness conservation into 3-D space.

Motion constraint in Fourier domain. The concept of image sequences as spatiotemporal images allows one to analyze motion in the corresponding *spatiotemporal frequency domain* (*Fourier domain*).

Let $g(\boldsymbol{x}, t)$ be an image sequence of any pattern moving with constant velocity, causing the optical flow $\boldsymbol{f}$ at any point in the image plane. The resulting spatiotemporal structure can be described by

$$g(\boldsymbol{x}, t) = g(\boldsymbol{x} - \boldsymbol{f}t) \tag{13.6}$$

The spatiotemporal Fourier transform $\hat{g}(\boldsymbol{k}, \omega)$ of Eq. (13.6) is given by [13]

$$\hat{g}(\boldsymbol{k}, \omega) = \hat{g}(\boldsymbol{k})\delta(\boldsymbol{k}^T\boldsymbol{f} - \omega) \tag{13.7}$$

where $\hat{g}(\boldsymbol{k})$ is the spatial Fourier transform of the pattern, and $\delta(\cdot)$ denotes Dirac's delta distribution. Equation (13.7) states that the 3-D Fourier spectrum of a pattern moving with constant velocity condenses to a plane in Fourier space. The 2-D Fourier spectrum of the pattern is being projected parallel to the temporal frequency ω onto the plane. Figure 13.4a shows the spatiotemporal image of a 1-D random pattern moving with 1 pixel/frame into positive x-direction. The corresponding Fourier (power) spectrum is shown in Fig. 13.4b.

The equation of the plane in Fourier domain is given by the argument of the delta distribution in Eq. (13.7):

$$\omega(\boldsymbol{k}, \boldsymbol{f}) = \boldsymbol{k}^T\boldsymbol{f} \tag{13.8}$$

The normal vector of the plane is pointing parallel to the 3-D vector $[f_1, f_2, 1]^T$. The plane constraint relation Eq. (13.8) is an equivalent formulation of the brightness change constraint equation, BCCE Eq. (13.2). It is the basis for all spatiotemporal energy-based techniques (Section 13.4) that attempt to fit a plane to the Fourier spectrum of an image sequence. From the inclination of the plane the optical flow can be estimated. Taking the derivatives of $\omega(\boldsymbol{k}, \boldsymbol{f})$ Eq. (13.8) with respect to k_x and k_y yields both components of the optical flow:

$$\nabla_k \omega(\boldsymbol{k}, \boldsymbol{f}) = \boldsymbol{f} \tag{13.9}$$

The Fourier transform does not necessarily have to be applied to the whole image. For local estimates, multiplication with an appropriate window function prior to transformation restricts the spectrum to a local neighborhood (Fig. 13.4c). It is, however, not possible to perform a Fourier transformation for a single pixel. The smaller the window, the more blurred the spectrum becomes [14] (compare Fig. 13.4b

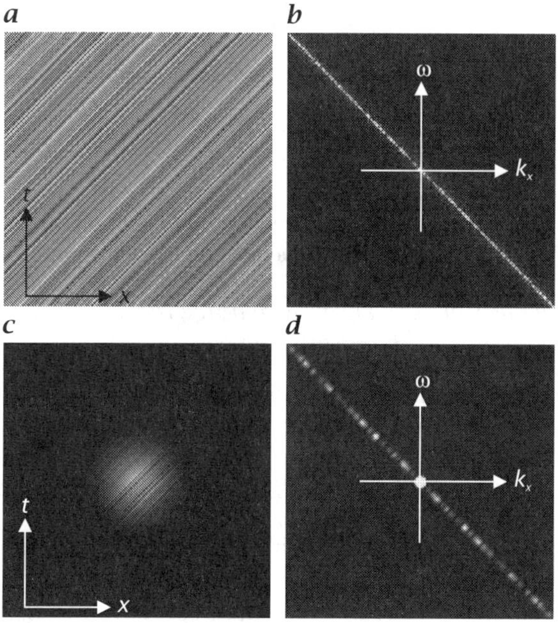

Figure 13.4: *Translating 1-D random pattern moving at 1 pixel/frame:* ***a*** *2-D xt-image (256 × 256);* ***b*** *power spectrum of the xt-image, with k_x and ω ranging from $-\pi$ to π. The star-shaped patterns are due to the finite size of the image;* ***c*** *windowed 2-D xt-image;* ***d*** *power spectrum of the windowed xt-image.*

with Fig. 13.4d). With the spatiotemporal window function $w(\boldsymbol{x}, t)$, the resulting Fourier spectrum is blurred by the Fourier transform of w, according to

$$\widehat{g \cdot w}(\boldsymbol{k}, \omega) = \hat{w}(\boldsymbol{k}, \omega) * [\hat{g}(\boldsymbol{k})\delta(\boldsymbol{k}\boldsymbol{f} - \omega)] \tag{13.10}$$

where $\hat{w}(\boldsymbol{k}, \omega)$ denotes the Fourier transform of the window function $w(\boldsymbol{x}, t)$, and $*$ defines the convolution

$$a(\boldsymbol{k}, \omega) * b(\boldsymbol{k}, \omega) = \int_{-\infty}^{\infty} a(\boldsymbol{k} - \boldsymbol{k}', \omega - \omega') b(\boldsymbol{k}', \omega') d\boldsymbol{k}' d\omega' \tag{13.11}$$

Without additional windowing, $w(\boldsymbol{x}, t)$ is given by the size of the image and the number of frames, that is, a box function with the size of the spatiotemporal image. Its Fourier transform corresponds to a 2-D sinc function, which can be observed in the star-shaped patterns of Fig. 13.4b.

Hence, the Fourier domain formulation Eq. (13.8) intrinsically extends the motion constraint to a local neighborhood of a pixel. In case

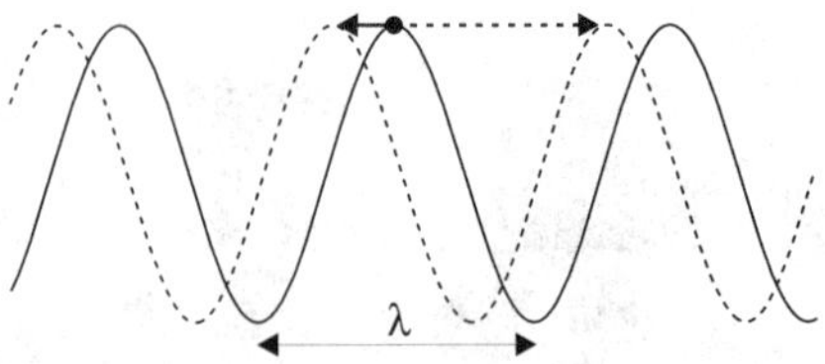

Figure 13.5: *Illustration of the temporal sampling theorem for a sinusoidal pattern of wavelength λ. Without restrictions on the magnitude of the displacement between two consecutive frames, both displacements indicated by arrows and all multiples of λ are equally likely to be the real displacement.*

of an *aperture problem*, the moving pattern shows spatial orientation within the local neighborhood. This causes the 3-D Fourier spectrum to reduce to a line instead of a plane. From the line, only one inclination angle can be extracted, corresponding to the normal optical flow.

Temporal sampling theorem. In all cases in which spatial and temporal derivatives are directly related, it is inherently assumed that the shift between two consecutive frames is small compared to the scale of the pattern. In other words: the time derivative has to be unambiguously related to the moving brightness pattern within a small spatiotemporal neighborhood. This corresponds to the fact that derivatives are always realized by finite differences in image sequence processing although they are defined as infinitesimal quantities. For overly large displacements, no coherent structures can be detected in the spatiotemporal image. How fast are patterns of a certain size allowed to move? The answer is given by the *temporal sampling theorem*.

Consider a moving sinusoidal pattern of wavelength λ (Fig. 13.5). If no restrictions on the magnitude of shifts within consecutive frames apply, the real shift cannot be unambiguously determined. It is further undetermined up to multiples of the wavelength λ. The displacement stays unambiguous if it can be restricted to less than half the wavelength λ. In this case the correct optical flow can be estimated by the *minimal motion*, indicated by the solid arrow in Fig. 13.5.

From the spatial sampling theorem we know that any periodic signal has to be sampled at least twice per wavelength (Section 2.4.2). For temporal periodic signals, the wavelength corresponds to the cycle T with $T = 2\pi/\omega$. Using Eq. (13.8) the temporal sampling theorem is given by

$$\Delta t < \frac{T}{2} = \frac{\pi}{\omega} = \frac{\pi}{\boldsymbol{k}^T \boldsymbol{f}} \tag{13.12}$$

where Δt denotes the minimum frame rate necessary to estimate the optical flow $\boldsymbol{f}$ of a periodical signal with wave number $\boldsymbol{k}$. The smaller the scale of a pattern, the more slowly it is allowed to move if the frame rate cannot be increased. As all patterns can be decomposed into periodic signals, Eq. (13.12) applies for any moving object. It is important to note that it is not the size of the object, but rather the smallest wave number contained in the Fourier spectrum of the object that is the limiting factor. A large disk-shaped object can suffer from temporal aliasing right at its edge, where high wave numbers are located.

If the temporal sampling theorem is violated by too large displacements, temporal aliasing appears. In spatiotemporal images it shows up as patterns with false inclinations or as distributed structures without any relation at all. A prominent example of temporal aliasing is one in which the wheels of horse-drawn carriages in movies seem to spin around in the wrong direction.

An interesting analogy exists in the human visual system. From psychophysical experiments with a random dot kinematogram [15] it was found that human observers tend to estimate a coherent minimal motion, independent from the scale of clusters within the random pattern. To explain these findings, Morgan [16] concludes that a coarse spatial filter precedes motion detection in the human visual pathway [15].

Performing a low-pass filtering to remove all small scale spatial frequencies beyond the critical limit is the basic idea of multiscale optical flow computation techniques (Chapter 14). Starting from coarse patterns, large displacements can be computed, which can be iteratively refined from smaller scales. Such an approach, however, assumes that patterns at all scales are moving with the same velocity. This is not true for physical processes showing dispersion, such as water surface waves.

It is important to note that the apparent motion, represented by the optical flow field $\boldsymbol{f}$, is the *sampled motion*, that is, the apparent motion after the spatiotemporal sampling process during image acquisition. If temporal aliasing persists, the real motion cannot be separated from the apparently moving structures, unless other constraints apply. Hence, optical flow computation or *low level motion* computation has to be treated separately from higher level algorithms that attempt to solve the problem of physical correspondence from visual correspondence.

13.2.2 Physical and visual correspondence

From the aperture problem we learned that only normal optical flow can be computed in the case of linear symmetry of the brightness distribution within a local neighborhood. Translations parallel to lines of constant gray values do not contribute to brightness variations and are thus not detectable. The temporal sampling theorem states that large displacements cannot be estimated from small-scale patterns. Both problems of motion estimation can be considered as special cases of a more general problem, commonly referred to as the *correspondence problem*. The motion of patterns does not always allow for relating corresponding features in consecutive frames in an unambiguous manner. The physical correspondence of features can remain undetectable due to an aperture problem, missing texture (recall the example of the spinning sphere in Fig. 13.1) or overly large displacements. Conversely, the apparent motion can lead to false correspondence. Variation in scene intensity may not be due to motion but instead may be caused by variations in illumination.

If local constraints are violated, *correspondence*-based techniques try to estimate a best match of features within consecutive frames (Chapter 13.5). Depending on the kind of features under consideration, these techniques can be classified into *correlation methods* and *token tracking* techniques [17]. Correlation techniques are computationally costly and therefore restricted to short-range displacements. Token tracking methods extract features, such as corners, straight line segments or blobs [18] and track them over time. The search can be extended to the entire image area, which enables estimates of long-range displacements. All correspondence-based techniques consider only two single images. They do not use any information about the continuous temporal domain.

13.2.3 Flow versus correspondence

There has been much discussion of the pros and cons of optical flow based techniques in contrast to correspondence-based techniques. We do not want to contribute to this dispute but rather recall which method seems to be best suited under certain circumstances.

In order to solve the aperture problem a variety of optical flow-based approaches have been proposed that try to minimize an objective function pooling constraints over a small finite area. An excellent overview of the current state of the art is given by Barron et al. [6]. They conclude that differential techniques, such as the local weighted least squares method proposed by Lucas and Kanade [19] (Section 13.3.1), perform best in terms of efficiency and accuracy. Phase-based methods [20] (Section 13.4.3) show slightly better accuracy but are less efficient in implementation and lack a single useful confidence measure. Bainbridge-Smith and Lane [9] come to the same conclusion in their comparison of the performance of differential methods. Performing analytical studies of various motion estimation techniques, Jähne [21] and [13] showed that the 3-D structure tensor technique (Section 13.3.2) yields the best results with respect to systematic errors and noise sensitivity. This could be verified by Jähne et al. [22], in their analysis of a calibrated image sequence with ground truth data provided by Otte and Nagel [8].

On the other hand, correspondence-based techniques (Section 13.5) are less sensitive to illumination changes. They are also capable of estimating long-range displacements of distinct features that violate the temporal sampling theorem. In this case any optical flow-based technique will fail. However, correlation-based approaches are extremely sensitive to periodic structures. With nearly periodic inputs (such as textures or bandpass filtered signals) they tend to find multiple local minima [6]. Comparative studies show that correlation-based techniques produce unpredictable output for straight edges (aperture problem), while optical-flow based techniques correctly estimate normal flow. Correlation techniques also perform less effectively in estimating subpixel displacements than do optical flow-based techniques [6, 23]. Especially at very small displacements in the order of less than 1/10 pixel/frame, optical flow-based techniques yield better results.

Before we turn towards a detailed description of the various techniques, we want to draw the conclusion that neither correlation nor optical flow-based techniques are perfect choices in any case. If the temporal sampling theorem can be assured to be fulfilled, optical flow-based techniques are generally the better choice. In other cases, when large displacements of small structures are expected, correlation-based approaches usually perform better.

For both kind of techniques, it is important to get *confidence measures* in addition to the optical flow. No technique is without errors in any case. Only if errors can be detected and quantified can the result be reliably interpreted. It also shows that differences in precision, attributable to details of the initial formulation, are, in fact, a result of different minimization procedures and a careful numerical discretization of the used filters.

13.3 Optical flow-based motion estimation

In this section we want to focus on common optical flow-based techniques. We can not detail all facets of the spectrum of existing techniques, but rather try to give a concise overview of the basic principles.

13.3.1 Differential techniques

Local weighted least squares. Assuming the optical flow f to be constant within a small neighborhood U Lucas and Kanade [19] propose a local weighted least squares estimate of the constraint Equation (13.2) on individual pixels within U. Similar approaches are reported by [24, 25, 26, 27]. The estimated optical flow is given by the solution of the following minimization problem:

$$\boldsymbol{f} = \arg\min\|\boldsymbol{e}\|_2^2, \quad \|\boldsymbol{e}\|_2^2 = \int_{-\infty}^{\infty} w(\boldsymbol{x}-\boldsymbol{x}')\left[(\nabla g)^T\boldsymbol{f}+g_t\right]^2 \mathrm{d}\boldsymbol{x}' \tag{13.13}$$

with a weighting function $w(\boldsymbol{x})$ selecting the size of the neighborhood. In practical implementations the weighting is realized by a Gaussian smoothing kernel. Additionally, w could weight each pixel according to some kind of confidence measure, for example, the magnitude of the gradient. In that way, *a priori* known errors are not propagated into the optical flow computation.

In the initial formulation of [19], Eq. (13.13) was given by a discrete sum of the squared *residuals* $(\nabla g)^T\boldsymbol{f}+g_t$, which have to be minimized. The mathematically equivalent *continuous least squares* formulation Eq. (13.13) replaces the weighted sum by a convolution integral [13, 21]. This formulation enables us to use linear filter theory, which allows, for example, optimizing the convolution kernels independently from the minimization procedure. In this way practical implementations of different approaches can be quantitatively compared without confusing discretization errors with intrinsic errors of the algorithms.

The minimization of Eq. (13.13) is carried out by standard least squares estimation. Both partial derivatives of $\|\boldsymbol{e}\|_2^2$ with respect to the two components f_1 and f_2 of the optical flow $\boldsymbol{f}$ have to equal zero at the minimum of $\|\boldsymbol{e}\|_2^2$:

$$\frac{\partial\|\boldsymbol{e}\|_2^2}{\partial f_1} = 2\int_{-\infty}^{\infty} w(\boldsymbol{x}-\boldsymbol{x}')g_x\left[(\nabla g)^T\boldsymbol{f}+g_t\right] \mathrm{d}\boldsymbol{x}' \stackrel{!}{=} 0 \tag{13.14}$$

$$\frac{\partial\|\boldsymbol{e}\|_2^2}{\partial f_2} = 2\int_{-\infty}^{\infty} w(\boldsymbol{x}-\boldsymbol{x}')g_y\left[(\nabla g)^T\boldsymbol{f}+g_t\right] \mathrm{d}\boldsymbol{x}' \stackrel{!}{=} 0 \tag{13.15}$$

If the optical flow $\boldsymbol{f}$ is assumed to be constant within the area of influence of w, it can be drawn out of the integral. Combining Eq. (13.14) and Eq. (13.15) yields the following linear equation system

$$\underbrace{\begin{bmatrix} \langle g_x g_x\rangle & \langle g_x g_y\rangle \\ \langle g_x g_y\rangle & \langle g_y g_y\rangle \end{bmatrix}}_{\boldsymbol{A}} \underbrace{\begin{bmatrix} f_1 \\ f_2 \end{bmatrix}}_{\boldsymbol{f}} = \underbrace{-\begin{bmatrix} \langle g_x g_t\rangle \\ \langle g_y g_t\rangle \end{bmatrix}}_{\boldsymbol{b}} \tag{13.16}$$

with the abbreviation

$$\langle a\rangle = \int_{-\infty}^{\infty} w(\boldsymbol{x}-\boldsymbol{x}')\, a\, \mathrm{d}\boldsymbol{x}' \tag{13.17}$$

In operator notation, the components of Eq. (13.16) are given by

$$\langle g_p\, g_q \rangle = \mathcal{B}(\mathcal{D}_p \cdot \mathcal{D}_q), \quad \text{and} \quad \langle g_p\, g_t \rangle = \mathcal{B}(\mathcal{D}_p \cdot \mathcal{D}_t) \tag{13.18}$$

where $\mathcal{B}$ is a smoothing operator and $\mathcal{D}_p$, $\mathcal{D}_q$, and $\mathcal{D}_t$ are discrete first-order derivative operators in the spatial directions p and q and in time direction t, respectively. The solution of Eq. (13.16) is given by

$$\boldsymbol{f} = \boldsymbol{A}^{-1}\boldsymbol{b} \tag{13.19}$$

provided the inverse of $\boldsymbol{A}$ exists. If all gradient vectors within U are pointing into the same direction, $\boldsymbol{A}$ gets singular. Then, the brightness distribution can be expressed locally as

$$g(\boldsymbol{x}) = g(\boldsymbol{d}^T\boldsymbol{x}) \tag{13.20}$$

where $\boldsymbol{d} = [d_1, d_2]^T$ is a vector pointing perpendicular to lines of constant brightness. From Eq. (13.20) the first-order partial derivatives can be computed as $g_x = d_1 g'$ and $g_y = d_2 g'$, where the abbreviation $g' = \partial g / \partial(\boldsymbol{d}^T\boldsymbol{x})$ is used. The determinant

$$\det(\boldsymbol{A}) = \langle g_x\, g_x \rangle \langle g_y\, g_y \rangle - \langle g_x\, g_y \rangle^2 \tag{13.21}$$

equals zero and $\boldsymbol{A}$ cannot be inverted. Thus, averaging Eq. (13.2) over a small neighborhood does not yield more information than a single point if the aperture problem persists within the neighborhood. In this case, only the normal flow $\boldsymbol{f}_\perp$ is computed according to Eq. (13.3).

Instead of zero determinant, singularity of $\boldsymbol{A}$ can be identified by analyzing the eigenvalues of the symmetric matrix $\boldsymbol{A}$ prior to inversion. While Simoncelli [27] suggests using the sum of eigenvalues, Barron et al. [6] conclude that the smallest eigenvalue constitutes a more reliable measure. In Section 13.7 we will compare common confidence and type measures of different approaches and show how they are related.

Jähne [13] shows that an extension of the integration in Eq. (13.13) into the temporal domain yields a better local regularization, provided that the optical flow is modeled constant within the spatiotemporal neighborhood U. However, this does not change the minimization procedure and results in the same linear equation system Eq. (13.16). All that needs to be changed are the components $\langle a \rangle$

$$\langle a \rangle = \int_{-\infty}^{\infty} w(\boldsymbol{x} - \boldsymbol{x}', t - t')\, a \, \mathrm{d}\boldsymbol{x}'\, \mathrm{d}t' \tag{13.22}$$

where both the integration as well as the window function w have been extended into the temporal domain.

While the presence of an aperture problem can be identified by the singularity of the matrix $\boldsymbol{A}$, the initial assumption of constant optical flow within U remains to be proved. In any case, an averaged optical flow will be computed by the solution of Eq. (13.19). This leads to over-smoothing of the optical flow field at motion discontinuities and false estimation at the presence of transparent motion overlay. Such cases lead to nonzero values of the expression $[(\nabla g)^T \boldsymbol{f} + g_t]$, which is called the measurement *innovation*, or the *residual*. The residual reflects the discrepancy between the predicted measurement $(\nabla g)^T \boldsymbol{f}$ and the actual measurement g_t. A residual of zero means that both are in complete agreement. Thus, a nonconstant optical flow field can be detected by analyzing the variance of the data σ^2, given by the squared magnitude of the residuals [13]

$$\sigma^2 = \|\boldsymbol{e}\|_2^2 = \left\langle \left[(\nabla g)^T \boldsymbol{f} + g_t \right]^2 \right\rangle \tag{13.23}$$

where $\boldsymbol{f}$ is the *estimated* optical flow. In case of constant $\boldsymbol{f}$ within U, the residuals in Eq. (13.23) vanish and σ^2 reduces to the variance cause by noise in the image. Thus, a variance significantly larger than the noise variance is a clear indicator for a violation of the assumption of constant optical flow. In real applications, $\boldsymbol{f}$ will never be constant over the whole image. If it varies smoothly over the image area, it can be considered locally constant and the local least squares estimate can be applied. Other models of the spatial distribution of $\boldsymbol{f}(\boldsymbol{x})$, such as linear (affine) motion, can be incorporated into the least squares approach as well. This will be the subject of Section 13.6.1.

From a probabilistic point of view, the minimization of Eq. (13.13) corresponds to a maximum likelihood estimation of the optical flow, given Gaussian-distributed errors at individual pixels [28]. Black and Anandan [12] show that the Gaussian assumption does not hold for motion discontinuities and transparent motions. By replacing the least squares estimation with robust statistics they come up with an iterative estimation of multiple motions (Section 13.6.2).

Second-order techniques. Instead of grouping constraints over a local neighborhood, it has been proposed to use second-order information to solve for both components of $\boldsymbol{f}$ [29, 30, 31]. This can be motivated by extending the brightness constancy assumption to an assumption on the conservation of the gradient ∇g under translation:

$$\frac{\mathrm{d}(\nabla g)}{\mathrm{d}t} = 0 \tag{13.24}$$

Evaluating Eq. (13.24) yields the following linear equation system for a single point:

$$\underbrace{\begin{bmatrix} g_{xx} & g_{xy} \\ g_{xy} & g_{yy} \end{bmatrix}}_{\boldsymbol{H}} \underbrace{\begin{bmatrix} f_1 \\ f_2 \end{bmatrix}}_{\boldsymbol{f}} = - \underbrace{\begin{bmatrix} g_{tx} \\ g_{ty} \end{bmatrix}}_{\boldsymbol{b}} \tag{13.25}$$

The matrix $\boldsymbol{H}$ is the *Hessian* of the image brightness function, containing all second-order partial spatial derivatives $g_{pq} = \partial^2 g/\partial p \partial q$. The second-order spatiotemporal derivatives in $\boldsymbol{b}$ are abbreviated by $g_{tp} = \partial^2 g/\partial t \partial p$. The linear equation system Eq. (13.25) can be solved by

$$\boldsymbol{f} = \boldsymbol{H}^{-1}\boldsymbol{b} \tag{13.26}$$

if the Hessian matrix is not singular. This happens if the determinant vanishes,

$$\det(\boldsymbol{H}) = g_{xx}g_{yy} - g_{xy}^2 = 0 \tag{13.27}$$

The trivial solution of Eq. (13.27) is given for vanishing second-order derivatives, $g_{xx} = g_{yy} = g_{xy} = 0$, that is, local planar brightness distribution. Equation (13.27) also holds, if the image brightness shows *linear symmetry* within the local area supporting the second-order derivative operators. In this case, the brightness distribution can be expressed locally as

$$g(\boldsymbol{x}) = g(\boldsymbol{d}^T\boldsymbol{x}) \tag{13.28}$$

where $\boldsymbol{d} = [d_1, d_2]^T$ is a vector pointing perpendicular to lines of constant brightness. From Eq. (13.28) the second-order partial derivatives can be computed as

$$g_{xx} = d_1^2 g'', \quad g_{yy} = d_2^2 g'', \quad \text{and} \quad g_{xy} = d_1 d_2 g'' \tag{13.29}$$

where the abbreviation $g'' = \partial^2 g/\partial(\boldsymbol{d}^T\boldsymbol{x})^2$ is used. With Eq. (13.29) the condition Eq. (13.27) is satisfied and the Hessian $\boldsymbol{H}$ cannot be inverted.

Thus, second-order techniques, just as first-order techniques, do not allow for estimating the 2-D optical flow field $\boldsymbol{f}$ in case of an aperture problem within a local neighborhood. Although no local averaging has been performed to obtain the solution Eq. (13.25), a local neighborhood is introduced by the region of support of the second-order derivative operators. In order to obtain second-order differential information, first-order properties of the image area need to be related over an increased area compared to first-order differentiation. From first-order information the full 2-D optical flow can only be extracted if the spatial orientation changes within the region of interest. Bainbridge-Smith and Lane [9] conclude that first-order differential techniques, such as proposed by Lucas and Kanade [19], are in fact generalized second-order techniques, because they implicitly require variation of the gradient within the region of support.

The initial assumption (Eq. (13.24)) requests that first-order (affine) motions, such as dilation, rotation or shear, are not allowed in the optical flow field. This constraint is much stronger than the brightness conservation assumption of Eq. (13.2) and is fulfilled only rarely for real motion fields. Hence, second-order techniques generally lead to sparser optical flow fields than those of first-order techniques [6]. If the assumption of conserved gradient is violated, the residual error

$$\|\boldsymbol{e}\|_2^2 = [\boldsymbol{H}\boldsymbol{f} - \boldsymbol{b}]^2 \tag{13.30}$$

will increase beyond the noise variance σ^2 (compare to Eq. (13.23)), which allows one to identify erroneous estimates of $\boldsymbol{f}$.

Global constraints. Local least squares techniques minimize the brightness change constraint equation Eq. (13.2) over a localized aperture, defined by the size of the spatial window function w (Eq. (13.13)).

Global constraint methods extend the integration to the entire image area and combine the local gradient constraint Eq. (13.2) with a spatial coherence assumption. The resulting objective function $\|\boldsymbol{e}_t\|_2^2$ to be minimized consists of two terms. The first one, $\|\boldsymbol{e}_d\|_2^2$, contains the local data (brightness) conservation constraint Eq. (13.2) at each pixel and a second one, $\|\boldsymbol{e}_s\|_2^2$, expresses the spatial relation between optical flow vectors:

$$\|\boldsymbol{e}_t\|_2^2 = \|\boldsymbol{e}_d\|_2^2 + \lambda^2\|\boldsymbol{e}_s\|_2^2 = \int\limits_D \left[(\nabla g)^T \boldsymbol{f} + g_t\right]^2 \, \mathrm{d}\boldsymbol{x}' + \lambda^2\|\boldsymbol{e}_s\|_2^2 \tag{13.31}$$

The integration is carried out over the domain D, which can be extended to the entire image. The parameter λ controls the influence of the spatial coherence term. The optical flow $\boldsymbol{f}$ is estimated by minimizing $\|\boldsymbol{e}_t\|_2^2$,

$$\boldsymbol{f} = \arg\min\|\boldsymbol{e}_t\|_2^2 \tag{13.32}$$

The introduction of a regularizing spatial coherence constraint $\|\boldsymbol{e}_s\|_2^2$ restricts the class of admissible solutions and makes the problem well-posed [12]. A variety of approaches have been proposed in the literature, dealing with the choice of an appropriate spatial constraint. In general, it should interpolate optical flow estimates at regions suffering from the aperture problem or without sufficient brightness variations. At the same time spatial oversmoothing of motion boundaries should be prevented. Both are competing requirements.

The most common formulation of $\|\boldsymbol{e}_s\|_2^2$ has been introduced by Horn and Schunk [10]. They propose a *global smoothness* constraint of the form

$$\|\boldsymbol{e}_s\|_2^2 = \int\limits_D \left[\left(\frac{\partial f_1}{\partial x}\right)^2 + \left(\frac{\partial f_1}{\partial y}\right)^2 + \left(\frac{\partial f_2}{\partial x}\right)^2 + \left(\frac{\partial f_2}{\partial y}\right)^2\right] \mathrm{d}\boldsymbol{x}' \tag{13.33}$$

Minimizing Eq. (13.32) by means of *Gauss-Seidel iteration* [32] yields an iterative solution for the optical flow $\boldsymbol{f}^{(k+1)}$ at time step $k+1$ given the flow $\boldsymbol{f}^{(k)}$ at time k:

$$\boldsymbol{f}^{(k+1)} = \left\langle \boldsymbol{f}^{(k)} \right\rangle - \nabla g \frac{\nabla g \left\langle \boldsymbol{f}^{(k)} \right\rangle + g_t}{\|\nabla g\|_2^2 + \lambda^2} \tag{13.34}$$

where $\left\langle \boldsymbol{f}^{(k)} \right\rangle$ denotes a local average of $\boldsymbol{f}^{(k)}$. The initial estimate $\boldsymbol{f}^{(0)}$ is usually set to zero for the entire image. It is important to note that the gradient ∇g apparently controls the influence of both terms in Eq. (13.34). If the gradient vanishes, that is, at regions with low spatial structure, the optical flow is interpolated from adjacent estimates. In regions with high contrast the local brightness change constraint (numerator of the right term in Eq. (13.34)) becomes dominant.

The propagation of the flow field into regions with low contrast is an important feature of Horn and Schunck's smoothness constraint. However, as no directional selectivity is included in Eq. (13.33) the resulting flow field is blurred over motion discontinuities. It also has the drawback that a localized error can have a far-reaching effect if the surrounding gradients are small [9].

In order to reduce smoothing across edges, Nagel [29, 33, 34] suggests an *oriented smoothness* constraint:

$$\|\boldsymbol{e}_s\|_2^2 = \int_D \frac{1}{\|\nabla g\|_2^2 + 2\delta} \left[E_1 + \delta E_2\right] \mathrm{d}\boldsymbol{x}' \tag{13.35}$$

$$E_1 = \left[\frac{\partial f_1}{\partial x} g_y - \frac{\partial f_1}{\partial y} g_x\right]^2 + \left[\frac{\partial f_2}{\partial x} g_y - \frac{\partial f_2}{\partial y} g_x\right]^2 \tag{13.36}$$

$$E_2 = \left(\frac{\partial f_1}{\partial x}\right)^2 + \left(\frac{\partial f_1}{\partial y}\right)^2 + \left(\frac{\partial f_2}{\partial x}\right)^2 + \left(\frac{\partial f_2}{\partial y}\right)^2 \tag{13.37}$$

The additional parameter δ controls the relative influence of the oriented smoothness term E_1 compared to E_2, which constitutes Horn and Schunck's global smoothness constraint. Again, the solution is given by an iterative Gauss-Seidel method. As an interesting feature, the rather complicated solution equations implicitly contain second-order derivatives.

In a more restrictive way, Hildreth [35, 36] reduce all computations to zero crossings of a Laplace-filtered image. Along these contour lines C, an objective function is defined according to

$$\|\boldsymbol{e}_t\|_2^2 = \int_C \left[(\nabla g)^T \boldsymbol{f} + g_t\right]^2 + \lambda^2 \left[\left(\frac{\partial f_1}{\partial s}\right)^2 + \left(\frac{\partial f_2}{\partial s}\right)^2\right] \mathrm{d}\boldsymbol{s}' \tag{13.38}$$

where the first term in the integral is given by the standard data conservation constraint Eq. (13.31) and $\partial f_p / \partial s$, denotes the directional derivative of f_p into the direction $\boldsymbol{s}$ along the contour C. In contrast to other approaches, all integrations are carried out along contour lines instead of by 2-D averaging. Thus, no information is smoothed across brightness edges. However, the approach inherently assumes that all edges belong to the same object. If contours of independently moving objects merge, the resulting optical flow field is blurred along the contour line as well.

All approaches incorporating global constraints have in common that they result in systems of differential equations relating spatial variations of the optical flow within the entire domain D. Such a system can only be solved iteratively using numerical iteration methods, such as *Gauss-Seidel iteration* or *successive overrelaxation* [28, 37]. Although efficient iterative solutions have been developed in numerical mathematics, they are still slower than closed solutions. Another problem of iterative solutions is the question of convergence, which may depend on image content. Further information on global constraints can be found in Chapter 16, where a general toolbox for variational approaches is proposed, together with an efficient numerical iteration scheme.

13.3.2 Tensor-based techniques

In Section 13.2.1 we have shown that optical flow computation can be formulated as orientation analysis in spatiotemporal images. A practical example of such a spatiotemporal image and the corresponding structures is shown in Fig. 13.6. This application example has been chosen for illustration because it demonstrates nicely how any moving gray-value structure causes inclined patterns, regardless of certain object properties.

In order to determine local orientation Bigün and Granlund [38] proposed a *tensor representation* of the local image brightness distribution. Starting with a different idea, Kass and Witkin [39] came to a solution that turned out to be equivalent to the tensor method. Searching for a general description of local orientation in multidimensional images, Knutsson [40, 41] concluded that local structure in an n-dimensional domain can be represented by a symmetric $n \times n$ tensor of second-order. In the analysis of data with a dimensionality higher than two it turns out that using scalars and vectors is no longer always convenient [42]. Tensors—a generalization of the vector concept—are perfectly suited to describe symmetries within local neighborhoods in multidimensional spatial and spatiotemporal signals.

This section outlines the practical application of tensor representations to optical flow computation and its relation to other optical flow-based techniques. We will show how a local least squares estimation

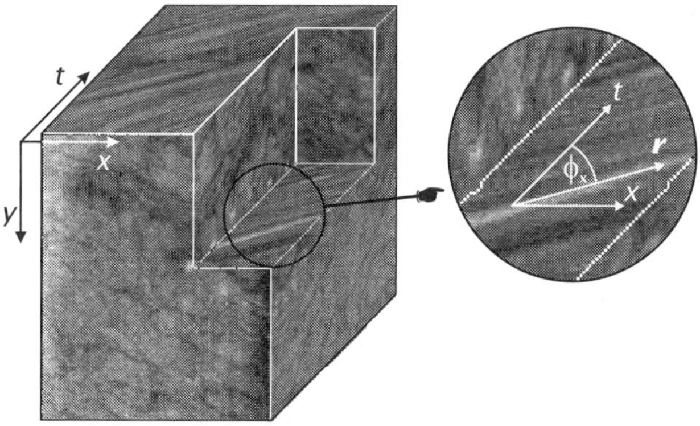

Figure 13.6: Illustration of the spatiotemporal brightness distribution of moving patterns. The sequence shows infrared images of the ocean surface moving mainly in positive x-direction. The upper right portion of the 3-D $\boldsymbol{x}t$*- cube has been cut off, revealing the internal structure of the spatiotemporal image.*

of optical flow, such as the approach of Lucas and Kanade [19], can be improved by using total least squares estimation instead of standard least squares. This leads directly to the *structure tensor technique* for optical flow computation [43, 44, 45, 46], which constitutes the most direct approach to linear symmetry detection in spatiotemporal images. Another tensor representation, based on combinations of quadrature filters, will be outlined in Section 13.4.2.

The structure tensor approach. The optical flow $\boldsymbol{f}$ and the direction $\boldsymbol{r}$ of constant brightness within a spatiotemporal image are related by $\boldsymbol{f} = r_3^{-1}\,[r_1, r_2]^T$ (Eq. (13.4)). Within a local neighborhood U, the vector $\boldsymbol{r}$ has to be as perpendicular as possible to the spatiotemporal gradient $\nabla_{\boldsymbol{x}t}g = \left[g_x, g_y, g_t\right]^T$. Thus, the scalar product $(\nabla_{\boldsymbol{x}t}g)^T\boldsymbol{r}$ has to vanish at any point within U for the optimum estimate of $\boldsymbol{r}$ (Eq. (13.5)). In a least squares sense, $\boldsymbol{r}$ can be found by minimizing

$$\boldsymbol{r} = \arg\min_{\boldsymbol{r}^T\boldsymbol{r}=1} \|e\|_2^2, \quad \|e\|_2^2 = \int_{-\infty}^{\infty} w(\boldsymbol{x}-\boldsymbol{x}')\left[(\nabla_{\boldsymbol{x}t}g)^T\boldsymbol{r}\right]^2 \,\mathrm{d}\boldsymbol{x}' \qquad (13.39)$$

which is equivalent to Eq. (13.13). In order to avoid the trivial solution $\boldsymbol{r} = 0$, the constraint $\boldsymbol{r}^T\boldsymbol{r} = 1$ has to be imposed on $\boldsymbol{r}$. The information within a local neighborhood U around the central point $\boldsymbol{x} = [x, y, t]^T$ is weighted by a window-function $w(\boldsymbol{x} - \boldsymbol{x}')$. In practical applications the size of the local neighborhood U represents the area over which the optical flow is averaged. Again, the spatial integration can be extended into the time domain for local regularization without changing the results of the following minimization procedure [13].

Using the abbreviation Eq. (13.17), the objective function $\|e\|_2^2$ can be transformed into

$$\|e\|_2^2 = \left\langle \left[(\nabla_{xt} g)^T \boldsymbol{r} \right]^2 \right\rangle = \left\langle \boldsymbol{r}^T (\nabla_{xt} g)(\nabla_{xt} g)^T \boldsymbol{r} \right\rangle \tag{13.40}$$

Under the assumption of constant $\boldsymbol{r}$ (that is, constant $\boldsymbol{f}$) within U, Eq. (13.40) reduces to the following quadratic form:

$$\|e\|_2^2 = \boldsymbol{r}^T \left\langle (\nabla_{xt} g)(\nabla_{xt} g)^T \right\rangle \boldsymbol{r} = \boldsymbol{r}^T \boldsymbol{J} \boldsymbol{r} \tag{13.41}$$

with the 3-D symmetric *structure tensor*

$$\boldsymbol{J} = \begin{bmatrix} \langle g_x \, g_x \rangle & \langle g_x \, g_y \rangle & \langle g_x \, g_t \rangle \\ \langle g_x \, g_y \rangle & \langle g_y \, g_y \rangle & \langle g_y \, g_t \rangle \\ \langle g_x \, g_t \rangle & \langle g_y \, g_t \rangle & \langle g_t \, g_t \rangle \end{bmatrix} \tag{13.42}$$

The components of $\boldsymbol{J}$ are given by

$$J_{pq} = \langle g_p \, g_q \rangle = \int_{-\infty}^{\infty} w(\boldsymbol{x} - \boldsymbol{x}') \, g_p g_q \, \mathrm{d}\boldsymbol{x}' \tag{13.43}$$

where g_p, $p \in \{x, y, t\}$, denotes the partial derivative along the coordinate p. The implementation of the tensor components can be carried out very efficiently by standard image processing operators. Identifying the convolution in Eq. (13.43) with a smoothing of the product of partial derivatives, each component of the structure tensor can be computed as

$$J_{pq} = \mathcal{B} \left(\mathcal{D}_p \cdot \mathcal{D}_q \right) \tag{13.44}$$

with the smoothing operator $\mathcal{B}$ and the differential operator $\mathcal{D}_p$ in the direction of the coordinate p.

The minimization of Eq. (13.41) subject to the constraint $\boldsymbol{r}^T \boldsymbol{r} = 1$ can be carried out by the method of *Lagrange multiplier*, minimizing the combined objective function $L(\boldsymbol{r}, \lambda)$

$$\boldsymbol{f} = \arg\min L(\boldsymbol{r}, \lambda), \quad L(\boldsymbol{r}, \lambda) = \boldsymbol{r}^T \boldsymbol{J} \boldsymbol{r} + \lambda \left(1 - \boldsymbol{r}^T \boldsymbol{r} \right) \tag{13.45}$$

The *Lagrange parameter* λ has to be chosen such that the partial derivatives of $L(\boldsymbol{r}, \lambda)$ with respect to all three components of $\boldsymbol{r}$ equal zero:

$$\frac{\partial L(\boldsymbol{r}, \lambda)}{\partial r_i} = 2 \sum_k J_{ik} r_k - 2\lambda r_i \stackrel{!}{=} 0, \quad i \in \{1, 2, 3\} \tag{13.46}$$

Combining the three equations in Eq. (13.46) yields the following linear equation system

$$\boldsymbol{J} \boldsymbol{r} = \lambda \boldsymbol{r} \tag{13.47}$$

Thus, the minimization reduces to an *eigenvalue problem* of the symmetric matrix $\boldsymbol{J}$. Once a minimizing $\boldsymbol{r}$ is found, Eq. (13.41) reduces to

$$\|e\|_2^2 = \boldsymbol{r}^T \boldsymbol{J} \boldsymbol{r} = \boldsymbol{r}^T \lambda \boldsymbol{r} = \lambda \tag{13.48}$$

which shows that the minimum of Eq. (13.41) is reached if the vector $\boldsymbol{r}$ is given by the *eigenvector* of the tensor $\boldsymbol{J}$ to the *minimum eigenvalue* λ.

Total least squares versus standard least squares. Although the local least squares technique (Eq. (13.13)) and the structure tensor technique (Eq. (13.39)) are based on the same initial formulation, the corresponding solutions Eqs. (13.19) and (13.47) are quite different. Practical implementations of both techniques also show that the structure tensor technique is more accurate (Section 13.8). Performing analytical studies Jähne [13] showed that the local least squares technique is biased towards lower values of $\boldsymbol{f}$ in the presence of noise, while the structure tensor technique yields an unbiased estimate for isotropic noise. What are the basic differences of both techniques and how are they related? In order to answer this question we have to examine the minimization procedure of Eqs. (13.13) and (13.39), respectively.

In a discrete formulation, both problems of local optical flow estimation constitute linear equation systems of the form

$$\underbrace{\begin{bmatrix} g_x(\boldsymbol{x}_1) & g_y(\boldsymbol{x}_1) \\ g_x(\boldsymbol{x}_2) & g_y(\boldsymbol{x}_2) \\ \vdots & \vdots \\ g_x(\boldsymbol{x}_N) & g_y(\boldsymbol{x}_N) \end{bmatrix}}_{\boldsymbol{X}} \underbrace{\begin{bmatrix} f_1 \\ f_2 \end{bmatrix}}_{\boldsymbol{f}} = - \underbrace{\begin{bmatrix} g_t(\boldsymbol{x}_1) \\ g_t(\boldsymbol{x}_2) \\ \vdots \\ g_t(\boldsymbol{x}_N) \end{bmatrix}}_{\boldsymbol{y}} \tag{13.49}$$

for N points within the local neighborhood U. The weighting coefficients $w(\boldsymbol{x}_i)$ have been set to unity in order to simplify the notation. However, this does not affect the algebraic relations of the following argumentation.

The task of optical flow estimation can be formulated in the following way: given a set of explanatory variables $\nabla g(\boldsymbol{x}_i)$ (data matrix $\boldsymbol{X}$) and a set of response variables $g_t(\boldsymbol{x}_i)$ (vector of observations $\boldsymbol{y}$), try to find a best estimate of the *true* but *unknown* model parameters $\boldsymbol{f} = [f_1, f_2]^T$, which are assumed to be constant within U. If Eq. (13.49) is overdetermined ($N > 2$), only approximate solutions can be found using either a *standard least squares* (LS) or a *total least squares* (TLS) approach. An excellent overview of the total least squares problem and practical applications can be found in [47].

Least squares The classical *least squares* (LS) approach assumes the explanatory variables of the data matrix $\boldsymbol{X}$ to be free of error, that is, measured with infinite precision. All errors are confined to the observation vector $\boldsymbol{y}$. To find the model parameter $\boldsymbol{f}$, the least squares estimate seeks to

$$\min \|\boldsymbol{y} - \boldsymbol{y}'\|_2^2, \quad \boldsymbol{y}' = \boldsymbol{X}\boldsymbol{f} \tag{13.50}$$

by searching for a minimizing $\boldsymbol{f}$. In minimizing Eq. (13.50) the gradients $\nabla g(\boldsymbol{x}_i)$ and the temporal derivatives $g_t(\boldsymbol{x}_i)$ are treated separately. A best estimate $\boldsymbol{f}$ is found by taking the derivatives of the quadratic objective function $\|\boldsymbol{y} - \boldsymbol{y}'\|_2^2$—which can be considered, as squared magnitude of a 2-D *residual error vector*—with respect to the two components f_1 and f_2.

Total least squares The *total least squares* (TLS) approach is motivated by the fact that errors due to sampling and noise may imply inaccuracies of the data matrix $\boldsymbol{X}$ as well. In the case of motion estimation both spatial and temporal derivatives may be corrupted. This fact can be accounted for by combining $\boldsymbol{X}$ and $\boldsymbol{y}$ to the *augmented data matrix* $\boldsymbol{C}$

$$\boldsymbol{C} = [\boldsymbol{X}; \boldsymbol{y}] = \begin{bmatrix} g_x(\boldsymbol{x}_1) & g_y(\boldsymbol{x}_1) & g_t(\boldsymbol{x}_1) \\ g_x(\boldsymbol{x}_2) & g_y(\boldsymbol{x}_2) & g_t(\boldsymbol{x}_2) \\ \vdots & \vdots & \vdots \\ g_x(\boldsymbol{x}_N) & g_y(\boldsymbol{x}_N) & g_t(\boldsymbol{x}_N) \end{bmatrix} \tag{13.51}$$

With Eq. (13.51) the linear equation system Eq. (13.49) reduces to

$$[\boldsymbol{X}; \boldsymbol{y}] \left[\boldsymbol{f}^T; 1\right]^T = r_3^{-1}\boldsymbol{C}\boldsymbol{r} = 0 \tag{13.52}$$

where the 3-D vector $\boldsymbol{r}$ is defined in Eq. (13.4). In order to find a best estimate of $\boldsymbol{r}$, we seek to

$$\min \|\boldsymbol{C}\boldsymbol{r}\|_2^2, \quad \text{subject to } \boldsymbol{r}^T\boldsymbol{r} = 1 \tag{13.53}$$

where the quadratic constraint $\boldsymbol{r}^T\boldsymbol{r} = 1$ is added to avoid the trivial solution $\boldsymbol{r} = 0$. In minimizing Eq. (13.53), the gradients $\nabla g(\boldsymbol{x}_i)$ and the temporal derivatives $g_t(\boldsymbol{x}_i)$ are treated on an equal basis. A best estimate for $\boldsymbol{r}$ is found by taking the derivatives of the quadratic objective function $\|\boldsymbol{C}\boldsymbol{r}\|_2^2$—which can be considered as squared magnitude of a 3-D *residual error vector*—with respect to *all three* components r_1, r_2, and r_3. This method of obtaining a linear relation between the columns of a matrix $\boldsymbol{C}$ is known as *linear orthogonal* l_2 *approximation* [48, 49], which is an alternative formulation of the total least squares estimation problem [47, 50].

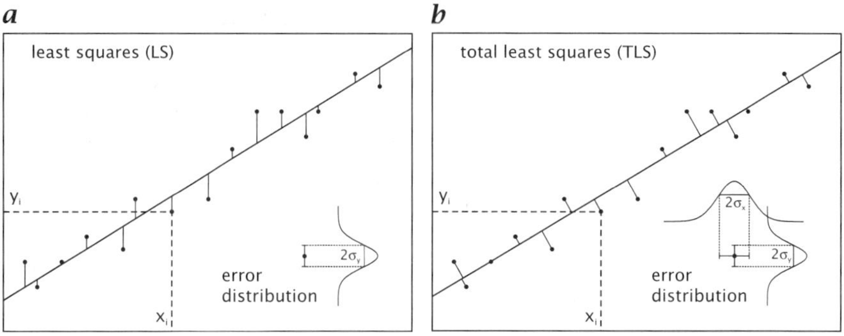

Figure 13.7: *Illustration of the difference between **a** standard least squares (LS) and **b** total least squares (TLS) estimation. Errors in the measured variables are indicated by Gaussian distributions. While LS assumes errors to be confined to the observables y_i, TLS allows errors in the variables x_i as well.*

The basic difference of least squares and total least squares can be illustrated by a simple regression problem fitting a straight line to measurements. Standard least squares minimizes the vertical deviation of the response variables to the estimated line, while total least squares minimizes the Euclidean distances of the points to the line (Fig. 13.7).

In terms of optical flow computation, using TLS instead of LS estimation implies two important differences on the results of either technique:

- Instead of only the two parameters f_1 and f_2, the total least squares technique varies all three parameters of the vector $\boldsymbol{r}$. This leads to a robust estimate of the spatiotemporal orientation in contrast to a fixed temporal component using standard least squares.
- Both techniques yield matrices with components of the form $\langle g_p g_q \rangle$, where g_p denotes partial derivatives in x, y, and t. Comparing the structure tensor Eq. (13.42) to the least squares solution Eq. (13.16) shows that the purely temporal component $\langle g_t g_t \rangle$ of Eq. (13.42) is missing in Eq. (13.16). This component, however, allows to separate isotropic noise, occlusions, and fast accelerations from coherent motion as shown in the following section. Such regions violating the model assumption of constant $\boldsymbol{f}$ within U have to be detected by analyzing the residual errors in the standard least squares estimation.

As a conclusion we note that the difference between the local least squares method of Lucas and Kanade [19] and the structure tensor formulation is neither imposed by the formulation of the minimization problem nor by the extension into the temporal domain, but rather by the minimization procedure.

Most recently, a number of authors have become aware of the subtle difference between the two minimization procedures, which leads to significant differences in the accuracy of a variety of optical flow techniques [51, 52]. An interesting extension of the TLS technique, referred to as *extended least squares technique* (ELS), was proposed by Srinivasan and Chellappa [52]. They show that the TLS optical flow solution is unbiased only if the error in estimating the temporal gradient is equal in variance to the error in estimating the spatial gradient. This, however, cannot always be satisfied, for example, if spatial and temporal derivative operators have different extensions. Using the ELS solution, this bias can be avoided.

All least squares techniques, however, intrinsically assume that the errors are Gaussian and independent with constant variance for all points within U [32]. This prerequisite leads directly to the quadratic form of the error function of either technique. The assumption of Gaussian error distributions is violated for multiple motions within U. In this case, quadratic objective functions tend to over-weight outliers, which can be reduced using robust error norms [12] (Section 13.6.2).

Eigenvalue analysis. In order to estimate optical flow from the structure tensor $\boldsymbol{J}$ we need to carry out an *eigenvalue analysis* of the symmetric 3×3 tensor (Eq. (13.47)). The symmetry of $\boldsymbol{J}$ implies that all three eigenvalues are real and it further implies that there is an orthonormal basis of eigenvectors [37]. These vectors are pointing into the directions of minimal and maximal brightness changes, respectively, spanning the principal-axes coordinate system of the local 3-D spatiotemporal neighborhood U. In the principal-axes system, the transformed structure tensor $\boldsymbol{J}'$ is diagonal and contains the eigenvalues of $\boldsymbol{J}$ as diagonal elements:

$$\boldsymbol{J}' = \begin{bmatrix} \lambda_1 & 0 & 0 \\ 0 & \lambda_2 & 0 \\ 0 & 0 & \lambda_3 \end{bmatrix} \tag{13.54}$$

Without restricting generality, the eigenvalues are sorted in descending order:

$$\lambda_1 \geq \lambda_2 \geq \lambda_3 \geq 0 \tag{13.55}$$

and the corresponding eigenvectors are denoted by $\boldsymbol{r}_1$, $\boldsymbol{r}_2$, and $\boldsymbol{r}_3$.

Eigenvalue analysis is a nontrivial but standard problem of numerical linear algebra for which a number of efficient solutions have been developed [28, 37]. A standard procedure in numerical eigenvalue analysis is the *Jacobi method*. It consists of a sequence of orthogonal similarity transformations designed successively to annihilate off-diagonal elements of the matrix. The Jacobi method is absolutely foolproof for all real symmetric matrices, such as the structure tensor (regardless of the image content).

Table 13.1: *Classification of motion types: rank (J), total coherency measure c_t and spatial coherency measure c_s.*

Motion type	c_t	c_s	rank (J)
Constant brightness, no apparent motion	0	0	0
Spatial orientation and constant motion (aperture problem)	1	1	1
Distributed spatial structure and constant motion	1	0	2
Distributed spatiotemporal structure (no coherent motion)	0	0	3

The structure tensor contains the entire information on the first-order structure of the brightness distribution within a local spatiotemporal neighborhood. Four different classes of 3-D spatiotemporal structures can be distinguished and identified by analyzing the rank of the structure tensor (Table 13.1), which is given by the number of nonzero eigenvalues. The eigenvalues of $\boldsymbol{J}$ constitute the squared partial derivatives of the spatiotemporal brightness structure along the corresponding principal axis (averaged over U). Thus, rank ($\boldsymbol{J}$) can be identified as the number of directions (principal axes) with non-zero brightness derivatives, which is directly related to the optical flow.

Constant brightness. In the case rank ($\boldsymbol{J}$) = 0, all eigenvalues are zero

$$\lambda_1 = \lambda_2 = \lambda_3 = 0 \tag{13.56}$$

that is, all partial derivatives along the principal axes vanish. Thus, the brightness distribution remains constant within U, and no optical flow can be estimated. This case can be identified by the sum of all eigenvalues, which equals the trace of $\boldsymbol{J}'$ (Eq. (13.54)). As the trace of a matrix stays constant under orthogonal similarity transformations,

$$\text{trace}\,(\boldsymbol{J}') = \text{trace}\,(\boldsymbol{J}) = \sum_{p=1}^{3} J_{pp} \tag{13.57}$$

these points can be detected by thresholding the trace of the structure tensor

$$\text{trace}\,(\boldsymbol{J}) < \gamma \tag{13.58}$$

prior to the eigenvalue analysis. For these points the eigenvalue analysis can be skipped completely. The threshold γ has to be chosen according to the noise level of the image sequence.

Normal optical flow. If rank ($\boldsymbol{J}$) = 1, an image structure with spatial orientation moves with a constant velocity, that is, the aperture problem remains within U. The spatiotemporal neighborhood consists of layered structures and only one eigenvalue λ_1 is larger than zero

$$\lambda_1 > 0, \quad \lambda_2 = \lambda_3 = 0 \tag{13.59}$$

The corresponding eigenvector $\boldsymbol{r}_1 = [r_{1,1}, r_{1,2}, r_{1,3}]^T$ is pointing normal to the planes of constant brightness and can be used to compute the normal optical flow $f_\perp$ (Eq. (13.3)):

$$\boldsymbol{f}_\perp = -\frac{r_{1,3}}{r_{1,1}^2 + r_{1,2}^2} \begin{bmatrix} r_{1,1} \\ r_{1,2} \end{bmatrix} \tag{13.60}$$

Two-dimensional optical flow. For $\operatorname{rank}(\boldsymbol{J}) = 2$, a distributed spatial brightness structure moves at constant velocity. No aperture problem is present within U. The spatiotemporal neighborhood consists of extruded structures and only one eigenvector has zero eigenvalue:

$$\lambda_1, \lambda_2 > 0, \quad \lambda_3 = 0 \tag{13.61}$$

The eigenvector $\boldsymbol{r}_3 = [r_{3,1}, r_{3,2}, r_{3,3}]^T$ to the smallest eigenvalue λ_3 is pointing into the direction of constant brightness in the spatiotemporal domain. This vector corresponds to the spatiotemporal orientation vector $\boldsymbol{r}$ (Eq. (13.4)) and can be used to compute the 2-D optical flow $\boldsymbol{f}$ according to:

$$\boldsymbol{f} = \frac{1}{r_{3,3}} \begin{bmatrix} r_{3,1} \\ r_{3,2} \end{bmatrix} \tag{13.62}$$

Distributed spatiotemporal structure. The case $\operatorname{rank}(\boldsymbol{J}) = 3$ represents no apparent linear motion. The brightness structure shows variations in all directions. Thus, all eigenvalues are larger than zero:

$$\lambda_1, \lambda_2, \lambda_3 > 0 \tag{13.63}$$

Confidence and type measures. Although the rank of the structure tensor proves to contain all information necessary to distinguish different types of motion it can not be used for practical implementations because it does not constitute a normalized measure of certainty. Additionally, it is only defined for integer values $0, \ldots, 3$. In real sequences mixtures between the types of motion usually occur and the presence of noise increases all eigenvalues simultaneously, increasing the isotropy of the 3-D gray-value structure. In this section we will introduce normalized measures to quantify the confidence and type of motion that are suited for practical implementations. In contrast to the rank, they yield real-valued numbers between zero and one.

Total coherency measure. In order to quantify the overall certainty of displacement estimation we define the normalized *total coherency measure*

$$c_t = \left(\frac{\lambda_1 - \lambda_3}{\lambda_1 + \lambda_3}\right)^2 \tag{13.64}$$

with λ_1 and λ_3 denoting the largest and smallest eigenvalue of the structure tensor, respectively. Table 13.1 shows the values of c_t for different cases of motion. For both types of apparent motion, that is, aperture problem and no aperture problem, c_t equals one. If no displacement can be computed it is identical to zero. With increasing noise level c_t approaches zero for all different types of motion.

Spatial coherency measure. While the total coherency c_t gives a normalized estimate for the certainty of local spatiotemporal orientation it does not allow identification of areas of apparent aperture problem. In order to quantify the presence of an aperture problem we define the *spatial coherency measure* (*edge measure*)

$$c_s = \left(\frac{\lambda_1 - \lambda_2}{\lambda_1 + \lambda_2}\right)^2 \tag{13.65}$$

where λ_2 denotes the second largest eigenvalue of the structure tensor. Table 13.1 shows the values of c_s for different cases of motion. Only if an aperture problem is present does c_s reach its maximum value of c_t. For all other types of motion it equals zero. The spatial coherency measure can be identified as the coherency measure of 2-D local orientation estimation (Volume 2, Section 10.6.7, Eq. (10.74)). Note that c_s is normalized between zero and c_t because it is not possible to detect the presence of an aperture problem more reliably than the overall certainty.

Corner measure. From the two independent measures c_t and c_s, a third number, which can be referred to as *corner measure* c_c, can be computed by $c_c = c_t - c_s$. It constitutes the counterpart of c_s, quantifying the absence of an aperture problem, that is, selecting points where both components f_1 and f_2 of the optical flow $\boldsymbol{f}$ can be reliably computed.

Figure 13.8 illustrates the coherency and type measures for a moving calibration target on a linear positioning table. The coherency measure shows the entire grid without regions of homogeneous brightness. These areas split up into the edges and crossing points of the grid for the edge and corner measure, respectively.

The importance of confidence and type measures for quantitative image sequence analysis are illustrated in Fig. 13.9 for a moving ring pattern with additive noise. The optical flow field shows random flow vectors in regions with homogeneous brightness. With the total coherency measure these regions can be identified. Further knowledge about the presence of an aperture problem allows reconstruction of the 2-D flow field from normal flow, using the local regularization technique outlined in the following section [44]. It has to be pointed out

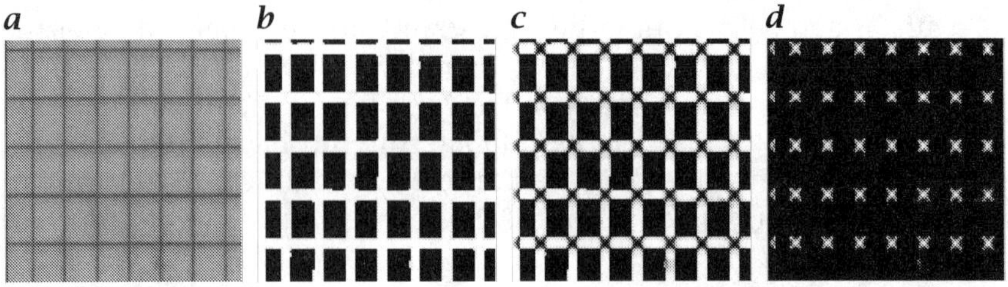

Figure 13.8: *Illustration of the confidence and type measures for a moving grid on a linear positioning table: **a** one frame of the sequence; **b** total coherency measure c_t; **c** spatial coherency (edge) measure c_s; **d** corner measure c_c.*

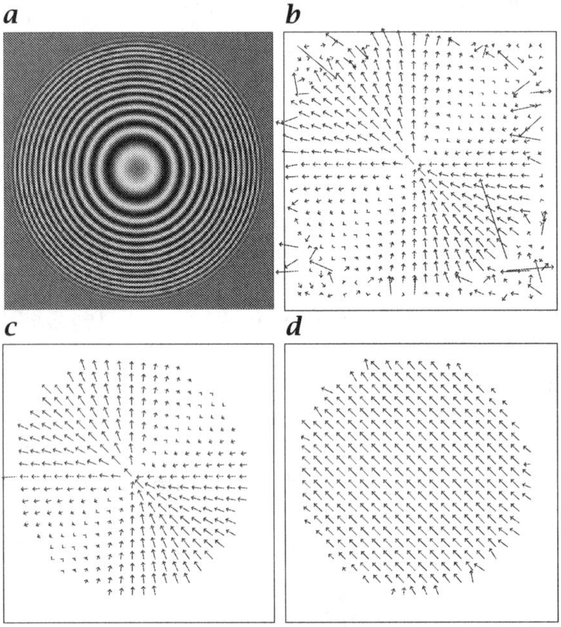

Figure 13.9: *Illustration of the importance of confidence and type measures for a ring pattern moving with (1,1) pixels/frame towards the upper left corner (with additive noise $\sigma_n = 1$): **a** one frame of the moving ring pattern; **b** optical flow computed for any image point without confidence and type measures; **c** optical flow masked by the confidence measure c_t; **d** local regularization incorporating confidence and knowledge about the presence of an aperture problem.*

that the confidence and type measures introduced in this section have to be used in conjunction with the trace of the structure tensor. Because they constitute normalized measures, high confidence may even occur when all eigenvalues are close to zero.

Two-dimensional flow from normal flow. For all image points with high values of the total coherency measure and simultaneously low values of the spatial coherency measure, that is, $(c_t - c_s) \approx c_t \approx 1$, the 2-D optical flow $\boldsymbol{f}$ can be computed according to Eq. (13.62). But how do we treat points suffering from the aperture problem, that is, $c_s \approx c_t \approx 1$?

It is important to note that an aperture problem does not introduce an erroneous optical flow field but only allows computation of partial information, eventually with high precision. As another important fact, more edge-like structures are statistically contained in images than isolated points or corners. Hence, it would be too much of a restriction to throw away all aperture problem pixels. On the other hand, long and straight lines are also less likely than slightly curved structures. Thus, it should be possible to reliably compute normal flow at edges and group it over an enlarged neighborhood to estimate the 2-D optical flow. The two measures c_s and c_t quantify the presence of an aperture problem as well as a certainty of the corresponding normal flow vector $\boldsymbol{f}_\perp$. Given this information and the previously computed normal flow $\boldsymbol{f}_\perp$, we try to find a best estimate of the 2-D optical flow $\boldsymbol{f}$.

For any point suffering from the aperture problem, the normal flow $\boldsymbol{f}_\perp$ is related to the optical flow $\boldsymbol{f}$ by

$$f_\perp = \boldsymbol{f}^T \hat{\boldsymbol{n}}, \quad \hat{\boldsymbol{n}} = \frac{\nabla g}{\|\nabla g\|} \tag{13.66}$$

where $\hat{\boldsymbol{n}} = [n_1, n_2]^T$ denotes a unit vector normal to lines of constant brightness in the image, that is, perpendicular to edges. The normal vector can be computed directly from the eigenvector of the structure tensor to the largest eigenvalue, $\boldsymbol{r}_1 = [r_{1,1}, r_{1,2}, r_{1,3}]^T$, by

$$\hat{\boldsymbol{n}} = \left(r_{1,1}^2 + r_{1,2}^2\right)^{-1/2} \begin{bmatrix} r_{1,1} \\ r_{1,2} \end{bmatrix} \tag{13.67}$$

using solely the spatial components of $\boldsymbol{r}_1$.

Similar to the local least squares approach of Lucas and Kanade [19], the search for a best estimate of $\boldsymbol{f}$ can be extended to a slightly larger neighborhood, $U' > U$, where U denotes the area of support of the smoothing kernel w used for the initial estimate of normal flow in Eq. (13.39) [44].

A local least squares estimate of $\boldsymbol{f}$ can be found by minimizing the following objective function with respect to both components f_1 and f_2:

$$\boldsymbol{f} = \arg\min \|\boldsymbol{e}\|_2^2 \tag{13.68}$$

with

$$\|\boldsymbol{e}\|_2^2 = \langle c \rangle^{-1} \int_{-\infty}^{\infty} w(\boldsymbol{x} - \boldsymbol{x}')c(\boldsymbol{x}') \left[\boldsymbol{f}^T \hat{\boldsymbol{n}}(\boldsymbol{x}') - f_\perp(\boldsymbol{x}')\right]^2 \mathrm{d}\boldsymbol{x}' \qquad (13.69)$$

and

$$\langle c \rangle = \int_{-\infty}^{\infty} w(\boldsymbol{x} - \boldsymbol{x}')c(\boldsymbol{x}') \, \mathrm{d}\boldsymbol{x}' \qquad (13.70)$$

The size of the local neighborhood is defined by a window function w, which can be chosen independently from the one in Eq. (13.39). The measure c incorporates any confidence measure, such as, for example, binary masks obtained by thresholding c_t and c_s, or analytical functions of c_t and c_s. Unequal weighting of individual pixels due to distributed confidence within U' formally requires a normalization of the objective function, given by $\langle c \rangle^{-1}$. This corresponds to a *normalized convolution*, introduced by Granlund and Knutsson [42]. However, $\langle c \rangle^{-1}$ constitutes a constant within U' that does not propagate into the following minimization procedure and, therefore, can be omitted in the practical implementation.

Solving Eq. (13.68) by standard least squares technique yields the linear equation system

$$\underbrace{\begin{bmatrix} \langle c n_1 n_1 \rangle & \langle c n_1 n_2 \rangle \\ \langle c n_1 n_2 \rangle & \langle c n_2 n_2 \rangle \end{bmatrix}}_{\boldsymbol{A}} \underbrace{\begin{bmatrix} f_1 \\ f_2 \end{bmatrix}}_{\boldsymbol{f}} = \underbrace{\begin{bmatrix} \langle c n_1 f_\perp \rangle \\ \langle c n_2 f_\perp \rangle \end{bmatrix}}_{\boldsymbol{b}} \qquad (13.71)$$

with

$$\langle c n_p n_q \rangle = \int_{-\infty}^{\infty} w(\boldsymbol{x} - \boldsymbol{x}')c(\boldsymbol{x}')n_p(\boldsymbol{x}')n_q(\boldsymbol{x}') \, \mathrm{d}\boldsymbol{x}' \qquad (13.72)$$

and

$$\langle c n_p f_\perp \rangle = \int_{-\infty}^{\infty} w(\boldsymbol{x} - \boldsymbol{x}')c(\boldsymbol{x}')n_p(\boldsymbol{x}')f_\perp(\boldsymbol{x}') \, \mathrm{d}\boldsymbol{x}' \qquad (13.73)$$

Equation (13.71) has a solution if the Matrix $\boldsymbol{A}$ can be inverted, which is the case only if

$$\det(\boldsymbol{A}) = \langle c n_1 n_1 \rangle \langle c n_2 n_2 \rangle - \langle c n_1 n_2 \rangle^2 \neq 0 \qquad (13.74)$$

If all normal vectors within U' are collinear, $\det(\boldsymbol{A}) = 0$. In this case the aperture problem remains within U' and Eq. (13.71) does not yield more information than a single value of $f_\perp$. As the vectors $\hat{\boldsymbol{n}}$ are normalized and $0 \leq c \leq 1$, the determinant $\det(\boldsymbol{A})$ is also normalized between 0 and 1. For orthogonal spatial distribution of $\hat{\boldsymbol{n}}$ and high confidence $c = 1$, it reaches the maximum value of 1. Thus, $\det(\boldsymbol{A})$ constitutes a normalized measure incorporating both the confidence c as well as the distribution of orientations of $\hat{\boldsymbol{n}}$ within U'.

Practical implementations showed that small changes in the orientation of $\hat{\boldsymbol{n}}$ within U' have already led to very precise estimates of $\boldsymbol{f}$. If the normal flow $\boldsymbol{f}_\perp$ can be precisely computed using, for example, the structure tensor technique, even the tangential components of $\boldsymbol{f}$ can be estimated if slight curvatures of the edges are present (Fig. 13.9d).

Finally, all integrations in the terms $\langle \cdot \rangle$ can be extended into the temporal domain for local regularization purpose.

13.3.3 Multifeature-based techniques

The basic problem of optical flow estimation is to solve the underconstrained brightness change constrained equation Eq. (13.2) for both components of $\boldsymbol{f}$. Two basic approaches to this problem have been introduced in this chapter. Second-order differential techniques extend the continuity of optical flow to the spatial gradient Eq. (13.24) to obtain two equations in two unknowns (Eq. (13.25)). Another approach was to model the optical flow and to group constraints over a local neighborhood (so far the model assumption was restricted to constant $\boldsymbol{f}$, which will be extended in Section 13.6). Both kinds of approaches fail, however, if the local neighborhood is subject to spatial orientation. In this case the matrices in the resulting algebraic equations—which are obtained by any technique—become singular. Thus, the aperture problem corresponds to a linear dependence of the rows in the corresponding solution matrix, that is, to linearly dependent constraint equations.

Multifeature (or multiconstraint) techniques try to use two or more features to obtain overconstrained equation systems at the same location. These features have to be linearly independent in order to solve for both components of $\boldsymbol{f}$. Otherwise the aperture problem remains, leading to singularities in the overconstrained system of equations. Multiple features can be obtained by:

- using multiple light sources and/or multispectral cameras;
- visualizing independent physical properties of the same object; and
- using results of (nonlinear) functions of the image brightness.

Of course, all features have to move with the same velocity. Otherwise the estimated optical flow exhibits the motion of the combined feature vector rather than the real object motion. This prerequisite can be violated for features showing different physical properties that are subject to *dispersion*.

Within the scope of this book, we can give only a concise overview of the principal possibilities of multifeature-based techniques, illustrated by two examples, which relate to the previous results of Section 13.3.

Augmented second-order solution. The second-order approach of Tretiak and Pastor [30] and Uras et al. [31] can be interpreted as a two-feature method, applying the optical flow constraint to the horizontal and vertical spatial derivative Eq. (13.24).

Equation (13.25) can be extended by incorporating the first-order BCCE Eq. (13.2) to form an overdetermined system of equations,

$$\begin{bmatrix} g_x & g_y \\ g_{xx} & g_{xy} \\ g_{xy} & g_{yy} \end{bmatrix} \begin{bmatrix} f_1 \\ f_2 \end{bmatrix} = - \begin{bmatrix} g_t \\ g_{xt} \\ g_{yt} \end{bmatrix} \tag{13.75}$$

The relative influence of first- and second-order terms in Eq. (13.75) can be changed by attaching weights to the corresponding equations. In a least squares sense this entails multiplying each side of Eq. (13.75) with

$$\boldsymbol{W} = \begin{bmatrix} g_x & g_y \\ g_{xx} & g_{xy} \\ g_{xy} & g_{yy} \end{bmatrix}^T \begin{bmatrix} w_1 & 0 & 0 \\ 0 & w_2 & 0 \\ 0 & 0 & w_2 \end{bmatrix} \tag{13.76}$$

where the diagonal matrix contains the weights w_1 and w_2 of the first- and second-order terms, respectively [9]. Using the fractional weight $w = w_1/w_2$ and carrying out the matrix multiplication yields the following system of equations

$$\begin{bmatrix} w g_x^2 + g_{xx}^2 + g_{xy}^2 & w g_x g_y + g_{xx} g_{xy} + g_{yy} g_{xy} \\ w g_x g_y + g_{xx} g_{xy} + g_{yy} g_{xy} & w g_y^2 + g_{yy}^2 + g_{xy}^2 \end{bmatrix} \begin{bmatrix} f_1 \\ f_2 \end{bmatrix}$$
$$= - \begin{bmatrix} w g_y g_t + g_{xx} g_{xt} + g_{xy} g_{yt} \\ w g_x g_t + g_{xy} g_{xt} + g_{yy} g_{yt} \end{bmatrix} \tag{13.77}$$

This approach is referred to as *augmented second-order technique* by Bainbridge-Smith and Lane [9]. They demonstrate that the first-order weighted least squares approach of Lucas and Kanade [19] (Eq. (13.13)) becomes equivalent to Eq. (13.77) if the aperture is restricted to a size where the brightness distribution can be adequately described by a second-order Taylor series. For larger apertures, the effect of higher-order derivatives leads to a more robust performance of the first-order local weighted least squares technique.

Multifeature structure tensor technique. The effect of linearly dependent constraint equations on the solubility of the corresponding algebraic equations, can be demonstrated by a simple example using the structure tensor technique.

Let $\mathbf{G}(\boldsymbol{x}) = [g(\boldsymbol{x}), h(\boldsymbol{x})]^T$ be a vector-valued image (e.g., color image) that contains only two components with 1-D horizontal and vertical brightness changes

$$\mathbf{G}(\boldsymbol{x}) = \begin{bmatrix} g(\boldsymbol{x}) \\ h(\boldsymbol{x}) \end{bmatrix} = \begin{bmatrix} ax \\ by \end{bmatrix} \tag{13.78}$$

moving with the velocity $\boldsymbol{u} = [u_1, u_2]^T$.

The temporal derivatives of g and h are given by the brightness change constraint equation Eq. (13.2), that is, $g_t = -(\nabla g)^T \boldsymbol{u} = -au_1$ and $h_t = -(\nabla h)^T \boldsymbol{u} = -bu_2$, with $\nabla g = [a, 0]^T$ and $\nabla h = [0, b]^T$. As all partial derivatives are constant over the entire image area, the structure tensor Eq. (13.42) of g and h computes directly to

$$\boldsymbol{J}_g = \begin{bmatrix} a^2 & 0 & -a^2u_1 \\ 0 & 0 & 0 \\ -a^2u_1 & 0 & a^2u_1^2 \end{bmatrix}, \quad \text{and} \quad \boldsymbol{J}_h = \begin{bmatrix} 0 & 0 & 0 \\ 0 & b^2 & -b^2u_2 \\ 0 & -b^2u_2 & b^2u_2^2 \end{bmatrix} \tag{13.79}$$

respectively. As one row equals zero and the two remaining rows are linearly dependent, $\mathrm{rank}(\boldsymbol{J}_g) = \mathrm{rank}(\boldsymbol{J}_h) = 1$. Thus, both components are subject to the aperture problem over the entire image area due to the linear brightness variation (Table 13.1). Estimating the optical flow from g and h independently yields $\boldsymbol{f}_g = [u_1, 0]^T$ and $\boldsymbol{f}_h = [0, u_2]^T$. Without further assumptions, the connection between $\boldsymbol{f}_g$ and $\boldsymbol{f}_h$ remains unknown.

The vector-valued image, $\mathbf{G}$, however, allows one to extract the 2-D optical flow in an unambiguous fashion. How can the information from both components be adequately combined to accomplish this?

Simply adding up both component images results in a third image with linear spatial brightness distribution

$$g(\boldsymbol{x}) + h(\boldsymbol{x}) = ax + by \tag{13.80}$$

which suffers from the aperture problem as well. This can be verified by computing the structure tensor $\boldsymbol{J}_{g+h}$

$$\boldsymbol{J}_{g+h} = \begin{bmatrix} a^2 & ab & -a(au_1 + bu_2) \\ ab & b^2 & -b(au_1 + bu_2) \\ -a(au_1 + bu_2) & -b(au_1 + bu_2) & (au_1 + bu_2)^2 \end{bmatrix} \tag{13.81}$$

where any two rows are collinear. Hence, $\mathrm{rank}(\boldsymbol{J}_{g+h}) = 1$, that is, the sum of both components does not yield additional information.

By adding up the structure tensors of both components (Eq. (13.79)), we obtain

$$\boldsymbol{J}_g + \boldsymbol{J}_h = \begin{bmatrix} a^2 & 0 & -a^2u_1 \\ 0 & b^2 & -b^2u_2 \\ -a^2u_1 & -b^2u_2 & -(a^2u_1^2 + b^2u_2^2) \end{bmatrix} \tag{13.82}$$

In this matrix the third row can be expressed by a linear combination of the two first rows, which reduces the rank by one. As no other linear dependency exists, rank $(\boldsymbol{J}_g + \boldsymbol{J}_h) = 2$, which allows for unambiguously determining the 2-D optical flow $\boldsymbol{f} = \boldsymbol{u}$ (Table 13.1).

This example demonstrates the importance of the order in which linear and nonlinear operations are carried out. Adding features with linear brightness variations retains the linear relationship. Adding up the structure tensors of individual components (which consists of non-linear operations), regularizes the combined structure tensor of linearly independent (uncorrelated) features. This technique can be easily extended to multiple features.

13.3.4 Accurate and efficient implementation

All optical flow-based techniques require combinations of partial derivatives of first- or higher-order and local smoothing. Both types of operations can be optimized for both speed-up and accuracy. Hence, any of the algorithms outlined in this section will benefit from a careful implementation. Comparative studies of different approaches are likely to be biased if different implementations of low-level operations have been used.

Using binomial operators, smoothing can be performed very efficiently by cascading elementary binomial kernels, as detailed in Chapter 7. If large kernels are required, the smoothing can be carried out on a multigrid data structure (Sections 4.4 and 7.5).

A more critical point is the choice of appropriate derivative operators. The numerical discretization of derivative filters is often taken for granted with a restriction to the standard symmetric difference filter 0.5 [1 0 -1]. It can be shown, however, that derivative filters optimized for a minimum deviation from the correct direction of the gradient vector reduce the errors in the optical flow by more than one order of magnitude.

Figure 13.10 illustrates this fact by a simple numerical study using the structure tensor technique. With the standard symmetric difference filter, large deviations from the correct displacements of more than 0.1 pixels/frame occur. With an optimized 3×3 Sobel-type filter [53], the error is well below 0.005 pixels/frame for displacements small enough to fulfill the temporal sampling theorem. This kernel results from a nonlinear approach for filter optimization, which will be detailed in Chapter 6.

Analyzing the impact of noise on differential least-squares techniques, Bainbridge-Smith and Lane [9] reported the same errors as in Fig. 13.10a and identified them as discretization errors of the derivative operators. In order to reduce these errors they used a combination of smoothing and derivative kernels for local regularization in only one

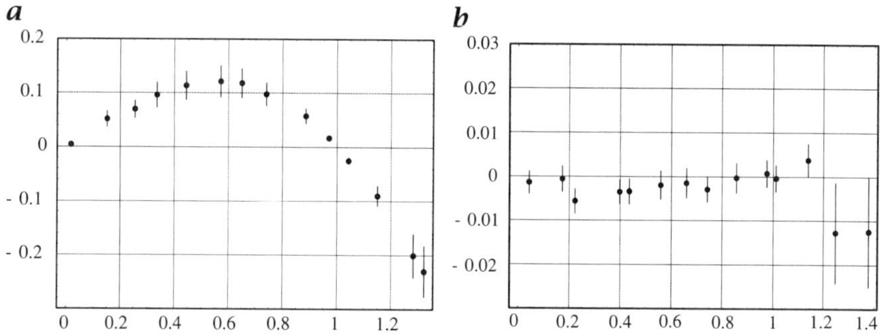

Figure 13.10: *Systematic error in the velocity estimate as a function of the interframe displacement of a moving random pattern. Derivatives have been computed with* ***a*** *the symmetric difference filter and* ***b*** *an optimized 3×3 Sobel filter [53] (Chapter 6).*

dimension. The error in the estimated optical flow decreases smoothly as the width of the smoothing kernel increases. In order to obtain errors in the same order of magnitude as those of the 2-D optimization in Fig. 13.10b, the 1-D regularization requires kernel sizes of at least 9 pixels.

13.4 Quadrature filter techniques

This section deals with different approaches based on the motion constraint in Fourier domain, detailed in Section 13.2.1. As the Fourier spectrum of moving patterns falls onto a plane (Eq. (13.7)), quadrature filter techniques try to estimate the orientation of this plane by using velocity-tuned filters in the Fourier domain. A variety of approaches have been proposed that differ in both the design of frequency-selective filters and the combination of the filter outputs. All approaches have in common that the 3-D frequency distribution is interpolated from the response of a finite number of smoothly varying window functions, subsampling the 3-D spectrum.

A certain wave number/frequency band can be extracted by multiplying the Fourier spectrum with an appropriate window function $\hat{w}(\boldsymbol{k}, \omega)$. The result of this operation, however, would be an oscillating signal with the selected wave numbers and frequencies, rather than quantification the "presence" of the selected frequency band. In order to reduce these oscillations and to omit zero crossings, we need to find a second signal with the same amplitude but a phase shift of $\pm\pi/2$ for every wave number and frequency. At zero crossings of the bandpass filtered signal, the phase-shifted signal shows extremes. A filter that performs such a phase shift is known as *Hilbert filter*. It has an imaginary transfer function with odd symmetry, while the bandpass filter has a real-valued transfer function with even symmetry.

A frequency selective filter and its Hilbert transform is called a *quadrature filter* (Section 4.2.2). The output $\boldsymbol{q}$ of the quadrature filter G is a complex valued number,

$$\boldsymbol{q} = G * g = q_+ - \mathrm{i} q_- \tag{13.83}$$

where g denotes the spatiotemporal image, q_+ the bandpass filtered signal and q_- its Hilbert transform, with the indices '+' and '-' referring to the even and odd symmetry of the corresponding filters. The magnitude

$$\|\boldsymbol{q}\| = q_+^2 + q_-^2 \tag{13.84}$$

minimizes the sensitivity to phase changes in the signal and provides an estimate of the *spectral density* or *energy* of the corresponding periodic image structure. For this reason, quadrature-filter-based approaches are commonly referred to as *spatiotemporal energy-based approaches* in the literature. For the simple case of a sinusoidal signal $a \sin(\boldsymbol{k}^T \boldsymbol{x} + \omega t)$ (corresponding to a delta peak in the Fourier spectrum), the magnitude of $\boldsymbol{q}$ will be completely phase invariant:

$$\boldsymbol{q} = \hat{w}(\boldsymbol{k}, \omega) a \sin(\boldsymbol{k}^T \boldsymbol{x} + \omega t) - \mathrm{i}\, \hat{w}(\boldsymbol{k}, \omega) a \cos(\boldsymbol{k}^T \boldsymbol{x} + \omega t) \tag{13.85}$$

$$\|\boldsymbol{q}\| = \hat{w}^2(\boldsymbol{k}, \omega) a^2 \left[\sin^2(\boldsymbol{k}^T \boldsymbol{x} + \omega t) + \cos^2(\boldsymbol{k}^T \boldsymbol{x} + \omega t)\right] = \hat{w}^2(\boldsymbol{k}, \omega) a^2$$

The most common quadrature filter pair is the *Gabor filter*. It selects a certain spatiotemporal frequency region with a Gaussian window function centered at $(\boldsymbol{k}_0, \omega_0)$ (Fig. 4.2, Section 4.2.2). The corresponding complex filter mask is given by

$$G(\boldsymbol{x}, t) = \exp\left[\mathrm{i}(\boldsymbol{k}_0 \boldsymbol{x} + \omega_0 t)\right] \exp\left[-\left(\frac{x^2}{2\sigma_x^2} + \frac{y^2}{2\sigma_y^2} + \frac{t^2}{2\sigma_t^2}\right)\right] \tag{13.86}$$

More detailed information about the basic concept of quadrature filters can be found in [13, 42]. In the following sections we will outline how these filters can be used for optical flow estimation.

13.4.1 Spatiotemporal energy models

One-dimensional optical flow. In order to estimate 1-D motion, Adelson and Bergen [54] proposed the use of three quadrature filters tuned for leftward motion $\boldsymbol{q}_L$, rightward motion $\boldsymbol{q}_R$, and static patterns $\boldsymbol{q}_S$, respectively. They noted that the output of quadrature filters is affected by the contrast of the signal (i. e., low signal contrast generates low response and vice versa) and suggested using ratios of filter responses to get a contrast-independent estimate of the 1-D optical flow [24, 54]:

$$f_1 = \frac{\|\boldsymbol{q}_R\| - \|\boldsymbol{q}_L\|}{\|\boldsymbol{q}_S\|} \tag{13.87}$$

This solution is closely related to the first-order local least squares technique of Lucas and Kanade [19]. For $g_y = 0$, the 1-D solution of Eq. (13.16) reduces to

$$f_1 = -\frac{\langle g_x g_t \rangle}{\langle g_x g_x \rangle} = -\frac{\mathcal{B}_{xt}\left(\mathcal{D}_x \cdot \mathcal{D}_t\right)}{\mathcal{B}_{xt}\left(\mathcal{D}_x \cdot \mathcal{D}_x\right)}, \tag{13.88}$$

where $\mathcal{B}_{xt}$ denotes a 2-D spatiotemporal binomial operator and $\mathcal{D}_x$ and $\mathcal{D}_t$ are first-order derivative operators along the indexed coordinate. Jähne [13] shows that a presmoothing of the image with $\mathcal{B}_{xt}$ prior to the computation of the derivatives yields a solution similar to Eq. (13.87). Replacing $\mathcal{D}_x$ by $\mathcal{D}_x \mathcal{B}_{xt}$ and $\mathcal{D}_t$ by $\mathcal{D}_t \mathcal{B}_{xt}$ in Eq. (13.88), the 1-D least squares solution is given by

$$f_1 = \frac{\mathcal{B}_{xt}\left(\mathcal{R} \cdot \mathcal{R} - \mathcal{L} \cdot \mathcal{L}\right)}{\mathcal{B}_{xt}\left(\mathcal{S} \cdot \mathcal{S}\right)} \tag{13.89}$$

where $\mathcal{R}$, $\mathcal{L}$, and $\mathcal{S}$ are combinations of derivatives of binomial filters:

$$\begin{aligned} \mathcal{R} &= \left(\mathcal{D}_x + \mathcal{D}_t\right) \mathcal{B}_{xt} \\ \mathcal{L} &= \left(\mathcal{D}_x - \mathcal{D}_t\right) \mathcal{B}_{xt} \\ \mathcal{S} &= 2 \mathcal{D}_x \mathcal{B}_{xt} \end{aligned} \tag{13.90}$$

Instead of the magnitude of quadrature filter responses, the squared output of derivative filters is used. The final smoothing of the squared signal, however, reduces the phase dependency and zero crossings if the scale of the local structure is smaller than the area of support of the smoothing operator.

Two-dimensional optical flow. A quadrature filter technique for the computation of 2-D optical flow was developed by Heeger [55, 56]. At each of several spatial scales, he used twelve Gabor filters tuned to different spatial orientation at three different temporal frequencies. The filters are arranged in three layers with cylindrical symmetry about the temporal frequency axis (Fig. 13.11a). The expected response of a Gabor filter (Eq. (13.86)) tuned to frequency (k_x, k_y, ω) for translating white noise, as a function of the velocity $\boldsymbol{f} = [f_1, f_2]^T$, is given by:

$$R_{\boldsymbol{k},\omega}(f_1, f_2) = \exp\left[-\frac{4\pi^2 \sigma_x^2 \sigma_y^2 \sigma_t^2 (f_1 k_x + f_2 k_y + \omega)}{(f_1 \sigma_x \sigma_t)^2 + (f_2 \sigma_y \sigma_t)^2 + (\sigma_x \sigma_y)^2}\right] \tag{13.91}$$

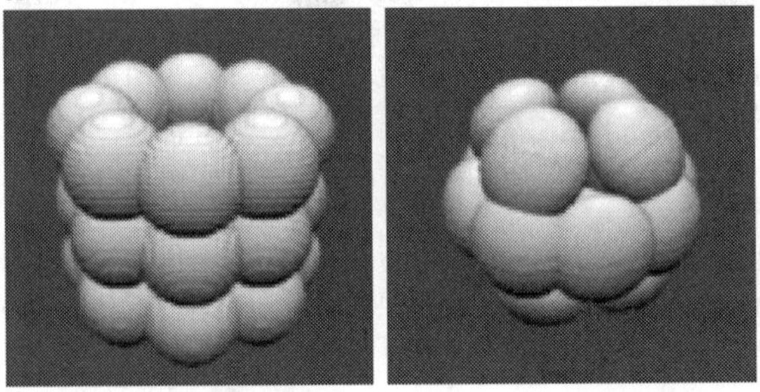

Figure 13.11: *Illustration of 3-D spatiotemporal filters in Fourier domain. Shown are level surfaces of the power spectra of the filters. Surfaces are rendered assuming a fixed point light source and a Lambertian surface:* ***a*** *arrangement of the twelve Gabor filters used in the approach of Heeger [55]. The ω axis is pointing along the cylindrical axis of symmetry;* ***b*** *spatiotemporal frequency spectra of the directional derivative filters used in the local least squares approach of Lucas and Kanade [19]. (Images courtesy of E. P. Simoncelli, New York University, [27].)*

In order to find the optical flow $\boldsymbol{f}$ that best fits the measured filter energy responses, Heeger [55] performed a least squares plane fit of the twelve different $R_{\boldsymbol{k},\omega}$, using a numerical optimization procedure.

The Gabor filters used in this approach are, however, not symmetrically arranged about the origin. This leads to systematic errors in velocity estimates if the wave number of the moving pattern does not match the center response of the filters [27]. The choice of Gabor filters has been motivated by the fact that they minimize a joint space-frequency localization criterion and have been suggested for use in biological vision modeling [27, 57, 58].

Similar to the 1-D case, the 2-D first-order least squares solution can be interpreted as a spatiotemporal energy-based approach. Simoncelli [27] showed that the components of Eq. (13.16) can be reformulated as local averages of squares of directional filters and differences of two such squares. This corresponds to eight different spatiotemporally oriented bandpass filters. Again, the local average of squared bandpass filters approximates the magnitude of quadrature filters. Level contours of the eight transfer functions are symmetrically arranged about the origin (Fig. 13.11b), in contrast to the Gabor filters of Heeger [55] (Fig. 13.11a). Thus, the velocity estimate computed with the first-order least squares solution will be invariant to scaling of the spatial frequency of the input signal.

Another interesting similarity between the first-order least squares solution and the plane constraint in Fourier domain can be found by transforming the objective function $\|e\|_2^2$ into Fourier domain. If the integration in Eq. (13.13) is extended to the entire image area, *Parseval's rule* allows us to find the corresponding formulation of the objective function in Fourier domain:

$$
\begin{aligned}
\|\boldsymbol{e}\|_2^2 &= \int_{-\infty}^{\infty} \left[g_x(\boldsymbol{x})f_1 + g_y(\boldsymbol{x})f_2 + g_t(\boldsymbol{x})\right]^2 \,\mathrm{d}\boldsymbol{x}\,\mathrm{d}t \\
&= \int_{-\infty}^{\infty} \left[k_1\hat{g}(\boldsymbol{k},\omega)f_1 + k_2\hat{g}(\boldsymbol{k},\omega)f_2 + \omega\hat{g}(\boldsymbol{k},\omega)\right]^2 \,\mathrm{d}\boldsymbol{k}\,\mathrm{d}\omega \\
&= \int_{-\infty}^{\infty} \left[\boldsymbol{k}^T\boldsymbol{f} + \omega\right]^2 \|\hat{g}(\boldsymbol{k},\omega)\|^2 \,\mathrm{d}\boldsymbol{k}\,\mathrm{d}\omega
\end{aligned}
\tag{13.92}
$$

which is exactly the form of a least squares planar regression error function, weighted by the image power spectrum, $\|\hat{g}(\boldsymbol{k},\omega)\|^2$ [27]. The term in brackets is the squared ω-distance between the point $(\boldsymbol{k},\omega)$ and the plane defined by $\boldsymbol{k}^T\boldsymbol{f} = -\omega$. This solution shows that the local least squares solution corresponds directly to a least squares plane fit in Fourier domain without the need for scale-selective quadrature filters. Using a local estimate by selecting a small image area with a window function does not change this solution.

13.4.2 Structure tensor from quadrature filter sets

In Section 13.3.2 we pointed out that tensors are perfectly suited to describe symmetries within local neighborhoods of spatiotemporal signals. In this section we discuss how to design optimal quadrature filters that detect both spatiotemporal orientation and wave number. We further show, how these filters can be combined to compute the *structure tensor* introduced in Section 13.3.2. This section is based on the work of Knutsson [40, 41], summarized in an excellent monograph by Granlund and Knutsson [42] detailing the theory of tensors for local structure analysis.

Spherically separable filters. In order to interpolate the spatiotemporal frequency distribution optimally from the frequency responses of directionally selective filters, they are required to have particular interpolation properties. Directional filters having the necessary properties were first suggested by Knutsson [40] for the 2-D case and further extended by Knutsson [41] for the 3-D case. He found that an optimal filter should be *polar separable*, that is, the transfer function should separate into a function of radius R and a function of direction D

$$
\hat{Q}(\boldsymbol{k}) = R(k)D(\bar{\boldsymbol{k}}) \quad \text{with} \quad \boldsymbol{k} = [k_1, k_2, \omega]^T \tag{13.93}
$$

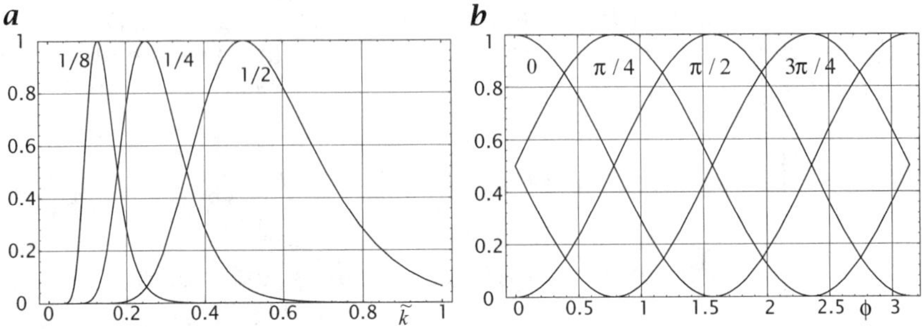

Figure 13.12: ***a*** *Radial and* ***b*** *angular part of the 2-D polar separable quadrature filter according to Eqs. (13.94) and (13.96) with $l = 1$ and $B = 2$ with different peak wave numbers k_0 and four directions (0°, 45°, 90°, and 125°)*

Here $\boldsymbol{k}$ denotes the 3-D spatiotemporal frequency vector. The arguments $k = \|\boldsymbol{k}\|$ and $\bar{\boldsymbol{k}} = \boldsymbol{k}/k$ are the magnitude of $\boldsymbol{k}$ and the unit directional vector, respectively.

The radial function $R(k)$ can be chosen arbitrarily without violating the basic requirements. Typically, $R(k)$ is a bandpass function with a certain center frequency and bandwidth. Knutsson et al. [59] suggested the following radial function:

$$R(k) = \exp\left[-\frac{(\ln k - \ln k_0)^2}{(B/2)^2 \ln 2}\right] \tag{13.94}$$

which is a *lognormal function*, that is, a Gaussian function on a logarithmic scale. The constant B is the relative bandwidth of the filter and k_0 the peak frequency.

The following directional function $D(\bar{\boldsymbol{k}})$ incorporating the necessary interpolation properties was suggested by Knutsson [41]:

$$D(\bar{\boldsymbol{k}}) = \begin{cases} (\bar{\boldsymbol{k}}^T \bar{\boldsymbol{d}}_i)^{2l} & \text{if } \bar{\boldsymbol{k}}^T \bar{\boldsymbol{d}}_i > 0 \\ 0 & \text{otherwise} \end{cases} \tag{13.95}$$

where $\bar{\boldsymbol{d}}_i$ is the unit vector pointing into the direction of the filter. The directional function has a maximum at the filter direction $\bar{\boldsymbol{d}}_i$ and varies as $\cos^{2l}(\phi)$, where ϕ is the difference in angle between an arbitrary direction $\boldsymbol{k}$ and $\bar{\boldsymbol{d}}_i$.

For the real even and the imaginary odd filter of the quadrature filter, the radial part R is the same and only the directional part D differs:

$$\begin{aligned} D_+(\bar{\boldsymbol{k}}) &= (\bar{\boldsymbol{k}}^T \bar{\boldsymbol{d}}_i)^{2l} \\ D_-(\bar{\boldsymbol{k}}) &= \mathrm{i}\,(\bar{\boldsymbol{k}}^T \bar{\boldsymbol{d}}_i)^{2l} \operatorname{sign}(\bar{\boldsymbol{k}}^T \bar{\boldsymbol{d}}_i) \end{aligned} \tag{13.96}$$

Figure 13.12 illustrates the transfer function of this quadrature filter with different peak wave number k_0 and in four directions.

Number and direction of filters. The filters used to compute local spatiotemporal structure have to be symmetrically distributed in the 3-D Fourier domain. It is shown in [41] that the minimum number of filters has to be greater than 4. However, as there is no way of distributing 5 filters symmetrically in 3-D space, the next possible number is 6. The orientations of these filters are given by the following 6 normal vectors:

$$\begin{array}{ll} \bar{\boldsymbol{d}}_1 = c\,[a, 0, b]^T & \bar{\boldsymbol{d}}_2 = c\,[-a, 0, b]^T \\ \bar{\boldsymbol{d}}_3 = c\,[b, a, 0]^T & \bar{\boldsymbol{d}}_4 = c\,[b, -a, 0]^T \\ \bar{\boldsymbol{d}}_5 = c\,[0, b, a]^T & \bar{\boldsymbol{d}}_6 = c\,[0, b, -a]^T \end{array} \tag{13.97}$$

where

$$a = 2, \; b = (1 + \sqrt{5}), \text{ and } c = (10 + 2\sqrt{5})^{-1/2} \tag{13.98}$$

Tensor construction. From the responses of the 6 directional filters, the *structure tensor* $\boldsymbol{J}$ (Section 13.3.2) can be computed. According to Granlund and Knutsson [42], $\boldsymbol{J}$ can be obtained by linear summation of the quadrature filter output magnitudes:

$$\boldsymbol{J}(\boldsymbol{x}) = \sum_{i=0}^{5} q_i \boldsymbol{M}_i, \quad \boldsymbol{M}_i = \left(\alpha \bar{\boldsymbol{d}}_i \bar{\boldsymbol{d}}_i^T - \beta \boldsymbol{I} \right) \tag{13.99}$$

where q_i is the magnitude of the complex-valued output of the quadrature filter in the direction $\bar{\boldsymbol{d}}_i$, $\boldsymbol{M}_i$ is a tensor associated with the quadrature filter i, and $\boldsymbol{I}$ is the identity tensor (matrix). The two constants are given by $\alpha = 5/4$ and $\beta = 1/4$. As the elements $\boldsymbol{M}_i$ are constant tensors, they can be precalculated. Thus, the structure tensor can be estimated by a weighted summation of the tensors $\boldsymbol{M}_i$, where the weights are the quadrature filter outputs q_i.

Optical flow computation. Given the structure tensor J, the optical flow can be computed analogously to that shown in Section 13.3.2. After an eigenvalue analysis of the structure tensor, the corresponding eigenvectors are pointing into the directions of minimal and maximal brightness changes, respectively. They can be used to compute either the normal flow $\boldsymbol{f}_\perp$ or the 2-D optical flow $\boldsymbol{f}$ depending on the distribution of the eigenvalues.

13.4.3 Phase techniques

Another class of techniques, based on the work of Fleet and Jepson [20], uses quadrature filters to estimate the local *phase* of the spatiotemporal image. The use of phase information is motivated by the fact that the phase component of a bandpass filtered signal is less sensitive to illumination changes than the amplitude component of the filter output

[60]. This corresponds to the fact that the phase of the Fourier transform carries the essential information: an image can still be recognized when the amplitude information is lost, but not vice versa [61].

Consider a planar spatiotemporal wave with a wave number $\boldsymbol{k}$ and a temporal frequency ω, corresponding to a delta peak in the 3-D Fourier domain:

$$g(\boldsymbol{x},t) = g_0 \exp\left[-\mathrm{i}\phi(\boldsymbol{x},t)\right] = g_0 \exp\left[-\mathrm{i}(\boldsymbol{k}^T\boldsymbol{x} - \omega t)\right] \tag{13.100}$$

This spatiotemporal signal corresponds to a planar 2-D wave, traveling with a phase speed $\boldsymbol{u}$, with $\omega = \boldsymbol{k}^T\boldsymbol{u}$ (Eq. (13.8)). The *phase* of the signal

$$\phi(\boldsymbol{x},t) = \boldsymbol{k}^T\boldsymbol{x} - \omega t = \boldsymbol{k}^T\boldsymbol{x} - \boldsymbol{k}^T\boldsymbol{u}t \tag{13.101}$$

varies linearly in space and time. The projection f_c of the 2-D velocity $\boldsymbol{u}$ onto the wave number unit vector $\bar{\boldsymbol{k}}$,

$$f_c = \bar{\boldsymbol{k}}^T\boldsymbol{u} = \frac{1}{\|\boldsymbol{k}\|}\boldsymbol{k}^T\boldsymbol{u} \tag{13.102}$$

is called *component velocity*. It is the instantaneous motion normal to level phase contours of a periodic structure (the output of a bandpass filter), as opposed to *normal velocity*, which constitutes the velocity component normal to the local intensity structure.

The component velocity $\boldsymbol{f}_c$ is pointing parallel to the phase gradient and can be computed by

$$\boldsymbol{f}_c = -\frac{\phi_t(\boldsymbol{x},t)}{\|\nabla\phi(\boldsymbol{x},t)\|}\frac{\nabla\phi(\boldsymbol{x},t)}{\|\nabla\phi(\boldsymbol{x},t)\|} \tag{13.103}$$

which can be directly verified using Eq. (13.101). Comparing Eq. (13.103) to Eq. (13.3) shows that, in fact, the phase-based technique is a differential technique applied to phase rather than intensity. The phase-based technique, however, allows one to estimate multiple component velocities at a single image location, compared to only one normal velocity in Eq. (13.3). If the wave-number vectors $\boldsymbol{k}$ of the different components are linear independent, the full 2-D optical flow can be recovered. Figure 13.13 illustrates the phase and component velocity for a simple pattern composed of two periodical signals.

The phase ϕ can be computed using a quadrature filter. As with any complex number, the argument arg($\boldsymbol{q}$) of the filter output represents the local phase of the signal:

$$\phi(\boldsymbol{x},t) = \arg(\boldsymbol{q}) = \arctan\frac{q_-(\boldsymbol{x},t)}{q_+(\boldsymbol{x},t)} \tag{13.104}$$

Unfortunately, a phase computed with the inverse tangent is restricted to the main interval $[-\pi,\pi[$ and jumps at the transition from $-\pi$ to π

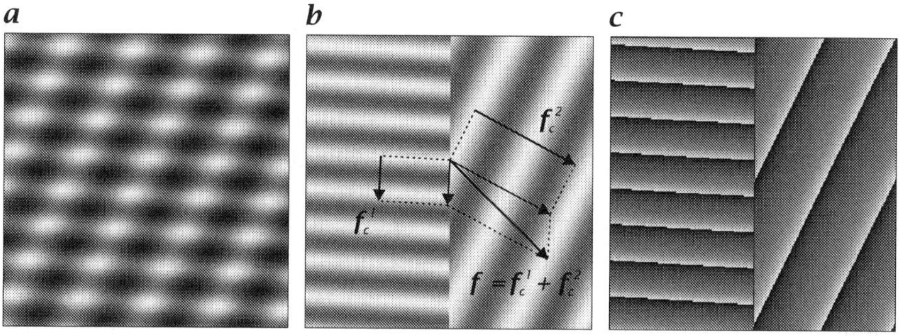

Figure 13.13: *Illustration of the phase technique:* ***a*** *sinusoidal plaid pattern composed of two sinusoids moving with the optical flow* $\boldsymbol{f}$*;* ***b*** *the two individual components allow one to extract the corresponding component velocities* $\boldsymbol{f}_c^1$ *and* $\boldsymbol{f}_c^2$*, respectively. The 2-D optical flow* $\boldsymbol{f}$ *is reconstructed from the component velocities;* ***c*** *phase images of the two sinusoidal patterns.*

(Fig. 13.13c). Computing the derivative of such a discontinuous signal would inevitably lead to errors in the velocity estimate.

Fleet and Jepson [20] found a solution to avoid this problem by directly computing the phase derivatives from the quadrature filter pair, without prior computation of the phase. This can be performed using the identity

$$\nabla_{xt}\phi(\boldsymbol{x},t) = \frac{q_+(\boldsymbol{x},t)\nabla_{xt}q_-(\boldsymbol{x},t) - q_-(\boldsymbol{x},t)\nabla_{xt}q_+(\boldsymbol{x},t)}{q_+^2(\boldsymbol{x},t) + q_-^2(\boldsymbol{x},t)} \tag{13.105}$$

where ∇_{xt} denotes the spatiotemporal gradient $\nabla_{xt}\phi = [\phi_x, \phi_y, \phi_t]^T$. Fleet and Jepson [20] propose to decompose the image into periodic structures by a set of Gabor filters. From the output of these filters, the component velocity of each bandpass filtered signal is computed by Eq. (13.103) using Eq. (13.105) for the partial derivatives. The 2-D optical flow is composed from these component velocities by a technique similar to the minimization procedure given in Eq. (13.68) (Section 13.3.2). The 2-D optical flow is estimated locally by solving a linear system of equations relating the component velocities to an affine model of optical flow (Section 13.6.1).

13.5 Correlation and matching

Differential and quadrature filter-based approaches are subject to errors, if the temporal sampling theorem is violated, that is, for large displacements of the moving pattern within two consecutive frames. Additionally, differential approaches and most quadrature filter techniques yield biased optical flow estimates, if the illumination changes within the temporal region of support.

Correspondence-based approaches are less sensitive to these error sources. They try to find the best match of a characteristic image feature and the corresponding feature in the consecutive frame. Correspondence techniques can be classified into *region-based matching* and *feature-based matching* techniques, respectively. Comprehensive overviews of feature-based matching techniques are given by Faugeras [62] and Murray [17]. These techniques—also referred to as *token tracking* techniques—are commonly extended into 3-D space to estimate disparity, recover 3-D motion (object motion and ego-motion), and to track objects. In this section we focus on region-based matching techniques, such as *cross correlation* and *distance minimization*.

Region-based matching techniques approximate the optical flow $\boldsymbol{f}$ by

$$\boldsymbol{f}(\boldsymbol{x}) = \frac{\boldsymbol{s}(\boldsymbol{x})}{t_2 - t_1} \tag{13.106}$$

where $\boldsymbol{s} = [s_1, s_2]^T$ is the displacement that yields the best match between two image regions in consecutive frames $g(\boldsymbol{x}, t_1)$ and $g(\boldsymbol{x} - \boldsymbol{s}, t_2)$. A best match is found by either *minimizing* a *distance measure*, or *maximizing* a *similarity measure*, with respect to the displacement $\boldsymbol{s}$.

13.5.1 Cross correlation

A suitable similarity measure of two image regions is given by the *cross-correlation function*

$$r(\boldsymbol{x}, \boldsymbol{s}) = \frac{\langle g(\boldsymbol{x}', t_1) g(\boldsymbol{x}' - \boldsymbol{s}, t_2)\rangle}{\left(\langle g^2(\boldsymbol{x}', t_1)\rangle \langle g^2(\boldsymbol{x}' - \boldsymbol{s}, t_2)\rangle\right)^{1/2}} \tag{13.107}$$

which has to be maximized over $\boldsymbol{s}$. The abbreviation Eq. (13.17) has been used in Eq. (13.107) to simplify notation. The window function w in the terms $< \cdot >$ determines the size of the region to be matched. The cross-correlation function is independent of illumination changes. It is zero for totally dissimilar patterns and reaches a maximum of one for similar features.

The cross-correlation function is a 4-D function, depending on both the position $\boldsymbol{x}$ within the image as well as on the shift $\boldsymbol{s}$. In order to restrict the number of admissible matches and to minimize computational costs, the search range of $\boldsymbol{s}$ is restricted to a finite search window.

To speed up computations, a fast maximum search strategy has been proposed by Jähne [13]. Assuming the cross-correlation function $r(\boldsymbol{s})$ to be appropriately approximated by a second-order polynomial in $\boldsymbol{s}$, he shows that the $\boldsymbol{s}^m$ maximizing $r(\boldsymbol{s})$ can be estimated by the following linear system of equations:

$$\begin{bmatrix} r_{s_1 s_1} & r_{s_1 s_2} \\ r_{s_1 s_2} & r_{s_2 s_2} \end{bmatrix} \begin{bmatrix} s_1^m \\ s_2^m \end{bmatrix} = - \begin{bmatrix} r_{s_1} \\ r_{s_2} \end{bmatrix} \tag{13.108}$$

with

$$r_{s_p} = \frac{\partial r}{\partial s_p} \quad \text{and} \quad r_{s_p s_q} = \frac{\partial^2 r}{\partial s_p \partial s_q} \tag{13.109}$$

The first- and second-order partial derivatives of r with respect to the components s_1 and s_2 are taken at $\boldsymbol{s} = 0$. However, the fast maximum search according to Eq. (13.108) will fail, if r cannot be approximated by a second-order polynomial within the search region of $\boldsymbol{s}$. In order to overcome this problem, an iterative coarse-to-fine strategy can be applied. Beginning at the coarsest level of a Laplacian pyramid (Section 4.4.3), where displacements are assumed to be in the order of 1 pixel/frame or less, maxima of r can be located within a small search space of only 1-3 pixels. Within this region the second-order approximation of r is appropriate. Subpixel displacements are successively computed from finer levels of the Laplacian pyramid, by a quadratic approximation of r about s^m from coarser levels.

13.5.2 Distance minimization matching

An alternative approach to maximizing the cross-correlation function is to minimize a distance measure, quantifying the dissimilarity between two image regions. A common distance measure is given by the *sum-of-squared difference* (SSD):

$$d_{1,2}(\boldsymbol{x}, \boldsymbol{s}) = \left\langle [g(\boldsymbol{x}', t_1) - g(\boldsymbol{x}' - \boldsymbol{s}, t_2)]^2 \right\rangle \tag{13.110}$$

The indices 1 and 2 refer to the time t_1 and t_2, respectively. Again the abbreviation Eq. (13.17) has been used to simplify notation. Interestingly, Eq. (13.110) is closely related to the approach of Lucas and Kanade [19]. Approximating $g(\boldsymbol{x}' - \boldsymbol{s}, t_2)$ in Eq. (13.110) by a truncated Taylor expansion about $\boldsymbol{s} = 0$ and skipping all terms above first-order yields the gradient-based formulation Eq. (13.13).

Approaches using SSD-based matching are reported by Anandan [63] and Singh [64, 65]. The matching technique of Anandan [63] uses a coarse-to-fine strategy based on a Laplacian pyramid. Similar to the maximum search for the cross-correlation function described in the preceding, the minimization of d is initially carried out on the coarsest level of the pyramid and then successively refined to subpixel accuracy.

An interesting extension of the two-frame matching techniques is proposed by Singh [64, 65]. He averages the SSD of two consecutive pairs of bandpass filtered images, that is, three frames, to average spurious SSD minima due to noise or periodic texture:

$$d_2(\boldsymbol{x}, \boldsymbol{s}) = d_{1,2}(\boldsymbol{x}, -\boldsymbol{s}) + d_{2,3}(\boldsymbol{x}, \boldsymbol{s}) \tag{13.111}$$

In a second stage, this error measure is converted into a probability response distribution using

$$R(\boldsymbol{x}, \boldsymbol{s}) = \exp\left[\frac{\ln(0.95) d_2(\boldsymbol{x}, \boldsymbol{s})}{\min(d_2(\boldsymbol{x}, \boldsymbol{s}))}\right] \tag{13.112}$$

The choice for an exponential function for converting error distribution into response distribution is motivated by the fact that the response obtained with an exponential function varies continuously between zero and unity over the entire range of error. Hence, finding a minimum of d_2 corresponds to maximizing the response function $R(\boldsymbol{x}, \boldsymbol{s})$ over $\boldsymbol{s}$. In order to avoid local maxima, Singh [65] suggests finding a best estimate $\boldsymbol{s}^m$ of the displacement $\boldsymbol{s}$ by computing the center of mass of R with respect to $\boldsymbol{s}$:

$$\boldsymbol{s}^m(\boldsymbol{x}) = \frac{\sum\limits_{n=0}^{N-1} R(\boldsymbol{x}, \boldsymbol{s}_n)\boldsymbol{s}_n}{\sum\limits_{n=0}^{N-1} R(\boldsymbol{x}, \boldsymbol{s}_n)} \tag{13.113}$$

where the summation is carried out over all N integer values $\boldsymbol{s}_n$ within the search window. The center of mass only approximates the maximum peak value if R is symmetrically centered about the peak. Thus, a coarse-to-fine strategy based on a Laplacian pyramid is used to ensure the surface of R to be centered close to the true displacement [6].

13.6 Modeling of flow fields

In all optical flow techniques detailed in this chapter, tight restrictions have been imposed on the optical flow field $\boldsymbol{f}(\boldsymbol{x})$. All techniques that group constraints over a local neighborhood U intrinsically assumed $\boldsymbol{f}$ to be constant within U. In order to fulfill this prerequisite, the local neighborhood tends to be chosen as small as possible to get a local estimate of $\boldsymbol{f}$. The larger the neighborhood gets, the more likely it is that $\boldsymbol{f}$ varies within U, or that U contains multiple motions. At the same time, U has to be chosen sufficiently large as to contain enough information to constrain the solution, that is, to overcome the aperture problem. This competition of requirements is commonly referred to as *generalized aperture problem* [66].

A variety of approaches use least-squares estimates (either LS or TLS) to group Eq. (13.2) or some other relation over a local neighborhood U. By using a quadratic objective function, they inherently assume Gaussian residual errors, locally independent with equal variance within U. The merit of this assumption is a fairly simple, closed solution. As soon as multiple motions (e. g., occlusion boundaries or transparent motion) are present within U, the residuals can not longer be considered Gaussian [12]. If these motions are independent, the error distribution might even become bimodal.

These considerations show that, in fact, we have already applied a model to optical flow computation, namely the most simple model of constant $\boldsymbol{f}$ and independent Gaussian errors within U. This section outlines two principal approaches to the forementioned problems. They try to model more appropriately the flow field and can be incorporated into techniques detailed so far. These approaches weaken the simple model assumptions by modeling both smooth spatial variations in the optical flow field as well as multiple motions.

13.6.1 Parameterization of flow fields

Parameterized flow field models assume the optical flow $\boldsymbol{f}(\boldsymbol{x})$ to be modeled according to some parametric function in the image coordinates. An appropriate optical flow technique has to estimate the model parameters $\boldsymbol{a}$, which include the mean optical flow, as well as spatial derivatives of $\boldsymbol{f}$. If the model appropriately describes the spatial variation of $\boldsymbol{f}$ within a certain area, the local neighborhood can be increased up to this size without violating the model assumption. In fact, the local region of support has to be increased (compared to constant $\boldsymbol{f}$ within U) in order to compute the model parameters reliably. The more parameters have to be estimated, the larger the local neighborhood has to be in order to regularize the solution. At the same time the computational complexity increases with the number of parameters.

Affine optical flow field. A more complicated model of the optical flow field assumes a linear variation of $\boldsymbol{f}$, that is, an *affine transformation* of local image regions:

$$\boldsymbol{f}(\boldsymbol{x}) = \begin{bmatrix} a_1 & a_2 \\ a_3 & a_4 \end{bmatrix} \begin{bmatrix} x \\ y \end{bmatrix} + \begin{bmatrix} a_5 \\ a_6 \end{bmatrix} = \boldsymbol{A}\boldsymbol{x} + \boldsymbol{t} \tag{13.114}$$

with

$$a_1 = \frac{\partial f_1}{\partial x}, \quad a_2 = \frac{\partial f_1}{\partial y}, \quad a_3 = \frac{\partial f_2}{\partial x}, \quad \text{and} \quad a_4 = \frac{\partial f_2}{\partial y} \tag{13.115}$$

This model appropriately describes the underlying optical flow field $\boldsymbol{f}(\boldsymbol{x})$, if it can be locally expressed by a first-order Taylor expansion,

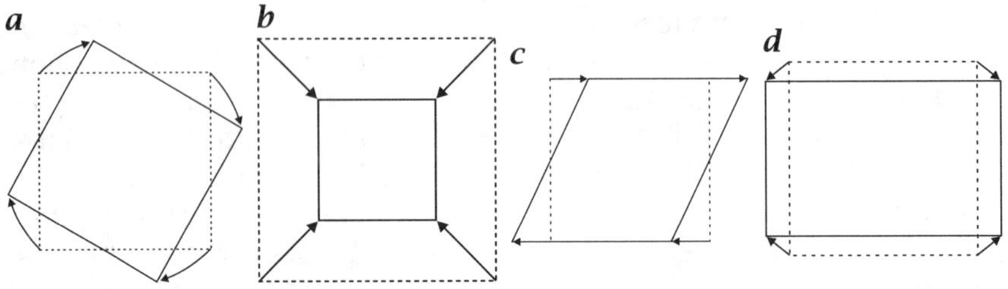

Figure 13.14: *Elementary geometric transformations of a planar surface element undergoing affine transformation:* ***a*** *rotation;* ***b*** *dilation;* ***c*** *shear;* ***d*** *stretching.*

which is always possible for smoothly varying $\boldsymbol{f}(\boldsymbol{x})$. The size of the local neighborhood U must be chosen such that it is small enough for the first-order condition to hold, and simultaneously large enough to constrain the solution.

The vector $\boldsymbol{t} = [a_5, a_6]^T$ represents the translation of the center of the local neighborhood and corresponds to the constant optical flow vector $\boldsymbol{f}$ used so far. From the four components $a_1, \ldots, a_4$ the four elementary geometric transformations of the local neighborhood can be computed (see also Eq. (16.34) in Chapter 16):

- If the optical flow field has nonzero *vorticity*, the local neighborhood is subject to *rotation*, as illustrated in Fig. 13.14a and Fig. 13.15c. Rotation (vorticity) can be computed from the nondiagonal elements of $\boldsymbol{A}$ by

$$\mathrm{rot}(\boldsymbol{f}) = \frac{\partial f_1}{\partial y} - \frac{\partial f_2}{\partial x} = a_3 - a_2 \qquad (13.116)$$

- If the optical flow field has nonzero *divergence*, the local neighborhood is subject to *dilation* (Fig. 13.14b and Fig. 13.15b). Dilation (divergence) can be computed by

$$\mathrm{div}(\boldsymbol{f}) = \frac{\partial f_1}{\partial x} + \frac{\partial f_2}{\partial y} = a_1 + a_4 \qquad (13.117)$$

  which corresponds to the trace of the matrix $\boldsymbol{A}$.

- The *shear* of the local neighborhood (Fig. 13.14c and Fig. 13.15d) can be computed by

$$\mathrm{sh}(\boldsymbol{f}) = \frac{\partial f_1}{\partial y} + \frac{\partial f_2}{\partial x} = a_2 + a_3 \qquad (13.118)$$

- The *stretching* of the local neighborhood (Fig. 13.14d and Fig. 13.15e) can be computed by

$$\mathrm{str}(\boldsymbol{f}) = \frac{\partial f_1}{\partial x} - \frac{\partial f_2}{\partial y} = a_1 - a_4 \qquad (13.119)$$

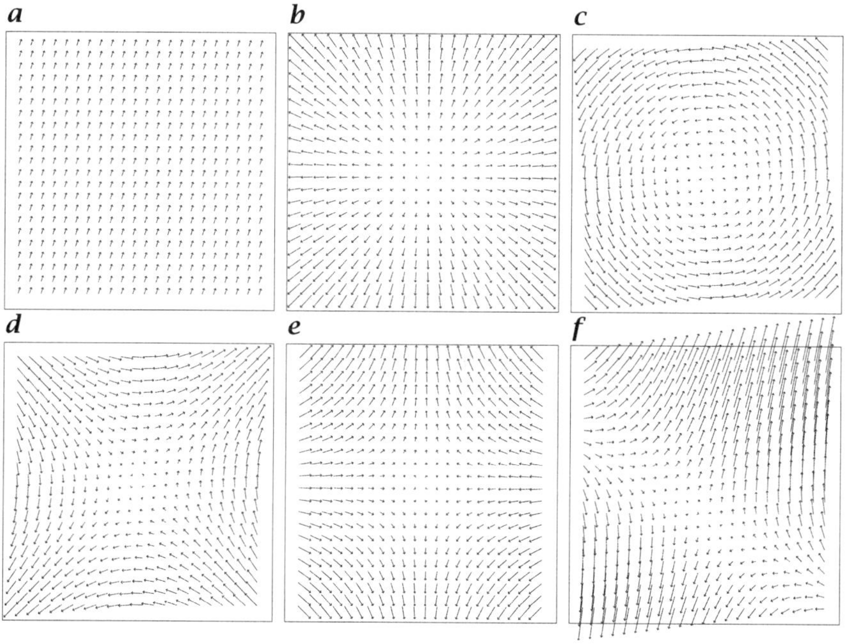

Figure 13.15: Elementary affine flow fields: ***a*** *pure translation ($\boldsymbol{t} = [1, 2]^T$);* ***b*** *pure divergence (div($\boldsymbol{f}$) = 1.0);* ***c*** *pure rotation (rot($\boldsymbol{f}$) = 1.0);* ***d*** *pure shear (sh($\boldsymbol{f}$) = 1.0);* ***e*** *pure stretching (str($\boldsymbol{f}$) = 1.0); and* ***f*** *example of a linear combination of all elementary transformations ($\boldsymbol{t} = [1, 2]^T$, div($\boldsymbol{f}$) = -1.0, rot($\boldsymbol{f}$) = 1.0, sh($\boldsymbol{f}$) = 0.3, str($\boldsymbol{f}$) = 0.8).*

In order to incorporate the affine model into optical flow estimation, we need to replace the constant flow vector $\boldsymbol{f}$ in the objective functions of any technique by the affine flow $\boldsymbol{f}(\boldsymbol{x}, \boldsymbol{a}) = \boldsymbol{A}\boldsymbol{x} + \boldsymbol{t}$, as illustrated in the two following examples:

Example 13.1: Local least squares estimate.

The brightness change constraint equation Eq. (13.2) for affine flow at the point $\boldsymbol{x}$ is given by

$$(\boldsymbol{A}\boldsymbol{x} + \boldsymbol{t})^T (\nabla g(\boldsymbol{x})) + g_t(\boldsymbol{x}) = 0 \tag{13.120}$$

Thus, a local least squares estimate corresponding to Eq. (13.13) can be obtained by the following minimization problem:

$$\boldsymbol{f}(\boldsymbol{x}) = \arg\min \|\boldsymbol{e}\|_2^2, \quad \|\boldsymbol{e}\|_2^2 = \left\langle \left[(\boldsymbol{A}\boldsymbol{x} + \boldsymbol{t})^T (\nabla g(\boldsymbol{x})) + g_t(\boldsymbol{x}) \right]^2 \right\rangle \tag{13.121}$$

with respect to the model parameters $\boldsymbol{a} = [a_1, \ldots, a_6]^T$.

Minimizing Eq. (13.121) by standard least squares technique yields a linear system of six equations in the six unknown parameters of $\boldsymbol{a}$ [13].

In order to reliably solve for all six parameters, the local neighborhood has to be sufficiently large to contain enough information about the spatial variation of $\boldsymbol{f}$ into all directions. For too small neighborhoods, only the translation vector $\boldsymbol{t}$ can be estimated. Fleet and Jepson [20] use least squares estimation together with an affine model of the optical flow field to estimate the 2-D flow from component velocities (Section 13.4.3).

Example 13.2: Region-based matching.

An affine model for the displacement vector field $\boldsymbol{s}(\boldsymbol{x})$ can also be incorporated into region-based matching techniques. Replacing the displacement vector $\boldsymbol{s}$ by the *affine displacement* $\boldsymbol{s}(\boldsymbol{x}, \boldsymbol{a})$,

$$\boldsymbol{s}(\boldsymbol{x}, \boldsymbol{a}^s) = \begin{bmatrix} a_1^s & a_2^s \\ a_3^s & a_4^s \end{bmatrix} \begin{bmatrix} x \\ y \end{bmatrix} + \begin{bmatrix} a_5^s \\ a_6^s \end{bmatrix} = \boldsymbol{A}^s \boldsymbol{x} + \boldsymbol{t}^s \tag{13.122}$$

$$\boldsymbol{a}^s = \left[a_1^s, \dots, a_6^s\right]^T = \boldsymbol{a}^s(t_2 - t_1) \tag{13.123}$$

yields the following modified sum-of-squared difference (SSD) measure Eq. (13.110):

$$\begin{aligned} d_{1,2}(\boldsymbol{x}, \boldsymbol{a}^s) &= \left\langle \left[g(\boldsymbol{x}', t_1) - g(\boldsymbol{x}' - \boldsymbol{A}^s \boldsymbol{x}' - \boldsymbol{t}^s, t_2)\right]^2 \right\rangle \\ &= \left\langle \left[g(\boldsymbol{x}', t_1) - g(\boldsymbol{D}\boldsymbol{x}' - \boldsymbol{t}^s, t_2)\right]^2 \right\rangle \end{aligned} \tag{13.124}$$

with $\boldsymbol{D} = \boldsymbol{I} - \boldsymbol{A}^s$. Please note that the translation vector $\boldsymbol{t}$ and the matrix $\boldsymbol{A}$ have been replaced by the mean displacement $\boldsymbol{t}^s$ and the matrix $\boldsymbol{A}^s$, which contains the spatial derivatives of the displacement $\boldsymbol{s}$, instead of the optical flow $\boldsymbol{f}$ (Eq. (13.122)). Minimization of Eq. (13.124) yields a linear 6×6 system, which has to be solved for the 6 parameters $\boldsymbol{a}^s$.

An affine region matching approach based on SSD-minimization has been proposed by Shi and Tomasi [18]. They point out that the matrix $\boldsymbol{A}^s$ is hard to estimate for small image regions U because the variations of $\boldsymbol{s}$ within U are small compared to the mean displacement $\boldsymbol{t}^s$. This, however, affects not only the parameters of $\boldsymbol{A}^s$, but also causes errors in the estimation of $\boldsymbol{t}^s$, because both parameter sets interact in the minimization procedure. They conclude that a constant flow model gives more reliable estimates for the translation of small image regions and propose an iterative two-model approach. An initial estimate for $\boldsymbol{t}^s$ is computed by assuming $\boldsymbol{A}^s$ to be zero. In a second step, the affine parameters $\boldsymbol{A}^s$ are estimated using the initial estimate $\boldsymbol{t}^s$.

Other approaches based on SSD using linear deformation have been reported in [67, 68], to mention only a few sources.

Lie group transformations. Affine flow is only one possible model of local image transformations. A mathematical generalization of the theory of transformations can be found by using the formalism of *Lie algebra*. In fact, the *affine group* is a subgroup of the *Lie group* of continuous transformations. Without detailing all mathematical prerequisites of Lie group theory, we approach this concept in terms of coordinate transformations from Cartesian image coordinates into generalized coordinates, and outline the practical application to optical flow computation. A more detailed treatment of Lie algebra is found in [50, 69].

In the following, we assume the image brightness pattern to undergo a spatial transformation within a time interval δt, which can be expressed by

$$g(\boldsymbol{x}, t) = g(\boldsymbol{x}', t - \delta t) = g(\boldsymbol{S}^{-1}(\boldsymbol{x}, \boldsymbol{a}), t - \delta t) \tag{13.125}$$

where $\boldsymbol{S} = [S_x, S_y]^T$ defines a 2-D invertible transformation acting on the image coordinates $\boldsymbol{x}$:

$$\boldsymbol{x} = \boldsymbol{S}(\boldsymbol{x}', \boldsymbol{a}), \quad \text{and} \quad \boldsymbol{x}' = \boldsymbol{S}^{-1}(\boldsymbol{x}, \boldsymbol{a}) \tag{13.126}$$

With $\boldsymbol{a} = [a_1, \ldots, a_p]^T$ we denote the p-dimensional parameter vector of the transformation, which is assumed to be constant within the time interval δt. If $\boldsymbol{S}$ is chosen to form a *Lie group of transformations* it is infinitely differentiable in $\boldsymbol{x}$ and analytic in $\boldsymbol{a}$. Applied to the image $g(\boldsymbol{x}, t)$ at a certain time instant t, it gives a transformed image $g(\boldsymbol{x}', t)$. Thus, successive application of the transformation $\boldsymbol{S}(\boldsymbol{x}, \boldsymbol{a}(t))$ defines a trajectory through the sequence, along which the brightness of g remains constant (although being treated as constant within δt, we allow $\boldsymbol{a}$ to slowly vary over longer periods).

As $\boldsymbol{S}$ is analytic with respect to the parameters a_i, we can expand the coordinate transformation in a first-order Taylor series about $\boldsymbol{a} = 0$, assuming the transformation to be infinitesimal within the time interval δt:

$$\boldsymbol{x} = \boldsymbol{x}' + \sum_{i=1}^{p} a_i \frac{\partial \boldsymbol{S}(\boldsymbol{x}', \boldsymbol{a})}{\partial a_i}, \quad \text{with} \quad \boldsymbol{x}' = \boldsymbol{S}(\boldsymbol{x}', \boldsymbol{a} = 0) \tag{13.127}$$

where $\boldsymbol{a} = 0$ is taken as the identity element of the transformation.

Using Eq. (13.127), we can determine how the spatiotemporal brightness distribution $g(\boldsymbol{x}, t)$ depends on the individual parameters a_i by taking the partial derivative

$$\frac{\partial g(\boldsymbol{x}, t)}{\partial a_i} = \frac{\partial g}{\partial x} \frac{\partial x}{\partial a_i} + \frac{\partial g}{\partial y} \frac{\partial y}{\partial a_i} = \frac{\partial g}{\partial x} \frac{\partial S_x}{\partial a_i} + \frac{\partial g}{\partial y} \frac{\partial S_y}{\partial a_i} \tag{13.128}$$

In operator notation, this expression can be reformulated for any $g(\boldsymbol{x}, t)$ as

$$\frac{\partial g(\boldsymbol{x}, t)}{\partial a_i} = \mathcal{L}_i g(\boldsymbol{x}, t) \tag{13.129}$$

$$\text{with} \quad \mathcal{L}_i = \frac{\partial S_x}{\partial a_i}\frac{\partial}{\partial x} + \frac{\partial S_y}{\partial a_i}\frac{\partial}{\partial y} = \xi_i^T \nabla, \quad \text{and} \quad \xi_i = \left[\frac{\partial S_x}{\partial a_i}, \frac{\partial S_y}{\partial a_i}\right]^T \tag{13.130}$$

The operator $\mathcal{L}_i$, $i \in \{1, \ldots, p\}$, is called an *infinitesimal generator* of the Lie group of transformations in a_i. As the explicit time dependency of g in Eq. (13.125) is formulated as 1-D "translation in time" with the fixed parameter $a_t = 1$, we can immediately infer the corresponding infinitesimal generator to be $\mathcal{L}_t = \partial/\partial t$.

An image sequence $g(\boldsymbol{x}, t)$ is called an *invariant function* under the group of transformations in the parameter a_i, if and only if

$$\mathcal{L}_i g(\boldsymbol{x}, t) = \frac{\partial g(\boldsymbol{x}, t)}{\partial a_i} = 0 \tag{13.131}$$

Thus, an invariant function remains constant if it is subject to a transformation with respect to the parameter a_i. Examples of such patterns and the corresponding transformations are the translation of a pattern with linear symmetry parallel to lines of constant brightness, or a pattern containing concentric circles rotated about the center of circular symmetry.

The set of parameters a_i, $i \in \{1, \ldots, p\}$, can be regarded as *generalized coordinates* of the transformation, also referred to as *canonical coordinates*, spanning a p-dimensional space. The unit vector $\bar{\eta}_i$ pointing along the direction of the canonical coordinate a_i is given in Cartesian (image) coordinates by

$$\bar{\eta}_i = \left|\frac{\partial \boldsymbol{x}}{\partial a_i}\right|^{-1} \frac{\partial \boldsymbol{x}}{\partial a_i} = \left|\frac{\partial \boldsymbol{S}}{\partial a_i}\right|^{-1} \frac{\partial \boldsymbol{S}}{\partial a_i} \tag{13.132}$$

The $\bar{\eta}_i(\boldsymbol{x})$, however, are depending on the position $\boldsymbol{x}$ and are not necessarily orthogonal in Cartesian coordinates (Example 13.5). For a one-parameter transformation ($p = 1$), $\bar{\eta}_1(\boldsymbol{x})$ is pointing into the direction of constant image brightness. For $p > 1$, the direction $\boldsymbol{r}(\boldsymbol{x})$ of constant brightness is given as linear combination of the directions $\bar{\eta}_i(\boldsymbol{x})$:

$$\boldsymbol{r}(\boldsymbol{x}) = \sum_{i=1}^{p} a_i \bar{\eta}_i(\boldsymbol{x}) \tag{13.133}$$

This immediately shows an important property of any Lie group of transformations: expressed in the canonical coordinates, the total transformation defined by $\boldsymbol{a}$ appears as a *translation*. Hence, Lie groups of transformations extend an arbitrary spatiotemporal transformation into a p-dimensional translation in the p canonical coordinates including the time t.

In a final step, we expand the spatiotemporal image at $g(\boldsymbol{x}, t)$ with respect to the parameters a_i, that is, we compose the transformation by the set of infinitesimal transformations:

$$g(\boldsymbol{x}, t) = g(\boldsymbol{x}', t - \delta t) + \sum_{i=1}^{p} a_i \frac{\partial g}{\partial a_i} = g(\boldsymbol{x}', t - \delta t) + \sum_{i=1}^{p} a_i \mathcal{L}_i g \quad (13.134)$$

With the initial assumption of brightness conservation (Eq. (13.125)), that is, $g(\boldsymbol{x}, t) = g(\boldsymbol{x}', t - \delta t)$, we immediately get the relation between the infinitesimal transformations and g:

$$\sum_{i=1}^{p} a_i \mathcal{L}_i g = 0, \quad \forall \boldsymbol{x} \quad (13.135)$$

Equation (13.135) has to be solved for the parameter vector $\boldsymbol{a}$. In order to avoid the trivial solution $\boldsymbol{a} = 0$, we need to add the constraint $\boldsymbol{a}^T \boldsymbol{a} = 1$, which is possible, as a scaling of $\boldsymbol{a}$ does not change the group of transformations.

It is important to note that the solution Eq. (13.135) constitutes a *generalization* of the standard brightness change constraint equation Eq. (13.2). Due to the presence of noise, Eq. (13.135) is usually not exactly satisfied. However, if we find an appropriate model for the optical flow field, which can be expressed by a Lie group of transformations, minimizing Eq. (13.135) with respect to the parameters $\boldsymbol{a}$ yields the underlying optical flow field. The minimization can be carried out by standard techniques of numerical linear algebra, such as LS and TLS estimation, as already pointed out earlier in this chapter.

An interesting relationship between Eq. (13.135) and previous approaches can be found, if we identify the sum in Eq. (13.135) by the scalar product

$$\boldsymbol{a}^T (\nabla_{\mathcal{L}} g), \quad \nabla_{\mathcal{L}} = [\mathcal{L}_1, \ldots, \mathcal{L}_p]^T \quad (13.136)$$

where $\nabla_{\mathcal{L}}$ denotes the *generalized gradient*. This notation obviously constitutes a generalized extension of the spatiotemporal gradient constraint Eq. (13.5), which has been directly used in the structure tensor technique (Eq. (13.39)) with $\boldsymbol{a} = \boldsymbol{r}$.

In the remainder of this section, we will illustrate how the Lie group formalism translates into practical application with the help of three simple examples.

Example 13.3: Static patterns

The trivial example of a flow field model is zero optical flow, that is, the assumption of static patterns. Hence,

$$g(\boldsymbol{x}, t) = g(\boldsymbol{x}, t - \delta t), \quad \forall \boldsymbol{x}, t \quad (13.137)$$

The only infinitesimal generator is the temporal translation $\mathcal{L}_t = \partial/\partial t$, with $a_t = 1$. Using Eq. (13.135) this yields the condition

$$\frac{\partial g(\boldsymbol{x},t)}{\partial t} = 0 \tag{13.138}$$

Example 13.4: Translation

Another simple example of a flow field model is a constant translation within a neighborhood U. The corresponding coordinate transformation reads

$$\boldsymbol{S}(\boldsymbol{x},\boldsymbol{t}) = \boldsymbol{x} + \boldsymbol{t} \tag{13.139}$$

where $\boldsymbol{t} = [t_1, t_2]^T$ denotes the translation vector, which has to be estimated. Letting $\boldsymbol{a} = [\boldsymbol{t}, 1]^T$, the infinitesimal generators can be computed by Eq. (13.130) as

$$\mathcal{L}_1 = \mathcal{L}_x = \frac{\partial}{\partial x}, \quad \mathcal{L}_2 = \mathcal{L}_y = \frac{\partial}{\partial y}, \quad \text{and} \quad \mathcal{L}_3 = \mathcal{L}_t = \frac{\partial}{\partial t} \tag{13.140}$$

Thus, Eq. (13.135) yields

$$t_1 \frac{\partial g}{\partial x} + t_2 \frac{\partial g}{\partial y} + \frac{\partial g}{\partial t} = 0 \tag{13.141}$$

which is nothing but the standard BCCE Eq. (13.2)!

Example 13.5: Rotation

A more complicated example of a flow field model is constant rotation within a neighborhood U. The corresponding coordinate transformation reads

$$\boldsymbol{S}(\boldsymbol{x},r) = [-ry, rx]^T, \quad r = \frac{1}{2}\mathrm{rot}(\boldsymbol{x}) \tag{13.142}$$

With the 2-D parameter vector $\boldsymbol{a} = [r, 1]^T$, the infinitesimal generators can be computed by Eq. (13.130) as

$$\mathcal{L}_1 = \mathcal{L}_r = -y\frac{\partial}{\partial x} + x\frac{\partial}{\partial y}, \quad \text{and} \quad \mathcal{L}_2 = \mathcal{L}_t = \frac{\partial}{\partial t} \tag{13.143}$$

which yields the condition Eq. (13.135)

$$rx\frac{\partial g}{\partial y} - ry\frac{\partial g}{\partial x} + \frac{\partial g}{\partial t} = 0 \tag{13.144}$$

The unit vector pointing into the direction of the canonical coordinate r is given by

$$\bar{\eta}_r(\boldsymbol{x}) = (x^2 + y^2)^{-1/2}[-y, x]^T$$

This vector is always pointing perpendicular to the position vector $\boldsymbol{x}$, corresponding to the pure rotational flow field, as illustrated in Fig. 13.15c.

Example 13.6: Affine flow

Finally, we are going to revisit affine flow fields in the context of Lie group transformations. The affine coordinate transformation is given by Eq. (13.114)

$$\boldsymbol{S}(\boldsymbol{x}, \boldsymbol{a}) = \begin{bmatrix} a_1 & a_2 \\ a_3 & a_4 \end{bmatrix} \begin{bmatrix} x \\ y \end{bmatrix} + \begin{bmatrix} a_5 \\ a_6 \end{bmatrix} = \boldsymbol{A}\boldsymbol{x} + \boldsymbol{t} \tag{13.145}$$

With $\boldsymbol{a} = [a_1, \ldots, a_6, 1]^T$, using Eq. (13.130), the infinitesimal generators can be derived as

$$\begin{gathered} \mathcal{L}_1 = x\frac{\partial}{\partial x}, \; \mathcal{L}_2 = y\frac{\partial}{\partial y}, \; \mathcal{L}_3 = x\frac{\partial}{\partial y}, \; \mathcal{L}_4 = y\frac{\partial}{\partial y} \\ \mathcal{L}_5 = \frac{\partial}{\partial x}, \; \mathcal{L}_6 = \frac{\partial}{\partial y}, \; \mathcal{L}_7 = \frac{\partial}{\partial t} \end{gathered} \tag{13.146}$$

The generators for the more intuitive transformations divergence, rotation, shear, and stretching can be obtained as the following linear combinations of $\mathcal{L}_1, \ldots, \mathcal{L}_4$:

$$\begin{aligned} \mathcal{L}_d &= \mathcal{L}_1 + \mathcal{L}_4 = x\frac{\partial}{\partial x} + y\frac{\partial}{\partial y}, \quad & \mathcal{L}_r &= \mathcal{L}_3 - \mathcal{L}_2 = x\frac{\partial}{\partial y} - y\frac{\partial}{\partial x} \\ \mathcal{L}_{st} &= \mathcal{L}_1 - \mathcal{L}_4 = x\frac{\partial}{\partial x} - y\frac{\partial}{\partial y}, \quad & \mathcal{L}_{sh} &= \mathcal{L}_2 + \mathcal{L}_3 = y\frac{\partial}{\partial x} + x\frac{\partial}{\partial y} \end{aligned} \tag{13.147}$$

where the indices d, r, sh, st denote the elementary transformations 'divergence', 'rotation', 'shear', and 'stretching', respectively. Thus, the Lie group formalism automatically decomposes the flow field into the elementary transformations, given the coordinate transformation Eq. (13.145).

The concept of Lie groups, outlined in this section, has been successfully used by Duc [50] for optical flow computation. Although more general than plain translation or affine flow, Lie groups of transformations do not account for brightness variations, as the image is only warped from the original image according to Eq. (13.125). They also do not model multiple motions and occlusions, a problem which can be addressed by using a robust estimation framework, which will be outlined in Section 13.6.2.

13.6.2 Robust estimates

Optical flow estimation is corrupted for all approaches pooling constraints over a finite-size spatial neighborhood in case it contains multiple motions, that is, at motion discontinuities and in the case of transparent motion overlay. Parameterized flow field models fail to handle these kinds of errors if they assume a smooth spatial transition of the optical flow field.

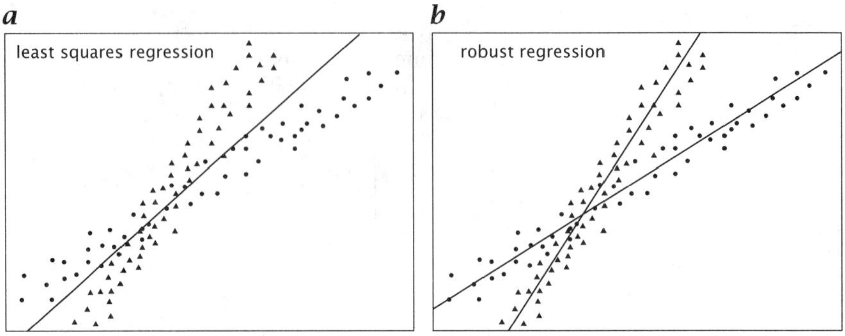

Figure 13.16: *Illustration of **a** least squares regression vs **b** robust regression of two independent data sets.*

The basic problem results from how the local constraints are combined. Least squares estimation tries to minimize the quadratic objective function

$$\|e\|_2^2 = \sum_{i=0}^{N-1} [e_i]^2 \tag{13.148}$$

where e_i denotes the residual error at point i. The summation is carried out over all N points within U. The influence of any residual error on the objective function can be computed as

$$\frac{\partial \|e\|_2^2}{\partial e_i} = 2e_i \tag{13.149}$$

which shows that the objective function $\|e\|_2^2$ depends linearly on the individual errors without bound. Hence, a single large error (outlier) is sufficient to corrupt the entire least squares solution.

By using a quadratic objective function, we inherently assume the residual errors to be Gaussian and independently distributed within the local neighborhood U, as already pointed out earlier in this chapter. If multiple, independent motions are present, we obtain an averaged optical flow $\boldsymbol{f}$. Deviations from this value at individual pixels are not Gaussian, but rather multimodal.

In a statistical context, only a fraction of the pixels within U fits to the model assumptions, while another fraction can be viewed as *outliers*. Thus, we need to recover the model parameters that best fit the majority of data while outliers have to be detected and rejected. This is the main goal of *robust statistics* [70], which has been increasingly used for a variety of computer vision applications [71]. Figure 13.16 illustrates the difference between standard least squares (LS) and robust estimation for the example of linear regression. While LS regression fits a line to the entire cloud of data points, disregarding individual clusters, robust regression techniques separate the clusters. An excellent introduction into robust estimation which addresses its application to the problem of optical flow computation, is given by Black and Anandan [12]. They propose a unified framework to account for the different optical flow techniques outlined in this chapter.

The basic idea of *robust estimation* is to replace the quadratic weighting of the residuals by another analytical expression $\rho(e_i)$, which is referred to as *M-estimator* in statistics. The ρ-function has to be designed to perform an unequal weighting depending on the magnitude of the residuals. Thus, we obtain the following minimization problem:

$$\boldsymbol{f} = \arg\min \|e\|_\rho, \quad \|e\|_\rho = \sum_{i=0}^{N-1} \rho(e_i, \sigma_s) \tag{13.150}$$

The optional scale parameter σ_s defines the range of residuals that are considered to belong to the set of 'inliers' (as opposed to 'outliers'). For a quadratic ρ, Eq. (13.150) corresponds to the standard least squares formulation.

In order to reduce the influence of outliers we search to minimize the influence of large residual errors on $\|e_\rho\|$. The influence of individual residuals is characterized by the *influence function* ψ, which is proportional to the derivative of the ρ-function [70]:

$$\psi(e_i, \sigma_s) = \frac{\partial \rho(e_i, \sigma_s)}{\partial e_i} \tag{13.151}$$

corresponding to Eq. (13.149) for a quadratic function. In order to be robust against outliers, ψ needs to be *redescending*, that is, it has to approach zero for large residuals after an initial increase for small values. Thus, the corresponding ρ-functions show an asymptotic behavior. One of the most simple ρ- functions is a truncated quadratic (Fig. 13.17a). The corresponding influence function drops to zero beyond a certain threshold (Fig. 13.17b). The truncated quadratic has to be compared to the standard quadratic with an unbounded ψ-function (Fig. 13.17a and b). Another commonly used ρ-function, proposed by Geman and McClure [72], is given by (Fig. 13.17c and d)

$$\rho(e_i, \sigma) = \frac{e_i^2}{\sigma + e_i^2}, \quad \psi(e_i, \sigma) = \frac{2\sigma e_i}{(\sigma + e_i^2)^2} \tag{13.152}$$

For practical application of the robust estimation framework to optical flow computation we simply need to replace the quadratic norm of the objective functions by a robust error norm ρ. As one example,

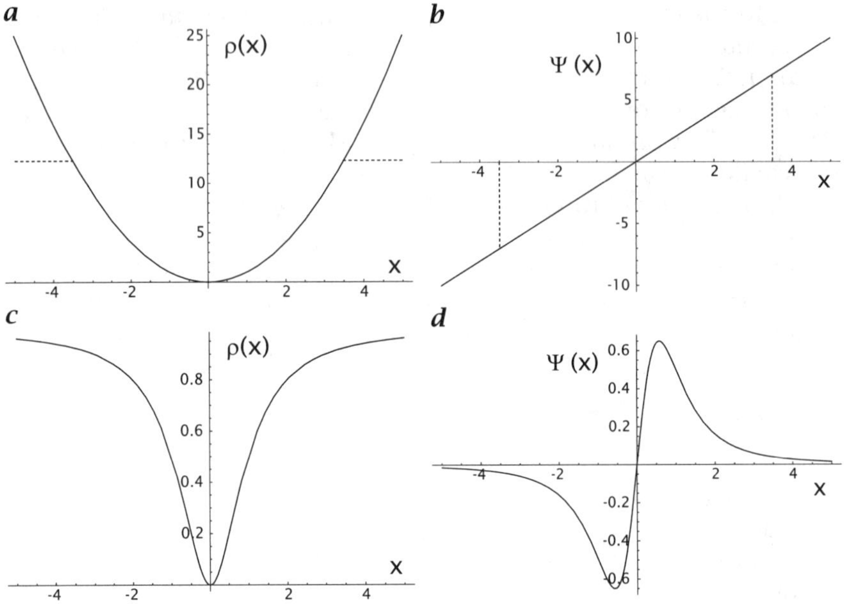

Figure 13.17: *Two examples of ρ and ψ functions:* ***a*** *quadratic (l_2 norm) and truncated quadratic (dashed);* ***b*** *derivative of the quadratic and truncated quadratic function;* ***c*** *Geman and McClure norm; and* ***d*** *derivative of the Geman and McClure norm [72].*

the local least squares technique Eq. (13.13) can be reformulated as

$$\boldsymbol{f} = \arg\min \|e\|_\rho, \quad \|e\|_\rho = \int_{-\infty}^{\infty} w(\boldsymbol{x} - \boldsymbol{x}')\, \rho\left((\nabla g)^T \boldsymbol{f} + g_t\right)\, d\boldsymbol{x}' \tag{13.153}$$

where ρ is a robust ρ-function. The discrete summation in Eq. (13.150) has been replaced by a weighted integration. Likewise, all other objective functions introduced in this chapter can be transformed into robust functions. Further details can be found in [12].

In general, robust formulations do not admit closed solutions and have to be solved iteratively. Black and Anandan [12] use over-relaxation techniques, such as the *Gauss-Seidel method*. This may be regarded as a disadvantage of robust estimation compared to LS estimation. It also has to be pointed out that robust techniques usually search for a dominant motion within U and attach a region of support to each motion. Although multiple motions can be iteratively found, the corresponding regions are disjoint. Thus, the image area is segmented into the individual motions, even in the case of transparency.

As an alternative to using robust M-estimators, Danuser and Stricker [73] propose a *generalized least-squares* technique to determine simultaneously an a priori unknown number of models and fit the data to these models. They argue that least squares (LS) estimation has considerable advantages over robust estimators, namely a significantly lower computational complexity and the fact that it can be proven to be the *best estimator* in absence of outliers and systematic errors (*Gauss-Markov conditions*). Furthermore, LS estimation can be efficiently complemented with error propagation (Section 13.7) by treating the input data as realizations of stochastic variables. It is, however, not robust enough as already pointed out at the beginning of this section.

By using generalized least squares estimation—a technique which is also referred to as *data snooping* [74]—LS estimation can be made more robust with respect to outliers. The goal is to search and eliminate observations that are perturbed by cross errors. The concept is similar to robust estimation with the difference that an observation with a significantly large residual error has absolutely no influence on the parameter estimation. The classification of the residuals is made based on a statistical test [73]. Förstner [68] was among the first exploiting the power of this technique for application in computer vision and pattern recognition. Danuser and Stricker [73] present a unified perspective of the application of generalized LS estimation to a general class of fitting problems.

13.7 Confidence measures and error propagation

Before we turn towards a comparative quantitative analysis of the results from different optical flow techniques, we want to revisit the availability and meaning of common *confidence measures*. We already pointed out several times during the course of this chapter that any optical flow estimation is subject to statistical and systematic errors depending on the noise level and image content. Thus, to quantify the reliability and precision of the results, optical flow estimation always needs to be combined with appropriate confidence measures to quantify the measurement precision.

13.7.1 General properties

Confidence measures can be classified into four principal tasks. In order to interpret the results of the optical flow computation, we need to:

1. Quantify the presence of image structure or features that allow information on motion to be obtained (as opposed to homogeneous areas).

2. Quantify statistical errors, such as random noise.
3. Quantify the presence of an aperture problem, which corresponds to the degree of singularity of the solution.
4. And finally, verify the underlying model assumptions.

Any good confidence measure needs to allow for the propagation of confidence into subsequent processing steps. There are two important ways to accomplish this task by using either *normalized measures* or *covariance matrices*.

Normalized measures. Normalized measures yield a real-valued output ranging from zero to unity from low to high confidence. As they are normalized, they can be directly used as weighting coefficients for individual estimates.

For example, if we need to average a property g over a local neighborhood U, we can incorporate the confidence c by using the concept of *normalized convolution* [42]:

$$\langle g \rangle_n = \frac{\langle c \cdot g \rangle}{\langle c \rangle} = \frac{W * [c \cdot g]}{W * c} \tag{13.154}$$

where W denotes an appropriate smoothing kernel. In fact, c does not necessarily have to be normalized, as the result is normalized by the denominator in Eq. (13.154) according to the individual weighting coefficients c within U. Normalized measures, however, are convenient to use in terms of interpretation. They quantify the confidence independent from the image contrast or other image properties.

Another alternative is to use an unbounded confidence measure, which can be thresholded according to some heuristic or computed value corresponding to high confidence. The resulting binary mask serves to mask reliable measurements or can be used as confidence in the normalized convolution Eq. (13.154).

Covariance matrices. The concept of covariance matrices is a powerful tool for error propagation, which has long been used in statistical estimation theory. However, this concept assumes Gaussian error distributions, which are not always present. If the real distribution deviates significantly from the Gaussian assumption, we need more parameters to parameterize it appropriately.

Let $\boldsymbol{a} = [a_1, \ldots, a_m]^T$ be an m-dimensional vector representing the measured parameters of the optical flow field. In the most simple case of plain translation it reduces to $\boldsymbol{a} = \boldsymbol{f}$ $(m = 2)$. If we assume $\boldsymbol{a}$ to be a random vector with a mean of $\boldsymbol{a}_0$, the *covariance matrix* $\Lambda^{\boldsymbol{a}}$ is given by

$$\Lambda^{\boldsymbol{a}} = \left\langle (\boldsymbol{a} - \boldsymbol{a}_0)(\boldsymbol{a} - \boldsymbol{a}_0)^T \right\rangle \tag{13.155}$$

where $\langle \cdot \rangle$ denotes a statistical (ensemble) average.

The covariance matrix represents the uncertainty in the measurements. On the diagonal, it contains the variances of the individual parameters, $\Lambda^{\boldsymbol{a}}_{ii} = \sigma^2(a_i)$. The off-diagonal elements contain cross errors given by the covariance of the model parameters.

As the covariance matrix is symmetric, it can be diagonalized, with the eigenvalues $\lambda_1 \geq \lambda_2$ as diagonal elements. These eigenvalues correspond to the variances of the model parameters in the principal axes coordinate system of the parameter space. In this coordinate system, the errors in the parameters are independent. If no aperture problem is present, we expect errors in both components of $\boldsymbol{f}$ to be of the same magnitude. In case of an aperture problem, however, the component perpendicular to the flow estimate is undefined. Hence, we expect $\lambda_1 \gg \lambda_2$.

A more detailed analysis of the covariance matrix and its relation to the least squares estimation can be found in [75].

From the parameters $\boldsymbol{a}$, we want to compute a resulting set of properties $\boldsymbol{b} = [b_1, \ldots, b_n]^T$ according to the functional relationship $\boldsymbol{b} = \boldsymbol{h}(\boldsymbol{a})$. How does the covariance of $\boldsymbol{a}$ translate into the covariance of $\boldsymbol{b}$?

A first-order Taylor expansion of $\boldsymbol{h}$ about $\boldsymbol{a}_0$ yields

$$\boldsymbol{h}(\boldsymbol{a}) = \boldsymbol{h}(\boldsymbol{a}_0) + \boldsymbol{Dh}(\boldsymbol{a}_0)(\boldsymbol{a} - \boldsymbol{a}_0) + \epsilon(\|\boldsymbol{a} - \boldsymbol{a}_0\|^2) \tag{13.156}$$

where $\boldsymbol{Dh}(\boldsymbol{a}_0)$ is the first-order derivative of $\boldsymbol{h}$ at $\boldsymbol{a}_0$, that is, the $m \times n$ *Jacobian matrix*. Using Eq. (13.156), we can find the covariance matrix of $\boldsymbol{b}$ to be [62]

$$\Lambda^{\boldsymbol{b}} = \boldsymbol{Dh}(\boldsymbol{a}_0)\Lambda^{\boldsymbol{a}}\boldsymbol{Dh}^T(\boldsymbol{a}_0) \tag{13.157}$$

It is important to note that the relation Eq. (13.157) constitutes only a first-order approximation resulting from the truncated first-order Taylor expansion of h.

An important application of this kind of error propagation is recursive least-squares estimation procedures, such as Kalman filtering [62, 76].

With these classifications and requirements in mind we are going to briefly revisit common confidence measures, as they have been proposed for the various optical flow techniques.

13.7.2 Interrelation of common confidence measures

Although being considered different, most confidence measures are closely related as they are motivated by the same requirements, usually the solubility of some kind of algebraic relation. This, however, corresponds to the aperture problem in disguise. We also need to know if any structure is available. This can be easily verified by computing the magnitude of the spatial gradient of the image. Even for techniques, that are missing any confidence measure, thresholding the results with the gradient improves the overall accuracy tremendously. Although the resulting flow field is sparse, the remaining flow vectors can be assured to be more reliable.

In his overview of optical flow techniques, Barron et al. [6] shows how confidence measures are obtained by the various implementations of optical flow techniques. In the following discussion, we focus on optical-flow-based approaches, where the interrelation of the various confidence measures can be demonstrated. For confidence measures of other techniques, such as correlation-based and phase-based approaches, we would like to refer to Barron et al. [77] and [6].

Structure tensor technique. Confidence measures for the structure tensor technique have been detailed in Section 13.3.2. They constitute normalized measures quantifying both the overall certainty the presence of an aperture problem.

Local least squares technique. Confidence measures for the local least squares approach have been defined by Barron et al. [6] and Simoncelli [27]. Both try to quantify the singularity of the matrix $\boldsymbol{A}$ in Eq. (13.16) by analyzing the eigenvalues of $\boldsymbol{A}$. While Simoncelli [27] proposes to threshold the sum of eigenvalues (trace of the matrix $\boldsymbol{A}$), Barron et al. [6] argue that the smallest eigenvalue proved to be more reliable in practical implementations. How are both measures related? In the following discussion we show that both measures are complementary and can be used in combination to obtain more information about the sources of errors.

In terms of local symmetry, the matrix $\boldsymbol{A}$ in Eq. (13.16) constitutes the *structure tensor* of a 2-D subspace of the spatiotemporal neighborhood and represents local orientation in 2-D images [38, 41]. Thus, it contains information about the presence of an aperture problem, as well as information about the presence of any structure at all. The trace of $\boldsymbol{A}$ is nothing but the squared gradient of the image and quantifies the presence of image structure, as opposed to constant brightness. The trace of a matrix stays invariant under orthogonal coordinate transformations. Thus, the sum of eigenvalues of $\boldsymbol{A}$ can be computed beforehand without explicitly solving the eigenvalue problem. This allows regions of low confidence to be identified before the computations have to be carried out. Hence, the confidence measure of Simoncelli [27] is perfectly suited to threshold the image before carrying out further computations. The same kind of measure has been used to perform an initial thresholding in the 3-D structure tensor technique [44] (Section 13.3.2).

For the remaining image points, we need to identify regions of apparent aperture problem. This can be done by analyzing the smallest eigenvalue of the 2-D structure tensor, that is, the eigenvalue of the matrix $\boldsymbol{A}$, as suggested by Barron et al. [6]. If the smallest eigenvalue is close to zero, then the aperture problem persists within U. Rather than thresholding the smallest eigenvalue, as suggested by Barron et al. [6], we can compute the *local orientation*, that is, the difference of the two eigenvalues, normalized to the sum of the eigenvalues [13, 21]. This corresponds to the *spatial coherency constraint* of the 3-D structure tensor technique (Section 13.3.2).

Both measures, based on the spatial gradients, do not allow for problems, such as isotropic noise, fast accelerations, and occlusions to be identified. They can be identified by using the total coherence measure of the 3-D structure tensor technique (Section 13.3.2). In order to detect these violations of the model assumptions, the local least squares technique needs to analyze the residual errors (Eq. (13.23)).

Second-order technique. For the second-order technique of Uras et al. [31], Barron et al. [6] propose a confidence measure by analyzing the spatial *Hessian* matrix. They suggest thresholding the determinant det($\boldsymbol{H}$). As we have shown in Section 13.3.1, the determinant becomes zero in case of an aperture problem (Eqs. (13.28) to (13.29)). It also vanishes in case of homogeneous brightness, that is, if all spatial gradients are zero.

Uras et al. [31] initially suggested using the condition number of the Hessian $\kappa(\boldsymbol{A}) \geq 1$ as confidence measure. This corresponds to the relative magnitude of the eigenvalues of the matrix $\boldsymbol{H}$ and also quantifies the relative distribution of gradients within a local neighborhood, that is, the presence of an aperture problem. The condition number represents the *elongation* of the *hyperellipsoid*, spanned by the two eigenvalues as principal axes. A condition number of 1 represents a well-conditioned matrix, that is, no aperture problem. If $\kappa(\boldsymbol{H})$ is large the matrix is *ill-conditioned*, that is, singular.

Barron et al. [6] found, however, that det($\boldsymbol{H}$) gives a more reliable measure than $\kappa(\boldsymbol{H})$.

13.8 Comparative analysis

This section tries to compare some of the previously introduced methods for optical flow computation. First of all it has to be noted that all algorithms have specific parameters that can be fine tuned to the given image data. This makes comparison rather difficult. Here a straightforward approach is chosen in that for each method a fixed parameter set is used regardless of the image content. Thus the results may not be optimal but can be used to compare across various types of input material. However, we believe that a method's sensibility to the parameter choice is also a relevant criterion if it is to be used in practical applications.

13.8.1 Test data

The test data used comprise computer-generated synthetic sequences, synthetic sequences with real world texture, and real, camera recorded, sequences. With the chosen material we try to capture some commonly encountered classes of problems.

Synthetic test sequences. To allow for a comparison of estimated and exact flow fields some synthetic sequences were used. Firstly we generate some test data so that parameters such as magnitude and direction of the flow fields can be controlled. Secondly we use some sequences provided in the literature that are generated based on realistic textures. We use four types of synthetic sequences, an example image of each of which is shown in Fig. 13.18:

Noise. On a uniform background of gray level 127 we added white noise with a standard deviation of 50 gray levels. Moving sequences are then computed from the Fourier spectra via the shift theorem as suggested by Bainbridge-Smith and Lane [9]. The nth frame in a sequence moving with constant velocity $\boldsymbol{u}$ is computed from

$$g(\boldsymbol{x}, n) = \int_{-\infty}^{\infty}\int_{-\infty}^{\infty} \hat{g}(\boldsymbol{k}, 0) \exp\left(2\pi \mathrm{i} n \boldsymbol{k}\boldsymbol{u}\right) \, \mathrm{d}^2 k \tag{13.158}$$

where $\hat{g}(\boldsymbol{k}, 0)$ is the Fourier transform of the original image $g(\boldsymbol{x}, 0)$. This test pattern consists of sharp peaks in the spatial domain and accordingly has a uniform power spectrum over the whole frequency domain.

Sinusoidal. Like Barron et al. [7], we use a sinusoidal plaid pattern which consists of two superposed sinusoidal plane-waves:

$$g(\boldsymbol{x}) = \sin(\boldsymbol{k}_1 \cdot \boldsymbol{x} + \omega_1 t) + \sin(\boldsymbol{k}_2 \cdot \boldsymbol{x} + \omega_2 t) \tag{13.159}$$

While showing large spatial extension there are only two wavelengths present within the Fourier spectra of these images.

Gaussian. Using a Gaussian-shaped object minimizes the trade-off between spatial and spectral extension. However, due to the low contrast in the outer areas this sequence does ask for reliable confidence measures that restrict the flow computation to the inner regions.

Grid. The grid is produced as a superposition of lines modeled with a narrow Gaussian profile, which may be sought as the point spread

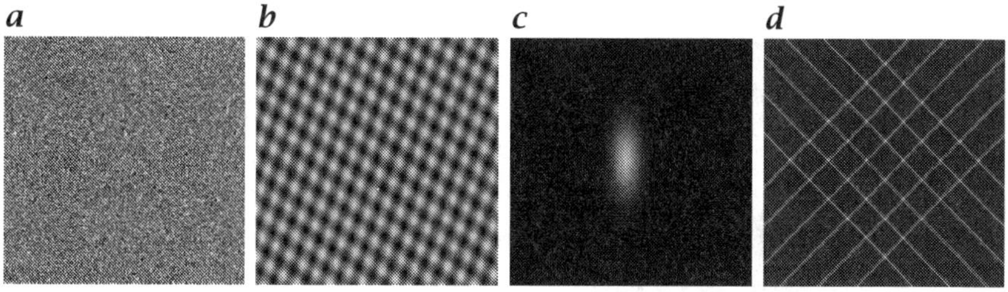

Figure 13.18: *Generated test sequences:* ***a*** *noise;* ***b*** *sinusoidal;* ***c*** *Gaussian; and* ***d*** *translating grid.*

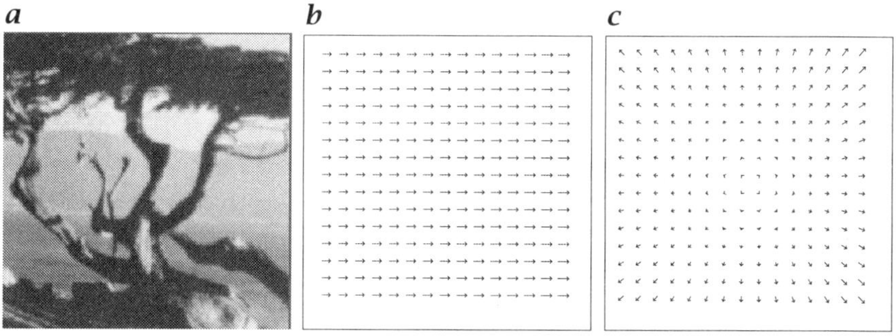

Figure 13.19: *Diverging and translating tree sequence:* ***a*** *example image;* ***b*** *correct translating flow; and* ***c*** *correct diverging flow .*

function acting during image acquisition. Thus spatially rather localized structures are obtained, which in turn introduces high frequencies in the spectrum. This is the typical situation that occurs at the boundaries of moving rigid objects.

In summary, the used sequences cover a wide range of possible spatial and frequency distributions and may be used as guidelines for a classification of the image material in a given application.

Semi-synthetic sequences with realistic textures. From an image of a tree, Fleet and Jepson [20] computed two sequences through warping with a translating and diverging flow field. This simulates camera movement along and normal to the cameras line of sight. The original image and the resulting correct flow fields are shown in Fig. 13.19. Another famous test sequence is given by the Yosemite sequence created by Lynn Quam at SRI (Fig. 13.20). This is a graphically generated sequence with the camera moving towards the valley. The result is a mainly divergent flow field with up to 5 pixels/frame movement in the lower left corner—the fractal-based clouds move left to right at 2 pixels/frame. The wide range of velocities together with occurring occlusion make this a complex scene to analyze.

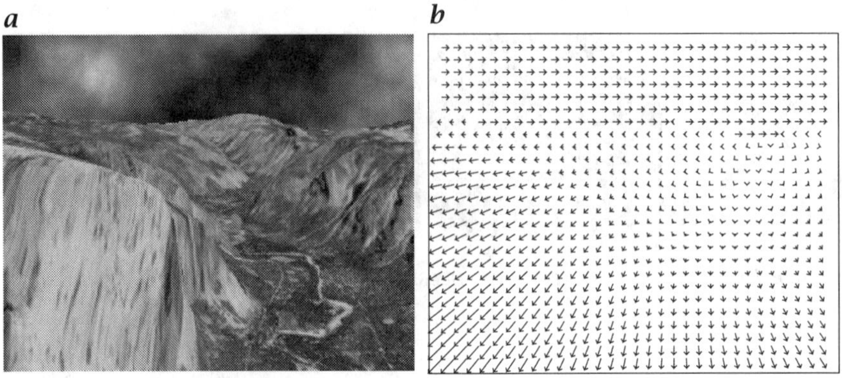

Figure 13.20: *Yosemite sequence:* ***a*** *example image; and* ***b*** *correct flow.*

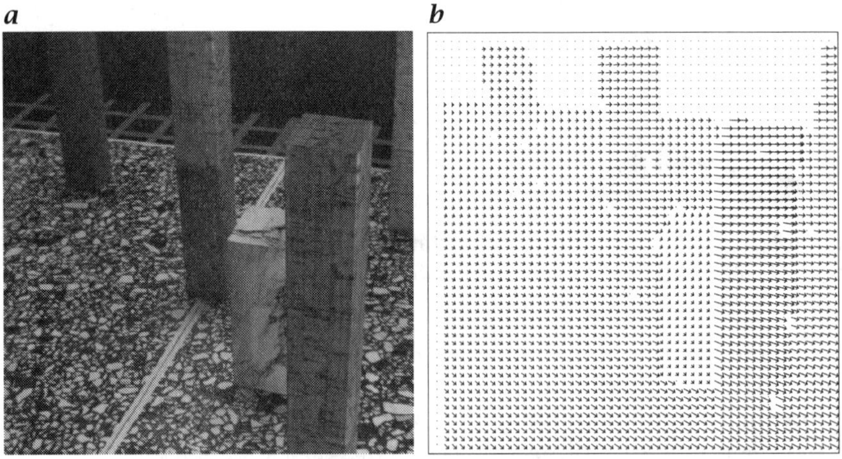

Figure 13.21: *Otte's block world:* ***a*** *example image; and* ***b*** *correct flow.*

Real test sequences. The ultimate test for any optical flow algorithm is its performance on real image data. However, even though there are many test sequences available it is usually not known what the actual motion was. Otte and Nagel [8] provided a calibrated sequence of which Fig. 13.21 shows image number 34 together with the actual flow field. This sequence was recorded by a camera mounted on a moving robot arm. The camera moves towards the scene, which is stationary apart from the lighter block which moves to the left.

Other real sequences we employed for testing are shown in Fig. 13.22. The Bonsai sequence (Fig. 13.22a) was recorded by rotating the tree around its axis in steps of one degree. Due to numerous occlusions of the small leaves this test case poses a challenging task. The rubic sequence of Fig. 13.22b shows a Rubik's cube rotating on a turntable.

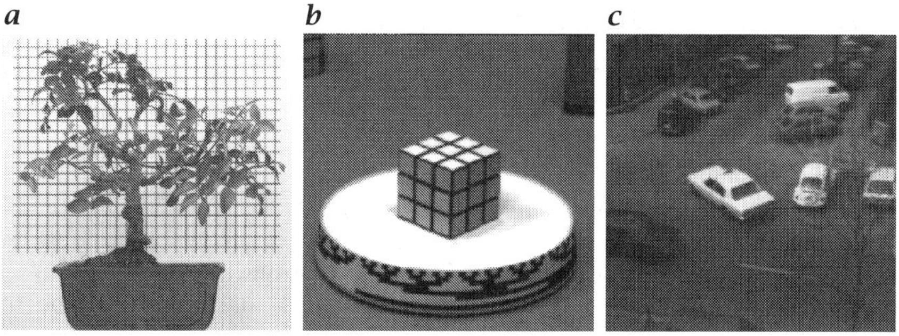

Figure 13.22: *Real test sequences:* ***a*** *bonsai sequence;* ***b*** *Rubic sequence; and* ***c*** *taxi sequence.*

This kind of movement results in a velocity range from 0.2 on the cube to 1.4 pixels/frame on the turntable. Street scenes are one possible application and an example scene is given by the Hamburg Taxi sequence (Fig. 13.22c). Here the taxi turns around the corner with the dark car in the lower left corner driving left to right. Furthermore, there is a moving pedestrian in the upper left corner and a van entering the scene from the right.

13.8.2 Error measures

While there is knowledge of the actual flow fields for the synthetic data, such ground truth is only available for real sequences taken in a controlled laboratory environment. If there is knowledge about the actual flow field $\boldsymbol{f}_a$ we use four measures to describe the deviations between this correct ground truth data and the estimated flow field $\boldsymbol{f}_e$:

Relative error. For errors in the estimated velocity magnitudes we use the relative error:

$$E_r = \frac{\| (\|\boldsymbol{f}_e\| - \|\boldsymbol{f}_a\|) \|}{\|\boldsymbol{f}_a\|} \cdot 100\,[\%] \tag{13.160}$$

This measure is particularly interesting for scientific applications where velocities have to be measured accurately over a sometimes wide range of magnitudes.

Direction error. Not only is the magnitude error of interest but also how well the direction of actual and estimated flow coincides. Thus a directional error in degrees is calculated as follows:

$$E_d = \arccos\left(\frac{\boldsymbol{f}_a^T \boldsymbol{f}_e}{\|\boldsymbol{f}_a\|\;\|\boldsymbol{f}_e\|}\right) \tag{13.161}$$

Angular error. If we consider a displacement vector not as a 2-D quantity but as a normalized 3-D entity $\bar{\boldsymbol{r}} = [r_1, r_2, r_3]^T / \sqrt{r_1^2 + r_2^2 + r_3^2}$ where $\boldsymbol{r}$ and $\boldsymbol{f}$ are related through $\boldsymbol{f} = r^{-3}[r_1, r_2]^T$ (Eq. (13.4)), it is natural to describe an error as an angle in 3D space:

$$E_a = \arccos\left(\bar{\boldsymbol{r}}_a^T \bar{\boldsymbol{r}}_e\right) \tag{13.162}$$

Where $\bar{\boldsymbol{r}}_a$ and $\bar{\boldsymbol{r}}_e$ are the 3-D directions corresponding to $\boldsymbol{f}_a$ and $\boldsymbol{f}_e$, respectively. This measure has the advantage that it combines both directional and magnitude errors simultaneously. Yet some bias is introduced. As shown in Fig. 13.23a, the relation between angular and relative error depends on speed. The angular error reaches a maximum for a given relative error at displacements around 1 pixel/frame. The use of E_a as error measure has also been criticized as symmetric deviations from the actual values do not lead to the same angular errors [8]. This effect can also be seen in Fig. 13.23a; while there is no bias for small displacements, the angular error is clearly higher for underestimated movements with a relative error above 10% and displacements greater than 0.5 pixel/frame.

The relation between directional and angular error with speed is given in Fig. 13.23b. For the same directional error the resulting angular error is significantly higher for larger displacements. Whether there is a positive or negative angle between estimated and actual flow has no influence on the angular error measure.

Bias. To estimate systematic over- or under-estimation a measure of bias is used, see also Section 14.6.1:

$$E_b = \frac{\boldsymbol{f}_a^T(\boldsymbol{f}_a - \boldsymbol{f}_e)}{\|\boldsymbol{f}_a\|} \tag{13.163}$$

This error measure captures the deviation (including sign) between estimated and actual flow in the direction of the actual flow.

The described error measures yield a value at each location where the velocity computation was successful. It is sometimes useful to view the thus-obtained error images in order to detect problematic regions. For comparison purposes, however, it is more convenient to compute an average error and corresponding standard deviation over the entire image. As Bainbridge-Smith and Lane [9] point out, this has the drawback that the mean error is easily dominated by a few large error values. Thus we also report the median error value, which is not sensitive to a few outliers.

For evaluation of the flow fields estimated on real imagery we proceed as follows. Otte's block world sequence was taken under a controlled environment. Thus the actual flow field can be computed from

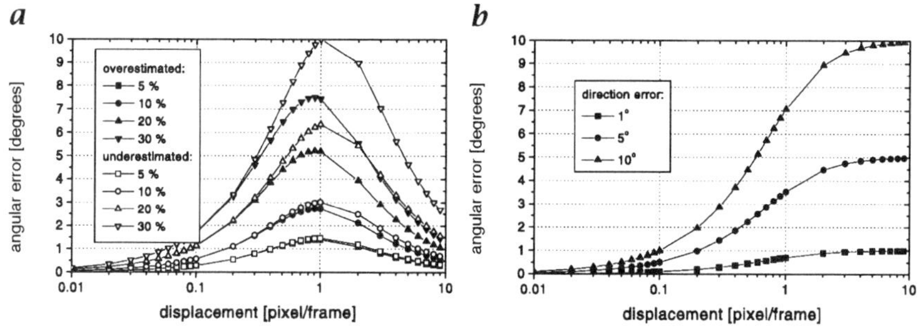

Figure 13.23: *Angular error measure as a function of the displacement:* ***a*** *for different relative errors; and* ***b*** *with varying directional error.*

geometric camera calibration and the errors are computed as already stated. For the remaining real sequences (Fig. 13.22) no ground truth data is available. In order to compare different algorithms on this test data we use an error measure calculated from warping the image, see Chapter 9, for which the flow was computed with the estimated flow field. The difference between a thus-obtained warped image $g'(\boldsymbol{x}) = \mathcal{W}(g(\boldsymbol{x}), \boldsymbol{f}(\boldsymbol{x}))$ and the original image $g(\boldsymbol{x})$ is parameterized by the root mean square error (rms):

$$E_{\mathrm{rms}} = \sqrt{\langle (g(\boldsymbol{x}) - g'(\boldsymbol{x}))^2 \rangle} \tag{13.164}$$

Here $\langle \cdot \rangle$ denotes averaging without windowing, where the averaging in this case is done only on those areas where the optical flow computation was successful. Hence the density of the calculated flow should also be taken into account when algorithms are compared to each other. We thus obtain a scalar quantity parameterizing the difference between original and warped image. This difference stems from both errors in the optical flow estimate and errors introduced through the warping procedure.

Lin and Barron [78] show that E_{rms} and the angular error E_a are well correlated. They compared various forward and backward interpolation schemes and conclude that backward bicubic spline interpolation with smoothed flow fields is one of the best methods. For the experiments reported in what follows, the 2-D binomial operator of 8th order $\mathcal{B}_{xy}^8$ is used to smooth the calculated flow fields.

This kind of error measure does have a significant drawback in that different absolute errors will result in different error values depending on the image content. Small displacement deviations lead to larger gray-value differences in areas with a high spatial gradient. To moderate this effect the difference between the two images is weighted by the magnitude of the spatial gradient. This leads to a normalized rms error measure:

$$E_{\mathrm{nrms}} = \sqrt{\left\langle \frac{(g(\boldsymbol{x}) - g'(\boldsymbol{x}))^2}{||\nabla g||^2} \right\rangle} \tag{13.165}$$

Again averaging is done only over pixels where the flow computation succeeded.

13.8.3 Comparison of methods and parameters

For an overview the following algorithms are used with the specific parameters stated here. Apart from the structure tensor the implementation uses the code provided by Barron et al. [6]; the choice of parameters is also strongly guided by theirs. In particular the amount of presmoothing and the filter kernels are similarly chosen. Unless otherwise stated, differentiation is done via four-point differences using the mask: $1/12\,[-1, 8, 0, -8, 1]$. Doing so, the differences between the various approaches are not obscured by the numerical accuracy of various differentiation kernels.

However, it is not obvious how a choice of filter kernel and the mask size used for matching are correlated. As all generated test sequences show homogeneous translational movement, increasing filter support and matching mask size yield better results. However, this is not usually the case in real applications and the choices used here are a common trade-off between necessary filter support and averaging over too large areas. In a certain application other choices of parameters will most likely yield better results. Here the intention is to compare some methods on common test data, not to fine-tune each method.

Differential techniques. For a detailed description of differential techniques see Section 13.3.1.

Local least squares (**lucas**, `/software/13/lucas`) as introduced by Lucas and Kanade [19] is used on images presmoothed with a Gaussian of standard deviation 1.5 pixel sampled to three standard deviations. To distinguish between normal and 2-D flow a threshold on the lower eigenvalue of 1.0 is used; see also Section 13.7.2.

Second-order optical flow (**uras**) is computed following Uras et al. [31]. Images are presmoothed with a spatial Gaussian of standard deviation 3.0 and a temporal Gaussian of standard deviation 1.5 pixel. A threshold of 1.0 on the spatial curvature, that is, the determinant of the Hessian matrix Eq. (13.27), is used to exclude unreliable measurements.

The global smoothness constraint Eq. (13.33) described by Horn and Schunk [10] (**horn**, `/software/13/horn`) is used with the influence parameter in Eq. (13.31) chosen to be $\lambda = 0.5$. Presmoothing is done by a Gaussian with spatiotemporal standard deviation of 1.5 pixel and maximal 100 iterations are run. This iteration is performed only on locations

where the spatial gradient exceeds a value of 5.0.
Oriented smoothness (**nagel**) as another global constraint method ([29]) is used with the parameter δ in Eq. (13.35) controlling the influence of the oriented smoothness term set to $\delta = 1.0$. Presmoothing and thresholding of the spatial gradient is done identically to the global regularization described previously. The number of iterations is also fixed to 100.

Tensor-based technique (tensor). The method is described in detail in Section 13.3.2 ([see also 44], `/software/13/tensor`). Instead of a sampled Gaussian a binomial operator is used for presmoothing, in particular we use the 8th-order operator $\mathcal{B}^8_{xyt}$. Averaging in the tensor itself (Eq. (13.44)) is done via a 4th-order binomial. Only pixels where the trace of the tensor exceeds 25 and the coherence measure Eq. (13.64) is above 0.9 are used.

Phase-based method (fleet). The algorithm developed by Fleet and Jepson [20], outlined in Section 13.4.3 is used as an example phase-based optical flow estimator. Again, spatiotemporal presmoothing with a Gaussian of standard deviation 1.5 pixel is done prior to any subsequent processing (2.5 pixel yields better results but needs more temporal support). A linear velocity model is fitted in a 5×5 window to the calculated component velocities Eq. (13.102) using a standard least squares technique. The thus-obtained 2-D estimates are only accepted if the condition number of the linear equation system is less than 10.0 and the residual error of the fit remains below 0.5.

Correlation techniques. Both matching techniques considered here use the sum-of-squared-differences (SSD) Eq. (13.110) as distance measure, see Section 13.5.2. Anandan [63] (**anandan**) employs a coarse-to-fine strategy on the Laplacian pyramid where we use four levels for the reported results. The relaxation to search for the minimum of the SSD is done on a 5×5 correlation window with 15 iterations.
Second, we use the method reported by Singh [64] (**singh**). The first SSD as defined in Eq. (13.111) is computed with a window size of 5×5. The center of mass for the probability response Eq. (13.112) is then computed from Eq. (13.113) on a 5×5 search window.

13.8.4 Results from generated synthetic data

We first report the results on the image sequences shown in Fig. 13.22, where we vary speed, direction, and artificial noise added to the images.

Total least squares vs least squares. Figure 13.24 shows a comparison of the least squares approach of Lucas and Kanade [19] and the total least squares (structure tensor) technique operating on the noise

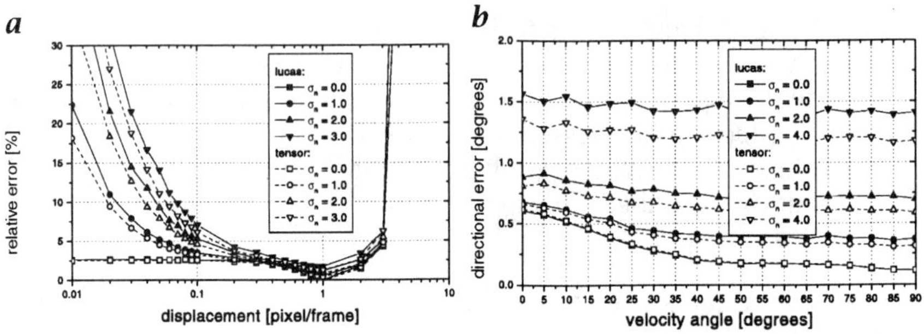

*Figure 13.24: Comparison of total least squares and least squares on the noise sequence: **a** relative error dependent on speed and noise; and **b** directional error dependent on direction and noise (displacement magnitude fixed at 0.4 pixel/frame).*

sequence (Fig. 13.22a). Without additional noise both perform equally well. When adding noise of increasing standard deviation to the images the total least squares method turns out to be more robust. Mainly for small displacements (< 0.1 pixel/frame), the relative error increases slightly less for the total least squares approach. However, the benefit of using total least squares becomes more evident for the directional error as shown in Fig. 13.24b, where a relatively larger displacement of 0.4 pixel/frame is used. In this case differentiation for both methods is done via the isotropy-optimized Sobel filter, see Section 13.3.4.

Errors in dependence of the velocity magnitude. Figure 13.25 shows the performance of the various approaches with increasing speed on the sinusoidal, Gaussian, and grid test patterns (Fig. 13.18b,c,d). No results for the phase-based method by Fleet are given, because it does not yield flow fields on these test images with the specified parameters. While both first- and second-order differential techniques yield good results for subpixel displacements, this is not the case for the matching methods (singh, anandan). With velocities closer to the temporal sampling limit the differential methods quickly degrade while the matching methods still recover the motion approximately. In particular, Singh's method captures integer pixel displacements accurately, the decrease in accuracy for movements exceeding 4 pixel/frame is due to the implementation where an upper limit on the displacement of 4 pixels is set within the matching procedure.

The results on the moving Gaussian (Fig. 13.25b) further indicates the usefulness of measures to distinguish between 2-D and normal flow. In particular the global smoothness methods (horn, nagel) integrate the unreliable velocity estimates from the low contrast outer regions, which reduces overall accuracy. This also accounts for the large errors for the second-order technique (uras), not reported in Fig. 13.25b, when no

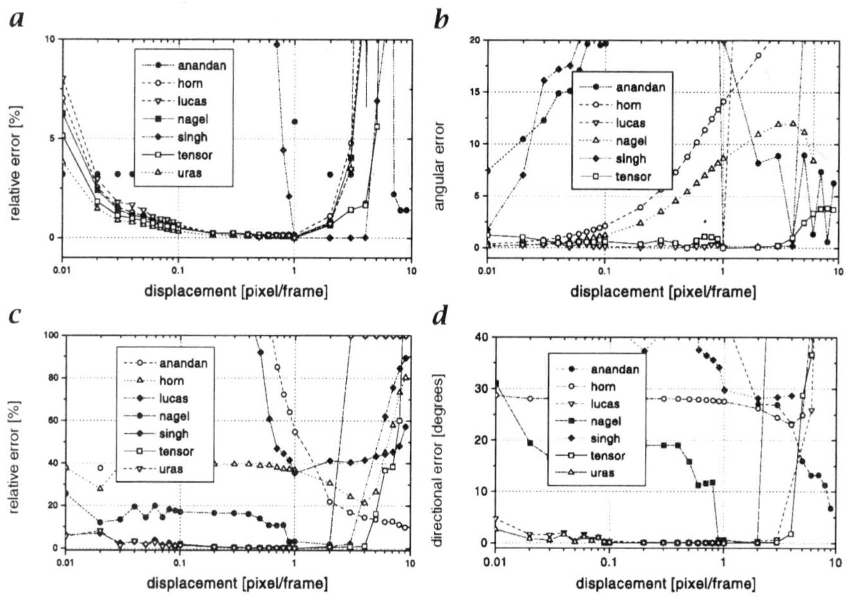

Figure 13.25: *Error in dependence of the velocity magnitude:* ***a*** *relative error for the sinusoidal;* ***b*** *angular error for the Gaussian;* ***c*** *relative error for the translating grid; and* ***d*** *directional error for the translating grid.*

threshold on the curvature is set. Applying a threshold of 1.0 as in the other examples leaves no areas where the flow is computed.

On the grid sequence similar effects can be observed. The matching techniques are unable to capture subpixel motion; however, they perform better for integral pixel displacements than the differential methods. Nonlocal methods (horn, nagel) have no means to decide if 2-D or normal velocities are computed. This leads to large differences between estimated and actual flow fields in this case, as the lines between the crossings suffer from the aperture problem. This is especially problematic in the auter regions where no crossing is close enough to be integrated. The resulting flow fields then show the normal flow as becomes evident from Fig. 13.26. Figure 13.25c also shows how a threshold on the gradient enables a selection of more reliable flow estimates.

Errors in dependence of the direction of the motion. Figure 13.27 shows the performance of the various approaches with changing direction of the moving sinusoidal test pattern, where the magnitude of the movement is set to 1 pixel/frame. It is remarkable that all methods show no dependence on the direction of movement apart from the fact that all yield best results in x- and y-direction. In this case the

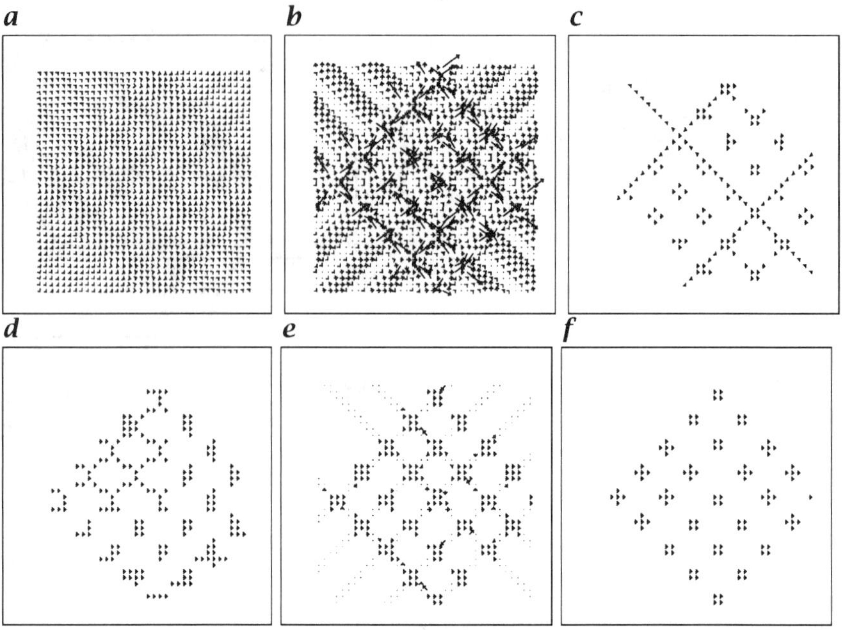

Figure 13.26: *Estimated flow fields on the translating grid sequence for a displacement of 0.6 pixel/frame:* ***a*** *nagel;* ***b*** *singh;* ***c*** *horn;* ***d*** *uras;* ***e*** *tensor; and* ***f*** *lucas.*

second-order method by Uras et al. [31] performs best, as will be seen in due course; this can be attributed to the nature of the test case. To be specific we have pure translational motion where the assumption of gradient conservation holds (Eq. (13.24)).

Errors in dependence of additional noise. To analyze the robustness of various algorithms with respect to additional noise in the images, white Gaussian noise of increasing standard deviation σ_n is added to the sinusoidal test pattern. The movement occurred with velocity $\boldsymbol{u} = \{0.47, 0.88\}$ pixel/frame. The relative and directional errors are shown in Fig. 13.28. All methods show nearly the same accuracy decline, which is quite large between no noise and noise of standard deviation 2 (note the logarithmic scale in Fig. 13.28). As noted before the phase-based method does not yield velocity estimates on this sequence for sensible threshold values; lowering these thresholds obviously forces the method to produce some flow fields. The result is reported in Fig. 13.28 with a significant performance penalty.

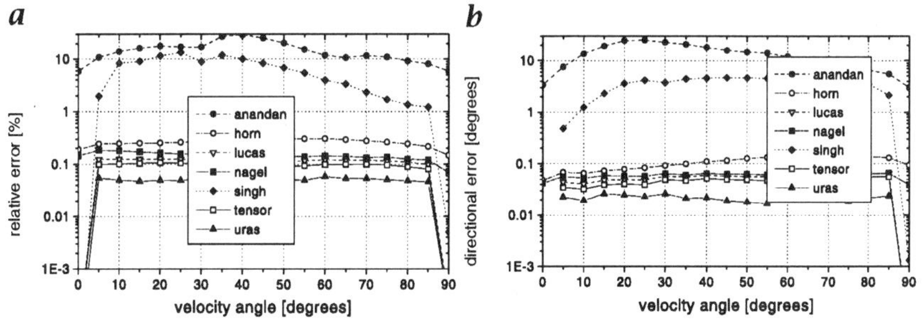

Figure 13.27: *Error in dependence of the velocity direction for the moving sinusoidal pattern:* ***a*** *relative error; and* ***b*** *directional error.*

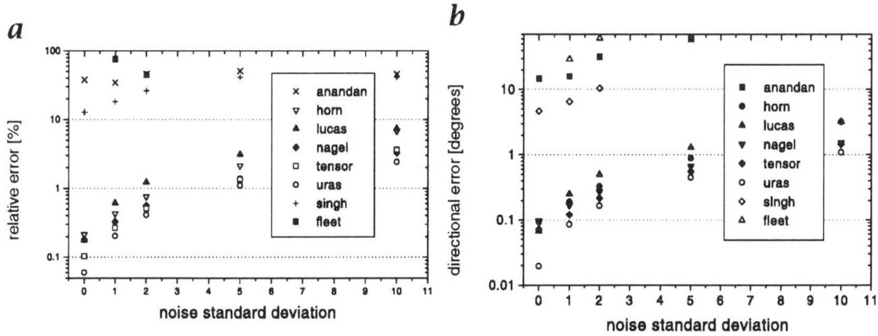

Figure 13.28: *Error in dependence of additional noise for the sinusoidal test pattern:* ***a*** *relative error; and* ***b*** *directional error.*

13.8.5 Results from realistic textures

Results on the translating and diverging tree and Yosemite sequences are given in Tables 13.2–13.4.

For the translating tree sequence (Fig. 13.19b) we obtain a similar result to that reported in the preceding, considering the fact that the motion is translational with a displacement close to 2 pixel/frame. Thus it is no surprise that the matching techniques (Anandan, Singh) also provide relatively good estimates. As before, the differential techniques give best estimates, yet it has to be pointed out that they yield only approximately half the density of the matching techniques. As differential methods reject any flow calculation on the homogeneous background their superiority can in this case be attributed to their ability to reject unreliable estimates. Interestingly, a simple threshold on the gradient magnitude, as done for the global smoothness constraint method (horn), is sufficient here. Doing so for the oriented smoothness method (nagel) also boosts the performance of this method significantly as reported by Barron et al. [6].

Table 13.2: *Results on the translating tree sequence; the values in parentheses are the median errors*

	E_r	E_d	E_a	E_b
A (100%)	7.8(6.4)±6.0	3.6(2.8)±3.1	4.1(3.6)±2.6	-0.02(-0.03)±0.19
S (100%)	3.8(2.7)±3.6	0.6(0.4)±3.9	1.2(0.8)±2.6	-0.02(0.00)±0.12
F (17.4%)	3.9(1.1)±11.1	3.0(0.3)±11.8	3.0(0.3)±10.5	0.06(-0.01)±0.30
U (38.2%)	0.9(0.7)±0.7	0.4(0.3)±0.4	0.5(0.4)±0.3	0.00(0.00)±0.02
N (100%)	7.1(2.8)±10.9	2.1(1.1)±2.8	3.1(1.5)±4.5	0.12(0.04)±0.24
L (46.0%)	1.4(1.0)±1.5	0.6(0.3)±0.7	0.6(0.4)±0.7	0.00(0.00)±0.04
H (53.2%)	4.3(1.9)±6.6	1.4(0.8)±2.0	1.9(1.0)±2.4	0.07(0.03)±0.14
T (69.8%)	1.4(1.1)±1.4	0.5(0.2)±0.7	0.6(0.4)±0.7	-0.02(-0.02)±0.03

Table 13.3: *Results on the diverging tree sequence; the values in parentheses are the median errors*

	E_r	E_d	E_a	E_b
A (100%)	28.9(18.0)±78.2	17.6(9.9)±16.2	10.0(8.9)±6.0	-0.01(-0.01)±0.19
S (100%)	26.2(20.0)±30.3	16.4(11.2)±18.5	10.2(8.9)±6.6	-0.02(-0.04)±0.18
F (32.2%)	3.1(1.5)±6.0	2.3(1.1)±4.5	1.4(0.9)±1.6	0.00(0.00)±0.04
U (53.0%)	8.9(6.8)±8.7	5.4(4.0)±6.4	3.8(3.5)±2.1	0.00(0.00)±0.07
N (100%)	7.4(4.1)±17.0	4.6(2.3)±9.1	2.8(1.9)±3.2	0.02(0.01)±0.09
L (54.4%)	5.5(2.9)±13.2	3.6(1.6)±8.9	2.0(1.5)±2.0	0.00(0.00)±0.04
H (53.5%)	5.5(2.6)±13.3	3.8(1.9)±8.5	2.2(1.5)±2.3	0.02(0.01)±0.06
T (59.8%)	5.4(2.6)±13.9	3.6(1.7)±7.6	2.1(1.5)±2.1	0.00(0.00)±0.04

Again the second-order method (uras) gives excellent results, even though with slightly less density than the other differential methods (lucas, tensor). Phase-based motion estimation (fleet) also yields good flow fields, even though at a smaller density. This can be seen as a general feature of this method: good but very sparse estimation.

Another interesting point to note is the large difference between mean and median error measures both for the phase-based (F), oriented smoothness (N) and global smoothness (H) methods. This suggests that they could yield better results if either a better, or just some way at all, could be found to remove unreliable estimates. Looking at the bias E_b it is noticeable that the same methods show some bias towards overestimating, which again is not the case for the median values.

For the diverging tree sequence (Fig. 13.19c) the situation presents itself a bit differently. Due to the divergent flow field the movements in the image center are far smaller than in the outer regions. As a result all

Table 13.4: Results on the Yosemite Sequence. The values in brackets are the median errors.

	E_r	E_d	E_a	E_b
A (100%)	42.9(25.6)±70.6	26.4(10.8)±37.7	19.7(12.9)±21.7	0.11(-0.06)±1.06
S (100%)	25.6(15.0)±27.7	15.8(6.3)±28.8	11.5(7.5)±15.0	0.17(0.04)±0.54
F (30.6%)	9.4(3.5)±17.3	8.3(1.8)±26.8	5.3(1.4)±14.3	0.10(-0.04)±0.47
U (14.5%)	14.1(6.9)±36.0	12.0(2.9)±33.4	7.6(2.6)±19.6	0.14(0.01)±0.57
N (92.2%)	27.4(13.0)±48.8	14.1(6.1)±22.6	12.7(6.2)±16.7	0.13(0.05)±0.91
L (39.8%)	9.4(4.1)±19.8	6.8(1.8)±22.6	4.5(1.8)±12.2	0.06(0.00)±0.37
H (32.9%)	11.7(5.2)±22.3	8.2(2.6)±23.3	5.5(2.0)±11.3	0.12(0.01)±0.37
T (62.2%)	27.4(5.4)±62.3	7.9(2.2)±20.1	7.4(2.2)±13.3	-0.26(-0.01)±1.22
T_2 (38.0%)	18.8(3.7)±48.7	4.6(1.7)±8.4	4.9(1.6)±8.4	-0.20(-0.02)±0.86

of the compared methods yield less accurate flow fields. In particular the matching methods (A, S) yield far worse results, as they can not reliably determine subpixel displacements.

Best results on this sequence are obtained with the phase-based method (F). Yet again only a smaller subset of the images is used, in particular the more difficult inner regions are omitted.

As already mentioned, the second-order differential method (U) yields less accurate flow fields in this case as the underlying assumption of gradient conservation does not hold any more. Interestingly, the density of the calculated flow is higher on the diverging than on the translating tree sequence for this method. Warping with a divergent flow field introduces some additional curvature into the image.

The global oriented smoothness (N) method also yields excellent results on the diverging tree sequence, taking into account that a 100% dense flow field is computed. The other differential methods (L,H,T) all yield almost identical error and density values.

Table 13.4 gives the results on the Yosemite sequence (Fig. 13.20). Here we observe relatively poor performance of all investigated algorithms, which may in part be attributed to the amount of temporal aliasing present in the sequence. Another difficulty with this sequence is the sky-mountain boundary, which introduces errors if averaged across.

In order to analyze the reasons why the various methods fail we show some of the relative error maps in Fig. 13.29. As mentioned here, the matching techniques are typically more robust to temporal aliasing; however, there are also large areas with slow dilational motion, which causes these methods to fail (Fig. 13.29). In particular, Singh's method accurately captures the motion, of the clouds where there is severe temporal aliasing. The fractal-based clouds do also change their shape

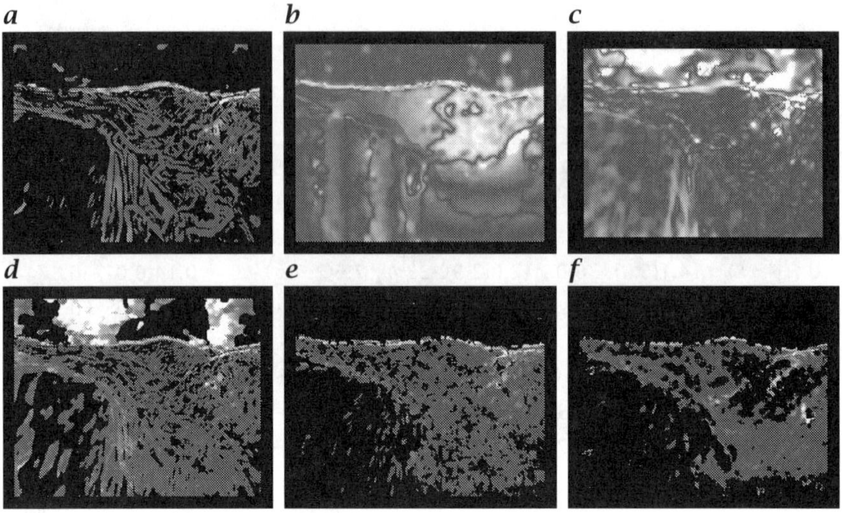

Figure 13.29: *Relative error on the Yosemite sequence, the error range* $\{0, 100\}[\%]$ *is mapped to the gray-value range* $\{100, 255\}$. *Areas where no velocity was computed are left black:* ***a*** *horn;* ***b*** *singh;* ***c*** *nagel;* ***d*** *tensor;* ***e*** *lucas; and* ***f*** *fleet.*

as they move, thus the rigidity assumption underlying all presented methods is violated. Under such circumstances matching methods are superior to differential approaches. As can be seen from Fig. 13.29c,d it is the sky where both the oriented smoothness (nagel) and the structure tensor produce erroneous flow fields. This also reflects itself in the median errors for these two methods.

On the Yosemite sequence the least squares method (lucas) and the phase-based method (fleet) perform best. This is due mainly to the fact that they manage to detect critical areas and, accordingly, exclude them from the flow computation (Fig. 13.29e,f). On this sequence the tensor method can also be made more accurate by rejecting regions without apparent linear motion (see Eq. (13.63). The results when requiring all eigenvalues to be greater than 0.03 are reported as T_2 in Table 13.4.

Image sequences, such as the Yosemite sequence, require a coarse-to-fine strategy if dense flow fields are to be computed reliably. Such a multiscale extension of the least squares approach is presented in Chapter 14.

Real image data. Error measures on the calibrated sequence of Fig. 13.21 are given in Table 13.5. The overall picture does not change, the differential techniques clearly outperform the matching techniques. This is not only due to the forced 100% density of the matching approaches as a comparison with the oriented smoothness method (N)

Table 13.5: *Results on Otte's block world (for image 34); the values in parentheses are the median errors*

	E_r	E_d	E_a	E_b
A (100%)	25.3(16.4)±30.5	17.8(11.2)±21.5	14.4(11.5)±11.6	0.05(0.04)±0.37
S (100%)	21.6(13.3)±26.8	20.0(11.9)±29.2	14.9(10.9)±14.3	0.12(0.06)±0.40
U (33.6%)	4.2(2.2)±12.5	4.4(4.0)±5.0	3.6(3.1)±3.6	-0.01(-0.01)±0.12
N (96.2%)	16.1(7.2)±34.1	8.2(4.7)±13.0	7.5(4.4)±8.9	0.01(-0.01)±0.33
L (54.3%)	6.8(3.1)±16.8	4.9(4.1)±5.8	4.2(3.4)±4.4	0.01(0.00)±0.17
H (46.0%)	7.6(3.7)±17.5	4.7(4.1)±4.5	4.4(3.4)±42	0.00(0.00)±0.17
T (60.7%)	10.8(4.5)±43.2	5.6(3.6)±4.0	4.9(3.1)±7.4	-0.05(-0.06)±0.38

shows. The actual motion (Fig. 13.21b) is mainly translational, which favors the second-order technique (U) as already stated here.

The overall performance across the various methods is not very good on this test sequence. However, this is due mainly to occlusion as opposed to temporal aliasing as encountered in the Yosemite sequence. Thus we conclude that the investigated methods would need to be extended to account for occlusion if such is present in the image data under consideration.

From the flow fields calculated on the uncalibrated real image sequences of Fig. 13.22 the root mean square error E_{rms} (Eq. (13.164)) takes the following values:

	A	S	F	U	N	L	H	T
bonsai	5.6	5.6	13.8	8.8	8.7	6.7	7.0	8.1
rubic	8.6	5.9	14.0	10.6	6.2	12.0	9.7	10.8
taxi	8.7	7.8	11.5	17.5	8.1	12.4	14.7	14.9

In comparison the normalized root mean square errors E_{nrms} (Eq. (13.165)) are found to be:

	A	S	F	U	N	L	H	T
bonsai	1.03	1.03	1.30	0.91	1.50	0.82	0.69	1.25
rubic	1.48	1.43	0.53	0.78	1.42	0.60	0.42	0.53
taxi	2.23	2.13	0.88	1.40	2.03	1.03	1.15	1.44

If we compare both error measures it becomes apparent that the oriented smoothness method (nagel) makes fewer errors in regions with higher gradient, in particular, at occlusion boundaries. Obviously this was the reason to introduce the orientation term in the first place.

Apparently the phase-based method (F) also has lower normalized error measures in comparison to the other methods. However, this

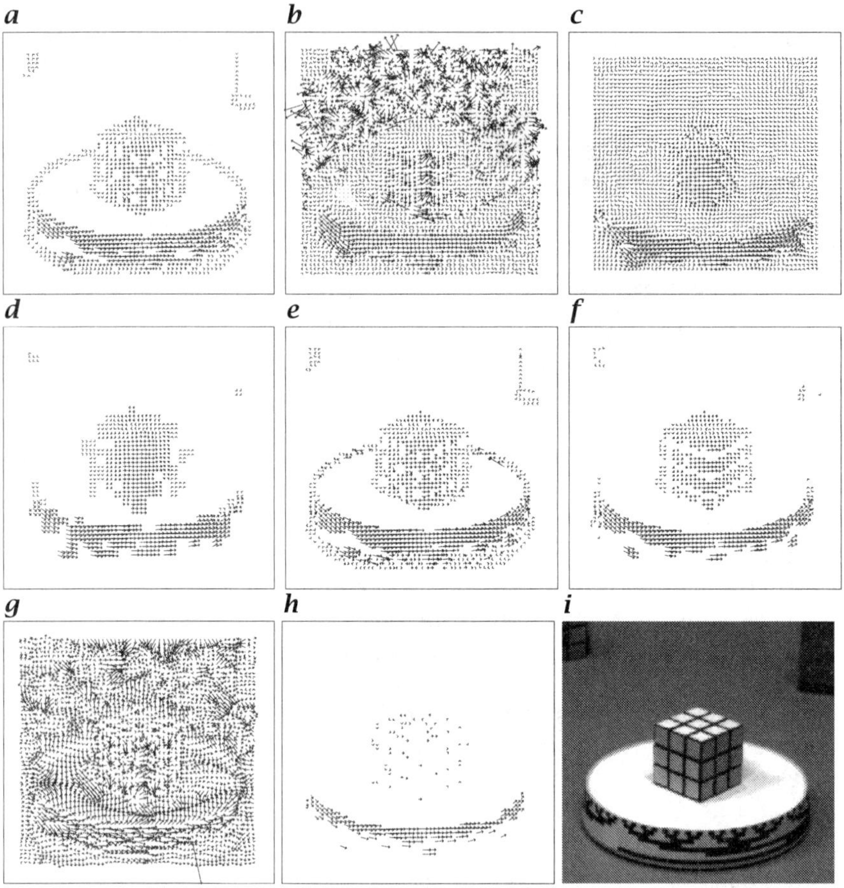

Figure 13.30: *Estimated flow fields on the rubic sequence:* ***a*** *horn;* ***b*** *singh;* ***c*** *nagel;* ***d*** *uras;* ***e*** *tensor;* ***f*** *lucas;* ***g*** *anandan;* ***h*** *fleet; and* ***i*** *original image.*

stems from the fact that here velocities are only computed at locations with high spatial gradient in the first place. Considering the density of the computed flow fields makes this method seem much less attractive. The percentages of the images for which the flow is calculated are:

	A	S	F	U	N	L	H	T
bonsai	100%	100%	2.2%	38.4%	100%	100%	64.4%	69.1%
rubic	100%	100%	6.9%	26.5%	100%	20.8%	31.5%	32.3%
taxi	100%	100%	11.8%	16.1%	100%	25.5%	23.2%	25.7%

In general the performance characteristics remain the same as in the preceding with the differential techniques providing the best trade-off between accuracy and density of the calculated flow fields. This also becomes evident when looking at the flow fields derived from the rotating Rubic's cube sequence as shown in Fig. 13.30. Obviously the forementioned absence of a means to distinguish reliable from unreliable flow results in large errors on the background. Another point worth noting is the similar structure of the flow computed at the frontal edge of the cube for the oriented smoothness and the second-order method (Fig. 13.30c,d). This can be attributed to the assumption of gradient conservation common to both methods. For rotational motion as is the case here this assumption is not valid and as a result the flow fields are smoothed out.

Figure 13.30b,d also shows a common problem that is encountered when matching techniques are used on areas with an aperture problem. Looking at the frontal edge of the cube, both methods seem to produce flow vectors almost at random. This may be attributed to the elongated minimum of the distance measure at this location. Within this minimum one location is chosen and most of the time this choice does not correspond to the normal flow that is computed by the differential methods in this case.

13.8.6 Summary

In general, good results on realistic data are not to be expected without a means to remove unreliable estimates. Depending on the image content, some way to distinguish normal from 2-D flow is essential for accurate motion estimation. Obviously, in cases without an aperture problem, such as the sinusoidal or noise test patterns, such a distinction is unnecessary.

In summary we found that the differential techniques give the best overall performance with respect to both accuracy and density. If a distinction between normal and 2-D flow has to be made, the local and total least squares approaches [19, 44] are clearly favored. It seems that the theoretical advantages of the total vs local least squares algorithm only becomes apparent for low signal-to-noise ratios and small displacements.

The second-order differential method by Uras et al. [31] performs very well for pure translational motion over all velocities up to the temporal sampling limit and regardless of the movement direction. However, for other types of motion, such as divergence or rotation, this method should not be used.

The phase-based method by Fleet and Jepson [20] provides accurate but rather sparse velocity fields. And the computational load for this method is far higher than for the other compared techniques.

Matching techniques are only useful for larger displacements, in particular for integer pixel displacements. However, in this case a differential multiscale approach as described in the next chapter might still be the better choice. Between the two compared matching techniques the method by Singh [64] was found to give more reliable results.

13.9 References

[1] Gibson, J. J., (1950). *The Perception of the Visual World.* New York: Houghton Mifflin.

[2] Horn, B. K. P., (1987). Motion fields are hardly ever ambiguous. *Int. J. of Computer Vision,* **1**:259–274.

[3] Horn, B. K., (1986). *Robot vision.* Cambridge, MA: MIT Press.

[4] Verri, A. and Poggio, T., (1987). Against quantitative optical flow. In *Proceedings ICCV'87, London,* pp. 171–180, IEEE. Washington, DC: Los Alamitos, CA: IEEE Computer Society Press.

[5] Verri, A. and Poggio, T., (1989). Motion field and optical flow: qualitative properties. *IEEE Trans. PAMI,* **11(5)**:490–498.

[6] Barron, J. L., Fleet, D. J., and Beauchemin, S. S., (1994). Performance of optical flow techniques. *Intern. J. Comput. Vis.,* **12(1)**:43–77.

[7] Barron, J. L., Fleet, D. J., Beauchemin, S. S., and Burkitt, T., (1992). Performance of optical flow techniques. In *Proc. Conf. Comp. Vis. Patt. Recogn., Champaign,* pp. 236–242.

[8] Otte, M. and Nagel, H.-H., (1994). Optical flow estimation: advances and comparisons. In *Computer Vision—ECCV '94,* J.-O. Eklundh, ed., pp. 51–60. Springer.

[9] Bainbridge-Smith, A. and Lane, R. G., (1997). Determining optical flow using a differential method. *Image and Vision Computing,* **15**:11–22.

[10] Horn, B. K. P. and Schunk, B. G., (1981). Determining optical flow. *Artificial Intelligence,* **17**:185–204.

[11] Jepson, A. and Black, M. J., (1993). Mixture models for optical flow computation. In *Proc. Computer Vision and Pattern Recognition, CVPR '93,* pp. 760–761. New York.

[12] Black, M. J. and Anandan, P., (1996). The robust estimation of multiple motions: parametric and piecewise-smooth flow fields. *Computer Vision and Image Understanding,* **63(1)**:75–104.

[13] Jähne, B., (1997). *Digital Image Processing-Concepts, Algorithms, and Scientific Applications, 4th edition.* New York: Springer.

[14] Bracewell, R., (1986). *The Fourier Transform and its Applications,* 2nd revised edition. New York: McGraw-Hill.

[15] McKee, S. P. and Wataminuk, S. N. J., (1994). The psychophysics of motion perception. In *Visual Detection of Motion,* A. T. Smith and R. J. Snowden, eds. Boston: Academic Press.

[16] Morgan, M. J., (1992). Spatial filtering precedes motion detection. *Nature,* **335**:344–346.

[17] Murray, B. F., D. W. Buxton, (1990). *Experiments in the Machine Interpretation of Visual Motion.* Cambridge, MA: MIT Press.

[18] Shi, J. and Tomasi, C., (1994). Good features to track. In *Proc. Conf. Comput. Vis. Patt. Recog.*, pp. 593–600. Seattle, Washington: IEEE Computer Society Press.

[19] Lucas, B. and Kanade, T., (1981). An iterative image registration technique with an application to stereo vision. In *DARPA Image Understanding Workshop*, pp. 121–130.

[20] Fleet, D. J. and Jepson, A. D., (1990). Computation of component image velocity from local phase information. *Intern. J. Comput. Vis.*, **5**:77–104.

[21] Jähne, B., (1993). *Spatio-temporal image processing.* Berlin: Springer.

[22] Jähne, B., Haussecker, H., Spies, H., Schmundt, D., and Schurr, U., (1998). Study of dynamical processes with tensor-based spatiotemporal image processing techniques. In *Computer Vision - ECCV '98.* Springer-Verlag, in press.

[23] Hering, F., Haussecker, H., Dieter, J., Netzsch, T., and Jähne, B., (1997). A comprehensive study of algorithms for multi-dimensional flow field diagnostics. In *Proc. ISPRS Intercommision V/III Symposium.* Zurich, Switzerland.

[24] Adelson, E. H. and Bergen, J. R., (1986). The extraction of spatiotemporal energy in human and machine vision. In *Proc. IEEE Workshop on Visual Motion*, pp. 151–156. Charleston.

[25] Kearney, J. K., Thompson, W. B., and Boley, D. L., (1987). Optical flow estimation: an error analysis of gradient-based methods with local optimization. *IEEE Trans. PAMI*, **9(2)**:229–244.

[26] Simoncelli, E. P., Adelson, E. H., and Heeger, D. J., (1991). Probability distributions of optical flow. In *Proc. Conf. Comput. Vis. Patt. Recog.*, pp. 310–315. Maui.

[27] Simoncelli, E. P., (1993). *Distributed Representation and Analysis of Visual Motion.* Dissertation, MIT.

[28] Press, W. H., Teukolsky, S. A., Vetterling, W., and Flannery, B., (1992). *Numerical Recipes in C: The Art of Scientific Computing.* New York: Cambridge University Press.

[29] Nagel, H., (1983). Displacement vectors derived from second-order intensity variations in image sequences. *Computer Vision, Graphics, and Image Processing (GVGIP)*, **21**:85–117.

[30] Tretiak, O. and Pastor, L., (1984). Velocity estimation from image sequences with second order differential operators. In *Proc. 7th Intern. Conf. Patt. Recogn., Montreal*, pp. 20–22.

[31] Uras, S., Girosi, F., Verri, A., and Torre, V., (1988). A computational approach to motion perception. *Biol. Cybern.*, **60**:79–97.

[32] Press, W. H., Vetterling, W. T., Teukolsky, S. A., and Flannery, B. P., (1994). *Numerical Recipes in C - The Art of Scientific Computing*, Second edition. Cambridge University Press.

[33] Nagel, H., (1986). Image sequences – ten (octal) years – from phenomenology towards a theoretical foundation. In *Proc. Int. Conf. Patt. Recogn., Paris 1986*, pp. 1174–1185. Washington: IEEE Computer Society Press.

[34] Nagel, H.-H., (1987). On the estimation of optical flow: relations between different approaches and some new results. *Artificial Intelligence*, **33**: 299–324.

[35] Hildreth, E. C., (1984). Computations underlying the measurement of visual motion. *Artificial Intelligence*, **23**:309–354.

[36] Hildreth, E. C., (1984). The computation of the velocity field. *Proc. Royal Soc. Lond.*, **B 221**:189–220.

[37] Golub, G. H. and Van Loan, C. F., (1989). *Matrix Computations*, second edition edition. Baltimore and London: The Johns Hopkins University Press.

[38] Bigün, J. and Granlund, G. H., (1987). Optimal orientation detection of linear symmetry. In *Proceedings ICCV'87, London 1987*, pp. 433–438, IEEE. Washington, DC: IEEE Computer Society Press.

[39] Kass, M. and Witkin, A., (1987). Analyzing oriented patterns. *Comp. Vision Graphics and Image Proc.*, **37**:362–385.

[40] Knutsson, H., (1982). *Filtering and Reconstruction in Image Processing.* Diss., Linköping Univ.

[41] Knutsson, H., (1998). Representing local structure using tensors. In *Proc. 6th Scandinavian Conf. on Image Analysis, Oulu, Finland*, pp. 244–251. Springer-Verlag.

[42] Granlund, G. H. and Knutsson, H., (1995). *Signal Processing for Computer Vision.* Kluwer.

[43] Bigün, J., Granlund, G. H., and Wiklund, J., (1991). Multidimensional orientation estimation with application to texture analysis and optical flow. *IEEE Trans. PAMI*, **13(8)**:775–790.

[44] Haussecker, H. and Jähne, B., (1997). A Tensor approach for precise computation of dense displacement vector fields. In *Mustererkennung 1997*, F. Wahl and E. Paulus, eds., pp. 199–208. Springer-Verlag.

[45] Haussecker, H., Spies, H., and Jähne, B., (1998). Tensor-based image sequence processing techniques for the study of dynamical processes. In *Proc. Intern. Symp. On Real-time Imaging and Dynamic Analysis*, Vol. 32(5), pp. 704–711. Hakodate, Japan: International Society of Photogrammetry and Remote Sensing, ISPRS, Commision V.

[46] Nagel, H.-H. and Gehrke, A., (1998). Spatiotemporal adaptive estimation and segmentation of OF-fields. In *Proc. Computer Vision - ECCV '98*, pp. 87–102. Lecture Notes in Computer Science, Springer-Verlag.

[47] Van Huffel, S. and Vandewalle, J., (1991). *The Total Least Squares Problem, Computational Aspects and Analysis.* Philadelphia: Society for Industrial and Applied Mathematics, SIAM.

[48] Späth, (1982). On discrete linear orthogonal L_p-approximation. *Z. Angew. Math. Mech.*, **62**:354–355.

[49] Watson, G. A., (1982). Numerical methods for linear orthogonal L_p approximation. *IMA J. Numer. Anal.*, **2**:221–237.

[50] Duc, B., (1997). *Feature Design: Applications to Motion Analysis and Identity Verification.* Dissertation, École Polytechnique Fédérale de Lausanne.

[51] Mühlich, M. and Mester, R., (1998). The role of total least squares in motion analysis. In *Proc. Computer Vision - ECCV '98*, pp. 305–321. Lecture Notes in Computer Science, Springer-Verlag.

[52] Srinivasan, S. and Chellappa, R., (1998). Optical flow using overlapped basis functions for solving global motion problems. In *Proc. Computer Vision - ECCV '98*, pp. 289–304. Lecture Notes in Computer Science, Springer-Verlag.

[53] Scharr, H., Körkel, S., and Jähne, B., (1997). Numerische Isotropieoptimierung von FIR-Filtern mittels Querglättung. In *Mustererkennung 1997*, F. Wahl and E. Paulus, eds., pp. 199–208. Springer-Verlag.

[54] Adelson, E. H. and Bergen, J. R., (1985). Spatio-temporal energy models for the perception of motion. *Jour. Opt. Soc. Am. A*, **2**:284–299.

[55] Heeger, D. J., (1987). Model for the extraction of image flow. *J. Opt. Soc. Am. A*, **4**:1455–1471.

[56] Heeger, D. J., (1988). Optical flow from spatiotemporal filters. *Int. J. Comp. Vis.*, **1**:279–302.

[57] Daugman, J. G., (1985). Uncertainty relation for resolution in space, spatial frequency, and orientation optimized by two-dimensional visual cortex filters. *J. Opt. Soc. Am. A*, **2(7)**:1160–1169.

[58] Gabor, D., (1941). Theory of communication. *J. IEE*, **93**:492–457.

[59] Knutsson, H., von Post, B., and Granlund, G. H., (1980). Optimization of arithmetic neighborhood operations for image processing. In *Proc. First Scandinavian Conference on Image Analysis*. Linköping, Sweden.

[60] Fleet, D. J. and Jepson, A. D., (1993). Stability of phase information. *IEEE Trans. PAMI*, **15(12)**:1253–1268.

[61] Lim, J. S., (1990). *Two-Dimensional Signal and Image Processing*. Englewood Cliffs, NJ: Prentice-Hall.

[62] Faugeras, O., (1993). *Three-Dimensional Computer Vision: A Geometric Viewpoint*. Cambridge, MA: MIT Press.

[63] Anandan, P., (1989). A computational framework and an algorithm for the measurement of visual motion. *Int. J. Comp. Vis.*, **2**:283–310.

[64] Singh, A., (1990). An estimation-theoretic framework for image-flow computation. In *Proceedings ICCV'90, Osaka, Japan*, pp. 168–177, IEEE. Washington, DC: IEEE Computer Society Press.

[65] Singh, A., (1992). *Optic Flow Computation: A Unified Perspective*. IEEE Computer Society Press.

[66] Black, M. J. and Anandan, P., (1993). A framework for the robust estimation of optical flow. In *Proceedings ICCV'93, Berlin*, pp. 231–236, IEEE. Washington, DC: IEEE Computer Society Press.

[67] Diehl, N. and Burkhardt, H., (1986). Planar motion estimation with a fast converging algorithm. In *Proc. 8th Intl. Conf. Pattern Recogn.*, pp. 1099–1102. IEEE Computer Society Press, Los Alamitos.

[68] Förstner, W., (1987). Reliability analysis of parameter estimation in linear models with applications to mensuration problems in computer vision. *Computer Vision, Graphics, and Image Processing*, **40**:273–310.

[69] Bluman, G. W. and Kumei, S., (1989). Symmetries and differential equations. *Applied Mathematical Sciences*, **81**.

[70] Hampel, F. R., Ronchetti, E. M., Rousseeuw, P. J., and Stahel, W. A., (1986). *Robust Statistics: The Approach Based on Influence Functions.* Wiley, New York.

[71] Meer, P., Mintz, D., and Rosenfeld, A., (1991). Robust regression methods for computer vision. *Int. J. Comp. Vision*, **6(1)**:59–70.

[72] Geman, S. and McClure, D. E., (1987). Statistical methods for tomographic image reconstruction. *Bull. Int. Statist. Inst.*, **LII-4**:721–741.

[73] Danuser, G. and Stricker, M., (1998). Parametric model fitting: from inlier characterization to outlier detection. *IEEE Trans. PAMI*, **20(3)**:263–280.

[74] Baarda, W., (1968). A testing procedure for use in geodetic networks. *Publications on Geodesy*, **2(5)**:1–97.

[75] Menke, W., (1984). *Geophysical data analysis: discrete inverse theory.* Orlando: Academic Press.

[76] Kalman, R. E., (1960). A new approach to linear filtering and prediction problems. *J. Basic Eng.*, **82D**:35–45.

[77] Barron, J. L., Fleet, D. J., and Beauchemin, S. S., (1993). *Performance of Optical Flow Techniques.* Technical Report, TR299, Dept. Of Computer Science, University of Western Ontario and RPL-TR-9107, Dept. of Computing Science, Queens University.

[78] Lin, T. and Barron, J., (1994). Image reconstruction error for optical flow. In *Vision Interface*, pp. 73–80.

14 Bayesian Multiscale Differential Optical Flow

Eero P. Simoncelli

Center for Neural Science, and
Courant Institute of Mathematical Sciences
New York University

14.1 Introduction

Images are formed as projections of the 3-D world onto a 2-D light-sensing surface. The brightness of the image at each point indicates how much light was absorbed by the surface at that spatial position at a particular time (or over some interval of time). When an object in the world moves relative to the sensor surface, the 2-D projection of that object moves within the image. The movement of the projection of each point in the world is referred to as the image velocity or the *motion field*.

The estimation of the image motion field is generally assumed to be the first goal of motion processing in machine vision systems. Motion

Handbook of Computer Vision and Applications
Volume 2
Signal Processing and Pattern Recognition

Copyright © 1999 by Academic Press
All rights of reproduction in any form reserved.
ISBN 0-12-379772-1/$30.00

estimation is also crucial for compression of image sequences (e.g., the MPEG video compression standard uses motion-compensated prediction). There is also evidence that this sort of computation is performed by biological systems. As an approximation to this, computer vision techniques typically compute an estimate of the motion field known as the *optical flow*. The idea is to measure the apparent motion of local regions of the *image brightness pattern* from one frame to the next. In doing this, one is assuming that these intensity patterns are preserved from frame to frame. As many authors have pointed out, the optical flow $\boldsymbol{f}$ is *not* always the same as the motion field $\boldsymbol{v}$ (e.g., [1, 2]).

There are many methods of computing optical flow. The most common are correlation, gradient, spatiotemporal filtering, and Fourier phase or energy approaches. Although based on somewhat different assumptions, these approaches are closely related, and can be made identical with proper formulation and choice of parameters [3, 4]. Correlation (usually over a local window) is by far the most prevalent technique. This is presumably due to a combination of intuitive directness and ease of hardware implementation. But a recent study by Barron et al. [5] suggests that gradient-based implementations have been the most accurate. In addition, the gradient solution is efficient (because the solution can be computed analytically rather than via optimization), and produces subpixel displacement estimates. A drawback of the gradient approach is that it may only be used for small displacements. But this difficulty can be alleviated using a multiscale coarse-to-fine algorithm. This chapter provides a practical description of a Bayesian multiscale gradient-based optical flow estimation algorithm, based on work previously published in [4, 6, 7].

14.2 Differential formulation

Gradient formulations of optical flow begin with the differential *brightness constancy constraint equation* [8]

$$\nabla^T g \, \boldsymbol{f} + g_t = 0 \tag{14.1}$$

where ∇g and g_t are the spatial image gradient and temporal derivative, respectively, of the image at a given spatial location and time (for notational simplicity, these parameters are omitted). The equation places a single linear constraint on the 2-D velocity vector $\boldsymbol{f}$ (at each point in space and time). As such, one cannot solve for velocity without imposing some additional constraint. This inherent indeterminacy is commonly known as the *aperture problem*.[1] In locations where the spatial

[1]The expression refers to the fact that the motion of a moving 1-D pattern viewed through a circular aperture is ambiguous. Actually, the problem is not really due to the aperture, but to the one-dimensionality of the spatial image structure.

gradient vanishes, the equation provides no constraint on the velocity vector. This is sometimes called the *blank wall problem*.

Typically, the aperture problem is overcome by imposing some form of smoothness on the field of velocity vectors. Many formulations use global smoothness constraints [8], which require global optimization[2]. Alternatively, one may assume locally constant velocity and combine linear constraints over local spatial (or temporal) regions [10]. This is accomplished by writing a weighted sum-of-squares error function based on the constraints from each point within a small region, where the points are indexed by a subscript $i \in \{1, 2, \dots n\}$

$$E(\boldsymbol{f}) = \sum_i w_i \left[\nabla^T g(\boldsymbol{x}_i, t)\boldsymbol{f} + g_t(\boldsymbol{x}_i, t) \right]^2 \tag{14.2}$$

where w_i is a set of *positive* weights.

To compute a linear least-squares estimate (LLSE) of $\boldsymbol{f}$ as a function of measurements ∇g and g_t, consider the gradient (with respect to $\boldsymbol{f}$) of this quadratic expression

$$\nabla_{\boldsymbol{f}} E(\boldsymbol{f}) = 2 \sum \nabla g \left[\nabla^T g \, \boldsymbol{f} + g_t \right] = 2\left[\boldsymbol{M}\boldsymbol{f} + \boldsymbol{b} \right] \tag{14.3}$$

where

$$\boldsymbol{M} = \sum \nabla g \nabla^T g = \begin{bmatrix} \sum g_x^2 & \sum g_x g_y \\ \sum g_x g_y & \sum g_y^2 \end{bmatrix}, \quad \boldsymbol{b} = \begin{bmatrix} \sum g_x g_t \\ \sum g_y g_t \end{bmatrix} \tag{14.4}$$

and all of the summations are over the patch, weighted by w_i as in Eq. (14.2). The (x, t) parameters have been omitted to simplify the notation.

Setting the gradient expression equal to the zero vector gives the least-squares velocity estimate

$$\hat{\boldsymbol{f}} = -\boldsymbol{M}^{-1}\boldsymbol{b} \tag{14.5}$$

assuming that the matrix $\boldsymbol{M}$ is invertible. Notice that matrix $\boldsymbol{M}$ and the vector $\boldsymbol{b}$ are both composed of blurred quadratic combinations of the spatial and temporal derivatives.

Despite the combination of information over the patch, it is important to recognize that the matrix $\boldsymbol{M}$ can still be singular. In particular, one cannot solve for the velocity in regions of the image where the intensity varies only one-dimensionally (the *extended aperture problem*) or zero-dimensionally (the *extended blank wall problem*). In addition, this basic formulation (where two motions can coexist within the same local region) has difficulties at occlusion boundaries or when image brightness changes are due to photometric effects.

[2]Although Weiss has recently shown that some solutions may be localized through the use of Green's functions [9].

Before introducing a model for uncertainty, it should be noted that the basic gradient approach may be extended in a number of ways. One can incorporate higher-order differential measurements (e.g., [11, 12]), or impose stronger constraints on the velocity field (e.g., affine motion or rigid-body motion [13]). A total least-squares formulation is given in Weber and Malik [14], although this solution is difficult to stabilize. The least-squares combination of local constraints may be replaced with a robust combination rule to give improved handling of occlusion boundaries [15]. The most promising recent development are techniques that simultaneously estimate motion and segment the scene into coherently moving regions (e.g., [9, 16, 17, 18, 19, 20]). Finally, gradient-based approaches have been shown to to be closely related to visual motion processing in mammals (e.g., [3, 21, 22, 23, 24]).

14.3 Uncertainty model

Each of the quantities in Eq. (14.1) is an idealization. First, we do not have the actual spatial or temporal derivatives, but *estimates* of these derivatives that are corrupted by image noise, filter inaccuracies, quantization, etc. Second, the equation is a constraint on the optical flow, but we are interested in estimating the *motion field.* As explained earlier, these two quantities often differ because changes in image intensities can be caused by nonmotion effects.

These idealizations can be made explicit by introducing a set of additive random variables. Define $\tilde{\boldsymbol{f}}$ as the optical flow, and $\boldsymbol{f}$ as the actual velocity field. The difference between these may be described using a random variable $\boldsymbol{n}_1$

$$\tilde{\boldsymbol{f}} = \boldsymbol{f} + \boldsymbol{n}_1$$

Similarly, let $\tilde{g}_t$ be the actual temporal derivative, and g_t the measured derivative. Then

$$g_t = \tilde{g}_t + n_2$$

with n_2 a random variable characterizing the uncertainty in this measurement relative to the true derivative. We assume that the spatial derivatives are measured more accurately than the temporal derivatives, and thus the equation does not include any term for uncertainty in these quantities.

Now the gradient constraint applies to the actual derivatives and the optical flow vector; thus we may write

$$\begin{aligned} 0 &= \nabla^T g\, \tilde{\boldsymbol{f}} + \tilde{g}_t \\ &= \nabla^T g(\boldsymbol{f} - \boldsymbol{n}_1) + g_t - n_2 \\ \Rightarrow \nabla^T g\, \boldsymbol{f} + g_t &= \nabla^T g\, \boldsymbol{n}_1 + n_2 \end{aligned} \tag{14.6}$$

This equation gives us a probabilistic relationship between the image *motion field* and the *measurements* of spatiotemporal gradient. It accounts for errors in our derivative measurements, and for deviations of the velocity field from the optical flow. But it still assumes that the underlying optical flow constraint is valid.

In order to make use of this formulation, we must characterize the random variables n_i in our definitions. It is desirable to choose these probability distributions such that $\boldsymbol{f}$ may be estimated analytically (as opposed to numerically). A common choice is to use independent zero-mean Gaussian distributions. The right-hand side of Eq. (14.6) is a zero-mean Gaussian random variable with variance equal to $\nabla^T g\, \boldsymbol{\Lambda}_1 \nabla g + \Lambda_2$, where $\boldsymbol{\Lambda}_1$ and Λ_2 are a covariance matrix and a variance corresponding to $\boldsymbol{n}_1$ and n_2, respectively. We interpret the equation as providing a conditional probability expression

$$\mathcal{P}(g_t|\boldsymbol{f}, \nabla g) \propto \exp\left\{-\frac{1}{2}(\nabla^T g\, \boldsymbol{f} + g_t)(\nabla^T g\, \boldsymbol{\Lambda}_1 \nabla g + \Lambda_2)^{-1}(\nabla^T g\, \boldsymbol{f} + g_t)\right\}$$

Bayes' rule may be used to write the desired conditional probability

$$\mathcal{P}(\boldsymbol{f} \mid \nabla g, g_t) = \frac{\mathcal{P}(g_t \mid \boldsymbol{f}, \nabla g)\mathcal{P}(\boldsymbol{f})}{\mathcal{P}(g_t)}$$

For the prior distribution $\mathcal{P}(\boldsymbol{f})$, we choose a zero-mean Gaussian with covariance $\boldsymbol{\Lambda}_p$. This imposes a preference for slower speeds[3].The denominator $\mathcal{P}(g_t)$ is only present for normalization purposes and does not affect the relative probabilities. The resulting distribution $\mathcal{P}(\boldsymbol{f}|\nabla g, g_t)$ is Gaussian

$$\begin{aligned}
&\mathcal{P}(\boldsymbol{f}|\nabla g, g_t) \\
&\propto \exp\left\{-\frac{1}{2}(\nabla^T g\, \boldsymbol{f} + g_t)^T(\nabla^T g\, \boldsymbol{\Lambda}_1 \nabla g + \Lambda_2)^{-1}(\nabla^T g\, \boldsymbol{f} + g_t)\right\} \\
&\quad \cdot \exp\left\{-\frac{1}{2}\boldsymbol{f}^T \boldsymbol{\Lambda}_p^{-1} \boldsymbol{f}\right\} \\
&= \exp\left\{-\frac{1}{2}\boldsymbol{f}^T\left[\nabla g(\nabla^T g\, \boldsymbol{\Lambda}_1 \nabla g + \Lambda_2)^{-1}\nabla^T g + \boldsymbol{\Lambda}_p^{-1}\right]\boldsymbol{f}\right. \\
&\qquad - g_t(\nabla^T g\, \boldsymbol{\Lambda}_1 \nabla g + \Lambda_2)^{-1}\nabla^T g\, \boldsymbol{f} \\
&\qquad \left. -\frac{1}{2} g_t(\nabla^T g\, \boldsymbol{\Lambda}_1 \nabla g + \Lambda_2) g_t\right\} \\
&= \exp\left\{-\frac{1}{2}(\boldsymbol{\mu}_f - \boldsymbol{f})^T \boldsymbol{\Lambda}_f^{-1}(\boldsymbol{\mu}_f - \boldsymbol{f})\right\}
\end{aligned} \tag{14.7}$$

[3]Such a preference has been suggested to play a role in human perception (e. g., Simoncelli [4], Weiss and Adelson [25])

The covariance matrix Λ_f and mean vector $\boldsymbol{\mu}_f$ may be derived by completing the square in the exponent

$$\begin{aligned}\Lambda_f &= \left[\nabla g(\nabla^T g\, \Lambda_1 \nabla g + \Lambda_2)^{-1} \nabla^T g + \Lambda_p^{-1}\right]^{-1} \\ \boldsymbol{\mu}_f &= -\Lambda_f \nabla g(\nabla^T g\, \Lambda_1 \nabla g + \Lambda_2)^{-1} g_t\end{aligned}$$

The advantage of the Gaussian form is that it is parameterized by these two quantities that are computed in analytic form from the derivative measurements.

If Λ_1 is assumed to be a diagonal matrix with diagonal entry λ_1, and the scalar variance of n_2 is rewritten as $\lambda_2 \equiv \Lambda_2$, then the solution becomes

$$\begin{aligned}\Lambda_f &= \left[\frac{\boldsymbol{M}}{(\lambda_1 \|\nabla g\|^2 + \lambda_2)} + \Lambda_p^{-1}\right]^{-1} \\ \boldsymbol{\mu}_f &= -\Lambda_f \frac{\boldsymbol{b}}{(\lambda_1 \|\nabla g\|^2 + \lambda_2)}\end{aligned} \tag{14.8}$$

where matrix $\boldsymbol{M}$ and vector $\boldsymbol{b}$ are defined as in Eq. (14.4), but without the summations. Note that multiplying Λ_p, λ_1 and λ_2 by a common scale factor will not affect the mean $\boldsymbol{\mu}_f$ of the distribution (although it *will* scale the variance).

The *maximum a posteriori estimate* (MAP) is simply the mean $\boldsymbol{\mu}_f$ because the distribution is Gaussian. This solution is very similar to that specified by Eq. (14.3). The differences are that: (1) the addition of the prior variance Λ_p ensures the invertibility of the matrix $\boldsymbol{M}$; and (2) the quadratic derivative terms in $\boldsymbol{M}$ and $\boldsymbol{b}$ are modified by a compressive nonlinearity. That is, for regions with low contrast (i.e., small $\|\nabla g\|^2$), the λ_2 term dominates the divisor of $\boldsymbol{M}$. For high-contrast regions, the $\lambda_1 \|\nabla g\|^2$ term will normalize the magnitude of the quadratic terms in $\boldsymbol{M}$. This seems intuitively reasonable; when the contrast (SNR) of the signal is low, an increase in contrast should increase our certainty of the velocity estimate. But as the contrast increases above the noise level of the signal, the certainty should asymptotically reach some maximum value rather than continuing to rise quadratically. The noise term n_2 accounts for errors in the derivative measurements. At low signal amplitudes, these will be the dominant source of error. The term $\boldsymbol{n}_1$ accounts for failures of the constraint equation. At high contrasts, these will be the dominant source of error.

The solution described thus far computes velocity for one point in isolation. As described in Section 14.2, the constraint at a single location is insufficient to uniquely specify a solution. We may therefore only compute the component of flow that is normal (perpendicular) to the local orientation. In the foregoing solution, the mean will be (approximately) the *normal flow* vector, and the width of these distributions in the direction perpendicular to the normal direction will be determined by Λ_p. The variance in the normal direction will be determined by both Λ_p and the trace of $\boldsymbol{M}$ (i.e., the sum of the squared magnitudes of the spatial derivatives).

If normal flow (along with variance information) does not provide a satisfactory input for the next stage of processing, then one can combine information in small neighborhoods (as in Eq. (14.2)). We now need an uncertainty model for the entire neighborhood of points. The simplest assumption is that the noise at each point in the neighborhood is independent. In practice this will not be correct. Nevertheless, as a first approximation, if we treat the uncertainties as pointwise-independent, then the resulting mean and variance are easy to calculate

$$\Lambda_f = \left[\sum_i \frac{w_i \boldsymbol{M}_i}{(\lambda_1 \|\nabla g(\boldsymbol{x}_i, t)\|^2 + \lambda_2)} + \Lambda_p^{-1} \right]^{-1} \tag{14.9}$$

$$\boldsymbol{\mu}_f = -\Lambda_f \sum_i \frac{w_i \boldsymbol{b}_i}{(\lambda_1 \|\nabla g(\boldsymbol{x}_i, t)\|^2 + \lambda_2)} \tag{14.10}$$

where, as before, w_i is a weighting function over the patch, with the points in the patch indexed by i. Here, the effect of the nonlinearity on the combination of information over the patch is to provide a type of gain control mechanism. If we ignore λ_2, the solution in the foregoing normalizes the information, equalizing the contribution from each point in the neighborhood by the magnitude of the spatial gradient. We will refer to this in later sections as the *basic* solution.

In the basic solution, information is combined over fixed size patches, using a fixed weighting function. An adaptive version of this algorithm could proceed by blurring over larger and larger regions (i.e., diffusion) until the magnitude of the variance (determinant of the variance matrix) is below some threshold. Because the variance matrix Λ_f describes a 2-D shape, this could be done directionally (i.e., anisotropic diffusion), averaging pixels that lie in the direction of maximal variance until the variance in this direction was below a threshold.

To illustrate the solution given in Eq. (14.10), we consider the response to a moving square. We have added a small amount of Gaussian-distributed white noise. Figure 14.1a shows one frame of the input image, along with the resulting distributions near the corner, on a side, and in the center. In the corner, the output is a fairly narrow distribution centered near the correct velocity. The error in the mean is due to the noise in the input. On the side, the ambiguity of the motion along the edge (i.e., the aperture problem) is indicated by the elongated shape of the distribution. In the center, the motion is completely ambiguous and the resulting distribution is essentially the prior. We also show the response for a low-contrast moving square, with the same amount of

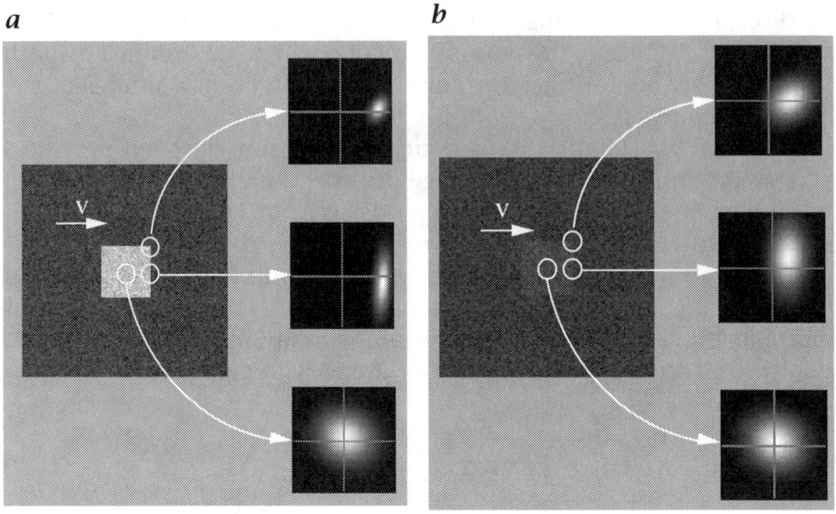

Figure 14.1: Output of the Bayesian algorithm in different regions of a moving square image at two different contrasts. Each plot shows a Gaussian density over the space of image velocities, computed using Eq. (14.10). The noise added to both sequences was of the same amplitude.

Gaussian noise, in Fig. 14.1b. Note that the velocity distribution corresponding to the corner is now substantially broader, as is that of the edge.

14.4 Coarse-to-fine estimation

The estimation of gradients from discretely sampled image sequences is prone to error. Some of the errors are due to poor choice of filter kernels; we address the issue of filter kernel design in the next section. For now, we focus on the problem of large translations. If motion from one frame of an image sequence to the next is too large (typically, more than 2 pixels), one cannot estimate the gradient accurately. The problem may be viewed easily in the Fourier domain, where it is evident as temporal aliasing. Consider a 1-D signal that is moving at a constant velocity. The power spectrum of this signal lies on a line through the origin [26]. We assume that the spatial sampling is dense enough to avoid aliasing (i.e., the images are spatially bandlimited before sampling, at a rate above the Nyquist limit). The temporal sampling of the imagery causes a replication of the signal spectrum at temporal frequency intervals of $2\pi/T$ radians, where T is the time between frames. This is illustrated in Fig. 14.2.

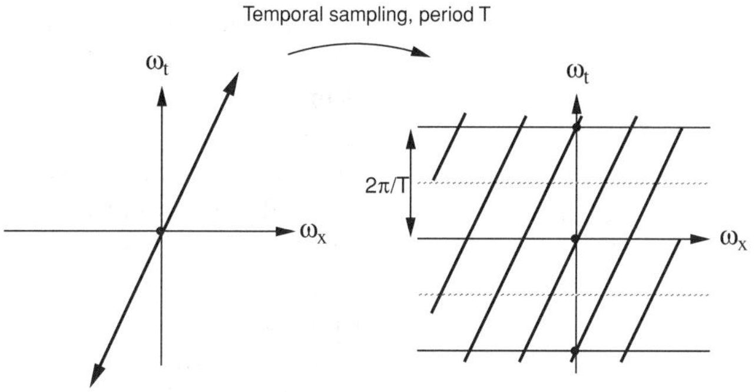

Figure 14.2: *Illustration of the temporal aliasing problem. On the left is an idealized depiction of the power spectrum of a 1-D pattern translating at speed v. The power spectrum is distributed along the heavy line, which has a slope of v. Temporally sampling the signal causes a replication of its power spectrum in the Fourier domain at temporal frequency intervals of $2\pi/T$. When the velocity of the signal is high, the replicas of the spectrum will interfere with the filter (gradient) measurements.*

Now consider the gradient-based estimation of optical flow in the Fourier domain. In particular, the energy function given in Eq. (14.2) may be rewritten

$$\begin{aligned} E(\boldsymbol{f}) &= \sum_{\boldsymbol{x}} \left| \boldsymbol{f}^T \nabla g + g_t \right|^2 \\ &= \sum_{\boldsymbol{k}} \left| \hat{g}(\boldsymbol{k})(\boldsymbol{f}^T \boldsymbol{k}) + \hat{g}(\boldsymbol{k})\omega \right|^2 \\ &= \sum_{\boldsymbol{k}} \left[(\boldsymbol{f}^T \boldsymbol{k}) + \omega \right]^2 \left| \hat{g}(\boldsymbol{k}) \right|^2 \end{aligned} \tag{14.11}$$

where the sum on the first line is over all image pixels and the sums on the latter two lines are over all frequencies $\boldsymbol{k}$. We have used Parseval's rule to switch to the Fourier domain, and the fact that the Fourier transform of the derivative operator in, for example, the $x-$ direction is ik_1. The term in square brackets is the squared ω-distance between the point $\boldsymbol{k}$ and the plane defined by $\boldsymbol{f}^T\boldsymbol{k} = -\omega$. This equation is precisely in the form of a least-squares planar regression error function, weighted by the image power spectrum $|\hat{g}(\boldsymbol{k})|^2$! Thus, the replicated spectra of Fig. 14.2 can confuse a motion estimation algorithm.

An important observation concerning this type of temporal aliasing is that it affects the higher spatial frequencies of an image. In particular, for a fixed global velocity, those spatial frequencies moving more than half of their period per frame will be aliased, but the lower spatial frequencies will be left intact. This suggests a simple but effective approach for avoiding the problem of temporal aliasing: estimate the velocity of a low-pass filtered copy of the image. Note that this "prefilter" must be quite large in spatial extent, in inverse proportion to its small spatial-frequency extent. Given imagery that contains only a single global motion, or a motion field that varies slowly, we could stop our computation at this point. But typical scenes contain more complex motion fields, which will not be captured by these low-frequency estimates.

In order to get better estimates of *local* velocity, higher-frequency bands must be used with spatially smaller filters. What we would like to do is use the coarse motion estimate to "undo" the motion, roughly stabilizing the position of the image over time. Then higher-frequency filters can be used to extract local perturbations to the large-scale motion. Specifically, we can use higher-frequency filters to estimate optical flow on the warped sequence, and this "optical flow correction" may then be composed with the previously computed optical flow to give a new optical flow estimate. This correction process may be repeated at finer and finer scales of a multiscale pyramid representation.

There are two mechanisms that one could imagine using to stabilize the image. In an interactive setting (i.e., a biological or robotically controlled visual system), the sensors can be moved so as to track a given point or object in the scene. This action reduces the image velocity of the object to zero.

Alternatively, in image-processing situations, where the image-gathering has already occurred, we can warp a spatially and temporally localized region of the image content in a direction opposite to the computed motion. For our purposes, we compute the warped image sequence

$$\mathcal{W}\{g, \boldsymbol{f}\}(\boldsymbol{x}, t + \Delta t) = g(\boldsymbol{x} - \boldsymbol{f}\Delta t, t + \Delta t)$$

where $\boldsymbol{f}$ is the warp vector field corresponding to the velocity estimated from the coarser scale measurements. Note that the warping only need be done over a range of Δt that covers the temporal extent of the derivative filters that will be applied.

We will concentrate on the warping approach here, although many of the observations apply to the tracking case as well. The warping procedure may be applied recursively to higher and higher-frequency sub-bands. This "coarse-to-fine" estimation process is illustrated in Fig. 14.3. This type of approach has been suggested and used by a number of authors [10, 27, 28, 29, 30].

As described in the foregoing, in order to generate estimates at different scales, we can apply the differential algorithm to low-pass prefilters of different bandwidth. To illustrate the effectiveness of this technique, consider a simple test pattern containing a disk of high-frequency texture moving at a fairly high velocity. This is illustrated in

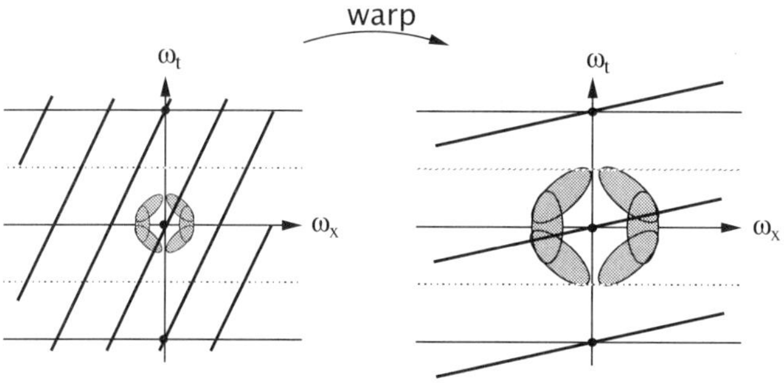

Figure 14.3: *Illustration of the coarse-to-fine approach for eliminating temporal aliasing. On the left is an idealized illustration of the (aliased) power spectrum of the signal. A low-frequency sub-band is used to estimate the motion of this signal. These estimates are then used to "undo" the motion, leaving a smaller, unaliased residual motion (shown on the right—note that the spectrum lies on a line of smaller slope). This motion may then be estimated using higher-frequency derivative filters.*

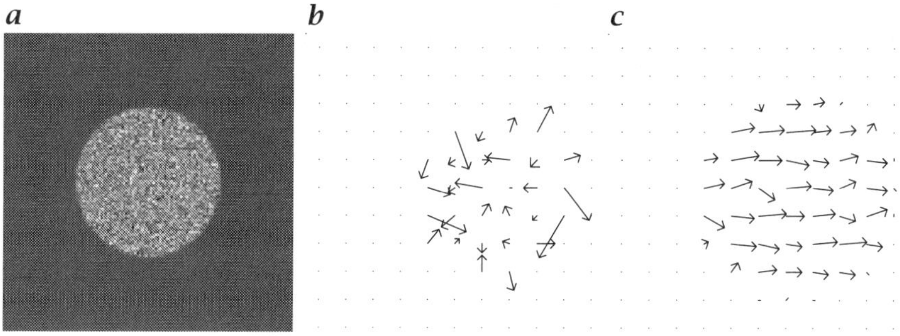

Figure 14.4: ***a*** *The stimulus, a rapidly moving disk containing fine-scale texture;* ***b*** *optical flow computed, direct gradient algorithm;* ***c*** *optical flow computed using coarse-to-fine gradient algorithm. The single dots correspond to optical flow vectors of length zero.*

Fig. 14.4. A local operator attempting to compute motion in the center of the disk would fail. But the multiscale algorithm is able to lock onto the coarse scale motion of the disk.

As we have described, a coarse-to-fine algorithm can be used to handle problems of temporal aliasing. It is also a technique for imposing a prior smoothness constraint (see, e. g., Szeliski [31]). This basic technique does, however, have a serious drawback. If the coarse-scale estimates are incorrect, then the fine-scale estimates will have no chance of correcting the errors.

To fix this, we must have knowledge of the error in the coarse-scale estimates. Because we are working in a probabilistic framework, and we have information describing the uncertainty of our measurements, we may use this information to properly combine the information from scale to scale. We define a *state evolution* equation with respect to scale

$$\boldsymbol{f}(l+1) = \boldsymbol{E}(l)\boldsymbol{f}(l) + \boldsymbol{n}_0(l), \qquad \boldsymbol{n}_0(l) \sim N(0, \Lambda_0)$$

where l is an index for scale (larger values of l correspond to finer scale), $\boldsymbol{E}(l)$ is the linear interpolation operator used to extend a coarse scale flow field to finer resolution, and $\boldsymbol{n}_0$ is a random variable corresponding to the certainty of the prediction of the fine-scale motion from the coarse-scale motion. We assume that the $\boldsymbol{n}_0(l)$ are independent, zero-mean, and normally distributed. This type of scale-to-scale Markov relationship has been explored in an estimation context in [32].

We also define the *measurement* equation

$$-g_t(l) = \nabla^T g(l)\boldsymbol{f}(l) + (n_2 + \nabla^T g(l)\boldsymbol{n}_1)$$

as in Section 14.3. We will assume, as before, that the random variables are zero-mean, independent and normally distributed. Remember that this equation is initially derived from the total derivative constraint for optical flow. This equation is a bit different than the measurement equation used in most estimation contexts. Here, the linear operator relating the quantity to be estimated to the measurement g_t is *also* a measurement.

Given these two equations, we may write down the optimal estimator for $\boldsymbol{f}(l+1)$, the velocity at the fine scale, given an estimate for the velocity at the previous coarse scale $\boldsymbol{\mu}_f(l)$ and a set of fine scale (gradient) measurements. The solution is in the form of a standard Kalman filter [33], but with the time variable replaced by the *scale* l

$$\begin{aligned}
\boldsymbol{\mu}_f(l+1) &= \boldsymbol{E}(l)\boldsymbol{\mu}_f(l) + \boldsymbol{\kappa}(l+1)\nu(l+1) \\
\Lambda_f(l+1) &= \Lambda'(l+1) - \boldsymbol{\kappa}(l+1)\nabla^T g(l+1)\Lambda'(l+1) \\
\boldsymbol{\kappa}(l+1) &= \frac{\Lambda'(l+1)\nabla g(l+1)}{\nabla^T g(l+1)\left[\Lambda'(l+1) + \Lambda_1\right]\nabla g(l+1) + \Lambda_2} \\
\nu(l+1) &= -g_t(l+1) - \nabla^T g(l+1)\boldsymbol{E}(l)\boldsymbol{\mu}_f(l) \\
\Lambda'(l+1) &= \boldsymbol{E}(l)\Lambda_f(l)\boldsymbol{E}(l)^T + \Lambda_0
\end{aligned}$$

Here, $\boldsymbol{\kappa}(l)$ is the *Kalman gain*, and $\nu(l)$ corresponds to an *innovations* process that represents the new information contributed by the measurements at level l.

The problem with the equations given in the foregoing is that we cannot compute the derivative measurements at scale l without making use of the velocity estimate at scale $l-1$, due to the temporal aliasing problem. In order to avoid this problem, we must write $\nu(l)$ in terms of derivatives of the warped sequence. We rewrite $\nu(l)$ as follows:

$$\begin{aligned}\nu(l+1) &= -g_t(l+1) - \nabla g(l+1)\cdot \boldsymbol{E}(l)\boldsymbol{\mu}_f(l)\\ &= -\frac{d}{dt} g\left(\boldsymbol{x} + t\boldsymbol{E}(l)\boldsymbol{\mu}_f(l), t\right)\\ &\approx -\frac{\partial}{\partial t}\mathcal{W}\{g(l+1), \boldsymbol{E}(l)\boldsymbol{\mu}_f(l)\}(x, y, t)\end{aligned}$$

Thus, the innovations process is computed as the temporal derivative of the image at scale $l+1$, after it has been warped with the interpolated flow field from scale l. In order to make the solution computationally feasible, we ignore the off-diagonal elements in $\Lambda'(l+1)$ (i.e., the correlations between adjacent interpolated flow vectors).

Now the Kalman solution may be put into the alternative "update" form by use of the following matrix identity [33]:

$$B^{-1} + C^T A^{-1} C = \left[B - BC^T(CBC^T + A)^{-1}CB\right]^{-1}$$

The left-hand side corresponds to the inverse of the updated covariance matrix given in the Kalman equations in the foregoing:

$$\begin{aligned}\Lambda_f(l+1) &= \left[\Lambda'(l+1)^{-1} + \nabla g(\nabla^T g\, \Lambda_1 \nabla g + \Lambda_2)^{-1}\nabla^T g\right]^{-1}\\ &= \left[\Lambda'(l+1)^{-1} + \frac{\boldsymbol{M}}{(\lambda_1\|\nabla g\|^2 + \lambda_2)}\right]^{-1}\end{aligned} \tag{14.12}$$

Similarly, we may rewrite the updated mean vector as

$$\begin{aligned}\boldsymbol{\mu}_f(l+1) &= \boldsymbol{E}(l)\boldsymbol{\mu}_f(l) + \Lambda_f(l+1)\nabla g(\nabla^T g\, \Lambda_1 + \Lambda_2)^{-1}\nu(l+1)\\ &= \boldsymbol{E}(l)\boldsymbol{\mu}_f(l) + \Lambda_f(l+1)\frac{\boldsymbol{b}'}{(\lambda_1\|\nabla g\|^2 + \lambda_2)}\end{aligned} \tag{14.13}$$

where the vector $\boldsymbol{b}'$ is defined by

$$\boldsymbol{b}' = \nabla g \nu(l+1)$$

These mean and covariance expressions are the same as those of Eq. (14.8) except that: (1) the prior covariance Λ_p has been replaced by $\Lambda'(l+1)$; (2) the vector $\boldsymbol{b}$ has been replaced by $\boldsymbol{b}'$, which is computed in the same manner but using the *warped* temporal derivative measurements; and (3) the mean $\boldsymbol{\mu}_f(l+1)$ is augmented by the interpolated estimate from the previous scale.

Figure 14.5 illustrates the effectiveness of this "Kalman filter over scale." The stimulus is a slowly moving textured disk, *with noise added.* The ordinary coarse-to-fine gradient algorithm gives terrible results because the noise leads to large errors in the coarse-scale velocity estimates that cannot be corrected at finer scales. The covariance-propagating version defined by Eqs. (14.12) and (14.13) produces better estimates (i. e., the mean vectors are closer to the actual flow), and the covariance information accurately indicates the more uncertain vectors.

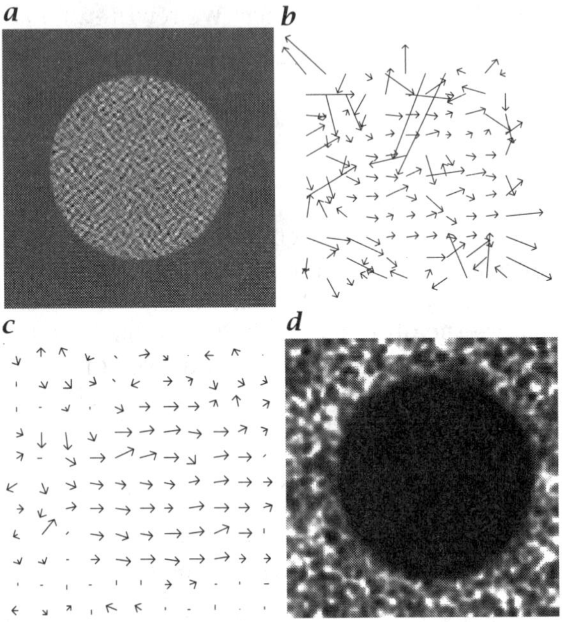

*Figure 14.5: Example using the covariance-propagating coarse-to-fine algorithm: **a** The stimulus, a slowly moving disk containing fine-scale texture in the presence of additive Gaussian white noise; **b** optical flow computed using standard coarse-to-fine gradient algorithm; **c** optical flow computed using Kalman-like coarse-to-fine gradient algorithm with covariance propagation; **d** the determinant of the terminal covariance matrix, indicating uncertainty of the estimate.*

Given that the derivative measurements will fail when the image velocity is too high, a more sophisticated version of this algorithm could prune the tree during the coarse-to-fine operation. That is, we can terminate the recursion at a given location (x, y, t) and level l if the interpolated covariance estimate from the previous scale $\Lambda'(l)$ is too large.

14.5 Implementation issues

In this section we will discuss some important issues that arise when implementing the algorithms discussed thus far.

14.5.1 Derivative filter kernels

The choice of convolution kernels used to estimate gradients can have a substantial impact on the accuracy of the estimates [34, 35], and yet many authors do not even describe the filters that they use. The most

Table 14.1: First-order derivative kernels. Shown are pairs of derivative (D) and interpolator (B) kernels of various sizes

^3B	0.223755	0.552490	0.223755			
^3D	-0.453014	0	0.453014			
^4B	0.092645	0.407355	0.407355	0.092645		
^4D	-0.236506	-0.267576	0.267576	0.236506		
^5B	0.036420	0.248972	0.429217	0.248972	0.036420	
^5D	-0.108415	-0.280353	0	0.280353	0.108415	
^6B	0.013846	0.135816	0.350337	0.350337	0.135816	0.013846
^6D	-0.046266	-0.203121	-0.158152	0.158152	0.203121	0.046266

common choice in the literature is a first-order difference. This type of differentiation arises naturally from the definition of continuous derivatives, and is reasonable when the spacing between samples is well below the Nyquist limit. But simple first-order differences are likely to produce poor results for the optical flow problem when applied directly to the input imagery, especially in highly textured regions (i. e., regions with much fine-scale content).

In the digital signal processing community, there has been a fair amount of work on the design of discrete differentiators (see, e.g., Oppenheim and Schafer [36]). This work is usually based on approximating the derivative of a continuous sinc function. The difficulty with this approach is that the resulting kernels typically need to be quite large in order to be accurate. In the computer vision literature, many authors have used sampled Gaussian derivatives that exhibit better differentiation properties than simple differences, but are less computationally expensive than sinc functions.

We have previously described a simple design procedure for matched pairs of 1-D kernels (a low-pass kernel and a differentiator) suitable for gradient estimation [4, 34, 35].[4] Let $\hat{B}(\boldsymbol{k})$ be the discrete Fourier transform (DFT) of the interpolator (often called the "prefilter"), and $\hat{D}(\boldsymbol{k})$ the DFT of the derivative filter. Then our design method attempts to meet the following requirements:

1. The derivative filters must be good approximations to the derivative of the prefilter. That is, for a derivative along the x-axis, we would like $jk_1\hat{B}(k) \approx \hat{D}(k)$, where k_1 is the component of the frequency coordinate in the x direction;
2. The low-pass prefilter should be symmetric, with $\hat{B}(0) = 1$;

[4]Fleet and Langley have designed recursive filters for these purposes [37].

3. For computational efficiency and ease of design, the prefilter should be separable. In this case, the derivatives will also be separable, and the design problem will be reduced to one dimension; and
4. The design algorithm should include a model for signal and noise statistics (e.g., Carlsson et al. [38]).

Table 14.1 gives sample values for a set of derivative kernels and their associated prefilters, at three different sizes [34]. These give significantly improved performance in optical flow or orientation estimation tasks.

14.5.2 Averaging filter kernels

The algorithm also requires averaging over a patch, which is equivalent to applying a low-pass filter. We desire this low-pass filter to have only positive weights as it will be used combine a set of squared constraints and should produce a positive value. There is a trade-off in choosing the spatial extent of the filter. A large filter will produce better power spectral estimates by combining information over a larger region. But it is also more likely to combine inconsistent motions. The question can only be properly settled given a knowledge of the statistics of the motion of the imagery to be analyzed. We experimented with binomial blurring filters and found that separable application of the kernel $[0.0625, 0.25, 0.375, 0.25, 0.0625]$ produced reliable results without overblurring.

14.5.3 Multiscale warping

In Section 14.4, we discussed the implementation of coarse-to-fine algorithms to reduce temporal aliasing. Conceptually, this approach operates by using prefilters of varying bandwidths.

A more efficient technique for generating multiscale representations is to construct an image pyramid [39], by recursively applying low-pass filtering and subsampling operations. In this case, the images at different scales are also represented at different sampling rates. Assuming the low-pass filter prevents aliasing, the effect of the subsampling in the Fourier domain is to stretch out the spectrum. This allows us to use the *same* derivative filters at each scale, rather than designing a whole family of derivative filters at different scales.

The algorithm begins by building a multiscale pyramid on each frame of the input sequence, and computing the optical flow on the sequence of top level (lowest frequency) images using the computation specified by Eq. (14.10). An upsampled and interpolated version of this coarse, low-resolution flow field must then be used to warp the sequence of images in the next pyramid level. We used a simple bilinear interpolator in this case because the optical flow is somewhat smooth due to the blurring operation. Optical flow is then computed on this warped sequence, and this "optical flow correction" is composed with the previously computed optical flow to give a new optical flow estimate. This correction process is repeated for each level of the pyramid until the flow fields are at the resolution of the original image sequence.

The warping equation is fairly unambiguous in the continuous case. But there are many ways in which one can implement a warping algorithm on discretely sampled image data. Consider the task of warping a frame at time t_1 back to time t_0. The primary issues are:

Indexing Should we use the velocity estimate at t_0 or t_1 (or a velocity estimate *between* the frames) as the warp field? Assuming that the velocity vectors are in units of pixels/frame, does the velocity estimate at position $(\boldsymbol{x}, t)$ correspond to the displacement of intensity at $(\boldsymbol{x} - \boldsymbol{f}, t - 1)$ to $(\boldsymbol{x}, t)$, or from $(\boldsymbol{x}, t)$ to $(\boldsymbol{x} + \boldsymbol{f}, t - 1)$?

Order If our filters are several frames long and thus require warping of several frames, should we use the velocity estimates at each of these frames, or just the velocity estimate of the central frame?

Interpolation Given that velocity vector components are typically not multiples of the pixel spacing, how should we interpolate the intensities of the warped images?

We compared several different variants and chose a simple and efficient warping scheme. We assume an odd-length temporal derivative filter of length $2N_t + 1$, and we use a velocity field estimate associated with the center frame. Because our derivative filters are separable, we apply the spatial portion to N_t frames centered at frame O. Let $g'(\boldsymbol{x}, t), -N_t \le t \le N_t$ be the set of spatially filtered frames. We then combine the temporal differentiation operation with the warping operation as follows:

$$g'_t(\boldsymbol{x}, 0) = \sum_{t=-N_t}^{N_t} d(t) I\left\{g'\left(\boldsymbol{x} + t\,\hat{\boldsymbol{f}}(\boldsymbol{x}, O),\ t\right)\right\}$$

where $d(t)$ is the temporal derivative kernel; $\hat{\boldsymbol{f}}$ is the previous estimate of optical flow; and $I\{\cdot\}$ is a bi-cubic spline interpolator used to evaluate g' at fractional-pixel locations.

14.5.4 Boundary handling

Convolution operations are used to compute the derivative filter responses, and to blur the energies. They are also used in coarse-to-fine schemes to construct the multiresolution image pyramid. Traditionally, convolution boundaries are handled by computing *circular* convolution. That is, the image is treated as one period of a periodic signal.

This often produces poor results because it associates the image content near one boundary with that near the opposite boundary.

There are many alternatives for handling edges. Let $h(n)$ be a 1-D signal, indexed by the discrete variable n, with $n = 0$ corresponding to the leftmost sample. Then we define an edge-handling mechanism (for the left edge) by assigning a value for the function f at negative values of n. Several example methods that we have experimented with are as follows:

1. Reflect the image about its edge pixel (or just beyond the edge pixel): $h(-n) = h(n)$ (or $h(-n) = h(n-1)$);
2. Imbed the image in a "sea of zeros": $h(-n) = 0$, for each $n > 0$;
3. Repeat the edge pixel: $h(-n) = h(0)$;
4. Reflect and invert (so as to preserve zeroth- and first-order continuity): $h(-n) = 2h(0) - h(n)$; and
5. Return zero for the convolution inner product whenever the filter kernel overhangs an edge of the image.

For the blurring and pyramid filtering operations we have found that reflection (item 1) is preferable. For the derivative operations, we choose to repeat the edge pixel (item 3).

14.6 Examples

We computed velocity field estimates for a set of synthetic and real image sequences in order to examine the behavior of the basic (first derivative) solution of Eq. (14.10).

14.6.1 Performance measures

In cases where the velocity field is known, we can analyze the errors in our estimates. There are a number of ways to do this. The simplest measure is the squared magnitude of the difference between the correct and estimated flow

$$E_{\text{mag2}} = |\hat{\boldsymbol{f}} - \boldsymbol{f}|^2$$

where $\boldsymbol{f}$ is the actual velocity, and $\hat{\boldsymbol{f}}$ is the estimate. Viewing an image containing these values at each spatial location often provides useful information about the spatial structure of the errors. Errors in optical flow are sometimes reported as a ratio of the error magnitude to magnitude of the actual flow, but this is problematic when the actual flow vectors are small.

Fleet and Jepson [40] used an error criterion based on the unit vector normal to the velocity plane in spatiotemporal frequency

$$E_{\text{angular}} = \arccos\left[\bar{\boldsymbol{u}}(\hat{\boldsymbol{f}}) \cdot \bar{\boldsymbol{u}}(\boldsymbol{f})\right]$$

where $\bar{\boldsymbol{u}}(\cdot)$ is a function producing a 3-D unit vector

$$\bar{\boldsymbol{u}}(\boldsymbol{f}) = \frac{1}{\sqrt{|\boldsymbol{f}|^2 + 1}} \begin{bmatrix} \boldsymbol{f}_1 \\ \boldsymbol{f}_2 \\ 1 \end{bmatrix}$$

and the resulting angular error is reported in units of degrees.

We also define a measure of bias in order to quantify characteristic over- or under- estimation of velocity magnitudes

$$E_{\text{bias}} = \frac{\boldsymbol{f} \cdot (\boldsymbol{f} - \hat{\boldsymbol{f}})}{|\boldsymbol{f}|}$$

Positive values of this measure, for example, indicate that the algorithm is overestimating the velocity magnitude.

In situations where we have estimated velocity field covariances Λ_f, as well as means $\boldsymbol{\mu}_f$, we can check that the covariance information adequately describes the errors in the flow estimates. The appropriate technique here is to normalize each of the errors according to the covariance information

$$E_{\text{normalized}} = \sqrt{(\boldsymbol{f}_{\text{actual}} - \boldsymbol{f}_{\text{est}})^T \Lambda_f^{-1} (\boldsymbol{f}_{\text{actual}} - \boldsymbol{f}_{\text{est}})}$$

If the flow field errors are exactly modeled by the additive Gaussian noise model, then a histogram of the values of the $E_{\text{normalized}}$ values should be distributed as a 2-D univariate Gaussian integrated over its angular coordinate

$$h(x) \propto x e^{-x^2/2}, \qquad x > 0$$

That is, a χ statistic.

14.6.2 Synthetic sequences

We generated a series of very simple synthetic test sequences to study the error behavior of the algorithm. These stimuli involve only translation of the image patterns, and therefore fully obey (modulo intensity quantization noise) the total derivative (Eq. (14.1)) for optical flow. Furthermore, because the entire image translates with a single velocity, the combination of information in a neighborhood is fully justified. Thus, these examples are primarily a test of the filters used to measure the

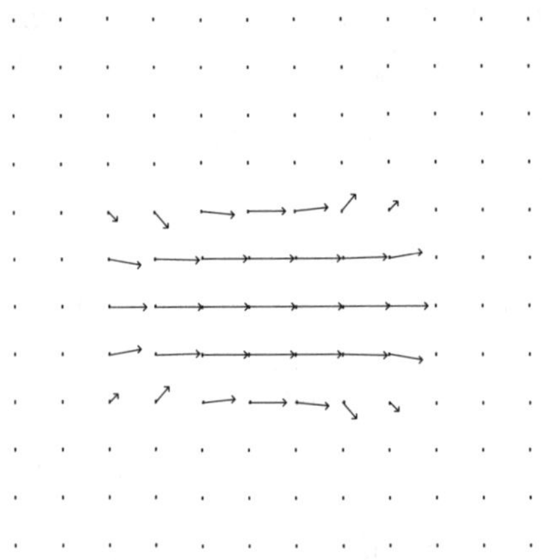

Figure 14.6: Velocity field estimated for a spatial impulse moving rightward at one pixel/frame. Dots correspond to zero velocity vectors.

derivatives, and the prior probability constraint used to determine a solution when there is an aperture or blank-wall problem. For this section, we used only the single-scale basic gradient algorithm, and we set the noise parameters as $\lambda_1 = 0, \lambda_2 = 1, \lambda_p = 1e^{-5}$.

To illustrate the spatial behavior of the algorithm, we estimated the velocity field of an impulse image moving at one pixel per frame. The flow field is shown in Fig. 14.6. The estimated velocity is correct in the center of the image (at the location of the impulse). The finite size of the derivative filters (five-tap kernels were used for this example) and the blurring of the energies leads to the situation shown, in which the impulse drags part of the background along. The velocity surrounding the impulse is consistent with the image intensities; because the image is zero everywhere except at the impulse, the motion is completely indeterminate.

Next, we examined a sinusoidal plaid pattern, taken from Barron et al. [5]. Two sinusoidal gratings with spatial frequency 6 pixels/cycle are additively combined. Their normal orientations are at 54° and −27° with speeds of 1.63 pixels/frame and 1.02 pixels/frame, respectively. The flow is computed using the multiscale algorithm. We built a one-level Gaussian pyramid on each frame, using the following five-tap kernel: $[0.0625, 0.25, 0.375, 0.25, 0.0625]$. Derivative filters used are the five-tap first derivative kernels given in Table 14.1. The covariance parameters were set as follows: $\lambda_1 = 0; \lambda_2 = 1; \lambda_p = 1e^{-5}$; and $\lambda_0 = 0.15$. One frame of the sequence, the estimated flow, and the error magnitude image are shown in Fig. 14.7.

Also shown is a table of error statistics. The errors compare quite favorably with the mean angular errors reported by Barron et al. [5]. Our mean angular error is an order of magnitude less than all the meth-

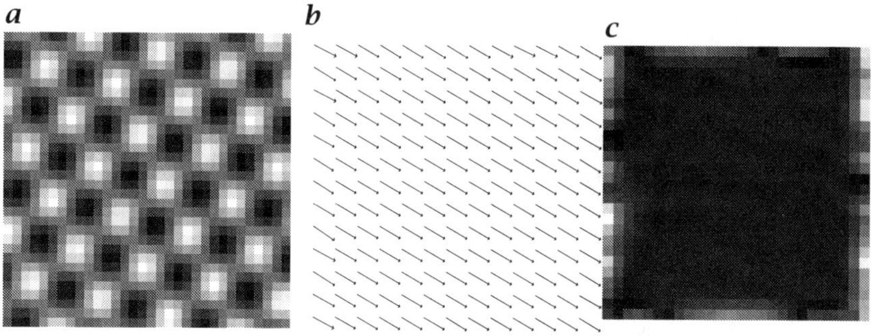

Mean E_{mag2}	$1.597 \cdot 10^{-4}$
Mean E_{angular}	0.2746°
St. dev. E_{angular}	0.300°
Mean E_{bias}	0.004378

Figure 14.7: *Velocity field estimates for sinusoidal plaid sequence:* ***a*** *example frame from the sequence;* ***b*** *estimated velocity field; and* ***c*** *error magnitude image. Note that the error is concentrated at the boundaries, where derivative measurement is difficult. Error statistics for this computation are given in the table (see text for definitions).*

ods examined, except for that of Fleet and Jepson [40] for which the value was 0.03°. But Barron *et al.* point out that the Fleet and Jepson results are computed with filters that are tuned for the sinusoids in the stimulus and that for a stimulus composed of different sinusoids, the algorithm would exhibit biases.

We also note that our algorithm is *significantly* more efficient than most of the algorithms in Barron et al. [5]. For example, the Fleet and Jepson algorithm is implemented with a set of 46 kernels. These are implemented separably as 75 convolutions with 1-D 21-tap kernels. Our solution requires eight convolutions (with 1-D kernels) for the first derivative measurements with kernels that are only three or five taps in length.

Moving one step closer to real imagery, we estimated velocity fields for a "texture-mapped" fly-through sequence of the Yosemite valley [5]. Starting with an aerial photograph and a range (height) map of the Yosemite valley, a sequence of images was rendered for a series of camera positions. Photometric effects are *not* included in this rendering process; the image pixel values are interpolated directly from the intensities of the original photograph. Thus, the sequence contains all of the standard problem sources except for lighting effects (i.e., sin-

[5] This sequence was generated by Lyn Quam at SRI International.

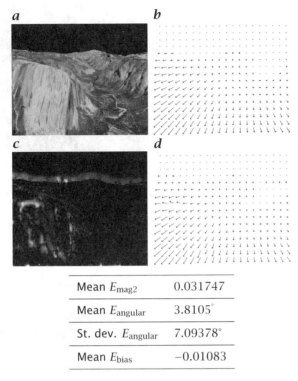

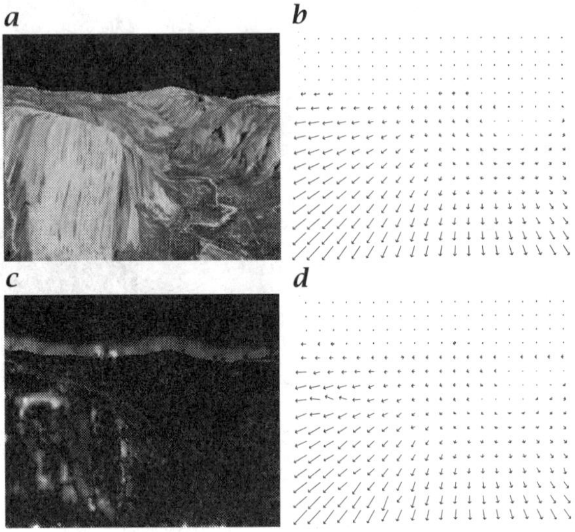

Mean E_{mag2}	0.031747
Mean E_{angular}	3.8105°
St. dev. E_{angular}	7.09378°
Mean E_{bias}	−0.01083

Figure 14.8: *Results of applying the algorithm to the synthetic "Yosemite" sequence:* ***a*** *example frame from the original sequence;* ***b*** *correct flow field;* ***c*** *estimated velocity field; and* ***d*** *error magnitude image. Note that errors are concentrated near occlusion boundaries.*

gular regions, temporal aliasing, and multiple motions at occlusions). Note that we have the camera motion and the depth of each point in the image, we can compute the *actual* image motion fields.

Again, we computed velocity fields using the multiscale solution. This time, we build a three-level Gaussian pyramid. Parameter settings were as follows: $\lambda_1 = 2\times10^{-5}$; $\lambda_2 = 0.004$; $\lambda_p = 0.5$; and $\lambda_0 = 0.15$. The results are illustrated in Fig. 14.8. We show a frame from the original sequence, the correct velocity field, the estimated velocity field, and the error magnitude image. Also given is a table of statistics. The statistics do not include the points closer than 10 pixels to the border.

The results are quite accurate, with most errors occurring (as expected) at occlusion boundaries, and at the borders of the image (which may be viewed as a type of occlusion boundary). But qualitative comparisons with the results of the Heeger or Fleet and Jepson algorithm indicate that the errors near these boundaries are contained within smaller regions near the boundaries because the support of the filters is much smaller.

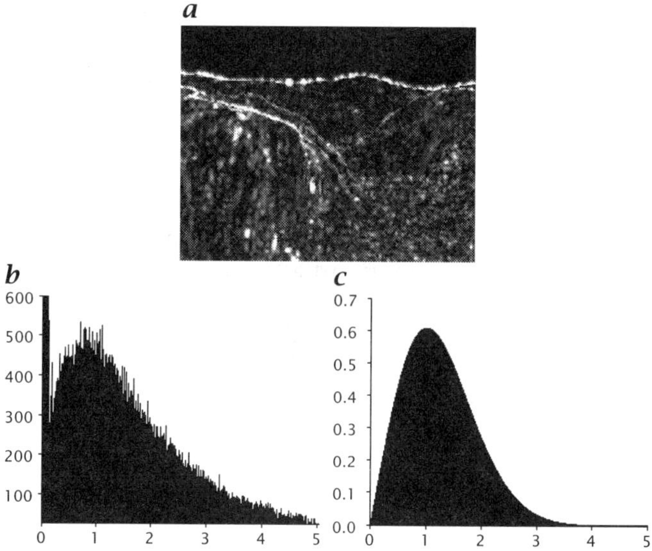

Figure 14.9: ***a*** *Image of* $E_{\text{normalized}}$ *for the Yosemite sequence velocity estimates;* ***b*** *histogram of* $E_{\text{normalized}}$ *values;* ***c*** *expected distribution* $h(x)$ *for this histogram (see text).*

Furthermore, the error statistics compare quite favorably to those reported in [5]. In particular, the best result reported is that of Lucas and Kanade, with a mean angular error of 3.55° and standard deviation of 7.09°. This is almost identical to our result, but the flow vector density is only 8.8%. The best result reported at 100% is that of Uras, which had a mean angular error of 10.44°, and standard deviation of 15.00°. The values given in Fig. 14.8 are significantly lower.

To analyze the appropriateness of the noise model, we computed an $E_{\text{normalized}}$ at each point. We show this image in Fig. 14.9, along with the histogram of values. If the flow field errors were exactly modeled by the simple additive Gaussian noise terms, then this histogram would be in the form of the χ statistic distribution (also plotted in Fig. 14.9). Qualitatively, the error histogram is seen to match, suggesting that the noise model is not unreasonable.

14.7 Conclusion

In this chapter, we described a Bayesian estimator for motion fields. We combine differential constraints over local spatial regions (thereby assuming a smooth motion field), and we assume a Gaussian prior probability density in which slower speeds are more likely. The output of the algorithm is a Gaussian distribution over the space of image velocities, at each position in the image. The mean of the distribution is a gain-controlled modification of the basic differential optical flow solution. The covariance matrix captures directional uncertainties, allowing proper combination of the output with other sources of information.

We developed a coarse-to-fine estimation algorithm for handling the problem of large displacements (temporal aliasing). Here we are able to take advantage of the uncertainty information provided by the covariance estimates, propagating this information using a Kalman filter over scale. Propagation of motion fields (and their covariances) over time has been described in [41]. We discussed the details of algorithm implementation, and showed several diagnostic examples designed to demonstrate the various strengths and weaknesses of the algorithm we have developed. We generated velocity field estimates for a number of synthetic sequences.

14.8 References

[1] Horn, B. K. P., (1986). *Robot Vision.* Cambridge, MA: MIT Press.

[2] Verri, A. and Poggio, T., (1989). Motion field and optical flow: Qualitative properties. *IEEE Pat. Anal. Mach. Intell.*, pp. 490–498.

[3] Adelson, E. H. and Bergen, J. R., (1986). The extraction of spatiotemporal energy in human and machine vision. In *Proc. IEEE Workshop on Visual Motion, Charlestown*, pp. 151–156. Los Alamitos, CA: IEEE Computer Society Press.

[4] Simoncelli, E. P., (1993). *Distributed Analysis and Representation of Visual Motion.* , Massachusetts Institute of Technology, Department of Electrical Engineering and Computer Science, Cambridge, MA. Also available as MIT Media Laboratory Vision and Modeling Technical Report #209.

[5] Barron, J. L., Fleet, D. J., and Beauchemin, S. S., (1994). Performance of optical flow techniques. *Intl. J. Comp. Vis.*, **12**(1):43–77.

[6] Simoncelli, E. P., (1993). Coarse-to-fine estimation of visual motion. In *Proc Eighth Workshop on Image and Multidimensional Signal Processing, Cannes, France*, pp. 128–129. Piscataway, NJ: IEEE Sig. Proc. Society.

[7] Simoncelli, E. P., Adelson, E. H., and Heeger, D. J., (1991). Probability distributions of optical flow. In *Proc. Conf. on Computer Vision and Pattern Recognition, Mauii, Hawaii*, pp. 310–315. Los Alamitos, CA: IEEE Computer Society Press.

[8] Horn, B. K. P. and Schunck, B. G., (1981). Determining optical flow. *Artificial Intelligence*, **17**:185–203.

[9] Weiss, Y., (1997). Smoothness in layers: Motion segmentation using nonparametric mixture estimation. In *Proc. IEEE Conf. Computer Vision and Pattern Recognition*, pp. 520–527. Los Alamitos, CA: IEEE Computer Society Press.

[10] Lucas, B. D. and Kanade, T., (1981). An iterative image registration technique with an application to stereo vision. In *Proceedings of the 7th Inter-*

national Joint Conference on Artificial Intelligence, Vancouver, pp. 674–679. San Francisco, CA: Morgan Kaufmann.

[11] Nagel, H. H., (1983). Displacement vectors derived from second order intensity variations in image sequences. *Computer Vision, Pattern Recognition, and Image Processing*, **21**:85–117.

[12] Uras, S., Girosi, F., Verri, A., and Torre, V., (1988). A computational approach to motion perception. *Biol. Cybern.*, **60**:79–87.

[13] Mendelsohn, J., Simoncelli, E., and Bajcsy, R., (1997). Discrete-time rigidity-constrained optical flow. In *Int'l Conf. Computer Analysis of Images and Patterns, Kiel, Germany*, pp. 255–262. Berlin: Springer.

[14] Weber, I. and Malik, J., (1996). Robust computation of optical flow in a multiscale differential framework. *Intl. J. Comp. Vis.*, **14**(1):67–81.

[15] Black, M. J. and Anandan, P. P., (1996). The robust estimation of multiple motions: Parametric and piecewise-smooth flow fields. *Computer Vision and Image Understanding*, **63**(1):75–104.

[16] Ayer, S. and Sawhney, H. S., (1995). Layered representation of motion video using robust maximum-likelihood estimation of mixture models and MDL encoding. In *Fifth Intl. Conf. Comp. Vis., Cambridge, MA*, pp. 777–784. Los Alamitos, CA: IEEE Computer Society Press.

[17] Darrell, T. J. and Simoncelli, E., (1994). Separation of transparent motion into layers using velocity-tuned mechanisms. In *European Conf. on Computer Vision*. New York: Springer.

[18] Hsu, S., Anandan, P. P., and Peleg, S., (1994). Accurate computation of optical flow by using layered motion representations. In *Proc. ICPR, Jerusalem, Israel*, pp. 743–746.

[19] Ju, S. X., Black, M. J., and Yacoob, Y., (1996). Skin and bones: Multilayer, locally affine, optical flow and regularization with transparency. In *IEEE Conf. CVPR, San Francisco, CA*, pp. 307–314. Los Alamitos, CA: IEEE Computer Society Press.

[20] Wang, J. Y. A. and Adelson, E. H., (1994). Representing moving images with layers. *IEEE Trans. Im. Proc.*, **3**(5):625–638.

[21] Heeger, D. J. and Simoncelli, E. P., (1992). Model of visual motion sensing. In *Spatial Vision in Humans and Robots*, L. Harris and M. Jenkin, eds., pp. 367–392. Cambridge, MA: Cambridge University Press.

[22] Koenderink, J. J. and van Doorn, A. J., (1987). Representation of local geometry in the visual system. *Biol. Cybern.*, **55**:367–375.

[23] Simoncelli, E. P. and Heeger, D. J., (1998). A model of neuronal responses in visual area MT. *Vision Research*, **38**(5):743–761.

[24] Young, R. A. and Lesperance, R. M., (1993). A physiological model of motion analysis for machine vision. In *Proc SPIE: Human Vision, Visual Processing, and Digital Display IV*, Vol. 1913, pp. 48–123. Bellingham, Washington: SPIE Publications.

[25] Weiss, Y. and Adelson, E. H., (1994). Slow and Smooth: A Bayesian theory for the combination of local motion signals in human vision. Technical Report 1624, AI Lab, Cambridge, MA: Massachusetts Institute of Technology.

[26] Watson, A. B. and Ahumada, A. J., (1983). A look at motion in the frequency domain. In *Motion: Perception and representation*, J. K. Tsotsos, ed., pp. 1–10. Baltimore: ACM.

[27] Anandan, P., (1989). A computational framework and an algorithm for the measurement of visual motion. *Intl. J. Computer Vision*, **2**:283–310.

[28] Battiti, R., Amaldi, E., and Koch, C., (1991). Computing optical flow across multiple scales: an adaptive coarse-to-fine strategy. *Intl. J. Comp. Vis.*, **6** (2):133–145.

[29] Enkelmann, W. and Nagel, H., (1988). Investigation of multigrid algorithms for estimation of optical flow fields in image sequences. *Computer Vision, Graphics, and Image Processing*, **43**:150–177.

[30] Quam, L., (1984). Hierarchical warp stereo. In *Proceedings of the DARPA Image Understanding Workshop*, pp. 149–155.

[31] Szeliski, R., (1990). Bayesian modeling of uncertainty in low-level vision. *Intl J. Computer Vision*, **5**(3):271–301.

[32] Chou, K. C., Willsky, A. S., Benveniste, A., and Basseville, M., (1989). Recursive and Iterative Estimation Algorithms for Multi-Resolution Stochastic Processes. Technical Report LIDS-P-1857, MIT Laboratory for Information and Decision Sciences.

[33] Gelb, A. (ed.), (1989). *Applied Optimal Estimation.* Cambridge, MA: MIT Press.

[34] Farid, H. and Simoncelli, E., (1997). Optimally rotation-equivariant directional derivative kernels. In *Int'l Conf Computer Analysis of Images and Patterns, Kiel, Germany*, pp. 207–214. Berlin: Springer-Verlag.

[35] Simoncelli, E. P., (1994). Design of multi-dimensional derivative filters. In *First Int'l Conf on Image Proc., Austin, Texas*, Vol. I, pp. 790–793. Piscataway, NJ: IEEE Sig. Proc. Society.

[36] Oppenheim, A. V. and Schafer, R. W., (1975). *Digital Signal Processing.* Englewood Cliffs, NJ: Prentice-Hall, Inc.

[37] Fleet, D. J. and Langley, K., (1995). Recursive filters for optical flow. *IEEE Pat. Anal. Mach. Intell.*, **17**(1):61–67.

[38] Carlsson, B., Ahlen, A., and Sternad, M., (1991). Optimal differentiators based on stochastic signal models. *IEEE Trans. Signal Proc.*, **39**(2).

[39] Burt, P. J. and Adelson, E. H., (1983). The Laplacian pyramid as a compact image code. *IEEE Trans. Comm.*, **COM-31**(4):532–540.

[40] Fleet, D. and Jepson, A., (1990). Computation of component image velocity from local phase information. *Intl. J. Comp. Vis.*, **5**(1):77–104.

[41] Singh, A., (1991). Incremental estimation of image-flow using a Kalman filter. In *Proceedings IEEE Workshop on Visual Motion, Princeton.* Los Alamitos, Ca: IEEE Computer Society Press.

15 Nonlinear Diffusion Filtering

Joachim Weickert

Department of Computer Science, University of Copenhagen, Denmark

Handbook of Computer Vision and Applications
Volume 2
Signal Processing and Pattern Recognition

Copyright © 1999 by Academic Press
All rights of reproduction in any form reserved.
ISBN 0-12-379772-1/$30.00

15.1 Introduction

Starting with Perona and Malik's pioneering work in 1987 [1, 2], *nonlinear diffusion* filtering has become a popular tool in medical imaging [3, 4, 5, 6, 7, 8, 9] as well as many other areas; it has been used for improved subsampling algorithms [10], postprocessing of fluctuating numerical data [11], blind image restoration [12], computer-aided quality control [13, 14], and segmentation of textures [15, 16] and remotely sensed data [17, 18]. In the meantime it has also entered commercial software packages such as the medical visualization tool Analyze[1].

Nonlinear diffusion filters regard the original image as the initial state of a diffusion process that adapts itself to the evolving image. Different adaptation strategies provide different ways to include *a priori* knowledge into the evolution. The embedding of the original image into a family of gradually smoother, simplified versions of it allows nonlinear diffusion filtering to be considered as a *scale-space* technique. The fact that the nonlinear adaptation may also enhance interesting structures such as edges relates them to image enhancement and image restoration methods.

The goal of the present chapter is to give an introduction to some selected key aspects of nonlinear diffusion filtering. We shall discuss some main ideas and study how they can be realized in practice by choosing adequate algorithms and suitable parameters. Questions of this type are often posed by practitioners, but are hardly addressed in the literature. This chapter is not intended as a state-of-the art review of the relevant literature in this area because descriptions in this direction are already available elsewhere [19, 20].

The chapter is organized as follows. Section 15.2 presents different nonlinear diffusion models. They comprise isotropic filters with a scalar-valued diffusivity as well as anisotropic ones with a diffusion matrix (diffusion tensor). In Section 15.3 we will be concerned with a continuous theory that establishes well-posedness and scale-space results for most of the previous models. Section 15.4 discusses some numerical algorithms for nonlinear diffusion filtering. We shall see that these discrete nonlinear diffusion filters can be regarded as iterated small averaging masks where the stencil weights are adapted to the evolving image. Section 15.5 describes a well-posedness and scale-space theory for discrete nonlinear diffusion filters that is in complete analogy to the continuous results.

The practically important question of how to select appropriate filter parameters is addressed in Section 15.6. In Section 15.7 some extensions are sketched, in particular, generalizations to multichannel images. The chapter is concluded with a summary in Section 15.8.

---

[1]Analyze is a registered trademark of Mayo Medical Ventures, 200 First Street SW, Rochester, MN 55905, U.S.A.

15.2 Filter design

15.2.1 The physics behind diffusion

Most people have an intuitive impression of diffusion as a physical process that equilibrates concentration differences without creating or destroying mass. This physical observation can be easily cast in a mathematical formulation. The equilibration property is expressed by *Fick's law*

$$\boldsymbol{j} = -\boldsymbol{D}\,\nabla u \tag{15.1}$$

This equation states that a concentration gradient ∇u causes a flux $\boldsymbol{j}$ that aims to compensate for this gradient. The relation between ∇u and $\boldsymbol{j}$ is described by the *diffusion tensor* $\boldsymbol{D}$, a positive-definite symmetric matrix. The case where $\boldsymbol{j}$ and ∇u are parallel is called *isotropic*. Then we may replace the diffusion tensor by a positive scalar-valued *diffusivity* D. In the general *anisotropic* case, $\boldsymbol{j}$ and ∇u are not parallel.

The observation that diffusion does only transport mass without destroying it or creating new mass is expressed by the *continuity equation*

$$\partial_t u = -\operatorname{div} \boldsymbol{j} \tag{15.2}$$

where t denotes the time. If we plug in Fick's law, Eq. (15.1), into the continuity equation, we end up with the *diffusion equation*

$$\partial_t u = \operatorname{div}(\boldsymbol{D}\,\nabla u) \tag{15.3}$$

This equation appears in many physical *transport processes* [21]. In the context of *heat transfer* it is called *heat equation*.

In image processing we may identify the concentration with the gray value at a certain location. If the diffusion tensor is constant over the whole image domain, one speaks of *homogeneous diffusion*, and a space-dependent filtering is called *inhomogeneous*. Often the diffusion tensor is a function of the differential structure of the evolving image itself. Such a feedback leads to *nonlinear diffusion filters*.

Sometimes the computer vision literature deviates from the preceding notations: It can happen that homogeneous filtering is named isotropic, and inhomogeneous blurring is called anisotropic, even if it uses a scalar-valued diffusivity instead of a diffusion tensor.

15.2.2 Limitations of linear diffusion filtering

Let us consider a 2-D (scalar-valued) image that is given by a continuous bounded mapping $g : \mathbb{R}^2 \to \mathbb{R}$. One of the most widely used methods

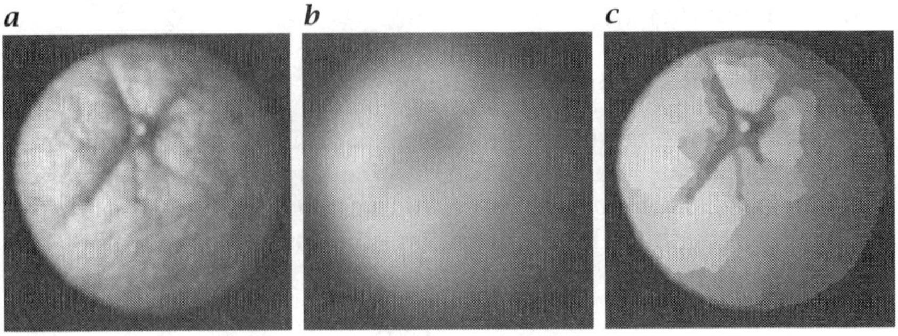

Figure 15.1: ***a*** *Orange,* 256 × 256 *pixels;* ***b*** *linear diffusion,* $t = 100$*;* ***c*** *Perona-Malik diffusion,* $\lambda = 3$, $t = 100$.

for smoothing g is to regard it as the initial state of a homogeneous linear diffusion process

$$\partial_t u = \partial_{xx} u + \partial_{yy} u \tag{15.4}$$

$$u(\boldsymbol{x}, 0) = g(\boldsymbol{x}) \tag{15.5}$$

From the literature on partial differential equations it is well known that its solution is given by the convolution integral

$$u(\boldsymbol{x}, t) = \begin{cases} g(\boldsymbol{x}) & (t = 0) \\ (K_{\sqrt{2t}} * g)(\boldsymbol{x}) & (t > 0) \end{cases} \tag{15.6}$$

where K_σ denotes a Gaussian with standard deviation σ

$$K_\sigma(\boldsymbol{x}) := \frac{1}{2\pi\sigma^2} \cdot \exp\left(-\frac{|\boldsymbol{x}|^2}{2\sigma^2}\right) \tag{15.7}$$

Linear diffusion filtering is the oldest and best-studied example of a scale-space. Usually, Witkin's 1983 work is regarded as the first reference to the linear scale-space idea [22], but linear scale-space has already been axiomatically derived by Iijima in 1962 [23, 24]. A detailed treatment of linear scale-space theory can be found in [25, 26, 27].

Figure 15.1a, b shows an example where an image depicting an orange is filtered by linear diffusion. In spite of its excellent smoothing properties, two disadvantages of linear diffusion filtering become apparent:

(a) Semantically useful information is eliminated in the same way as noise. Because linear diffusion filtering is designed to be uncommitted, one cannot incorporate image-driven information in order to bias the scale-space evolution towards a desired task, for instance, edge detection; and

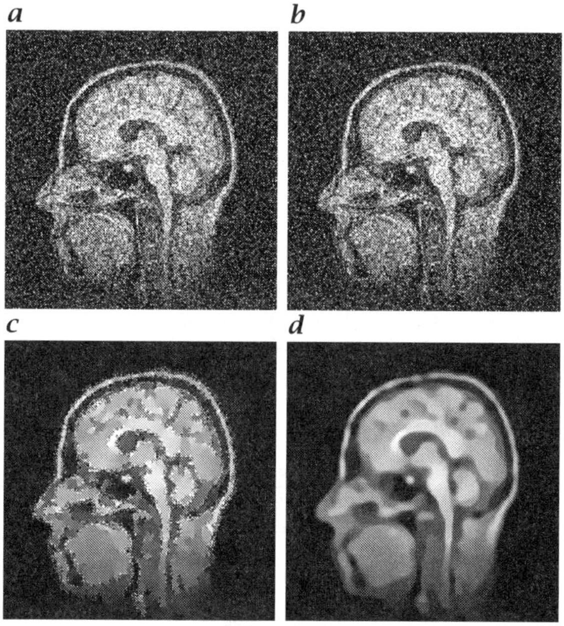

Figure 15.2: ***a*** *MR image degraded by additive Gaussian noise with zero mean,* 256×256 *pixels, signal-to-noise ratio: 1;* ***b*** *Perona-Malik diffusion,* $\lambda = 4$, $t = 25$; ***c*** *regularized isotropic nonlinear diffusion,* $\lambda = 4$, $\sigma = 2$, $t = 25$; ***d*** *edge enhancing anisotropic diffusion,* $\lambda = 4$, $\sigma = 2$, $t = 25$.

(b) Linear diffusion filtering dislocates structures when moving from finer to coarser scales. Hence, structures that are identified at a coarse scale have to be traced back to the original image in order to get their correct location [22, 28]. In practice, this may be difficult to handle and give rise to instabilities.

15.2.3 Isotropic nonlinear diffusion

Basic Idea. In order to avoid the blurring and localization problems of linear diffusion filtering, Perona and Malik proposed a nonlinear diffusion method [1, 2]. Their nonuniform process (which they name anisotropic[2]) reduces the diffusivity at those locations that have a larger likelihood to be edges, that is, which have larger gradients.

Let Ω denote a rectangular image domain and consider an image $g(\boldsymbol{x}) : \Omega \to \mathbb{R}$. Perona and Malik obtain a filtered image $u(\boldsymbol{x}, t)$ as the

[2]In our terminology, the Perona-Malik filter is regarded as an isotropic model because it reveals a scalar-valued diffusivity and not a diffusion tensor.

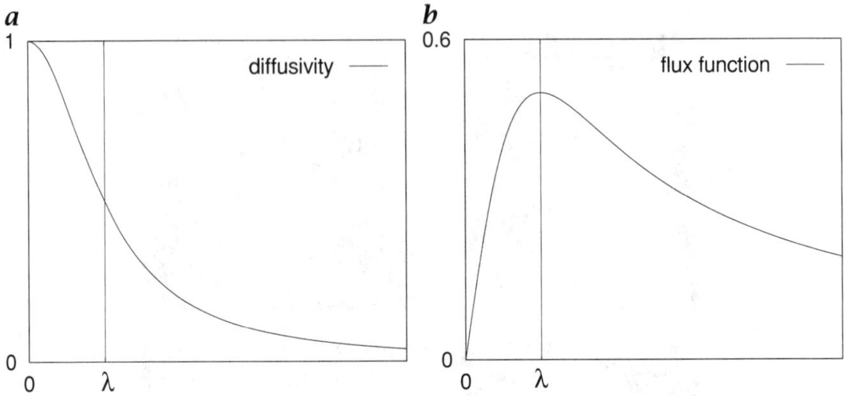

Figure 15.3: ***a*** *Diffusivity* $D(s^2) = 1/(1 + s^2/\lambda^2)$; ***b*** *flux* $\Phi(s) = s/(1 + s^2/\lambda^2)$. *From Weickert [19].*

solution of the diffusion equation[3]

$$\partial_t u = \operatorname{div}(D(|\nabla u|^2)\,\nabla u) \qquad \text{on} \qquad \Omega \times (0, \infty) \tag{15.8}$$

with the original image as initial condition

$$u(\boldsymbol{x}, 0) = g(\boldsymbol{x}) \qquad \text{on} \qquad \Omega \tag{15.9}$$

and reflecting boundary conditions (∂_n denotes the derivative normal to the image boundary $\partial\Omega$)

$$\partial_n u = 0 \qquad \text{on} \qquad \partial\Omega \times (0, \infty) \tag{15.10}$$

Among the *diffusivities* they propose is

$$D(|\nabla u|^2) = \frac{1}{1 + |\nabla u|^2/\lambda^2} \qquad (\lambda > 0) \tag{15.11}$$

The experiments of Perona and Malik were visually impressive in that edges remained stable over a very long time. Edge detection based on this process clearly outperformed the linear Canny edge detector, even without applying nonmaximum suppression and hysteresis thresholding. This is due to the fact that diffusion and edge detection interact in one single process instead of being treated as two independent processes that are to be applied subsequently. However, the Perona-Malik approach reveals some problems that we shall discuss next.

Forward-backward diffusion. To study the theoretical behavior of the Perona-Malik filter, let us for simplicity of notation restrict ourselves to the 1-D case.

[3]For smoothness reasons we write $|\nabla u|^2$ instead of $|\nabla u|$.

For the diffusivity Eq. (15.11) it follows that the *flux function* $\Phi(s) := sg(s^2)$ satisfies $\Phi'(s) \geq 0$ for $|s| \leq \lambda$, and $\Phi'(s) < 0$ for $|s| > \lambda$ (see Fig. 15.3). As Eq. (15.8) can be rewritten as

$$\partial_t u = \partial_x(\Phi(\partial_x u)) = \Phi'(\partial_x u)\, \partial_{xx} u \tag{15.12}$$

we observe that (in spite of its nonnegative diffusivity) the Perona-Malik model resembles a *forward diffusion*

$$\partial_t u = \partial_{xx} u \tag{15.13}$$

for $|\partial_x u| \leq \lambda$, and the *backward diffusion*

$$\partial_t u = -\partial_{xx} u \tag{15.14}$$

for $|\partial_x u| > \lambda$. Hence, λ plays the role of a *contrast parameter* separating forward (low contrast) from backward (high contrast) diffusion areas. In the same way as the forward diffusion smoothes contrasts, the backward diffusion enhances them. Thus, the Perona–Malik model may enhance gradients whose absolute value is larger than λ; see Perona and Malik [2] for more details on *edge enhancement*.

The *forward-backward diffusion* behavior is explicitly intended in the Perona-Malik method, as it gives the desirable result of blurring small fluctuations and sharpening edges. Two other examples for diffusivities where a contrast parameter λ separates forward from backward diffusion are

$$g(s^2) = \exp\left(\frac{-s^2}{2\lambda^2}\right) \tag{15.15}$$

$$g(s^2) = \begin{cases} 1 & (s^2 = 0) \\ 1 - \exp\left(\dfrac{-3.31488}{(s/\lambda)^8}\right) & (s^2 > 0) \end{cases} \tag{15.16}$$

Experiments indicate that the latter example often gives more "segmentation-like" results. Figure 15.1c shows an example where the last diffusivity has been used. Its edge-enhancing potential is clearly visible at the contours of the orange.

An obvious practical problem of the Perona-Malik filter is that it misinterprets large gradients due to noise as semantically important edges that it should preserve. It is thus unsuited for denoising severely degraded images. This problem is illustrated in Fig. 15.2b.

Besides this practical problem, there is also a theoretical one. A reasonable requirement for an evolution process in image analysis is that of *well-posedness*, that is, the problem should have a unique solution that depends continuously on the initial image.

Unfortunately, forward-backward diffusion equations of Perona-Malik type reveal *ill-posedness* aspects; although there are some conjectures [29, 30] that they might have generalized solutions[4], until now nobody was able to prove their existence. If they exist, there is evidence that their steady states do not depend continuously on the original image [31].

However, the practical behavior of finite difference approximations is much better than one would expect from the forementioned theory: One can easily calculate a discrete solution for all times, and this solution converges to a flat image for $t \to \infty$. The mainly observable instability is the so-called *staircasing effect*, where a sigmoid edge evolves into piecewise-linear segments that are separated by jumps. A discrete explanation for this so-called *Perona-Malik paradox* [30] has been given in Weickert and Benhamouda [32]. They proved that a standard spatial finite difference discretization is sufficient to turn the Perona-Malik process into a well-posed system of nonlinear ordinary differential equations. If a simple explicit time discretization is applied, then the resulting scheme is *monotonicity preserving* in the 1-D case [33], that is, a monotone function remains monotone after filtering. Thus, oscillations cannot appear and artifacts are restricted to staircasing. In this sense, a naive implementation of the Perona-Malik filter often works reasonably well because of the regularizing[5] effect of the discretization. Different discretizations, however, may lead to strongly differing results. Thus, it seems to be more natural to introduce the regularization directly into the continuous Perona-Malik equation in order to become more independent of the numerical implementation [34, 35]. This shall be done next.

Regularized isotropic nonlinear diffusion. In 1992, Catté, Lions, Morel and Coll [34] proposed a regularization of the Perona-Malik process that has a unique solution, and which is even infinitely times differentiable. Besides this theoretical advantage, their modification is also more robust under noise.

They propose to regularize the gradient within the diffusivity D by convolving it with a Gaussian K_σ with standard deviation $\sigma > 0$. Thus, their filter uses

$$\partial_t u = \operatorname{div}(D(|\nabla u_\sigma|^2)\ \nabla u) \tag{15.17}$$

where $u_\sigma := K_\sigma * u$. Experiments showed that this regularization leads to filters that can still *enhance edges* [33], produces less *staircasing* [35], and that are less sensitive to the discretization [36].

[4] A generalized solution satisfies a generalized (integral) formulation of the diffusion equation. In particular, a generalized solution does not have to be twice differentiable in x.

[5] A regularization of an ill-posed problem is a well-posed approximation to it.

The regularizing effect of the modification by Catté et al. [34] is due to the fact that ∇u_σ remains bounded. Moreover, the convolution with a Gaussian K_σ makes the filter insensitive to structures at scales smaller than σ. Therefore, when regarding Eq. (15.17) as an image-restoration equation, it reveals (besides the contrast parameter λ) an additional *noise scale* σ. This avoids a shortcoming of the genuine Perona-Malik process that misinterprets strong oscillations due to noise as edges that should be preserved or even enhanced. This is illustrated in Fig. 15.2c. Noise within a region can be eliminated very well, but at edges, $|\nabla u_\sigma|$ is large and the diffusion is inhibited. Therefore, this regularization is not optimal in the vicinity of noisy edges.

To overcome this problem, a desirable method should prefer diffusion along edges to diffusion perpendicular to them. This cannot be done with a scalar-valued diffusivity, one has to use a diffusion matrix (diffusion tensor) instead. This leads us to anisotropic diffusion filters.

15.2.4 Edge-enhancing anisotropic diffusion

An anisotropic diffusion filter for edge-enhancing diffusion does not only take into account the contrast of an edge, but also its direction.

This can be achieved by constructing the orthonormal system of eigenvectors $\boldsymbol{v}_1$, $\boldsymbol{v}_2$ of the diffusion tensor $\boldsymbol{D}$ such that $\boldsymbol{v}_1 \parallel \nabla u_\sigma$ and $\boldsymbol{v}_2 \perp \nabla u_\sigma$. In order to prefer smoothing along the edge to smoothing across it, one can choose the corresponding eigenvalues λ_1 and λ_2 as [11]

$$\lambda_1 := D(|\nabla u_\sigma|^2) \tag{15.18}$$

$$\lambda_2 := 1 \tag{15.19}$$

In general, ∇u is not parallel to one of the eigenvectors of $\boldsymbol{D}$ as long as $\sigma > 0$. Hence, the behavior of this model is really anisotropic. If we let the regularization parameter σ tend to 0, we end up with the isotropic Perona–Malik process.

There is an interesting relation between the regularized isotropic Diffusion in Eq. (15.17) and edge-enhancing anisotropic diffusion. While the former uses a scalar-valued diffusivity

$$D(|\nabla u_\sigma|^2) = D(\nabla u_\sigma^T \nabla u_\sigma) \tag{15.20}$$

one can formally write the diffusion tensor of edge-enhancing diffusion as

$$\boldsymbol{D}(\nabla u_\sigma) = D(\nabla u_\sigma \nabla u_\sigma^T) \tag{15.21}$$

This can be seen as follows. If D can be represented as a globally convergent power series

$$D(s) = \sum_{k=0}^{\infty} \alpha_k s^k \tag{15.22}$$

we can regard $D(\nabla u_\sigma \nabla u_\sigma^T)$ as the matrix-valued power series

$$D(\nabla u_\sigma \nabla u_\sigma^T) = \sum_{k=0}^{\infty} \alpha_k (\nabla u_\sigma \nabla u_\sigma^T)^k \tag{15.23}$$

The matrix $(\nabla u_\sigma \nabla u_\sigma^T)^k$ has eigenvectors ∇u_σ and $\nabla u_\sigma^\perp$ with corresponding eigenvalues $|\nabla u_\sigma|^{2k}$ and 0. From this it follows that D has the eigenvectors ∇u_σ and $\nabla u_\sigma^\perp$ with corresponding eigenvalues $D(|\nabla u_\sigma|^2)$ and $D(0) = 1$.

Figure 15.2d depicts a result of edge-enhancing anisotropic diffusion. We observe that it is capable of reducing noise at edges.

15.2.5 Coherence-enhancing anisotropic diffusion

A second motivation for introducing anisotropy into diffusion processes arises from the wish to process 1-D features such as line-like structures. We shall now investigate a modification of a model by Cottet and Germain [37], which is specifically designed for the enhancement of coherent flow-like structures [14].

For this purpose one needs more sophisticated structure descriptors than ∇u_σ. A good descriptor for local orientation is the *structure tensor (second-moment matrix, scatter matrix, interest operator)* [38, 39]

$$J_\rho(\nabla u_\sigma) := K_\rho * (\nabla u_\sigma \nabla u_\sigma^T) \tag{15.24}$$

and its equivalent approaches [40, 41]. The component-wise convolution with the Gaussian K_ρ averages orientation information over an *integration scale* ρ. Because J_ρ is a symmetric positive-semidefinite matrix, there exists an orthonormal basis of eigenvectors v_1 and v_2 with corresponding eigenvalues $\mu_1 \geq \mu_2 \geq 0$. The eigenvalues measure the average contrast (gray-value variation) in the eigendirections within a scale ρ. Therefore, v_1 is the orientation with the highest gray-value fluctuations, and v_2 gives the preferred local orientation, the *coherence direction*. The expression $(\mu_1 - \mu_2)^2$ is a measure of the local coherence. If one wants to enhance coherent structures, one should smooth mainly along the coherence direction v_2 with a diffusivity λ_2 that increases with respect to the coherence $(\mu_1 - \mu_2)^2$. This can be accomplished by designing $\boldsymbol{D}$ such that it possesses the same eigenvectors $\boldsymbol{v}_1, \boldsymbol{v}_2$ as $\boldsymbol{J}_\rho$ and choosing its corresponding eigenvalues as

$$\lambda_1 := \alpha \tag{15.25}$$

$$\lambda_2 := \begin{cases} \alpha & \text{if } \mu_1 = \mu_2, \\ \alpha + (1-\alpha)\exp\left(\dfrac{-c}{(\mu_1 - \mu_2)^2}\right) & \text{else} \end{cases} \tag{15.26}$$

where $c > 0$. The small positive parameter $\alpha \in (0, 1)$ is mainly introduced for theoretical reasons, as we will see in Section 15.3. It keeps the diffusion tensor uniformly positive-definite.

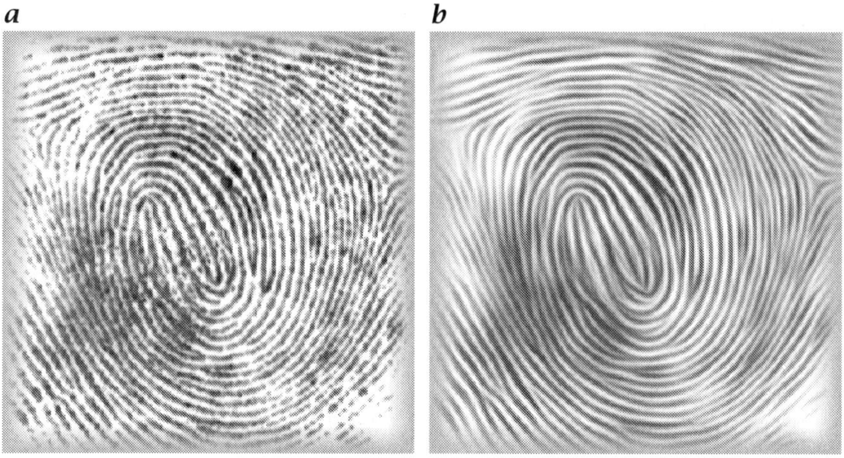

Figure 15.4: ***a*** *Fingerprint,* 256×256 *pixels;* ***b*** *coherence-enhancing anisotropic diffusion* $c = 1$, $\sigma = 0.5$, $\rho = 4$, $t = 20$. *From Weickert [14].*

Figure 15.4 shows the *restoration* properties of coherence-enhancing anisotropic diffusion when being applied to a fingerprint image. The diffusion filter encourages smoothing along the coherence orientation v_2 and is therefore well-suited for closing interrupted lines. Due to its reduced diffusivity at noncoherent structures, the locations of the semantically important singularities in the fingerprint remain the same. It should be noted that this filter cannot be regarded as a regularization of a Perona-Malik process. Moreover, a pure local analysis cannot detect interrupted lines. This requires *semilocal* information from the structure tensor that averages orientation information over an integration scale ρ.

15.3 Continuous theory

Interestingly, all of the previously mentioned diffusion filters can be cast in the form

$$\partial_t u = \operatorname{div}(\boldsymbol{D}(\boldsymbol{J}_\rho)\,\nabla u) \tag{15.27}$$

Evidently, coherence-enhancing diffusion uses $\boldsymbol{D} = \boldsymbol{D}(\boldsymbol{J}_\rho(\nabla u_\sigma))$, but also the diffusion tensor for edge-enhancing diffusion can be written as

$$\boldsymbol{D} = D(\nabla u_\sigma \nabla u_\sigma^T) = D(\boldsymbol{J}_0(\nabla u_\sigma)) \tag{15.28}$$

and regularized isotropic nonlinear diffusion uses

$$\boldsymbol{D} = D(|\nabla u_\sigma|^2)\,\boldsymbol{I} = D(\operatorname{trace}(\boldsymbol{J}_0(\nabla u_\sigma)))\,\boldsymbol{I} \tag{15.29}$$

and linear diffusion corresponds to $\boldsymbol{D} = \boldsymbol{I}$.

This gives rise to the question as to whether these filters can be treated within a unifying theoretical framework. The answer is: yes. Let us consider the following filter structure:

> Assume that g is bounded, $\rho \geq 0$, and $\sigma > 0$. Consider the problem
>
> $$\begin{aligned} \partial_t u = \operatorname{div}(\boldsymbol{D}(\boldsymbol{J}_\rho(\nabla u_\sigma))\, \nabla u) \quad & \text{on} \quad \Omega \times (0,\infty) \\ u(\boldsymbol{x},0) = g(\boldsymbol{x}) \quad & \text{on} \quad \Omega \\ \langle D(\boldsymbol{J}_\rho)\nabla u, \boldsymbol{n}\rangle = 0 \quad & \text{on} \quad \partial\Omega \times (0,\infty) \end{aligned}$$
>
> where the diffusion tensor $\boldsymbol{D} = (d_{ij})$ satisfies the following properties:
>
> (C1) Smoothness:
> $\boldsymbol{D}(\boldsymbol{J}_\rho(v))$ is component-wise in $C^\infty(\Omega)$ for all v that are component-wise in $C^\infty(\Omega)$;
>
> (C2) Symmetry:
> $d_{12}(J) = d_{21}(J)$ for all symmetric matrices $\boldsymbol{J} \in \mathbb{R}^{2\times 2}$; and
>
> (C3) Uniform positive-definiteness:
> If $\boldsymbol{v} \in \mathbb{R}^2$ is bounded by some constant K, then there exists a positive lower bound $c(K)$ for the eigenvalues of $\boldsymbol{D}(\boldsymbol{J}_\rho(v))$.
>
> (P_c)

For this class the following theoretical results can be shown:[6]

(a) *(Well-posedness and smoothness)*
There exists a unique weak solution $u(\boldsymbol{x},t)$ that is infinitely times differentiable for $t > 0$, and which depends continuously on f with respect to the $L^2(\Omega)$ norm;

(b) *(Extremum principle)*
Let $a := \inf_\Omega f$ and $b := \sup_\Omega f$. Then, $a \leq u(\boldsymbol{x},t) \leq b$ on $\Omega \times [0,\infty)$;

(c) *(Average gray-level invariance)*
The average gray level $\mu := \frac{1}{|\Omega|}\int_\Omega f(\boldsymbol{x})\, d\boldsymbol{x}$ is not affected by nonlinear diffusion filtering: $\frac{1}{|\Omega|}\int_\Omega u(\boldsymbol{x},t)\, d\boldsymbol{x} = \mu$ for all $t > 0$;

(d) *(Lyapunov functionals)*
$E(u(t)) := \int_\Omega r(u(\boldsymbol{x},t))\, d\boldsymbol{x}$ is a Lyapunov function for all convex $r \in C^2[a,b]$: $E(u(t))$ is decreasing and bounded from below by $\int_\Omega r(\mu)\, dx$:

---

[6] The spaces $L^p(\Omega)$, $1 \leq p < \infty$ consist of the functions w, for which the (Lebesgue) integral $\int_\Omega |w(x)|^p\, dx$ exists. They are supplemented with the norm $\|w\|_{L^p(\Omega)} := (\int_\Omega |w(x)|^p\, dx)^{1/p}$.

(e) *(Convergence to a constant steady state)*
$\lim_{t\to\infty} u(\boldsymbol{x},t) = \mu$ in $L^p(\Omega)$, $1 \le p < \infty$.

The existence, uniqueness and regularity proof goes back to Catté et al. [34], all other results are proved in Weickert [20].

What do these results mean? A solution that is infinitely times differentiable for $t > 0$ shows a strong smoothing property, which is characteristic for diffusion processes; even if the bounded initial image is discontinuous, the filtered result becomes smooth immediately.

Continuous dependence of the solution on the initial image is of significant practical importance, as it guarantees stability under perturbations. This is of importance when considering stereo images, image sequences or slices from medical CT or MR sequences, because we know that similar images remain similar after filtering.

Many smoothing scale-space properties are closely related to extremum principles; Hummel [42], for instance, shows that under certain conditions the maximum principle for diffusion processes is equivalent to the property that the corresponding scale-space never creates additional level-crossings for $t > 0$.

Average gray-level invariance is a property that distinguishes diffusion filters from morphological scale-spaces as treated in Alvarez et al. [43]. The latter cannot be written in divergence form and, thus, they are not conservative. Moreover, average gray-level invariance is required in scale-space-based segmentation algorithms such as the hyperstack [44]. In addition to this invariance it is evident that (P_c) satisfies classical scale-space invariances similarly to invariances under gray-level shifts, contrast reversion, translations and rotations. Usual architectural properties of scale-spaces (e. g., the semigroup property) are satisfied as well.

The Lyapunov functionals introduced in the forementioned item (d) show that the considered evolution equation is a simplifying, information-reducing transform with respect to many aspects. Indeed, the special choices $r(s) := |s|^p$, $r(s) := (s-\mu)^{2n}$ and $r(s) := s \ln s$, respectively, imply that all L^p norms with $2 \le p \le \infty$ are decreasing (e. g., the energy $\|u(t)\|^2_{L^2(\Omega)}$), all even *central moments* are decreasing (e. g., the variance), and the *entropy* $S[u(t)] := -\int_\Omega u(\boldsymbol{x},t) \ln(u(\boldsymbol{x},t))\, d\boldsymbol{x}$, a measure of uncertainty and missing information, is increasing with respect to t [11]. Using Parseval's equality we know that a decreasing energy is equivalent to a decreasing sum of the squared Fourier coefficients. Thus, in spite of the fact that the filters may act as image enhancers, their global smoothing properties in terms of Lyapunov functionals can be interpreted in a deterministic, stochastic, information-theory-based and Fourier-based manner. The temporal evolution of Lyapunov-like expressions such as the entropy has also been used for *selecting* the most important scales [45, 46], and there are interesting relations between Lyapunov functionals, generalized entropies and fractal theory [47].

The result item (e) tells us that, for $t \to \infty$, this simplifying scale-space representation tends to the most global image representation that is possible; a constant image with the same average gray level as f.

15.4 Algorithmic details

Usually, the differential equations for nonlinear diffusion cannot be solved analytically. Hence one has to use numerical approximations. *Finite difference* (FD) methods *finite difference methods* are mainly used, as they are relatively easy to implement and a digital image already provides information on a regular rectangular pixel grid. Good introduction to these methods can be found in Morton and Mayers [48] and Mitchell and Griffiths [49]. Finite difference methods replace all derivatives by finite differences. To illustrate the principle, we have to introduce some notations first. Let h_1 and h_2 denote the pixel size in x and y direction, respectively, and τ the time step size. We set $x_m := (m - 1/2)\, h_1$, $y_n := (n - 1/2)\, h_2$, $t_k := k\tau$ and denote by U_{mn}^k an approximation of $u(x_m, y_n, t_k)$. In image processing, it is often assumed that $h_1 = h_2 = 1$.

15.4.1 Regularized isotropic diffusion

Let us start with the Catté/Lions/Morel/Coll equation

$$\partial_t u = \partial_x \left(D(|\nabla u_\sigma|^2)\, \partial_x u \right) + \partial_y \left(D(|\nabla u_\sigma|^2)\, \partial_y u \right) \tag{15.30}$$

A simple finite-difference approximation to $\partial_t u$ in (x_m, y_n, t_k) is given by

$$\partial_t u \approx \frac{U_{mn}^{k+1} - U_{mn}^k}{\tau} \tag{15.31}$$

By expanding $u(x_m, y_n, t_{k+1})$ in a Taylor series around (x_m, y_n, t_k), it may be verified that this approximation has an error of order $O(\tau)$. This first-order error is characteristic for one-sided approximations.

The spatial derivatives can be approximated in the following manner:

$$\begin{aligned} \partial_x(D\,\partial_x u) &\approx \frac{(D\,\partial_x u))_{m+1/2,n}^k - (D\,\partial_x u))_{m-1/2,n}^k}{h_1} \\ &\approx \frac{1}{h_1} \left(\frac{D_{m+1,n}^k + D_{mn}^k}{2}\, \frac{U_{m+1,n}^k - U_{mn}^k}{h_1} - \frac{D_{mn}^k + D_{m-1,n}^k}{2}\, \frac{U_{mn}^k - U_{m-1,n}^k}{h_1} \right) \end{aligned} \tag{15.32}$$

This is a second-order approximation in space because it uses central differences; D^k_{mn} is given by

$$D^k_{mn} := D\left(\sqrt{\left(\frac{V^k_{m+1,n} - V^k_{m-1,n}}{h_1}\right)^2 + \left(\frac{V^k_{m,n+1} - V^k_{m,n-1}}{h_2}\right)^2}\right) \tag{15.33}$$

where V^k_{mn} is a Gaussian-smoothed version of U^k_{mn}.

The preceding approximations lead to the scheme

$$\begin{aligned}\frac{U^{k+1}_{mn} - U^k_{mn}}{\tau} &= \frac{1}{h_1}\left(\frac{D^k_{m+1,n} + D^k_{mn}}{2}\,\frac{U^k_{m+1,n} - U^k_{mn}}{h_1} - \frac{D^k_{mn} + D^k_{m-1,n}}{2}\,\frac{U^k_{mn} - U^k_{m-1,n}}{h_1}\right)\\ &+ \frac{1}{h_2}\left(\frac{D^k_{m,n+1} + D^k_{mn}}{2}\,\frac{U^k_{m,n+1} - U^k_{mn}}{h_2} - \frac{D^k_{mn} + D^k_{m,n-1}}{2}\,\frac{U^k_{mn} - U^k_{m,n-1}}{h_2}\right)\end{aligned} \tag{15.34}$$

As a result, the unknown U^{k+1}_{mn} can be calculated explicitly as a weighted mean of known values at level k. In stencil notation, the averaging mask is as follows:

0	$\tau\,\frac{D^k_{m,n+1} + D^k_{m,n}}{2h_2^2}$	0
$\tau\,\frac{D^k_{m-1,n} + D^k_{m,n}}{2h_1^2}$	$1 - \tau\,\frac{D^k_{m-1,n} + 2D^k_{m,n} + D^k_{m+1,n}}{2h_1^2} - \tau\,\frac{D^k_{m,n-1} + 2D^k_{m,n} + D^k_{m,n+1}}{2h_2^2}$	$\tau\,\frac{D^k_{m+1,n} + D^k_{m,n}}{2h_1^2}$
0	$\tau\,\frac{D^k_{m,n-1} + D^k_{m,n}}{2h_2^2}$	0

(15.35)

This example illustrates that nonlinear diffusion filtering can be realized by iteratively applying a 3×3 *averaging mask*, where the stencil weights are adapted to the underlying image structure via the diffusivity D. The weights have to be updated at each iteration step, as D depends on the evolving image.

It should be noted that the stencil weights sum up to 1. One can guarantee *stability* if one can ensure that all weights are nonnegative, because then the averaging operation calculates U^{k+1}_{mn} as a convex combination of values at time level k. This avoids over- and undershoots.

Nonnegativity is always satisfied for the noncentral weights. If $h_1 = h_2 = 1$ and the diffusivity D does not exceed 1 (as in all our examples), then the central stencil weight is nonnegative for

$$\tau \leq \frac{1}{4} \tag{15.36}$$

This time-step size restriction ensures stability of the scheme.

15.4.2 Anisotropic nonlinear diffusion

Let the diffusion tensor be represented by $\boldsymbol{D} = \begin{pmatrix} A & B \\ B & C \end{pmatrix}$, where all entries may depend on the underlying image structure. The functions A, B and C can be expressed in terms of the eigenvalues and eigenvectors of D

$$A = \lambda_1 \cos^2\psi + \lambda_2 \sin^2\psi \tag{15.37}$$

$$B = (\lambda_1 - \lambda_2)\sin\psi\cos\psi \tag{15.38}$$

$$C = \lambda_1 \sin^2\psi + \lambda_2 \cos^2\psi \tag{15.39}$$

For *edge-enhancing anisotropic diffusion* the eigenvalues λ_1 and λ_2 are given by Eq. (15.18) and Eq. (15.19), respectively, and the first eigenvector $(\cos\psi, \sin\psi)^T$ is parallel to ∇u_σ.

In the case of *coherence-enhancing anisotropic diffusion* we have to perform a principal component analysis of the structure tensor $\boldsymbol{J}_\rho = \begin{pmatrix} J_{11} & J_{12} \\ J_{12} & J_{22} \end{pmatrix}$ first. Its eigenvalues are given by

$$\mu_1 = \frac{1}{2}\left(J_{11} + J_{22} + \sqrt{(J_{11} - J_{22})^2 + 4J_{12}^2}\right) \tag{15.40}$$

$$\mu_2 = \frac{1}{2}\left(J_{11} + J_{22} - \sqrt{(J_{11} - J_{22})^2 + 4J_{12}^2}\right) \tag{15.41}$$

and the first eigenvector $(\cos\psi, \sin\psi)^T$ satisfies

$$\begin{pmatrix} \cos\psi \\ \sin\psi \end{pmatrix} \parallel \begin{pmatrix} 2J_{12} \\ J_{22} - J_{11} + \sqrt{(J_{11} - J_{22})^2 + 4J_{12}^2} \end{pmatrix} \tag{15.42}$$

The diffusion tensor uses identical eigenvectors and its eigenvalues are calculated via Eqs. (15.25) and (15.26) from the eigenvalues of the structure tensor.

An anisotropic diffusion filter can be written as

$$\begin{aligned} \partial_t u &= \operatorname{div}(\boldsymbol{D}\nabla u) = \operatorname{div}\begin{bmatrix} A\,\partial_x u + B\,\partial_y u \\ B\,\partial_x u + C\,\partial_y u \end{bmatrix} \\ &= \partial_x(A\,\partial_x u) + \partial_x(B\,\partial_y u) + \partial_y(B\,\partial_x u) + \partial_y(C\,\partial_y u) \end{aligned} \tag{15.43}$$

Compared to isotropic nonlinear diffusion, the main novelty of this process is the mixed derivative expression $\partial_x(B\,\partial_y u) + \partial_y(B\,\partial_x u)$. The standard central difference approximations to these terms are

$$\begin{aligned} \partial_x(B\,\partial_y u) &\approx \frac{1}{2h_1}\left(B_{m+1,n}\frac{U_{m+1,n+1} - U_{m+1,n-1}}{2h_2} - B_{m-1,n}\frac{U_{m-1,n+1} - U_{m-1,n-1}}{2h_2}\right) \\ \partial_y(B\,\partial_x u) &\approx \frac{1}{2h_2}\left(B_{m,n+1}\frac{U_{m+1,n+1} - U_{m-1,n+1}}{2h_1} - B_{m,n-1}\frac{U_{m+1,n-1} - U_{m-1,n-1}}{2h_1}\right) \end{aligned} \tag{15.44}$$

If the other derivatives are approximated as in Section 15.4.1, we obtain the averaging mask

$\tau \frac{-B^k_{m-1,n}-B^k_{m,n+1}}{4h_1h_2}$	$\tau \frac{C^k_{m,n+1}+C^k_{m,n}}{2h_2^2}$	$\tau \frac{B^k_{m+1,n}+B^k_{m,n+1}}{4h_1h_2}$
$\tau \frac{A^k_{m-1,n}+A^k_{m,n}}{2h_1^2}$	$1-\tau \frac{A^k_{m-1,n}+2A^k_{m,n}+A^k_{m+1,n}}{2h_1^2}$ $-\tau \frac{C^k_{m,n-1}+2C^k_{m,n}+C^k_{m,n+1}}{2h_2^2}$	$\tau \frac{A^k_{m+1,n}+A^k_{m,n}}{2h_1^2}$
$\tau \frac{B^k_{m-1,n}+B^k_{m,n-1}}{4h_1h_2}$	$\tau \frac{C^k_{m,n-1}+C^k_{m,n}}{2h_2^2}$	$\tau \frac{-B^k_{m+1,n}-B^k_{m,n-1}}{4h_1h_2}$

(15.45)

For sufficiently small τ, this mask reveals the sign pattern

?	+	?
+	+	+
?	+	?

(15.46)

It should be noted that b may have any sign. Thus, ? may become negative, and we cannot guarantee the stability of this scheme by regarding it as a convex combination.

Although this scheme may create some over- and undershoots, it is experimentally quite stable if the time step size τ does not exceed 0.25 for $h_1 = h_2 = 1$. This scheme is popular because of its simplicity.

It is possible to construct provably stable schemes where all stencil weights are nonnegative. They are, however, more complicated. More details can be found in Weickert [20, pp. 88-95].

15.5 Discrete theory

It would be desirable that the continuous well-posedness and scale-space properties also carry over to the discrete case. In order to establish similar results, it is instructive to write the explicit scheme (Eq. (15.34)) in a shorter and more abstract form. Instead of representing a pixel by a double index (m, n), we may also use a single index $i(m, n)$. Then Eq. (15.34) can be written as

$$u_i^{k+1} = u_i^k + \tau \sum_{l=1}^{2} \sum_{j \in \mathcal{N}_l(i)} \frac{D_j + D_i}{2h_l^2} (u_j - u_i) \tag{15.47}$$

where $\mathcal{N}_l(i)$ denotes the neighbors of pixel i in l-direction. This also takes into account the zero flux boundary conditions if we allow only inner neighbors. In vector-matrix notation, the preceding scheme gives

$$\boldsymbol{u}^{k+1} = \boldsymbol{Q}(\boldsymbol{u}^k)\,\boldsymbol{u}^k \tag{15.48}$$

where $\boldsymbol{Q}(\boldsymbol{u}) = (Q_{ij}(\boldsymbol{u}))_{ij}$ satisfies

$$Q_{ij} := \begin{cases} \tau \frac{D_i+D_j}{2h_l^2} & (j \in \mathcal{N}_l(i)) \\ 1 - \tau \sum\limits_{l=1}^{2} \sum\limits_{j\in\mathcal{N}_l(i)} \frac{D_i+D_j}{2h_l^2} & (j = i) \\ 0 & (\text{else}) \end{cases} \tag{15.49}$$

In order to interpret this scheme within a general framework, we study a filter class satisfying the subsequent requirements:

Let $\boldsymbol{g} \in \mathbb{R}^N$. Calculate a sequence $(\boldsymbol{u}^{(k)})_{k\in\mathbb{N}_0}$ of processed versions of $\boldsymbol{g}$ by means of

$$\begin{aligned} \boldsymbol{u}^0 &= \boldsymbol{g}, \\ \boldsymbol{u}^{k+1} &= \boldsymbol{Q}(\boldsymbol{u}^k)\,\boldsymbol{u}^k, \qquad \forall\, k \in \mathbb{N}_0, \end{aligned}$$

where $\boldsymbol{Q} = (Q_{ij})$ has the following properties: (P_d)

(D1)	continuity in its argument	
(D2)	symmetry:	$Q_{ij} = Q_{ji} \quad \forall\, i,j$
(D3)	unit row sum:	$\sum_j Q_{ij} = 1 \quad \forall\, i$
(D4)	nonnegativity:	$Q_{ij} \geq 0 \quad \forall\, i,j$
(D5)	irreducibility	
(D6)	positive diagonal	

$\boldsymbol{Q}$ is irreducible, if any two pixels are connected by a path with nonvanishing matrix elements. Formally: For any i, j there exist $k_0,\dots,k_r$ with $k_0 = i$ and $k_r = j$ such that $Q_{k_p k_{p+1}} \neq 0$ for $p = 0,\dots,r-1$.

Under these prerequisites one can establish results that are in complete analogy to the continuous setting [20]:

(a) *(Continuous dependence on initial image)*
For every $k > 0$ the unique solution $\boldsymbol{u}^k$ of (P_d) depends continuously on the initial image $\boldsymbol{f}$;

(b) *(Extremum principle)*
Let $a := \min_j f_j$ and $b := \max_j f_j$. Then, $a \leq u_i^k \leq b$ for all i and k;

(c) *(Average gray-level invariance)*
The average gray level $\mu := \frac{1}{N}\sum_j f_j$ is not affected by the discrete diffusion filter: $\frac{1}{N}\sum_j u_j^k = \mu$ for all $k \in \mathbb{N}_0$;

(d) *(Lyapunov sequences)*
$E(\boldsymbol{u}^k) := \sum_i r(u_i^k)$ is a Lyapunov sequence for all convex $r \in C[a,b]$: $E(\boldsymbol{u}^k)$ is decreasing in k and bounded from below by $\sum_i r(\mu)$;

(e) *(Convergence to a constant steady state)*
$\lim_{k \to \infty} u_i^k = \mu$ for all i.

Remarks:

(a) It is easy to see that Eq. (15.48) satisfies (D1)–(D6) for $\tau < 0.25$: Indeed, (D1)–(D3) are automatically satisfied by the construction of $\boldsymbol{Q}$. A positive diagonal of $\boldsymbol{Q}$ requires $\tau < 0.25$. All other elements of $\boldsymbol{Q}$ are automatically nonnegative, and the irreducibility follows from the fact that all pixels are connected with their neighbors through nonvanishing diffusivities;

(b) The standard discretization of the mixed derivative terms for anisotropic diffusion filters violate the nonnegativity requirement (D4). In Weickert [20], however, it is shown that one can construct more sophisticated discretizations that allow satisfying (D1)–(D6). Hence, the discrete scale-space theory is also applicable to anisotropic filters.

(c) The preceding explicit discretizations suffer from a restriction of their time-step-size τ. In practice, this restriction can be quite severe, requiring a large number of iterations with small step sizes in order to end up at an "interesting" time. This may lead to poor efficiency.
It is, however, possible to design absolutely stable schemes that do not suffer from any step-size limitations. The price one has to pay for this absolute stability is the solution of linear systems of equations. A recently established class of *additive operator splitting* (AOS) schemes [50] is an efficient representative of this class. They lead to very simple linear systems that can be solved in linear complexity by recursive filtering, and they separate each iteration step into 1-D diffusions that are summed up afterwards. They treat all axes equally, they satisfy (D1)–(D6), and (under typical accuracy requirements) they are about one order of magnitude more efficient than explicit schemes. A further speed-up by another order of magnitude is possible by implementing them on a *parallel computer* [51]. They are also applicable to anisotropic filters [20]. A detailed description of AOS algorithms can be found in Weickert et al. [50].

15.6 Parameter selection

The preceding model contains several parameters that have to be specified in practical situations. The goal of this section is to clarify their meaning and to present some empirical guidelines for their selection.

Because the time t is an inherent parameter in each continuous diffusion process, it has nothing to do with its discretization. The common tradition in image analysis, however, is to assign unit length to a pixel. In this case, a different discretization has to be regarded as a rescaling of the image domain. The scaling behavior of diffusion processes implies that a spatial rescaling that replaces x by βx, has to replace t by $\beta^2 t$. This means, for instance, that a subsampling in each image direction by a factor 2 results in a four times faster image evolution. Moreover, typical finite-difference implementations reveal a computational effort that is proportional to the pixel number. This gives another speed-up by a factor 4, such that the whole calculation becomes 16 times faster.

There remains another question to be addressed: what is a suitable *stopping time* t of the process? It should be observed that this question only appears when regarding the diffusion process as a *restoration method.* Considering it as a *scale-space* means that one is interested in the entire evolution. In a linear scale-space representation based on the diffusion process $\partial_t u = \Delta u$, the time t corresponds to a convolution with a Gaussian of standard deviation $\sigma = \sqrt{2t}$. Thus, specifying at spatial smoothing radius σ immediately determines the stopping time t.

In the nonlinear diffusion case, the smoothing is nonuniform and the time t is not directly related to a spatial scale. Other intuitive measures, such as counting the number of extrema, are also problematic for diffusion filters, as it is well known that for linear and nonlinear diffusion filters in dimensions ≥ 2, the number of local extrema does not necessarily decrease monotonically, that is, creation of extrema is not an exception but an event that happens generically [52].

However, there's another possibility to define an average measure for the simplicity or globality of the representation. This can be constructed by taking some *Lyapunov functional* $E(u(t))$ and investigating the expression

$$\Psi(u(t)) := \frac{E(g) - E(u(t))}{E(g) - E(\mu)} \tag{15.50}$$

We observe that $\Psi(u(t))$ increases monotonically from 0 to 1. It gives the average globality of $u(t)$ and its value can be used to measure the distance of $u(t)$ from the initial state g and its constant steady-state μ. Prescribing a certain value for Ψ provides us with an *a posteriori* criterion for the stopping time of the nonlinear diffusion process. Moreover, this strategy frees the users from any recalculations of the stopping time, if the image is resampled. Last but not least, Ψ can also be used to synchronize different nonlinear diffusion scale-spaces in order to ease the comparison of results. Practical applications to the restoration of medical images have demonstrated the usefulness and simplicity of this criterion [51, 53]. They use the variance as Lyapunov functional.

For the Perona-Malik filter, it is evident that the "optimal" value for the *contrast parameter* λ has to depend on the problem. One possibility to determine a good practical value for λ is to calculate a cumulate histogram for $|\nabla g|^2$ and to set λ to a certain quantile of this histogram. Perona and Malik use the 90% quantile, that is, 90% of all gradients are smaller than λ. Often one can get better results by staying more in the backward diffusion region, for example, by choosing a 50 % quantile. The smaller the quantile, however, the slower the diffusion. Other proposals for choosing λ use statistical properties of a training set of regions that are considered as flat [54], or estimate it by means of the local image geometry [7].

Regularized isotropic nonlinear diffusion and edge-enhancing anisotropic diffusion use another parameter besides λ, namely the *noise scale* σ. Because these filters are insensitive to scales smaller than σ, one should adapt σ to the noise. Useful values range from less than one pixel size for "noiseless" images to several pixels for more degraded images.

Coherence-enhancing anisotropic diffusion uses three other parameters: α, c, and ρ.

We have already seen that the regularization parameter α was introduced to ensure a small amount of isotropic diffusion. This parameter is mainly important for theoretical reasons. In practice, it can be fixed to a small value (e.g., 0.001), and no adaptation to the actual image material is required.

The parameter c is a threshold parameter playing a similar role as the contrast parameter λ in the other processes. Structures with coherence measures $(\mu_1 - \mu_2)^2 \ll c$ are regarded as almost isotropic, and the diffusion along the coherence direction v_2 tends to α. For $(\mu_1 - \mu_2)^2 \gg c$, the diffusion along the coherence direction v_2 tends to its maximal value, which is limited by 1. Therefore, c can be estimated by calculating a cumulate $(\mu_1 - \mu_2)^2$ histogram for g, and by setting c to a certain quantile. If one estimates that 95 % of the image locations have strongly preferred 1-D structures, one may set c to the 95 % quantile of the process.

The *integration scale* ρ of the structure tensor should reflect the texture scale of the problem. For instance, for a fingerprint image, it should not be smaller than the distance between two neighboring lines. Because overestimations are by far less critical than underestimations [20], it is often not very difficult to find parameter estimates that work well over the whole image domain. For coherence-enhancing diffusion, it is important that the noise scale σ is significantly smaller than the integration scale ρ; too large values for σ results in a cancellation of opposite gradient, and the orientation information in the texture is destroyed.

The suggestions in this section are intended as first guidelines. It is often reported that people who start using nonlinear diffusion filters quickly develop a good intuition for selecting appropriate parameters.

15.7 Generalizations

15.7.1 Similarity terms

Diffusion filters with a constant steady state require that a *stopping time* T be specified if one wants to get nontrivial results. A method to obtain nontrivial steady states consists of adding a reaction term that keeps the steady-state solution close to the original image [55, 56]

$$\partial_t u = \mathrm{div}(D(|\nabla u|^2)\, \nabla u) + \beta(g - u) \qquad (\beta > 0) \tag{15.51}$$

It should be noted that the additional similarity term does not solve the parameter selection problem; instead of specifying a stopping time T, one has to determine β. However, diffusion–reaction methods can be related to the minimization of *energy functionals*. These relations are discussed in Chapter 16.

15.7.2 Higher dimensions

It is easily seen that many of the previous results can be generalized to higher dimensions. This may be useful when considering, for example, CT or MR image sequences arising from medical applications or when applying diffusion filters to the postprocessing of fluctuating higher-dimensional numerical data. Spatially regularized 3-D nonlinear diffusion filters have been investigated by Gerig et al. [4] in the isotropic case, and by Rambaux and Garçon [57] in the edge-enhancing anisotropic case. Experiments with 3-D coherence-enhancing diffusion are presented in Weickert [58]. It should be noted that the entire continuous and discrete well-posedness and scale-space theory is applicable in any dimension.

15.7.3 Vector-valued models

Vector-valued images can arise either from devices measuring multiple physical properties or from a feature analysis of one single image. Examples for the first category are color images, multispectral Landsat exposures and multispin echo MR images, whereas representatives of the second class are given by statistical moments or the jet space induced by the image itself and its partial derivatives up to a given order. Feature vectors play an important role for tasks such as texture segmentation.

The simplest idea of how to apply diffusion filtering to *multichannel images* would be to diffuse all channels separately and independently from each other. This leads to the undesirable effect that edges may be formed at different locations for each channel. In order to avoid this, one should use a common diffusivity that combines information from

Figure 15.5: ***a*** *Forest scene, 226×323 pixels;* ***b*** *regularized isotropic nonlinear diffusion* $\sigma = 2$, $\lambda = 10$, $t = 25$; ***c*** *coherence-enhancing anisotropic diffusion* $c = 1$, $\sigma = 0.5$, $\rho = 5$, $t = 10$. *From Weickert [60].*

all channels. *Nonlinear isotropic vector-valued diffusion models* were studied by Gerig et al. [4] and Whitaker [15] in the context of medical imagery. They use filters of type

$$\partial_t u_i = \operatorname{div}\left(D\Big(\sum_{j=1}^{m} |\nabla u_{j,\sigma}|^2\Big)\,\nabla u_i\right) \qquad (i = 1, ..., m) \tag{15.52}$$

where the vector $[u_1(x,t), \ldots, u_m(x,t)]^T$ describes the multichannel image. It is assumed that all channels use a similar intensity range.

A corresponding *vector-valued edge-enhancing anisotropic diffusion* process is given by Weickert [59]

$$\partial_t u_i = \operatorname{div}\left(D\Big(\sum_{j=1}^{m} \nabla u_{j,\sigma}\,\nabla u_{j,\sigma}^T\Big)\,\nabla u_i\right) \qquad (i = 1, ..., m) \tag{15.53}$$

Vector-valued coherence-enhancing diffusion uses a common structure tensor that results from the sum of the structure tensors in all channels [60]

$$\partial_t u_i = \operatorname{div}\left(\boldsymbol{D}\Big(\sum_{j=1}^{m} J_\rho(\nabla u_{j,\sigma})\Big)\,\nabla u_i\right) \qquad (i = 1, ..., m) \tag{15.54}$$

Figure 15.5 illustrates the effect of Eqs. (15.52) and (15.54) on a color image.

15.8 Summary

In this chapter we have investigated several models for nonlinear diffusion filtering that serve as examples of how one can incorporate *a priori* knowledge in a scale-space evolution. These filters may also be regarded as enhancement methods for features such as edges or flow-like structures. We have discussed a general continuous well-posedness and scale-space theory, which also carries over to the algorithmically important discrete setting. Standard finite-difference algorithms allow realization of nonlinear diffusion filters by iterated avaraging with small masks where the stencil weights are adapted to the evolving image. Such methods are not difficult to implement and they can be generalized to filters for higher-dimensional data sets as well as vector-valued images.

This chapter is intended as an introduction to the topic. The area is very vivid, and much research is in progress with respect to theoretical foundations, highly efficient algorithms, relations between nonlinear diffusion and other image-processing methods such as curve evolutions, morphology, and snakes. For further studies of this and related areas, the reader is referred to Weickert [20], Caselles et al. [61], ter Haar Romeny [62], ter Haar Romeny et al. [63] and the references therein.

Acknowledgment

This work has been supported by the EU-TMR network VIRGO. The forest image has been kindly provided by Dr. Martin Reißel.

15.9 References

[1] Perona, P. and Malik, J., (1987). Scale space and edge detection using anisotropic diffusion. In *Proc. IEEE Comp. Soc. Workshop on Computer Vision, Miami Beach, Nov. 30 - Dec. 2, 1987*, pp. 16–22. Washington DC: IEEE Computer Society Press.

[2] Perona, P. and Malik, J., (1990). Scale space and edge detection using anisotropic diffusion. *IEEE Trans. Pattern Anal. Mach. Intell.*, **12**:629–639.

[3] Bajla, I., Marušiak, M., and Šrámek, M., (1993). Anisotropic filtering of MRI data based upon image gradient histogram. In *Computer analysis of images and patterns*, D. Chetverikov and W. Kropatsch, eds., Vol. 719 of *Lecture Notes in Comp. Science*, pp. 90–97. Berlin: Springer.

[4] Gerig, G., Kübler, O., Kikinis, R., and Jolesz, F., (1992). Nonlinear anisotropic filtering of MRI data. *IEEE Trans. Medical Imaging*, **11**:221–232.

[5] Lamberti, C., Sitta, M., and Sgallari, F., (1992). Improvements to the anisotropic diffusion model for 2-D echo image processing. In *Proc. An-*

nual Int. Conf. of the IEEE Engineering in Medicine and Biology Society, Vol. 14, pp. 1872-1873.

[6] Loew, M., Rosenman, J., and Chen, J., (1994). A clinical tool for enhancement of portal images. In *Image processing, SPIE*, M. Loew, ed., Vol. 2167, pp. 543-550.

[7] Luo, D.-S., King, M., and Glick, S., (1994). Local geometry variable conductance diffusion for post-reconstruction filtering. *IEEE Trans. Nuclear Sci.*, **41**:2800–2806.

[8] Sijbers, J., Scheunders, P., Verhoye, M., A. Van, d. L., Dyck, D. V., and Raman, E., (1997). Watershed-based segmentation of 3D MR data for volume quantization. *Magnetic Resonance Imaging*, **15**:679–688.

[9] Steen, E. and Olstad, B., (1994). Scale-space and boundary detection in ultrasonic imaging using nonlinear signal-adaptive anisotropic diffusion. In *Image Processing, SPIE*, M. Loew, ed., Vol. 2167, pp. 116–127.

[10] Ford, G., Estes, R., and Chen, H., (1992). Scale-space analysis for image sampling and interpolation. In *ICASSP-92, Proc. IEEE Int. Conf. Acoustics, Speech and Signal Processing, San Francisco, March 23–26, 1992*, Vol. 3, pp. 165-168.

[11] Weickert, J., (1996). Theoretical foundations of anisotropic diffusion in image processing. In *Theoretical Foundations of Computer Vision, Computing Suppl. 11*, W. Kropatsch, R. Klette, and F. Solina, eds., pp. 221–236. Wien: Springer.

[12] You, Y.-L. and Kaveh, M., (1996). Anisotropic blind image restoration. In *Proc. IEEE Int. Conf. Image Processing, ICIP-96, Lausanne, Sept. 16–19, 1996*, Vol. 2, pp. 461-464.

[13] Weickert, J., (1994). Anisotropic diffusion filters for image processing based quality control. In *Proc. Seventh European Conf. on Mathematics in Industry*, A. Fasano and M. Primicerio, eds., pp. 355–362. Stuttgart: Teubner.

[14] Weickert, J., (1995). Multiscale texture enhancement. In *Computer Analysis of Images and Patterns*, V. Hlaváč and R. Šára, eds., Vol. 970 of *Lecture Notes in Comp. Science*, pp. 230–237. Berlin: Springer.

[15] Whitaker, R., (1993). Geometry limited diffusion in the characterization of geometric patches in images. *CVGIP: Image Understanding*, **57**:111–120.

[16] Whitaker, R. and Gerig, G., (1994). Vector-valued diffusion. In *Geometry-Driven Diffusion in Computer Vision*, B. ter Haar Romeny, ed., pp. 93–134. Dordrecht: Kluwer.

[17] Acton, S., Bovik, A., and Crawford, M., (1994). Anisotropic diffusion pyramids for image segmentation. In *IEEE Int. Conf. Image Processing, Austin, Nov. 13–16, 1994*, Vol. 3, pp. 478–482. Los Alamitos: IEEE Computer Society Press.

[18] Acton, S. and Crawford, M., (1992). A mean field solution to anisotropic edge detection of remotely sensed data. In *Proc. 12th Int. Geoscience and Remote Sensing Symposium, Houston, May 26–29, 1992*, Vol. 2, pp. 845–847.

[19] Weickert, J., (1997). A review of nonlinear diffusion filtering. In *Scale-Space Theory in Computer Vision*, B. ter Haar Romeny, L. Florack, J. Koenderink, and M. Viergever, eds., Vol. 1252 of *Lecture Notes in Computer Science*, pp. 3–28. Berlin: Springer.

[20] Weickert, J., (1998). *Anisotropic Diffusion in Image Processing.* Stuttgart: Teubner-Verlag.

[21] Crank, J., (1975). *The Mathematics of Diffusion.* 2nd edition. Oxford: Oxford University Press.

[22] Witkin, A., (1983). Scale-space filtering. In *Proc. Eight Int. Joint Conf. on Artificial Intelligence, IJCAI '83, Karlsruhe, Aug. 8–12, 1983*, Vol. 2, pp. 1019–1022.

[23] Iijima, T., (1962). Basic theory on normalization of pattern (in case of typical one-dimensional pattern). *Bulletin of the Electrotechnical Laboratory (in Japanese)*, **26**:368–388.

[24] Weickert, J., Ishikawa, S., and Imiya, A., (1997). On the history of Gaussian scale-space axiomatics. In *Gaussian Scale-Space Theory*, J. Sporring, M. Nielsen, L. Florack, and P. Johansen, eds., pp. 45–59. Dordrecht: Kluwer.

[25] Florack, L., (1997). *The Structure of Scalar Images.* Dordrecht: Kluwer.

[26] Lindeberg, T., (1994). *Scale-Space Theory in Computer Vision.* Boston: Kluwer.

[27] Sporring, J., Nielsen, M., Florack, L., and Johansen, P. (eds.), (1997). *Gaussian Scale-Space Theory.* Dordrecht: Kluwer.

[28] Bergholm, F., (1987). Edge focusing. *IEEE Trans. Pattern Anal. Mach. Intell.*, **9**:726–741.

[29] Kawohl, B. and Kutev, N., (1997). *Maximum and Comparison Principles for Anisotropic Diffusion (Preprint).* Cologne, Germany: Mathematical Institute, University of Cologne.

[30] Kichenassamy, S., (1997). The Perona-Malik paradox. *SIAM J. Appl. Math.*, **57**:1343–1372.

[31] You, Y.-L., Xu, W., Tannenbaum, A., and Kaveh, M., (1996). Behavioral analysis of anisotropic diffusion in image processing. *IEEE Trans. Image Proc.*, **5**:1539–1553.

[32] Weickert, J. and Benhamouda, B., (1997). A semidiscrete nonlinear scale-space theory and its relation to the Perona–Malik paradox. In *Advances in Computer Vision*, F. Solina, W. Kropatsch, R. Klette, and R. Bajcsy, eds., pp. 1–10. Wien: Springer.

[33] Benhamouda, B., (1994). *Parameter Adaptation for Nonlinear Diffusion in Image Processing.* Master thesis, Dept. of Mathematics, University of Kaiserslautern, Germany.

[34] Catté, F., Lions, P.-L., Morel, J.-M., and Coll, T., (1992). Image selective smoothing and edge detection by nonlinear diffusion. *SIAM J. Numer. Anal.*, **29**:182–193.

[35] Nitzberg, M. and Shiota, T., (1992). Nonlinear image filtering with edge and corner enhancement. *IEEE Trans. Pattern Anal. Mach. Intell.*, **14**:826–833.

[36] Fröhlich, J. and Weickert, J., (1994). *Image Processing using a Wavelet Algorithm for Nonlinear Diffusion. Report No. 104, Laboratory of Technomathematics.* Kaiserslautern, Germany: University of Kaiserslautern.

[37] Cottet, G.-H. and Germain, L., (1993). Image processing through reaction combined with nonlinear diffusion. *Math. Comp.*, **61**:659–673.

[38] Förstner, M. and Gülch, E., (1987). A fast operator for detection and precise location of distinct points, corners and centres of circular features. In *Proc. ISPRS Intercommission Conf. on Fast Processing of Photogrammetric Data, Interlaken, 1987.*

[39] Rao, A. and Schunck, B., (1991). Computing oriented texture fields. *CVGIP: Graphical Models and Image Processing*, **53**:157–185.

[40] Bigün, J. and Granlund, G., (1987). Optimal orientation detection of linear symmetry. In *Proc. First Int. Conf. on Computer Vision (ICCV), London, June 8-11, 1987*, pp. 433–438. Washington: IEEE Computer Society Press.

[41] Kass, M. and Witkin, A., (1987). Analyzing oriented patterns. *Computer Vision, Graphics, and Image Processing*, **37**:362–385.

[42] Hummel, R., (1986). Representations based on zero-crossings in scale space. In *Proc. IEEE Comp. Soc. Conf. Computer Vision and Pattern Recognition, CVPR '86, Miami Beach, June 22–26, 1986*, pp. 204–209. Washington: IEEE Computer Society Press.

[43] Alvarez, L., Guichard, F., Lions, P.-L., and Morel, J.-M., (1993). Axioms and fundamental equations in image processing. *Arch. Rational Mech. Anal.*, **123**:199–257.

[44] Niessen, W., Vincken, K., Weickert, J., and Viergever, M., (1997). Nonlinear multiscale representations for image segmentation. *Computer Vision and Image Understanding*, **66**:233–245.

[45] Jägersand, M., (1995). Saliency maps and attention selection in scale and spatial coordinates: an information theoretic approach. In *Proc. Fifth Int. Conf. on Computer Vision, ICCV '95, Cambridge, June 20–23, 1995*, pp. 195–202. Los Alamitos: IEEE Computer Society Press.

[46] Sporring, J., (1996). The entropy of scale-space. In *Proc. 13th Int. Conf. Pattern Recognition, ICPR 13, Vienna, Aug. 25–30, 1996*, Vol. A, pp. 900–904.

[47] Sporring, J. and Weickert, J., (1997). On generalized entropies and scale-space. In *Scale-Space Theory in Computer Vision*, B. ter Haar Romeny, L. Florack, J. Koenderink, and M. Viergever, eds., Vol. 1252 of *Lecture Notes in Computer Science*, pp. 53–64. Berlin: Springer.

[48] Morton, K. and Mayers, D., (1994). *Numerical Solution of Partial Differential Equations.* Cambridge: Cambridge University Press.

[49] Mitchell, A. and Griffiths, D., (1980). *The Finite Difference Method in Partial Differential Equations.* Chichester: Wiley.

[50] Weickert, J., ter Haar Romeny, B., and Viergever, M., (1998). Efficient and reliable schemes for nonlinear diffusion filtering. *IEEE Trans. Image Proc.*, **7**:398–410.

[51] Weickert, J., Zuiderveld, K., ter Haar Romeny, B., and Niessen, W., (1997). Parallel implementations of AOS schemes: a fast way of nonlinear diffu-

sion filtering. In *Proc. 1997 IEEE International Conference on Image Processing, ICIP-97, Santa Barbara, Oct. 26–29, 1997*, Vol. 3, pp. 396–399. Piscataway, NJ: IEEE Signal Processing Society.

[52] Rieger, J., (1995). Generic evolution of edges on families of diffused gray value surfaces. *J. Math. Imag. Vision*, **5**:207–217.

[53] Niessen, W., Vincken, K., Weickert, J., and Viergever, M., (1998). Three-dimensional MR brain segmentation. In *Proc. Sixth Int. Conf. on Computer Vision, ICCV '98, Bombay, Jan. 4–7, 1998*, pp. 53–58.

[54] Yoo, T. and Coggins, J., (1993). Using statistical pattern recognition techniques to control variable conductance diffusion. In *Information Processing in Medical Imaging*, H. Barrett and A. Gmitro, eds., Vol. 687 of *Lecture Notes in Computer Science*, pp. 459–471. Berlin: Springer.

[55] Nordström, N., (1990). Biased anisotropic diffusion—a unified regularization and diffusion approach to edge detection. *Image Vision Comput.*, **8**: 318–327.

[56] Schnörr, C., (1994). Unique reconstruction of piecewise smooth images by minimizing strictly convex non-quadratic functionals. *Jour. Math. Imag. Vision*, **4**:189–198.

[57] Rambaux, I. and Garçon, P., (1994). *Nonlinear Anisotropic Diffusion Filtering of 3-D Images.* Project work, Département Génie Mathématique, INSA de Rouen and Laboratory of Technomathematics, University of Kaiserslautern, Kaiserslautern, Germany.

[58] Weickert, J., (1999). Coherence-enhancing diffusion filtering. *To appear in Int. J. Comput. Vision.*

[59] Weickert, J., (1994). *Scale-Space Properties of Nonlinear Diffusion Filtering with a Diffusion Tensor.* Report No. 110, Laboratory of Technomathematics, University of Kaiserslautern, Kaiserslautern, Germany.

[60] Weickert, J., (1997). Coherence-enhancing diffusion of color images (Extended version to appear in Image and Vision Computing). In *Pattern Recognition and Image Analysis, VII NSPRIA, Barcelona, April 21–25, 1997*, A. Sanfeliu, J. Villanueva, and J. Vitrià, eds., pp. 239–244. Barcelona: Centro de Visió per Computador.

[61] Caselles, V., Morel, J., Sapiro, G., and A. Tannenbaum (eds.), (1998). Partial differential equations and geometry-driven diffusion in image processing and analysis. *IEEE Trans. Image Proc.*, **7(3)**.

[62] ter Haar Romeny, B. (ed.), (1994). *Geometry-Driven Diffusion in Computer Vision.* Dordrecht: Kluwer.

[63] ter Haar Romeny, B., Florack, L., Koenderink, J., and Viergever, M. (eds.), (1997). *Scale-space theory in computer vision*, Vol. 1252 of *Lecture Notes in Computer Science*, Berlin. Springer.

16 Variational Methods for Adaptive Image Smoothing and Segmentation

Christoph Schnörr

Lehrstuhl für Bildverarbeitung, Fakultät für Mathematik und Informatik
Universität Mannheim, Germany

16.1 Introduction

This chapter explains variational techniques for the adaptive processing of 2-D and 3-D images, vector-valued images, and image sequences for the purpose of nonlinear smoothing, segmentation, extraction of local image structure (homogeneous regions, edges, characteristic points), noise suppression and restoration, and computation of optical flow. For each category of image data, the exposition provides:

Handbook of Computer Vision and Applications
Volume 2
Signal Processing and Pattern Recognition

Copyright © 1999 by Academic Press
All rights of reproduction in any form reserved.
ISBN 0-12-379772-1/$30.00

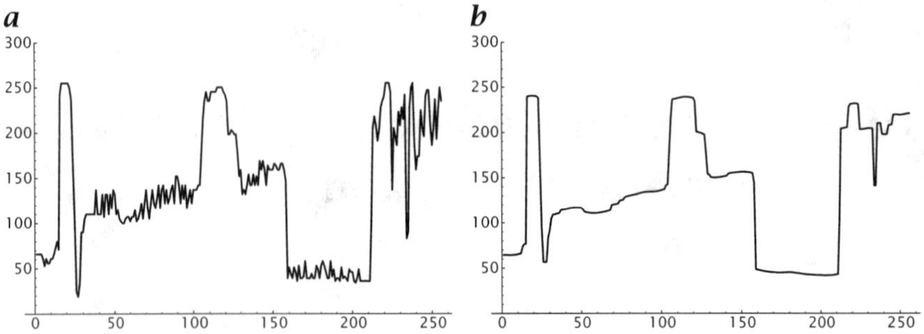

Figure 16.1: ***a*** *Data from a real image;* ***b*** *the data from* ***a*** *adaptively smoothed.*

- a description of a variational approach,
- a consistent discretization of the approach (results are provided in terms of computational molecules),
- an iterative scheme to solve the resulting system of nonlinear equations numerically, and
- examples computed to indicate the range of applications.

The material presented introduces the reader to a specific research field of image processing and computer vision and should enable him to integrate these techniques into solution approaches to diverse application problems.

16.1.1 Motivation and general problem formulation

Consider the data in Fig. 16.1a and the result of applying a variational technique in Fig. 16.1b. Obviously, small signal variations have been smoothed out whereas the coarse signal structure in terms of more distinct signal variations has been preserved. Thus, the data have been processed by a smoothing process that is capable of adapting itself to the local signal structure. The need for this kind of unsupervised (pre-)processing arises in numerous applications involving real data.

In a more general way, the following important issues underlie the design of variational techniques for adaptive image processing:

- Data reduction by adaptively suppressing image details (local signal variations), as illustrated in Fig. 16.1.
- Partitioning of the image domain into locations with significant signal variations and homogeneous regions (image segmentation). Localization of signal variations is important along with the robust contrast information of regions.
- Optimality of segmentations in terms of measures of "strength of local signal variation" and "homogeneity."

- Discretization and consistency. Many useful concepts and properties like "level lines of functions" or "rotational invariance" are meaningful only for continuous problem formulations. Approximate problem formulations that preserve such concepts and properties in the limit of increasingly fine discretizations are called *consistent*.
- Computational architecture and parallelism. As is obvious from Fig. 16.1, the result at a certain location cannot be computed by just taking two neighboring data points into consideration. Rather, a local context of several data points has to be considered. Nevertheless, all approaches described in this chapter can be realized on fine-grained parallel architectures with nearest-neighbor communication.

In general, a *variational approach* is formulated by considering input data $g \in S_1$ and the processed data $v_g \in S_2$ as elements of some spaces S_1, S_2 of functions defined over the given image domain A, and by defining v_g as a solution of a minimization problem:

$$v_g = \arg\min_{v \in S_2} J(v)\,, \quad J(v) = \int_A L(g, v)\,\mathrm{d}\boldsymbol{x} \tag{16.1}$$

where the function L depends on the problem at hand. In most cases, the right-hand side of Eq. (16.1) can be decomposed as follows:

$$J(v) = \int_A L_g(g, v)\,\mathrm{d}\boldsymbol{x} + \int_{A_r} L_r(v)\,\mathrm{d}\boldsymbol{x} + \int_{A_t} L_t(v)\,\mathrm{d}\boldsymbol{x} \tag{16.2}$$

Here, the sets A_r and A_t define a partition of the image domain A into *regions* and *transitions* and are implicitly defined by local properties of the functions v, like the magnitude of the gradient, for example. As a consequence, the optimal segmentation of A is obtained by computing the minimum v_g of the functional J in Eq. (16.1).

16.1.2 Basic references to the literature

In this section, references are given to some important research papers as well as to other fields related to the contents of this chapter. No attempt, however, has been made to survey any aspect of variational modeling in image processing and early computer vision. The general references given here will be supplemented by more specific references in subsequent sections.

A clear-cut mathematical definition of the image segmentation problem has been given by [1]:

$$J_{MS}(v, K) = \alpha \int_A (v - g)^2\,\mathrm{d}\boldsymbol{x} + \int_{A \setminus K} |\nabla v|^2\,\mathrm{d}\boldsymbol{x} + \beta \mathcal{L}(K) \tag{16.3}$$

Given some image data g, a piecewise smooth function v_g, which may have jumps along a 1-D discontinuity set $K \subset A$, has to be determined such that the functional J in Eq. (16.3) attains a local minimum. According to the general form of Eq. (16.2), the functional Eq. (16.3) comprises three terms: The first term measures the distance between v and the data g with respect to the $L^2(A)$-norm, the second term measures the homogeneity of v in terms of the magnitude of the gradient of v:

$$|\nabla v| = \left\| \begin{bmatrix} v_x \\ v_y \end{bmatrix} \right\| = \left(v_x^2 + v_y^2\right)^{1/2}, \quad \text{for} \quad \boldsymbol{x} = \begin{bmatrix} x \\ y \end{bmatrix} \in \mathcal{R}^2$$

and the third term measures the length of the discontinuity set K. The relative influence of these terms depends on two global parameters α and β that can be controlled by the user. The reader should note that dropping any term in Eq. (16.3) would lead to meaningless minimizers and segmentations, respectively.

The variational segmentation approach of Mumford and Shah provides a mathematically sound definition of what most conventional segmentation approaches (see, e.g., [2, 3]) try to achieve. This has been demonstrated in a recent review [4]. On the other hand, the approach of Eq. (16.3) turned out to be mathematically rather involved, and it is by no means straightforward to specify consistent discrete approximations of it (see [4, 5], and [6] for a simplified version of the approach of Eq. (16.3)). For these reasons, we confine ourselves in Section 16.2 to mathematically simpler yet practically useful variational problems that, in some sense, approximate the approach Eq. (16.3) of Mumford and Shah.

Rather influential results in the field of image segmentation and restoration have been presented by Geman and Geman [7]. Their approach can be seen as a discrete counterpart of the Mumford-Shah model given here. Furthermore, their seminal paper describes a probabilistic problem/solution formulation in terms of *Markov random fields*, *Gibbs distributions*, and Gibbs sampling, which turned out to be basic to much subsequent work. Gibbs distributions are nowadays widely used across several disciplines in order to model spatial context. This broader probabilistic viewpoint, however, will not be pursued in this chapter. We merely point to the fact that all functionals J considered here induce Gibbs distributions over the space S_2 in Eq. (16.1) in a natural way by means of:

$$p(v) = \frac{1}{Z} \exp\left(-J(v)\right)$$

with a normalizing constant Z. For a recent review we refer to Li [8], and for a more mathematically oriented account to Geman [9] and Winkler [10].

Further important work has been reported by Blake and Zisserman [11]. In particular, their Graduated-Non-Convexity approach introduced the idea of homotopy-like deterministic minimization algorithms to the field of computer vision. The related concept of mean-field annealing has been presented by Geiger and Girosi [12]. See also Geiger and Yuille [13] for a review of variational segmentation approaches. Anticipating Section 16.2.3, let us mention that we do not pursue these concepts, which amount to solving sequences of *nonlinear* systems of equations, here. Rather, we explain a minimization algorithm in terms of sequences of *linear* systems of equations, which, from our point of view, is more compatible with current concepts of parallel computing.

Another important current research field is known under the keyword "*images and PDEs*" [14] (PDE = partial differential equation). The connection to this field is given by the Euler-Lagrange equation, which corresponds to the functional Eq. (16.1) (see Section 16.2.1). This nonlinear diffusion equation may be used to describe how a starting point approaches a minimizer of the functional J. In the field "images and PDEs," however, more general types of *nonlinear diffusion* equations are investigated. Corresponding research topics include nonlinear smoothing schemes for edge-detection and image enhancement, extensions of the linear scale-space paradigm and invariance principles, and equations describing the evolution of active contours (so-called 'snakes'). For further details and surveys we refer to [15, 16, 17, 18, 19, 20] and Volume 2, Chapter 15.

Within this field, the nonlinear smoothing schemes described in this chapter form a special class. The distinguishing feature is that each approach obeys a global optimality criterion Eq. (16.1) that makes explicit how different criteria Eq. (16.2) are combined in order to compute an optimal segmentation of given image data. Note that Euler-Lagrange equations are not needed for implementing a variational technique. Furthermore, there are many well-posed variational approaches, like that of Eq. (16.3) for example, the functionals of which are not smooth enough to admit an equivalent description in terms of PDEs.

16.2 Processing of two- and three-dimensional images

This section describes variational techniques for the processing of scalar-valued images. In Section 16.2.1, a variational principle is presented and related mathematical issues are discussed. In particular, we distinguish convex from nonconvex minimization approaches. Section 16.2.2 shows how these approaches are converted into nonlinear systems of equations. An algorithm to numerically compute a solution to these equations is described in Section 16.2.3. Finally, some representative numerical examples are presented in Section 16.2.4.

16.2.1 Variational principle

We consider a family of functionals Eq. (16.1) of the following form:

$$J(v) = \frac{1}{2}\int_A \left\{(v-g)^2 + \lambda(|\nabla v|)\right\} \mathrm{d}\boldsymbol{x} \tag{16.4}$$

This formulation has been introduced by Nordström [22]. Among various possibilities, we choose two particular definitions of the function λ (see Fig. 16.2):

$$\lambda_c(t) = \begin{cases} \lambda_{c,\mathrm{low}}(t) = \lambda_h^2 t^2 & , 0 \le t \le c_\rho \\ \lambda_{c,\mathrm{high}}(t) = \epsilon_c^2 t^2 + (\lambda_h^2 - \epsilon_c^2) c_\rho (2t - c_\rho) & , 0 < c_\rho \le t \end{cases} \tag{16.5}$$

and

$$\lambda_{nc}(t) = \begin{cases} \lambda_{nc,\mathrm{low}}(t) = \lambda_h^2 t^2 & , 0 \le t \le c_\rho \\ \lambda_{nc,\mathrm{high}}(t) & , 0 < c_\rho \le t \end{cases} \tag{16.6}$$

where

$$\lambda_{nc,\mathrm{high}}(t) = \begin{cases} \frac{1}{2\delta t}\Big[(\epsilon_{nc} - 2\lambda_h^2 c_\rho)t^2 \\ \quad +(2\lambda_h^2(c_\rho + \delta t) - \epsilon_{nc}) c_\rho (2t - c_\rho)\Big] & , t \le c_\rho + \delta t \\ \epsilon_{nc}\left(t - c_\rho - \frac{\delta t}{2}\right) + c_\rho \lambda_h^2 (c_\rho + \delta t) & , c_\rho + \delta t \le t \end{cases}$$

$0 < \epsilon_c, \delta t \ll 1$, and $\epsilon_{nc} < 2\lambda_h^2 c_\rho$. These functions are continuously differentiable, and the essential parameters to be specified by the user are λ_h and c_ρ. Definitions Eq. (16.5) and Eq. (16.6) lead to representative examples of *convex* and *nonconvex* variational approaches, respectively, as they exhibit the essential features of other definitions that have been reported in the literature (see the list in [23], for example),

According to Eq. (16.2), the functional Eq. (16.4) takes the form:

$$J(v) = \frac{1}{2}\int_A (v-g)^2 \,\mathrm{d}\boldsymbol{x} + \frac{1}{2}\int_{A_r} \lambda_{\mathrm{low}}(|\nabla v|)\,\mathrm{d}\boldsymbol{x} + \frac{1}{2}\int_{A_t} \lambda_{\mathrm{high}}(|\nabla v|)\,\mathrm{d}\boldsymbol{x} \tag{16.7}$$

where the region and transition sets A_r and A_t are defined by low and high magnitudes of the gradient of v, respectively:

$$A_r = \{x \in A : |\nabla v| \le c_\rho\} \tag{16.8}$$

$$A_t = \{x \in A : |\nabla v| > c_\rho\} \tag{16.9}$$

Let us briefly discuss some major differences between the convex and nonconvex case of Eq. (16.4):

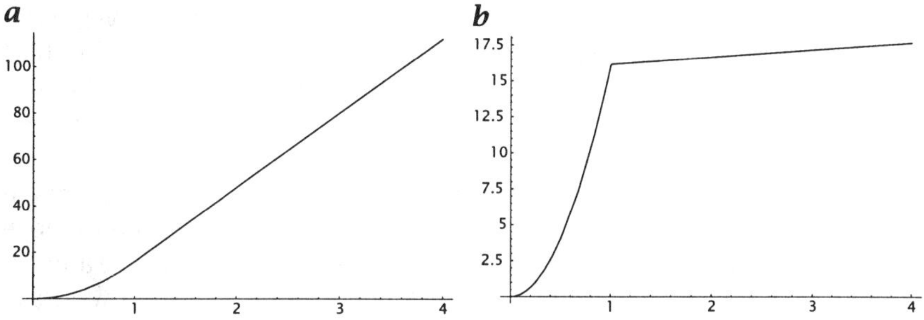

Figure 16.2: ***a*** *Graph of λ_c, which is a convex combination of a quadratic and a linear function ($\lambda_h = 4, c_\rho = 1, \epsilon_c = 0.1$);* ***b*** *graph of λ_{nc}, which quadratically combines a quadratic function with a linear function of slope $\epsilon_{nc}(\lambda_h = 4, c_\rho = 1, \delta t = 0.01, \epsilon_{nc} = 0.5)$.*

Convex case. In this case the continuous problem formulation Eq. (16.4) is well-posed for a certain choice of function spaces S_1, S_2 in Eq. (16.1), and for each given image data g there is a unique function v_g minimizing the functional J in Eq. (16.1) with $\lambda = \lambda_c$ from Eq. (16.5). With other words, the intrinsic properties of the approach are well-defined and do not depend on discrete concepts used for modeling sensors and computation. Furthermore, any discrete solution $v_{h,g}$ computed as shown in subsequent sections approximates the function v_g in the sense that, as the resolution of the sensor becomes increasingly better, we have:

$$\|v_g - v_{h,g}\|_{S_2} \to 0$$

Convex variational approaches have been advocated by several researchers (e.g., [24, 25, 26]), mainly due to uniqueness of the solution. Our definition Eq. (16.5) given in the preceding follows Schnörr [25]. We note, however, that in addition to uniqueness of the solution, convex variational approaches exhibit favorable properties like continuous dependence of the solution on the data and parameters, for example. Furthermore, a comparison of Eq. (16.7), regarded as an approximation of the Mumford-Shah model, with Eq. (16.3) reveals that using $\lambda_{c,\text{high}}$ for the transition measure in Eq. (16.7) does not mean to make a bad compromise in order to achieve convexity. Rather, the length of the discontinuity set of v in Eq. (16.3) is replaced by length of level lines of v, which are summed up over the contrast at locations where v rapidly varies. This is a meaningful measure for real signals with bounded gradients [27].

Nonconvex case. In this case, to our knowledge, no continuous and well-posed problem formulation of Eq. (16.4) has been reported in the literature. This means that, strictly speaking, the variational approach of Eq. (16.4) with λ_{nc} from Eq. (16.6) makes sense mathematically only after having discretized the approach. In contrast to the convex case, the resulting approach depends on the particular discretization method used. Our definition Eq. (16.6) given here follows closely Blake and Zisserman [11] who thoroughly investigated a discrete version of the nonconvex approach of Eq. (16.4).

In general, there are multiple local minima $\{v_g\}$ for given image data g, making the approach dependent on the starting point and more sensitive against perturbations of the input image data and parameter values. A comparison of the nonconvex version of Eq. (16.4) with the Mumford-Shah model Eq. (16.3) shows that the 1-D discontinuity measure in Eq. (16.3) is approximated by the area of regions with a large gradient of v. In contrast to the convex case discussed here, however, further properties of v are not "measured" within these regions. A numerical example in Section 16.2.4 illustrates this point.

For the purpose of discretization in Section 16.2.2, we set the first variation of the functional Eq. (16.4) at the point v_g equal to zero, as a necessary condition for v_g to be a local minimizer of J. $\forall v \in S_2$:

$$\frac{\mathrm{d}}{\mathrm{d}\tau} J(v_g + \tau v)\big|_{\tau=0} = \int_A \left\{(v_g - g)v + \rho(|\nabla v_g|)\nabla v_g^T \nabla v\right\} \mathrm{d}\boldsymbol{x} = 0 \qquad (16.10)$$

where we introduced the so-called diffusion coefficient:

$$\rho(t) = \frac{\lambda'(t)}{2t}, \quad t \geq 0 \qquad (16.11)$$

Note that in the convex case, Eq. (16.10) uniquely determines the global minimizer v_g of J in Eq. (16.4).

For the following it will be convenient to write Eq. (16.10) in a more compact form. To this end, we use the customary notation for the *linear* action of some functional q on a function v:

$$\langle q, v\rangle := q(v) \qquad (16.12)$$

Equation (16.10) may then be written as follows:

$$\langle A(v_g), v\rangle = \langle f, v\rangle, \quad \forall v \in S_2 \qquad (16.13)$$

with a nonlinear operator A mapping v_g to the linear functional $A(v_g)$:

$$\langle A(v_g), v\rangle = \int_A \left\{v_g v + \rho(|\nabla v_g|)\nabla v_g^T \nabla v\right\} \mathrm{d}\boldsymbol{x} \qquad (16.14)$$

and the linear functional f:

$$\langle f, v\rangle = \int_A g v \,\mathrm{d}\boldsymbol{x} \qquad (16.15)$$

Equation (16.13) is the starting point for the discretization with the *finite element method* (FEM) to be described in Section 16.2.2.

16.2.2 Finite element method discretization

We first explain the basic scheme that can be applied mechanically to obtain a proper discretization of all variational approaches described in this chapter. Next we illustrate the application of this scheme for the case of 1-D signals. Finally, the results of discretizing the 2-D and 3-D cases are described.

The material presented in this Section is fairly standard. A more general introduction and further details can be found in numerous textbooks on the *finite element method*.

Basic scheme. The first step is to triangulate the underlying domain A and to choose piecewise linear basis functions $\phi_i(\boldsymbol{x}), i = 1, \dots, N$. Examples will be given in the following sections. These basis functions define a linear subspace:

$$S_h := \operatorname{span}\{\phi_1, \dots, \phi_N\} \subset S_2$$

and we approximate problem Eq. (16.13) by restricting it to this subspace. Let $v_{h,g}, v_h \in S_h$ denote representatives of the functions $v_g, v \in S_2$ (h denotes the discretization parameter related to the mesh-width of the triangulation):

$$v_{h,g} = \sum_{i=1}^{N} \boldsymbol{v}_{g,i} \phi_i(\boldsymbol{x}) \,, \qquad v_h = \sum_{i=1}^{N} \boldsymbol{v}_i \phi_i(\boldsymbol{x}) \tag{16.16}$$

Then our task is to solve the following equation for a minimizing function $v_{h,g}$:

$$\langle A(v_{h,g}), v_h \rangle = \langle f, v_h \rangle \,, \quad \forall v_h \in S_h \tag{16.17}$$

Inserting Eq. (16.16) yields (recall from Eq. (16.12) that the left-hand quantities in Eq. (16.17) act *linearly* on v_h):

$$\sum_{i=1}^{N} \boldsymbol{v}_i \langle A(v_{h,g}), \phi_i \rangle = \sum_{i=1}^{N} \boldsymbol{v}_i \langle f, \phi_i \rangle \,, \quad \forall v_h \in S_h$$

This equation has to be satisfied for *arbitrary* functions $v_h \in S_h$. Hence, we conclude that:

$$\langle A(v_{h,g}), \phi_i \rangle = \langle f, \phi_i \rangle \,, \quad i = 1, \dots, N \tag{16.18}$$

Eq. (16.18) is a system of N nonlinear equations that has to be solved for the N real numbers $\boldsymbol{v}_{g,j}, j = 1, \dots, N$, that determine a minimizing function $v_{h,g}$ in Eq. (16.16). Again we note that in the convex case, this nonlinear vector equation has a unique solution $\boldsymbol{v}_g$. Numerical schemes to compute $\boldsymbol{v}_g$ are the subject of Section 16.2.3.

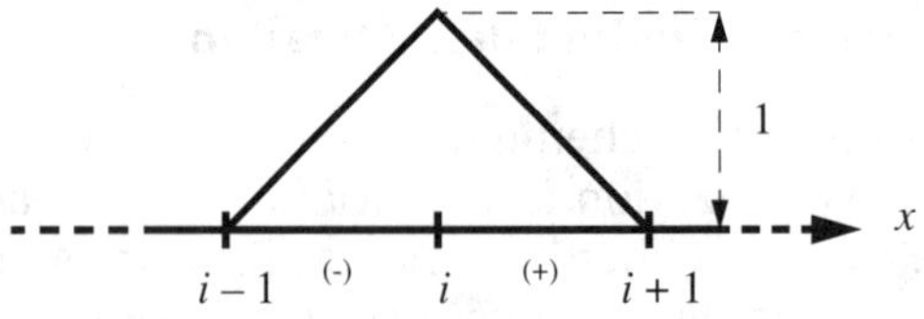

Figure 16.3: *A piecewise linear basis function for the 1-D case.*

Introductory Example: 1-D signals. Suppose the input signal g is given on a regularly spaced mesh as shown in Fig. 16.1a. To each node $i = 1, \ldots, N$ we assign a basis function ϕ_i as depicted in Fig. 16.3. Note that the function ϕ_i is uniquely defined by the following three conditions:

- ϕ_i is piecewise linear,
- $\phi_i = 1$ at node i, and
- $\phi_i = 0$ at all nodes $j \neq i$.

This holds true in the 2-D and 3-D case, too (see in what follows). Furthermore, we set without loss of generality the distance between adjacent pixels equal to 1.

Next we wish to compute the i-th equation of Eq. (16.18). To this end, we represent g in the same way as $v_{h,g}$:

$$g(x) = \sum_{i=1}^{N} \boldsymbol{g}_i \phi_i(x)$$

Furthermore, we denote the two constant values of $\rho(|v'_{h,g}(x)|)$ within the intervals around node i with $\rho_{(+)}$ and $\rho_{(-)}$, respectively (see Fig. 16.3). For example, for any x in the interval $(+)$ we have:

$$\rho_{(+)} = \rho\left(\left|\sum_{j=1}^{N} \boldsymbol{v}_{g,j}\phi'_j(x)\right|\right) = \rho(|\boldsymbol{v}_{g,i+1} - \boldsymbol{v}_{g,i}|)$$

Using this notation and Eqs. (16.14) and (16.15), the i-th equation of Eq. (16.18) then reads:

$$\frac{1}{6}\boldsymbol{v}_{g,i-1} + \frac{2}{3}\boldsymbol{v}_{g,i} + \frac{1}{6}\boldsymbol{v}_{g,i+1} + \rho_{(-)}(\boldsymbol{v}_{g,i} - \boldsymbol{v}_{g,i-1}) - \rho_{(+)}(\boldsymbol{v}_{g,i+1} - \boldsymbol{v}_{g,i})$$

$$= \frac{1}{6}\boldsymbol{g}_{i-1} + \frac{2}{3}\boldsymbol{g}_i + \frac{1}{6}\boldsymbol{g}_{i+1}, \quad i = 2, \ldots, N-1 \tag{16.19}$$

Note that at the boundary node only the half support of ϕ_1 and ϕ_N, respectively, lie within the domain A. As a consequence, the *natural*

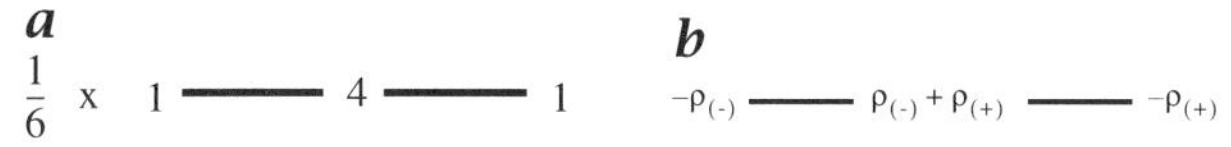

Figure 16.4: *1-D case:* ***a*** *first; and* ***b*** *second stencil.*

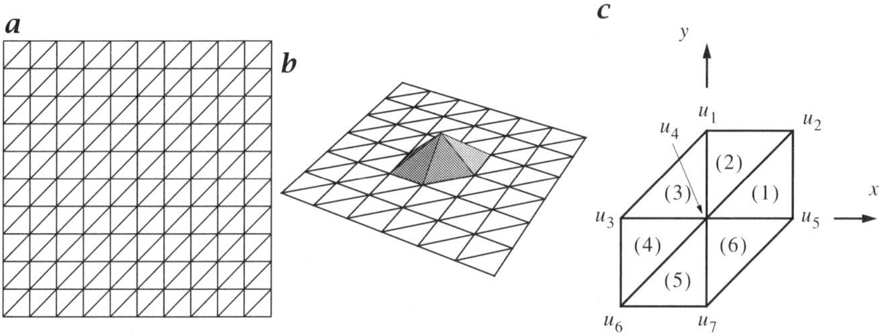

Figure 16.5: *2-D case:* ***a*** *uniform triangulated domain A;* ***b*** *a piecewise linear basis function; and* ***c*** *local labeling of nodal variables and triangular elements.*

boundary conditions are automatically incorporated just by computing Eq. (16.18). We obtain:

$$\frac{1}{3}\boldsymbol{v}_{g,1} + \frac{1}{6}\boldsymbol{v}_{g,2} - \rho_{(+)}(\boldsymbol{v}_{g,2} - \boldsymbol{v}_{g,1}) = \frac{1}{3}\boldsymbol{g}_1 + \frac{1}{6}\boldsymbol{g}_2\,, \quad i = 1$$

$$\frac{1}{6}\boldsymbol{v}_{g,N-1} + \frac{1}{3}\boldsymbol{v}_{g,N} + \rho_{(-)}(\boldsymbol{v}_{g,N} - \boldsymbol{v}_{g,N-1}) = \frac{1}{6}\boldsymbol{g}_{N-1} + \frac{1}{3}\boldsymbol{g}_N\,, \quad i = N$$

In the 2-D and 3-D case, the corresponding equations are rather lengthy. Therefore, we prefer a graphic notation in terms of stencils specifying the coefficients of nodal variables. Figure 16.4 illustrate this for Eq. (16.19) using two stencils, the first one for the first term on the left-hand side of Eq. (16.19) (Fig. 16.4a; we get the same stencil for the right-hand side of Eq. (16.19)), and the second one for the second term on the left-hand side of Eq. (16.19) (Fig. 16.4b).

2-D images. The 2-D case runs completely analogous to the 1-D case here. In most applications a uniform *triangulation* of the underlying domain A suffices (Fig. 16.5a; see, e.g., [27] for an application using less regular grids). The corresponding piecewise linear basis function is depicted in Fig. 16.5b.

The support of a basis function together with a labeling of neighboring nodal variables and triangular regions is shown in Fig. 16.5c (we use a dummy function u here playing the role of either v_g or g). Using this notation we have, for example:

$$\rho_{(1)} = \rho\Big(\big[(\boldsymbol{u}_5 - \boldsymbol{u}_4)^2 + (\boldsymbol{u}_2 - \boldsymbol{u}_5)^2\big]^{1/2}\Big)$$

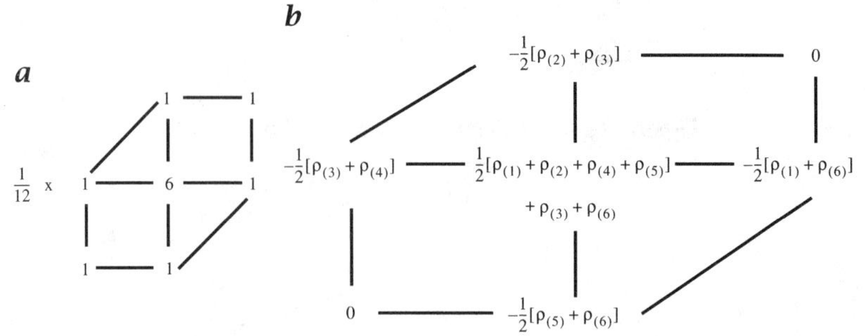

Figure 16.6: *2-D case:* ***a*** *first; and* ***b*** *second stencil.*

The resulting two stencils for an arbitrary interior node are shown in Fig. 16.6. As shown in the last Section, appropriate modifications of these stencils at boundary nodes are automatically obtained by choosing the correct domain of integration in Eq. (16.18). It can easily be seen that for ρ = constant the stencil in Fig. 16.6b gives the familiar 5-point stencil of the Laplacian operator. In the nonlinear case, this stencil tries to capture the rotational invariance of the underlying continuous problem formulation. Hence, this discretization is less directionally biased than just using separate horizontal and vertical first-order differences.

3-D images. The 3-D case, again, runs completely analogous to the 1-D case. However, the partitioning of the underlying domain A becomes slightly more complicated if we still wish to use piecewise *linear* basis functions. For segmentation problems it is reasonable to do so because then merely element-by-element threshold operations are involved (see Eqs. (16.8) and (16.9)).

We associate with each given voxel $\boldsymbol{g}_i$ a node of a regular 3-D mesh covering the underlying domain A. Each cube-cell of this mesh is subdivided into 5 tetrahedra as shown in Fig. 16.7. In each tetrahedron, functions are represented by linearly interpolating the nodal variables associated with the 4 vertices. FEM theory requires that adjacent elements have in common either complete faces or complete edges or vertices. Therefore, the orientation of the subdivision has to change like a checkerboard in each coordinate direction (Fig. 16.8).

To illustrate this in more detail, we consider the interior tetrahedron depicted in Fig. 16.9a, the treatment of which is not as straightforward as with the remaining four tetrahedra. Suppose the nodal values $\boldsymbol{u}_0, \ldots, \boldsymbol{u}_3$ of some function u is given. To obtain some value $u(\boldsymbol{x})$ within the tetrahedron, we make the linear ansatz:

$$u(\boldsymbol{x}) = c_0 + \begin{bmatrix} c_1 \\ c_2 \\ c_3 \end{bmatrix}^T \begin{bmatrix} x \\ y \\ z \end{bmatrix}$$

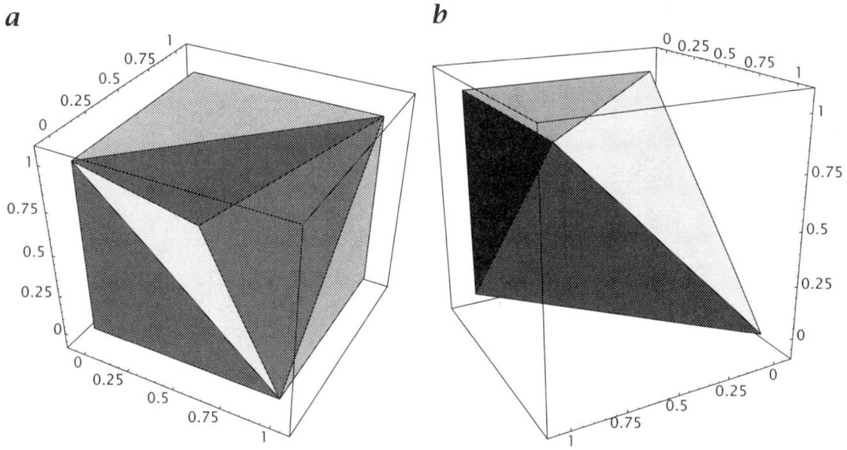

Figure 16.7: *3-D case: subdividing the cube between 8 nodes into 5 tetrahedra:* ***a*** *the cube with the two tetrahedra shown in* ***b*** *removed.*

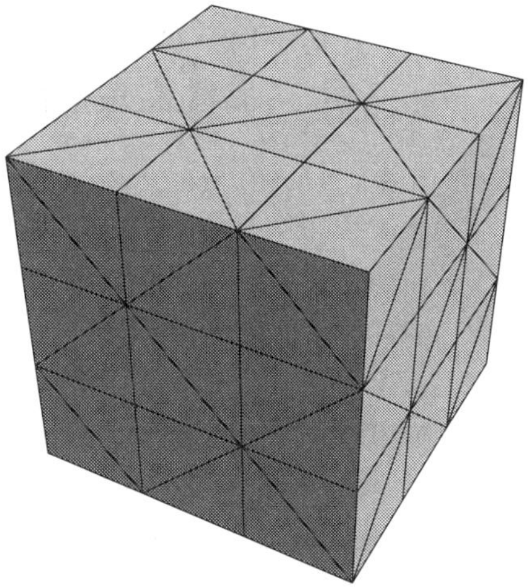

Figure 16.8: *3-D case: partitioning the domain A.*

The interpolation conditions read:

$$\begin{bmatrix} \boldsymbol{u}_0 \\ \boldsymbol{u}_1 \\ \boldsymbol{u}_2 \\ \boldsymbol{u}_3 \end{bmatrix} = \begin{bmatrix} 1 & \boldsymbol{p}_0^T \\ 1 & \boldsymbol{p}_1^T \\ 1 & \boldsymbol{p}_2^T \\ 1 & \boldsymbol{p}_3^T \end{bmatrix} \begin{bmatrix} c_0 \\ c_1 \\ c_2 \\ c_3 \end{bmatrix}$$

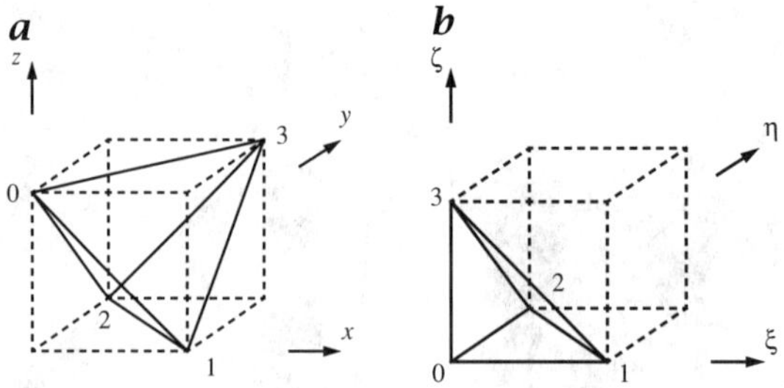

Figure 16.9: *Mapping an interior tetrahedron:* ***a*** *onto a reference tetrahedron;* ***b*** *(see text).*

where the vectors $\boldsymbol{p}_0, \ldots, \boldsymbol{p}_3$ give the vertices' positions. Solving for the coefficients c_i yields:

$$u(x, y, z) = \frac{1}{2} \begin{bmatrix} 1 \\ x \\ y \\ z \end{bmatrix}^T \begin{bmatrix} 1 & 1 & 1 & -1 \\ -1 & 1 & -1 & 1 \\ -1 & -1 & 1 & 1 \\ 1 & -1 & -1 & 1 \end{bmatrix} \begin{bmatrix} \boldsymbol{u}_0 \\ \boldsymbol{u}_1 \\ \boldsymbol{u}_2 \\ \boldsymbol{u}_3 \end{bmatrix}$$

Note that the representation of a basis function ϕ_i centered at node i is obtained by setting $\boldsymbol{u}_i = 1$ and $\boldsymbol{u}_j = 0$ for $i \neq j$.

Integrals appearing in Eq. (16.18) are best carried out by mapping the interior tetrahedron T_{int} in Fig. 16.9a onto a reference tetrahedron T_{ref} shown in Fig. 16.9b:

$$\boldsymbol{x} = \boldsymbol{p}_0 + \underbrace{[\boldsymbol{p}_1 - \boldsymbol{p}_0, \boldsymbol{p}_2 - \boldsymbol{p}_0, \boldsymbol{p}_3 - \boldsymbol{p}_0]}_{\boldsymbol{A}} \boldsymbol{\xi}$$

Accordingly, using the chain rule, derivatives of some function u transform:

$$\nabla_{\boldsymbol{x}} u = \boldsymbol{A}^{-T} \nabla_{\boldsymbol{\xi}} u$$

Integrating some function u over the interior tetrahedron then becomes:

$$\int_{T_{\text{int}}} u(\boldsymbol{x}) \, \mathrm{d}\boldsymbol{x}$$

$$= \int_{T_{\text{ref}}} u(x(\xi, \eta, \zeta), y(\xi, \eta, \zeta), z(\xi, \eta, \zeta)) \underbrace{\left| \frac{\partial(x, y, z)}{\partial(\xi, \eta, \zeta)} \right|}_{=2} \mathrm{d}\xi \, \mathrm{d}\eta \, \mathrm{d}\zeta$$

$$= 2 \int_0^1 \int_0^{1-\zeta} \int_0^{1-\eta-\zeta} u(\boldsymbol{\xi}) \, \mathrm{d}\xi \, \mathrm{d}\eta \, \mathrm{d}\zeta$$

We conclude this section by specifying the two stencils for an interior node, analogous to the 1-D and 2-D case cited here. Note however that, according to Fig. 16.8, we have two types of nodes.

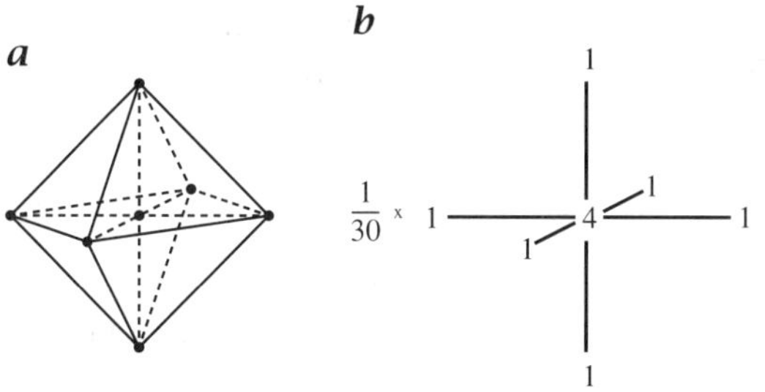

Figure 16.10: *Interior node of type 1: **a** adjacent tetrahedra; **b** first stencil.*

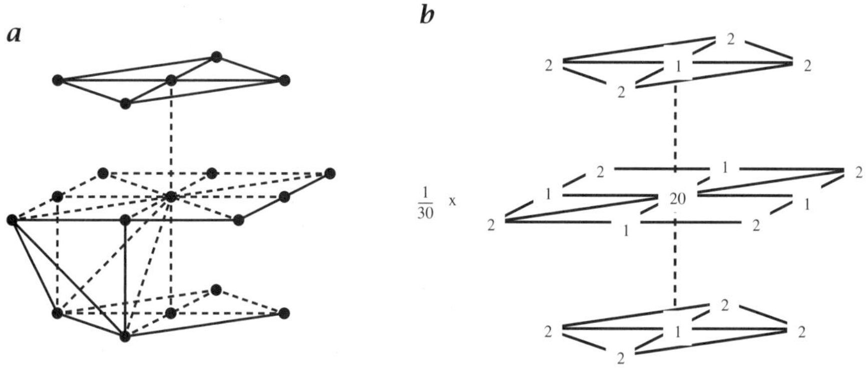

Figure 16.11: *Interior node of type 2: **a** ajacent tetrahedra (for better visibility only 4 of 32 tetrahedra have been drawn); **b** first stencil.*

Figure 16.10a shows the first type of interior nodes along with the adjacent tetrahedra. Figure 16.10b shows the first stencil for such a node. For the second stencil, we have only two different coefficients, analogous to Fig. 16.6b. The first coefficient is for the interior node in Fig. 16.10a:

$$\frac{1}{2}\sum_{i=1}^{8}\rho_{(i)}$$

where the sum is running over all adjacent tetrahedra. The second coefficient is the same for each exterior node in Fig. 16.10a:

$$-\frac{1}{6}\sum_{i=1}^{4}\rho_{(i)}$$

where the sum is running over all tetrahedra adjacent to both the interior and the considered exterior node.

Figure 16.11a shows the second type of interior nodes along with the adjacent tetrahedra. Figure 16.11b shows the first stencil for such a node. For the second stencil, we have again two different coefficients. The first coefficient is for the interior node in Fig. 16.11a:

$$\frac{1}{4}\sum_{i=1}^{32}\rho_{(i)}$$

where the sum is running over all adjacent tetrahedra. The second coefficient is the same for each exterior node i in Fig. 16.11a:

$$-\frac{1}{12}\sum_{j=1}^{n(i)}\rho_{(j)}$$

where the sum is running over all $n(i)$ tetrahedra adjacent to both the interior and the considered exterior node i.

16.2.3 Algorithm

This section describes a class of algorithms that can be used to solve the nonlinear system of equations Eq. (16.18) numerically. The design of such an algorithm is based on a technique that replaces the original nonlinear system by a sequence of linear systems of equations, which can be solved efficiently with various linear solvers. Only the linearization technique is described here. Algorithms for the solution of the resulting sparse linear systems can be found in numerous excellent textbooks (e.g., [28, 29]). For additional details, an investigation of alternative approaches and parallel implementations we refer to [30, 31].

In the following, it will be more convenient to specify modifications of Eq. (16.13) rather than Eq. (16.18). According to the discretization of Eq. (16.13) described in Section 16.2.2, the corresponding modifications of Eq. (16.18) are then immediate.

Minimization of convex functionals. Consider Eq. (16.13). This nonlinear equation becomes linear if we "freeze" its nonlinear part by using the solution of the previous iteration step as its argument. With Eqs. (16.14) and (16.15), Eq. (16.13) thus becomes (k counts the iteration steps):

$$\int_A \left\{ v_g^{k+1} v + \rho(|\nabla v_g^k|)(\nabla v_g^k)^T \nabla v \right\} \mathrm{d}\boldsymbol{x} = \int_A g v \,\mathrm{d}\boldsymbol{x}\,, \quad \forall v \in S_2 \tag{16.20}$$

To our knowledge, this approach was introduced as the so-called *Kačanov method* in the field of mathematical elasticity 25 yr ago (see [32, 33, 34]). In the case of convex functionals Eq. (16.4) with λ from Eq. (16.5), it can be shown that the sequence v_g^k according to Eq. (16.20) converges to the global minimizer v_g, that is, the unique solution of Eq. (16.13), irrespective of the starting point v_g^0 [31, 35].

Minimization of nonconvex functionals. A linearization technique closely related to that of the previous section has been proposed by Geman and Reynolds [36] (see also Charbonnier et al. [37]). The idea is to rewrite the original functional Eq. (16.4) using an auxiliary function w:

$$J_{\text{aux}}(v, w) = \frac{1}{2} \int_A \left\{ (v - g)^2 + w|\nabla v|^2 + \psi(w) \right\} \mathrm{d}\boldsymbol{x} \tag{16.21}$$

and to update, iteratively, v_g and w:

$$v_g^{k+1} = \arg\min_v J_{\text{aux}}(v, w^k) \tag{16.22}$$

and

$$w^{k+1} = \arg\min_w J_{\text{aux}}(v_g^{k+1}, w) \tag{16.23}$$

Note that w^k is fixed in Eq. (16.22), so that v_g^{k+1} is computed as the solution of the linear equation:

$$\int_A \left\{ v_g^{k+1} v + w^k (\nabla v_g^{k+1})^T \nabla v \right\} \mathrm{d}\boldsymbol{x} = \int_A g v \, \mathrm{d}\boldsymbol{x}, \quad \forall v \in S_2 \tag{16.24}$$

To make step Eq. (16.23) more explicit, we have to explain how the function ψ in Eq. (16.21) is chosen. ψ is chosen such that:

$$\lambda(t) = \inf_w \left(w t^2 + \psi(w) \right)$$

with λ from the original minimization problems Eqs. (16.4) and (16.6). If λ is such that ρ in Eq. (16.11) is strictly monotone and decreasing (as in Eq. (16.6)), then it is not difficult to show that step Eq. (16.23) reduces to:

$$w^{k+1} = \rho(|\nabla v_g^{k+1}|) \tag{16.25}$$

that is, ψ is not needed explicitly to carry out Eq. (16.23). As a result, we have the iteration Eq. (16.20) again, with ρ now defined by some nonconvex function λ. As ρ defined by Eqs. (16.11) and (16.5) illustrates, it is possible to weaken the assumptions slightly and to consider functions ρ that are (not strictly) monotone decreasing, too.

According to nonconvexity, only a local minimum can be expected after convergence of the iteration from the preceding. Furthermore, this minimum generally depends on the starting point v_g^0.

16.2.4 Applications

In this section, we demonstrate various aspects of the variational approach Eq. (16.4) with a few numerical examples. In all experiments we used the convex case Eq. (16.5), with one exception (Fig. 16.17) to

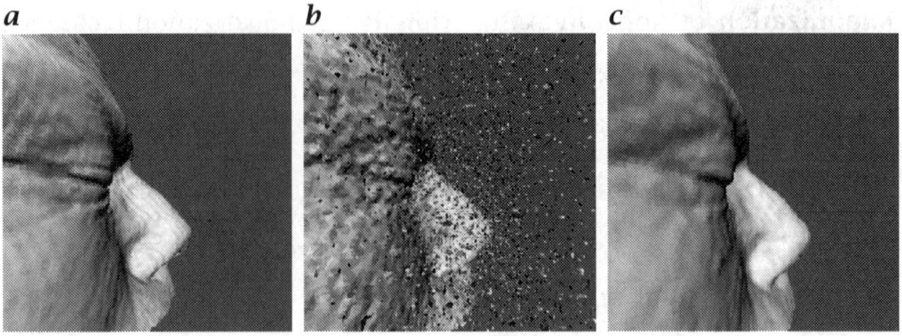

Figure 16.12: ***a*** *Isocontour surface of 3-D data set;* ***b*** *contaminated with noise;* ***c*** *after adaptive smoothing of the data shown in* ***b*** *(see text).*

exhibit some differences to the nonconvex case. As a convergence criterion the following threshold with respect to the maximum residuum of the nonlinear Eq. (16.18) was used:

$$\max_{i\in\{1,\ldots,N\}} \left| \langle A(v_{h,g}) - f, \phi_i \rangle \right| \le 0.1$$

Adaptive smoothing. We first illustrate the adaptive smoothing behavior with an academic example. Figure 16.12 shows an isocontour surface of a real 3-D data set in ***a***, superimposed with noise in ***b***, and ***c*** shows the corresponding isocontour surface of the minimizing function v_g by processing the noisy data g shown in ***a***. Two aspects can be seen here: First, noise can be eliminated without destroying significant signal structure in terms of large gradients. Second, whereas smoothing stops locally along the gradient direction (i. e., normal to the surface), smoothing still occurs along the surface, as can be seen from the small ripples of the surface in Fig. 16.12a that have been eliminated in c. One main advantage of variational approaches is that such complex, locally adaptive smoothing behavior emerges from a global optimization principle and does not have to be encoded explicitly.

As a realistic application case, Fig. 16.13 shows a slice through a noisy 3-D CT data set ***a*** and sections with some object ***b*** and ***c***. Figure 16.14 illustrates how adaptive variational smoothing of the 3-D image data eliminates noise without destroying the fairly complex signal structure. As a result, detection of the object by a simple threshold operation becomes robust.

Segmentation and feature extraction. In this section, we illustrate the segmentation of images into homogeneous regions Eq. (16.8) and transition regions Eq. (16.9). Figure 16.15 shows a Lab scene g in ***a*** and the processed image v_g in ***b***. According to definitions Eqs. (16.8) and (16.9), v_g implicitly encodes a partition of the image plane as shown in

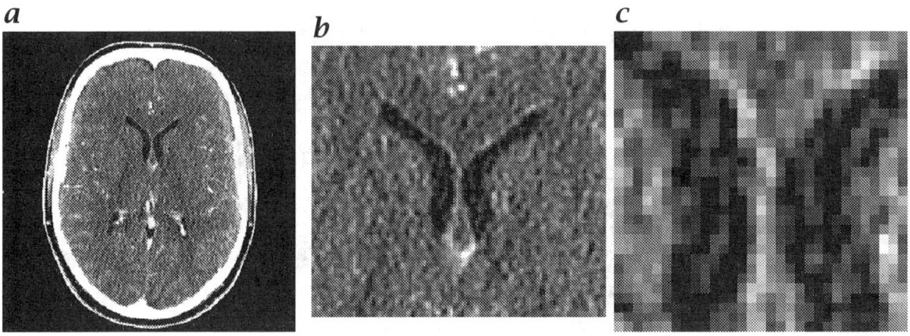

Figure 16.13: ***a*** *Slice of a 3-D CT image data set;* ***b, c*** *sections with an object of interest.*

Fig. 16.15c. By choosing a smaller value for the scale parameter λ_h in Eq. (16.5), finer details can be resolved at the cost of less smoothing (i.e., noise suppression) within homogeneous regions (Fig. 16.15d). This latter aspect, that is feature detection through anisotropic locally adaptive processing while simultaneously smoothing within nonfeature regions, is a main feature of variational approaches. Figure 16.16 illustrates this aspect in more detail. As a result, local contrast information around signal transitions becomes robust.

Finally, let us consider some differences between convex Eq. (16.5) and nonconvex Eq. (16.6) variational processing. Figure 16.17 shows the corresponding results for the image shown in Fig. 16.17a. Noise suppression along with region formation can be clearly seen for both approaches, whereas contrast is better preserved using the nonconvex version. However, as can be seen in Fig. 16.17d and e, the formation of transition regions is more susceptible to noise for the nonconvex than for the convex approach. This is due to the fact that smoothing almost completely stops in the nonconvex case, whereas in the convex case smoothing still continues in directions perpendicular to the gradient direction. From our viewpoint, this fact together with the existence of multiple local minima and the dependency on the starting point reduces the attractivity of nonconvex approaches, in particular in the context of image sequence processing where gradual changes of the input image data may not lead to gradual changes of corresponding image segmentations.

Noise suppression and restoration. For large gradients $|\nabla v|$, the convex smoothness term of the functional Eq. (16.4), Eq. (16.5) is dominated by the so-called total variation measure, which for admissible functions with respect to problem Eq. (16.4) takes the simple form:

$$\int_{A_t} \lambda(|\nabla v|)\,\mathrm{d}\boldsymbol{x} \sim \int_{A_t} |\nabla v|\,\mathrm{d}\boldsymbol{x}$$

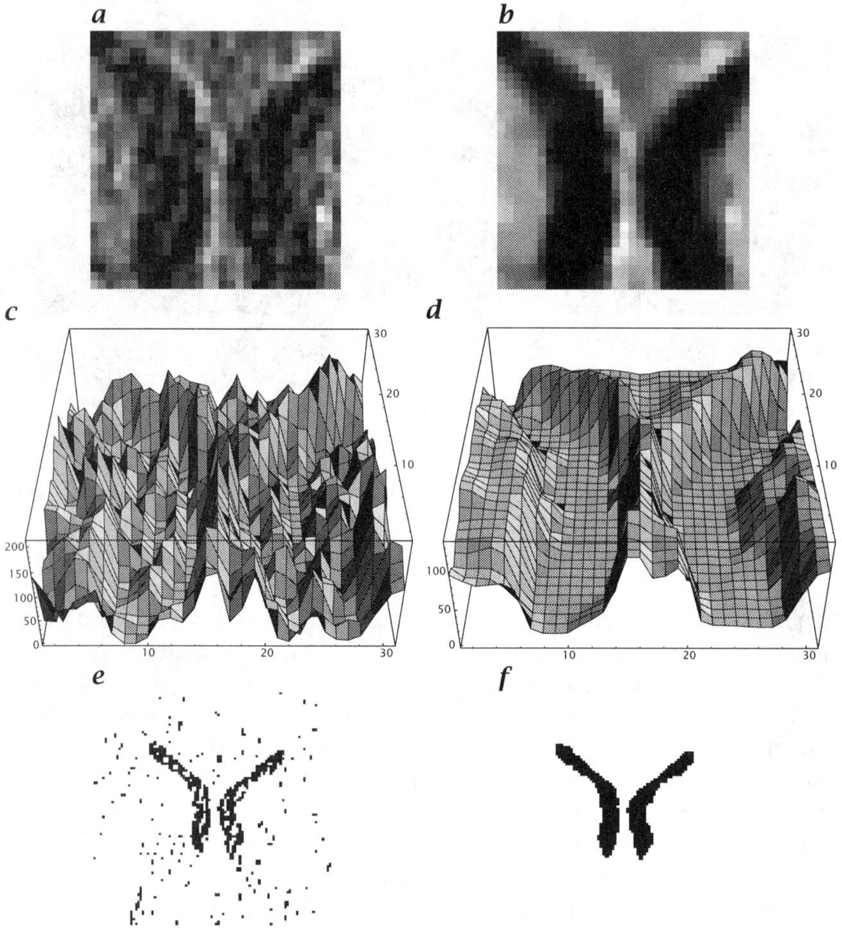

Figure 16.14: *Left column: Original data. Right column: Adaptively smoothed data:* ***a,b*** *section of Fig. 16.13;* ***c,d*** *3-D plot of* ***a*** *and* ***b****, respectively;* ***e,f*** *result of threshold operation.*

As an alternative to restoring signal transitions in the context of image segmentation, this measure can also be used to restore entire images by the variational approach [38, 39, 40, 41]. This powerful approach can be simulated by choosing a small value for the parameter c_ρ in Eq. (16.5). Figure 16.18 shows as an example the restoration of a mammogram. We note, however, that a proper adaptation of the approach Eq. (16.4) to restoration tasks requires in general the inclusion of a blurring operator K into the first term of Eq. (16.4) which models the point spread function of the imaging device:

$$\int_A (Kv - g)^2 \, d\boldsymbol{x}$$

a b c d
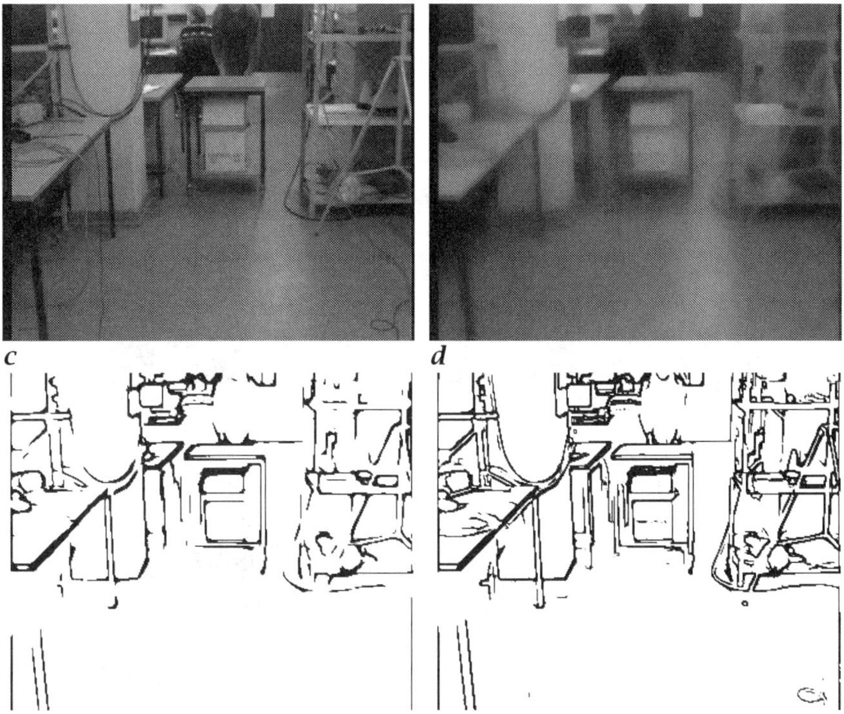

Figure 16.15: ***a*** *Lab scene* g; ***b*** *the unique minimizer* v_g *to Eq. (16.4);* ***c*** *the segmentation encoded by* v_g *according to Eqs. (16.8) and (16.9);* ***d*** *choosing a smaller scale parameter* λ_h *in Eq. (16.5) enables the computation of finer details.*

16.3 Processing of vector-valued images

This section extends the variational approach of Eq. (16.4) to vector-valued images. We describe a straightforward extension appropriate for the processing of color images, for example. A variation of this approach that is useful for some image sequence processing tasks is presented in Section 16.4.

16.3.1 Variational principle

Let

$$\boldsymbol{g} : \boldsymbol{x} \in A \subset \mathcal{R}^d \rightarrow \mathcal{R}^n \tag{16.26}$$

denote a vector-valued image. For example, we have $d = 2$ and $n = 3$ for color images. For the gradient of vector-valued functions $\boldsymbol{v}$ we use

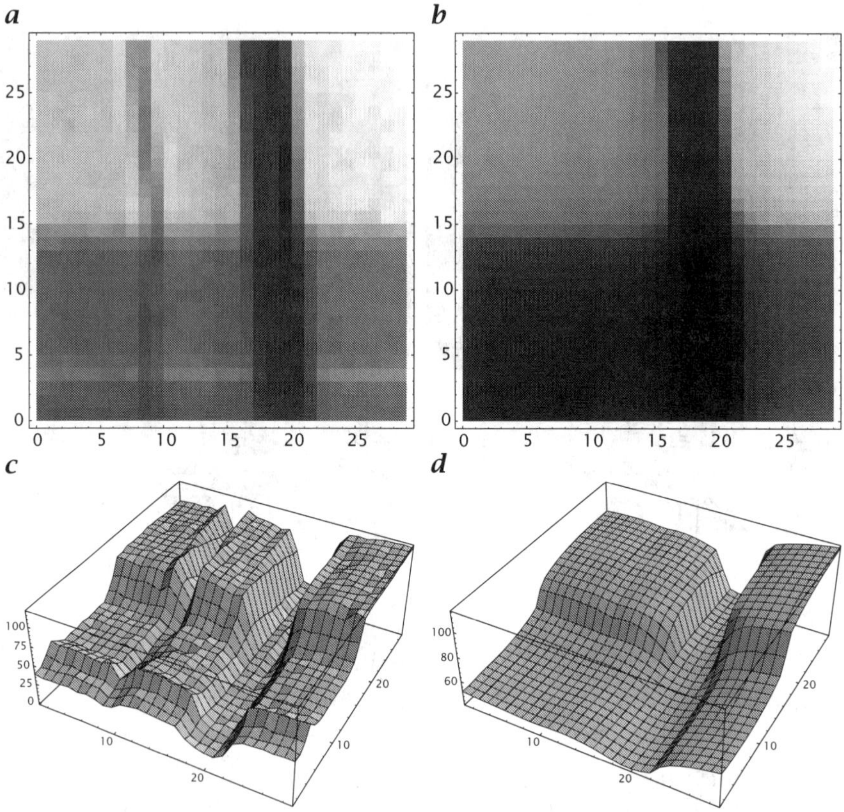

Figure 16.16: ***a*** *Section of the Lab scene shown in Fig. 16.15;* ***b*** *detection and localization of signal structure is not affected very much by elimination of smaller details. As a result, local contrast information around signal transitions becomes robust;* ***c, d*** *3-D plots of* ***a*** *and* ***b****, respectively.*

the symbol:

$$D\boldsymbol{v} := \left[\ \nabla v_1, \ldots, \nabla v_n\ \right]$$

The corresponding inner product and norm are denoted as:

$$(D\boldsymbol{u}, D\boldsymbol{v}) = \operatorname{trace}(D\boldsymbol{u}^T D\boldsymbol{v}) , \qquad \|D\boldsymbol{v}\| = (D\boldsymbol{v}, D\boldsymbol{v})^{1/2}$$

The variational approach—analog to Eq. (16.4)—then reads ([42]):

$$J(\boldsymbol{v}) = \frac{1}{2}\int_A \left\{ |\boldsymbol{v} - \boldsymbol{g}|^2 + \lambda(\|D\boldsymbol{v}\|) \right\} \mathrm{d}\boldsymbol{x} \tag{16.27}$$

Computing the first variation, we again obtain a variational equation of the form Eq. (16.13) that, for λ defined by Eq. (16.5), uniquely determines the global minimizer $\boldsymbol{v}_g$ of the functional Eq. (16.27), where

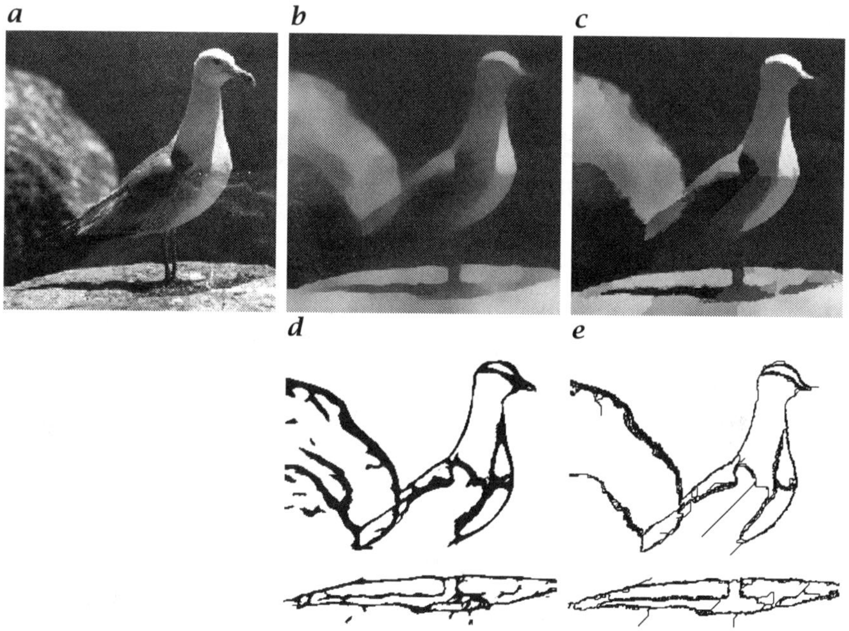

Figure 16.17: ***a*** *Real image;* ***b*** *unique minimum of the convex variational approach;* **c** *local minimizer of the nonconvex variational approach. Contrast is better preserved by the nonconvex approach;* ***d, e*** *segmentations according to* ***b*** *and* **c***, respectively. Transitions detected by the convex approach are more robust against noise because smoothing does not stop completely.*

(see definitions Eq. (16.14) and Eq. (16.15) in the scalar case):

$$\langle A(\boldsymbol{v}_g), \boldsymbol{v} \rangle = \int_A \left\{ \boldsymbol{v}_g^T \boldsymbol{v} + \rho(\|D\boldsymbol{v}_g\|)(D\boldsymbol{v}_g, D\boldsymbol{v}) \right\} \mathrm{d}\boldsymbol{x} \tag{16.28}$$

and

$$\langle f, \boldsymbol{v} \rangle = \int_A \boldsymbol{g}^T \boldsymbol{v} \, \mathrm{d}\boldsymbol{x} \tag{16.29}$$

Alternatively, one may use definition Eq. (16.6) in order to formulate a nonconvex variational approach. An alternative meaningful extension of the standard smoothness term in Eq. (16.4) to the case of vector-valued images is discussed in Sapiro and Ringach [43].

16.3.2 Finite element method discretization

For simplicity, we consider the case of color images, that is, $d = 2$ and $n = 3$ in Eq. (16.26). Each component function of a vector-valued image is represented as in Eq. (16.16). For example, for the three components

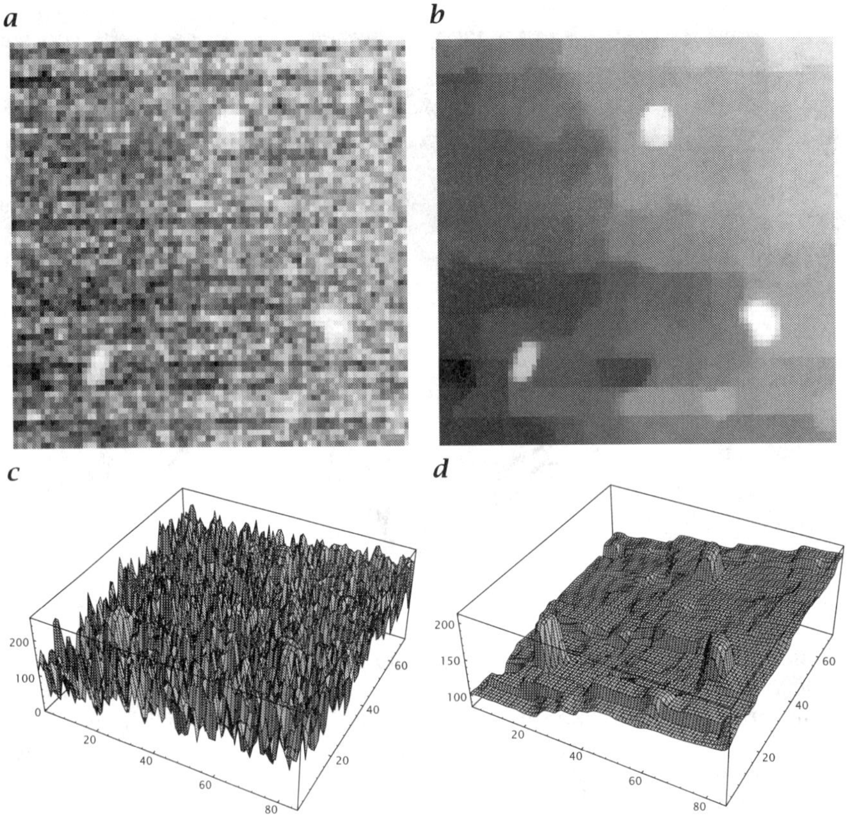

Figure 16.18: ***a*** *Section of a mammogram;* ***b*** *restored image;* ***c, d*** *3-D plots of* ***a, b*** *.*

of $\boldsymbol{v}_h$ this means:

$$v_{h,i} = \sum_{j=1}^{N} \boldsymbol{v}_{i,j}\phi_j(\boldsymbol{x}) \,, \quad i = 1, \ldots, 3 \tag{16.30}$$

and similarly for the components of $\boldsymbol{g}_h$ and $\boldsymbol{v}_{h,\boldsymbol{g}}$. Inserting these representations into Eq. (16.13) (using the definitions Eqs. (16.28) and (16.29)), we obtain a nonlinear system of equations analogous to Eq. (16.18) where each equation corresponds to a variable $\boldsymbol{v}_{i,j}$, $i = 1, \ldots, 3$, $j = 1, \ldots, N$ (see the derivation of Eq. (16.18) in Section 16.2.2). As a consequence, the stencil presented for the case of 2-D images in Section 16.2.2 can be used. The only difference concerns the argument of the functions $\rho_{(i)}$, which now is $\|D\boldsymbol{v}_{h,\boldsymbol{g}}\|$ instead of $|\nabla v_{h,g}|$ in the scalar case. Correspondingly, the resulting nonlinear system of equations can be solved by a sequence of linear systems of equations by successively "freezing" the argument of ρ for one iteration step (see Section 16.2.3).

Figure 16.19: ***a*** *Color image;* **c,d** *the minimizer* $\boldsymbol{v}_g$ *computed at a small and a larger scale, respectively;* **b** *the segmentation corresponding to* **c***; topologically connected regions are marked with the mean color, transitions are marked with black.*

16.3.3 Numerical example: color images

Figure 16.19 shows a color image $\boldsymbol{g}$ and the minimizer $\boldsymbol{v}_g$ to Eq. (16.27) computed at a small ($\lambda_h = 2$) and a larger scale ($\lambda_h = 9$), respectively. The preservation of image structure as well as the formation of homogeneous regions is clearly visible.

16.4 Processing of image sequences

In this section, we describe a specific alternative to the smoothness term of the functional Eq. (16.27) adapted to the estimation of motion fields. A *motion field* is a vector field that describes the instantaneous velocity of projected scene points in the image plane. Estimates of the motion field for a fixed time point are referred to as *optical flow* fields $\boldsymbol{f}$ in the literature (see Chapters 13 and 14).

16.4.1 Preprocessing

To compute $\boldsymbol{f}$, local constraints due to the spatiotemporal variation of the image data $g(\boldsymbol{x}, t)$ may be used:

$$\frac{\mathrm{d}g}{\mathrm{d}t} = \nabla g^T \boldsymbol{f} + \frac{\partial g}{\partial t} = 0 \tag{16.31}$$

Here, the assumption has been made that g behaves like a "conserved quantity." As this assumption is often severely violated under realistic illumination conditions, g is replaced by more robust quantities related to the output of bandpass filters. Furthermore, multiple constraint equations similar to Eq. (16.31) can be used (see, e.g., [44, 45, 46, 47]). For more information related to the topic "optical flow" the reader is referred to Chapters 13 and 14. A survey of current problems in the field of image sequence analysis has been presented by Mitiche and Bouthemy [48].

16.4.2 Variational principle

In the following we focus on variational approaches to the computation of optical flow fields $\boldsymbol{f}$. The classical approach is due to [49]:

$$J(\boldsymbol{f}) = \frac{1}{2} \int_A \left\{ \left(\nabla g^T \boldsymbol{f} + g_t \right)^2 + \lambda^2 \left(|\nabla f_1|^2 + |\nabla f_2|^2 \right) \right\} \mathrm{d}\boldsymbol{x} \ , \ \lambda \in \mathcal{R} \tag{16.32}$$

which has been considerably generalized in the literature (see, e.g., [50] and references therein). Formally, $\boldsymbol{f}$ may be regarded as a vector-valued image, so the nonquadratic smoothness term in Eq. (16.27),

$$\frac{1}{2} \int_A \lambda(\|D\boldsymbol{f}\|) \, \mathrm{d}\boldsymbol{x} \tag{16.33}$$

with λ from Eq. (16.5) or Eq. (16.6), can be used to replace the terms with derivatives of f_1, f_2 in Eq. (16.32). By this, the computation of $\boldsymbol{f}$ by minimizing the functional J becomes adaptive to so-called *motion boundaries*, that is, significant changes of the structure of the optical flow $\boldsymbol{f}$.

An alternative to Eq. (16.33) that may be useful in some applications is given by [51]:

$$\frac{1}{4} \int_A \left\{ \lambda_d(|\mathrm{div}(\boldsymbol{f})|) + \lambda_r(|\mathrm{rot}(\boldsymbol{f})|) + \lambda_s(|\mathrm{sh}(\boldsymbol{f})|) \right\} \mathrm{d}\boldsymbol{x} \tag{16.34}$$

where:

$$\begin{aligned} \operatorname{div}(\boldsymbol{f}) &= f_{1,x} + f_{2,y} , \\ \operatorname{rot}(\boldsymbol{f}) &= f_{2,x} - f_{1,y} , \\ \operatorname{sh}(\boldsymbol{f}) &= \left[f_{2,y} - f_{1,x}, f_{1,y} + f_{2,x} \right]^T \end{aligned}$$

denote the component's divergence, vorticity, and shear of the vector-gradient $D\boldsymbol{f}$. The functions λ_d, λ_r and λ_s are defined by Eq. (16.5) (or Eq. (16.6)). Parameter values may differ for each function. Using definition Eq. (16.5) makes the functional Eq. (16.34) together with the first data term in Eq. (16.32) convex so that the minimizing $\boldsymbol{f}$ is unique [52]. For $c_\rho \to \infty$ in Eq. (16.5) the functional Eq. (16.34) becomes identical to the smoothness term in Eq. (16.32) due to the identity:

$$\|D\boldsymbol{f}\|^2 = \frac{1}{2}\left(\operatorname{div}^2(\boldsymbol{f}) + \operatorname{rot}^2(\boldsymbol{f}) + |\operatorname{sh}(\boldsymbol{f})|^2\right)$$

16.4.3 Finite element method discretization

In this section, we describe how the nonlinear system of equations corresponding to the functional Eq. (16.34) is computed, analogous to Eq. (16.18). Note that these equations have to be supplemented according to some data term (like the first term of the right-hand side in Eq. (16.32), for example) chosen by the user, the discretization of which proceeds in the same manner (see also Section 16.2.2).

Analogous to Section 16.2.1 and Section 16.3.1 (see, e. g., Eq. (16.28)), let $\boldsymbol{f}_g$ denote the minimizer of Eq. (16.34), and let $\boldsymbol{f}$ denote arbitrary admissible vector fields. Computing the first variation of Eq. (16.34) in the direction of a vector field $\boldsymbol{f}$ yields:

$$\frac{1}{2}\int_A \Big\{\rho_d(|\operatorname{div}(\boldsymbol{f}_g)|)\operatorname{div}(\boldsymbol{f}_g)\operatorname{div}(\boldsymbol{f}) + \rho_r(|\operatorname{rot}(\boldsymbol{f}_g)|)\operatorname{rot}(\boldsymbol{f}_g)\operatorname{rot}(\boldsymbol{f}) + \rho_s(|\operatorname{sh}(\boldsymbol{f}_g)|)\operatorname{sh}(\boldsymbol{f}_g)^T\operatorname{sh}(\boldsymbol{f})\Big\}\,d\boldsymbol{x} \tag{16.35}$$

where (see Eq. (16.11)):

$$\rho_d(t) = \frac{\lambda_d'(t)}{2t}, \quad \rho_r(t) = \frac{\lambda_r'(t)}{2t}, \quad \rho_s(t) = \frac{\lambda_s'(t)}{2t}$$

Next, vector fields $\boldsymbol{f}_g, \boldsymbol{f}$ are represented as in Eq. (16.30) by functions $\boldsymbol{f}_{h,g}, \boldsymbol{f}_h$, which, in turn, are represented by variables $\boldsymbol{f}_{1,g,i}, \boldsymbol{f}_{2,g,i}$ and $\boldsymbol{f}_{1,i}, \boldsymbol{f}_{2,i}$, for $i = 1, \ldots, N$. Inserting into Eq. (16.35) yields a nonlinear equation for each variable $\boldsymbol{f}_{1,i}, \boldsymbol{f}_{2,i}$ in terms of the variables $\boldsymbol{f}_{1,g,j}, \boldsymbol{f}_{2,g,j}$ representing the minimizing vector field $\boldsymbol{f}_g$ (see Section 16.2.2). We summarize the result by specifying the stencils in Figures 16.20 and

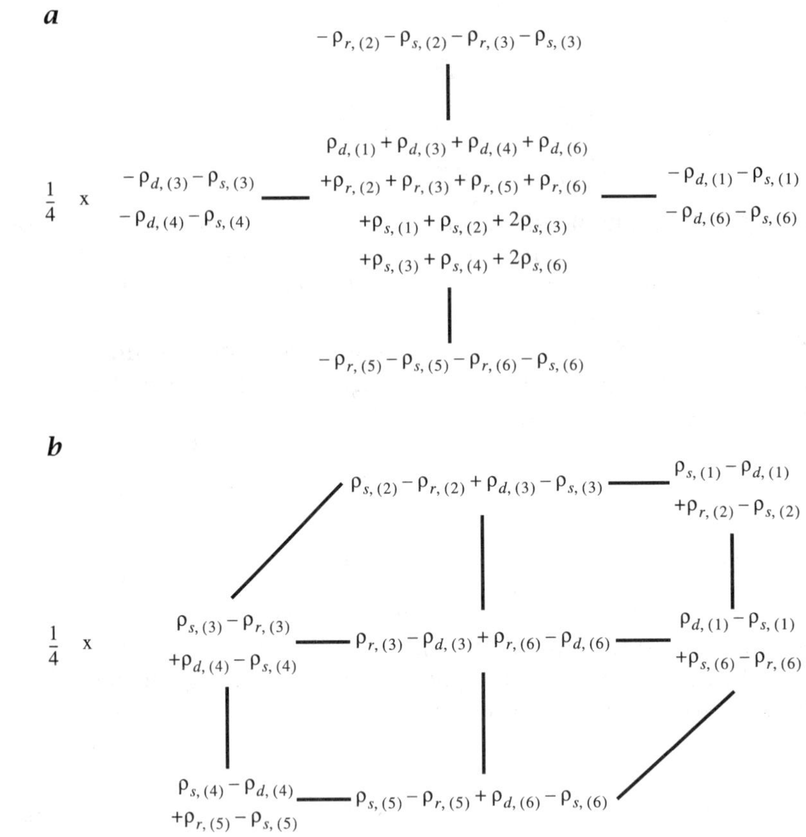

Figure 16.20: ***a*** *Stencil w.r.t. variables* $\boldsymbol{f}_{1,g,j}$ *of the equation corresponding to a variable* $\boldsymbol{f}_{1,i}$*;* ***b*** *stencil w.r.t. variables* $\boldsymbol{f}_{2,g,j}$ *of the equation corresponding to a variable* $\boldsymbol{f}_{1,i}$*.*

16.21 of equations that correspond to interior variables $\boldsymbol{f}_{1,i}$ and $\boldsymbol{f}_{2,i}$, respectively.

At boundary locations, appropriate modifications of these stencils are automatically obtained by carrying out the integral in Eq. (16.35). Recall from Section 16.2.2 that these stencils depict the coefficients of the variables $\boldsymbol{f}_{1,g,j}, \boldsymbol{f}_{2,g,j}$ around node i. Due to nonlinearity, these coefficients are themselves functions of $\boldsymbol{f}_{1,g,j}, \boldsymbol{f}_{2,g,j}$. Using the notation introduced in Section 16.2.2, and denoting for notational simplicity the variables corresponding to

$$\boldsymbol{f}_g = \begin{bmatrix} f_{1,g} \\ f_{2,g} \end{bmatrix}$$

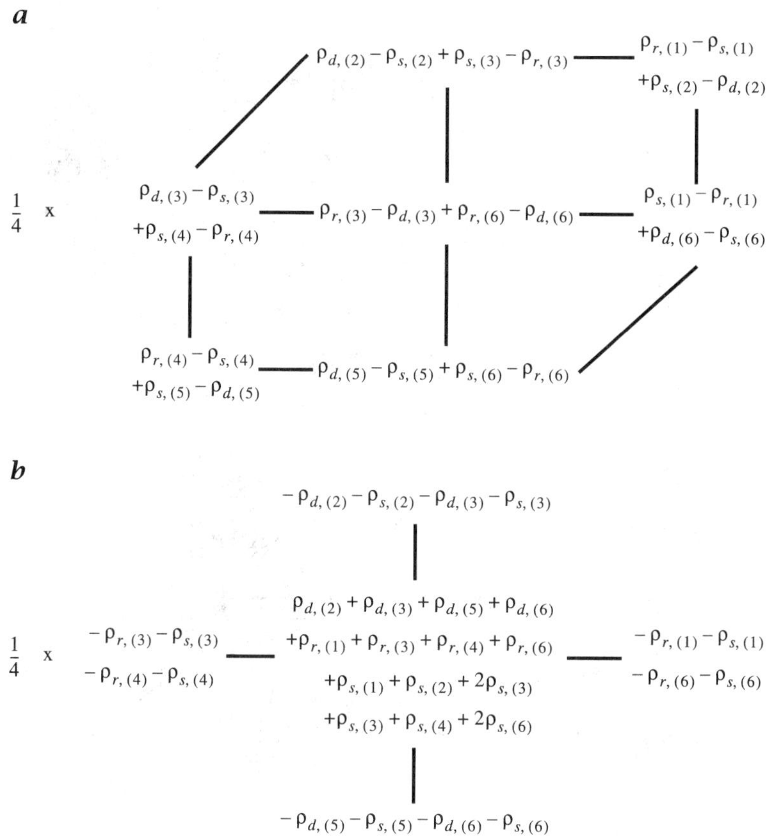

Figure 16.21: ***a*** *Stencil w.r.t. variables* $\boldsymbol{f}_{1,\boldsymbol{g},j}$ *of the equation corresponding to a variable* $\boldsymbol{f}_{2,i}$; ***b*** *stencil w.r.t. variables* $\boldsymbol{f}_{2,\boldsymbol{g},j}$ *of the equation corresponding to a variable* $\boldsymbol{f}_{2,i}$.

with $\boldsymbol{u}1_j, \boldsymbol{u}2_j$ (instead of $\boldsymbol{f}_{1,\boldsymbol{g},j}, \boldsymbol{f}_{2,\boldsymbol{g},j}$), then $\rho_{d,(1)}$, for example, means (see Fig. 16.5c):

$$\begin{aligned} \rho_{d,(1)} &= \rho_d\Big(\,|\operatorname{div}(\boldsymbol{f}_{h,\boldsymbol{g}})|\,\Big)_{\text{within element}(1)} \\ &= \rho_d\Big(\,|\boldsymbol{u}1_5 - \boldsymbol{u}1_4 + \boldsymbol{u}2_2 - \boldsymbol{u}2_5|\,\Big) \end{aligned}$$

16.4.4 Numerical examples

Because the preprocessing step, that is, the evaluation of constraint equations like Eq. (16.31) is not the topic of the present chapter, we restrict ourselves to illustrate the effect of using the smoothness term of Eq. (16.34). To this end, we generated noisy vector fields $\boldsymbol{f}_d$ and

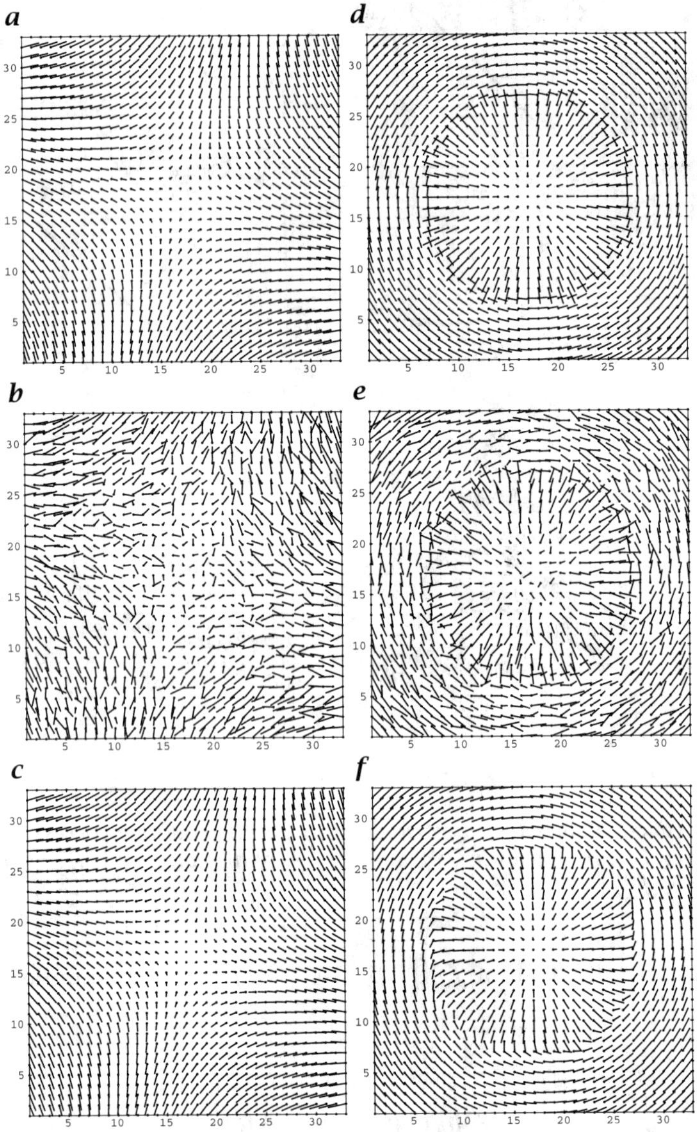

Figure 16.22: *Left column: Structure-selective smoothing:* ***a*** *computer-generated vector field; only the shear-term of the gradient is different from zero;* ***b*** *noisy input data;* ***c*** *reconstructed vector field by filtering divergent and rotational components. Right column: Structure-adaptive smoothing;* ***d*** *computer-generated vector field comprising a divergent and a rotational component;* ***e*** *noisy input data;* ***f*** *restored vector field. The smoothness term Eq. (16.34) automatically adapts to the local vector field structure.*

supplemented Eq. (16.34) with the data term:

$$\frac{1}{2}\int_A |\boldsymbol{f} - \boldsymbol{f}_d|^2 \,\mathrm{d}\boldsymbol{x}$$

The main difference between the standard smoothness measure of Eq. (16.33) and Eq. (16.34) is that the first term favors piecewise constant vector fields whereas the latter term admits vector fields with richer local structure. This is illustrated in Fig. 16.22 with vector fields being nowhere constant.

Acknowledgment. Image data depicted in Fig. 16.13 was kindly provided by ICS-AD from Philips Medical Systems, Best, and Philips Research Labs, Hamburg, courtesy of W.P.Th.M. Mali, L. Ramos, and C.W.M. van Veelen, Utrecht University Hospital. The author gratefully acknowledges comments by Josef Heers.

16.5 References

[1] Mumford, D. and Shah, J., (1989). Optimal approximations by piecewise smooth functions and associated variational problems. *Comm. Pure Appl. Math.*, **42**:577–685.

[2] Haralick, R. and Shapiro, L., (1985). Image segmentation techniques. *Comp. Vision, Graphics, and Image Proc.*, **29**:100–132.

[3] Pal, N. and Pal, S., (1993). A review on image segmentation techniques. *Patt. Recog.*, **9**:1277–1294.

[4] Morel, J.-M. and Solimini, S., (1995). *Variational Methods in Image Segmentation.* Boston: Birkhäuser.

[5] Richardson, T. and Mitter, S., (1994). Approximation, computation, and distortion in the variational formulation. In ter Haar Romeny [18], pp. 169–190.

[6] Koepfler, G., Lopez, C., and Morel, J., (1994). A multiscale algorithm for image segmentation by variational method. *SIAM J. Numer. Anal.*, **31**(1): 282–299.

[7] Geman, S. and Geman, D., (1984). Stochastic relaxation, Gibbs distributions, and the Bayesian restoration of images. *IEEE Trans. Patt. Anal. Mach. Intell.*, **6**(6):721–741.

[8] Li, S., (1995). *Markov Random Field Modeling in Computer Vision.* Tokyo: Springer.

[9] Geman, D., (1990). Random fields and inverse problems in imaging. In *École d'Été de Probabilités de Saint-Flour XVIII - 1988*, P. Hennequin, ed., Vol. 1427 of *Lect. Notes in Math.*, pp. 113–193. Berlin: Springer.

[10] Winkler, G., (1995). *Image Analysis, Random Fields and Dynamic Monte Carlo Methods*, Vol. 27 of *Appl. of Mathematics.* Heidelberg: Springer.

[11] Blake, A. and Zisserman, A., (1987). *Visual Reconstruction.* Cambridge, MA: MIT Press.

[12] Geiger, D. and Girosi, F., (1991). Parallel and deterministic algorithms from MRF's: surface reconstruction. *IEEE Trans. Patt. Anal. Mach. Intell.*, **13**(5):401–412.

[13] Geiger, D. and Yuille, A., (1991). A common framework for image segmentation. *Int. J. of Comp. Vision*, **6**(3):227–243.

[14] Alvarez, L., (1996). Images and PDE's. In Berger et al. [53], pp. 3–14.

[15] Alvarez, L., Guichard, F., Lions, P., and Morel, J., (1993). Axioms and fundamental equations of image processing. *Arch. Rat. Mech. Anal.*, **123**: 199–257.

[16] Caselles, V., Kimmel, R., Sapiro, G., and Sbert, C., (1997). Minimal surfaces based object segmentation. *IEEE Trans. Patt. Anal. Mach. Intell.*, **19**(4): 394-398.

[17] Sapiro, G. and Tannenbaum, A., (1993). Affine invariant scale-space. *Int. J. of Comp. Vision*, **11**(1):25–44.

[18] ter Haar Romeny, B. M. (ed.), (1994). *Geometry-Driven Diffusion in Computer Vision*, Dordrecht, The Netherlands. Kluwer Academic Publishers.

[19] Weickert, J., (1997). A review of nonlinear diffusion filtering. In ter Haar Romeny et al. [21], pp. 3–28.

[20] Malladi, R., Sethian, S., and Vemuri, B., (1996). A fast level set based algorithm for topology-independent shape modeling. *Jour. Math. Imag. Vision*, **6**(2/3):269–289.

[21] ter Haar Romeny, B., Florack, L., Koederink, J., and Viergever, M. (eds.), (1997). *Scale-space theory in computer vision*, Vol. 1252 of *Lect. Not. Comp. Sci.* Berlin: Springer.

[22] Nordström, N., (1990). Biased anisotropic diffusion—a unified regularization and diffusion approach to edge detection. *Image and Vis. Comp.*, **8** (4):318–327.

[23] Black, M. and Rangarajan, A., (1996). On the unification of line processes, outlier rejection, and robust statistics with applications in early vision. *Int. J. of Comp. Vision*, **19**(1):57–91.

[24] Li, S., (1995). Convex energy functions in the DA model. In *Proc. Int. Conf. Image Proc.*

[25] Schnörr, C., (1994). Unique reconstruction of piecewise smooth images by minimizing strictly convex non-quadratic functionals. *Jour. Math. Imag. Vision*, **4**:189–198.

[26] Stevenson, R., Schmitz, B., and Delp, E., (1994). Discontinuity preserving regularization of inverse visual problems. *IEEE Trans. Systems, Man and Cyb.*, **24**(3):455–469.

[27] Schnörr, C., (1998). A study of a convex variational diffusion approach for image segmentation and feature extraction. *Jour. of Math. Imag. and Vision*, **8**(3):271–292.

[28] Hackbusch, W., (1993). *Iterative Solution of Large Sparse Systems of Equations*. Berlin: Springer.

[29] Kelley, C., (1995). *Iterative Methods for Linear and Nonlinear Equations*. Philadelphia: SIAM.

[30] Heers, J., Schnörr, C., and Stiehl, H., (1998). A class of parallel algorithms for nonlinear variational image segmentation. In *Proc. Noblesse Workshop on Non-Linear Model Based Image Analysis (NMBIA'98), Glasgow, Scotland.*

[31] Heers, J., Schnörr, C., and Stiehl, H., (1998). *Investigating a class of iterative schemes and their parallel implementation for nonlinear variational image smoothing and segmentation.* Technical report FBI-HH-M 283/98, Comp. Sci. Dept., AB KOGS, University of Hamburg, Hamburg, Germany.

[32] Fučik, S., Kratochvil, A., and Nečas, J., (1973). Kačanov-Galerkin method. *Comment. Math. Univ. Carolinae,* **14**(4):651–659.

[33] Nečas, J. and Hlaváček, I., (1981). *Mathematical Theory of Elastic and Elasto-Plastic Bodies.* Amsterdam: Elsevier.

[34] Zeidler, E., (1985). *Nonlinear Functional Analysis and its Applications,* Vol. III. Berlin: Springer.

[35] Schnörr, C., (1998). *Variational approaches to image segmentation and feature extraction.* Habilitation thesis, University of Hamburg, Comp. Sci. Dept., Hamburg, Germany. In German.

[36] Geman, D. and Reynolds, G., (1992). Constrained restoration and the recovery of discontinuities. *IEEE Trans. Patt. Anal. Mach. Intell.,* **14**(3): 367–383.

[37] Charbonnier, P., Blanc-Féraud, L., Aubert, G., and Barlaud, M., (1997). Deterministic edge-preserving regularization in computed imaging. *IEEE Trans. in Image Proc.,* **6**(2):298–311.

[38] Rudin, L., Osher, S., and Fatemi, E., (1992). Nonlinear total variation based noise removal algorithms. *Physica D,* **60**:259–268.

[39] Rudin, L., Osher, S., and Fu, C., (1996). Total variation based restoration of noisy, blurred images. *SIAM J. Numer. Analysis.* submitted.

[40] Chan, T., Golub, G., and Mulet, P., (1996). A nonlinear primal-dual method for Total Variation-based image restoration. In Berger et al. [53], pp. 241–252.

[41] Dobson, D. and Vogel, C., (1997). Convergence of an iterative method for total variation denoising. *SIAM J. Numer. Anal.,* **34**:1779–1791.

[42] Schnörr, C., (1996). Convex variational segmentation of multi-channel images. In Berger et al. [53], pp. 201–207.

[43] Sapiro, G. and Ringach, D., (1996). Anisotropic diffusion of multivalued images. In Berger et al. [53], pp. 134–140.

[44] Fleet, D. and Jepson, A., (1990). Computation of component image velocity from local phase information. *Int. J. of Comp. Vision,* **5**(1):77–104.

[45] Singh, A., (1992). *Optic Flow Computations: A Unified Perspective.* Los Alamitos, California: IEEE Comp. Soc. Press.

[46] Srinivasan, M., (1990). Generalized gradient schemes for the measurement of two-dimensional image motion. *Biol. Cybernetics,* **63**:421–431.

[47] Weber, J. and Malik, J., (1995). Robust computation of optical flow in a multi-scale differential framework. *Int. J. of Comp. Vision,* **14**(1):67–81.

[48] Mitiche, A. and Bouthemy, P., (1996). Computation and analysis of image motion: A synopsis of current problems and methods. *Int. J. of Comp. Vision*, **19**(1):29–55.

[49] Horn, B. and Schunck, B., (1981). Determining optical flow. *Artif. Intell.*, **17**:185–203.

[50] Black, M. and Anandan, P., (1996). The robust estimation of multiple motions: Parametric and Piecewise-Smooth Flow Fields. *Comp. Vis. Graph. Image Proc.: IU*, **63**(1):75–104.

[51] Schnörr, C., (1994). Segmentation of Visual Motion by Minimizing Convex Non-Quadratic Functionals. In *12th Int. Conf. on Pattern Recognition*. Jerusalem, Israel.

[52] Schnörr, C., Sprengel, R., and Neumann, B., (1996). A variational approach to the design of early vision algorithms. *Computing Suppl.*, **11**:149–165.

[53] Berger, M.-O., Deriche, R., Herlin, I., Jaffré, J., and Morel, J.-M. (eds.), (1996). *12th Int. Conf. on Analysis and Optim. of Systems: Images, Wavelets and PDEs*, Vol. 219 of *Lect. Notes in Control and Information Sciences*, Berlin. Springer.

17 Stereopsis - Geometrical and Global Aspects

Hanspeter A. Mallot

Max-Planck-Institut für biologische Kybernetik, Tübingen, Germany

17.1 Introduction

Stereopsis is the perception of depth from the parallactic differences between the images seen by the left and the right eye. Wheatstone [1], using his mirror-stereoscope, was the first to demonstrate that image difference, or *disparity*, is indeed the crucial carrier of information.

Much work in stereovision has been devoted to one particular type of image differences, namely the position differences of the images of individual points in the two cameras or eyes. In order to measure these point disparities, an image matching procedure is required as reviewed for example, by Dhond and Aggarwal [2], Förstner [3], Jenkin et al. [4]. Image matching and the associated correspondence problem [5, 6] will not be dealt with in this chapter. The traditional view that correspondence is the central problem in stereopsis has been challenged by recent psychophysical findings indicating that other types of disparity as well

Handbook of Computer Vision and Applications
Volume 2
Signal Processing and Pattern Recognition

Copyright © 1999 by Academic Press
All rights of reproduction in any form reserved.
ISBN 0-12-379772-1/$30.00

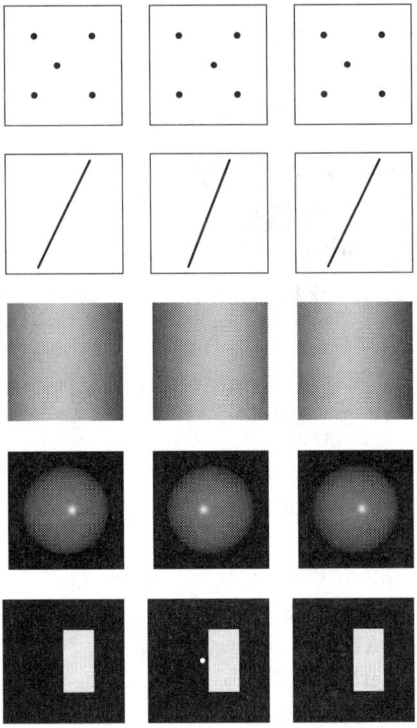

Figure 17.1: *Types of image differences or disparities:* ***a*** *point disparities;* ***b*** *orientation disparities;* ***c*** *intensity disparities;* ***d*** *disparate highlights (photometric disparities);* ***e*** *monocular occlusion ("amodal stereopsis"). For crossed fusion, use the left two columns, for uncrossed fusion the right ones. Readers not used to free stereoscopic fusion should cover up the left column and place a piece of cardboard vertically between the right two columns. By placing the head symmetrically over the cardboard, each eye is allowed to view one column only. In this situation, fusion is easily obtained.*

as global image comparisons play an important part at least in human vision [7, 8].

The different viewpoints used for recording the two half-images of a stereogram result in a number of different types of image differences, some of which are illustrated in Fig. 17.1. A comprehensive discussion is given in Arndt et al. [9] and Howard and Rogers [10].

1. *Horizontal disparity* is the horizontal offset of the images of an individual point projected into the two cameras. It can be measured as an angle or as a distance on the camera target (Fig. 17.1a).
2. *Vertical disparity* is the analogous offset in the vertical image direction. Because the stereo baseline between the two cameras is usually horizontal, vertical disparities are usually rather small. They van-

ish in nonverging camera systems, that is, systems with parallel view axes.

3. *Orientation disparities* occur if oblique lines are imaged. Generally, the resulting lines in the two images will have different slope (Fig. 17.1b). Related higher-order disparities include the projected movement of a point moving in space or the deformation (size, shear, rotation) of a planar figure.

4. *Disparate shading* as shown in Fig. 17.1c,d may result for purely geometrical reasons. Fig. 17.1c shows a Lambertian shaded cylinder with horizontal disparities that cannot be pinpointed to feature points in the image. Still, depth perception is obtained. Figure 17.1d shows a more complicated case where disparities are due to specular reflection, that is, to the fact that the same surface point looks different when observed from different directions. It is interesting to note that even though the highlight is the virtual image of the light source and its disparity therefore corresponds to a point behind the spherical surface, human observers are able to make correct use of disparate highlights. That is to say, they perceive a protruding surface when the highlight's disparity is uncrossed [11].

5. *Monocular occlusion*, also called amodal or *DaVinci stereopsis*, is another example of stereopsis without feature correspondence. In the case shown in Fig. 17.1e, the dot seems to float behind the rectangle as if it was occluded in the right image. When exchanging the two half-images, perceived depth is not inverted.

The image differences illustrated in Fig. 17.1a-c can be formalized by a so-called *disparity map*, that is, a continuous, one-to-one function $\delta(x', y')$ such that

$$I_r(x', y') = I_l(x' - \delta_1(x', y'), y' - \delta_2(x', y')) \qquad (17.1)$$

where the components of δ are the horizontal and vertical disparities. Using first-order derivatives of δ leads to the orientation and deformation disparities. The global disparity map exists only if the imaged surface is completely visible from both eyes (no monocular occlusion) and if shading is Lambertian. It does not in general exist at the most interesting image regions, that is, at depth discontinuities.

17.2 Stereo geometry

In this Section, we review the *geometry of binocular space*, as it has been developed in psychophysics and optometry [12]. We will argue that the formulation presented here is also advantageous for technical stereoheads. We will assume throughout this chapter that the view

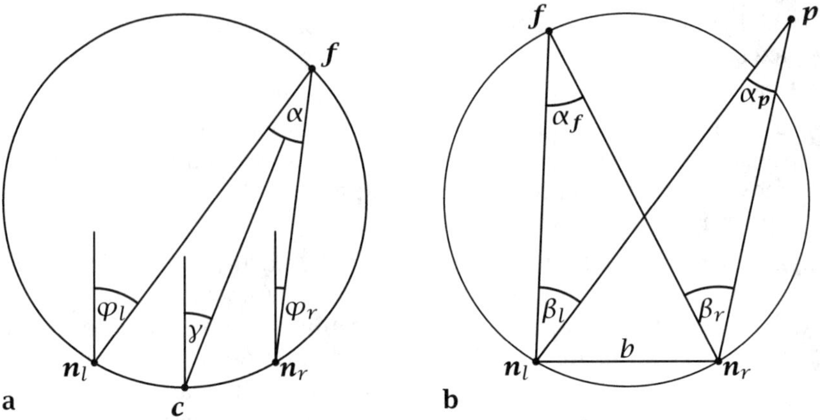

Figure 17.2: *Naming conventions for binocular geometry:* ***a*** *view axes and fixation;* ***b*** *image position of peripheral points.* $\boldsymbol{f}$*: Fixation point.* $\boldsymbol{n}_l, \boldsymbol{n}_r$*: nodal points.* $\boldsymbol{c}$*: "Cyclopean point" halfway between the nodal points.* b*: baseline distance.* φ_r, φ_l*: azimuth angles of the cameras (viewing directions) in a head-centered system.* $\alpha = \alpha_f$*: Vergence.* γ*: Version.* $\boldsymbol{p}$*: arbitrary point viewed while fixating at* $\boldsymbol{f}$*.* $\alpha_{\boldsymbol{p}}$*: target vergence of* $\boldsymbol{p}$*.* β_l, β_r*: azimuth angles of point* $\boldsymbol{p}$ *in camera-centered coordinate system.*

axes of the two cameras meet at some point in space, called the fixation point. The case of parallel camera axes is contained as a limiting case.

World coordinates will be given in a Cartesian system (x, y, z) whose origin is the midpoint of the camera nodal points. The horizontal x axis points to the right, the vertical y axis points upward, and the horizontal z axis marks the depth direction away from the observer. This coordinate system is not the head coordinate system in that it does not rotate with the head; it is, however, centered at the head. Image coordinates are denoted by (x'_l, y'_l) for the left and (x'_r, y'_r) for the right camera.

17.2.1 Hering coordinates

The basic variables describing a binocular head are illustrated in Fig. 17.2a. The heading direction is normal to the baseline connecting the camera nodal points and the pan-axis of the head. We assume for now that the nodal points are located at $\boldsymbol{n}_l = (-b/2, 0, 0)$ and $\boldsymbol{n}_r = (+b/2, 0, 0)$, respectively; the length of the baseline therefore is b. We consider first the geometry of the horizontal (epipolar, (x, z)) plane; for a more complete discussion, see Howard and Rogers [10]. The viewing directions of the camera φ_l and φ_r are defined with respect to the heading direction and positive turns are to the right. Rather than using these viewing directions themselves, we introduce the quantities

$$\alpha = \varphi_l - \varphi_r \tag{17.2}$$

$$\gamma = \frac{1}{2}(\varphi_l + \varphi_r) \tag{17.3}$$

These quantities are known as the (Hering)-*vergence* (α) and (Hering)-*version* (γ), respectively.

Vergence takes the value 0 if the camera axes are parallel. Negative values do not occur as long as the axes converge, that is, as long as there is an intersection point of the viewing axes. For each vergence $\alpha > 0$, a circle can be drawn through the nodal points and the intersection point of the two camera axes. This circle has the radius

$$R = \frac{b}{2 \sin \alpha} \tag{17.4}$$

and the center

$$\boldsymbol{v} = \left[0, 0, \frac{b}{2} \cot \alpha\right]^T \tag{17.5}$$

It is called the *Vieth-Müller circle* (VMC) of vergence α. As an application of the theorem of Thales, it is easy to show that whenever fixating a point on a fixed VMC, the same vergence angle α will result, that is, the VMCs are the iso-vergence lines.

Version as defined in Eq. (17.4) is the average, or "cyclopean," viewing direction of the two cameras. More formally, when fixating a point $\boldsymbol{f}$ with some vergence α, consider the corresponding Vieth-Müller-circle. The point on the circle halfway between the two nodal points may be called the "cyclopean point" $\boldsymbol{c}$; the visual direction from this point to the fixation point is Hering's version, γ (see Fig. 17.2). To see this, consider the three triangles $\Delta \boldsymbol{n}_l \boldsymbol{f} \boldsymbol{n}_r$ (apical angle α), $\Delta \boldsymbol{n}_l \boldsymbol{f} \boldsymbol{c}$ (apical angle α_l), $\Delta \boldsymbol{c} \boldsymbol{f} \boldsymbol{n}_r$ (apical angle α_r), all of which are inscribed into the same VMC. Therefore, from Eq. (17.4)

$$\frac{b}{2 \sin \alpha} = \frac{b_l}{2 \sin \alpha_l} = \frac{b_r}{2 \sin \alpha_r}$$

where b_l and b_r denote the length of the chords $\overline{\boldsymbol{n}_l, \boldsymbol{c}}$ and $\overline{\boldsymbol{c}, \boldsymbol{n}_r}$, respectively. If $b_l = b_r$, that is, if $\boldsymbol{c}$ is centered between $\boldsymbol{n}_l$ and $\boldsymbol{n}_r$, it follows that $\alpha_l = \alpha_r$. Since, from simple trigonometry, $\alpha_l = \varphi_l - \gamma$ and $\alpha_r = \gamma - \varphi_r$, this implies $\gamma = \frac{1}{2}(\varphi_l + \varphi_r)$.

Note that $\boldsymbol{c}$ depends on the current vergence angle. The lines of constant version are the so-called *hyperbolas of Hillebrand*. Simple trigonometric considerations yield the transformation rule from Hering

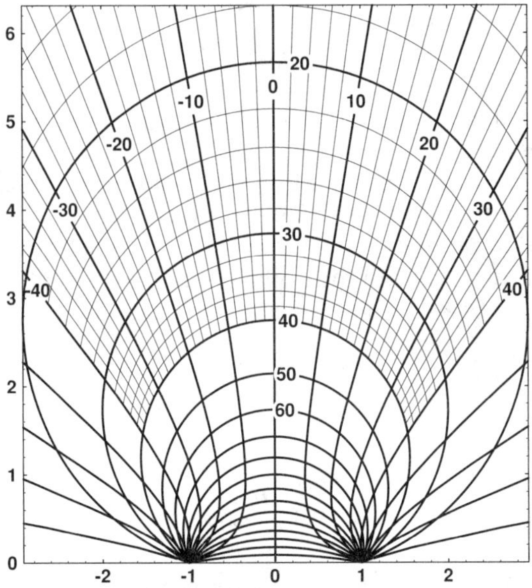

Figure 17.3: *Curves of iso-vergence (Vieth-Müller circles) and iso-version (hyperbolas of Hillebrand). The nodal points are located at* $\boldsymbol{n} = (\pm 1, 0)$. *The bold lines are spaced at 10° both for version and vergence. The light line spacing is 2°.*

vergence and version to Cartesian x, y, z coordinates:

$$
\begin{aligned}
H(\alpha, \gamma) = \begin{bmatrix} x \\ y \\ z \end{bmatrix} &= \frac{b}{2\sin\alpha} \begin{bmatrix} \sin 2\gamma \\ 0 \\ \cos\alpha + \cos 2\gamma \end{bmatrix} \\
&= R \begin{bmatrix} \cos\varphi_r \sin\varphi_l - \cos\varphi_l \sin\varphi_r \\ 0 \\ 2\cos\varphi_r \cos\varphi_l \end{bmatrix}
\end{aligned}
\tag{17.6}
$$

The iso-curves of this transformation for constant vergence (circles) and constant version (hyperbolas) are plotted in Fig. 17.3.

17.2.2 Horizontal disparity

So far, we have considered only the camera axes and their intersection points. As camera movements are mostly rotations, the angular description seems rather natural. We now turn to points that are not currently fixated and to their images in the two cameras, and will show

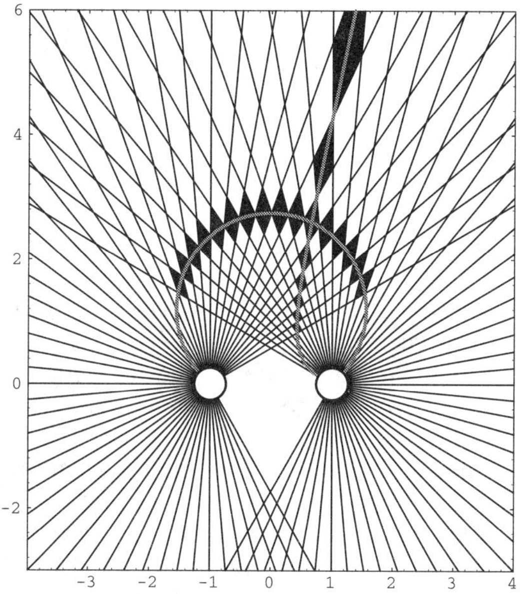

Figure 17.4: Stereo geometry for collimated imaging devices (complex eyes). Each quadrangle corresponds to one pair of image points. Points in 3-D space can be distinguished if they fall into different quadrangles. A Vieth-Müller circle and an iso-version hyperbola are marked for comparison with Fig. 17.3. (Redrawn based on figures from Burkhardt et al. [13])

that the angular formulation applies here as well. Let the system fixate a point $\boldsymbol{f}$ and consider a second point $\boldsymbol{p}$. The angles between the optical axis of each camera and the ray through point $\boldsymbol{p}$ will be called β_l and β_r, respectively (see Fig. 17.2b). They correspond to the image coordinates of the projection of $\boldsymbol{p}$, which is given by $x'_{l,r} = f \tan \beta_{l,r}$ where f is the focal length of the camera. The *disparity* of the point $\boldsymbol{p}$ is defined by angular difference:

$$\delta = \beta_l - \beta_r \tag{17.7}$$

Likewise, we define the average eccentricity

$$\eta = \frac{1}{2}(\beta_l + \beta_r) \tag{17.8}$$

It is quite clear that disparity δ depends on the current vergence angle of the system. If this is changed such as to fixate $\boldsymbol{p}$, δ is obviously reduced to zero. To stress this dependence of disparity on vergence, δ is sometimes called *relative* disparity. Let us now denote by $\alpha_{\boldsymbol{p}}$ the vergence angle obtained when fixating $\boldsymbol{p}$, sometimes also called the *target vergence* of $\boldsymbol{p}$. Let us further denote by $\delta_f(\boldsymbol{p})$ the disparity of point $\boldsymbol{p}$ when fixating $\boldsymbol{f}$. It is then easy to show that

$$\delta_f(\boldsymbol{p}) = \alpha_f - \alpha_{\boldsymbol{p}} \tag{17.9}$$

Analogously, we have:

$$\eta_f(\boldsymbol{p}) = \gamma_f - \gamma_{\boldsymbol{p}} \tag{17.10}$$

With these relations, we can also use the coordinate system derived for eye movements for disparities. For example, when fixating a point with Hering-coordinates (α_f, γ_f), the Cartesian coordinates of a point with disparity $\delta_f(\boldsymbol{p})$ and eccentricity $\eta_f(\boldsymbol{p})$ are $H(\alpha_f + \delta_f(\boldsymbol{p}), \gamma_f + \eta_f(\boldsymbol{p}))$, where H is the transformation defined in Eq. 17.6. In Fig. 17.3 disparities with respect to an arbitrary fixation point are immediately given by the distance from the fixation point in vergence direction. Hering coordinates thus provide a means for a unified evaluation of disparities at changing vergence conditions. As a consequence, we have shown that for each vergence state of the system, the corresponding VMC is the (theoretical) *horopter*, that is, the geometrical locus of all points having disparity zero with respect to the fixation point.

Figure 17.4 shows an alternative account of binocular geometry in the plane. While this approach applies most clearly to collimated imaging systems such as the complex eyes of insects [13], it is also useful for discussions of stereo resolution [14]. Resolution is inversely proportional to the size of the quadrilaterals in Fig. 17.4.

17.2.3 Vertical disparity and epipolar lines

So far, we have considered only the horizontal plane together with camera movements about axes orthogonal to this plane. In this case, disparities are completely described by Eqs. (17.7) to (17.9). Points outside this plane are imaged to positions that may differ both in their horizontal and vertical coordinates. As an example, consider a point at height h above the horizontal plane. Its vertical coordinate in the two image planes will depend on the distance of the point from the camera nodal points. Therefore, disparity will have a vertical component.

Vertical disparities are closely related to the notion of epipolar lines (see Fig. 17.5). Consider a point $\boldsymbol{p}_l$ in the left image plane. The geometrical locus of all points $\boldsymbol{p}$ in 3-D space generating an image at point $\boldsymbol{p}_l$ is a ray from the left nodal point containing $\mathbf{p}_l$. When observed from the right camera, this ray is imaged at a certain line in the image. The plane spanned by all rays from the right nodal point to the ray of possible positions of $\boldsymbol{p}$ is identical to the plane passing through the two nodal points and $\boldsymbol{p}_l$ or any one of its generators $\boldsymbol{p}$; it is called the

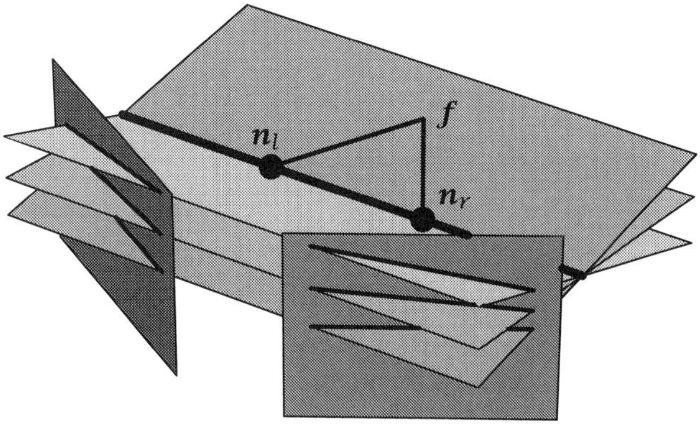

Figure 17.5: *Epipolar lines and vertical disparities in a verging stereo system. $\boldsymbol{n}_l, \boldsymbol{n}_r$: left and right nodal points. $\boldsymbol{f}$ fixation. The image planes are orthogonal to the "optical axes" $\overline{\boldsymbol{n}_l \boldsymbol{f}}$ and $\overline{\boldsymbol{n}_r \boldsymbol{f}}$, respectively. The epipolar lines diverge towards the midline of the system.*

epipolar plane of $\boldsymbol{p}$. The intersections of the epipolar plane with the image planes form a pair of epipolar lines. Any point imaged on some epipolar line in one image must be imaged on the corresponding epipolar line in the other image. That is to say that horizontal and vertical disparity have a constant ratio, which corresponds to the slope of the epipolar lines. All epipolar lines of one image meet at a common intersection point, which is also the intersection of the image plane with the baseline connecting the two nodal points of the camera system. If the vergence angle is zero, that is, if the camera axes are parallel to each other and orthogonal to the base line, the epipolar lines become parallel and horizontal and all vertical disparities vanish.

Epipolar lines are important in two respects. First, if the coordinates of the fixation point are known, epipolar lines can be predicted from camera geometry. In the stereo-matching process, this information can be used to simplify the matching process because corresponding image points must be localized along the respective epipolar lines. One way to do this is by means of the so-called *epipolar transformation* [15], a collineation applied to the images to make epipolar lines horizontal.

A second application of epipolar lines is the calibration of stereo camera systems. If vergence is symmetric, the vergence angle can be infered from a single known stereo correspondence with nonzero vertical disparity. In symmetric vergence, the epipolar lines of the two half-images are mirror-symmetric with respect to the vertical midline of the images. The intersection points of all epipolar lines are located on the x' axis of the image coordinate system at $y'_{r,l} = \pm f \cot \alpha/2$

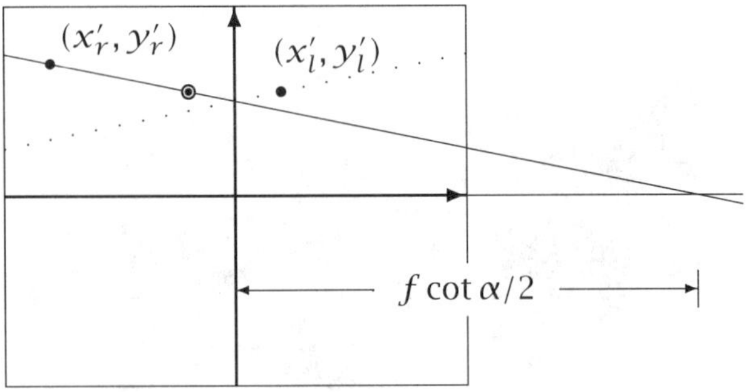

Figure 17.6: *Slope of an epipolar line in symmetrical vergence. The figure shows the two image planes superimposed. If a pair of corresponding points* $((x'_l, y'_l), (x'_r, y'_r))$ *is known, the slope of the right epipolar line can be determined by mirroring the point from the left image at the vertical image midline (*y' *axis), which results in a point* $(-x'_l, y'_l)$*, shown by an open dot. The line through* (x'_r, y'_r) *and* $(-x'_l, y'_l)$ *is the epipolar line. From its intersection with the horizontal axis, the vergence angle* α *(Eq. (17.2)) can be inferred.*

for the left and right image, respectively (see Fig. 17.6). As before, α denotes vergence and f is the focal length of the camera. If a pair of corresponding points is given by (x'_r, y'_r) in the right image and (x'_l, y'_l) in the left image, the slope of the epipolar line in the right image is

$$s_r = \frac{y'_r - y'_l}{x'_r + x'_l} \tag{17.11}$$

The epipolar line crosses the horizontal image axis at $x_r - y_r/s_r$. From this, we obtain:

$$\alpha = 2 \arctan \frac{y'_r - y'_l}{x'_l y'_r + x'_r y'_l} \tag{17.12}$$

Note that the enumerator of the fraction in this equation is the vertical disparity in Cartesian coordinates. Equation (17.12) is undefined for points on the horizontal or vertical image axes. In conclusion, in symmetrically verging systems, one pair of corresponding image points suffices to determine the absolute position of the point in space, even if the vergence of the camera system is allowed to change.

17.2.4 Binocular camera movements

So far, we have considered cases where the camera rotation was confined to a pair of axes orthogonal to the horizontal plane. If we now turn to general fixation points, we first have to discuss the degrees of freedom of the required turns. The possible arrangements and naming conventions are summarized in Fig. 17.7. The human eye moves according to the Listing system shown in Fig. 17.7c.

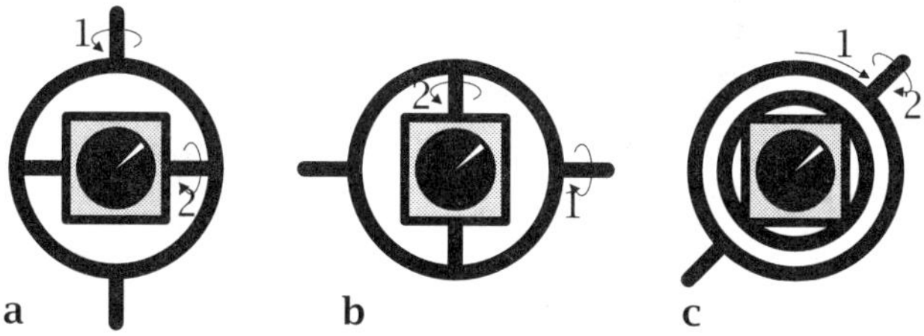

Figure 17.7: *Degrees of freedom of rotation for technical and biological camera systems. The central square with the pupil marks the camera.* ***a*** *Fick system. The first turn is about the vertical axis, the second about a horizontal one.* ***b*** *Helmholtz system. The first turn is about a vertical axis, the second turn about an axis orthogonal moving axis.* ***c*** *Listing system. The camera is placed in a bearing. In the first rotation the outside ring is moved, thereby selecting an axis for the second turn. All systems include a roll movement about the view axis as a third step. It is not shown here.*

We give rotation matrices for the three systems that rotate a space direction $[a, b, c]^T$ with $a^2+b^2+c^2 = 1$ and $c \neq 1$ into the straight ahead direction of the camera, $[0, 0, 1]^T$. Additional roll movement about that axis of gaze is not included in these matrices.

In the *Fick system* (Fig. 17.7a), the first rotation is around a vertical axis, while the second uses a horizontal one. Technically, this is realized by two independent pan-tilt camera systems. The equation reads:

$$\boldsymbol{F}_{(a,b,c)} = \begin{bmatrix} c/\sqrt{a^2+c^2} & 0 & -a/\sqrt{a^2+c^2} \\ -ab/\sqrt{a^2+c^2} & \sqrt{a^2+c^2} & -bc/\sqrt{a^2+c^2} \\ a & b & c \end{bmatrix} \tag{17.13}$$

The *Helmholtz system* starts with a turn about a fixed horizontal axis (Fig. 17.7b). *Stereo heads* using the Helmholtz geometry can thus be built with a common tilt axis. Additional turns are about an axis orthogonal to this tilt axis. The matrix is:

$$\boldsymbol{H}_{(a,b,c)} = \begin{bmatrix} \sqrt{b^2+c^2} & -ab/\sqrt{b^2+c^2} & -ac/\sqrt{b^2+c^2} \\ 0 & c/\sqrt{b^2+c^2} & -b/\sqrt{b^2+c^2} \\ a & b & c \end{bmatrix} \tag{17.14}$$

Finally, in the *Listing system*, movement starts by choosing an axis of rotation. The second step is a turn about that axis moving the gaze direction from the start to the goal position on a great circle. All possible axes lie in what is called Listing's plane, a plane orthogonal to the principal (straight ahead) direction passing through the center of the

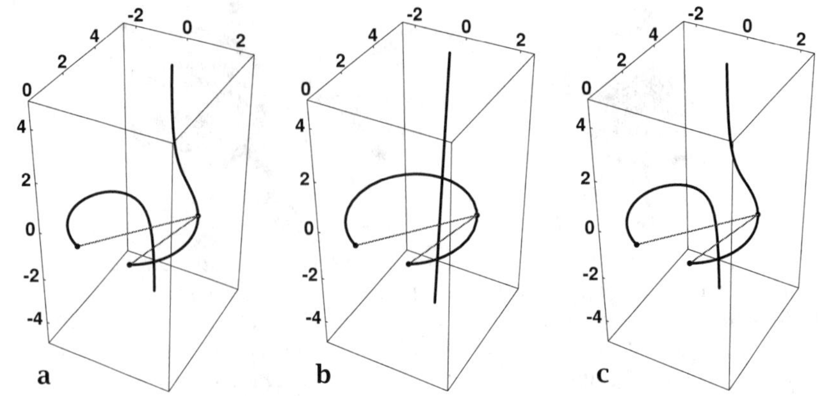

Figure 17.8: *Space horopter for a stereo camera system with nodal points* $(\pm 1, 0, 0)^\top$ *fixating at* $(2.0, 0.3, 3.0)^\top$*:* ***a*** *Fick system;* ***b*** *Helmholtz system;* ***c*** *Listing system.*

eye:

$$
\boldsymbol{L}_{(a,b,c)} = \begin{bmatrix} (a^2c + b^2)/(1 - c^2) & -ab/(1 + c) & -a \\ -ab/(1 + c) & (a^2 + b^2c)/(1 - c^2) & -b \\ a & b & c \end{bmatrix} \tag{17.15}
$$

In human vision, Listing's law states that the roll position at any one viewing direction is as if the eye had moved to this direction along a great circle from the straight ahead position. Roll is independent of the actual way by which the current position is reached.

17.2.5 The space horopter

An important concept for understanding stereo geometry is the space *horopter*, that is, the set of points in the 3-D world whose vertical and horizontal disparity vanish simultaneously. It is clear that the space horopter passes through the point of fixation. Because the vanishing of both horizontal and vertical disparity poses a 2-D constraint on the horopter, one would expect it to be a curve, or some 1-D manifold. With the rotation matrices given in the foregoing, the problem can be formulated as follows.

Let $\boldsymbol{f} = [f_1, f_2, f_3]^T$ denote a fixation point with $f_3 > 0$. Let $\boldsymbol{M}$ denote one of the forementioned rotation matrices. We write

$$
\boldsymbol{M}_l = \boldsymbol{M}_{\boldsymbol{f}-\boldsymbol{n}_l}; \quad \boldsymbol{M}_r = \boldsymbol{M}_{\boldsymbol{f}-\boldsymbol{n}_r} \tag{17.16}
$$

where the camera nodal points are denoted by $\boldsymbol{n}_l$ and $\boldsymbol{n}_r$, respectively. $\boldsymbol{M}_l(\boldsymbol{p} - \boldsymbol{n}_l)$ thus describes the coordinate transformation of a point $\boldsymbol{p}$

Table 17.1: Examples for stereo camera heads with various degrees of freedom. In the DoF column, the first number applies to the cameras, the second to the head, and the third to a further support system (body, vehicle, etc.)

DoF	Type	Examples
	HELMHOLTZ architectures (common tilt axis)	
$1+4+0$	symmetric vergence + head tilt, pan, x, y-translation	U Penn; Krotkov [17]
$1+2+0$	symmetric vergence + head tilt and pan (symmetric Helmholtz)	Harvard head; Clark and Ferrier [18]
$2+1+6$	camera pan + yoked tilt + Puma arm	Rochester head; Coombs and Brown [19]
	FICK architectures (independent tilt and pan)	
$4+2+0$	camera pan and tilt about nodal points + eccentric pan and tilt of neck module	KTH head; Pahlavan and Eklundh [20]
$4+0+2$	camera pan and tilt + turn and z-translation of vehicle	Seelen et al. [21]
	LISTING architecture (camera movement on great circles)	
$6+6+6$		human head

from world coordinates into the coordinate system centered around the left camera. A point on the horopter must then satisfy the equation

$$\boldsymbol{M}_l(\boldsymbol{p} - \boldsymbol{n}_l) = \lambda \boldsymbol{M}_r(\boldsymbol{p} - \boldsymbol{n}_r) \tag{17.17}$$

Where λ is a positive real variable describing the ratio of the distances of point $\boldsymbol{p}$ to the two nodal points.

Figure 17.8 shows solutions of Eq. (17.17) for the three systems of camera axes. For the Helmholtz system, the space horopter is composed of a Vieth-Müller circle in a plane tilted away from the horizontal by the common elevation angle, and a medial line perpendicular to the circle. In the other cases, the space horopter is a space curve that degenerates to the circle plus line arrangement for fixation points in the horizontal or medial plane. For a derivation of the space horopter in the Listing case, see Solomons [16].

17.2.6 Stereo camera heads

The discussion of stereo geometry presented so far applies to stereo camera systems with a fair number of degrees of freedom to move. In

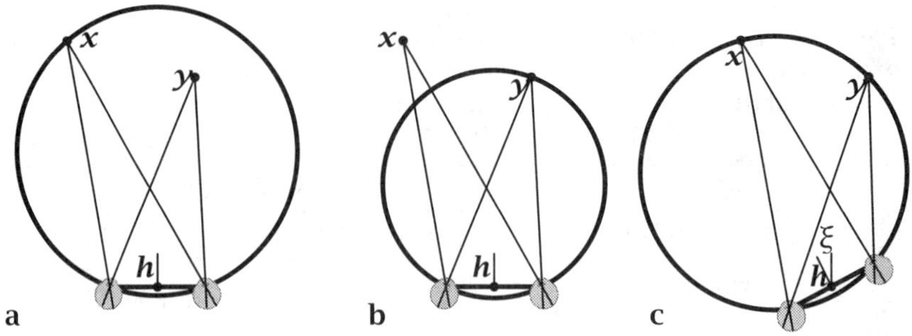

Figure 17.9: Comparison of camera heads with two degrees of freedom. The center of rotation of the camera head is marked by **h**: ***a*** *and* ***b*** *head with independently moving camera* ((φ_l, φ_r) *system);* ***c*** *head with symmetric version and yoked pan movements* ((α, ξ) *system). In the* (φ_l, φ_r) *system, the zero-disparity circle can be made passing through just one point* (**x** *or* **y**) *at any one time. In the* (α, ξ) *system, the disparity of both points can be compensated simultaneously. Note that the spatial relation of* $\boldsymbol{x}$, $\boldsymbol{y}$ *and* **h** *is the same in all panels.*

human vision, these are the yoked variables, vergence and version, for the movements within the horizontal plane; for movements outside the horizontal plane, Listing's law applies. Mechanically, each eye has the full three degrees of freedom of rotation. Movements of head and body give additional flexibility to the system.

An overview of some technical camera heads is given in Table 17.1; for a more comprehensive discussion, see Murray et al. [22]. As an example of the design questions arising in the design of camera heads, we discuss one simple geometrical property of verging camera systems that seems to have been overlooked previously.

Consider a simple camera head with two degrees of freedom. These can be either the two viewing directions (pan) φ_l and φ_r of the individual cameras, or the symmetric vergence of the system α and the heading direction ξ. For simplicity, we assume that the head turns around a vertical axis through the midpoint between the two camera nodal points and the cameras turn around parallel axes through their respective nodal points. Note that ξ is not identical to the version angle γ introduced in Section 17.2.1. Two criteria could be the following:

C1 Is it possible to fixate any point in the plane, thereby reducing its disparity to zero?

C2 Given two points in the plane, is it possible to simultaneously reduce both disparities to zero? In this case, a smooth surface passing through the two points would have low disparity values throughout.

With respect to criterion 1, the (φ_l, φ_r) system has a problem with points on the base line. The (α, ξ) system can fixate any point in the plane without restriction. With respect to criterion 2, it is quite clear that for the (φ_l, φ_r) system, simultaneous disparity reduction of two points is possible only if the two points happen to be on a circle passing through the two nodal points. In the (α, ξ) system, however, simultaneous disparity reduction is always possible as long as the line through the two points $\boldsymbol{x}$ and $\boldsymbol{y}$ is neither the baseline nor the horizontal midline of the system. The corresponding settings for the camera head are:

$$\xi = \arctan \frac{(4\boldsymbol{x}^2 - b^2)y_2 - (4\boldsymbol{y}^2 - b^2)x_2}{(4\boldsymbol{y}^2 - b^2)x_1 - (4\boldsymbol{x}^2 - b^2)y_1} \tag{17.18}$$

$$\begin{aligned} \alpha &= \arctan \frac{b(x_1 \sin \xi + x_2 \cos \xi)}{\boldsymbol{x}^2 - b^2/4} \\ &= \arctan \frac{b(y_1 \sin \xi + y_2 \cos \xi)}{\boldsymbol{y}^2 - b^2/4} \end{aligned} \tag{17.19}$$

An example of this relationship is shown in Fig. 17.9c.

17.3 Global stereopsis

17.3.1 Global disparity

In this section, we will briefly discuss global image difference as one interesting variable in stereo vision. We will assume that the left and right images are related to each other by a 1-D disparity map $\delta(x', y')$ such that

$$I_r(x', y') = I_l(x' - \delta(x', y'), y') \tag{17.20}$$

Vertical disparities will be neglected in this analysis.

We will prove in this section that the global disparity or image shift minimizing the overall image difference equals the averaged true disparity, weighted by local image contrast. To see this, we introduce the global image *correlation*

$$\Phi(D) := \int\int [I_l(x', y') - I_r(x' + D, y')]^2 \, dx' \, dy' \tag{17.21}$$

Setting $I(x', y') := I_l(x', y')$ and substituting Eq. (17.20) into Eq. (17.21), we obtain:

$$\Phi(D) = \int\int [I(x', y') - I(x' - \delta(x', y') + D, y)]^2 \, dx' \, dy' \tag{17.22}$$

The minimization is now performed by calculating the derivative $\Phi'(D)$. Application of the chain rule yields:

$$\Phi'(D) = 2\int\int I_{x'}(x' - \delta(x',y') + D, y') \\ [I(x',y') - I(x' - \delta(x',y') + D, y')]\,\mathrm{d}x'\,\mathrm{d}y' \tag{17.23}$$

Setting $\Phi'(D^*) = 0$ and linearly approximating the term in square brackets, we obtain:

$$0 \approx \int\int I_{x'}(x',y')[(D^* - \delta(x',y'))I_{x'}(x',y')]\,\mathrm{d}x'\,\mathrm{d}y' \tag{17.24}$$

This yields the final result:

$$D^* \approx \frac{\int\int \delta(x',y') I_{x'}^2(x',y')\,\mathrm{d}x'\,\mathrm{d}y'}{\int\int I_{x'}^2(x',y')\,\mathrm{d}x'\,\mathrm{d}y'} \tag{17.25}$$

As stated above, Eq. (17.25) shows that the global disparity, that is, the image shift maximizing overall correlation between the left and the right image, is equivalent to the average of the local disparities, weighted by the squared partial derivative of the image intensity function $I_{x'}^2(x',y')$, which may be considered a measure of image contrast in the "disparity direction."

In verging camera systems, global disparities can be used to adjust the vergence angle and thus the working point of stereopsis to some point of interest in space. In biological vision, disparities are considered only in a narrow range around zero, called *Panum's fusional area*. The advantage of this is that high disparity resolution can be deployed to regions in space where it is actually needed. In terms of stereo correspondence algorithms, the ability to verge results in a smaller required search space for disparities. Global image correlation as defined in Eq. (17.21) has been used for vergence control, for example, by Ahuja and Abbott [23]. In human vergence movements, an averaging mechanism as described by Eq. (17.25) has been demonstrated by Mallot et al. [24]. Phase-based approaches to global disparity estimation have been discussed by Theimer and Mallot [25].

17.3.2 Inverse perspective mapping

As one example of a technical application of global stereopsis, we briefly discuss *obstacle avoidance* by *inverse perspective mapping* [26, 27]. Here, prior to disparity calculations, the images are transformed in a way that makes global disparity an even more interesting variable. The basic idea is illustrated in Fig. 17.10. Consider two stereoscopic views of a scene as depicted in Fig. 17.10a,b. If no obstacle were around, the

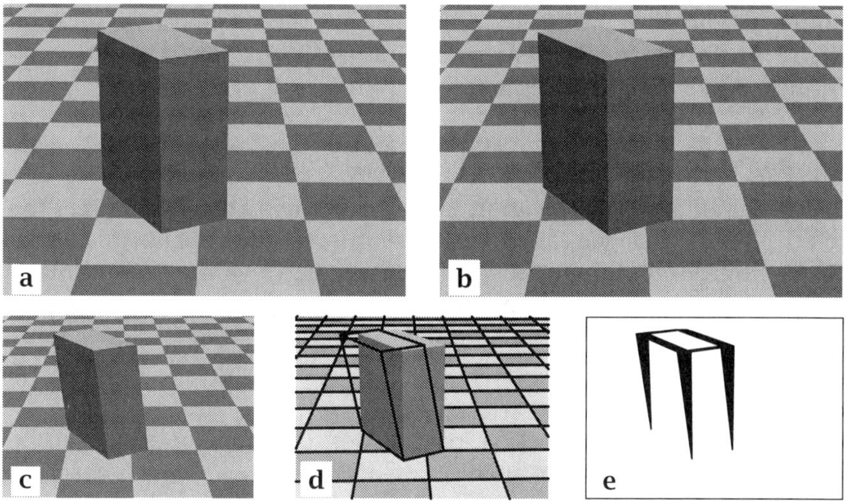

Figure 17.10: *Obstacle avoidance by inverse perspective mapping:* ***a,b*** *left and right images of a scene;* **c** *predicted right view based on inverse perspective mapping of the left view;* ***d*** *comparison of actual and predicted right image. The actual image is shown as gray values, whereas the prediction is shown by contours. The images coincide in the ground plane, but deviate increasingly for objects raising above the plane;* **e** *difference image of actual and predicted right image. The obstacle can easily be segmented from the ground plane.*

right image could be predicted from the left by a perspective remapping technique. This remapping is a projective collineation that can be obtained by projecting the right image back to the ground plane and imaging the result with the left camera. Comparing the original and the predicted right image, one obtains deviations in those image regions where something is protruding or receding from the horizontal plane, that is, in obstacle regions. If both images are identical, no obstacle is present. An intuitive way to think of this is that inverse perspective mapping creates a zero-disparity plane (for comparisons of the right and the predicted right image) that coincides with the ground plane. Whenever a "disparity" occurs, an obstacle must be present.

The technique is not sensitive to cast shadows and other image structure as long as it is confined to the plane. Disparity is zero for points in the ground plane and increases with obstacle elevation. Inverse perspective mapping has been applied successfully in autonomous robots [21], [28] as well as to driver support systems on the highway [29], [30].

Inverse perspective mapping is a projective collineation, most suitably formalized in terms of homogeneous coordinates. Let $\tilde{\boldsymbol{x}}_l$ and $\tilde{\boldsymbol{x}}_r$ denote the homogeneous representations of the left and right image points $\boldsymbol{x}_l$ and $\boldsymbol{x}_r$. Intuitively, $\tilde{\boldsymbol{x}}_l$ and $\tilde{\boldsymbol{x}}_r$ are the rays passing through the respective image points. Inverse perspective mapping is then described by a 3×3 matrix $\boldsymbol{Q}$ with

$$\tilde{\boldsymbol{x}}_r = \boldsymbol{Q}\tilde{\boldsymbol{x}}_l \tag{17.26}$$

which depends on the rotation between the two cameras $\boldsymbol{M}_l\boldsymbol{M}_r^T$, the relative position of the camera nodal points, $\boldsymbol{n}_l - \boldsymbol{n}_r$, the normal of the assumed ground plane $\boldsymbol{g}$, and the distance between the ground plane and the left camera nodal point d. The relation reads:

$$\boldsymbol{Q} = \boldsymbol{M}_l\boldsymbol{M}_r^T + \frac{(\boldsymbol{n}_l - \boldsymbol{n}_r)\boldsymbol{g}^\top}{d} \tag{17.27}$$

For a proof, see Faugeras [31], proposition 6.1. Similar ideas can be applied to the monocular analysis of optical flow, in which case the inverse perspective mapping goes from the image plane to the assumed ground plane [26]. As compared to the stereoscopic case, optical flow has the disadvantage that it works only when the observer is moving, requiring faster motions when more reliable obstacle information is sought.

17.4 References

[1] Wheatstone, C., (1838). Some remarkable phenomena of vision. I. *Philosophical Trans. Royal Society*, **13**:371–395.

[2] Dhond, U. R. and Aggarwal, J. K., (1989). Structure from stereo—a review. *IEEE Trans. Systems, Man, and Cybernetics*, **19**:1489–1510.

[3] Förstner, W., (1992). Image Matching. In *Computer and Robot Vision*, R. M. Haralick and L. G. Shapiro, eds., Vol. 2, Chapter 16. Reading, MA: Addison Wesley.

[4] Jenkin, M. R. M., Jepson, A. D., and Tsotsos, J. K., (1991). Techniques for disparity measurement. *Computer Vision Graphics and Image Processing: Image Understanding*, **53**:14–30.

[5] Julesz, B., (1971). *Foundations of Cyclopean Perception.* Chicago and London: Chicago University Press.

[6] Marr, D. and Poggio, T., (1979). A computational theory of human stereo vision. *Proc. Royal Society (London) B*, **204**:301–328.

[7] Anderson, B. L. and Nakayama, K., (1994). Toward a general theory of stereopsis: Binocular matching, occluding contours, and fusion. *Psychological Review*, **101**:414–445.

[8] Mallot, H. A., Arndt, P. A., and Bülthoff, H. H., (1996a). A psychophysical and computational analysis of intensity-based stereo. *Biological Cybernetics*, **75**:187–198.

[9] Arndt, P. A., Mallot, H. A., and Bülthoff, H. H., (1995). Human stereovision without localized image-features. *Biological Cybernetics*, **72**:279–293.

[10] Howard, I. P. and Rogers, B. J., (1995). *Bionocular Vision and Stereopsis.* Number 29 in Oxford Psychology Series. New York, Oxford: Oxford University Press.

[11] Blake, A. and Bülthoff, H. H., (1990). Does the brain know the physics of specular reflection? *Nature*, **343**:165–168.

[12] Helmholtz, H. v., (1909–1911). *Handbuch der physiologischen Optik*, 3. edition. Hamburg: Voss.

[13] Burkhardt, D., Darnhofer-Demar, B., and Fischer, K., (1973). Zum binokularen Entfernungssehen der Insekten. I. Die Struktur des Sehraums von Synsekten. *Zeitschrift für vergleichende Physiologie*, **87**:165–188.

[14] Völpel, B. and Theimer, W. M., (1995). Localization uncertainty in area-based stereo algorithms. *IEEE Trans. Systems, Man, and Cybernetics*, **25**: 1628–1634.

[15] Caprile, B. and Torre, V., (1990). Using vanishing points for camera calibration. *International Journal of Computer Vision*, **4**:127–139.

[16] Solomons, H., (1975). Derivation of the space horopter. *British Jour. Physiological Optics*, **30**:56–90.

[17] Krotkov, E. P., (1989). *Active Computer Vision by Cooperative Focus and Stereo.* Berlin: Springer.

[18] Clark, J. J. and Ferrier, N. J., (1992). Attentive Visual Servoing. In *Active Vision*, A. Blake and A. Yuille, eds. Cambridge, MA: The MIT Press.

[19] Coombs, D. and Brown, C., (1993). Real-time binocular smooth pursuit. *International Journal of Computer Vision*, **11**:147–164.

[20] Pahlavan, K. and Eklundh, J.-O., (1992). A head-eye system—analysis and design. *Computer Vision Graphics and Image Processing: Image Understanding*, **56**:41–56.

[21] Seelen, W. v., Bohrer, S., Kopecz, J., and Theimer, W. M., (1995). A neural architecture for visual information processing. *International Journal of Computer Vision*, **16**:229–260.

[22] Murray, D. W., Du, F., McLauchlan, P. F., Reid, I. D., Sharkey, P. M., and Brady, M., (1992). Design of stereo heads. In *Active Vision*, A. Blake and A. Yuille, eds. Cambridge, MA: MIT Press.

[23] Ahuja, N. and Abbott, A. L., (1993). Active Stereo: Integrating disparity, vergence, focus, aperture, and calibration for surface estimation. *IEEE Trans. Pattern Analysis and Machine Intelligence*, **15**:1007–1029.

[24] Mallot, H. A., Roll, A., and Arndt, P. A., (1996b). Disparity-evoked vergence is driven by interocular correlation. *Vision Research*, **36**:2925–2937.

[25] Theimer, W. and Mallot, H. A., (1994). Phase-based binocular vergence control and depth reconstruction using active vision. *Computer Vision Graphics and Image Processing: Image Understanding*, **60**:343–358.

[26] Mallot, H. A., Bülthoff, H. H., Little, J. J., and Bohrer, S., (1991). Inverse perspective mapping simplifies optical flow computation and obstacle detection. *Biological Cybernetics*, **64**:177–185.

[27] Mallot, H. A., Schulze, E., and Storjohann, K., (1989). Neural network strategies for robot navigation. In *Neural Networks from Models to Applications*, L. Personnaz and G. Dreyfus, eds., pp. 560–569. Paris: I.D.S.E.T.

[28] Košecka, J., Christensen, H. I., and Bajcsy, R., (1995). Discrete event modeling of visually guided behaviors. *International Journal of Computer Vision*, **14**:179–191.

[29] Zielke, T., Storjohann, K., Mallot, H. A., and Seelen, W. v., (1990). Adapting computer vision systems to the visual environment: topographic mapping. In *Computer Vision—ECCV 90 (Lecture Notes in Computer Science 427)*, O. Faugeras, ed., INRIA. Berlin: Springer.

[30] Luong, Q.-T., Weber, J., Koller, D., and Malik, J., (1995). An integrated stereo-based approach to automatic vehicle guidance. In *5th International Conference on Computer Vision*, pp. 52–57. Los Alamitos, CA: IEEE Computer Society Press.

[31] Faugeras, O., (1993). *Three-Dimensional Computer Vision. A Geometric Viewpoint.* Cambridge, MA: MIT Press.

18 Stereo Terrain Reconstruction by Dynamic Programming

Georgy Gimel'farb

Computer Science Department, The University of Auckland, New Zealand

18.1 Introduction

Photogrammetric terrain reconstruction from aerial and space stereopairs of images occupies a prominent place in cartography and remote sensing of the Earth's surface. Traditional analytical photogrammetry, based on human stereopsis, involves the following two main steps. First, several ground control points (GCP) are detected in the images for placing these latter in such a way as to visually perceive a *stereo model* of the 3-D surface and embed it into a reference 3-D coordinate system. This step is called *image orientation* or *calibration* [1] (see also Chapter 17). Then, the perceived stereo model is visually traced along x- or

Handbook of Computer Vision and Applications
Volume 2
Signal Processing and Pattern Recognition

Copyright © 1999 by Academic Press
All rights of reproduction in any form reserved.
ISBN 0-12-379772-1/$30.00

y-profiles (3-D lines with constant y- or x-coordinates, respectively) or along horizontals (lines with constant z-coordinates).

A dense set of regularly or irregularly spaced 3-D points of the profiles or horizontals form a *digital surface model* (DSM) of the terrain. On-line or posterior visual exclusion of particular "noncharacteristic" objects, such as forest canopy or buildings, converts a DSM into a *digital terrain model* (DTM), *digital elevation model* (DEM), or *triangulated irregular network* (TIN)[1].

Digital photogrammetry uses (interactive) computational methods both to orient the images by detecting the GCPs and to reconstruct the terrains [3, 4]. The *computational binocular stereo* models a "low-level" human stereopsis that is based on the one-to-one correspondence between 3-D coordinates of the visible terrain points and 2-D coordinates of the corresponding pixels in stereo images (for more detail, see Chapter 17). Under a known optical geometry of binocular stereo viewing, found by calibration, 3-D coordinates of each spatial point are computed from differences between 2-D coordinates of the corresponding pixels. The difference of x-coordinates is called a *horizontal disparity*, or x-parallax. The difference of y-coordinates is a *vertical disparity*, or y-parallax. The disparities can be presented as a *digital parallax map* (DPM) that specifies all the correspondent pixels in a given stereo pair. A DSM is computed from a DPM using the calibration parameters.

Each binocularly visible terrain area is represented by (visually) similar corresponding regions in a given stereo pair, and the correspondences can be found by searching for the similar regions in the images. As human stereo vision finds these similarities so easily and, at most, reliably hides the principal *ill-posedness* of the binocular stereo, there always exist a multiplicity of optical 3-D surfaces giving just the same stereo pair [5]. Therefore, it is impossible to reconstruct precisely the real terrain from a single pair, and the computational reconstruction pursues a more limited goal of bringing surfaces close enough to those perceived visually or restored by traditional photogrammetric techniques from the same stereo pair.

Natural terrains possess a large variety of geometric shapes and photometric features, thus the computational reconstruction assumes only a very general prior knowledge about the optical 3-D surfaces to be found (at most, specifications of allowable smoothness, discontinuities, curvature, and so forth). Long-standing investigations have resulted in numerous stereo methods (see, for instance, [6, 7, 8, 9, 10, 11]. Some of them, mostly, simple correlation or least-square image matching [12, 13, 14] have already found practical use in modern photogrammetric

[1]A DEM contains 3-D points (x, y, z) supported by a regular (x, y)-lattice; a DTM either means just the same as the DEM or incorporates also some irregular characteristic topographic features, and a TIN approximates the surface by adjacent nonoverlapping planar triangles with irregularly spaced vertices (x, y, z) [2].

devices. But there is still the need to develop more efficient and robust methods to be implemented in practice.

18.1.1 Intensity-based stereo: basic features

To measure the similarity between stereo images, both photometric and geometric distortions including discontinuities due to partial occlusions should be taken into account. *Photometric distortions* are due to nonuniform albedo of terrain points, nonuniform and noisy transfer factors over a *field-of-view* (FOV) of each image sensor, and so forth. Because of these distortions, the corresponding pixels in stereo images may have different signal values. *Geometric distortions* are due to projecting a 3-D surface onto the two image planes and involve: (*i*) spatially variant disparities of the corresponding pixels; and (*ii*) partial occlusions of some terrain points. As a result, the corresponding regions may differ in positions, scales, and orientations. Partial occlusions lead to only monocular visibility of certain terrain patches so that some image regions have no stereo correspondence. If a terrain is continuous, then, the geometric distortions preserve the natural x- and y-order of the binocularly visible points (BVP) in the images.

Due to occlusions, even without photometric distortions, two or more terrain variants are in full agreement with the same stereo pair. Therefore, terrain reconstruction, as an ill-posed problem, must involve a proper regularization [5, 15, 16].

Today's approaches to computational stereo differ in the following features: (*i*) similarities that are measured for matching the images; (*ii*) the extent to which the image distortions are taken into account; (*iii*) the regularizing heuristics that are involved; and (*iv*) how the stereo pair is matched as a whole. All the approaches exploit the image signals, that is, gray values (intensities) or, generally, colors (signal triples in RGB or other color scale) or multiband signatures (signals in several and not only visible spectral bands). But with respect to image matching, they are usually classified as *feature-based* and *intensity-based* stereo.

The first group relies on specific image features (say, edges, isolated small areas, or other easily detectable objects) to be found in both stereo images by preprocessing. Then, only the features are tested for similarity. Usually, a natural terrain has a relatively small number of such characteristic features, and in most cases the intensity-based approaches where image similarity is defined directly in terms of the signal values (gray levels, colors, or multiband signatures) are used to reconstruct terrains.

The intensity-based approaches are based on mathematical models that relate optical signals of the surface points to the image signals in the corresponding pixels. The model allows one to deduce a particular measure of similarity between the corresponding pixels or regions in the images to be used for stereo matching. The similarity measure takes account of the admissible geometric and photometric image distortions.

The simplest model assumes: (*i*) no local geometric distortions; and (*ii*) either no photometric distortions or only spatially uniform contrast and offset differences between the corresponding image signals. More specifically, it is assumed that a horizontal planar patch of a desired terrain is viewed by (photometrically) ideal image sensors and produces two relatively small corresponding rectangular windows in both stereo images. Then, the similarity between the two windows is measured by summing squared differences between the signals or by computing the cross correlation [7, 8, 17].

The forementioned model is easily extended to take account of varying x-slopes of a surface patch: by exhausting relative x-expansions and contractions of both the windows and searching for the maximum similarity [14]. An alternative way is to adapt the window size until the simplifying assumption about a horizontal surface patch is justified [18].

More elaborated models compute similarity under various nonuniform photometric distortions of the images. In particular, to partially exclude the nonuniformity either only phases of the Fourier transforms of both the windows are matched [19], or outputs of Gabor wavelet filters are used to isolate illumination perturbances of the images from variations of the surface reflectance attributed to orientations of the terrain patches [20]; or cepstrums, that is, amplitudes of the Fourier transforms of the logarithmic Fourier transforms of the windows, are used to isolate the surface reflectance variations from the perturbations caused by the noisy linear optical stereo channels that transfer the signals [21], and so forth. On frequent occasions complex combinations of intensity- and feature-based techniques are used to obtain a robustness to typical image distortions [22].

Alternative and computationally less complex signal models in [23, 24] allow one to take into account both the varying surface geometry and the nonuniform signal distortions along a single terrain profile. The models admit arbitrary changes of the corresponding gray values provided that ratios of the corresponding gray-level differences remain in a given range. Section 18.3 presents these models in more detail.

18.1.2 Global versus local optimization

A terrain is reconstructed by searching for the maximum similarity between the corresponding regions or pixels in a given stereo pair. A similarity measure takes account of the admissible image distortions and includes some regularizing heuristics to deal with the partial occlusions. Generally, there exist two possible scenarios for reconstructing a terrain: to exhaust all possible variants of a visible surface (a *global optimization*) or to successively search for each next small surface patch, given the previously found patches (a *local optimization*). For a continuous terrain, both the variants are guided by the visibility constraints.

The local optimization is widely used in practice because in many cases it needs less computation and easily takes into account both x- and y-disparities of the corresponding pixels. But, it has the following drawback. If each local decision is taken independently from others, then the patches found may form an invalid 3-D surface violating the visibility constraints. But if each next search is guided by the previously found patches, then the local errors are accumulated and, after a few steps, the "guidance" may result in completely wrong matches. In both cases, the local optimization needs an intensive interactive on-line or post-editing of a *DPM* or *DSM* to fix the resulting errors.

The global optimization is less subject to the local errors. But it is feasible only if the direct exhaustion of the surface variants can be avoided. In particular, this is possible when a terrain is reconstructed in a profile-by-profile mode and an additive similarity measure allows the use of dynamic programming techniques for the global optimization. Historically, this approach was first proposed in [25] (see also the comprehensive review [7]) and then extended in [23, 24, 26, 27]. Dynamic programming algorithms, but mostly for a feature-based stereo, were studied in many subsequent works, such as [28, 29, 30, 31, 32]. The symmetric *dynamic programming stereo* in [23, 24, 33] uses the maximum likelihood or Bayesian decision rule, derived from a particular probability model of the initial stereo images and desired surfaces, and takes into account:

- the geometric symmetry of stereo channels (image sensors);
- basic regular and random nonuniform distortions of the images; and
- discontinuities in the images because of occlusions in each channel.

18.2 Statistical decisions in terrain reconstruction

In this section, we review the symmetric geometry of binocular stereo and discuss the influence of the visibility constraints on optimal statistical decisions for terrain reconstruction [34]. We restrict our consideration to an ideal horizontal stereo pair (in the general case, stereo geometry is discussed in Chapter 17). For considerations of probabilistic models and optimal statistical decisions in more detail, see Chapter 26.

A *DSM* is considered as a bunch of epipolar profiles obtained by crossing a surface by a fan of epipolar planes. An epipolar plane contains the base-line connecting the optical centers of stereo channels.

Traces of an epipolar plane in the images, that is, two corresponding *epipolar (scan) lines*, represent any *epipolar profile* in this plane. Thus, to reconstruct a profile only the signals along the epipolar lines have to be matched [12, 13].

18.2.1 Symmetric stereo geometry

Both images of an ideal stereo pair are in the same plane. Let $\boldsymbol{L}$ and $\boldsymbol{R}$ denote two square lattices supporting a digital stereo pair in this plane. The pixels have integer x and y coordinates with steps of 1. The corresponding epipolar lines coincide with the x-lines having the same y-coordinate in the two images, and a DPM contains only the x-parallaxes of the corresponding pixels.

Figure 18.1 shows a cross section of a digital surface by an epipolar plane. Lines $o_L x_L$ and $o_R x_R$ represent the corresponding x-lines in the images. The correspondence between the signals in the profile points and in the image pixels is given by the symbolic labels "a" - "k." Notice that both the solid and the dashed profiles give just the same labels in the images if the signals for these profiles have the shown labels.

Let $[X, y, Z]^T$ be the symmetric 3-D coordinates of a point in the DSM. Here, $y = y_L = y_R$ denotes the y-coordinate of the epipolar lines that specify an epipolar plane containing the point and $[X, Z]^T$ are the Cartesian 2-D coordinates of the point in this plane. The X-axis coincides with the stereo base-line that links optical centers O_L and O_R of the channels and is the same for all the planes. The Z-axis lies in the plane y. The origin O of the symmetric (X, Z) coordinates is midway between the centers [24]. If spatial positions of the origin O and plane y are known, the symmetric coordinates $[X, y, Z]^T$ are easily converted into any given Cartesian 3-D coordinate system.

Let pixels $[x_L, y]^T \in \boldsymbol{L}$ and $[x_R, y]^T \in \boldsymbol{R}$ correspond to a surface point $[X, y, Z]^T$. Then the x-parallax $p = x_L - x_R$ is inversely proportional to the depth (distance, or height) Z of the point $[X, Z]^T$ from the base-line OX: $p = bf/Z$. Here, b denotes the length of the base-line and f is the focal length for the channels.

Each digital profile in the epipolar plane y is a chain of the isolated 3-D points $[X, y, Z]^T$ that correspond to the pixels $[x_L, y]^T \in \boldsymbol{L}$ and $[x_R, y]^T \in \boldsymbol{R}$. The *DSM* points $[X, y, Z]^T$, projected onto the image plane through the origin O, form the auxiliary "central" lattice $\boldsymbol{C}$. This lattice has x-steps of 0.5 and y-steps of 1.

A symmetric *DPM* on the lattice $\boldsymbol{C}$ is obtained by replacing the coordinates X and Z of a DSM in the epipolar plane y with the corresponding (x, y)-coordinates in $\boldsymbol{C}$ and the x-parallaxes, respectively. If the pixels $[x_L, y]^T \in \boldsymbol{L}$ and $[x_R, y]^T \in \boldsymbol{R}$ in a stereo pair correspond to a surface point with the planar coordinates $[x, y]^T \in \boldsymbol{C}$, then the

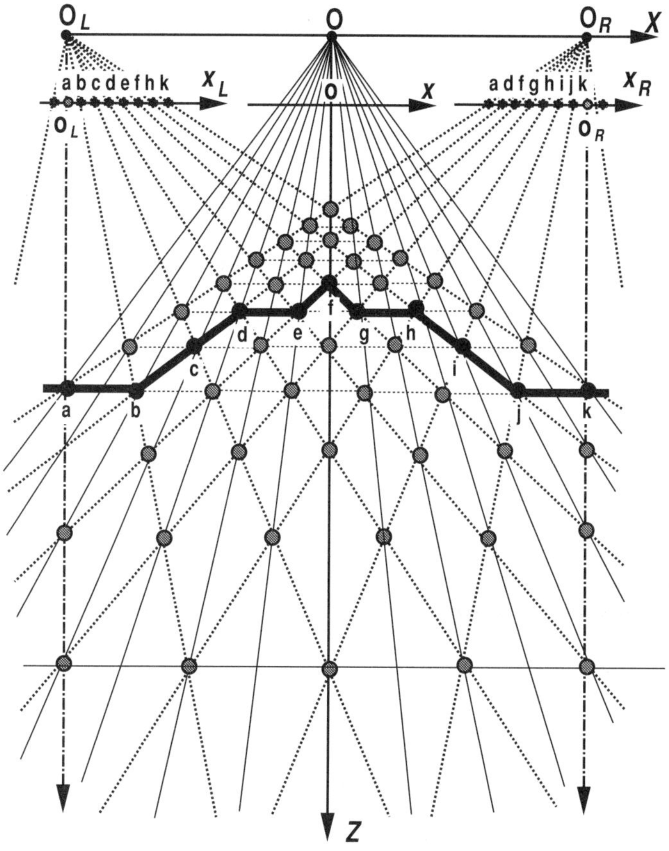

***Figure 18.1:** Digital terrain profile in the epipolar plane.*

following simple relations hold:

$$x_L = x + \frac{p}{2}; \;\; x_R = x - \frac{p}{2} \tag{18.1}$$

Figure 18.2 shows the epipolar plane of Fig. 18.1 in the symmetric (x, p) coordinates. Figure 18.3 presents two more profiles giving rise to the same distribution of the corresponding pixels along the epipolar lines under the shown labels of the points.

We will consider an extended *DPM* $(\boldsymbol{p}, \boldsymbol{g})$ that contains a digital surface $\boldsymbol{p} : \boldsymbol{C} \to \boldsymbol{P}$ and an ortho-image $\boldsymbol{g} : \boldsymbol{C} \to \boldsymbol{Q}$ of the surface in the symmetric 3-D coordinates. Here, $\boldsymbol{P} = [p_{\min}, p_{\min} + 1, \ldots, p_{\max}]$ is a finite set of the x-parallax values and $\boldsymbol{Q} = [0, 1, \ldots, q_{\max}]$ is a finite set of the signal values (say, gray levels).

The ortho-image $\boldsymbol{g}$ represents the optical signals $\boldsymbol{g}(x, y) \in \boldsymbol{Q}$ in the surface points $[x, y, p = \boldsymbol{p}(x, y)]^T$; $(x, y) \in \boldsymbol{C}$. The digital sur-

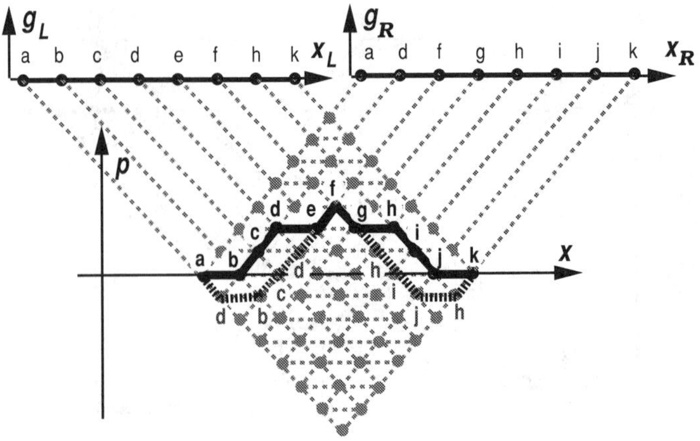

Figure 18.2: *Epipolar profiles in (x, p) coordinates giving the same image signals.*

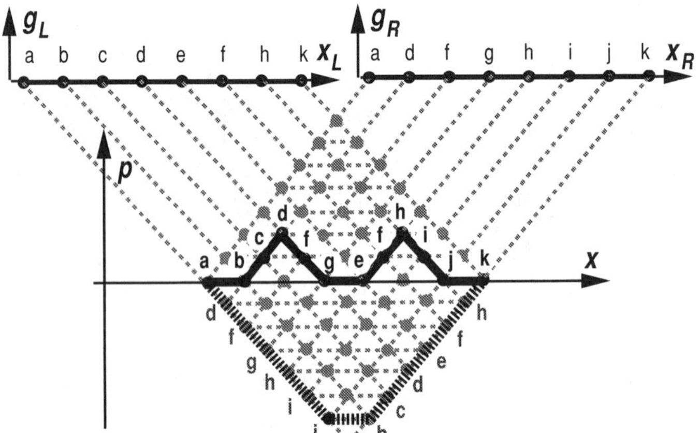

Figure 18.3: *Epipolar profiles in (x, p) coordinates giving the same image signals.*

face $\boldsymbol{p}$ consists of the *epipolar profiles* $\boldsymbol{p}_y$. Each profile has a fixed y-coordinate of the points and is represented by the two *epipolar lines* $\boldsymbol{g}_{L,y}$ and $\boldsymbol{g}_{R,y}$ with the same y-coordinate of the pixels in the images.

18.2.2 Simple and compound Bayesian decisions

Partial occlusions of the surface points impose the following strict visibility constraints on the x-parallaxes along an epipolar line in a symmetric DPM:

$$\mathbf{p}(x-0.5,y)-1 \le \mathbf{p}(x,y) \le \mathbf{p}(x-0.5,y)+1 \tag{18.2}$$

Let $\mathcal{P}$ be the parent population of all the DPMs $\mathbf{p}$ that satisfy the constraints Eq. (18.2). The constraints result in specific statistical decisions for reconstructing a DPM $\mathbf{p} \in \mathcal{P}$ from a given stereo pair.

Let an error be defined as any discrepancy between the true and the reconstructed surface. The conditional Bayesian MAP-decision that minimizes the error probability by choosing a surface $\mathbf{p} \in \mathcal{P}$ with the maximum *a posteriori* probability is as follows:

$$\mathbf{p}^{\text{opt}} = \arg\max_{\mathbf{p}\in\mathcal{P}} \Pr(\mathbf{p}|\mathbf{g}_L,\mathbf{g}_R) \tag{18.3}$$

Here, $\Pr(\mathbf{p}|\mathbf{g}_L,\mathbf{g}_R)$ is the *a posteriori* probability distribution (p.d.) of the surfaces for a given initial stereo pair.

If the probability model of a terrain and stereo images allows only the prior p.d. $\Pr(\mathbf{g}_L,\mathbf{g}_R|\mathbf{p})$ of the images to be obtained, then the conditional maximum likelihood decision can be used instead of the conditional MAP-decision:

$$\mathbf{p}^{\text{opt}} = \arg\max_{\mathbf{p}\in\mathcal{P}} \Pr(\mathbf{g}_L,\mathbf{g}_R|\mathbf{p}) \tag{18.4}$$

Let a pointwise error be a difference between the true and the reconstructed x-parallax value in a particular surface point. Compound Bayesian decisions are more adequate to the low-level stereo than the simple rules in Eqs. (18.3) and (18.4) because they minimize either the expected number of the pointwise errors:

$$\mathbf{p}^{\text{opt}} = \arg\max_{\mathbf{p}\in\mathcal{P}} \sum_{(x,y)\in\mathbf{C}} \Pr_{x,y}(\mathbf{p}(x,y)|\mathbf{g}_L,\mathbf{g}_R) \tag{18.5}$$

or the mean magnitude of the pointwise errors, that is, the variance of the obtained DPM about the true one

$$\mathbf{p}^{\text{opt}} = \arg\max_{\mathbf{p}\in\mathcal{P}} \sum_{(x,y)\in\mathbf{C}} (p(x,y) - \mathcal{E}\{\mathbf{p}(x,y)|\mathbf{g}_L,\mathbf{g}_R\})^2 \tag{18.6}$$

Here, $\Pr_{x,y}(p|\mathbf{g}_L,\mathbf{g}_R)$ denotes a posterior marginal probability of the surface point $[x,y,p=\mathbf{p}(x,y)]^T$ for a given stereo pair and $\mathcal{E}\{\ldots\}$ is a posterior expectation of the surface point, that is, the expected x-parallax value in the surface point with the planar coordinates (x,y)

$$\mathcal{E}\{\mathbf{p}(x,y)|\mathbf{g}_L,\mathbf{g}_R\} = \sum_{p\in\mathbf{P}} p\Pr_{x,y}(p|\mathbf{g}_L,\mathbf{g}_R) \tag{18.7}$$

Due to the constraints Eq. (18.2), the rule in Eq. (18.5) with the maximum sum of the posterior marginal probabilities of the surface points (the MSPM-decision) is not reduced to the well-known pointwise MPM-decision with the maximal posterior marginal probability of each profile point [16]. Likewise, the rule in Eq. (18.6) with minimal variance of these points about the posterior expectations (the MVPE-decision) is not reduced to the well-known PE-decision that chooses the posterior expectations as the reconstructed points [35].

Both the conditional simple decisions in Eqs. (18.3) and (18.4) and the conditional compound MSPM- and MVPE-decisions in Eqs. (18.5) and (18.6) allow for the dynamic programming reconstruction of an epipolar profile (see Section 18.4).

18.3 Probability models of epipolar profiles

This section presents geometric and photometric probability models describing the initial stereo images and the desired surfaces. Geometric models [26, 27] represent an *epipolar profile* by a *Markov chain* of admissible transitions between the vertices in a planar graph of profile variants (GPV). Figures 18.2 and 18.3 show examples of the GVP. Radiometric models [23, 24, 25, 33] describe basic regular and random photometric distortions of stereo images $\boldsymbol{g}_L$ and $\boldsymbol{g}_R$ with respect to the optical signals, that is, to the ortho-image of a surface [2].

18.3.1 Prior geometric model

Transitions between the GPV-vertices in the coordinates x, p represent all profile variants with at least the MVPs [23, 24]. Each GPV-vertex $\boldsymbol{v} = [x, p, s]$ has three visibility states s indicating the binocular ($s = B$) or only monocular ($s = M_L$ or M_R) observation by the stereo channel L or R. It is obvious that only the eight transitions shown in Fig. 18.4 are allowed in a GPV.

The Markov chain model with a stationary p.d. describes the expected shape and smoothness of a profile by transition and marginal probabilities of the visibility states. This allows for probabilistic ordering of the profile variants in Figs. 18.2 and 18.3 that have the same similarity with respect to image signals. Let $\Pr(\boldsymbol{v}|\boldsymbol{v}')$ be a probability of transition from a preceding vertex $\boldsymbol{v}'$ to a current vertex $\boldsymbol{v}$. The differences $x - x'$ and $p - p'$ between the x-coordinates and x-parallaxes in these GPV-vertices are uniquely specified by the visibility states s and s'. Therefore, the transition probabilities can be denoted as $\Pr(s|s')$. If the Markov chain has the stationary p.d. of the visibility states in the equilibrium, then only seven of the allowable transitions have nonzero

[2]In the following, the abbreviations BVP and MVP denote the binocularly and the only monocularly visible surface points, respectively.

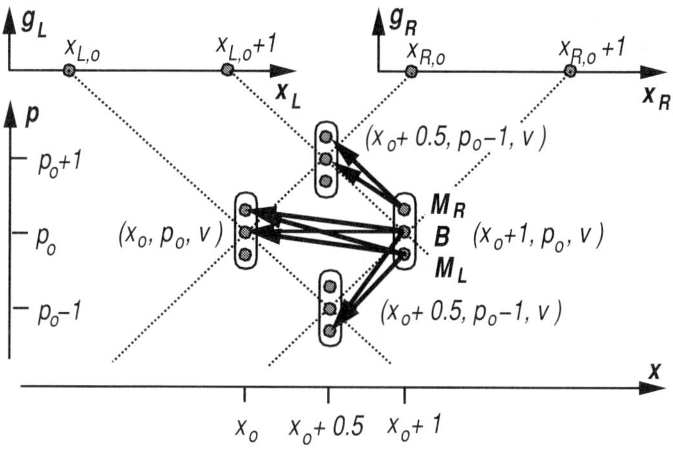

Figure 18.4: *Admissible transitions in the GPV.*

probability and the transition $M_R \to M_L$ is absent

$$\Pr(M_L|M_R) \equiv \Pr(x, p, M_L|x-1, p, M_R) = 0$$

The GPV in Fig. 18.5 with a narrow "tube" of x-parallaxes demonstrates both the uniform internal transitions and specific uppermost/lowermost transitions that allow the equilibrium conditions to be preserved. Let M substitute for both M_L or M_R so that

$$\Pr(M_L|B) = \Pr(M_R|B) \equiv \Pr(M|B); \qquad \Pr(B|M_L) = \Pr(B|M_R) \equiv \Pr(B|M);$$
$$\Pr(M_L|M_L) = \Pr(M_R|M_R) \equiv \Pr(M|M); \qquad \Pr(M_L|M_R) \equiv \Pr^\circ(M|M)$$

The transition probabilities $\Pr(B|M)$ and $\Pr(M|B)$ and the resulting marginal probabilities of the visibility states $\Pr(B)$ and $\Pr(M)$ in the generated profiles are expressed in terms of the two transition probabilities $\Pr(B|B)$ and $\Pr(M|M)$ as follows:

$$\Pr(M|B) = \frac{1-\Pr(B|B)}{2}; \quad \Pr(B|M) = 1-\Pr(M|M); \quad \Pr^\circ(M|M) = 0;$$
$$\Pr(B) = \frac{1-\Pr(M|M)}{2-\Pr(B|B)-\Pr(M|M)}; \quad \Pr(M) = \frac{0.5(1-\Pr(B|B))}{2-\Pr(B|B)-\Pr(M|M)} \tag{18.8}$$

To retain the equilibrium conditions at the boundaries of the GPV in Fig. 18.5 and the marginal probabilities $\Pr(B)$ and $\Pr(M)$ for the internal GPV-vertices, the transition probabilities for the extreme GPV-vertices at the uppermost boundary are as follows:

$$\begin{aligned} &\Pr_{\text{upp}}(B|B) = 1-\Pr(M); \qquad \Pr_{\text{upp}}(M|B) = \Pr(M); \\ &\Pr_{\text{upp}}(B|M) = 1; \qquad \Pr_{\text{upp}}(M|M) = 0; \qquad \Pr^\circ_{\text{upp}}(M|M) = 0 \end{aligned} \tag{18.9}$$

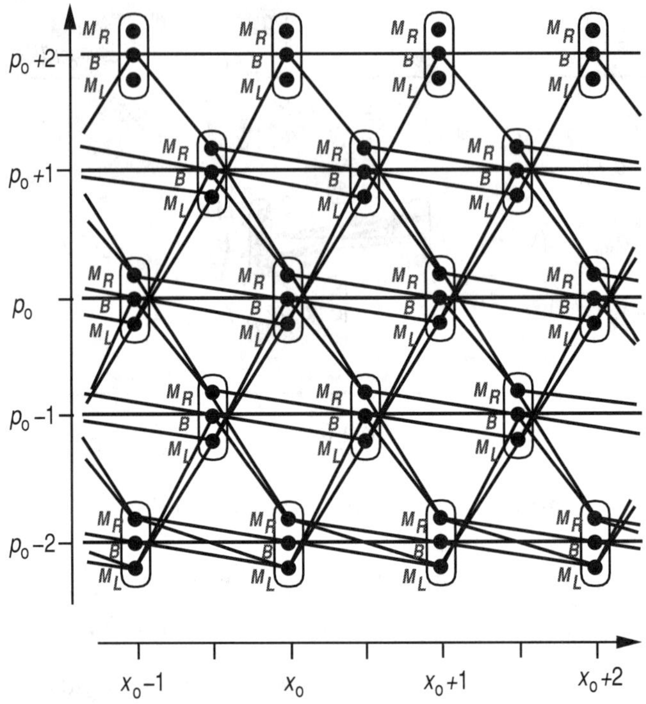

Figure 18.5: *GPV for the symmetric DP stereo.*

At the lowermost boundary there are the following transition probabilities:

$$\Pr_{\text{low}}(B|B) = 1 - \frac{\Pr(M)}{\Pr(M)}; \quad \Pr_{\text{low}}(M|B) = \frac{\Pr(M)}{\Pr(B)}; \quad \Pr_{\text{low}}(B|M) = 1;$$
$$\Pr_{\text{low}}(M|M) = 0; \quad \Pr^{\circ}_{\text{low}}(M|M) = 0 \quad \text{if} \quad \Pr(M) \le \Pr(B)$$

and

$$\Pr_{\text{low}}(B|B) = 0; \quad \Pr_{\text{low}}(M|B) = 1; \quad \Pr_{\text{low}}(B|M) = \frac{\Pr(B)}{\Pr(M)};$$
$$\Pr_{\text{low}}(M|M) = 0; \quad \Pr^{\circ}_{\text{low}}(M|M) = 1 - \frac{\Pr(B)}{\Pr(M)} \quad \text{if} \Pr(M) > \Pr(B)$$

18.3.2 Prior photometric models

A symmetric photometric model specifies the basic distortions of the images $\boldsymbol{g}_L$ and $\boldsymbol{g}_R$ with respect to the ortho-image $\boldsymbol{g}$ of a *DPM*. The distortions are described by positive transfer factors that vary over a FOV of each stereo channel and by a random noise in the channels

$$q_L = a_L q + r_L; \quad q_R = a_R q + r_R \tag{18.10}$$

Here, $q = \boldsymbol{g}(x, y)$ is the signal $q \in \boldsymbol{Q}$ in the point $[x, y, p = \boldsymbol{p}(x, y)]^T$ of a surface represented by a DPM $(\boldsymbol{p}, \boldsymbol{g})$, and $q_L = \boldsymbol{g}_L(x_L, y)$ and $q_R = \boldsymbol{g}_R(x_R, y)$ are the signal values in the corresponding image pixels. The transfer factors $a_L = \boldsymbol{a}_L(x_L, y)$, $a_L = \boldsymbol{a}_R(x_R, y)$ and the random noise $r_L = \boldsymbol{r}_L(x_L, y)$, $r_R = \boldsymbol{r}_R(x_R, y)$ present the multiplicative and the additive parts of the ortho-image distortions, respectively. The transfer factors $\boldsymbol{a}_L$ and $\boldsymbol{a}_R$ vary in a given range $A = [a_{\min}, a_{\max}]$ such that $0 < a_{\min} \leq (a_L, a_R) \leq a_{\max}$.

Transfer factors represent the most regular part of the image distortions that cannot be independent for the adjacent BVPs to retain a visual resemblance between the stereo images. To describe these interdependencies, the symmetric difference model [23, 24] involves a direct proportion between each gray-level difference in the adjacent BVPs and the two corresponding differences in the stereo images to within the additive random noise:

$$a_L q - a'_L q' = e_L (q - q'); \quad a_R q - a'_R q' = e_R (q - q') \tag{18.11}$$

Here, $q = \boldsymbol{g}(x, y)$ and $q' = \boldsymbol{g}(x', y')$ are the signal values in the neighboring BVPs along the same epipolar profile ($y = y'$) or in the two adjacent profiles ($|y - y'| = 1$) in the DPM; $\boldsymbol{p}$ and e_L, e_R denote the positive "difference" transfer factors. These factors describe local interactions between the "amplitude" factors a_j over the FOVs and can vary within a given range $E = [e_{\min}, e_{\max}]$ where $0 < e_{\min} \leq (e_L, e_R) \leq e_{\max}$. The difference model in Eq. (18.11) admits large deviations between the corresponding gray levels but retains the visual resemblance of the images by preserving the approximate direct proportions between the corresponding gray-level differences.

For the independent p.d. of the ortho-image signals and the independent random noise $\boldsymbol{r}_L$, $\boldsymbol{r}_R$ in the stereo images, Eq. (18.11) results in a *Markov chain* of the image signals corresponding to the BVPs and in the independent image signals corresponding to the MVPs along a given profile, respectively.

Under a given surface geometry $\boldsymbol{p}$, different statistical estimates of the surface ortho-image $\boldsymbol{g}$ and transfer factors $\boldsymbol{a}_L$, $\boldsymbol{a}_R$ can be deduced using particular assumptions about a p.d. of the random noise and variations of the transfer factors. The estimates are based on the corresponding image signals for the BVPs of a surface. The match between the estimated ortho-image and the initial stereo images to within a given range of the transfer factors forms a theoretically justified part of a quantitative intensity-based measure of similarity between the stereo images.

A heuristic part of the measure corresponds to the MVPs because the model in Eq. (18.10) does not indicate how to estimate parameters of the image distortions without prior assumptions about their links with similar parameters for the neighboring BVPs.

18.3.3 Posterior model of a profile

The geometric model (Eq. (18.8)) and the photometric model (Eq. (18.11)) describe a terrain profile $\boldsymbol{p}_y \in \boldsymbol{p}$ and signals $\boldsymbol{g}_{L,y}, \boldsymbol{g}_{R,y}$ along the corresponding epipolar lines in the images by particular *Markov chains*. As a result, both the prior p.d. $\Pr(\boldsymbol{g}_{L,y}, \boldsymbol{g}_{R,y} | \boldsymbol{p}_y)$ of the signals for a given profile and the posterior p.d. $\Pr(\boldsymbol{p}_y | \boldsymbol{g}_{L,y}, \boldsymbol{g}_{R,y})$ of the profiles for given image signals can be assumed to expand in the products of conditional transition probabilities.

For brevity, the index y is omitted below. Let $\Pr(\boldsymbol{g}_L, \boldsymbol{g}_R | \boldsymbol{v}_{i-1}, \boldsymbol{v}_i)$ denote the transition probability of the image signals for two given successive GPV-vertices along a profile. Let $\Pr(\boldsymbol{v}_i | \boldsymbol{v}_{i-1}; \boldsymbol{g}_L, \boldsymbol{g}_R)$ be the transition probability of the two successive GPV-vertices along the profile for given corresponding image signals. Then the forementioned prior and posterior p.d. are as follows:

$$\Pr(\boldsymbol{g}_L, \boldsymbol{g}_R | \boldsymbol{p}_y) = \Pr_0(\boldsymbol{g}_L, \boldsymbol{g}_R | \boldsymbol{v}_0) \prod_{i=1}^{N-1} \Pr(\boldsymbol{g}_L, \boldsymbol{g}_R | \boldsymbol{v}_{i-1}, \boldsymbol{v}_i) \tag{18.12}$$

$$\Pr(\boldsymbol{p} | \boldsymbol{g}_L, \boldsymbol{g}_R) = \Pr_0(\boldsymbol{v}_0 | \boldsymbol{g}_L, \boldsymbol{g}_R) \prod_{i=1}^{N-1} \Pr(\boldsymbol{v}_i | \boldsymbol{v}_{i-1}; \boldsymbol{g}_L, \boldsymbol{g}_R) \tag{18.13}$$

Here, i denotes serial numbers of the GPV-vertices along a profile, N is the total number of these points, $\Pr_0(\boldsymbol{g}_L, \boldsymbol{g}_R | \boldsymbol{v}_0)$ is the marginal probability of the image signals for a given starting GPV-vertex $\boldsymbol{v}_0$, and $\Pr_0(\boldsymbol{v}_0 | \boldsymbol{g}_L, \boldsymbol{g}_R)$ is the marginal probability of the starting GPV-vertex $\boldsymbol{v}_0$ for given image signals. The transition probabilities in Eqs. (18.12) and (18.13) are derived from the photometric model of Eq. (18.11), but the transition probabilities in Eq. (18.13) depend also on the geometric model of Eq. (18.8).

The marginal probabilities of the GPV-vertices are calculated in succession along the GPV by the obvious relations that follow directly from Figs. 18.4 and 18.5:

$$\Pr(\boldsymbol{v} | \boldsymbol{g}_L, \boldsymbol{g}_R) = \sum_{\boldsymbol{v}' \in \omega(\boldsymbol{v})} \Pr(\boldsymbol{v}' | \boldsymbol{g}_L, \boldsymbol{g}_R) \Pr(\boldsymbol{v} | \boldsymbol{v}'; \boldsymbol{g}_L, \boldsymbol{g}_R) \tag{18.14}$$

Here, $\omega(\boldsymbol{v})$ denotes a set of the nearest neighboring GPV-vertices $\boldsymbol{v}'$ that precede the current vertex $\boldsymbol{v}$. Generally, the set contains the following GPV-vertices shown in Fig. 18.4:

$$\begin{aligned}
\omega(x, p, M_L) &= \{(x-1, p, B),\ (x-0.5, p-1, M_L)\} \\
\omega(x, p, B) &= \{(x-1, p, B),\ (x-1, p, M_R);\ (x-0.5, p-1, M_L)\} \\
\omega(x, p, M_R) &= \{(x-0.5, p+1, B),\ (x-0.5, p+1, M_R)\}
\end{aligned} \tag{18.15}$$

Transitional probabilities $\Pr(\boldsymbol{v}_i|\boldsymbol{v}_{i-1};\boldsymbol{g}_L,\boldsymbol{g}_R)$ in Eq. (18.13) are related by the photometric model of Eq. (18.11) to the maximum residual deviations of each stereo image $\boldsymbol{g}_L$, $\boldsymbol{g}_R$ from the estimated ortho-image $\boldsymbol{g}$. The deviations are obtained by transforming the estimated ortho-image in such a way as to find the best approximation of each stereo image to within a given range E of the difference transfer factors. Let i be ordinal number of a GPV-vertex along the profile. Let

$$q_{L,i} = \boldsymbol{g}_L(x_{L,i}, y) \quad \text{and} \quad q_{R,i} = \boldsymbol{g}_R(x_{R,i}, y)$$

be the gray values in the pixels

$$[x_{L,i}, y]^T \in \boldsymbol{L} \quad \text{and} \quad [x_{R,i}, y]^T \in \boldsymbol{R}$$

corresponding to the GPV-vertex $\boldsymbol{v}_{i,B} = [x_i, p_i, s_i = B]$. Let $u_{L,i}$ and $u_{R,i}$ be the gray values that approximate $q_{L,i}$ and $q_{R,i}$, respectively, in the transformed ortho-images. The ortho-image is transformed to approximate the images $\boldsymbol{g}_L$ and $\boldsymbol{g}_R$ by minimizing the maximum square deviation from both the images.

Under a particular p.d. of the random noise, the transition probabilities for the neighboring BVPs are as follows [24, 33]:

$$\Pr(\boldsymbol{v}_{i,B}|\boldsymbol{v}_{i-1,B};\boldsymbol{g}_L,\boldsymbol{g}_R) \propto \Pr(B|B) \exp\left(-\gamma d(q_{L,i}, q_{L,i-1}, q_{R,i}, q_{R,i-1})\right) \tag{18.16}$$

where the factor γ is inversely proportional to the expected variance of the residual minimax deviations $\delta_{L,i} = q_{L,i} - u_{L,i} \equiv -\delta_{R,i} = u_{R,i} - q_{R,i}$ of the approximation. The local dissimilarity $d(...) = (\delta_{L,i})^2$ in the exponent depends on the corresponding gray-level differences $\Delta_{L:i,i-1} = q_{L,i} - q_{L,i-1}$ and $\Delta_{R:i,i-1} = q_{R,i} - q_{R,i-1}$ in the images, on the current estimate e^{opt} of the difference transfer factors, and on the residual errors as follows:

$$\begin{aligned} \delta_{L,i} &= \delta_{L,i-1} + \Delta_{L:i,i-1} - e^{\text{opt}}(\Delta_{L:i,i-1} + \Delta_{R:i,i-1}) \\ e^{\text{opt}} &= \arg\min_{e \in E} \left\{ \left(\delta_{L,i-1} + \Delta_{L:i,i-1} - e(\Delta_{L:i,i-1} + \Delta_{R:i,i-1})\right)^2 \right\} \end{aligned} \tag{18.17}$$

Here, $e = e_L/(e_L + e_R)$ is the normed transfer factor and E denotes its range: $E = [e_{\min}, e_{\max}]$ where $0 < e_{\min} \leq 0.5 \leq e_{\max} = 1 - e_{\min} < 1$.

The transition probability $\Pr(\boldsymbol{v}_{i,B}|\boldsymbol{v}_{i-1,M};\boldsymbol{g}_L,\boldsymbol{g}_R)$ for the transition $M \to B$ (that is, $s_{i-1} = M$ and $s_i = B$) has similar form except for using the nearest preceding BVP along the profile instead of the adjacent MVP $\boldsymbol{v}_{i-1}$ to get the dissimilarity value $d(...)$ of Eqs. (18.16) and (18.17). The relations in Eq. (18.17) are derived from the model in Eq. (18.11) by minimizing the maximum pixelwise error of adjusting the ortho-image to the stereo images. It is easily shown that the gray value q_i for the BVP $\boldsymbol{v}_i$ is estimated by averaging the corresponding image signals:

$q_i = (q1_i + q2_i)/2$. The ortho-image is then transformed to approximate each stereo image by changing the gray-level differences for the successive BVPs within a given range E of the transfer factors.

But, additional heuristics are essential to define the transition probabilities for the transitions $M \to M$ and $B \to M$ because the MVPs do not allow one to estimate the transfer factors and ortho-image signals. If the transfer factors and additive noise in Eq. (18.10) vary rather smoothly over the FOVs there are several possible ways to introduce these heuristics:

- constant value of a residual square deviation $d(\ldots) = d_0 \equiv \delta_0^2 > 0$ for all the MVPs [23, 24];
- extension of a deviation computed for a current BVP on the subsequent MVPs [24]; and
- extension of a relative deviation of the approximation $\lambda_{L,i} = \delta_{L,i}/q_{L,i}$ for a current BVP on the subsequent MVPs: $\delta_{L,k} = \max\{\delta_0, \lambda_{L,i}q_{L,k}\}$; $k = i+1, i+2, \ldots$, as long as $s_k = M_L$ or M_R, and so forth.

18.4 Dynamic programming reconstruction

This section reviews the *dynamic programming terrain reconstruction* based on the optimal statistical decisions Eqs. (18.3) to (18.6). The additive similarity measures, obtained by taking the logarithm of the p.d. in Eqs. (18.12) and (18.13), allow one to implement the maximum likelihood rule of Eq. (18.4) or the Bayesian MAP decision of Eq. (18.3), respectively. The relations in Eqs. (18.14) and (18.15) allow one to compute the additive similarity measures of Eqs. (18.5) and (18.6) for the compound Bayesian rules. Each similarity measure is maximized by dynamic programming to take account of the visibility constraints of Eq. (18.2) [23, 24, 33].

Some heuristics are embedded into the similarity measures to cope with discontinuities in the images due to occlusions and reduce the resulting multiplicity of the surfaces that are consistent with the images. Also, confidences of the reconstructed terrain points have to be estimated for evaluating and validating the obtained results.

18.4.1 Unified dynamic programming framework

Equations (18.12) to (18.14) provide a unified dynamic programming framework for terrain reconstruction in a profile-by-profile mode. Each epipolar profile $\boldsymbol{p}_y$ is reconstructed as a continuous path in the GPV maximizing an additive similarity measure

$$\boldsymbol{p}^{\text{opt}} = \arg\max_{\boldsymbol{p}} W(\boldsymbol{p}|\boldsymbol{g}_L, \boldsymbol{g}_R) \tag{18.18}$$

The similarity measure $W(...)$ is represented as follows:

$$W(\boldsymbol{p}|\boldsymbol{g}_L, \boldsymbol{g}_R) = \sum_{i=1}^{n-1} w(\boldsymbol{v}_{i-1}; \boldsymbol{v}_i|\boldsymbol{g}_L, \boldsymbol{g}_R) \tag{18.19}$$

where the local similarity term $w(...)$ describes the transition between the GPV-vertices $\boldsymbol{v}_{i-1}$ and $\boldsymbol{v}_i$. In particular, such a term can be obtained from the transition probabilities in Eqs. (18.16) and (18.17).

Dynamic programming search for the global maximum of the similarity measure in Eq. (18.19) involves a successive pass along the x-axis of the GPV. At any current x-coordinate x_c, all the possible GPV-vertices $\boldsymbol{v}_c = (x_c, p_c, s_c)$ are examined to calculate and store, for each, the vertex, the local potentially optimal backward transition $\boldsymbol{v}_c \to \boldsymbol{v}_p = t(\boldsymbol{v}_c)$ to one of the preceding vertices $\omega(\boldsymbol{v}_c)$ listed in Eq. (18.15).

Let $[x_b, x_e]$ be a given range of the x-coordinates of the GPV-vertices. Let $W_{x_c}(\boldsymbol{v}_c)$ denote the similarity value accumulated along a potentially optimal part of the profile with x-coordinates between x_b and x_c that ends in the GPV-vertex $\boldsymbol{v}_c$. Then the basic dynamic programming recurrent computation is as follows:

$$\begin{aligned} t(\boldsymbol{v}_c) &= \arg \max_{\boldsymbol{v}_p \in \omega(\boldsymbol{v}_c)} \left\{ W_{x_p}(\boldsymbol{v}_p) + w(\boldsymbol{v}_p; \boldsymbol{v}_c|\boldsymbol{g}_L, \boldsymbol{g}_R) \right\} \\ W_{x_c}(\boldsymbol{v}_c) &= W_{x_p}(t(\boldsymbol{v}_c)) + w(t(\boldsymbol{v}_c); \boldsymbol{v}_c|\boldsymbol{g}_L, \boldsymbol{g}_R) \end{aligned} \tag{18.20}$$

After passing a given range of the x-coordinates, the desired profile $\boldsymbol{p}^{\text{opt}}$ of Eq. (18.18) is obtained by the backward pass using the stored potentially-optimal transitions $t(\boldsymbol{v})$ for the GPV-vertices

$$\begin{aligned} \boldsymbol{v}_{N-1}^{\text{opt}} &= \arg \max_{\boldsymbol{v}_e} \{W_{x_e}(\boldsymbol{v}_e)\} \\ \boldsymbol{v}_{i-1}^{\text{opt}} &= t(\boldsymbol{v}_i^{\text{opt}}); \;\; i = N-1, ..., 1 \end{aligned} \tag{18.21}$$

The maximum accumulated similarity value in Eq. (18.21) corresponds to the desired global maximum of the similarity value in Eq. (18.18):

$$W(\boldsymbol{p}^{\text{opt}}|\boldsymbol{g}_L, \boldsymbol{g}_R) = W_{x_e}(\boldsymbol{v}_{N-1}^{\text{opt}}) \tag{18.22}$$

By embedding calculations of the corresponding marginals of Eq. (18.14) into this search one can implement in a similar way the compound decisions in Eqs. (18.5) and (18.6).

18.4.2 Regularizing heuristics

The similarity measure of Eq. (18.19), deduced from the probabilistic models of the surface and stereo images, does not overcome the inherent ambiguity of terrain reconstruction. Figures 18.2 and 18.3 show that visually the least appropriate "pit-like" dotted profile in Fig. 18.3, even with no photometric distortions, concurs successfully with other, much more natural profiles. This variant is excluded either by setting proper parameters of the geometric model of Eq. (18.8) or by using a simple heuristic based on the expected surface smoothness. The latter is rather straightforward: under the equal signal similarity, the most smooth profile, that is, with the maximum number of the BVPs, has to be chosen. This heuristic, easily implemented by dynamic programming, counts in favor of the solid profile in Fig. 18.2 with the five BVPs.

But there are visually less appropriate variants that cannot be excluded using only the numbers of the BVPs or the probability ordering of Eq. (18.8). Therefore, additional heuristics have to be introduced to obtain the terrains that mostly agree with the visual reconstruction. Such a heuristic can be based on an assumption that the more photometric transformations (even the admissible ones) are required to convert one stereo image into another in line with a given surface, the less appropriate is the surface. For example, the conversion of the epipolar line $\boldsymbol{g}_L$ into the corresponding line $\boldsymbol{g}_R$ in accord with the solid or the dashed profile in Fig. 18.2 results in two gaps, size of 2 and 1 or of 4 and 1, respectively, to be interpolated. In the first case, the $\boldsymbol{g}_L$-signals ("f,""h") and ("h,""k") have to be interpolated for fitting the $\boldsymbol{g}_R$-signals ("f-g-h") and ("h-i-j-k"). In the second case, the $\boldsymbol{g}_L$-signals ("a,""f") and ("f,""k") are compared to the $\boldsymbol{g}_R$-signals ("a-d-f") and ("f-g-h-i-j-k").

The solid and the dashed profiles in Fig. 18.3 involve two gaps of size 2 or one gap of size 6, respectively. The desired heuristic should take account of the signal matches after such a transformation. The latter heuristic is embedded in Gimel'farb [27] to the MAP-decision of Eq. (18.3) by summing the two weighted similarity measures

$$\boldsymbol{p}^{\text{opt}} = \arg\max_{\boldsymbol{p}} \{\alpha W(\boldsymbol{p}|\boldsymbol{g}_L, \boldsymbol{g}_R) + (1-\alpha) W_{\text{reg}}(\boldsymbol{p}|\boldsymbol{g}_L, \boldsymbol{g}_R)\} \tag{18.23}$$

Here, α is a relative weight of the heuristic part ($0 \le \alpha \le 1$), $W(\boldsymbol{p}|\boldsymbol{g}_L, \boldsymbol{g}_R)$ denotes the similarity measure of Eq. (18.19) between the epipolar lines $\boldsymbol{g}_L$ and $\boldsymbol{g}_R$ in the stereo images under a profile $\boldsymbol{p}$, and $W_{\text{reg}}(\boldsymbol{p}|\boldsymbol{g}_L, \boldsymbol{g}_R)$ is the similarity measure between the two lines $\boldsymbol{g}_L$ and $\boldsymbol{g}_R$ matched in accord with the profile $\boldsymbol{p}$. The second measure estimates the magnitude of deformations that transform one of the images into another image. The magnitude is given by a sum of square differences between the corresponding intensity changes along the profile $\boldsymbol{p}$

$$W_{\text{reg}}(\boldsymbol{p}|\boldsymbol{g}_L, \boldsymbol{g}_R) = \sum_{i=1}^{n-1} \left(\Delta_{L:i,b(i)} - \Delta_{R:i,b(i)}\right)^2 \tag{18.24}$$

Here, $b(i)$ is the closest BVP that precedes the GPV-vertex $\boldsymbol{v}_i$ along the profile $\boldsymbol{p}$ and $\Delta_{L:i,k} = \boldsymbol{g}_L(x_{L,i}, y) - \boldsymbol{g}_L(x_{L,k}, y)$ and $\Delta_{R:i,k} = \boldsymbol{g}_L(x_{R,i}, y) -$

$g_R(x_{R,k}, y)$ denote the gray-level differences between the two pixels in each stereo image. The pixels correspond to the GPV-vertices $\boldsymbol{v}_i$ and $\boldsymbol{v}_k$; $k < i$, along the epipolar profile.

The weighted similarity measure in Eq. (18.23) decides in favor of the profile giving the highest resemblance between the stereo images transformed one into the other, all other factors being equal. Thus, it tries to suppress the pit-like profile variants that may cause large differences between the corresponding parts of the transformed images.

18.4.3 Confidence of the digital parallax map

Computational stereo does nothing more than match stereo images. Even if the geometric constraints and regularizing heuristics allow the elimination of some geometric ambiguities shown in Figs. 18.2 and 18.3, there still exist the photometric ambiguities, that is, the places with no signal variations to guide the matching. A BVP of a terrain is confident if it is represented by a specific visual pattern that gives no multiple good matches in a close vicinity of the corresponding points in the images.

Only in this case can human visual reconstruction be used for validating the computed *DPM* or *DSM*. But, if the detectable pattern is present only in a single image due to partial occlusions, or is absent at all because the signal values are almost equal, then the computed surface points have very low or even zero confidence. Such places can hardly be compared to the GCPs, even if these latter exist due to field surveys or have been found by photogrammetric visual reconstruction.

Let $\boldsymbol{S} = \boldsymbol{C} \to [0, S_{\max}]$ denote a *confidence map* for a DPM with a conditional confidence range $0 \le \boldsymbol{S}(x, y) \le S_{\max}$. The confidence measure has to be derived from the image signals used for stereo matching: the more discriminative the image features, the more confident the reconstructed terrain point.

Generally, the confidence measures reflect not only the image and terrain features but also the features of stereo matching. For example, in [36] two confidence measures for a DPM obtained by a correlation-based local optimization are considered. The first measure is based on a difference $\boldsymbol{p}(x, y) - \boldsymbol{p}'(x, y)$ between the best-match disparity $\boldsymbol{p}(x, y)$ in the DPM and the second-best-match disparity $\boldsymbol{p}'(x, y)$ for the same planar position $(x, y) \in \boldsymbol{C}$ in the DPM. The second measure exploits the ratio of the cross correlation, giving the best match to the autocorrelation threshold. Experiments with these measures have shown that low-confident terrain areas must be excluded both from stereo matching and stereo evaluation.

We restrict our consideration to a simple confidence measure that does not take into account a matching algorithm. This measure is more convenient for evaluating different stereo techniques because the confidence map is computed only from the initial stereo images and the obtained DPM.

The basic photometric distortions in Eq. (18.11) are specified by a given range of relative changes of the gray-level differences in both images: each gray-level difference between two neighboring BVPs in the profile can be changed in each image to within this range. Therefore, in the simplest case, the gray-level differences estimated for the BVPs in the reconstructed DPM may serve as the confidence measure: the higher the difference, the more definite the matching and the greater the confidence. Let $(b(x), y)$ denote the planar coordinates of a BVP that precedes a BVP with the planar coordinates (x, y) in the reconstructed DPM $(\boldsymbol{p}, \boldsymbol{g})$. Then, $\boldsymbol{S}(x, y) = |\boldsymbol{g}(x, y) - \boldsymbol{g}(b(x), y)|$. It should be noted that the "vertical" gray-level differences take no part in the forementioned confidences only because of the adopted independent line-by-line DPM reconstruction.

The obtained confidence map allows the confident and nonconfident parts of a DPM to be separated by simple thresholding. A more elaborated approach involves a separate linear approximation of the gray levels in the stereo images that correspond to the BVPs before and after a current BVP. The obtained $\vee$- or $\wedge$-shaped gray-level approximations and variations of the image signals with respect to them allow a rough estimate of a fiducial interval for the x-disparities in this point. The greater the interval, the smaller the confidence.

18.5 Experimental results

Experiments with real aerial and ground stereo pairs (a few of them are presented in [27, 33, 37]) indicate that the symmetric dynamic programming approach gives dense DPMs that agree closely with the visually perceived surfaces. To exclude outliers caused by inexact epipolar geometry of the images or by low-contrast image regions, the reconstruction involves online median filtering over several adjacent profiles.

In [33] the accuracy of the DPM the size of $1124(x) \times 450(y)$ points reconstructed from a stereo pair of highland was verified using 433 GCPs with x-parallaxes found by an analytic photogrammetric device. The profiles were reconstructed within the range $\boldsymbol{P} = [-50, 50]$ in the profile-by-profile mode. The histogram of absolute deviations between the computed and manually perceived DPMs in the GCPs is shown in Table 18.1, the mean absolute deviation being 1.47 of the x-parallax unit.

Because of difficulties in obtaining the GCPs for the available stereo pairs, we have used in most cases the simplified performance evaluation method of [11]. This method checks the computed x-parallaxes against the ones that are visually found for some arbitrarily chosen

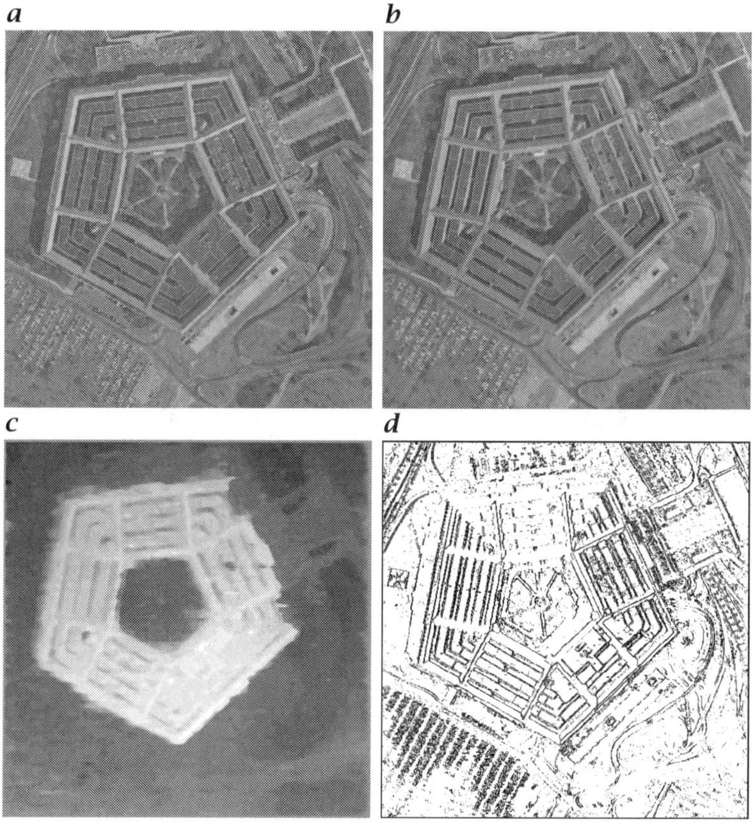

Figure 18.6: ***a*** *,* ***b*** *512× 512 stereo pair "Pentagon;"* ***c*** *the reconstructed DPM; and* ***d*** *the thresholded confidence map.*

characteristic terrain points. In our experiments, generally about 60 to 70% of the computed x-parallaxes are within the ± 1 range with respect to the chosen control values. Most significant errors occur in shaded, vastly occluded, or highly textured terrain regions.

For example, Figs. 18.6 and 18.7 show the initial stereo pairs "Pentagon" and "Mountain," range images of the reconstructed *DPMs*, and the thresholded confidence maps. The threshold θ is set as to choose 20% of all the DPM points as the confident ones with $\boldsymbol{S}(x, y) \geq \theta$. These latter are shown by black pixels in Fig. 18.6d and Fig. 18.7d.

The range images Fig. 18.6c and Fig. 18.7c represent the x-parallax map by gray-scale coding (from the nearest white pixels to the most distant black pixels). The x-parallax map is reduced to the left stereo image, that is, to the lattice $\boldsymbol{L}$. The *DPMs* are obtained by using the similarity measure of Eq. (18.23) with the following basic parameters: the weight $w = 0.5$ (variations in a broad range $0.2 \leq w \leq 0.8$ have

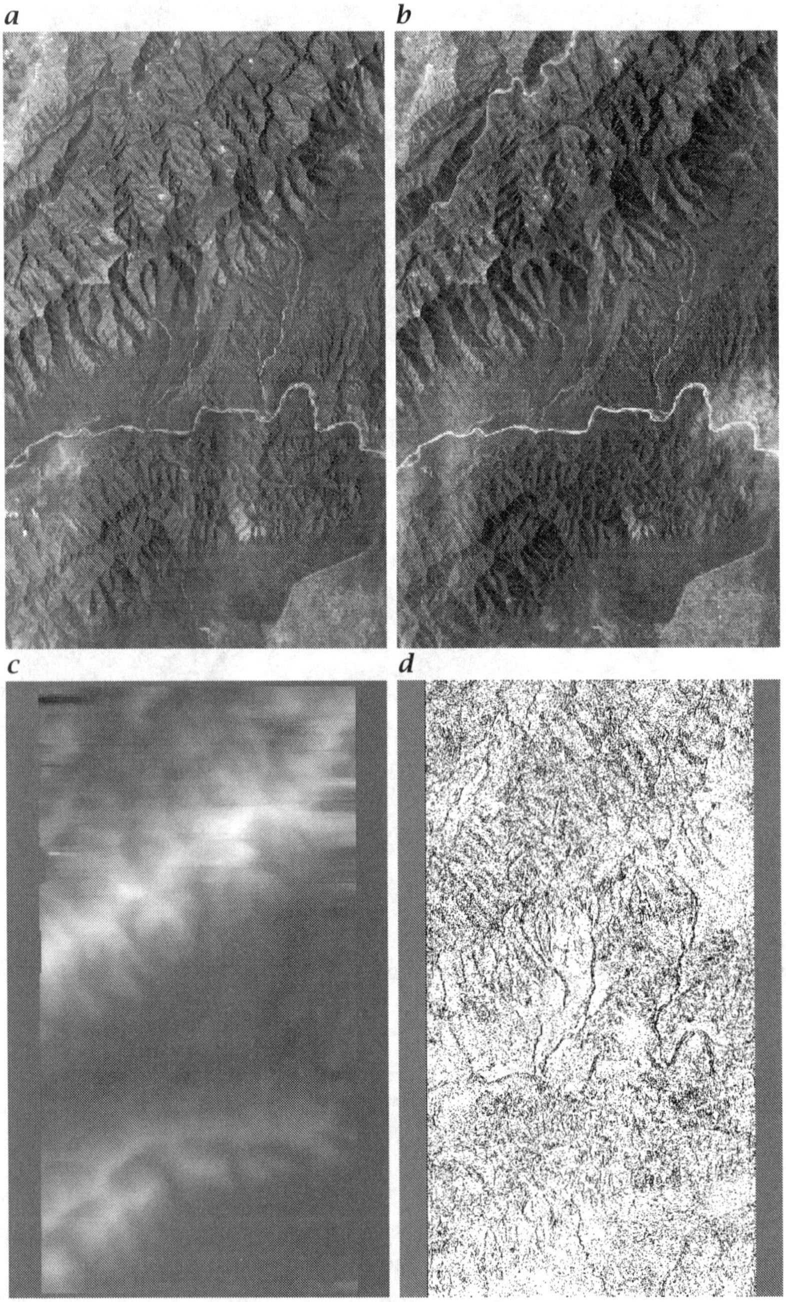

Figure 18.7: ***a*** *,* ***b*** *700× 1100 stereo pair "Mountain;"* **c** *the reconstructed DPM; and* ***d*** *the thresholded confidence map.*

Table 18.1: *Absolute deviations of x-parallaxes for the 433 GCPs in the reconstructed DPM*

Deviation	0	≤ 1	≤ 2	≤ 3	≤ 4	≤ 8
Number of the GCPs	98	257	356	403	421	433
% of the GCPs	23	60	82	93	97	100

Table 18.2: *Processing time for reconstructing the DPM "Pentagon"*

Algorithm	[24, 27]	[22]	[20]
Computer (*OS*)	HiNote VP Series 500 (Windows-95)	Symbolics 3650 (Genera 7.2)	IBM RS/6000 (*N/A*)
Language	MS Visual C++	Lisp	*N/A*
DPM size	512×512	512×512	256×256
Time	$38s$	$22h\,44m\,16s$	$20m$

almost no effect on the resulting DPMs), the range $E = [0.2, 0.8]$ of the normed transfer factor in Eq. (18.17), and the residual square deviation $d_0 = 100$ for the MVPs.

On the whole, the obtained range images correspond rather closely to the visual depth perception of these scenes, and the chosen confident points represent main topographic landmarks of these terrains. But, there are a few local depth errors: mainly along the upper right edge of the Pentagon building in Fig. 18.6 and in a small textured region at the upper left part of Fig. 18.7. The errors in Fig. 18.6 are caused by a strip of the wall along this edge, which is seen in the right image but is occluded (and, thus, has no stereo correspondence) in the left image. This strip is grouped in the reconstructed profiles with the similar neighboring roof's details that are observed in both images.

These errors illustrate the main drawbacks of the simplified symmetric binocular stereo used in the experiments: (*i*) it takes no account of the possibly inexact epipolar geometry of the images; (*ii*) it takes no account of y-interactions between the signals because of the independent profile-by-profile reconstruction mode; (*iii*) the regularizing heuristics do not overcome in full measure all the errors caused by the MVPs that match closely the neighboring BVPs.

Nonetheless, in spite of the local errors, the overall quality of the reconstruction of the observed surfaces is fairly good. Also, this dynamic programming approach greatly surpasses many other algorithms in time complexity. Table 18.2 shows the processing times for reconstructing the same scene "Pentagon" by our dynamic programming approach and by the algorithms of Cochran and Medioni [22] and Chen et al. [20].

These and other experimental results show that the efficient and fast *dynamic programming terrain reconstruction* can be obtained by integration of the theoretical image/surface models, the optimal statistical decision rules, and the regularizing heuristics that take into account the ill-posedness of the problem.

18.6 References

[1] Haralick, R. M. and Shapiro, L. G., (1993). *Computer and Robot Vision*, Vol. 2. Reading, MA: Addison-Wesley.

[2] Maune, D. F., (1996). Introduction to digital elevation models (DEM). In *Digital Photogrammetry: An Addendum to the Manual of Photogrammetry*, C. Greve, ed., pp. 131–134. Bethesda: ASPRS.

[3] Ackermann, F., (1996). Techniques and Strategies for DEM Generation. In *Digital Photogrammetry: An Addendum to the Manual of Photogrammetry*, C. Greve, ed., pp. 135–141. Bethesda: ASPRS.

[4] Schenk, A. F., (1996). Automatic generation of DEMs. In *Digital Photogrammetry: An Addendum to the Manual of Photogrammetry*, C. Greve, ed., pp. 145–150. Bethesda: ASPRS.

[5] Kyreitov, V. R., (1983). Inverse Problems of Photometry. Novosibirsk: Computing Center of the Academy of Sciences of the USSR, Siberian Branch [In Russian].

[6] Barnard, S. T. and Fischler, M. A., (1982). Computational stereo. *ACM Computing Surveys*, **14**:553–572.

[7] Baker, H. H., (1984). Surfaces from mono and stereo images. *Photogrammetria*, **39**:217–237.

[8] Hannah, M. J., (1988). Digital stereo image matching techniques. *International Archives on Photogrammetry and Remote Sensing*, **27**:280–293.

[9] Dhond, U. R. and Aggarwal, J. K., (1989). Structure from stereo—a review. *IEEE Trans. Systems, Man, and Cybernetics*, **19**:1489–1510.

[10] Gülch, E., (1991). Results of test on image matching of ISPRS WG III/4. *ISPRS Journal of Photogrammetry and Remote Sensing*, **46**:1–18.

[11] Hsieh, Y. C., McKeown, D. M., and Perlant, F. P., (1992). Performance evaluation of scene registration and stereo matching for cartographic feature extraction. *IEEE Trans. Pattern Analysis and Machine Intelligence*, **14**:214–238.

[12] Helava, U. V. and Chapelle, W. E., (1972). Epipolar scan correlation. *Bendix Technical Jour.*, **5**:19–23.

[13] Scarano, F. A. and Brumm, G. A., (1976). A digital elevation data collection system. *Photogrammetric Engineering and Remote Sensing*, **42**:489–496.

[14] Helava, U. V., (1988). Object space least square correlation. *Photogrammetric Engineering and Remote Sensing*, **54**:711–714.

[15] Poggio, T., Torre, V., and Koch, C., (1985). Computational vision and regularization theory. *Nature*, **317**:314–319.

[16] Marroquin, J., Mitter, S., and Poggio, T., (1987). Probabilistic solution of ill-posed problems in computational vision. *Jour. American Statistical Association*, **82**:76–89.

[17] Förstner, W., (1993). Image matching. In *Computer and Robot Vision, Chapter 16*, R. M. Haralick and L. G. Shapiro, eds., pp. 289–378. Reading, MA: Addison-Wesley.

[18] Kanade, T. and Okutomi, M., (1994). A stereo matching algorithm with an adaptive window: theory and experiment. *IEEE Trans. Pattern Analysis and Machine Intelligence*, **16**:920–932.

[19] Wenig, J., (1993). Image matching using the windowed Fourier phase. *International Journal of Computer Vision*, **11**:211–236.

[20] Chen, T.-Y., Klarquist, W. H., and Bovik, A. C., (1994). Stereo vision using Gabor wavelets. In *Proc. IEEE Southwest Symposium on Image Analysis and Interpretation, April 21-24, 1994, Dallas, Texas*, pp. 13–17. Los Alamitos: IEEE Computer Society Press.

[21] Ludwig, K.-O., Neumann, H., and Neumann, B., (1994). Local stereoscopic depth estimation. *Image and Vision Computing*, **12**:16–35.

[22] Cochran, S. T. and Medioni, G., (1991). 3D surface description from binocular stereo. *IEEE Transactions on Pattern Analysis and Machine Intelligence*, **14**:981–994.

[23] Gimel'farb, G. L., (1979). Symmetric approach to the problem of automating stereoscopic measurements in photogrammetry. *Kibernetika*, **2**:73–82. In Russian; English translation: *Cybernetics*, **15(2)**: 235-247, 1979.

[24] Gimel'farb, G. L., (1991). Intensity-based computer binocular stereo vision: signal models and algorithms. *International Journal of Imaging Systems and Technology*, **3**:189–200.

[25] Gimel'farb, G. L., V.B.Marchenko, and Rybak, V., (1972). An algorithm for automatic identification of identical sections on stereopair photographs. *Kibernetika*, **2**:118–129. In Russian; English translation: *Cybernetics*, **8(2)**: 311-322, 1972.

[26] Gimel'farb, G. L., (1994). Regularization of low-level binocular stereo vision considering surface smoothness and dissimilarity of superimposed stereo images. In *Aspects of Visual Form Processing*, C. Arcelli, L. P. Cordella, and G. S. di Baja, eds., pp. 231–240. Singapore: World Scientific.

[27] Gimel'farb, G. L., (1996). Symmetric bi- and trinocular stereo: tradeoffs between theoretical foundations and heuristics. In *Theoretical Foundations of Computer Vision, Computing Supplement 11*, W. Kropatsch, R. Klette, and F. Solina, eds., pp. 53–71. Wien: Springer.

[28] Baker, H. H. and Binford, T. O., (1981). Depth from edge and intensity based stereo. In *Proc. 7th Intern. Joint Conf. Artificial Intelligence, August 24-28, 1981, Vancouver, Canada*, P. J. Hayes, ed., Vol. 2, pp. 631–636. San Mateo: William Kaufmann.

[29] Ohta, Y. and Kanade, T., (1985). Stereo by intra- and inter-scan line search using dynamic programming. *IEEE Trans. Pattern Analysis and Machine Intelligence*, **7**:139–154.

[30] Lloyd, S. A., (1986). Stereo matching using intra- and inter-row dynamic programming. *Pattern Recognition Letters*, **4**:273–277.

[31] Raju, G. V. S., Binford, T., and Shekar, S., (1987). Stereo matching using Viterbi algorithm. In *Proc. DARPA Image Understanding Workshop, February 23-25, 1987, Los Angeles, CA*, Vol. 2, pp. 766–776. San Mateo: Morgan Kaufmann.

[32] Cox, I. J., Hingorani, S. L., and Rao, S. B., (1996). A maximum likelihood stereo algorithm. *Computer Vision and Image Understanding*, **63**:542–567.

[33] Gimel'farb, G. L., Krot, V. M., and Grigorenko, M. V., (1992). Experiments with symmetrized intensity-based dynamic programming algorithms for reconstructing digital terrain model. *Intern. Jour. Imaging Systems and Technology*, **4**:7–21.

[34] Gimel'farb, G. L., (1994). Intensity-based bi- and trinocular stereo vision: Bayesian decisions and regularizing assumptions. In *Proc. 12th IAPR Intern. Conf. Pattern Recogn., October 9-13, 1994, Jerusalem, Israel*, Vol. 1, pp. 717–719. Los Alamitos: IEEE Computer Society Press.

[35] Yuille, A. L., Geiger, D., and Bülthoff, H., (1990). Stereo integration, mean field theory and psychophysics. In *Computer Vision—ECCV 90*, O. Faugeras, ed., Lecture Notes in Computer Science 427, pp. 73–82. Berlin: Springer.

[36] Bolles, R. C., Baker, H. H., and Hannah, M. J., (1993). The JISCT stereo evaluation. In *Proc. DAPRA Image Understanding Workshop, April 18-21, 1993, Washington, D.C.*, pp. 263–274. San Mateo: Morgan Kaufmann.

[37] Gimel'farb, G. L., Malov, V. I., Gayda, V. B., Grigorenko, M. V., Mikhalevich, B. O., and Oleynik, S. V., (1996). Digital photogrammetric station "Delta" and symmetric intensity-based stereo. In *Proc. 13th IAPR Intern. Conf. Pattern Recogn., August 25-29, 1996, Vienna, Austria*, Vol. III, pp. 979–983. Los Alamitos: IEEE Computer Society Press.

19 Reflectance-Based Shape Recovery

Reinhard Klette[1], Ryszard Kozera[2], and Karsten Schlüns[3]

[1]The University of Auckland, Auckland, New Zealand
[2]University of Western Australia, Perth, Australia
[3]Humboldt Universität, Berlin, Germany

Handbook of Computer Vision and Applications
Volume 2
Signal Processing and Pattern Recognition

Copyright © 1999 by Academic Press
All rights of reproduction in any form reserved.
ISBN 0-12-379772-1/$30.00

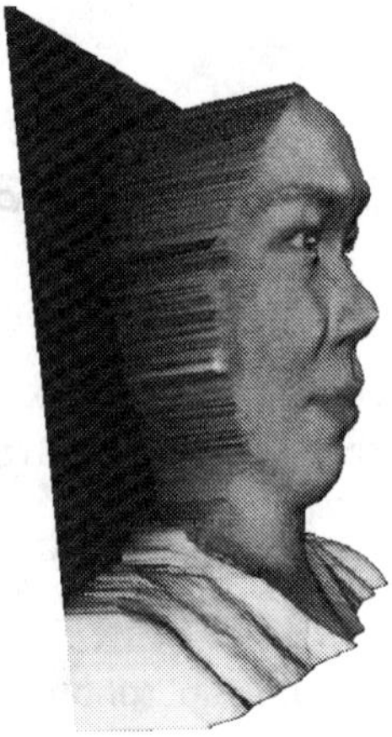

Figure 19.1: *Reconstructed face using photometric stereo.*

19.1 Introduction

Reflectance-based shape recovery of nonplanar surfaces from one or several irradiance images is a classic task in computer vision [1, 2]. The goal is to reconstruct the 3-D shape of an object from its irradiances by using its reflection properties. The problem is called *shape from shading* (SFS) if just one irradiance image is used as input for the reconstruction process [3]. The term *photometric stereo method* (*PSM*) or just *photometric stereo* refers to the extension of shape from shading to a class of methods that use two (2S PSM) or more (3S PSM, etc.) images for shading-based 3-D shape recovery.

A broad spectrum of techniques is available to approach reflectance-based shape recovery in appropriate fields of application (see, e.g., Klette et al. [4]). For example, 3S PSM may be used for generating height maps of a human face, a human hand, etc. (see Fig. 19.1). Using colored illumination [5, 6] this 3-D reconstruction may even be achieved for dynamic scenes several times per second. The use of inexpensive equipment (three light sources and a video camera), not dangerous radiation (as in case of laser light) and a reasonable performance are some advantages of PSM. Furthermore, the image values of (one of) the acquired images may be used for texture mapping without any additional need to register height and texture data, because the generated height values are located at the same pixel position as the acquired image values.

This field of reflectance-based shape recovery also contains serious mathematical problems (see, e.g., proofs of existence or uniqueness of object surfaces [7], or analysis of shadows or interrefections [8, 9]). This chapter reports the advances in applied and in theoretical work.

19.1.1 Shape from shading and photometric stereo

There are a number of factors that influence the measured irradiances of an image. First, the image that is acquired by the sensor depends on the geometrical and spectral distribution of the light source that illuminates the observed scene. The individual objects of the scene are characterized by their geometry and by their reflection properties. The geometry and the reflection properties affect the light falling on the imaging sensor. The imaging system converts the light to measured image irradiances.

Shape from shading (SFS) methods try to infer the geometry of an object from a single image. For this inversion, the mentioned factors and their influences have to be considered for the conceptual design of an SFS method. The only *a prioi* constraint is that the geometry has to be extracted from the image. An additional goal could be to extract the reflection properties from the given image, and, as well, to obtain a more complete description of the visible surface.

It is impossible to infer unambiguous geometrical properties of objects from image irradiances without restricting the general problem. The design of SFS methods that allow a mathematical proof of existence, uniqueness or convergence of a solution, is a field of ongoing active research.

Common assumptions to ensure an unambiguous surface reconstruction from a single or several images are as follows:

(i) The *irradiance* E_0 and the *direction* $\boldsymbol{s}$ *of the illumination* are known. There are no intraobject or interobject interreflections, that is, scene objects do not act as secondary light sources. In general, a light source is assumed that emits parallel light of a constant irradiance E_0 from a constant and known illumination direction $\boldsymbol{s} = [s_1, s_2, s_3]^T$. If the illumination direction $\boldsymbol{s}$ coincides with the viewer direction $\boldsymbol{v}$, that is, $\boldsymbol{s} = [0, 0, -1]^T$, then SFS simplifies significantly. Some SFS methods exist that assume a close point light source, hence the light rays cannot be modeled as parallel. Approaches that assume diffuse illumination (e.g., sky illumination) comprise another special case. Furthermore, the effects of the inverse square law (see, e.g., [4]) are usually disregarded;

(ii) The *reflection properties* of the object surfaces are known. For additional simplification, linearly reflecting surfaces or Lambertian surfaces are often assumed where the *albedo* ρ is constant and known for the entire object;

(iii) The modeling by *reflectance maps* assumes that a unique scene radiance value is assigned to each *surface orientation* $\boldsymbol{n} = [n_1, n_2, n_3]^T$. Often the *reflectance map* is assumed to be known. For example, it is assumed that the reflectance map can be approximated as being locally or globally linear;

(iv) For the *object surface geometry* it is assumed that faces can be approximated by continuous or continuously differentiable functions u in classes as C^1 or C^2. Some methods exist that are especially designed to reconstruct polyhedral objects. In general, it has to be assumed that height values of respective orientations are known at a few (singular) points in advance. Of special interest are boundary points showing zero irradiances (occluding boundaries) and points of maximal irradiance. Sometimes it is assumed that the surface can be locally approximated as a plane (facet model) or as a sphere;

(v) The *sensor* is linear; and

(vi) Shading-based shape recovery methods usually assume an orthographic *projection of scene objects* into the xy−image plane. This allows taking in account surface functions $u(x, y)$ with first-order derivatives u_x, u_y and normals $\boldsymbol{n} = [u_x, u_y, -1]^T$. There are also methods that assume perspective projection.

These assumptions can be reduced by extracting from the scene some parameters that were expected to be known. For example, usually only the product of the irradiance E_0 of the light source and the albedo ρ has to be determined and not their individual values. Under the assumptions of parallel illumination, a Lambertian reflection, and an orientation $\boldsymbol{n}_0$ in the scene that coincides with the illumination direction $\boldsymbol{s}$, it follows that the product $E_0\rho$ can be read from the maximal irradiance value. Also, in practice, many of the constraints (except two of them) prove to be rather uncritical restrictions. The *critical assumptions* are that the albedo ρ is restricted to be constant over the whole object (or even over the whole image), which corresponds to a uniform coloring, and the limitation to Lambertian surfaces because, in addition to the diffuse component, many materials exhibit a considerable amount of specular reflection. A *genuine Lambertian surface* allows a representation by a graph of a function u.

Assume parallel and constant illumination from lighting direction $\boldsymbol{s} = [s_1, s_2, s_3]^T$, a genuine Lambertian surface, constant albedo ρ, and a known product $E_0\rho$. According to *Lambert's cosine law* and the *image irradiance equation* it holds that

$$E = E_0\rho\cos(\alpha) \tag{19.1}$$

with $\alpha = \angle(\boldsymbol{n}, \boldsymbol{s})$, for the measured irradiance E and a surface normal $\boldsymbol{n} = [u_x, u_y, -1]^T$. The term $\cos(\alpha)$ and hence the angle α can be calculated from the known quantities. All vectors that subtend the angle α with the illumination direction are solutions to Eq. (19.1).

The *Gaussian sphere* is useful in representing these solutions. Without loss of generality, we can restrict the surface orientations to *unit surface normals* $\bar{\boldsymbol{n}}$. Then the solution vectors $\bar{\boldsymbol{n}}$ form the lateral area of a right circular cone. The vertex of the cone lies at the center of the Gaussian sphere. The orientation of the cone (vector of the cone axis) is determined by the illumination direction $\boldsymbol{s}$. The boundary of the circular base of the cone is incident with the surface of the Gaussian sphere. All these points on the Gaussian sphere are surface orientations satisfying the equation for the image irradiance function E.

For *Lambertian surfaces* often we consider image irradiance equations

$$E_i(x,y) = \rho(x,y)\frac{u_x(x,y)p_i + u_y(x,y)q_i - r_i}{\sqrt{u_x(x,y)^2 + u_y(x,y)^2 + 1}\,\sqrt{p_i^2 + q_i^2 + r_i^2}} \tag{19.2}$$

defined over domains $\Omega_i = \{[x,y]^T \in \mathbb{R}^2 : 0 \le E_i(x,y) \le 1\}$, for light sources $i = 1,2,3,\ldots$, with irradiances $E_{0,i} = 1$ and orientations $[p_i, q_i, r_i]^T$, and image coordinates $[x,y]^T$.

Shape from shading (SFS) methods are extended to PSM if several irradiances are known for every image point and the corresponding surface point. Because of the larger amount of data an improvement of the reconstruction results and furthermore a reduction of the necessary assumptions can be expected. Photometric stereo methods first recover surface orientations and can be combined with an integration method to calculate a *height* or *depth map*. Even without a subsequent integration step the surface orientations can be used, for example, to determine curvature parameters of object surfaces or to recognize objects.

To acquire images for photometric stereo the object is consecutively illuminated by several light sources. Each image E_i is taken with only one light source being switched on. Movement inside the system consisting of the object, the light sources, and the sensor is not allowed. Therefore, more than one irradiance value can be assigned to a projected surface point without encountering a correspondence problem. Each acquired image corresponds to one light source.

We distinguish between albedo-dependent photometric stereo methods and albedo-independent methods. The property of *albedo-dependent methods* is that the albedo ρ of the surface material or the product $E_0\rho$ has to be known for every image point (x,y). This is especially true for all SFS methods. *Albedo-independent methods* have the property that the albedo has theoretically no influence on the reconstruction of orientations or height values as long as $\rho > 0$.

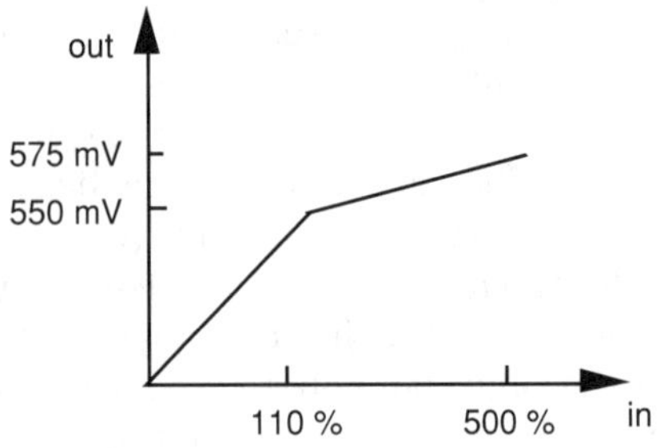

Figure 19.2: *Example of pre-kneeing to preserve the dynamic range.*

19.1.2 Linear sensor

Modern cameras suitable for image processing are usually based on semiconductor sensors, the so-called *charge coupled device* (CCD) chips. Several properties of these cameras are of interest for measuring irradiances (see, e.g., [10]).

A linear behavior of the imaging sensor is assumed in shading-based techniques such as SFS, 2S PSM or 3S PSM. For these techniques it is assumed that the gray values (or the color values) in the image have a *direct linear relation* to the measured *image irradiances* (the radiation entering the camera lens, see also Volume 1, Chapters 2 and 5). First, we briefly mention that signal attenuation caused by a pre-knee circuit, clipping, and blooming already lead to a nonlinear camera response. Further reasons for nonlinear camera behavior are explained in the following and a sketch of a linearization technique is given.

Attenuation of the signal occurs if more photons fall on the CCD chip than the image acquisition system is able to process. This can be caused by different factors when the image signal is processed in analog form (voltages) in the camera or when the signal is digitized in the frame grabber. One reason for attenuation is the limited *dynamic range* of the components in the imaging system. The analog component of the camera system causes an attenuation if the electric signal is processed by a so-called *pre-knee circuit*. Figure 19.2 shows the characteristics of the pre-knee circuit of the Sony three-chip camera DXC-930P. The voltage of the signal is linearly attenuated starting at a certain level of the input signal. As a result, the signal is no longer globally linear.

Furthermore, *clipping* of the input signal occurs whenever the analog signal exceeds the highest processable voltage, for example when the analog signal is converted to a digital signal (a gray value for each color channel) in the frame grabber. Usually, the clipping level (*white level*) of the analog/digital converter can be controlled by programming the frame grabber.

If the intensity of the incoming light at a CCD cell exceeds a certain level that is several times higher than the clipping level, then the CCD cell is no longer able to accumulate more charge per time unit. The additional charge is spread into the neighboring CCD cells. This effect is called *blooming* and appears as a white streak or blob around the affected pixels in the image. Blooming is particularly noticeable in scene analysis when specular highlights occur on the surface of the object that has to be reconstructed. For interline transfer sensors blooming starts at about 600 % overload according to [11].

In principle, CCD chips possess the property of having a high linearity because photons are transformed directly into charge in a CCD cell. But CCD cameras usually delinearize the signal for display requirements. It has to be guaranteed that the light received by the camera is transformed into a proportional amount of light emitted by a monitor screen. The input voltage U of a cathode ray tube in a monitor and the emitted radiant intensity I are in exponential relationship $I \approx U^{\gamma}$ where γ is the *gamma value*. Therefore, a circuit is integrated in the camera for the *gamma correction*. The circuit adjusts the *linear* CCD camera signal U_{in} to the *nonlinear* monitor characteristic

$$U_{\text{out}} = U_{\max}^{(1-1/\gamma)} U_{\text{in}}^{1/\gamma} \tag{19.3}$$

where $U_{\max}$ is the maximum voltage. The gamma value γ depends on the monitor and the video standard of the television system.

Therefore, the gamma correction has to be inverted to linearize the camera characteristic. This gamma re-correction can be done through substituting γ by $1/\gamma$ if the gamma value of the camera is known. This leads to the equation

$$E_{\text{out}} = G_{\max}^{(1-\gamma)} E_{\text{in}}^{\gamma} \tag{19.4}$$

which transforms the measured image irradiance values (gray values) from E_{in} to E_{out}. For many CCD cameras it is possible to switch the gamma value through the camera control unit to 1. This avoids a gamma re-correction procedure.

If neither the gamma value is known nor the gamma correction can be switched off, then the gamma value has to be calculated by using a calibration image. A calibration image for this purpose usually contains a number of gray and/or matte color patches of known reflection properties (see [12, 13] for one example of a calibration chart). The spectral reflectance factors of gray patches of such a calibration chart are constant over the visible wavelength interval of the light. The constant reflectance factors (*albedos*) can be represented as percentages that describe how much light the gray patches reflect. The percentages are properties of the patches and are independent from the illumination and the camera. The relationship between these percentages and the measured image irradiances describes directly the camera behavior with respect to linearity. Because a model of the nonlinear characteristic of the camera is known (see Eq. (19.4)) the gamma value can be estimated.

Besides the gamma correction that causes a nonlinear camera behavior the *black level* has to be considered. A CCD cell generates electrons even if no light (photons) is falling on the light-sensitive area caused by thermal energy within the CCD chip. The current generated by these electrons is called *dark current*. The analog/digital converter transforms the associated voltage into an image gray value (measured image irradiance). The gray value that is a result of the dark current is called *black level*. It can be modeled as being an additive offset to the camera signal and must be subtracted from the gray values. Actually the black level does not lead to a nonlinear characteristic but the goal is to produce a camera curve that is directly linear, that means a totally black gray patch having 0 % reflection should generate the gray value 0. Often the black level can be adjusted by a knob at the camera control unit called master black control.

A further factor playing an important role with respect to color reproduction is the overall scaling of the three color channels. A gray object taken under white illumination produces a gray image, hence the color channels have identical gray values v. Therefore, the gray value triple $\boldsymbol{c} = [v, v, v]^T$ is assigned to each pixel when we assume idealized image acquisition. Although called "white," the color of white light sources, such as daylight, fluorescent lamps, and usual light bulbs, produce different white tones, expressed in color temperature values. To get "white" for these different light sources a so-called *white balance* has to be performed. A manual white balance is done by exposing a white object to the color camera and pushing the white balance button at the camera control unit.

19.1.3 Illumination parameters

The 3S PSM approach (as discussed later on) can also be employed for the calculation of an *illumination direction* (see [1]). Assume that we have acquired the irradiance images of a curved calibration object having a Lambertian surface of known geometry (e. g., a sphere) and having uniform albedo ρ. The 3S PSM assumes that three positive irradiance values $\boldsymbol{E} = [E_1, E_2, E_3]^T$ can be measured for every image point $[x, y]^T$ with respect to three illumination directions $\boldsymbol{p}$, $\boldsymbol{q}$, and $\boldsymbol{r}$; 3S PSM is then directed on calculating a (unit) surface normal $\bar{\boldsymbol{n}}$ from such an irradiance triplet by using the known illumination parameters.

Now we consider a one-point light source. For the calculation of one illumination direction $\boldsymbol{s}$ the calibration object has to ensure (at least) three depicted and illuminated surface points with known and noncoplanar surface (unit) normals $\bar{\boldsymbol{n}}_1$, $\bar{\boldsymbol{n}}_2$, and $\bar{\boldsymbol{n}}_3$. These three known surface normals are combined into a matrix $\boldsymbol{N} = [\bar{\boldsymbol{n}}_1, \bar{\boldsymbol{n}}_2, \bar{\boldsymbol{n}}_3]$. Further, assume a diagonal matrix $\boldsymbol{D}$ that contains in its diagonal positions the irradiance values of the light source at the considered image points. In practice we can assume that these light-source irradiances are constant over the object, that is, $\boldsymbol{D}$ contains the same positive value in all three diagonal positions. This leads to the following system of *image irradiance equations*:

$$\boldsymbol{E} = \rho \boldsymbol{D} \boldsymbol{N} \bar{\boldsymbol{s}}^T \tag{19.5}$$

The unit vector of the illumination direction that is scaled by the albedo ρ can be determined with

$$\bar{\boldsymbol{s}}^T = \boldsymbol{N}^{-1} \frac{1}{\rho} \boldsymbol{D}^{-1} \boldsymbol{E} \tag{19.6}$$

This shows that in practice the matrix $\boldsymbol{D}$ can simply be the identity matrix. Because the meaning of being given or unknown data is exchanged for the surface normals and the illumination directions in comparison to 3S PSM, this method is also referred to as *inverse 3S PSM*. The robustness can be improved by including more than three surface normals.

19.2 Reflection and gradients

The amount of light encoded into the gray value of a particular pixel of a digital image can be seen as the result of interactions between surface materials and light sources. Vision-based shape-recovery methods are influenced by the lighting and by the reflection characteristics of the observed objects. Therefore it is necessary to model the properties of both the illumination and the object materials. A discussion of radiometric and photometric quantities that are relevant to computer vision is presented in Klette et al. [4], Haralick and Shapiro [14].
Vision-based shape recovery normally leads to reconstructions of gradient maps. These gradient maps have to be integrated for generating depth or height maps. This section deals with reflection models [15] and gradient integration. Both topics are interesting subproblems in shading-based shape recovery.

19.2.1 Reflectance distribution functions and maps

The *bidirectional reflectance-distribution function* (BRDF) describes reflection characteristics (see also Volume 1, Chapter 3). The BRDF was defined in 1977 by the National Bureau of Standards, USA, for the standardization of reflection representations [16]. The BRDF describes how

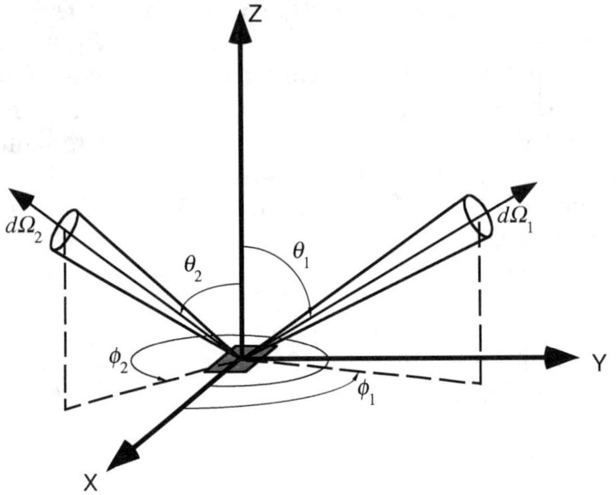

Figure 19.3: *Geometry of the bidirectional reflectance-distribution function (BRDF).*

"bright" a differential surface dA of a material appears when it is observed from a general direction and illuminated from a particular direction (see Fig. 19.3). The BRDF

$$f_r(\theta_2, \phi_2; \theta_1, \phi_1) = \frac{dL_1(\theta_2, \phi_2; \theta_1, \phi_1; E_2)}{dE_2(\theta_2, \phi_2)} \tag{19.7}$$

is defined as the ratio between the reflected differential radiance dL_1 in viewer direction and the differential irradiance dE_2 coming from an illumination direction. The BRDF is expressed in sr^{-1} (1 / *steradian*). The term "direction" in this definition should be interpreted as a differential solid angle in a direction given by spherical coordinates. The letter θ denotes the slant angle and the letter ϕ stands for the tilt angle. The spherical coordinates of the BRDF refer to a right-handed coordinate system where the origin coincides with the surface point and whose z-axis coincides with the surface orientation. The tilt angle is taken counterclockwise by looking onto the surface patch.

If the differential irradiance dE_2 is described in the foreshortened portion of the illumination over the differential solid angle $d\Omega_2$ by using the radiance that is received by the surface, the BRDF can be formulated as

$$f_r(\theta_2, \phi_2; \theta_1, \phi_1) = \frac{dL_1(\theta_2, \phi_2; \theta_1, \phi_1; E_2)}{L_2(\theta_2, \phi_2)\cos(\theta_2)\, d\Omega_2} \tag{19.8}$$

If we integrate over the entire observed solid angle Ω_2 of the incoming radiation the reflected radiance L_1 is represented by

$$L_1 = \int_{\Omega_2} f_r\,(\theta_2,\phi_2;\theta_1,\phi_1)\,L_2\,(\theta_2,\phi_2)\cos(\theta_2)\;\mathrm{d}\Omega_2 \tag{19.9}$$

The irradiance $\mathrm{d}E_2$ depends on a direction because it holds

$$\mathrm{d}E_2\,(\theta_2,\phi_2) = L_2\,(\theta_2,\phi_2)\cos(\theta_2)\;\mathrm{d}\Omega_2 \tag{19.10}$$

A perfectly *diffuse reflecting surface* appears equally bright when observed from any arbitrary direction. Furthermore, this feature is also independent from the type of illumination. If a surface emits the entire incoming energy through reflection, then it is called a *Lambertian reflector* and neither absorption nor transmission of radiation takes place. It follows that the entire radiance L_1 that is reflected over the visible hemisphere is equal to the incoming irradiance E_2. A Lambertian reflector has three important properties:

(i) The reflected radiance L_1 does not depend on the direction (isotropic) and is constant, that is, $L_1\,(\theta_1,\phi_1) = L_1 = \text{const}$;

(ii) The BRDF is constant, that is, $f_r\,(\theta_2,\phi_2,\theta_1,\phi_1) = f_r = \text{const}$; and

(iii) The radiant emittance M is equal to the irradiance E_2.

The radiant emittance M can now be expressed as the integral of the reflected radiance L_1 over the visible hemisphere

$$M = \int_{\Omega_1} L_1\;\mathrm{d}\Omega_1 = L_1\,\pi = E_2 \tag{19.11}$$

From this it follows that

$$f_r = \frac{L_1}{E_2} = \frac{1}{\pi} \tag{19.12}$$

holds for the Lambertian reflector. If the Lambertian reflector is illuminated by a light source that has the radiance $L_2(\theta_2,\phi_2)$ we get

$$L_1 = \frac{1}{\pi}\int_{\Omega_2} L_2(\theta_2,\phi_2)\cos(\theta_2)\;\mathrm{d}\Omega_2 \tag{19.13}$$

as reflected radiance. This equation contains *Lambert's cosine law*

$$L_1 = \frac{E_0}{\pi}\cos(\theta_2) \tag{19.14}$$

for the reflected radiance L_1 of a Lambertian reflector illuminated by a parallel radiating light source of irradiance E_0. The index 0 usually

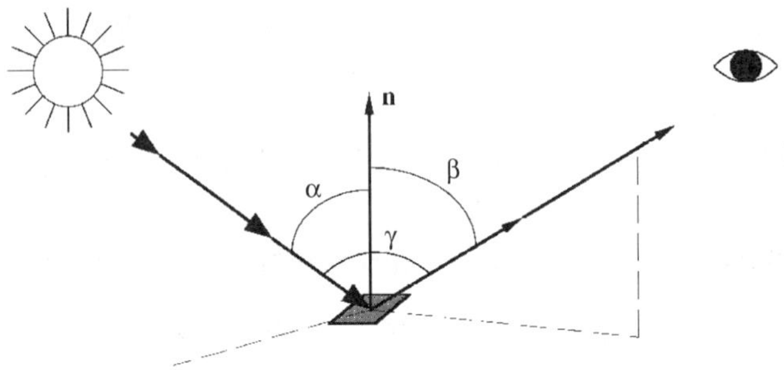

Figure 19.4: *Definition of three photometric angles* α, β, *and* γ. *Each arrow marks the direction of one light ray.*

denotes a quantity related to the light source. It is assumed that illumination directions outside of the interval

$$0 \leq \theta_2 < \frac{\pi}{2} \tag{19.15}$$

do not cause reflections.

According to its definition the Lambertian reflector does not absorb any radiation for any wavelength. The *albedo* ρ is used to describe surfaces that possess all properties of a Lambertian reflector apart from a partial absorption of the incoming radiation (*Lambertian surfaces*). It describes the relative portion of the radiation that is reflected by the surface. The albedo can be seen as a scaling factor that lies usually in the interval $[0, 1]$. The definition of the albedo can be extended to non-Lambertian surfaces.

The three *photometric angles* α, β, and γ are defined with respect to the surface normal $\boldsymbol{n}$ (see Fig. 19.4), where α is the angle between the surface normal and the illumination direction (*incident angle*), β is the angle between the surface normal and the reflection direction (*emittance angle*), and γ is the angle between the illumination direction and the reflection direction (*phase angle*). Without loss of generality, the reflection direction can be aligned to the viewer direction (optical axis of sensor).

The viewer direction is described by a vector $\boldsymbol{v}$ that points to the viewer (camera). Generally, an orthographic projection is assumed so that the viewer direction reduces to $\boldsymbol{v} = [0, 0, -1]^T$. This is the standard viewer direction. The illumination direction is also simply described by a vector $\boldsymbol{s}$ that points to the light source.

The radiance equation for a Lambertian reflector can be extended for a *general Lambertian surface* not being necessarily a Lambertian reflector. Let us assume that the surface has albedo ρ and is illuminated by a parallel radiating light source with irradiance E_0 under the incident

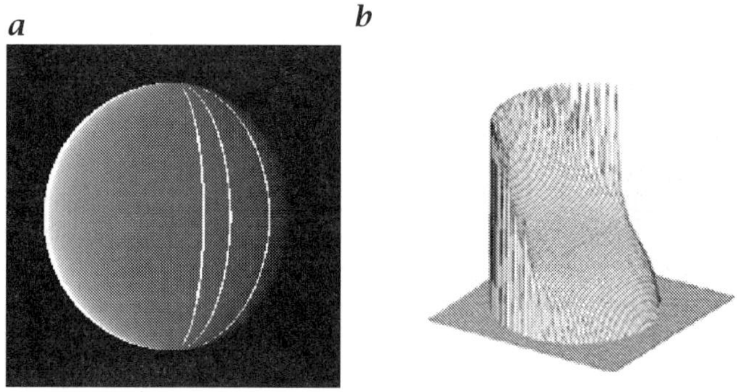

Figure 19.5: *Irradiance image of a linearly shaded sphere using the illumination orientation* $\boldsymbol{s} = [-0.5, 0, -1]^T$*:* ***a*** *three overlaid isoirradiance curves; and* ***b*** *a grid representation of the irradiances.*

angle α. Then the corresponding radiance equation is

$$L_1 = \frac{E_0}{\pi} \rho \cos(\alpha) = \frac{E_0}{\pi} \rho \cos \angle (\boldsymbol{n},\ \boldsymbol{s}) \tag{19.16}$$

Considering surface reflection properties and assuming nonvarying illumination directions $\boldsymbol{s}$ and viewer directions $\boldsymbol{v}$ variations in the reflected radiation are solely caused by changes of the surface orientation. Horn [17] introduced the *reflectance map* to model this relationship. Reflectance maps can be defined as continuous or discrete functions. Usually, the *gradient space* representing the surface gradients $[p, q]^T = [u_x, u_y]^T$ is chosen for reflectance maps because of its simplicity. In this case the reflectance map function is $R(p, q)$. Another useful representation are stereographic coordinates $[f, g]^T$ and reflectance maps $R_s(f, g)$. Furthermore, a general reflectance map $R_n(\bar{\boldsymbol{n}})$ can be defined by using the unit surface normal $\bar{\boldsymbol{n}}$. As an example,

$$R(p, q) = E_0 \rho \frac{s_1 p + s_2 q - s_3}{\left\| [s_1, s_2, s_3]^T \right\|} \tag{19.17}$$

is a *linear reflectance map*, for illumination direction $\boldsymbol{s} = [s_1, s_2, s_3]^T$ and using gradient space representation. The shading of a sphere that has linear reflectance is shown in Fig. 19.5.

Constant scaling factors are usually eliminated from the representation of reflectance maps, as the factor $1/\pi$ for the Lambertian reflectance maps. Consequently, the reflectance map

$$R(p, q) = E_0 \rho \cos \angle \left([p,\ q,\ -1]^T,\ \boldsymbol{s} \right), \quad R_n(\bar{\boldsymbol{n}}) = E_0 \rho \bar{\boldsymbol{n}} \bar{\boldsymbol{s}}^T$$
$$\text{or} \quad R_s(f, g) = \frac{E_0 \rho \, [4f,\ 4g,\ f^2 + g^2 - 4]^T \bar{\boldsymbol{s}}}{4 + f^2 + g^2} \tag{19.18}$$

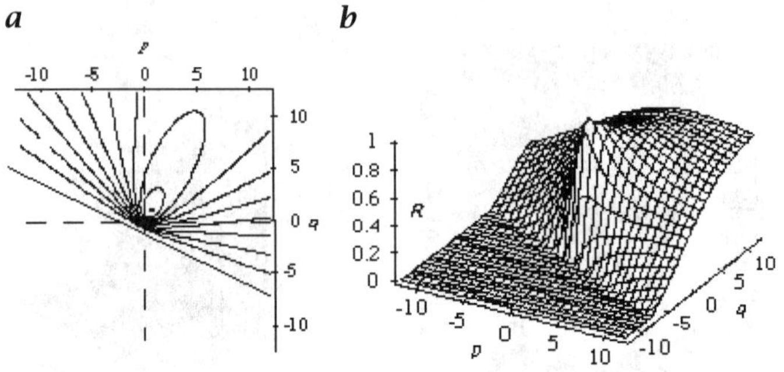

Figure 19.6: *Reflectance map of a Lambertian surface in gradient space with illumination direction* $\boldsymbol{s} = [0.5, 1, -1]^T$*:* ***a*** *isoradiance contour plot;* ***b*** *3-D plot.*

corresponds to a Lambertian surface (see Fig. 19.6). A rotationally symmetric *Lambertian reflectance map* is given by

$$R(p,q) = E_0\rho \frac{1}{\left\|[p,\ q,\ -1]^T\right\|}, \text{ where } \boldsymbol{s} = \bar{\boldsymbol{s}} = \boldsymbol{v} = \bar{\boldsymbol{v}} = [0,\ 0,\ -1]^T \tag{19.19}$$

Lambertian reflectance maps with $\boldsymbol{s} \neq \boldsymbol{v}$ are not rotationally symmetric. The left-hand side of Fig. 19.6 shows the reflectance map as isoradiance plot thus every curve shows orientations of equal scene radiance values (*isoradiance curves*). The second-order isoradiance curves in these maps describe a point, a circle, an ellipse, a parabola, a hyperbola, or a straight line. Every isoradiance curve defines the location of equal irradiances in a captured image. Consequently, these curves are also called *isoirradiance curves*.

The point in the isoradiance plot represents the gradient that is identical to the gradient $[p_s, q_s]^T$ of the illumination direction and hence takes the maximal radiance value. The gradients lying on the straight line represent those surface normals, which are orthogonal to the illumination direction. The function value zero is assigned to them because surface patches oriented in this way cannot receive light from the light source. This straight line is called *self-shadow line.*

It holds an algebraic duality that the distance between the illumination gradient $[p_s, q_s]^T$ and the origin is reciprocal to the distance between the self-shadow line and the origin. The illumination gradient and the self-shadow line are located on different sides of the origin. It follows that the self-shadow line is uniquely defined by the illumination gradient. The self-shadow line is called the *dual line* to this gradient.

For isotropically reflecting surface materials with unknown reflection characteristics the mapping of an orientation to a radiance value can be determined using a calibration object (see [4]). The following assumptions are made: the calibration object has the same surface material as the surface that has to be reconstructed later on by using SFS or PSM. Note that only one surface material can be characterized by a single reflectance map.

19.2.2 Reflection and image irradiance equation

The simple reflection representation in the form of reflectance maps allows the description of the large class of isotropic reflecting materials. However, for more general cases it is of benefit to use analytical reflection models in a more general way than already done for the Lambertian reflection [18]. An analytical reflection model should satisfy the requirements of simplicity and should be physically plausible as much as possible. In general, *hybridly reflecting surfaces* have to be considered where reflection is an additive composition of *diffuse* or *body reflection* L_b and of *specular* or *interface reflection* L_s.

The diffuse reflection component is usually modeled by Lambert's cosine law though there exists no complete physical explanation of Lambert's cosine law. By contrast, many models exist for the description of the specular reflection component. In principle, there are two different ways to describe specular reflection, approaches that use physical optics (wave optics) and approaches that apply models from geometrical optics [19]. Approaches of physical optics use the electromagnetic theory for the analysis of the reflection where the Maxwell equations constitute the mathematical basis. The application of geometrical optics is a lot simpler, but it can be used only if the wavelength of the incoming light is small compared to the roughness of the material. Consequently, reflection models that are derived from geometrical optics can always be approximations of the wave-optical reflection models. Two general representatives of these approaches are the Beckmann-Spizzichino model (physical optics) and the Torrance-Sparrow model (geometrical optics) (see [20]). Simplifications of both reflection models are used in computer vision and computer graphics to describe the specular component.

The *Beckmann-Spizzichino model* describes the specular reflection by two additively overlapping components usually called specular spike and specular lobe. The specular spike-component models a portion of the reflection that only occurs in a very narrow range of angles around the direction of perfect specular (mirror-like) reflection. The diffuse portion of the specular reflection is modeled by the lobe component. It describes the scattering reflection caused by the surface roughness.

The *Torrance-Sparrow model* describes the specular reflection for surfaces whose roughness is large compared to the wavelength of the light. It models the surface by planar, perfectly specular reflecting microfacets whose orientations are normally distributed around the

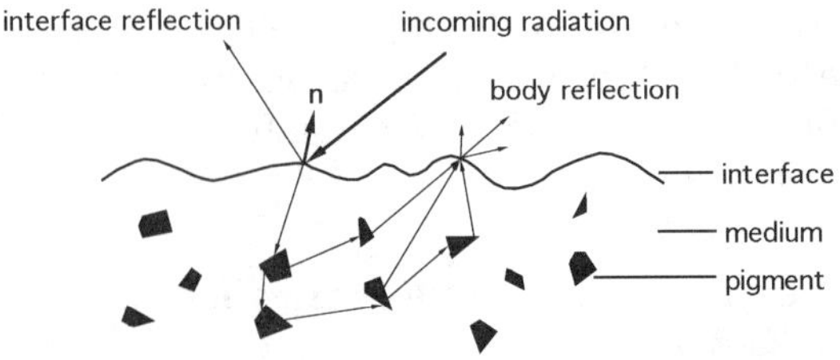

Figure 19.7: *Simple model of an inhomogeneous dielectric material.*

macroscopic surface orientation that is visually inferable. The mathematical formula mainly comprises a Fresnel term, the geometrical attenuation factor, and a Gaussian normal distribution. The Fresnel term describes the reflection behavior depending on the illumination direction $\boldsymbol{s}$, on the viewer direction $\boldsymbol{v}$, and on the refraction index of the surface material. Note that the refraction index depends on the wavelength. Besides a simplified Torrance-Sparrow model the *Phong model* is used in computer vision and in computer graphics [21].

A model that describes hybrid reflection properties without specifying the diffuse and the specular reflection component explicitly is the *dichromatic reflection model* (DRM). This model can be used for inhomogeneous dielectric materials whose surface structure can be modeled as being composed of an interface and an optically neutral medium containing color pigments (see [22]). Fig. 19.7 illustrates the principal structure of such an inhomogeneous dielectric.

The interface separates the surface from the environment that is usually air. If the distribution of the color pigments is uniform and the pigments display the same optical behavior, then it can be assumed that the penetrating light does not have a specific direction when it leaves the surface (body or diffuse reflection). Part of the radiation falling on the object surface does not penetrate the medium and is reflected by the interface (interface or specular reflection). The DRM models the specular reflection component with microfacets. Mathematically, the DRM can be formulated in the following way:

$$\begin{aligned} L(\lambda, \boldsymbol{n}, \boldsymbol{s}, \boldsymbol{v}) &= L_s(\lambda, \boldsymbol{n}, \boldsymbol{s}, \boldsymbol{v}) + L_b(\lambda, \boldsymbol{n}, \boldsymbol{s}, \boldsymbol{v}) \\ &= m_s(\boldsymbol{n}, \boldsymbol{s}, \boldsymbol{v}) c_s(\lambda) + m_b(\boldsymbol{n}, \boldsymbol{s}, \boldsymbol{v}) c_b(\lambda) \end{aligned} \tag{19.20}$$

where the modeled scene radiance L is a quantity that depends on the wavelength λ.

The essential assumption of the DRM is that both reflection components can be factorized into a geometrical component and a spectral component as given in Eq. (19.20). The geometrical components are m_s and m_b. The spectral components are c_s and c_b. The factor c_s is called *interface reflection color* and c_b is the *body reflection color*.

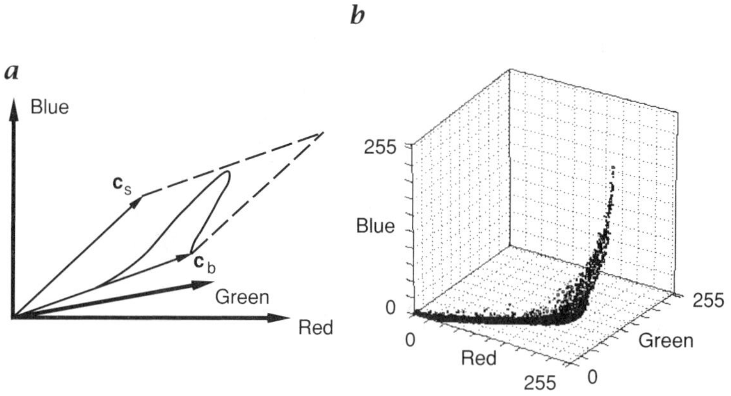

Figure 19.8: ***a*** *Dichromatic plane of a curved, hybridly reflecting object showing one color;* ***b*** *an L-shaped color cluster of a real watering can (see Fig. 19.9, left).*

The factorization of the interface reflection only holds under specific assumptions [4]. The factorization of the body reflection is feasible without any further significant restrictions.

With the additional assumption of a neutral reflecting interface, c_s describes the spectral distribution (color) of the light source. This special case of the DRM is called the *neutral interface reflection model* (NIRM). The geometrical component m_s can be made explicit by the formulas of a simplified Torrance-Sparrow model, the Phong model or other models. But the particular advantage of the DRM is that the geometric component of the specular reflection does not have to be modeled explicitly to apply the DRM for various tasks. The scaling factor m_b can be usually modeled by Lambert's cosine law.

If the description of the scene radiance L is restricted to three narrow wavelength bands in the red, green, and blue spectral range of the visible light, then the scene radiance can be represented as a 3-D color vector

$$\boldsymbol{L} = m_s(\boldsymbol{n}, \boldsymbol{s}, \boldsymbol{v})\boldsymbol{c}_s + m_b(\boldsymbol{n}, \boldsymbol{s}, \boldsymbol{v})\boldsymbol{c}_b \tag{19.21}$$

Because from the mathematical point of view, m_s and m_b represent arbitrary scaling factors, the vectors $\boldsymbol{c}_s$ and $\boldsymbol{c}_b$ form a 2-D subspace (a plane) in the RGB color space (*dichromatic plane, color-signal plane*).

It can be observed that the colors in the dichromatic plane form T- and L-shaped clusters if the object has sufficiently many and different surface orientations. Figure 19.8 shows on the left the outline of a typical L-shaped cluster and on the right the cluster for the real orange watering can (see Fig. 19.9, left). If the object shows several hybridly reflecting materials one cluster arises for every material. The repre-

Figure 19.9: ***a*** *Image of a real watering can showing a large highlight;* ***b*** *picture of the watering can after removal of the specular reflection. The six gray patches in the bottom line were used to linearize the camera (compare Section 19.1.2).*

sentations shown in Fig. 19.8 are called *color histograms*. Contrary to gray-value histograms, color histograms only have binary values. Color histograms only code whether or not a certain color exists in the image. Both the DRM and the NIRM are of great importance in physics-based computer vision. For example, it is possible to separate the reflection components and hence to remove the specular reflection component (highlights) from images by analyzing color histograms [9, 22, 23].

Figure 19.9 displays an example of such a highlight removal. The left picture shows the original image of a watering can. The right picture shows the watering can after the elimination of the specular reflection component using the DRM. These reflection models can also be used to remove interreflections [8], for color image segmentation, color classification, and color object recognition.

Now we discuss the relation between the radiance reflected from the object surfaces (scene radiance) to its counterpart, the measured image irradiance of the imaging sensor. It can be shown [24] that (under a few assumptions, see also [4]) the relation between the reflected radiance L and the image irradiance E can be approximated by

$$E = L \frac{\pi}{4} \frac{d^2}{f^2} \cos^4(\psi) \tag{19.22}$$

where d is the diameter of the lens, f is its focal length, and ψ is the angle between the optical axis and the light ray going through the center of the observed small solid angle.

This relationship in conjunction with a reflectance map R leads to the *image irradiance equation*

$$E(x, y) = cR(p, q) \tag{19.23}$$

where c is a scaling factor. Because the surface gradient (p, q) depends on world coordinates but the image irradiance E is given in terms of image coordinates, this equation implicitly contains the assumption of an orthographic projection as it was already assumed for defining the reflectance map.

If, additionally, the image irradiance is proportional to the values measured by the imaging sensor and the digitization system, then the relationship between the scene radiance and the measured image irradiance (gray value) of the image is linear, too. Normal video cameras have a built-in gamma recorrection (compare Section 19.1.2) that is a nonlinear mapping between the image irradiances and the gray values. Therefore a photometric calibration must be carried out to linearize the camera before the image irradiance equation can be applied. For simplification purposes the image irradiance equation is often represented in the literature by

$$E(x, y) = R(p, q) \tag{19.24}$$

Therefore, the function $E(x, y)$ in this equation can be regarded as an image irradiance function and as a measured image irradiance function. The image irradiance equation is the most important tool to describe the relationship between irradiances, scene radiances, and surface gradients.

19.2.3 Depth maps from gradient maps

The models of surface geometry are also used in shading-based shape recovery, besides the models of surface reflection. Classes of C^n *functions* are suitable to describe curved surfaces. These classes model continuity, respectively, of differentiability assumptions. Generally, $C^n(\Omega)$ denotes the class of all functions that are defined on a domain Ω, for $n \geq 0$. These functions are continuous, and their derivatives exist up to and including the nth order and are continuous as well. In this chapter either the real plane $\Re^2$ or a bounded subset of this plane is assumed to be the definition domain Ω. Accordingly, often we refrain from stating the definition domain. Furthermore, only the sets C^1 or C^2 are relevant in this chapter. Functions of these sets are called C^1-continuous, respectively, C^2-continuous surface functions.

A surface function $u = u(x, y)$ is also characterized by the validity or invalidity of the *integrability condition*

$$\frac{\partial^2 u(x, y)}{\partial x \partial y} = \frac{\partial^2 u(x, y)}{\partial y \partial x} \tag{19.25}$$

for all $[x, y]^T \in \Omega$. As a special corollary from Frobenius' theorem in mathematical analysis it follows that the validity of this condition $u_{xy} = u_{yx}$ is "approximately equivalent" to C^2-continuity (see [4]).

Function $u = u(x, y)$ is an *antiderivative of a vector field* $\mathbf{w}(x, y) = [p(x, y), q(x, y)]^T$ over a domain Ω if

$$p(x, y) = \frac{\partial u}{\partial x}(x, y) = u_x(x, y) \text{ and } q(x, y) = \frac{\partial u}{\partial y}(x, y) = u_y(x, y) \tag{19.26}$$

hold for all $[x, y]^T \in \Omega$. Mathematical analysis offers (in principle) ways to calculate such an antiderivative. For example, the *integration of vector fields* can be based on arbitrarily specified *integration paths*, that is, on piecewise C^1-curves

$$\gamma : \quad [a, b] \rightarrow \Re^2, \gamma(t) = [\gamma_1(t), \gamma_2(t)]^T = [x(t), y(t)]^T \tag{19.27}$$

that lies inside the region Ω, with $a < b$, $\gamma(a) = [x_0, y_0]^T$, and $\gamma(b) = [\hat{x}, \hat{y}]^T$. For such a curve it holds that

$$u(\hat{x}, \hat{y}) = u(x_0, y_0) + \int_\gamma p(x, y)\, \mathrm{d}x + q(x, y)\, \mathrm{d}y \tag{19.28}$$

where the result at position $[\hat{x}, \hat{y}]^T$ is independent from the integration path. The *depth map*, the *height map*, and the *gradient map*, respectively, are functions over the *image grid*

$$\left\{[x, y]^T : 1 \le x \le M \wedge 1 \le y \le N\right\}$$

In the ideal case at each point $[x, y]^T$ a depth map for surface function u states the *depth* $u(x, y)$ of those surface points that are projected into this image point. A height map is defined relatively to an assumed background plane (of height zero), which is parallel to the image plane. In the ideal case at each point $[x, y]^T$ the height value is equal to the (scaled) height of those surface point that is projected into this image point. Height is measured with respect to the chosen background plane. A given depth or height map allows us to reconstruct object faces in 3-D space within a subsequent computation step of a general backprojection approach. In this chapter we consider depth or height maps as the ultimative goal of *single-view shape recovery*.

Shading-based shape recovery techniques normally provide gradient values for a discrete set of visible points on object surfaces. This requires a subsequent integration step to achieve (within possible limits) the specified ultimative goal of (relative) depth or height maps.

The general remarks about integration paths support *local integration techniques*: Assume a scan algorithm that passes through all image points of the image grid (e.g., known under names as meander scan, Hilbert scan, or Peano scan, etc.). Starting with initial depth values this

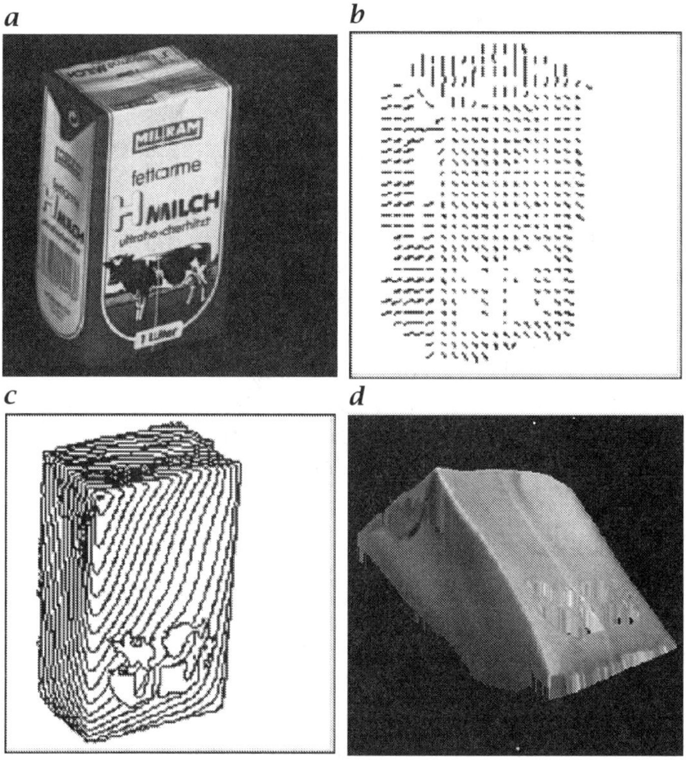

Figure 19.10: ***a*** *Object;* ***b*** *reconstructed gradient map using 3S PSM;* ***c*** *contour plot and* ***d*** *shaded surface with Lambertian texture for the lighting direction* $\mathbf{s} = [0, 0, -1]^T$ *of reconstruction results using the Frankot-Chellappa algorithm.*

algorithm can be used to propagate depth values according to a local approximation rule (e.g., based on the 4-neighborhood) using the given gradient data. Such a calculation of relative depth values can be done within repeated scans (i.e., using different scan algorithms). Finally, resulting depth values can be determined by averaging operations. Initial depth values have to be provided or assumed for the start positions of the different runs.

Several proposals follow this general scheme of local propagations (for a review, see [25]). A *global integration method*, based on results of Frankot and Chellappa [26] and presented in Klette et al. [4], leads, in practice to considerably better results for the task of calculating depth from gradients. The solution calculated by this *Frankot-Chellappa algorithm* is optimal in the sense of the quadratic error function between ideal and given gradient values. It only provides a relative height function up to an additive constant. See Fig. 19.10 for an example of a reconstructed surface.

19.3 Three light sources

This section discusses 3S PSM where it is assumed that no motion occurs inside the system consisting of the object, the light sources, and the sensor. Therefore, three irradiances (an irradiance triplet) can be assigned to every object point that is projected into the image plane. It is assumed that all irradiances are positive, which means that shadows are excluded from the analysis. The smaller the angle between the illumination directions, the more object portions are covered simultaneously by all light sources. On the other hand, with smaller angles the sensitivity with respect to noise in the measurements of the irradiances during the image acquisition increases. The same holds for the sensitivity with respect to the inaccurate estimation of other fixed parameters, for example, the illumination directions. Thus, no optimal choice of illumination directions exists for 3S methods.

19.3.1 Albedo-dependent analysis

We begin our discussion of shape recovery with the assumption of a Lambertian surface. The shape of a smooth genuine Lambertian surface with uniform albedo can be uniquely determined by 3S PSM (see [1] or [7]).

Three irradiance values are measured for any visible surface point where each value corresponds to the case that exactly one of the light sources was switched on. We assume a Gaussian sphere representation of the reflectance maps, that is, each measured irradiance corresponds to a circle on the sphere representing all possible unity normals at the given surface point. This requires the assumption that for all three light sources the products $E_0\rho$ of the light source irradiances and the albedo are known. On the Gaussian sphere the true orientation at the given surface point is represented by the intersection point of all these three circles on the Gaussian sphere (assuming noncoplanar light source orientations).

If the three illumination directions are not coplanar and the three image irradiances are consistent with each other, then 3S PSM leads to a unique solution. The orientation of a point on a Lambertian surface can be recovered uniquely with three image irradiances independent of the neighborhood of the considered image point. We do not have to introduce smoothness assumptions or integrability constraints. The reconstruction of the surface orientations is carried out point-locally by analyzing irradiance triplets. But note that so far this is the ideal case in theory.

The pair of gradients of an irradiance pair is given by the intersection of two conic sections in the gradient space for a Lambertian surface. The left picture in Fig. 19.11 illustrates the intersection of two conic

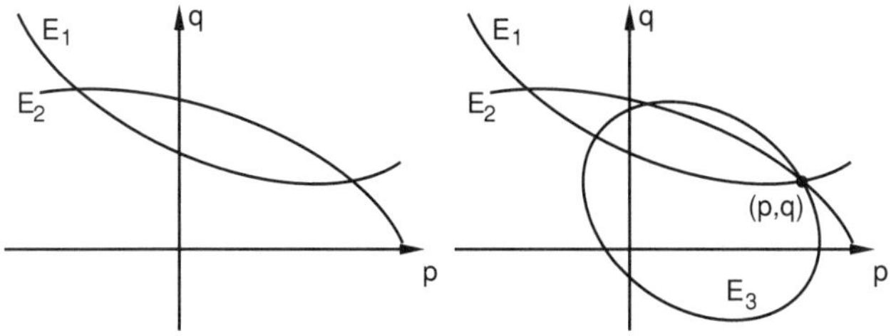

Figure 19.11: *Isoirradiance curves of 2S (left) and 3S (right) PSM.*

sections. When an additional light source is introduced that generates the image irradiance E_3, then the three conic sections intersect at a unique point. The intersection (p, q) in gradient space represents the desired orientation.

However, when the irradiances are measured for a real surface point, then basically there never exists a unique intersection due to noise and other errors. But even in this case two gradients would exist for each consistent pair of irradiances. If three consistent irradiance pairs are used to calculate the solution pairs, then six intersections occur. Three of the six intersections should represent orientations that point approximately into the same direction similar to the sought-after surface normal $\boldsymbol{n} = [p, q, -1]^T$. Finally, not the gradients themselves but the orientations should be compared to determine an approximate orientation.

Furthermore, the recovery of the solution can also be achieved without explicitly calculating the solution candidates, simply by generating the intersection curves nonanalytically. For this approach the reflectance maps are represented as image matrices. For this purpose, first, a generation of the discrete reflectance maps (for all three light sources) can be performed. The use of a calibration object has the advantage that neither the illumination directions nor the products $E_{0i}\rho$ have to be known. Then the selection of the orientations can be carried out through simple threshold segmentations of the reflectance maps. The three irradiances measured in the image are taken to specify the thresholds. The segmentation result consists of three regions that represent the orientations that are consistent with the image irradiances. Finally, the binarized reflectance maps are intersected (binary AND operation). The centroid of the resulting region can be used to represent approximately the orientation at the considered image point. Note that the stereographic projection is a more convenient 2-D representation of the orientations because it causes less distortions. The width W of the segmentation interval $[E_i - W/2, E_i + W/2]$, with $i = 1, 2, 3$, can be adapted to the noise level in the image acquisition system and to expected variations in the albedo.

This described *threshold segmentation for 3S PSM* has the advantage that it is easily applicable to surfaces that have no Lambertian reflection properties because we do not have to solve a system of nonlinear equations. For reflectance maps that are synthetically generated and parameterized by a set of real parameters, ambiguous solutions can easily be detected for a certain accuracy without a uniqueness proof. If the reflectance maps are generated by using a calibration object, then we do not have to determine the reflection parameters, that is, the surface roughness and the ratio of the diffuse and the specular reflection component.

For a *look-up table solution to 3S PSM* note that an irradiance triplet that is measured in the images can be regarded as a point in a Cartesian coordinate system $E_1E_2E_3$ where each of the three axes (irradiance axis) represents the image irradiances of one light source. A surface orientation is uniquely assigned to every possible irradiance triplet; thus the generation of a 3-D look-up table is possible. The generation of the look-up table can be carried out in two different ways. If the illumination directions and irradiances of the light sources are known, then the look-up table can be built by applying explicit equations. Moreover, a calibration object can be employed for the generation. Again, it is advantageous that the directions and irradiances of the light sources as well as the reflection parameters do not have to be known explicitly. A surface orientation is determined by looking up the entry that corresponds to the measured irradiance triplet. The look-up table entry contains either a 2-D representation of the surface orientation or it is empty. If the image irradiances are digitized with 8-bit accuracy and the surface orientations are encoded with 2×4 Bytes, then the look-up table needs 128 MB (!) of memory.

Figure 19.12 illustrates two different views of a look-up table for a real sphere showing Lambertian reflection characteristics. The estimated illumination directions for the sphere are

$$\begin{aligned} \boldsymbol{s}_1 &= [-0.312, -0.231, -1]^T \\ \boldsymbol{s}_2 &= [0.049, 0.304, -1]^T \\ \boldsymbol{s}_3 &= [0.411, -0.236, -1]^T \end{aligned}$$

The estimated ratios of the light source irradiances are 1.0 : 1.022 : 0.772. A total number of 41717 triplets with positive 8-bit irradiances were measured on the sphere having a radius of 123 pixels. For the sake of clarity, the illustrations only display 1303 irradiance triplets. Fig. 19.12 on the right shows an orthographic projection of the look-up table.

It can easily be seen that the irradiances describe an ellipsoidal surface. In this example, the density of the look-up table is only approximately 3 % with respect to the number of its entries. It can be shown

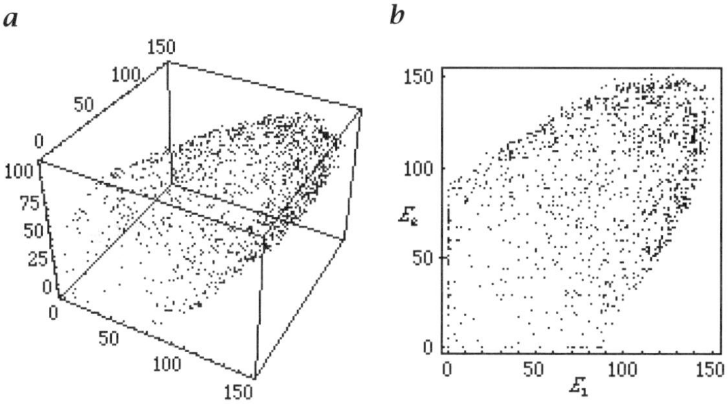

Figure 19.12: ***a*** *The 3-D oblique view of a real look-up table in a coordinate system that is spanned by three irradiances originating from three different light sources;* ***b*** *orthogonal projection along the irradiance axis* E_3.

that in the ideal case this point distribution describes in fact the surface of an ellipsoid [6]. The center of this ellipsoid is located at the origin of the $E_1E_2E_3$ coordinate system. The ellipsoid is restricted to the first octant of the coordinate system because only positive irradiances make sense. Each irradiance restricts the other two irradiance values to an ellipse in the $E_1E_2E_3$ space. Hence a unique solution is found by intersecting the three orthogonal ellipses.

The lengths of the three semiaxes of the ellipsoid are proportional to the albedo of the surface material. Moreover, the orientation of the ellipsoid is albedo-independent and determined by the three illumination directions. Every ray in the $E_1E_2E_3$ space passing through the origin represents a unique orientation. From the mentioned properties it follows that the look-up table can be made albedo-independent by propagating each entry along a ray. Thus, a valid surface orientation is assigned to every look-up table entry.

19.3.2 Albedo-independent analysis

In the following it will be assumed that the albedo ρ remains unknown. At first we note that a pair of irradiances constrains the gradients of a Lambertian surface with unknown albedo to a straight line in gradient space (see [27]). Under parallel illumination the two image irradiance equations of a Lambertian surface can be represented as

$$E_1 = E_{01}\rho\frac{\boldsymbol{n}^T\boldsymbol{s}_1}{\|\boldsymbol{n}\|\;\|\boldsymbol{s}_1\|} \text{ and } E_2 = E_{02}\rho\frac{\boldsymbol{n}^T\boldsymbol{s}_2}{\|\boldsymbol{n}\|\;\|\boldsymbol{s}_2\|} \tag{19.29}$$

resulting in the equation

$$\rho \boldsymbol{n}^T (E_{01} E_2 \|\boldsymbol{s}_2\| \boldsymbol{s}_1 - E_{02} E_1 \|\boldsymbol{s}_1\| \boldsymbol{s}_2) = 0 \tag{19.30}$$

which can be interpreted as a scaled scalar product. If $\rho \neq 0$, then the albedo can be eliminated from the equation that leads to albedo independence. By collecting the known quantities in $E_{0a,b} = E_{0a} E_b \|\boldsymbol{s}_b\|$ the equation can be represented as the simplified scalar product

$$\boldsymbol{n}^T (E_{01,2} \boldsymbol{s}_1 - E_{02,1} \boldsymbol{s}_2) = 0 \tag{19.31}$$

The representation

$$\boldsymbol{n}^T (\boldsymbol{s}_{1,2} - \boldsymbol{s}_{2,1}) = 0, \text{ with } \boldsymbol{s}_{a,b} = E_{0a,b} \boldsymbol{s}_a = E_{0a} E_b \|\boldsymbol{s}_b\| \boldsymbol{s}_a \tag{19.32}$$

is even more compact. The vector difference $\boldsymbol{s}_{1,2} - \boldsymbol{s}_{2,1}$ consists of known quantities and lies in the *symmetry plane* defined by the illumination directions $\boldsymbol{s}_1$ and $\boldsymbol{s}_2$. For a given illumination geometry the variables of the vector difference $\boldsymbol{s}_{1,2} - \boldsymbol{s}_{2,1}$ are just the two image irradiances E_1 and E_2. The vector $\boldsymbol{s}_1 \times \boldsymbol{s}_2$ is perpendicular to the set of vectors defined by $\boldsymbol{s}_{1,2} - \boldsymbol{s}_{2,1}$. The solutions of the foregoing equation are vectors $\boldsymbol{n}$, for which the scalar product becomes zero. From this it follows that all those vectors $\boldsymbol{n}$ satisfy the equation that is oriented orthogonal to the vector difference $\boldsymbol{s}_{1,2} - \boldsymbol{s}_{2,1}$. The gradients of the possible vector differences $\boldsymbol{s}_{1,2} - \boldsymbol{s}_{2,1}$ lie in the gradient space on a determinable straight line h that is constant for a given illumination geometry. The straight line h is the line that is dual to the gradient $(p_s, q_s) = (p(\boldsymbol{s}_1 \times \boldsymbol{s}_2), q(\boldsymbol{s}_1 \times \boldsymbol{s}_2))$. A unique point on h is assigned to each irradiance pair (E_1, E_2). From the relationship

$$\boldsymbol{n}^T (\boldsymbol{s}_{1,2} - \boldsymbol{s}_{2,1}) = 0 \tag{19.33}$$

it follows that each gradient on the straight line h has a dual straight line k that represents the possible solutions $\boldsymbol{n}$ of Eq. (19.33).

The straight line h can be described explicitly by the equation

$$q_h = h(p_h) = -\frac{p_s}{q_s} p_h - \frac{1}{q_s} \tag{19.34}$$

The set of straight lines generated by the straight line h can be represented explicitly by

$$q_k = k(p_k) = \frac{q_s}{1 + p_s p_h}(1 + p_h p_k) \tag{19.35}$$

The variable p_h itself depends on the measured image irradiance pair (E_1, E_2) and can be calculated by

$$p_h = p(\boldsymbol{w}), \text{ with } \boldsymbol{w} = E_{01} E_2 \|\boldsymbol{s}_2\| \boldsymbol{s}_1 - E_{02} E_1 \|\boldsymbol{s}_1\| \boldsymbol{s}_2 \tag{19.36}$$

Thus, all gradients that are consistent with any arbitrary irradiance pair can be calculated by using Eq. (19.33). It can be shown that the gradient (p_s, q_s) lies on the straight line k. The albedo ρ can be found for every gradient by substituting a solution into any of the two image irradiance equations.

Similar equations to Eq. (19.33) can be formulated for the irradiance pairs (E_1, E_3) and (E_2, E_3). For the pair (E_1, E_3) the equation

$$\boldsymbol{n}^T(E_{01}E_3 \,\|\boldsymbol{s}_3\|\, \boldsymbol{s}_1 - E_{03}E_1 \,\|\boldsymbol{s}_1\|\, \boldsymbol{s}_3) = 0 \tag{19.37}$$

arises, which can be combined with the equation for the image irradiance pair (E_1, E_2). The terms in parentheses are vectors that are orthogonal to the desired surface orientation $\boldsymbol{n}$. After calculating the vector product

$$\boldsymbol{w} = (E_{01}E_2 \,\|\boldsymbol{s}_2\|\, \boldsymbol{s}_1 - E_{02}E_1 \,\|\boldsymbol{s}_1\|\, \boldsymbol{s}_2) \times (E_{01}E_3 \,\|\boldsymbol{s}_3\|\, \boldsymbol{s}_1 - E_{03}E_1 \,\|\boldsymbol{s}_1\|\, \boldsymbol{s}_3) \tag{19.38}$$

a vector results that is collinear to the surface normal $\boldsymbol{n}$. Therefore, $\boldsymbol{n} = s\boldsymbol{w}$. The scaling factor s must have such a sign that the surface normal $\boldsymbol{n}$ obtains a negative z-component. Besides the surface normal the albedo can be point-locally recovered by substituting the normalized vector $\bar{\boldsymbol{n}}$ into one of the three image irradiance equations. When the equation is divided by one of the three irradiances of the light sources, for example, by E_{03}, then the direction of the calculated vector

$$\left(\frac{E_{01}}{E_{03}}E_2 \,\|\boldsymbol{s}_2\|\, \boldsymbol{s}_1 - \frac{E_{02}}{E_{03}}E_1 \,\|\boldsymbol{s}_1\|\, \boldsymbol{s}_2\right) \times \left(\frac{E_{01}}{E_{03}}E_3 \,\|\boldsymbol{s}_3\|\, \boldsymbol{s}_1 - E_1 \,\|\boldsymbol{s}_1\|\, \boldsymbol{s}_3\right) \tag{19.39}$$

does not change with respect to $\boldsymbol{w}$. This property is helpful for the realization of an albedo-independent photometric stereo method because it means that only the ratios of the irradiances of the light sources have to be known. This leads to a different scaling of the albedo value.

Figure 19.13 shows three input images of a synthetic Mozart statue for the described 3S photometric stereo method. The images were generated by using Lambertian reflectance maps. A light source setup having the *slant angles* $\sigma(\boldsymbol{s}_1) = \sigma(\boldsymbol{s}_2) = \sigma(\boldsymbol{s}_3) = 20°$ and the *tilt angles* $\theta(\boldsymbol{s}_1) = 90°$, $\theta(\boldsymbol{s}_2) = -150°$, $\theta(\boldsymbol{s}_3) = -30°$ were chosen for rendering. Relatively small slant angles for the illumination directions guarantee that no strong self-shadows arise. The ratios of the irradiance values E_{0i} of the light sources are equal to one.

Figure 19.14 illustrates the shape recovery results for the Mozart statue. The integration of the height map was carried out using the Frankot-Chellappa algorithm, see Section 19.2.3. The left picture of Fig. 19.14 shows a grid representation of the reconstruction. Because detail information gets lost in this representation the right-hand picture presents the same surface by using texture mapping. The texture image

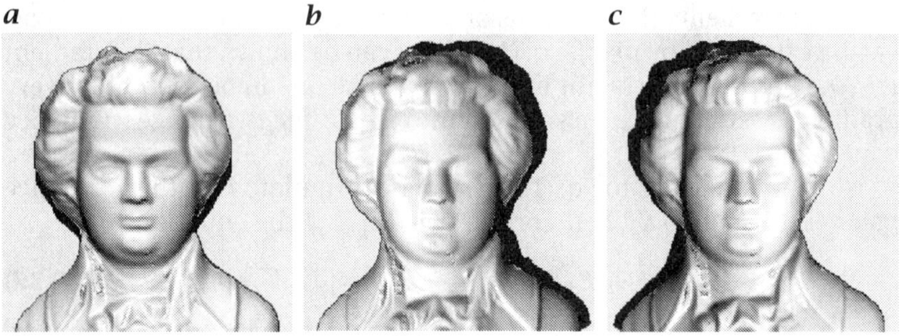

Figure 19.13: *Image triplet of a synthetic Mozart statue for 3S photometric stereo. In the text the indices 1, 2, and 3 are assigned to the images from left to right.*

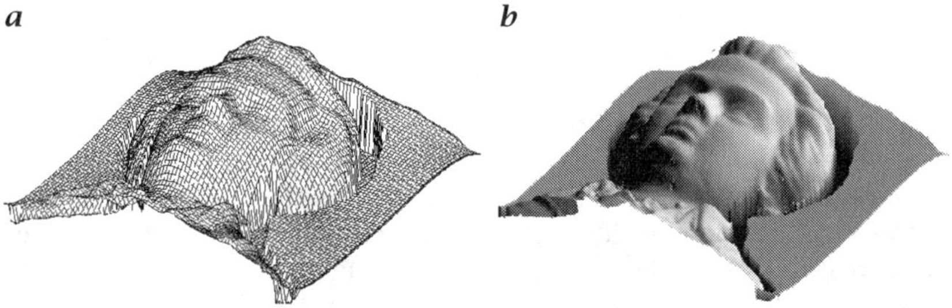

Figure 19.14: *Surface reconstruction results:* ***a*** *grid representation; and* ***b*** *texture mapping.*

was calculated from the recovered surface normals by using a Lambertian reflectance map with the illumination direction $\boldsymbol{s} = [1, 1, -1]^T$.

The image triplet of a real hand shown in Fig. 19.15 is an example of an object with a nonconstant albedo (different blood circulation). The ratios of the light source irradiances were estimated as 1.0 : 0.638 : 0.640. Estimations for the illumination directions of the three hand images are

$$\begin{aligned} \boldsymbol{s}_1 &= [-0.370, -0.028, -1]^T \\ \boldsymbol{s}_2 &= [0.044, 0.472, -1]^T \\ \boldsymbol{s}_3 &= [0.420, 0.043, -1]^T \end{aligned}$$

The 3-D plots presented in Fig. 19.16 show that a good surface reconstruction is possible by using 3S photometric stereo. Artifacts can occur when the hand is not entirely still and when the specular reflection component (caused by the transpiration) is not taken into account by the reflection model. In the right picture of Fig. 19.16 the first input image is mapped onto the 3-D reconstruction.

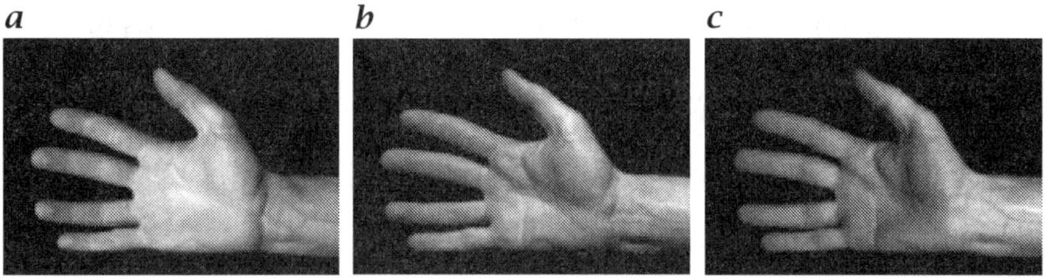

Figure 19.15: *An image triplet of a real hand used as input for a 3S photometric stereo method. The images 2 and 3 were brightened for visualization purposes where the indices 1, 2, and 3 are assigned to the images from left to right.*

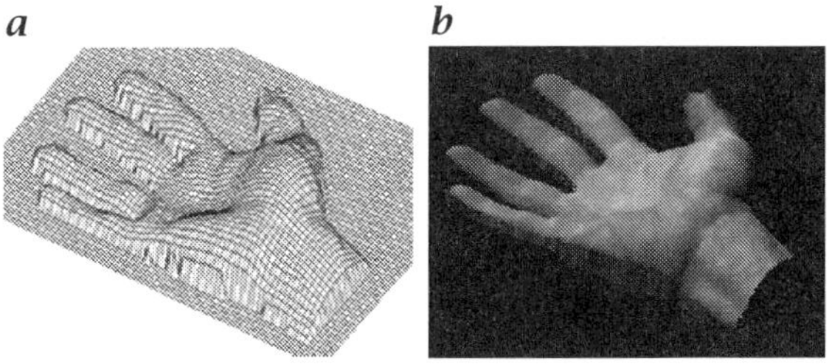

Figure 19.16: *Surface reconstruction results:* ***a*** *grid representation;* ***b*** *first input image was chosen for texture mapping.*

19.4 Two light sources

A more complex task is given if only two light sources are used to accomplish the task of unique surface recovery. The illumination directions $\boldsymbol{p}$ and $\boldsymbol{q}$ of the two light sources are assumed to be not collinear. In order to prevent an interference of the irradiances of the two light sources, the two pictures have to be taken consecutively. The object and the camera have a fixed position and orientation. Thus, an irradiance pair $[E_1, E_2]^T$ is assigned to each image point and the corresponding surface point for 2S PSM.

19.4.1 Albedo-dependent analysis

This section focuses on fundamentals of situations when the shape of a smooth Lambertian surface is uniquely determined by a pair of images. More applied results for 2S PSM can be found in Klette et al. [4]. First, we discuss gradient computation and then we analyze the corresponding uniqueness and existence problems. For more detailed texts an interested reader is referred to [7, 28] or Onn and Bruckstein [29]. A 2S PSM algorithm is formulated and discussed in Klette et al. [4] following Kozera [7], Onn and Bruckstein [29]. The second stage of the shape recovery process involves gradient integration as already discussed in Section 19.2.

Suppose that a genuine Lambertian surface represented by the graph of a function u of class C^1 defined over a domain $\Omega = \Omega_1 \cap \Omega_2$ is illuminated from two linearly independent directions $\boldsymbol{p} = [p_1, p_2, p_3]^T$ and $\boldsymbol{q} = [q_1, q_2, q_3]^T$. The captured images are E_1 and E_2, respectively. We assume that the albedo $\rho(x, y)$ is constant over the entire domain Ω with $\rho(x, y) \equiv c$ and $0 < c \leq 1$. Note that $\langle \boldsymbol{p}|\boldsymbol{q}\rangle$ is the dot product of both vectors. We then have the following (see [7] and [29]):

Theorem 19.1 *The first derivatives u_x and u_y of function u can be expressed in terms of E_1, E_2, $\boldsymbol{p}$, and $\boldsymbol{q}$, where $\|\boldsymbol{p}\| = \|\boldsymbol{q}\| = 1$, in the following form $u_x = e_1/e_3$ and $u_y = e_2/e_3$, where*

$$\begin{aligned} e_1 &= (q_1\langle \boldsymbol{p}|\boldsymbol{q}\rangle - p_1)E_1 + (p_1\langle \boldsymbol{p}|\boldsymbol{q}\rangle - q_1)E_2 + (p_3q_2 - p_2q_3)\varepsilon\sqrt{\Lambda}, \\ e_2 &= (q_2\langle \boldsymbol{p}|\boldsymbol{q}\rangle - p_2)E_1 + (p_2\langle \boldsymbol{p}|\boldsymbol{q}\rangle - q_2)E_2 + (p_1q_3 - p_3q_1)\varepsilon\sqrt{\Lambda}, \\ e_3 &= (p_3 - q_3\langle \boldsymbol{p}|\boldsymbol{q}\rangle)E_1 + (q_3 - p_3\langle \boldsymbol{p}|\boldsymbol{q}\rangle)E_2 + (p_1q_2 - p_2q_1)\varepsilon\sqrt{\Lambda} \end{aligned} \tag{19.40}$$

and where $\Lambda = \Lambda(x, y) = [1 - E_1^2(x, y) - E_2^2(x, y)] - \langle \boldsymbol{p}|\boldsymbol{q}\rangle[\langle \boldsymbol{p}|\boldsymbol{q}\rangle - 2E_1(x, y)E_2(x, y)]$, and $\varepsilon = \varepsilon(x, y)$ is a function taking values ± 1 so that $f(x, y) = \varepsilon(x, y)\sqrt{\Lambda(x, y)}$ is a continuous function.

The case when $\Lambda > 0$: When Λ is positive over Ω, the function ε appearing in Eq. (19.40) must take one of the values 1 or -1 because the gradient (u_x, u_y) has to be a continuous function. As an immediate consequence, Theorem 19.1 implies that there exist at most two C^2/C^1 solutions to the system (Eq. (19.2)).

The next theorem formulates necessary and sufficient conditions for the existence of exactly two solutions of class C^2 (and so of class C^1) to the system Eq. (19.2) (see also [7] and [29]).

Theorem 19.2 *Let E_1 and E_2 be functions of class C^1 over a simply connected region Ω of $\Re^2$ with values in $(0, 1]$ and let e_1, e_2, and e_3 be defined by Eq. (19.40). Suppose that $\Lambda > 0$ on Ω and that, for each choice of sign, $\sigma^{\pm} = (p_3 - q_3\langle \boldsymbol{p}|\boldsymbol{q}\rangle)E_1 + (q_3 - p_3\langle \boldsymbol{p}|\boldsymbol{q}\rangle)E_2 \pm (p_1q_2 - p_2q_1)\sqrt{\Lambda}$ does not vanish over Ω. Then*

$$(e_1/e_3)_y = (e_2/e_3)_x \tag{19.41}$$

is a necessary and sufficient condition for the existence of exactly two solutions of class C^2 to Eq. (19.2), for each choice of sign.

Consequently, if both vector fields $\left[u_x^+, u_y^+\right]^T$ where $\varepsilon(x, y) \equiv 1$, and $\left[u_x^-, u_y^-\right]^T$ where $\varepsilon(x, y) \equiv -1$ are integrable (see Eq. (19.41)), then there exist exactly two C^2 class solutions to Eq. (19.2) over Ω.

Now we analyze the meaning of Eq. (19.41) for images E_1 and E_2 generated by a C^2 Lambertian surface, that is, when Eq. (19.2) is satisfied for a certain function u of class C^2. We have the following (see also [28] and [29]):

Theorem 19.3 *Let $\boldsymbol{p} = [0,0,-1]^T$ and $\boldsymbol{q} = [q_1, q_2, q_3]^T$ be such that $q_1^2 + q_2^2 > 0$ and $\|\boldsymbol{q}\| = 1$, and let u be a function of class C^2 on a simply connected open subset Ω of $\Re^2$. Suppose that functions E_1 and E_2 are given by Eq. (19.2). Suppose, moreover, that $\Lambda > 0$ over Ω. In order that there exist a solution of class C^2 to Eq. (19.2) different from u, it is necessary and sufficient that u satisfies*

$$q_1 q_2 (u_{yy} - u_{xx}) + (q_1^2 - q_2^2) u_{xy} = 0 \tag{19.42}$$

As Eq. (19.42) is generically not satisfied by function u, a C^2 class uniqueness, in the case when $\Lambda > 0$ over Ω, is therefore in most cases ensured. In other words, the integrability condition (Eq. (19.42)) disambiguates surface reconstruction for two image patterns and essentially ascertains *a generic uniqueness* for 2S PSM.

In connection with the previous theorem a natural question arises about the possible analytic and geometric relationship between these two solutions (if both exist). Clearly, each of them has to satisfy an additional constraint imposed by Eq. (19.42). A *standard method of characteristics* (see the classical theory of the second-order partial differential equations [30], applied to Eq. (19.42)) yields (see [7]):

Theorem 19.4 *Suppose that $q_1^2 + q_2^2 > 0$. Any solution u of class C^2 to Eq. (19.42) over an open convex region Ω is given by*

$$u(x,y) = \begin{cases} \phi(q_1 x + q_2 y) + \psi(q_1 x - q_2 y) & \text{if } q_1 q_2 \neq 0 \\ \phi(x) + \psi(y) & \text{if } q_1 q_2 = 0 \end{cases} \tag{19.43}$$

for some functions ϕ and ψ of class C^2. Conversely, for any functions ϕ and ψ of class C^2, the foregoing formula defines a solution of class C^2 to Eq. (19.42). In addition, if a C^2 class function u satisfying Eq. (19.42) is determined, then the corresponding functions ϕ and ψ can be found by using the following formulas:

$$\phi(x) = \begin{cases} u(q_1 x/(q_1^2 + q_2^2), q_2 x/(q_1^2 + q_2^2)) - c & \text{if } q_1 q_2 \neq 0 \\ u(x,0) - c & \text{if } q_1 q_2 = 0 \end{cases} \tag{19.44}$$

$$\psi(x) = \begin{cases} u(-q_2 x/(q_1^2 + q_2^2), q_1 x/(q_1^2 + q_2^2)) + c & \text{if } q_1 q_2 \neq 0 \\ u(0,x) + c & \text{if } q_1 q_2 = 0 \end{cases} \tag{19.45}$$

where c is an arbitrary constant.

The last theorem implies that if there exist two C^2 class solutions to Eq. (19.42) (which is a rare case), then each of them can be decomposed as a sum of two single-variable C^2 class functions. A natural question arises about the relationship between pairs $[\phi_u, \psi_u]^T$ and $[\phi_v, \psi_v]^T$. This is answered by the following (see [28]):

Theorem 19.5 *Let* $\boldsymbol{p} = [0,0,-1]^T$ *and* $\boldsymbol{q} = [q_1, q_2, q_3]^T$ *be such that* $q_1^2 + q_2^2 > 0$ *and* $\|\boldsymbol{q}\| = 1$. *Let* u *be a function of class* C^2 *defined over and open convex region* Ω, *satisfying Eq. (19.2) and*

$$u(x,y) = \begin{cases} \phi(q_1 x + q_2 y) + \psi(q_1 x - q_2 y) & \text{if } q_1 q_2 \neq 0 \\ \phi(x) + \psi(y) & \text{if } q_1 q_2 = 0 \end{cases} \tag{19.46}$$

for some functions ϕ *and* ψ *of class* C^2. *Then the second solution* v *to Eq. (19.2) of class* C^2 *can be expressed in the form:*

$$v(x,y) = \begin{cases} \phi(q_1 x + q_2 y) - \psi(q_1 x - q_2 y) & \text{if } q_1 q_2 \neq 0 \\ -\phi(x) + \psi(y) & \text{if } q_1 = 0 \\ \phi(x) - \psi(y) & \text{if } q_2 = 0 \end{cases} \tag{19.47}$$

The last two theorems determine *analytic representations* of two C^2 class solutions as well as establish the corresponding relationship between these representations. Furthermore, one can derive now two alternative schemes for finding those two solutions (if both exist). First, as indicated in Theorem 19.1 and Theorem 19.2 one can recover both functions u and v by calculating the corresponding contour integrals. However, only one contour integration is in fact necessary. Having found the first solution u, we can apply Theorem 19.4 and decompose u in terms of a pair of C^2 class functions (ϕ, ψ). Finally, Theorem 19.5 renders the second solution v, represented uniquely in terms of a pair of functions $[\phi, \psi]^T$.

In addition, a geometric relationship between the graphs of two solutions u and v can also be now established. Namely, as easily verified, the Gaussian curvature $K_u(x,y)$ of the graph of function u calculated at point $[x, y, u(x,y)]^T$, and the Gaussian curvature $K_v(x,y)$ of the graph of function v calculated at point $[x, y, v(x,y)]^T$ satisfy $K_u(x,y) = -K_v(x,y)$.

The immediate consequence of this fact is that there is no $\pm u + c$ ambiguity in 2S PSM when both Λ and the Gaussian curvature of at least one solution do not vanish. Such a symmetry is characteristic for the single-image shape recovery when a point light-source is positioned overhead. However, one can expect nonuniqueness (in two point light-source photometric stereo) resulting from replacing u by $-u + c$ for the graphs with zero Gaussiam curvature. Note also that, if an admissible class of shapes contains only *convex/concave surfaces* consisting exclusively of elliptic points the second solution (if it exists) consists exclusively of *hyperbolic points*. Such a theoretical solution is considered not physically plausible as being *a priori* excluded from an admissible class of surfaces. Consequently, any restriction of class of admissible solutions, might also disambiguate a possible case of nonuniqueness in 2S PSM.

Example 19.1: Lambertian surface

Let $\boldsymbol{p} = [0, 0, -1]^T$ and $\boldsymbol{q} = [1/\sqrt{3}, 1/\sqrt{3}, -1/\sqrt{3}]^T$, and let $E_1(x, y) = (x^2+y^2+1)^{-1/2}$ and $E_2(x, y) = (x+y+1)[3(x^2+y^2+1)]^{-1/2}$. Consider the corresponding two image irradiance equations for 2S PSM:

$$\begin{aligned} \frac{1}{\sqrt{u_x^2 + u_y^2 + 1}} &= \frac{1}{\sqrt{x^2 + y^2 + 1}} \\ \frac{u_x + u_y + 1}{\sqrt{3}\sqrt{u_x^2 + u_y^2 + 1}} &= \frac{x + y + 1}{\sqrt{3}\sqrt{x^2 + y^2 + 1}} \end{aligned} \tag{19.48}$$

defined over $\Sigma = \{[x, y]^T \in \Re^2 : x + y + 1 \geq 0,\ x < y\}$. An easy inspection shows that Λ vanishes only along the line $x = y$ and thus Λ is positive over Σ. Applying Theorems 19.1 and 19.2 yields that both vector fields $\left[u_x^+, u_y^+\right]^T = [y, x]^T$ and $\left[u_x^-, u_y^-\right]^T = [x, y]^T$ are C^2 integrable. Moreover, the corresponding C^2/C^1 class solutions to Eq. (19.48), defined over Σ, are given up to a constant as $u^+(x, y) = xy$ and $u^-(x, y) = 1/2(x^2 + y^2)$. Alternatively, we can first integrate one of the vector fields, say, $\left[u_x^+, u_y^+\right]^T$, and verify that u^+ satisfies Eq. (19.42). Hence the second vector field $\left[u_x^-, u_y^-\right]^T$ is also C^2 integrable. By Eq. (19.43), the function $u^+(x, y) = \phi(1/\sqrt{3}(x + y)) + \psi(1/\sqrt{3}(y - x))$. Furthermore, formulae Eq. (19.44) and Eq. (19.45) yield

$$\phi(x) = u^+((\sqrt{3}x/2), (\sqrt{3}x/2)) - c = (3/4)x^2 - c$$

and

$$\psi(x) = u^+(-(\sqrt{3}x/2), (\sqrt{3}x/2)) + c = -(3/4)x^2 + c$$

Using Theorem 19.5 results in

$$u^-(x, y) = \phi(1/\sqrt{3}(x + y)) - \psi(1/\sqrt{3}(y - x)) = (x^2 + y^2)/2$$

which obviously coincides with the second solution, already determined by using a standard contour gradient integration method. Observe that u^- also satisfies Eq. (19.42). Note, moreover, that the graph of u^+ consists exclusively of hyperbolic points with negative Gaussian curvature $K_{u^+}(x, y) = -(1 + x^2 + y^2)^{-2}$, whereas the graph of u^- consists exclusively of elliptic points with positive Gaussian curvature $K_{u^-}(x, y) = (1 + x^2 + y^2)^{-2}$.

Hence, the equation $K_u(x, y, u(x, y)) = -K_v(x, y, v(x, y))$ is clearly also fulfilled. The reconstructed surfaces coincide with the Lambertian paraboloid and hyperboloid, respectively.

The case when $\Lambda \equiv 0$: We consider the case when Λ introduced in Theorem 19.1 vanishes for given E_1 and E_2 defined (captured) over some domain Ω.

An immediate consequence of Theorem 19.1 is that there is at most one C^2/C^1 class solution to the system Eq. (19.2). The next theorem formulates a necessary and sufficient condition for existence of exactly one solution u of class C^2 to the system Eq. (19.2) (see [7]).

Theorem 19.6 *Let E_1 and E_2 be functions of class C^1 over a simply connected region Ω of $\Re^2$ with values in $(0,1]$. Suppose that $\Lambda \equiv 0$ on Ω and that $\sigma = (p_3 - q_3\langle \boldsymbol{p}|\boldsymbol{q}\rangle)E_1 + (q_3 - p_3\langle \boldsymbol{p}|\boldsymbol{q}\rangle)E_2$ does not vanish over Ω. Then a necessary and sufficient condition for the existence of exactly one class C^2 solution u of Eq. (19.2) is $(g_1/g_3)_y = (g_2/g_3)_x$, where*

$$\begin{aligned} g_1 &= (q_1\langle \boldsymbol{p}|\boldsymbol{q}\rangle - p_1)E_1 + (p_1\langle \boldsymbol{p}|\boldsymbol{q}\rangle - q_1)E_2 \\ g_2 &= (q_2\langle \boldsymbol{p}|\boldsymbol{q}\rangle - p_2)E_1 + (p_2\langle \boldsymbol{p}|\boldsymbol{q}\rangle - q_2)E_2 \\ g_3 &= (p_3 - q_3\langle \boldsymbol{p}|\boldsymbol{q}\rangle)E_1 + (q_3 - p_3\langle \boldsymbol{p}|\boldsymbol{q}\rangle)E_2 \end{aligned}$$

Furthermore, in case of Λ vanishing over Ω, it can be shown that the graph of u constitutes *a developable surface of cylindrical type* and that the vectors $\boldsymbol{n} = [u_x, u_y, -1]^T$, $\boldsymbol{p}$, and $\boldsymbol{q}$ are co-planar, for each $[x,y]^T \in \Omega$. For a more detailed analysis an interested reader is referred to [28].

We close this subsection with an example highlighting another important aspect appearing in 2S PSM. As it turns out, the uniqueness problem is not a mere function of an unknown surface but also depends on the mutual position of vectors $\boldsymbol{n} = [u_x, u_y, -1]^T$, $\boldsymbol{p}$, and $\boldsymbol{q}$. This is explicitly illustrated in the following example:

Example 19.2: Lambertian surface

Let $\boldsymbol{q} = \left[q_1(q_1^2+q_2^2+1)^{-1/2}, q_2(q_1^2+q_2^2+1)^{-1/2}, -(q_1^2+q_2^2+1)^{-1/2}\right]^T$ and $\boldsymbol{p} = [0,0,-1]^T$, and let
$E_1(x,y) = (a^2+b^2+1)^{-1/2}$
and
$E_2(x,y) = (aq_1+bq_2+1)(a^2+b^2+1)^{-1/2}(q_1^2+q_2^2+1)^{-1/2}$.
Assume that the vectors $\boldsymbol{p}$ and $\boldsymbol{q}$ are linearly independent. Consider now the corresponding two image irradiance equations for 2S PSM:

$$\begin{aligned} \frac{1}{\sqrt{u_x^2+u_y^2+1}} &= \frac{1}{\sqrt{a^2+b^2+1}} \\ \frac{q_1u_x+q_2u_y+1}{\sqrt{q_1^2+q_2^2+1}\sqrt{u_x^2+u_y^2+1}} &= \frac{q_1a+q_2b+1}{\sqrt{q_1^2+q_2^2+1}\sqrt{a^2+b^2+1}} \end{aligned} \tag{19.49}$$

A straightforward calculation shows that Λ vanishes over Ω, if

$$aq_2 - bq_1 = 0$$

The latter happens only and only if the three vectors $\boldsymbol{n} = [u_x, u_y, -1]^T$, $\boldsymbol{p}$, and $\boldsymbol{q}$ are co-planar, that is, when they are linearly dependent. Theorem 19.6 yields the existence of exactly one C^2/C^1 solution to Eq. (19.49) defined as $u(x,y) = ax + by + c$. If, in turn, $aq_2 - bq_1 \neq 0$ (i.e., vectors $\boldsymbol{n}$, $\boldsymbol{p}$, and $\boldsymbol{q}$ are linearly independent) then Λ is positive over Ω. Thus, the Theorem 19.2 ensures the existence of exactly two C^2/C^1 solutions: $u^+(x,y) = ax + by + c$ and $u^-(x,y) = Ax + By + c$, where $A = (a(q_1^2 - q_2^2) + 2bq_1q_2)/(q_1^2 + q_2^2)$ and $B = (b(q_2^2 - q_1^2) + 2aq_1q_2)/(q_1^2 + q_2^2)$. As expected, the condition Eq. (19.42) is satisfied by both u^+ and u^- and

$$K_{u^+}(x,y,u^+(x,y)) = -K_{u^-}(x,y,u^-(x,y)) = 0$$

Note, finally, that each reconstructed surface coincides with a Lambertian plane.

The case when $\Lambda \geq 0$: So far, we have considered the cases in which Λ is either positive or vanishes over a given domain Ω. Now we shall treat the situation in which Λ is nonnegative. Our analysis will not be complete as we shall confine ourselves to the specific case concerning the topology of the zero sets of Λ. Namely, we assume that region $\Omega = D_1 \cup D_2 \cup \Gamma$, where subdomains D_1 and D_2, and a smooth curve Γ are mutually disjoint, Λ is positive over $D_1 \cup D_2$, and Λ vanishes over Γ. It can be verified that this special topological case is obeyed by most pairs of images and pairs of point light-source directions.

Assume that there exists at least one solution u of class C^2 to Eq. (19.2) and that the irradiance functions E_1, E_2 appearing in these equations are C^1 class over Ω. Suppose that the set $\{[x,y]^T \in \Omega : \Lambda = 0\}$ is a smooth curve Γ such that $\Omega \setminus \Gamma = D_1 \cup D_2$, where D_1 and D_2 are disjoint open subsets of Ω, on which, of course, Λ is positive. By Theorem 19.2, there exist at most two solutions $\left[u_1^1, u_1^2\right]^T$ to Eq. (19.2) of class C^2 over D_1 and at most two solutions (u_2^1, u_2^2) to Eq. (19.2) of class C^2 over D_2, respectively.

We do not exclude the possibility that $u_i^1 = u_i^2$ for either $i = 1$, or $i = 2$, or $i = 1$ and $i = 2$. Clearly, the restriction of u to D_i coincides with either u_i^1 or u_i^2 for $i = 1, 2$.

Conversely, suppose that for some i and j with $i, j = 1, 2$ and some constant c the limits

$$\begin{aligned} &\lim_{[x',y']^T \in D_1 \to [x,y]^T \in \Gamma} u_1^i(x',y') = \\ &\lim_{[x',y']^T \in D_2 \to [x,y]^T \in \Gamma} (u_2^j(x',y') + c) = g^{ij}(x,y) \end{aligned}$$

exist for each $[x,y]^T \in \Gamma$. Set

$$v_{ij}(x,y) = \begin{cases} u_1^i(x,y) & \text{if } [x,y]^T \in D_1 \\ g^{ij}(x,y) & \text{if } [x,y]^T \in \Gamma \\ u_2^j(x,y) + c & \text{if } [x,y]^T \in D_2 \end{cases} \tag{19.50}$$

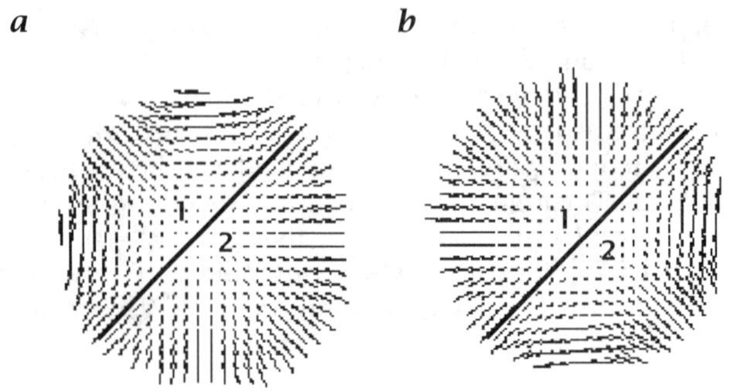

*Figure 19.17: Needle map pair illustrating the surface normal pairs of a sphere calculated in an albedo dependent 2S PSM. The straight-line segment drawn in bold illustrates locations of unique solutions (set Γ). The labels identify the regions D_1 of u_1^i and D_2 of u_2^j: **a** pair of positive solutions; **b** pair of negative solutions.*

and suppose that for each $[x, y]^T \in \Gamma$ the function v_{ij} is of class C^2. Then v_{ij} is a class C^2 solution of Eq. (19.2) over Ω and in such a case we say that the functions u_1^i and u_2^j *bifurcate* along Γ in the C^2 class. It is clear that, up to a constant, one can define in this way at most four solutions of class C^2 to Eq. (19.2) over Ω.

As an example, assume a synthetic sphere with a radius of 100 pixels and Lambertian reflectance maps having the illumination directions $\boldsymbol{p} = [-0.3, -0.3, -1]^T$ and $\boldsymbol{q} = [0.3, 0.3, -1]^T$. Possible solutions of 2S PSM are shown in Fig. 19.17. The set Γ is shown as a straight-line segment. In region D_1 lying left of the straight-line segment the negative solutions are the correct gradients, whereas in region D_2 the positive solutions correspond to the intended solution. The other solutions are not integrable, respectively. Each of the two regions contains approximately 12,000 image points. Thus, for the synthetic sphere we can robustly distinguish between the integrable and the nonintegrable solution.

For image pairs of more complex objects such as the synthetic Lambertian Mozart statue that was already used in the previous section the selection of the correct solution is more difficult. Illumination directions $\boldsymbol{p}$ and $\boldsymbol{q}$ having the spherical coordinates

$$\sigma(\boldsymbol{p}) = \sigma(\boldsymbol{q}) = 20°, \ \theta(\boldsymbol{p}) = -150° \text{ and } \theta(\boldsymbol{q}) = -30°$$

were chosen to render the statue. The two irradiance images of the Mozart statue are displayed in Fig. 19.13 (center **b** and right **c** picture). For a discrete image a threshold has to be defined that indicates which orientations are considered as belonging to the symmetry plane. A

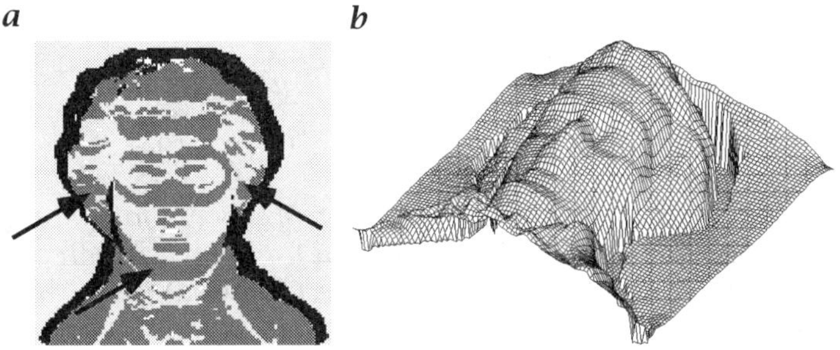

Figure 19.18: ***a*** *Labeled image of a synthetic Mozart statue. For the coding of the four gray values refer to the text. The arrows indicate regions with incorrectly selected surface normals;* ***b*** *3-D plot of the recovered Mozart statue where the Frankot-Chellappa algorithm was used for gradient map integration.*

simple and useful criterion is to measure the angle that is subtended by the symmetry plane and the examined orientation. If the angle is smaller than a threshold, then the solution is classified as being unique. A threshold of 10° was applied for the Mozart statue.

The left picture of Fig. 19.18 shows a labeled segmentation result. In the black regions one of the two irradiances is zero so that no orientation can be determined. The light-gray regions characterize locations whose orientations were classified as belonging to the symmetry plane. Dark-gray regions represent locations for which the integrability criterion could be calculated. White regions indicate locations that were left untouched because they are too close to the boundary, the irradiances are too low, or the gradients are too steep.

A wrong selection of a positive or negative solution occurs in some regions. The largest areas where the wrong solution was selected are indicated by arrows. The right-hand picture of Fig. 19.18 shows the recovered surface of the Mozart statue. Because for integration of the surface the global Frankot-Chellappa method [26] and [4] was used, the incorrectly recovered surface normals have only a minor effect on the overall result. Visible errors occur at the chin where a double chin appears. The recovery result can be improved by adaptive segmentation.

The next result establishes necessary and sufficient conditions that a bifurcation takes place (Kozera [7])

Theorem 19.7 *Let* $\boldsymbol{p} = [0, 0, -1]^T$ *and let* $\boldsymbol{q} = [q_1, q_2, q_3]^T$ *be such that* $q_1^2 + q_2^2 > 0$ *and* $\|\boldsymbol{q}\| = 1$. *For a pair of* C^1 *class functions* E_1 *and* E_2 *defining a system Eq. (19.2), suppose that the set* $\{[x, y]^T \in \Omega : \Lambda = 0\}$ *is a smooth curve* Γ *such that* $\Omega \setminus \Gamma = D_1 \cup D_2$, *where* D_1 *and* D_2 *are disjoint open subsets of* Ω. *Assume that there exist two different solutions of class* C^2 *to Eq. (19.2) over* D_1 *and two different solutions of class* C^2 *to Eq. (19.2) over* D_2, *respectively. Let* u *be a solution over* D_1 *and* v *be a* *solution over D_2 such that*

$$\begin{aligned} g(x,y) &= \lim_{[x',y']^T \in D_1 \to [x,y]^T \in \Gamma} u(x',y') \\ &= \lim_{[x',y']^T \in D_2 \to [x,y]^T \in \Gamma} (v(x',y') + c) \end{aligned}$$

for some choice of constant c. Assume, moreover, that the triplet of functions $[u,v,g]^T$ defines in Eq. (19.50) a C^1 class function z over Ω. If $q_1^2 - q_2^2 \neq 0$, then the function z is of class C^2 over Ω if and only if, for each $[x,y]^T \in \Gamma$

$$\begin{aligned} \lim_{(x',y') \in D_1 \to [x,y]^T \in \Gamma} u_{xx}(x',y') &= \lim_{(x',y') \in D_2 \to [x,y]^T \in \Gamma} v_{xx}(x',y') \\ \lim_{(x',y') \in D_1 \to [x,y]^T \in \Gamma} u_{yy}(x',y') &= \lim_{(x',y') \in D_2 \to [x,y]^T \in \Gamma} v_{yy}(x',y') \end{aligned}$$

If $q_1^2 - q_2^2 = 0$, then the function z is of class C^2 over Ω if and only if, for each $[x,y]^T \in \Gamma$, either

$$\begin{aligned} \lim_{(x',y') \in D_1 \to [x,y]^T \in \Gamma} u_{xx}(x',y') &= \lim_{(x',y') \in D_2 \to [x,y]^T \in \Gamma} v_{xx}(x',y') \\ \lim_{(x',y') \in D_1 \to [x,y]^T \in \Gamma} u_{xy}(x',y') &= \lim_{(x',y') \in D_2 \to [x,y]^T \in \Gamma} v_{xy}(x',y') \end{aligned}$$

or

$$\begin{aligned} \lim_{(x',y') \in D_1 \to [x,y]^T \in \Gamma} u_{yy}(x',y') &= \lim_{(x',y') \in D_2 \to [x,y]^T \in \Gamma} v_{yy}(x',y') \\ \lim_{(x',y') \in D_1 \to [x,y]^T \in \Gamma} u_{xy}(x',y') &= \lim_{(x',y') \in D_2 \to [x,y]^T \in \Gamma} v_{xy}(x',y') \end{aligned}$$

It should be emphasized that a similar result establishing sufficient conditions for C^1 class bifurcations can be derived. As shown in [7] such bifurcations are generically feasible. Furthermore, it can also be proved that, if there exist exactly two C^2 class solutions to Eq. (19.2), defined over D_1 and D_2, then only an even number of C^2 class bifurcations is possible. This combined with the case of having exactly one C^2 solution over D_1 and/or D_2 permits having either zero, one, two, or four C^2 class solutions to Eq. (19.2), defined globally over Ω. Recall, however, that the existence of a unique solution of class C^2, over D_1 and D_2, is generically ensured (see the subsection covering the case when $\Lambda > 0$). Therefore, a global generic uniqueness result for C^2 class functions, considered over Ω can also be ascertained.

An interested reader is referred to [28] for a more detailed discussion of this case. We present now an example in which a different number of C^2/C^1 class bifurcations appear in 2S PSM.

Example 19.3: One bifurcation—a generic case

Assume that $\boldsymbol{p} = [0,0,-1]^T$ and $\boldsymbol{q} = [q_1, q_2, q_3]^T$ are linearly independent and that $\|\boldsymbol{q}\| = 1$. It is easy to show that for the corresponding two images of a Lambertian hemisphere

$$u_h(x,y) = -\sqrt{1 - x^2 - y^2}$$

the function Λ vanishes along $\Gamma = \{[x,y]^T \in \Omega : q_2x - q_1y = 0\}$. Clearly, the curve Γ decomposes Ω into two disjoints subdomains D_1 and D_2, over which Λ is positive. As the condition Eq. (19.42) is not satisfied by u_h over both D_1 and D_2, Theorem 19.3 ensures that there exists exactly one C^2 class solution over each D_1 and D_2 that is u_h. Thus, there can be maximum one C^2 class solution over Ω, subject to the existence of a successful C^2 class bifurcation along the curve Γ. As the hemisphere u_h constitutes a global C^2 class solution over Ω, the existence of at least one C^2 class bifurcation is therefore ascertained. Summing up, two images of a Lambertian hemisphere can be uniquely interpreted within the set of C^2 class functions.

Two bifurcations: Consider two image irradiance equations introduced in Example 19.2. Let Ω be a simply connected set containing the $D_1 = \{[x,y]^T \in \Omega : x < y\}$, $D_2 = \{[x,y]^T \in \Omega : x > y\}$, and $\Gamma = \{[x,y]^T \in \Omega : x = y\}$. As mentioned before Λ vanishes along Γ and, moreover, there exist exactly two C^2 class solutions to Eq. (19.48), over D_1 and D_2, defined as follows: $u^+(x,y) = xy$ and $u^-(x,y) = (x^2+y^2)/2$. An easy inspection shows that only two C^2 class bifurcations succeed. Namely, by using Eq. (19.50), $u(x,y) = xy$ and $v(x,y) = (x^2+y^2)/2$ yield two C^2 class functions defined globally over entire Ω. The remaining two other functions (introduced in Eq. (19.50))

$$w(x,y) = \begin{cases} xy & \text{if } [x,y]^T \in D_1 \\ x^2 & \text{if } [x,y]^T \in \Gamma \\ (x^2+y^2)/2 & \text{if } [x,y]^T \in D_2 \end{cases}$$

$$z(x,y) = \begin{cases} (x^2+y^2)/2 & \text{if } [x,y]^T \in D_1 \\ x^2 & \text{if } [x,y]^T \in \Gamma \\ xy & \text{if } [x,y]^T \in D_2 \end{cases}$$

are not of class C^2 along the line Γ. A simple verification shows, however, that both functions w and z are still C^1 class functions over Γ. Hence there exist exactly two (four) C^2 (C^1) class solutions to Eq. (19.48) considered over entire Ω.

Four bifurcations: Let $\boldsymbol{p} = [0,0,-1]^T$ and $\boldsymbol{q} = [0, 1/\sqrt{2}, -1/\sqrt{2}]^T$, and let $E_1(x,y) = (1+x^8)^{-1/2}$ and $E_2(x,y) = (2(1+x^8))^{-1/2}$ be defined over $\Omega = \Re^2$. A straightforward calculation shows that for the corresponding two image irradiance equations a function Λ vanishes only along the line $x = 0$, that is, over the y–axis. Moreover, there exist, over both $D_1 = \{[x,y]^T \in \Re^2 : x > 0\}$ and $D_2 = \{[x,y]^T \in \Re^2 : x < 0\}$, exactly two C^2 class solutions: $u(x,y) = x^5/5$ and $v(x,y) = -x^5/5$. It is a matter of simple calculation to show that four functions: v_{11}, v_{12}, v_{21}, and v_{22} (defined with the aid of Eq. (19.50)) are of class C^2 over Γ. Therefore, there exist exactly four C^2 class solutions over entire Ω. Note that, if Ω does not contain y–axis, then there exist only two C^2 class solutions to the corresponding 2S PSM problem, namely, u and v, and in this case there is no possibility of having bifurcations.

It is evident now, that bifurcations can either reduce or increase the number of global C^2/C^1 class solutions over the entire domain Ω. However, a reduction case, due to the condition Eq. (19.42), is generic. Note finally, that if none of the integrability conditions is fulfilled or none of the bifurcations succeeds, a pair of such spurious images cannot be generated by a genuine Lambertian surface (see [7]).

19.4.2 Albedo-independent analysis

As discussed for Eq. (19.36), all gradients that are consistent with any 2S PSM irradiance pair can be calculated by using Eq. (19.36). If we look at the corresponding points on the Gaussian sphere, then every pair of positive irradiances restricts the orientations to a half of a great circle because the latter is represented in the gradient space by a straight line. In contrast to the gradient space the representation of orientations using the Gaussian sphere is independent from the viewer direction $\boldsymbol{v}$. Therefore, the number of solutions reduces implicitly from a great circle to a half of a great circle because only those orientations are relevant.

The perimeter of the circles can be seen as a measure of the cardinality of the orientations that are consistent with the irradiances. The larger the irradiance value, the smaller the perimeter of the circle. The irradiance E and the perimeter of the circle are related through the equation

$$U = 2\pi \left(1 - \left(\frac{E}{E_0 \rho}\right)^2\right) \tag{19.51}$$

On the other hand, the perimeter of the circle of albedo-independent 2S methods remains always equal to 2π for all irradiance pairs and therefore it is in general larger than the circles in SFS methods while keeping the viewer direction and the restriction of the orientations by the illumination directions in mind. Besides the surface orientation, another unknown variable, the albedo ρ, exists for 2S methods. Neighboring orientations on the surface are often linked together through smoothness assumptions as discussed in Section 19.4.1. From a formal point of view, such assumptions would also be sensible for the albedo. But for real-world objects discontinuous albedo changes are more likely. Usually, discontinuous albedo variations occur more often than smooth color-value changes or gray-value changes.

Assume that a unique gradient map of a Lambertian surface has to be recovered from a pair of irradiance images without knowing the albedo value ρ. Assume that the two illumination directions $\boldsymbol{s}_1$ and $\boldsymbol{s}_2$ are known associated with the irradiance images.

Lee and Rosenfeld [31] propose a 3-D shape recovery method for Lambertian surfaces that can be approximated locally by spheres. Under the assumption of a locally spherical surface it can be shown that the possible orientations can be restricted to a straight line in the gradient space for a given single image irradiance value E. This is even possible without knowledge of the $E_0\rho$ term. The restriction to a straight line follows by using the irradiance changes for the considered image point. It can be shown that this straight line can be represented by the equation

$$E_y p - E_x q = \tan(\sigma(\mathbf{s}))\,(\cos(\theta(\mathbf{s}))E_y - \sin(\theta(\mathbf{s}))E_x) \qquad (19.52)$$

As for linear reflectance maps two irradiances are sufficient to recover the gradient $[p,q]^T = [u_x,u_y]^T$ uniquely by intersecting two straight lines for each image point. This solution is not only independent of the albedo ρ, it can be calculated so that the solution becomes independent of the absolute irradiances of the light sources, as well. In practice this makes the determination of the illumination parameters easier. As a conclusion the knowledge of the ratio E_{01}/E_{02} of the irradiances values is sufficient. For the numerical determination of the partial derivatives of the image irradiance function $E(x,y)$ it has to be assumed that the albedo ρ does not change in the immediate neighborhood of an image point.

19.5 Theoretical framework for shape from shading

Approaches in shading-based shape recovery transform measured irradiance values into data about surface functions u. These transformations are based on models about light sources, sensors, surface geometry or surface reflectance. Within a given context the theoretical fundamentals are specified by problems as:

(i) existence of solutions u within a class of surface functions (as C^1 or C^2, or convex surfaces) and with respect to used models;

(ii) uniqueness of solutions u;

(iii) analytic or geometric relationships between several solutions (as possible decompositions into "similar" components);

(iv) methods for calculating such solutions u;

(v) algorithms for implementing such methods; and

(vi) features of these algorithms as stability, domain of influence, or convergence of iterative solutions towards the proper solution u.

So far, we reviewed results related to topics (i) ... (v) in this chapter.

As an illustration to results to topic (vi) we discuss briefly the convergence of algorithms for *linear SFS* (see [32]).

We assume discrete irradiance values $E(x,y)$ at exactly all grid point positions within a rectangular domain Ω. The grid resolution is specified by a grid constant 2^{-r}, for $r = 0, 1, 2, \ldots$ and the resulting grid points are called *r-grid points*. We assume $N_r \times N_r$ r-grid points in Ω, say, with $N_r = 2^r(N_0 + 1) - 1$. These measured image irradiances are assumed to correspond to reflectance properties of a projected object surface satisfying a *linear image irradiance equation*

$$a\frac{\partial u}{\partial x}(x, y) + b\frac{\partial u}{\partial y}(x, y) = E(x, y) \tag{19.53}$$

We assume an integrable function u on Ω and $(a, b) \neq (0, 0)$. The task is to calculate a function u over Ω based on the available input set of discrete irradiance values $E(x, y)$ at r-grid points, and based on a specified boundary condition, where u satisfies Eq. (19.53).

More precisely, we are interested in a numerical solution of the following *Cauchy problem*: If $\mathrm{sgn}(ab) \geq 0$ then

$$u(x, 0) = f(x), \quad \text{for} \quad 0 \leq x \leq N_0 + 1$$

is given as boundary condition, and if $\mathrm{sgn}(ab) < 0$ then

$$u(x, N_0 + 1) = f(x), \quad \text{for} \quad 0 \leq x \leq N_0 + 1$$

is given. Furthermore, also

$$\chi(0, y) = g(y), \quad \text{for} \quad 0 \leq y \leq N_0 + 1$$

is assumed to be known.

The functions f, g are integrable on $[0, N_0 + 1]$ and satisfy $f(0) = g(0)$ if $\mathrm{sgn}(ab) \geq 0$, or $f(0) = g(N_0 + 1)$ if $\mathrm{sgn}(ab) < 0$. This Cauchy problem is given in "digital form," that is, only values at r-grid point positions are given for functions $p = u_x$, $q = u_y$, E, f, and g.

A linear partial differential equation may be solved with the aid of the finite difference method. Assuming normed function spaces on Ω the sequence of r-grids allows us to define corresponding normed r-grid spaces; see Kozera and Klette [32] for details. A *finite difference scheme* (FDS) is defined for all r-grids, for $r = 0, 1, 2, \ldots$, and basically it characterizes an operator R_r mapping an unknown function defined on Ω, as u in our case, into a function u_r

$$R_r(u) = u_r, \quad \text{with} \quad u_r(i, j) \approx u(i2^{-r}, j2^{-r})$$

defined on r-grid points that is considered to be an approximation of the unknown function.

For example, applying a (simple) *forward difference approach* together with Taylor's expansion yields

$$\left.\frac{\partial u}{\partial x}\right|_r^{(i,j)} = \frac{u_r(i + 1, j) - u(i, j)}{2^{-r}} + O(2^{-r})$$

in the x-direction, and

$$\left.\frac{\partial u}{\partial y}\right|_r^{(i,j)} = \frac{u_r(i,j+1) - u(i,j)}{2^{-r}} + O(2^{-r})$$

in the y-direction. A (simple) *backward difference approach* in x-direction is given by

$$\left.\frac{\partial u}{\partial x}\right|_r^{(i,j)} = \frac{u(i,j) - u(i-1,j)}{2^{-r}} + O(2^{-r})$$

just to mention a further example. The differences are normalized by the distance 2^{-r} between neighboring r-grid points, in x- or in y-direction. Larger neighborhoods could be used for defining more complex forward or backward approaches, and further approaches may also be based on symmetric, or unbalanced neighborhoods of r-grid points. Finally, a finite difference scheme is characterized by selecting one approach for the $x-$, and another one for the y-direction.

The *forward-forward FDS* transforms the given differential equation into

$$a\frac{u_r(i+1,j) - u_r(i,j)}{2^{-r}} + b\frac{u_r(i,j+1) - u_r(i,j)}{2^{-r}} + O(2^{-r}) = E(i2^{-r}, j2^{-r})$$

and this equation may be simplified as

$$\tilde{u}_r(i,j+1) = \left(1 + \tfrac{a}{b}\right)\tilde{u}_r(i,j) - \tfrac{a}{b}\tilde{u}_r(i+1,j) + \tfrac{2^{-r}}{b}E(i2^{-r}, j2^{-r})$$

where $\tilde{u}_r(i,j)$ is used as an approximation for function $u_r(i,j)$. The *backward-forward FDS* leads to

$$\tilde{u}_r(i,j+1) = \left(1 - \tfrac{a}{b}\right)\tilde{u}_r(i,j) + \tfrac{a}{b}\tilde{u}_r(i-1,j) + \tfrac{2^{-r}}{b}E(i2^{-r}, j2^{-r})$$

the *forward-backward FDS* leads to

$$\tilde{u}_r(i+1,j) = \left(1 - \tfrac{b}{a}\right)\tilde{u}_r(i,j) + \tfrac{b}{a}\tilde{u}_r(i,j-1) + \tfrac{2^{-r}}{a}E(i2^{-r}, j2^{-r})$$

and the *backward-backward FDS* leads to

$$\tilde{u}_r(i,j) = \tfrac{1}{1+c}\tilde{u}_r(i,j-1) + \tfrac{c}{1+c}\tilde{u}_r(i-1,j) + \tfrac{2^{-r}}{b(1+c)}E(i2^{-r}, j2^{-r})$$

where $c = \frac{a}{b} \neq -1$, and for $c = -1$ to

$$\tilde{u}_r(i-1,j) = \tilde{u}_r(i,j-1) + \tfrac{2^{-r}}{b}E(i2^{-r}, j2^{-r})$$

These schemes are studied in Kozera and Klette [32].

A finite difference scheme is *consistent* with an initial boundary value problem if the error of approximation in representing the original problem converges to zero as $2^{-r} \to 0$. The listed four schemes are consistent. A finite difference scheme is *convergent* to the solution u_r (if it exists) if the digitization error converges to zero as $2^{-r} \to 0$. A further notion of stability for linear difference schemes was defined by *Rjabenki* and *Filippov*. A linear difference scheme is *RF stable* if the operators

$$\left\{R_r^{-1}\right\}_{r=0,1,2,\ldots}$$

are *uniformly bounded* as $2^{-r} \to 0$. A consistent and RF stable finite difference scheme is convergent to the solution of the given Cauchy problem if such a solution exists.

For the convergence analysis of the given schemes let $c = a/b$ assuming that $b \neq 0$, and $d = b/a$ assuming that $a \neq 0$.

Theorem 19.8 [32] *The forward-forward FDS is RF stable iff* $-1 \le c \le 0$. *The backward-forward FDS is RF stable iff* $0 \le c \le 1$. *The forward-backward FDS is RF stable iff* $0 \le d \le 1$. *The backward-backward FDS is RF stable iff* $c \ge 0$ *or* $c = -1$.

Consequently, in these positive cases the sequences of functions

$$\{\tilde{u}_r\}_{r=0,1,2,\ldots}$$

are convergent to the solution of the specified Cauchy problem.

19.6 Shape from shading

The SFS problem is the hardest in the class of shading-based shape recovery problems. The given information is a single image E and a reflectance model [33, 34].

It was shown by [1] that the SFS problem for a Lambertian surface with constant albedo corresponds to that of solving the following first-order partial differential equation:

$$E(x, y) = \frac{p_1 u_x + p_2 u_y - p_3}{\sqrt{p_1^2 + p_2^2 + p_3^2}\sqrt{u_x^2 + u_y^2 + 1}} \tag{19.54}$$

defined over a domain Ω. We consider here the case when the albedo is constant; see Eq. (19.54). Given $0 \le E(x, y) \le 1$, the questions of the existence and uniqueness of solutions to Eq. (19.54) arise naturally. Existence corresponds to the problem of whether a given shading pattern with intensity between 0 and 1 is generated by a genuine Lambertian surface. Uniqueness corresponds to that of whether a shading pattern is due to one and only one Lambertian shape (given up to a constant). We shall analyze in this section only the case when $\mathbf{s} = [0, 0, -1]^T$. Then one can rewrite Eq. (19.54) as the *eikonal equation*

$$u_x^2 + u_y^2 = \mathcal{E}(x, y) \tag{19.55}$$

with $\mathcal{E}(x, y) = E(x, y)^{-2} - 1$.

In this section we present first two different classes of images for which there are no genuine shapes. In the second part of this section we refer to the uniqueness problem for the eikonal equation Eq. (19.55). Lastly, we briefly discuss a number of methods recovering the unknown surface from its single image.

19.6.1 Images without solution

Let R be either a positive number or $+\infty$. Let f be a nonnegative continuous function on the interval $[0, R)$ vanishing exactly at zero. Consider Eq. (19.55) with

$$\mathcal{E}(x, y) = f(\sqrt{x^2 + y^2}) \tag{19.56}$$

given over $D(R) = \{[x, y]^T \in \Re^2 : x^2 + y^2 < R^2\}$. With this special form of image, the class of circularly symmetric solutions is of the form $\pm U + k$, where

$$U(x, y) = \int_0^{\sqrt{x^2+y^2}} \sqrt{f(\sigma)}\, d\sigma \tag{19.57}$$

A condition on f guaranteeing that all solutions to the corresponding eikonal equation are unbounded may readily be formulated. Clearly, in the class of circularly symmetric solutions, this sufficient condition is

$$\int_0^R \sqrt{f(\sigma)}\, d\sigma = +\infty \tag{19.58}$$

It is less evident, though true, that the same condition is sufficient in the general case. In fact, we have the following (see [35, 36]):

Theorem 19.9 *Let f be a nonnegative continuous function on $[0, R)$ vanishing exactly at zero and satisfying Eq. (19.58). Then there is no bounded C^1 solution in $D(R)$ to Eq. (19.55) with E given by $E(x, y) = f(\sqrt{x^2 + y^2})$.*

Interestingly, condition Eq. (19.58) is not only sufficient but also necessary for the unboundedness of all solutions to the equation in question. We have the following theorem (see [35, 36]):

Theorem 19.10 *Let f be a nonnegative continuous function in $[0, R)$ vanishing exactly at zero and satisfying $\int_0^R \sqrt{f(\sigma)}\, d\sigma < +\infty$. Then every solution in $D(R)$ to Eq. (19.55) with $E(x, y) = f(\sqrt{x^2 + y^2})$ is bounded.*

Observe that whether the integral $\int_0^R \sqrt{f(\sigma)}\, d\sigma$ is finite or infinite depends exclusively on the behavior of f near R. The integral will be infinite if, for example, $f(r)$ diverges to infinity sufficiently rapidly as r tends to R. This means that, in the context of real images of Lambertian surfaces illuminated by an overhead point light-source, a circularly symmetric image cannot be derived from a genuine shape if it gets dark too quickly as the image boundary is approached.

We now establish the existence of images E for which there is no solution whatsoever to Eq. (19.55); see also [37, 38].

Theorem 19.11 *Let Ω be a bounded open-connected subset of the $\Re^2$ with boundary $\partial\Omega$ being a piecewise C^1 curve of length $\ell_{\partial\Omega}$. Let $[x_0, y_0]^T$ be a point in Ω and r be a positive number such that the closed disk $\bar{D}(x_0, y_0, r)$ of radius r centered at $[x_0, y_0]^T$ is contained in Ω. Suppose E is a nonnegative continuous function on the closure of Ω, positive in Ω, such that*

$$4r\sqrt{E_1} > \ell_{\partial\Omega}\sqrt{E_2} \quad \text{with} \quad \begin{aligned} E_1 &= \min\{E(x,y) : [x,y]^T \in \bar{D}(x_0,y_0,r)\} \\ E_2 &= \max\{E(x,y) : [x,y]^T \in \partial\Omega\} \end{aligned} \tag{19.59}$$

Then there is no C^1 solution to Eq. (19.55) in Ω.

Note that the theorem is of local character: if Ω is a subset of a domain Δ and E is a nonnegative function on Δ whose restriction to Ω satisfies Eq. (19.59) for some choice of $\bar{D}(x_0, y_0, r)$ in Ω, then, obviously, there is no C^1 solution to Eq. (19.55) in Δ. Reformulated in terms of Lambertian shading, this locality property can be expressed as saying that no genuine image can admit too dark a spot on too bright a background, assuming that the background does not contain a point having unit brightness. The precise balance between the qualifications "too dark" and "too bright" is, of course, given by condition Eq. (19.59).

19.6.2 Ambiguous shading patterns

The second part of this section refers to the uniqueness problem for the eikonal equation Eq. (19.55). Uniqueness of this kind has been demonstrated in the case where $E(x, y) = (x^2 + y^2)(1 - x^2 - y^2)^{-1}$. Deift and Sylvester [39], proved that $\pm(1 - x^2 - y^2)^{1/2} + k$ are the only C^2 solutions to this equation over the unit disk $D(1)$. All of these solutions are hemispherical in shape. In an effort to obtain a more general result, Bruss [40] asserted the following: if $D(R)$ is the disk in the xy-plane with radius R centered at the origin, and f is a continuous function on

$[0, R)$ of class C^2 over $(0, R)$ satisfying the following conditions:

(i) $f(0) = 0$ and $f(r) > 0$ for $0<r<R$;
(ii) $\lim_{r \to 0} f'(r) = 0, \lim_{r \to 0} f''(r)$ exists and is positive; and
(iii) $\lim_{r \to R} f(r) = +\infty$.

Then all solutions of class C^2 to Eq. (19.55) in $D(R)$ with

$$E(x, y) = f(\sqrt{x^2 + y^2})$$

take the form

$$\pm \int_0^{\sqrt{x^2+y^2}} \sqrt{f(\sigma)}\, d\sigma + k \tag{19.60}$$

and thus are circularly symmetric with common shape. It is possible to show that Bruss' claim is invalid (for the construction of the specific counterexample, see [36, 37]). Similarly, in Kozera [41] it was recently shown that Brooks' uniqueness results [42, 43] concerning the images of the Lambertian plane and hemisphere have been erroneously proved. Some new uniqueness results have also been established in Oliensis [44] and Rouy and Tourin [45]. It should be noted, however, that these results introduce additional uniqueness enforcement conditions that cannot be easily obtained as the initial data from a mere single image.

We shall present now a number of surface reconstruction algorithms for a single-image shape recovery and will briefly discuss their intrinsic limitations.

19.6.3 Method of characteristic strips

This method is based on the classical approach from the theory of the first-order partial differential equations applied to the equation

$$F(x, y, u, p, q) = 0 \tag{19.61}$$

where $F(x, y, u, p, q) = p^2 + q^2 - \mathcal{E}(x, y)$ over image Ω. This was first introduced in the shape-from-shading literature by [1]. For a more detailed theory discussing the general case of F involving n-independent variables, an interested reader is referred to [30]. We shall briefly now outline the basics of the *method of characteristic strips* in the context of the shape-from-shading problem.

Given an initial curve $\gamma \subset \Re^2$ in the image (image boundary) Ω and surface height over γ, the unknown surface $S(t, s)$ is generated along the so-called *base characteristics* $[x(t, s), y(t, s)]^T$ expressed in a parametric form depending on (t, s)-variables (see the first two equations in Eq. (19.62)). Here, variable s parameterizes initial curve γ and variable

t parameterizes the evolution of the surface $S(t,s)$ along base characteristic direction (i. e., whenever s is fixed). In other words, the surface S is swept out by the family of characteristics of the form

$$t \to [x(t,s), y(t,s), u(t,s), p(t,s), q(t,s)]^T$$

satisfying the corresponding system of five ordinary differential equations (called also characteristic equations)

$$\begin{aligned} x_t(t,s) &= 2p(t,s) \\ y_t(t,s) &= 2q(t,s) \end{aligned} \qquad \begin{aligned} u_t(t,s) &= 2\mathcal{E}(x(t,s), y(t,s)) \\ p_t(t,s) &= \mathcal{E}_x(x(t,s), y(t,s)) \\ q_t(t,s) &= \mathcal{E}_y(x(t,s), y(t,s)) \end{aligned} \tag{19.62}$$

It is assumed here that the function u defined over *generalized initial curve* $\tilde{\gamma} \in R^5$

$$\begin{aligned} x(0,s) &= x_0(s) \\ y(0,s) &= y_0(s) \end{aligned} \qquad \begin{aligned} u(0,s) &= u_0(s) \\ p(0,s) &= p_0(s) \\ q(0,s) &= q_0(s) \end{aligned} \tag{19.63}$$

satisfies an eikonal equation and a chain-rule along $\tilde{\gamma}$

$$\begin{aligned} p_0^2(s) + q_0^2(s) &= \mathcal{E}(x_0(s), y_0(s)) \\ \dot{u}_0(s) &= p_0(s)\dot{x}_0(s) + q_0(s)\dot{y}_0(s) \end{aligned} \tag{19.64}$$

and that the curve γ obeys the so-called *noncharacteristic condition*

$$\dot{x}_0 F_q - \dot{y}_0 F_p \neq 0 \tag{19.65}$$

for all $[x_0(s), y_0(s)]^T \in \gamma(s)$. The last condition excludes the case when the initial curve γ coincides with the base characteristic direction. In such a situation the solution would collapse to a single curve in $\Re^3$. Note also that, if $p_0(s_0)$ and $q_0(s_0)$ are *a priori* given, then by using implicit function theorem and condition Eq. (19.65) one can find $p_0(s)$ and $q_0(s)$, defined in some neighborhood of s_0. Assuming that γ is non-characteristic and that F and γ are of class C^2, the following result (due to Cauchy; see, for example, [30]) can be established:

Theorem 19.12 *There exists, in some strip neighborhood of* γ*, exactly one* C^1 *solution* $[x(t,s), y(t,s), u(t,s), p(t,s), q(t,s)]^T$ *of the Cauchy problem (Eq. (19.62) and Eq. (19.63)) such that*

$$\tilde{u}(x(t,s), y(t,s)) = u(t(x,y)s(x,y))$$

defines a unique C^2 *solution to the problem (Eq. (19.61))*

With the aid of the foregoing theorem, one can transform a given first-order partial differential equation into an equivalent system of five mutually coupled ordinary differential equations. Such transformation, in general, renders still a diffucult task for finding an exact analytic solution to a corresponding Cauchy problem, Eqs. (19.62) and (19.63). To see it, note that the unknown functions appearing in left-hand sides of Eq. (19.62), reappear also in the right-hand sides of the same system in a nonlinear form. The alternative, is to resort, for example, to the finite-difference approximations of the derivatives applied to the left-hand sides of the system Eq. (19.62). Consequently, by using a forward-difference derivative approximation, the following sequential scheme can be derived:

$$\begin{aligned} x(t^{n+1},s^k) &= x(t^n,s^k) + 2\Delta t p(t^n,s^k) \\ y(t^{n+1},s^k) &= y(t^n,s^k) + 2\Delta t q(t^n,s^k) \\ u(t^{n+1},s^k) &= u(t^n,s^k) + 2\Delta t \mathcal{E}(x(t^n,s^k),y(t^n,s^k)) \\ p(t^{n+1},s^k) &= p(t^n,s^k) + \Delta t \mathcal{E}_x(x(t^n,s^k),y(t^n,s^k)) \\ q(t^{n+1},s^k) &= q(t^n,s^k) + \Delta t \mathcal{E}_y(x(t^n,s^k),y(t^n,s^k)) \end{aligned} \tag{19.66}$$

where each $\left[t^n,s^k\right]^T$ represents the corresponding point on the grid expressed in the $[t,s]^T$ coordinate system. It is clear that given Eq. (19.66) and Dirichlet and Neumann boundary conditions Eq. (19.63) one can sequentially find a numerical solution to Eq. (19.62). The following convergence and stability results for the forementioned numerical scheme can be established (see, for example, Gear [46]):

Theorem 19.13 *Assume that function $\mathcal{E} \in C^2(\bar{\Omega})$ is defined over compact $\bar{\Omega}$. Then, if $0 \le t \le b$, the numerical solution to Eq. (19.66) is convergent to the solution $[x(t,s),y(t,s),u(t,s),p(t,s),q(t,s)]^T$ of the Cauchy problem, Eqs. (19.62) and (19.63). Moreover, a corresponding finite-difference Eq. (19.66) is stable with the stability upper-bound constant equal to e^{bL}, where*

$$\begin{aligned} \alpha_1 &= 2\sup_{[x,y]^T\in\Omega}\{|\mathcal{E}_x(x,y)| + |\mathcal{E}_y(x,y)|\} \\ \alpha_2 &= \sup_{[x,y]^T\in\Omega}\{|\mathcal{E}_{xx}(x,y)| + |\mathcal{E}_{yx}(x,y)|\} \\ \alpha_3 &= \sup_{[x,y]^T\in\Omega}\{|\mathcal{E}_{xy}(x,y)| + |\mathcal{E}_{yy}(x,y)|\} \end{aligned}$$

and constant $L = \max_{1\le i\le 3}\{2,|\alpha_i|\}$.

The main problem with the method of characteristic strips stems from the fact that the surface should not be reconstructed over $[t,s]^T$ coordinate system but in the standard Cartesian $[x,y]^T$ coordinate system. The corresponding transformation between two coordinate systems usually changes the rectangular grid (expressed in $[t,s]^T$ variables) to the curvilinear Cartesian grid. Hence, the coverage of the image domain by base characteristics $[x(t,s), y(t,s)]^T$ tends to be uneven, resulting in an inhomogeneous density of the reconstructed surface. The next problem is that the coverage of the image domain will only be extensive if the initial curve and surface are appropriately chosen. Furthermore, the method is not amenable to parallelism and should not be applied in the neighborhood of the occluding boundary, where constant $L = \infty$. Note, however, that for any fixed constant L, a strong stability condition can be enforced by shrinking Δt, respectively. The latter ensures that the computed numerical solution to Eq. (19.66) is "close" to the ideal solution to Eq. (19.66), and thus, by the last convergence result, "close" to the solution of the Cauchy problem, Eqs. (19.62) and (19.63). Finally, it should be pointed out that the method of characteristic strips requires Dirichlet and Neumann boundary conditions, which, in the case if not *a priori* given, might not be easily obtainable from a mere image Ω.

We close this section with an example illustrating some difficulties that might appear in solving the Cauchy problem, Eqs. (19.62) and (19.63), analytically even in special simple cases of eikonal equation.

Example 19.4:

Consider the following eikonal equation

$$u_x^2(x,y) + u_y^2(x,y) = c \tag{19.67}$$

where $c > 0$ is an arbitrary constant. With no extra boundary conditions the problem is ill-posed as the family of functions $v(x,y) = ax + by$, where $a^2 + b^2 = c$, constitutes different C^2 class solutions to Eq. (19.67). Let us now incorporate Dirichlet and Neumann boundary conditions along the Y–axis: $v(0,y) = \bar{b}y$, $v_x(0,y) = \bar{a}$, and $v_y(0,y) = \bar{b}$, where $(\bar{a},\bar{b}) \neq (0,0)$, $\bar{a} \neq 0$, and $\bar{a}^2 + \bar{b}^2 = c$. The corresponding Cauchy problem, Eqs. (19.62) and (19.63) takes the following form:

$$\begin{array}{ll} (a)\ x_t(t,s) = 2p(t,s) & (c)\ u_t(t,s) = 2c \\ (b)\ y_t(t,s) = 2q(t,s) & (d)\ p_t(t,s) = 0 \\ & (e)\ q_t(t,s) = 0 \end{array} \tag{19.68}$$

with the corresponding boundary conditions defined as

$$\begin{array}{ll} (a)\ x(0,s) = 0 & (c)\ u(0,s) = \bar{b}s \\ (b)\ y(0,s) = s & (d)\ p(0,s) = \bar{a} \\ & (e)\ q(0,s) = \bar{b} \end{array} \tag{19.69}$$

Note that the conditions from Eq. (19.64) are here clearly satisfied. Furthermore, Eq. (19.68)(d,e) combined with Eq. (19.69)(d,e) yield $p(t,s) = \bar{a}$ and $q(t,s) = \bar{b}$. By coupling Eq. (19.68)(a) and Eq. (19.69)(a) together with Eq. (19.68)(b) and Eq. (19.69)(b) we obtain that $x(t,s) = 2\bar{a}t$ and $y(t,s) = 2\bar{b}t + s$. Thus, $t(x,y) = x/2\bar{a}$ and $s(x,y) = y - (\bar{b}/\bar{a})x$. With the aid of Eq. (19.68)(c) and Eq. (19.69)(c) we arrive at $u(t,s) = ct + \bar{b}s$. Putting $t(x,y)$ and $s(x,y)$ back into $u(t,s)$, and bearing in mind that $c = \bar{a}^2 + \bar{b}^2$, we finally obtain $u(t,s) = \tilde{u}(x(t,s), y(t,s)) = \bar{a}x + \bar{b}y$. Theorem 19.12 ensures also, that the latter forms a unique C^2 class solution to Cauchy problem, Eqs. (19.68) and (19.69). A moment reflection reveals, however, that finding an exact analytic solution for $u_x^2(x,y) + u_y^2(x,y) = x^2 + y^2$, by using the method of characteristic strips, is much more complicated.

19.6.4 Method of equal-height contours

This method is a variant of the method of characteristic strips. Namely, it is assumed here that $\gamma(s)$ (where $s \in (a,b)$) is a smooth (piecewise-smooth) *equal-height contour* contained in the image Ω (i. e., $\tilde{u}(x,y) = C$ over γ). By imposing such special Dirichlet boundary conditions it is possible to determine the Neumann boundary conditions, up to two pairs of gradients defined along curve γ. In case of equal-height contour a corresponding solution $\tilde{u}$ is generated along the evolution of equal-height contours γ_t, for which $\gamma_0 = \gamma$. In other words, the unknown surface is swept out by $[\gamma_t, \tilde{u}(\gamma_t)]^T$, where the family

$$\gamma_t(s) = \{[x(t,s), y(t,s)]^T : [s,t]^T \in (a,b) \times (c,d)\}$$

of equal-height contours is generated by solving the following Cauchy problem:

$$\begin{aligned} x_t(t,s) &= \pm \frac{y_s(t,s)}{\sqrt{\mathcal{E}(x(t,s), y(t,s))(x_s^2(t,s) + y_s^2(t,s))}} \\ y_t(t,s) &= \mp \frac{x_s(t,s)}{\sqrt{\mathcal{E}(x(t,s), y(t,s))(x_s^2(t,s) + y_s^2(t,s))}} \\ x(0,s) &= x_0(s) \\ y(0,s) &= y_0(s) \end{aligned} \tag{19.70}$$

and $\gamma_0(s) = [x(0,s), y(0,s)]^T$ is the initial equal-height contour. A final solution $\tilde{u}$ is given here by

$$\tilde{u}(x(t,s), y(t,s)) = u(t,s) = t + C \tag{19.71}$$

where $u(0,s) = C$. The choice of appropriate pair of signs $(+,-)$ or $(-,+)$ in Eq. (19.70), governs the direction of evolution of equal-height contours (either outwards or inwards).

Note that, if we differentiate $\tilde{u}(x(t,s), y(t,s)) = t$ over the parameter s, the chain rule yields $p(t,s)x_s(t,s) + q(t,s)y_s(t,s) = 0$. This combined with the fact that $p^2(t,s) + q^2(t,s) = \mathcal{E}(x(t,s), y(t,s))$ implies that

$$\begin{aligned} p(t,s) &= \pm\frac{y_s(t,s)\sqrt{\mathcal{E}(x(t,s),y(t,s))}}{\sqrt{x_s^2(t,s)+y_s^2(t,s)}} \\ q(t,s) &= \mp\frac{x_s(t,s)\sqrt{\mathcal{E}(x(t,s),y(t,s))}}{\sqrt{x_s^2(t,s)+y_s^2(t,s)}} \end{aligned} \tag{19.72}$$

In particular, for $s = 0$, there exist exactly two choices of Neumann boundary conditions guaranteeing—in each case—the existence of a unique C^2 class solution to a corresponding Cauchy problem (see Theorem 19.12). Indeed, let u be a C^2 class solution to Eqs. (19.70) and (19.71) with Dirichlet boundary condition set to $u(\gamma) = C$. An easy inspection shows that function $v = -u + 2C$ satisfies $u_x^2 + u_y^2 = \mathcal{E}(x,y)$, Dirichlet boundary conditions $v(\gamma) = C$, and one of the Neumann boundary conditions Eq. (19.72). Thus, we have *an essential duality* in solving a Cauchy problem, Eqs. (19.70) and (19.71), which is ambiguous up to a vertical shift and mirror-like reflection.

Note, that Eqs. (19.70) to (19.72) can be transformed into an equivalent system of five characteristic strip equations:

$$\begin{aligned} x_t(t,s) &= \frac{p(t,s)}{p^2(t,s)+q^2(t,s)} \\ y_t(t,s) &= \frac{q(t,s)}{p^2(t,s)+q^2(t,s)} \\ u_t(t,s) &= 1 \\ p_t(t,s) &= \frac{\mathcal{E}_x(x(t,s),y(t,s))}{2(p^2(t,s)+q^2(t,s))} \\ q_t(t,s) &= \frac{\mathcal{E}_y(x(t,s),y(t,s))}{2(p^2(t,s)+q^2(t,s))} \end{aligned} \tag{19.73}$$

The last system differs from the system of characteristic strips by the speed of evolution along the base characteristic direction. Thus, both systems are equivalent and render the same solution. This variant of the method of characteristic strips was mentioned in shape-from-shading literature by Bruckstein [47] and later re-introduced by Kimmel and Bruckstein [48, 49]. For a more detailed mathematical analysis of this method an interested reader is also referred here to Osher [50], Sethian [51]. The corresponding discrete method of equal-height contour evolution is analyzed in Osher and Sethian [52], Sethian [53]. Recently, a *fast marching level set method* has been applied to the eikonal equation over a rectangular grid [54]. An interested reader is also referred to [32], where convergence, stability, and performance of various finite-difference schemes (applied over a rectangular grid to the linear shape from shading problem) have been discussed.

Note finally, that the knowledge of the initial equal-height contour (which is a clear drawback of this method), as opposed to the general case of extracting general Dirichlet and Neumann boundary conditions (necessary for applying a method of characteristic strips) can, in certain cases, be obtainable. The latter happens, for example, if the surface is positioned on the horizontal plane and disappears continuously from the viewing direction.

We close this subsection with an example illustrating the equal-height contour method.

Example 19.5:

Consider the eikonal equation introduced in Eq. (19.67). Let the initial height contour $y_0(s)$ be $x(0,s) = s/a$, $y(0,s) = -s/b$, along which $u(0,s) = 0$, and $ab \neq 0$. We search for $\tilde{u}(x(t,s), y(t,s)) = u(t,s) = t$, where the pair $[x(t,s), y(t,s)]^T$ satisfies the following system:

$$\begin{aligned} x_t(t,s) &= \frac{-y_s(t,s)}{\sqrt{c(x_s^2(t,s) + y_s^2(t,s))}} \qquad & u(t,s) &= t \\ & & x(0,s) &= x_0(s) \\ y_t(t,s) &= \frac{x_s(t,s)}{\sqrt{c(x_s^2(t,s) + y_s^2(t,s))}} & y(0,s) &= y_0(s) \end{aligned} \tag{19.74}$$

In order to solve Eq. (19.74), pertinent Neumann boundary conditions have to be incorporated. Choosing in Eq. (19.72) a pair $(-,+)$ we obtain:

$$p(t,s) = \frac{-y_s(t,s)\sqrt{c}}{\sqrt{x_s^2(t,s) + y_s^2(t,s)}} \quad \text{and} \quad q(t,s) = \frac{x_s(t,s)\sqrt{c}}{\sqrt{x_s^2(t,s) + y_s^2(t,s)}}$$

Thus $p(0,s) = a$ and $q(0,s) = b$ along initial equal-height contour $y_0(s)$ and therefore the last two equations of Eq. (19.73) yields $p(t,s) = a$ and $q(t,s) = b$. This, together with the first two equations of Eq. (19.73) yields $x(t,s) = (a/c)t + s/a$ and $y(t,s) = (b/c)t - s/b$. Hence, $t(x,y) = ax + by$. As $\tilde{u}(x(t,s), y(t,s)) = u(t,s) = t$ we finally arrive at one of two C^2 class solutions to Eq. (19.74). Choosing, in turn, the second pair $(+,-)$ in Eq. (19.72) we obtain the second C^2 class solution $\tilde{v}(\bar{x}(t,s), \bar{y}(t,s)) = -a\bar{x} - b\bar{y}$ to Eq. (19.74).

19.6.5 Direct variational method

The methods of Ikeuchi and Horn [55], Horn [1] and Bruckstein [47] rely in a crucial way on provision of prior information (Dirichlet or Neumann boundary conditions). The amount of necessary information usually exceeds the minimal amount of initial data required by various theoretical uniqueness results. This is so because the algorithms based on differential equations cannot proceed by starting from singular points (i.e., for the point for which $\mathcal{E}(x_0, y_0) = 0$), which, as it turns out, are important clues for the shape recovery process.

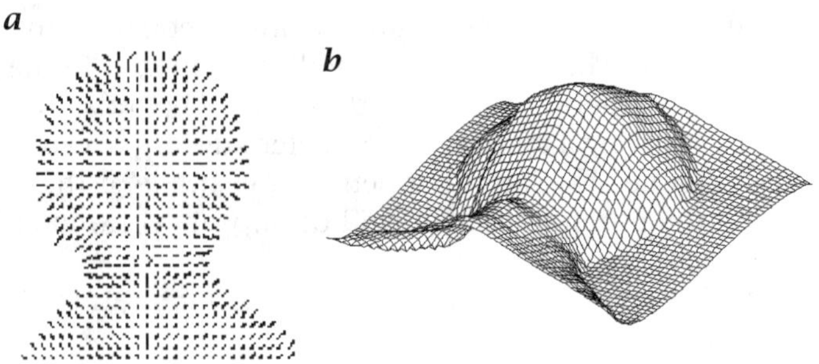

Figure 19.19: *Reconstruction result of the synthetic Mozart statue by using the method by Ikeuchi and Horn [55], using a weighting factor equal to 1.0 and 300 iterations:* ***a*** *needle map visualization of the reconstructed gradient field;* ***b*** *3-D plot of the recovered Mozart statue where the Frankot-Chellappa algorithm was used for gradient map integration.*

An iterative SFS method with functional minimization developed by Ikeuchi and Horn [55] is discussed in Klette et al. [4]. The method has one parameter (a weighting factor). To compare the performance with previous results shown for the synthetic Mozart statue an example is shown in Fig. 19.19 for 300 iterations.

In this section we only outline *a direct variational method* by analyzing the simplest case. For a more general case see [56]. We assume here that a domain Ω has exactly one *singular point* $S_0 = [x_0, y_0]^T$. A direct variational method discussed in [56] is based on the following crucial result.

Theorem 19.14 *If a function u satisfies an eikonal equation Eq. (19.55) over a domain Ω, and X and Y are points in Ω that can be joined by the base characteristic curve wholly contained in Ω, then the relative depth $|u(X) - u(Y)|$ between points of the graph of u is given by*

$$|u(X) - u(Y)| = \min_{\gamma} \int_{\gamma} \sqrt{\mathcal{E}} dl \tag{19.75}$$

where the minimum is taken over all piecewise-smooth curves γ in Ω joining X and Y, and the integration is meant with respect to standard measure.

The proof of Theorem 19.14 reveals that a minimal value of Eq. (19.75) is attained along the base characteristic direction (i.e., along gradient direction). It can be shown that for the *convex (concave)* Lambertian surface the corresponding image has exactly one singular point S_0 (where $u_x(S_0) = u_y(S_0) = 0$) and that each point of the image $X \in \Omega$ can be joined by the base characteristic curve with S_0. Consequently, the previous theorem yields

$$u(X) = u(S_0) - \min_{\mathcal{Y}} \int_{\mathcal{Y}} \sqrt{\mathcal{E}} dl \quad \text{and} \quad u(X) = u(S_0) + \min_{\mathcal{Y}} \int_{\mathcal{Y}} \sqrt{\mathcal{E}} dl \tag{19.76}$$

whenever the surface is convex/concave. Note that, for the saddle-like function $u(x, y) = xy$ the base characteristic pattern (which in case of arbitrary eikonal equation coincides with the gradient direction) does not have the forementioned property. Consequently, the method presented here can only be applicable to the convex (concave) surfaces. In an effort of extending this result for an image containing more than one singular point a generalization of the notion of the convex (concave) surface is necessary. It is useful at this stage to consider those smooth surfaces having base characteristic curves pointing outward (or inward) at the periphery of the domain. They are called *convex skirt* surfaces (see [56] or [44]). In addition, it is assumed that the convex skirt function, in the neighborhood of the singular point S_0, has a nonvanishing Hessian. By using *index theory* (see [56]) it can be shown that the number of singular points has to be odd. Moreover, if N_+ denotes the number of concave singular surface points, N_- denotes the number of convex singular surface points, and $N_\pm$ denotes the number of saddle singular surface points, then it can be shown that any convex skirt surface with nonvanishing Hessian has to satisfy the following condition $N_+ + N_- - N_\pm = 1$. The latter imposes a clear constraint on the number of possible solutions. For $n = 1$, we have only two possible cases: $N_+ = 1$ together with its mirror-like reflection $N_- = 1$. For the case when $n = 3$, there are four possible solutions. An interested reader is referred here to [56], where a method of finding a convex skirt solution (generalizing Theorem 19.14) together with explicit shape recovery algorithm is presented. A similar topic is also discussed by [57].

Finally, we point out that in order to derive a computational scheme for Eq. (19.76) Dijkstra's greedy algorithm for finding the shortest path from the single source to any other node on a weighted graph can be used [58]. The source here, will be a singular point S_0, the nodes of the graph coincide with the rectangular grid points and the edges are the straight lines joining the eight neighboring points with any point at the grid. Assuming that the grid increment is h, the corresponding weight function $\omega([x_i, y_j]^T, [x_k, y_l]^T)$ assigned to each existing edge $([(x_i, y_j]^T, [x_k, y_l]^T)$ can be defined as

$$\omega = \begin{cases} \frac{h}{2}(\sqrt{\mathcal{E}(x_i, y_j)} + \sqrt{\mathcal{E}(x_k, y_l)}), \text{if } |k-i| + |l-j| = 1 \\ \frac{h}{\sqrt{2}}(\sqrt{\mathcal{E}(x_i, y_j)} + \sqrt{\mathcal{E}(x_k, y_l)}), \text{if } |k-i| + |l-j| = 2 \end{cases} \tag{19.77}$$

For more detailed analysis concerning numerical schemes for Eq. (19.76) an interested reader is referred to [56] and [58].

The use of the forementioned optimization method reduces the number of initial information necessary to ascertain well-posedness of a given shape-from-shading problem (e.g., no boundary conditions are here requested). Similarly to the case of photometric stereo, the unknown function u is found, up to an arbitrary constant. In addition, the computational scheme for Eq. (19.76) can be derived over a fixed rectangular grid. The major disadvantage stems, however, from the necessity of tightening the original class of C^1 class surfaces to convex/concave skirt C^1 class surfaces. Such a restriction appears neither in photometric stereo nor in other single image shape reconstruction algorithms. The latter is, however, achieved by imposing additional constraints such as multiple illuminations or accessibility of boundary conditions.

19.7 Concluding remarks

Shape from shading methods require a strong restriction of the object surfaces because the problem to recover a surface from a single image is extremely underdetermined. Therefore, SFS is an ill-posed problem. Assumptions on the surface properties support finding a unique solution to a certain extent. But with every additional restriction the practical use of such methods declines as well. Very critical simplifications are the following three assumptions:

(i) The term $E_0\rho$ is known and constant;

(ii) The surfaces are at least C^1-continuous; and

(iii) 3-D coordinates of singular points and/or singular orientations are known.

This chapter informed about 2S and 3S PSM techniques that allow refraining from assumptions (i) and (iii). Assumption (ii) is also related to the discrete integration problem as briefly discussed in Section 19.2.3. Photometric stereo methods can be improved further by using colored light sources [5, 6], or by integration of shadow information [9, 59].

This chapter also informed about theoretical work, and here we can state a situation where SFS or albedo-dependent 2S PSM are analyzed in greater detail as 3S PSM so far. However, there exist more contributions to fundamentals of 3S PSM as cited in this chapter. In comparison to different shape recovery techniques, as, for example, stereo image analysis (see Chapters 17 and 18), based on structured lighting [4], on focus (see Chapter 20), or on motion and occluding boundaries (see, for example, [4]), shading-based shape recovery has special benefits as, for example, the use of inexpensive equipment, reconstruction of smooth surfaces, and no use of dangerous radiation. It offers reasonable accuracy and time-efficient reconstructions for selected applications.

19.8 References

[1] Horn, B. K. P., (1986). *Robot vision.* Cambridge, MA: MIT Press.

[2] Woodham, R. J., (1978). Photometric stereo: a reflectance map technique for determining surface orientation from image intensity. *Image Understanding Systems & Industrial Applications, SPIE,* **155**:136–143.

[3] Horn, B. K. P. and Brooks, M. J., (1989). *Shape from Shading.* Cambridge, MA: MIT Press.

[4] Klette, R., Schlüns, K., and Koschan, A., (1998). *Computer Vision—Spatial Data from Images (German edition: Vieweg, Wiesbaden 1996).* Singapore: Springer.

[5] Drew, M. S., (1994). Robust specularity detection from a single multi-illuminant color image. *CVGIP: Image Understanding,* **59**:320–327.

[6] Woodham, R. J., (1994). Gradient and curvature from the photometric-stereo method, including local confidence estimation. *J. Optical Society America,* **A 11**:3050–3068.

[7] Kozera, R., (1991). Existence and uniqueness in photometric stereo. *Applied Mathematics and Computation,* **44(1)**:1–103.

[8] Rumpel, D. and Schlüns, K., (1995). Szenenanalyse unter Berücksichtigung von Interreflexionen und Schatten. In *Proc. DAGM-Symposium, Bielefeld, Germany, 1995,* pp. 218–227, DAGM. Berlin: Springer.

[9] Schlüns, K., (1997). Shading Based 3-D Shape Recovery in the Presence of Shadows. In *Proc. Intern. Conf. on Digital Image& Vision Computing, Albany, Auckland, New Zealand,* pp. 195–200.

[10] Hashimoto, Y., Yamamoto, M., and Asaida, T., (1995). Cameras and display systems. *Proc. IEEE,* **83**:1032–1043.

[11] Lenz, R., (1989). Image data acquisition with CCD cameras. In *Optical 3-D Measurement Techniques,* A. Gruen and H. Kahmen, eds., pp. 22–34. Karlsruhe, Germany: Wichmann.

[12] McCamy, C. S., Marcus, H., and Davidson, J. G. ., (1976). A color-rendition chart. *J. Applied Photographic Engineering,* **2**:95–99.

[13] Meyer, G. W., (1988). Wavelength selection for synthetic image generation. *Computer Vision, Graphics and Image Processing,* **41**:57–79.

[14] Haralick, R. M. and Shapiro, L. G., (1993). *Computer and Robot Vision,* Vol. II. Reading, MA: Addison-Wesley.

[15] Schlick, C., (1994). A survey of shading and reflectance models. *Computer Graphics Forum,* **13**:121–131.

[16] Nicodemus, F. E., Richmond, J. C., Hsia, J. J., Ginsberg, I. W., and Limperis, T., (1977). *Geometrical Considerations and Nomenclature for Reflectance.* Monograph 160, U.S. Department of Commerce, National Bureau of Standards, Washington.

[17] Horn, B. K. P., (1977). Understanding image intensities. *Artificial Intelligence,* **8**:201–231.

[18] Nayar, S. K. and Oren, M., (1995). Generalization of the Lambertian Model and Implications for Machine Vision. *Int. J. Computer Vision*, **14**:227–251.

[19] Hecht, E., (1997). *Optics*, 3rd edition. Reading, MA: Addison-Wesley.

[20] Nayar, S. K., Ikeuchi, K., and Kanade, T., (1991). Shape from interreflections. *Int. J. Computer Vision*, **6**:173–195.

[21] Foley, J. D., van Dam, A., Feiner, S. K., and Hughes, J. F., (1990). *Computer Graphics—Principles and Practice*, 2nd edition. Reading, MA: Addison-Wesley.

[22] Klinker, G. J., Shafer, S. A., and Kanade, T., (1990). A physical approach to color image understanding. *Int. J. Computer Vision*, **4**:7–38.

[23] Klinker, G. J., Shafer, S. A., and Kanade, T., (1988). The measurement of highlights in color images. *Int. J. Computer Vision*, **2**:7–32.

[24] Horn, B. K. P. and Sjoberg, R. W., (1979). Calculating the reflectance map. *Applied Optics*, **18**:1770–1779.

[25] Klette, R. and Schlüns, K., (1996). Height data from gradient fields. *SPIE Proc. Photonics East*, **2908**:204–215.

[26] Frankot, R. T. and Chellappa, R., (1988). A method for enforcing integrability in shape from shading algorithms. *IEEE Trans. Patt. Anal. and Mach. Int., PAMI*, **10**:439–451.

[27] Lee, C.-H. and Rosenfeld, A., (1984). An approximation technique for photometric stereo. *Pattern Recognition Letters*, **2**:339–343.

[28] Kozera, R., (1992). On shape recovery from two shading patterns. *Internat. J. Pattern Recognition and Artificial Intelligence*, **6(4)**:673–698.

[29] Onn, R. and Bruckstein, A. M., (1990). Integrability disambiguates surface recovery in two-image photometric stereo. *Internat. J. Computer Vision*, **5(1)**:105–113.

[30] John, F., (1971). *Partial Differential Equation*, Vol. 1. New York: Springer.

[31] Lee, C.-H. and Rosenfeld, A., (1985). Improved methods of estimating shape from shading using the light source coordinate system. *Artificial Intelligence*, **26**:125–143.

[32] Kozera, R. and Klette, R., (1997). Finite difference based algorithms for a linear shape from shading. *Machine Graphics and Vision*, **6(2)**:157–201.

[33] Horn, B. K. P., (1990). Height and gradient from shading. *Int. J. of Computer Vision*, **5**:37–75.

[34] Zhang, R., Tsai, P. S., Cryer, J. E., and Shah, M., (1994). Analysis of shape from shading techniques. In *Proc. Computer Vision and Pattern Recognition, Seattle, Washington, U.S.A.*, pp. 377–384.

[35] Brooks, M. J., Chojnacki, W., and Kozera, R., (1992). Shading without shape. *Quarterly of Applied Mathematics*, **50(1)**:27–38.

[36] Brooks, M. J., Chojnacki, W., and Kozera, R., (1992). Circularly symmetric eikonal equations and non-uniqueness in computer vision. *J. Math. Analysis and Applications*, **165(1)**:192–215.

[37] Brooks, M. J., Chojnacki, W., and Kozera, R., (1992). Impossible and ambiguous shading patterns. *Internat. J. Computer Vision*, **7(2)**:119–126.

[38] Horn, B. K. P., Szeliski, R., and Yuille, A., (1989). Private communication.

[39] Deift, P. and Sylvester, J., (1981). Some remarks on the shape-from-shading problem in computer vision. *Math. Analysis and Applications*, **84(1)**:235–248.

[40] Bruss, A. R., (1982). The eikonal equation: some results applicable to computer vision. *J. Math. Physics*, **23(5)**:890–896.

[41] Kozera, R., (1997). Uniqueness in shape from shading revisited. *J. Math. Imaging and Vision*, **7(2)**:123–138.

[42] Brooks, M. J., (1983). *Shape from Shading Discretely*. PhD thesis, Essex University, England.

[43] Brooks, M. J., (1983). Two results concerning ambiguity in shape from shading. *Proc. Nat. Conf. on Artificial Intelligence*, pp. 26–39.

[44] Oliensis, J., (1991). Uniqueness in shape from shading. *International Journal of Computer Vision*, **6(2)**:75–104.

[45] Rouy, E. and Tourin, A., (1992). A viscosity solutions approach to shape-from-shading. *SIAM Journal on Numerical Analysis*, **29**:867–884.

[46] Gear, C. W., (1971). *Numerical Initial Value Problems in Ordinary Differential Equations*. Englewood Cliffs, NJ: Prentice-Hall Inc.

[47] Bruckstein, A. M., (1988). On shape from shading. *Computer Vision, Graphics and Image Processing*, **44(2)**:139–154.

[48] Kimmel, R. and Bruckstein, A., (1994). Tracking level set by level sets: a method for solving the shape from shading problem. *Computer Vision and Image Understanding*, **62(2)**:47–58.

[49] Kimmel, R. and Bruckstein, A., (1995). Global shape from shading. *Computer Vision and Image Understanding*, **62(3)**:360–369.

[50] Osher, S. J., (1993). A level set formulation for the solution of the Dirichlet problem for Hamilton-Jacobi equations. *SIAM J. Math. Analysis*, **24(5)**: 1145–1152.

[51] Sethian, J. A., (1985). Curvature and the evolution of fronts. *Communications in Mathematical Physics*, **101**:487–499.

[52] Osher, S. J. and Sethian, J. A., (1988). Fronts propagating with curvature dependent speed: algorithms based on Hamilton-Jacobi formulations. *J. Computational Physics*, **79**:12–49.

[53] Sethian, J. A., (1990). Numerical algorithms for propagating interfaces: Hamilton-Jacobi equations and conservation laws. *Journal of Differential Geometry*, **31**:131–161.

[54] Sethian, J. A., (1996). *Level Set Methods: Evolving Interfaces in Geometry, Fluid Mechanics, Computer Vision and Material Science*. Cambridge: Cambridge University Press.

[55] Ikeuchi, K. and Horn, B. K. P., (1981). Numerical shape from shading and occluding boundaries. *Artificial Intelligence*, **17**:141–184.

[56] Brooks, M. J. and Chojnacki, W., (1994). Direct computation of shape from shading. In *Proceedings 12th Internat. Conf. Pattern Recognition, Jerusalem, Israel, Oct. 9-13, 1994*, pp. 114–119. Los Alamitos, CA: IEEE Computer Society Press.

[57] Oliensis, J. and Dupuis, P., (1993). A global algorithm for shape from shading. In *Proc. Internat. Conf. on Comuter Vision, Berlin, Germany, 1993*, pp. 692–701. Los Alamitos, CA: IEEE Computer Society Press.

[58] Cormen, T. H., Leiserson, C. E., and Rivest., R. L., (1990). *Introduction to algorithms.* Cambridge, MA: MIT Press.

[59] Solomon, F. and Ikeuchi, K., (1996). Extracting the shape and roughness of specular lobe objects using four light photometric stereo. *IEEE Trans. Pattern Analysis and Machine Intelligence*, **18**:449–454.

20 Depth-from-Focus

Peter Geißler and Tobias Dierig

Interdisziplinäres Zentrum für Wissenschaftliches Rechnen (IWR)
Universität Heidelberg, Germany

Handbook of Computer Vision and Applications
Volume 2
Signal Processing and Pattern Recognition

Copyright © 1999 by Academic Press
All rights of reproduction in any form reserved.

ISBN 0-12-379772-1/$30.00

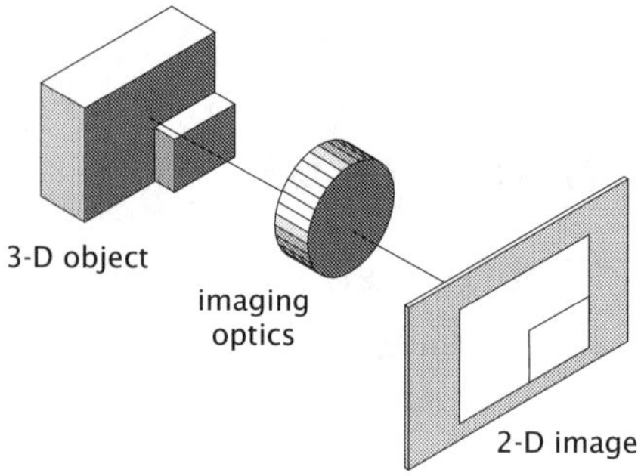

Figure 20.1: *Loss of depth information caused by the projection of a 3-D scene onto a 2-D image.*

20.1 Introduction

Image acquisition always contracts the 3-D information of the scene to 2-D information of the image due to the projection on the 2-D image plane. Therefore the reconstruction of the depth information from 2-D images is a fundamental problem in computer vision applications.

Many different approaches to the problem are known, including *stereo* (Dhond and Aggarwal [1], Chapters 17 and 18) or its generalization to multiview imaging, *shape from shading* and *photogrammetric stereo* (Chapter 19, shape from motion, texture analysis and depth from focus.

Depth from focus addresses the reconstruction of the depth information by using the fact that images usually contain blur. A typical situation is well known from photographs taken with the lens focused to a close distance. While the foreground is well focused, objects in the background appear blurred. In general, the blur increases with increasing distance from the location of focus. In this sense the depth-from-focus technique can be classified as a *triangulation* technique (Volume 1, Section 18.4).

The basic idea of depth from focus is to correlate the grade of the blurring with the distance of the objects and therefore estimate their 3-D positions from the defocus. Unfortunately, defocus is not the only source of blur, but can also be feigned by smooth brightness changes in the scene. Therefore, depth-from-focus either requires multiple views of the same scene in order to distinguish defocus from blur, or making use of known properties of the scene and the lens setup. Both approaches lead to different realizations of depth recovery and will be discussed later in this chapter.

20.2 Basic concepts

20.2.1 Defocused imaging

Defocused imaging has been discussed in detail in Volume 1, Chapter 4. Therefore, only a brief overview is given here in order to summarize the most important terms and definitions.

Depth of field. A paraxial lens of focal length f focuses all rays emerging from a point P onto its corresponding point P' in image space according to the basic lens equation

$$\frac{1}{f} = \frac{1}{d_0} + \frac{1}{d_i} \tag{20.1}$$

Therefore only objects located at a given distance d_0 are imaged well focused onto the image plane at the fixed position d_i, whereas objects at other distances d_0' appear blurred. The distance range in which the blur does not exceed a certain value is called the depth of field. A good value to characterize the depth of field is f-number $f/2R$, which gives the ratio of the focal length to the diameter of the lens. As a zero-order approximation, blurring is described by the radius ϵ of the blur circle for an object point at $d_0' = d_0 + \Delta d_0$, which is controlled by the ratio of the image distances

$$\frac{\epsilon}{R} = \frac{d_i}{d_i'} - 1 = d_i \frac{\Delta d_0}{d_0 d_0'} \tag{20.2}$$

The depth of field is now determined by the choice of a maximal radius of the blur circle, the so-called circle of confusion. If ϵ_c denotes the circle of confusion, the depth of field can be expressed in terms of the magnification $M = d_i/d_0$, the f-number $O = f/2R$, and the object distances

$$\Delta d_0 = \frac{2O}{Mf} d_0' \epsilon_c = \frac{d_0}{\frac{Mf}{2O\epsilon_c} - 1} \tag{20.3}$$

In Eqs. (20.2) and (20.3) we combined the two distinct cases of Δd_0 being positive or negative by understanding ϵ as having the same sign as Δd_0. Distinguishing between positive and negative signs shows the inherent asymmetry for the depth of field, caused by the nonlinearity of Eq. (20.1)

$$|\Delta d_0| = \frac{2O}{Mf} d_0' |\epsilon_c| = \frac{d_0}{1 \mp \frac{Mf}{2O\epsilon_c}} \tag{20.4}$$

Therefore it is a common practice to assume $MR \gg \epsilon_c$, leading to the approximation of $d_0' \approx d_0$ in Eq. (20.3) and removing the asymmetry.

Depth of focus. Moving the image plane instead of the object plane also causes a defocused image. Equivalent to the depth of field in object space the term depth of focus in image space denotes the maximal dislocation of the image plane with respect to a given circle of confusion. Again, with the approximation of the circle of confusion being small compared to the lens radius, the depth of focus is given by

$$\Delta d_i = \frac{2O}{f} d_i \epsilon_c \tag{20.5}$$

The relation between depth of focus and depth of field is given by the longitudinal magnification M^2

$$\Delta d_0 = M^2 \Delta d_i \tag{20.6}$$

Point spread function of optical systems. The point spread function is one of the central terms in depth-from-focus, because it describes the effect of image blur in a quantitative way. The image of an object is the superposition of the images of all object points. An ideal, aberration-free optics would image every object point onto its conjugate point in the image plane. In the case of defocus the rays emerging from the object point no longer meet at the image plane, but at the plane conjugate to the actual object plane. The image of the object point is therefore an intensity distribution at the image plane, which is is called the *point spread function* (PSF) of the lens. Under certain assumptions, which are described in detail in Volume 1, Section 4.7, the effect of blurring can be described as a convolution of the well-focused image, as it would be achieved by a pinhole camera, with the PSF

$$g(\boldsymbol{x}') = \int f(\boldsymbol{x}(\vec{\xi}'))\mathrm{PSF}(\vec{\xi}' - \boldsymbol{x}')\,\mathrm{d}^2\xi' = f(\boldsymbol{x}(\boldsymbol{x}')) * \mathrm{PSF}(\boldsymbol{x}') \tag{20.7}$$

In many cases, we can assume that the shape of the PSF remains unchanged for every object point, independent of its distance from the plane of best focus. Then, the PSF can be described by a shape function S and a scaling factor σ, which varies with the distance g'

$$\mathrm{PSF}_Z(\boldsymbol{x}) = \frac{S\left(\frac{\boldsymbol{x}}{\sigma(Z)}\right)}{\int S\left(\frac{\boldsymbol{x}}{\sigma(Z)}\right)\,\mathrm{d}^2x} \tag{20.8}$$

The denominator normalizes the PSF to $\int \mathrm{PSF}_Z(\boldsymbol{x})\,\mathrm{d}^2x = 1$, forcing gray-value preservation. In many cases it is sufficient to replace σ by the radius of the blur circle ϵ. The shape function can be completely different for different optical setups. Nevertheless, only a few shape functions are sufficient in order to describe the main properties of standard optics. These are:

- **circular box function** This PSF is used for optical systems with circular aperture stop, which are not dominated by wave optics;
- **noncircular box function** This PSF is used for optical systems with noncircular aperture stop, which are not dominated by wave optics;
- **Gaussian** Widely used in order to describe the PSF; and
- **Airy disk** Used for optical systems that are dominated by wave optics, with coherent and monochromatic illumination, mainly microscopic systems

The details of the various point spread functions can be found in Volume 1, Section 4.7.1

20.2.2 Defocus in the Fourier domain

In Fourier space, the convolution turns into a multiplication of the Fourier transform of the object function with the Fourier transform of the PSF. The latter is called the *optical transfer function (OTF)*. Its values give the transfer coefficient for spatial structures of different wavelength through the optical system. A value of zero indicates that this particular wavelength cannot be seen by the optics. A typical OTF will act as a low-pass filter, eliminating higher spatial frequencies, that is, high resolution details.

20.3 Principles of depth-from-focus algorithms

As Eq. (4.46) shows, defocus appears as multiplication in Fourier space. Because of its commutativity, there is no distinction between the PSF and the object function. This has serious implications for depth-from-focus algorithms, because it means that the gray-value structure depends on both object properties as well as the PSF. A smooth gray-value transition may arise from either a massive defocus or merely reflects a non-uniform object surface. On the other hand, depth estimation from defocus requires the effect of blur caused by the PSF to be separated from other sources. Two different approaches to solve this problem are possible:

Multiple-view approaches. Using multiple cameras viewing the same scene with different focal or aperture settings results in a set of images with the same object function, but taken with different PSFs. Separation of the object properties from the PSF effects becomes possible. A variety of realization of these approaches is possible:

- **Focus series** A series of images is taken with a single camera while varying the focusing of the lens. Within the focus series, at each image point the image with the maximum sharpness is selected from the series, resulting in a depth map. Of course, this is only possible with static objects that are not moving during the image acquisition.

- **Dual focus view** Using two cameras with different object planes results in two images taken with different PSFs for every plane in between the two object planes. Only at the very center do the two PSFs become identical, thus leading to the same images at this position. Using cameras with different optics, for example different focal length, eliminates this problem.
- **Multiple aperture view** Instead of using different focusing, two or more cameras can be focused at the same object while having different f-numbers, resulting in different blurring. As a special case, consider a combination of a pinhole camera with a camera of finite aperture. The image from the pinhole camera shows no blurring, thus giving the object function. With this information, the influence of the PSF can be calculated from the other image.

Single-view approaches. Solving the depth-from-focus problem by using a single image instead of multiple views allows the observation of fast moving objects with little effort. To discriminate object function and PSF, *a priori* knowledge about the object function and the PSF is necessary. This class of algorithms therefore requires either the objects to be restricted to known shapes or the selection of regions, wherein the object features are known, for example, step edges or point objects.

Ambiguity of depth estimation. It is important to notice that there may be an ambiguity in depth estimation by depth from focus, due to the fact that the size of the PSF has its minimum at the plane of best focus, increasing in both directions: towards and farther away from the camera position. If no special arrangements are made, this results in an ambiguity of the depth estimation, because two positions of the object are possible and cannot be distinguished. This has to be taken into account especially with single-view methods, but also with multiple-view methods because there is only a certain distance range in which no ambiguity occurs.

20.4 Multiple-view depth-from-focus

Multiple-view approaches use sets of views of the same scene, taken with different camera settings, and mainly with different focusing. Considering the changing camera parameter as an additional dimension of the image data, they start with an already 3-D data set. These data are transformed in order to achieve the desired depth information. These approaches are used most commonly with focus series.

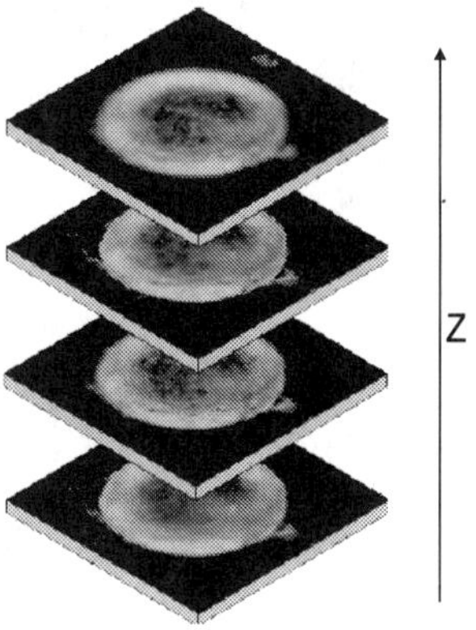

Figure 20.2: Focus series of a machine screw used for depth recovery.

20.4.1 Introduction to focus series

Focus series are a common approach for the investigation of motionless objects, and are often used in microscopy. The focus of a single camera is changed to a number of settings, resulting in a series of images taken with different planes of best focus (Fig. 20.2). The depth value of each pixel can be found directly from selecting the image showing the less blur from the series. This is done be calculating a sharpness measure on each image of the stack, and then for each pixel or small region of the image, finding the maximum of the sharpness measure along the depth axis. Unfortunately, usually the number of images is limited, resulting in a poor depth resolution. Interpolation of the sharpness measure between the images is therefore required in order to increase depth resolution.

The quality of the depth map is mainly given by the method used to located the image of best focus within the series, and the interpolation that is done in between these images.

20.4.2 Sharpness measure

As pointed out in Volume 1, Section 4.7.1, defocus causes suppression of higher spatial frequencies in the power spectrum of the image. Any filter sensitive to high spatial frequencies in a local neighborhood is therefore suitable as a sharpness filter. Obviously, a large variety of such filters exists, but most of the filters belong to the two main classes of contrast operators or bandpass filters. In the following, an example of each filter class is given.

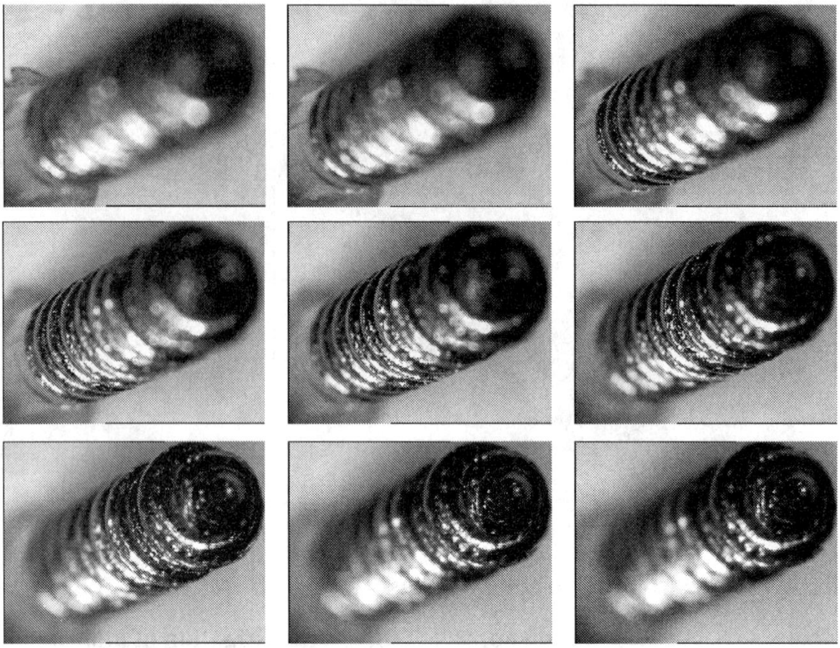

Figure 20.3: Focus series of a metric screw taken with a telecentric optics with an object to image ratio of 20.

Contrast filter. Contrast filters allow a fast implementation of the sharpness measure. They measure the range of gray values available in a neighborhood N of the pixel. Because the lack of high spatial frequencies results in slower gray-value changes, the local contrast also decreases with increasing defocus. As contrast detector, either the local contrast operator

$$C_l(\boldsymbol{x}) = \max_{\boldsymbol{x}' \in N} g(\boldsymbol{x}') - \min_{\boldsymbol{x}' \in N} g(\boldsymbol{x}') \tag{20.9}$$

or the normalized contrast

$$C_n(\boldsymbol{x}) = \frac{\max_{\boldsymbol{x}' \in N} g(\boldsymbol{x}') - \min_{\boldsymbol{x}' \in N} g(\boldsymbol{x}')}{\max_{\boldsymbol{x}' \in N} g(\boldsymbol{x}') + \min_{\boldsymbol{x}' \in N} g(\boldsymbol{x}')} \tag{20.10}$$

can be used. These filters are very sensitive to contrast changes, but also sensitive to isolated noise pixels. They can be improved by replacing the minimum and maximum operator by rank filters, for example, p-quantile filters. The p-quantile $Q(p)$ value in an neighborhood N is defined as the gray value at which the pth fraction of all gray values in N are below $Q(p)$ and the $1 - p$th fraction of gray values is above

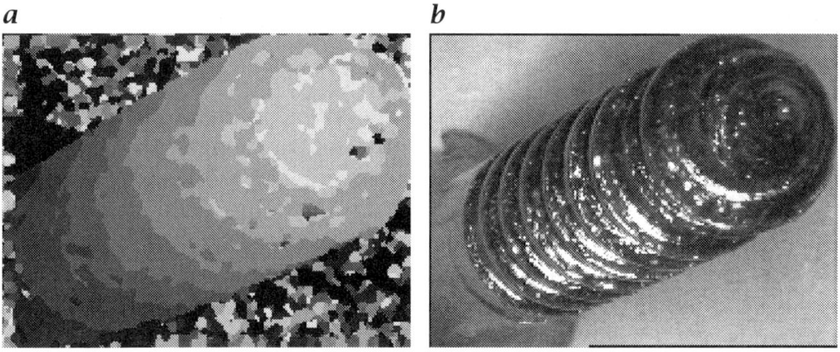

Figure 20.4: ***a*** *Depth map of a machine screw calculated by the variance method;* ***b*** *overall sharp image calculated from the original images using the depth map.*

$Q(p)$. This can be expressed by the local gray-value histogram $H(g)$ of the neighborhood N as

$$Q(p) = F^{-1}(p) \qquad \text{with} \quad F(g) = \sum_{-\infty}^{g} H(g) \tag{20.11}$$

$F(g)$ is the cumulative distribution function (CDF) [2] of the gray-value distribution.

As a contrast filter, it is used with a value of $p < 0.5$ in the following manner as a local p-quantile filter:

$$C_p(\boldsymbol{x}) = Q(1-p, Vx) - Q(p, Vx) \tag{20.12}$$

or as the corresponding normalized filter

$$C_p(\boldsymbol{x}) = \frac{Q(1-p, Vx) - Q(p, Vx)}{Q(1-p, Vx) + Q(p, Vx)} \tag{20.13}$$

As the p-quantile is a generalization of minimum and maximum operators, the local contrast operator Eq. (20.9) is the p-quantile of $p = 0$. In order to achieve high processing speed, a variance-based method has been implemented by one of the authors. The results of this method, applied to a focus series of a screw (Fig. 20.3) are shown in Fig. 20.4a. To give a first estimate of the position, for each region of 16×16 pixel the image with the highest local contrast has been chosen. In addition, an overall sharp image is calculated by selecting each pixel from the image previously found to have the highest contrast at this position (see Fig. 20.4b).

Bandpass filter. In order to find image regions containing high spatial frequencies, high-pass and bandpass filters can be used. Although the high-pass filters seem to be optimal in selecting high frequencies, they tend to fail due to their noise sensitivity. Therefore they are combined with a low-pass filter, which cuts the wavelength above the cut wavelength of the high-pass filter to form a bandpass. Bandpass filters select a range of spatial frequencies from the Fourier transform of the image. The center wave number and width of the filter can be optimized to meet the requirements of the image material. A bandpass filter can easily be constructed from the difference of two Gaussian filters, as the well-known Difference of Gaussian (DoG) filter

$$DoG_{\sigma_1,\sigma_2}(\boldsymbol{x}) = \frac{1}{\sqrt{2\pi}\sigma_1} e^{-\frac{x^2}{2\sigma_1{}^2}} - \frac{1}{\sqrt{2\pi}\sigma_2} e^{-\frac{x^2}{2\sigma_2{}^2}} \tag{20.14}$$

As an effective implementation, pyramid decompositions of the images can preferably be used. Darell and Wohn [3] report an algorithm using first a bandpass decomposition of the image by a Laplacian pyramid, adequate for DoG filtering. In order to average the results over a larger area, a Gaussian pyramid is constructed on each level of the Laplacian pyramid, resulting in a dual pyramid structure $I^{k,l}$

$$I^{k,l} = \mathcal{E} G^{(k)} L^{(l)} I \tag{20.15}$$

where I is the image, $G^{(k)}$ is the operator for the kth level of the Gaussian pyramid, $L^{(l)}$ is the operator for the lth level of the Laplacian pyramid, and $\mathcal{E}$ is the expansion operator suitable to interpolate the subsampled image back to the original image size. This is used as the final sharpness measure. Figure 20.5 shows the results of calculating the depth from the depth series in Fig. 20.3 using different levels for both the Gaussian as the Laplacian pyramid. For these images, the combination of the 0-th level of the Laplacian pyramid with the second level of the Gaussian pyramid selects the optima wave-number range.

20.4.3 Three-dimensional reconstruction

So far, all methods result in a depth map, giving a distance value for each pixel in the image, also called a 2.5D reconstruction. Therefore, only opaque surfaces can be surveyed with this method, as they appear in many technical applications. However, microscopic imaging typically deals with transparent or semitransparent objects. The question arises whether it is possible to perform a fully 3-D reconstruction of the object from depth series. This can be done by deconvolving the image stack with the inverse of the 3-D point spread function of the microscope.

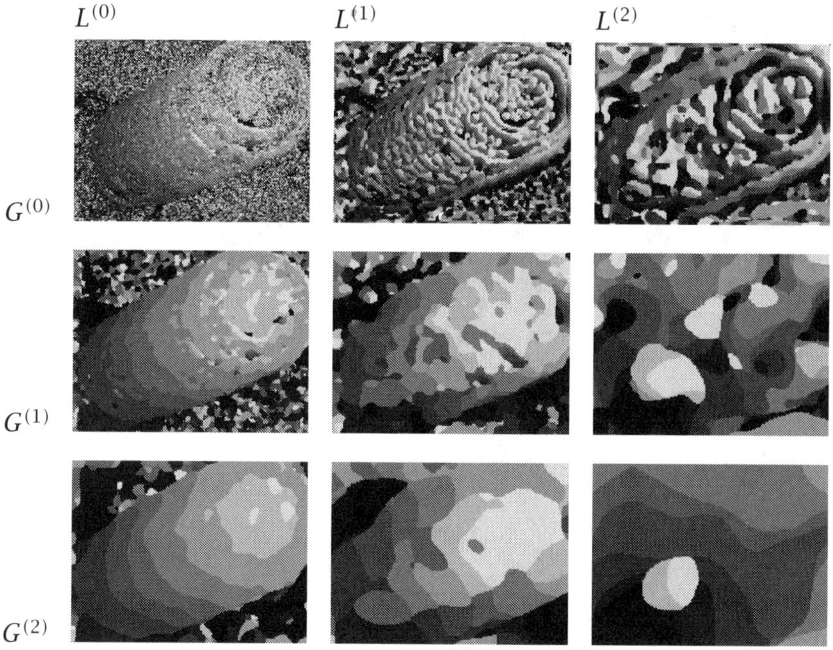

Figure 20.5: *Depth map calculated from different combinations of levels of the Laplacian and Gaussian pyramid. The best results are obtained from the combination of the 0-th level of the Laplacian pyramid with the first and second level of the Gaussian pyramid.*

20.5 Dual-view depth-from-focus

The basic idea of dual-view depth-from-focus techniques is to take two images of the same scene, but with different parameters of the optical setup to realize different point spread functions. To ensure that the image pair is taken at the same time, beamsplitters and folding mirrors are used as illustrated in Fig. 20.6.

20.5.1 Dual aperture

In order to achieve a depth estimate at a position $\boldsymbol{x}_0$, a region centered at this point is considered. The choice of the size of this region determines the spatial resolution of the depth map. Pentland [4] developed a method based on the assumption of a Gaussian point spread function, which will be summarized here. Denoting the two images by g_i, the object function by O_i, and the variances of the two Gaussian PSFs by

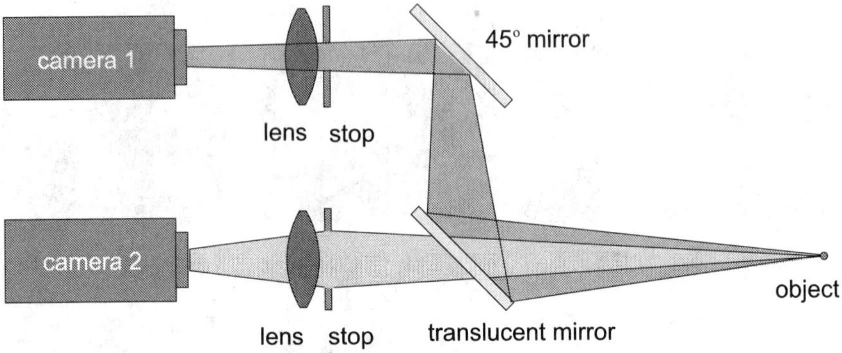

Figure 20.6: *Optical setup for a dual aperture camera system. One beamsplitter and a folding mirror are necessary to simultaneously acquire two images with different aperture of the same object.*

σ_i, the relation of the two images is given by

$$\frac{g_1(\boldsymbol{x})}{g_2(\boldsymbol{x})} = \frac{O_1(\boldsymbol{x}) * G_{\sigma_1}(\boldsymbol{x})}{O_2(\boldsymbol{x}) * G_{\sigma_2}(\boldsymbol{x})} \tag{20.16}$$

It is important to note that there is no matching problem, because the two camera setups are identical except for the f-number. Therefore the object functions are identical. In Fourier space, the convolution turns into a multiplication. By dividing the Fourier transforms instead of the images, the result becomes independent of the object functions

$$\frac{\hat{g}_1(\boldsymbol{k})}{\hat{g}_2(\boldsymbol{k})} = \frac{\hat{O}(\boldsymbol{k})\hat{G}_{\sigma_1}(\boldsymbol{k})}{\hat{O}(\boldsymbol{k})\hat{G}_{\sigma_1}(\boldsymbol{k})} = \frac{\sigma_2^2 G_{\sigma_1'}(\boldsymbol{k})}{\sigma_1^2 G_{\sigma_1'}(\boldsymbol{k})} \quad \text{with } \sigma_i' = \frac{1}{\sigma_i} \tag{20.17}$$

or

$$\frac{\hat{g}_1(\boldsymbol{k})}{\hat{g}_2(\boldsymbol{k})} = \frac{\sigma_2^2}{\sigma_1^2} e^{-\frac{k^2}{2}(\sigma_1^2-\sigma_2^2)} \sim G_\sigma(\boldsymbol{k}) \quad \text{with } \sigma = \frac{1}{\sigma_1^2 - \sigma_2^2} \tag{20.18}$$

The ratio of the Fourier transforms of the two images therefore is a Gaussian with variance σ, which can be estimated with standard algorithms. From Eq. (20.2) the depth d_0' is known to be

$$\frac{\epsilon}{R} = \frac{d_i}{d_0} - \frac{d_i}{d_0'} \Rightarrow d_0' = \frac{d_i f}{d_i - f - 2O\epsilon} \tag{20.19}$$

Pentland [4] uses ϵ as a direct estimate for σ. If only two cameras are used, one has to be a pinhole camera in order to fix σ_1 to zero. Using three or more cameras with finite aperture results in a set of estimates of the differences of the σ-values

$$S_{ij} = \sigma_i^2 - \sigma_j^2 \tag{20.20}$$

and therefore allows for the solution of Eq. (20.19).

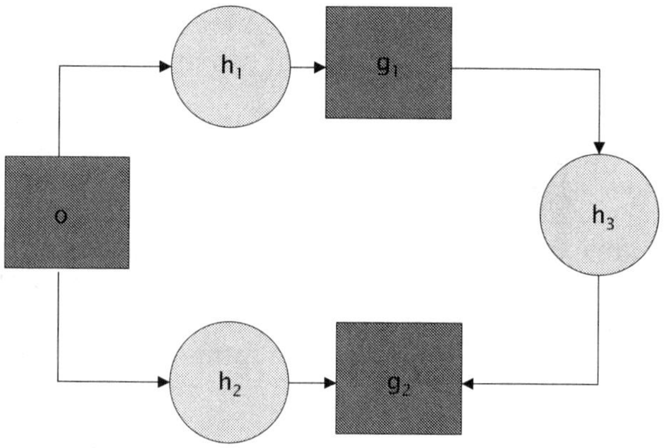

Figure 20.7: Illustration of the convolution ratio of the two PSFs h_1 and h_2.

20.5.2 Dual aperture and focus

In fact, is possible to reconstruct depth information from only two cameras without the limitations to pinhole setups. Assuming again identical optics but for the aperture settings of the both cameras, two images are taken from the same scene O by the convolution with two different, now arbitrarily shaped point spread functions h_1 and h_2

$$g_1(\boldsymbol{x}) = O(\boldsymbol{x}) * h_1(\boldsymbol{x}), \qquad g_2(\boldsymbol{x}) = O(\boldsymbol{x}) * h_2(\boldsymbol{x}) \tag{20.21}$$

Convolution ratio. As introduced by Ens and Lawrence [5], the *convolution ratio* h_3 of two defocus operators is defined as the convolution kernel that transforms the low aperture (and therefore less blurred) image g_1 into the high aperture image g_2, as indicated in Fig. 20.7

$$g_2(\boldsymbol{x}) = g_1(\boldsymbol{x}) * h_3(\boldsymbol{x}) \tag{20.22}$$

Now, g_2 can be expressed either in terms of h_2 or h_1 and h_3

$$g_2(\boldsymbol{x}) = O(\boldsymbol{x}) * h_1(\boldsymbol{x}) * h_3(\boldsymbol{x}) = O(\boldsymbol{x}) * h_2(\boldsymbol{x}) \tag{20.23}$$

which is equivalent to

$$h_1(\boldsymbol{x}) * h_3(\boldsymbol{x}) = h_2(\boldsymbol{x}) \tag{20.24}$$

Depth recovery now requires two separate steps. First, the convolution ratio has to be computed from the image pair. Second, it has to be correlated with the true depth information. Ens and Lawrence [6] give a method based on inverse filtering to compute the convolution ratio. The windowed Fourier transform of the two images is given by

$$\begin{aligned} g_i(\boldsymbol{x})w_i(\boldsymbol{x}) &= (O(\boldsymbol{x}) * h_1(\boldsymbol{x}))w_i(\boldsymbol{x}) \text{ space domain} \\ \hat{g}_i(\boldsymbol{k}) * \hat{w}_i(\boldsymbol{k}) &= (\hat{O}(\boldsymbol{k})\hat{h}_1(\boldsymbol{k})) * \hat{w}_i(\boldsymbol{k}) \text{ Fourier domain} \end{aligned} \tag{20.25}$$

with the window functions $w_i(\boldsymbol{x})$. Windowing is necessary in order to calculate spatial resolved depth maps instead of a global depth estimate for the complete scene.

To isolate the convolution ratio, the ratio of the two Fourier transforms is taken

$$\frac{\hat{g}_2(\boldsymbol{k}) * \hat{w}_2(\boldsymbol{k})}{\hat{g}_1(\boldsymbol{k}) * \hat{w}_1(\boldsymbol{k})} = \frac{(\hat{O}(\boldsymbol{k})\hat{h}_2(\boldsymbol{k})) * \hat{w}_2(\boldsymbol{k})}{(\hat{O}(\boldsymbol{k})\hat{h}_1(\boldsymbol{k})) * \hat{w}_1(\boldsymbol{k})} \tag{20.26}$$

Selection of the size of the window. The convolution ratio can be computed by means of Fourier transformation

$$h_3(\boldsymbol{x}) = \mathcal{FT}^{-1}\left[\frac{\hat{w}_2(\boldsymbol{k}) * \hat{h}_2(\boldsymbol{k})}{\hat{w}_1(\boldsymbol{k}) * \hat{h}_1(\boldsymbol{k})}\right] \tag{20.27}$$

The size of the window function is critical for the quality of the depth estimation, because larger sizes of the window improve the Fourier transformations, but, on the other hand, decrease the resolution of the depth maps. In addition, if the size of the window is large, only slow depth transitions can be detected. In the 1-D case, Ens and Lawrence [6] compute the correlation of accuracy and window size with a numerical simulation.

Window size	Error
4	66 %
8	24 %
16	6 %
32	1 %

For this calculation, a step edge scene $O = \{..., 0, 0, 1, 1, ...\}$ has been used with a defocus operator of a pinhole camera $h_1 = \{0, 1, 0\}$ and a defocus operator $h_2 = \{1, 1, 1\}$. Using a Gaussian window function, it can be seen that the error decreases as the size of the window function increases. To achieve smaller error, the window size has to be one order of magnitude larger than the PSF. If the size of w is small in order to guarantee a good spatial resolution of the depth map, its Fourier transform $\hat{w}$ can assumed to be constant, thus Eq. (20.27) turns into the simpler representation

$$h_3(\boldsymbol{x}) = \mathcal{FT}^{-1}\left[\frac{\hat{h}_2(\boldsymbol{k})}{\hat{h}_1(\boldsymbol{k})}\right] \tag{20.28}$$

A common problem with inverse filtering are zero crossings of the Fourier transform, because these wave numbers cannot be reconstructed. The image functions $g_i = O * h_i$ have two kinds of zero crossings. The zero crossings of the object function O occur in both image functions, while the zero crossings of the defocus operators h_1 and h_2 differ. Unfortunately, the convolution of $\hat{O}$ with the Fourier transforms $\hat{h}_i$ can change the location of the zero crossings. The next sections introduce several algorithms suitable to solve the problems associated with zero crossing shifts.

Constraint inverse filtering. By using regularization, the problems with inverse filtering can be reduced. Therefore, the inverse filtering can be constrained by least squares fitting $\hat{h}_3(\boldsymbol{k})$ to a model. In this approach a quadratic model ($\hat{h}_3(\boldsymbol{k}) = a\boldsymbol{k}^2 + b$) is used, because it has been shown that the characteristic part of $\hat{h}_3(\boldsymbol{x})$ is a quadratic-type shape. Equation (20.28) can be written as

$$\hat{h}_1(\boldsymbol{k})\hat{h}_3(\boldsymbol{k}) - \hat{h}_2(\boldsymbol{k}) = 0 \tag{20.29}$$

With $\boldsymbol{H}_1$ is a matrix with $\hat{h}_1(\boldsymbol{k})$ stacked along its diagonal and $\boldsymbol{h}_{2,3}$ stacked vectors formed from $\hat{h}_{2,3}(\boldsymbol{k})$; Eq. (20.29) can be denoted in matrix notation

$$\boldsymbol{H}_1\boldsymbol{h}_3 - \boldsymbol{h}_2 = 0 \tag{20.30}$$

The regularized form of Eq. (20.30) minimized the functional

$$\|\boldsymbol{H}_1 \cdot \boldsymbol{h}_3 - \boldsymbol{h}_2\|^2 + \lambda\|\boldsymbol{C}\boldsymbol{h}_3\|^2 = \min \tag{20.31}$$

where

- λ is a scalar parameter, which adjusts between fitting $\boldsymbol{h}_3$ more to the data or to the quadratic shape; and
- $\boldsymbol{C}$ is a matrix that minimizes the second term if $\boldsymbol{h}_3$ has quadratic shape.

To get the solution for this minimization problem and derive the best-fitted $\boldsymbol{h}_3$, the Euler equation (Bertero and Poggio [7]) for Eq. (20.31) is solved for $\boldsymbol{h}_3$

$$\begin{aligned} &\boldsymbol{H}_1^T\boldsymbol{H}_1\boldsymbol{h}_3 - \boldsymbol{H}_1^T\boldsymbol{h}_2 + \lambda\boldsymbol{C}^T\boldsymbol{C}\boldsymbol{h}_3 = 0 \quad \rightsquigarrow \\ &\boldsymbol{h}_3 = \left(\boldsymbol{H}_1^T\boldsymbol{H}_1 + \lambda\boldsymbol{C}^T\boldsymbol{C}\right)^{-1}\boldsymbol{H}_1^T\boldsymbol{h}_2 \end{aligned} \tag{20.32}$$

From this the parameter to the best-fitted quadratic can be derived. By comparing the zero crossing of the quadratic and of the theoretically derived $\hat{h}_3$, that is, the Airy function mentioned in Section 20.2.1, the depth can be calculated.

Matrix methods. A different approach is the matrix-based method, which was introduced by Ens and Lawrence [6]. This method characterizes the depth-from-focus problem as a system of linear equations. To write the convolution from Eq. (20.22) as matrix-vector multiplication, a special matrix type will be required. First, the 1-D case will be discussed, therefore it is assumed that g_1, g_2 are $1 \times (m+n-1)$ images and h_3 is a $1 \times m$-filter mask. To write $g_1 * h_3 = g_2$ in matrix notation, from g_1 a Toeplitz matrix $\boldsymbol{G}_1$ is contructed as follows:

$$\boldsymbol{G}_1 = \begin{bmatrix} g_1(m) & g_1(m+1) & & \ldots & g_1(m+n-1) \\ g_1(m-1) & g_1(m) & g_1(m+1) & & \vdots \\ \vdots & g_1(m-1) & g_1(m) & \ddots & \vdots \\ \vdots & & g_1(m-1) & \ddots & g_1(m+1) \\ \vdots & & & \ddots & g_1(m) \\ \vdots & & & & g_1(m-1) \\ \vdots & & & & \vdots \\ g_1(1) & & & & g_1(n) \end{bmatrix} \tag{20.33}$$

where the row i of the matrix contains the i times shifted 1-D-image. The image g_2 and the filter mask h_3 are stacked into column vectors $\boldsymbol{g}_2$ and $\boldsymbol{h}_3$, so the matrix notation is

$$\boldsymbol{G}_1 \boldsymbol{h}_3 = \boldsymbol{g}_2 \tag{20.34}$$

In the 2-D case $\boldsymbol{G}_1$ is a block Toeplitz matrix

$$\boldsymbol{G}_1 = \begin{bmatrix} \boldsymbol{G}_{1,M} & \boldsymbol{G}_{1,M+1} & & \ldots & \boldsymbol{G}_{1,M+N-1} \\ \boldsymbol{G}_{1,M-1} & \boldsymbol{G}_{1,M} & \boldsymbol{G}_{1,M+1} & & \vdots \\ \vdots & \boldsymbol{G}_{1,M-1} & \boldsymbol{G}_{1,M} & \ddots & \vdots \\ \vdots & & \boldsymbol{G}_{1,M-1} & \ddots & \boldsymbol{G}_{1,M+1} \\ \vdots & & & \ddots & \boldsymbol{G}_{1,M} \\ \vdots & & & & \boldsymbol{G}_{1,M-1} \\ \vdots & & & & \vdots \\ \boldsymbol{G}_{1,1} & & & & \boldsymbol{G}_{1,N} \end{bmatrix} \tag{20.35}$$

where each $\boldsymbol{G}_{1,i}$ is $m \times n$ Toeplitz matrix that is constructed from the ith image row of $g_1(\boldsymbol{x})$. The vectors $\boldsymbol{g}_2$ and $\boldsymbol{h}_3$ contain the image rows of $g_2(\boldsymbol{x})$ and $h_3(\boldsymbol{x})$ put next to each other

$$\begin{aligned}\boldsymbol{g}_2 = [\ & g_2(1,1),\ldots,g_2(n,1),\\ & g_2(1,2),\ldots,g_2(n,2),\\ & \ldots,\\ & g_2(1,m),\ldots,g_2(n,m)]^T\end{aligned} \tag{20.36}$$

Now Eq. (20.22) can be written in matrix notation

$$\boldsymbol{G}_1\boldsymbol{h}_3 = \boldsymbol{g}_2 \tag{20.37}$$

and solved for $\boldsymbol{h}_3$

$$\boldsymbol{h}_3 = \boldsymbol{G}_1^{-1}\boldsymbol{g}_2 \tag{20.38}$$

which can be done exactly for the case that there is no noise and one image is not blurred because it was taken with a pinhole camera. When noise is added the problem becomes ill-posed. Small changes in the input data $g_1(\boldsymbol{x})$ can produce large fluctuations in the matrix $\boldsymbol{G}_1^{-1}$.

As in the foregoing paragraph about constrained inverse filtering, additional information can be used to make the calculation more robust. Because $h_1(\boldsymbol{x})$ and $h_2(\boldsymbol{x})$ can be theoretically or experimentally derived and referred to Eq. (20.24), $\boldsymbol{h}_3(\boldsymbol{x})$ must belong to a family of patterns. Therefore, a regularization approach can be used and the following functional, the regularized form of Eq. (20.35), must be minimized:

$$\|\boldsymbol{G}_1\boldsymbol{h}_3 - \boldsymbol{g}_2\|^2 + \lambda\|\boldsymbol{C}\boldsymbol{h}_3\|^2 = \min \tag{20.39}$$

where λ is a scalar parameter and $\boldsymbol{C}$ is a matrix minimizing the second term if $\boldsymbol{h}_3$ belongs to the family of patterns. The Euler equation for Eq. (20.39) is

$$\boldsymbol{G}_1^T\boldsymbol{G}_1\boldsymbol{h}_3 - \boldsymbol{G}_1^T\boldsymbol{g}_2 + \lambda\boldsymbol{C}^T\boldsymbol{C}\boldsymbol{h}_3 = 0 \tag{20.40}$$

which can be solved for $\boldsymbol{h}_3$

$$\boldsymbol{h}_3 = \left(\boldsymbol{G}_1^T\boldsymbol{G}_1 + \lambda\boldsymbol{C}^T\boldsymbol{C}\right)^{-1}\boldsymbol{G}_1^T\boldsymbol{g}_2 \tag{20.41}$$

Unfortunately, it is computationally expensive to solve Eq. (20.41), and additionally it is only easy to find the matrix $\boldsymbol{C}$ for simple patterns of $\boldsymbol{h}_3$ as, for example, quadratic.

For geometric optics $h_1(\boldsymbol{x})$ and $h_2(\boldsymbol{x})$ are unique indicators of scene depth, therefore using Eq. (20.24) is also a unique indicator of depth.

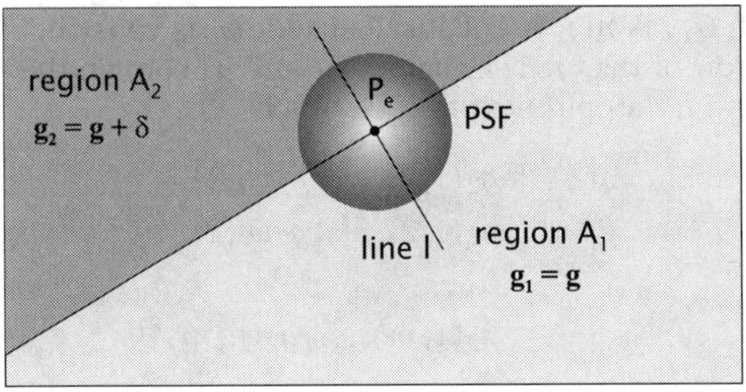

Figure 20.8: *Geometry at the step edge.*

Now for each depth a $h_3(\boldsymbol{x})$ pattern can be calculated *a priori* and put together in a table. To achieve higher depth resolution the depth discretization is made finer and the pattern table becomes larger. From Eq. (20.22) we get

$$g_1(\boldsymbol{x}) * h_3(\boldsymbol{x}) - g_2(\boldsymbol{x}) = 0 \tag{20.42}$$

which will be satisfied for the exact $h_3(\boldsymbol{x})$, but not for $\check{h}_3(\boldsymbol{x})$ from the pattern table. To find the best $\check{h}_3(\boldsymbol{x})$, the table is searched for the $\check{h}_3(\boldsymbol{x})$ that minimizes the following equation:

$$\sum_{\boldsymbol{x}} \left[g_1(\boldsymbol{x})\check{h}_3(\boldsymbol{x}) - g_2(\boldsymbol{x}) \right]^2 = \min \tag{20.43}$$

The depth value that belongs to the best $\check{h}_3(\boldsymbol{x})$ is the depth of the scene, with respect to the discretization error of the table.

20.6 Single-view depth-from-focus

Single-view depth-from-focus requires only one image of the scene to be taken. Therefore, it is necessary to know properties either of the object function or of the point spread function. Even if the shape of the PSF is completely known, restrictions to the object function are necessary in order to solve the depth-from-focus problem. A common approach is to calculate depth estimates only at image regions, whose properties can be estimated from the image itself, for example, line edges. This results in sparse depth maps, where values are given only at these positions. Often, the point spread function is approximated by box functions or Gaussians.

20.6.1 Sharp discontinuities

Step edges in the gray value are ideal in order to separate the defocus from the image. For the implementation of such depth-from-focus algorithms, first, a detection of step edges has to be made. The actual depth estimation can only be performed in the neighborhood of these edges. This section will describe several approaches for the depth recovery near linear step edges. A step edge of height γ along a straight line is defined by

$$O(\boldsymbol{x}) = \begin{cases} g_0 + \gamma & : \ \boldsymbol{x} \in A_2 \\ g_0 & : \ \boldsymbol{x} \in A_1 \end{cases} \tag{20.44}$$

The spatial constant. An important prerequisite of the methods described here is that the point spread function is of known shape, and, in addition, has rotational symmetry. Furthermore, we assume the point spread function to be of Gaussian shape with variance $\sigma(z)^2$, where σ depends on the distance z of the object to the plane of best focus; σ is often denoted as the *spatial constant*. Because of the symmetry, images of objects located in front or behind this plane are indistinguishable. Therefore, the object position has to be limited to one side of the focal plane.

Estimation of the spatial constant. As the gray values in the neighborhood of a step edge are determined by the height of the step g_1 and g_2 and the spatial constant σ, the analysis of the gray-value changes close to the edge provides a way to estimate σ. Algorithms of this kind have been introduced first by Pentland [8] and Grossman [9] who coined the term *depth-from-focus* to denote these methods.

Direct estimation of the spatial constant. The approach of Pentland [4] focuses on the estimation of σ from the gray value along a line l perpendicular to the edge, as indicated in Fig. 20.8.

Without loss of generality, the edge line may be in the y-direction at the position x_0 for the further computations. Therefore, instead of Eq. (20.44) we use $O_x(\boldsymbol{x})$ unless otherwise noted.

$$O_x(\boldsymbol{x}) = \begin{cases} g_0 + \gamma & : \ x > x_0 \\ g_0 & : \ x < x_0 \end{cases} \tag{20.45}$$

We define the sharpness measure $C(\boldsymbol{x})$ as the Laplacian of the image, which itself is the convolution of the object function O with a

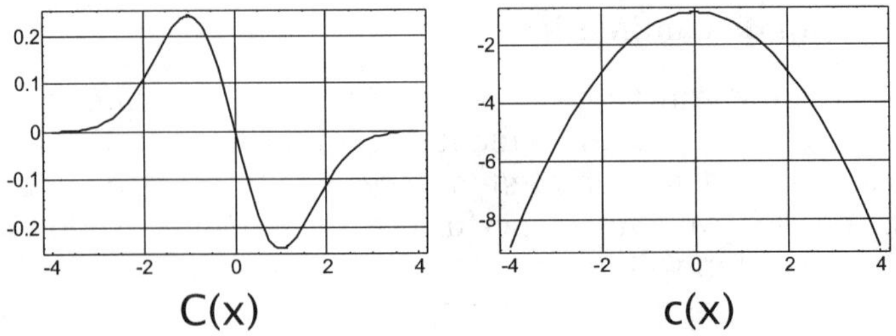

Figure 20.9: *Sharpness measures $C(x)$ and $c(x)$ along the line l.*

Gaussian G_σ

$$\begin{aligned} C(\boldsymbol{x}) &= \Delta(G_\sigma * O_x) \\ &= \int \Delta G_\sigma(\sqrt{\boldsymbol{x} - \boldsymbol{x}'}) O_x(\boldsymbol{x}')\, \mathrm{d}^2 x' \\ &= \delta\left[\frac{\mathrm{d}}{\mathrm{d}x} G^1_\sigma(x - x_0)\right] \end{aligned} \tag{20.46}$$

Herein G^1 denotes a 1-D Gaussian. The position of the step edge in the blurred image is defined as the zero crossing of the Laplacian of the image. At this very position, we obtain

$$C(\boldsymbol{x}) = \delta\left[\frac{\mathrm{d}}{\mathrm{d}x} G^1_\sigma(x)\right] = -\frac{\delta x}{\sqrt{2\pi}\sigma^3} e^{-\frac{x^2}{2\sigma^2}} \tag{20.47}$$

From

$$\ln\left|\frac{C(\boldsymbol{x})}{x}\right| = \ln\frac{\delta}{\sqrt{2\pi}\sigma^3} - \frac{x^2}{2\sigma^2} \tag{20.48}$$

we obtain an equation linear in x^2 as seen in Fig. 20.9

$$ax^2 + b = c \quad \text{with} \quad a = -\frac{1}{2\sigma^2} \quad b = \ln\frac{\delta}{\sqrt{2\pi}\sigma^3} \quad c = \ln\left|\frac{C(\boldsymbol{x})}{x}\right| \tag{20.49}$$

A standard linear regression then yields an estimate of σ, which is correlated to the depth.

Decomposition of the spatial constant. Analyzing the gray values along lines perpendicular to the edges require precise edge finders. Especially, errors in the edge direction introduce deviations in the spatial constant and therefore lead to errors in the depth estimations. Lai et al. [10] extended Pentland's algorithms without requiring an exact determination of the line direction.

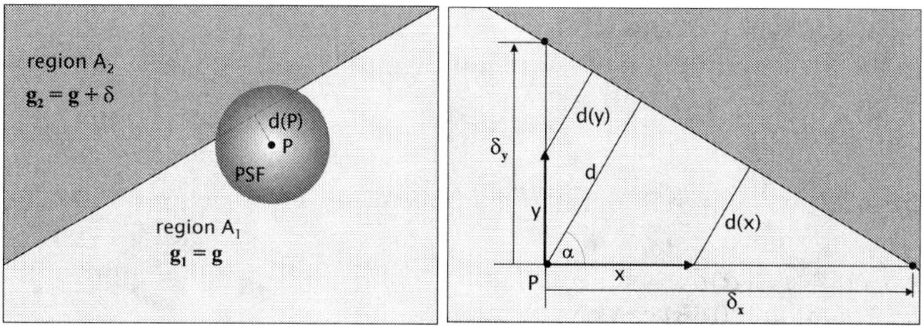

Figure 20.10: *Definitions of the horizontal and vertical edge distances.*

We start with a step edge

$$O(\boldsymbol{x}) = \begin{cases} g_0 + \gamma & : \quad x < a + by \\ g_0 & : \quad x > a + by \end{cases} \tag{20.50}$$

in an arbitrary direction, given by the line $x = a + by$. Again, assuming a Gaussian PSF, the gray value at a point P can be expressed by its distance d perpendicular to the edge

$$\begin{aligned} g(\boldsymbol{x}) = G_\sigma * O &= g_1 \int\limits_{\boldsymbol{x} \in A_1} G_\sigma(\boldsymbol{x})\, \mathrm{d}^2 x + g_2 \int\limits_{\boldsymbol{x} \in A_2} G_\sigma(\boldsymbol{x})\, \mathrm{d}^2 x \\ &= g_1 E\left(\frac{d(\boldsymbol{x})}{\sigma}\right) + g_2 E\left(-\frac{d(\boldsymbol{x})}{\sigma}\right) \end{aligned} \tag{20.51}$$

with

$$E(x) = \int_{-\infty}^{x} G_1^1(x')\, \mathrm{d}x' \tag{20.52}$$

The main idea of Lai et al. [10] is to decompose the spatial constant σ into two components σ_x and σ_y for the horizontal and vertical axis, and then derive equations for the horizontal and vertical gray-value changes. It is convenient to split the 2-D equation Eq. (20.51) into two 1-D equations, using the horizontal and vertical edge distances δ_x and δ_y, as defined in Fig. 20.10.

To simplify matters, the origin of coordinate system shall be located at the currently investigated point P. Using $d = \cos\alpha(\delta_x - x)$ for solely horizontal movements and $d = \sin\alpha(\delta_y - y)$ for vertical ones, the gray value can be written as

$$
\begin{aligned}
g_{(x)}(x) &= g(x, y=0) = g_1 E\left(\frac{\delta_x - x}{\sigma_x}\right) + g_2 E\left(-\frac{\delta_x - x}{\sigma_x}\right) \\
g_{(y)}(y) &= g(x=0, y) = g_1 E\left(\frac{\delta_y - y}{\sigma_y}\right) + g_e E\left(-\frac{\delta_y - y}{\sigma_y}\right)
\end{aligned}
\tag{20.53}
$$

with $\sigma = \cos(\alpha)\sigma_x = \sin(\alpha)\sigma_y$.

Equation (20.53) can be rewritten as

$$
\begin{aligned}
g_{(x)} &= g_2 + \Delta g N\left(\frac{\delta_x - x}{\sigma_x}\right) \\
g_{(y)} &= g_2 + \Delta g N\left(\frac{\delta_y - y}{\sigma_y}\right)
\end{aligned}
\tag{20.54}
$$

According to Eq. (20.54), σ can be calculated by estimating the 1-D spatial constants σ_x and σ_y and combing them to

$$
\sigma = \frac{\sigma_x \sigma_y}{\sqrt{\sigma_x^2 \sigma_y^2}}
\tag{20.55}
$$

To solve the depth estimation problem, either the spatial constant σ or its decompositions σ_x and σ_y must be estimated from a suitable region of the image. First, this region has to be chosen in the neighborhood of step edges. The most general method is to formulate an optimization problem, either from Eq. (20.51) for direct estimation of σ or from Eq. (20.54) for the decomposed spatial constants. It can be formulated as

$$
C(g_1, g_2, \sigma_i) = \sum\left(g(\boldsymbol{x}) - g_2 - \Delta g E\left(\frac{\delta_x - x}{\sigma_x}\right)^2\right) \rightarrow \min
\tag{20.56}
$$

or, equivalently

$$
\frac{\partial C(g_1, g_2, \sigma_i)}{\partial g_1} = 0 \qquad \frac{\partial C(g_1, g_2, \sigma_i)}{\partial g_2} = 0 \qquad \frac{\partial C(g_1, g_2, \sigma_i)}{\partial \sigma_1} = 0
\tag{20.57}
$$

Lai et al. [10] use a standard Newton method to solve Eqs. (20.56) and (20.57).

Edge detection. Edge detection is a basic step in image processing for these algorithms (Chapter 10). Therefore, its accuracy should be as good as possible in order to eliminate errors in the depth estimation (Chapter 6). Besides simple edge filters as first- and second-order derivatives, Lai et al. [10] prefer the *Laplace of Gaussian* (LoG) filter first proposed by Marr and Hildreth [11] and Hildreth [12] (see also Section 10.4.2). According to Haralick [13], it can be written as

$$\Delta g(\boldsymbol{x}) = \frac{1}{4\pi\sigma^4}\left(2 - \frac{|\boldsymbol{x}|^2}{\sigma^2}\right)\exp\left(-\frac{|\boldsymbol{x}|^2}{2\sigma^2}\right) \tag{20.58}$$

Estimating depth. Depth estimation is carried out by correlating the spatial constant σ with the actual distance of the object. This is done by establishing an analytical relation between the spatial constant and depth, and by performing a calibration of the image acquisition system. As a first-order approximation blurring is described by the blur circle, for example, a point spread function of uniform value (Subbarao and Gurumoorthy [14]). The radius of the blur circle is calculated assuming paraxial and aberration-free optics. As known from Eq. (20.2), the radius ϵ_c of the blur circle is given by

$$\frac{\epsilon_c}{R} = d_i \frac{\Delta d_o}{d_o d_o'} \tag{20.59}$$

Therefore, the depth D is given by

$$D = d_o' = d_o + \Delta d_o = \frac{d_i f}{d_i - f - 2O\epsilon_c} \tag{20.60}$$

with f being the focal length of the lens, O is its F-number, and d_i is the distance from the lens to the image plane. The assumption of a Gaussian point spread function instead of the blur circle can be expressed by replacing ϵ_c by the spatial constant σ and an adaptation factor k as $\epsilon_c = k\sigma$. According to Subbarao [15], k is in the range of $0 \leq k \leq 0.5$. Equation (20.60) can further be simplified to

$$D = \frac{A}{B - k\sigma} \quad \text{with} \quad A = k\frac{d_i f}{O} \quad \text{and} \quad B = k\frac{d_i - f}{O} \tag{20.61}$$

where A and B can be seen as system constants, which are to be derived by the calibration procedure. This can be done easily be estimating σ for several points of known distance D and performing an optimization problem on Eq. (20.61).

20.6.2 Object-based depth-from-focus

Object-based algorithms represent a different approach for single-view depth-from-focus. These algorithms are of special interest when observing fast-moving objects. They assume that the images contain only a limited number of object classes, which can be clearly distinguished by image segmentation. Because the object properties are known, depth reconstruction becomes possible with only one image. In

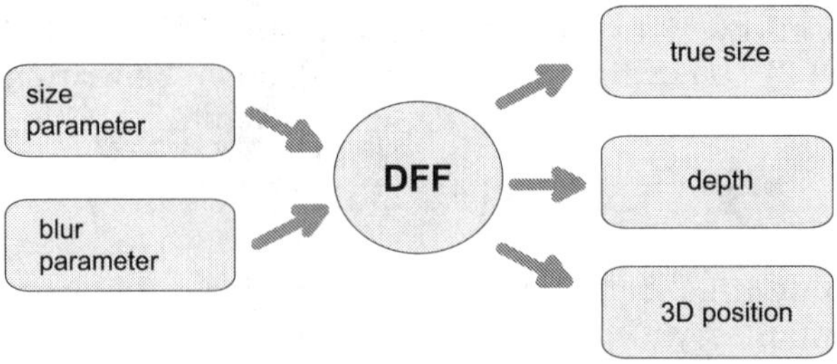

Figure 20.11: *Overview of the input and output parameters of the object-based depth-from-focus algorithm.*

fact, provided that an appropriate calibration has been done, not even the shape of the point spread function has to be known. Object-based algorithms have to be seen in clear contrast to the algorithms described so far. These provide a depth map, which may be dense or spare, on the image, while object-based approaches first segment the image in order to find and classify objects, and result in a depth estimate for each single object.

In this section, two different approaches of object-based depth-from-focus will be discussed. Because of the different nature of the objects the two methods use different object features in order to solve the depth-recovery problem.

Object feature-based algorithm. This algorithm has been developed by Jähne and Geißler [16] for objects of circular shape, but arbitrary size. In general, the algorithm can be applied to any objects of given shape, which are distinguished only in their size, that is, a scaling factor. Besides the depth the algorithm results in a correct measurement of the size of the objects, even if they undergo massive blur. The basic idea of the algorithm is to establish a robust measure of both size and blur, and then correlate these parameters by means of a suitable calibration, thus giving correct size and depth as the result (Fig. 20.11)
Shape of objects and PSF. As the first step of the algorithm, the shape of the objects has to be parameterized. An object is represented by its shape function and a scaling factor. For the application the algorithm has been developed, the shape function is a circular box function. Thus, an object of radius r is described by

$$I(\boldsymbol{x}) = \Pi\left(\frac{|\boldsymbol{x}-\boldsymbol{x}_0|}{2r'})\right) * \mathrm{PSF}(\boldsymbol{x})_Z \tag{20.62}$$

with the box function

$$\Pi(x) = \begin{cases} 1 & : \quad |x| \in [0, 1/2] \\ 0 & : \quad \text{otherwise} \end{cases} \tag{20.63}$$

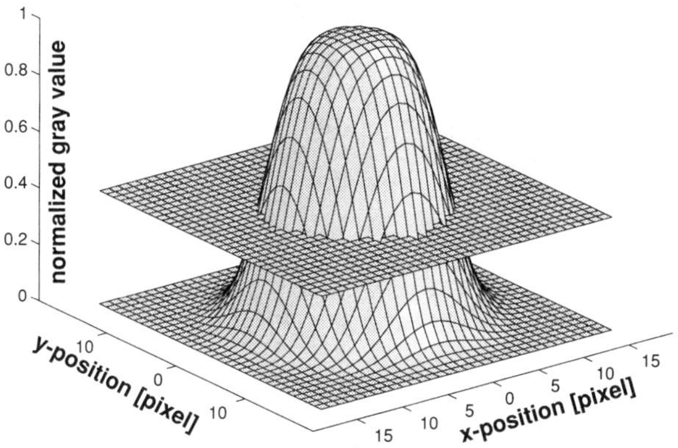

Figure 20.12: *Definition of the* $1/q$*-area as the size of blurred objects.*

Hereby, the object is already blurred due to its defocused position at the depth $z \neq 0$. As known from Section 20.2.1, the point spread function can be described by a shape function, which remains unchanged for every defocus, and a scaling parameter that describes the amount of blur. In the following, we assume the image gray values to be normalized in such a manner that a well-focused object has a minimum gray value of zero and a maximum gray value of 1.0. Furthermore, for the following calculations, we will assume the point spread function being of rotational symmetry.

Size parameter. Besides the scaling due to the magnification of the imaging optics, defocus itself changes the size of the objects, because there is no inescapable definition of the size of an object with blurred edges. Therefore, as the preliminary size of a blurred object, Jähne and Geißler [17] chose the equivalent radius of the $1/q$-area of the object. The $1/q$-area is hereby defined as the area over which the gray value of the object is larger than $1/q$ of the peak gray value (Fig. 20.12).

Now, an optimal value of q has to be chosen. For a linear edge, the value $q = 0.5$ leads to a constant (normalized) gray value of 0.5 at the object boundary, as long as the scope of the PSF does not exceed the size of the object, because

$$g_{\text{object edge}} = \int\limits_{x \leq 0} \text{PSF}(x, y) \; \mathrm{d}x \, \mathrm{d}y \tag{20.64}$$

due to the symmetry of the PSF.

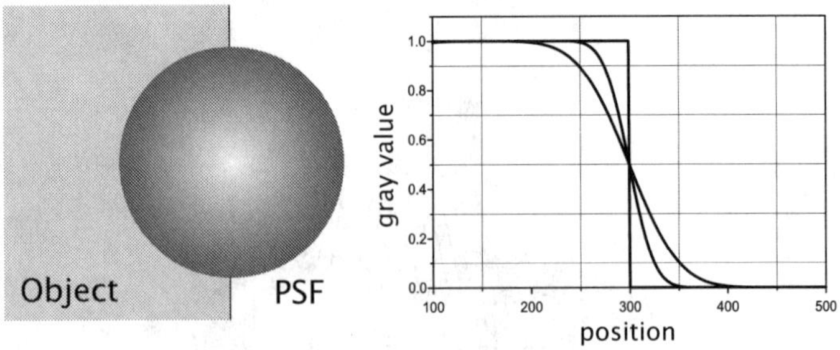

Figure 20.13: *As long as the PSF is of point symmetric shape, the gray value at the object edge remains unchanged if the object is convoluted with the PSF.*

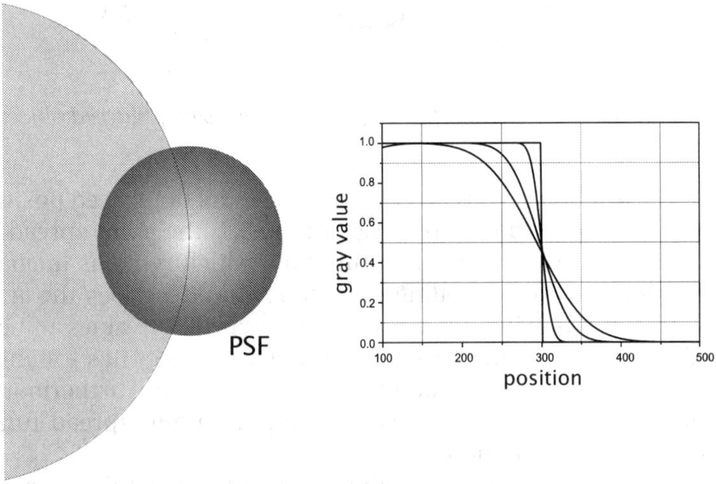

Figure 20.14: *Influence of the edge curvature to the edge gray value.*

Unfortunately, the objects are of circular shape. This leads to a smaller integration area than in Eq. (20.64), causing a slight decrease of the gray values at the object edges. This is illustrated in Fig. 20.14.

The change of the edge gray value with increasing defocus depends on the shape function of the PSF. The more the PSF is concentrated towards its center, the less distinct is the effect. Figure 20.15 illustrates this with a box-shaped and a Gaussian-shaped PSF, where the latter shows less variation.

Any value for q will therefore cause deviations in the size estimate of blurred objects. Therefore, there is no optimal value at all. In the following, we will choose 0.5, but this is for convenience only. This will cause the size shift as shown in Fig. 20.16 In the depth-from-focus correlation of the input parameters, the correct size will be calculated.

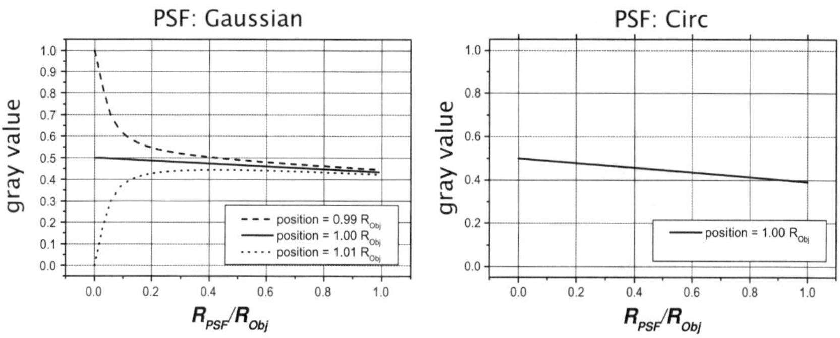

Figure 20.15: Gray value at the object edge for a Gaussian- and box-shaped point spread function.

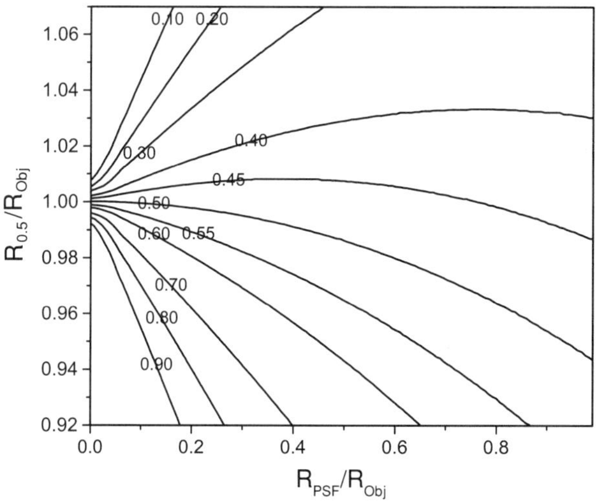

Figure 20.16: Dependence of the 1/0.5 equivalent radius from the defocus.

Defocus parameter. As the measure of blur, the mean gray value g_m on the $1/q$-area is suitable. Due to the normalization of the gray values, g_m is also normalized and ranges from 0 to 1. Because the integral gray-value sum $\int g(\boldsymbol{x})d^2x$ is independent of defocus, the mean gray value decreases with increasing defocus. Thus, it provides a normalized and monotonic measure.

At this point, depth recovery could be done by establishing a calibration matrix, which correlates the $1/q$-area, and the mean gray value on it with the actual depth. However, it is possible to use the uniform shape of objects and PSF to reduce the calibration matrix to a 1-D calibration vector. This is explained in the next section.

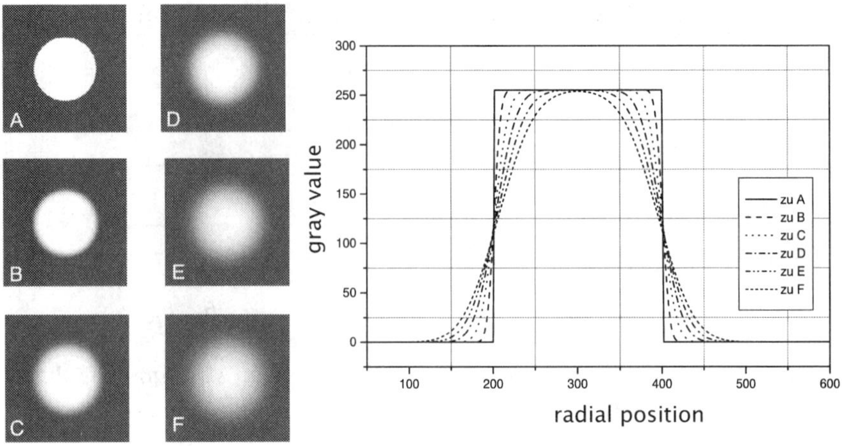

Figure 20.17: *Increasing defocus of an object of 100 pixel radius. Besides the images of the objects, the right part of the illustration shows the radial gray value cross section. The defocus increases from A to F.*

Similarity condition. For a better analysis of g_m we use the fact that the depth dependence of the PSF can be approximated by a scale factor $\eta(Z)$ and a shape function $\mathcal{P}$

$$\mathrm{PSF}_Z(\boldsymbol{x}) = \frac{\mathcal{P}\left(\dfrac{\boldsymbol{x}}{\eta(Z)}\right)}{\displaystyle\int \mathcal{P}\left(\dfrac{\boldsymbol{x}}{\eta(Z)}\right)\,\mathrm{d}^2x} \tag{20.65}$$

The division by the integral of the shape function forces the normalization of the PSF to $\int PSF_Z(\boldsymbol{x})d^2x = 1$, which denotes $\boldsymbol{x}$ coordinates on the image plane, while Z denotes the distance of the object point to the plane of focus. As already pointed out, all objects are of the same shape. Denoting the magnification of the optics by $V(Z)$, they are described by their shape function $\mathcal{O}$ and their radius R

$$G(\boldsymbol{x}) = \mathcal{O}\left(\frac{\boldsymbol{x}}{V(Z)R}\right) \tag{20.66}$$

The image of an object, which may be defocused, is therefore given by

$$n(\boldsymbol{x}) = G(\boldsymbol{x}) * \mathrm{PSF}_Z(\boldsymbol{x}) \sim \mathcal{O}\left(\frac{\boldsymbol{x}}{V(Z)R}\right) * \mathcal{P}\left(\frac{\boldsymbol{x}}{\eta(Z)}\right) \tag{20.67}$$

Images of object with the same ratio between the scale factors $V(Z)R$ of the object function and the scale factor $\eta(Z)$ of the point spread function are distinguished only in scaling, but not in shape. In particular, the mean gray value remains unaffacted. Therefore, the similarity condition Eq. (20.68) holds as follows:

$$\frac{\eta(Z)}{V(Z)R} = \text{const} \quad \Leftrightarrow \quad g_m = \text{const} \tag{20.68}$$

In addition, g_m can be expressed as

$$g_m(Z,R) = g_m\left(\frac{\eta(Z)}{V(Z)R}\right) \tag{20.69}$$

With a telecentric optics, this can be further simplified. With this setup, explained in Volume 1, Section 4.6.3, the scaling of the PSF then becomes linear and symmetric in Z, and can be approximated as $\eta(Z) \sim |Z|$. In addition, $V(Z)$ remains constant over Z. Finally, the mean gray value depends only on the *normalized distance* $|Z|/R$

$$g_m(Z,R) = g_m\left(\frac{|Z|}{R}\right) \tag{20.70}$$

Similar considerations lead to the similarity condition for the equivalent radius. Images of objects with the same ratio Z/R are distinguished by a scale factor only, which has to be given by the object size. Therefore

$$R_{1/2} = R\rho\left(\frac{|Z|}{R}\right) \Leftrightarrow \frac{R_{1/2}}{R} = \rho\left(\frac{|Z|}{R}\right) \tag{20.71}$$

Depth estimation.

With Eqs. (20.69) and (20.71) the depth estimation is carried out by the following steps:

- **Segmentation.** The image is segmented in order to find the objects and to determine their $1/q$-area and respective mean gray value;
- **Normalized depth.** From the defocus measure g_m the normalized depth $|Z|/R$ is calculated according to the inversion of Eq. (20.70);
- **True radius.** From the $1/q$-equivalent radius $R_{1/q}$ and Eq. (20.71) the true radius R is obtained.
- **Depth estimation.** From the normalized depth $|Z|/R$ and the radius R the depth $|Z|$ can be calculated easily.

The relations between normalized depth, ratio of radii $R_{1/q}/R$ and mean gray value have to be obtained by a calibration procedure. Figure 20.18 shows the result of the calibration used for the depth-from-focus method. The application of the method to particle size and concentration measurements is described in detail in Volume 3, Chapter 29.

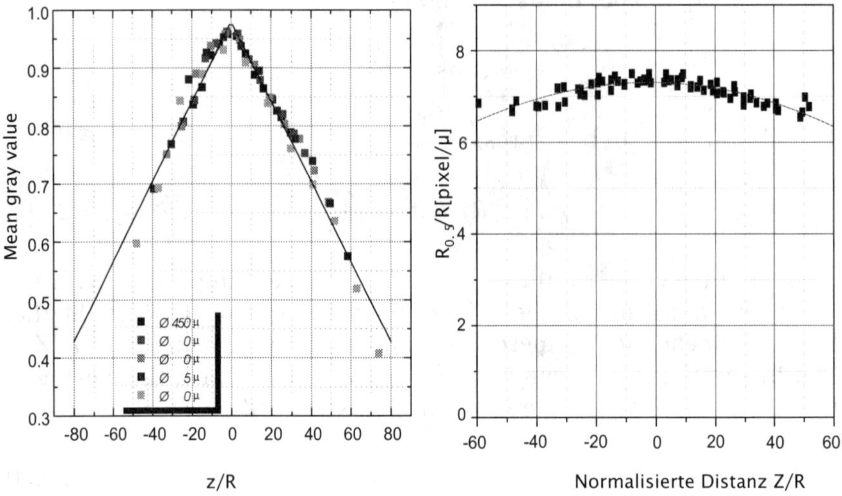

Figure 20.18: *Calibration data used for the depth-from-focus approach: left) calibration of mean gray value versus normalized depth; right) calibration of radius versus normalized depth.*

Pyramid-based depth-from-focus. As already pointed out, defocus can be measured by analyzing the suppression of high spatial frequencies. This has been used by Scholz et al. [18] and Suhr et al. [19] in order to solve the depth-from-focus problem for a biotechnological application. The application itself is described in detail in Volume 3, Section 29.4. Here we focus on the depth-from-focus algorithm. A Laplacian pyramid is defined as the difference of the levels of the Gaussian pyramid ([20],Burt [21], see also Section 4.4.3), thus consisting of a sequence of DoG filters in octave steps, combined with subsampling to save memory and time. Therefore each level $L^{(P)}$ of the Laplacian pyramid is obtained by

$$\begin{aligned} L^{(P)} &= G^{(P)} - \mathcal{E}^{(P+1)} G^{(P+1)} \\ &= \left[\mathcal{I}^{(P+1)} - \mathcal{E}^{(P+1)} (\mathcal{R}\mathcal{B})^{(P)} \right] \left(\prod_{p=0}^{P-1} (\mathcal{R}\mathcal{B})^{(p)} \right) G^{(0)} \end{aligned} \qquad (20.72)$$

with $G^{(0)}$ as the lowest level of the Gaussian pyramid, which is the original image, $\mathcal{B}$ as smoothing operator, the reduction operator $\mathcal{R}$ and the expansion operator $\mathcal{E}$ (Jähne [22]). The transfer functions of the first four levels of the pyramid are shown in Fig. 20.19. As a result, only the fine scales, removed by the smoothing operation, remain in the finer level.

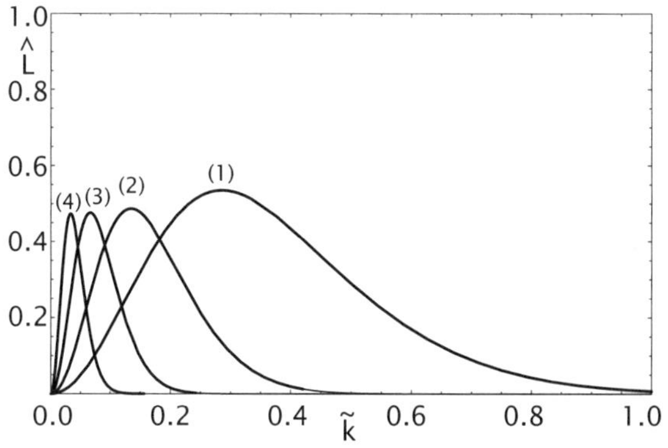

Figure 20.19: *Transfer functions of the first four levels of the Laplacian pyramid using a B^{16} binomial convolution kernel.*

Because the application deals with the detection of cells in a fluid medium, it concerns objects of similar shape and size. Due to the properties of the cells and the imaging technique used, all cells appear as approximately Gaussian-shaped objects of very similar size, but different brightness. The basic idea of the algorithm is to calculate a feature vector for each object observed. The feature vector is defined as the squared filter response on each level of the Laplacian pyramid

$$|L^{(k)}|^2 = \sum_{i=0}^{M-1} \sum_{j=0}^{N-1} (L_{i,j}^{(k)})^2 \tag{20.73}$$

whereby $L^{(k)}$ denotes the kth level of the Laplacian pyramid. The feature vector is then

$$\boldsymbol{F} = (F_0, F_1, ..) = (|L^{(0)}|^2, |L^{(1)}|^2, |L^{(2)}|^2, ...|L^{(n)}|^2) \tag{20.74}$$

The orientation of $\boldsymbol{F}$ is independent of the brightness of the object, therefore the ratios of the components of the feature vector

$$O_{i,j} = \tan \phi_{i,j} = \frac{|L^{(j)}|^2}{|L^{(i)}|^2} \qquad i, j \in [0, 1, ..., n] \qquad \forall i \neq j \tag{20.75}$$

are normalized with respect to the brightness of the object. Each of the directional components $O_{i,j}$ is a measure of the defocus, and is sensitive to a certain wave-number range.

In order to achieve the actual depth estimation, first, a calibration has to be done in order to correlate the feature vector with the actual depth of the objects (Scholz et al. [23]). The calibration data are stored in lookup tables for the depth recovery of the measured objects.

20.7 References

[1] Dhond, U. R. and Aggarwal, J. K., (1989). Structure from stereo—a review. *IEEE Trans. Sys. Man. and Cyb.*, **19**(6):1489–1510.

[2] Rice, J. A., (1988). *Mathematical Statistics and Data Analysis.* Pacific Grove, California: Wadsworth & Brooks/Cole Advanced Books & Software.

[3] Darell, T. and Wohn, K., (1990). Depth from focus using a pyramid architecture. *Pattern Recognition Letters*, **11**:787–796.

[4] Pentland, A. P., (1987). A new sense for depth of field. *IEEE Trans. Pattern Analysis and Machine Intelligence*, **9**:523–531.

[5] Ens, J. and Lawrence, P., (1991). A matrix based method for determining depth from focus. *Pattern Recognition Letters*, **12**.

[6] Ens, J. and Lawrence, P., (1993). An investigation of methods for determining depth from focus. *IEEE Trans. Pattern Analysis and Machine Intelligence*, **15**(2):97–108.

[7] Bertero, M. and Poggio, R. A., (1988). Ill-posed problems in early vision. *Proc. IEEE*, **76**(8):869–889.

[8] Pentland, A. P., (1985). A new sense for depth of field. In *Proc. International Joint Conference on Artificial Intelligence*, pp. 988–994.

[9] Grossman, P., (1987). Depth from focus. *Pattern Recognition Letters*, **5**: 63–69.

[10] Lai, S. H., Fu, C. W., and Chang, S. Y., (1992). A generalized depth estimation algorithm with a single image. *IEEE Trans. Pattern Analysis and Machine Intelligence*, **14**(6):405–411.

[11] Marr, D. and Hildreth, E. C., (1980). Theory of edge detection. *Proc. Royal Soc. London Ser. B*, **207**:187–217.

[12] Hildreth, E. C., (1983). The detection of intensity changes by computer and biological vision systems. *Comput. Vision Graphics Image Processing*, **22**:1–27.

[13] Haralick, R. M., (1984). Digital step edges from zero crossings of second directional derivatives. *IEEE Trans. Patt. Anal. Machine Intell.*, **PAMI-6**: 58–68.

[14] Subbarao, M. and Gurumoorthy, N., (1998). Depth recovery from blurred edges. *IEEE Computer Society Conf. Comput. Vision Pattern Recognition*, pp. 498–503.

[15] Subbarao, M., (1997). Direct recovery of depth map I: Differential methods. *Proc. IEEE Computer Society Workshop Comput. Vision*, pp. 58–65.

[16] Jähne, B. and Geißler, P., (1994). Depth from focus with one image. In *Proc. IEEE Conference on Computer Vision and Pattern Recognition 1994, Seattle*, pp. 713–717. Los Alamitos, CA: IEEE Computer Society Press.

[17] Jähne, B. and Geißler, P., (1994). An imaging optical technique for bubble measurements. In *Sea Surface Sound '94 - Proceedings of the Third International Meeting on Natural Physical Related to Sea Surface Sound, Lake Arrowhead, California, March 7–11*, M. J. Buckingham and J. R. Pot-

ter, eds., pp. 290–303. Singapore: World Scientific Publishing Co. Pte. Ltd. ISBN 981-02-1891-5.

[18] Scholz, T., Jähne, B., Suhr, H., Wehnert, G., Geißler, P., and Schneider, K., (1994). A new depth-from-focus technique for in situ determination of cell concentration in bioreactors. In *Proceedings of the 16th DAGM Symposium, Wien*, pp. 145–154. DAGM.

[19] Suhr, H., Bittner, C., Geißler, P., Jähne, B., Schneider, K., Scheper, T., Scholz, T., and Wehnert, G., (1995). In situ microscopy for on-line characterization of cell-populations in bioreactors, including cell-concentration measurements by Depth from Focus. *Biotechnology and Bioengineering*, **47**:106–116.

[20] Burt, P. J. and Adelson, E. H., (1983). The Laplacian pyramid as a compact image code. *IEEE Trans. COMM*, **31**:532–540.

[21] Burt, P. J., (1984). The pyramid as a structure for efficient computation. In *Multiresolution Image Processing and Analysis*, A. Rosenfeld, ed., Vol. 12 of *Springer Series in Information Sciences*, pp. 6–35. New York: Springer.

[22] Jähne, B., (1997). *Digital Image Processing—Concepts, Algorithms and Scientific Applications*, 4th edition. Berlin: Springer.

[23] Scholz, T., Jähne, B., Suhr, H., Wehnert, G., Geißler, P., and Schneider, K., (1995). In situ determination of cell concentration in bioreactors with a new depth-from-focus technique. In *Computer Analysis of Images and Patterns—Proceedings of the 6th International Conference , CAIP '95, September 6-8, Prague, Czech Republic*, V. Hlaváč and R. Šára, eds., Lecture Notes in Computer Science, pp. 392–399. Berlin: Springer.

[24] Bove, V. M., (1989). Discrete Fourier transform based depth from focus. *Image Understanding and Machine Vision, Technical Digest Series, Optical Society of America and Air Force Office of Scientific Research*, **14**:118–121.

[25] Krotkov, E., (1987). Focusing. *Internat. Jour. Computer Vision*, **1**:223–237.

Part IV

Object Analysis, Classification, Modeling, Visualization

21 Morphological Operators

Pierre Soille

Silsoe Research Institute, Silsoe, Bedfordshire, United Kingdom

Handbook of Computer Vision and Applications
Volume 2
Signal Processing and Pattern Recognition

Copyright © 1999 by Academic Press
All rights of reproduction in any form reserved.
ISBN 0-12-379772-1/$30.00

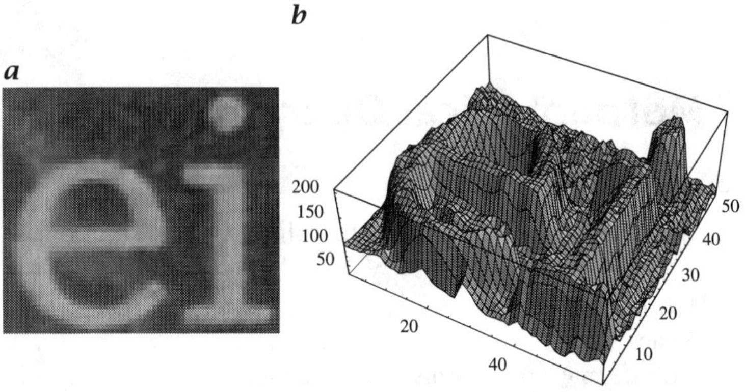

Figure 21.1: ***a*** *A gray-scale image and* ***b*** *its topographic or set representation called subgraph generated by associating each point of the image with an elevation value proportional to its gray-level.*

21.1 Introduction

Mathematical morphology (*MM*) or simply *morphology* can be defined as a theory for the analysis of spatial structures [1]. It is called morphology because it aims at analyzing the shape and form of objects. Mathematical morphology is not only a *theory*, but also a powerful image analysis *technique*. The purpose of this chapter is to introduce the morphological operators used in practical applications[1]. The emphasis is therefore put on the technique rather than the theory.

Morphological operators belong to the class of nonlinear neighborhood operators (Chapter 5). The neighborhood used for a given morphological operator is called *structuring element*. The operators are then defined by testing whether the structuring element fit or does not fit the image objects considered as sets of an n-dimensional space. A set representation of a binary image is trivial because it is already defined as a set of black pixels and its *complement*, the set of white pixels. For gray-scale images, a set representation can be achieved by considering the set of points lying below the image intensity surface and above the image definition domain. The resulting set is called *subgraph*. The subgraph of a 2-D gray-scale image is shown in Fig. 21.1. From this figure, it can be seen that a gray-scale image is viewed as a topographic surface, the brighter the gray-tone level of a pixel, the higher the elevation of the terrain point corresponding to this pixel. In practice, set operators such as union and intersection can be directly generalized to gray-scale images of any dimension by considering the point-wise maximum and minimum operators.

[1]A comprehensive description of the principles and applications of morphological image analysis can be found in Soille [2].

Morphological operators are best suited to the selective extraction or suppression of image structures. The selection is based on their shape, size, and orientation. In this sense, morphological operators are low-level image operators that already integrate some knowledge about the image objects that are under study. For instance, line segment structuring elements should be considered for the morphological processing of thin elongated objects such as glass fibers in materials sciences or roads in satellite images.

By combining elementary morphological operators, important image processing tasks can also be achieved. For example, there exist combinations leading to the definition of morphological edge sharpening, contrast enhancement, and gradient operators. A morphological segmentation operator integrating region growing and boundary detection techniques is also available.

Morphological operators are not restricted to the processing of 2-D images. They are well suited for n-dimensional binary and gray-scale images. Likewise, multicomponent images are handled by processing each component separately. Although most of the examples in this chapter deal with 2-D images, all morphological operations discussed in this chapter can also be applied to multichannel images and higher-dimensional images.

The chapter is organized as follows. The basics of morphological operators and background notions useful for defining and characterizing them are discussed in Section 21.2. A brief description of the fundamental morphological transformations follows in Section 21.3 including erosion and dilation (Section 21.3.1), morphological gradients (Section 21.3.2), and opening and closing (Section 21.3.3). Morphological operators requiring two rather than a unique input image are called geodesic and detailed in Section 21.3.6. Operators such as the hit-or-miss transform requiring two rather than a unique structuring element are presented in Section 21.3.9. While Section 21.4 deals with efficient computation of morhpological operations, Section 21.3 demonstrats their application to nonlinear filtering, segmentation and other elementary image processing tasks. A survey of scientifical and technical applications solved using morphological operators is presented in Volume 3, Chapter 12.

21.2 Basics

21.2.1 Image transforms and cross sections

In mathematical terms, a gray-tone image f is a mapping of a subset $\mathcal{D}_f$ of $\mathbb{Z}^n$ called the definition domain of f into a finite chain of nonnegative integers:

$$f : \mathcal{D}_f \subset \mathbb{Z}^n \longrightarrow \{0, 1, \ldots, t_{\max}\}$$

where $t_{\max}$ is the maximum value of the data type used for storing the image (i. e.„ $2^n - 1$ for pixels coded on n bits). There is no need to consider negative values because usual morphological operators do preserve the dynamic range of the input image. Note that a binary image is nothing but a gray-scale image with only two gray-scale levels (0 for the background and 1 for the foreground).

Morphological image transformations are image-to-image transformations, that is, the transformed image has the same definition domain as the input image and it is still a mapping of this definition domain into the set of nonnegative integers. We use the generic notation Ψ for such mappings. The *identity transform* I is a trivial example of image-to-image transformation.

A widely used image-to-image transformation is the threshold operator T, which sets all pixels $\boldsymbol{x}$ of the input image f whose values lie in the range $[t_i, t_j]$ to 1 and the other ones to 0:

$$[T_{[t_i,t_j]}(f)](\boldsymbol{x}) = \begin{cases} 1, & \text{if } t_i \le f(\boldsymbol{x}) \le t_j \\ 0, & \text{otherwise} \end{cases}$$

It follows that the threshold operator maps any gray-tone image into a binary image.

The *cross section* of a gray-tone image f at level t is the set of pixels of the image whose values are greater than or equal to t. In image transformation terms, the cross-section operator CS_t maps a gray-tone image into a binary image as follows:

$$CS_t = T_{[t,t_{\max}]} \tag{21.1}$$

The subgraph of a gray-tone image (see example in Fig. 21.1b) corresponds to the stacking of its successive cross sections. Hence, we can decompose a gray-tone image into the sum of its cross sections, starting at level 1:

$$I = \sum_{t=1}^{t_{\max}} CS_t$$

The decomposition of a gray-scale image into the sum of its successive cross sections is often referred to as the threshold decomposition or threshold superposition principle [3]. An image-to-image transformation Ψ is *invariant to threshold decomposition* if it can be written as the sum of the transformations of the cross sections:

$$\Psi, \text{ invariant to threshold decomposition} \Leftrightarrow \quad \Psi = \sum_{t=1}^{t_{\max}} \Psi\, CS_t.$$

21.2.2 Set operators

The basic set operators are the *union* $\cup$ and the *intersection* $\cap$. For gray-tone images, the union becomes the *point-wise maximum* operator $\vee$ and the intersection is replaced by the *point-wise minimum* operator $\wedge$:

$$\begin{array}{ll} \text{union:} & (f \vee g)(\boldsymbol{x}) = \max[f(\boldsymbol{x}), g(\boldsymbol{x})] \\ \text{intersection:} & (f \wedge g)(\boldsymbol{x}) = \min[f(\boldsymbol{x}), g(\boldsymbol{x})] \end{array} \quad (21.2)$$

Another basic set operator is *complementation*. The complement of an image f, denoted by f^c, is defined for each pixel x as the maximum value of the data type used for storing the image minus the value of the image f at position x:

$$f^c(\boldsymbol{x}) = t_{\max} - f(\boldsymbol{x}) \quad (21.3)$$

The complementation operator is denoted by $\complement$: $\complement(f) = f^c$.

The *set difference* between two sets X and Y, denoted by $X \setminus Y$, is defined as the intersection between X and the complement of Y: $X \setminus Y = X \cap Y^c$

The *transposition* of a set B corresponds to its symmetric set with respect to its origin:

$$\check{B} = \{-\boldsymbol{b} \mid \boldsymbol{b} \in B\}. \quad (21.4)$$

A set B with an origin O is symmetric if and only if $B = \check{B}$.

21.2.3 Order relationships

The set inclusion relationship allows us to determine whether two sets are ordered, that is, whether the first is included in the second or vice versa. In this section, we show how to extend ordering relationships to gray-scale images and to image transformations.

An image f is less than or equal to an image g with the same definition domain if the value of f is less than or equal to the value of g at all pixels $\boldsymbol{x}$ in the common domain of definition. Equivalently, for all gray-scale levels t, the cross section of f at level t is included in the cross section of g at the level t:

$$f \le g \Leftrightarrow \forall \boldsymbol{x},\ f(\boldsymbol{x}) \le g(\boldsymbol{x}) \Leftrightarrow \forall t,\ CS_t(f) \subseteq CS_t(g)$$

Order relationships for image transformations are defined by analogy: a transformation Ψ_1 is less than or equal to a transformation Ψ_2 if and only if, for all images f, $\Psi_1(f)$ is less than or equal to $\Psi_2(f)$:

$$\Psi_1 \le \Psi_2 \Leftrightarrow \forall f,\ \Psi_1(f) \le \Psi_2(f)$$

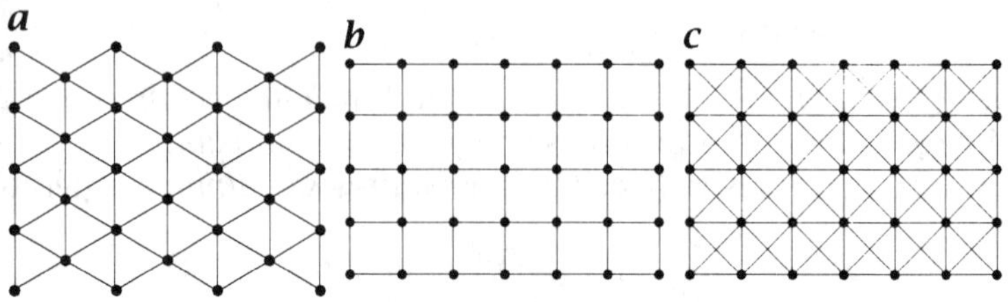

Figure 21.2: *The points of a digitization network are considered as the vertices of a graph. The arcs or edges of the graph define the neighbors of each vertex:* ***a*** *hexagonal graph;* ***b*** *4-connected graph;* ***c*** *8-connected graph.*

21.2.4 Graph, path, and connectivity

Important notions of discrete geometry have already been presented in Section 2.3. Graph theoretical concepts for image processing are discussed in Chapter 24. Thus this section just summaries the basic definitions and concepts used in morphology.

A nonoriented graph $\mathcal{G}$ associated to a digitization network is a pair (V, E) of *vertices* V and *edges* E, where

$V = (v_1, v_2, \ldots, v_n)$	is a set of vertices or points of the digitization network,
$E = (e_1, e_2, \ldots, e_m)$	is a family of unordered pairs (v_i, v_j) of vertices represented by edges or arcs.

A graph is said to be *simple* if it does not contain any loop (i.e., (v_i, v_i)-type edge) and if there exists no more than one arc linking any given pair of vertices. A graph is planar if it can be drawn in the plane without intersecting any pair of edges. The three most common graphs used in image analysis are the hexagonal graph for the triangular network and the 4- and 8-connected graphs for the square network (see Fig. 21.2).

These graphs are also referred to as *grids*. For 3-dimensional images digitized according to a cubic network, common graphs are 6-, 16-, or 26-connected. Other useful networks for 3-dimensional images are the centred cubic and face-centred networks. In the following, the neighbors of a pixel v in a graph $\mathcal{G} = (V, E)$ are denoted by $N_{\mathcal{G}}(v)$:

$$N_{\mathcal{G}}(v) = \{v' \in V \mid (v, v') \in E\}$$

For each digitized set X, there corresponds a graph whose vertices are the points of X and whose edges are the pairs (v_i, v_j) such that v_i is a neighbor of v_j in the considered digitization graph.

A sequence $v_0, v_1, \ldots, v_l$ of distinct vertices of a graph $\mathcal{G}$ is a *path* $\mathcal{P}$ of length l if v_i and v_{i+1} are neighbors for all i in $0, 1, \ldots, l-1$. A set is *connected* if each pair of its points can be joined by a path all of whose points are in the set.

21.2.5 Discrete distances and distance functions

Definitions. The concept of *distance* is widely used in image analysis and especially in mathematical morphology. There exist many discrete distances satisfying the three axioms of a metric (compare discussion in Section 2.3). The choice of a given *metric* depends on the application speed, memory load, and accuracy requirements.

The discrete distance d_G between two pixels p and q in a graph or grid $\mathcal{G}$ is the smallest length of the paths $\mathcal{P}$ linking p to q:

$$d_{\mathcal{G}}(p,q) = \min\{L(\mathcal{P}) \mid \mathcal{P} \text{ path linking } p \text{ to } q \text{ in } \mathcal{G}\} \tag{21.5}$$

The path(s) corresponding to the smallest length is (are) called shortest path(s) or *geodesics.* If the underlying graph is 4-connected, the metric is known as the *city-block metric* which is denoted by d_b. The 8-connected graph defines the *chess board metric* d_c. An alternative approach is to consider the points of the digitization network as if they were embedded into the Euclidean space $\mathbb{R}^n$. By doing so, the neighborhood relationships between points of the image definition domain are not taken into account and the actual *Euclidean distance* d_e is considered. In practice, Euclidean distances are often rounded to their nearest integer value. The rounded Euclidean distance function $d_{e'}$ is a semimetric because it does not satisfy the triangle inequality axiom of a metric [4].

The *distance function* D on a binary image f associates each pixel $\boldsymbol{x}$ of the definition domain $\mathcal{D}_f$ of f with its distance to the nearest zero-valued pixel:

$$[D(f)](\boldsymbol{x}) = \min\{d(\boldsymbol{x},\boldsymbol{x}') \mid f(\boldsymbol{x}') = 0\} \tag{21.6}$$

The distance function is sometimes referred to as the *distance transform.* Depending on whether d_e or $d_{\mathcal{G}}$ is used in Eq. (21.6), one defines a Euclidean or a discrete distance function.

The link existing between distance transforms and morphological operations will be highlighted in Section 21.3.1. In fact, we will see that distance functions are widely used in morphology for analyzing objects of binary images. A distance function on a binary image of cells is shown in Fig. 21.3.

Skeleton by influence zones. The set of pixels of a binary image that are closer to a given connected component than any other connected component defines the influence zone of the considered connected component. For example, the influence zones of a collection of points are the Voronoï polygons associated with these points. In mathematical terms, let X be a binary image or set and $K_1, K_2, \ldots, K_n$ the connected components of X. The *influence zone* IZ of a connected

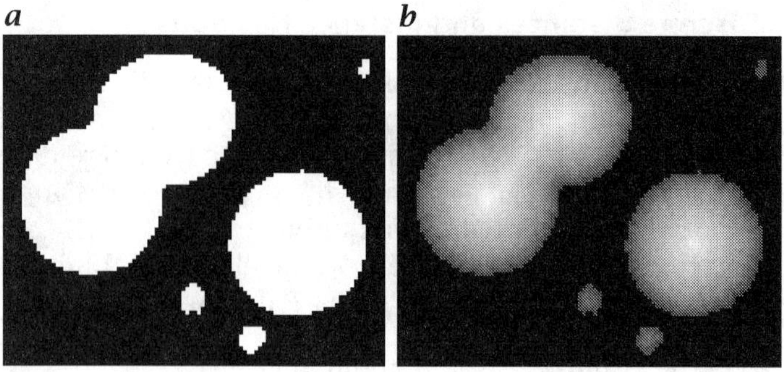

Figure 21.3: *Distance function on a binary image of cells. Note that the high values of the distance function correspond to the center of the cells:* ***a*** *binary image of cells;* ***b*** *rounded Euclidean distance function on (a).*

component K_i is the set of pixels of the image definition domain, which is closer to K_i than any other particle of X:

$$IZ(K_i) = \{\boldsymbol{x} \mid \forall j \in \{1, \dots, n\}, i \neq j \Rightarrow d(\boldsymbol{x}, K_i) < d(\boldsymbol{x}, K_j)\} \quad (21.7)$$

The skeleton by influence zones or $SKIZ$ is defined as the points that do not belong to any influence zone:

$$SKIZ(X) = \complement[\bigcup_i IZ(K_i)]$$

Hence, the $SKIZ$ of a set is equivalent to the boundary of its influence zones.

21.2.6 Image operator properties

The properties of an image operator allows us to predict its behavior. Hence they are very helpful for choosing the appropriate operators when developing a methodology for solving an image analysis problem. The properties of linear shift-invariant image operators have already been described in Section 5.3. Morphological operators are nonlinear shift-invariant filters that may satisfy some other properties:

Idempotence. A transformation Ψ is idempotent if applying it twice to any image is equivalent to applying it only once:

$$\Psi, \text{ idempotent } \Leftrightarrow \Psi\Psi = \Psi$$

It therefore makes no sense to apply an idempotent transformation twice. Removing all objects of a given surface area on a binary image is an example of an idempotent transformation. Idempotence is a key property of a morphological filter. Ideal bandpass filters are also idempotent operators.

Extensivity. A transformation Ψ is extensive if it is greater than or equal to the identity transform I:

$$\Psi,\ \text{extensive}\ \Leftrightarrow\ I \leq \Psi$$

Anti-extensivity. A transformation Ψ is anti-extensive if it is less than or equal to the identity transform I:

$$\Psi,\ \text{anti-extensive}\ \Leftrightarrow\ I \geq \Psi$$

Increasingness. A transformation Ψ is increasing if it preserves the order relationships between images:

$$\Psi,\ \text{increasing}\ \Leftrightarrow\ \forall f, g,\ f \leq g \Rightarrow \Psi(f) \leq \Psi(g) \tag{21.8}$$

Any increasing operator defined for binary images can be directly extended to gray-scale images using the threshold superposition principle. Consider for instance the binary operator that removes all connected components with a surface area smaller than a given threshold value. This operator is increasing and can be extended to gray-scale images by applying the operator to each cross section and stacking them back to get the transformed gray-scale image.

Duality. Two transformations Ψ and Φ are dual with respect to complementation if applying Ψ to an image is equivalent to applying Φ to the complement of the image and taking the complement of the result:

$$\Psi \text{ and } \Phi \text{ dual with respect to complementation } \complement\ \Leftrightarrow\ \Psi = \complement\Phi\complement \tag{21.9}$$

For example, setting to 0 all foreground connected components whose surface area is less than a given threshold value λ is the dual transformation of setting to 1 all background-connected components whose surface area is less than λ.

Self-duality. A transformation Ψ is self-dual with respect to complementation if its dual transformation with respect to the complementation is Ψ itself:

$$\Psi,\ \text{self-dual with respect to complementation } \complement\ \Leftrightarrow\ \Psi = \complement\Psi\complement$$

Linear shift-invariant filters (i.e., convolutions) are all self-dual operators. When a transformation is not self-dual, a symmetric processing can only be approximated by applying the transformation and then its dual (see Section 21.5.3).

21.2.7 Structuring element

An SE is nothing but a small set used to probe the image under study. An origin must also be defined for each SE so as to allow its positioning at a given point or pixel: an SE at point $\boldsymbol{x}$ means that its origin coincides with $\boldsymbol{x}$. The elementary isotropic SE of an image is defined as a point and its neighbors, the origin being the central point. For instance, it is a centered 3×3 window for a 2-D image defined over an 8-connected grid. In practice, the shape and size of the SE must be adapted to the image patterns that are to be processed. Some frequently used SEs are discussed hereafter.

Digital approximations of line segments. Line segments are often used to remove or extract elongated image structures. There are two parameters associated with line SEs: length and orientation. The latter has degree units and the former is usually given in number of pixels. This number should be set according to the actual width or length of the objects that are to be processed. In a square grid, there are only $2k - 2$ possible orientations for a line segment having an odd extent of k pixels.

Periodic lines. Digital connected line segments at arbitrary orientation are only broad approximations of Euclidean line segments. This led Jones and Soille [5, 6] to introduce the concept of *periodic* lines by considering those points of the Euclidean line that fall exactly on grid points. A periodic line $P_{\lambda,\vec{v}}$ with the following equation:

$$P_{\lambda,\vec{v}} = \bigcup_{i=0}^{i=\lambda} i\vec{v} \qquad (21.10)$$

where $\lambda + 1 > 0$ is the number of points in the periodic line and $\vec{v}$ is a constant vector called the *periodicity* of the line. Periodic line structuring elements have proven their utility for filtering linear image features and generating better approximations of disk-like SEs from cascades of periodic lines.

Digital approximations of the disk. Due to their isotropy, disks and spheres are very attractive SEs. Unfortunately, they can only be approximated in a digital grid. The larger the neighborhood size is, the better the approximation is. Radial decomposition of disks (Section 21.4.2) can be obtained by cascading periodic lines in various directions.

Pair of points. A pair of points is nothing but a periodic line having only 2 points: $P_{1,\vec{v}}$. In the case of binary images, an erosion with a pair of points can be used to estimate the probability that points separated by a vector $\vec{v}$ are both object pixels, that is, by measuring the number of object pixels remaining after the erosion. By varying the modulus of $\vec{v}$, it is possible to highlight periodicities in the image (Section 21.5.2).

Composite structuring elements. A composite or two-phase SE contains two non-overlapping SEs sharing the same origin. Composite SEs are considered for performing hit-or-miss transforms (Section 21.3.9). The first is used for an erosion and the second for a dilation, both transformations being computed in parallel.

Elementary symmetric structuring elements. Many morphological transformations consist in iterating fundamental operators with the elementary symmetric SE, that is, a pixel and its neighbors in the considered neighborhood graph.

Further structuring elements. Elementary triangles are sometimes considered in the hexagonal grid and 2×2 squares in the square grid. In fact, the 2×2 square is the smallest isotropic SE of the square grid but it is not symmetric in the sense that its center is not a point of the digitization network. Such small, non-symmetric SEs will be used for filtering fine image structures using opening and closing transformations (Section 21.3.3).

21.3 Morphological operators

Morphological operators aim at extracting relevant structures of the image. This can be achieved by probing the image with another set of given shape called the *structuring element* (SE), see Section 21.2.7. Erosions and dilations are the two fundamental morphological operators because all other operators are based on their combinations.

21.3.1 Erosion and dilation

Erosion. The first question that may arise when we probe a set with a structuring element is *"Does the structuring element fit the set?"* The eroded set is the locus of points where the answer to this question is affirmative. In mathematical terms, the *erosion* of a set X by a structuring element B is denoted by $\varepsilon_B(X)$ and is defined as the locus of points $\boldsymbol{x}$, such that B is included in X when its origin is placed at $\boldsymbol{x}$:

$$\varepsilon_B(X) = \{x \mid B_{\boldsymbol{x}} \subseteq X\} \tag{21.11}$$

Equation 21.11 can be rewritten in terms of an intersection of set translations, the translations being determined by the SE:

$$\varepsilon_B(X) = \bigcap_{\boldsymbol{b} \in B} X_{-\boldsymbol{b}}$$

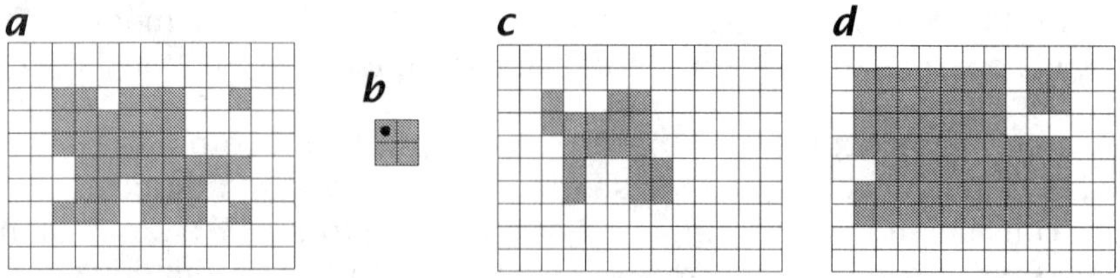

Figure 21.4: Erosion ε and dilation δ of a set X by a 2 × 2 structuring element whose origin is the upper left pixel. ***a*** *A binary image X.* ***b*** *A structuring element B.* ***c*** *Erosion of X by B.* ***d*** *Dilation of X by B.*

This latter definition itself can be directly extended to binary and gray-scale images: the erosion of an image f by a structuring element B is denoted by $\varepsilon_B(f)$ and is defined as the minimum of the translations of f by the vectors $-\boldsymbol{b}$ of B:

$$\varepsilon_B(f) = \bigwedge_{\boldsymbol{b}\in B} f_{-\boldsymbol{b}} \tag{21.12}$$

Hence, the eroded value at a given pixel $\boldsymbol{x}$ is the minimum value of the image in the window defined by the structuring element when its origin is at $\boldsymbol{x}$:

$$[\varepsilon_B(f)](\boldsymbol{x}) = \min_{\boldsymbol{b}\in B} f(\boldsymbol{x}+\boldsymbol{b}) \tag{21.13}$$

To avoid the erosion of the image structures from the border of the image, we assume that the image values outside the definition domain are set to $t_{\max}$.

Dilation. The *dilation* is the dual operator of the erosion and is based on the following question: *"Does the structuring element hit the set?"* The dilated set is the locus of points where the answer to this question is affirmative.

The dilation of a set X by a structuring element B is denoted by $\delta_B(X)$ and is defined as the locus of points $\boldsymbol{x}$ such that B hits X when its origin coincides with $\boldsymbol{x}$:

$$\delta_B(X) = \{\boldsymbol{x} \mid B_{\boldsymbol{x}} \cap X \neq \emptyset\} \tag{21.14}$$

The dilation and erosion of a discrete binary image are illustrated in Fig. 21.4.

Equation (21.14) can be rewritten in terms of a union of set translations, the translations being defined by the SE:

$$\delta_B(X) = \bigcup_{\boldsymbol{b}\in B} X_{-\boldsymbol{b}} \tag{21.15}$$

This latter definition can be directly extended to binary and gray-scale images: the dilation of an image f by a structuring element B is denoted by $\delta_B(f)$ and is defined as the maximum of the translation of f by the vectors $-\boldsymbol{b}$ of B:

$$\delta_B(f) = \bigvee_{\boldsymbol{b} \in B} f_{-\boldsymbol{b}} \tag{21.16}$$

In other words, the dilated value at a given pixel $\boldsymbol{x}$ is the maximum value of the image in the window defined by the structuring element when its origin is at $\boldsymbol{x}$:

$$[\delta_B(f)](\boldsymbol{x}) = \max_{\boldsymbol{b} \in B} f(\boldsymbol{x} + \boldsymbol{b}) \tag{21.17}$$

When dilating an image, borders effects are handled by assuming a zero-extension of the image. Gray-scale erosion and dilation are illustrated in Fig. 21.6.

We denote by nB a structuring element of size n, that is, an SE B that has been dilated n times by its transposed $\check{B}$ (see Eq. (21.4)):

$$nB = \delta_{\check{B}}^{n}(B). \tag{21.18}$$

Notice that if $B = \check{B}$ then the following relationship holds: $\delta_B^n = \delta_{nB}$.

Properties. The dilation and the erosion are dual transformations with respect to complementation. This means that any erosion of an image is equivalent to a complementation of the dilation of the complemented image with the same structuring element (and vice versa). This duality property illustrates the fact that erosions and dilations do not process the objects and their background symmetrically: the erosion *shrinks* the objects but *expands* their background (and vice versa for the dilation).

Erosions and dilations are invariant to translations and to threshold decomposition. They also preserve the order relationships between images, that is, they are increasing transformations.

The dilation distributes the point-wise maximum operator $\vee$ and the erosion distributes the point-wise minimum operator $\wedge$:

$$\delta(\bigvee_i f_i) = \bigvee_i \delta(f_i)$$
$$\varepsilon(\bigwedge_i f_i) = \bigwedge_i \varepsilon(f_i)$$

For example, the point-wise maximum of two images dilated with an identical structuring element can be obtained by a unique dilation of the point-wise maximum of the images. This results in a gain of speed.

The two following equations concern the composition of dilations and erosions:

$$\delta_{B_2}\delta_{B_1} = \delta_{(\delta_{\breve{B}_2} B_1)} \tag{21.19}$$

$$\varepsilon_{B_2}\varepsilon_{B_1} = \varepsilon_{(\delta_{\breve{B}_2} B_1)} \tag{21.20}$$

These two properties are very useful in practice as they allow us to decompose a morphological operation with a large SE into a sequence of operations with smaller SEs. For example, an erosion with a square SE of side n in pixels is equivalent to an erosion with a horizontal line of n pixels followed by an erosion with a vertical line of the same size. It follows that there are $2(n-1)$ min comparisons per pixel with decomposition and $n^2 - 1$ without, that is, $O(n)$ resp. $O(n^2)$ algorithm complexity.

The decomposition property is also important for hardware implementations where the neighborhood size is fixed (e.g., fast 3×3 neighborhood operations). By cascading elementary operations, larger neighborhood size can be obtained. For example, an erosion by a square of width $2n+1$ pixels is equivalent to n successive erosions with a 3×3 square.

Erosion and distance function. The elementary erosion of size n of a set X with a diamond ♦ or square ■ can be obtained by thresholding the corresponding distance function on X for all values strictly greater than n:

$$\varepsilon^n_{\blacklozenge}(X) = \{\boldsymbol{x} \in X \mid D_b(\boldsymbol{x}) > n\} = T_{[n+1,t_{\max}]}[D_b(X)]$$
$$\varepsilon^n_{\blacksquare}(X) = \{\boldsymbol{x} \in X \mid D_c(\boldsymbol{x}) > n\} = T_{[n+1,t_{\max}]}[D_c(X)]$$

Pseudo-Euclidean erosions, that is, erosions by the best digital approximation of a disk of a given size, can be obtained by thresholding the rounded Euclidean distance function:

$$\varepsilon^n_{e'}(X) = \{\boldsymbol{x} \in X \mid D_{e'}(\boldsymbol{x}) > n\} = T_{[n+1,t_{\max}]}[D_{e'}(X)]$$

Minkowski operators. The Minkowski subtraction of a set B to a set X is the intersection of the translations of X by the vectors of B and is denoted by $\ominus$: $X \ominus B = \bigcap_{\boldsymbol{b}\in B} X_{\boldsymbol{b}}$. By inspecting Eq. (21.11), it can be seen that $\varepsilon_B(X) = X \ominus \breve{B}$. The erosion is therefore equivalent to the Minkowski subtraction if and only if the SE is symmetric with respect to its origin (i.e., $B = \breve{B}$). The same developments apply for the Minkowski addition $\oplus$: $X \oplus B = \bigcup_{\boldsymbol{b}\in B} X_{\boldsymbol{b}}$, and therefore $\delta_B(X) = X \oplus \breve{B}$.

21.3.2 Morphological gradients

A common assumption in image analysis consists of considering image objects as regions of rather homogeneous gray-levels. It follows that object boundaries or edges are located where there are high gray-level variations. Morphological gradients are operators enhancing intensity pixel variations within a neighborhood. The erosion/dilation outputs for each pixel the minimum/maximum value of the image in the neighborhood defined by the SE. Variations are therefore enhanced by combining these elementary operators.

The basic morphological gradient, also called *Beucher gradient* [7, 8], is defined as the arithmetic difference between the dilation and the erosion with the elementary structuring element B of the considered grid. This morphological gradient is denoted by ρ:

$$\rho_B = \delta_B - \varepsilon_B. \tag{21.21}$$

From this latter equation, it can be seen that the morphological gradient outputs the maximum variation of the gray-level intensities within the neighborhood defined by the SE rather than a local slope.

In Fig. 21.5b, it can be seen that the thickness of step edge detected by a morphological gradient equals two pixels: one pixel on each side of the edge. A zero thickness can be achieved with inter-pixel approaches or by defining the edge as the interface between two adjacent regions. Alternatively, half-gradients can be used to detect either the internal or the external boundary of an edge. These gradients are one-pixel thick for a step edge.

The *half-gradient by erosion* or *internal gradient* ρ^- is defined as the difference between the identity transform and the erosion:

$$\rho_B^- = I - \varepsilon_B \tag{21.22}$$

The internal gradient enhances internal boundaries of objects brighter than their background and external boundaries of objects darker than their background. For binary images, the internal gradient will provide a mask of the internal boundaries of the objects of the image.

The *half-gradient by dilation* or *external gradient* ρ^+ is defined as the difference between the dilation and the identity:

$$\rho_B^+ = \delta_B - I \tag{21.23}$$

Note that the following relationships hold: $\rho^- = \rho^+ \complement$ and $\rho^+ + \rho^- = \rho$. In Fig. 21.5, internal and external gradients are compared to the morphological gradient.

The choice between internal or external gradient depends on the nature of the objects to be extracted. For instance, an external gradient applied to a thin dark structure will provide a thin edge whereas an internal gradient will output a double edge.

Morphological, external, and internal gradients are illustrated in Fig. 21.6. Note the effect of half-gradients on thin bright and dark features.

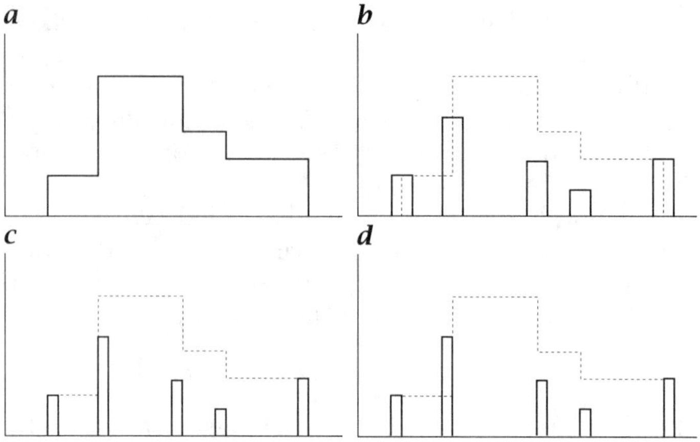

Figure 21.5: *Morphological gradients of a 1-D digital signal f with sharp transitions between homogeneous regions:* ***a*** *Original 1-D signal f;* ***b*** *Beucher's gradient $\rho(f) = \delta_B(f) - \varepsilon_B(f)$;* **c** *Internal gradient $\rho^-(f) = f - \varepsilon_B(f)$;* ***d*** *External gradient $\rho^+(f) = \delta_B(f) - f$.*

21.3.3 Opening and closing

The erosion of an image not only removes all structures that cannot contain the structuring element but it also shrinks all the other ones. The search for an operator recovering most structures lost by the erosion leads to the definition of the morphological opening operator. The principle consists in dilating the image previously eroded using the same structuring element. In general, not all structures are recovered. For example, objects completely destroyed by the erosion are not recovered at all. The dual operator of the morphological opening is the morphological closing. Both operators are the basis of the morphological approach to image filtering developed in Section 21.5.3.

Morphological opening. Once an image has been eroded, there exists in general no inverse transformation to get the original image back. The idea behind the morphological opening is to dilate the eroded image to recover as much as possible the original image.

The opening γ by a structuring element B is denoted by γ_B and is defined as the erosion by B followed by the dilation with the transposed SE $\check{B}$:

$$\gamma_B = \delta_{\check{B}} \varepsilon_B \tag{21.24}$$

In Eq. (21.24), it is essential to consider the transposed SE for the dilation. Indeed, an erosion corresponds to an intersection of translations. It follows that a union of translations in the opposite direction (i.e., a dilation by the transposed SE) must be considered when attempting to

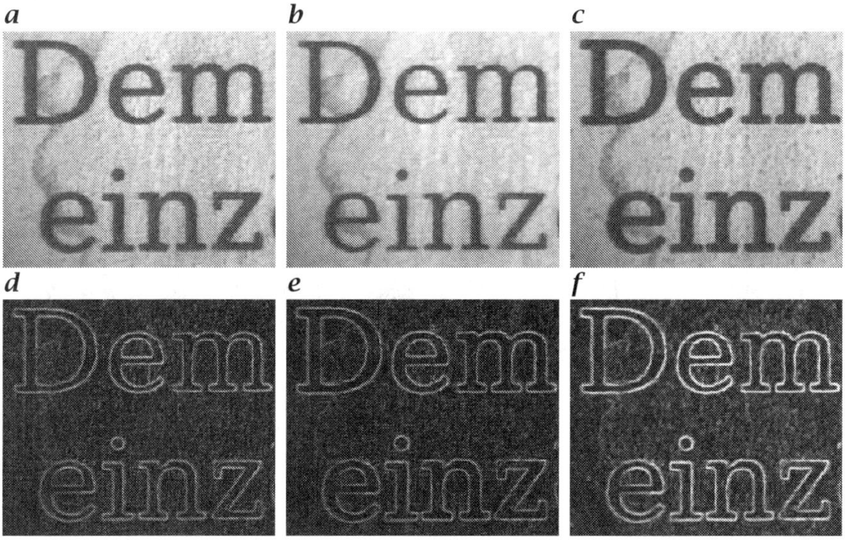

Figure 21.6: *Morphological gradients or how to combine erosion and dilation for enhancing object boundaries:* ***a*** *original image* f*;* ***b*** *dilated image* $\delta(f)$*;* ***c*** *eroded image* $\epsilon(f)$*. Edge images:* ***d*** $\rho^+(f) = \delta(f) - f$*;* ***e*** $\rho^-(f) = f - \varepsilon(f)$*;* ***f*** $\rho(f) = \delta(f) - \varepsilon(f)$*. In this figure, the SE B is a* 3×3 *square.*

recover the original image. Consequently, the opening of an image is independent from the origin of the SE.

Although the opening is defined in terms of erosions and dilations in Eq. (21.24), it possesses a geometric formulation in terms of SE fit using the question already introduced for the erosions: *"Does the structuring element fit the set?"* Each time the answer to this question is affirmative, the *whole* SE must be kept (for the erosion, it is the origin of the SE that is kept). Therefore, the opened set is the union of all SEs fitting the set:

$$\gamma_B(X) = \bigcup\{B \mid B \subseteq X\} \tag{21.25}$$

Morphological closing. The idea behind the morphological closing is to build an operator tending to recover the initial shape of the image structures that have been dilated. This is achieved by eroding the dilated image.

The closing by a structuring element B is denoted by ϕ_B and is defined as the dilation with a structuring element B followed by the erosion with the transposed structuring element $\check{B}$:

$$\phi_B = \varepsilon_{\check{B}}\delta_B \tag{21.26}$$

Using set formalism, we have the following question for defining a closing: *"Does the SE fit the background of the set?"* If yes, then all points

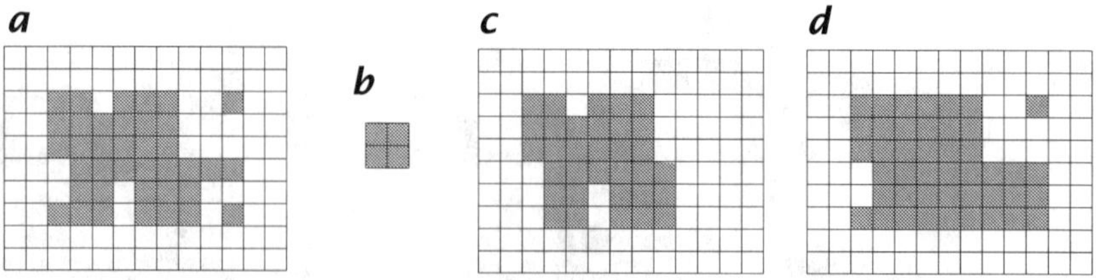

Figure 21.7: *Opening and closing of a 13×10 discrete binary image by a 2 × 2 square structuring element (the object pixels are the gray pixels):* ***a*** *a binary image X;* ***b*** *a structuring element B;* ***c*** *opening of X by B;* ***d*** *closing of X by B.*

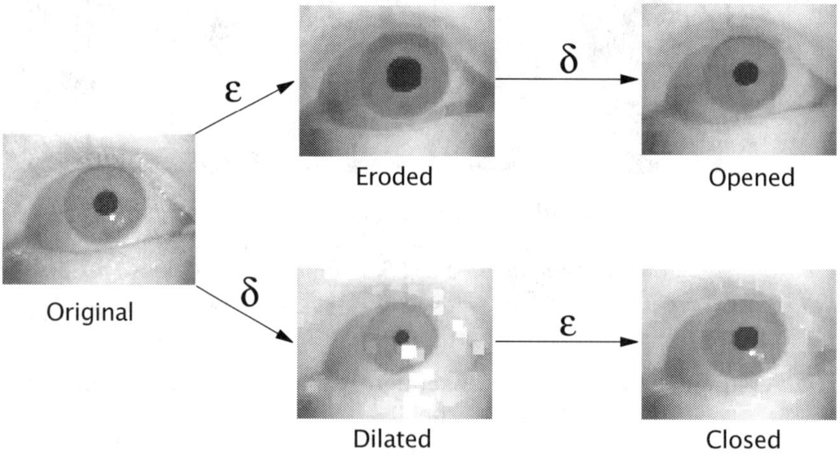

Figure 21.8: *Opening and closing of a gray-scale image with a 5 × 5 square SE.*

of the SE belong to the complement of the closing of the set:

$$\phi_B(X) = \complement[\bigcup\{B \mid B \subseteq X^c\}] = \bigcap\{B^c \mid X \subseteq B^c\}$$

Contrary to the opening, the closing filters the set from the outside. The opening and closing of a discrete image by a 2 × 2 square SE is shown in Fig. 21.7.

Note that the opening removes all object pixels that cannot be covered by the structuring element when it fits the object pixels while the closing fills all background structures that cannot contain the structuring element. In Fig. 21.8, the closing of a gray-scale image is shown together with its opening.

Properties. When we open a set, we probe it from the inside because the SE has to fit the set. More precisely, an opening *removes the object pixels* that cannot be covered by the SE translations that fit the image objects. The closing has the opposite behavior because it *adds the background pixels* that cannot be covered by the SE translations that fit the background of the image. In other words, openings and closings are dual transformations with respect to set complementation.

The fact that openings and closings are not self-dual transformations means that one or the other transformation should be used depending on the relative brightness of the image objects we would like to process. The relative brightness of an image region defines whether it is a background or foreground region. Background regions have a low intensity value compared to their surrounding regions and vice versa for the foreground regions. Openings filter the foreground regions from the inside. Closings have the same behavior on the background regions. For instance, if we want to filter noisy pixels with high intensity values an opening should be considered.

We have already stated that openings are anti extensive transformations (some pixels are removed) and closings are extensive transformations (some pixels are added). Therefore, the following ordering relationships always hold:

$$\gamma \leq I \leq \phi$$

Morphological openings γ and closings ϕ are both increasing transformations. This means that openings and closings preserve order relationships between images. Moreover, successive applications of openings or closings do not further modify the image. Indeed, they are both idempotent transformations: $\gamma\gamma = \gamma$ and $\phi\phi = \phi$. The idempotence property is often regarded as an important property for a filter because it ensures that the image will not be further modified by iterating the transformation. It corresponds well to a sifting operation: Once we have sifted materials through a sieve, sifting the materials once more using the same sieve will not further sieve these materials.

Algebraic opening and closing. If an increasing, idempotent, and anti extensive transformation can be defined as an erosion by a structuring element followed by a dilation with the transposed structuring element, it is referred to as a *morphological* opening. A transformation having the same properties, but that cannot be written as a unique erosion followed by a dilation with the transposed SE, is called an *algebraic* opening. Its dual transformation is an algebraic closing. Matheron [9] has shown that any algebraic opening can be defined as the supremum of a family of morphological openings. A useful algebraic opening is the surface area opening γ_λ [10, 11]. It can be defined as the union of all openings with connected SEs whose size in number of pixels equals λ:

$$\gamma_\lambda = \bigvee_i \{\gamma_{B_i} \mid \text{Area}(B_i) = \lambda\}$$

The surface area opening of a binary image comes down to removing all connected components whose surface area in number of pixels is smaller than a given threshold value λ.

21.3.4 Top-hats

The choice of a given morphological filter is driven by the available knowledge about the shape, size, and orientation of the structures we would like to filter. For example, we may choose an opening by a 2×2 square SE to remove impulse noise or a larger square to smooth the object boundaries. Morphological top-hats [12] proceed *a contrario*. Indeed, the approach undertaken with top-hats consists in using knowledge about the shape characteristics that are *not* shared by the relevant image structures. An opening or closing with an SE that does not fit the relevant image structures is then used to *remove* them from the image. These structures are recovered through the arithmetic difference between the image and its opening or between the closing and the image. These arithmetic differences are at the basis of the definition of morphological top-hats. The success of this approach is due to the fact that there is not necessarily a one-to-one correspondence between the knowledge about what an image object is and what it is not. Moreover, it is sometimes easier to remove relevant image objects than to try to suppress the irrelevant objects.

The white top-hat or *top-hat by opening* WTH of an image f is the difference between the original image f and its opening γ:

$$WTH = I - \gamma \tag{21.27}$$

As the opening is an anti extensive image transformation, the gray-scale values of the white top-hat are always greater or equal to zero.

The *black top-hat* or *top-hats by closing* BTH of an image f is defined as the difference between the closing ϕ of the original image and the original image:

$$BTH = \phi - I \tag{21.28}$$

It follows that $BTH = WTH\complement$. Due to the extensivity property of the closing operator, the values of the black top-hat images are always greater or equal to zero. The application of top-hat transforms to the correction of illumination is discussed in Section 21.5.1.

21.3.5 Granulometries

Principle. The concept of a *granulometry* [13], or size distribution, may be likened to the sifting of rocks in a gravel heap. The rocks are sifted through screens of increasing size, leaving only the rocks that are too big to pass through the sieve. The process of sifting the rocks at a particular size is analogous to the opening of an image using a particular size of structuring element. The residue after each opening is often collated into a granulometric curve, revealing useful information about the distribution of object sizes in the image.

In mathematical terms, a granulometry is defined by a transformation having a size parameter λ and satisfying the three following axioms:

- *Antiextensivity:* the rocks that remain in the sieve are a subset in the initial rocks.
- *Increasingness:* When sifting a subset of a heap of rocks, the rocks remaining in the sieve are a subset of those remaining after sifting the whole heap.
- *Absorption:* Let us consider a sifting transformation Φ at two different sizes λ and ν. Sifting with Φ_λ and then with Φ_ν will give the same result as sifting with Φ_ν prior to Φ_λ. It is only the size of the largest sieve that determines the result. This property is called *absorption*:

$$\Phi_\lambda \Phi_\nu = \Phi_\nu \Phi_\lambda = \Phi_{\max(\lambda,\nu)} \tag{21.29}$$

Note that for $\lambda = \nu$ the idempotence property is a particular case of the absorption property.

By definition, all openings satisfy the two first properties. However, not all openings with SEs of increasing size satisfy the absorption property. Disk-like SEs or line segments of increasing size are usually considered (families based on cascades of periodic lines are detailed in [6]). Figure 21.9 illustrates a granulometry with a family of square SEs of increasing size. Note that the size distribution does not require the particles to be disconnected.

Granulometries are interpreted through granulometric curves. Three kinds of granulometric curves are currently used:

1. Number of particles of Φ_λ vs. λ
2. Surface area of Φ_λ vs. λ
3. Loss of surface area between Φ_λ and $\Phi_{\lambda+1}$ vs. λ

The latter type of granulometric curve is often referred to as the *pattern spectrum* [14] of the image. A large impulse in the pattern spectrum at a given scale indicates the presence of many image structures at that scale. The granulometric curve associated with the granulometry presented in Fig. 21.9 is provided in Fig. 21.10 together with its pattern spectrum.

Granulometries also apply to gray-tone images. In this latter case, the surface area measurement should be replaced by the volume.

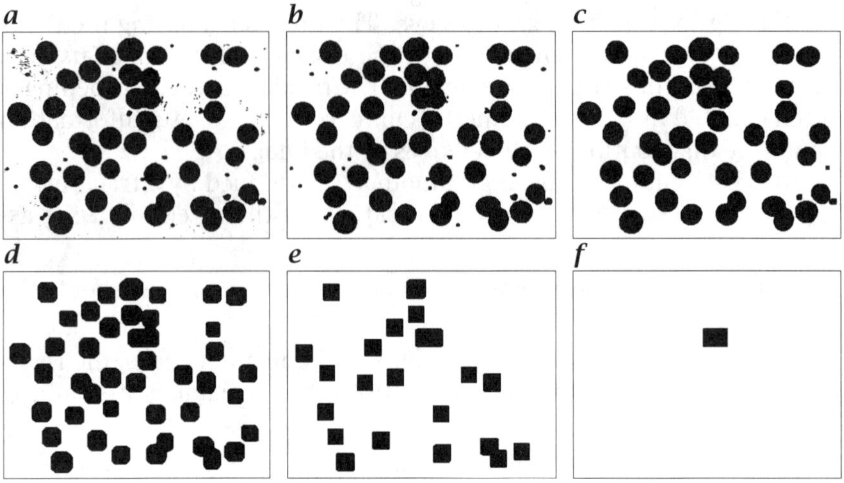

Figure 21.9: *Successive openings of a binary image of blood cells or granulometry (using square SEs of increasing size):* ***a*** *Original image* f; ***b*** *Opening of size 1:* $\gamma_B(f)$; ***c*** $\gamma_{3B}(f)$; ***d*** $\gamma_{9B}(f)$; ***e*** $\gamma_{13B}(f)$; ***f*** $\gamma_{15B}(f)$.

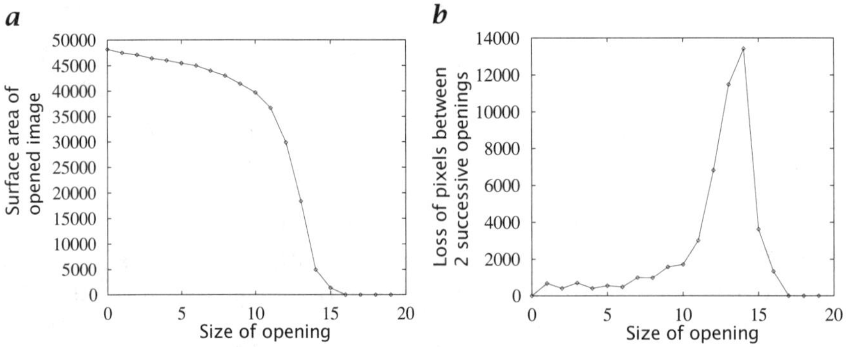

Figure 21.10: *Granulometric curves corresponding to Fig. 21.9.* ***a*** *Surface area of the opening vs size of the opening.* ***b*** *Derivative of* ***a****. The high peak observed in the pattern spectrum (b) indicates that most cells of Fig. 21.9a are at this size.*

21.3.6 Geodesic operators

All morphological operators discussed so far involved combinations of *one* input image with specific structuring elements. The approach taken with geodesic operators is to consider *two* input images. A morphological operator is applied to the first image and it is then forced to remain either greater than or lower to the second image. Authorized morphological operators are restricted to elementary erosions and dilations. The choice of specific structuring elements is therefore eluded. In practice, geodesic transformations are iterated until stability making

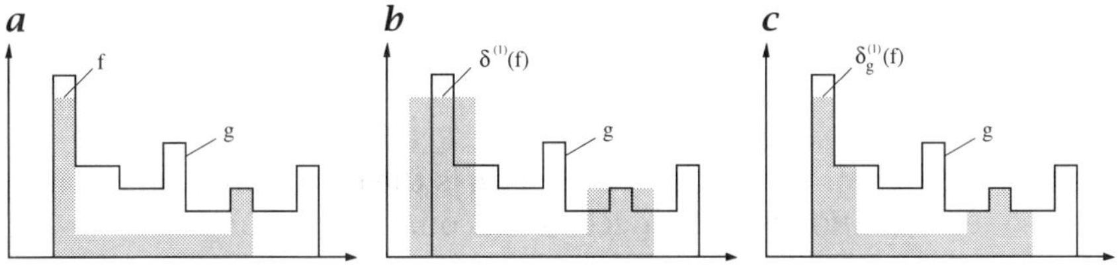

Figure 21.11: *Geodesic dilation of a 1-D marker signal f with respect to a mask signal g. Due to the point-wise minimum operator, all pixels of the elementary dilation of f having values greater than g are set to the value of g:* ***a*** *1-D marker signal f and mask signal g, $f \leq g$:* ***b*** *Elementary dilation $\delta^{(1)}(f)$;* ***c*** *Geodesic dilation $\delta_g^{(1)}(f)$.*

the choice of a size unnecessary. It is the combination of appropriate pairs of input images which produces new morphological primitives. These primitives are at the basis of formal definitions of many important image structures for both binary and gray-scale images.

Geodesic dilation. A geodesic dilation involves two images: a marker image and a mask image. By definition, both images must have the same domain of definition and the mask image must be larger than or equal to the marker image. The marker image is first dilated by the elementary isotropic structuring element. The resulting dilated image is then forced to remain below to the mask image. The mask image acts therefore as a limit to the propagation of the dilation of the marker image.

Let denote by f the marker image and by g the mask image ($f \leq g$). The *geodesic dilation* of size 1 of the marker image f with respect to the mask image g is denoted by $\delta_g^{(1)}(f)$ and is defined as the point-wise minimum between the mask image and the elementary dilation $\delta^{(1)}$ of the marker image:

$$\delta_g^{(1)}(f) = \delta^{(1)}(f) \wedge g \tag{21.30}$$

When dealing with binary images, the mask image is often referred to as the geodesic mask and the marker image the marker set. The geodesic dilation is illustrated on 1-D signals in Fig. 21.11.

The geodesic dilation of size n of a marker image f with respect to a mask image g is obtained by performing n successive geodesic dilations of f with respect to g:

$$\delta_g^{(n)}(f) = \delta_g^{(1)}[\delta_g^{(n-1)}(f)]$$

It is essential to proceed step-by-step and to apply the point-wise minimum operator after each elementary geodesic dilation in order to control the expansion of the marker image. Indeed, the geodesic dilation is lower or equal to the corresponding conditional dilation:

$$\delta_g^{(n)}(f) \leq \delta^{(n)}(f) \wedge g$$

Geodesic erosion. The *geodesic erosion* is the dual transformation of the geodesic dilation with respect to set complementation:

$$\varepsilon_g^{(1)}(f) = \varepsilon^{(1)}(f) \vee g \tag{21.31}$$

where $f \geq g$ and $\varepsilon^{(1)}$ is the elementary erosion. Hence, the marker image is first eroded and second the point-wise maximum with the mask image is calculated.

The geodesic erosion of size n of a marker image f with respect to a mask image g is obtained by performing n successive geodesic erosions of f with respect to g:

$$\varepsilon_g^{(n)}(f) = \varepsilon_g^{(1)}[\varepsilon_g^{(n-1)}(f)]$$

Morphological reconstruction. Geodesic dilations and erosions of a given size are seldom used in practice. However, when iterated until stability, they allow the definition of powerful morphological reconstruction algorithms.

Definition. The *reconstruction by dilation* of a mask image g from a marker image f ($f \leq g$) is defined as the geodesic dilation of f with respect to g until stability and is denoted by $R_g(f)$:

$$R_g(f) = \delta_g^{(i)}(f)$$

where i is such that $\delta_g^{(i)}(f) = \delta_g^{(i+1)}(f)$.

The reconstruction by dilation on 1-D gray-tone signals is illustrated in Fig. 21.12. In this figure, stability is reached after the fifth geodesic dilation.

The morphological reconstruction by dilation of a mask image from a given marker image is an increasing ($f_1 \leq f_2 \Rightarrow R_g(f_1) \leq R_g(f_2)$), antiextensive ($R_g(f) \leq g$), and idempotent ($R_{R_g(f)}(f) = R_g(f)$) transformation. It is therefore an algebraic opening.

The *reconstruction by erosion* of a mask image g from a marker image f ($f \geq g$) is defined as the geodesic erosion of f with respect to g until stability is reached. It is denoted by $R_g^{\star}(f)$:

$$R_g^{\star}(f) = \varepsilon_g^{(i)}(f)$$

where i is such that $\varepsilon_g^{(i)}(f) = \varepsilon_g^{(i+1)}(f)$

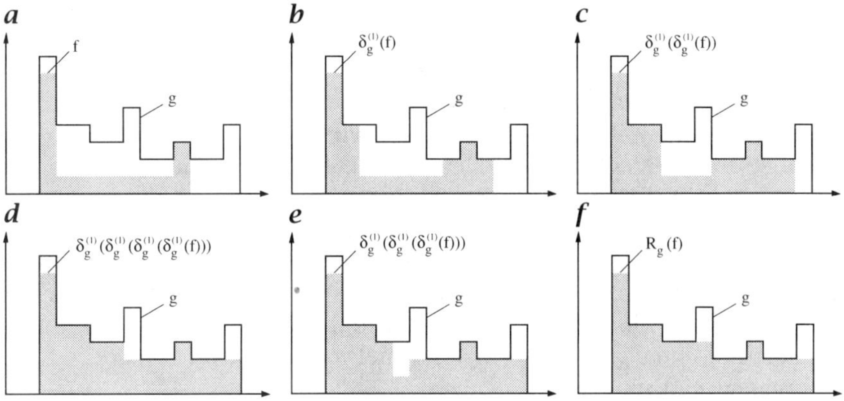

Figure 21.12: *Morphological reconstruction by dilation of a 1-D signal g from a marker signal f. The geodesic dilation of size 5 of the marker signal with respect to the mask signal g is equivalent to the reconstruction of g from f since further geodesic dilations do not modify the result anymore:* ***a*** *1-D marker signal f and mask signal g;* ***b*** *geodesic dilation of size 1 of f with respect to g;* ***c*** *geodesic dilation of size 2 of f with respect to g;* ***d*** *geodesic dilation of size 3 of f with respect to g;* ***e*** *geodesic dilation of size 4 of f with respect to g;* ***f*** *geodesic dilation of size 5 of f with respect to g.*

On the choice of the mask and marker images. Morphological reconstruction algorithms are at the basis of numerous valuable image transformations. These algorithms do not require choosing an SE nor setting its size. The main issue consists in selecting an appropriate pair of mask/marker images. The image under study is usually used as mask image. A suitable marker image is then determined using:

1. Knowledge about the expected result
2. Known facts about the image or the physics of the object it represents
3. Some transformations of the mask image itself
4. Other image data if available (i. e., multispectral and multitemporal images)
5. Interaction with the user (i.e., markers are manually determined)

One or usually a combination of these approaches is considered. The third one is the most utilized in practice but it is also the most critical: one has to find an adequate transformation or even a sequence of transformations. As the marker image has to be greater (respectively, less) than the mask image, extensive (respectively, antiextensive) transformations are best suited for generating them.

21.3.7 Reconstruction-based operators

Particles connected to the image border. In many applications it is necessary to remove all particles connected to the image border. Indeed, they may introduce some bias when performing statistics on particle measurements. Particles connected to the image border are extracted using the input image as mask image and the intersection between the input image and its border as marker image. The marker image contains therefore seeds for each particle connected to the image border and the reconstruction outputs the image of all these particles. Note that large blobs have a higher probability to intersect the image border than small blobs. Statistical methods must be considered for compensating this bias.

The removal of objects connected to the image border can be extended to gray-scale images. In this latter case, the marker image equals zero everywhere except along its border where the values of the input image are considered.

Removal of holes of a binary image. We define the holes of a binary image as the set of background components that are not connected to the image border. It follows that the complement of the background component(s) that touch(es) the image border outputs an image whose holes have been suppressed. This can be achieved with a reconstruction by erosion where the mask image equals the input image and the marker image an image of constant value $t_{\max}$ having the same border values as the input image. This definition is suited to the processing of gray-tone images (see example in Volume 3, Chapter 19).

Double threshold. The *double threshold operator DBLT* consists in thresholding the input image for two ranges of gray-scale values, one being included in the other. The threshold for the narrow range is then used as a seed for the reconstruction of the threshold for the wide range:

$$DBLT_{[t_1 \le t_2 \le t_3 \le t_4]}(f) = R_{T_{[t_1,t_4]}(f)}[T_{[t_2,t_3]}(f)]$$

The resulting binary image is much cleaner than that obtained with a unique threshold. Moreover, the result is more stable to slight modifications of threshold values. The double threshold technique is sometimes called *hysteresis threshold* [15].

Regional extrema. Image minima and maxima are important morphological features. They often mark relevant image objects: minima for dark objects and maxima for bright objects. In morphology, the term minimum is used in the sense of regional minimum, that is, a minimum whose extent is not necessarily restricted to a unique pixel: A

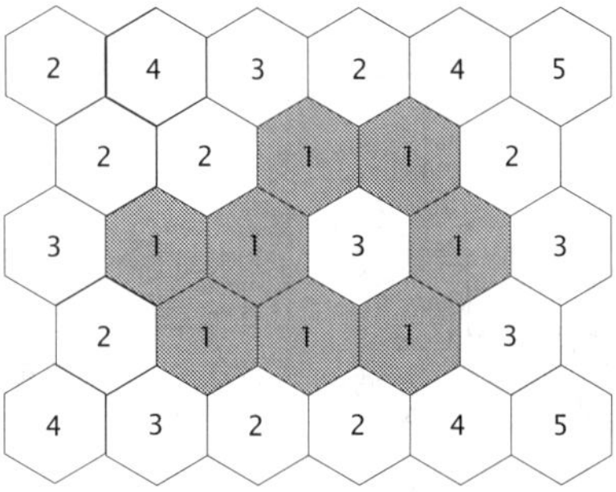

Figure 21.13: *A regional minimum at level 1 in the hexagonal grid.*

regional minimum M of an image f at elevation t is a connected component of pixels with the value t whose external boundary pixels have a value strictly greater than t. An example of regional minimum is given in Fig. 21.13. We denote by RMIN the operator extracting all regional minima of an image.

The regional maxima RMAX of an image are equivalent to the regional minima of the complement of this image: $\mathrm{RMAX} = \mathrm{RMIN}\,\complement$. The extrema of an image are defined as the union of its regional minima and maxima.

The set of all regional maxima RMAX of an image f can be obtained by performing the following morphological reconstruction by dilation:

$$\mathrm{RMAX}(f) = f - R_f(f - 1) \tag{21.32}$$

If the image data type does not support negative values, the following equivalent definition should be considered:

$$\mathrm{RMAX}(f) = f + 1 - R_{f+1}(f) \tag{21.33}$$

Similarly, the regional minima RMIN of an image f are given by

$$\mathrm{RMIN}(f) = R_f^{\star}(f + 1) - f \tag{21.34}$$

The detection of minima is illustrated in Fig. 21.14.

Minima imposition. The minima imposition technique [16] concerns the filtering of the image minima. It assumes that markers of relevant image features have been determined. The marker image f_m is then defined as follows for each pixel x:

$$f_m(x) = \begin{cases} 0, & \text{if } x \text{ belongs to a marker} \\ t_{\max}, & \text{otherwise} \end{cases}$$

The imposition of the minima of the input image g is performed in two steps. First, the point-wise minimum between the input image and the

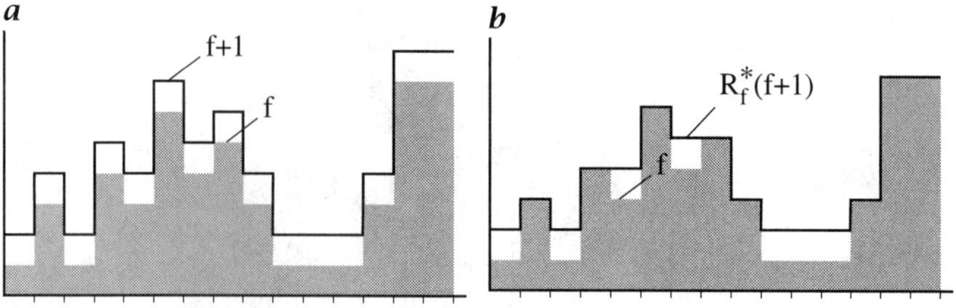

Figure 21.14: *Minima detection by reconstruction: subtracting f from $R_f^\star(f+1)$ provides a mask of the minima of f:* ***a*** *1-D signal f;* ***b*** *Reconstruction by erosion of f from $f+1$.*

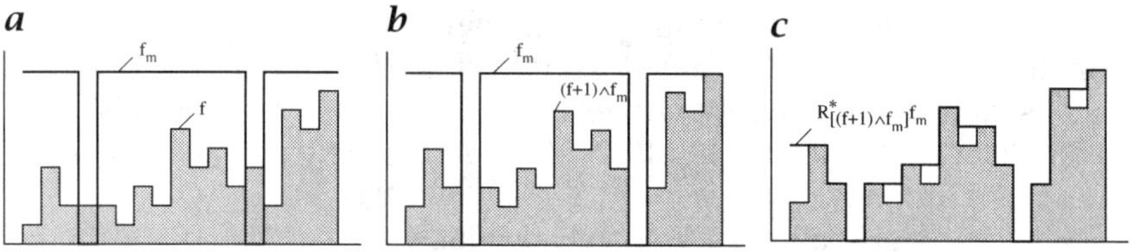

Figure 21.15: *Minima imposition technique. The input signal f contains 7 minima. The two minima of the marker signal f_m are imposed to the input signal by using a morphological reconstruction by erosion:* ***a*** *Input signal f and marker signal f_m;* ***b*** *Point-wise minimum between $f+1$ and f_m: $(f+1)\wedge f_m$* ***c*** *Reconstruction of $(f+1)\wedge f_m$ from the marker function f_m.*

marker image is computed: $f \wedge f_m$. By doing so, minima are created at locations corresponding to the markers (if they do not already exist) and we make sure that the resulting image is lower or equal to the marker image. Moreover, two minima to impose may already belong to a minima of f at level 0. It is therefore necessary to consider $(f+1)\wedge f_m$ rather than $f \wedge f_m$. The second step consists in a morphological reconstruction by erosion of $(f+1)\wedge f_m$ from the marker image f:

$$R^\star_{[(f+1)\wedge f_m]}(f_m)$$

The imposition of minima is illustrated in Fig. 21.15 on a 1-D signal. The same developments apply for maxima imposition techniques.

Opening/closing by reconstruction. The opening by reconstruction of size n an image f is defined as the reconstruction of f from the erosion of size n of f:

$$\gamma_R^{(n)}(f) = R_f[\varepsilon^{(n)}(f)] \tag{21.35}$$

It is an algebraic opening. Contrary to the morphological opening, the opening by reconstruction preserves the shape of the components that

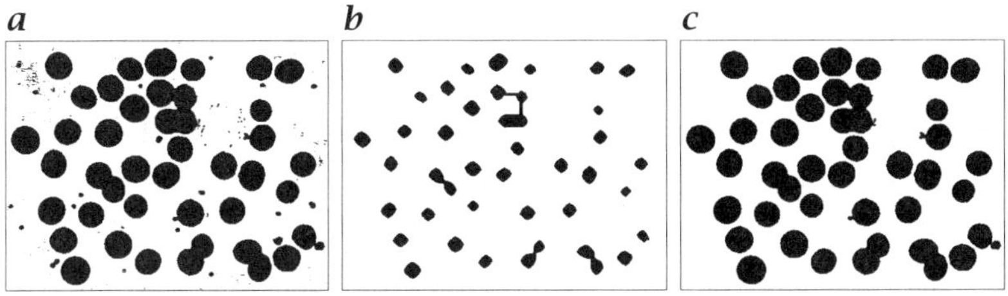

Figure 21.16: *Opening by reconstruction of a binary image:* **c** *the output image is the reconstruction of* **a** *the original image f using* **b** *the erosion as marker image (erosion of f by a square SE).*

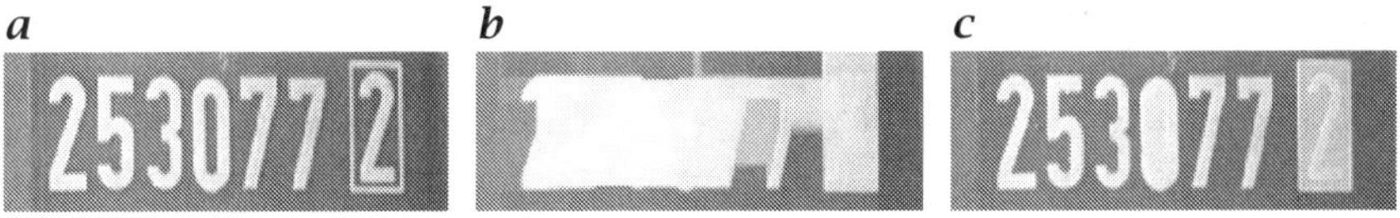

Figure 21.17: *Morphological closing and morphological closing by reconstruction of an image of a container plate:* **a** *Image of a container plate f;* **b** *Closing of f by a 15×15 square;* **c** *Closing by reconstruction of f with the same square.*

are not removed by the erosion: All image features that cannot contain the structuring element are removed, the others being unaltered. This is illustrated in Fig. 21.16 for a binary image. The original image (Fig. 21.16a) is first eroded (Fig. 21.16b). The eroded sets are then used as seeds for a reconstruction of the original image. This leads to Fig. 21.16c.

Closings by reconstruction are defined by duality:

$$\phi_R^{(n)}(f) = R_f^\star[\delta^{(n)}(f)] \tag{21.36}$$

The morphological closing and closing by reconstruction of a container plate is shown in Fig. 21.17.

The structuring element considered for both closings is a large square. The dark image structures that have been completely filled by the morphological closing remain closed after the reconstruction. This happens for the 0 and the 2 surrounded by a rectangle box.

The following order relationships hold:

$$\gamma \leq \gamma_R \leq I \leq \phi_R \leq \phi.$$

Opening and closing by reconstruction are used for processing signals of at least two dimensions. Indeed, the opening (respectively closing) by reconstruction of 1-D signals is always equivalent to its morphological opening (respectively closing).

21.3.8 Geodesic distance and skeleton by influence zones

Binary geodesic transformations have been first introduced in image analysis using the concept of geodesic distance [17, 18]: the *geodesic distance* $d_A(p,q)$ between two pixels p and q in A is the minimum of the length L of the path(s) $\mathcal{P} = (p_1, p_2, \ldots, p_l)$ joining p and q and included in A:

$$d_A(p,q) = \min\{L(\mathcal{P}) \mid p_1 = p,\ p_l = q \text{ and } \mathcal{P} \subseteq A\}$$

The *geodesic skeleton by influence zones* [18] stems directly from the definition of the geodesic distance. Let X be a set composed of the union of connected components K_i and included in a larger connected set A. The geodesic influence zone $IZ_A(K_i)$ of a connected component K_i of X in A is the locus of points of A whose geodesic distance to K_i is smaller than their geodesic distance to any other component of X:

$$IZ_A(K_i) = \{p \in A, \forall\, j \in [1,N] \setminus \{i\}, d_A(p,K_i) < d_A(p,K_j)\}$$

The use of geodesic distances for interpolating the deformation of a curve into another is detailed in Volume 3, Section 19.2. Geodesic influence zones are at the basis of the definition of the *watershed transformation* presented in Section 21.5.4.

21.3.9 Hit-or-miss

Hit-or-miss transformations [1] involve SEs composed of two sets: the first has to fit the object under study while the second has to miss it. Hence, the name *fit-and-miss* would have been more appropriate. Hit-or-miss transformations are applied to binary images for extracting neighborhood configurations such as those corresponding to isolated background and foreground pixels. Adding all pixels having a given configuration to an image leads to the definition of thickenings and subtracting them from the image defines the thinning operator. Thinnings are at the basis of discrete algorithms for computing the skeleton of a set.

The basic idea behind the hit-or-miss transform consists in extracting image pixels of a binary image having a given neighboring configuration such as a foreground pixel surrounded by background pixels (i. e.,, an isolated foreground pixel). The neighboring configuration is therefore defined by two disjoint sets, the first for the object pixels and the second for the background pixels. These two sets form what we call a composite SE that has a unique origin, that is, both sets share the same origin.

In order to perform a hit-or-miss transform, the SE is set to every possible position of the image. At each position, the following question

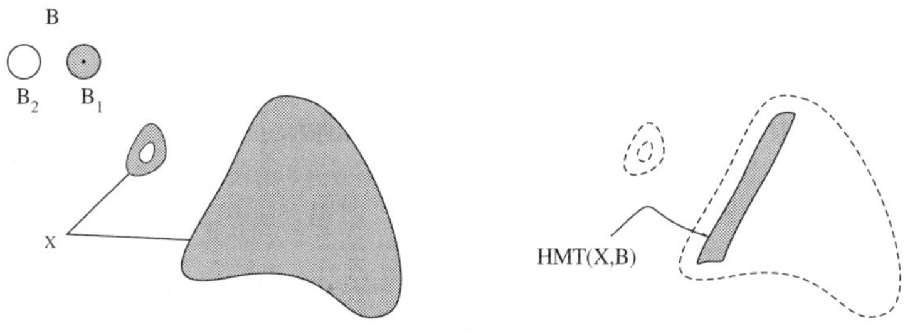

Figure 21.18: *Hit-or-miss transformation HMT of a set X by a composite structuring element B (B_1 is the gray disk and B_2 the white disk, the origin of both disks is located at the center of B_1).*

is considered *"Does the first set* fit *the foreground while, simultaneously, the second set* misses *it (i.e., fits the background)?".* If the answer is affirmative, then the point defined by the origin of the SE is a point of the hit-or-miss transformation of the image. Let us now formalize this definition in terms of morphological transformations.

The hit-or-miss transformation HMT of a set X by a composite structuring element $B = (B_1, B_2)$ is the set of points, $\boldsymbol{x}$, such that when the origin of B coincides with $\boldsymbol{x}$, B_1 fits X and B_2 fits X^c:

$$HMT_B(X) = \{\boldsymbol{x} \mid (B_1)_{\boldsymbol{x}} \subseteq X,\ (B_2)_{\boldsymbol{x}} \subseteq X^c\} \tag{21.37}$$

The hit-or-miss transformation of a set X by a composite structuring element B is sometimes denoted by $X \circledast B$. Using the definition of the erosion Eq. (21.11), the HMT can be written in terms of an intersection of two erosions:

$$HMT_B(X) = \varepsilon_{B_1}(X) \cap \varepsilon_{B_2}(X^c) \tag{21.38}$$

By definition, B_1 and B_2 have the *same* origin. They also need to be disjoint sets (i.e., $B_1 \cap B_2 = \emptyset$), otherwise the hit-or-miss would output the empty set whatever X.

An example is provided in Fig. 21.18. Both SEs of the composite SE B are disks but they have a common origin located at the center of the gray disk B_1.

It follows that B_2 does not contain its origin. Points of the hit-or-miss transform of the set X by the composite SE B (see right-hand side of the figure) are such that when the origin of B coincides with each of these points, the disk B_1 fits X and, simultaneously, the disk B_2 fits the background of X. Hence, the hit-or-miss transformation extracts all points of the image having a neighborhood configuration as defined by the composite SE B.

21.3.10 Thinning and Thickening

Thinnings consist in removing the object pixels having a given configuration. In other words, the hit-or-miss transform of the image is subtracted from the original image. Contrary to hit-or-miss transforms, there exists a definition of thinnings for gray-scale images.

Binary case. The thinning of a set or binary image X by a composite SE B is denoted[2] by $X \bigcirc B$ and defined as the set difference between X and the hit-or-miss transform of X by B:

$$X \bigcirc B = X \setminus HMT_B(X) \tag{21.39}$$

The origin of the SE must belong to B_1 the set of object pixels, otherwise the operation comes down to the identity transform. By definition, thinnings are antiextensive and nonincreasing operators.

Gray-scale case. Due to their nonincreasingness, thinnings defined in Eq. (21.39) cannot be extended to gray-scale images using the threshold decomposition principle. However, there exists a definition for gray-scale image that comes down to Eq. (21.39) when applied to binary images [19] and Beucher [20], Beucher [7]. The principle is the following. The gray scale value of the image at position x is set to the largest value of the image within the neighborhood defined by the background pixels of the SE if and only if the smallest value of the image within the neighborhood defined by the object pixels of the SE equals the image value at position x, otherwise the gray-scale value of the image at position x is not modified (remember that, for a thinning, the origin of the SE must belong to the set B_1 of object pixels of the SE):

$$(f \bigcirc B)(x) = \begin{cases} [\delta_{B_2}(f)](x) & \text{if } [\delta_{B_2}(f)](x) < f(x) \text{ and} \\ & f(x) = [\varepsilon_{B_1}(f)](x) \\ f(x) & \text{otherwise} \end{cases} \tag{21.40}$$

In this equation, the dilated value can be smaller than the original value because the SE B_2 does not contain its origin. The definition for binary images is a particular case of this definition. Indeed, the dilation by B_2 equals zero if all points of B_2 fit the background of the set and the erosion by B_1 equals one if and only if all points of B_1 fit the foreground.

Thickenings consist in adding background pixels with a specific configuration to the set of object pixels.

[2]Beware that in the literature, the symbol $\circ$ is sometimes used for the morphological opening operator (and $\bullet$ for the morphological closing).

Binary case. The thickening of a binary image or set X by a composite SE B is denoted by $X \odot B$ and defined as the union of X and the hit-or-miss transform of X by B:

$$X \odot B = X \cup HMT_B(X)$$

For a thickening, the origin of the SE must belong to the set B_2 of background pixels. Thickenings are extensive and nonincreasing transformations. Thinnings and thickenings are dual transformations:

$$X \odot B = (X^c \bigcirc B^c)^c \tag{21.41}$$

where $B = (B_1, B_2)$ and $B^c = (B_2, B_1)$

Gray-scale case. The thickening of a gray-scale image by a composite SE B at a pixel x is defined as the eroded value of the image by B_2 if this value is larger than the original image value at x and if the dilated value by B_1 is equal to this original image value; otherwise the thickening remains at the original value:

$$(f \odot B)(x) = \begin{cases} [\varepsilon_{B_2}(f)](x), & \text{if } [\delta_{B_1}(f)](x) = f(x) \text{ and } f(x) < [\varepsilon_{B_2}(f)](x), \\ f(x), & \text{otherwise} \end{cases}$$

21.4 Efficient computation of morphological operators

21.4.1 Distance transforms

The reference sequential algorithm for computing city-block and chessboard distance functions (see Section 21.2.5) is due to Rosenfeld and Pfaltz [21]. It requires one forward and one backward image sequential scan. Backward neighbors N_G^- are considered for forward scans and forward neighbors N_G^+ for backward scans. Backward neighbors of a pixel are the already processed neighbors of this pixel when performing a forward scan (and vice versa for the forward neighbors). For example, the 4-connected backward neighbors N_4^- of a pixel are its left and top neighbors, the 4-connected forward neighbors N_4^+ being the right and down pixels. Once the two scans have been performed, the input binary image f holds the distance function:

1. Forward image scan
2.   if $f(p) = 1$
3. $f(p) \leftarrow 1 + \min\{f(q) \mid q \in N_G^-(p)\}$
4. Backward image scan
5.   if $f(p) \neq 0$

6. $f(p) \leftarrow \min[f(p), 1 + \min\{f(q) \mid q \in N_G^+(p)\}]$

The reference sequential algorithm for computing Euclidean distance transforms is due to Danielsson [22]. Distance transforms in arbitrary dimensions are discussed in [23].

21.4.2 Erosions and dilations

The raw algorithm for computing erosions or dilations consists in considering for every pixel all the neighbors defined by the SE and calculating the min or max value among them (see Eqs. 21.13 and 21.17). There are therefore $n - 1$ min/max comparisons per image pixel for an SE of n pixels. This number of operations can often be reduced drastically by using appropriate algorithms and data structures. These techniques are reviewed hereafter.

Linear structuring elements. In the case of linear structuring elements, van Herk [24] has proposed a *recursive algorithm* requiring three min/max comparisons per image pixel whatever the length of the SE. In his implementation, a 1-D input array f of length nx is divided into blocks of size k, where k is the length of the SE in number of pixels. The elements of f are indexed by indices running from 0 to $nx - 1$. It is also assumed that nx is a multiple of k. Two temporary buffers g and h of length nx are also required. In the case of dilation, the maximum is taken recursively inside the blocks in both the right and left directions. When both g and h have been constructed, the result for the dilation r at any index x is given by considering the maximum value between g at position x and h at position $x+k-1$. This recursive dilation algorithm can be written as follows:

$$
\begin{aligned}
g(x) &= \begin{cases} f(x) & \text{if } x = 0, k, \ldots, (m-1)k \\ \max[g(x-1), f(x)] & \text{otherwise} \end{cases} \\
h(x) &= \begin{cases} f(x) & \text{if } x = mk-1, (m-1)k-1, \ldots, k-1 \\ \max[h(x+1), f(x)] & \text{otherwise} \end{cases} \\
r(x) &= \max[h(x), g(x+k-1)]
\end{aligned}
$$

This algorithm has also been presented by Gil and Werman [25]. It has been extended to plain and periodic lines at arbitrary angles in [26].

Decomposition of SEs. Decompositions of structure elements as per Eqs. (21.19) and (21.20) are used to speed up the computations of erosions and dilations. For example, dilating or eroding an image with a hexagon having n pixels along its sides is equivalent to dilating or eroding the image successively with three line segments of n pixels (see Fig. 21.19).

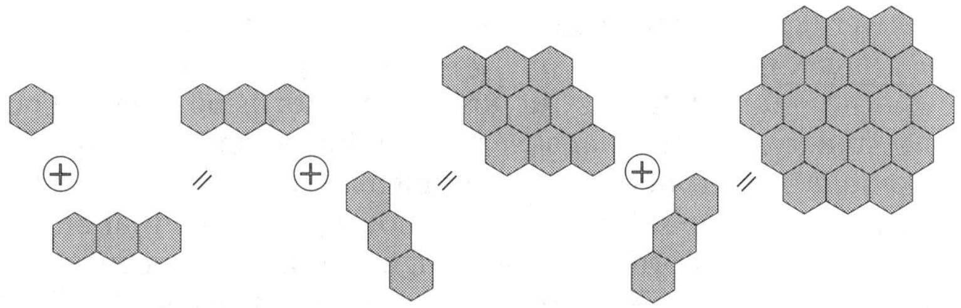

Figure 21.19: Generation of an hexagon of size 2 by cascading three line segment dilations.

This reduces the number of comparisons from $3(n^2 - n)$ to $3(n-1)$ or even 9 when using the recursive procedure described in the previous section. A *logarithmic decomposition* of convex sets has been proposed by van den Boomgaard and van Balen [27] and is based on the definition of the extreme sets of a convex set [28].

Moving histogram technique. The frequency distribution of the gray-scale values falling within the structuring element is computed and used for determining the minimum or maximum values of the image within this window. When processing the following pixel, the histogram is updated by taking into account the pixels that come out of the window and those that come in. For example, in the case of a line segment structuring element, there are only 2 such pixels whatever the length of the line segment. The scanning order of the image pixels should be chosen so as to minimize the number of pixels coming in and out.

This idea stems from the work of Huang et al. [29] on median and rank filters. An adaptation to arbitrary-shaped structuring elements is proposed in [30].

Fast binary erosions and dilations. As n pixels can be stored in an n-bit data type word, a logical operator can be simultaneously applied to n pixels using a unique bitwise operator. A description of this technique can be found for example in [27]. Moreover, the contours of the objects of a dilated binary image can be obtained by processing the contours of the original objects rather than processing the whole image pixels. Zamperoni [31] implemented a technique for dilating and eroding binary images using the Freeman boundary coding scheme [32]. Vincent [33] has shown that these ideas can be extended to arbitrary SEs.

Ragnemalm [34] developed an algorithm for fast erosion and dilation by contour processing and thresholding of distance maps using a queue of stacks for an ordered peeling of a set. A version of the algorithm implementing Euclidean peelings is also presented. van Vliet and Verwer [35] developed a queue-based contour processing method for fast binary neighborhood operation. Finally, Ji et al. [36] propose a fast algorithm for arbitrary structuring elements using interval coding.

In summary, a careful analysis of the image and structuring element should be considered before implementing a morphological operator. Moreover, we will see in the following sections that advanced morphological transformations although defined from combinations of erosions and dilations are often speeded up by using specific algorithmic techniques. A comparison between parallel, sequential, chain-code-based, and queue-based implementations is discussed in [37].

21.4.3 Openings and granulometries

Openings. By definition, morphological openings and closings can be obtained from the erosion and dilation primitives discussed in the previous section. In some cases [38], faster algorithms can be obtained by implementing the geometric interpretation of the definition of openings, Eq. (21.25).

Algebraic openings cannot be defined as an erosion followed by a dilation with the transposed SE nor in terms of SE fits. The implementation of the definition of the area opening in terms of a union of openings with all connected SEs having a given number of pixels would require a too large number of erosions and dilations as the number of connected SEs with n pixels grows exponentially with n. This led Vincent [39] to propose an efficient algorithm based on priority queue or heap data structures. An evaluation of several implementations of these data structures for computing morphological transformations can be found in [40].

Granulometries. The opening of size $\lambda+1$ of an image f can be written as follows:

$$\gamma_{(\lambda+1)B} = \delta_{(\lambda+1)B}\varepsilon_B\varepsilon_{\lambda B} \qquad (21.42)$$

Provided that the erosion at the previous step has been stored, the opening requires an erosion of size 1 and a dilation of size $\lambda + 1$. If the SE is obtained by cascading line segments, the recursive procedure described in Section 21.4.2 should be used because the processing time for computing an opening will be the same whatever the size of the SE.

Granulometries of binary images with a family of isotropic SEs can be further speeded up by computing the *opening function* of the input binary image. The opening function OF maps each pixel of the input binary image X with the size of the opening that removes it from X:

$$[OF(X)](\boldsymbol{x}) = \max\{\lambda \mid \boldsymbol{x} \in \gamma_{\lambda B}(X)\}$$

Therefore, the histogram of the opening function is equivalent to the derivative of the granulometric curve of the original binary image. This technique is detailed in [41] together with a fast implementation based on a sequential algorithm similar to that used for computing distance functions. It has been extended by Nacken [42] to opening functions based on chamfer metrics and Vincent [43] to granulometries along horizontal, vertical, or diagonal lines in gray-scale images. A fast implementation of local gray-scale granulometries using tree data structures is proposed in [44].

21.4.4 Geodesic transforms

Fast morphological reconstruction. The raw algorithm for implementing a morphological reconstruction by dilation of a mask image g from a marker image f consists in iterating sequences of elementary dilations and point-wise image transformations. This algorithm is best suited for parallel processors. On sequential computers, a better approach is to perform the point-wise minimum while computing the dilation. In this latter case, a succession of forward and backward image sequential scans are necessary. Backward neighbors N_G^- are considered for forward scans and forward neighbors N_G^+ for backward scans. During each scan, the dilated value of each pixel of the marker image is computed using the appropriate set of neighbors and it is directly updated by the point-wise minimum with the corresponding pixel of the mask image. By doing so, already processed pixels are taken into account for processing further pixels. When stability is reached, the marker image holds the desired reconstruction:

1. Repeat until stability
2. Forward scan of all pixels p
3. $f(p) \leftarrow \min[g(p), \max\{f(q) \mid q \in N_G^-(p) \cup p\}]$
4. Backward scan of all pixels p
5. $f(p) \leftarrow \min[g(p), \max\{f(q) \mid q \in N_G^+(p) \cup p\}]$

Using this algorithm, any reconstruction of a 1-D signal can be performed in only two scans (forward and backward scans). On 2-D images, a higher number of scans is usually required to reach stability. This number is image dependent. A detailed description of parallel, sequential, and queue-based implementations is provided in [45].

Fast regional extrema detection. A fast algorithm for setting to the minimum image value $t_{\min}$ all image pixels which does not belong to a regional maximum has been proposed in [46]. The input image f is first copied into the output image g (step 1). The procedure continues by scanning the image (step 2) and checking, for each pixel of g having a value different from $t_{\min}$ (step 3), whether it has a neighbor of higher intensity value (step 4). If yes, then all pixels connected to this pixel and having the same intensity are set to zero (step 5):

1. $g \leftarrow f$
2. Scan of all pixels x
3. if $(g(x) \neq t_{\min})$
4. if $(\exists\, y \in N_G(x) \mid f(y) > f(x))$
5. $g(z) \leftarrow t_{\min},\ \forall\, z \in \gamma_x\{w \mid g(w) = f(x)\}$

At the end of this procedure, the pixels belonging to the regional maxima keep their original value, the other ones being set to $t_{\min}$. In the algorithm, γ_x refers to the *connected opening*: $\gamma_x(X)$ is reconstruction of the connected component of X marked by x. Fast connected opening γ_x can be implemented using stack data structures.

21.5 Morphological image processing

21.5.1 Correction of uneven illumination

An illumination gradient occurs when a scene is unevenly illuminated. There is a need for correcting this effect because gray-scale measurements and global threshold techniques cannot be applied to images of unevenly illuminated scenes. The best solution is to optimize the lighting system so as to acquire evenly illuminated images but still this is impossible in many practical situations. For instance, the background 'illumination' of an x-ray image of a manufactured metallic part of uneven width is directly proportional to the width of this part and is therefore uneven: the larger the width, the darker the output intensity level.

If the image objects have all the same local contrast, that is, if they are either all darker or brighter than the background, *top-hat* transforms can be used for mitigating illumination gradients. Indeed, a top-hat with a large isotropic structuring element acts as a high-pass filter. As the illumination gradient lies within the low frequencies of the image, it is removed by the top-hat. White top-hats are used for dark backgrounds and black top-hats for bright backgrounds.

For example, Fig. 21.20a shows an badly illuminated image of seeds. A closing with a large structuring element removes the seeds but preserves the illumination function. The black top-hat or subtraction of the original image from the closing provides us with an evenly illuminated image (Fig. 21.20c). A more contrasted image can be obtained by dividing the original image with its closing (Fig. 21.20d).

Note that in quality control applications where a series of objects are acquired at a fixed position, another solution consists in capturing first

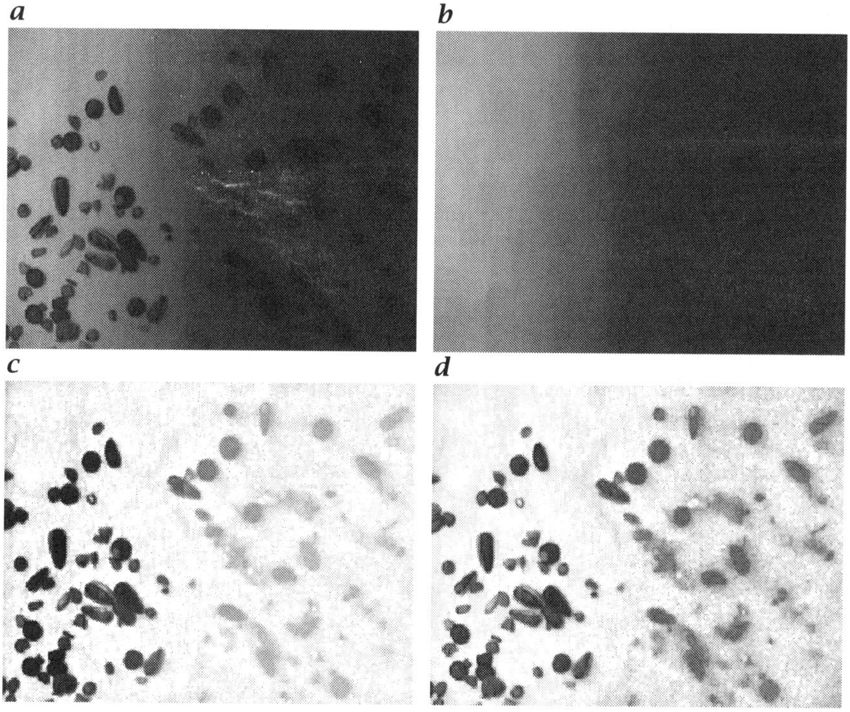

Figure 21.20: *Use of top-hat for mitigating inhomogeneous illumination:* ***a*** *Original image f;* ***b*** *Closing of f with a large square: $\phi(f)$;* ***c*** *Black top-hat: $BTH(f) = \phi(f) - f$;* ***d*** *Division of f by $\phi(f)$.*

an image without any object and then perform the point-wise division of further image captures with this background image.

21.5.2 An erosion-based image measurement

An image measurement consists in reducing the image to some meaningful numerical values. In this section, we show that erosions by a pair of points can be used for extracting information such the direction of oriented image structures or the periodicity of periodic image structures.

The *covariance* K of an image consists in measuring the *volume*[3] of the image eroded by a *pair of points* $P_{1,\vec{v}}$ Eq. (21.10):

$$K(f; P_{1,\vec{v}}) = \mathrm{Vol}[\varepsilon_{P_{1,\vec{v}}}(f)] \tag{21.43}$$

In the case of binary images, the covariance is nothing but the surface area of the intersection of the image with the image translated by a

[3]The volume of an image equals the sum of the gray-level intensities of all its pixels.

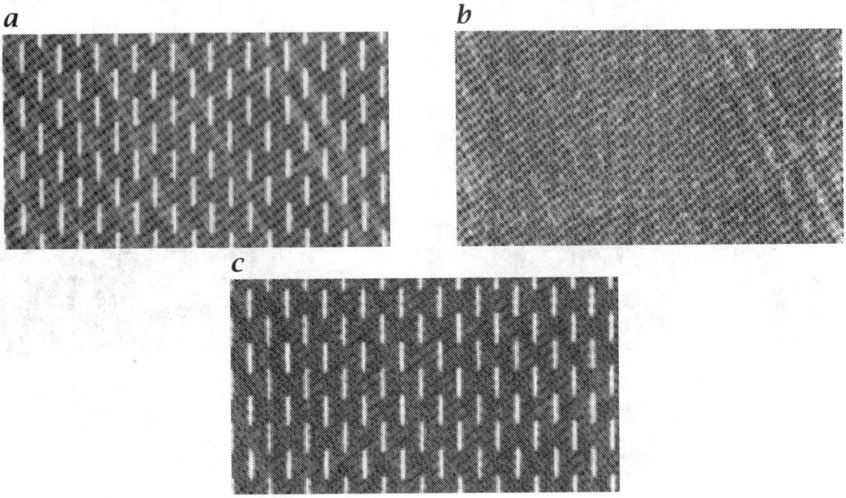

Figure 21.21: Erosion of an image with points separated by an increasing distance along the horizontal direction. When the distance equals the periodicity of the dashed lines, these are not eroded: ***a*** *An image f with periodic dashed lines;* ***b*** $\varepsilon_{P_{1,(11,0)}}(f)$; ***c*** $\varepsilon_{P_{1,(21,0)}}(f)$.

vector $\vec{v}$:

$$K(X; P_{1,\vec{v}}) = \text{Area}(X \cap X_{\vec{v}})$$

An example of erosion by a pair of points is provided in Fig. 21.21.

In practice, a family of pair of points is considered such as a pair of points in a given direction separated by an increasing distance. A diagram "Volume of erosion by a pair of points vs distance between these points" is then plotted and interpreted for determining the periodicity of periodic image structures. For example, the sum of the gray-levels for erosions by points separated by an increasing distance along the horizontal direction applied to Fig. 21.21a is shown in Fig. 21.22. The peaks of this diagram are located at multiple of the distance separating two successive dashed lines, that is, about 21 pixels (Fig. 21.21c).

The covariance can also be used to determine the orientation of image structures automatically by considering a family of erosions by a pair of equidistant points in various directions.

21.5.3 Filtering

Morphological filters are nonlinear filters suited to the selective removal of image structures, the selection being based on their shape and local contrast[4]. Contrary to linear filters, morphological filters preserve sharp edges.

[4]The local contrast of an object tells us whether it is a dark object on a bright background or vice versa.

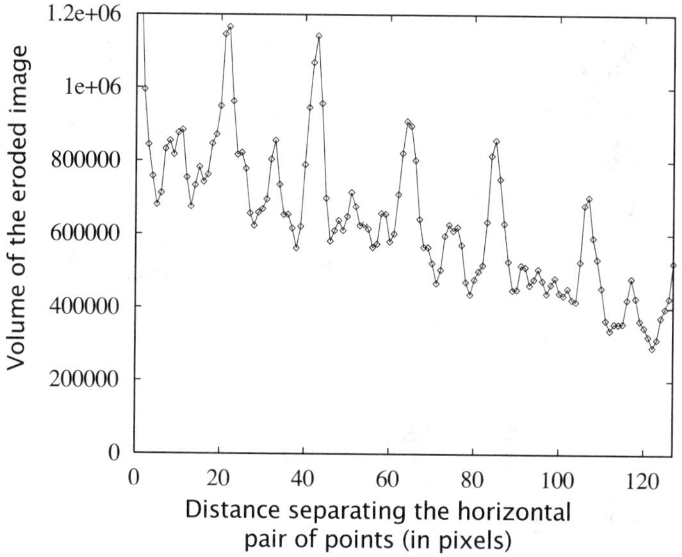

Figure 21.22: *Use of covariance for determining the periodicity of periodic image structures: sum of gray-levels of erosion of Fig. 21.21a by the horizontal pair of points $P_{1,(i,0)}$ vs i (i denotes the distance separating the pair of points).*

Morphological filter definitions. The basic idea behind a morphological filter is to suppress image structures selectively. These structures are either noise or irrelevant image objects. It follows that the structures that are preserved should not be modified by further applications of the same filter. This illustrates a key property of a morphological filter: the idempotence. In this sense, a morphological filtering operation can be compared with the sifting of materials through a sieve: Once the materials have been sifted, they will not be further sifted by passing them through the same sieve. A morphological filter also shares the increasing property of a sifting process. This property ensures that the order relationships between images are preserved.

The idempotence and increasing properties are necessary and sufficient conditions for an image transformation to be a *morphological* filter:

$$\Psi, \text{ morphological filter} \Leftrightarrow \Psi \text{ is increasing and idempotent.}$$

Consequently, closings are extensive morphological filters and openings are antiextensive morphological filters. They are the basic morphological filters.

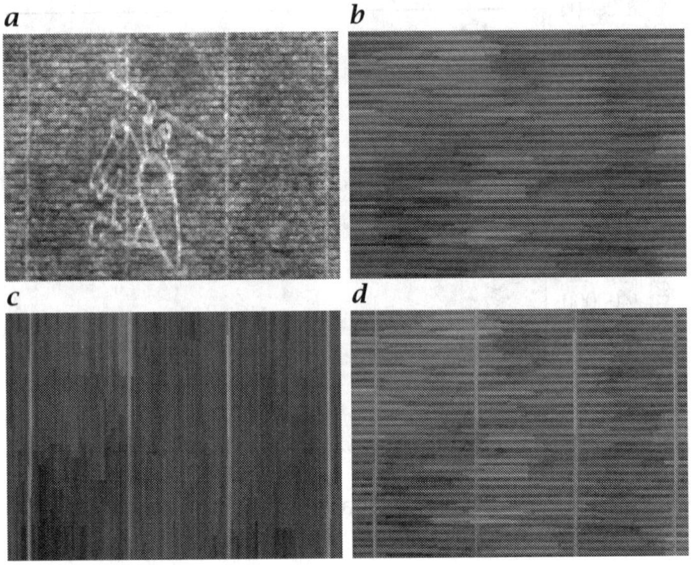

Figure 21.23: Opening as a union of openings: ***a*** *The input image represents a watermark on paper containing laid (horizontal) and chain (vertical) lines. The union of openings shown in* ***d*** *using* ***b*** *horizontal and* ***c*** *vertical structuring elements is an opening that can be used to extract laid and chain lines while suppressing the watermark.*

Design of a morphological filter. New filters can be designed by combining elementary filters. However, all combinations are not allowed. For instance, the composition of two openings is generally not an opening nor a filter. In fact, the composition of two idempotent transformations is not necessarily an idempotent operation. In this section, we detail parallel and sequential combinations of existing filters leading to new filters.

Parallel combinations. Let us consider for example the image of a watermark shown at the left of Fig. 21.23. Assume that we would like to design a filter extracting both laid and chain lines while removing the watermark. This can be simply achieved by calculating the union of two openings performed in parallel: the first with a horizontal SE and the second with a vertical SE.

It can be shown that this union of openings is extensive, idempotent, and increasing. It follows that it is still an opening (in the algebraic sense). This example illustrates an important way of building new openings from existing ones because any union of a series of openings is still an opening. The dual rule applies for closings:

1. Any union (or point-wise maximum) of openings is an opening: $(\bigvee_i \gamma_i)$ is an opening.
2. Any intersection (or point-wise minimum) of closings is a closing: $(\bigwedge_i \phi_i)$ is a closing.

Such parallel combinations are often used for filtering elongated image structures. In this case, openings (for bright objects) or closings (for dark objects) with line segments in several directions are considered (the longer the SE, the larger the number of directions).

Sequential combinations. We have already mentioned that the composition of two openings is not necessarily a filter. However, the composition of two ordered filters is always a filter. The pair of ordered filters considered is often an opening γ and the dual closing ϕ. An opening filters out bright image structures while a closing has the same filtering effect but on the dark image structures. If the image is corrupted by a symmetrical noise function, it is therefore interesting to use a sequential combination such as an opening followed by a closing or vice versa, the selection depending on the local contrast of the image objects that should be extracted.

Compositions of ordered filters leading to new filters are given hereafter:

$$\gamma\phi,\ \phi\gamma,\ \gamma\phi\gamma,\ \text{and } \phi\gamma\phi \text{ are filters}$$

This rule is called the *structural theorem* [47]. Moreover, the following ordering relationships are always satisfied:

$$\gamma \le \gamma\phi\gamma \le \begin{matrix}\gamma\phi \\ \phi\gamma\end{matrix} \le \phi\gamma\phi \le \phi$$

The $\phi\gamma$ filter is often called an open-close filter as it consists of an opening followed by a closing. Close-open filters are defined by duality. Although open-close and close-open filters have almost the same filtering effect, they are not equivalent. Moreover, there exists no order relationship between $\gamma\phi$ and $\phi\gamma$ nor between $\gamma\phi$ and I or $\phi\gamma$ and I.

Consecutive applications of openings and closings are at the basis of the alternating sequential filters described in the next section.

Alternating sequential filters. As detailed in the previous section, the filtering of an image corrupted by dark and bright noisy structures can be achieved by a sequence of either close-open or open-close filters. When the level of noise is high in the sense that it contains noisy structures over a wide range of scales, a unique close-open or open-close filter with a large SE does not lead to acceptable results. For example, Fig. 21.24a shows a noisy interferogram that is filtered by open-close (Fig. 21.24b) and close-open (Fig. 21.24c) filters with 5×5

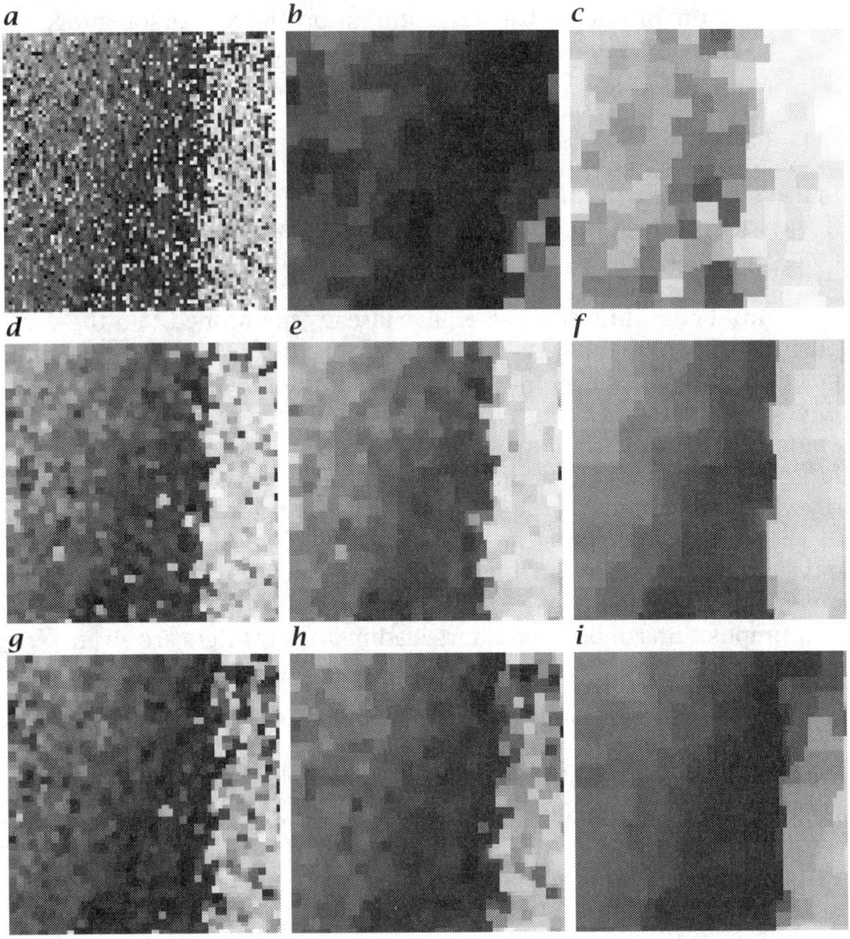

Figure 21.24: *Alternating sequential filters:* ***a*** *the original image is a subset of a noisy interferogram. The first row shows a direct application of* **b** *an open-close or* **c** *close-open filter with a* 5×5 *square;* ***d*** *to* ***f*** *display a series of ASFs of increasing size and starting with a closing;* ***g*** *to* **i** *show ASFs starting with an opening.*

square. Due to the high level of noise, the opening of the open-close filter removes almost all structures leading thereby to an almost dark image (Fig. 21.24b). The dual behavior is obtained with the close-open filter (Fig. 21.24c).

A solution to this problem is to alternate closings and openings, beginning with a small structuring element and then proceeding with ever increasing structuring elements until a given size is reached. This sequential application of open-close (or close-open) filters is called an *alternating sequential filter* [48, 49].

Definition. Let γ_i be an opening and ϕ_i be the dual closing of size i. Following the structural theorem the following combinations are all morphological filters:

$$
\begin{aligned}
m_i &= \gamma_i \phi_i, \; r_i = \phi_i \gamma_i \phi_i \\
n_i &= \phi_i \gamma_i, \; s_i = \gamma_i \phi_i \gamma_i
\end{aligned}
$$

An alternating sequential filter of size i is defined as the sequential combination of one of these filters, starting the sequence with the filter of size 1 and terminating it with the filter of size i:

$$
\begin{aligned}
M_i &= m_i \cdots m_2 m_1, \; R_i = r_i \cdots r_2 r_1 \\
N_i &= n_i \cdots n_2 n_1, \quad S_i = s_i \cdots s_2 s_1
\end{aligned}
$$

It can be proved that alternating sequential filters (ASFs) are all morphological filters. Moreover, they satisfy the following absorption law:

$$
i \le j \Rightarrow ASF_j ASF_i = ASF_j \text{ and } ASF_i ASF_j \le ASF_j
$$

Note that M_i and N_i constitute a pair of dual filters that are not ordered. The final result depends therefore on whether an opening or the dual closing is used as first filter in the sequence. Although ASFs are not self-dual, they act in a much more symmetrical way than closings and openings. The ASFs are particularly suited to noise reduction before applying other morphological operators like gradients and top-hats.

Example. Examples of ASFs are given in the two last rows of Fig. 21.24. The goal is to filter the noisy interferogram shown in Fig. 21.24a. The used structuring elements are squares of width equal to $2i + 1$ pixels where i denotes the size of the ASF. Figure 21.24d to f show ASF of type M. The ASF of type N are illustrated in Fig. 21.24g to i. Notice that both filters suppress noisy structures of the original image. The larger the size of the ASF, the larger the size of the structures that are removed.

Toggle mappings. The idea of toggle mappings stems from associating an image with:

1. a series of transformations ψ_i
2. a toggling criterion, that is, a decision rule that determines at each pixel x which ψ_i must be considered.

A trivial example of a toggle mapping is the threshold operator. The primitives are the white and black images, and the decision rule involves at pixel x, the value $f(x)$ and that of a constant, namely the threshold level. In general, the primitives are derived from the function f itself and the toggling criterion is chosen in order to optimize either noise reduction or contrast enhancement.

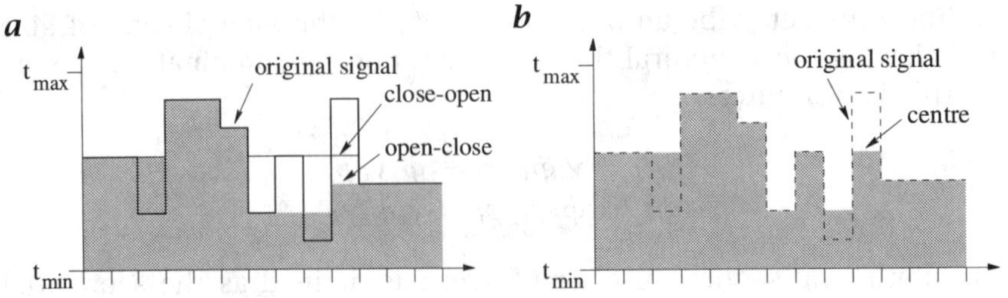

Figure 21.25: *Morphological center based on two primitives:* ***a*** *A 1-D signal together with its open-close and close-open filters by an SE of 2 pixels.* ***b*** *The corresponding morphological center.*

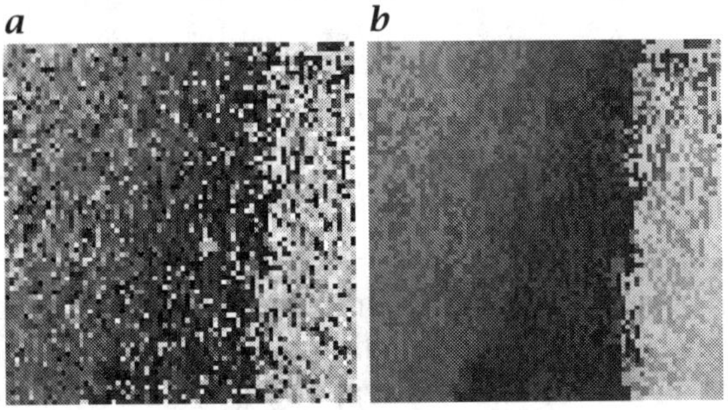

Figure 21.26: ***b*** *Morphological center of the interferogram shown in* ***a*** *using the dual pair of ASFs M_5 (Fig. 21.24f) and N_5 (Fig. 21.24i) as primitives. This filter is self-dual.*

Morphological center. Starting from a pair of image transformations, the output value of the morphological center [50, 51] at a given pixel is the median value of the triplet defined by the original image value and the two transformed values. By doing so, it can be seen that the output value will be different from the original value if and only if *both* transformed values are larger (or smaller) than the original image value. In this latter case, the output value will always be the value that is closer to the original image value. A formal definition suited to a series of transformations is presented hereafter.

Let $\{\psi_1, \psi_2, \ldots, \psi_n\}$ be a family of mappings. The morphological center β with respect to this family is defined as follows:

$$\beta = (I \vee \bigwedge_i \psi_i) \wedge \bigvee_i \psi_i \tag{21.44}$$

When there are only two mappings, the morphological center at point x is nothing but the *median* value of f, $\psi_1(f)$, and $\psi_2(f)$ at x. This is illustrated in Fig. 21.25 for a 1-D signal.

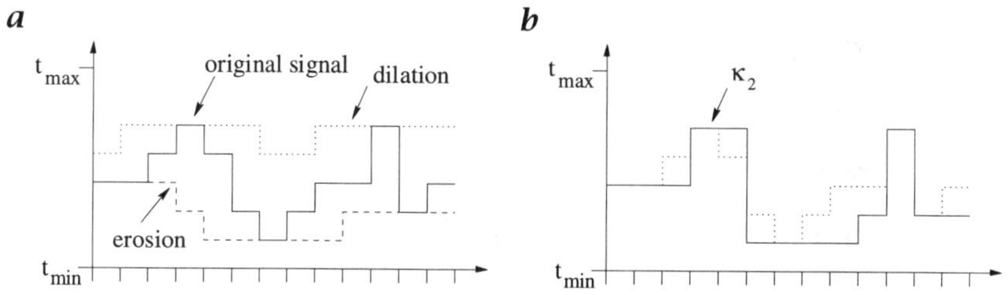

Figure 21.27: *Two-state toggle contrast κ^2 of a 1-D signal using an erosion and a dilation with a line segment of 5 pixels as primitives. Note that steeper edge slopes are obtained without smoothing effect.*

The morphological center is not an idempotent transform. When the ψ_i's are all increasing mappings, they transmit to β their increasing property. Moreover, if pairs of dual transformations are used for the ψ_i's, the resulting center is self-dual. The self duality of an operator means that it processes dark and bright image structures symmetrically. Note that using an opening and a closing as primitives does not make sense because the morphological center will be the identity transform. In practice, one has to consider dual pairs of compositions such as $\{\phi\gamma, \gamma\phi\}$, $\{\gamma\phi\gamma, \phi\gamma\phi\}$, or even an ASF and its dual as primitives, that is, pair of dual filters that are not ordered with respect to the identity transform. The morphological center of the noisy interferogram shown in Fig. 21.24a and using the dual pair of ASF filters M_5 and N_5 as primitives is shown in Fig. 21.26.

Toggle contrast. Contrary to morphological centers, toggle contrast mappings κ modify the image f at pixel x only when $f(x)$ lies *within* the interval defined by the minimum and the maximum of all $\psi_i(f)$ at pixel x [52, 53, 54]. Let us for instance define the two-state toggle contrast κ^2 with an antiextensive transformation ψ_1 and an extensive transformation ψ_2 as primitives:

$$\kappa^2(x) = \begin{cases} \psi_2(x), & \text{if } \psi_2(x) - I(x) < I(x) - \psi_1(x) \\ \psi_1(x), & \text{otherwise} \end{cases} \tag{21.45}$$

In other words, at each point x, κ^2 equals the value of the transform that is the closest to the original function. An example is provided in Fig. 21.27 for a 1-D signal and on an image in Fig. 21.28.

Toggle contrasts based on erosions and dilations sharpen the edges much more than those based on openings and closings. Contrary to top-hat contrast operators [55], erosion/dilation toggle contrasts sharpen the edges but do not boost the contrast of image structures smaller

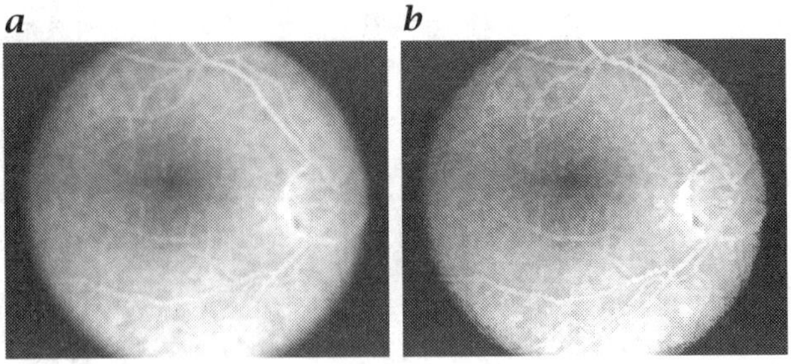

Figure 21.28: *Two-state toggle contrast κ^2 for sharpening a blurred fluorescein angiogram of the eye. The primitives are the erosion and dilation by a 3×3 square:* ***a*** *original angiogram f;* ***b*** $\kappa^2(f)$.

than the considered SE. Also, they preserve the dynamic range of the input data but do destroy many image structures.

21.5.4 Segmentation

Assuming that image objects are connected regions of rather homogeneous intensity levels, one should be able to extract these regions by using some neighborhood properties rather than purely spectral properties as for histogram-based segmentation techniques. Indeed, a high gray-scale variation between two adjacent pixels may indicate that these two pixels belong to different objects.

The morphological approach to image segmentation combines region growing and edge detection techniques: It groups the image pixels around the regional minima of the image and the boundaries of adjacent groupings are precisely located along the crest lines of the gradient image. This is achieved by a transformation called the *watershed transformation.*

The watershed transformation. Let us consider the topographic representation of a gray-level scale image. Now, let a drop of water fall on such a topographic surface. According to the law of gravitation, it will flow down along the steepest slope path until it reaches a minimum. The whole set of points of the surface whose steepest slope paths reach a given minimum constitutes the *catchment basin* associated with this minimum. The *watersheds* are the zones dividing adjacent catchment basins. This is illustrated in Fig. 21.29a.

Provided that the input image has been transformed so as to output an image whose minima mark relevant image objects and whose crest lines correspond to image object boundaries, the watershed transformation will partition the image into meaningful regions. This approach to the segmentation of gray-scale images is detailed below.

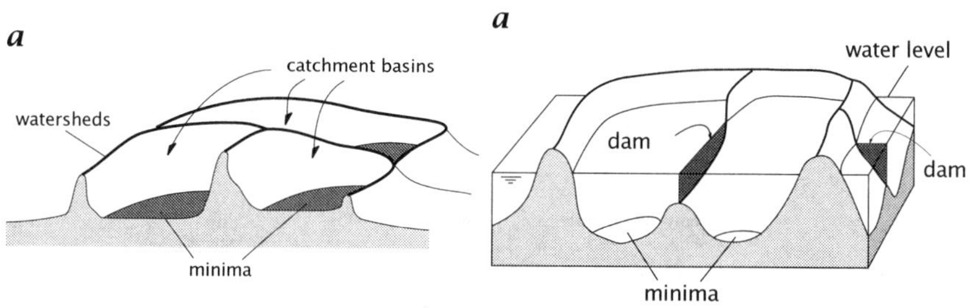

Figure 21.29: ***a*** *Minima, catchment basins, and watersheds on the topographic representation of a gray-scale image.* ***b*** *Building dams at the places where the water coming from two different minima would merge.*

Definition in terms of flooding simulations. The definition of the watersheds in terms of water flows is not well-suited to an algorithmic implementation as there are many cases where the flow direction at a given point is not determined (e. g., flat regions or pixels having more than one neighbor pixel with the lowest gray-scale value). However, a definition in terms of flooding simulations alleviates all these problems. Consider again the gray tone image as a topographic surface and assume that holes have been punched in each regional minima of the surface. The surface is then slowly immersed into a lake. Starting from the minima at the lowest altitude, the water will progressively flood the catchment basins of the image. In addition, dams are erected at the places where the waters coming from two different minima would merge (see Fig. 21.29b). At the end of this flooding procedure, each minimum is completely surrounded by dams, which delineate its associated catchment basin. The resulting dams correspond to the watersheds. They provide us with a partition of the input image into its different catchment basins.

In other words, the set of the catchment basins CB of the gray-scale image f is equal to the set $X_{h_{\max}}$, that is, once all levels have been flooded:

(i) $X_{h_{\min}} = T_{h_{\min}}(f)$

(ii) $\forall\ h \in [h_{\min}, h_{\max} - 1],\ \ X_{h+1} = \mathrm{RMIN}_{h+1}(f) \cup IZ_{T_{t \le h+1}(f)}(X_h)$

where $\mathrm{RMIN}_h(f)$ denotes the regional minima of f at level h. The *watersheds* WS of f correspond to the boundaries of the catchment basins of f. An efficient queue-based algorithm is detailed in [56, 57].

Marker-controlled segmentation. The basic idea behind the marker-controlled segmentation is to transform the input image in such a way that the watersheds of the transformed image correspond to meaningful object boundaries. The transformed image is called the *segmentation function.* In practice, a direct computation of the watersheds

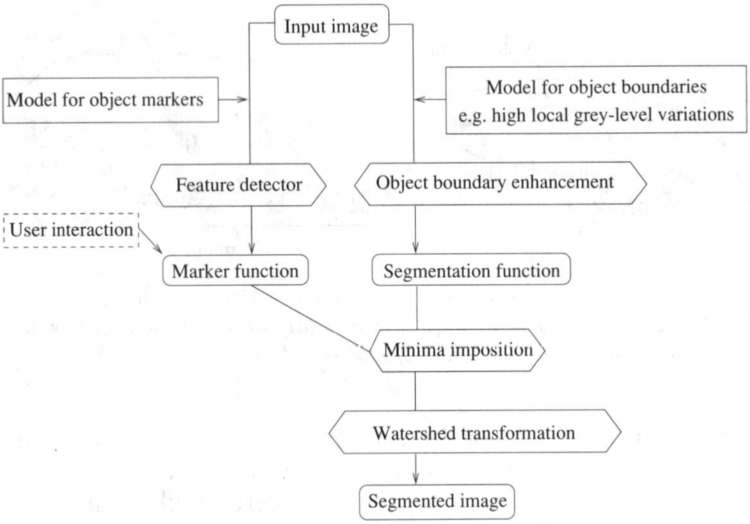

Figure 21.30: *Morphological paradigm for image segmentation. Image understanding is done at the very first stages of the process. The 'intelligent' part of the process is when it generates the marker and the segmentation functions. Then, the rest of the procedure is non-parametric.*

of the segmentation function produces an over-segmentation, which is due to the presence of spurious minima. Consequently, the segmentation function must be filtered *before* computing its watersheds. Any filtering technique may be considered. However, the minima imposition technique described in Section 21.3.7 is the best filter in most applications. This technique requires the determination of a *marker function* marking the relevant image objects and their background. The corresponding markers are then used as the set of minima to impose to the segmentation function. The schematic of this approach is summarized in Fig. 21.30.

The object markers are extracted from the image using some feature detectors. The choice of appropriate feature detectors relies on some *a priori* knowledge or assumptions about the properties of an image object. Common features include image extrema, flat zones (i. e., connected components of pixels of constant gray-level value), zones of homogeneous texture, etc. In some applications, the markers may be defined manually. One marker per region is necessary as there will be a one-to-one correspondence between the markers and the segments of the final partition. However, if the class of object marked by each marker is known, several markers of the same class may be considered for each image object. The size of a marker can range from a unique pixel to a large connected component of pixels. When processing noisy images, large markers perform better than small ones.

The determination of the segmentation function is based on a model for the definition of an object boundary. For example, if the image objects are defined as regions of rather constant gray-scale values, a *morphological gradient* operator will enhance the object boundaries. If the image objects are regions of homogeneous texture, operators highlighting the transition between two textures should be considered.

The object markers are then used as the set of markers to impose to the segmentation function. Finally, the object boundaries are obtained by computing the watersheds of the filtered segmentation function.

Meyer [58] proposed an extension of the watershed algorithm presented in [57]. It consists in combining the minima imposition and the computation of the watersheds into a unique step. This is achieved by using a priority queue or an array of queues, one for each priority. The flooding simulation is initiated from the external boundaries of the markers, each pixel being inserted in a queue with a priority equal to its gray-level in the original image. The flooding is then simulated by processing the pixels at the lowest priority and successively inserting their nonprocessed neighbors in the queue whose priority corresponds to their gray-level (or the current priority level if the pixel value is less than this priority level). The markers being labeled beforehand, an image of labeled catchment basins is created while simulating the flooding process. Further details can be found in [16].

Application to the separation of overlapping blobs. Images of round objects like cells or coffee beans can be segmented by simple thresholding techniques provided that the object gray-scale values are different from those of the background. However, it may be that the resulting blobs are connected or overlap each other. This is illustrated by the image of cells shown in Fig. 21.3a. Granulometries can be used to estimate the average size of the cells as well as their number. However, shape description of the individual blobs requires the prior separation of all connected blobs. The marker-controlled segmentation provides us with a powerful tool for solving this problem. Its principle is summarized in Fig. 21.31.

The top left-hand side of the figure represents three blobs we would like to separate. The inverse of the distance transform of these blobs is an appropriate segmentation function because there is a one-to-one correspondence between the regional minima of the inverted distance function and the number of blobs. Moreover, the watershed lines of this inverted distance function provide us with a suitable separation of the blobs. Usually, the distance function must be filtered to remove irrelevant maxima before applying the watershed transformation. Ad-

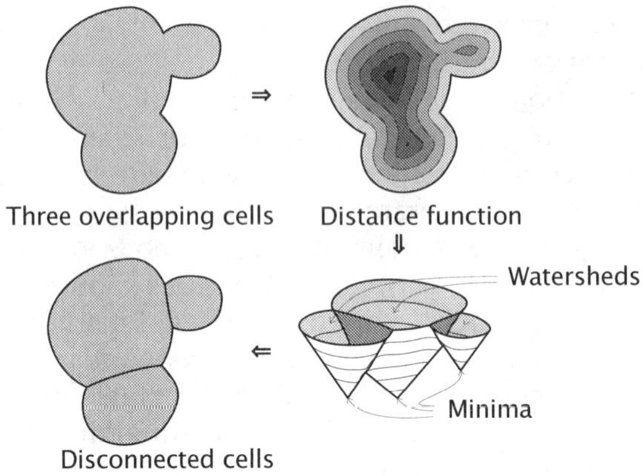

Figure 21.31: *Segmentation of overlapping blobs by watershedding the complement of their distance function [57].*

ditional applications of the watershed transformation to the segmentation of binary and gray-tone images are given in Volume 3, Chapters 12, 19, and 39.

21.6 References

[1] Serra, J., (1982). *Image analysis and mathematical morphology.* London: Academic Press.

[2] Soille, P., (1999). *Morphological Image Analysis—Principles and Applications.* Berlin: Springer.

[3] Shih, F. and Mitchell, O., (1989). Threshold decomposition of gray-scale morphology into binary morphology. *IEEE Transactions on Pattern Analysis and Machine Intelligence,* **11**(1):31–42.

[4] Rosenfeld, A. and Pfaltz, J., (1968). Distance functions on digital pictures. *Pattern Recognition,* **1**:33–61.

[5] Jones, R. and Soille, P., (1996). Periodic lines and their applications to granulometries. In *Mathematical Morphology and its Applications to Image and Signal Processing,* P. Maragos, W. Schafer, and M. Butt, eds., pp. 264–272. Kluwer Academic Publishers.

[6] Jones, R. and Soille, P., (1996). Periodic lines: Definition, cascades, and application to granulometries. *Pattern Recognition Letters,* **17**(10):1057–1063.

[7] Beucher, S., (1990). *Segmentation d'images et morphologie mathématique.* PhD thesis, Ecole des Mines de Paris.

[8] Rivest, J.-F., Soille, P., and Beucher, S., (1993). Morphological gradients. *Journal of Electronic Imaging,* **2**(4):326–336.

[9] Matheron, G., (1975). *Random sets and integral geometry.* Wiley.

[10] Cheng, F. and Venetsanopoulos, A., (1992). An adaptive morphological filter for image processing. *IEEE Transactions on Image Processing*, **1**(4): 533–539.

[11] Vincent, L., (1992). Morphological area openings and closings for greyscale images. In *Proc. Shape in Picture '92, NATO Workshop*. Berlin: Springer.

[12] Meyer, F., (1986). Automatic screening of cytological specimens. *Computer Vision, Graphics, and Image Processing*, **35**:356–369.

[13] Matheron, G., (1967). *Eléments pour une théorie des milieux poreux*. Paris: Masson.

[14] Maragos, P., (1989). Pattern spectrum and multiscale shape representation. *IEEE Transactions on Pattern Analysis and Machine Intelligence*, **11** (7):701–716.

[15] Canny, J., (1986). A computational approach to edge detection. *IEEE Transactions on Pattern Analysis and Machine Intelligence*, **8**(6):679–698.

[16] Beucher, S. and Meyer, F., (1993). The morphological approach to segmentation: the watershed transformation. In *Mathematical morphology in image processing*, E. Dougherty, ed., chapter 12, pp. 433–481. Marcel Dekker.

[17] Lantuéjoul, C. and Beucher, S., (1980). Geodesic distance and image analysis. *Mikroskopie*, **37**:138–142.

[18] Lantuéjoul, C. and Beucher, S., (1981). On the use of the geodesic metric in image analysis. *Journal of Microscopy*, **121**:39–49.

[19] Goetcherian, V., (1980). From binary to grey tone image processing using fuzzy logic concepts. *Pattern Recognition*, **12**:7–15.

[20] Beucher, S., (1981). *Ligne de partage des eaux : comment l'expliquer en termes de transformation fonctionnelle ?* Technical Report N-699, Ecole des Mines de Paris.

[21] Rosenfeld, A. and Pfaltz, J., (1966). Sequential operations in digital picture processing. *J. Assoc. Comp. Mach.*, **13**(4):471–494.

[22] Danielsson, P.-E., (1980). Euclidean distance mapping. *Computer Graphics and Image Processing*, **14**:227–248.

[23] Borgefors, G., (1984). Distance transformations in arbitrary dimensions. *Computer Vision, Graphics, and Image Processing*, **27**:321–345.

[24] van Herk, M., (1992). A fast algorithm for local minimum and maximum filters on rectangular and octogonal kernels. *Pattern Recognition Letters*, **13**:517–521.

[25] Gil, J. and Werman, M., (1993). Computing 2-D min, median and max filters. *IEEE Transactions on Pattern Analysis and Machine Intelligence*, **15**(5):504–507.

[26] Soille, P., Breen, E., and Jones, R., (1996). Recursive implementation of erosions and dilations along discrete lines at arbitrary angles. *IEEE Transactions on Pattern Analysis and Machine Intelligence*, **18**(5):562–567.

[27] van den Boomgaard, R. and van Balen, R., (1992). Methods for fast morphological image transforms using bitmapped binary images. *Computer*

Vision, Graphics, and Image Processing: Graphical Models and Image Processing, **54**(3):252–258.

[28] Pecht, J., (1985). Speeding up successive Minkowski operations. *Pattern Recognition Letters*, **3**(2):113–117.

[29] Huang, T., Yang, G., and Tang, G., (1979). A fast two-dimensional median filtering algorithm. *IEEE Transactions on Acoustics, Speech and Signal Processing*, **27**(1):13–18.

[30] Van Droogenbroeck, M. and Talbot, H., (1996). Fast computation of morphological operations with arbitrary structuring elements. *Pattern Recognition Letters*, **17**(14):1451–1460.

[31] Zamperoni, P., (1980). Dilatation und Erosion von konturcodierten Binärbildern. *Microscopica Acta*, **Suppl. 4**:245–249.

[32] Freeman, H., (1961). On the encoding of arbitrary geometric configurations. *IRE Transactions on Electronic Computers*, **10**:260–268.

[33] Vincent, L., (1991). Morphological transformations of binary images with arbitrary structuring elements. *Signal Processing*, **22**(1):3–23.

[34] Ragnemalm, I., (1992). Fast erosion and dilation by contour processing and thresholding of distance maps. *Pattern Recognition Letters*, **13**:161–166.

[35] van Vliet, L. and Verwer, B., (1988). A contour processing method for fast binary neighbourhood operations. *Pattern Recognition Letters*, **7**:27–36.

[36] Ji, L., Piper, J., and Tang, J.-Y., (1989). Erosion and dilation of binary images by arbitrary structuring elements using interval coding. *Pattern Recognition Letters*, **9**:201–209.

[37] Vincent, L., (1993). Morphological algorithms. In *Mathematical morphology in image processing*, E. Dougherty, ed., chapter 8, pp. 255–288. Marcel Dekker.

[38] Van Droogenbroeck, M., (1994). On the implementation of morphological operations. In *Mathematical morphology and its applications to image processing*, J. Serra and P. Soille, eds., pp. 241–248. Kluwer Academic Publishers.

[39] Vincent, L., (1993). Grayscale area openings and closings, their efficient implementation and applications. In *Proc. EURASIP workshop on Mathematical morphology and its applications to signal processing*, J. Serra and P. Salembier, eds., pp. 22–27. Barcelona.

[40] Breen, E. and Monro, D., (1994). An evaluation of priority queues for mathematical morphology. In *Mathematical morphology and its applications to image processing*, J. Serra and P. Soille, eds., pp. 249–256. Kluwer Academic Publishers.

[41] Laÿ, B., (1987). Recursive algorithms in mathematical morphology. *Acta Stereologica*, **6**(3):691–696.

[42] Nacken, P., (1996). Chamfer metrics, the medial axis and mathematical morphology. *Journal of Mathematical Imaging and Vision*, **6**(2/3):235–248.

[43] Vincent, L., (1994). Fast grayscale granulometry algorithms. In *Mathematical morphology and its applications to image processing*, J. Serra and P. Soille, eds., pp. 265–272. Kluwer Academic Publishers.

[44] Vincent, L., (1996). Local grayscale granulometries based on opening trees. In *Mathematical morphology and its applications to image and signal processing*, P. Maragos, R. Schafer, and M. Butt, eds., pp. 273–280. Boston: Kluwer Academic Publishers.

[45] Vincent, L., (1993). Morphological grayscale reconstruction in image analysis: applications and efficient algorithms. *IEEE Transactions on Image Processing*, **2**(2):176–201.

[46] Breen, E. and Jones, R., (1996). Attribute openings, thinnings, and granulometries. *Computer Vision and Image Understanding*, **64**(3):377–389.

[47] Matheron, G., (1988). Filters and Lattices. In *Image analysis and mathematical morphology. Volume 2: theoretical advances*, J. Serra, ed., chapter 6, pp. 115–140. Academic Press.

[48] Sternberg, S., (1986). Grayscale morphology. *Computer Graphics and Image Processing*, **35**:333–355.

[49] Serra, J., (1988). Alternating sequential filters. In *Image analysis and mathematical morphology. Volume 2: theoretical advances*, J. Serra, ed., chapter 10, pp. 203–214. Academic Press.

[50] Meyer, F. and Serra, J., (1989). Filters: from theory to practice. In *Acta Stereologica*, Vol. 8. Freiburg im Breisgau.

[51] Serra, J., (1988). Measurements on numerical functions. In *Image analysis and mathematical morphology. Volume 2: theoretical advances*, J. Serra, ed., chapter 14, pp. 297–315. Academic Press.

[52] Kramer, H. and Bruckner, J., (1975). Iterations of non-linear transformations for enhancement on digital images. *Pattern Recognition*, **7**:53–58.

[53] Lester, J., Brenner, J., and Selles, W., (1980). Local transforms for biomedical image analysis. *Computer Graphics and Image Processing*, **13**:17–30.

[54] Meyer, F. and Serra, J., (1989). Contrasts and activity lattice. *Signal Processing*, **16**:303–317.

[55] Soille, P., (1998). *Morphologische Bildverarbeitung*. Berlin: Springer.

[56] Soille, P. and Vincent, L., (1990). Determining watersheds in digital pictures via flooding simulations. In *Visual Communications and Image Processing'90*, M. Kunt, ed., Vol. SPIE-1360, pp. 240–250. Lausanne.

[57] Vincent, L. and Soille, P., (1991). Watersheds in digital spaces: an efficient algorithm based on immersion simulations. *IEEE Transactions on Pattern Analysis and Machine Intelligence*, **13**(6):583–598.

[58] Meyer, F., (1991). Un algorithme optimal de ligne de partage des eaux. In *Reconnaissance des Formes et Intelligence Artificielle, 8e congrès*, pp. 847–857. Lyon-Villeurbanne: AFCET.

22 Fuzzy Image Processing

Horst Haußecker[1] and Hamid R. Tizhoosh[2]

[1] Interdisziplinäres Zentrum für Wissenschaftliches Rechnen (IWR)
Universität Heidelberg, Germany
[2] Lehrstuhl für Technische Informatik, Universität Magdeburg, Germany

Handbook of Computer Vision and Applications
Volume 2
Signal Processing and Pattern Recognition

Copyright © 1999 by Academic Press
All rights of reproduction in any form reserved.
ISBN 0-12-379772-1/$30.00

22.1 Introduction

Our world is *fuzzy*, and so are images, projections of the real world onto the image sensor. Fuzziness quantifies vagueness and ambiguity, as opposed to crisp memberships. The types of uncertainty in images are manifold, ranging over the entire chain of processing levels, from pixel-based grayness ambiguity over fuzziness in geometrical description up to uncertain knowledge in the highest processing level.

The human visual system has been perfectly adapted to handle uncertain information in both data and knowledge. It would be hard to define quantitatively how an object, such as a car, has to look in terms of geometrical primitives with exact shapes, dimensions, and colors. Instead, we are using a descriptive language to define features that eventually are subject to a wide range of variations. The interrelation of a few such "fuzzy" properties sufficiently characterizes the object of interest. Fuzzy image processing is an attempt to translate this ability of human reasoning into computer vision problems as it provides an intuitive tool for inference from imperfect data.

Where is the transition between a gray-value slope and an edge? What is the border of a blurred object? Which gray values exactly belong to the class of "bright" or "dark" pixels? These questions show, that image features almost naturally have to be considered fuzzy. Usually these problems are just overruled by assigning thresholds—heuristic or computed—to the features in order to classify them. Fuzzy logic allows one to quantify appropriately and handle imperfect data. It also allows combining them for a final decision, even if we only know heuristic rules, and no analytic relations.

Fuzzy image processing is special in terms of its relation to other computer vision techniques. It is not a solution for a special task, but rather describes a new class of image processing techniques. It provides a new methodology, augmenting classical logic, a component of any computer vision tool. A new type of image understanding and treatment has to be developed. Fuzzy image processing can be a single image processing routine, or complement parts of a complex image processing chain.

During the past few decades, fuzzy logic has gained increasing importance in control theory, as well as in computer vision. At the same time, it has been continuously attacked for two main reasons: It has been considered to lack a sound mathematical foundation and to be nothing but just a clever disguise for probability theory. It was probably its name that contributed to the low reputation of fuzzy logic. Meanwhile, fuzzy logic definitely has matured and can be considered to be a mathematically sound extension of multivalued logic. Fuzzy logical reasoning and probability theory are closely related without doubt.

They are, however, *not* the same but *complementary*, as we will show in Section 22.1.3.

This chapter gives a concise overview of the basic principles and potentials of state of the art fuzzy image processing, which can be applied to a variety of computer vision tasks.

22.1.1 A brief history

In 1965, Zadeh introduced the idea of *fuzzy sets*, which are the extension of classical crisp sets [1]. The idea is indeed simple and natural: The membership of elements of a set is a matter of grade rather than just zero or one. Therefore, membership grade and membership functions play the key role in all systems that apply the idea of fuzziness. Prewitt was the first researcher to detect the potentials of fuzzy set theory for representation of digital images [2]:

> "... a pictorial object is a fuzzy set which is specified by some membership function defined on all picture points. From this point of view, each image point participates in many memberships. Some of this uncertainty is due to degradation, but some of it is inherent. The role of object extraction in machine processing, like the role of figure/ground discrimination in visual perception, is uncertainty-reducing and organizational. In fuzzy set terminology, making figure/ground distinctions is equivalent to transforming from membership functions to characteristic functions."

In 1969, Ruspini introduced the fuzzy partitioning in clustering [3]. In 1973, the first fuzzy clustering algorithm called fuzzy *c* means was introduced by Bezdek [4]. It was the first fuzzy approach to pattern recognition. Rosenfeld extended the digital topology and image geometry to fuzzy sets at the end of the 70s and beginning of the 80s [5, 6, 7, 8, 9, 10, 11]. It was probably the most important step toward the development of a mathematical framework of fuzzy image processing because image geometry and digital topology play a pivotal role in image segmentation and representation, respectively. One of the pioneers of fuzzy image processing is S. K. Pal. Together with coworkers, he developed a variety of new fuzzy algorithms for image segmentation and enhancement [12, 13, 14, 15, 16, 17, 18, 19, 20, 21, 22, 23]. In the past decades, many other researchers have also investigated the potentials of fuzzy set theory for developing new image processing techniques. The width and depth of these investigations allow us to speak of a *new methodology* in computer vision: fuzzy image processing. But many questions should be answered: What actually is fuzzy image processing? Why should we use it? Which advantages and disadvantages have fuzzy algorithms for image processing? In following sections of this chapter, we will try to answer these questions.

22.1.2 Basics of fuzzy set theory

The two basic components of fuzzy systems are *fuzzy sets* and *operations on fuzzy sets*. *Fuzzy logic* defines rules, based on combinations of fuzzy sets by these operations. This section is based on the basic works of Zadeh [1, 24, 25, 26, 27].

Crisp sets. Given a universe of discourse $X = \{x\}$, a crisp (conventional) set A is defined by enumerating all elements $x \in X$

$$A = \{x_1, x_2, \ldots, x_n\} \tag{22.1}$$

that belong to A. The membership can be expressed by a function f_A, mapping X on a binary value:

$$f_A : X \longrightarrow \{0, 1\}, \quad f_A = \begin{cases} 1 \text{ if } x \in A \\ 0 \text{ if } x \notin A \end{cases} \tag{22.2}$$

Thus, an arbitrary x either belongs to A, or it does not, partial membership is not allowed.

For two sets A and B, combinations can be defined by the following operations:

$$\begin{aligned} A \cup B &= \{x \,|\, x \in A \text{ or } x \in B\} \\ A \cap B &= \{x \,|\, x \in A \text{ and } x \in B\} \\ \bar{A} &= \{x \,|\, x \notin A, \ x \in X\} \end{aligned} \tag{22.3}$$

Additionally, the following rules have to be satisfied:

$$A \cap \bar{A} = \varnothing, \quad \text{and} \quad A \cup \bar{A} = X \tag{22.4}$$

Fuzzy sets. Fuzzy sets are a generalization of classical sets. A fuzzy set A is characterized by a *membership function* $\mu_A(x)$, which assigns each element $x \in X$ a real-valued number ranging from zero to unity:

$$A = \{(x, \mu_A(x)) \,|\, x \in X\} \tag{22.5}$$

where $\mu_A(x) : X \to [0, 1]$. The *membership function* $\mu_A(x)$ indicates to which extend the element x has the attribute A, as opposed to the binary membership value of the mapping function f_A for crisp sets Eq. (22.2).

The choice of the shape of membership functions is somewhat arbitrary. It has to be adapted to the features of interest and to the final goal of the fuzzy technique. The most popular membership functions are given by piecewise-linear functions, second-order polynomials, or trigonometric functions.

Figure 22.1 illustrates an example of possible membership functions. Here, the distribution of an optical flow vector (Chapter 13),

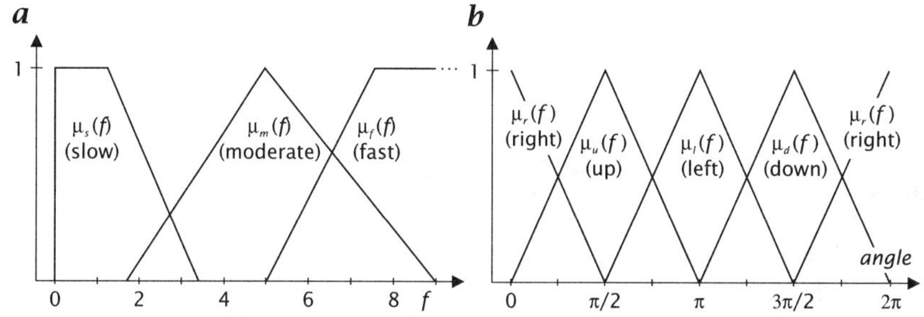

***Figure 22.1:** Possible membership functions for **a** the magnitude and **b** the direction of an optical flow vector $\boldsymbol{f}$.*

is characterized by fuzzy magnitude, $f = \|\boldsymbol{f}\|$, and fuzzy orientation angle, given by two independent sets of membership functions.

It is important to note that the membership functions do not necessarily have to add up to unity:

$$\mu_A(x) + \mu_B(x) + \ldots \neq 1 \tag{22.6}$$

as opposed to relative probabilities in stochastic processes.

A common notation for fuzzy sets, which is perfectly suited for fuzzy image processing, has been introduced by Zadeh [26]. Let X be a finite set $X = \{x_1, \ldots, x_n\}$. A fuzzy set A can be represented as follows:

$$A = \frac{\mu_A(x_1)}{x_1} + \ldots + \frac{\mu_A(x_n)}{x_n} = \sum_{i=1}^{n} \frac{\mu_A(x_i)}{x_i} \tag{22.7}$$

For infinite X we replace the sum in Eq. (22.7) by the following integral:

$$A = \int_X \frac{\mu_A(x)}{x} dx \tag{22.8}$$

The individual elements $\mu_A(x_i)/x_i$ represent fuzzy sets, which consist of one single element and are called *fuzzy singletons*. In Section 22.3.1 we will see how this definition is used in order to find a convenient fuzzy image definition.

Operations on fuzzy sets. In order to manipulate fuzzy sets, we need to have operations that enable us to combine them. As fuzzy sets are defined by membership functions, the classical set theoretic operations have to be replaced by function theoretic operations. Given two fuzzy

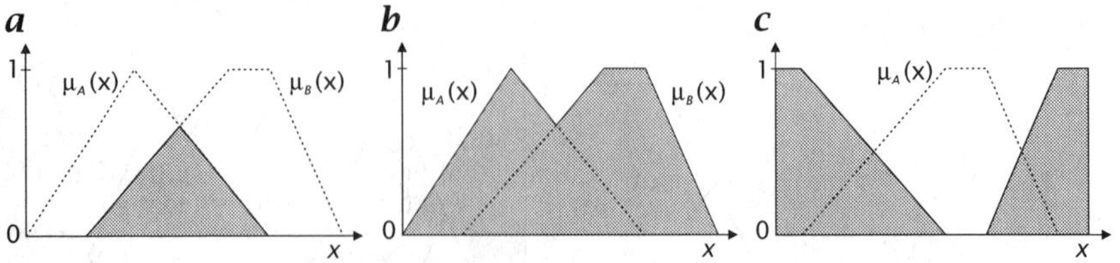

Figure 22.2: *Operations on fuzzy sets. The boundary of the shaded curves represent the* ***a*** *intersection $\mu_{A \cap B}$ of the fuzzy sets μ_A and μ_B,* ***b*** *the union $\mu_{A \cup B}$ of the fuzzy sets μ_A and μ_B, and* ***c*** *complement $\mu_{\bar{A}}$ of the fuzzy set μ_A.*

sets A and B, we define the following pointwise operations ($\forall x \in X$):

$$
\begin{array}{llll}
\text{equality} & A = B & \Leftrightarrow & \mu_A(x) = \mu_B(x) \\
\text{containment} & A \subset B & \Leftrightarrow & \mu_A(x) \le \mu_B(x) \\
\text{complement} & \bar{A}, & & \mu_{\bar{A}}(x) = 1 - \mu_A(x) \\
\text{intersection} & A \cap B, & & \mu_{A \cap B}(x) = \min\{\mu_A(x), \mu_B(x)\} \\
\text{union} & A \cup B, & & \mu_{A \cup B}(x) = \max\{\mu_A(x), \mu_B(x)\}
\end{array}
\tag{22.9}
$$

It can be easily verified that the conditions of Eq. (22.4) are no longer satisfied

$$
\begin{array}{lll}
A \cap \bar{A} & = & \min\{\mu_A(x), 1 - \mu_A(x)\} \neq \emptyset \\
A \cup \bar{A} & = & \max\{\mu_A(x), 1 - \mu_A(x)\} \neq X
\end{array}
\tag{22.10}
$$

for $\mu(x) \neq 1$, due to the partial membership of fuzzy sets.

The results of the complement, intersection, and union operations on fuzzy sets is illustrated in Fig. 22.2. The operations defined in Eq. (22.9) can be easily extended for more than two fuzzy sets and combinations of different operations.

Linguistic variables. An important feature of fuzzy systems is the concept of *linguistic variables*, introduced by Zadeh [26]. In order to reduce the complexity of precise definitions, they make use of words or sentences in a natural or artificial language, to describe a vague property.

A linguistic variable can be defined by a discrete set of membership functions $\{\mu_{A_1}, \ldots, \mu_{A_N}\}$ over the set $\{x\} = U \subset X$. The membership functions quantify the variable x by assigning a partial membership of x with regard to the terms A_i. An example of a linguistic variable could be the property "velocity," composed of the terms "slow," "moderate," and "fast." The individual terms are numerically characterized by the membership functions μ_s, μ_m, and μ_f. A possible realization is shown in Fig. 22.1a.

Linguistic hedges. Given a linguistic variable x represented by the set of membership functions $\{\mu_{A_i}\}$, we can change the meaning of a linguistic variable by modifying the shape (i. e., the numerical representation) of the membership functions. The most important linguistic hedges are *intensity modification*, μ^i, *concentration*, μ^c, and *dilation*, μ^d:

$$\begin{aligned}
\mu^i(x) &= \begin{cases} 2\mu^2(x) & \text{if } 0 \le \mu(x) \le 0.5 \\ 1 - 2[1-\mu(x)]^2 & \text{otherwise} \end{cases} \\
\mu^c(x) &= \mu^2(x) \\
\mu^d(x) &= \sqrt{\mu(x)}
\end{aligned} \tag{22.11}$$

An application example using dilation and concentration modification is shown in Fig. 22.19.

Fuzzy logic. The concept of linguistic variables allows us to define combinatorial relations between properties in terms of a language.

Fuzzy logic—an extension of classical *Boolean logic*—is based on linguistic variables, a fact which has assigned fuzzy logic the attribute of *computing with words* [28].

Boolean logic uses *Boolean operators*, such as AND ($\wedge$), OR ($\vee$), NOT ($\neg$), and combinations of them. They are defined for binary values of the input variables and result in a binary output variable. If we want to extend the binary logic to a combinatorial logic of linguistic variables, we need to redefine the elementary logical operators. In fuzzy logic, the Boolean operators are replaced by the operations on the corresponding membership functions, as defined in Eq. (22.9).

Let $\{\mu_{A_i}(x_1)\}$ and $\{\mu_{B_i}(x_2)\}$ be two linguistic variables of two sets of input variables $\{x_1\}$ and $\{x_2\}$. The set of output variables $\{x_3\}$ is characterized by the linguistic variable $\{\mu_{C_i}(x_3)\}$. We define the following basic combinatorial rules:

if $(A_j \wedge B_k)$ **then** C_l:

$$\mu'_{C_l}(x_3) = \left(\min\left\{\mu_{A_j}(x_1), \mu_{B_k}(x_2)\right\}\right)\mu_{C_l}(x_3) \tag{22.12}$$

if $(A_j \vee B_k)$ **then** C_l:

$$\mu'_{C_l}(x_3) = \left(\max\left\{\mu_{A_j}(x_1), \mu_{B_k}(x_2)\right\}\right)\mu_{C_l}(x_3) \tag{22.13}$$

if $(\neg A_j)$ **then** C_l:

$$\mu'_{C_l}(x_3) = \left(1 - \mu_{A_j}(x_1)\right)\mu_{C_l}(x_3) \tag{22.14}$$

Thus, the output membership function $\mu_{C_i}(x_3)$ is modified (weighted) according to the combination of A_i and B_j at a certain pair (x_1, x_2). These rules can easily be extended to more than two input variables. A fuzzy inference system consists of a number of if-then rules, one for any membership function μ_{C_i} of the output linguistic variable $\{\mu_{C_i}\}$.

Given the set of modified output membership functions $\{\mu'_{C_i}(x_3)\}$, we can derive a single output membership function $\mu_C(x_3)$ by *accumulating* all μ'_{C_i}. This can be done by combining the μ'_{C_i} by a logical OR, that is, the maximum operator:

$$\mu_C(x_3) = \max_i \left\{\mu'_{C_i}(x_3)\right\} \tag{22.15}$$

Defuzzification. The resulting output membership function $\mu_C(x_3)$ can be assigned a numerical value $x \in \{x\}$ by *defuzzification*, reversing the process of fuzzification. There are a variety of approaches to get a single number from a membership function reported in the literature. The most common techniques are computing the *center of area* (center of mass) or the *mean of maxima* of the corresponding membership function. Applications examples are shown in Section 22.4.3.

The step of defuzzification can be omitted if the final result of the fuzzy inference system is given by a membership function, rather than a crisp number.

22.1.3 Fuzzy logic versus probability theory

It has been a long-standing misconception that fuzzy logic is nothing but another representation of probability theory. We do not want to contribute to this dispute, but rather try to outline the basic difference.

Probability describes the uncertainty in the occurrence of an event. It allows predicting the event by knowledge about its relative frequency within a large number of experiments. After the experiment has been carried out, the event either has occurred or not. There is no uncertainty left. Even if the probability is very small, it might happen that the unlikely event occurs. To treat stochastic uncertainty, such as random processes (e. g., noise), probability theory is a powerful tool, which has conquered an important area in computer vision (Chapter 26).

There are, however, other uncertainties, that can not be described by random processes. As opposed to probability, fuzzy logic represents the *imperfection* in the informational content of the event. Even after the measurement, it might not be clear, if the event has happened, or not.

For illustration of this difference, consider an image to contain a single edge, which appears at a certain rate. Given the probability distribution, we can predict the likelihood of the edge to appear after a certain number of frames. It might happen, however, that it appears in every image or does not show up at all. Additionally, the edge may be corrupted by noise. A noisy edge can appropriately be detected with probabilistic approaches, computing the likelihood of the noisy measurement to belong to the class of edges. But how do we define the edge? How do we classify an image that shows a gray-value slope? A noisy slope stays a slope even if all noise is removed. If the slope is extended over the entire image we usually do not call it an edge. But if the slope is "high" enough and only extends over a "narrow" region, we tend to call it an edge. Immediately the question arises: How large is "high" and what do we mean with "narrow?"

In order to quantify the shape of an edge, we need to have a model. Then, the probabilistic approach allows us to extract the model parameters, which represent edges in various shapes. But how can we treat this problem, without having an appropriate model? Many real world applications are too complex to model all facets necessary to describe them quantitatively. Fuzzy logic does not need models. It can handle vague information, imperfect knowledge and combine it by heuristic rules—in a well-defined mathematical framework. This is the strength of fuzzy logic!

22.2 Why fuzzy image processing?

In computer vision, we have different theories, methodologies, and techniques that we use to solve different practical problems (e. g., digital geometry, mathematical morphology, statistical approaches, probability theory, etc.). Because of great diversity and complexity of problems in image processing, we always require new approaches. There are some reasons to use fuzzy techniques as a new approach. We briefly describe two of them [29].

22.2.1 Framework for knowledge representation/processing

The most important reason why one should investigate the potentials of fuzzy techniques for image processing is that fuzzy logic provides us with a powerful mathematical framework for representation and processing of expert knowledge. Here, the concept of linguistic variables and the fuzzy if-then rules play a key role. Making a human-like processing possible, fuzzy inference engines can be developed using expert knowledge. The rule-based techniques, for example, have the general form:

If condition A_1, **and** condition A_2, **and** ..., **then** action B

In real applications, however, the conditions are often partially satisfied (e.g., the question of homogeneity in a neighborhood can not always be

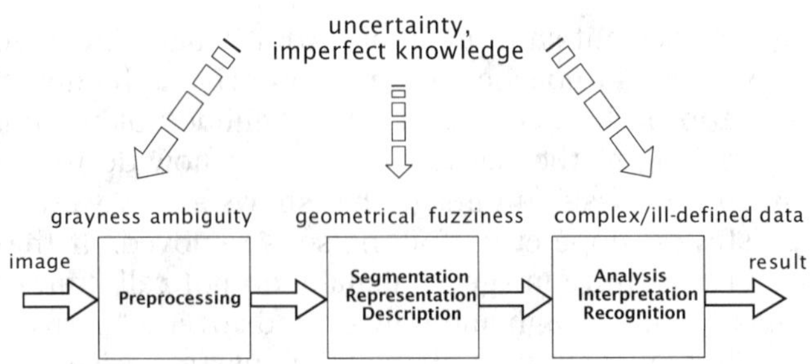

Figure 22.3: *Imperfect knowledge in image processing (similar to [29]).*

answered with a crisp yes or no). Fuzzy if-then rules allow us to perform actions also partially.

22.2.2 Management of vagueness and ambiguity

Where is the boundary of a region? Is the region homogeneous? Which gray level can serve as a threshold? Should we apply noise filtering, edge enhancement, or smoothing technique? What is a road or a tree in a scene analysis situation? These and many other similar questions arise during image processing—from low-level through high-level processing—and are due to vagueness and ambiguity. There are many reasons why our knowledge in such situations is imperfect. Imprecise results, complex class definitions, different types of noise, concurring evidences, and finally, the inherent fuzziness of many categories are just some sources of uncertainty or imperfect knowledge.

Distinguishing between low-level, intermediate-level, and high-level image processing, the imperfect knowledge is due to grayness ambiguity, geometrical fuzziness, and imprecision/complexity (Fig. 22.3). Fuzzy techniques offer a suitable framework for management of these problems.

22.3 Fuzzy image understanding

To use the fuzzy logic in image processing applications, we have to develop a new image understanding. A new image definition should be established, images and their components (pixels, histograms, segments, etc.) should be fuzzified (transformation in membership plane), and the fundamental topological relationships between image parts should be extended to fuzzy sets (fuzzy digital topology).

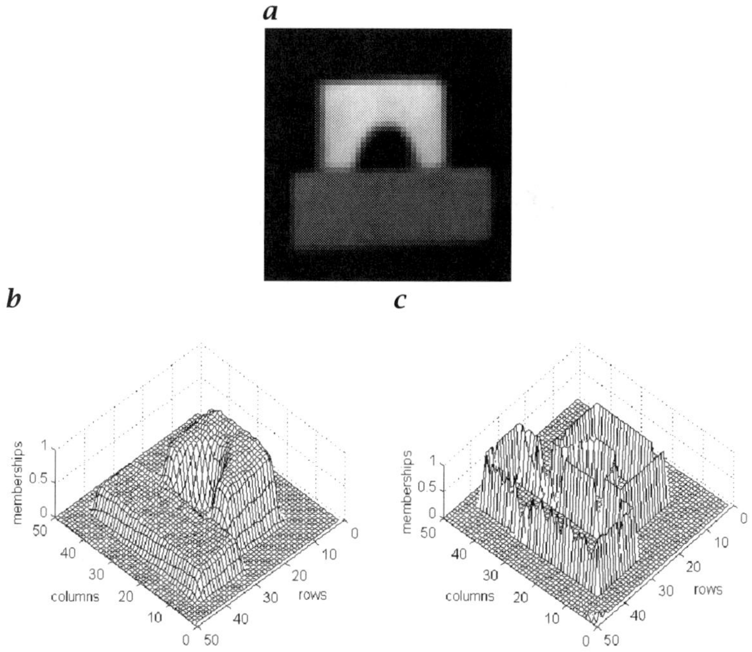

***Figure 22.4:** Images as an array of fuzzy singletons. **a** test image as a fuzzy set regarding **b** brightness (bright pixels have higher memberships), and **c** edginess (edge pixels have higher memberships).*

22.3.1 A new image definition: Images as fuzzy sets

An image G of size $M \times N$ with L gray levels can be defined as an array of fuzzy singletons (fuzzy sets with only one supporting point) indicating the membership value μ_{mn} of each image point x_{mn} regarding a predefined image property (e.g., brightness, homogeneity, noisiness, edginess, etc.) [13, 15, 29]:

$$G = \bigcup_{m=1}^{M} \bigcup_{n=1}^{N} \frac{\mu_{mn}}{x_{mn}} \tag{22.16}$$

The definition of the membership values depends on the specific requirements of particular application and on the corresponding expert knowledge. Figure 22.4 shows an example where brightness and edginess are used to define the membership grade of each pixel.

22.3.2 Image fuzzification: From images to memberships

Fuzzy image processing is a kind of nonlinear image processing. The difference to other well-known methodologies is that fuzzy techniques

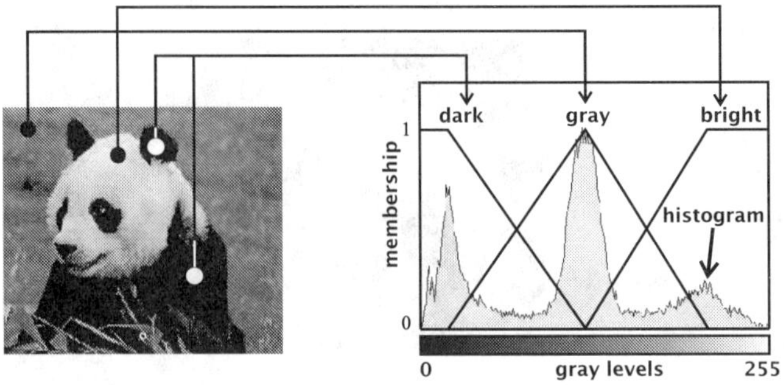

Figure 22.5: Histogram-based gray-level fuzzification. The location of membership functions is determined depending on specific points of image histogram (adapted from [31]).

operate on membership values. The image fuzzification (generation of suitable membership values) is, therefore, the first processing step. Generally, three various types of image fuzzification can be distinguished: histogram-based gray-level fuzzification, local neighborhood fuzzification, and feature fuzzification [29].

As in other application areas of fuzzy set theory, the fuzzification step should be sometimes optimized. The number, form, and location of each membership function could/should be adapted to achieve better results. For instance, genetic algorithms are performed to optimize fuzzy rule-based systems [30].

Histogram-based gray-level fuzzification [29]. To develop any point operation (global histogram-based techniques), each gray level should be assigned with one or more membership values regarding to the corresponding requirements.

Example 22.1: Image brightness

The *brightness* of an image can be regarded as a fuzzy set containing the subsets *dark*, *gray*, and *bright* intensity levels (of course, one may define more subsets such as very dark, slightly bright, etc.). Depending on the normalized image histogram, the location of the membership functions can be determined (Fig. 22.5). It should be noted that for histogram-based gray-level fuzzification some knowledge about image and its histogram is required (e.g., minimum and maximum of gray-level frequencies). The detection accuracy of these histogram points, however, should not be very high as we are using the concept of fuzziness (we do not require precise data).

Local neighborhood fuzzification [29]. Intermediate techniques (e.g., segmentation, noise filtering etc.) operate on a predefined neighborhood of pixels. To use fuzzy approaches to such operations, the fuzzi-

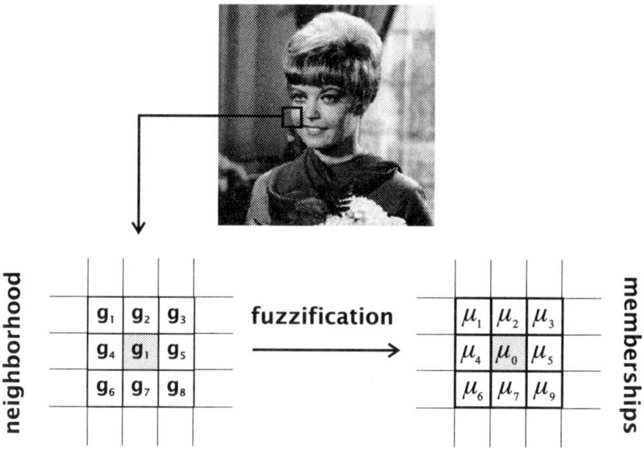

Figure 22.6: *On local neighborhood fuzzification [31].*

fication step should also be done within the selected neighborhood (Fig. 22.6). The local neighborhood fuzzification can be carried out depending on the task to be done. Of course, local neighborhood fuzzification requires more computing time compared with histogram-based approach. In many situations, we also need more thoroughness in designing membership functions to execute the local fuzzification because noise and outliers may falsify membership values.

Example 22.2: Edginess

Within 3×3-neighborhood U we are interested in the degree of membership of the center point to the fuzzy set *edge pixel.* Here, the edginess μ_e is a matter of grade. If the 9 pixels in U are assigned the numbers $0, \ldots 8$ and G_0 denotes the center pixel, a possible membership function can be the following [29]:

$$\mu_e = 1 - \left[1 + \frac{1}{\Delta} \sum_{i=0}^{8} \|G_0 - G_i\| \right]^{-1} \tag{22.17}$$

with $\Delta = \max_U(G_i)$.

Example 22.3: Homogeneity

Within 3×3-neighborhood U, the homogeneity is regarded as a fuzzy set. The membership function μ^h can be defined as:

$$\mu_h = 1 - \frac{G^{max,l} - G^{min,l}}{G^{max,g} - G^{min,g}} \tag{22.18}$$

where $G^{min,l}$, $G^{max,l}$, $G^{min,g}$, and $G^{max,g}$ are the local and global minimum and maximum gray levels, respectively.

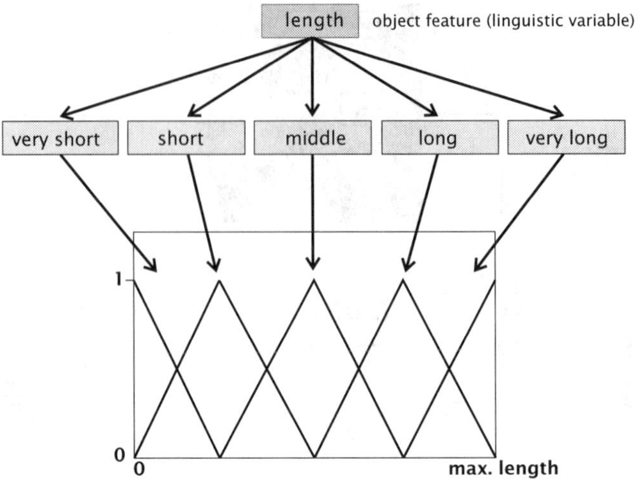

Figure 22.7: Feature fuzzification using the concept of linguistic variables [29].

Feature fuzzification [29]. For high-level tasks, image features should usually be extracted (e.g., length of objects, homogeneity of regions, entropy, mean value, etc.). These features will be used to analyze the results, recognize the objects, and interpret the scenes. Applying fuzzy techniques to this tasks, we need to fuzzify the extracted features. It is necessary not only because fuzzy techniques operate only on membership values but also because the extracted features are often incomplete and/or imprecise.

Example 22.4: Object length

If the length of an object was calculated in a previous processing step, the fuzzy subsets *very short*, *short*, *middle-long*, *long* and *very long* can be introduced as terms of the linguistic variable *length* in order to identify certain types of objects (Fig. 22.7).

22.3.3 Fuzzy topology: Noncrisp definitions of topological relationships

Image segmentation is a fundamental step in all image processing systems. However, the image regions can not always be defined crisply. It is sometimes more appropriate to consider the different image parts, regions, or objects as fuzzy subsets of the image. The topological relationships and properties, such as *connectedness* and *surroundedness*, can be extended to fuzzy sets. In image analysis and description, the digital topology plays an important role. The topological relationships between parts of an image are conventionally defined for (crisp) subsets of image. These subsets are usually extracted using different types

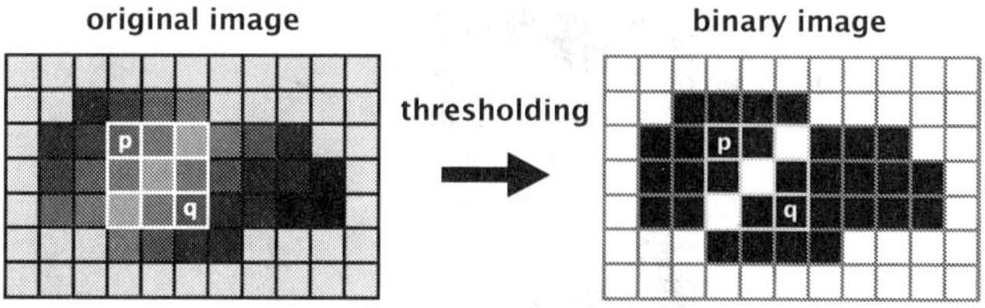

Figure 22.8: On crisp and fuzzy connectedness. The pixels p and q are fuzzy connected in original image, and not connected in the binary image.

of segmentation techniques (e. g., thresholding). Segmentation procedures, however, are often a strong commitment accompanied by loss of information. In many applications, it would be more appropriate to make soft decisions by considering the image parts as fuzzy subsets. In these cases, we need the extension of (binary) digital topology to fuzzy sets. The most important topological relationships are connectedness, surroundedness and adjacency. In the following, we consider an image g with a predefined neighborhood $U \subset g$ (e.g., 4- or 8-neighborhood).

Fuzzy connectedness [5]. Let p and $q \in U(\subset g)$ and let μ be a membership function modeling G or some regions of it. Further, let δ_{pq} be paths from p to q containing the points r. The degree of *connectedness* of p and q in U with respect to μ can be defined as follows (Fig. 22.8):

$$\text{connectedness}_{\mu}(p,q) \equiv \max_{\delta_{pq}} \left[\min_{r \in \delta_{pq}} \mu(r) \right] \tag{22.19}$$

Thus, if we are considering the image segments as fuzzy subsets of the image, the points p and q are connected regarding to the membership function μ if the following condition holds:

$$\text{connectedness}_{\mu}(p,q) \geq \min\left[\mu(p), \mu(q)\right] \tag{22.20}$$

Fuzzy surroundedness [5, 11, 32]. Let μ_A, μ_B and μ_C be the membership functions of fuzzy subsets A, B and C of image G. The fuzzy subset C separates A from B if for all points p and r in $U \subset G$ and all paths δ from p to q, there exists a point $r \in \delta$ such that the following condition holds:

$$\mu(C)(r) \geq \min\left[\mu_A(p), \mu_B(q)\right] \tag{22.21}$$

In other words, B surrounds A if it separates A from an unbounded region on which $\mu_A = 0$. Depending on particular application, appropriate membership functions can be found to measure the surroundedness. Two possible definitions are given in Example 22.5, where $\mu_{B \odot A}$

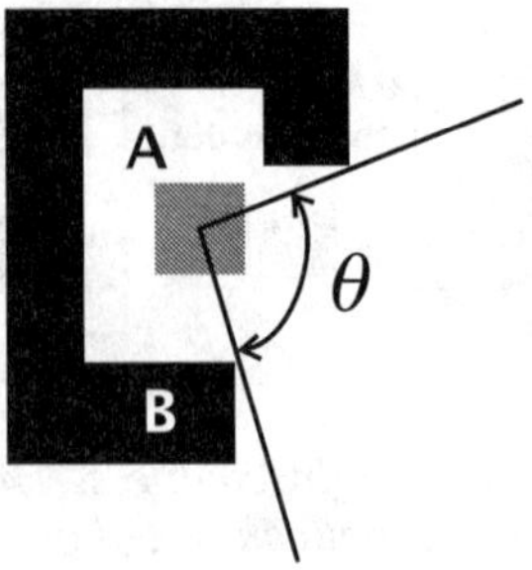

Figure 22.9: Example for calculation of fuzzy surroundedness.

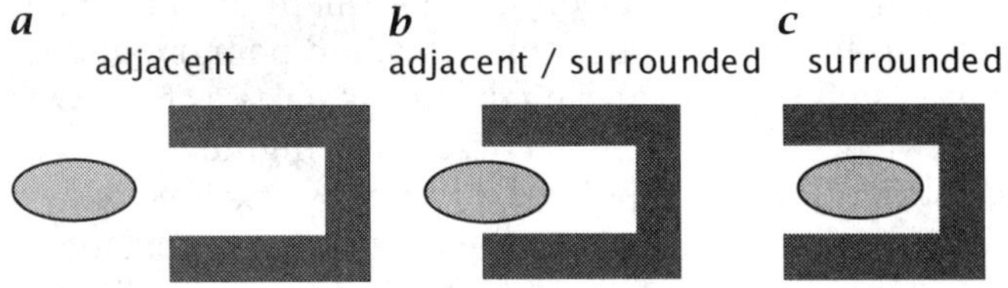

Figure 22.10: Relationship between adjacency and surroundedness.

defines the membership function of the linguistic variable '*B* surrounds *A*' (Fig. 22.9) [29, 32].

Example 22.5: Surroundedness

$$\mu_{B \odot A}(\theta) = \begin{cases} \dfrac{\pi - \theta}{\pi} & 0 \le \theta < \pi \\ 0 & \text{otherwise} \end{cases}, \quad \mu_{B \odot A}(\theta) = \begin{cases} \cos^2\left(\dfrac{\theta}{2}\right) & 0 \le \theta < \pi \\ 0 & \text{otherwise} \end{cases}$$

Fuzzy adjacency [5, 11, 17]. The adjacency of two disjoint (crisp) sets is defined by the length of their common border. Following, a brief description of generalization of this definition to fuzzy sets.

Let μ_1 and μ_2 be piecewise-constant fuzzy sets of G. The image G can be partitioned in a finite number of bounded regions G_i, meeting pairwise along arcs, on each of which $\mu_1(i)$ and $\mu_2(j)$ are constant. If μ_1 and μ_2 are disjoint then in each region G_i either $\mu_1 = 0$ or $\mu_2 = 0$. Let $A(i, j, k)$ be the k-th arc along which G_i and G_j meet. Then the adjacency of μ_1 and μ_2 can be defined as follows:

$$\text{adjacency}(\mu_1, \mu_2) = \sum_{i,j,k\ i \neq j} \mu_1(i)\mu_2(j)\|A(i, j, k)\| \tag{22.22}$$

where $\|A(i, j, k)\|$ indicates the length of the k-th arc. This definition may not fully agree with our intuition in some situations. For instance, consider the following cases:

1. $\mu_1 = 0.1$, $\mu_2 = 0.15 \longrightarrow$ adjacency = 0.015
2. $\mu_1 = 0.7$, $\mu_1 = 0.75 \longrightarrow$ adjacency = 0.525

The difference of membership values is the same in both cases, namely 0.05. Intuitively, one may expect that the adjacency should also be the same in both cases. Therefore, it may be useful to use other definitions of fuzzy adjacency:

$$\text{adjacency}(\mu_1, \mu_2) = \sum_{i,j,k} \frac{\|A(i,j,k)\|}{1 + \|\mu_1(i)\mu_2(j)\|} \tag{22.23}$$

Now, to introduce a definition for degree of adjacency for fuzzy image subsets, let us consider two segments S_1 and S_2 of an image G. Further, let $B(S_1)$ be the set of border pixels of S_1, and p an arbitrary member of B. The degree of adjacency, can be defined with respect to the definition of adjacency in Eq. (22.22) as follows:

$$\text{degree of adjacency}(\mu_1, \mu_2) = \sum_{p \in B(S_1)} \frac{1}{1 + d(p)} \tag{22.24}$$

where $d(p)$ is the shortest distance of pixel p from the border of segment S_2. Considering the adjacency definition in Eq. (22.23), the degree of adjacency can also be defined as follows:

$$\text{degree of adjacency}(\mu_1, \mu_2) = \sum_{p \in B(S_1)} \frac{1}{1 + \|\mu_1(i)\mu_2(j)\|} \frac{1}{1 + d(p)} \tag{22.25}$$

where $p \in S_1$ and $q \in S_2$ are border pixels, and $d(p)$ is the shortest distance between p and q. Here, it should be noted that there exists a close relationship between adjacency and surroundedness (Fig. 22.10a,b). Depending on particular requirements, one may consider one or both of them to describe spatial relationships.

22.4 Fuzzy image processing systems

Fuzzy image processing consists (as all other fuzzy approaches) of three stages: fuzzification, suitable operations on membership values, and, if necessary, defuzzification (Fig. 22.11). The main difference to other methodologies in image processing is that input data (histograms, gray levels, features, ...) will be processed in the so-called membership plane where one can use the great diversity of fuzzy logic, fuzzy set theory and fuzzy measure theory to modify/aggregate the membership values, classify data, or make decisions using fuzzy inference. The new membership values are retransformed in the gray-level plane

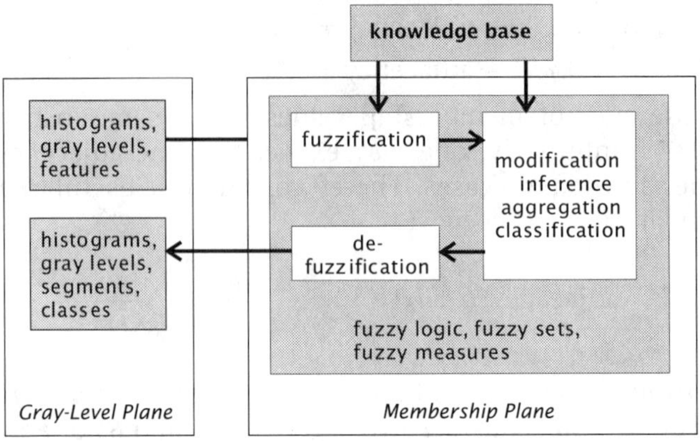

Figure 22.11: *General structure of fuzzy image processing systems [29].*

Table 22.1: *On relationships between imperfect knowledge and the type of image fuzzification [29].*

Problem	Fuzzification	Level	Examples
Brightness ambiguity/ vagueness	histogram	low	thresholding
Geometrical fuzziness	local	intermediate	edge detection, filtering
Complex/ill-defined data	feature	high	recognition, analysis

to generate new histograms, modified gray levels, image segments, or classes of objects. In the following, we briefly describe each processing stage.

22.4.1 Fuzzification (coding of image information)

Fuzzification is in a sense a type of input data coding. It means that membership values are assigned to each input (Section 22.3.2). Fuzzification does mean that we assign the image (its gray levels, features, segments, ...) with one or more membership values with respect to the properties of interest (e. g., brightness, edginess, homogeneity). Depending on the problem we have (ambiguity, fuzziness, complexity), the suitable fuzzification method, should be selected. Examples of properties and the corresponding type of fuzzification are given in Table 22.1.

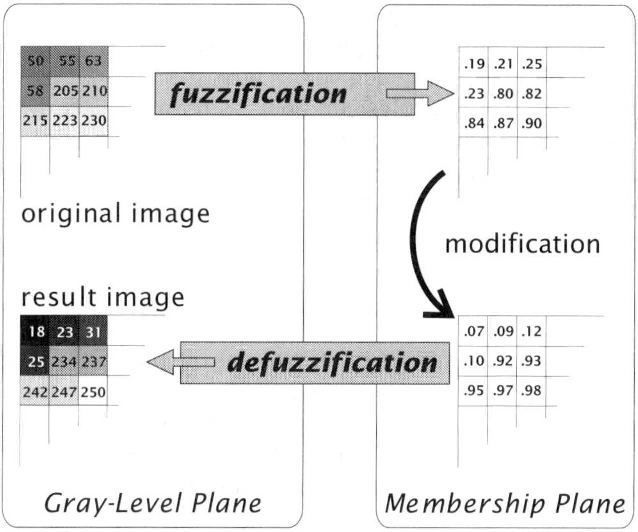

Figure 22.12: *Example for modification-based fuzzy image processing [29].*

22.4.2 Operations in membership plane

The generated membership values are modified by a suitable fuzzy approach. This can be a modification, aggregation, classification, or processing by some kind of if-then rules.

Aggregation. Many fuzzy techniques aggregate the membership values to produce new memberships. Examples are fuzzy hybrid connectives, and fuzzy integrals, to mention only some of them. The result of aggregation is a global value that considers different criteria, such as features and hypothesis, to deliver a certainty factor for a specific decision (e. g., pixel classification).

Modification. Another class of fuzzy techniques modify the membership values in some ways. The principal steps are illustrated in Fig. 22.12. Examples of such modifications are linguistic hedges, and distance-based modification in prototype-based fuzzy clustering. The result of the modification is a new membership value for each fuzzified feature (e. g., gray level, segment, object).

Classification. Fuzzy classification techniques can be used to classify input data. They can be numerical approaches (e. g., fuzzy clustering algorithms, fuzzy integrals, etc.) or syntactic approaches (e. g., fuzzy grammars, fuzzy if-then rules, etc.). Regarding to the membership values, classification can be a kind of modification (e. g., distance-based adaptation of memberships in prototype-based clustering) or aggregation (e. g., evidence combination by fuzzy integrals).

Inference. Fuzzy if-then rules can be used to make soft decisions using expert knowledge. Indeed, fuzzy inference can also be regarded as a kind of membership aggregation because they use different fuzzy connectives to fuse the partial truth in premise and conclusion of if-then rules.

22.4.3 Defuzzification (decoding of the results)

In many applications we need a crisp value as output. Fuzzy algorithms, however, always deliver fuzzy answers (a membership function or a membership value). In order to reverse the process of fuzzification, we use defuzzification to produce a crisp answer from a fuzzy output feature. Depending on the selected fuzzy approach, there are different ways to defuzzify the results. The well-known defuzzification methods such as *center of area* and *mean of maximum* are used mainly in inference engines. One can also use the inverse membership function if point operations are applied. Figure 22.12 illustrates the three stages of fuzzy image processing for a modification-based approach.

22.5 Theoretical components of fuzzy image processing

Fuzzy image processing is knowledge-based and nonlinear. It is based on fuzzy logic and uses its logical, set-theoretical, relational and epistemic aspects. The most important theoretical frameworks that can be used to construct the foundations of fuzzy image processing are: fuzzy geometry, measures of fuzziness/image information, rule-based approaches, fuzzy clustering algorithms, fuzzy mathematical morphology, fuzzy measure theory, and fuzzy grammars. Any of these topics can be used either to develop new techniques, or to extend the existing algorithms [29]. In the following, we give a brief description of each field. Here, the soft computing techniques (e. g., neural fuzzy, fuzzy genetic) are not mentioned due to space limitations.

Combined approaches, such as neural fuzzy and fuzzy genetic techniques are not considered here because of space limitations. In Sections 22.5.1–22.5.7 we will briefly introduce each of these topics.

22.5.1 Fuzzy geometry

Geometrical relationships between the image components play a key role in intermediate image processing. Many geometrical categories such as area, perimeter, and diameter, are already extended to fuzzy sets [5, 6, 7, 8, 9, 10, 11, 16, 17]. The geometrical fuzziness arising

Table 22.2: *Theory of fuzzy geometry [5, 6, 7, 8, 9, 10, 11, 16, 17, 29]*

Aspects of fuzzy geometry	Examples of subjects and features
digital topology	connectedness, surroundedness, adjacency
metric	area, perimeter, diameter, distance between fuzzy sets
derived measures	compactness index of area coverage, elongatedness
convexity	convex/concave fuzzy image subsets
thinning/medial axes	shrinking, expanding, skeletonization
elementary shapes	fuzzy discs, fuzzy rectangles, fuzzy triangles

during segmentation tasks can be handled efficiently if we consider the image or its segments as fuzzy sets. The main application areas of fuzzy geometry are feature extraction (e. g., in image enhancement), image segmentation, and image representation ([12, 16, 17, 29, 29, 33], see also Table 22.2).

Fuzzy topology plays an important role in fuzzy image understanding, as already pointed out earlier in this chapter. In the following, we describe some fuzzy geometrical measures, such as compactness, index of area coverage, and elongatedness. A more detailed description of other aspects of fuzzy geometry can be found in the literature.

Fuzzy compactness [7]. Let G be an image of size MN, containing one object with the membership values $\mu_{m,n}$. The *area* of the object—interpreted as a fuzzy subset of the image—can be calculated as:

$$\text{area}(\mu) = \sum_{m=0}^{M} \sum_{n=0}^{N} \mu_{m,n} \tag{22.26}$$

The *perimeter* of the object can be determined as

$$\text{perimeter}(\mu) = \sum_{m=1}^{M} \sum_{n=1}^{N-1} \|\mu_{m,n} - \mu_{m,n+1}\| + \sum_{m=1}^{M-1} \sum_{n=1}^{N} \|\mu_{m,n} - \mu_{m+1,n}\| \tag{22.27}$$

The *fuzzy compactness*, introduced by Rosenfeld [7] can be defined as

$$\text{compactness}(\mu) = \frac{\text{area}(\mu)}{[\text{perimeneter}(\mu)]^2} \tag{22.28}$$

In the crisp case, the compactness is maximum for a circle. It can be shown that the compactness of fuzzy sets is always more than a corresponding case. Many fuzzy techniques are, therefore, developed for image segmentation, which minimizes the fuzzy compactness.

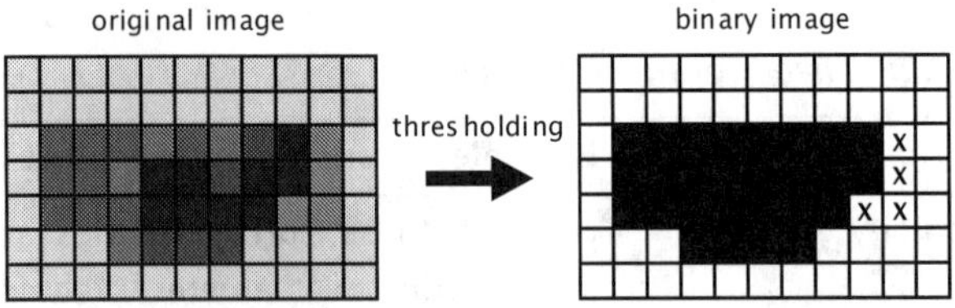

Figure 22.13: Calculation of elongatedness of crisp image subsets is often accompanied with loss of information (pixels marked with "x" are lost during the thresholding task).

Index of area coverage [16, 17]. The *index of area coverage* of a fuzzy image subset μ, introduced by Pal and Ghosh [16], represents the fraction of the maximum image area actually covered by this subset. It is defined as follows:

$$\mathrm{ioac}(\mu) = \frac{\mathrm{area}(\mu)}{\mathrm{length}(\mu)\mathrm{breadth}(\mu)} \tag{22.29}$$

Here, the length and breadth of the fuzzy image subset are calculated as follows:

$$\mathrm{length}(\mu) = \max_m \left\{ \sum_n \mu_{m,n} \right\} \tag{22.30}$$

$$\mathrm{breadth}(\mu) = \max_n \left\{ \sum_m \mu_{m,n} \right\} \tag{22.31}$$

The definition of the index of area coverage is very similar to compactness. For certain cases, it can be shown that there exists a relationship between the two definitions.

Fuzzy elongatedness [7]. As an example for cases that have no simple generalization to fuzzy sets, we briefly explain the *elongatedness* of an object. The elongatedness can serve as a feature to recognize a certain class of objects. Making strong commitments to calculate such geometrical features (e. g., thresholding), it can lead to loss of information and falsification of final results (Fig. 22.13).

Let μ be the characteristic function of a crisp image subset. The elongatedness can be defined as follows:

$$\mathrm{elongatedness}(\mu) = \frac{\mathrm{area}(\mu)}{[\mathrm{thickness}(\mu)]^2} \tag{22.32}$$

Now, letting μ be the membership function of a fuzzy image subset, a closely related definition of fuzzy elongatedness is introduced by

Rosenfeld [5]:

$$\text{fuzzy elongatedness}(\mu) = \max_{\delta>0} \frac{\text{area}(\mu - \mu_{-\delta})}{(2\delta)^2} \tag{22.33}$$

Here, μ_δ denotes the result of a shrinking operation in a given distance δ, where the local "min" operation can be used as a generalization of shrinking.

22.5.2 Measures of fuzziness and image information

Fuzzy sets can be used to represent a variety of image information. A central question dealing with uncertainty is to quantify the "fuzziness" or uncertainty of an image feature, given the corresponding membership function. A goal of fuzzy image processing might be to minimize the uncertainty in the image information.

Index of fuzziness. The intersection of a crisp set with its own complement always equals zero (Eq. (22.4)). This condition no longer holds for two fuzzy sets. The more fuzzy a fuzzy set is, the more it intersects with its own complement. This consideration leads to the definition of the *index of fuzziness* γ. Given a fuzzy set A with the membership function μ_A defined over an image of size $M \times N$, we define the *linear index of fuzziness* γ_l as follows:

$$\gamma_l(G) = \frac{2}{MN} \sum_{m,n} \min(\mu_{mn}, 1 - \mu_{mn}) \tag{22.34}$$

Another possible definition is given by the *quadratic index of fuzziness* γ_q defined by

$$\gamma_q(G) = \frac{1}{\sqrt{MN}} \left[\left(\sum_{m,n} \min(\mu_{mn}, 1 - \mu_{mn}) \right)^2 \right]^{1/2} \tag{22.35}$$

For binary-valued (crisp sets) both indices equal zero. For maximum fuzziness, that is, $\mu_{mn} = 0.5$ they reach the peak value of 1.

Fuzzy entropy. An information theoretic measure quantifying the information content of an image is the *entropy*. The counterpart in fuzzy set theory is given by the *fuzzy entropy*, quantifying the uncertainty of the image content. The *logarithmic fuzzy entropy* H_{log}, is defined by [34]

$$H_{log}(G) = \frac{1}{MN \ln 2} \sum_{m,n} S_n(\mu_{mn}) \tag{22.36}$$

where

$$S_n(\mu_{mn}) = -\mu_{mn}\ln(\mu_{mn}) - (1-\mu_{mn})\ln(1-\mu_{mn}) \tag{22.37}$$

Another possible definition, called the *exponential fuzzy entropy* has been proposed by Pal and Pal [21]:

$$H_{exp}(G) = \frac{1}{MN(\sqrt{e}-1)}\sum_{m,n}\left\{\mu_{mn}e^{(1-\mu_{mn})} + (1-\mu_{mn})e^{\mu_{mn}} - 1\right\} \tag{22.38}$$

The fuzzy entropy also yields a measure of uncertainty ranging from zero to unity.

Fuzzy correlation. An important question in classical classification techniques is the *correlation* of two different image features. Similarly, the *fuzzy correlation* $K(\mu_1, \mu_2)$ quantifies the correlation of two fuzzy features, defined by the membership functions μ_1 and μ_2, respectively. It is defined by [13]

$$K(\mu_1, \mu_2) = 1 - \frac{4}{\Delta_1 + \Delta_2}\sum_{m,n}(\mu_{1,mn} - \mu_{2,mn})^2 \tag{22.39}$$

where

$$\Delta_1 = \sum_{m,n}(2\mu_{1,mn} - 1)^2, \quad \text{and} \quad \Delta_2 = \sum_{m,n}(2\mu_{2,mn} - 1)^2 \tag{22.40}$$

If $\Delta_1 = \Delta_2 = 0$, K is set to unity. Fuzzy correlation is used either to quantify the correlation of two features within the same image or, alternatively, the correlation of the same feature in two different images. Examples of features are brightness, edginess, texturedness, etc.

More detailed information about the theory on common measures of fuzziness can be found in [13, 14, 21, 35, 36, 37, 38]. A variety of practical applications are given by [19, 20, 29, 39, 40, 41, 42].

22.5.3 Rule-based systems

Rule-based systems are among the most powerful applications of fuzzy set theory. They have been of utmost importance in modern developments of fuzzy-controllers. Thinking of fuzzy logic usually implies dealing with some kind of rule-based inference, in terms of incorporating expert knowledge or heuristic relations. Whenever we have to deal with combining uncertain knowledge without having an analytical model, we can use a rule-based fuzzy inference system. Rule-based approaches incorporate these techniques into image processing tasks.

Rule-based systems are composed of the following three major parts: *fuzzification*, *fuzzy inference*, and *defuzzification*.

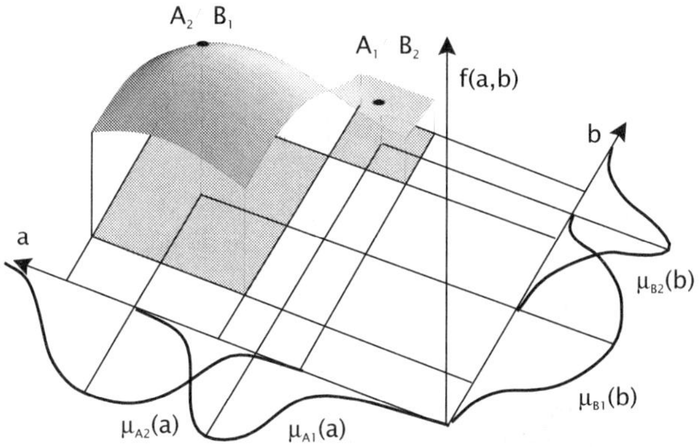

Figure 22.14: *The rules of a fuzzy-inference system create* fuzzy patches *in the product space $A \times B$. These regions constitute the support of the function $\mu_C(a,b)$.*

We outlined the components fuzzification and defuzzification earlier in this chapter. They are used to create fuzzy sets from input data and to compute a crisp number from the resulting output fuzzy set, respectively.

The main part of rule-based systems is the *inference engine*. It constitutes the brain of the fuzzy technique, containing the knowledge about the relations between the individual input fuzzy sets and the output fuzzy sets. The fuzzy inference system comprises a number of rules, in terms of if-then conditions, which are used to modify the membership functions of the corresponding output condition according to Eqs. (22.12) to (22.14). The individual output membership functions are accumulated to a single output fuzzy set using Eq. (22.15).

An interesting aspect of rule-based systems is that they can be interpreted as a nonlinear interpolation technique approximating arbitrary functions from partial knowledge about relations between input and output variables. Consider $f(a,b)$ to be a function of the two variables a, and b. In case we do not know the analytical shape of f we need an infinite number of relations between a, b, and $f(a,b)$ in order to approximate f. If we quantify a and b by fuzzy sets A_i and B_i, it is sufficient to know the relations between the finite number of pairs (A_i, B_j). The continuous function f over the entire parameter space $A \times B$ can be interpolated, as illustrated in Fig. 22.14. In control theory, the function $f(a,b)$ is called the *control surface*. It is, however, necessary to carefully choose the shape of the membership functions μ_{A_i} and μ_{B_i}, as they determine the exact shape of the interpolation between the sparse support points, that is, the shape of the control surface.

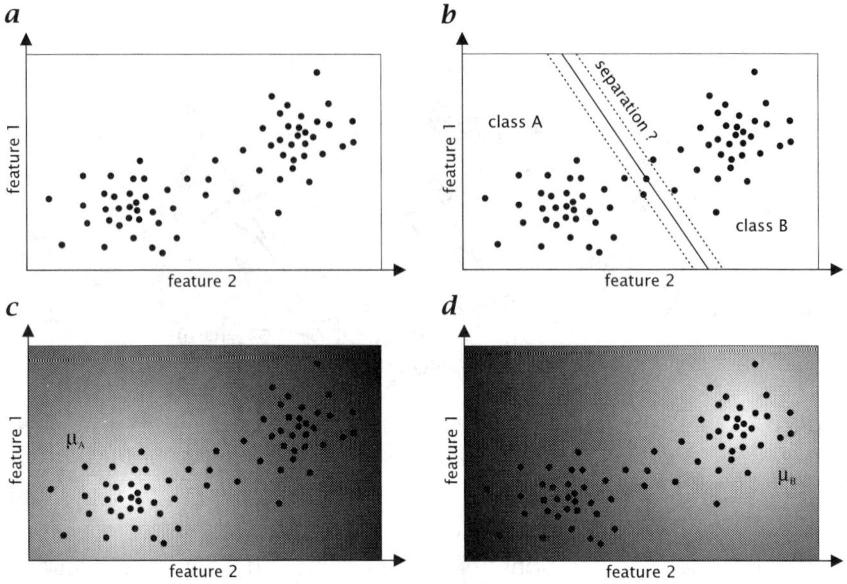

Figure 22.15: *Crisp versus fuzzy classification.* ***a*** *Set of feature points.* ***b*** *Crisp classification into two sets A and B. Features close to the separation line are subject to misclassification.* ***c*** *Fuzzy membership function μ_A and μ_B used for fuzzy clustering.*

More detailed information about the theory on rule-based systems can be found in [24, 25, 26, 27]. A variety of practical applications are given by [29, 43, 44, 45, 46, 47].

22.5.4 Fuzzy/possibilistic clustering

In many image processing applications, the final step is a classification of objects by their features, which have been detected by image processing tools. Assigning objects to certain classes is not specific to image processing but a very general type of technique, which has led to a variety of approaches searching for *clusters* in an n-dimensional *feature space*.

Figure 22.15a illustrates an example of feature points in a 2-D space. The data seem to belong to two clusters, which have to be separated. The main problem of all clustering techniques is to find an appropriate partitioning of the feature space, which minimizes misclassifications of objects. The problem of a crisp clustering is illustrated in Fig. 22.15b. Due to a long tail of "outliers" it is not possible to unambiguously find a separation line, which avoids misclassifications. The basic idea of *fuzzy clustering* is not to classify the objects, but rather to quantify the partial membership of the same object to more than one class, as illustrated in Fig. 22.15. This accounts for the fact that a small transition in the feature of an object—eventually crossing the separation line—should only lead to a small change in the membership, rather than changing the final classification. The membership functions can be used in subsequent processing steps to combine feature properties until, eventually, a final classification has to be performed.

Within the scope of this handbook we are not able to detail all existing clustering techniques. More detailed information about the theory of fuzzy-clustering and the various algorithms and applications can be found in the following publications [4, 29, 48, 49, 50, 51, 52, 53, 54, 55, 56, 57].

22.5.5 Fuzzy morphology

Fuzzy morphology extends the concept of classical morphology (Chapter 21) to fuzzy sets. In the following we assume the image to be represented by a fuzzy membership function μ. In addition to the membership function at any pixel of the image of size $M \times N$, we need a "fuzzy" *structuring element*, ν. The structuring element can be thought of as the membership function. The shape of the structuring element, that is, the values of the membership function ν_{mn}, determine the spatial area of influence as well as the magnitude of the morphological operation.

Without going into details of the theoretical foundations, we show two possible realizations of the two basic morphological operations *fuzzy dilation* and *fuzzy erosion*, respectively [29].

Example 22.6: Fuzzy erosion

1. [58, 59]:

$$E_\nu(x) = \inf \max \left[\mu(y), (1 - \nu(y - x)) \right], \quad x, y \in X \tag{22.41}$$

2. [60]:

$$E_\nu(x) = \inf \left[\mu(y)\nu(y - x) + 1 - \nu(y - x) \right], \quad x, y \in X \tag{22.42}$$

Example 22.7: Fuzzy dilation

1. [58, 59]:

$$E_\nu(x) = \sup \min \left[\mu(y), \nu(y - x) \right], \quad x, y \in X \tag{22.43}$$

2. [60]:

$$E_\nu(x) = \sup \left[\mu(y)\nu(y - x) \right], \quad x, y \in X \tag{22.44}$$

Other realizations and more detailed information about the theory of morphology can be found in the following publications [29, 61, 62, 63, 64, 65, 66, 67, 68, 69].

22.5.6 Fuzzy measure theory

Fuzzy sets are useful to quantify the inherent vagueness of image data. Brightness, edginess, homogeneity, and many other categories are a matter of degree. The class boundaries in these cases are not crisp. Thus, reasoning should be performed with partial truth and incomplete knowledge. Fuzzy set theory and fuzzy logic offer the suitable framework to apply heuristic knowledge within complex processing tasks.

Uncertainty arises in many other situations as well, even if we have crisp relationships. For instance, the problem of thresholding is not due to the vagueness because we have to extract two classes of pixels belonging to object and background, respectively. Here, the main problem is that the decision itself is uncertain—namely assigning each gray level with membership 1 for object pixels and membership 0 for background pixels. This uncertainty, however, is due to the ambiguity, rather than to vagueness. For this type of problems, one may take into account *fuzzy measures* and *fuzzy integrals*.

Fuzzy measure theory—introduced by Sugeno [70]—can be considered as a generalization of classical measure theory [71]. *Fuzzy integrals* are nonlinear aggregation operators used to combine different sources of uncertain information [29, 72, 73, 74, 75, 76, 77, 78, 79, 80, 81, 82].

Fuzzy measures. Let X be a universe of discourse (a set of features, algorithms, images of different sources, etc.). A fuzzy measure

$$g : 2^X \longrightarrow [0,1] \tag{22.45}$$

over the set X in a measurable space (X, K), satisfies the following conditions (K is the power set of X):

1. Boundedness:

$$g(\emptyset) = 0 \quad \text{and} \quad g(X) = 1 \tag{22.46}$$

2. Monotony:

$$A \in K, \; B \in K, \; A \subset B \;\Rightarrow\; g(A) \leq g(B) \tag{22.47}$$

3. Lower continuity:

$$\{A_n\} \subset K, \; A_1 \subset A_2 \subset \ldots, \; \bigcup_{n=1}^{\infty} A_n \in K \;\Rightarrow\; \lim_{n \to \infty} g(A_n) = g\left(\bigcup_{n=1}^{\infty} A_n\right) \tag{22.48}$$

4. Upper continuity:

$$\{A_n\} \subset K, \; A_1 \supset A_2 \supset \ldots, \; \bigcap_{n=1}^{\infty} A_n \in K, \;\Rightarrow\; \lim_{n \to \infty} g(A_n) = g\left(\bigcap_{n=1}^{\infty} A_n\right) \tag{22.49}$$

A fuzzy measure is a set function and represents the (subjective) estimation of importance of each information source. Sugeno [70] introduced a class of fuzzy measures, called λ-fuzzy measures, also referred to as *Sugeno measures*. A fuzzy measure g_λ is a Sugeno measure in (X, K) if it satisfies the following rule (λ-rule):

1. A, B, and $A \cup B \in K$, $A \cap B = \emptyset$
2. $g_\lambda(A \cup B) = g_\lambda(A) + g_\lambda(B) + \lambda g_\lambda(A) g_\lambda(B)$
3. $\lambda \in (-1/\sup g_\lambda(A), \infty) \cup \{0\}$

In pattern recognition and image processing applications, we generally have to deal with finite numbers of elements. The λ-rule can be formulated as follows:

$$g_\lambda\left(\bigcup_{i=1}^{n} A_i\right) = \begin{cases} \sum_{i=1}^{n} g_\lambda(A_i) & \text{if } \lambda = 0 \\ \frac{1}{\lambda}\left[\prod_{i=1}^{n}(1 + \lambda g_\lambda(A_i)) - 1\right] & \text{if } \lambda \neq 0 \end{cases} \tag{22.50}$$

The Sugeno measure can be completely constructed if the value of λ is known. Assuming the universe of discourse $X = \{x_1, x_2, \ldots, x_n\}$, we consider the case that the Sugeno measure is not a probability measure ($\lambda \neq 0$):

$$g_\lambda(X) = \frac{1}{\lambda}\left[\prod_{i=1}^{n}(1 + \lambda g_\lambda(\{x_i\})) - 1\right] \tag{22.51}$$

The value of λ can be calculated from the following equation:

$$1 + \lambda g_\lambda(X) = \prod_{i=1}^{n}(1 + \lambda g_\lambda(\{x_i\})) \tag{22.52}$$

For the case that $g_\lambda(X) = 1$ we receive the following polynomial expression:

$$1 + \lambda = \prod_{i=1}^{n}(1 + \lambda \mu(\{x_i\})) \tag{22.53}$$

Example 22.8:

Let $X = \{a, b, c\}$. Suppose that a fuzzy measure g is defined as follows:

$$g(x) = \begin{cases} 0.0 \text{ if } x = \emptyset \\ 0.4 \text{ if } x = \{a\} \\ 0.2 \text{ if } x = \{b\} \\ 0.3 \text{ if } x = \{c\} \\ 1.0 \text{ if } x = \{a, b, c\} = X \end{cases} \tag{22.54}$$

We solve Eq. (22.52) to find the corresponding λ-fuzzy measure:

$$1 + \lambda = (1 + 0.4\lambda)(1 + 0.2\lambda)(1 + 0.3\lambda) \tag{22.55}$$

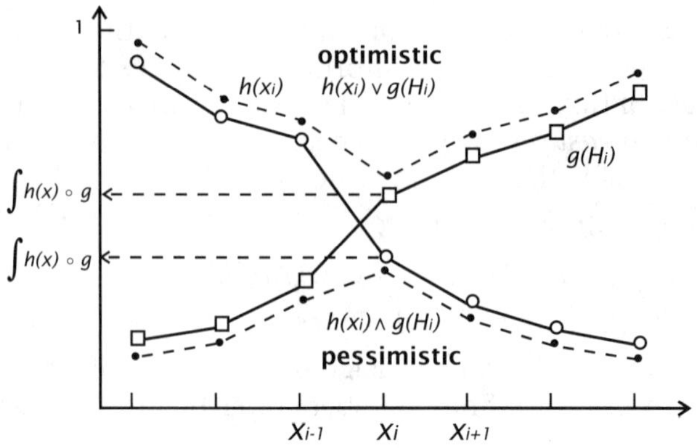

***Figure 22.16:** Illustration of the fuzzy integral.*

which has the two solutions $\lambda_1 = 0.372$ and $\lambda_2 = -11.2$, respectively. The only useful solution is given by λ_1, as $\lambda_2 < -1$. The fuzzy λ-fuzzy measure can be completely constructed:

$$
\begin{aligned}
g_\lambda(\{\varnothing\}) &= g(\{\varnothing\}) &&= 0.0,\\
g_\lambda(\{a\}) &= g(\{a\}) &&= 0.4,\\
g_\lambda(\{b\}) &= g(\{b\}) &&= 0.2,\\
g_\lambda(\{c\}) &= g(\{c\}) &&= 0.3,\\
g_\lambda(\{a,b\}) &= g(\{a\}) + g(\{b\}) + \lambda g(\{a\})g(\{b\}) &&= 0.63,\\
g_\lambda(\{a,c\}) &= g(\{a\}) + g(\{c\}) + \lambda g(\{a\})g(\{c\}) &&= 0.74,\\
g_\lambda(\{b,c\}) &= g(\{b\}) + g(\{c\}) + \lambda g(\{b\})g(\{c\}) &&= 0.52,\\
g_\lambda(\{a,b,c\}) &= g(\{X\}) &&= 1.0.
\end{aligned}
$$

Fuzzy integrals. The fuzzy integral of a function $h : X \longrightarrow [0,1]$ over X, with respect to the fuzzy measure g is defined as follows:

$$\int h(x) \circ g = \sup_{a \in [0,1]} [\alpha \wedge g(F_\alpha)] \tag{22.56}$$

where $F(\alpha) = \{x | h(x) \geq \alpha\}$. Some basic properties of fuzzy integrals are

1. $\int a \circ g = a$, $a \in [0,1]$,
2. $\int h_1 \circ g \leq \int h_2 \circ g$, if $h_1 \leq h_2$,
3. $\int_A h \circ g \leq \int_B h \circ g$, if $A \subset B$.

Let X be a set with a finite numbers of elements $x_1, x_2, \ldots, x_n$. Further let h be a decreasing function of x:

$$h(x_1) \geq h(x_2) \geq \ldots \geq h(x_n) \tag{22.57}$$

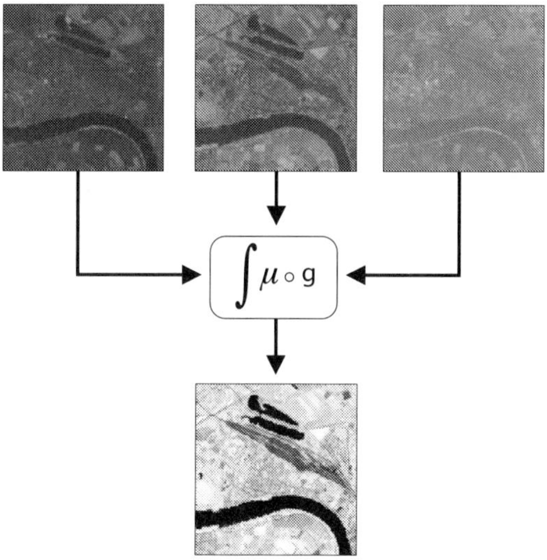

Figure 22.17: Segmentation by fusion of multispectral images [29].

The fuzzy integral can be reformulated as follows:

$$\int h(x) \circ g = \bigvee_{i=1}^{n} \left[h(x_i) \wedge g(H_i) \right] \tag{22.58}$$

where $H_i = \{x_1, x_2, \ldots, x_i\}$. The operators $\vee$ and $\wedge$ represent the maximum and minimum operator, respectively. This reformulation of fuzzy integral reduces the computational cost from 2^n to n calculations, taking into account that the function h should be sorted in a previous step.

The calculation of the fuzzy integral in Eq. (22.58) can be regarded as a *pessimistic fusion* of *objective evidence* (value of the function h) and *subjective importance* of the information source (fuzzy measure g). One may develop a more optimistic fusion by exchanging the order of maximum and minimum operators (Fig. 22.16).

Applications. Fuzzy integrals as nonlinear aggregation operators can be applied to different problems in image processing and pattern recognition. The main application areas are the fusion of different decisions (differing experts, algorithms, etc.) and fusion of different sensors [72, 73, 74, 75, 76, 77, 78, 80, 81]. For instance, Keller et al. [78] used fuzzy integration for image segmentation. Tizhoosh [29] applied the fuzzy integral to segment images by fusing multispectral images (Fig. 22.17) [29] and for fusion of subjective image quality evaluations in medical applications [82].

One of the problems using fuzzy integral as an aggregation operator relates to constructing the underlying fuzzy measure. The most simple way is to interpret the subjective evaluation of the expert as fuzzy densities. This way, however, is not possible in many applications. Therefore, in the literature some techniques are introduced for construction of fuzzy measures. For instance, the use of a confusion matrix [72, 78], a genetic approach [83], or an approach based on relations equations [84], are some examples for automatic generation of fuzzy measures.

22.5.7 Fuzzy grammars

Language is a powerful tool to describe patterns. The structural information can be qualitatively described without a precise numerical quantification of features. The theory of formal languages has been used for speech recognition before it has been considered to be relevant for pattern recognition. The main reason was that formal languages have been criticized for being not flexible enough for an application in pattern recognition, especially for dealing with disturbances such as noise or unpredictable events.

Fuzzy grammars, introduced by Zadeh and Lee [85], are an extension of classical formal languages that are able to deal with uncertainties and vague information. Fu [86] uses the theory of fuzzy grammars for the first time in image processing. Theoretical and practical aspects of fuzzy languages are detailed by [87, 88, 89, 90]. Practical examples can be found in [23, 91, 92].

22.6 Selected application examples

22.6.1 Image enhancement: contrast adaptation

Image enhancement tries to suppress disturbances, such as noise, blurring, geometrical distortions, and illumination corrections, only to mention some examples. It may be the final goal of the image processing operation to produce an image, with a higher contrast or some other improved property according to a human observer. Whenever these properties cannot be numerically quantified, fuzzy image enhancement techniques can be used. In this section we illustrate the example of *contrast adaptation* by three different algorithms.

In recent years, some researchers have applied the concept of fuzziness to develop new algorithms for contrast enhancement. Here, we briefly describe following fuzzy algorithms:

1. Minimization of image fuzziness
2. Fuzzy histogram hyperbolization
3. Rule-based approach

*Figure 22.18: Example for contrast enhancement based on minimization of fuzziness: **a** original image; and **b** contrast enhanced image.*

Example 22.9: Minimization of image fuzziness [15, 18, 33]

This method uses the intensification operator to reduce the fuzziness of the image that results in an increase of image contrast. The algorithm can be formulated as follows:

1. setting the parameters (F_e, F_d, g_{max}) in Eq. (22.59)
2. fuzzification of the gray levels by the transformation G:

$$\mu_{mn} = G(g_{mn}) = \left[1 + \frac{g_{max} - g_{mn}}{F_d}\right]^{-F_e} \tag{22.59}$$

3. recursive modification of the memberships ($\mu_{mn} \longrightarrow \mu'_{mn}$) by following transformation (intensification operator [24]):

$$\mu'_{mn} = \begin{cases} 2\,[\mu_{mn}]^2 & 0 \le \mu_{mn} \le 0.5 \\ 1 - 2\,[1 - \mu_{mn}]^2 & 0.5 \le \mu_{mn} \le 1 \end{cases} \tag{22.60}$$

4. generation of new gray levels by the inverse transformation G^{-1}:

$$g'_{mn} = G^{-1}(\mu'_{mn}) = g_{max} - F_d\left((\mu'_{mn})^{-1/F_e} - 1\right) \tag{22.61}$$

Figure 22.18 shows an example for this algorithm. The result was achieved after three iterations.

Example 22.10: Fuzzy histogram hyperbolization [29, 42]

Due to the nonlinear human brightness perception, this approach modifies the membership values of original image by a logarithmic function. The algorithm can be formulated as follows (Fig. 22.19):

1. setting the shape of membership function
2. setting the value of fuzzifier β (Fig. 22.19)
3. calculation of membership values
4. modification of the membership values by β

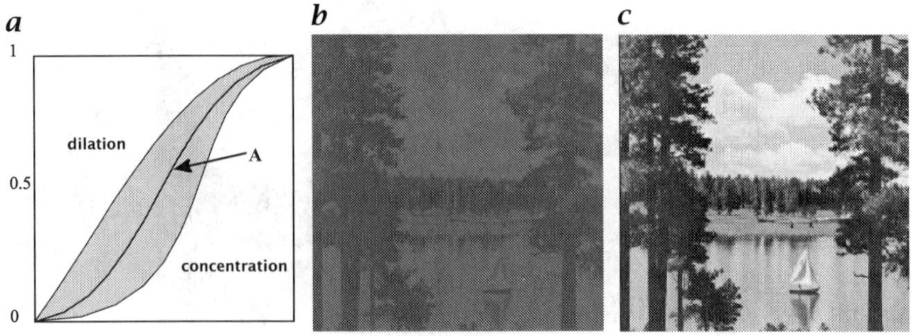

Figure 22.19: ***a*** *Application of dilation (β = 0.5) and concentration (β = 2) operators on a fuzzy set. The meaning of fuzzy sets may be modified applying such operators. To map the linguistic statements of observers in the numerical framework of image processing systems, linguistic hedges are very helpful.* ***b*** *and* ***c*** *are examples for contrast enhancement based on hyperbolization (β = 0.9).*

5. generation of new gray levels by following equation:

$$g'_{mn} = \left(\frac{L-1}{\exp(-1)-1}\right)\left(\exp\left(-\mu^{\beta}(g_{mn})\right)-1\right) \tag{22.62}$$

Example 22.11: Fuzzy rule-based approach [29, 42]

The fuzzy rule-based approach is a powerful and universal method for many tasks in the image processing. A simple rule-based approach to contrast enhancement can be formulated as follows (Fig. 22.20):

1. setting the parameter of inference system (input features, membership functions, ...)
2. fuzzification of the actual pixel (memberships to the dark, gray and bright sets of pixels, see Fig. 19)
3. inference (if dark then darker, if gray then gray, if bright then brighter)
4. defuzzification of the inference result by the use of three singletons

22.6.2 Edge detection

Another important application example of fuzzy techniques is *edge detection.* Edges are among the most important features of low-level image processing. They can be used for a variety of subsequent processing steps, such as object recognition and motion analysis.

The concept of fuzziness has been applied to develop new algorithms for edge detection, which are perfectly suited to quantify the presence of edges in an intuitive way. The different algorithms make use of various aspects of fuzzy theory and can be classified into the following three principal approaches:

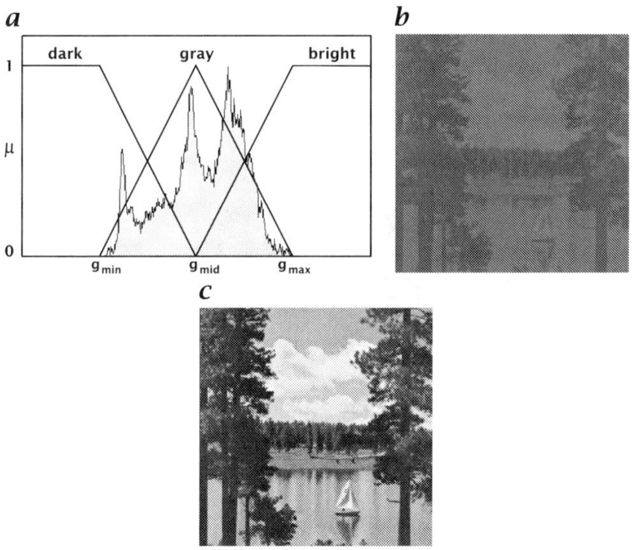

Figure 22.20: ***a*** *Input membership functions for rule-based enhancement based on the characteristic points of image histogram;* ***b*** *and* ***c*** *example for contrast enhancement based on fuzzy if-then rules.*

1. Edge detection by optimal fuzzification [93]
2. Rule-based edge detection [46, 47]
3. Fuzzy-morphological edge detection [29]

Here, we briefly describe the rule-based technique, which is the most intuitive approach using fuzzy logic for edge detection. Other approaches to fuzzy-based edge detection can be found in [43, 44].

Example 22.12: Rule-based edge detection [46, 47]

A typical rule for edge extraction can be defined as follows:

if a pixel belongs to an edge
then it is assigned a dark gray value
else it is assigned a bright gray value

This rule base is special in terms of using the "else" rule. In that way only one explicit logical relation is used and anything else is assigned the complement. It would be harder and more costly to specify all possible cases that can occur.

The input variables are differences between the central point P of a small 3×3 neighborhood U and all neighbors $P_i \in U$. Instead of computing all possible combinations of neighboring points, only eight different clusters of three neighboring points are used [29]. Each of the eight differences is fuzzified according to a membership function μ_i, $i = \{1, \ldots, 8\}$.

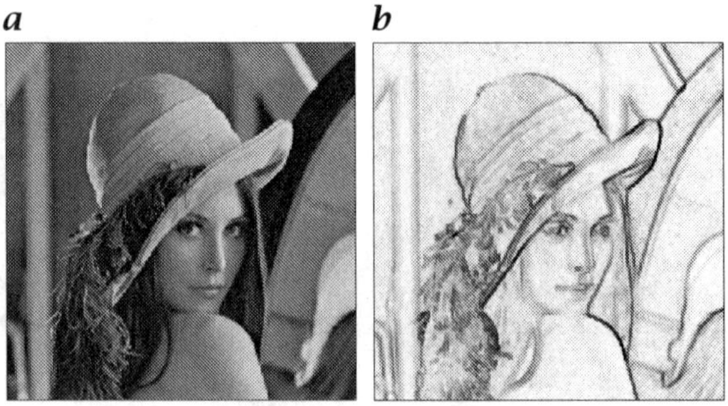

Figure 22.21: *Example for rule-based edge detection:* ***a*** *original image; and* ***b*** *fuzzy edge image.*

The output membership function μ_e corresponding to "edge" is taken as a single increasing wedge. The membership function μ_n of "no edge" is its complement, that is, $\mu_n = 1 - \mu_e$.

The fuzzy inference reduces to the following simple modification of the output membership functions:

$$\mu_e = \max\{\mu_i; i = 1, \ldots, 8\}, \quad \text{and} \quad \mu_n = 1 - \mu_e \tag{22.63}$$

Figure 22.21 illustrates the result of this simple rule-based approach. The final mapping of edges onto gray values of an edge image can be changed by modifying the shape of the individual membership functions. If small differences are given less weight, the noise of the input image will be suppressed. It is also very straightforward to construct directional selective edge detectors by using different rules according to the orientation of the neighboring point clusters.

22.6.3 Image segmentation

The different theoretical components of fuzzy image processing provide us with diverse possibilities for development of new segmentation techniques. The following description gives a brief overview of different fuzzy approaches to image segmentation [29].

Fuzzy rule-based approach If we interpret the image features as linguistic variables, then we can use fuzzy if-then rules to segment the image into different regions. A simple fuzzy segmentation rule may seem as follows: IF the pixel is dark AND its neighborhood is also dark AND homogeneous, THEN it belongs to the background.

Fuzzy clustering algorithms Fuzzy clustering is the oldest fuzzy approach to image segmentation. Algorithms such as fuzzy c-means (FCM, [49]) and possibilistic c-means (PCM, [55]) can be used to build clusters (segments). The class membership of pixels can be interpreted as similarity or compatibility with an ideal object or a certain property.

Measures of fuzziness and image information Measures of fuzziness (e. g., fuzzy entropy) and image information (e. g., fuzzy divergence) can also be used in segmentation and thresholding tasks (see the example that follows).

Fuzzy geometry Fuzzy geometrical measures such as fuzzy compactness [5] and index of area coverage [16] can be used to measure the geometrical fuzziness of different regions of an image. The optimization of these measure (e. g., minimization of fuzzy compactness regarding the cross-over point of membership function) can be applied to make fuzzy and/or crisp pixel classifications.

Fuzzy integrals Fuzzy integrals can be used in different forms:

1. Segmentation by weighting the features (fuzzy measures represent the importance of particular features)
2. Fusion of the results of different segmentation algorithms (optimal use of individual advantages)
3. Segmentation by fusion of different sensors (e. g., multispectral images, fuzzy measures represent the relevance/importance of each sensor)

Example 22.13: Fuzzy thresholding

In many image processing applications, we often have to threshold the gray-level images to generate binary images. In these cases, the image contains a background and one or more objects. The production of binary images serves generally the feature calculation and object recognition. Therefore, image thresholding can be regarded as the simplest form of segmentation, or more general, as a two-class clustering procedure. To separate the object gray levels g_0 from the background gray levels g_B, we have to determine a threshold T. The thresholding can be carried out by the following decision:

$$g = \begin{cases} g_0 = 0 & \text{if } 0 \le g_i \le T \\ g_B = 1 & \text{if } T \le g_i \le L-1 \end{cases} \tag{22.64}$$

The basic idea is to find a threshold T that minimizes/maximizes the amount of image fuzziness. To answer the question of how fuzzy the image G of size $M \times N$ and L gray levels $g = 0, 1, ..., L-1$ is, measures of fuzziness-like fuzzy entropy [34]:

$$H = \frac{1}{MN\ln 2}\sum_{g=0}^{L-1} h(g)\left[-\mu(g)\ln(\mu(g)) - (1-\mu(g))\ln(1-\mu(g))\right] \tag{22.65}$$

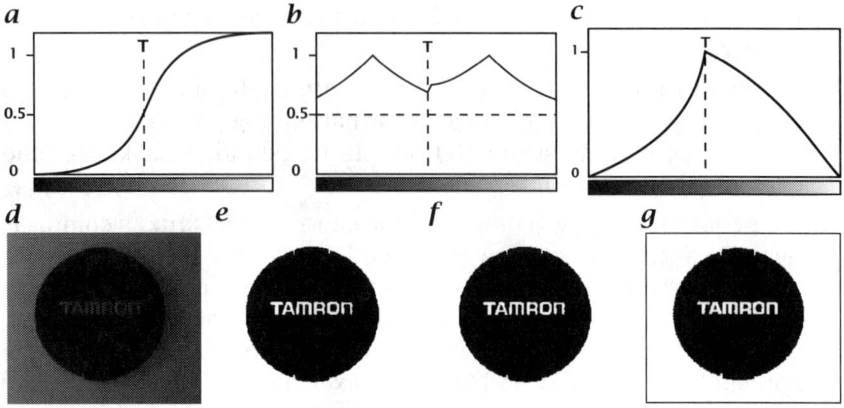

*Figure 22.22: Different membership functions for fuzzy thresholding applied by: **a** Pal and Murthy [20]; **b** Huang and Wang [39]; and **c** [29]; **d** original image; Results of thresholding: **e** Pal and Murthy [20]; **f** Huang and Wang [39]; and **g** Tizhoosh [41].*

or index of fuzziness [38]

$$\gamma = \frac{2}{MN} \sum_{g=0}^{L-1} h(g) \min\left(\mu(g), 1 - \mu(g)\right) \tag{22.66}$$

can be used, where $h(g)$ denotes the histogram value and $\mu(g)$ the membership value of the gray level g, respectively.

The general procedure for fuzzy thresholding can be summarized as follows:

1. Select the type of membership function (Fig. 22.22)
2. Calculate the image histogram
3. Initialize the membership function
4. Move the threshold and calculate in each position the amount of fuzziness using fuzzy entropy or any other measure of fuzziness
5. Find out the position with minimum/maximum fuzziness
6. Threshold the image with the corresponding threshold

The main difference between fuzzy thresholding techniques is that each of them uses different membership function and measures of fuzziness, respectively. Figure 22.22 illustrated three examples of fuzzy membership functions applied to thresholding together with the corresponding results on a test image. For the analytical form of the various membership functions, we would like to refer to the literature [20, 33, 39, 41].

Table 22.3: The practical and theoretical ripeness of different fuzzy approaches [29]

Fuzzy approach	Theoretical/practical ripeness
rule-based systems	extensively investigated
fuzzy-clustering	↓ ↓ ↓ ↓ ↓ ↓ ↓
measures of fuzziness	↓ ↓ ↓ ↓ ↓ ↓
fuzzy geometry	↓ ↓ ↓ ↓ ↓
neural fuzzy approaches	↓ ↓ ↓ ↓
fuzzy genetic approaches	↓ ↓ ↓
fuzzy measures/integrals	↓ ↓
fuzzy grammars	↓
fuzzy morphology	more investigations necessary

22.7 Conclusions

Among all publications on fuzzy approaches to image processing, fuzzy clustering and rule-based approaches have the greatest share. Measures of fuzziness and fuzzy geometrical measures are usually used as features within the selected algorithms. Fuzzy measures and fuzzy integrals seem to become more and more an interesting subject of research. The theoretical research on fuzzy mathematical morphology seems still to be more important than practical reports. Only a few applications of fuzzy morphology can be found in the literature. Fuzzy grammars, finally, seem to be still as unpopular as its classical counterpart. Table 22.3 gives an overview of theoretical/practical ripeness of different fuzzy approaches (here, the ripeness, as a fuzzy number, may also be interpreted as degree of popularity measured by number of corresponding publications).

The topics detailed in Sections 22.4.1–22.5.7 can also be used to extend the existing image processing algorithms and improve their performance. Some examples are: *fuzzy Hough transform* [94], fuzzy mean filtering [95], and fuzzy median filtering [96].

Besides numerous publications on new fuzzy techniques, the literature on introduction to fuzzy image processing can be divided into overview papers [13, 14, 77, 97], collections of related papers [49], and textbooks [15, 29, 31, 56, 72].

Fuzzy clustering algorithms and rule-based approaches will certainly play an important role in developing new image processing algorithms. Here, the potentials of fuzzy if-then rule techniques seem to be greater than already estimated. The disadvantage of rule-based approach, however, is its expensive computing in local operations. Hardware developments will be presumably a subject of investigations. Fuzzy integrals will find more and more applications in image data fusion. The theoretical research on fuzzy morphology will be completed with regard to its fundamental questions, and more practical reports will be published in this area. Fuzzy geometry will be further investigated and play an indispensable part of fuzzy image processing.

It is not possible (and also not meaningful) to do everything in image processing with fuzzy techniques. Fuzzy image processing will mainly play a supplementary role in computer vision. Its part will be possibly small in many applications; its role, nevertheless, will be a pivotal and decisive one.

22.8 References

[1] Zadeh, L. A., (1965). Fuzzy sets. *Information and Control*, **8**:338–353.

[2] Prewitt, J. M. B., (1996). Object enhancement and extraction. In *Picture Processing and Psychopictorics*, B. Lipkin and A. Rosenfeld, eds., pp. 75–149. New York: Academic Press.

[3] Ruspini, E. H., (1969). A new approach to clustering. *Information and Control*, **15**(1):22–32.

[4] Bezdek, J. C., (1981). *Pattern Recognition with Fuzzy Objective Function Algorithms*. New York: Plenum Press.

[5] Rosenfeld, A., (1979). Fuzzy digital topology. *Information and Control*, **40**:76–87.

[6] Rosenfeld, A., (1984). The diameter of a fuzzy set. *Fuzzy Sets and Systems*, **13**:241–246.

[7] Rosenfeld, A., (1984). The fuzzy geometry of image subsets. *Pattern Recognition Letters*, **2**:311–317.

[8] Rosenfeld, A., (1990). Fuzzy rectangles. *Pattern Recognition Letters*, **11**: 677–679.

[9] Rosenfeld, A. and Haber, S., (1985). The perimeter of a fuzzy set. *Pattern Recognition*, **18**:125–130.

[10] Rosenfeld, A. and Janos, L., (1982). Some results on fuzzy digital convexity. *Pattern Recognition*, **15**:379–382.

[11] Rosenfeld, A. and Klette, R., (1985). Degree of adjacency or surroundedness. *Pattern Recognition*, **18**(2):169–177.

[12] Pal, S. K., (1989). Fuzzy skeletonization of an image. *Pattern Recognition Letters*, **10**:17–23.

[13] Pal, S. K., (1992). Fuzziness, image information and scene analysis. In *An introduction to Fuzzy Logic Applications in Intelligent Systems*, R. Yager and L. Zadeh, eds., pp. 147–184. Dordrecht: Kluwer Academic Publishers.

[14] Pal, S. K., (1994). Fuzzy sets in image processing and recognition. In *Fuzzy Logic Technology and Applications*, R. J. Marks, ed., pp. 33–40. Piscataway: IEEE Technical Activities Board.

[15] Pal, S. K. and Dutta Majumder, D., (1986). *Fuzzy Mathematical Approach to Pattern Recognition.* New York: John Wiley & Sons.

[16] Pal, S. K. and Ghosh, A., (1990). Index of area coverage of fuzzy image subsets and object extraction. *Pattern Recognition Letters*, **11**:831-841.

[17] Pal, S. K. and Ghosh, A., (1992). Fuzzy geometry in image analysis. *Fuzzy Sets and Systems*, **48**:23-40.

[18] Pal, S. K. and King, R. A., (1981). Histogram equalization with S and p functions in detecting x-ray edges. *Electronics Letters*, **17**(8):302-304.

[19] Pal, S. K. and Kundu, M. K., (1990). Automatic selection of object enhancement operator with quantitative justification based on fuzzy set theoretic measures. *Pattern Recognition Letters*, **11**:811-829.

[20] Pal, S. K. and Murthy, C. A., (1990). Fuzzy thresholding: mathematical framework, bound functions and weighted moving average technique. *Pattern Recognition Letters*, **11**:197-206.

[21] Pal, S. K. and Pal, N. K., (1991). Entropy: a new definition and its applications. *IEEE Trans. System, Man and Cybernetics*, **21**(5):1260-1270.

[22] Pal, S. K. and Pal, N. K., (1992). Higher order fuzzy entropy and hybrid entropy of a set. *Information Science*, **61**(3):211-231.

[23] Pal, S. K. and Pathak, A., (1991). Fuzzy grammars in syntactic recognition of skeletal maturity from x-rays. *IEEE Trans. System, Man and Cybernetics*, **16**(5):657-667.

[24] Zadeh, L. A., (1972). A fuzzy-set-theoretic interpretation of linguistic hedges. *Jour. Cybernetics*, **2**:4-34.

[25] Zadeh, L. A., (1973). Outline of a new approach to the analysis of complex systems and decision processes. *IEEE Trans. System, Man and Cybernetics*, **3**(1):28-44.

[26] Zadeh, L. A., (1975). The concept of a linguistic variable and its applications to approximate reasoning. *Information Science*, **8**:199-249.

[27] Zadeh, L. A., (1975). The concept of a linguistic variable and its applications to approximate reasoning. *Information Science*, **9**:43-80.

[28] Zadeh, L. A., (1996). Fuzzy logic = computing with words. *IEEE Trans. Fuzzy Systems*, **4**(2):103-111.

[29] Tizhoosh, H. R., (1997). *Fuzzy Image Processing (in German).* Berlin: Springer.

[30] Ishibuchi, H., Nozaki, K., and Yamamoto, N., (1993). Selecting fuzzy rules by genetic algorithms for classification. In *Proc. 2nd IEEE International Conference on Fuzzy Systems*, Vol. 2, pp. 1119-1124. San Francisco.

[31] Tizhoosh, H. R., (1997). A systematical introduction to fuzzy image processing (in German). In *AFN '97*, pp. 39-45. Magdeburg, Germany: University of Magdeburg.

[32] Wang, X. and Keller, J. M., (1997). Fuzzy surroundedness. In *Proc. FUZZ-IEEE'97, Barcelona, Spain*, Vol. 2, pp. 1173-1178.

[33] Rosenfeld, A. and Pal, S. K., (1988). Image enhancement and thresholding by optimization of fuzzy compactness. *Pattern Recognition Letters*, **7**: 77-86.

[34] De Luca, A. and Termini, S., (1972). A definition of a nonprobalistic entropy in the setting of fuzzy set theory. *Information and Control*, **20**: 301–312.

[35] Bhandari, D., Pal, N. R., and Majumder, D. D., (1992). Fuzzy divergence: a new measure for image segmentation. In *Proceedings 2nd International Conference on Fuzzy Logic & Neural Networks, Iizuka, Japan*, pp. 645–648.

[36] Bhandari, D., Pal, N. R., and Majumder, D. D., (1992). Fuzzy divergence, probability measure of fuzzy events and image threshold. *Pattern Recognition Letters*, **13**:857–867.

[37] Friedman, M., Kandel, A., and Schneider, M., (1989). The use of weighted fuzzy expected value (WFEV) in fuzzy expert systems. *Fuzzy Sets and Systems*, **31**:37–45.

[38] Kaufman, A., (1975). *Introduction to the Theory of Fuzzy Subsets - Fundamental Theoretical Elements*, Vol. 1. New York: Academic Press.

[39] Huang, L. K. and Wang, M. J., (1995). Image thresholding by minimizing the measure of fuzziness. *Pattern Recognition*, **28**:41–51.

[40] Kandel, A., Friedman, M., and Schneider, M., (1989). The use of weighted fuzzy expected value (WFEV) in fuzzy expert systems. *Fuzzy Sets and Systems*, **31**:37–45.

[41] Tizhoosh, H., (1998). On image thresholding and potentials of fuzzy techniques *(in German)*. In *Informatik '98: Informatik zwischen Bild und Sprache*, R. Kruse and J. Dassow, eds., pp. 97–106. Berlin: Springer.

[42] Tizhoosh, H. R., Krell, G., and Michaelis, B., (1997). On fuzzy image enhancement of megavoltage images in radiation therapy. In *Proc. 6th IEEE International Conference on Fuzzy Systems*, Vol. 3, pp. 1399–1404. Barcelona, Spain.

[43] Keller, J. M., (199). Fuzzy logic rules in low and mid level computer vision tasks. In *Proc. NAFIPS'96*, pp. 19–22.

[44] Law, T., Itoh, H., and Seki, H., (1996). Image filtering, edge detection, and edge tracing using fuzzy reasoning. *IEEE Trans. Pattern Analysis and Machine Intelligence*, **18**(5):481–491.

[45] Miyajima, K. and Norita, T., (1992). Region extraction for real image based on fuzzy reasoning. In *Proc. FUZZ-IEEE'92*, pp. 229–236. San Diego.

[46] Russo, F., (1992). A user-friendly research tool for image processing with fuzzy rules. In *Proc. 1st IEEE International Conference on Fuzzy Systems*, pp. 561–568. San Diego.

[47] Russo, F. and Ramponi, G., (1994). Edge extraction by FIRE operators. In *Proc. 3rd IEEE International Conference on Fuzzy Systems*, Vol. I, pp. 249–253.

[48] Bezdek, J. C., Hall, L. O., Clark, M., Goldgof, D., and Clarke, L. P., (1996). Segmenting medical images with fuzzy methods: An update. In *Fuzzy Information Engineering: A Guided Tour of Applications*, R. Yager, D. Dubois, and H. Prade, eds., pp. 69–92. New York: John Wiley & Sons.

[49] Bezdek, J. C. and Pal, S. K. (eds.), (1992). *Fuzzy Models For Pattern Recognition*. Piscataway, NJ: IEEE Press.

[50] Dave, R. and Krishnapuram, R., (1997). Robust Clustering Methods: A Unified View. *IEEE Trans. Fuzzy Systems*, **5**(2):270–293.

[51] Dave, R. N., (1989). Use of the adaptive fuzzy clustering algorithms to detect lines in digital images. *Intelligent Robots and Computer Vision*, **1192**(2):600–611.

[52] Dave, R. N., (1992). Boundary Detection through fuzzy clustering. In *Proceedings FUZZ-IEEE 1992, International Conference on Fuzzy Systems*, pp. 127–134.

[53] Dave, R. N., (1992). Generalized fuzzy c-shells clustering and detection of circular and elliptical boundaries. *Pattern Recognition*, **25**(7):127–134.

[54] Krishnapuram, R. and Keller, J. M., (1993). A possibilistic approach to clustering. *IEEE Trans. Fuzzy Systems*, **1**(2):98–110.

[55] Krishnapuram, R. and Keller, J. M., (1996). The possibilistic c-means algorithm: insights and recommendations. *IEEE Trans. Fuzzy Systems*, **4**(3): 385–393.

[56] Kruse, R., Höppner, F., and F., K., (1997). *Fuzzy-Clusteranalyse.* Braunschweig: Vieweg.

[57] Pal, N. R., Pal, K., and Bezdek, J. C., (1997). A mixed c-means clustering model. In *Proc. FUZZ-IEEE'97*, pp. 11–21.

[58] Bloch, I., Pellot, C., Sureda, F., and Herment, A., (1996). Fuzzy modelling and fuzzy mathematical morphology applied to 3D Reconstruction of blood vessels by multi-modality data fusion. In *Fuzzy Information Engineering*, D. Dubois, H. Prade, and R. Yager, eds., pp. 92–110. New York: John Wiley & Sons.

[59] De Baets, B., (1997). Fuzzy mathematical morphology: A logical approach. In *Uncertainty Analysis in Engineering and Science: Fuzzy Logic, Statistics, and Neural Network Approach*, B. Ayyub and M. Gupta, eds., pp. 53–67. Dordrecht: Kluwer Academic Publisher.

[60] Bloch, I. and Maitre, H., (1995). Fuzzy mathematical morphologies: A comparative study. *Pattern Recognition*, **28**(9):1341–1387.

[61] Bloch, I. and Maitre, H., (1993). Mathematical morphology on fuzzy sets. In *International Workshop on Mathematical Morphology and Its Applications to Signal Processing*, pp. 1303–1308. Barcelona.

[62] De Baets, B. and Kerre, E., (1993). An introduction to fuzzy mathematical morphology. In *Proc. NAFIPS 93*, pp. 129–133.

[63] Gader, P. D., (1997). Fuzzy spatial relations based on fuzzy morphology. In *Proc. FUZZ-IEEE 97*, Vol. 2, pp. 1179–1183. Barcelona.

[64] Goetcherian, V., (1980). From binary to gray tone image processing using fuzzy logic concepts. *Pattern Recognition*, **12**:7–15.

[65] Maccarone, M. C., (1994). Fuzzy mathematical morphology: concepts and applications. In *Vision Modeling and Information Coding, Vistas in Astronomy, Special issue*, A. Bijaoui, ed., Vol. 40, pp. 469–477.

[66] Nakatsuyama, M., (1993). Fuzzy mathematical morphology for image processing. In *Proc. ANZIIS*, pp. 75–78.

[67] Serra, J., (1982). *Image Analysis and Mathematical Morphology*, Vol. 1. London: Academic Press.

[68] Sinha, D. and Dougherty, E. R., (1992). Fuzzy mathematical morphology. *Jour. Visual Communication and Image Representation*, **3**(3):286–302.

[69] Sinha, D. and Dougherty, E. R., (1993). Fuzzification of set inclusion. In *Proc. SPIE 93*. Orlando, USA.

[70] Sugeno, M., (1974). *Theory of Fuzzy Integrals and Its Applications*. PhD thesis, Tokyo Institute of Technology, Japan.

[71] Wang, Z. and Klir, G. J., (1992). *Fuzzy Measure Theory*. New York: Plenum Press.

[72] Chi, Z., Yan, H., and Pham, T., (1996). *Fuzzy Algorithms with Applications to Image Processing and Pattern Recognition*. Singapore: World ScientificPublishing.

[73] Gader, P. D., Mohamed, M. A., and Keller, J. M., (1996). Fusion of handwritten word classifiers. *Pattern Recognition Letters*, **17**:577–584.

[74] Grabisch, M., (1996). Fuzzy measures and integrals: A survey of applications and recent issues. In *Fuzzy Information Engineering: A Guided Tour of Applications*, R. Yager, D. Dubois, and H. Prade, eds., pp. 507–530. New York: John Wiley & Sons.

[75] Grabisch, M., Nguyen, H. T., and Walker, E. A., (1995). *Fundamentals of Uncertainty Calculi with Applications to Fuzzy Inference*. Dordrecht: Kluwer Academic Publishers.

[76] Grabisch, M. and Nicolas, J. M., (1994). Classification by fuzzy integral: performance and tests. *Fuzzy Sets and Systems*, **65**:255–271.

[77] Keller, J. and Krishnapuram, R., (1994). Fuzzy decision models in computer vision. In *Fuzzy Sets, Neural Networks and Soft Computing*, R. Yager and L. Zadeh, eds., pp. 213–232. New York: Van Nostrand Reinhold.

[78] Keller, J. M., Gader, P., Tahani, H., Chiang, J. H., and Mohamed, M., (1994). Advances in fuzzy integration for pattern recognition. *Fuzzy Sets and Systems*, **65**:273–283.

[79] Keller, J. M., Qiu, H., and Tahani, H., (1986). Fuzzy logic rules in low and mid level computer vision tasks. In *Proc. NAFIPS'96*, pp. 324–338.

[80] Pham, T. D. and Yan, H., (1996). Color image segmentation: a fuzzy integral mountain-clustering approach. In *Proc. Image Segmentation Workshop 1996, The Australian Pattern Recognition Society*, pp. 27–32. Sydney.

[81] Tahani, H. and Keller, J. C., (1992). The fusion of information via fuzzy integration. In *Proc. NAFIPS'92*, pp. 468–477. Puerto Vallarta, Mexico.

[82] Tizhoosh, H. and Michaelis, B., (1998). Improvement of image quality based on subjective evaluation and Fuzzy aggregation techniques. In *EUFIT'98, Aachen, Germany*, Vol. 2, pp. 1325–1329.

[83] Wang, Z. and Wang, J., (1996). Using genetic algorithm for extension and fitting of belief measures and plausibility measures. In *Proc. NAFIPS'96*, pp. 348–350. Berkeley, USA.

[84] Yuan, B. and Klir, J. K., (1996). Constructing fuzzy measures—A new method and its application to cluster analysis. In *Proc. NAFIPS'96*, pp. 567–571. Berkeley, USA.

[85] Zadeh, L. A. and Lee, E. T., (1969). Note on fuzzy languages. *Information Science*, **1**:421–434.

[86] Fu, S., (1982). *Syntactic Pattern Recognition and Application.* Englewood Cliffs, NJ: Prentice Hall.

[87] DePalma, G. F. and Yau, S. S., (1975). Fractionally fuzzy grammars with application to pattern recognition. In *Fuzzy Sets and Their Applications to Cognitive and Decision Processes,* Z. L. A., K. S. Fu, K. Tanaka, and M. Shimura, eds., pp. 329–351. London: Academic Press.

[88] Majumder, A. K., Ray, A. K., and Chatterjee, B., (1982). Inference of fuzzy regular language using formal power series representation. In *Proc. Indian Statistical Institute Golden Jubilee Conference on Advances in Information Science and Technology,* pp. 155–165. Calcutta.

[89] Majumder, D. D. and Pal, S. K., (1977). On fuzzification, fuzzy languages and pattern recognition. In *Proc. 7th IEEE Int. Conf. on Cybern. and Soc.,* pp. 591–595. Washington.

[90] Tamura, S. and Tanaka, K., (1973). Learning of fuzzy formal language. *IEEE Trans. System, Man and Cybernetics,* **3**.

[91] Kickert, W. J. M. and Koppelaar, H., (1976). Application of fuzzy set theory to syntactic pattern recognition of handwritten capitals. *IEEE Trans. System, Man and Cybernetics,* **6**:148–151.

[92] Parizeau, M. and Plamondon, R., (1995). A fuzzy-syntactic approach to allograph modeling for cursive script recognition. *IEEE Trans. Pattern Analysis and Machine Intelligence,* **17**(7):702–712.

[93] Gupta, M. M., Knopf, G. K., and Nikiforuk, P. N., (1988). Edge perception using fuzzy logic. In *Fuzzy Computing—Theory, Hardware and Applications,* M. M. Gupta and T. Yamakawa, eds., pp. 35–51. Amsterdam: Elsevier Science Publishers.

[94] Han, J., Koczy, L., and Poston, T., (1994). Fuzzy Hough Transforms. *Pattern Recognition Letters,* **15**:649–658.

[95] Lee, C.-S., Y.-H., K., and Yau, P.-T., (1997). Weighted fuzzy mean filter for image processing. *Fuzzy Sets and Systems,* **89**(2):157–180.

[96] Taguchi, A., (1996). A design method of fuzzy weighted median filters. In *Proc. ICIP'96.*

[97] Krishnapuram, R. and Keller, J. M., (1992). Fuzzy set theoretic approach to computer vision: an overview. In *Proc. FUZZ-IEEE'92,* pp. 135–142. San Diego.

23 Neural Net Computing for Image Processing

Anke Meyer-Bäse

Department of Electrical Engineering and Computer Science, University of Florida

23.1 Introduction

Neural networks have been successfully employed to solve a variety of computer vision problems. They are systems of interconnected simple processing elements. There exist many types of neural networks that solve a wide range of problems in the area of image processing. There are also many types of neural networks and they are determined by the type of connectivity between the processing elements, the weights (*synapses*) of the connecting links, the processing elements' characteristics, and training or learning rules. These rules specify an initial set of weights and indicate how weights should be modified during the learning process to improve network performance.

Handbook of Computer Vision and Applications
Volume 2
Signal Processing and Pattern Recognition

Copyright © 1999 by Academic Press
All rights of reproduction in any form reserved.
ISBN 0-12-379772-1/$30.00

The theory and representation of the various network types is motivated by the functionality and representation of biological neural networks. In this sense, processing units are usually referred to as *neurons*, while interconnections are called synaptic connections. Although different neural models are known, all have these basic components in common [1]:

1. A finite set of *neurons* $a(1), a(2), \ldots, a(n)$ with each neuron having a specific neural value at time t, which will be denoted by $a_t(i)$.
2. A finite set of *neural connections* $\boldsymbol{W} = (w_{ij})$, where w_{ij} denotes the strength of the connection of neuron $a(i)$ with neuron $a(j)$.
3. A *propagation rule* $\tau_t(i) = \sum_{j=1}^{n} a_t(j) w_{ij}$.
4. An *activation function* f, which takes τ as an input and produces the next state of the neuron $a_{t+1}(i) = f(\tau_t(i) - \theta)$, where θ is a threshold and f a hard limiter, threshold logic, or sigmoidal function, which introduces a nonlinearity into the network.

23.2 Multilayer perceptron (MLP)

Multilayer perceptrons (MLP) are one of the most important types of neural nets because many applications are successful implementations of MLPs. Typically the network consists of a set of processing units that constitute the *input layer*, one or more *hidden layers*, and an *output layer*. The input signal propagates through the network in a forward direction, on a layer-by-layer basis. Figure 23.1 illustrates the configuration of the MLP.

A node in a hidden layer is connected to every node in the layer above and below it. In Fig. 23.1 weight w_{ij} connects input node x_i to hidden node h_j and weight v_{jk} connects h_j to output node o_k. Classification begins by presenting a pattern to the input nodes x_i, $1 \le i \le l$. From there data flows in one direction through the perceptron until the output nodes o_k, $1 \le k \le n$, are reached. Output nodes will have a value of either 0 or 1. Thus, the perceptron is capable of partitioning its pattern space into 2^n classes.

The steps that govern the data flow through the perceptron during *classification* are [1]:

1. Present the pattern $\boldsymbol{p} = [p_1, p_2, \ldots, p_l] \in \mathcal{R}^l$ to the perceptron, that is, set $x_i = p_i$ for $1 \le i \le l$.
2. Compute the values of the hidden-layer nodes as it is illustrated in Fig. 23.2.

$$h_j = \frac{1}{1 + \exp - \left(w_{0j} + \sum_{i=1}^{l} w_{ij} x_i\right)} \qquad 1 \le j \le m \tag{23.1}$$

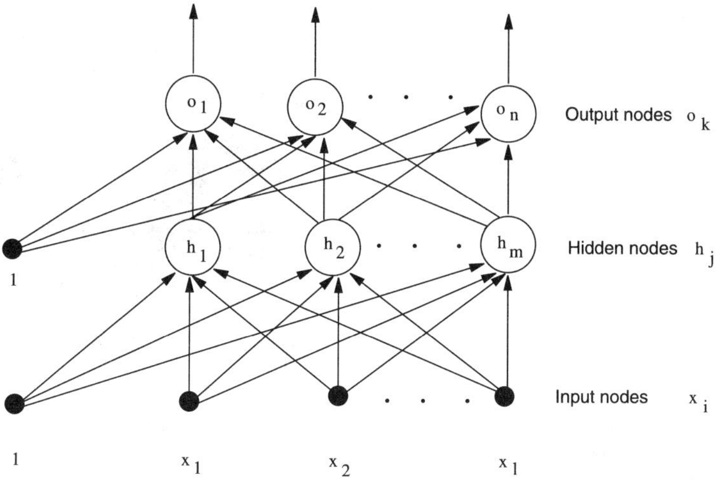

Figure 23.1: *Two-layer perceptron.*

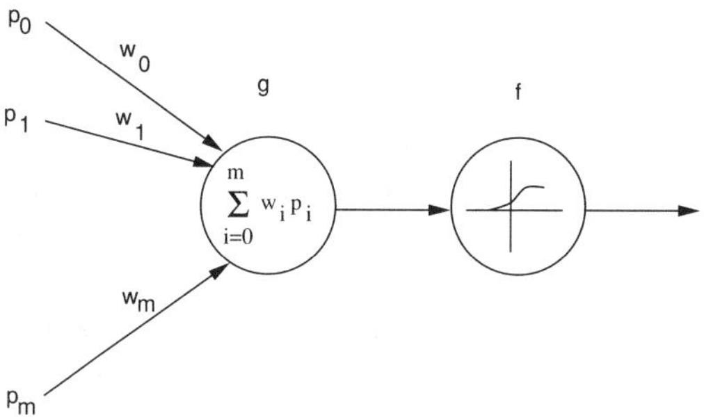

Figure 23.2: *Propagation rule and activation function for the MLP network.*

3. Calculate the values of the output nodes according to

$$o_k = \frac{1}{1 + \exp\left(v_{0k} + \sum_{j=1}^{m} v_{jk} h_j\right)} \qquad 1 \leq k \leq n \tag{23.2}$$

4. The class $\boldsymbol{c} = [c_1, c_2, \ldots, c_n]$ that the perceptron assigns $\boldsymbol{p}$ must be a binary vector. So o_k must be the threshold at some level τ and depends on the application.
5. Repeat Steps 1,2,3, and 4 for each pattern that is to be classified.

Multilayer perceptrons (MLPs) are highly nonlinear interconnected structures and are, therefore, ideal candidates for both nonlinear function approximation and *nonlinear classification* tasks. A classical problem that can be solved only by the MLP is the *XOR-problem.* While a linear classifier is able to partition $\mathcal{R}^m$ into regions separated by a hy-

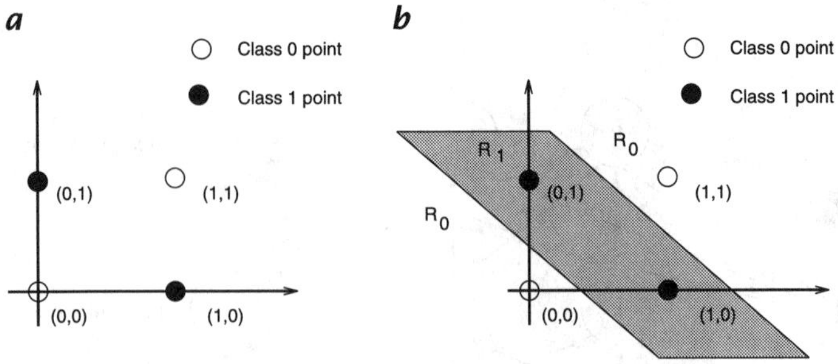

Figure 23.3: XOR-problem and solution strategy using the MLP.

perplane, the MLP is able to construct very complex decision boundaries as illustrated in Fig. 23.3.

Multilayer perceptrons have been applied to a variety of problems in image processing, including *optical character recognition* [2] and *medical diagnosis* [3, 4].

23.2.1 Backpropagation-type neural networks

Multilayer perceptrons (MLPs) have been applied successfully to solve some difficult and diverse problems by training them in a supervised manner with a highly popular algorithm known as the error backpropagation algorithm. This process consists of two passes through the different layers of the network: a forward and a backward pass. During the forward pass a training pattern is presented to the *perceptron* and classified.

The backward pass recursively, level by level, determines error terms used to adjust to the perceptron's weights. The error terms at the first level of the recursions are a function of $\boldsymbol{c}^t$ and output of the perceptron $(o_1, o_2, \ldots, o_n)$. After all the errors have been computed, weights are adjusted using the error terms that correspond to their level. The algorithmic description of the *backpropagation* is given here [1]:

1. **Initialization:** Initialize the weights of the perceptron randomly with numbers between -0.1 and 0.1; that is,

$$
\begin{aligned}
w_{ij} &= \text{random}([-0.1, 0.1]) \quad 0 \le i \le l, 1 \le j \le m \\
v_{jk} &= \text{random}([-0.1, 0.1]) \quad 0 \le j \le m, 1 \le k \le n
\end{aligned}
\tag{23.3}
$$

2. **Presentation of training examples:** Present $\boldsymbol{p}^t = \left[p_1^t, p_2^t, \ldots, p_l^t\right]$ from the training pair $(\boldsymbol{p}^t, \boldsymbol{c}^t)$ to the perceptron and apply steps 1, 2, and 3 from the perceptron classification algorithm described earlier.

3. **Forward computation:** Compute the errors $\delta_{ok}, 1 \leq k \leq n$ in the output layer using

$$\delta_{ok} = o_k(1 - o_k)(c_k^t - o_k) \tag{23.4}$$

where $\boldsymbol{c}^t = \left[c_1^t, c_2^t, \ldots, c_n^t\right]$ represents the correct class of $\boldsymbol{p}^t$. The vector $(o_1, o_2, \ldots, o_n)$ represents the output of the perceptron.

4. **Forward computation:** Compute the errors δ_{hj}, $1 \leq j \leq m$, in the hidden-layers nodes using

$$\delta_{hj} = h_j(1 - h_j) \sum_{k=1}^{n} \delta_{ok} v_{jk} \tag{23.5}$$

5. **Backward computation:** Let v_{jk} denote the value of weight v_{jk} after tth training pattern has been presented to the perceptron. Adjust the weights between the output layer and the hidden layer using

$$v_{jk}(t) = v_{jk}(t-1) + \eta \delta_{ok} h_j \tag{23.6}$$

The parameter $0 \leq \eta \leq 1$ represents the learning rate.

6. **Backward computation:** Adjust the weights between the hidden layer and the input layer according to

$$w_{ij}(t) = w_{ij}(t-1) + \eta \delta_{hj} p_i^t \tag{23.7}$$

7. **Iteration:** Repeat steps 2 through 6 for each element of the training set. One cycle through the training set is called an iteration.

Design considerations. MLPs construct global approximations to nonlinear input-output mapping. Consequently they are capable of generalization in regions of the input space where little or no data are available.

The size of a network is an important consideration from both the performance and computational points of view. It has been shown [5] that one hidden layer is sufficient to approximate the mapping of any continuous function.

The number of neurons in the input layer is equal to the length of the feature vector. Likewise, the number of nodes in the output layer is usually the same as the number of classes. The number of subsequent hidden layers and the number of neurons in each layer are design choices. In most applications, the latter number is a small fraction of the number of neurons in the input layer. It is usually desirable to keep this number small to reduce the danger of overtraining. On the other hand, too few neurons in the hidden layer may make it difficult for the network to converge to a suitable partitioning of a complex feature space. Once a network has converged, it can be shrunk in size and retrained, often with an improvement in overall performance.

Data used for training must be representative of the population over the entire feature space and training patterns should be presented randomly. The network must be able to generalize to the entire training set as a whole, not to individual classes one at a time.

23.2.2 Convolution neural networks (CNN)

Convolution neural networks (CNN) represent a well-established method in medical image processing [6, 7]. The difference between a CNN and an MLP applied to image classification is that a CNN works directly with images and not with extracted features. The basic structure of a CNN is shown in Fig. 23.4, which represents a four-layer CNN with two input images, three image groups in the first hidden layer, two groups in the second hidden layer and a real-valued output [7]. The number of layers and the number of groups in each layer are implementation-oriented. The image propagates from input to output by means of convolution with trainable weight kernels.

Forward Propagation. Let $H_{l,g}$ denote the gth image group at layer l, and let $N(l)$ be the number of such groups. Image propagation from the input layer ($l = 1$) to the output layer ($l = L$) proceeds as follows [7]. The image $H_{l,g} (l \geq 2)$ is obtained by applying a point-wise *sigmoid nonlinearity* to an intermediate image $I_{l,g}$, that is,

$$H_{l,g}(i,j) = \frac{1}{1 + \exp(-I_{l,g}(i,j))}, \quad g = 1,\ldots,N(l) \tag{23.8}$$

The intermediate image $I_{l,g}$ is equal to the sum of the images obtained from the convolution of $H_{l-1,g'}$ at layer $l - 1$ with trainable *kernel of weights* $w_{l-1,g,g'}$. More precisely

$$I_{l,g} = \sum_{g'=1}^{N(l-1)} H_{l-1,g'} * * w_{l-1,g,g'} \tag{23.9}$$

where $**$ denotes two-dimensional (2-D) convolution, and $w_{l-1,g,g'}$ denotes the kernel of weights connecting the $g'th$ group in the $(l - 1)$th layer of the gth group in the lth layer.

The *spatial width* $S_w(l-1)$ of the *weight kernel* $w_{l-1,g,g'}$ defines the *receptive field* for the layer l. The spatial width $S_H(l)$ of an image at layer l is related to the image width at the layer $l - 1$ by

$$S_H(l) = S_H(l-1) - S_w(l-1) + 1 \tag{23.10}$$

Consequently the image width becomes smaller as the layer number increases. The edge effect in convolution is avoided by using this definition. The width of the receptive field of a given node in the lth layer

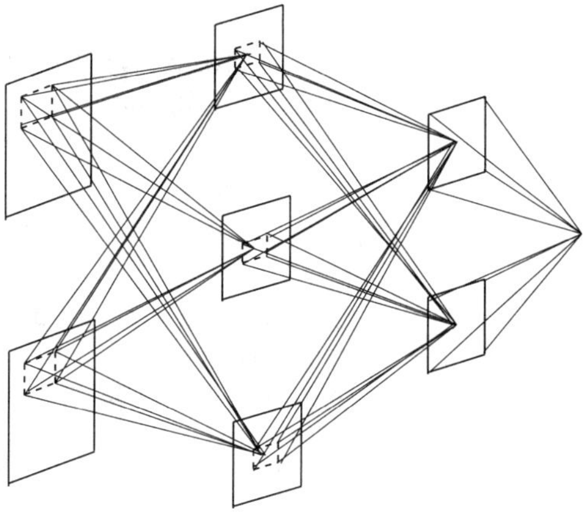

Figure 23.4: *Convolution neural network.*

is equal to the sum of the kernel widths of the proceeding layers minus $(l-2)$. The spatial width of the image at the output layer ($l = L$) is one. The output of the CNN, defined as $O(g) \equiv H_{L,g}(0,0)$, is thus a real number.

Note that an MLP is a special case of a CNN. If for the weight kernels and image groups in a CNN we substitute real numbers, then we get ordinary MLP weights for the weight kernels and nodes for the images. The underlying equations in both networks are the same.

Backpropagation. Like the MLP the CNN learns through backpropagation. For each training image p (or set p of training images in case the input layer processes more than one image) we can define the desired-output value $O_d^{(p)}(g)$, where $g = 1, \ldots, N(L)$ denotes the output node number. At each training epoch t, training images are applied to the CNN and the actual CNN outputs $O_a^{(p)}[t]$ are computed using Eqs. (23.8) and (23.9). The CNN output error for training image p at training epoch t is defined as

$$E^p[t] = \frac{1}{2}\sum_{g=1}^{N(L)}(O_d^{(p)}(g) - O_a^{(p)}(g)[t])^2 \tag{23.11}$$

and the cumulative CNN error during training epoch t is defined as

$$E[t] = \sum_{p=1}^{P} E^{(p)}[t] \tag{23.12}$$

where p is the total number of training samples.

It can be shown that both for an MLP and for a CNN, the computation of the partial derivatives needed for weights updating can be carried out as a backpropagation process.

23.3 Self-organizing neural networks

In a *self-organizing map*, the neurons are placed at the nodes of a lattice that is usually 1-D or 2-D. The neurons become selectively tuned to various input patterns or classes of input patterns in the course of a competitive learning process. The location of the neurons so tuned (i. e., the winning neurons) tend to become ordered with respect to each other in such a way that a meaningful coordinate system for different input features is created over the lattice [8]. A self-organizing *feature map* is therefore characterized by the formation of a topographic map of the input patterns, in which the spatial locations (i. e., coordinates) of the neurons in the lattice correspond to intrinsic features of the input patterns, hence the name "self-organizing feature map" [9].

23.3.1 Kohonen maps

The principal goal of a Kohonen self-organizing map is to transform an incoming signal pattern of arbitrary dimension into a 1-D or 2-D discrete map, and to perform this transformation adaptively in a topological ordered fashion. Many activation patterns are presented to the network, one at a time. Typically, each input presentation consists simply of a localized region of activity against a quiet background. Each such presentation causes a corresponding localized group of neurons in the output layer of the network to be active.

The essential components of such a network are [9]:

1. A 1-D or 2-D *lattice of neurons* that computes simple discriminant functions of inputs received from an input of arbitrary dimension as shown in Fig. 23.5a.
2. A procedure that compares these discriminant functions and selects the neuron with the largest discriminant function value ("winner neuron").
3. An interactive network that activates the selected neuron and its neighbors simultaneously. The neighborhood $\Lambda_{i(\boldsymbol{x})}(n)$ of the winning neuron is chosen to be a function of the discrete time n. Figure 23.5b illustrates such a neighborhood, which usually first includes all neurons in the network and then shrinks gradually with time.

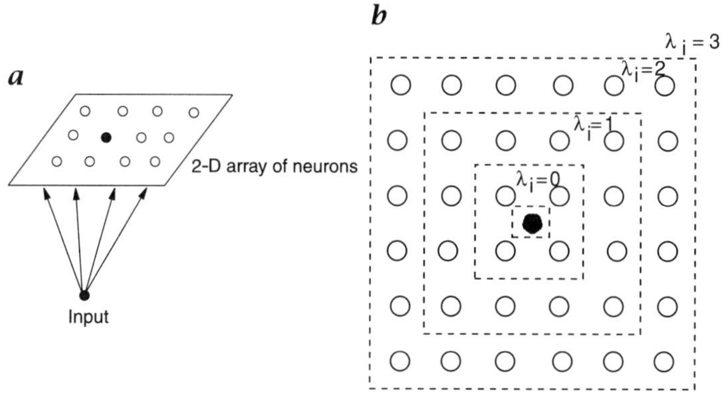

*Figure 23.5: **a** Kohonen neural network; and **b** neighborhood Λ_i, of varying size, around "winning" neuron i, identified as a black circle.*

4. An adaptive process that enables the activated neurons to increase their discriminant function values in relation to the input signals.

The learning algorithm of the self-organized map is simple and is outlined here:

1. **Initialization**: Choose random values for the initial *weight vectors* $\boldsymbol{w}_j(0)$ to be different for $j = 1, 2, \ldots, N$, where N is the number of neurons in the lattice. The magnitude of the weights should be small.
2. **Sampling**: Draw a sample $\boldsymbol{x}$ from the input distribution with a certain probability, the vector $\boldsymbol{x}$ represents the input.
3. **Similarity Matching**: Find the best matching *(winning) neuron* $i(\boldsymbol{x})$ at time n, using the minimum-distance Euclidean criterion:

$$i(\boldsymbol{x}) = \underset{j}{argmin} \; ||\boldsymbol{x}(n) - \boldsymbol{w}_j(n)||, \quad j = 1, 2, \ldots, N \tag{23.13}$$

4. **Updating**: Adjust the synaptic weight vectors of all neurons, using the update formula

$$\boldsymbol{w}_j(n+1) = \begin{cases} \boldsymbol{w}_j(n) + \eta(n)[\boldsymbol{x}(n) - \boldsymbol{w}_j(n)], & j \in \Lambda_{i(\boldsymbol{x})}(n) \\ \boldsymbol{w}_j(n) & \text{otherwise} \end{cases} \tag{23.14}$$

where $\eta(n)$ is the learning-rate parameter, and $\Lambda_{i(\boldsymbol{x})}(n)$ is the *neighborhood function* centered around the winning neuron $i(\boldsymbol{x})$; both $\eta(n)$ and $\Lambda_{i(\boldsymbol{x})}$ are varied dynamically during learning for best results.

5. **Continuation**: Continue with step 2 until no noticeable changes in the feature map are observed.

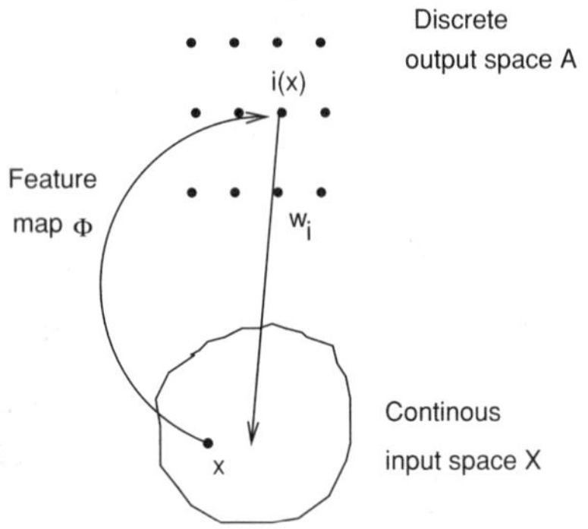

Figure 23.6: *Mapping between input space X and output space $\mathcal{A}$.*

The presented learning algorithm has some interesting properties, which are explained based on Fig. 23.6. To begin with, let X denote a spatially continuous input (sensory) space, the topology of which is defined by the metric relationship of the vectors $\boldsymbol{x} \in X$. Let $\mathcal{A}$ denote a spatially discrete output space, the topology of which is endowed by arranging a set of neurons as the computation nodes of a lattice. Let Φ denote a nonlinear transformation called a feature map, which maps the input space X onto the output space $\mathcal{A}$, as shown by

$$\Phi : X \to \mathcal{A} \tag{23.15}$$

Property 1: Approximation of the input space: The self-organizing feature map Φ, represented by the set of synaptic weight vectors $\{\boldsymbol{w}_j | j = 1, 2, \ldots, N\}$, in the input space $\mathcal{A}$, provides a good approximation to the input space X.

Property 2: Topological ordering: The feature map Φ computed by the learning algorithm is topologically ordered in the sense that the spatial location of a neuron in the lattice corresponds to a particular domain or feature of input patterns.

Kohonen maps have been applied to a variety of problems in image processing, including texture segmentation [10] and medical diagnosis [11].

Design considerations. The success of the map formation is critically dependent on how the main parameters of the algorithm, namely, the *learning-rate parameter* η and the *neighborhood function* Λ_i, are selected. Unfortunately, there is no theoretical basis for the selection of these parameters. But there are some practical hints [12]:

The learning-rate parameter $\eta(n)$ used to update the *synaptic vector* $\boldsymbol{w}_j(n)$ should be time-varying. For the first 100 iterations $\eta(n)$ should begin with a value close to unity and decrease thereafter gradually, but stay above 0.1.

For topological ordering of the weight vectors $\boldsymbol{w}_j$ to take place, careful consideration has to be given to the neighborhood function Λ_i. Λ_i can take many geometrical forms but should include always the winning neuron in the middle. The neighborhood function Λ_i usually begins such that all neurons in the network are included and then it gradually shrinks with time. During the first 1000 iterations the radius of the neighborhood function Λ_i shrinks linearly with time n to a small value of only a couple of neighboring neurons.

23.3.2 Learning vector quantization

Vector quantization [9] is a technique that exploits the underlying structure of input vectors for the purpose of data compression. Specifically, an input space is split into a number of distinct regions, and for each region a reconstruction vector is defined. When the quantizer is presented a new input vector, the region in which the vector lies is first determined, and it is represented by the reproduction vector of that region. Thus, by using an encoded version of this reproduction vector for storage in place of the original input vector, considerable savings can be realized. The collection of possible reconstruction vectors is called a reconstruction *codebook* and its members are called *codewords*.

A vector quantizer with minimum encoding distortion is called a *Voronoi quantizer* (for a detailed discussion of Voronoi diagrams, see Sections 24.4 and 25.1. An input space is divided into four Voronoi cells with associated Voronoi vectors as shown in Fig. 23.7. Each Voronoi cell contains those points of the input space that are the closest to the Voronoi vector among the totality of such points.

Learning vector quantization (LVQ) is a supervised learning technique that uses class information to move the Voronoi vectors slightly, so as to improve the quality of the classifier decision regions. An input vector $\boldsymbol{x}$ is picked at random from the input space. If the class labels of the input vector $\boldsymbol{x}$ and a Voronoi vector $\boldsymbol{w}$ agree, then the Voronoi vector is moved in the direction of the input vector $\boldsymbol{x}$. If, on the other hand, the class labels of the input vector $\boldsymbol{x}$ and the Voronoi vector $\boldsymbol{w}$ disagree, the Voronoi vector $\boldsymbol{w}$ is moved away from the input vector $\boldsymbol{x}$.

Let $\{\boldsymbol{w}_j | j = 1, 2, \ldots, N\}$ denote the set of Voronoi vectors, and $\{\boldsymbol{x}_i || 1, 2, \ldots, L\}$ denote the set of input vectors. We assume that there are more input vectors than Voronoi vectors. The learning vector quantization (LVQ) algorithm proceeds as follows [9]:

1. Suppose that the Voronoi vector $\boldsymbol{w}_c$ is the closest to the input vector $\boldsymbol{x}_i$. Let $C_{\boldsymbol{w}_c}$ denote the class associated with the Voronoi vector $\boldsymbol{w}_c$, and $C_{\boldsymbol{x}_i}$ denote the class label of the input vector $\boldsymbol{x}_i$. The Voronoi

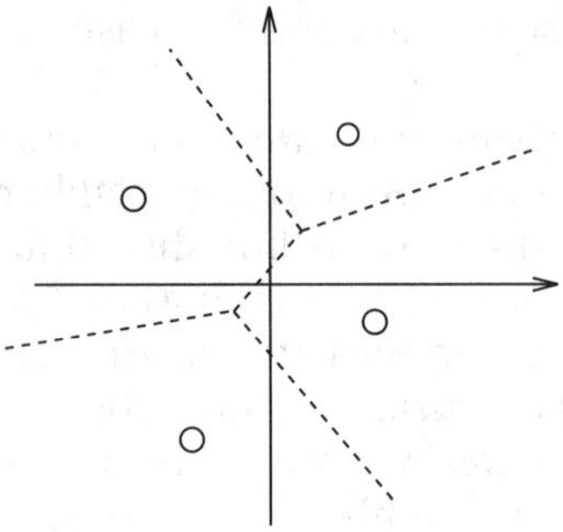

Figure 23.7: *Voronoi diagram involving four cells.*

vector $\boldsymbol{w}_c$ is adjusted as follows:

$$\boldsymbol{w}_c(n+1) = \begin{cases} \boldsymbol{w}_c(n) + \alpha_n[\boldsymbol{x}_i - \boldsymbol{w}_c(n)] & C_{\boldsymbol{w}_c} = C_{\boldsymbol{x}_i} \\ \boldsymbol{w}_c(n) - \alpha_n[\boldsymbol{x}_i - \boldsymbol{w}_c(n)] & \text{otherwise} \end{cases} \tag{23.16}$$

where $0 < \alpha_n < 1$.

2. The other Voronoi vectors are not modified.

The learning constant α_n should decrease monotonically with the number of iterations n. The relative simplicity of the LVQ, its ability to work in *unsupervised mode* has made it a useful tool for image segmentation problems [11].

23.4 Radial-basis neural networks (RBNN)

23.4.1 Regularization networks

The design of a *supervised network* may be accomplished in many different ways. The backpropagation algorithm for the design of a multilayer perceptron can be viewed as an application of an *optimization method* known in statistics as *stochastic approximation.* In this section we present a different approach by viewing the design of a neural network as an approximation problem in a high-dimensional space. In the context of a neural network, the hidden units provide a set of "functions" that constitute an arbitrary "basis" for the input patterns (vectors) when they are expanded into the hidden-unit space; these functions are called *radial-basis functions.* Major contributions to the theory, design, and application of radial-basis function networks include papers by Moody and Darken [13] and Poggio and Girosi [14].

The construction of a radial-basis function (RBF) network in its most basic form involves three different layers. For a network with N hidden neurons, the output of the ith output node $f_i(\boldsymbol{x})$ when the n-dimensional input vector $\boldsymbol{x}$ is presented, is given by

$$f_i(\boldsymbol{x}) = \sum_{j=1}^{N} w_{ij}\Psi_j(\boldsymbol{x}) \tag{23.17}$$

where $\Psi_j(\boldsymbol{x}) = \Psi(||\boldsymbol{x} - \boldsymbol{m}_j||/\sigma_j)$ is a suitable *radially-symmetric function* that defines the output of the jth hidden node. Often $\Psi(.)$ is chosen to be the *Gaussian function* where the width parameter σ_j is the standard deviation. $\boldsymbol{m}_j$ is the location of the jth centroid, where each centroid is represented by a kernel/hidden node, and w_{ij} is the weight connecting the jth kernel/hidden node to the ith output node. Figure 23.8a illustrates the configuration of the network.

The steps that govern the data flow through the radial-basis function network during classification are:

1. Present the pattern $\boldsymbol{p} = [p_1, p_2, \ldots, p_n] \in \mathcal{R}^l$ to the RBF network, that is, set $x_i = p_i$ for $1 \le i \le n$.
2. Compute the values of the hidden-layer nodes as it is illustrated in Fig. 23.8b.

$$\psi_i = \exp\left(-d(\boldsymbol{x}, \boldsymbol{m}^i, \boldsymbol{K}^i)/2\right) \tag{23.18}$$

The *shape matrix* $\boldsymbol{K}^i$ is positive definite and its elements k^i_{jk}

$$k^i_{jk} = \frac{h^i_{jk}}{\sigma^i_j * \sigma^i_k} \tag{23.19}$$

represent the correlation coefficients h^i_{jk} and σ^i_j the standard deviation.
We have for h^i_{jk}: $h^i_{jk} = 1$ for $j = k$ and $|h^i_{jk}| \le 1$ otherwise.
3. Calculate the values of the output nodes according to

$$f_{oj} = \phi_j = \sum_i w_{ji}\psi_i \tag{23.20}$$

4. The class $\boldsymbol{c} = [c_1, c_2, \ldots, c_n]$ that the RBF network assigns $\boldsymbol{p}$ must be a binary vector.
5. Repeat Steps 1,2,3, and 4 for each pattern that is to be classified.

The learning process undertaken by an RBF network may be viewed as follows. The linear weights associated with the output units of the network tend to evolve on a different "time scale" compared to the nonlinear activation functions of the hidden units. The weight adaptation process is a linear process compared to the nonlinear parameter adaptation of the hidden layer neurons. As the different layers of an RBF

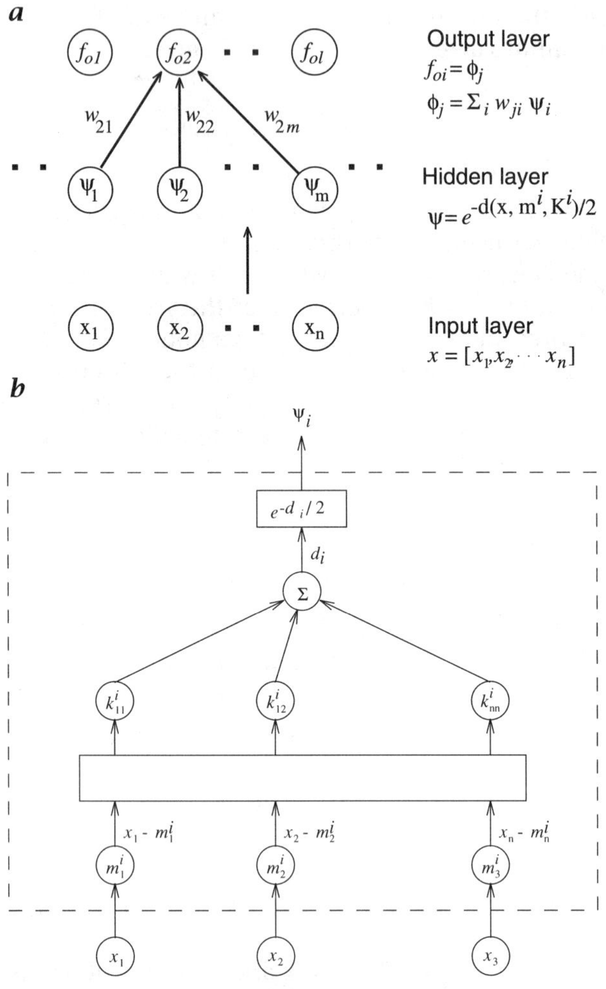

Figure 23.8: RBF network: ***a*** *three-layer model; and* ***b*** *the connection between input layer and hidden layer neuron.*

network are performing different tasks, it is reasonable to separate the optimization of the hidden and output layers by using different techniques. The output layer's weights are adjusted according to a simple delta rule as shown in the MLP case.

There are different strategies we can follow in the design of an RBF network, depending on how the centers of the RBF network are specified [9]:

1. Fixed centers selected at random: It is the simplest approach to assume fixed radial-basis functions defining the activation functions

of the hidden units. Specifically, the locations of the centers may be chosen randomly from the training set.

2. Self-organized selection of centers: The locations of the centers of the hidden units are permitted to move in a self-organized fashion, whereas the linear weights of the output layer are computed using a supervised learning rule. The self-organized component of the learning process serves to allocate network resources in a meaningful way by placing the centers of the radial-basis functions in only those regions of the input space where significant data are present.
3. Supervised selection of centers: The centers and all other free parameters of the network undergo a supervised learning process; in other words, the RBF network takes on its most generalized form. A natural candidate for such a process is *error-correction learning*, which is most conveniently implemented using a *gradient-descent procedure* that represents a generalization of the *LMS algorithm*.

RBF networks have been applied to a variety of problems in image processing, like *image coding* and analysis [15] and also in medical diagnosis [16].

Design considerations. The RBF networks construct local approximations to nonlinear input-output mapping, with the result that these networks are capable of fast learning and reduced sensitivity to the order of presentation of training data. In many cases, however, we find that in order to represent a mapping to some desired degree of smoothness, the number of radial-basis functions required to span the input space adequately may have to be very large. This fact can be very inappropriate in many practical applications.

The RBF network has only one hidden layer and the number of basis functions and their shape is problem-oriented and can be determined on-line during the learning process [17, 18]. The number of neurons in the input layer is equal to the length of the feature vector. Likewise, the number of nodes in the output layer is usually the same as the number of classes.

23.5 Transformation radial-basis networks (TRBNN)

The selection of appropriate features is an important precursor to most statistical pattern recognition methods. A good feature selection mechanism helps to facilitate classification by eliminating noisy or nonrepresentative features that can impede recognition. Even features that provide some useful information can reduce the accuracy of a classifier when the amount of training data is limited. This so-called "curse of dimensionality," along with the expense of measuring and including features, demonstrates the utility of obtaining a minimum-sized set of features that allow a classifier to discern pattern classes well. Well-known methods in literature applied to feature selection are the floating search methods [19] and genetic algorithms [20].

Radial-basis neural networks are excellent candidates for feature selection. It is necessary to add an additional layer to the traditional architecture (e. g., Moody and Darken [13]) to obtain a representation of relevant features. The new paradigm is based on an explicit definition of the relevance of a feature and realizes a linear transformation of the feature space.

Figure 23.9 shows the structure of a radial-basis neural network with the additional layer 2, which transforms the feature space linearly by multiplying the input vector and the center of the nodes by the matrix $\boldsymbol{B}$. The covariance matrices remain unmodified.

$$\boldsymbol{x}' = \boldsymbol{B}\boldsymbol{x}, \quad \boldsymbol{m}' = \boldsymbol{B}\boldsymbol{m}, \quad \boldsymbol{C}' = \boldsymbol{C} \tag{23.21}$$

The neurons in layer 3 evaluate a kernel function for the incoming input while the neurons in the output layer perform a weighted linear summation of the kernel functions:

$$\boldsymbol{y}(\boldsymbol{x}) = \sum_{i=1}^{N} w_i \exp\left(-d(\boldsymbol{x}', \boldsymbol{m}_i')/2\right) \tag{23.22}$$

with

$$d(\boldsymbol{x}', \boldsymbol{m}_i') = (\boldsymbol{x}' - \boldsymbol{m}_i')^T \boldsymbol{C}_i^{-1} (\boldsymbol{x}' - \boldsymbol{m}_i') \tag{23.23}$$

Here, N is the number of neurons in the second hidden layer, $\boldsymbol{x}$ is the n-dimensional input pattern vector, $\boldsymbol{x}'$ is the transformed input pattern vector, $\boldsymbol{m}_i'$ is the center of a node, w_i are the output weights and $\boldsymbol{y}$ represents the m-dimensional output of the network. The $n \times n$ covariance matrix $\boldsymbol{C}_i$ is of the form

$$C_{jk}^i = \begin{cases} \dfrac{1}{\sigma_{jk}^2} & \text{if} \quad m = n \\ 0 & \text{otherwise} \end{cases} \tag{23.24}$$

where σ^{jk} is the standard deviation. Because the centers of the *Gaussian potential function units* (GPFU) are defined in the feature space, they will be subject to transformation by $\boldsymbol{B}$ too. Therefore, the exponent of a GPFU can be rewritten as:

$$d(\boldsymbol{x}) = (\boldsymbol{x} - \boldsymbol{m}_i)^T \boldsymbol{B}^T \boldsymbol{C}_i^{-1} \boldsymbol{B} (\boldsymbol{x} - \boldsymbol{m}_i) \tag{23.25}$$

and is in this form similar to Eq. (23.23).

For the moment, we will regard $\boldsymbol{B}$ as the unit matrix. The network models the distribution of input vectors in the feature space by the weighted summation of Gaussian normal distributions, which are provided by the Gaussian Potential Function Units (GPFU) Ψ_j. To measure the difference between these distributions, we define the relevance ρ_n for each feature x_n:

$$\rho_n = \frac{1}{PJ} \sum_p \sum_j \frac{(x_{pn} - m_{jn})^2}{2\sigma_{jn}^2} \tag{23.26}$$

where P is the size of the training set and J is the number of the GPFUs. If ρ_n falls below the threshold ρ_{th}, one will decide to discard feature x_n. This criterion will not identify every irrelevant feature: If two features are correlated, one of them will be irrelevant, but this cannot be indicated by the criterion.

Learning paradigm for the transformation radial-basis neural network. We follow the idea of Lee and Kil [17] for the implementation of the neuron allocation and learning rules for the TRBNN. The network generation process starts initially without any neuron.

The mutual dependency of correlated features can often be approximated by a linear function, which means that a linear transformation of the input space can render irrelevant features.

First we assume that layers 3 and 4 have been trained so that they comprise a model of the pattern generating process while $\boldsymbol{B}$ is the unit matrix. Then the coefficients B_{nr} can be adapted by gradient descent with the relevance ρ_n' of the transformed feature x_n' as the target function. Modifying B_{nr} means changing the relevance of x_n by adding x_r to it with some weight B_{nr}. This can be done online, that is, for every training vector $\boldsymbol{x}_p$ without storing the whole training set. The diagonal elements B_{nn} are constrained to be constant 1, because a feature must not be rendered irrelevant by scaling itself. This in turn guarantees that no information will be lost. B_{nr} will only be adapted under the condition that $\rho_n < \rho_p$, so that the relevance of a feature can be decreased only by some more relevant feature. The coefficients are adapted by the learning rule:

$$B_{nr}^{new} = B_{nr}^{old} - \mu \frac{\partial \rho_n}{\partial B_{nr}} \tag{23.27}$$

with the learning rate μ and the partial derivative:

$$\frac{\partial \rho_n}{\partial B_{nr}} = \frac{1}{PJ} \sum_p \sum_j \frac{(x_{pn}' - m_{jn}')}{\sigma_{jn}^2} (x_{pr}' - m_{jr}') \tag{23.28}$$

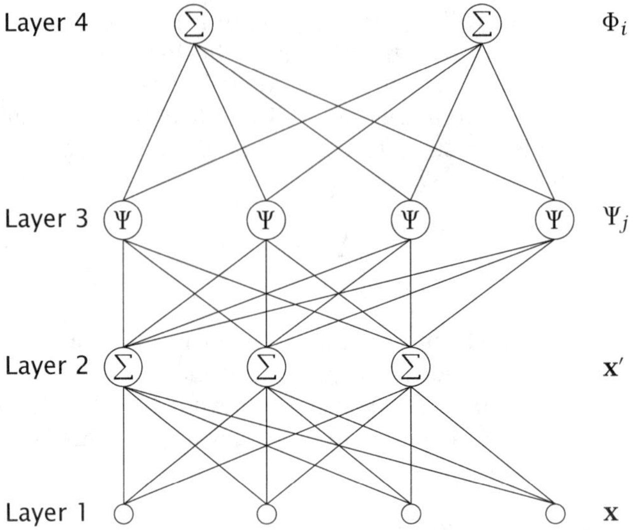

Figure 23.9: *Linear transformation radial-basis neural network.*

In the learning procedure, which is based on, for example, Lee and Kil [17], we minimize according to the LMS criterion the target function:

$$E = \frac{1}{2} \sum_{p=0}^{P} |y(\boldsymbol{x}) - \Phi(\boldsymbol{x})|^2 \tag{23.29}$$

where P is the size of the training set. The neural network has some useful features as *automatic allocation of neurons*, discarding of degenerated and inactive neurons and variation of the learning rate depending on the number of allocated neurons.

The relevance of a feature is optimized by gradient descent:

$$\rho_i^{new} = \rho_i^{old} - \eta \frac{\partial E}{\partial \rho_i} \tag{23.30}$$

Based on the new introduced relevance measure and the change in the architecture we get the following correction equations for the neural network:

$$\begin{aligned} \frac{\partial E}{\partial w_{ij}} &= -(y_i - \Phi_i)\Psi_j \\ \frac{\partial E}{\partial m_{jn}} &= - \quad \textstyle\sum_i \quad (y_i - \Phi_i) w_{ij} \Psi_j \textstyle\sum_k \quad (x'_k - m'_{jk}) \frac{B_{kn}}{\sigma_{jk}^2} \\ \frac{\partial E}{\partial \sigma_{jn}} &= - \quad \textstyle\sum_i \quad (y_i - \Phi_i) w_{ij} \Psi_j \frac{(x'_n - m'_{jn})^2}{\sigma_{jn}^3} \end{aligned} \tag{23.31}$$

In the transformed space the hyperellipses have the same orientation as in the original feature space. Hence they do not represent the same distribution as before. To overcome this problem, layers 3 and 4 will be adapted at the same time as $\boldsymbol{B}$. Converge these layers fast enough, they can be adapted to represent the transformed training data, providing a model on which the adaptation of $\boldsymbol{B}$ can be based. The adaptation with two different target functions (E and ρ) may become unstable if $\boldsymbol{B}$ is adapted too fast, because layers 3 and 4 must follow the transformation of the input space. Thus μ must be chosen $\ll \eta$. A large gradient has been observed causing instability when a feature of extreme high relevance is added to another. This effect can be avoided by dividing the learning rate by the relevance, that is, $\mu = \mu_0/\rho_r$.

23.6 Hopfield neural networks

23.6.1 Basic architecture considerations

A pattern, in parlance of a N node *Hopfield neural network*, is an N-dimensional vector $\boldsymbol{p} = [p_1, p_2, \ldots, p_N]$ from the space $\mathbf{P} = \{-1, 1\}^N$. A special subset of $\mathbf{P}$ is the set of patterns $\mathbf{E} = \{\boldsymbol{e}^k : 1 \le k \le K\}$, where $\boldsymbol{e}^k = [e_1^k, e_2^k, \ldots, e_N^k]$. The Hopfield net associates a vector from $\mathbf{P}$ with an exemplar pattern in $\mathbf{E}$. The neural net partitions $\mathbf{P}$ into classes whose members are in some way similar to the exemplar pattern that represents the class. The Hopfield network finds a broad application area in image restoration and segmentation.

As already stated in the introduction, neural networks have four common components. For the Hopfield net we have the following:

Neurons: The Hopfield network has a finite set of neurons $\boldsymbol{x}(i), 1 \le i \le N$, which serve as processing units. Each neuron has a value (or state) at time t denoted by $\boldsymbol{x}_t(i)$. A neuron in the Hopfield net has one of the two states, either -1 or +1; that is, $\boldsymbol{x}_t(i) \in \{-1, +1\}$.

Synaptic Connections: The cognition of a neural net resides within the interconnections between its neurons. For each pair of neurons, $\boldsymbol{x}(i)$ and $\boldsymbol{x}(j)$, there is a connection w_{ij} called the synapse between $\boldsymbol{x}(i)$ and $\boldsymbol{x}(j)$. The design of the Hopfield net requires that $w_{ij} = w_{ji}$ and $w_{ii} = 0$. Figure 23.10a illustrates a 3-node network.

Propagation Rule: It defines how states and connections influence the input of a neuron. The propagation rule $\tau_t(i)$ is defined by

$$\tau_t(i) = \sum_{j=1}^{N} \boldsymbol{x}_t(j) w_{ij} - b_i \tag{23.32}$$

Activation Function: The activation function f determines the next state of the neuron $\boldsymbol{x}_{t+1}(i)$ based on the value $\tau_t(i)$ calculated by

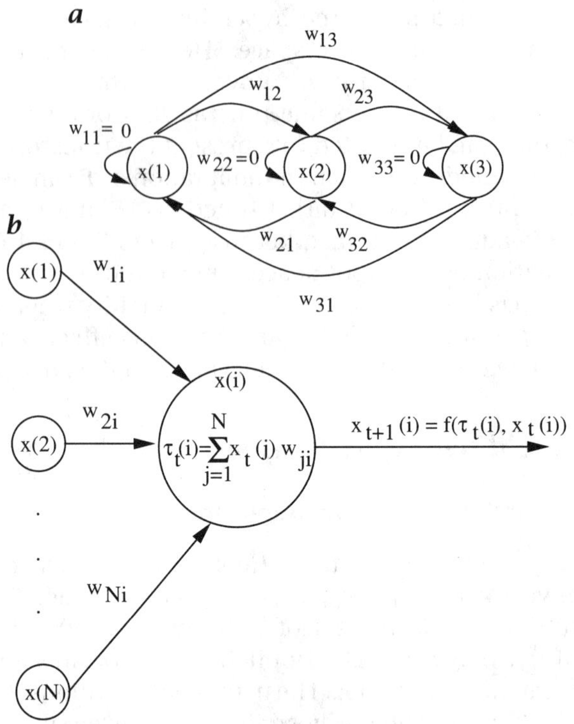

Figure 23.10: ***a** Hopfield neural network; and **b** propagation rule and activation function for the Hopfield network.*

the propagation rule and the current value $\boldsymbol{x}_t(i)$. Figure 23.10b illustrates this fact. The activation function for the Hopfield net is the hard limiter defined here:

$$\boldsymbol{x}_{t+1}(i) = f(\tau_t(i), \boldsymbol{x}_t(i)) = \begin{cases} 1, & \text{if} \quad \tau_t(i) > 0 \\ -1, & \text{if} \quad \tau_t(i) < 0 \end{cases} \tag{23.33}$$

The network learns patterns that are N-dimensional vectors from the space $\mathbf{P} = \{-1, 1\}^N$. Let $\boldsymbol{e}^k = [e_1^k, e_2^k, \ldots, e_n^k]$ denote the kth exemplar pattern where $1 \le k \le K$. The dimensionality of the pattern space determines the number of nodes in the net, such that the net will have N nodes $\boldsymbol{x}(1), \boldsymbol{x}(2), \ldots, \boldsymbol{x}(N)$.

The training algorithm of the Hopfield neural network.

1. Assign weights w_{ij} to the synaptic connections:

$$w_{ij} = \begin{cases} \sum_{k=1}^{K} e_i^k e_j^k, & \text{if} \quad i \ne j \\ 0, & \text{if} \quad i = j \end{cases} \tag{23.34}$$

Keep in mind that $w_{ij} = w_{ji}$, so it is necessary to perform the preceding computation only for $i < j$.

2. Initialize the net with the unknown pattern. The pattern to be learned is now presented to the net. If $\boldsymbol{p} = [p_1, p_2, \ldots, p_N]$ is the unknown pattern, put

$$\boldsymbol{x}_0(i) = p_i, \quad 1 \le i \le N \tag{23.35}$$

3. Iterate until convergence. Using the propagation rule and the activation function we get for the next state

$$\boldsymbol{x}_{t+1}(i) = f\left(\sum_{j=1}^{N} \boldsymbol{x}_t(j) w_{ij}, \boldsymbol{x}_t(i)\right) \tag{23.36}$$

This process should be continued until any further iteration will produce no state change at any node.

4. Continue the classification process. For learning another pattern, repeat steps 2 and 3.

The convergence property of Hopfield's network depends on the structure of $\boldsymbol{W}$ (the matrix with elements w_{ij}) and the updating mode. An important property of the Hopfield model is that if it operates in a sequential mode and $\boldsymbol{W}$ is symmetric with non-negative diagonal elements, then the energy function

$$\begin{aligned} E_{hs}(t) &= \frac{1}{2}\sum_{i=1}^{n}\sum_{j=1}^{n} w_{ij} x_i(t) x_j(t) - \sum_{i=1}^{n} b_i x_i(t) \\ &= -\frac{1}{2}\boldsymbol{x}^T(t)\boldsymbol{W}\boldsymbol{x}(t) - \boldsymbol{b}^T\boldsymbol{x}(t) \end{aligned} \tag{23.37}$$

is nonincreasing [21]. The network always converges to a fixed point.

23.6.2 Modified Hopfield network

The problem of restoring *noisy-blurred images* is important for many applications ([22, 23, 24], see also Chapter 16). Often, the image degradation can be adequately modeled by a linear blur and an additive white Gaussian process. Then the degradation model is given by

$$\boldsymbol{z} = \boldsymbol{D}\boldsymbol{x} + \eta \tag{23.38}$$

where $\boldsymbol{x}, \boldsymbol{z}$ and η represent the ordered original and degraded images and the additive noise. The matrix $\boldsymbol{D}$ represents the linear spatially invariant or spatially varying distortion.

The purpose of *digital image restoration* is to operate on the degraded image $\boldsymbol{z}$ to obtain an improved image that is as close to the original image $\boldsymbol{x}$ as possible, subject to a suitable optimality criterion. A common optimization problem is:

$$\text{minimize} \quad f(\boldsymbol{x}) = \frac{1}{2}\boldsymbol{x}^T\boldsymbol{T}\boldsymbol{x} - \boldsymbol{b}^T\boldsymbol{x} \quad \text{subject to} \quad 0 \le x_i \le 255 \tag{23.39}$$

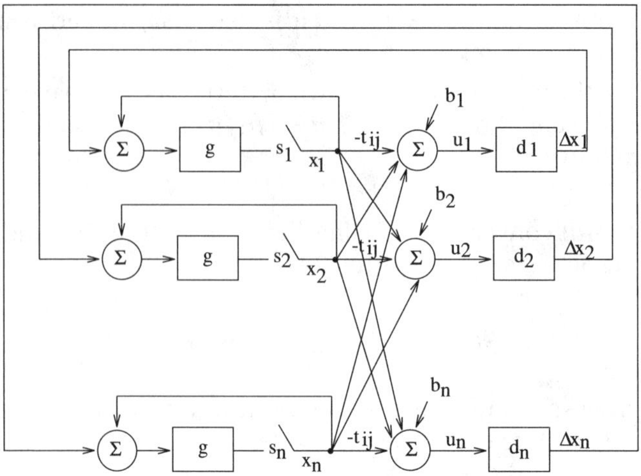

***Figure 23.11:** Block diagram of the modified Hopfield network model applied to image restoration.*

where x_i denotes the ith element of the vector $\boldsymbol{x}$, $\boldsymbol{b} = \boldsymbol{D}^T\boldsymbol{z}$ and $\boldsymbol{T}$ is a symmetric, positive semidefinite matrix equal to

$$\boldsymbol{T} = \boldsymbol{D}^T\boldsymbol{D} + \lambda\boldsymbol{C}^T\boldsymbol{C} \tag{23.40}$$

In Eq. (23.40), $\boldsymbol{C}$ is a high-pass filter and λ, the regularization parameter, controls the tradeoff between deconvolution and noise smoothing. Comparing Eq. (23.39) and Eq. (23.37) it is clear that the function $f(\boldsymbol{x})$ to be minimized for the restoration problem equals E_{hs} for $\boldsymbol{W} = -\boldsymbol{T}$ and $\boldsymbol{x} = \boldsymbol{v}$.

Updating rule. The modified Hopfield network for image restoration that was proposed in [25] is shown in Fig. 23.11 and is given by the following equations:

$$x_i(t+1) = g(x_i(t) + \Delta x_i), \quad i = 1, \ldots, n \tag{23.41}$$

where

$$g(v) = \begin{cases} 0, & v < 0 \\ v, & 0 \le v \le 255 \\ 255, & v > 255 \end{cases} \tag{23.42}$$

$$\Delta x_i = d_i(u_i) = \begin{cases} -1, & u_i < -\theta_i \\ 0, & -\theta_i \le u_i \le \theta_i \\ 1, & u_i > \theta_i \end{cases} \quad \text{with} \tag{23.43}$$

$$\theta_i = \tfrac{1}{2}t_{ii} > 0 \quad \text{and} \quad u_i = b_i - \textstyle\sum_{j=1}^{n} t_{ij}x_j(t)$$

The degraded image $\boldsymbol{z}$ is used as the initial condition for $\boldsymbol{x}$. x_i are the states of neuron, which take discrete values between 0 and 255, instead of binary values. This consideration is possible because the interconnections are determined in terms of pixel locations and not gray-level values, as can be seen from Fig. 23.11.

In the following, an algorithm is presented that sequentially updates each pixel value according to the updating rule. For the analysis to be followed let $l(t)$ denote a partition of the set $\{1, \ldots, n\}$. The algorithm has the following form:

1. $\boldsymbol{x}(0) = \boldsymbol{D}^T \boldsymbol{z}; t := 0$ and $i := 1$.
2. Check termination.
3. Choose $l(t) = \{i\}$.
4. temp $= g(x(t) + \Delta x_i e_i)$ where Δx_i is given by Eq. (23.43).
5. If temp $\neq x(t)$ then $x(t+1) :=$ temp and $t := t + 1$.
6. $i; = i + 1$ (if $i > n, i = i - n$) and go to step 1.

In step 3 of the preceding algorithm, the function $g(.)$ is used with a vector as an input. In this case $g(\boldsymbol{x}) = [g(x_1), \ldots, g(x_n)]$, where $g(x_i)$ is defined by Eq. (23.42).

23.7 References

[1] Ritter, G. X. and Wilson, J. N., (1996). *Handbook of Computer Vision Algorithms in Image Algebra.* Boca Raton: CRC Press.

[2] Säckinger, E., Boser, B. E., Bromley, J., LeCun, Y., and Jackel, L. D., (1992). Application of an ANNA neural network chip to high-speed character recognition. *IEEE Trans. Neural Networks,* **3**:498–505.

[3] Dhawan, A. P., Chitre, Y., Kaiser, C., and Moskowitz, M., (1996). Analysis of mammographic microcalcifications using gray-level image structure features. *IEEE Trans. Medical Imaging,* **15**:246–259.

[4] Dhawan, A. P. and LeRoyer, E., (1988). Mammographic feature enhancement by computerized image processing. *Computer Methods and Programs in Biomedicine,* pp. 23–25.

[5] Hartman, E. J., Keeler, J. D., and Kowalski, J. M., (1990). Layered neural networks with Gaussian hidden units as universal approximations. *Neural Computation,* **2**:210–215.

[6] Lo, S. B., Chan, H. P., Lin, J., Freedman, M. T., and Mun, S. K., (1995). Artificial convolution neural network for medical image pattern recognition. *Neural Networks,* **8**:1201–1214.

[7] Sahiner, B., Chan, H. P., Petrick, N., Wei, D., Helvie, M. A., Adler, D., and Goodsitt, M. M., (1996). Classification of mass and normal breast tissue: A convolution neural network classifier with spatial domain and texture images. *IEEE Trans. Medical Imaging,* **15**:598–610.

[8] Kohonen, T., (1988). *Self-Organization and Associative Memory.* New York: Springer.

[9] Haykin, S., (1994). *Neural Networks.* New York: Maxwell Macmillan Publishing Company.

[10] Oja, E., (1992). Self-organizing maps and computer vision. *Neural Networks for Perception,* **1**:368–385.

[11] Kotropoulos, C., Magnisalis, X., Pitas, I., and Strintzis, M. G., (1994). Nonlinear Ultrasonic Image Processing Based on Signal-Adaptive Filters and Self-Organizing Neural Networks. *IEEE Trans. Image Processing,* **3**:65–77.

[12] Kohonen, T., (1982). Self-organized formation of topologically correct feature maps. *Biological Cybernetics,* **43**:59–69.

[13] Moody, J. and Darken, C., (1989). Fast learning in networks of locally-tuned Processing Units. *Neural Computation,* **1**:281–295.

[14] Poggio, T. and Girosi, F., (1990). Networks for approximation and learning. *Proceedings of the IEEE,* **78**:1481–1497.

[15] Saha, A., Christian, D. S., Tang, D. S., and Wu, C. L., (1991). Oriented non-radial basis functions for image coding and analysis. *Touretky's Connectionist Summer School,* **2**:728–734.

[16] Zong, X., Meyer-Bäse, A., and Laine, A., (1997). Multiscale segmentation through a radial basis neural network. *IEEE Int. Conf. on Image Processing,* **I**:400–403.

[17] Lee, S. and Kil, R. M., (1991). A Gaussian potential function network with hierarchically self-organizing learning. *Neural Networks,* **4**:207–224.

[18] Platt, J., (1991). A resource-allocating network for function interpolation. *Neural Computation,* **3**:213–225.

[19] Pudil, P., Novovicova, J., and Kittler, J., (1994). Floating search methods in feature selection. *Pattern Recognition Letters,* **15**:1119–1125.

[20] Siedlecki, W. and Sklansky, J., (1989). A note on genetic algorithms for large-scale feature selection. *Pattern Recognition Letters,* **10**:335–347.

[21] Hopfield, J. J., (1982). Neural networks and physical systems with emergent collective computational abilities. *Proc. National Academy of Science,* **79**:2554–2558.

[22] Figueiredo, M. A. T. and Leitao, J. M. N., (1994). Sequential and parallel image restoration: neural network implementations. *IEEE Trans. Neural Networks,* **3**:789–801.

[23] Katsaggelos, A. G., (1991). *Digital Image Processing.* Berlin: Springer.

[24] Sun, Y., Li, J. G., and Wu, S. Y., (1995). Improvement on performance of modified Hopfield neural network for image restoration. *IEEE Trans. Image Processing,* **4**:688–692.

[25] Paik, J. K. and Katsagellos, A. K., (1992). Image restoration using a modified Hopfield network. *IEEE Trans. Image Processing,* **1**:49–63.

24 Graph Theoretical Concepts for Computer Vision

D. Willersinn[1], E. Bertin[2], C. Klauck[3], R. Eils[4]

[1]Fraunhofer-Institut für Informations- und Datenverarbeitung (IITB) Karlsruhe, Germany
[2]Laboratoire de Statistique et d'analyses de données, Université Pierre Mendès, Grenoble, France,
[3]Institut für Elektrotechnik und Informatik, Fachhochschule Hamburg, Hamburg, Germany,
[4]Interdisziplinäres Zentrum für Wissenschaftliches Rechnen, Universität Heidelberg, Germany

Handbook of Computer Vision and Applications
Volume 2
Signal Processing and Pattern Recognition

Copyright © 1999 by Academic Press
All rights of reproduction in any form reserved.
ISBN 0-12-379772-1/$30.00

24.1 Introduction

Graphs are important data structures for computer vision. They are widely used to represent the neighborhood relations that exist in the discrete sensor images that we obtain from the world. At the same time, we use graphs to represent the scenes captured by the sensor as well as the relational structure of our knowledge about the world. Both representations are combined by image understanding techniques.

An important aspect for the representation of image structure is the duality that holds between regions and their boundaries. The image representations we cover in this chapter can represent this duality relation explicitly. The chapter starts with Section 24.2, which contains the basic notions from graph theory that will be used during the rest of the chapter. Section 24.3 discusses two alternative ways to represent 2-D digital images by a pair of dual graphs. Section 24.4 is devoted to Voronoi diagrams and Delaunay graphs, dual representations for higher dimensional images. Section 24.5 gives an overview of matching algorithms.

Knowledge representations and their use in computer vision are only partly covered in this Chapter. Section 24.6 describes graph grammars, formalisms that allow deriving a new graph from an old one, and that are used in the knowledge-based system for image retrieval IRIS described in Chapter 25. Additional knowledge-based image understanding techniques involving operations on graphs are covered in Chapter 27.

24.2 Basic definitions

The definitions from graph theory that are contained in this section can be found in standard textbooks on graph theory (e.g., those by Berge [1], Christofides [2], Harary [3], Thulasiraman and Swamy [4]).

Section 24.2.1 defines graphs as sets of vertices and edges, as well as the concepts of adjacency and degree. More complex notions like connectedness of graphs and subgraphs are defined in Section 24.2.2.

Section 24.2.3 and Section 24.2.4 are devoted to duality between graphs.

24.2.1 Graphs, vertices, edges

Definition 24.1 *A* **graph** $G = (V, E)$ *consists of two sets: a finite set* V *of elements called* **vertices** *and a finite set* E *of elements called* **edges**. *Each edge creates a binary relation between a pair of vertices.*

We use the symbols $v_1, v_2, v_3, \ldots$ to represent the vertices and the symbols $e_1, e_2, e_3, \ldots$ to represent the edges of the graph.

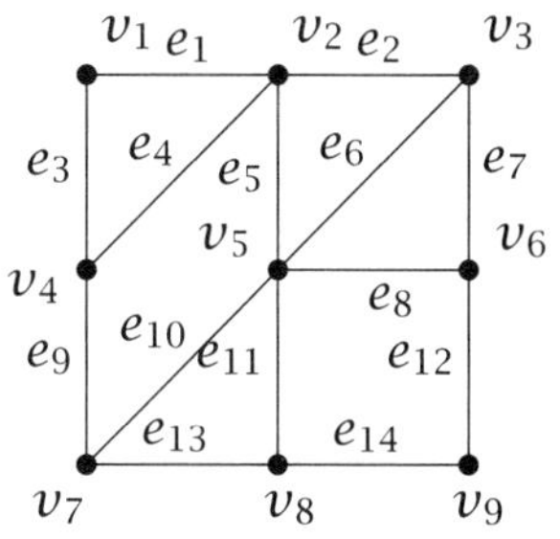

Figure 24.1: *Pictorial representation of a graph $G(V,E)$.*

Figure 24.1 shows the example of a graph. Vertices are represented by black spots (•), edges by straight lines.

Definition 24.2 *The vertices v_i and v_j associated with an edge e_l are called the* **end vertices** *of e_l; e_l is said to be incident to its end vertices. The edge is denoted as $e_l = (v_i, v_j)$.*

Definition 24.3 *More than one edge in a graph $G(V,E)$ may have the same pair of end vertices. All edges having the same pair of end vertices are called* **parallel edges**.

Definition 24.4 *An edge e_l is called a* **self-loop** *at vertex v_i if its end vertices are identical, that is, $e_l = (v_i, v_i)$.*

Definition 24.5 *Two* **edges** *are* **adjacent** *if they have a common end vertex.*

Definition 24.6 *Two* **vertices** *are* **adjacent** *if they are the end vertices of some edge.*

Definition 24.7 *The number of edges incident to a vertex v of a graph $G(V,E)$ is called its* **degree** *or its* **valency**. *It is denoted by $d(v)$. A self-loop at a vertex v increases the degree of v by two.*

Definition 24.8 *A vertex of degree 1 is called a* **pendant vertex**.

Definition 24.9 *The edge incident to a pendant vertex is called a* **pendant edge**.

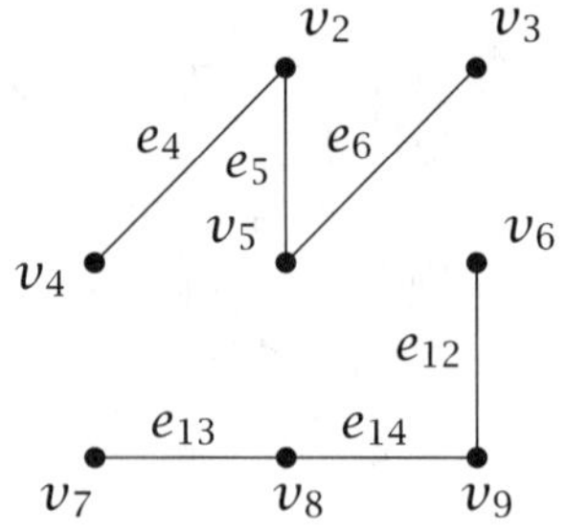

Figure 24.2: *Two paths of G.*

24.2.2 Paths, subgraphs, and components of a graph

Definition 24.10 *A* **path** $\mathcal{K}$ *in a graph is a finite alternating sequence of vertices and edges* $v_0, e_1, v_1, e_2, \ldots, v_{k-1}, e_k, v_k$ *such that*

1. *vertices* v_{i-1} *and* v_i *are the end vertices of the edge* e_i, $1 \le i \le k$;
2. *all edges are distinct;*
3. *all vertices are distinct.*

Vertices v_0 *and* v_k *are called* **end vertices of the path**, *and we refer to it as* $v_0 - v_k$ *path. The number of edges in a path is called the* **length of the path**.

Figure 24.2 shows two examples of paths of the graph G in Fig. 24.1.

Definition 24.11 *A graph G is* **connected** *if there exists a path between every pair of vertices in G.*

Definition 24.12 *Consider a graph* $G = (V, E)$. $G' = (V', E')$ *is a* **subgraph** *of G if* V' *and* E' *are, respectively, subsets of V and E such that an edge* (v_i, v_j) *is in* E' *only if* v_i *and* v_j *are in* V'.

Definition 24.13 *Let* V' *be a subset of the vertex set V of a graph* $G = (V, E)$. *Then the subgraph* $G' = (V', E')$ *is the induced subgraph of G on the vertex set* V' *(or simply* **vertex-induced subgraph** $\langle V' \rangle$ *of G) if* E' *is a subset of E such that an edge* (v_i, v_j) *is in* E' *if and only if* v_i *and* v_j *are in* V'.

Definition 24.14 *A* **clique** *of a graph* $G(V, E)$ *is a set* $S \subseteq V$ *such that in* $\langle S \rangle$ *every pair of vertices is adjacent.*

Definition 24.15 *If* e_l *is an edge of a graph* $G = (V, E)$, *then* $G - e_l$ *is the subgraph of G that results after* **removing** *the edge* e_l *from G. Note that the end vertices of* e_l *are not removed from G. The removal of a set of edges from a graph is defined as the removal of single edges in succession.*

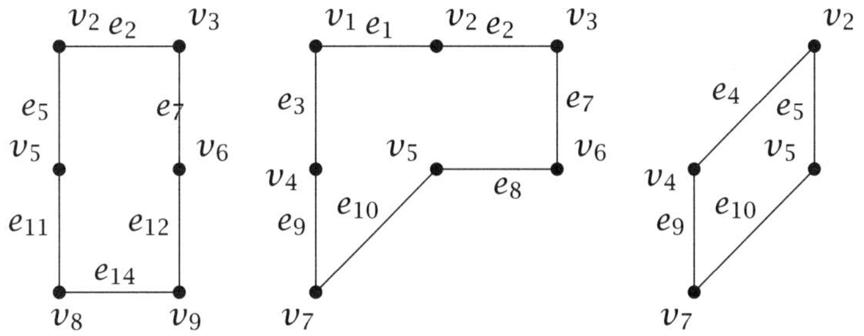

Figure 24.3: *Three examples of circuits of G.*

Definition 24.16 *A set V is said to be* **partitioned** *into subsets $V_1, V_2, \ldots, V_p$, if*

$$V_i \neq \emptyset, 1 \leq i \leq p;$$
$$V_1 \cup V_2 \cup \ldots \cup V_p = V, \text{ and}$$
$$V_j \cap V_k = \emptyset, \forall\, j,k;\; j \neq k$$

We refer to subsets $V_1, V_2, \ldots, V_p$ as a **partition** *of V.*

Definition 24.17 *Consider a graph $G(V,E)$ which is not connected. Then the vertex set V of G can be partitioned into subsets $V_1, V_2, \ldots, V_p$ such that the vertex-induced subgraphs $\langle V_i \rangle$, $i = 1,2,\ldots,p$, are connected and no vertex in subset V_i is connected to any vertex in subset V_j, $i \neq j$. We call subgraphs $\langle V_i \rangle$, $i = 1,2,\ldots,p$,* **connected components** *or simply* **components** *of G.*

24.2.3 Circuits, cutsets, cuts, and dual graphs

Definition 24.18 *A* **circuit** *is a path the end vertices of which are identical.*

Figure 24.3 shows three circuits of the graph G in Fig. 24.1.

Definition 24.19 *A* **cutset** *C of a connected graph G is a minimal set of edges of G with respect to inclusion ($\subseteq$) such that its removal from G disconnects G, that is, the graph $G - C$ is disconnected.*

Figure 24.4 shows graph G of Fig. 24.1 after removal of the cutset $C = \{e_9, e_{10}, e_{11}, e_{12}\}$: $G - C$ is disconnected and consists of exactly two components $\langle\{v_1, v_2, v_3, v_4, v_5, v_6\}\rangle$ and $\langle\{v_7, v_8, v_9\}\rangle$ A notion that is closely related to the one of a cutset is that of a cut.

Definition 24.20 *Consider a connected graph $G(V,E)$ with vertex set V. Let V_1 and V_2 be a partition of V. Then the set C of all edges having one end vertex in V_1 and the other end vertex in V_2 is called a* **cut** *of G.*

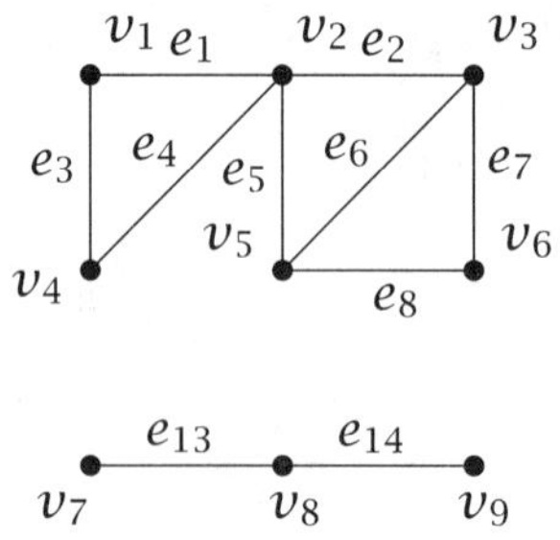

Figure 24.4: *G after removal of the cutset* $\{e_9, e_{10}, e_{11}, e_{12}\}$.

According to [4, p. 44], we denote a cut by $\langle V_1, V_2 \rangle$. The relationship between a cut and a cutset is stated more formally in Theorems 24.1 and 24.2, the proofs of which can be found in [4, p. 45].

Theorem 24.1 *A cut in a connected graph G is a cutset or union of edge-disjoint cutsets.*

Theorem 24.2 *A cut* $\langle V_1, V_2 \rangle$ *of a connected graph G is a cutset of G if the induced subgraphs of G on the vertex sets* V_1 *and* V_2 *are connected. If S is a cutset of a connected graph G, and* V_1 *and* V_2 *are the vertex sets of the two components of* $G - S$*, then* $S = \langle V_1, V_2 \rangle$.

Circuits and cutsets are used to define an important relationship between pairs of graphs.

Definition 24.21 *A graph* $\overline{G}$ *is a* **combinatorial dual** *of a graph G if there is a one-to-one correspondence between the edges of* $\overline{G}$ *and those of G such that a set of edges in* $\overline{G}$ *is a circuit if and only if the corresponding set of edges in G is a cutset.*

Duality is a symmetric relation, as we formally state in Theorem 24.3.

Theorem 24.3 *Consider two graphs G and* $\overline{G}$. *If* $\overline{G}$ *is a dual of G, then G is a dual of* $\overline{G}$.

The proof can be found in [4, p. 189].

24.2.4 Planar graphs and geometrical duals

Definition 24.21 defines the combinatorial dual of a graph. For pictorial representations of dual graphs we use a different way of defining dual graphs based on drawings of graphs on surfaces.

Definition 24.22 *A graph is said to be* **embeddable** *into a surface S if it can be drawn on S so that its edges intersect only at their end vertices.*

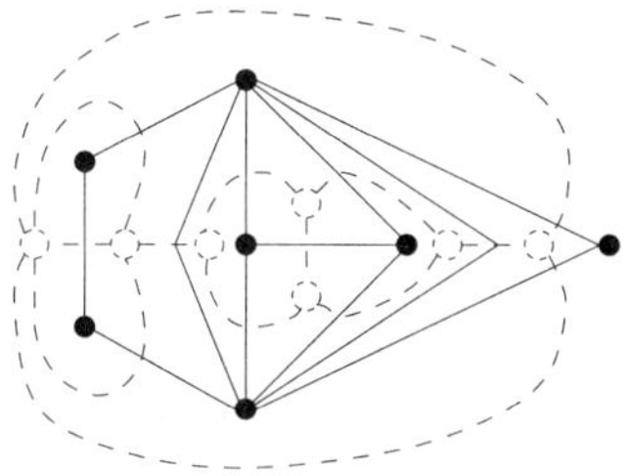

Figure 24.5: A graph G (solid lines) and its geometrical dual $\overline{G}$ (dashed lines).

Definition 24.23 *A graph G is said to be* **planar** *if it can be embedded into a plane. Such a drawing of a planar graph G is called a* **planar embedding** *of G or simply a* **plane graph**.

Definition 24.24 *An embedding of a planar graph into a plane divides the plane into* **regions** *or* **faces**. *A region or face is* **finite** *if the area it encloses is finite; otherwise it is* **infinite**.

Definition 24.25 *The edges on the boundary of a face contain exactly one circuit, and this circuit is said to enclose the face. Let $f_1, f_2, f_3, \ldots, f_r$ be the faces of a planar graph with f_r as the exterior face. We denote by $C_i, 1 \leq i \leq r$, the circuit on the boundary of region f_i. The circuits $C_1, C_2, \ldots, C_{r-1}$, corresponding to the finite faces, are called* **meshes** *or* **cycles**. *Like Harary ([3], p. 103), we will refer to a cycle corresponding to a face f_i as the cycle of f_i, and we will denote it as $C(f_i)$.*

Definition 24.26 specifies how to obtain a dual graph from a planar embedding of a graph.

Definition 24.26 *Let G be a plane graph. Then the* **geometrical dual** $\overline{G}$ *of G is constructed as follows:*

1. *place a vertex $\overline{v_i}$ in each face f_i of G, including the exterior region;*
2. *if two regions f_i and f_j have an edge e in common, then join the corresponding vertices $\overline{v_i}$ and $\overline{v_j}$ by a line crossing only e; this line represents edge $\overline{e} = (\overline{v_i}, \overline{v_j})$.*

Figure 24.5 shows a simple example of a pair of dual graphs. Note the correspondence between vertices of $\overline{G}$ and faces of G. Also, each edge of G corresponds to one edge of $\overline{G}$, indicated in the drawing by one dashed line crossing exactly one solid line.

Geometrical and combinatorial duals are equivalent as proved by Whitney [5, 6, loc. cit. [3]], who formulated Theorem 24.4 concerning the equivalence between planarity and the existence of a combinatorial dual. We cite Theorem 24.4 from [3, p. 115].

Theorem 24.4 *A graph is planar if and only if it has a combinatorial dual.*

24.2.5 Trees and rooted trees

Definition 24.27 *A graph is said to be* **acyclic** *if it has no circuits. A* **tree** *is a connected acyclic graph. A* **rooted tree** *is one which has a distinguished vertex, called the* **root**.

24.3 Graph representation of two-dimensional digital images

In a **region adjacency graph** [7], regions can be referred to as units, and adjacency relations between regions are represented explicitly. Ballard and Brown [7, p. 159] use the dual of a region adjacency graph to represent region boundaries explicitly.

In this section we propose a dual graph representation of a digital image that is complete in the sense that it also represents the image boundary explicitly.

24.3.1 Digital images

The processing of images by computers requires that images are supplied in some digital form. Definitions 24.28 and 24.29 of images and digital images are adopted from Haralick and Shapiro [8].

Definition 24.28 *A* **2-D image** *is a spatial representation of an object, a 2-D or 3-D scene. It may be abstractly thought of as a continuous function I of two variables defined on some bounded and usually rectangular region of a plane. The value of the image located at spatial coordinates (r, c) is denoted by $I(r, c)$.*

Definition 24.29 differs from the original definition found in [8].

Definition 24.29 *A* **2-D digital image** *is an image in digital format and is obtained by partitioning the area of the image into a finite set of small mutually exclusive convex polygons called* **resolution cells**. *Each resolution cell has a representative image value assigned to it. The number of resolution cells of an image is called its* **size**.

In contrast to Haralick and Shapiro, we do not assume an array structure of a digital image. In the remainder of this contribution, we may sometimes refer to 2-D digital images simply as images for convenience.

Kovalevsky [9] points out that the essential difference between an image and a set of resolution cells consists in adjacency relations between cells.

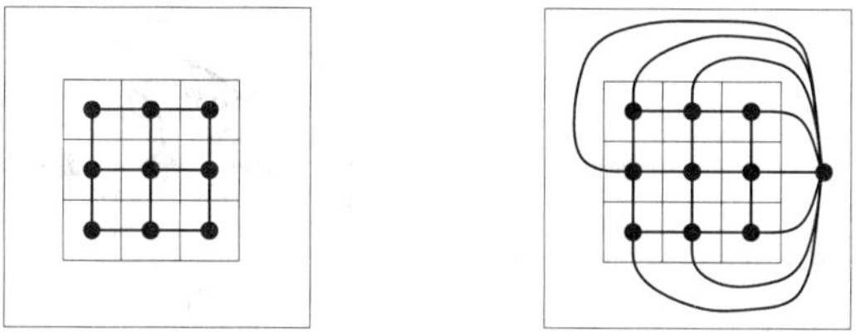

Figure 24.6: *Two different ways of representing image structure by a graph.*

Definition 24.30 *Two resolution cells are adjacent if they have a common side. A resolution cell is adjacent to itself.*

24.3.2 The representation of the image

Figure 24.6 shows two different ways of constructing a graph that represents neighborhood relations in a digital image. In this particular example the image contains nine square resolution cells. The left part of Fig. 24.6 shows a graph that is minimal in the sense that all neighborhood relations between resolution cells are represented by an edge in the image.

The graph displayed in the right part of Fig. 24.6 is derived from the same image, but it also represents resolution cell sides of the image boundary β. This is important for the correct representation of those regions of an image that have contours containing sides of the image boundary. The boundary of such regions would not be represented completely by the graph shown in the left part of Fig. 24.6.

In this thesis the second image representation is selected for its ability to reflect the topological properties of the image in a more complete way. Definition 24.31 specifies the corresponding algorithm for the construction of a plane graph $G(V,E)$ and its geometrical dual $\overline{G}(\overline{V},\overline{E})$ from a digital image.

Definition 24.31 *Let I be a 2-D digital image, and let the resolution cells of I be denoted as c_i. Let further each cell $c_i \in I$ be assigned to an equivalence class k_i. Then a graph $G(V,E)$ and its geometrical dual $\overline{G}(\overline{V},\overline{E})$ is obtained from I by the following process:*

1. *Place a vertex $v_i \in V$ in every resolution cell c_i and assign v_i to the equivalence class k_i of c_i. Place one vertex v_E in the plane surrounding I;*
2. *if two cells c_i, c_j have a common side, then draw a line between vertices v_i and v_j in such a way that the common side is intersected; this line represents the edge $(v_i, v_j) \in E$;*

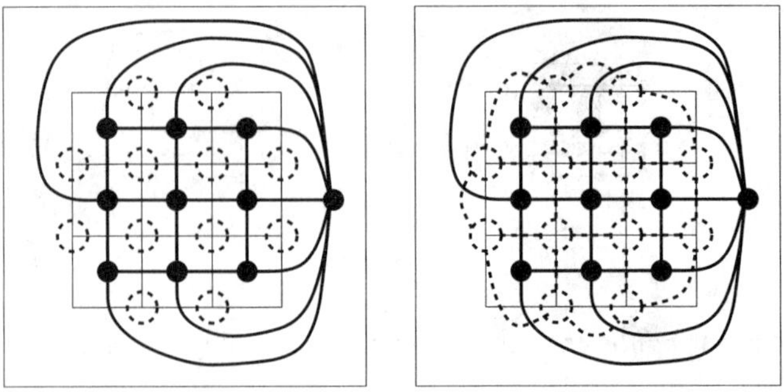

Figure 24.7: *Construction of the face graph.*

3. *if a cell c_i is on the boundary of I, then draw a line between vertices v_i and v_E such that a side common to c_i and the plane surrounding I is intersected; this line represents the edge $(v_i, v_E) \in E$;*
4. *construct the geometrical dual $\overline{G}$ of G according to Definition 24.26.*

We refer to graph G as the **neighborhood graph** *as its edges explicitly represent adjacency between elements of the representation of I. Graph $\overline{G}$ is called* **face graph** *because vertices $\overline{v} \in \overline{V}$ represent faces of a planar embedding of G.*

Figure 24.7 illustrates the construction of the dual graph (dashed lines). Note that each resolution cell corner that is common to at least two cells corresponds to a mesh of three or more in length in the neighborhood graph G. Each vertex of the face graph $\overline{G}$ corresponds to one face of G. For this reason there is also a correspondence between resolution cell corners and vertices of $\overline{G}$, illustrated in Fig. 24.7 by the fact that each dashed circle encloses one resolution cell corner. The right part of Fig. 24.7 shows the final result of the construction process of Definition 24.31.

A dual graph representation obtained from a digital image according to Defintion 24.31 can be transformed into a topologically correct and minimal representation of the image regions by a massively parallel process [10].

24.4 Voronoi diagrams and Delaunay graphs

The history of Voronoi diagrams goes back to Descartes (1664) in astronomy. Later, Dirichlet (1850) exploited Voronoi diagrams in $\mathbb{R}^2$ and $\mathbb{R}^3$, and Voronoi (1905) in higher dimensions in the study of reducibility of positive definite quadratic forms. One can notice that Voronoi diagrams have been discovered in many fields under different names such as Dirichlet regions, Thiessen polygons (1911), and Wigner and Seitz zones (1933) ([11, 12, 13]).

In this section we give some definitions and properties of Voronoi diagrams and Delaunay graphs. Proofs will not be given here for the sake of shortness. A comprehensive cover of the topics can be found for example, in [14, 15, 16]. Let φ be a finite set of distinct points in $\mathbb{R}^k$, $k \in \mathbb{N}^*$.

Definition 24.32 (Voronoi diagram) *Let x be a point of φ. The Voronoi region $VR(x|\varphi)$ associated with x is the set of points nearer from x than from any of the other points of φ:*

$$VR(x|\varphi) = \{z \in \mathbb{R}^k, d(z,x) \leq d(z,y), \forall z \in \varphi\}$$

where d is the Euclidean distance. The Voronoi diagram of φ is the union of the Voronoi regions:

$$VD(\varphi) = \bigcup_{x \in \varphi} VR(x|\varphi)$$

According to this definition, one can see that each Voronoi region is polyhedral and convex as an intersection of half-hyperplanes. More precisely, if $H(x,y)$ denotes the half-hyperplane that is the perpendicular bissector of the segment $[x,y]$ containing x then

$$VD(x|\varphi) = \bigcap_{y \in \varphi \setminus \{x\}} H(x,y)$$

($H(x,y)$ is called the dominance region of x over y). Furthermore the Voronoi diagram is a "partition" of $\mathbb{R}^k$ in such a way:

$$\bigcup_{x \in \varphi} V(x) = \mathbb{R}^k \text{ and } [V(x) \setminus \partial V(x)] \cap [V(y) \setminus \partial V(y)] = \emptyset, \quad x, y \in \varphi$$

In $\mathbb{R}^2$ a Voronoi vertex is defined as a point where three or more Voronoi polygons meet (see Fig. 24.8). However, one has to distinguish the case where one or more Voronoi edges degenerate to a point:

Definition 24.33 *If there exists at least a Voronoi vertex which is incident to more than $k+1$ edges, the Voronoi diagram is called degenerate. Otherwise, it is called nondegenerate (see Fig. 24.9).*

One can see that a Voronoi diagram is not degenerate if we assume that the set of points φ is in general position (no $k+2$ points lie on the same hypersphere and no $l+1$ points lie on a $l-1$ dimensional affine subspace of $\mathbb{R}^k$, $l = 2, \cdots, k$) [12].

According to the Definition 24.32, the following property is rather trivial:

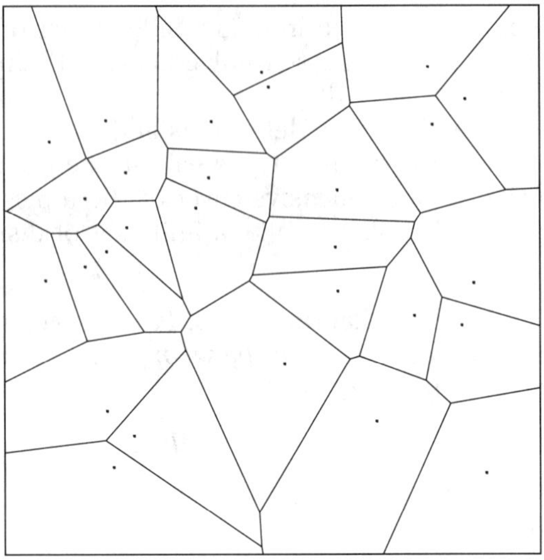

Figure 24.8: *Voronoi diagram.*

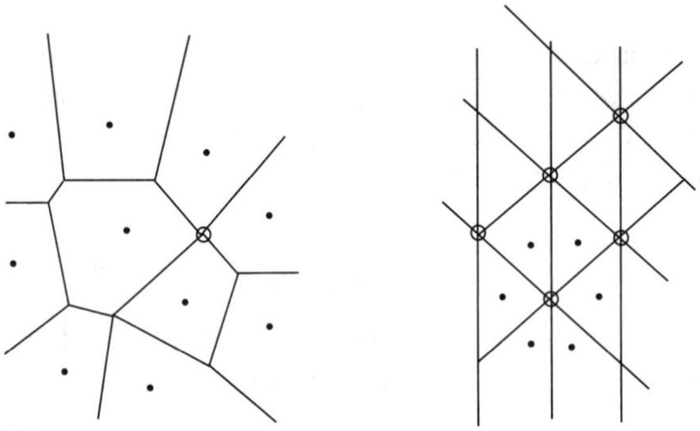

Figure 24.9: *Degenerate Voronoi diagrams. The vertices indicated by open circles have more than three edges.*

Property 24.1 *The point $x \in \varphi$ is the nearest point from point $\tilde{x}$ if and only if $\tilde{x}$ is contained in $Vor(x|\varphi)$.*

This property is related to the following problem [17]:

Problem 1 (The nearest neighbor search problem) *Given a set of distinct points φ, find the nearest neighbor point among φ from a given point $\tilde{x}$ ($\tilde{x}$ is not necessarily a point in φ).*

A straightforward method to solve problem 1 would be to calculate and compare all distances $\|\tilde{x} - x\|, x \in \varphi$. Although this is not very complex for only one point, it might become tedious with increasing

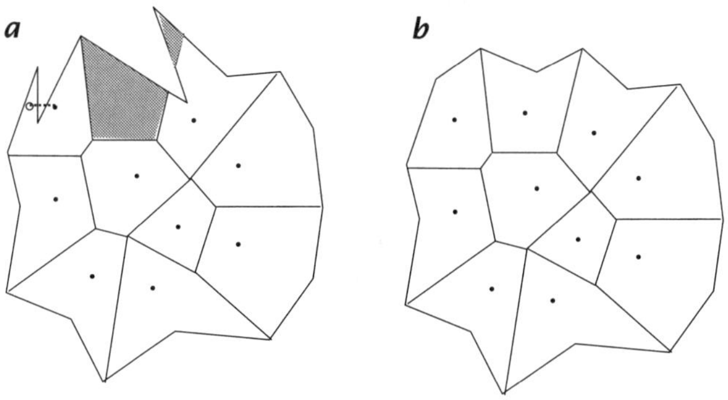

Figure 24.10: *Bounded Voronoi diagrams:* ***a*** *a disconnected boundary Voronoi region (shaded); and* ***b*** *Boundary Voronoi polygons (star-shaped with respect to their points)*

number of point probes. Thus, if the same set of points φ is repeatedly used for (minimum) distance calculations, it is reasonable to calculate the Voronoi diagram first and then use the Voronoi diagram to solve the *point-location problem* (i.e., to find the region in which a point $\tilde{x}$ falls).

In practical applications we consider a Voronoi diagram in a bounded region S.

Definition 24.34 *Let $Vor(\varphi)$ be a Voronoi diagram in $\mathbb{R}^k$, $S \subset \mathbb{R}^k$ and*

$$Vor(\varphi) \cap S = \{Vor(x_1|\varphi) \cap S, Vor(x_2|\varphi) \cap S, \ldots, V(x_n) \cap S\} \tag{24.1}$$

The set $Vor(\varphi) \cap S$ is called a bounded Voronoi diagram. If a Voronoi polytope $Vor(x|\varphi)$ shares the boundary of S and if it is connected, $Vor(x|\varphi)$ is called a boundary polytope. If it is disconnected, it is called a boundary region (see Fig. 24.10).

Since polytope in a k-dimensional Voronoi diagram may be unbounded, Voronoi edges may be infinitely long. Thus, strictly spoken, the k-dimensional Voronoi diagram is not a graph. However, as we will see, any Voronoi diagram may be transferred to a Voronoi graph by simply adding a point in an unbounded region.

The following definition was given by Delaunay in 1934.

Definition 24.35 (Delaunay graph) *The Delaunay graph $DG(\varphi)$ is a graph composed of simplexes in which the interior of the hypersphere $S(\psi)$ circumscribed by every simplex ψ of $DG(\varphi)$ does not contain any point of φ: $\forall \psi \in DG(\varphi), \partial(S(\psi)) \cap \varphi = \emptyset$.*

We assume that the set of points φ is in general position in a way to ensure the existence and unicity of the Delaunay graph. In this case,

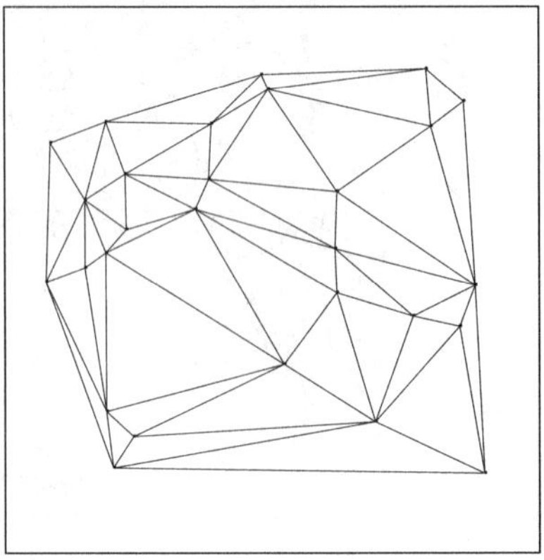

Figure 24.11: *Delaunay graph.*

the Delaunay graph and the Voronoi diagram are dual in a graph theoretical sense as there is a one-to-one correspondence between the $(k-l)$–facets of $VD(\varphi)$ and the l–facets of $DG(\varphi)$, $0 \le l \le k$ [12]. Furthermore, $DG(\varphi)$ is a partition of the convex-hull of φ, denoted by $CH(\varphi)$ (see Fig. 24.11).

The Delaunay graph contains various interesting subgraphs for computer vision as the Gabriel graph, the relative neighbor graph, the minimum spanning tree and the nearest neighbor graph [11].

Definition 24.36 (Gabriel graph) *Two points x and y are said to be in the Gabriel graph $GG(\varphi)$ if and only if the interior of the hypersphere with $[x, y]$ in diameter does not contain any point of φ.*

One can show that two points x and y are in $GG(\varphi)$ if x and y are Delaunay neighbors and the Delaunay edge joining x and y intersect the hyperface between the two Voronoi polytopes $VD(x|\varphi)$ and $VD(y|\varphi)$ (see Fig. 24.12).

Definition 24.37 (Relative neighbor graph) *Two points x and y are said to be in the relative neighbor graph $RNG(\varphi)$ if and only if the interior of the hyperspheres centered in x (respectively, y) with $d(x, y)$ in radius do not contain any point of φ (see Fig. 24.13).*

Definition 24.38 (Euclidean minimum spanning tree) *An Euclidean minimum spanning tree $EMST(\varphi)$ is a tree such that the nodes are given by the points of φ and the sum of the length of the edges is minimal (see Fig. 24.14).*

The algorithm to compute the minimum spanning tree is based on the following lemma:

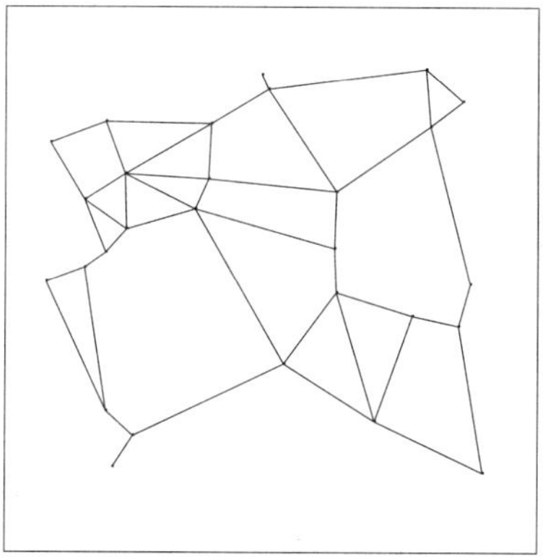

Figure 24.12: *Gabriel graph.*

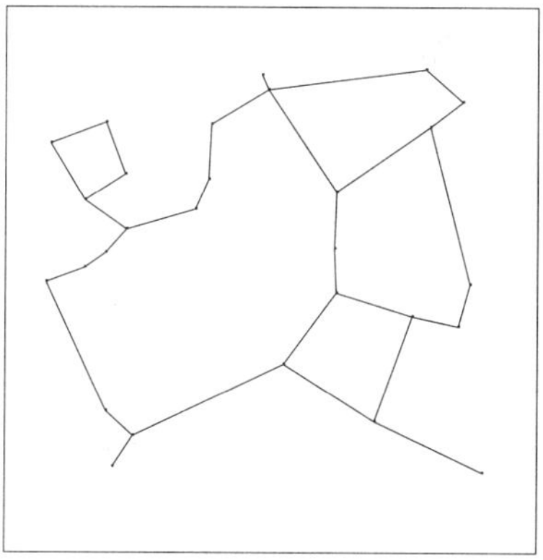

Figure 24.13: *Relative neighbor graph.*

Lemma 24.1 *Let $\{\varphi_1, \varphi_2\}$ be a partition of the set of points φ. There is a Euclidean minimum spanning tree of φ that contains the shortest edge joining φ_1 and φ_2.*

The *EMST* algorithm will handle, at each step, a forest of tree. The initial forest is the set of points. The general step of the algorithm is:

1. Select a tree T in the forest;
2. Find an edge (x', y') such that $d(x', y') = \min_{x \in T,\ y \in \varphi \setminus T} d(x, y)$;
3. If T' is the tree containing y', merge T and T' by binding them with edge (x', y').

The algorithm terminates when the forest consists of a single tree EMST(φ). The second step of the algorithm is computed with the help of the Voronoi diagram.

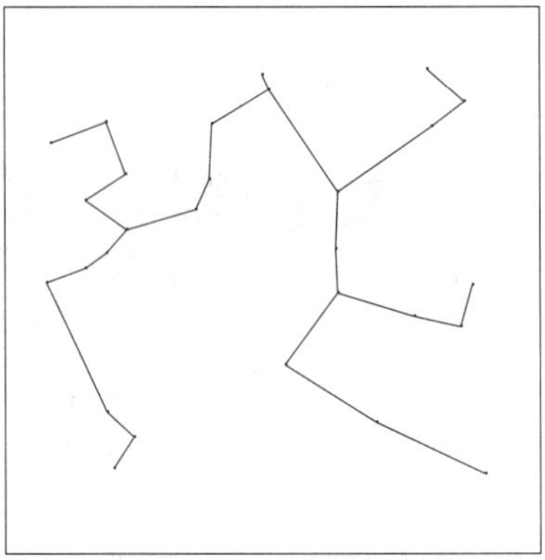

Figure 24.14: *Minimum spanning tree.*

One can notice that the $EMST$ is related to the following problem:

Problem 2 (The closest pair problem) *Given a set of distinct points φ, find the closest pair (i.e., the pair $\{x, y\}, x, y \in \varphi$ with minimum distance among all possible pairs in φ).*

In fact the closest pair of φ is an edge of $EMST(\varphi)$.

Definition 24.39 (Nearest neighbor graph) *The nearest-neighbor graph $NNG(\varphi)$ is the directed graph defined by the following directed relation:*

$$x \underset{\varphi}{\rightsquigarrow} y \Leftrightarrow d(x, y) = \min_{y \in \varphi \setminus \{x\}} d(x, y)$$

When the Euclidean distances $d(x, y)$ and $d(x, z)$ are equal, y and z are ordered in terms of nearness of x according to the lexicographic order on the polar coordinates (see Fig. 24.15).

The computation of the nearest neighbor graph is closely related to the Voronoi diagram according to the following property:

Property 24.2 *The nearest neighbor from x is the point of $\varphi \setminus \{x\}$ whose Voronoi polyhedra share the $(k-1)$-Voronoi faces of $Vor(x|\varphi)$.*

More generally, y is a directed neighbor of x in the l–**nearest neighbor graph**, $l \in \mathbb{N}^*$, if there exists i, $i \le l$ such that y is the i–th nearest neighbor of x in the set of points $\varphi \setminus \{x\}$. One can notice that the l–nearest neighbor graph of φ is not a subgraph of $DT(\varphi)$ for $l \ge 2$ in the general case. Meanwhile, we have the following proposition, which is very interesting to compute the l–nearest neighbor graph from the Delaunay graph:

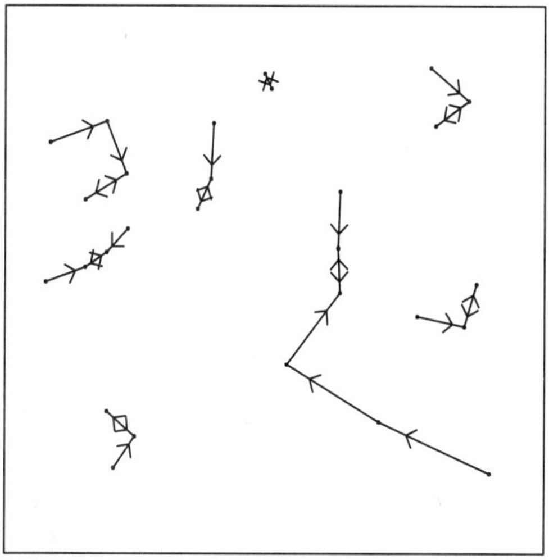

Figure 24.15: *Nearest neighbor graph.*

Proposition 24.1 *The minimum path in the Delaunay graph $DG(\varphi)$ between a point $x \in \varphi$ and its ith nearest neighbor is at most of length i ($\#\varphi \geq i$).*

Proposition 24.2 $NNG(\varphi) \subset MST(\varphi) \subset RNG(\varphi) \subset GG(\varphi) \subset DG(\varphi)$. The proof is given in [16]. As a tree is a connecting graph, the Gabriel graph and the relative neighbor graph are also connecting graphs. Unfortunately, the nearest neighbor graph is not a connecting graph in the general cases.

One can show that the Gabriel graph, the relative neighbor graph, the minimum spanning tree and the nearest neighbor graph can be computed in $O(n)$ from the Delaunay graph in the plane according to the Proposition 24.2 [16].

In the following, some other basic properties of the k-dimensional Voronoi diagram are stated. In order to describe topological properties of a Voronoi diagram in the plane with respect to the number of Voronoi vertices, Voronoi edges and Voronoi polygons, first the Voronoi diagram has to be transferred to a (planar) graph. In graph theory edges are not allowed to be infinitely long. Hence, a dummy point q_0 is placed sufficiently far away from the convex hull $CH(\varphi)$ (see Fig. 24.16). Subsequently, each infinite Voronoi edge is cut at a certain point and connected to the dummy point q_0. Let Q_{+1} denote the set of Voronoi vertices including the dummy point p_0 and E_b denote the set of the (manipulated) Voronoi edges. The so-obtained graph $G(Q_{+1}, E_b)$ forms a planar graph and is called the *Voronoi graph* induced from the Voronoi diagram. The Euler formula (see e.g., [18]) can be applied to the Voronoi

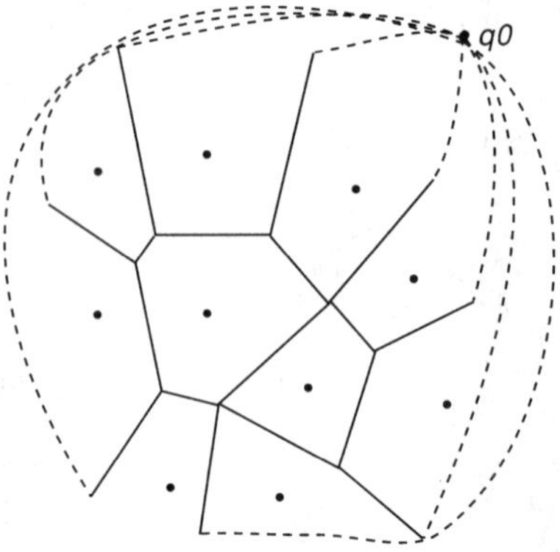

Figure 24.16: A Voronoi graph induced from a Voronoi diagram by the addition of a dummy point outside the convex hull of the set of points φ.

graph. Since the number of vertices n_v is incremented by 1 for the added dummy point, the Euler formula leads to:

Proposition 24.3 *Let n, n_e and n_v denote the number of points, Voronoi edges and Voronoi vertices of a 2-D Voronoi diagram, respectively. Then*

$$n_v - n_e + n = 1 \tag{24.2}$$

More generally Euler-Schlaefli's equation (see e.g., [19]) for the k-dimensional case leads to:

Proposition 24.4 *Let n_l be the number of l-dimensional Voronoi faces in a k-dimensional Voronoi diagram. Then*

$$\sum_{l=0}^{k}(-1)^l n_l = (-1)^k \tag{24.3}$$

In the following some estimates of the number of Voronoi edges and vertices are given. They can be easily deduced from Euler's equation (Eq. (24.2)).

Proposition 24.5 *Let n, n_e and n_v be the numbers of points, Voronoi edges and Voronoi vertices of a 2-D Voronoi diagram, respectively. Further let n_c be the number of infinite Voronoi polygons and let $3 \le n < \infty$. Then*

$$\begin{array}{ll} n_e \le 3n - 6 & n_e \ge 3n_v + n_c - 3 \\ n_v \le 2n - 5 & n_v \ge \frac{1}{2}(n - n_c) + 1 \end{array} \tag{24.4}$$

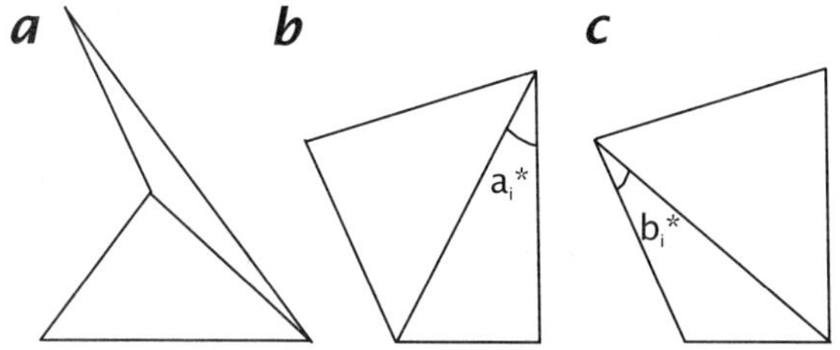

Figure 24.17: *In triangulation* ***a****, the quadrangle is nonconvex. Thus, there is no alternative triangulation to the one shown. In triangulations* ***b*** *and* ***c****, the quadrangle is convex and does not degenerate into a triangle. Thus, there are two possible triangulations. The minimum angle among six angles in the two triangles in triangulations* ***b*** *and* ***c*** *is a_i^* and b_i^*, respectively. The minimum angle a_i^* in triangulation* ***b*** *is larger than the minimum angle b_i^* in triangulation* ***c****. Thus, triangulation* ***b*** *is regarded as locally better according the local max-min angle criterion.*

Other results are given for the stationary Poisson point process in $\mathbb{R}^k$ in [12] where φ "locally finite" (for all bounded Borel B set of $\mathbb{R}^k$, $\#(B \cap \varphi) < +\infty$).

To complete this section some interesting geometrical properties of Delaunay triangulations will be presented. For a given set φ of points there are many possible triangulations spanning φ. Sometimes, one would like to obtain a triangulation, which is as closely equiangular as possible. One way to achieve such a triangulation is to demand that the minimum angle in a triangulation is as large as possible. This criterion is (locally) achieved applying the *local max-min angle criterion*: (see Fig. 24.17).

The local max-min angle criterion: For a triangulation $\mathcal{T}$ of $CH(\varphi)$ spanning φ, let $\triangle x_{i1}x_{i2}x_{i3}$ and $\triangle x_{i1}x_{i2}x_{i4}$ be two triangles sharing an internal edge $\overline{x_{i1}x_{i2}}$ in $CH(\varphi)$. For a convex quadrangle $x_{i1}x_{i3}x_{i2}x_{i4}$, which does not degenerate into a triangle, let $\alpha_{ij}, j \in \{1, \cdots, 6\}$ be six angles in $\triangle x_{i1}x_{i2}x_{i3}$ and $\triangle x_{i1}x_{i2}x_{i4}$; $\beta_{ij}, j \in \{1, \cdots, 6\}$ be six angles in $\triangle x_{i1}x_{i3}x_{i4}$ and $\triangle x_{i2}x_{i3}x_{i4}$. If the relation

$$\min_j\{\alpha_{ij}, j \in \{1, \cdots, 6\}\} \geq \min_j\{\beta_{ij}, j \in \{1, \cdots, 6\}\} \tag{24.5}$$

holds, then the edge satisfies the *local max-min angle criterion*. Furthermore, if the quadrangle is nonconvex or degenerates into a triangle, then $\overline{x_{i1}x_{i2}}$ is also said to satisfy the local max-min angle criterion.

It can now be shown that the Delaunay triangulation satisfies the local max-min angle criterion and that any triangulation satisfying this criterion is the Delaunay triangulation:

Proposition 24.6 (local max-min theorem) *Let φ be a set of distinct points*

$$\varphi = \{x_1, \ldots, x_n\} \subset \mathbb{R}^2 (3 \leq n < \infty)$$

which satisfies the noncosphericity assumption (compare Definition 24.33); $\mathcal{T}(\varphi)$ be further a triangulation of $CH(\varphi)$. $\mathcal{T}(\varphi)$ is the Delaunay triangulation spanning φ if and only if every internal edge in $\mathcal{T}(\varphi)$ satisfies the local max-min angle criterion.

Note that the local max-min angle theorem gives rise to a constructive algorithm which provides a Delaunay triangulation spanning a given set φ. This procedure is referred to as the swapping procedure or, alternatively, the locally optimal procedure [20] and the locally equiangular triangulation [21]. Generally, in these procedures starting with an arbitrary triangulation spanning φ every edge that does not fulfill the local max-min angle criterion is swapped as illustrated in Fig. 24.17.

The Delaunay triangulation is the triangulation with the lexicographically largest angle vector. Intuitively this means that in the Delaunay triangulation elongated and thin triangles are avoided. Thus, it can be expected that the distance $D(x, y)$ of two points $x, y \in \varphi$ in the Delaunay graph (i.e., the length of the shortest path between these two points) provides a good estimate of the Euclidean distance. This proposition is described by the following property which is due to [22].

Proposition 24.7 *For any $x, y \in \varphi$*

$$D(x, y) \leq c \cdot d(x, y) \tag{24.6}$$

where $d(x, y)$ denotes the Euclidean distance between x and y and

$$c = \frac{2\pi}{3\cos(\pi/6)} \approx 2.42$$

On the other hand, Chew shows that c can be arbitrarily close to $\pi/2 \approx 1.57$ [23]. Note that for n points there are $O(n^2)$ pairs of points whereas there are only $O(n)$ edges in the Delaunay triangulation. Thus, according to Proposition 24.7 for a large set of points the distance network of these points can be efficiently approximated by the Delaunay triangulation with only $O(n)$ storage requirements.

Recently Baccelli, Tchoumatchenko and Zuyev show that for the Delaunay graph constructed with respect to a Poisson process, c is asymptotically less than $4/\pi \approx 1.27$ [24]. Simulations nevertheless show that the asymptotic ratio c is approximately 1.05 for the Poisson-Delaunay graph [24].

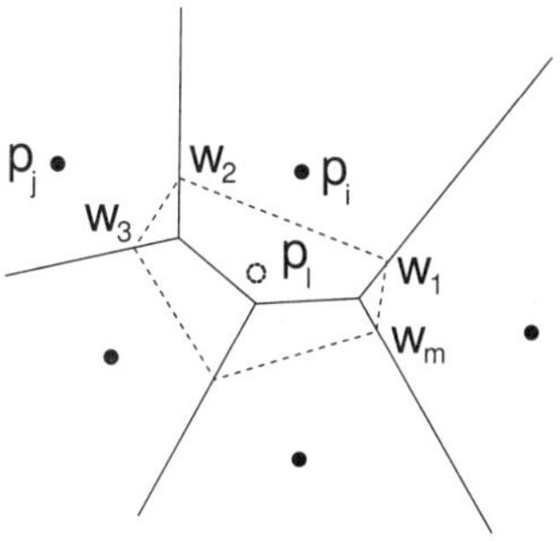

Figure 24.18: *Addition of a new point p_l (open circle) into a Voronoi diagram with five points (filled circles). Dashed lines indicate the Voronoi polygon associated with the new point p_l.*

24.4.1 Approaches for the computation of Voronoi diagrams

An algorithm for computing a Voronoi diagram should provide a full topological description of the resulting geometrical structure (e.g., a list of vertices and edges that belong to one polygon as well as a list of all contiguous polygons). This way of representation, however, requires an unreasonable amount of memory. A data structure that allows the retrieval of a variety of topological information with a minimum of memory requirements is the *winged-edge data structure* that is commonly used in geometric modeling and computer graphics [7, 25, 26]. The complexity of this data structure for n points in the plane is $O(n)$, as the number of vertices and edges in a 2-D Voronoi diagram is $O(n)$ (Proposition 24.5). The retrieval of edges and vertices surrounding a polygon can be performed in $O(n)$ time.

The computation of Voronoi diagrams in higher dimensional space is clearly more complex than in the plane. As the number n_l of l-faces of the Voronoi diagram ($0 \leq l \leq k$) for n points in a k-dimensional space is of $O(n^{\min\{k+1-l, \lceil k/2 \rceil\}})$ [13], the lower bound of the worst-case time complexity of an algorithm for constructing the k-dimensional Voronoi diagram of n points is $O(n \log n + n^{\lceil k/2 \rceil})$.

The most famous algorithms to compute the Voronoi diagram and the Delaunay graph are the *divide and conquer* [16] and the *incremental* [27] ones. The idea of the divide-and-conquer algorithm is to divide the problem recursively into subproblems and then, merge the results obtained. The main advantage of this algorithm is its $O(n \log n)$ optimal complexity in $\mathbb{R}^2$ and $O(n^2)$ optimal complexity in $\mathbb{R}^3$ [28]. The incremental algorithm works by local modification of the Voronoi diagram after insertion of a new point in the structure. We start with only one point in the structure and then we add one point after the other (see Fig. 24.18). Although its worst-case time complexity is $O(n^2)$ in $\mathbb{R}^2$ for the computation of planar Voronoi diagrams, its average time complex-

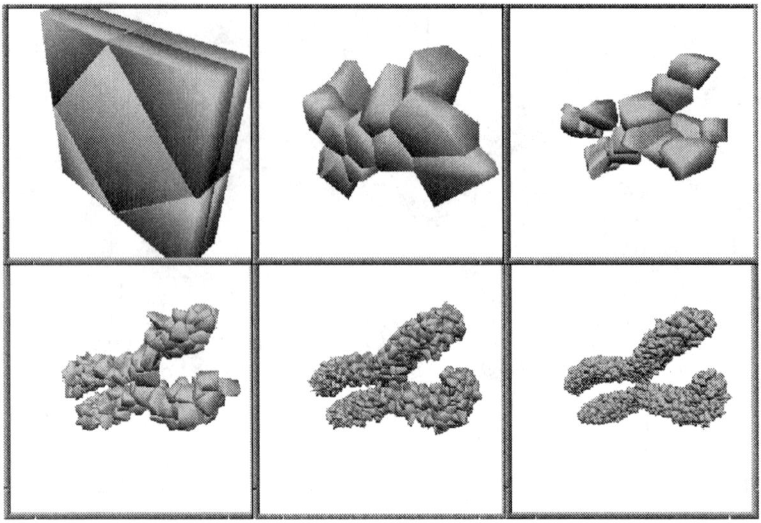

Figure 24.19: Split step in Voronoi polyedra of a volume data: 9 polyhedra, 45 polyhedra, 331 polyhedra, 1023 polyhedra, 3456 polyhedra, and 7000 polyhedra (convergence).

ity can be reduced to $O(n)$ when the data are (not too far) uniformly distributed [29]. In $\mathbb{R}^k$ the reader may refer to [30, 31, 32]. Practically we use the incremental technique because it is important to add or to remove a polytope without computing the whole structure again.

24.4.2 Applications

The concepts of Voronoi diagram and Delaunay graph are used extensively in many fields (see [13] and references therein).

One can find an application for convex partitioning of a gray-level image in 2-D and 3-D. Our algorithm is a generalization of the split-and-merge algorithm on octree regular structures [33], extended to Voronoi irregular structures [34, 35, 36]. The global principle results in the steps of the following algorithm (cf. Definitions 24.40 and 24.41):

1. Select a small number of points in the image using a Poisson process.
2. Compute the Voronoi diagram and the Delaunay graph from the selected point.
3. Compute mean gray value and standard deviation of each polygon.
4. For all polyhedra, split if the polyhedron is not homogeneous (Definition 24.40).
5. Repeat 2-4 until convergence (all the polyhedra are homogeneous).
6. Merge: suppression of the useless polyhedra (Definition 24.41).

The proof of convergence is straightforward (in the worst case all the polygons have one pixel in their interior, which gives a variance equal to zero).

Definition 24.40 *A region enclosed by a polyhedron is said to be homogeneous if and only if the variance in the region is less than a given threshold.*

Definition 24.41 *A polyhedra $VD(x|\varphi)$ is said to be useless if and only if all the neighbors of $VD(x|\varphi)$ have almost equal gray-level means.*

An illustration of the split-and-merge algorithm is given in Fig. 24.19, where the size of the image is $128 \times 128 \times 31$ with 256 gray values.

The convex partitioning obtained is useful in several applications:

- Image segmentation using irregular pyramid [37, 38];
- Fractal image compression [39];
- Quantitative information for chromosome territories in the cell nuclei [40, 41] and for the spatial distribution of the AgNOR proteins to discriminate malignant tumor pathology [42].

An application of spatial Delaunay Gibbs point processes models in biology in the context of stochastic geometry is given in [43, 44]. Indeed, an image of the piece of prostatic tissue is reproduced in Fig. 24.20a. The architecture presents some cancer on the left side and some normal hyperplasia type on the right side of the image. One can easily grasp the difference of architecture on which the pathological diagnostic is based (Gleason grade). Once the image is segmented in a way to extract the center of the cell nuclei (result of the image segmentation in Fig. 24.20b), the Voronoi region yields somehow a natural way to represent the region of influence of each cell [45, 46, 47] (Fig. 24.20c). Indeed, under Definition 24.32, the Voronoi region associated with the center of the cell x is the set of points of $\mathbb{R}^2$ closer to x than to any of the other cell centers. Thus the Delaunay graph (Fig. 24.20d) associated with a potential function depicts the neighborhood relationships in between cells.

24.5 Matching

Matching techniques are widely used in computer vision to relate structural descriptions. The relations that are established by matching techniques can be grouped in two classes, relations between image structures, and relations between an image structure and structured knowledge about scenes. The latter class of relations are established to solve image understanding problems.

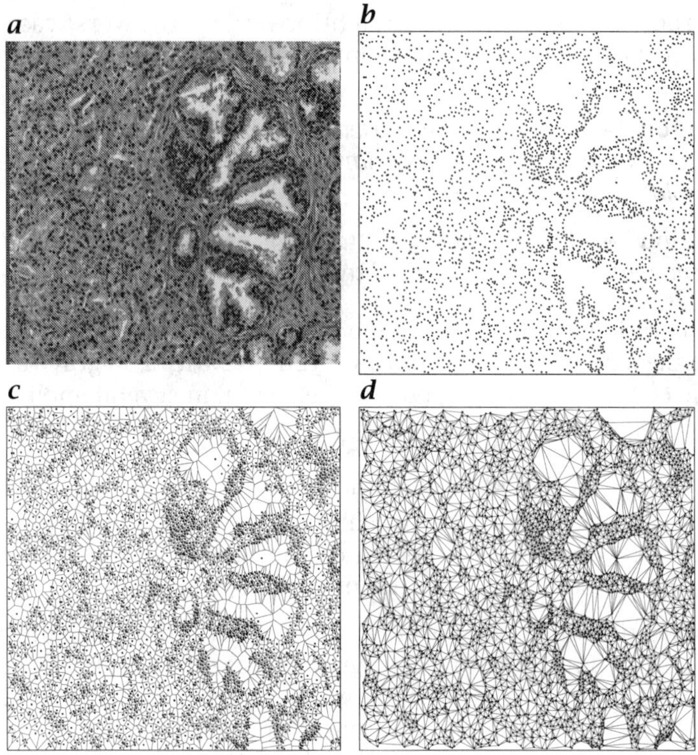

Figure 24.20: ***a*** *Image of a prostatic tissue;* ***b*** *cell nuclei segmentation;* ***c*** *Voronoi diagram;* ***d*** *Delaunay triangulation.*

24.5.1 Graph isomorphisms and matchings

Ballard and Brown [7] propose the notion of isomorphism to formally express the matching problem in graph-theoretical terms (Definitions 24.42, 24.43, and 24.44). For the sake of completeness, we add the formal Definitions 24.5.1, 24.46, and 24.47 of matchings that can be found in, for example, Thulasiraman and Swamy [4].

Definition 24.42 *Given two graphs* (V_1, E_1) *and* (V_2, E_2)*, find a 1:1 and onto mapping (an* **isomorphism***)* f *between* V_1 *and* V_2 *such that for* $v_1, v_2 \in V_1, V_2, f(v_1) = v_2$ *and for each edge of* E_1 *connecting any pair of nodes* v_1 *and* $v_1' \in V_1$ *there is an edge of* E_2 *connecting* $f(v_1)$ *and* $f(v_1')$.

Definition 24.43 *Find isomorphisms between a graph* (V_1, E_1) *and a subgraph* (V_2, E_2) *of another graph (a* **subgraph isomorphism***).*

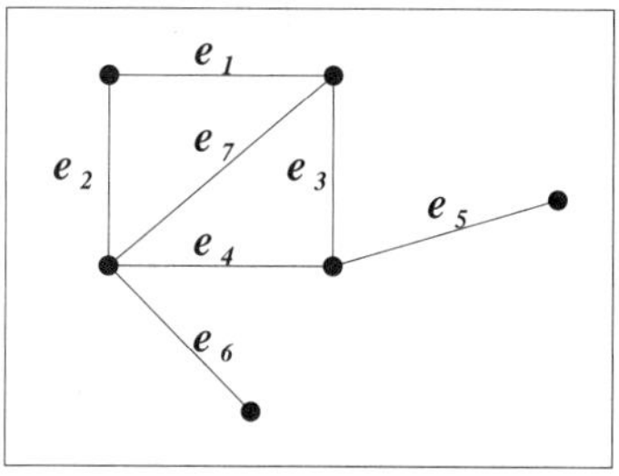

Figure 24.21: Illustration of matchings.

Definition 24.44 *Find all isomorphisms between subgraphs of a graph (V_1, E_1) and subgraphs of another graph (V_2, E_2) (a* **"double"subgraph isomorphism***).*

In graph theory, matchings are defined as particular sets of edges.

Definition 24.45 *Two edges in a graph are said to be* **independent** *if they do not have any common vertex. Edges $e_1, e_2, \ldots$ are said to be* **independent** *if no two of them has a common vertex. A* **matching** *in a graph is a set of independent edges.*

Reference [4] uses the graph drawn in Fig. 24.21 to illustrate matchings, for example, the set $\{e_1, e_4\}$ in Fig. 24.21 is a matching.

Definition 24.46 *A* **maximal matching** *is a maximal set of independent edges; a matching with the largest number of edges is called a* **maximum matching**.

Set $\{e_1, e_4\}$ in Fig. 24.21 is a maximal matching, $\{e_5, e_6\}$ is not.
Set $\{e_1, e_5, e_6\}$ is a maximum matching of the graph in Fig. 24.21.

Definition 24.47 *Let M be a matching in a graph. A vertex is said to be* **saturated** *in M if it is an end vertex of an edge in M. A matching saturating all the vertices of a graph G is called a* **perfect matching** *of G.*

Both the graph isomorphism problem and the subgraph isomorphism problem are "notoriously hard in general" [48, p. 574]. Although NP-complete in general, the subgraph isomorphism problem can be solved in polynomial time if both graphs are rooted trees [48, p. 575]. For the definition of computational complexity and NP completeness, we recommend the study of Garey and Johnson [49].

For the solution of the graph isomorphism problem, more "easy" cases exist in which efficient algorithms can solve the problem. Besides the case of rooted trees, for which an $O(n)$ algorithm exists for the graph isomorphism problem, van Leeuwen [48, pp. 576] mentions planar graphs.

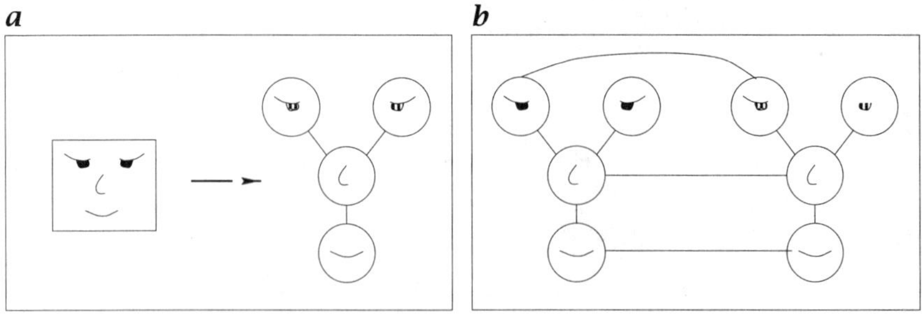

Figure 24.22: ***a*** *Construction of a model graph with image features as attributes;* ***b*** *matching of model graph and graph representing the structure of an image.*

24.5.2 Matching in computer vision: problem statement

The matching illustrated by Fig. 24.21 connects vertices of one graph. In computer vision matchings usually connect vertices of two graphs. The vertices of the graphs carry attributes that represent features extracted from images. Figure 24.22a shows an example of how a graph may be derived from an image. The left part represents an image that shows perceptionally significant features of a face: the eyes, the nose, and the mouth. If the computer vision task is face recognition, then it is reasonable to extract these features from the image and to store them as attributes of vertices. The vertices may then be connected by edges according to the spatial relationships of their attributes in the image domain, thus yielding the graph represented in the right part of Fig. 24.22.

Note that the edges of graphs derived from images do not necessarily represent spatial relationships of image features, but may represent their relationships in more general terms. Figure 24.22b illustrates the matching problem of computer vision by means of the graph displayed in Fig. 24.22a, and which is represented as a model in the left part of the image.

The right part of Fig. 24.22b contains a graph that has been derived from a new image. Dashed lines in Fig. 24.22b represent edges of a matching. These edges establish relations between vertices of both the model graph and the graph derived from the new image. In practice a vertex n of the new graph is connected to a vertex m of the model graph if the attributes of n and m are similar according to an application-specific measure of similarity.

A general problem encountered in computer vision is the presence of noise and occlusions. One consequence of noise and occlusion is illustrated in Fig. 24.22b: not all of the vertices of the displayed graphs are saturated. The feature of the left eye's signature derived from the new image differs from the features stored with any vertex of the model graph. The similarity measure computed to establish the matching is insufficient to establish a relation between the unsaturated vertices, thus hindering a perfect matching.

Another problem caused by noise and occlusions consists in ambiguities. Based on the similarity measure used to compute the matching, a vertex of one graph may be found similar to more than one vertex of the other graph. This may lead to several possible matchings and requires a decision for the optimal matching.

24.5.3 Matching by association graph construction

A popular approach to solving the matching problem in computer vision is by construction of an **association graph** [7, 50, 51]. It is adopted in many fields of computer vision [52, 53, 54, 55, 56, 57, 58].

In an association graph, each edge m of a matching M is represented by a vertex that carries the end vertices of m as attributes. By construction, the association graph represents all possible matchings relating two graphs. All vertices representing the edges of one matching are connected to form a clique. Thus, each individual matching is represented by a clique in the association graph, and the search of the best possible matching corresponds to a search of the clique with the largest number of vertices in the association graph. We report here the construction process given by Ballard and Brown [7]. Recently, Pelillo et al. [59] have extended the method to cope with the problem of finding correct matchings between hierarchical structures.

Definition 24.48 *Given two attributed graphs $G_1(V_1, E_1)$ and $G_2(V_2, E_2)$, the association graph $G(V, E)$ is constructed as follows. For each pair $v_i \in V_1, v_j \in V_2$ of similar vertices, define a vertex $v \in V$ that carries the label (v_i, v_j). Vertices v_i and v_j are similar if their respective attributes are similar.*

Consider two vertices u and v of G carrying labels (v_k, v_l) and (v_i, v_j), respectively. u and v are connected by an edge $e \in E$ if they have "compatible" topological relationships, that is, the edges $(v_i, v_k) \in E_1$ and $(v_j, v_l) \in E_2$ exist, or if the vertices of the v_i, v_k-path in G_1 and the vertices of the v_j, v_l-path in G_2 are all pairwise similar.

Cliques in the association graph can be found using the following procedure:

Definition 24.49 *Let $G(V, E)$ be an association graph. The following recursive procedure finds all cliques in G, starting from $X = \emptyset$:*

```
Cliques(X, V-X) :=
  if (no vertex in V-X is connected to all elements of X,
     then {X};
     else
        Cliques (X + {v}, V) + Cliques(X, V - {v}),
        where v is connected to all elements of X.
```

24.6 Graph grammars

The graph grammar formalism presented in this section is based mainly on the work of Kreowski and Rozenberg [60]. According to requirements coming up from the application to knowledge representation this formalism has been extended with some features, such as attributes and semantic relations. Surveys and detailed introduction to graph grammars can be found, for example, in [60, 61, 62, 63].

24.6.1 Graph

Definition 24.50 *Let Σ_E, Σ_R be two finite sets of labels.*

1. *A tuple $BP = (E, R, s, t, k_E, k_R)$ is a* **labeled graph**, *in this section shortly called graph, with*
   - *$E \neq \emptyset$ is a finite set of* **entities**, *normally called vertices,*
   - *$R \subseteq E \times E$ is a finite set of* **relations**, *normally called edges,*
   - *$s, t : R \to E$ are* **direction mappings**, *which assign to each relation $r \in R$ a* **source** *$s(r) \in E$ and a* **target** *$t(r) \in E$,*
   - *$k_E : E \to \Sigma_E$ and $k_R : R \to \Sigma_R$ are mappings called* **entity and relation labeling**, *which assign to each entity $e \in E$ a* **label** *$\sigma_e \in \Sigma_E$ or to each relation $r \in R$ a* **label** *$\sigma_r \in \Sigma_R$.*
2. *A graph G with $E = \emptyset$ is called* **empty** *and is denoted by λ.*
3. *Let G_1 and G_2 be graphs. G_2 is called a* **subgraph** *of G_1, denoted by $G_2 \subseteq G_1$, if $R_{G_2} \subseteq R_{G_1}, E_{G_2} \subseteq E_{G_1}$, and the mappings $s_{G_2}, t_{G_2}, k_{E_{G_2}}, k_{R_{G_2}}$ are restrictions of the corresponding mappings of G_1 to R_{G_2} and E_{G_2}.*
4. *Let G_1 and G_2 be graphs. Let $V \subseteq G_1$ and $W \subseteq G_2$ be subgraphs. Let $g : V \to W$ be a graph homomorphism[1] with $g(V) = W$. Then G_1 and G_2 can be glued together along the* **gluing parts** *V* **and** *W according to g yielding the new graph U, called the* **(g-)gluing of** *G_1* **and** *G_2, which is defined as follows:*
   (a) *$E_U = E_{G_2} + (E_{G_1} - E_V), R_U = R_{G_2} + (R_{G_1} - R_V)$*

[1] Two mappings $g_E : E_{G_1} \to E_{G_2}$, $g_R : R_{G_1} \to R_{G_2}$ form a graph homomorphism $g : G_1 \to G_2$ if they preserve incidences and labels; for details see [60].

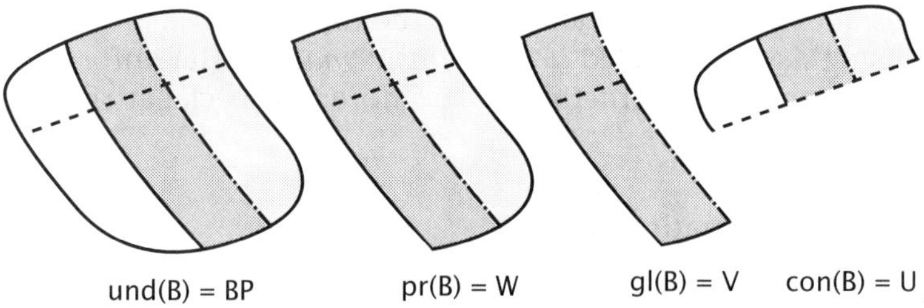

Figure 24.23: *A structured graph (see Kreowski and Rozenberg [60]).*

(b) $s_U, t_U : R_U \to E_U, k_{E_U} : E_U \to \Sigma_{E_U}, k_{R_U} : R_U \to \Sigma_{R_U}$ *are defined for all* $r \in R_U$ *and* $e \in E_U$ *by*
$f_U(r) =$ *if* $r \in E_{G_2}$ *then* $f_{G_2}(r)$ *else if* $f_{G_1}(e) \in E_V$ *then* $g(f_{G_1}(e))$ *else* $f_{G_1}(e)$, *where* $f \in \{s, t\}$, *and* $k_{E_U}(e) =$ *if* $e \in E_{G_2}$ *then* $k_{E_{G_2}}(e)$ *else* $k_{E_{G_1}}(e)$. *and* $k_{R_U}(r) =$ *if* $r \in R_{G_2}$ *then* $k_{R_{G_2}}(r)$ *else* $k_{R_{G_1}}(r)$.

The gluing of G_1 *and* G_2 *is called the* **disjoint union** *of graphs, if the gluing parts are empty, i.e.,* $V = W = \lambda$.

5. *Let* G *be a graph and* $V \subseteq G$ *a subgraph of* G. *Then the pair* $A = (G, V)$ *is called a* **weakly structured graph**; G *is called* **underlying structure** *of A (denoted by und(A)), and* V *is called the* **gluing part** *of A (denoted by gl(A)).*
6. *Let* G *be a graph and* $V \subseteq W \subseteq G$, *that is,* V *a subgraph of* W, *and* W *a subgraph of* G. *Let also* $U \subseteq G$ *be a discrete*[2] *subgraph of* G. *Then the 4-tuple* $B = (G, U, W, V)$ *is called a* **structured graph**; G *is called* **underlying structure** *of B (denoted by und(B)),* U *is called* **contact part** *of B (denoted by con(B)),* W *is called* **protected part** *of B (denoted by pr(B)), and* V *is called the* **gluing part** *of B (denoted by gl(B)).*

An abstract example of a structured graph is given in Fig. 24.23. In this figure the general relations of the graphs G, U, W, V are shown by relations of shapes. Kreowski and Rozenberg mainly distinguish the different transformation rules in [60] according to the protected part of the left-hand side:

Comment 24.6.1 *If a rule protects nothing, that is,* $pr(B) = \lambda$, *then it is called* **destructive**; *if a rule protects the connecting part, that is,* $con(B) \subseteq pr(B) \neq \lambda$, *it is called* **protecting**. *The subgraph* $pr(B) \setminus gl(B)$ *is called in this section the* context *of the structured graph B.*

In order to structure complex graph entities we will split them in our formalism into smaller parts and iterate this graph resulting in a hierarchically distributed graph. The dynamical aspects of a graph structured in that hierarchically and distributed way are described by *graph*

[2] $R_U = \emptyset$.

transformations [64] that can change the topology of a graph. In our formalism this will be called *graph transformation*. The "informations" about the hierarchical structure will be stored in special attributes, the so-called *roles*.

24.6.2 Transformation rules

The notion of a transformation rule[3] and its application to a graph is described in general.

Definition 24.51 *A tuple* $tr = (B, A, apt, \gamma, IM)$ *is a* **transformation rule**, *with*

- B *is a structured graph, called* **left-hand side** *of* tr,
- A *is a weakly structured graph, called* **right-hand side** *of* tr,
- $apt : gl(A) \to gl(B)$ *is an isomorphism, called* **gluing adaptor**,
- $\gamma = (\gamma_{in}, \gamma_{out})$ *is an ordered pair of two relations* $\gamma_{in}, \gamma_{out} \subseteq E \times \Sigma_R \times E \times \Sigma_R \times E$, *called* **embedding specification** *of* tr *Sometimes it is better to have a function for the embedding specification, which creates the* $(\gamma_{in}, \gamma_{out})$*-pair* on the fly. *Then* γ *denotes this function*[4]*:* $\gamma($*<important input>*$) \to (\gamma_{in}, \gamma_{out})$[5].
- IM *is a set of application conditions, represented as equations, called the* **information management** *specifications of* tr.

Our transformation rules will be applied in different applications. The semantics of the right- and left- hand side as well as the semantics of the information management specifications change according to these different applications. Some examples for the different applications are given:

hierarchy As already mentioned here, we will use these rules to describe hierarchically distributed graphs. In this case the left-hand side, that is, the state *before* the application of the rule specifies the graph, which will be refined. The right- hand side, that is, the state *after* the application of the rule, specifies the refined graph. In the information management specifications pre- and postconditions of this refinement step are described. These conditions can be proofed by external domains, like calendar systems, arithmetic calculus etc.

optimization We also use these rules to find nonoptimized graphs, specified by the left-hand side. The right-hand side and the information management specifications describe how this graph is optimized.

[3]In [60] these rules are called *structured graph rewriting rules*.

[4]In the IRIS-system described in this book a function is used.

[5] A horrible part resulting from the "'application marshlands"': Sometimes the embedding depends on the current state of the real world.

analysis We use standard algorithms, for example, [65], to check the specified rules for soundness and correctness. The rules themselves are used to analyze a given graph, that is, a given graph G is describable by a set of transformation rules.

execution A given graph G is executed by applying a special set of transformation rules, which are called *execution rules*. There the left-hand side describes the preconditions and the right- hand side the postconditions of an elementary execution step. The information management specifications describe additional pre- and postconditions and the "effects," which should be performed if the execution is performed. In the IRIS system described in this book we execute the graph to recognize objects.

simulation The simulation of a given graph is handled like the execution of a graph; instead of calling the real systems, dummies will be used to simulate the real world.

According to [60] we split the application of a transformation rule tr to a graph G into five basic steps (see Fig. 24.24 on page 785).

Definition 24.52 *Let G be a graph and $tr = (B, A, apt, \gamma, IM)$ be a transformation rule. Then the* **application** *of tr to G is done by executing the following five steps.*

choose *Choose a graph homomorphism $g : und(B) \to G$, that is, choose an occurrence of B in the graph G, denoted by $g(and(B))$. g is called* **locating homomorphism**. *(syntactical check)*

check *The rule tr is* **g-applicable** *to G if the following conditions are satisfied:*

1. *if a graph entity $e \in E_{g(und(B))}$ is incident[6] with a relation $r \in R_G \setminus R_{g(und(B))}$, then $e \in E_{g(con(B))}$.*
2. *The application conditions of IM are satisfyable.*

(semantics check)

remove *If tr is g-applicable to G, then construct the* **remainder graph**, *denoted by $G \setminus g(und(B))$ as a subgraph of G such that*

$$E_{G\setminus g(und(B))} = (E_G \setminus E_{g(und(B))}) \cup E_{g(pr(B))}$$

and

$$\begin{aligned} R_{G\setminus g(und(B))} &= \{r \in (R_G \setminus (R_{g(und(B))}) \cup R_{g(pr(B))}) \\ &\quad \| s_G(r), t_G(r) \in E_{G\setminus g(und(B))}\} \end{aligned}$$

add *$f : gl(A) \to g(gl(B))$ is defined by*

[6]If for two graph entities $a, b \in E$ and a graph relation $r \in R$: $s(r) = a, t(r) = b$, then a, b are called **incident** with relation r.

- *$\forall e \in E_{gl(A)} : f_E(e) = g_e(apt_E(e))$ and*
- *$\forall r \in R_{gl(A)} : f_R(r) = g_r(apt_R(r))$.*

Then construct the f-gluing of $und(A)$ and $G \setminus g(und(B))$; the resulting graph is denoted by $(G \setminus g(und(B))) \uplus und(A)$.

connect *Add to $(G \setminus g(und(B))) \uplus und(A)$ new relations according to the following rules:*

1. *For each removed relation $r \in R_G$ connecting $s_G(r) \in E_G \setminus E_{g(und(B))}$ and $t_G(r) \in E_{g(und(B))} \setminus E_{g(pr(B))}$, and for each added graph entity $e \in E_{und(A)} \setminus E_{gl(A)}$ a new relation r' leading from $s_G(r)$ to e, labeled by $\sigma_{r'}$, is established provided that*

$$(s_G(r), \sigma_*, t_G(r), \sigma_{r'}, e) \in C_{in}$$

   where $\sigma_* \geq_\Sigma \sigma_r$.

2. *For each removed graph $r \in R_G$ connecting $s_G(r) \in E_{g(und(B))} \setminus E_{g(pr(B))}$ and $t_G(r) \in E_G \setminus E_{g(und(B))}$, and for each added graph entity $e \in E_{und(A)} \setminus E_{gl(A)}$ a new relation r' leading from e to $t_G(r)$, labeled by $\sigma_{r'}$, is established provided that*

$$(s_G(r), \sigma_r, e, \sigma_{r'}, t_G(r)) \in C_{out}$$

   where $\sigma_* \geq_\Sigma \sigma_r$.

3. *If γ denotes a function, then apply this function to create the connecting relations.*

The resulting graph is denoted by G'.

G_1 **directly derives** *a graph G_2* **through** *tr if G_2 is isomorphic to G'_1. A direct derivation is denoted by $G_1 \Rightarrow G_2$; a sequence of derivation is denoted by $G_1 \Rightarrow^*_{KB} G_2$, where KB is a set of transformation rules, our knowledge base.*

An abstract example of a direct derivation is given in Fig. 24.24. The specifications of IM may be executed in the connect-step; this is the case when the specifications are used to pass or generate information, that is, when the specifications are assignments.

In the case in which we use a destructive transformation rule the embedding of the right-hand side is done by the connector only. In the other case, that is, we use a protecting transformation rule, the embedding of the right-hand side is done by the gluing mechanism only.

As mentioned here, we use different sets of transformation rules—in the following defined as *graph grammar*—to describe different applications within our formalism, like optimization, analysis etc. In the terminology of the research in Artificial Intelligence these grammars are describing our *knowledge base* about general and/or individual graphs, their disadvantages, how these disadvantages can be bridged, how the graph itself can be optimized and so forth.

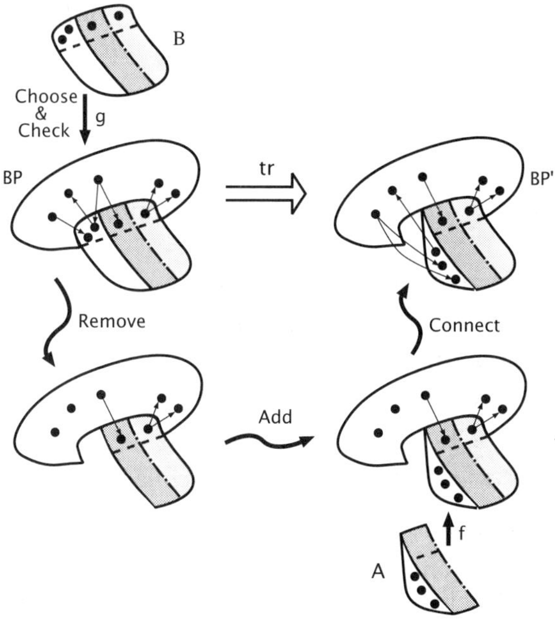

Figure 24.24: *A derivation step yielding G′ from G (see Kreowski and Rozenberg [60]).*

Definition 24.53 *A* **structured graph grammar** *is a system $PG = (\Sigma, T, KB, SG)$, where*

- $\Sigma = (\Sigma_E, \Sigma_R)$ *is a pair of labels,*
- $T = (T_E, T_R)$ *is a pair of* **terminal objects,** *where $T_E \subseteq \Sigma_E$ and $T_R \subseteq \Sigma_R$,*
- *KB is a finite set of transformation rules, and*
- *SG is a graph, called* **start graph.**

graph entities Coming up from the realization, that objects or any other graph entities strongly depend on (context) specific conditions, we offer to represent all this information, that is, all necessary *knowledge*, in one uniform formalism. The advantage of this integrated representation is that in any application of our formalism, for example, analysis, execution, optimization etc., it is possible to use any *knowledge*. This will lead to a qualitatively better and extensive handling of knowledge.

In this section we specify the different graph entities to offer the integrated representation. This is done mainly by establishing specific attributes to our graph entities.

Definition 24.54 *A* **complex graph entity** $e \in E$ *of label* $s = \sigma(e)$ *is a tuple* $e = (e_{imp}, e_{exp}, e_{body}, e_i, e_e, e_{vis}, e_{user})$, *with*

- e_{imp} *is a set of* **import pegs,**
- e_{exp} *is a set of* **export pegs,**
- $e_{body} \neq \emptyset$ *is a set of alternative graphs, called* **detailed graphs** *of* e,
- $e_i : e_{imp} \to e_{body}$ *and* $e_e : e_{body} \to e_{exp}$ *are* **import/export attaching functions,**
- e_{vis} *is a set of* **visibility specifications,**
- e_{user} *is a set of user defined informations/attributes.*

An **atomic graph entity** $e \in E$ *is a tuple* $e = (e_{imp}, e_{exp}, e_{body}, e_i, e_e, e_{vis}, e_{user})$, *with*

- e_{imp}, e_{exp}, e_i, e_e, e_{vis}, *and* e_{user} *as above,*
- $e_{body} \neq \emptyset$ *is a set of alternative nodes, called* **basics** *of* e.

Note that the body of a graph entity is not directly coupled to the export part but uses an intermediate *interface part*. In this way, specifications may be developed independently from each other and mapping of required import resources to actually existing export resources may be done afterwards by means of relations.

e_{user} are user defined attributes usable in the information specifications to pass, verify and/or generate any kind of information. External domains, like arithmetic, etc., are integrated in our formalism by using these attributes and the information specifications.

In distributed applications it is important to have a kind of *information hiding principle*, that is, a set of visibility specifications, realized by e_{vis}. Any graph entity has its own private state, that is, its information may be declared as invisible for a set of users and visible for another set of users such as, for example, the access mode in UNIX.

24.7 References

[1] Berge, C., (1991). *Graphs*, 3rd edition. North-Holland.

[2] Christofides, N., (1975). *Graph Theory: An Algorithmic Approach.* New York: Academic Press.

[3] Harary, F., (1972). *Graph Theory.* Reading, MA: Addison-Wesley.

[4] Thulasiraman, K. and Swamy, M. N. S., (1992). *Graphs: Theory and Algorithms.* New York: Wiley-Interscience.

[5] Whitney, H., (1932). The coloring of graphs. *Ann. Math.*, **2**(33):688–718.

[6] Whitney, H., (1932). Non-separable and planar graphs. *Trans. Amer. Math. Soc.*, **34**:339–362.

[7] Ballard, D. and Brown, C., (1982). *Computer Vision.* Englewood Cliffs, NJ: Prentice-Hall.

[8] Haralick, R. M. and Shapiro, L. G., (1991). Glossary of computer vision terms. *Pattern Recognition*, **24**(1):69–93.

[9] Kovalevsky, V. A., (1989). Finite topology as applied to image analysis. *Computer vision, graphics and image processing*, **46**:141–161.

[10] Willersinn, D., (1995). *Dual Irregular Pyramids.* Number 377 in VDI Fortschrittsberichte, Reihe 10. VDI Verlag.

[11] Aurenhammer, F., (1991). Voronoi diagrams—a survey of a fundamental geometric data structure. *ACM Computing Surveys*, **33**(3):345–405.

[12] Møller, J., (1994). Lectures on random Voronoi tessellations. In *Lecture Notes in Statistics*, Vol. 87. New York: Springer.

[13] Okabe, A., Boots, B., and Sugihara, K., (1992). *Spatial Tesselations: Concept and Applications of the Voronoi Diagram.* New York: John Wiley and Sons.

[14] Boissonnat, J.-D. and Yvinec, M., (1995). *Géométrie Algorithmique.* Paris: Ediscience international.

[15] Edelsbrunner, H., (1988). Algorithms in combinatorial geometry. In *Texts and Monographs in Computer Science.* New York: Springer.

[16] Preparata, F. and Shamos, M., (1988). *Computational Geometry, an Introduction.* New York: Springer.

[17] Knuth, D., (1973). *The Art of Computer Programming. Volume III: Sorting and Searching.* Reading, MA: Addison Wesley.

[18] Bollobas, B., (1990). *Graph Theory: An Introductory Course.* Berlin, Heidelberg, New York, Tokyo: Springer.

[19] Mäntylä, M. J., Sulonen, R., and Gutwin, C., (1982). A solid modeler with Euler operators. *IEEE Comput. Graph. Appl.*, **2**:17–31.

[20] Lee, D. and Schachter, B., (1980). Two algorithms for constructing the Delaunay triagulation. *Int J. Comp. Inf. Science*, **3**:219–242.

[21] Sibson, R., (1978). Locally equiangular triangulations. *The Computer Journal*, **21**:243–245.

[22] Keil, M. and Gutwin, C., (1989). The Delaunay triangulation closely approximates the complete Euclidean graph. In *Lecture Notes in Computer Science*, G. Goos and J. Hartmanis, ed., Vol. 382. Berlin, Heidelberg, New York: Springer.

[23] Chew, P., (1986). There is a planar graph almost as good as the complete graph. In *Proc. of the* 2nd *Symposium on Computational Geometry, The Hague*, pp. 169–177. Yorktown Heights, NY: ACM.

[24] Baccelli, F., Tchoumatchenko, K., and Zuyev, S., (1998). *Markov Paths on the Poisson-Delaunay Graph.* Technical Report 3420, INRIA, Sophia Antipolis.

[25] Baumgart, B., (1975). A polyhedron representation for computer vision. In *IFIPS Conference Proceedings*, Vol. 44, pp. 589–596. Amsterdam: North Holland.

[26] Hoffmann, C., (1989). *Geometric and Solid Modelling - An Introduction.* San Mateo: Morgan Kaufmann Pub.

[27] Green, P. and Sibson, R., (1978). Computing Dirichlet tessellation in the plane. *Computer Journal*, **21**:168–173.

[28] Elbaz, M., (1992). *Sur les diagrammes de Voronoï et de Delaunay dans le plan et dans l'espace.* PhD thesis, Université de Haute Alsace.

[29] Mauss, A., (1984). Delaunay triangulation and the convex hull of N points in expected linear time. *BIT*, **24**:151–163.

[30] Bertin, E. and Chassery, J.-M., (1991). Diagramme de Voronoï 3D: Construction et applications en imagerie 3D. In *Proc. du* 8ème *Congrès RFIA, AFCET-INRIA ed., Lyon-Villeurbanne*, pp. 803–808.

[31] Bowyer, A., (1981). Computing Dirichlet tessellation. *Computer Journal*, **24**(2):162–166.

[32] Watson, D., (1981). Computing the n-dimensional Delaunay tessellation with application to Voronoi polytopes. *Computer Journal*, **24**(2):167–172.

[33] Preston, K. and Siderits, R., (1992). New techniques for three-dimensional data analysis in histopatology. *Analytical and Quantitative Cytology and Histology*, **14**(5):398–406.

[34] Ahuja, N., An, B., and Schachter, B., (1985). Image representation using Voronoi tessellation. *Computer Vision, Graphics, and Image Processing*, **29**:286–295.

[35] Bertin, E., Parazza, F., and Chassery, J.-M., (1993). Segmentation and measurement based on 3D Voronoi diagram: application to confocal microscopy. *Special Issue in Computerized Medical Imaging and Graphics*, **17**(3):175–182.

[36] Chassery, J.-M. and Melkemi, M., (1991). Diagramme de Voronoï appliqué à la segmentation d'images et à la détection d'évenements en imagerie multi-source. *Traitement du Signal*, **8**(3):155–164.

[37] Bertin, E., Bischof, H., and Bertolino, P., (1996). Voronoi Pyramid controlled by Hopfield Neural Networks. *Computer Vision and Image Understanding*, **63**(3):462–475.

[38] Willersinn, D., Bertin, E., and Kropatsch, W., (1994). *Dual Irregular Voronoi Pyramids and Segmentation.* Technical Report PRIP-TR-27, PRIP, TU Wien.

[39] Davoine, F., Bertin, E., and Chassery, J.-M., (1997). A flexible partitionning scheme for fractal image compression. *Fractals*, **5**:243–256.

[40] Eils, R., Bertin, E., Saracoglu, K., Rinke, B., Schröck, E., Parazza, F., Robert-Nicoud, Y. U. M., Stelzer, E., Chassery, J.-M., Cremer, T., and Cremer, C., (1995). Morphology of territories of chromosome X and 7 in amniotic fluid cell nuclei determined by laser confocal sectioning and 3D Voronoi diagrams. *Jour. Microscopy*, **177**(2):150–161.

[41] Eils, R., Dietzel, S., Bertin, E., Schröck, E., Speicher, M., Ried, T., Robert-Nicoud, M., Cremer, C., and Cremer, T., (1996). Three-dimensional reconstruction of painted human interphase chromosomes : active and inactive X-chromosome territories have similar volumes but differ in shape and surface structure. *The Journal of Cell Biology*, **135**(6):1427–1440.

[42] Parazza, F., Bertin, E., Wozniack, Z., and Usson, Y., (1995). Tools for the analysis of the spatial distribution of AgNor using simultaneous confocal laser fluorescence and transmitted light microscopy. *Jour. Microscopy*, **178**(3):521–560.

[43] Bertin, E., Billiot, J.-M., and Drouilhet, R., (1997). *Spatial Delaunay Gibbs point processes.* Technical Report RR-97-1, Université Pierre Mendès France, LABSAD.

[44] Bertin, E., Billiot, J.-M., and Drouilhet, R., (1998). Existence of "Nearest-Neighbour" Gibbs point models. *Advances in Applied Probability*, **31(4)**: accepted.

[45] Honda, H., (1978). Description of cellular patterns by Dirichlet domains: the two dimensional case. *J. Theor. Biol.*, **75**:523–543.

[46] Marcelpoil, R. and Bertin, E., (1993). Cellules en Société. *Science et Vie*, **184**:68–74.

[47] Marcelpoil, R. and Usson, Y., (1992). Methods for the study of cellular sociology: Voronoi diagrams and parametrization of the spatial relationships. *Jour. Theor. Biol.*, **154**:359–369.

[48] van Leeuwen, J., (1990). *Handbook of Theoretical Computer Science*, Vol. A, Algorithms and Complexity, chapter 10 Graph Algorithms, pp. 525–632. Amsterdam: Elsevier.

[49] Garey, M. R. and Johnson, D. S., (1979). *Computers and Intractability: A Guide to the Theory of NP-Completeness.* New York: W.H. Freeman and Company.

[50] Ambler, A. P., Barrow, H. G., Brown, C. M., Burstall, R. M., and Popplestone, R. J., (1973). A versatile computer-controlled assembly system. In *Proceedings of the 3rd International Conference on Artificial Intelligence, Stanford, California*, pp. 298–307. Menlo Park, CA: Stanford Research Institute.

[51] Barrow, H. G. and Burstall, R. M., (1976). Subgraph isomorphism, matching relational structures, and maximal cliques. *Information Processing Letters*, **4**(4):83–84.

[52] Horaud, R. and Skordas, T., (1989). Stereo correspondence through feature grouping and maximal cliques. *IEEE Trans. Pattern Analysis and Machine Intelligence*, **11**(11):1168–1180.

[53] Lohmann, G. and von Cramon, D. Y., (1998). Automatic detection and labeling of the human cortical folds in magnetic resonance data sets. In *5th European Conference on Computer Vision, Proceedings Volume II*, H. Burkhardt and B. Neumann, eds., number 1407 in Lecture Notes in Computer Science, pp. 369–381. Freiburg: Springer.

[54] Ogawa, H., (1986). Labeled point pattern matching by Delaunay triangulation and maximal cliques. *Pattern Recognition*, **19**:35–40.

[55] Pla, F. and Marchant, J. A., (1997). Matching feature points in image sequences through a region-based method. *Computer Vision and Image Understanding*, **66**:271–285.

[56] Radig, B., (1984). Image sequence analysis using relational structure. *Pattern Recognition*, **17**:161–167.

[57] Venkateswar, V. and Chellappa, R., (1995). Hierarchical stereo and motion correspondence using feature groupings. *International Jour. Computer Vision*, **15**:245–269.

[58] Yang, B., Snyder, W. E., and Bilbro, G. L., (1989). Matching oversegmented 3D images using association graphs. *Image and Vision Computing*, **7**: 135–143.

[59] Pelillo, M., Siddiqi, K., and Zucker, S. W., (1998). Matching hierarchical structures using association graphs. In *5th European Conference on Computer Vision, Proceedings Volume II*, H. Burkhardt and B. Neumann, eds., number 1407 in Lecture Notes in Computer Science, pp. 3–16. Freiburg: Springer.

[60] Kreowski, H.-J. and Rozenberg, G., (1990). On structured graph grammars I. *Information Sciences*, **52**:185–210.

[61] Corradini, A. and Montanari, U. (eds.), (1995). *Joint COMPUGRAPH/SEMAGRAPH Workshop on Graph Rewriting and Computation, Vol. 2*, Electronic Notes in Theoretical Computer Science, Volterra / Pisa, Italy.

[62] Cuny, J. J. et al. (eds.), (1996). *Graph grammars and their application to computer science: 5th international workshop, Williamsburg, VA, USA, November 13-18, 1994: selected papers*, Vol. 1073 of *Lecture Notes in Computer Science*, New York, NY. Springer.

[63] Kreowski, H.-J. and Rozenberg, G., (1990). On structured graph grammars II. *Information Sciences*, **52**:221–246.

[64] Taentzer, G., (1994). Hierarchically distributed graph transformations. In *Proceedings of the 5th International Workshop on Graph Grammars and their Application to Computer Science*, pp. 430–435. Berlin, New York: Springer.

[65] Drobot, V., (1989). *Formal Language and Automata Theory.* Rockville, MD: Computer Science Press.

25 Shape Reconstruction from Volumetric Data

Roland Eils[1] and Kurt Sätzler[2,1]

[1]Interdisziplinäres Zentrum für Wissenschaftliches Rechnen (IWR)
Universität Heidelberg, Germany
[2]Max-Planck-Institut für Medizinische Forschung, Heidelberg, Germany

25.1 Introduction

Virtually all objects in life sciences are 3-D. Imaging techniques such as light microscopy, electron microscopy or x-ray tomography provide a sequence of 2-D serial cross sections through those 3-D objects. The problem is to reconstruct the 3-D shape from the set of serial sections. The shape representation should allow a rapid 3-D display, the simulation of arbitrary cuts and the analysis of geometrical parameters of the object. This problem is similar to image sequence analysis, where an

Handbook of Computer Vision and Applications
Volume 2
Signal Processing and Pattern Recognition

Copyright © 1999 by Academic Press
All rights of reproduction in any form reserved.
ISBN 0-12-379772-1/$30.00

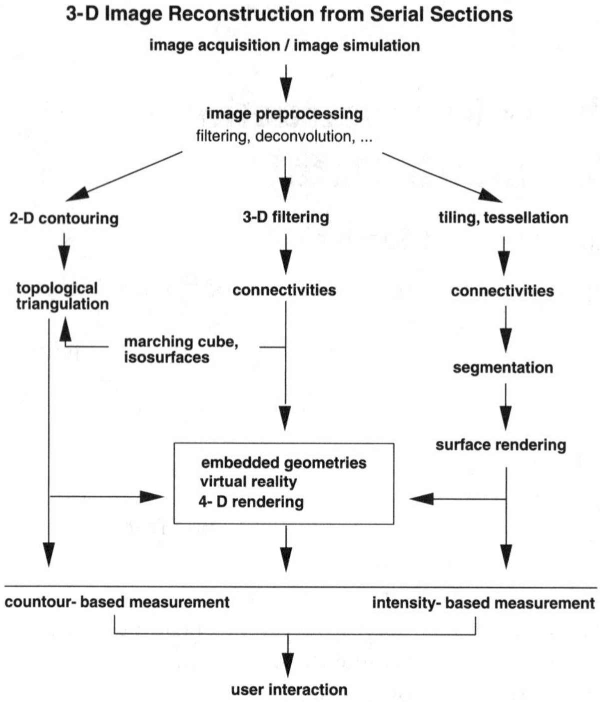

Figure 25.1: *Three different approaches to shape reconstruction from serial sections.*

object needs to be reconstructed in time space. The problem of matching different time images, interpolation of movement and deformation of objects can be considered as a 3-D shape reconstruction problem.

Several solutions to the shape reconstruction problem have been proposed in the literature. Basically, three different classes of shape reconstruction approaches can be identified (Fig. 25.1). In the first class, the 3-D image data stack is considered to be built up by a set of independent serial sections. This situation occurs in applications where the object is physically sectioned as in electron microscopy. The problem is then to first extract a contour of the object of interest in each of the sections. The shape reconstruction problem may be considered as a spatial interpolation problem. Based on topological considerations, the 3-D triangulation of the object based on the 2-D contour information needs to be constructed.

In the second class of shape reconstruction approaches, the image volume is considered as a continuous space made up by image voxels. This situation occurs in applications where the object is optically sectioned as in light microscopy. Due to the optical imaging properties, the different sections must not be considered independently, as each section contains additional information from the section below and above it (see Volume 1, Section 21.4.1). In this case; the problem is to find surfaces within the continuous image space. This problem is referred to as the *tiling* or *tessellation* problem.

A third class of algorithms is closely related to the tiling approach. Instead of finding surfaces in the continuous image space, the object is first segmented into sets of connected voxels by appropriate filtering techniques. The problem is then to extract and follow the faces of the voxels on the object boundary. Based on combinatorial considerations on boundary voxels, object surfaces are constructed (marching cube algorithms, for review see Watt and Watt [1]). This class of algorithms has been extensively used for shape reconstruction in computer tomography.

In this chapter, a unified geometrical concept to solve the shape reconstruction problem from serial sections is presented. The shape reconstruction approach is based on the *Voronoi diagram* and its dual *Delaunay graph* (for a detailed description of these structures in computer vision see Section 24.4). The Delaunay construction, given a set of points, decomposes the m-dimensional Euclidean space into non-overlapping spacefilling *simplexes*. Thus, the space is tessellated using tiles that are identical to each other up to linear transformations. The Voronoi construction decomposes the space into polyhedral cells of much less uniform character with variable number of faces. The concept of Voronoi diagrams, however, is simple and appealingly intuitive. Given a finite set of distinct, isolated points in the Euclidean space of m dimensions, all locations in that space are associated with the closest (not necessarily unique) member of this set. These two structures, the Delaunay and the Voronoi construction, are mutually dual: Two points are joint in the Delaunay tessellation if and only if their respective Voronoi polyhedra share an $(m-1)$-dimensional face.

Voronoi diagrams have been exploited in numerous fields of applications including crystallography, astronomy, urban planning and also in mathematics, particularly in combinatorics and computational geometry. In this chapter, we will show how Voronoi diagrams might be used to solve the shape reconstruction problems of types I and II (see preceding text). This approach provides a powerful instrument for rapid shape reconstruction and quantitative evaluation of serially sectioned objects. In Section 25.3, an approach to shape reconstruction from serial sections based on 2-D contours (shape reconstruction problem I) is described, whereas in Section 25.4 an approach to volumetric shape reconstruction in continuos image space (shape reconstruction problem II) is presented. Both shape reconstruction approaches will be illustrated by applications in the field of biology. This chapter will conclude with a discussion of the different shape reconstruction approaches in Section 25.5.

25.2 Incremental approach

Among many other methods, the incremental method is one of the most important and efficient methods for the computation of Voronoi diagrams (Section 25.2; for comprehensive review see Okabe et al. [2]). Although its worst-case time complexity is $O(n^2)$ for the computation of planar Voronoi diagrams, its average time complexity can be reduced to $O(n)$ by applying algorithmic techniques such as the bucketing method. Hence, it is optimal in an average sense and has outperformed $O(n \log n)$-methods as the divide-and-conquer method.

The basic idea of the incremental method is subsequently to add new seeds into the Voronoi diagram (see Fig. 24.18). This is done by first finding the nearest neighbor of the new seed in the set of generators of the previous step (i. e., the Voronoi polygon in which the new generator is located; compare Step 1 in Algorithm 25.1). In the second step, the Voronoi diagram is updated in the neighborhood of the nearest generator (compare Algorithm 25.3). Precisely, let $\mathcal{V}_{l-1}$ be the Voronoi diagram of the $(l-1)$ generators $p_1, p_2, \ldots, p_{l-1}$. Then, the Voronoi diagram $\mathcal{V}_l$ of the $(l-1)$ and the new generator p_l is created as follows:

Algorithm 25.1 (Incremental method)

Input: Voronoi diagram $\mathcal{V}_{l-1}$ and new generator p_l

Output: Voronoi diagram $\mathcal{V}_l$

Procedure: Step 1. Search for the Voronoi polyhedron in which the new generator is located, that is, search for the generator point p_i, $i \in \{1 \ldots l-1\}$ being closest to the new generator p_l.

Step 2. To obtain $\mathcal{V}_l$ modify the Voronoi diagram $\mathcal{V}_{l-1}$ in a neighborhood of p_i by inserting the new generator p_l.

The main part of the incremental method is Step 2, which will be described in further detail in Algorithm 25.3. Step 1 of the incremental method can be done by:

Algorithm 25.2 (Nearest neighbor search)

Input: l generators $p_1, p_2, \ldots, p_l$, Voronoi diagram $\mathcal{V}_{l-1}$ and initial guess p_k, $k \in \{1 \ldots l-1\}$

Output: the generator p_i, $i \in \{1 \ldots l-1\}$ being closest to p_l

Procedure: Step 1. In the set of adjacent generators of p_k find the generator p_j with minimum distance to p_l

Step 2. If $d(p_k, p_l) \le d(p_j, p_l)$ return p_k, else $p_k \leftarrow p_j$ and go to step 1.

Obviously, the preceding algorithm terminates in finite time with the closest generator p_i of p_l. The worst-case time complexity of the algorithm is $O(l)$, because any of the l generators will be visited at most once. The average time required by the preceding algorithm, however, strongly depends on the choice of the initial guess. A good initial guess may be achieved with quaternary tree bucketing (see Ohya et al. [3] for a 2-D solution). Applying this approach, the average time complexity of the nearest neighbor search is reduced to $O(1)$.

Step 2 of the incremental method can be completed by the *boundary growing procedure* (see the algorithm that follows, which is given in a "pseudo" programming language). The algorithm is explained for the 2-D case, but can be easily transferred to the 3-D case [4, 5]. The main idea of this method is to divide the vertices of the Voronoi diagram of the former step into two classes:

The class of vertices that are closer to the new generator than to any other generator and the class of vertices that are closer to one of the old generators than to the new one (open circles in Fig. 24.18). The first set of vertices will be suppressed as they fall into the Voronoi polygon defined by the new generator. Accordingly, the set of edges is divided into three classes: The first class consists of edges that are incident to vertices which are to be suppressed (e.g., e_1 in Fig. 24.18). These edges will also be suppressed in the new Voronoi diagram. The corresponding generating seeds of these edges will not be neighbors in the new Voronoi diagram, as their common edge was suppressed (e.g., s_1 and s_2 in Fig. 24.18).

The second class consists of edges that are not incident to any of the suppressed vertices (e.g., e_2 in Fig. 24.18). These edges will be retained and the neighborhood relationship between the corresponding generating seeds will not be changed. The third class consists of hybrid edges, that is, edges that are incident to one vertex to be suppressed and one to be retained (e.g., s_3 in Fig. 24.18). These edges will be changed during the update of the Voronoi diagram, as one of the incident vertices is to be suppressed. However, the corresponding generating seeds of these edges will remain neighbors in the new Voronoi diagram.

Algorithm 25.3 (Boundary growing procedure)

Input: Voronoi diagram $\mathcal{V}(P_{l-1})$

Output: Voronoi diagram $\mathcal{V}(P_l)$

Step 1 Current generator p = nearest generator to p_l. The vertices of polygon of the current generator which are closer to p_l have to be suppressed [6].

Step 2 Divide the set of vertices of the current polygon $V(p)$ into two sets: The set of vertices $\mathcal{I}$ that have to be suppressed and the set of vertices that have to be kept.

Step 3 Insert the current generator p into the list of already treated generators.

Step 4 **For all** neighbors $\tilde{p}$ of the current generator which do not appear in the list of already treated generators **do**

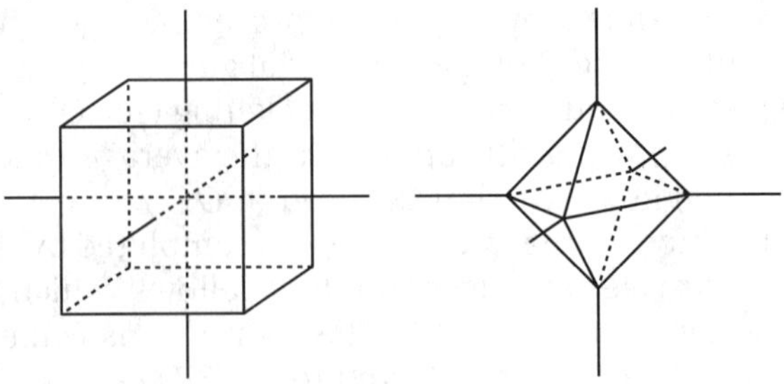

Figure 25.2: *Illustration of the initializing configuration of a 3-D Voronoi diagram: Left: Eight generators are placed at the vertices of a cube circumscribing the convex hull of P. Right: The resulting first polyhedron is created by a generator inside the cube. This polyhedron is bounded.*

Step 4a Intersect the two sets $V(p)$ (set of points of the current generator) and $V(\tilde{p})$ (set of points of the neighboring generator): $V(p) \cap V(\tilde{p}) = (A_1, A_2)$. In 3-D, the intersection would be a polygon, whereas in 2-D one directly obtains an edge. Thus, in 3-D the algorithm has to branch in order to decide which edges of the polygon constitute the new polyhedron $V(\tilde{p})$.

Step 4b **If** ($\mathcal{I} \supseteq V(p) \cap V(\tilde{p})$) **then** p and $\tilde{p}$ are no longer neighbors. The common edge between p and $\tilde{p}$ is to be suppressed; thus, p and $\tilde{p}$ are no longer neighbors.

Step 4c **elseif** ($\mathcal{I} \not\supseteq V(p) \cap V(\tilde{p})$ **and** $V(\tilde{p}) \cap \mathcal{I} \neq \emptyset$) **then** One of the vertices of the intersection edge is to be suppressed, whereas the other one is to be kept.

Step 4d Insert $\tilde{p}$ in the list of generators to be treated.

Step 4e The new vertex is calculated as the intersection between the line (A_1, A_2) and the medial line between p_l and p. This new point is added to the list of vertices of $V(p_l)$. The new generator p_l is assigned neighbor of p and $\tilde{p}$ and vice versa.

Step 5 Continue while the list of generators to be treated is not empty.

The above algorithm only works well for bounded polyhedra. To avoid exceptional branching within the algorithm, all polyhedra are forced to be finite using a simple trick: Recalling that a Voronoi polyhedron is infinite if and only if the respective generator is on the boundary of the convex hull $CH(P)$ spanning the set of generators P. Thus, by adding artificial generators in the background (i.e., sufficiently far away from the convex hull), the only infinite polyhedra will be those of the artificial generators, whereas all other polyhedra are bounded. For this purpose four initial generators are added in 2-D such that all generators to be added are placed within the convex hull of the four initial generators. In 3-D eight initial generators are added, which lie on the vertices of a cube circumscribing the convex hull of P (compare Fig. 25.2).

The time complexity of the region growing procedure obviously depends on the size of the substructure that has to be deleted. As the average number of vertices of a 2-D Voronoi polygon is six or less (recall Section 24.5), one could expect that the size of structure to be deleted should be constant. However, under certain conditions the number of vertices to be deleted might depend on the number of generators. Thus, to restrict the average size of the substructure to be constant, one has to take care that before starting the incremental method the generators are reordered in such a way that they are as uniformly distributed as possible. For this purpose, the bucketing technique may also be applied. Ohya et al. [3, 7]) showed that the construction of the quaternary tree and the reordering of the generators can be done in linear time. In addition, the nearest neighbor search method as well as the deletion of the substructure can be expected to be completed in $O(1)$ time applying the bucketing method. Thus, in total the average time complexity of the incremental method could be reduced from $O(n^2)$ to $O(n)$.

25.3 Three-dimensional shape reconstruction from contour lines

In this section the 3-D image data stack is considered to be built up by a set of independent serial sections. The shape reconstruction problem may then be considered as an interpolation problem between the extracted contours in each individual section. Based on topological considerations, the 3-D triangulation of the object based on the 2-D contour information needs to be constructed.

Several solutions have been proposed in the literature. In Keppel [8] and Fuchs et al. [9] the problem is reduced to the reconstruction of a sequence of surfaces between each pair of adjacent contours. The surfaces are constructed as elementary triangles between two vertices on one contour and another vertex on the adjacent contour. It can be shown that this shape reconstruction problem is equivalent to the search of a path in a directed graph. Associating a weight to the edges of that graph a classical shortest path algorithm will produce an optimal shape reconstruction (for review of different choices of weights see Boissonnat [10]). Because of the existence of different weights this shape reconstruction approach was used in a wide range of applications. However, it was pointed out in Sloan and Hrechanyk [11] that the tiling algorithms are not suited for the shape reconstruction of objects with rapid topological changes. For example the shape reconstruction of a convex contour in one plane and a spiral like contour in the adjacent plane would result in a surface intersecting itself. In addition, this approach cannot handle the topologically important case of (multiple) hierachical contours (see Section 25.3.3).

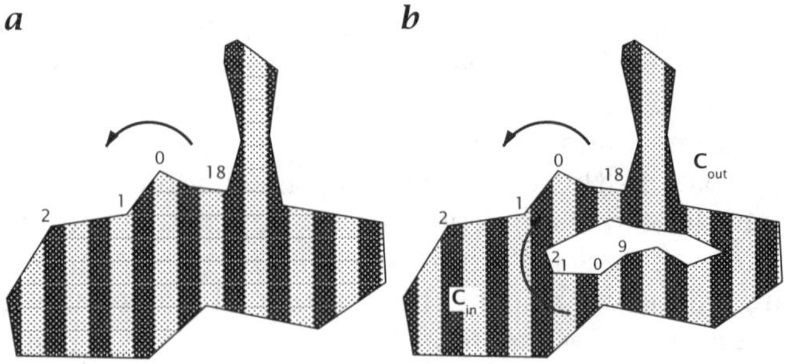

Figure 25.3: ***a*** *Representation of a cross-sectional contour and the neighborhood on the contour specifying inside and outside of the shape by the sense of orientation;* ***b*** *hierarchically structured contours: The two contours are topologically connected contours, as they contribute to the surface of one and the same object.*

Here we will present an alternative approach based on the Delaunay graph for 3-D shape reconstruction of serial contour data first suggested by Boissonnat [10]. The principal idea is to compute a tetrahedral representation of the object. The object will be reconstructed section by section. The contour vertices will suit as Voronoi seeds. The Voronoi diagram and its dual Delaunay graph are then computed by a split-and-merge approach described in Section 25.4.2. The set of intermediate reconstructions from each pair of neighboring contours will be combined into a final shape reconstruction. Contours that mark the start or end of a bifurcation and thus do not show an overlap in two consecutive sections will not be linked in the reconstruction (Fig. 25.4). This approach not only provides a triangulated surface of the reconstructed object but also a volumetric representation of the reconstructed object.

25.3.1 Topological prerequisites

First we need to formalize the contour definition to obtain the correct topological representation of the sectioned object. A contour is defined as a closed, cyclic and planar polygon circumscribing the object of interest. This definition induces a bidirectional neighborhood on the contour.

Note that the object might include holes or complicated bifurcations (see Fig. 25.3). Since *inside* and *outside* of a sectioned object is given by the sense of orientation of the contour vertices, holes are given an inverse sense of orientation as the regular outlining contours (see Fig. 25.3).

With these topological prerequisites the Voronoi diagram and its dual structure, the Delaunay graph, may be computed for the set of

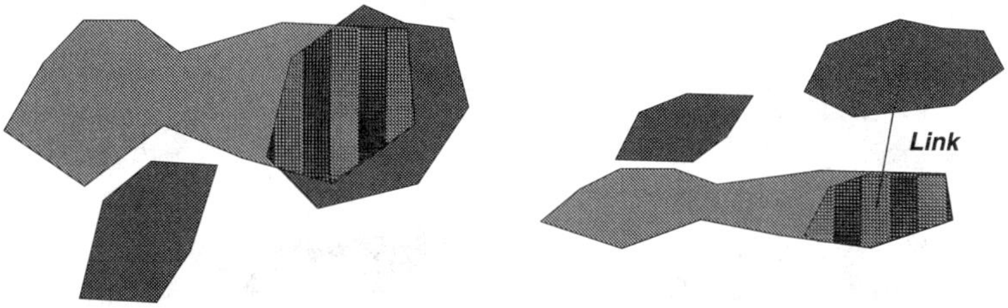

Figure 25.4: *Schematic representation of overlapping contours: Two contours that show an overlap when being projected on each other will be linked. Left: top view; right: side view.*

contour vertices taken as Voronoi seeds. However, when reconstructing the 3-D object by the Delaunay approach neighboring vertices on the contours also need to be neighbors in the Delaunay graph. It was shown [10] that this condition can be met for arbitrary contour lines by adding a finite number of vertices to the contour. Hence, in the following we will assume that neighboring vertices on the contour will also be neighbors in the Delaunay graph.

25.3.2 Classification of tetrahedra

For each pair of consecutive sections the Voronoi diagram is computed on the set of contour vertices as Voronoi seeds. By this a tetrahedrization of the 3-D image space made up by two serial sections is obtained. In order to extract objects in the Delaunay tetrahedrization the Delaunay tetrahedra have to be classified as *in* or *out*. Inside tetrahedra constitute to the object while outside tetrahedra belong to the background. The object surface is made up by triangular facets between *in* and *out* tetrahedra. Furthermore, the direction of the surface normal is given by the sense of orientation on the contours.

In this subsection we will deal only with the case of simple contours, that is, a contour does not contain holes. The more general case of hierachical contours will be dealt with in the following subsection. For a classification of tetrahedra as *in* or *out* we first distinguish four intermediate classes of tetrahedra (Fig. 25.5):

1. exactly three out of the four vertices of a tetrahedron belong to one and the same contour;
2. two pairs of vertices of a tetrahedron belong to two different contours;
3. two vertices belong to one contour, the remaining two vertices belong to two different contours; and
4. all four vertices belong to different contours.

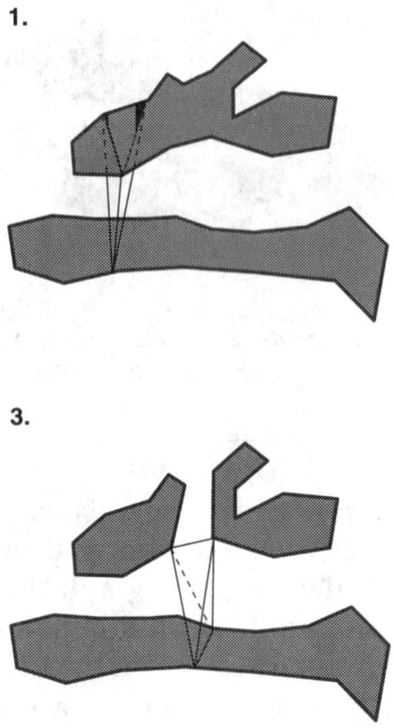

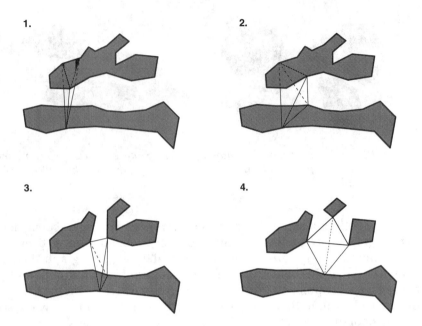

Figure 25.5: *Four classes of Delaunay tetrahedra.*

A final classification of tetrahedra as *in* or *out* will then be achieved on the basis of the intermediate classification specified here and the following additional conditions:

1. Tetrahedra of class 1: If the triangle defined by the three contour vertices lies within the contour, then the tetrahedron will be considered as *in* (else *out*).
2. Tetrahedra of class 2: the two pairs of contour vertices form an edge. We now have to distinguish the following cases:
   (a) The two vertices are neighbors on the contour, that is, the edge is part of the contour polygon. Those tetrahedra are indefinite and will be classified by an iterative approach. The set of indefinite tetrahedra will be iteratively visited. Each tetrahedron having two or more neighboring inside tetrahedra will be labeled as inside. The remaining set of still indefinite tetrahedra will be classified as *out*.
   (b) If one of the two edges is inside (or outside) the contour, then the tetrahedron will be considered as *in* (or *out*).
3. Tetrahedra of types 3 and 4 will be considered as *out*.

25.3.3 Generalization for hierarchical contours

In the previous subsection we described only the case of simple contours. Here a generalization to the topologically important case of hierarchical contours induced by holes within the object (Fig. 25.3b) will be provided. In the foregoing classifications the concept of (simple) contours needs to be replaced by the concept of *topologically connected* contours. Two contours are called *topologically connected* if they contribute to the surface of one and the same object.

25.3.4 Refinement of the Delaunay tetrahedrization

The set of contour vertices may not be sufficient to describe rapid topological changes between adjacent contours. Hence the Delaunay surface representation might not lead to an appropriate topological representation of the object shape. Therefore additional points must be inserted into the Delaunay graph. Different approaches to a solution of this interpolation problem have been suggested (see Boissonnat and Geiger [12], Oliva et al. [13]).

Here the 3-D outside skeleton of the initial object is applied to insert additional points for the Delaunay tetrahedrization. The outside skeleton is defined as the set of lines between the Voronoi vertices corresponding to two neighboring outside tetrahedra. If large topological changes occur such as, for example, bifurcations and birth of holes, the outside skeleton intersects the initial object.

The gravity center of the common triangular face between two tetrahedra defined by the intersection criterion was shifted into a medial plane. This new point suits as a new seed for the refined Delaunay tetrahedrization. The result of this process is shown in Fig. 25.6. So called *nonsolid connections* [12], which can be seen in Fig. 25.6a at the border line, can be eliminated by introducing seeds at the medial plane. Therefore a disconnection of the internal skeleton is avoided and the neighborhood structure on the closing planes is not influenced.

25.3.5 Shape reconstruction of multiple cross sections

To reconstruct an object consisting of multiple cross sections, we apply the presented algorithm pairwise to consecutive sections. The reconstructed surface slices are then merged to one object by stacking the surface slices one above another. As we used a Delaunay tetrahedrization of the object and because the triangulated closing plane shared by two consecutive cross sections is identical [10], the neighborhood representation given by the individual surface slices is conserved from one reconstructed slice to the other. The neighborhood information is still conserved after refinement of the Delaunay tetrahedrization by

a *b*

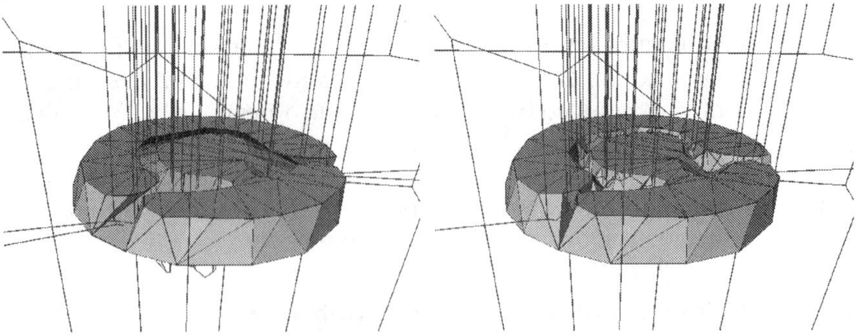

Figure 25.6: ***a*** *The light gray lines represent the 3-D outer skeleton which intersects the object (see small black spots on the surface);* ***b*** *same after adding new seeds.*

adding new seeds in the medial plane (see Fig. 25.6). We can easily link the identical medial surfaces together and therefore get a Delaunay-like neighborhood representation throughout the whole object. Note however that the refined tetrahedrization of the object is generally not a Delaunay type tetrahedrization. Exploiting the neighborhood structure connected components can easily be found and, therefore, volume, surface and Gouraud normals can be computed.

25.3.6 Applications

The reconstruction algorithm for cross-sectional contours was applied to the shape reconstruction of peroxisomes in rat hepatocytes (Fig. 25.8, data obtained from Grabenbauer [14]) or rat brain material (Fig. 25.7, data from Schwegler, University of Magdeburg, FRG). Ultra thin sections of rat liver (approx. 40-60 nm section thickness) were imaged by electron microscopy. The images were digitized and transfered to a Silicon Graphics workstation. After alignment and contouring of serial sections a 3-D shape reconstruction was computed within a few seconds as described in the foregoing text. The reconstructed shapes were displayed online using the Computer Aided Reconstruction software package (MiniCAR, Sätzler and Eils, unpublished).

25.4 Three-dimensional shape reconstruction from volumetric data

In this section the 3-D image volume is considered as a continuous image space (Chapter 2). The shape reconstruction problem is hence to find surfaces within the continuous image space. Here we will describe

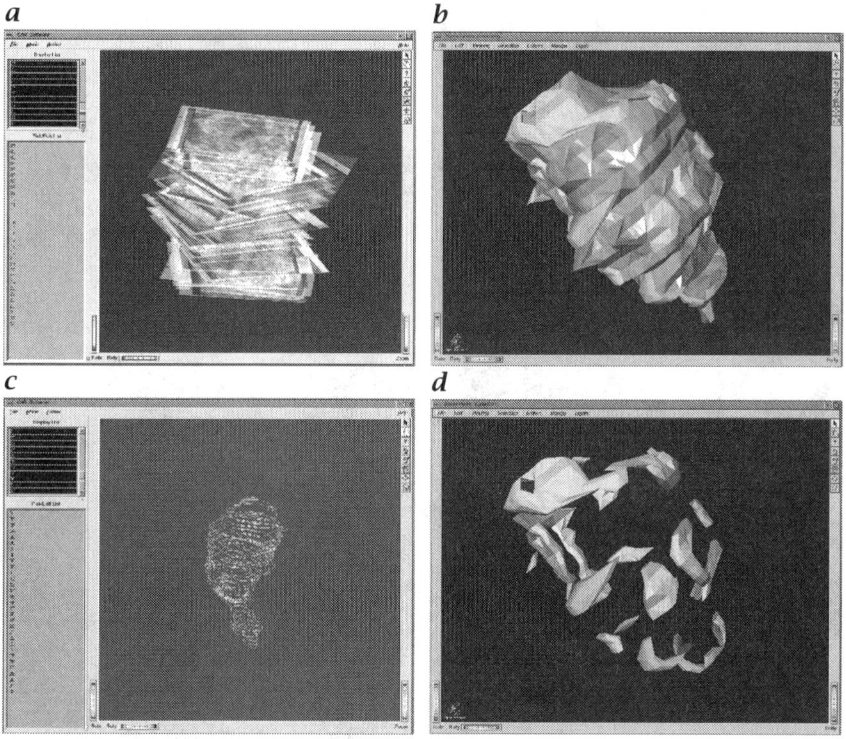

Figure 25.7: ***a*** *Shows a side view of an aligned image stack of electron microscopical sections through a spine;* ***c*** *shows the outlined contours from the spine shown in* ***a*** *and its optical densities (active zones);* ***b*** *shows the shape reconstruction of the spine and its optical densities;* ***d*** *shows the reconstructed shape of the active zones only.*

an approach that is based on the Voronoi diagram. In a first step the image space is subdivided into simple geometric entities, that is, Voronoi polyhedra made up by image voxels with similar image information. Thereafter, objects are segmented as sets of connected polyhedra exploiting the dual Delaunay graph structure. A surface representation as well as morphological parameters such as volume or surface area of segmented objects can be easily extracted from the geometric shape representation. In the following subsection a motivation for the geometric model as an appropriate model for 3-D shape reconstruction of serial sections in light microscopy is given. In Section 25.4.2 a split-and-merge approach to 3-D shape reconstruction will be introduced. In Section 25.4.3 some applications of the split-and-merge approach for quantitative image analysis in cell biology will be given.

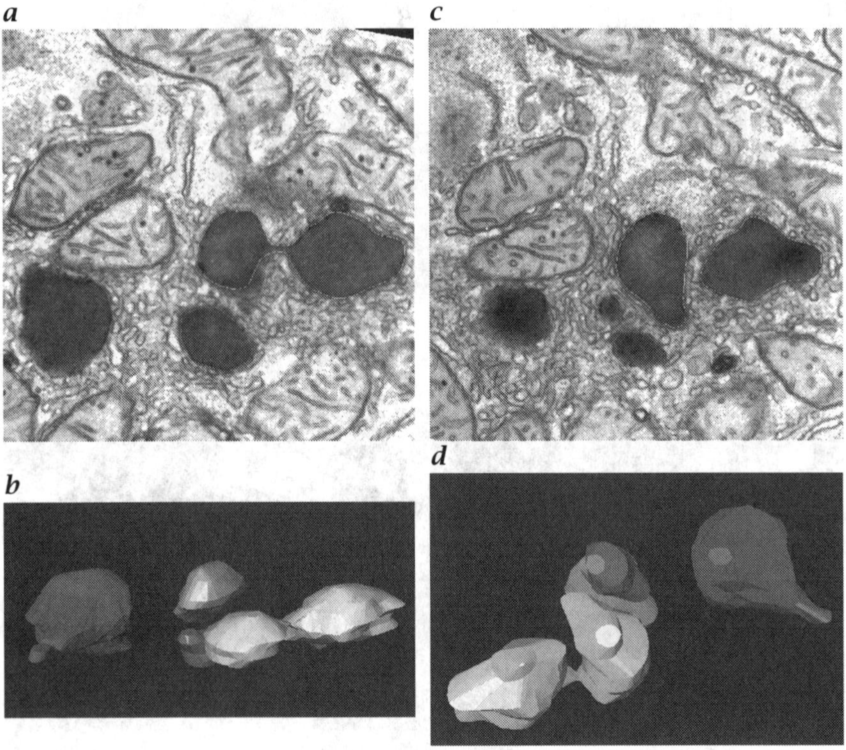

*Figure 25.8: **a** and **b** show serial sections from a rat liver recorded on an electron microscope. The peroxisomes of the rat hepatocytes are outlined; **c** and **d** show two different views of the reconstructed peroxisomes.*

25.4.1 The geometrical model for three-dimensional shape reconstruction of serial sections in light microscopy

In image processing two different approaches to segmentation might be distinguished (see, e.g., Jähne [15]): Point-oriented methods and region-oriented methods. The point-oriented methods decide for each point, regardless of its neighborhood, whether it belongs to the object (*foreground*) or *background*.

In the design of appropriate imaging methods for shape reconstruction of microscopical images one has to consider the following obstacles (see Volume 1, Chapter 21):

- The objects are smeared by the imaging properties of the microscope. This process is usually modeled by a convolution of the original object with the so-called point spread function of the microscope.
- The imaging process induces considerable noise in the image.

- The resolution along the optical axis is worse than in the focal plane.

Although point oriented methods such as thresholding are widely used for segmentation of serial sections in light microscopy, such methods appear to be inappropriate for the following reasons: The histograms of the images usually do not show a bimodal behavior because of the smearing property of the microscopical system. In addition, the biological objects of interest do not have a distinct but a fuzzy boundary. Furthermore, the noisy image structure requires the incorporation of a noise model. These considerations argue for a region-oriented model for image segmentation.

In the next subsection a split-and-merge approach for image segmentation [4, 5, 16, 17, 18] based on the incremental construction of the 3-D Voronoi diagram (see Section 25.2) is presented. The image volume is divided into subunits consisting of Voronoi polyhedra. Each of these subunits represents a volume with a homogeneous gray value distribution, that is, the standard deviation of the gray-value distribution inside the subunit does not exceed the overall standard deviation of the gray-value distribution of the whole image volume. The large amount of image data is thus compressed to a small amount of subunits. Furthermore, the geometrical structure of the polyhedra is well-suited for computational processing. Based on simple geometrical considerations geometrical parameters such as volume or surface area and the distance between different objects (i.e., the distance between two opposing facets) may be easily calculated. Additionally, facets of polyhedra may be easily decomposed into triangles (i.e., the smallest entities in computer graphics), providing the basis for rapid visualization of segmented objects.

25.4.2 The split-and-merge approach for image segmentation

The split-and-merge approach is based on a geometrical model. The basic idea is to partition the image volume consisting of serial sections into convex polyhedra, thus building the 3-D Voronoi diagram. For the decomposition each polyhedron is associated with a generator and each image point (voxel) is assigned to a polyhedron. The neighborhood information is contained in the Delaunay graph, which is dual to the Voronoi graph. The construction of the Voronoi diagram and the dual Delaunay graph follows the incremental approach (compare Algorithm 25.1). With this approach the image guides the evolution of the Voronoi diagram by adding generators in those regions of the image space with a high variance of gray values. As there is no *a priori* knowledge of the location of the generators, the Voronoi diagram must be built dynamically (compare Fig. 25.9):

Algorithm 25.4 *The split-and-merge method*

1. **Split:**
   (a) Initialization:
   In a first step approximately 30-70 generators depending on the size of the image volume are randomly placed in the image space according to a Poisson process. For these initializing generators the Voronoi diagram and the Delaunay graph are built. For each Voronoi polyhedron, parameters such as volume, surface area, mean, and variance of gray values of the voxels (*volume elements*) belonging to the respective polyhedron are calculated. Those parameters are used for further refinement of the tessellation.
   (b) Propagation:
   In the following step, each polyhedron obtained in the previous step is tested for homogeneity. In principle, a wide variety of homogeneity criteria can be chosen. Here a polyhedron is regarded as homogeneous, if one of the following criteria holds:
   - The standard deviation of the gray-value distribution of all voxels belonging to the respective polyhedron is below the overall standard deviation of the gray values of the image volume.
     The *noise* inside a geometrical unit (i.e., a polyhedron) cannot be expected to be smaller than the *noise* in the whole image volume.
   - The volume of the respective polyhedron is below a preset limit.
     The minimum size of a polyhedron is limited as a polyhedron should not be smaller in volume than the smallest unit that can be resolved depending on the resolution of the image acquisition system.

   If a polyhedron is homogeneous within the preset limits it must not be further subdivided and is retained. If a polyhedron is still regarded as being inhomogeneous, a new generator is added at the gravity center of the common facet between two neighboring inhomogeneous generators (for a 2-D demonstration see Fig. 25.10). For the new set of generators the Voronoi diagram and the Delaunay graph are computed. For each Voronoi polyhedron, the preceding described parameters are calculated again.
   (c) Convergence:
   The propagation step is iterated until all polyhedra are regarded as being homogeneous.
   Apparently, the rate of convergence depends on the choice of homogeneity criteria. Robust analytical parameters such as gradient or Laplacian may be added to the variance criteria. Additionally, the surface area of the common facet between adjacent polyhedra could be used to decide whether a further subdivision of these polyhedra is useful.

2. **Merge:**
   If all neighbors of a polyhedron P with generator p are homogeneous and have an almost equal average gray value, then the respective generator p is deleted. This deletion step is described in detail in Bertin and Chassery [16].

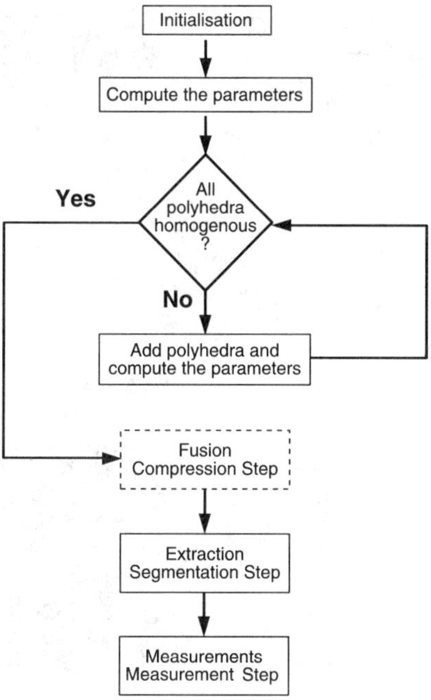

Figure 25.9: *Flowchart of the Split-and-Merge method.*

25.4.3 Segmentation and measurements

In this subsection some applications of the split-and-merge approach to 3-D shape reconstruction and quantitative image analysis are given. After computing the Voronoi diagram the objects of interest such as tessellated chromosome territories have to be segmented in the Voronoi diagram. According to the geometrical model objects are defined as sets of neighboring polyhedra, which are similar according to a chosen similarity criterion. For this purpose the Delaunay graph is modified to a weighted graph in the following way:

Definition 25.1 *The (binary) weighted Delaunay graph*
*Let $\mathcal{D}(P, E_D)$ be a Delaunay graph on the set of generators P with a set of edges E_D. Further, let $\mathcal{V}(P, E_V)$ be the dual Voronoi graph. Each of the Voronoi generators p_i, $i = 1 \dots n$, is assigned to a (characteristic) value by a mapping $f_c : P \mapsto \Re$. Further, let $f_r : f_c(P) \times f_c(P) \mapsto \{0, 1\}$ be a (*similarity*) relation on the pairs of characteristic values of the generators p_i. Then the weighted Delaunay graph $\mathcal{D}_w(P, E_w)$ is obtained from the Delaunay graph $\mathcal{D}$ by assigning all edges $e_l \in E_D$ the value $f_r(f_c(p_i), f_c(p_j))$ where p_i and p_j are incident to the edge e_l. For convenience an edge with the weight 1 (0) will be termed a 1-edge (0-edge), the generators incident to a 1-edge 1-neighbors and a component consisting of only 1-edges a 1-component.*

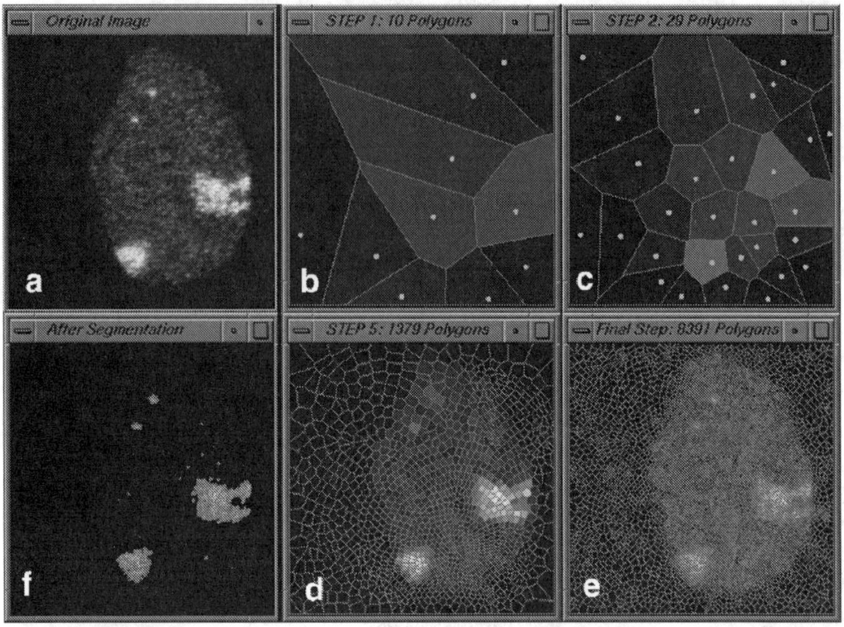

Figure 25.10: *Application of the iterative Voronoi tessellation procedure to one light optical section of a human female cell nucleus with two painted X-territories:* ***a*** *original image of one section of a nucleus with two painted X-chromosomes;* ***b*** *initial Voronoi tessellation. The dots demonstrate the locations of the generating Voronoi seeds. Each image point contained in a polygon is closer to its generating seed than to any other Voronoi seed;* ***c, d*** *Voronoi-tessellation step nos. 2 and 5;* ***e*** *final Voronoi tessellation;* ***f*** *a geometric representation of each object is obtained as a connected component in the weighted Delaunay graph (see Definition 25.1). Note that a 2-D tessellation is demonstrated here for simplicity, while a true 3-D Voronoi tessellation was applied to the stack of light optical serial sections obtained for each nucleus.*

There are several possibilities for choosing the similarity criterion (expressed by f_r), ranging from statistical conditions (e.g., mean, variance or gradient of gray values) to geometrical constraints (e.g., volume, surface, roundness, curvature). In this thesis the characteristic value of a generator p_i is the mean gray value of all image voxels belonging to the respective polyhedron P_i. Furthermore, the relation f_r is defined as follows:

$$f_r(f_c(p_i), f_c(p_j)) = \begin{cases} 0 & : \quad f_c(p_k) < t \quad k = i \vee k = j \\ 1 & : \quad f_c(p_k) \geq t \quad k \in \{i, j\} \end{cases} \tag{25.1}$$

where $t \in \Re$ is a preset (threshold) value. Literally, the foregoing definition means that the edge between two generators is weighted by 0, if the mean gray value of either P_i or P_j (or both P_i and P_j) is less than the preset threshold (i.e., at least one of the two polyhedra assigned to the generators p_i and p_j belongs to the background). Accordingly, a weight 1 of the edge incident to two generators means that both associated polyhedra belong to one and the same foreground object (recall that two generators are neighboring in the Delaunay graph if and only if their associated Voronoi polyhedra share a common edge).

In terms of graph theory the search for neighboring polyhedra with a mean gray value not less than a preset threshold is equivalent to a search for 1-components in the weighted Delaunay graph. (recall Definiton 24.17 for definition of components).

Polyhedra whose generators are 1-neighbors in the weighted Delaunay graph are considered to belong to the same object. Hence, the set of polyhedra in a given 1-component constitutes one object. Starting with an arbitrary generator in the Voronoi diagram fulfilling the constraint (e.g., whose associated mean gray value exceeds the preset threshold), a search for 1-neighbors is performed simultaneously in all directions. Each generator already assigned to an object is labeled to avoid double assignment. For all labeled generators a search for 1-neighbors is performed in the same way giving a 1-component of the weighted Delaunay graph. At this stage, the extraction of the first object is finished. Subsequently, another unlabeled, that is, untreated generator fulfilling the constraint is selected in the Voronoi diagram. For this generator, again a search for a 1-component is performed in the same way as described here, thus yielding the second object. This procedure is iterated until there are no more unlabeled generators fulfilling the constraint (i. e., all 1-components of the Delaunay graph are found):

Algorithm 25.5 *Method for the determination of 1-components in the weighted Delaunay graph*

Input List P of n unlabeled generators; Voronoi diagram $\mathcal{V}(P)$ $i = 0$

Output: k lists of labeled generators P_i (each list corresponds to one 1-component in the Delaunay graph)

Repeat the following steps until all generators are labeled:

Step 1 Increment i

Step 2a Find an unlabeled generator.

Step 2b Assign a label to this generator and insert it into the list P_i

Step 3 Repeat the following step until no more unlabeled 1-neighbors of generators contained in P_i are found.

Step 4 Label and add all unlabeled 1-neighbors of the generators contained in the list P_i to this list.

Note that the forementioned extraction algorithm is very fast, as it basically consists of insertion of generators into the list of components P_i and of labeling of generators, which is done in constant time. Moreover, as any polyhedron can only belong to one and only one object, the average time complexity of the algorithm does not exceed $O(n)$.

In the following the computation of morphological parameters such as volume and surface area of objects extracted in the 3-D Voronoi diagram will be described. To calculate the volume O of this object one simply adds the volume of all polyhedra P_i belonging to this object (i.e., all polyhedra whose associated generators are part of the respective 1-component). The volume $[\mathrm{vol}(P_i)]$ of a single polyhedron is computed by counting all image voxels v whose centers c_v lie inside the polyhedron. The volume $\mathrm{vol}(P_i)$ of a polyhedron P_i is then obtained by multiplying the number of voxels v by the volume vol_{voxel} of a single voxel:

$$[\mathrm{vol}(O)] = \sum_{p_i \in O} [\mathrm{vol}(P_i)] \quad \text{and} \quad [\mathrm{vol}(P_i)] = \sum_{c_v \in P_i} \mathrm{vol}_{\mathrm{voxel}} \tag{25.2}$$

The surface area $\mathrm{surf}(O)$ of an object can be estimated by the sum of surface areas of all facets that constitute to the boundary of the object:

$$[\mathrm{surf}(O)] = \sum_{p_i \in O \text{and incident to a 0-edge}} \mathrm{surface}(p_i, p_j) \tag{25.3}$$

The determination of such facets consists of two steps. In the first step the generators p_i of the object O which are incident to a 0-edge (see the preceding data) are searched. These generators are associated with a polyhedron, which is the neighbor of a polyhedron p_j not belonging to the object and thus shares a common (surface) facet with this background polyhedron. In the second step the common facet $\mathrm{surface}(p_i, p_j)$ is calculated. Finally, the third step decomposes this facet into triangles and the surface areas of the triangles are calculated analytically:

Algorithm 25.6 *Surface area estimation*

Input: Voronoi diagram $\mathcal{V}(P)$ of a set P of unlabeled generators p_i; Object $0 \subset P$

Output: Surface area of the object 0

Repeat the following steps until all generators incident to a 0-edge are labeled:

Step 1 Find and label $p_i \in O$ which is incident to a 0-edge in the weighted Delaunay graph

Step 2 Compute the common facet between the polyhedron associated with the generator p_i found in Step1 and the polyhedron associated with its 0-neighbor.

Step 3 a) Decompose the facets determined in Step 2 into triangles.

b) Compute the surface area of the facet as the sum of the surface areas of its triangles.

c) Add the surface area of the facet to the surface area of the object

25.4.4 Applications

The split-and-merge approach to shape reconstruction has been widely used for image analysis in light microscopy (see, e.g., Eils et al. [17, 18], Dietzel et al. [19, 20], Eils et al. [21]). Here, some applications of the Voronoi tessellation procedure to obtain quantitative morphological data for chromosome territories in human cell nuclei are demonstrated. As a model system, chromosomes 7 and X were visualized in human female amniotic fluid cell nuclei by chromosomal in situ suppression hybridization with chromosome specific composite probes [21]. Chromosome territories were segmented by the split-and-merge approach and visualized on a Silicon Graphics workstation (Fig. 25.11). The morphology of chromosome territories was described by three parameters, that is, volume, surface area, and a roundness factor (shape factor). The complete evaluation of a nucleus including calculation of the Voronoi diagram, 3-D visualization of extracted territories using computer graphical methods, and quantitative image analysis was carried out on a Silicon Graphics workstation in generally less than five min. The geometric information obtained by this procedure revealed that both X- and 7-chromosome territories were similar in volume. Roundness factors indicated a pronounced variability in interphase shape for both pairs of chromosomes. Surface estimates showed a significant difference between the two X-territories but not between chromosome 7-territories [21].

In a second application the 3-D morphology of human X chromosome territories was studied in more detail by a four color experiment [20]. According to this study the bended structure of the inactive X chromosome territory cannot be explained by a tight telomere-telomere association (Fig. 25.11).

25.5 Summary

In this chapter we presented a unified geometrical concept for shape reconstruction from serial sections. This concept was based on a fundamental structure in computational geometry, that is, the Voronoi diagram. In combination with its dual Delaunay graph, the Voronoi diagram provides a powerful tool for shape reconstruction of serial sections and extraction of morphological parameters from the reconstructed objects.

In shape reconstruction problem I we did not have any 3-D structure (such as image voxels). The information about the 3-D object consisted solely of (planar) contours obtained from the cross-sectional images. In this case the shape reconstruction problem can be considered as an interpolation problem between the sequential object contours. Considering the contour points as Voronoi seeds a volumetric representation

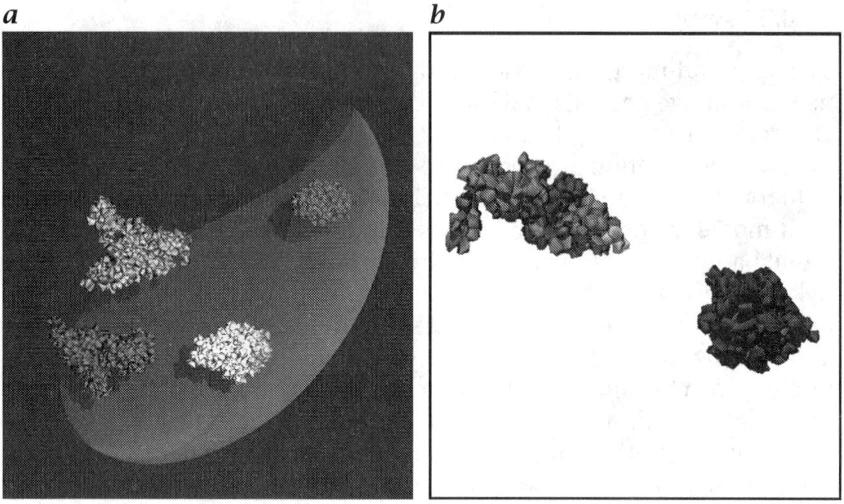

Figure 25.11: ***a*** *Computer graphic visualization of segmented chromosome territories of a typical female, human cell nucleus by ray tracing. The extracted territories have been colored in red (top right domain, X_i), yellow (buttom right, X_a), light blue and dark blue (top and bottom left, 7). The cell nucleus was modeled by an ellipsoid. As the nucleus was not counterstained in this experiment, the size of the ellipsoid reflects the average size of amniotic fluid cell nuclei measured in other experiments;* ***b*** *provide enlarged 3-D reconstruction of two X-territories in a female, human cell nucleus. The centromere region has been colored in magenta, the telomere region (Xpter) of the short arm in light gray and the telomere region (Xqter) of the long arm region in green.*

by Delaunay tetrahedra of the 3-D image volume was obtained. Using the sense of orientation of contour points and the neighborhood information on contours, tetrahedra were classified as *in* or *out*. Objects were then identified as connected sets of inside tetrahedra.

To handle rapid topological changes between two consecutive contours additional intermediate points were inserted using the 3-D *outside skeleton* of the initial object. The outside skeleton was defined as the set of lines between Voronoi vertices corresponding to two neighboring outside tetrahedra. If topological changes occurred as, for example, bifurcations and birth of holes, the outside skeleton intersected the initial object.

The gravity center of the common triangular face between two tetrahedra defined by the intersection criterion was shifted into a medial plane. Using these points as additional Voronoi seeds a refined Delaunay tetrahedrization was computed. With this approach we were able to eliminate nonsolid connections. Hence, objects from planar contours even with large topological changes between sequential contours could be reconstructed in a topologically correct way.

In shape reconstruction problem of type II the object was defined as a set of image voxels. The shape reconstruction problem was then to compute a 3-D Voronoi tessellation of the continuous image space. We used the incremental method for the computation of the 3-D Voronoi diagram. Although its worst-case time complexity is inferior to other methods, it is optimal in an average sense and has thus outperformed other approaches such as the divide-and-conquer method. The basic idea of the incremental method is to subsequently add new seeds into the Voronoi diagram. The Voronoi diagram is updated in a *local* neighborhood of the new generator by an efficient boundary growing procedure. The incremental approach was integrated into a split-and-merge approach to shape reconstruction and segmentation. In a split step the Voronoi tessellation of the 3-D image space is iteratively refined. Thereafter, neighboring *similar* Voronoi polyhedra are merged, thus reducing the complexity of the resulting Voronoi tessellation. Objects were identified as components in the weighted Delaunay graph, that is, sets of neighboring polyhedra with similar image information.

The reconstruction approaches described herein are integrated into user friendly software packages. Using the geometrical graph structure of the Voronoi diagram, morphological parameters such as surface area and volume can be easily computed for extracted objects. In combination with the possibility of rapid visualization and animation of extracted objects, both shape reconstruction approaches provide a powerful instrument for the morphological analysis of 3-D structures in a wide range of applications.

Acknowledgments

We would like to acknowledge early contributions by E. Bertin, University of Grenoble, France, to the split-and-merge approach to multidimensional Voronoi tessellation. The groups of T. Cremer, University of Munich, and D. Fahimi, University of Heidelberg, provided the image data used for shape reconstruction in this chapter. We further thank D. Willersinn, Fraunhofer-Institut für Informations- und Datenverarbeitung (IITB), Karlsruhe, for careful reading of the manuscript. Finally, we would like to thank W. Jäger, IWR, University of Heidelberg, for the steady support of our Biocomputing research group.

25.6 References

[1] Watt, A. and Watt, M., (1992). *Advanced Animation and Rendering Techniques*, 1 edition. New York: Addison-Wesley.

[2] Okabe, A., Boots, B., and Sugihara, K., (1992). *Spatial Tessellations—Concepts and Applications of Voronoi Diagrams*. New York: John Wiley.

[3] Ohya, T., Iri, M., and Murota, K., (1984). A fast Voronoi-diagram algorithm with quaternary tree bucketing. *Information Processing Letters*, **18**:227-231.

[4] Bertin, E., Marcelpoil, R., and Chassery, J., (1992). Morphological algorithms based on Voronoi Delaunay graphs: microscopic and medical applications. In *Image Algebra and Morphological Image Processing III*, pp. 356–357. San Diego: SPIE.

[5] Bertin, E., Parazza, F., and Chassery, J., (1993). Segmentation and measurement based on 3D Voronoi diagram: Application to confocal microscopy. *Comput. Med. Imag.Graph*, **17**(3):175–182.

[6] Bowyer, A., (1981). Computing Dirichlet tessellations. *The Computer Journal*, **24**:162–166.

[7] Ohya, T., Iri, M., and Murota, K., (1984). Improvements of the incremental method for the Voronoi diagram with computational comparison of various algorithms. *Jour. Operations Research Society of Japan*, **27**:306–336.

[8] Keppel, E., (1975). Approximating complex surfaces by triangulation of contour lines. *IBM J. Res. Develop.*, **19**:2–11.

[9] Fuchs, H., Kedem, Z., and Uselton, S., (1977). Optimal surface reconstruction from planar contours. *Commun. ACM*, **20**:693–702.

[10] Boissonnat, J. D., (1988). Shape reconstruction from planar cross-sections. *Computer Vision, Graphics, and Image Processing*, **44**:1–29.

[11] Sloan, K. and Hrechanyk, L., (1981). Surface reconstruction from sparse data. In *IEEE Conf. on Pattern Recognition and Image Processing*, pp. 45–48. New York: IEEE.

[12] Boissonnat, J. D. and Geiger, B., (1992). *Three-dimensional reconstruction of complex shapes based on the Delaunay triangulation.* Technical Report No. 1697, INRIA.

[13] Oliva, J.-M., Perrin, M., and Coquillart, S., (1996). 3D Reconstruction of complex polyhedral shapes from contours using a simplified generalized Voronoi diagram. In *EUROGRAPHICS '96*, pp. C 397–408.

[14] Grabenbauer, M., (1997). *Dreidimensionale Strukturanalyse der Peroxisomen in humanen Hepatoblastomzellen (HepG2) und Vergleich mit der normalen Rattenleber.* Master's thesis, Institut für Anatomie und Zellbiologie, Heidelberg.

[15] Jähne, B., (1997). *Digital Image Processing*, 4 edition. Berlin: Springer.

[16] Bertin, E. and Chassery, J., (1991). Diagramme de Voronoi 3D: Construction et applications en imagerie 3D. In *AFCET, 8me Congres Reconnaissance des formes et intelligence artificielle, Lyon-Villeurbanne 2*, pp. 803–808.

[17] Eils, R., Bertin, E., Saracoglu, K., Rinke, B., Schröck, E., Parazza, F., Usson, Y., Robert-Nicoud, M., Stelzer, E. H. K., Chassery, J. M., Cremer, T., and Cremer, C., (1995). Application of laser confocal microscopy and 3D-Voronoi diagrams for volume and surface estimates of interphase chromosomes. *Jour. Microscopy*, **177**:150–161.

[18] Eils, R., Saracoglu, K., Münkel, C., Imhoff, J., Sätzler, K., Bertin, E., Dietzel, S., Schröck, E., Ried, T., Cremer, T., and Cremer, C., (1995). Three-

dimensional imaging approaches and Monte Carlo simulations: development of tools to study the morphology and distribution of chromosome territories and subchromosomal targets in human cell nuclei. In *Zoological Studies*, P. C. Cheng, ed., Vol. 34, pp. 7–10. New Jersey, London, Singapore: World Scientific Publishing.

[19] Dietzel, S., A.Jauch, Kienle, D., Qu, G., Holtgreve, H., Eils, R., Münkel, C., Bittner, Meltzer, P., Trent, J., and Cremer, T., (1997). Chromosome arm painting discloses separate and variably shaped domains in human cell nuclei. *Chromosome Res.*, pp. 25–33.

[20] Dietzel, S., Eils, R., Sätzler, K., Bornfeld, H., Jauch, A., Cremer, C., and Cremer, T., (1998). Evidence against a looped structure of the inactive human X-chromosome territory. *Exp. Cell Res.*, p. 239.

[21] Eils, R., Dietzel, S., Bertin, E., Schröck, E., Speicher, M. R., Ried, T., Robert-Nicoud, M., Cremer, C., and Cremer, T., (1996). Three-dimensional reconstruction of painted human interphase chromosomes: active and inactive X-chromosome territories have similar volumes but differ in shape and surface structure. *Jour. Cell Biol.*, **135**(6):1427–1440.

26 Probabilistic Modeling in Computer Vision

Joachim Hornegger[1,2], Dietrich Paulus[1], and Heinrich Niemann[1]

[1]Lehrstuhl für Mustererkennung, Universität Erlangen-Nürnberg
[2]Robotics Laboratory, Stanford University, Stanford, CA, U.S.

26.1 Introduction

The mapping of real world objects to the image plane including the geometric and the radiometric parts of image formation is basically well understood [1, 2]. From an abstract point of view, a camera is thought of as a geometric engine that projects the 3-D world to the 2-D image space. The resulting image data and *prior knowledge* on the considered application are the major sources of information for various vision issues. Common examples are image restoration, filtering, segmentation, reconstruction, modeling, *detection*, *recognition* or *pose estimation* algorithms. The most challenging and still not sufficiently solved problems in computer vision, however, are especially related to

Handbook of Computer Vision and Applications
Volume 2
Signal Processing and Pattern Recognition

Copyright © 1999 by Academic Press
All rights of reproduction in any form reserved.
ISBN 0-12-379772-1/$30.00

object recognition [3]. Up to now, there have been no general algorithms that allow the automatic learning of arbitrary 3-D objects and their recognition and localization in complex scenes. State-of-the-art approaches dealing with high-level vision tasks are essentially dominated by model-based object recognition methods [4]. Generally speaking, segmentation algorithms decompose given images in primitives, reference models are matched to observations, and distance measures are the basis for class decisions and pose estimates. The selection of discriminating image features and the adequate representation of object models define herein the vital problems. The overall performance of vision systems is basically biased by these components.

In the past, numerous applications have led to various types of representations for object models that allow the implementation of excellent systems showing the required run-time behavior; several recent systems are reported in [5]. Many image processing and computer vision algorithms are characterized by prevailing *ad hoc* solutions. Most techniques apply intuitive ideas specified for the given application and neglect the exploration of precisely defined mathematical models. There exists no unified theoretical formalization that provides the framework for the analytical analysis of designed complete systems. For the most part, it is left to empirical studies to justify the usage of the chosen representation scheme.

It is beyond the scope of this chapter to provide an exhaustive overview and a lucid discussion of models successfully applied in computer vision. We also cannot introduce general models that fit all requirements of conceivable applications, but we do present some probabilistic modeling schemes and their basic features, which have been shown to be proper for a wide range of vision problems. Theoretical aspects that unnecessarily complicate the presentation of substantial concepts are disclaimed and left to references. The applied researcher will get some understanding of ideas that form the basis of probabilistic modeling techniques and the methods used to deal with these models in practice. This overview will hopefully inspire further developments and applications of statistical techniques in computer vision.

The organization of the chapter is as follows: The next section summarizes arguments for a probabilistic formulation of computer vision modules and introduces the basic requirements for object models. The formal definitions of the considered vision problems that have to be solved using *probabilistic models* are summarized in Section 26.3.

Following the abstract framework, we introduce a family of probabilistic models. We start with a general modeling scheme and specialize this to various probabilistic models such as *histograms* (Section 26.4.1), *intensity-based models* (Section 26.4.2), mixtures of densities with incorporated feature transforms (Section 26.4.3), or *Markov random fields* (Section 26.4.4). Section 26.5 addresses automatic *model generation* including *parameter estimation* techniques and structural learning. Those who will apply statistical methods to computer vision will notice that the usage of *probabilistic models* is painstaking and necessitates a huge amount of engineering to fit particular requirements. In Section 26.6 we will give several hints for solving problems that are usually related to probabilistic models, and how these can be solved in many cases—either heuristically or by means of theoretically well-understood techniques. The chapter concludes with a summary and a brief discussion.

26.2 Why probabilistic models?

An immediate question is why we should prefer a probabilistic setup to any other recognition algorithms. In fact, both from a pragmatic and a theoretical point of view, the advantages of a statistical framework are persuasive:

- Sensor signals and associated features show a probabilistic behavior due to sensor noise, varying illumination conditions or segmentation errors;
- Generally, pattern recognition routines should use all available sources of information including *prior knowledge* and empirical data. A unified mathematical formulation incorporating all modules is desirable. In a probabilistic setting for computer vision, *prior knowledge* is encoded in prior probabilities of objects or of multiple object appearance in more complex scenes (probabilistic scene modeling). Stochastic properties of empirical data are summarized in densities characterizing pattern classes [6, 7]. According to Bayes' theorem posteriors finally combine both prior and class probabilities in a unified manner by a simple multiplication [8];
- Another fundamental argument supporting statistical methods is that decision theory guarantees the optimality of *Bayesian classifiers*, which maximize posterior probabilities (see also Section 26.3). All classifiers attempt to give models for designing (theoretically) optimal decisions. Essentially, this corresponds to the approximation of posterior probabilities estimated from the given training data [6]. The use of probabilistic models is straightforward and seems to be the most *natural* one;
- The design of learning algorithms can utilize comprehensive results in statistics and statistical learning theory [9, 10]. If, for instance, approximations of posterior distributions are based on parametric density functions, standard *parameter estimation* techniques can be applied for model generation such as those in [9, 11].

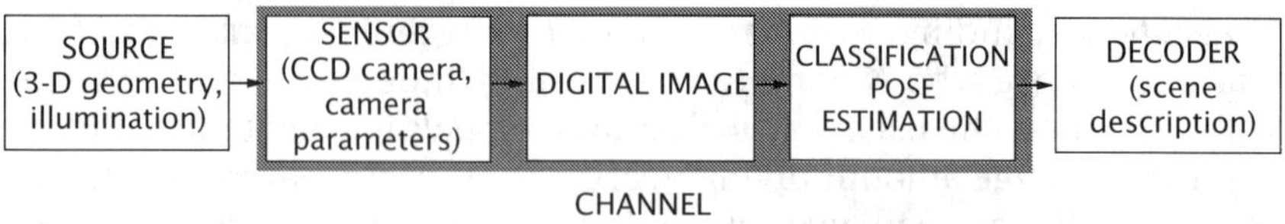

Figure 26.1: *The source channel model for scene analysis.*

- Object recognition and scene analysis can be considered in terms of communication (according to [12]). Figure 26.1 shows the object recognition problem incorporated into the source channel model, which is well known from information theory [13]. In computer vision applications, the system engineer can strongly influence both the signal generator and the decoder. For instance, the acquisition of data can be affected in terms of viewing direction, number of views and resolution. The decoding is basically determined by used models and associated *inference* and recognition algorithms. According to the source channel model and the use of a probabilistic framework, we conclude that *active vision* algorithms, which basically act on source coding, can make use of all theoretical results provided by information theory. In contrast to other pattern recognition applications such as speech processing, the source channel model in computer vision is not yet well established [14], and there seems an immense potential for future algorithms that will advantageously use this analogy; and
- Finally, the success of probabilistic models in different areas of applied pattern recognition also motivate the use of statistical methods. Speech recognition and handwritten character recognition systems based on *hidden Markov models* have already left the research stage and have led to commercial products. Probabilistic methods indisputably represent the state-of-the-art techniques in these fields and provide the most powerful known algorithms [12].

In addition to these general as well as fundamental advantages, a probabilistic setting introduces some valuable tools for simplification and for the increase of computational tractability; the incorporation of independency assumptions regarding observed features leads to compromise solutions and paves the way to eliminate the trade-off between computational efficiency and models that are still rich enough to provide the required discriminating power. Marginalizations, that is the elimination of random variables by integration, reduce the complexity, allow the usage of probabilistic models, if the input data are incomplete, and provide techniques to define hierarchical modeling schemes.

In practice, the design and usage of probabilistic models should follow the general guideline: as much theory as necessary, and as simple as possible.

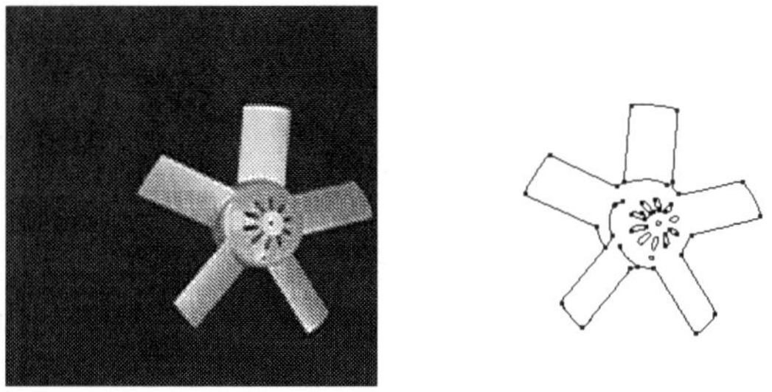

Figure 26.2: *Gray-level image and the result of line and corner detection.*

26.3 Object recognition: classification and regression

Most computer vision problems can be considered in terms of standard pattern recognition problems related to *classification* and *regression*. A digital image $\boldsymbol{f}$ is mathematically considered as a matrix of discrete intensity values $\boldsymbol{f} = [f_{m,n}]_{1 \le m \le M, 1 \le n \le N}$. For further processing, most high-level vision tasks require the labeling or segmentation of images. The labeling is defined by a discrete mapping of intensity values to categorical variables. Examples are the assignment of binary values to back and foreground pixels or the association of image elements with regions. In low-level image processing an important task is especially the segmentation of images into lines or corners. Apart from segmentation errors, these geometric features allow the use of known relationships between the 3-D world and the 2-D observation; they form the basis of most known 3-D recognition and *pose estimation* systems [3, 15]. From an abstract point of view, the detection of geometric features also maps an image to a matrix of the same size where each entry is, for instance, either assigned to the label *element of a line* or *no element*. Figure 26.2 illustrates an example of segmented point and line features. These basic low-level operations show that formally we have to find an appropriate function that assigns image data to a set of labels.

In a unified manner also the solution of object identification problems can be considered as a labeling procedure [16]. A given image $\boldsymbol{f}$ (or the result of any preprocessing and segmentation steps) is assigned to a single class Ω_κ, which is an element of the set of considered classes $\Omega = \{\Omega_1, \Omega_2, \ldots, \Omega_K\}$.[1] If more objects are present, the classifier is expected to compute the set of corresponding classes. An image is thus mapped to a set of classes. Of course, there are different ways to associate pattern classes with objects. It usually depends on the given

[1]In the text the authors mostly prefer to denote a pattern class by Ω_κ instead of using the integer κ to reveal that classes are categorical variables without any ordering. Integers would imply the natural ordering, which is indeed not present.

application and the used features, whether or not types of objects are considered to represent instances of the same class. For example, objects can share the same 3-D shape and differ in color. A restriction to geometry-like corners or lines leads to recognition algorithms where objects of different colors belong to the same class, if their 3-D shape is identical. These geometric features are almost invariant with respect to colors. A green cube will result in the same corners as a red cube. Another problem is caused by objects that are considered to be elements of different classes but share a common view, that is, there exist viewing directions where you cannot distinguish between these objects.

Including image segmentation, the task of object recognition, that is, the discrete mapping of images to pattern classes, is a composition of various labeling (respectively, classification) processes. The mapping from the original image to discrete classes is mostly subdivided into the following stages (with variations [7]):

1. *Preprocessing*: in the preprocessing stage images are filtered. Domain and range of these image transforms are discrete intensity values;
2. *Segmentation*: the segmentation maps the image matrix to a matrix that defines, for instance, geometric primitives. In the most general case, segmentation algorithms transform images to parameters that define geometric features uniquely, for example, start and end points of straight line segments. In this case a single image point can belong to different geometric primitives. Examples are points where lines intersect; and
3. *Classification*: the final classification stage maps segmentation results to classes.

The discussion so far reveals that the basic problem in object recognition can be stated as follows: We have to define and to provide a modeling scheme that allows one to compute a mapping δ from images to labels or classes, dependent on the given application. Without loss of generality, we restrict the description to classes and omit identical formulas for labels. The *classification* is in fact defined by $\delta(\boldsymbol{f}) = \kappa \in \{1, 2, \ldots, K\}$. This mapping ζ characterizes the so-called *decision rule* of the classifier. It is not obvious for system design how to choose the decision rule and how to select an appropriate representation of objects that allow the comparison of models and observations. Due to our ultimate goal of implementing reliable object recognition systems, it is a natural consequence that we seek classifiers with minimum error rates. For that purpose, let us define a *loss function* $L(\lambda, \kappa)$ that penalizes *classification* errors. The function $L(\lambda, \kappa)$ measures the price we pay for classifying an observation belonging to class Ω_λ to Ω_κ. Herein, we take for granted that correct decisions are cheaper than misclassifications. Now we choose the decision rule δ^* that minimizes the expected *classification* loss. With respect to this objective, the optimal classifier results from solving the minimization problem

$$\delta^*(\boldsymbol{f}) = \operatorname{argmin}_{\delta(\boldsymbol{f})} \sum_{\lambda=1}^{K} L(\lambda, \delta(\boldsymbol{f}))\, p(\lambda|\boldsymbol{f}) \tag{26.1}$$

where $p(\lambda|\boldsymbol{f})$ is the *a posteriori* probability for observing class Ω_λ given the image $\boldsymbol{f}$. Having especially a 0-1 loss function, where we charge classification errors by 1, the objective function in Eq. (26.1) takes its minimal value if we fade out the highest summand by correct decisions. Therefore, we determine that class of highest posterior probability, and the optimal decision rule minimizing the average loss is

$$\delta^*(\boldsymbol{f}) = \operatorname{argmax}_\kappa\, p(\kappa|\boldsymbol{f}) = \operatorname{argmax}_\kappa\, p(\kappa)p(\boldsymbol{f}|\kappa) \tag{26.2}$$

Classifiers applying this decision rule are called *Bayesian classifiers*. The observation that Bayesian classifiers minimize the expected loss and therefore the misclassification rate is the major reason for the introduction of probabilistic models in computer vision and other fields of pattern recognition [6, 11, 12]. We get an excellent classifier if we are able to characterize the statistical properties of objects appearing in sensor data. But usually this is a highly nontrivial task and represents the fundamental problem in probabilistic modeling: the definition and computation of posteriors based on empirical data. Without appropriate probabilistic models and accurate approximations of posteriors, there is no way to implement an optimal object recognition system.

Besides classification also the position and orientation of objects with respect to a reference coordinate system are of potential interest. For instance, a robot that has to grasp objects requires pose parameters of high accuracy. Let us assume the intrinsic camera parameters are known. Thus *pose estimation* of objects is confined to the computation of rotation and translation. These transforms are referred to the world coordinate system. In the following we denote rotation by $\boldsymbol{R} \in \mathbb{R}^{3\times 3}$ and the translation by $\boldsymbol{t} \in \mathbb{R}^3$. Details concerning the representation of the orthogonal rotation matrix are omitted, and we refer to [17]. For simplicity, the six degrees of freedom determining the pose are denoted by the vector $\boldsymbol{\theta}$. In contrast to the classification problem, the input data are no longer mapped to discrete variables such as class numbers, but to a real-valued vector $\boldsymbol{\theta}$. In terms of statistical decision theory, *pose estimation* thus corresponds to a *regression problem*. With regard to optimal regression, we introduce analogously to classification a penalty function for estimates. Pose parameters have to be determined such that the mean loss is observed. Here, the loss function $L(\boldsymbol{\theta}, \eta_\kappa(\boldsymbol{f}))$ charges the errors in pose estimates, where the *regression function* η_κ maps the observation to pose parameters. This function depends on the actual class Ω_κ of the shown object and is therefore indexed by κ, that is, $\eta_\kappa(\boldsymbol{f}) = \boldsymbol{\theta} \in \mathbb{R}^6$. The most commonly used loss function in

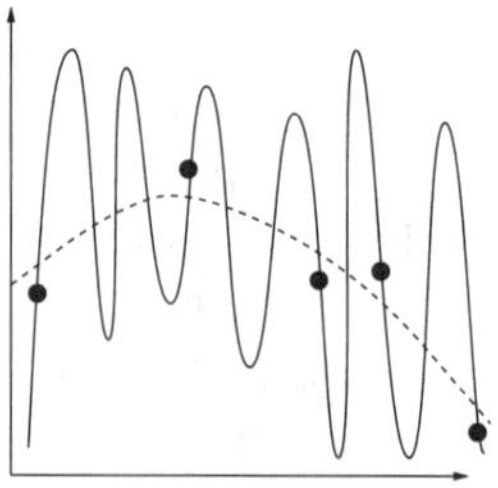

Figure 26.3: *An example of over-fitting (solid line: over-fitting with no errors regarding training samples; dashed line: smooth approximation with errors).*

regression is the square error, which is defined by $||\boldsymbol{\theta} - \eta_\kappa(\boldsymbol{f})||^2$. The regression problem associated with *pose estimation* is generally stated as the minimization task

$$\eta^*_\kappa(\boldsymbol{f}) = \operatorname{argmin}_{\eta_\kappa(\boldsymbol{f})} \int L(\boldsymbol{\theta}, \eta_\kappa(\boldsymbol{f}))\, p(\boldsymbol{\theta}|\boldsymbol{f}, \kappa)\, d\boldsymbol{\theta} \tag{26.3}$$

where $p(\boldsymbol{\theta}|\boldsymbol{f}, \kappa)$ is the probability density function of $\boldsymbol{\theta}$ given the image $\boldsymbol{f}$ and the class Ω_λ. A similar argument to *Bayesian classifiers* shows that the optimal estimate regarding the square error loss function is given by the conditional expectation $\eta^*_\kappa(\boldsymbol{f}) = E[\theta|\boldsymbol{f}, \kappa]$.

In practice, the major problem is the representation of the *regression* function, and many applications restrict the forementioned conditional expectation to a parametric family of functions. In these cases, the minimization Eq. (26.3) reduces to *parameter estimation* problems. Commonly used parametric functions in statistics are, for example, linear functions [18]. In addition to parameterization, further constraints to regression functions can (and often should) be incorporated by regularization. For instance, we can also claim that the average curvature of the regression function in combination with the square error has to be minimized [10]. If the regression function is not restricted to a specific parametric family and regularization is unconsidered, the regression problem is generally ill-posed, and we observe an over-fitting to training data. Figure 26.3 illustrates the problem of over-fitting; the filled bullets represent the sample data and the solid and the dashed line show different approximations of the sampled function. In the case of over-fitting (solid line), the function values between sample data tend to be inaccurate and rough.

A general rule of thumb is to incorporate all available knowledge into the model and recognition process. Notably, the relation between the observation and pose parameters can be defined if the 3-D structure of objects and the projection properties of the chosen sensor are known. We suggest the *regression* of probability density functions for observations that are parameterized regarding the pose $\boldsymbol{\theta}$. From a theoretical point of view, we thus consider a generalization of the earlier-defined square error loss, and obviously the negative likelihood value of the parametric density function for given observations acts as the loss value of the estimated pose. Assuming a uniform distribution of pose parameters, the optimal pose parameters $\boldsymbol{\theta}^*$ result from the maximum likelihood estimate

$$\boldsymbol{\theta}^* = \operatorname{argmax}_{\boldsymbol{\theta}}\; p(\boldsymbol{f}|\kappa;\boldsymbol{\theta}) \tag{26.4}$$

In this case, the pose estimation using probabilistic models corresponds to a standard *parameter estimation* problem.

The discussion shows that recognition and *pose estimation* are finally a combination of two familiar problems in statistical decision theory—*classification* and *regression.* We conclude this section by summarizing the guidelines for the construction and usage of probabilistic models in object recognition and localization:

- We have to provide prior distributions $p(\kappa)$, $\kappa = 1, 2, \ldots, K$, which include all available knowledge regarding the given classes and their appearance in images; and
- The probabilities $p(\boldsymbol{f}|\kappa;\boldsymbol{\theta})$, $\kappa = 1, 2, \ldots, K$, of observed images $\boldsymbol{f}$ (or features) have to be defined. Especially, if we are also interested in object localization, the probability density function has to be parameterized with respect to pose parameters denoted by $\boldsymbol{\theta}$. The specification of these probability density functions constitutes the hardest problem within the design of probabilistic models. In the following sections, the class density $p(\boldsymbol{f}|\kappa;\boldsymbol{\theta})$ is also referenced by the term *model density*.

Related to the abstract mathematical structure of probabilistic models, there are several related computational aspects of practical importance:

- We have to provide learning algorithms that allow the automatic training of probability density functions from empirical data. From scratch, the training includes both the acquisition of the concrete model structure, for instance, the automatic decision for the required family of distributions, and the estimation of associated model parameters. Both theoretical and empirical results are necessary, which give hints how to select the sample data for model acquisition, and which validation methods are advantageous to judge generated models; and
- In view of runtime efficiency it is very important to implement sophisticated (in terms of low complexity and high efficiency) *inference* strategies, which allow the fast evaluation of posteriors $p(\kappa|\boldsymbol{f};\boldsymbol{\theta})$ for given observations $\boldsymbol{f}$ and usually unknown pose parameters $\boldsymbol{\theta}$.

We begin the discussion of various probabilistic modeling schemes by a generic definition of model densities.

26.4 Parametric families of model densities

The discrete image matrix $\boldsymbol{f} = [f_{m,n}]_{1\le m\le M, 1\le n\le N}$ is formally considered as a random matrix. Each entry $f_{m,n}$ of the matrix $\boldsymbol{f}$ is characterized by three components: the position in the image defined by the 2-D grid coordinates $[m, n]^T$ and the associated pixel value $f_{m,n}$. For some reasons, which will become clear later, we take the image matrix $\boldsymbol{f}$ by a set of random vectors

$$\left\{[m, n, f_{m,n}]^T \mid 1 \le m \le M, 1 \le n \le N\right\} \tag{26.5}$$

and define both 2-D grid points and intensity values as potential random measures. Depending on the used image type, the intensity $f_{m,n}$ can be a color vector, a gray level or more generally a vector including any other label. Independent of the concrete dimension and interpretation of pixel values, the induced random vectors Eq. (26.5) can be characterized by a conditional probability density function, which depends on the present pattern class Ω_κ. Because the appearance of objects in the image plane changes with the object pose, the density will also be parameterized regarding the pose $\boldsymbol{\theta}$.[2] Generally, we get for the whole image the probability density

$$p\left(\left\{ [m, n, f_{m,n}]^T \,\middle|\, 1 \le m \le M, 1 \le n \le N\right\} | \kappa; \boldsymbol{\theta}\right) \tag{26.6}$$

which depends on the present object belonging to Ω_κ (or any other type of labels).

Example 26.1: Dimension of parameter space

For discrete-valued random variables, that is, both the grid point coordinates and the intensity values are quantized, the use of the discrete probability function Eq. (26.6) is beyond its practical application. An example clarifies the necessity of simplifications: Let us assume we consider for a single set of pose parameters $\boldsymbol{\theta}$ the discrete distribution of gray levels in the image plane. To assign probabilities to a 512×512 8-bit gray-level image would require more than 2×10^6 discrete measures. Obviously, an immense training set would be necessary to estimate these probabilities even for a single pose vector. Inevitably we will also encounter problems with the curse-of-dimensionality [19], which originally prohibits the effective usage and computational tractability of this modeling scheme (see also Section 26.6).

This example shows that the model density (Eq. (26.6)) is far too general, not computationally feasible, and too abstract for any application. Nevertheless, it is the source of a broad class of model densities.

---

[2] We point out that $\boldsymbol{\theta}$ is considered as a parameter and not as a random variable. This is also indicated in expressions by a separating semicolon.

The introduction of additional constraints, the consideration of dependencies of bounded order, the incorporation of specializations, and the usage of continuous instead of discrete random variables are basic tools that will induce reduced parameter sets. Conceivable, simple, and well-studied continuous probability density functions are Gaussian densities and convex combinations of Gaussians [7]. Evident specializations are marginals and the introduction of independencies. The right combination of these techniques pushes the dimension of the final parameter space to mathematical feasibility and the curse-of-dimensionality can be beaten.

26.4.1 Histograms

An extreme case of marginalization and independency are *histograms* of intensity values. Relative frequencies of intensities represent a non-trivial probabilistic model of images given a pattern class Ω_κ. We compute the discrete probabilities of intensity values independently of their position in the image grid. To derive histograms from Eq. (26.6), first we decompose the probability density function according to the assumption that all intensity values are mutually independent; thus, we obtain the factorization

$$
\begin{aligned}
& p\left(\left\{[m,n,f_{m,n}]^T \,|1 \le m \le M, 1 \le n \le N\right\} \middle| \, \kappa;\boldsymbol{\theta})\right) \\
&= \prod_{m=1}^{M}\prod_{n=1}^{N} p\left([m,n,f_{m,n}]^T\,|\kappa;\boldsymbol{\theta}\right)
\end{aligned}
\tag{26.7}
$$

The marginal over the image coordinates leads to the demanded discrete probabilities

$$
p\left(\boldsymbol{f}|\kappa;\boldsymbol{\theta}\right) = \prod_{m=1}^{M}\prod_{n=1}^{N}\left(\sum_{m'=1}^{M}\sum_{n'=1}^{N} p\left([m',n',f_{m,n}]\,|\kappa;\boldsymbol{\theta}\right)\right) \tag{26.8}
$$

Histograms show several obvious advantages: they are generated easily and these discrete probability mass functions show some useful invariance properties. Assuming that we have normalized images, planar rotations and translations of objects will not (drastically) change the distribution of gray levels. Therefore, the pose parameters in the histogram can be reduced by these three degrees of freedom. The pose parameters include only out-of-plane rotations, denoted by φ_x and φ_y, and 1-D translations t_z along the optical axis. We gather from this example the important fact that clever marginals can reduce the dimension of pose parameters. Marginals provide a powerful technique for efficient *pose estimation* algorithms based on probabilistic models [20].

Histograms are accepted as simple and useful probabilistic models that are widely and successfully applied in computer vision [14].

However, discrete probabilities of intensities are also marginals that drastically simplify the real probability density function of object appearances in images. Marginalization is known to reduce the discriminatory power. Histograms only record the overall intensity composition of images. As a consequence, there is an increase of the rate of misclassifications. Histograms show tremendous invariances. Based on histograms, for instance, all images where we just permute pixels, lead to identical distributions of gray levels and thus the same classification results. Many applications defuse this property by restricting the computation of histograms to local window frames. But even in local histograms, the invariance to permutations is present. Remarkably, despite this extreme kind of invariance histograms are proper for a wide range of applications.

Example 26.2: Object recognition using histograms

Let us consider a single $(M \times N)$ 8-bit gray-level image $\boldsymbol{f}$ for reduced pose parameters $\boldsymbol{\theta}'$, which include out-of-plane rotations and the translation along the z-axis. The histogram of this image is computed based on relative frequencies. For an arbitrary intensity value f, for instance, we get the discrete probability

$$p(f|\kappa;\boldsymbol{\theta}') = \frac{\#\{f_{m,n} = f | 1 \leq m \leq M, 1 \leq n \leq N\}}{NM} \tag{26.9}$$

where $\#\{\cdot\}$ denotes the cardinality of the set $\{\cdot\}$. Let us consider single planar objects under constant illumination. The background is assumed to be constant and no occlusion occurs. If the chosen objects do not show identical histograms, that is, there exists no permutation of pixels, which maps one image of an object to the image of another object, the classification simply based on distributions of gray levels is efficient and reliable. Figure 26.4 shows four different industrial objects that can be classified using histograms: for constant illumination, for a fixed distance between objects and camera it is possible to use a histogram-based recognition procedure, which classifies these objects with a recognition rate of 100 % (no pose estimation). The rotations and translations, however, are restricted to 2-D transforms, and we took 90 sample views of each object to generate the histograms, and a disjoint set of 87 images of each object for *classification*.

The dependency on illumination can be eliminated or minimized if we do not consider intensities but the result of filtering operations such as wavelets, Gabor filtering or high-pass filters [14].

26.4.2 Probabilistic modeling of intensities and image points

The major disadvantage of histograms for solving *classification* and *pose estimation* issues is due to invariance properties and the assumed independency of grid positions. A first step to generalize relative frequencies of intensity values is an isolated modeling of intensities dependent on grid points, that is, we do not consider the probability of

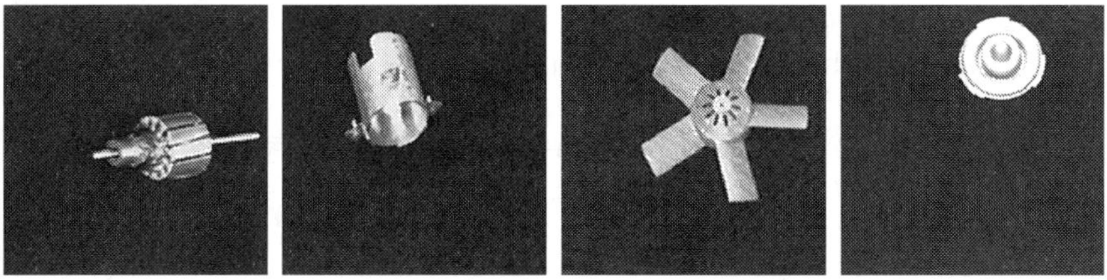

Figure 26.4: Industrial objects.

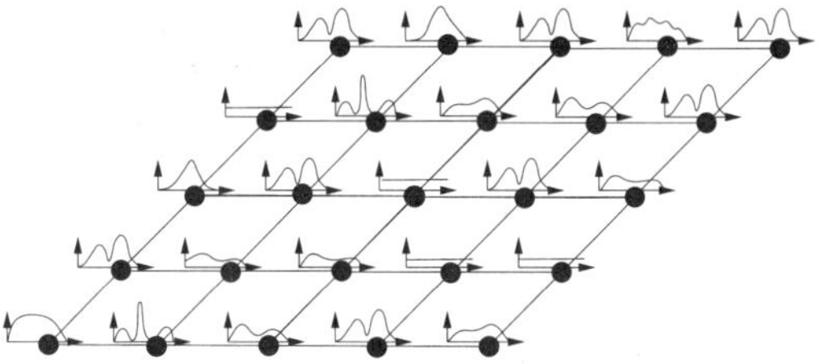

Figure 26.5: Explicit modeling of intensity distribution in the image grid.

observing a special intensity value in the image, but the probability of a certain intensity at a given grid point. Instead of eliminating grid points by marginalization, we thus compute the joint probability of the intensity value f at the randomly selected image point $[m, n]$. This probability density function is given by $p(m, n|\kappa)\, p(f|m, n, \kappa; \boldsymbol{\theta})$, where $\boldsymbol{\theta}$ denotes the pose parameter. Assuming mutually independent intensity values and image points, the density of the complete image $\boldsymbol{f}$ is obtained by the product

$$p(\boldsymbol{f}|\kappa; \boldsymbol{\theta}) = \prod_{m=1}^{M} \prod_{n=1}^{N} p(m, n|\kappa)\, p(f_{m,n}|m, n, \kappa; \boldsymbol{\theta}) \tag{26.10}$$

The priors of grid points are set equal if all image points are considered. Therefore, the probabilities $p(m, n|\kappa)$ in Eq. (26.10) include no additional information and can be omitted. Figure 26.5 illustrates the basic idea of the chosen model: all image points are separately modeled and mutually independent.

Example 26.3: Explicit modeling of sensor noise

Let us assume that pose parameters remain constant, that is, we omit the parameter $\boldsymbol{\theta}$ and illumination conditions do not change. In this case, the randomness of intensity values in real images is basically influenced by sensor noise. Without additional information, sensor noise is well modeled by a white, zero mean, Gaussian density, that is, formally we consider the random variable f as a continuous measure. In consequence of this observation, we define the intensity value f

at the grid point $[m,n]^T$ for a given class Ω_κ to be $p(f|m,n;\kappa)$, a normally distributed random variable

$$p(f|m,n,\kappa) = \mathcal{N}(f;\boldsymbol{\mu}_{\kappa,m,n},\Sigma_{\kappa,m,n}) = \frac{1}{\sqrt{\det 2\pi\Sigma_{\kappa,m,n}}}\exp(a) \tag{26.11}$$

$$\text{where} \quad a = -\tfrac{1}{2}(f-\boldsymbol{\mu}_{\kappa,m,n})^T\Sigma_{\kappa,m,n}^{-1}(f-\boldsymbol{\mu}_{\kappa,m,n})$$

Here, $\boldsymbol{\mu}_{\kappa,m,n}$ denotes the mean vector and $\Sigma_{\kappa,m,n}$ the positive semidefinite, symmetric covariance matrix of the intensity value at the grid point $[m,n]^T$ of an object belonging to class Ω_κ. All density functions corresponding to image points are thus parameterized with respect to means and covariances of intensity values. Instead of estimating the discrete probability for each intensity level at a single image point, only the computation of mean and covariance is required. This example shows an important advantage of continuous random variables: it often reduces the number of free parameters. Additionally, we can decrease the dimension of the parameter space drastically if the chosen noise model is homogeneous in terms of showing identical covariances for all pixels of the given sensor. In that case, the Gaussians at all grid points $[m,n]$ distinguish in means, but share the same covariance Σ of intensity values, that is, we set $\Sigma_{\kappa,m,n} = \Sigma$. This technique is called *parameter tying* (see also Section 26.6): Different random measures have partially the same parameters. Parameter tying is a widely applied technique in statistics. It provides robust estimates especially in the presence of sparse training data, because a reduction of the parameter space induces estimates of higher reliability.

The introduced modeling scheme based on mutually independent image entries raises several questions:

- The first problem is the incorporation of pose parameters. Variations in position and orientation of objects have to be incorporated into this model. Because an object is modeled based on distributions where the intensities are included as continuous random variables and the grid points as discrete ones, even the simplest transforms in the image plane cause problems. Generally, planar rotations and translations define no discrete mapping of grid points. To deal with this problem, obviously resampling is required. In case of in-plane transforms, in [21] it is suggested to use linear interpolation between intensity values.
- Another fair criticism on this modeling scheme is due to the independency constraint of neighboring pixel values. Obviously, this independency assumption does not fit to the real-world situation. Widely used constraints such as the smoothness criterion, which states that neighboring pixels share similar intensity values, require the explicit incorporation of dependencies.

An alternative probabilistic model, which resolves some of forementioned problems, results from a different factorization of the original

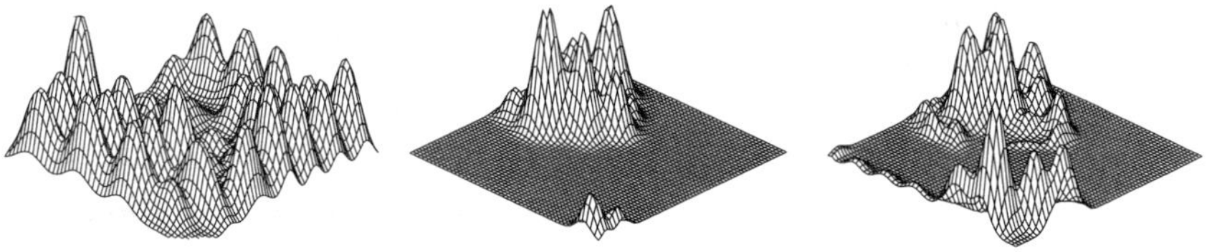

Figure 26.6: *Probability densities of image points conditioned on three different intensity values.*

probability $p([m, n, f_{m,n}]^T|\kappa; \boldsymbol{\theta})$ and a different interpretation of random variables: Now we consider the intensity values as discrete measures, the coordinates of grid points as continuous random variables. Instead of

$$p([m, n, f_{m,n}]^T|\kappa; \boldsymbol{\theta}) = p(m, n|\kappa)\, p(f|m, n, \kappa; \boldsymbol{\theta}) \tag{26.12}$$

we use the decomposition

$$p([m, n, f_{m,n}]^T|\kappa; \boldsymbol{\theta}) = p(f_{m,n}|\kappa)\, p(m, n|f_{m,n}, \kappa; \boldsymbol{\theta}) \tag{26.13}$$

Assuming again mutual independency of random vectors, the joint probability density function of the complete image showing class Ω_κ is now given by

$$p(\boldsymbol{f}|\kappa; \boldsymbol{\theta}) = \prod_{m=1}^{M} \prod_{n=1}^{N} p(f_{m,n}|\kappa)\, p(m, n|f_{m,n}, \kappa; \boldsymbol{\theta}) \tag{26.14}$$

Figure 26.6 shows three density functions. Each of these densities corresponds to a single intensity value, and visualizes the distribution of grid points showing a certain intensity value.

In the case of modeling distributions of intensities at image points, we were able to incorporate explicit knowledge on the sensor noise model (Example 26.3). The density function $p(m, n|f, \kappa; \boldsymbol{\theta})$, however, is the probability measure that the image point $[m, n]$ appears showing the specific intensity value f. Therefore, this density characterizes the spatial distribution of a particular intensity in the image plane. For the parametric representation of grid point distributions conditioned on an intensity value, a single Gaussian is obviously not an adequate approximation. The density associated with grid points is expected to be a multimodal and thus concave function. Therefore, we suggest the use of mixtures of densities [22]

$$p(m, n|f, \kappa; \boldsymbol{\theta}) = \sum_{i=1}^{l_f} p_i\, p(m, n|\boldsymbol{B}_{f,\kappa}; \boldsymbol{\theta}) \tag{26.15}$$

where l_f denotes the order of the *mixture density*, the coefficients p_i sum up to 1, and the densities $p(m,n|\boldsymbol{B}_{f,\kappa})$ are parameterized in $\boldsymbol{B}_{f,\kappa}$. If, for instance, the mixture base densities are Gaussians, these parameters correspond to mean vectors and covariance matrices. Convex combinations of probability density functions are generally advantageous, because they show good approximation properties of multimodal functions, and they are not restricted to discrete values of $[m,n]^T$. This model obviously avoids interpolation for grid points if the object is rotated and translated in the image plane.

Example 26.4: Spatial distribution of intensities

The prior probabilities $p(f|\kappa)$ of intensities are a minor problem and can be defined by relative frequencies Eq. (26.9). In this case, however, the parameter $\boldsymbol{\theta}'$ is not required because we use a simplified model and assume that this probability does not depend on the object's pose. The basic issue in defining an appropriate model using the representation suggested in Eq. (26.14) is the right choice of the density $p(m,n|f_{m,n},\kappa;\boldsymbol{\theta})$ based on convex combinations. We neglect the pose parameters and consider a mixture representation of this density: A widely applied approximation method for multimodal functions is based on linear combinations of Gaussians [22]. Once the number l_f of mixture components associated with a certain intensity value f is known, the multi-modal density is represented by

$$p(m,n|f,\kappa) = \sum_{i=1}^{l_f} p_i \mathcal{N}([m,n]^T; \boldsymbol{\mu}_{\kappa,i}, \Sigma_{\kappa,i}) \qquad (26.16)$$

where $p_i \geq 0$, $\sum_{i=1}^{l_f} p_i = 1$, and $\boldsymbol{\mu}_{\kappa,i} \in \mathbb{R}^2$ and $\Sigma_{\kappa,i} \in \mathbb{R}^{2\times 2}$ denote the mean vector and covariance matrix of the ith mixture component associated with the gray-level f.

The extension of this model based on Gaussian mixtures with respect to pose parameters is straightforward if pose parameters $\boldsymbol{\theta}$ define an affine mappings. Let the affine mapping be given by the matrix $\boldsymbol{R}$ and the vector $\boldsymbol{t}$. If an arbitrary normally distributed random variable with mean vector $\boldsymbol{\mu}$ and and covariance matrix Σ is transformed by this affine mapping, the resulting random variable is again Gaussian. The corresponding mean vector is defined by $\boldsymbol{R}\boldsymbol{\mu} + \boldsymbol{t}$ and the covariance matrix by $\boldsymbol{R}\Sigma\boldsymbol{R}^T$ [8]. Using this example, at least in-plane transformations are easily built in Eq. (26.16): For given 2-D rotations and translations we get the density

$$p(m,n|f,\kappa;\boldsymbol{R},\boldsymbol{t}) = \sum_{i=1}^{l_f} p_i \mathcal{N}([m,n]^T; \boldsymbol{R}\boldsymbol{\mu}_{\kappa,i} + \boldsymbol{t}, \boldsymbol{R}\Sigma_{\kappa,i}\boldsymbol{R}^T) \qquad (26.17)$$

The probabilistic models so far are substantially restricted to 2-D images, and out-of-plane rotations and translations are still an open problem; the statistical characterization of 3-D objects and their appearance in the image plane including six degrees of freedom is not yet possible. The simplest way to extend these models is to quantize the pose and formally consider each 2-D view of an object as a separate class. This appearance-based strategy, however, shows the disadvantage that for each discrete set of pose parameters single probabilistic models have to be computed, and we have to deal with quantization errors in pose parameters. In [21], the authors suggest interpolating those density parameters that define the 2-D views and in-plane transformations dependent on pose parameters. Without additional geometric knowledge, regression (Section 26.3) provides the only way to generalize the given 2-D models to arbitrary pose parameters. The selection of an appropriate regression function, however, is a crucial and nontrivial issue.

Example 26.5: Model parameters and regression

As we have already mentioned in our discussion of histograms, pose parameters $\boldsymbol{\theta}$, which define a 3-D rotation and translation, are partitioned into two subsets:

- $[\varphi_z, t_x, t_y]$: transformations in the image plane; these include rotations around the optical axis and translations in the 2-D image plane, that is, three degrees of freedom; and
- $[\varphi_x, \varphi_y, t_z]$: out-of-plane rotations around the horizontal and vertical axes and translations along the optical axis represent the other parameters.

The incorporation of in-plane affine transformations was already mentioned in Example 26.4. The extension of these models with respect to the additional pose parameters $[\varphi_x, \varphi_y, t_z]$ is not obvious. According to Section 26.3 we have to use regression to generalize our models such that we can deal with arbitrary pose parameters.

Let us consider the model suggested in Example 26.3. We estimate mean vectors and covariance matrices of all image points for a given set of nonplanar rotations and translations represented by the vector $[\varphi_x, \varphi_y, t_z]$. Furthermore, we simplify the problem and assume that the covariance matrices are independent of rotations and translations. This is acceptable because we expect no change in sensor noise with varying pose parameters. Only mean vectors are parameterized, that is, for a given grid point $[m, n]^T$ the parameterized mean vectors are $\boldsymbol{\mu}_{m,n}(\varphi_x, \varphi_y, t_z)$, $1 \leq m \leq M$ and $1 \leq n \leq N$.

Due to these restrictions, we have to estimate the mean vectors dependent on pose parameters $[\varphi_x, \varphi_y, t_z]$. For that purpose, we define for each image point a parametric regression function that is computed such that the following sum of square errors is minimal:

$$\epsilon = \sum_{\varphi_x, \varphi_y, t_z} ||\boldsymbol{\mu}(\varphi_x, \varphi_y, t_z) - \eta_\kappa(\varphi_x, \varphi_y, t_z)||^2 \tag{26.18}$$

For simplicity, we omitted the indices m and n that identify the considered grid point. As an example of parametric regression we can choose trivariate polynomials defined by

$$\eta_\kappa(\varphi_x, \varphi_y, t_z) = \sum_{s\geq 0} \sum_{i_1+i_2+i_3=s} a_{i_1,i_2,i_3}\, {\varphi_x}^{i_1} {\varphi_y}^{i_2} {t_z}^{i_3} \qquad (26.19)$$

where a_{i_1,i_2,i_3} are the real-valued coefficients of the basis monomials ${\varphi_x}^{i_1} {\varphi_y}^{i_2} {t_z}^{i_3}$. Of course, the degree of this polynomial can be selected such that there are no approximation errors, but it is expected that the induced over-fitting (see Fig. 26.3) will lead to insufficient results. An implementation and experimental evaluation of this regression technique for 3-D pose estimation applied to the model introduced in Example 26.3 is discussed in [21]. The used pixel values, however, are not intensities but the result of Gabor filters. The authors restrict the regression function to a univariate polynomial of low degree (8 addends) and therefore avoid an explicit regularization. The error using a quantization of 10° for out-of-plane-rotations leads to a mean error of 4.6° without providing explicit 3-D information. Planar rotations show a mean error of 2.1°.

The regression based on polynomials or arbitrarily selected parametric functions appears incidentally and without any geometric justification. A more obvious way would be to compute the distribution of the appearing object using the knowledge of the 3-D structure, the illumination model, and the mapping from the 3-D world to the image plane. An incorporation of the overall geometric relationships seems worthwhile. However, the major problem with respect to this issue is that the projection from 3-D to 2-D can be computed explicitly, not its inverse. But there is some hope: There exist first results towards the incorporation of geometry in probabilistic models if we use geometric features instead of intensities [20, 23, 24]. The next section considers segmentation results of images as random measures for pose estimation and summarizes existing probabilistic models using geometric features instead of intensity values or results of any preprocessing operations.

26.4.3 Model densities using geometric features

Let us assume that preprocessing and segmentation algorithms map the observed image to a set of 2-D points. The information provided by the whole image is thus reduced to a comparatively small set of features. We denote the set of points by $\boldsymbol{O} = \{\boldsymbol{o}_k | k = 1, 2, \ldots, m\}$, where $\boldsymbol{o}_k \in \mathbb{R}^2$. Some examples for the segmentation of gray-level images into point features are shown in Fig. 26.7. Here the corners are features attached to the associated 3-D object. If we rotate and translate the corresponding 3-D points of the object in the 3-D space, this linear transform, the object geometry, and the projection to the image plane characterize the resulting 2-D features—apart from noise,

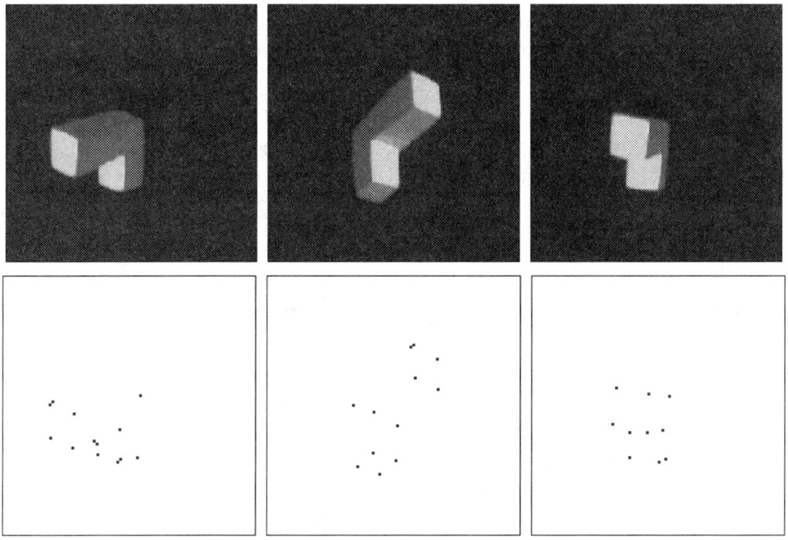

Figure 26.7: *Gray-level images and sparse sets of computed point features.*

occlusion, and segmentation errors. If the correspondences of 3-D and 2-D points are known, the transform can be written in a single equation. We denote the assignment of 2-D features $\boldsymbol{o}_k$ in the image to the index of the corresponding feature of the 3-D object by ζ_κ. The identifier ζ_κ in this context is not incidental. In fact, the assignment of 2-D and 3-D points can formally be considered as a *classification* or, in other words, all points get a label indicating the correspondence. If there are m observed features and n_κ 3-D points for class Ω_κ, the discrete mapping ζ_κ is defined by

$$\zeta_\kappa : \begin{cases} \boldsymbol{O} & \rightarrow \{1, 2, \ldots, n_\kappa\} \\ \boldsymbol{o}_k & \mapsto \qquad i_k \end{cases} \tag{26.20}$$

We get the probability observing a set of single points with a given assignment function ζ_κ by the following substitutions in our generic density Eq. (26.6): The grid coordinates $[m, n]^T$ are now represented by the grid coordinates of segmented point features $\boldsymbol{o}_k$, and instead of the intensity value $f_{m,n}$ characterizing each image point, we use $\zeta_\kappa(\boldsymbol{o}_k)$ in the argument triple. Based on this substitution and considering the assignment as discrete random variables we obtain

$$p(\{(\boldsymbol{o}_k, \zeta_\kappa(\boldsymbol{o}_k))|k = 1, 2, \ldots, m\}|\kappa; \boldsymbol{\theta}) = \prod_{k=1}^{m} p(\zeta_\kappa(\boldsymbol{o}_\kappa))\, p(\boldsymbol{o}_k|\zeta_\kappa, \kappa; \boldsymbol{\theta}) \tag{26.21}$$

if independent point features are assumed.

Unlike the intensity values f in the corresponding density Eq. (26.14), the assignment $\zeta_\kappa(\boldsymbol{o}_k)$ of single-point features is unknown. We have *no information* on the correspondence between 3-D points and 2-D observations. Because the assignment is modeled as a random variable, we make use of the power of statistical framework and eliminate this random measure by marginalization. We sum Eq. (26.21) over all possible assignments. This yields the model density of the observed 2-D points without knowing the originally required correspondence defined by ζ_κ

$$p(\{\boldsymbol{o}_k|k=1,2,\ldots,m\}|\kappa;\boldsymbol{\theta}) = \sum_{\zeta_\kappa}\prod_{k=1}^{m} p(\zeta_\kappa(\boldsymbol{o}_k))\, p(\boldsymbol{o}_k|\zeta_\kappa,\kappa;\boldsymbol{\theta}) \quad (26.22)$$

Example 26.6: Point features under orthographic projection

Statistical tests show that point features in images are approximately normally distributed [24]. The mapping from the 3-D world to 2-D images is defined by an orthographic projection. If a 3-D point $\boldsymbol{c}$ is rotated, translated and projected orthographically, this mapping is known to be affine [1]. There exists a matrix $\boldsymbol{R} \in \mathbb{R}^{2\times 3}$ and a translation vector $\boldsymbol{t} \in \mathbb{R}^2$, which map the 3-D point $\boldsymbol{c}$ to the 2-D point $\boldsymbol{o}$

$$\boldsymbol{o} = \boldsymbol{R}\boldsymbol{c} + \boldsymbol{t} \quad (26.23)$$

The constraint that 2-D point features observed in the image are normally distributed still holds if we assume the corresponding 3-D point features to be Gaussian (see Eq. (26.17)). Let $\boldsymbol{\mu}_{\kappa,\zeta_\kappa(\boldsymbol{o}_k)}$ be the 3-D mean vector of the 3-D model point indexed by $\zeta_\kappa(\boldsymbol{o}_k)$ of class Ω_κ, which corresponds to $\boldsymbol{o}_k$. If the orthographic projection is known, these two vectors are related by Eq. (26.23), and the 2-D mean vector of the image point is defined by

$$\boldsymbol{\mu}'_{\kappa,\zeta_\kappa(\boldsymbol{o}_k)} := \boldsymbol{R}\boldsymbol{\mu}_{\kappa,\zeta_\kappa(\boldsymbol{o}_k)} + \boldsymbol{t}$$

Analogously, the (2×2) covariance matrix is given by

$$\boldsymbol{\Sigma}'_{\kappa,\zeta_\kappa(\boldsymbol{o}_k)} := \boldsymbol{R}\boldsymbol{\Sigma}_{\kappa,\zeta_\kappa(\boldsymbol{o}_k)}\boldsymbol{R}^T$$

where $\boldsymbol{R}\boldsymbol{\Sigma}_{\kappa,\zeta_\kappa(\boldsymbol{o}_k)}\boldsymbol{R}^T$ denotes the (3×3) covariance matrix of the 3-D model point. The model density of observed 2-D point features in the presence of unknown assignments is therefore

$$\begin{aligned} & p(\{\boldsymbol{o}_k|k=1,2,\ldots,m\}|\kappa;\boldsymbol{\theta}) \\ & = \sum_{\zeta_\kappa}\prod_{k=1}^{m} p(\zeta_\kappa(\boldsymbol{o}_k))\,\mathcal{N}(\boldsymbol{o}_k;\boldsymbol{\mu}'_{\kappa,\zeta_\kappa(\boldsymbol{o}_k)},\boldsymbol{\Sigma}'_{\kappa,\zeta_\kappa(\boldsymbol{o}_k)}) \end{aligned} \quad (26.24)$$

This model density is experimentally studied in [20]. The empirical evaluation uses 4 polyhedral objects as shown in Fig. 26.8. The parameters of the model density are estimated automatically (see also

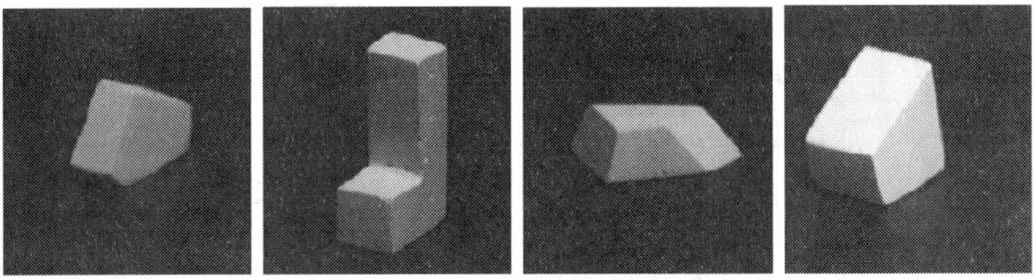

Figure 26.8: *Polyhedral 3-D objects.*

Section 26.5 and Example 26.12), where training images contain 400 views of each object. The disjoint test set also includes 400 samples of each class, and the achieved recognition rate based on sparse point features is 70 %. An example where this probabilistic model is used for pose estimation is illustrated in Fig. 5.2, Chapter 5. In consideration of the tremendous reduction of information using only 2-D point features instead of complete images this result represents a lower bound of the achievable recognition rate. Features of higher discriminatory power, which also incorporate implicit 3-D information—such as the available models that use point features—will reduce misclassifications.

The probabilistic models introduced so far use intensity images or segmentation results as input data, and in fact they represent extreme cases concerning independency assumptions; we have always used mutually independent random variables; either grid points, intensities, assignments or point features were independent and the corresponding densities properly factorized. In the following we will discuss statistical representations that also incorporate dependencies of higher (i. e., arbitrary) order.

26.4.4 Markov random fields

Very popular and widely used probabilistic models in image processing and computer vision are *Markov random fields* (MRFs) [16, 25, 26] (Section 12.2.13). MRFs in general allow the use of locally bounded dependencies. We introduce the basic concepts of MRFs in an abstract manner, and illustrate these using concrete examples out of the field of computer vision.

Let $X = \{X_i | i = 1, 2, \ldots, L\}$ define a set of random variables. We suppose that for each random variable X_i there exists a well-defined neighborhood. The set of neighbors of X_i is commonly denoted by [26]

$$\partial(X_i) = \{X_j | \; X_i \text{ and } X_j \text{ are neighbors}\} \tag{26.25}$$

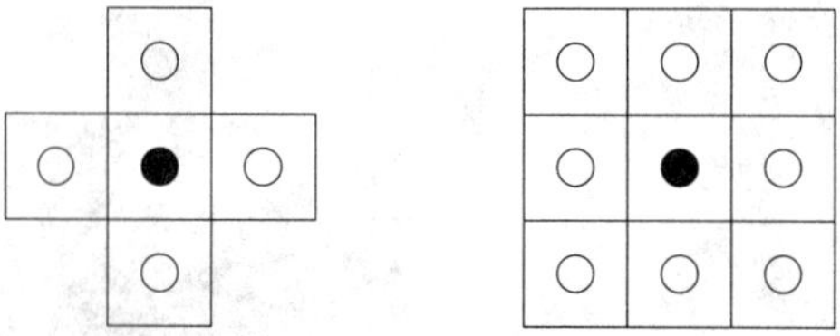

Figure 26.9: *Neighborhoods of first (left) and second (right) order.*

Example 26.7: First- and second-order neighbors

In image processing applications the random measures X_i are usually intensity values, and local *neighborhood* is based on the given structure of the image grid. For instance, we can consider each random measure associated with a pixel to be a neighbor of a certain random variable if the Euclidean distance of grid coordinates is one (*first-order neighborhood*) or lower or equal to $\sqrt{2}$ (*second-order neighborhood*). Figure 26.9 illustrates first- and second-order neighborhoods.

The introduction of neighborhoods based on the topology of image grids is most common in image processing. Because we interpret each image point as a triple $[m, n, f_{m,n}]^T$, the definition of contra-intuitive neighborhood relations also is possible: analoguos to intensities, we can also consider the grid point $[m, n]^T$ associated with an intensity value f as a random variable. Now a neighborhood relationship can be induced using intensities. For instance, if we consider gray-level images, we define grid points to be neighbors if the absolute difference between their gray levels is bounded by a threshold. This neighborhood shows no obvious geometric interpretation in the image plane because pixels that are far apart in the image grid are considered to be neighbors.

Mathematically, MRFs are defined by two basic properties:

1. *Positivity:* The probability of observing an arbitrary set of random variables X is nonzero, that is,

$$p(X) > 0 \tag{26.26}$$

2. *Markov property:* The probability of observing a certain random variable $X_i \in X$ depends only on its neighbors $\partial(X_i)$, that is,

$$p(X_i | \{X_1, X_2, \ldots, X_{i-1}, X_{i+1}, \ldots, X_L\}) = p(X_i | \partial(X_i)) \tag{26.27}$$

The Markov property introduces statistical dependencies of bounded order and defines the local characteristics of the MRF. The order of dependency is herein the cardinality of the set of neighbors. The preceding used neighborhood system induces a graph structure on the random variables, and therefore it enables us to use the language of graph theory in the context of Markov random fields; the vertices of the graph are defined by the random variables, and two vertices are connected by

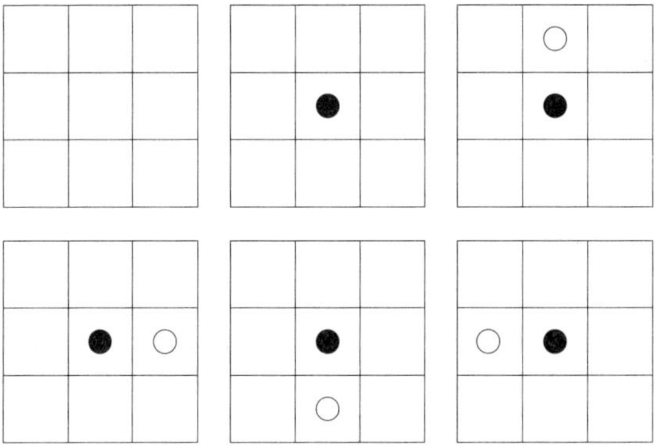

Figure 26.10: *Cliques corresponding to first-order neighborhoods.*

an edge if the corresponding random variables are neighbors. This analogy between neighborhoods, random variables and graphs also allows the notion of cliques. In graph theory a *clique* is defined as a set of vertices in which all pairs are mutual neighbors, that is, a clique defines a complete subgraph.

Example 26.8: Cliques of first- and second-order neighborhoods

Unconsciously, we already made use of the analogy of neighborhood systems and graphs in Example 26.7 where we have visualized dependencies between image points. Obviously, only pairs of vertices connected by an edge satisfy the clique definition, which requires a mutual neighborhood relation between all vertices. Figure 26.10 shows the cliques to the graph associated with the first-order neighborhood. Note also that the empty graph is by definition a clique.

Equipped with the neighborhood systems and the concept of cliques, now we are able to compute the joint density of MRFs with the most current tools: The *equivalence theorem* for MRFs [26] states that the joint density $p(X)$ over all random variables X is proportional to a product of real-valued functions associated with cliques of the graph. The clique functions, however, have to be symmetric in their arguments, that is, whenever we change the order of input variables, the output is not affected. If $C = \{C_1, C_2, \ldots, C_P\}$ denotes the set of cliques and X_{C_i} the random variables belonging to clique C_i, then there exists a set of clique functions $\phi_{C_i}(X_{C_i})$, $i = 1, 2, \ldots, P$, such that

$$p(X) = \frac{1}{Z} \prod_{C_i \in C} \phi_{C_i}(X_{C_i}) \tag{26.28}$$

The denominator Z is a normalization factor, which guarantees that the integral over the complete domain of the density function turns out to be unity; Z is constant and due to its definition, is independent of the actual random variable X. Fortunately, the positivity constraint Eq. (26.26) allows writing this product in *Gibbsian form.* For the set of random variables X, the overall density leads to the so-called *Gibbs field*

$$p(X) = \frac{1}{Z} \exp\left(- \sum_{C_i \in C} V_{C_i}(X_{C_i}) \right) = \frac{1}{Z} \exp(-U(X)) \tag{26.29}$$

Gibbs distributions are well studied in statistical physics and according to physicists we call the function V_{C_i} *potential function*, which maps the set of random variables belonging to clique C_i to real values; the sum $U(X)$ of potentials is the *energy function.* In case of discrete random variables, here Z is defined by the marginal

$$Z = \sum_{Y} \exp(-U(Y)) \tag{26.30}$$

The computation of conditional densities using Gibbs distributions is surprisingly simple. If the Markov field is given in Gibbsian form, the conditional dependency for observing any random variable X_j satisfies

$$\begin{aligned} p(X_j | X_1, \ldots, X_{j-1}, X_{j+1}, X_L) &= \frac{\exp\left(\sum_{C_i \in C} V_{C_i}(X_{C_i})\right)}{\sum_{X_j} \exp\left(\sum_{C_i \in C} V_{C_i}(X_{C_i})\right)} \\ &= \frac{\exp\left(\sum_{C_i \in C(X_j)} V_{C_i}(X_{C_i})\right)}{\sum_{X_j} \exp\left(\sum_{C_i \in C(X_j)} V_{C_i}(X_{C_i})\right)} \end{aligned} \tag{26.31}$$

where $C(X_j)$ is the set of all cliques including random variable X_j. All factors of the numerator and denominator cancel that do not contain an element of the clique C_j to which the random variable X_j belongs. This shows that the conditional density of random variable X_j depends on its local neighborhood—as required by the Markov property.

Most computer vision researchers are usually less familiar with statistical physics, and therefore the use of the Gibbs fields seems inconvenient and apparently not necessarily advantageous. However, we have seen in (26.31) that this notation is advantageous for the computation of conditional probabilities, and we abate the first skepticism on Gibbs distributions looking at a familiar but also degenerated example:

Example 26.9: A trivial Markov random field

Again, we consider the probabilistic image model as introduced in Eq. (26.10). There we proposed the idealized assumption that all intensity values $f_{m,n}$ in the image grid are mutually independent. This independency structure induces a trivial neighborhood system on the image grid: the set of nontrivial cliques is defined by empty singletons.

According to the definition of MRFs, Eq. (26.10) defines a Markov random field if the positivity constraint is valid. The latter is obviously true if we model the distributions of intensity values at each image point by Gaussians. Because positivity guarantees the equivalence between Markov random and Gibbs fields, there has to exist a clique representation of the joint density $p(\boldsymbol{f}|\kappa;\boldsymbol{\theta})$ based on Gibbsian forms. Originally we had the product over all singletons

$$p(\boldsymbol{f}|\kappa;\boldsymbol{\theta}) = \frac{1}{Z}\prod_{m=1}^{M}\prod_{n=1}^{N} p(f_{m,n}|m,n,\kappa;\boldsymbol{\theta}) \tag{26.32}$$

where $p(f_{m,n}|\kappa;\boldsymbol{\theta})$ denotes the probability density of intensities at $[m,n]^T$. The restriction to Gaussians (Eq. (26.11)) shows that the representation in Eq. (26.32) already complies with a Gibbs distribution Eq. (26.29). Therefore, Eq. (26.10) defines an MRF.

Unfortunately, Gibbs distributions do not provide a unique representation of MRFs. In fact, arbitrary positive densities $p(X)$ can be transformed to an infinite set of Gibbsian forms: For an arbitrary strictly positive scalar c we define

$$U(X) = -\log\,(c \cdot p(X)) \tag{26.33}$$

and

$$Z = \sum_{Y}\exp(-U(Y)) = \sum_{Y} c \cdot p(Y) = c \tag{26.34}$$

since $\log(\cdot)$ and $\exp(\cdot)$ are mutually inverse. This simple procedure leads to a Gibbsian representation of $p(X)$.

So far, we have seen that MRFs define a Gibbs field. The equivalence theorem states that this is also true in reverse order: each Gibbs field induces a Markov random field. This remarkable correspondence between Markov random and Gibbs fields was discovered by Hammersley and Clifford. The rather technical proof of the Gibbs-Markov equivalence is omitted and beyond the scope of this chapter. The interested reader will find a pretty elegant version in [26].

In practice, the knowledge of the equivalence theorem reveals two options to define priors and model densities based on MRF:

1. We ignore the result on Gibbs distributions and compute the joint density for a set of random variables by standard manipulations. One example are 1-D Markov chains that are extensively used in speech recognition [12]. There, the probability of observing a set of random variables $p(X)$ is usually computed using the factorization

$$p([X_1, X_2, \ldots, X_L]) = p(X_1)\prod_{i=2}^{L} p(X_i|X_{i-1}) \tag{26.35}$$

Two random variables X_i and X_j are considered to be neighbors if the difference of indices is ± 1. In the context of Markov chains the explicit factorization based on clique functions in Gibbsian form is quite uncommon, and learning corresponds here to the immediate estimation of $p(X_1)$ and the transition probabilities $p(X_i|X_{i-1})$ instead of estimating potential functions. In case of bounded dependency, we have the identity

$$p(X_j|X_1,\ldots,X_{j-1},X_{j+1},\ldots,X_L) = p(X_j|X_{j-1})p(X_{j+1}|X_j) \quad (26.36)$$

and therefore X_j depends only on its neighbors $\partial(X_j) = \{X_{j-1}, X_{j+1}\}$ This yields:

$$p(X_j|X_1,\ldots,X_{j-1},X_{j+1},\ldots,X_L) = p(X_j|\partial(X_j)) \quad (26.37)$$

2. According to the given application we define a neighborhood system, consider the associated graph, and define the energy function in terms of clique potentials. The evaluation of the density for a given observation is done by multiplying clique functions Eq. (26.37). If, for instance, a parametric representation of clique potentials is selected, learning is restricted to the estimation of these degrees of freedom.

Both strategies—the explicit use of conditional densities and the application of Gibbsian densities—are in fact equivalent and useful in practice. It obviously depends on the concrete problem and the given model as to which representation is advantageous. Let us consider two examples based on the Gibbsian form of Markov random fields that define prior densities of images, and a 2-D Markov chain model that is applied to image segmentation.

Example 26.10: The Ising model

One of the most referenced and nontrivial introductory examples of MRFs is the Ising model, which was invented by the physicist E. Ising. It is a statistical model to explain empirical observations on ferromagnetism theoretically. We state this model in terms of images and intensity values, as we are more familiar with this terminology. Let us consider images as a 2-D square lattice. We induce a graph structure according to neighbors of first order. The range of discrete intensity values $f_{m,n}$ is restricted to $\{\pm 1\}$. In the physical model these intensity values describe the *spin* at the considered lattice point. The energy of the complete random field is supposed to be minimal if all spins are identical. This is obviously valid for the energy function

$$U(\boldsymbol{f}) = -\alpha\left(\sum_{m=1}^{M-1}\sum_{n=1}^{N} f_{m,n}f_{m+1,n} + \sum_{m=1}^{M}\sum_{n=1}^{N-1} f_{m,n}f_{m,n+1}\right) \quad (26.38)$$

where $\alpha > 0$.

Ising's model, however, does not weight singleton cliques (see also Fig. 26.9) by zero as suggested in Eq. (26.38), but incorporates these

***Figure 26.11:** Two images maximizing the prior defined by Eq. (26.39).*

singleton potentials in the energy function as an additive term weighted by β

$$U(\boldsymbol{f}) = -\alpha\left(\sum_{m=1}^{M-1}\sum_{n=1}^{N} f_{m,n}f_{m+1,n} + \sum_{m=1}^{M}\sum_{n=1}^{N-1} f_{m,n}f_{m,n+1}\right) + \beta\sum_{m=1}^{M}\sum_{n=1}^{N} f_{m,n} \tag{26.39}$$

We omit the physical interpretation of α and β, which basically depend on the temperature and the chosen material. For different choices of these parameters we get different binary images that maximize the density function of this Gibbs field. Figure 26.11 shows some examples.

Example 26.11: Third-order Markov random field

A remarkable and rich subclass of Markov random fields are *third-order Markov mesh fields* as introduced by Abend et al. [27]. Third-order Markov mesh fields of an image $\boldsymbol{f}$ are defined by the conditional densities

$$p(f_{m,n}|\{f_{k,l}|k < m \quad \text{or} \quad l < n\}) = p\left(f_{m,n}\,\middle|\,\begin{matrix} f_{m-1,n-1} & f_{m-1,n} \\ f_{m,n-1} & \end{matrix}\right) \tag{26.40}$$

where the spatial ordering of the conditional random variables visualizes the chosen neighborhood. In analogy to 1-D Markov chains, these conditional probabilities require a special treatment at the boundaries. The boundary densities are given by the marginals

$$p\left(f_{m,n}\,\middle|\,\begin{matrix} f_{m-1,n-1} & f_{m-1,n} \\ f_{m,n-1} & \end{matrix}\right) = \begin{cases} p(f_{m,n}) & , \quad \text{if} \quad m = n = 1 \\ p(f_{m,n}|f_{m,n-1}) & , \quad \text{if} \quad n > m = 1 \\ p(f_{m,n}|f_{m-1,n}) & , \quad \text{if} \quad m > n = 1 \end{cases} \tag{26.41}$$

The joint probability for observing an image $\boldsymbol{f}$ is obtained by the product

$$p(\boldsymbol{f}) = \prod_{m=1}^{M}\prod_{n=1}^{N} p\left(f_{m,n}\,\middle|\,\begin{matrix} f_{m-1,n-1} & f_{m-1,n} \\ f_{m,n-1} & \end{matrix}\right) \tag{26.42}$$

If we also assume that all transition probabilities are spatially homogeneous, that is, the probabilities in Eq. (26.40) are independent from the position defined by $[m, n]^T$ in the image grid, we can estimate the number of discrete probabilities required to define this random field: for G discrete intensity values we need G^4 discrete probabilities. Using the Gibbsian form of MRF it is straightforward to show that the forementioned definition leads to the Markov property [27] (see also Eq. (26.37))

$$p(f_{m,n}|\{f_{k,l}|k \neq m, l \neq m\}) = p\left(f_{m,n} \left| \begin{array}{ccc} f_{m-1,n-1} & f_{m-1,n} & f_{m-1,n+1} \\ f_{m,n-1} & & f_{m,n+1} \\ f_{m+1,n-1} & f_{m-1,n} & f_{m+1,n+1} \end{array} \right. \right) \tag{26.43}$$

This is a basic result, which states that Eqs. (26.40) and (26.41) and the Markov property Eq. (26.43) define the same random fields.

Up to now we have considered MRFs in general and the given examples have shown that MRFs can be used to define priors (Example 26.10 and Example 26.11); we can define a probability density for a given set of observations. The *Bayesian classifier*, however, requires the definition of posterior probabilities including priors and model densities.

Major applications of Markov random field models do not deal with object recognition and pose estimation, but with image labeling [16, 26]. Based on prior models and observations a labeled image is computed using Bayesian labeling: this can be a restored image [25], a transformation into line segments [28], or texture segmentation [29].

26.5 Automatic model generation

We have introduced various probabilistic models. With the exception of histograms the discussion has neglected the problem of model generation. Of course, the explicit construction of model densities by human interaction has to be avoided. In general, the objective of learning is to generate a probability density function that best describes the statistical behavior of training samples. As already stated in the Introduction, learning of probabilistic models conceptually includes both automatic acquisition of the *structure* and the *model parameters* based on empirical data. Both subproblems interact, and cannot be considered as mutually independent parts. Variations of the model structure, obviously, change the number of parameters. The common principle of structural and parametric learning is as follows:

- we define a search space;
- choose an objective function that scores the actual structure or parameter set;

- use a search algorithm that guides the navigation in the search space; and
- terminate learning, if no improvement occurs.

In spite of fitting into this general framework, the overall complexity of both learning problems is completely different. While the estimation of parameters usually corresponds to optimization problems of continuous functions, structural optimization implies a search problem in a combinatorial space of exponential size. At the beginning of the discussion of training algorithms, let us assume the structure of the model density is known, and learning reduces to a *parameter estimation* problem.

26.5.1 Parameter estimation

There exists a vast literature on *parameter estimation* techniques, and the basic problem is the definition of an accurate objective function, which has to be optimized with respect to model parameters. The most popular *parameter estimation* techniques are the maximum likelihood (ML) and the maximum *a posteriori* (MAP) estimation [9]. We will not summarize these standard techniques, but present a more general *parameter estimation* algorithm, which is applied especially in the presence of incomplete sample data and which has an excellent reputation for model generation. Indeed, most estimation problems in computer vision have to deal with incomplete information: missing depth information; self occlusion; segmentation errors; unknown correspondences of features; etc. In 1977, Dempster et al. came up with the *expectation maximization algorithm* (EM algorithm, [30, 31]), which is especially constructed for estimation problems with latent data and is in fact a generalized version of ML estimation.

The basic idea of the *EM algorithm* uses the *missing information principle*. In colloquial speech the available training data are constituted by the equation:

$$\begin{aligned}\text{observable information} &= \text{complete information}\\ &\quad - \text{missing information}\end{aligned}$$

This difference can be rewritten in terms of classical information theory: Let X be the random variable for the observable data. The aleatory variable Y denotes the missing data. Thus the complete information is represented by the pair (X, Y). All these random variables are associated with parametric distributions: $p(X;\boldsymbol{B})$; $p(Y;\boldsymbol{B})$; and $p(X, Y;\boldsymbol{B})$, where the shared parameter set is summarized by $\boldsymbol{B}$. Obviously, we can apply Bayes' rule and get: $p(X;\boldsymbol{B}) = p(X, Y;\boldsymbol{B})/p(Y|X;\boldsymbol{B})$ In a straightforward manner the application of the logarithm induces the difference

$$(-\log p(X|\boldsymbol{B})) = (-\log p(X, Y|\boldsymbol{B})) - (-\log p(Y|X, \boldsymbol{B})) \tag{26.44}$$

Here, the negative log-likelihood function $(-\log p(X; \boldsymbol{B}))$ denotes the observable, the term $(-\log p(X, Y; \boldsymbol{B}))$ the complete, and $(-\log p(Y| X; \boldsymbol{B}))$ the missing information. We conclude that the informal principle in Eq. (26.44) corresponds to the forementioned colloquial description.

The maximization of the log-likelihood function $\log p(X; \boldsymbol{B})$ with respect to the parameter set $\boldsymbol{B}$ results in a maximum likelihood estimation. Instead of maximizing $\log p(X|\boldsymbol{B})$, we could also minimize the difference on the right-hand side of Eq. (26.44). This observation leads to an iterative estimation technique for the parameter set $\boldsymbol{B}$:

Assume that $\widehat{\boldsymbol{B}}^{(0)}$ is the initial estimate of $\boldsymbol{B}$, and $\widehat{\boldsymbol{B}}^{(i)}$ denotes the estimated value of the ith iteration step. Now we consider Eq. (26.44) in the $(i+1)$-st iteration. The multiplication of both sides by the conditional density $p(Y|X; \widehat{\boldsymbol{B}}^{(i)})$ and the marginalization over the non-observable part Y, results into the *key-equation* of the *EM algorithm*

$$
\begin{aligned}
&\underbrace{\int \left(\log p(X|\widehat{\boldsymbol{B}}^{(i+1)})\right) p(Y|X, \widehat{\boldsymbol{B}}^{(i)})\, dY}_{(a)} = \\
&\qquad \underbrace{\int \left(\log p(X, Y|\widehat{\boldsymbol{B}}^{(i+1)})\right) p(Y|X, \widehat{\boldsymbol{B}}^{(i)})\, dY}_{(b)} \\
&\qquad - \underbrace{\int \left(\log p(Y|X, \widehat{\boldsymbol{B}}^{(i+1)})\right) p(Y|X, \widehat{\boldsymbol{B}}^{(i)})\, dY}_{(c)}
\end{aligned}
\qquad (26.45)
$$

This equation shows some remarkable properties [30]:

a) Since $\log p(X|\widehat{\boldsymbol{B}}^{(i+1)})$ is independent of Y, the variable of the integral, we get

$$
\int \left(\log p(X|\widehat{\boldsymbol{B}}^{(i+1)})\right) p(Y|X, \widehat{\boldsymbol{B}}^{(i)})\, dY = \log p(X|\widehat{\boldsymbol{B}}^{(i+1)}) \qquad (26.46)
$$

the log-likelihood function of Eq. (26.44). The multiplication and marginalization have no effect on the left-hand side of Eq. (26.44).

b) The term

$$
Q(\widehat{\boldsymbol{B}}^{(i+1)}|\widehat{\boldsymbol{B}}^{(i)}) := \int \left(\log p(X, Y|\widehat{\boldsymbol{B}}^{(i+1)})\right) p(Y|X, \widehat{\boldsymbol{B}}^{(i)})\, dY \qquad (26.47)
$$

is a conditional expectation for the complete information, if $\widehat{\boldsymbol{B}}^{(i)}$ and X are known. In the following, we call this expectation *Q-function* or *Kullback-Leibler statistics* in accordance with [30].

c) The last term

$$
H(\widehat{\boldsymbol{B}}^{(i+1)}|\widehat{\boldsymbol{B}}^{(i)}) := \int \left(\log p(Y|X, \widehat{\boldsymbol{B}}^{(i+1)})\right) p(Y|X, \widehat{\boldsymbol{B}}^{(i)})\, dY \qquad (26.48)
$$

denotes the negative entropy of the missing information. A consequence of Jensen's inequality is that Eq. (26.48) decreases within each iteration, that is,

$$H(\widehat{\boldsymbol{B}}^{(i+1)}|\widehat{\boldsymbol{B}}^{(i)}) - H(\widehat{\boldsymbol{B}}^{(i)}|\widehat{\boldsymbol{B}}^{(i)}) \leq 0 \tag{26.49}$$

These conclusions suggest an iterative approximation of the maximum likelihood estimation: instead of the maximization of the log-likelihood, we iteratively maximize the Kullback-Leibler statistics (Eq. (26.47)), which automatically decreases (Eq. (26.48)). This iterative process of maximizing (M-step) the expectation (Eq. (26.47)) (E-step) characterizes the *expectation maximization algorithm.*

The advantages of the EM algorithm are versatile. The basic idea is motivated by the *parameter estimation* problem with missing information. Mostly, the EM algorithm decouples the estimation process in a manner that fits well with the modular structures of the chosen statistical models. The high-dimensional optimization problems are often decomposed in lower-dimensional independent search problems, which result in closed-form iteration formulas or optimization problems of the Q-function with iterative inner loops.

In most applications the EM technique yields simple and elegant algorithms, which have low storage requirements due to its iterative nature, and are easily implemented. With respect to numerical stabilities, the maximization of Kullback-Leibler statistics has proven to be more robust than direct ML estimation [22].

Despite these arguments, the EM algorithm shows some major disadvantages: It is known to be a local optimization method with a linear convergence rate [30]. Thus the success of the *parameter estimation* depends greatly on the chosen initial value $\widehat{\boldsymbol{B}}^{(0)}$. If the initialization is not close to the global optimum of the likelihood function, the EM iterations will not succeed and terminate in a local maximum of the log-likelihood function. There are several modifications of the EM algorithm for improving the low convergence rate [9], but they are omitted here.

This general introduction of the EM algorithm opens a wide range of applications, and the intuitive introduction based on the missing information principle will simplify the usage of EM to solve specific parameter estimation problems.

We conclude this subsection on parameter estimation by demonstrating the power of the EM algorithm using a concrete probability model introduced in Example 26.6:

Example 26.12: Estimation of mean vectors from projections in the presence of unknown assignments

Let us assume we have to estimate the mean vectors of normally distributed 3-D points based on 2-D points from different viewpoints; see Fig. 26.7 for some example views. The mapping of 3-D points to the 2-D space is supposed to be orthogonal, and the correspondence between the observed 2-D and 3-D points is unknown. Training data using multiple views include:

- the set of point features of each view, which are denoted by ${}^{\varrho}\boldsymbol{O} = \{{}^{\varrho}\boldsymbol{o}_1, \ldots, {}^{\varrho}\boldsymbol{o}_{{}^{\varrho}m}\}$ for the ϱth view. Here, ${}^{\varrho}n_{\kappa}$ is the number of point features of the ϱth view; and
- for each training view the pose parameters. These are affine transform, and represented by the matrix ${}^{\varrho}\boldsymbol{R} \in \mathbb{R}^{2\times 3}$ and the vector ${}^{\varrho}\boldsymbol{t} \in \mathbb{R}^2$ for each sample view indexed by ϱ.

We assume that the model density introduced in Eq. (26.24) characterizes the appearance of observations in the image. The estimation of 3-D mean vectors has to be done unsupervised with respect to these correspondences, as they are not part of observations. Obviously, this is a parameter estimation problem based on latent data. The application of the EM algorithm requires the successive maximization of the Kullback-Leibler statistics. Here, the observable random variables are the 2-D points (i. e., X=$\boldsymbol{O}$) and the *hidden variables* are represented by the assignment between 2-D and 3-D points, (i. e., $Y = [\zeta_{\kappa}(\boldsymbol{o}_1), \ldots, \zeta_{\kappa}(\boldsymbol{o}_m)]$). We omit the technical computation of the Kullback Leibler statistics; for details we refer to [20]. We get the final iteration formula, which successively maximizes the Q-function with respect to the 3-D mean vector $\boldsymbol{\mu}_{\kappa,j}$ belonging to the jth 3-D feature of class Ω_{κ}

$$\widehat{\boldsymbol{\mu}}_{\kappa,j}^{(i+1)} = \left(\sum_{\varrho} \sum_{k=1}^{{}^{\varrho}m} p(\varrho,k)\, {}^{\varrho}\boldsymbol{R}^T ({}^{\varrho}\boldsymbol{R} \widehat{\boldsymbol{\Sigma}}_{\kappa,j}^{(i+1)}\, {}^{\varrho}\boldsymbol{R}^T)^{-1}\, {}^{\varrho}\boldsymbol{R} \right)^{-1} \sum_{\varrho} \sum_{k=1}^{{}^{\varrho}m} p(\varrho,k)\, {}^{\varrho}\boldsymbol{R}^T ({}^{\varrho}\boldsymbol{R} \widehat{\boldsymbol{\Sigma}}_{\kappa,j}^{(i+1)}\, {}^{\varrho}\boldsymbol{R}^T)^{-1} ({}^{\varrho}\boldsymbol{o}_k - {}^{\varrho}\boldsymbol{t}) \tag{26.50}$$

where

$$p(\varrho,k) = \frac{\widehat{p}^{(i)}(j)\, p({}^{\varrho}\boldsymbol{o}_k | \widehat{\boldsymbol{\mu}}_{\kappa,j}^{(i)}, \widehat{\boldsymbol{\Sigma}}_{\kappa,j}^{(i)}, {}^{\varrho}\boldsymbol{R}, {}^{\varrho}\boldsymbol{t})}{\sum_{l=1}^{{}^{\varrho}n_{\kappa}} \widehat{p}^{(i)}(l)\, p({}^{\varrho}\boldsymbol{o}_k | \widehat{\boldsymbol{\mu}}_{\kappa,j}^{(i)}, \widehat{\boldsymbol{\Sigma}}_{\kappa,j}^{(i)}, {}^{\varrho}\boldsymbol{R}, {}^{\varrho}\boldsymbol{t})} \tag{26.51}$$

This iteration formula allows the estimation of 3-D mean vectors using 2-D observations without knowing the assignment. Although this formula seems quite complicated it is can be reduced to the well-known estimator for mean vectors by specialization: Assume the object is respresented by a single feature in each view, that is, ${}^{\varrho}m = 1$ for all ϱ, and there is no feature transform, that is, the affine transform is equal to the identity, and re-evaluate Eq. (26.50).

26.5.2 Automatic learning of model structure

The methods for *learning* the structure of probabilistic models are far beyond the available results in parameter estimation. In structural learning, we have to find:

- the dependency structure of random variables; and
- the number of stochastic processes incorporated in the probabilistic model.

As in parameter estimation the most obvious criterion for optimization is the likelihood function, but it has to be used cautiously. Without any regularization, structural optimization tends to over-fit the sample data in the sense that the resulting structure adapts to sample data perfectly. The estimated model structure is usually far too complex as the following example shows:

Example 26.13: Over-fitting in structural learning

Suppose we know that two features $\boldsymbol{o}_1$ and $\boldsymbol{o}_2$ belonging to one object are mutually independent. Each feature can be detected with the probability 0.5. Based on the maximum likelihood criterion, structural learning now decides whether or not these features are mutually independent in the observation. For all observations we will get the ML estimate that exactly fits the observation, specifically, we select the probability that considers both features as mutually dependent random measures. Convince yourself using a sample set of 1000 images resulting in the following data and maximize the likelihood function:

- the pair $(\boldsymbol{o}_1, \boldsymbol{o}_2)$ is observed 200 times;
- only feature $\boldsymbol{o}_1$ show 300 images;
- the single feature $\boldsymbol{o}_2$ was detected in 250 images; and
- the segmentation algorithm was not able to compute any feature in 250 images.

Due to this observation of model over-fitting, it is suggested that an objective function be introduced that combines the maximum likelihood function with a scoring function for the model complexity [32]. In terms of Bayesian estimation, we maximize the *a posteriori* probability instead of the likelihood function. The prior probability for models therein measures the model complexity. The optimization has to be done using combinatorial search techniques such as genetic algorithms (see also Chapter 27, Section 27.5).

Because we have considered parameter estimation problems in the presence of latent training data, procedures for structural learning also have to be provided that work on incomplete training data. A variant of the EM algorithm—the *structural EM algorithm*—was recently developed and allows the training of model structures in the presence of incomplete training data [33]. The basic idea herein is to estimate missing variables using the actual structure and the available empirical data. The estimates are plugged in and we start structural optimization with a complete data set. The best structure (or a set including structures with highest scores) of this step is used for refining estimates of missing variables. The refinement of estimates and the optimization of the model structure are repeated until the procedure converges.

26.6 Practical issues

Before we conclude this chapter with a brief summary, we comment on some practical issues generally related to the usage of probabilistic models in computer vision.

The most critical decisions in probabilistic modeling are related to the dependency structure of considered random variables and the number of parameters in the chosen model. If probabilistic models do not result in satisfactory recognition rates, the most obvious problem might be caused by inaccurate independency assumptions and by the selection of inappropriate parametric distributions. The increase of dependencies and the related growth of free parameters suggest more accurate models. In fact, for many applications this is a totally false conclusion that is related to a fundamental problem in pattern recognition [19, 34]: the *curse-of-dimensionality*. Indeed it can be shown that:

- in high-dimensional spaces it is impossible to get large sample sets, that is, with increasing dimension an exponentially increasing number of data points is required to guarantee a densely sampled Euclidean space;
- all interpoint distances are large and rather equal;
- nearest neighborhoods are not local; and
- all data points are close to the boundary of the considered space.

The natural consequence of this principle is that a careless increase of model complexity will end in insufficient classification results. These are hard to understand if the engineer is not aware of the curse. The only way to avoid problems related to the curse-of-dimensionality is to restrict the considered functions to a special class of parametric functions. Reasonable high-dimensional models require some locally restricted structure or reduced parameters enforced by parameter tying; otherwise parametric models are not practical. But this strategy is two edged: Often probabilistic models are criticized because of incorporated independency assumptions—regardless of convincing experimental results. For a wide range of *classification* problems, however, even *naive Bayes* [11], which approximates class conditional densities of random vectors by the product of its marginals, is surprisingly successful. Theoretically, it is not yet completely solved and clear why these simple techniques often are superior to more sophisticated ones, but certainly one reason is the curse-of-dimensionality.

Another matter is based on the *bias variance trade-off* in parameter estimation. If a parameter set $\boldsymbol{B}$ has to be estimated using empirical data, the mean square error between the real value $\boldsymbol{B}_0$ and its estimate $\hat{\boldsymbol{B}}$ is a measure for the quality of the estimation procedure

$$E[(\boldsymbol{B}_0 - \hat{\boldsymbol{B}})^2] = (\boldsymbol{B}_0 - E[\hat{\boldsymbol{B}}])^2 + E[(\hat{\boldsymbol{B}} - E[\hat{\boldsymbol{B}}])^2] \tag{26.52}$$

The first term $(\boldsymbol{B}_0 - E[\hat{\boldsymbol{B}}])$ herein denotes the *bias* and $E[(\hat{\boldsymbol{B}} - E[\hat{\boldsymbol{B}}])^2]$ is the *variance* of the estimator. Typically, bias and variance interact: low bias induces high variance, low variance high bias. If the parametric model is correct, then the estimation is unbiased and even the variance will be low. However, if the chosen model does not exactly fit, we observe usually low bias but high variance, and minor changes in the training samples cause high variations in estimates. For that reason, restricted parametric models of lower variance are often preferred to more complex and highly parameterized density functions [35]. The high variance of these estimates also explains the success of the *bootstrap* [36], where the training set is sampled by replacement. Instead of using the training set as is, we randomly choose a subset of empirical data, estimate the parameters, and repeat this process several times. At the end the computed models are averaged and finally show a lower variance [37].

We assume implicitly that training data are sufficient for estimating the required parameters. The dimension of the chosen parameter space, the curse-of-dimensionality, the bootstrap, and the fact that we observe only samples of a subset of the real set of events are hints that this basic assumption is possibly wrong. Our models also have to consider and to predict random measures with a probability nonequal to zero, which are not part of the observation. At first glance, this seems awkward and most unrealistic. A simple example, however, shows its necessity: If we model objects by histograms it might happen that some intensity values are never observed. The histogram will include the probability 0 and whenever we observe this intensity value during runtime, the complete product of probabilities (Eq. (26.8)) will annihilate. This example shows that we also have to attend to methods that can deal with sparse training samples. Statistical models used for speech recognition have been used widely in this field. In many applications techniques such as *deleted interpolation* or *Good-Turing estimates* provide reliable estimates [12], and these methods will also support and improve probabilistic models in computer vision. Good estimates of parametric models are the crucial prerequisite for the successful use of probabilistic models.

26.7 Summary, conclusions, and discussion

This chapter provided an overview on probabilistic models in computer vision and related algorithms. The basic arguments that suggest a preference for probabilistic modeling schemes over others have been summarized. *Bayesian classifiers* allow the unified incorporation of prior knowledge and class-specific densities. However, it is a fundamental problem to define adequate statistical models that solve the trade-off between independency assumptions, the dimension of the parameter space, the curse-of-dimensionality, the size of available sample data, and the discriminatory power. The generic point of view starting with a general probabilistic model has proven to be advantageous: independencies and marginalization are powerful tools to switch between different levels of model densities. We have shown that mixture density models, hidden Markov models, Markov random fields, and others, have the same roots in the generic model of sensor data.

In the authors' opinion there is an immense potential for *probabilistic models* with regard to robust learning techniques, excellent classifiers, and a systematic and theoretically well-founded approach to active vision.

Acknowledgments

The authors gratefully acknowledge the fruitful discussions with William M. Wells (MIT, Harvard University) and Carlo Tomasi (Stanford University). This work was supported by the Deutsche Forschungsgemeinschaft (DFG), grants Ho 1791/2-1 and SFB 603.

26.8 References

[1] Faugeras, O., (1993). *Three-Dimensional Computer Vision—a Geometric Viewpoint.* Cambridge, MA: MIT Press.

[2] Xu, G. and Zhang, Z., (1996). *Epipolar Geometry in Stereo, Motion and Object Recognition—a Unified Approach,* Vol. 6 of *Computational Imaging and Vision.* Dordrecht: Kluwer Academic Press.

[3] Trucco, E. and Verri, A., (1998). *Introductory Techniques for 3-D Computer Vision.* New York: Prentice Hall.

[4] Jain, A. K. and Flynn, P. J. (eds.), (1993). *Three-Dimensional Object Recognition Systems.* Amsterdam: Elsevier.

[5] Ponce, J., Zisserman, and Hebert, M. (eds.), (1996). *Object Representation in Computer Vision,* Vol. 1144 of *Lecture Notes in Computer Science.* Heidelberg: Springer.

[6] Devroye, L., Györfi, L., and Lugosi, G., (1996). *A Probabilistic Theory in Pattern Recognition,* Vol. 31 of *Applications of Mathematics, Stochastic Modeling and Applied Probability.* Heidelberg: Springer.

[7] Niemann, H., (1990). *Pattern Analysis and Understanding*, Vol. 4 of *Springer Series in Information Sciences.* Heidelberg: Springer.

[8] Papoulis, A., (1991). *Probability, Random Variables, and Stochastic Processes*, 3 edition. Electrical Engineering: Communications and Signal Processing. New York: McGraw-Hill.

[9] Tanner, M. A., (1996). *Tools for Statistical Inference: Methods for the Exploration of Posterior Distributions and Likelihood Functions*, 3rd edition. Springer Series in Statistics. Heidelberg: Springer.

[10] Vapnik, V. N., (1996). *The Nature of Statistical Learning Theory.* Heidelberg: Springer.

[11] Ripley, B. D., (1996). *Pattern Recognition and Neural Networks.* Cambridge: Cambridge University Press.

[12] Jelinek, F., (1998). *Statistical Methods for Speech Recognition.* Cambridge, MA: MIT Press.

[13] Cover, T. M. and Thomas, J. A., (1991). *Elements of Information Theory.* Wiley Series in Telecommunications. New York: Wiley.

[14] Schiele, B. and Crowley, J. L., (1998). Transinformation for active object recognition. In *Proceedings of the* 6th *International Conference on Computer Vision (ICCV), Bombay*, pp. 249–254. Los Alamitos, CA: IEEE Computer Society Press.

[15] Shi, J. and Tomasi, C., (1994). Good features to track. In *Proceedings of Computer Vision and Pattern Recognition, Seattle, Washington*, pp. 593–600. Los Alamitos, CA: IEEE Computer Society Press.

[16] Li, S. Z., (1996). *Markov Random Field Modeling in Computer Vision.* Heidelberg: Springer.

[17] Altmann, S. L., (1986). *Rotations, Quaternions, and Double Groups.* Oxford: Oxford University Press.

[18] Green, P. and Silverman, B., (1994). *Nonparametric Regression and Generalized Linear Models: A Roughness Penalty Approach*, Vol. 58 of *Monographs on Statistics and Applied Probability.* New York: Chapman and Hall.

[19] Bellman, R. E., (1961). *Adaptive Control Process.* Princeton: Princeton University Press.

[20] Hornegger, J., (1996). *Statistische Modellierung, Klassifikation und Lokalisation von Objekten.* Aachen: Shaker.

[21] Pösl, J. and Niemann, H., (1997). Wavelet Features for Statistical Object Localization without Segmentation. In *Proceedings of the International Conference on Image Processing (ICIP), Santa Barbara, California, USA*, Vol. 3, pp. 170–173. Los Alamitos, CA: IEEE Computer Society Press.

[22] Redner, R. A. and Walker, H. F., (1984). Mixture densities, maximum likelihood and the EM algorithm. *Society for Industrial and Applied Mathematics Review*, **26**(2):195–239.

[23] Hornegger, J. and Niemann, H., (1995). Statistical Learning, Localization, and Identification of Objects. In *Proceedings of the* 5th *International Conference on Computer Vision (ICCV), Boston*, pp. 914–919. Los Alamitos, CA: IEEE Computer Society Press.

[24] Wells III, W. M., (1997). Statistical Approaches to Feature-Based Object Recognition. *International Journal of Computer Vision*, **21**(2):63–98.

[25] Geman, S. and Geman, D., (1984). Stochastic relaxation, Gibbs distributions, and the Bayesian restoration of images. *IEEE Trans. Pattern Analysis and Machine Intelligence*, **6**(6):721–741.

[26] Winkler, G., (1995). *Image Analysis, Random Fields and Dynamic Monte Carlo Methods*, Vol. 27 of *Applications of Mathematics*. Heidelberg: Springer.

[27] Abend, K., Hareley, T., and Kanal, L. N., (1965). Classification of binary random patterns. *IEEE Trans. Information Theory*, **IT**(11):538–544.

[28] Devijver, P. A. and Dekesel, M., (1987). Learning the Parameters of a Hidden Markov Random Field Image Model: A Simple Example. In *Pattern Recognition Theory and Applications*, P. A. Devijver and J. Kittler, eds., Vol. 30 of *NATO ASI Series F: Computer and System Sciences*, pp. 141–163. Heidelberg: Springer.

[29] Dubes, R. C. and Jain, A. K., (1993). Random Field Models in Image Analysis. In *Statistics and Images*, Vol. 1 of *Advances in Applied Statistics*, pp. 121–154. Abingdon: Carfax Publishing Company.

[30] Dempster, A., Laird, N., and Rubin, D., (1977). Maximum likelihood from incomplete data via the EM algorithm. *Jour. Royal Statistical Society, Series B (Methodological)*, **39**(1):1–38.

[31] Moon, T. K., (1996). The expectation-maximization algorithm. *Signal Processing*, **13**(6):47–60.

[32] Heckerman, D., (1995). *A Tutorial on Learning Bayesian Networks*. Technical Report MSR-TR-95-06, Microsoft Research Advanced Technology Division, Microsoft Corporation, Redmond, WA 98052.

[33] Friedman, N., (1998). The Bayesian structural EM algorithm. In *Proceedings of 14th Conf. on Uncertainty in Artificial Intelligence, Madison, Wisconsin*, p. to appear. Los Alamitos, CA: IEEE Computer Society Press.

[34] Bishop, C. M., (1995). *Neural Networks for Pattern Recognition*. Oxford: Oxford University Press.

[35] Hastie, T. and Tibshirani, R., (1990). *Generalized Linear Models*, Vol. 43 of *Monographs on Statistics and Applied Probability*. New York: Chapman and Hall.

[36] Efron, B. and Tibshirani, R., (1994). *An Introduction to the Bootstrap*, Vol. 57 of *Monographs on Statistics and Applied Probability*. New York: Chapman and Hall.

[37] Shao, J. and Tu, D., (1995). *The Jackknife and Bootstrap*. Springer Series in Statistics. Heidelberg: Springer.

27 Knowledge-Based Interpretation of Images

Heinrich Niemann

Lehrstuhl für Mustererkennung, Universität Erlangen-Nürnberg, Germany

27.1 Introduction

27.1.1 General remarks

The problem of image understanding is to transform a sensor signal, that is, an image or image sequence, into a task-specific symbolic description. This should be done not just somehow, but in an *optimal* manner, where optimality is still to be defined. It is not necessary to extract all information contained in the images but to provide the *relevant* information in a format that suits the subsequent usage, either by man or by machine. Usually, information is not required as arrays or subarrays of pixels, but in some symbolic and condensed format. An example is given in Fig. 27.1. Processing must be done within a time defined by the application. The provided results must be sufficiently reliable and processing must be robust with respect to various adverse

Handbook of Computer Vision and Applications
Volume 2
Signal Processing and Pattern Recognition

Copyright © 1999 by Academic Press
All rights of reproduction in any form reserved.
ISBN 0-12-379772-1/$30.00

conditions. It may be necessary to adapt automatically to changing properties of the images and imaging conditions. There may be time and equipment for an active exploration of an environment in order to optimize viewpoints for interpretation, as may be the case in service robotics, or there may be no (or very little) time and equipment to do so, as is usually the case in autonomous car driving. For such systems profitable applications are waiting or are already being exploited in areas like production automation, quality control, medical image interpretation, traffic control and guidance, remote sensing, inspection of machines or buildings or traffic routes, and sensor controlled autonomous robots and vehicles, to name a few.

Interpretation of sensory inputs can only be done with respect to an internal *model* or with respect to internal *knowledge* of the environment, where in principle the observations may in turn modify the internal model. Hence, all interpretation is model-based or knowledge-based.

We present an approach to represent a model of the task domain or the *a priori* knowledge about it in a *semantic network* and to compute an interpretation that is optimal with respect to a given judgment function. From among the different approaches to optimization we consider an algorithm based on *graph search* and we show that the optimization problem can also be solved iteratively by *combinatorial optimization.*

An early example of an operational system using this approach was described by Niemann et al. [1] and in the textbook by Sagerer and Niemann [2]. Related work on semantic networks can be found, for example, in Kumar [3], Niemann et al. [4], Shastri [5], and Sowa [6]. Other approaches to knowledge representation are rule-based systems, [7, 8, 9, 10], fuzzy rules, [11, 12], relational structures, [13, 14], or formal logic, [15, 16, 17]. We see the advantages of semantic networks in that they allow a well-structured representation of knowledge that approaches human intuition, that relations between elements of the knowledge base are made explicit and hence can be used efficiently, that context-dependent relations can be modeled and used for interpretation, that alternatives of processing and uncertain results can be handled via standard optimization procedures, and that usage of knowledge is possible by task-independent control algorithms having a sound theoretical basis. For knowledge representation in semantic networks several slightly different definitions were developed. We will outline here the approach developed in [2, 18] and refer the reader to the foregoing references for other definitions.

Algorithms and programs for information processing will require a lot of specialized knowledge from its designer, for example, knowledge about signal processing, statistical decision making, object-oriented programming, and the like. Therefore, sometimes almost anything is called "knowledge-based." In general, and in this contribution, the

a *b*

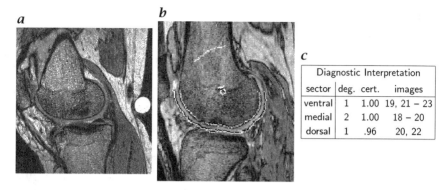

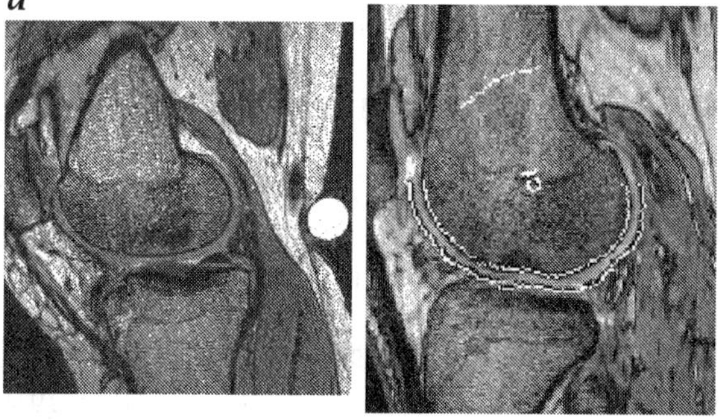

c

Diagnostic Interpretation			
sector	deg.	cert.	images
ventral	1	1.00	19, 21 – 23
medial	2	1.00	18 – 20
dorsal	1	.96	20, 22

Figure 27.1: ***a*** *An example (of a section) of an image from a magnetic resonance (MR) image sequence;* ***b*** *extracted contours of the cartilage; and* ***c*** *an automatically computed diagnostic interpretation showing also the degree of arthrosis and the certainty of the interpretation.*

term knowledge-based interpretation is reserved for an approach where task-specific knowledge is *explicitly* represented in the system for interpretation and where this knowledge is used by a *separate* and mainly *task-independent* control algorithm to compute an optimal interpretation. The representation of knowledge is treated in Section 27.2, optimal interpretation is defined in Section 27.3, control algorithms are treated in Section 27.4 and Section 27.5, general ideas for judgment functions are given in Section 27.6, and some extensions and remarks on applications are given in Section 27.7. Due to limitations of space, the presentation has to omit many details and formal definitions; these can be found in Sagerer and Niemann [2].

27.1.2 Overview of the approach

Based on statistical decision theory, the classification of 2-D and 3-D objects as well as spoken words and utterances traditionally is treated as an optimization problem, for example, see Section 26.3. Based on logic inferences, knowledge-based interpretation often is still related to rule-based and heuristic approaches. It is shown here that interpretation also can be formulated and solved as an optimization problem.

In any case, given an image the task is to compute a symbolic description which

- optimally fits to the observed images;
- is maximally compatible with explicitly represented task-specific knowledge;
- and contains all, or at least most of, the information requested by the user, which may be a human or a machine (see Fig. 27.1).

Therefore, image understanding basically is an *optimization problem.*

Two main phases of processing are assumed, that is, a phase of mainly data-driven processing and a phase of mainly model-driven processing. However, it is not assumed in general that these two phases are strictly sequential in the sense that the first phase must be finished before the second may start. Rather it is assumed that the timing of the phases, the data used by them, and the order of switching between phases is determined by a control strategy implemented by a *control module* or control algorithm. During data-driven processing no explicitly represented task-specific knowledge is used (e.g., no knowledge about cars or diseases of the knee), whereas during model-driven processing this knowledge is the essential part.

This view is motivated by the fact that the human visual system also seems to have two processing phases. One phase is mainly data-driven and subconscious, for example, when perceiving immediate cues like shades of gray, color, depth, or motion. The other phase works with conscious scrutiny, for example, when looking for a certain person or evaluating a medical image. In addition, present day image understanding systems start with some data-driven preprocessing and segmentation before going into model-driven processing.

We assume that the process of image understanding starts with some preprocessing (e.g., filtering, morphological operation, or normalization) transforming an image, that is, an array of pixels $\boldsymbol{f}$, into another image $\boldsymbol{h}$. We will not treat this step here. The next step is the computation of an *initial segmentation*

$$\mathcal{A} = \langle O \rangle \tag{27.1}$$

of the image. The initial segmentation $\mathcal{A}$ is given as a network of segmentation objects O, for example, lines, vertices, regions, together with their attributes, for example, length, color, velocity, and space coordinates. A segmentation object is a structure

$$\begin{aligned} O = [&D : T_O, && \texttt{name} \\ &(A : (T_A, \mathcal{R} \cup V_T))^*, && \texttt{attributes} \\ &(P : O)^*, && \texttt{parts} \\ &(S(A_O, A_P) : \mathcal{R})^*, && \texttt{relations} \\ &G : \mathcal{R}^n] && \texttt{judgment} \end{aligned} \tag{27.2}$$

For example, a segmentation object O may be "right angle," its attributes the coordinates of a circumscribing rectangle, its parts the two lines forming a right angle, the relation a fuzzy relation defining the degree of fulfilment of the predicate right angle, and the judgment a combination of edge strength and fulfilment of the relation. Initial segmentation will not be treated here. The interested reader can find material in this volume.

The phase of mainly data-driven processing is followed by a model-driven phase, where we assume that a *model* $\mathcal{M}$ of the task domain is given and that this model is represented by a network of concepts C

$$\mathcal{M} = \langle C \rangle \tag{27.3}$$

The model has to contain all the information relevant to solve a given task of image understanding and to compute from an image the information requested by a user, but need not contain anything else. The structure of a concept is defined below in Eq. (27.4).

The segmentation objects O and concepts C give a "natural" interface between segmentation and understanding. There must be so-called *primitive concepts*, which can be linked directly to results of segmentation. For example, assume a model $\mathcal{M}$ for the diagnostic interpretation of MR images of the knee contains, among others, concepts defining the cartilage by curved contour lines. In this case segmentation should extract appropriate curved contour lines that may be assigned to the primitive concepts of the cartilage. This way segmentation and model are interfaced. An object-oriented implementation of $\mathcal{A}$ and $\mathcal{M}$ is advantageous, [19], and material on this is given in Volume 3, Chapter 5.

In principle, the border between parts of the system implemented in a semantic network and parts of a system implemented, for example, by a network of procedures, can be chosen arbitrarily. For example, in Weierich et al. [20] everything, starting with the input image and including initial segmentation, is defined in concepts; in Salzbrunn et al. [21] initial segmentation is implemented by procedures and the semantic network starts with the definition of objects. As a rough "rule of thumb" one may say that preprocessing and initial segmentation are well handled by procedures, knowledge-based inferences by a semantic network, and object recognition and localization either by a semantic network (if the search complexity is low, for example, in the images shown in Fig. 27.1) or by algorithms tailored to object recognition, for example, statistical approaches or neural networks.

27.2 Model of the task domain

As mentioned here, knowledge about the task domain is explicitly represented in a model $\mathcal{M}$, which is a network of concepts C. In order to make possible a *task-independent* control algorithm, which uses the model (and the initial segmentation $\mathcal{A}$) to interpret an image, all concepts representing whichever item of knowledge have the *same* syntax. This is defined in the next subsection.

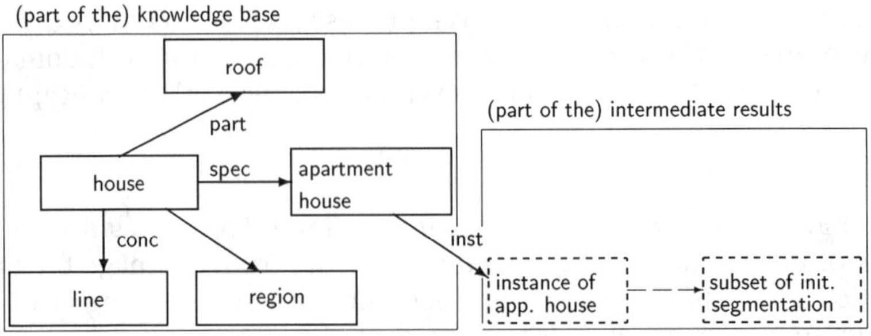

Figure 27.2: *Three links (spec, part, and conc) are provided to relate a concept to other concepts defining it and one link (inst) to relate it to instances of the concept found in an image.*

27.2.1 Definition of a concept

We start from some colloquial and usually ambiguous natural language conception, such as "car," "accident," "drive," "big," and so on. This conception is represented internally (in the computer) by a recursive formal data structure that contains the information relevant to the task domain. For example, for autonomous driving of cars on a highway the price of a car will not be relevant, but the size and shape. The internal formal representation is called a *concept*. The concept is referenced by a name that may be identical to the colloquial conception. For example, the conception "car" is represented internally by a concept named "car" (or "Auto"). If some subset of pixels is computed to meet the definition of a concept C with sufficient reliability, an *instance* $I(C)$ of the concept is found, linked to this concept C, and stored in a memory of intermediate results. In order to allow for a well-structured representation of knowledge, the three links or relations "part," "concrete," and "specialization" are introduced, see also Fig. 27.2. The structure of a concept C is defined by

$$
\begin{aligned}
C &= (D : T_C, && \texttt{name} \\
&\quad [H_{\text{obl}}, H_{\text{opt}}]^*, && \texttt{sets of modality} \\
&\quad (V : C)^*, && \texttt{specializations} \\
&\quad (L : I)^*, && \texttt{instances} \\
&\quad (A : (T_A \mapsto F))^*, && \texttt{attributes} \\
&\quad (S(A_C, A_P, A_K) \mapsto F)^*, && \texttt{relations} \\
&\quad (G \mapsto F)) && \texttt{judgment} \\
H &= ((P_{\text{ci}} : C^+)^*, && \texttt{context}\textbf{indep}\texttt{. parts} \\
&\quad (P_{\text{cd}} : C^+)^*, && \texttt{context}\textbf{depend}\texttt{. parts} \\
&\quad (K : C^+)^*) && \texttt{concretizations}
\end{aligned}
\qquad (27.4)
$$

The main defining components of a concept are *sets of modality* consisting of obligatory and optional elements H_{obl} and H_{opt}, respectively. The notation $[H_{\text{obl}}, H_{\text{opt}}]^*$ indicates that there may be zero, one, or more such sets. Obligatory elements must be present in order to compute an instance of a concept in the image, optional ones may be present. The sets of modality facilitate a compact representation of knowledge because slight modifications, for example, chairs with three, four, or five legs, can be represented in the same concept by different sets of modality. The defining components of an element H are its context-*in*dependent and context-*de*pendent *parts* $P_{\text{ci}}, P_{\text{cd}}$ and *concretes* K. The distinction between parts and concretes allows one to represent relations between different *levels of abstraction* or different conceptual systems. For example, a "wheel" is a physical part of a "car" (attached to the concept "car" by the link "part"), which naturally is in the conceptual system of "cars." The same holds for a "house" and its "roof." A wheel may "rotate," but a rotation is not a physical part of a car or a wheel but a special type of "motion." Hence, a wheel would be related to a rotation as a concrete by the link "conc." Another view of a concretization is that it is closer to the pixel data, for example, a "line" as a concrete of a "house" is closer to the pixels, see Fig. 27.2.

The distinction between context-independent and -dependent parts allows one to handle context-dependent relations between objects and their parts. With respect to the usage of a knowledge base this means that a context-independent part may be detected or inferred *without* having the superior concept, whereas a context-dependent part can only be inferred *after* having the superior concept. For example, the "hood" of a car usually can be detected in an image without having the car, but a "leg of a chair" usually can be inferred from straight lines only if the chair as a context has been established.

In order to have compact knowledge bases and to define hierarchies of conceptions it is possible to introduce a concept as the *specialization* of some other (more general) concept. It is common to imply that all defining elements (parts, concretes, attributes, relations) of a more general concept are handed down to the more special one or are *inherited* by it unless explicitly defined otherwise. For example, an "apartment house" is a special "house" related to it by the link "spec."

According to the preceding definition a concept C has a set of *attributes* (or features, properties) A, each one referencing a function (or procedure) F, which can compute the value of the corresponding attribute. The notation $(A : \ldots)^*$ indicates that there may be an arbitrary number (including zero) of attributes in a concept.

In general there may be *structural relations* S between the attributes A_C of a concept or between attributes A_P and A_K of its parts and concretes, respectively. Since in image processing noise and processing errors are inevitable, relations usually can only be established with limited precision. Therefore, each relation references a function F computing a measure of the degree of fulfilment of this relation, for example, in the sense of a fuzzy relation.

Finally, every concept C has an attached function F computing a *judgment* $G(I(C))$ of an instance $I(C)$. The judgment may be a goodness or value or alternatively a cost or loss, but obviously this does not make an esential difference. Some general remarks on judgment are given in Section 27.6. The judgment G may be a scalar or a vector.

The active elements of the model are the functions computing values during instantiation. The concepts and links may be viewed as *declarative knowledge*, the functions as *procedural knowledge*. It is mentioned that some additional elements were introduced in the references given in Section 27.1 but have to be omitted here due to space limitations.

In order to facilitate a task-independent and efficient control algorithm it is useful to request that a model $\mathcal{M}$ of a task domain is *cycle-free*, that is, there is no path in the semantic network leading from a concept C via links of different type back to C, and *consistent*, that is, between two concepts there cannot be links of different type. The designer of a model has to ensure these restrictions, which are also meaningful for knowledge representation. A *model* represented by a *semantic network* then is a special type of graph having three types on links, the part, the concrete, and the specialization and one type of node, the concept. During processing two more node types are used, the modified concept and the instance.

27.2.2 Instance and modified concept

In knowledge-based image analysis one tries to determine which objects and so on are actually present in the image. The occurrence of an object is represented by an *instance* $I(C)$ of the corresponding concept C, see also Fig. 27.3. The relation between the concept and its instance is represented by a link L from C to $I(C)$. An instance is represented by a structure identical to Eq. (27.4) except that references to functions are replaced by the actual values computed by those functions from the image. Since due to noise and processing errors the occurrence of an instance can only be inferred with limited certainty and precision, a *judgment* G is computed for every instance of a concept.

There may be the situation that some instances have been computed and allow the restriction of attribute values of a concept C, which cannot yet be instantiated. In this case a so called *modified concept* $Q(C)$ is created. For example, the detection of one "wheel" of a "car" constrains both the location of the car (bottom-up) and of the other wheels (top-down). This way *constraints* are propagated bottom-up and top-down. Modified concepts improve both the efficiency and reliability of interpretation. An example of some concepts is given in Fig. 27.3, taken from Salzbrunn et al. [21], to illustrate the definition Eq. (27.4).

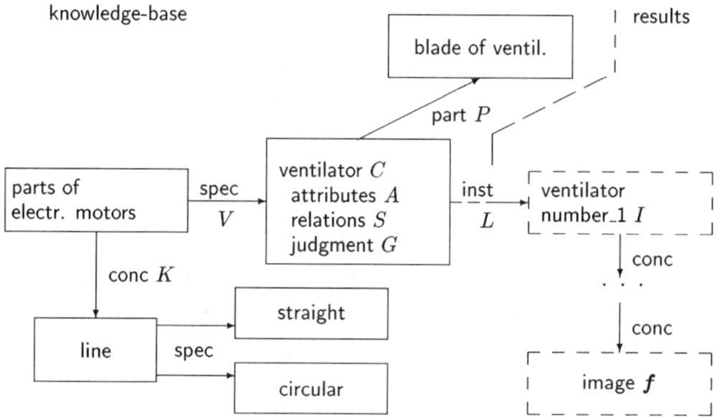

Figure 27.3: *Examples of concepts linked to other concepts and modeling industrial parts*

The general concept "parts of electric motors" is useful if there are several more special concepts, like "ventilator," "rotor," and so on. Then all concepts can be accessed via the general one, and by inheritance all special concepts as well as their parts are defined by "lines" which in turn may be "straight" or "circular." Since in this example the concept "line" does not have parts or concretes, it is a *primitive concept*. The instantiation of primitive concepts is done, by definition, by means of segmentation results, as mentioned already in Section 27.1.2.

The process of instantiation can be defined and implemented by task-independent rules. They define the conditions to compute a partial instance (which is necessary to handle context-dependent parts), to instantiate a concept, to enlarge an instance by optional components H_{opt}, to compute a modified concept top-down or bottom-up, or to compute modified concepts from initial segmentation results. Details of the instantiation of concepts have to be omitted here. In principle, in order to compute an instance of a concept, first its obligatory context-independent parts and its obligatory concretes must be instantiated. If this is the case, an instance can be created and its attributes, relations, and judgment computed. An obligatory context-dependent part can only be instantiated if a partial instance of its superior concept is available. The instance may be extended by computing instances of optional parts and concretes.

27.2.3 Function-centered representation

Facing both the large amount of data and the limited processing time in the image understanding tasks outlined in the foregoing, the exploitation of parallelism provides a promising way to achieve the processing rates neccessary to keep up with the sensory input. Most parallel semantic network systems employ an isomorphic mapping between the processors of a parallel hardware and the nodes and links of a knowledge base, which turned out to be a feasible approach if both concepts and inferences are simple [5].

However, as in our formalism a concept may have an arbitrary number of attributes and structural relations, complex concepts may become a bottleneck in instantiation. Therefore, we employ a representation of a semantic network based on the functions F in the concept definition Eq. (27.4). This is natural because the functions for computing values of attributes, relations, and judgments are the active elements in the model. Each computation by a function needed during instantiation is represented by a node of a directed acyclic graph that may be mapped to a multiprocessor system for purposes of parallel processing. Basically, from the arguments of the functions F a dependency structure is created showing which functions may be computed in parallel and which sequentially because their arguments need results provided from other functions. The details of the automatic conversion of a model to this dependency structure are given in Fischer and Niemann [22].

27.3 Interpretation by optimization

The result of interpretation is a *symbolic description*

$$\mathcal{B} = \langle I(C) \rangle \qquad (27.5)$$

which is a network of instances of concepts defined in the model. It contains both a condensed "summary" in the form of instantiated goal concepts as well as details in the form of instances of parts and concretes down to primitive concepts.

Every primitive concept is instantiated by a segmentation result, and every object, event, situation, motion or whatever is relevant to the task domain is defined by a concept in the model $\mathcal{M}$. In particular, the goal (or the goals) of interpretation is also defined in a concept, the goal concept C_g. Intermediate results of processing give rise to, possibly competing, instances $I_i(C)$ of a concept C. Every concept has, among other defining items, an associated judgment G, which allows the computation of the score, value, or alternatively of the cost, of an instance $I(C)$. Therefore, also the goal concept has an associated judgment.

A natural definition of image interpretation then is to require the determination of the best scoring instance $I^*(C_g)$ of the goal concept, that is

$$I^*(C_g) = \arg \max_{\{I(C_g)\}} \{G(I(C_g) \mid \mathcal{M}, \mathcal{A}\} \qquad (27.6)$$

The actual computation of interpretations is done by the control module as outlined in Sections 27.4 and 27.5.

The dependence of Eq. (27.6) on the model $\mathcal{M}$ ensures that the interpretation is compatible with *a priori* knowledge and contains all the information required by a subsequent user. The dependence on the initial segmentation $\mathcal{A}$ ensures that the interpretation is compatible with the observed data. Finally, the computation of the best scoring instance ensures that from among competing interpretations the best one is selected. Hence, the requirements of Section 27.1.2 are met and image interpretation is formulated and solved as an optimization problem.

27.4 Control by graph search

In general, the task of a *control module* is to compute an efficient strategy for the interpretation of an image, given a model. This requires in particular to determine which available processing algorithm should be applied to which subset of intermediate results. In the foregoing context this requires the computation of an optimal instance $I^*(C_g)$ of the goal concept. One approach to do this is by graph search. Because our model consists only of concepts with identical syntactic definition, the control algorithm can be implemented task-independently. Only the judgment functions G defining the quality of instances are task-dependent.

When using graph search, every state of analysis, characterized by the current intermediate results, is associated with a node v in a search tree. If a node is not a goal node v_g of the search process, new nodes are generated by applying transformations. In our context the transformations are given by the rules mentioned at the end of Section 27.2.2. We thus have an implicitly defined graph, which is given by a start node and by transformations to generate new nodes from a given node. Clearly, we are only interested in generating as few nodes of the search tree as are necessary to find an optimal instance $I^*(C_g)$ of the goal concept. Therefore, an algorithm for graph search is needed to find the optimal path efficiently, that is, the minimal cost path, to the goal node.

Let v_0 be the start node of the search tree, v_i the current node, and v_g the goal node. Let $\varphi(v_i)$ be the cost of an *optimal path* from v_0 to v_g via v_i, $\psi(v_i)$ the cost of an optimal path from v_0 to v_i, and $\chi(v_i)$ the cost of an optimal path from v_i to v_g. Then the additive combination

$$\varphi(v_i) = \psi(v_i) + \chi(v_i) \qquad (27.7)$$

must hold. As one usually does not know the true costs, they are replaced by their estimates $\hat{\varphi}(v_i)$, $\hat{\psi}(v_i)$, $\hat{\chi}(v_i)$. The estimate $\hat{\chi}(v_i)$ must be *optimistic*, that is,

$$\hat{\chi}(v_i) \le \chi(v_i) \qquad \text{for } \textit{all } v_i \qquad (27.8)$$

An obvious optimistic estimate is $\hat{\chi}(v_i) = 0$. However, more efficient search can be expected if an estimate $0 < \hat{\chi}(v_i) \leq \chi(v_i)$ is known. In addition it is required that the estimate is *monotone* in the sense

$$\hat{\chi}(v_j) - \hat{\chi}(v_k) \leq r(v_j, v_k) \tag{27.9}$$

where $r(v_j, v_k)$ are the true costs of an optimal path from v_j to a successor v_k. A graph search algorithm meeting these constraints is called an *A*-algorithm*, [18, 23]. The operation of this algorithm is:

1. Given a nonempty set V_s of start nodes, a nonempty set V_g of goal nodes, a judgment function $\hat{\varphi}(v)$ for a node v, and a set T of transformations to generate successor nodes of a node v. A list *OPEN* is initialized by $V_s \cup v_0$, and a list *CLOSED* by v_0.
2. Remove from *OPEN* the best scoring node v_k and put it on *CLOSED*.
3. If $v_k \in V_g$, then STOP with *"success,"* that is the best scoring path to a goal node was found; and otherwise expand v_k to generate the set V_k of successor nodes. If no successors can be generated, then STOP with *"failure,"* that is, no goal node can be reached.
4. Compute the scores of the nodes in V_k, and add to *OPEN* those successor nodes not yet on *OPEN* and not on *CLOSED*. Determine if a better path to a node in *OPEN* was found and adjust the scores on *OPEN* accordingly.
5. Continue with step 2.

It is known that this algorithm will terminate if a path to a goal node exists, and that it will always terminate for finite graphs. The *admissibility* has been proven, that is, if there is a path to a goal node, the algorithm will terminate with the *optimal path* in the sense of the judgment function. If the judgment function is monotone, Eq. (27.9), then the algorithm has already found the optimal path to each node v_i chosen for expansion; this means that in this case $\hat{\psi}(v_i) = \psi(v_i)$. Finally, it is mentioned that the A*-algorithm has exponential complexity in the worst case. But it is also known that for "good" scoring functions its complexity may only be linear. Hence, the design of a proper judgment is essential for the feasibility of this approach.

In the problem of computing an optimal instance of the goal concept in a semantic network, an elementary control algorithm is as follows. Elementary control by graph search starts with the top-down expansion of the goal C_g until primitive concepts are reached. Primitive concepts do not have parts and/or concretes and can be instantiated by results of initial segmentation. This expansion is independent of the input image and can be done once for the knowledge base. The result of expansion is the *instantiation path*, which is a list of concepts. All concepts on this list must be instantiated in order to instantiate the goal C_g. After expansion the concepts on the instantiation path are

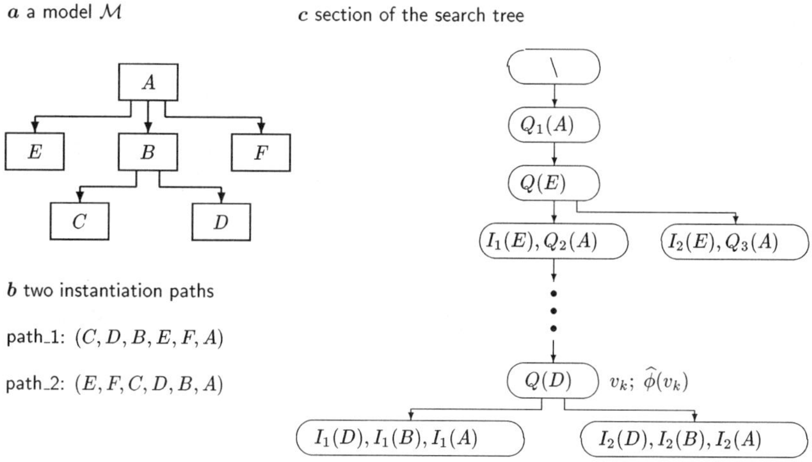

Figure 27.4: *An example of:* ***a*** *a model;* ***b*** *instantiation paths; and* ***c*** *search tree nodes.*

instantiated bottom-up until the goal is reached. Of course, this step depends on the input image. Due to alternative definitions of a concept, due to competing instances, and due to a combinatorial multiplicity of assigning results of initial segmentation to primitive concepts, it is necessary to concentrate the instantiation on the most promising alternatives. Clearly, this can be done by the A*-algorithm.

With reference to Fig. 27.4 let the goal of processing be to compute an optimal instance of the concept A in model $\mathcal{M}$. A search tree is initialized with an empty root node as shown in the figure. Next the goal of processing, that is, concept A is put on a new search tree node. Because it is useful to only deal with modified concepts and instances, A is modified to $Q(A)$ before putting it on the node, even though at this stage of processing the modification is "no modification." The instantiation algorithm notices that instantiation of A at first needs an instance of E (see path_2 in Fig. 27.4), and, therefore, $Q(E)$ is put on a new search tree node. Since E is a primitive concept, it can be instantiated. It is assumed that there are two competing instances $I_1(E), I_2(E)$ causing two new modifications $Q_2(A), Q_3(A)$. The judgment of the two new search tree nodes is computed. It is assumed that the node containing $I_1(E)$ has the best judgment, therefore, search continues at this node.

The process of putting modified concepts from the model and newly computed instances and modifications on the search tree continues until A is finally instantiated. In the example, two competing instances $I_1(A), I_2(A)$ are shown. It is realized that at this state of computation some nodes have successors, that is, they were already selected for expansion, and some do not yet have successors. Let us assume that from among the unexpanded nodes the one containing $I_2(A)$ has the best score. If we used an optimistic and monotone judgment function as outlined here, the properties of the A^*-algorithm assure us that search is finished, that is, no better instance than $I_2(A)$ can be found. If some unexpanded node *not* containing an instance of A (for example, the node containing $I_2(E)$ and $Q_3(A)$) had had a better judgment, search would have continued at that node, because a better scoring goal node might be found in the following. This approach is sufficiently powerful to interpret, for example, scintigraphic or MR image sequences. Extensions are mentioned in Section 27.7.

27.5 Control by combinatorial optimization

An alternative to the foregoing approach to design a *control module* is to convert the network of concepts into a network of functions as outlined in Section 27.2.3. A particular assignment of segmentation results to primitive concepts and a particular assignment of concept definitions (i.e., sets of modality) is considered as a state in a combinatorial optimization problem by means of which one computes an optimal assignment. This can be done by algorithms like simulated annealing, great deluge, or genetic programming. Details are given, for example, in Fischer [24].

The function-centered representation of a semantic network originally was developed to speed up analysis by the parallel computation of instances. In addition it provides an approximate interpretation at every iteration and therefore supports the fast computation of suboptimal interpretations, which may be used by other processing modules if less processing time is available—the so-called *any time property*.

The algorithm may be divided into two stages. In the first one, a bottom-up instantiation is executed, values and judgments are computed for each attribute, structural relation, link, or concept of the function network. Initially this will lead to many competing interpretations having low values of judgment. In the second stage interpretations obtained from bottom-up instantiation are iteratively improved by applying a combinatorial optimization procedure. Ideally, this will lead to a unique interpretation having a high value of judgment.

As indicated by its name, bottom-up instantiation proceeds from the bottom to the top of the network, starting with the computation of attributes that provide an interface to the initial segmentation, and finishing with the judgment of goal concepts. As a result of bottom-up instantiation we obtain instances for the goal concepts, each provided with a judgment $G(I(C_g))$. From the best-scored instances we create a

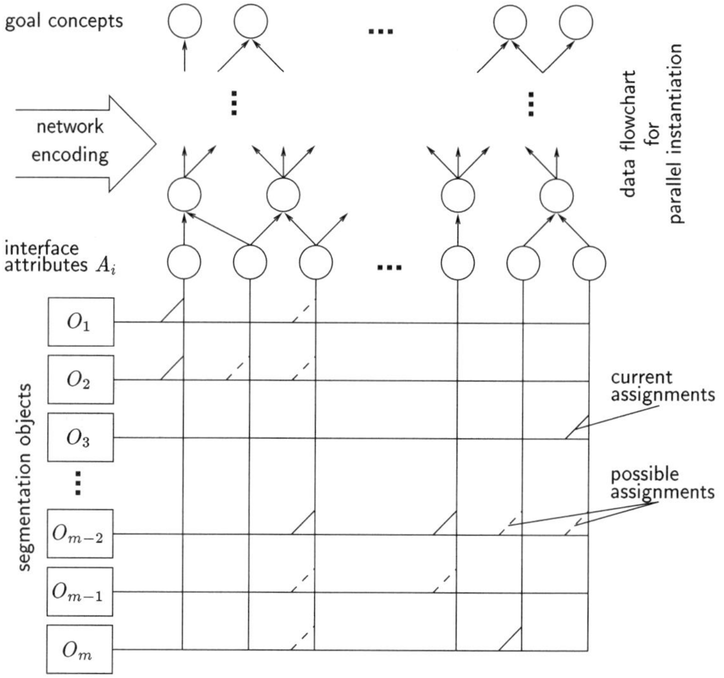

Figure 27.5: *The principle of bottom-up instantiation. Hypotheses resulting from actual matches between initial attributes and segmentation objects are propagated through the data flowchart, resulting in a judgment of goal concepts.*

vector

$$\boldsymbol{g} = (G(I^*(C_{g_1}), \ldots, G(I^*(C_{g_n})) \tag{27.10}$$

representing the final result of a single iteration step.

From Fig. 27.5, which depicts the principle of bottom-up instantiation, it becomes evident that the computation of instances and their judgment is completely determined by assigning to each interface (attribute) node A_i a (possibly empty) subset $\{O_j^{(i)}\}$ of segmentation objects and selecting for each concept node C_l a unique set of modality $H_l^{(k)}$. This allows us to characterize the *current state of analysis* by a vector

$$\boldsymbol{r}_c = \left[(A_i, \{O_j^{(i)}\}) \mid i = 1, \ldots, m \, ; \; (C_k, H_l^{(k)}) \mid k = 1, \ldots, m' \right] \tag{27.11}$$

where m is the number of interface nodes and m' the number of concepts having more than one member in its set of modality. Hence, Eq. (27.10) is a function of the current state $\boldsymbol{r}_c$, that is, $\boldsymbol{g} = \boldsymbol{g}(\boldsymbol{r}_c)$.

Treating the vector $\boldsymbol{r}_c$ as the current state of analysis, the computation of an optimal instance according to Eq. (27.6) may be identified as a combinatorial optimization problem whose optimum is defined by a suitable cost function ϕ; its choice will be given in Section 27.6. This approach was used, for example, to find street markers in image sequences of traffic scenes [24].

27.6 Judgment function

Judgment functions for graph search may be scalar functions or vector-valued functions. In the last case the evaluation of the best scoring instance is done in lexicographic order. An examples of a scalar function will be presented. In the case of combinatorial optimization the judgment function mainly measures the deviation between the current state and the desired state as outlined in what follows.

Judgment deals with the quantitative treatment of alternative, uncertain, or imprecise results that may arise during segmentation as well as during knowledge-based processing. Therefore, judgment has to take place in both phases of processing outlined in Section 27.1.2. In this section we will briefly give an idea of the scoring of segmentation and recognition results and then treat the judgment of instances and states of analysis that may occur during graph search.

Results of initial segmentation are either scored heuristically or forwarded to knowledge-based processing without a judgment of quality. Heuristic scores are based, for example, on the contrast and length of a line, the error of approximating a set of points by a straight line, or the homogeneity of a region.

Judgment of assignments between results of initial segmentation and primitive concepts of the knowledge base are obtained, for example, from the fit between computed segmentation objects and expected model elements. This may be done by fuzzy functions or distance measures. The former are useful for scoring the agreement between attributes, for example, for the diameter of a circle stored in the model and the diameter of a circle found in an image. The latter are useful for scoring straight or curved lines.

Graph search. During knowledge-based processing we have to distinguish between the judgment $G(I(C))$ of an instance $I(C)$ of a concept C and the judgment $\phi(v)$ of a node v in the search tree. The score of an instance in principle is always based on the quality of the match between data and model or on the quality of fulfilment of fuzzy inference rules. The score of a search tree node is always based on the current estimate of the quality of an instance of the associated *goal concept* as is requested and evident from graph search, Eq. (27.7), as well as combinatorial optimization, Eq. (27.10). Therefore, instantiation is always directed towards *optimal* instantiation of a *goal concept* C_g as requested in Eq. (27.6).

In general the judgment of an instance of a concept is a combination of the judgments of its parts, concretes, attributes, and relations

$$G(I(C)) = G(I(P_i)) \circ G(I(K_j)) \circ G(A_k) \circ G(S_l) \tag{27.12}$$

For example, the operation $\circ$ may be a sum- or a max-operation in the case that the judgment measures costs.

Let the goal concept be C_g and C be some concept having the set $D_i, i = 1, \ldots, n$ of parts and concretes. Let G be a measure of cost normalized to $0 \le G \le G_{\max}$. Then an estimate of the cost of an instance of the goal C_g associated with a node v in the search tree and denoted by $\hat{G}(I_v(C_g))$ can be computed at every stage of analysis from the recursive definition of the goodness of a instance $I_v(C)$ associated with v by

$$\hat{G}(I_v(C)) = \begin{cases} G(I_v(C)) & \text{if } C \text{ is instantiated and } I_v(C) \text{ is the} \\ & \text{instance associated with } v \\ 0 & \text{if } C \text{ is primitive and still uninstantiated} \\ \hat{G}(\hat{G}(I_v(D_1)), \ldots, \hat{G}(I_v(D_n)) \mid C) & \\ & \text{if } C \text{ is still uninstantiated and instances} \\ & I_v(D_1), \ldots, I_v(D_n) \text{ are associated with } v \end{cases}$$

Due to the requirements of the A*-algorithm we then use

$$\phi(v) = \hat{G}(I_v(C_g)) \tag{27.13}$$

as an optimistic estimate of the cost of an instance of the goal concept in node v.

Combinatorial optimization. To design a *cost function* ϕ suited for combinatorial optimization, we assume that an error-free segmentation would support a single interpretation, and therefore results in an ideal judgment $G(I^*(C_{g_i})) = 1.0$ for the correct goal concept. On the other hand, at the same time this segmentation would give no evidence to any other goal concept, that is, $G(I^*(C_{g_j})) = 0.0,\ j \neq i$. Therefore, we would obtain the i-th unit vector $\boldsymbol{e}_i$ as an ideal result of instantiation, if the i-th goal concept provides the desired symbolic description. We approximate this behavior and define

$$\begin{aligned} \phi(\boldsymbol{r}_c) &= \min\nolimits_{1 \le i \le n} \{(\boldsymbol{e}_i - \tilde{\boldsymbol{g}}(\boldsymbol{r}_c))^2\} \\ \tilde{\boldsymbol{g}}(\boldsymbol{r}_c) &= \frac{\boldsymbol{g}(\boldsymbol{r}_c)}{||\boldsymbol{g}(\boldsymbol{r}_c)||} \end{aligned} \tag{27.14}$$

as a cost function, that computes the minimum distance from $\boldsymbol{g}(\boldsymbol{r}_c)$, see Eq. (27.10), to the unit vectors $\boldsymbol{e}_i$. Note that this function provides a problem-independent measure of costs because no assumptions on the contents of the knowledge base are made, and that there is a correspondence to the judgment of a search tree node in Section 27.4 because both evaluate the expected quality of goal achievement.

27.7 Extensions and remarks

In addition to the basic definitions and properties of semantic networks presented here, several extensions and modifications are presented in the references. These include, for example: the inclusion of additional links to facilitate the automatic construction of concepts from camera views or the interpretation of elliptic sentences; the definition of priorities for the instantiation of concepts on the instantiation path; the inclusion of adjacency matrices to define a time order of concepts; the definition of holistic concepts, which can be instantiated either from classification of feature vectors or from segmentation results; the definition of vector-valued goodness functions; the formulation of a control algorithm alternating between phases of top-down expansion and bottom-up instantiation; the updating of an instance representing one object in a time-sequence of images instead of computing a new instance of the same object at every image; details are available from Sagerer and Niemann [2].

The approach outlined here was used, for example: to interpret scintigraphic time-sequences of images of the heart [1]; to interpret MR volume-sequences of images of the knee [20]; to generate models for industrial parts and to recognize them [21, 25]; to understand speech and to carry out a spoken dialog [26, 27]; to interpret time-sequences of images for car driving [28, 29]; to evaluate remote sensing data [30, 31, 32]; or to compute protein-docking [33]. Additional references on image understanding systems are available from Crevier and Lepage [34].

It thus can be concluded that semantic networks combined with a task-independent control algorithm are a flexible, powerful, and successful approach to knowledge-based image understanding.

27.8 References

[1] Niemann, H., Bunke, H., Hofmann, I., Sagerer, G., Wolf, F., and Feistel, H., (1985). A knowledge-based system for analysis of gated blood pool studies. *TransPAMI*, 7:246–259.

[2] Sagerer, G. and Niemann, H., (1997). *Semantic Networks for Understanding Scenes*. Advances in Computer Vision and Machine Intelligence. New York and London: Plenum Press.

[3] Kumar, D. (ed.), (1990). *Current Trends in SNePS—Semantic Network Processing Systems*, Vol. 437 of *Lecture Notes of AI*. Berlin, Heidelberg: Springer.

[4] Niemann, H., Sagerer, G., Schröder, S., and Kummert, F., (1990). ERNEST: A semantic network system for pattern understanding. *TransPAMI*, **9**: 883–905.

[5] Shastri, L., (1988). *Semantic Networks: An Evidential Formalization and its Connectionist Realization*. London: Pitman.

[6] Sowa, J. (ed.), (1991). *Principles of Semantic Networks*. San Mateo, CA: Morgan Kaufmann.

[7] Matsuyama, T. and Hwang, V., (1990). *SIGMA: A Knowledge-based Aerial Image Understanding System*. New York: Plenum Press.

[8] Newell, A., (1973). Production systems: Models of control structures. In *Visual Information Processing*, W. C. Chase, ed., pp. 463–526. New York: Academic Press.

[9] Sohn, A. and Gaudiot, J.-L., (1990). Representation and processing of production systems in connectionist architectures. *IJPRAI*, **4**:199–214.

[10] Stilla, U. and Michaelsen, E., (1997). Semantic modeling of man-made objects by production nets. In *Automatic Extraction of Man-Made Objets from Aerial and Space Images (II)*, A. Gruen, E. Baltsavias, and O. Henricsson, eds., pp. 43–52, Ascona Workshop. Basel: Birkhäuser.

[11] Zadeh, L., (1983). Commonsense knowledge representation based on fuzzy logic. *IEEE Computer*, **16**(10):61–65.

[12] Zadeh, L., (1989). Knowledge representation in fuzzy logic. *IEEE Trans. Knowledge and Data Engineering*, **1**:89–100.

[13] Radig, B., (1984). Image sequence analysis using relational structures. *Pattern Recognition*, **17**:161–167.

[14] Zhang, S., Sullivan, G., and Baker, K., (1993). The automatic construction of a view-independent relational model for 3D object recognition. *IEEE Trans. PAMI*, **15**:531–544.

[15] A. Deliyanni, A. and R. A. Kowalski, R., (1979). Logic and semantic networks. *Comm. ACM*, **22**:184–192.

[16] Dahl, V., (1983). Logic programming as a representation of knowledge. *IEEE Computer*, **16**(10):106–111.

[17] Dubois, D. and Prade, H., (1991). Possibilistic logic, preferential models, non-monotonicity and related issues. In *Proc. 12. Int. Joint Conf. on Artificial Intelligence*, pp. 419–424. Darling Harbour, Sydney, Australia.

[18] Niemann, H., (1990). *Pattern Analysis and Understanding*, 2nd edition. Springer Series in Information Sciences 4. Berlin: Springer.

[19] Paulus, D. and Hornegger, J., (1997). *Pattern Recognition of Images and Speech in C++*. Advanced Studies in Computer Science. Braunschweig: Vieweg.

[20] Weierich, P., Wetzel, D., Niemann, H., and Glückert, K., (1993). AUDIGON—A medical expert system with new judgement functions for the fuzzy rulebase. In *Proc. First European Congress on Fuzzy and Intelligent Tech-*

nologies EUFIT'93, pp. 472–477. Aachen, Germany: Verlag der Augustinus Buchhandlung.

[21] Salzbrunn, R., Niemann, H., M., H., and Winzen, A., (1992). Object recognition by a robust matching technique. In *Advances in Structural and Syntactic Pattern Recognition*, H. Bunke, ed., pp. 481–495. Singapore: World Scientific.

[22] Fischer, V. and Niemann, H., (1993). Parallelism in a semantic network for image understanding. In *Parallelrechner: Theorie, Hardware, Software, Anwendungen*, A. Bode and M. Dal Cin, eds., Lecture Notes in Computer Science. Berlin, Heidelberg, New York: Springer.

[23] Nilsson, N., (1982). *Principles of Artificial Intelligence.* Berlin, Heidelberg, New York: Springer.

[24] Fischer, V., (1995). *Parallelverarbeitung in einem semantischen Netzwerk für die wissensbasierte Musteranalyse*, Vol. 95 of *DISKI.* Sankt Augustin: infix Verlag.

[25] Niemann, H., Brünig, H., Salzbrunn, R., and Schröder, S., (1990). A knowledge-based vision system for industrial applications. *Machine Vision and Applications*, **3**:201–229.

[26] Mast, M., Kummert, F., Ehrlich, U., Fink, G., Kuhn, T., Niemann, H., and Sagerer, G., (1994). A speech understanding and dialog system with a homogeneous linguistic knowledge base. *TransPAMI*, **16**:179–194.

[27] Sagerer, G., (1990). *Automatisches Verstehen gesprochener Sprache*, Vol. 74 of *Reihe Informatik.* Mannheim: BI Wissenschaftsverlag.

[28] Wetzel, D., (1996). *Wissensbasierte Verkehrsszenenanalyse zur Fahrerunterstützung*, Vol. 109 of *DISKI.* Sankt Augustin: infix Verlag.

[29] Wetzel, D., Niemann, H., and Richter, S., (1994). A robust cognitive approach to traffic scene analysis. In *Proc. of Second IEEE Workshop on Applications of Computer Vision, Sarasota, Florida*, pp. 65–72. Los Alamitos, CA: IEEE Computer Society Press.

[30] Kunz, D., Schilling, K.-J., and Vögtle, T., (1997). A new approach for satellite image analysis by means of a semantic network. In *Semantic Modeling*, W. Förstner and L. Plümer, eds., pp. 20–36. Basel: Birkhäuser.

[31] Liedtke, C.-E., Bückner, J., Grau, O., Growe, S., and Tönjes, R., (1997). AIDA: A system for the knowledge based interpretation of remote sensing data. In *Proc. Third International Airborne Remote Sensing Conference and Exhibition.* Copenhagen.

[32] Quint, F. and Stiess, M., (1995). Map-based semantic modeling for the extraction of objects from aerial images. In *Automatic Extraction of Man-Made Objects from Aerial and Space Images*, A. Grün, O. Kübler, and P. Agouris, eds., pp. 307–316. Basel: Birkhäuser.

[33] Ackermann, F., Herrmann, G., Posch, S., and Sagerer, G., (1996). Evaluierung eines Protein-Dockingsystems durch Leave-One-Out-Test. In *Mustererkennung 1996. Proc. 18. DAGM-Symposium*, B. Jähne, P. Geißler, H. Haußecker, and F. Hering, eds., pp. 130–137. Heidelberg: Springer.

[34] Crevier, D. and Lepage, R., (1997). Knowledge-based image understanding systems: a survey. *CVIU*, **67**(2):161–185.

28 Visualization of Volume Data

Jürgen Hesser and Christoph Poliwoda

Informatik V, Universität Mannheim, Germany

Handbook of Computer Vision and Applications
Volume 2
Signal Processing and Pattern Recognition

Copyright © 1999 by Academic Press
All rights of reproduction in any form reserved.
ISBN 0-12-379772-1/$30.00

Visualization is a means of representing structure information from volume data sets by presenting the graphical objects as if they were real. These data sets can be generated by various sources like computed tomography (CT), magnetic resonance imaging (MRI), ultrasound, confocal microscopes, etc. but sources like time series of 2-D images may be used as well. What characterizes these data is that each element is assigned to a node in a three or higher dimensional grid. Rectilinear grids are assumed for the following discussion because they play the most relevant role in practice; further discussions of general models can, for example, be found in specific papers [1, 2, 3].

This chapter has the scope of presenting both an overview of current state of the art rendering algorithms for volume data, and how to use them most efficiently. The latter should allow the practitioner to prepare the data set accordingly to see the desired information.

28.1 Theoretical foundations of selected visualization techniques

Theoretical foundations of volume rendering in simplified physical models are a trade off between accurate physical simulation of illumination and resulting rendering speed. This trade off is solved by the assumptions of geometric optics and by limiting the discussion to models that rely only on reflection/refraction, and absorption of light. Two models in computer graphics that describe this interaction are presented in the following. They are the foundations of most commonly used rendering methods like radiosity, ray-tracing, surface rendering, and volume rendering.

28.1.1 The rendering equation

Our basic starting point for discussing the propagation of light is the known *rendering equation* of Kajiya [4]. Let us consider the reflection (or refraction) of light at an arbitrary surface point $\boldsymbol{x}$ in the virtual scene (see also Chapter 2). The bidirectional reflectivity $\rho(\boldsymbol{x}', \boldsymbol{x}, \boldsymbol{x}'')$ describes the fraction of intensity of incoming light $I(\boldsymbol{x}, \boldsymbol{x}'')$ from a visible neighboring point $\boldsymbol{x}''$ that is reflected or refracted to another visible neighboring point $\boldsymbol{x}'$ (see also Fig. 28.1). By integration over all such points $\boldsymbol{x}''$ one obtains the overall light intensity reflected by surface point $\boldsymbol{x}$ towards $\boldsymbol{x}'$: $\int \rho(\boldsymbol{x}', \boldsymbol{x}, \boldsymbol{x}'') I(\boldsymbol{x}, \boldsymbol{x}'') d\boldsymbol{x}''$.

Besides indirect reflection, $\boldsymbol{x}'$ can also be illuminated by light sources positioned at $\boldsymbol{x}$. Its intensity is described by $q(\boldsymbol{x}', \boldsymbol{x})$. Finally, the factor $g(\boldsymbol{x}', \boldsymbol{x})$ denotes the visibility of $\boldsymbol{x}'$ from $\boldsymbol{x}$: A surface in between

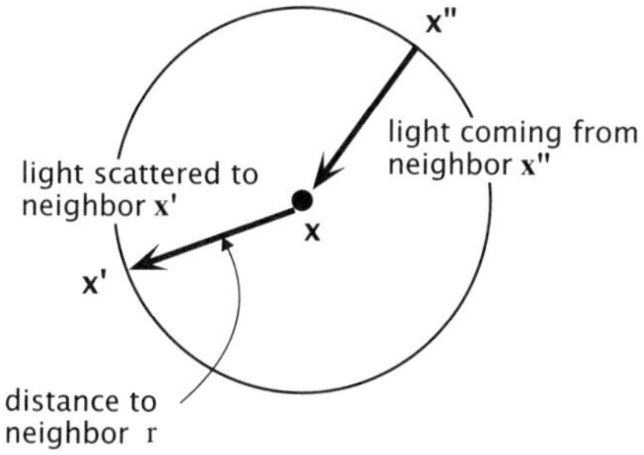

Figure 28.1: *The volume element $\boldsymbol{x}$ is illuminated by light from its neighboring volume elements $\boldsymbol{x}''$ and reflects light to the local neighbor $\boldsymbol{x}'$.*

both points can block the light ($g(\boldsymbol{x}', \boldsymbol{x}) = 0$) or not[1]. In the latter case $g(\boldsymbol{x}', \boldsymbol{x}) = 1/r^2$ because the reflection point $\boldsymbol{x}$ can be considered as a point light source leading to a quadratic attenuation of intensity as a function of the distance to this source. Thus the rendering equation reads:

$$I(\boldsymbol{x}', \boldsymbol{x}) = g(\boldsymbol{x}', \boldsymbol{x}) \left(q(\boldsymbol{x}', \boldsymbol{x}) + \int \rho(\boldsymbol{x}', \boldsymbol{x}, \boldsymbol{x}'') I(\boldsymbol{x}, \boldsymbol{x}'') \, \mathrm{d}\boldsymbol{x}'' \right) \tag{28.1}$$

Solving this rendering equation (e.g., by *Monte Carlo* methods) is very time consuming. For two exceptions, however, it can be simplified significantly.

In the first exception all surfaces are ideally diffuse reflectors. The reflectivity $\rho(\boldsymbol{x}', \boldsymbol{x}, \boldsymbol{x}'')$ depends on only $\boldsymbol{x}$ and $\boldsymbol{x}'$. Therefore the rendering equation reads:

$$I(\boldsymbol{x}', \boldsymbol{x}) = g(\boldsymbol{x}', \boldsymbol{x}) \left(q(\boldsymbol{x}', \boldsymbol{x}) + \rho(\boldsymbol{x}', \boldsymbol{x}) \int I(\boldsymbol{x}, \boldsymbol{x}'') \, \mathrm{d}\boldsymbol{x}'' \right) \tag{28.2}$$

With $I(\boldsymbol{x}) = \int_S I(\boldsymbol{x}, \boldsymbol{x}'') \, \mathrm{d}\boldsymbol{x}''$ the rendering equation Eq. (28.2) simplifies to:

$$I(\boldsymbol{x}') = \int g(\boldsymbol{x}', \boldsymbol{x}) \left(q(\boldsymbol{x}', \boldsymbol{x}) + \rho(\boldsymbol{x}', \boldsymbol{x}) I(\boldsymbol{x}) \right) \mathrm{d}\boldsymbol{x} \tag{28.3}$$

which—assuming a discrete set of flat surface elements—leads to a set of linear equations that can be solved by standard methods of numerical mathematics. This approach is known as the *radiosity method.*

[1]Initially, absorption is not considered by this contribution but can be added as well.

The other exception is ideally specular surfaces. These surfaces reduce the number of contributing reflecting sources to three:

$$
\begin{aligned}
I(\boldsymbol{x}',\boldsymbol{x}) = {} & g(\boldsymbol{x}',\boldsymbol{x})[q(\boldsymbol{x}',\boldsymbol{x}) \\
& +\rho(\boldsymbol{x}',\boldsymbol{x},\boldsymbol{x}''_r)I(\boldsymbol{x},\boldsymbol{x}''_r) \\
& \rho(\boldsymbol{x}',\boldsymbol{x},\boldsymbol{x}''_t)I(\boldsymbol{x},\boldsymbol{x}''_t) \\
& \rho(\boldsymbol{x}',\boldsymbol{x},\boldsymbol{x}''_{\text{Phong}})I_0]
\end{aligned}
\tag{28.4}
$$

where $\boldsymbol{x}''_r$ is the point that reflects light onto $\boldsymbol{x}$ to $\boldsymbol{x}'$ by ideal reflection; $\boldsymbol{x}''_t$ is the point that is reached by ideal transmission, $\boldsymbol{x}''_{\text{Phong}}$ is the contribution of the light source, modeled by the Phong illumination model (see Section 3.3.5), and I_0 is the initial light intensity of the considered light source[2]. This second solution, Eq. (28.4), is known as *ray-tracing*.

Ray-tracing and radiosity approaches are very expensive methods to display 3-D objects defined by surfaces. The reason is that multiple reflections have to be considered. By neglecting light from multiple reflections or refractions the rendering equation can be simplified further. From the equation for ray-tracing there remains only the third contribution, $I(\boldsymbol{x}',\boldsymbol{x}) = g(\boldsymbol{x}',\boldsymbol{x})\rho(\boldsymbol{x}',\boldsymbol{x},\boldsymbol{x}''_{\text{Phong}})I_0$, whereby it is assumed that the viewer does not look directly into a light source and blocking of incoming light I_0 does not occur. The bidirectional reflectivity ρ can be modeled by the Phong illumination model and $g(\boldsymbol{x}',\boldsymbol{x})$ determines the visible surfaces in the case of nontransparent objects.

This simplified version of 3-D rendering is the starting point of OpenGL (see Section 28.3.1) that can allow for real-time visualization.

28.1.2 Particle model approach

Krüger's particle model [5] is another description for modeling the physical interactions of light with matter; and it will lead to an algorithm for volume data, volume rendering. Krüger's approach considers the change of intensity $I(\boldsymbol{x},\boldsymbol{s},\nu)$ as a function of the frequency ν of the light ray, the current point in the volume $\boldsymbol{x}$, and the current ray direction $\boldsymbol{s}$.

Solely inelastic and elastic scattering are considered to be the causes for effects like absorption, emittance, and dispersion. In mathematical terms, the interactions are described by the Boltzmann equation [6], which is a special case of transport theory problems [7].

[2]For ray-tracing the eventual blocking of incoming light I_0 is tested as well.

In this approach the local change of the intensity ∇I in direction $\boldsymbol{s}$ is given by

$$
\begin{aligned}
\boldsymbol{s}\nabla I(\boldsymbol{x},\boldsymbol{s},\nu) &= -\sigma_t(\boldsymbol{x},\nu)I(\boldsymbol{x},\boldsymbol{s},\nu) + q(\boldsymbol{x},\boldsymbol{s},\nu) \\
&- S_{\text{in}}\frac{\partial I(\boldsymbol{x},\boldsymbol{s},\nu)}{\partial \nu} \\
&+ \sigma_s(\boldsymbol{x},\nu)\int d\Omega \cdot \rho(\boldsymbol{x},\boldsymbol{s}' \to \boldsymbol{s})I(\boldsymbol{x},\boldsymbol{s}',\nu)
\end{aligned}
\tag{28.5}
$$

with:

- $\sigma_t = \sigma_s + \sigma_a$ as the intensity loss due to scattering, described by factor σ_s; and absorption, described by factor σ_a.
- q is the intensity of a local light source.
- S_{in} describes the loss due to inelastic scattering like dispersion.

The last term is the contribution to I by scattering on other surfaces. It corresponds to the integral term in the rendering equation Eq. (28.1):

- $\rho(\boldsymbol{x},\boldsymbol{s}' \to \boldsymbol{s})$ is hereby the amount of light that is scattered from direction $\boldsymbol{s}'$ into direction $\boldsymbol{s}$ at point $\boldsymbol{x}$. This contribution can be, for example, modeled by the Phong illumination model.
- $d\Omega$ is the solid angle around $\boldsymbol{s}$.

By formal integration one obtains the following integro-differential equation:

$$
\begin{aligned}
I(\boldsymbol{x},\boldsymbol{s},\nu) &= I_s(\boldsymbol{x}-R'\boldsymbol{s},\boldsymbol{s},\nu)\exp(-\tau(R)) \\
&+ \int_0^R \exp[-(\tau(R)-\tau(R'))]Q(\boldsymbol{x}-R'\boldsymbol{s},\boldsymbol{s},\nu)\,\mathrm{d}R'
\end{aligned}
\tag{28.6}
$$

$I_s(\boldsymbol{x}-R'\boldsymbol{s},\boldsymbol{s},\nu)$ is the incident light intensity, τ is the optical length, defined by:

$$
\tau(R) = \int_0^R dR'\sigma_t(\boldsymbol{x}-R'\boldsymbol{s},\boldsymbol{s},\nu) \tag{28.7}
$$

with Q as the generalized source, defined by:

$$
Q(\boldsymbol{x},\boldsymbol{s},\nu) = q(\boldsymbol{x},\boldsymbol{s},\nu) + \sigma_s(\boldsymbol{x},\nu)\int p(\boldsymbol{x},\boldsymbol{s}' \to \boldsymbol{s})I(\boldsymbol{x},\boldsymbol{s},\nu)\,\mathrm{d}\Omega \tag{28.8}
$$

For the derivation of the volume rendering algorithms, Eq. (28.6) is first simplified by restricting the generalized source (see Eq. (28.8)) to a single source q (neglect of refraction and multiple reflections). The second simplification of Eq. (28.6) is the omission of absorption from incident light energy: $I_s(\boldsymbol{x}-R'\boldsymbol{s},\boldsymbol{s},\nu)\exp(-\tau(R)) = 0$. It follows:

$$
I(\boldsymbol{x},\boldsymbol{s},\nu) = \int_0^R \exp[-(\tau(R)-\tau(R'))]q(\boldsymbol{x}-R'\boldsymbol{s},\boldsymbol{s},\nu)\,\mathrm{d}R' \tag{28.9}
$$

By inserting the τ-term:

$$I(\boldsymbol{x},\mathbf{s},\nu) = \int_0^R \mathrm{d}R' \exp\left(-\int_R^{R'} \mathrm{d}R''\sigma_t(\boldsymbol{x}-R''\mathbf{s},\mathbf{s},\nu)\right) q(\boldsymbol{x}-R'\mathbf{s},\mathbf{s},\nu) \tag{28.10}$$

Equation (28.10) is known as the *volume rendering equation* [8]. The discretization of this formula gives:

$$\begin{aligned} I(\boldsymbol{x},\mathbf{s},\nu) &= \sum_{z=0}^{Z} \exp\left(-\sum_{k=z+1}^{Z} \sigma_t(k)\Delta z\right) q(z)\Delta z \\ &= \sum_{z=0}^{Z} q(z)\Delta z \prod_{k=z+1}^{Z} \exp(-\sigma_t(k)\Delta z) \end{aligned} \tag{28.11}$$

As a common simplification, $\exp(-\sigma_t(k)\Delta z)$ is approximated by $1-\alpha(P,k)$ and $q(z)\Delta z$ by $C(P,z)\alpha(P,z)$, where P is the considered ray, α is the opacity of the corresponding voxel and C is the voxel color.

The standard ray-casting formula states now (whereby $C(P)$ replaces $I(\boldsymbol{x},\mathbf{s},\nu)$):

$$C(P) = \sum_{z=0}^{Z} C(P,z)\alpha(P,z) \prod_{k=z+1}^{Z} (1-\alpha(P,k)) \tag{28.12}$$

28.2 Basic concepts and notation for visualization

The discussion and the application of rendering methods requires the introduction of some basic concepts and notations. We assume the following configuration. A viewer located at point $\mathbf{V}$ looks at an artificial scene built up of geometric objects and those represented by volume data sets (see Fig. 28.2). The image he sees is generated on the *projection plane* by rendering algorithms. To define this projection plane one requires one point on the plane, the *view reference point* $\mathbf{V}_{vrp}$, and a normal vector, the *view plane normal* $\mathbf{V}_{vpn}$ pointing to the viewer.

In order to define a unique coordinate system on this plane, one additional vector is necessary. It is the projection $\mathbf{v}$ of the view up vector $\mathbf{V}_{vup}$ onto the projection plane. This vector $\mathbf{v}$ defines the up-direction in the rendered image. The second coordinate direction $\mathbf{u}$ is defined by the cross product of $\mathbf{v}$ with the view plane normal $\mathbf{V}_{vpn}$: $\mathbf{u} = \mathbf{v}\times\mathbf{V}_{vpn}$.

From the artificial scene the viewer sees only a part that is later displayed in a graphical window on the computer screen. The visible region of the scene is defined by the viewing frustum as shown in

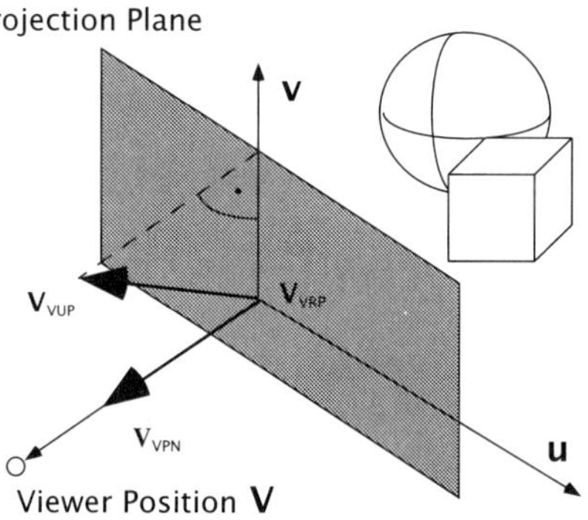

Figure 28.2: *Definition of basic notations for a 3-D view.*

Fig. 28.2. All objects outside are considered as transparent and are clipped accordingly.

The objects in the virtual scene are either defined by their geometric shape or by a volume data set. Geometric shapes are represented, for example, by polygon nets, Bezier surfaces or NURBS. Data sets are defined by grids. In this chapter we concentrate on rectilinear grids since they are often used and fast rendering algorithms have been developed for them. Each grid point is called *VOXEL* that comes from VOlume piXEL. It is assumed to be a result of resampling an object by imaging devices and it is assumed to be at most 16 bit wide. For example, CT, MRI, ultrasound, and even confocal microscopes fulfill these demands.

28.3 Surface rendering algorithms and OpenGL

28.3.1 OpenGL

In this section, one of two different approaches is presented that allows to render volume data sets. It is based on surface rendering motivated as a simplification of the rendering equation in Section 28.1.1. For this rendering approach there has evolved a *de facto* application programming interface (API). This is OpenGL that is shortly sketched in the following.

OpenGL, derived from Iris GL of Silicon Graphics Inc., has its roots in the programming of dedicated graphics hardware. Its definition as a state machine still forces the programmer to obey or take advantage of many side effects during programming. In the following a brief description of its processing model is given, but for a full reference the reader is referred to special literature [9, 10].

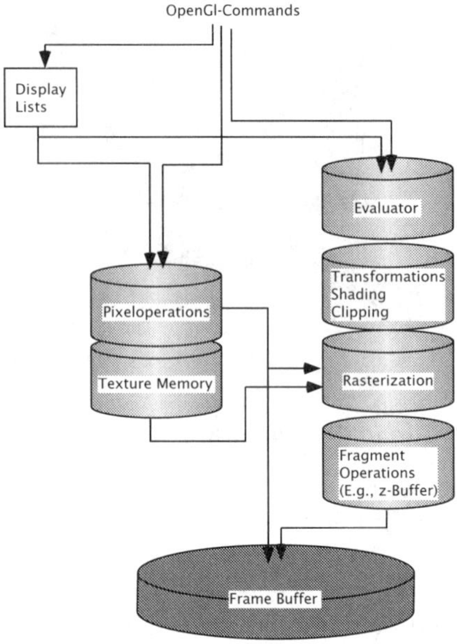

Figure 28.3: *Sketch of the OpenGL architecture.*

OpenGL's visualization process can be described by two pipelines that are filled by single or grouped OpenGL commands (Fig. 28.3). Groups of commands, so-called display lists, have been introduced to allow for a faster processing. The pipelines, in particular, are the geometry and the pixel pipeline.

Geometry pipeline. Although OpenGL allows describing the shape of objects by surface patches like Bezier or NURBS surfaces, for efficiency reasons these higher-order surface representations are mapped into polygon nets in the first stage of the OpenGL geometry pipeline. After this evaluator stage all objects are described by polygons and their respective vertices.

Operations like geometric transformations, shading, and clipping are applied to these vertices. Among the geometric transformations are, for example, rotation, scaling, shearing, translation, and perspective projection. For shading the Phong illumination model is applied. And clipping planes determine the visible half-spaces in the virtual environment. The result are polygon vertices within the viewing frustum that are projected onto the projection plane and which have a color (red, green, blue, abbreviated as RGB) and eventually an opacity (A).

In the subsequent rasterization stage polygons are filled with pixels in the screen coordinate system. This is called rasterization where the pixels are arranged at raster points of a virtual raster display. During this rasterization the color values of the vertices have to be translated into pixel RGB values. This is done by either flat shading, that is, the polygon has a uniform color, or Gouraud shading, in which the color of the vertices is linearly interpolated within the polygon. Additionally, texture mapping can be applied. It maps a predefined pattern, stored in a texture buffer of the pixel pipeline onto the polygon. For each raster point the texture color is interpolated and either replaces the polygon color or is blended with it.

The last stage in the geometry pipeline is the fragment stage. Fragments are the pixel's RGB(A) values that are generated in the rasterization stage. There are several processing modes that can be enabled. Most important is the z-buffering that determines the visible surface (it corresponds to the function $g(\boldsymbol{x}', \boldsymbol{x})$ of Section 28.1.1). After this stage, the final image is stored in the frame buffer that can be directly read to display the result on the computer screen.

Pixel pipeline. The second pipeline is for pixel processing and texturing. Pixels can be manipulated in the fragment phase in the geometry pipeline and on the frame buffer. Texturing information maps 2-D images on the rasterized polygons. In newer extensions of Silicon Graphics Inc. [11] OpenGL specification 3-D texture mapping is possible. Here, individual slices are resampled from a volumetric regular data set and then blended using the **over** operator as defined in the next section.

Surface rendering algorithms specified, for example, by sets of OpenGL commands have been integrated into specialized high-performance rendering engines [12] and many graphics cards [13, 14, 15]. These systems allow scenes with several thousand to million polygons per second to be rendered. For this reason, surface-based algorithms have been considered to be ideal for real-time rendering engines operating on volumetric data sets. It is the reason why much research has been dedicated into this direction [16].

28.3.2 Iso-surface extraction by marching cubes

The question that now arises is how to apply surface rendering to volumetric data sets. The solution to this problem is quite straightforward. One has to define each object in the volume data by surfaces that form the object's boundary. This thin surface can be determined by segmentation procedures that have been described in this book (see Chapter 25). In medicine automatic segmentation is a very difficult and mostly unsolved task. The method that is mostly applied is the segmentation using a global gray-value threshold. It leads directly to the extraction of iso-surfaces in the gray-value data set.

An algorithm for iso-surface extraction in volume data sets is the *marching cubes*marching cube algorithm [16]. Basically, it assumes that the gray values between grid points vary linearly. This way iso-surfaces lead to polygon nets. The polygon's vertices are hereby located on the edges between two neighboring nodes in the grid, one being above and one being below the user-defined threshold. The vertex position on the edge is determined by linear interpolation. After this interpolation of the polygon net's vertices a precalculated look-up table serves for assigning them to individual polygons.

After this generation of a polygon net, the objects can be rendered by OpenGL, that is, standard rendering techniques. Unfortunately, the number of polygons that are generated can be very high. For example, the extraction of the surface of a CT data set of a human jaw (an example is shown in Fig. 28.4) requires about 900,000 polygons whereby the full data set contains 8 million voxels. As a remedy the number of polygons is reduced, that is, neighboring polygons are fused if the generated errors are below a given bound (methods for mesh decimation are described in Schroeder [17]).

28.4 Volume rendering

28.4.1 Ray-casting

Iso-surfacing as described in the previous section suffers from several problems that are connected with the extraction of a surface. For example, if the threshold is chosen too high, relevant but poorly defined structures are not extracted as a separate object. Lowering the threshold, however, leads to an extraction of noise. Moreover, some structures, for example, a tumor that infiltrates surrounding healthy tissue, cannot be described by surfaces in principle. Indeed, the basic problem is the underlying extraction of a surface that displays only a limited amount of information that is in the data set[3].

In order to overcome these problems one has to overcome the difficulty to extract surfaces, that is, a volume-oriented approach is necessary. In the following we discuss this approach more thoroughly as it allows for a more flexible representation of objects in data sets without being forced to describe them by surfaces. This approach is called ray-casting.

[3]This does not mean that surface rendering is unsuited to display the object's shape. On the contrary, if the object surface can be determined and if this surface correctly describes the object, surface rendering should be chosen. However, in many volume data sets, especially due to noise in the image, surface extraction is difficult and thus volume rendering is often superior.

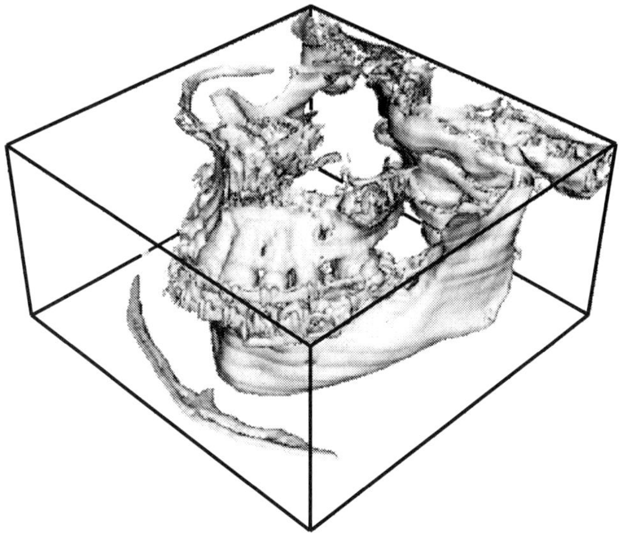

Figure 28.4: *CT scan of a human head (256 × 256 × 128 voxels). Extraction of the bone surface by Marching Cubes (vtk Toolkit [18]). Threshold: 1500, image size 800 × 800. Image generated by Marco Heidl.*

The basic starting point of ray-casting is the volume rendering equation Eq. (28.12). It describes how the light is accumulated to generate an image. Its algorithmic realization can be characterized by four phases.

First, primary or viewing rays are cast into the virtual scene (see Fig. 28.5). The viewing rays are perpendicular to the compositing plane and are equidistantly arranged on a regular 2-D grid on this compositing plane. Similarly, the grid points of this 2-D grid later coincide with the pixels shown on the screen.

Second, each ray is sampled at equidistant points; these are the sample points (see Fig. 28.5). For sampling, the gray value of the sample point is interpolated from the data set's neighboring voxel gray values. Trilinear interpolation is most frequently used for that purpose (see Lacroute [8] and also Chapter 8). The result of this resampling is a resampled data set, which is a rectilinear cube as well.

Third, at each sample point a gradient is estimated by difference or gradient filters (see Fig. 28.6 and Section 10.3). The gradient is nor-

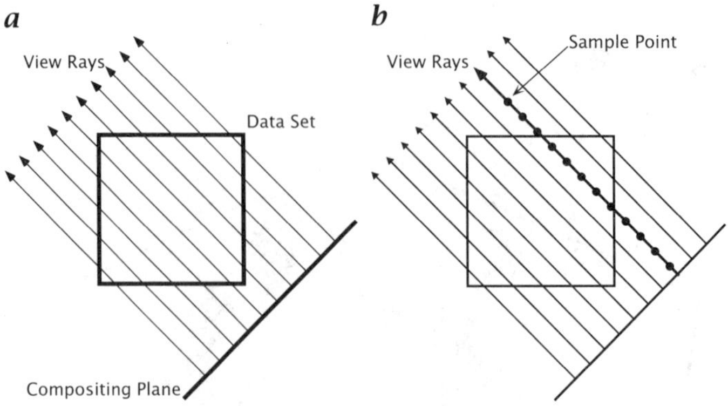

Figure 28.5: ***a*** *First step of ray-casting: By viewing the data set from various directions, the compositing plane can be oriented arbitrarily to the data set, which is assumed to be a rectilinear grid. Rays are cast from this plane into the volume whereby the rays are equidistant and orthogonal to the plane. Each starting point of the rays thus coincides with the pixels in the final projection.* ***b*** *Second step of ray-casting: Sample points at equidistant positions are sampled in the second step along each ray.*

malized by the gradient magnitude. Moreover, it delivers the normal direction of a potential surface near the sample point in the data set.

Gray value and gradient magnitude are used to derive opacity and RGB (red, green, blue) values via look-up tables (LUTs). It is assumed that both input values of the LUT are equally influential for differentiating between different objects, which thereby allows them to be displayed with appropriate colors and opacities.

Gradient values are taken along with the viewer and light source directions to perform shading. Phong shading, which is most frequently used [8], calculates the amount of incoming light that is reflected in the viewer direction.

The fourth stage is compositing (also called alpha-blending). It uses a recursive formulation of the volume rendering equation Eq. (28.12). With the following *over operator* the recursive procedure determines the intensity of light that reaches the compositing plane:

$$\begin{aligned} C_{\text{out}} &= C(P,z)\alpha(P,z) + C_{\text{in}}(1-\alpha(P,z)) \\ &=: (C(P,z)\alpha(P,z)) \text{ over } C_{\text{in}} \end{aligned} \tag{28.13}$$

where C_{out} and C_{in} are the outgoing and incoming color intensities for voxel z of ray P, $\alpha(P,z)$ is the corresponding opacity of this voxel, and $C(P,z)$ is the light intensity the voxel reflects.

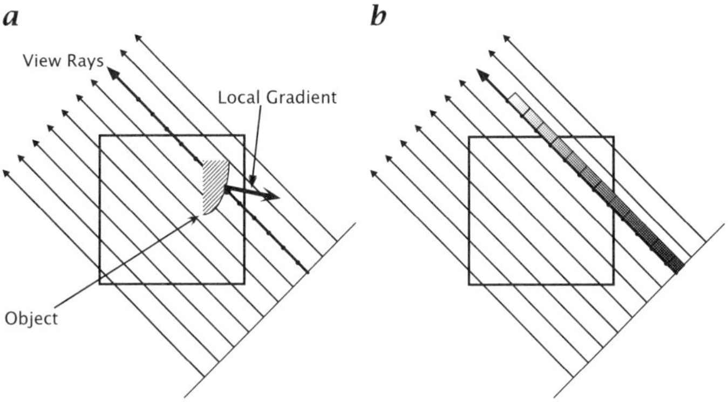

Figure 28.6: ***a*** *Third stage: gradients are determined in the third step using local difference filters either on the original data or on the sampled data.* ***b*** *Fourth stage: in the compositing step of ray-casting the light reflected in the viewer direction is attenuated on its way through the data set and the intensities of all sample points of the ray are composited to the final pixel value.*

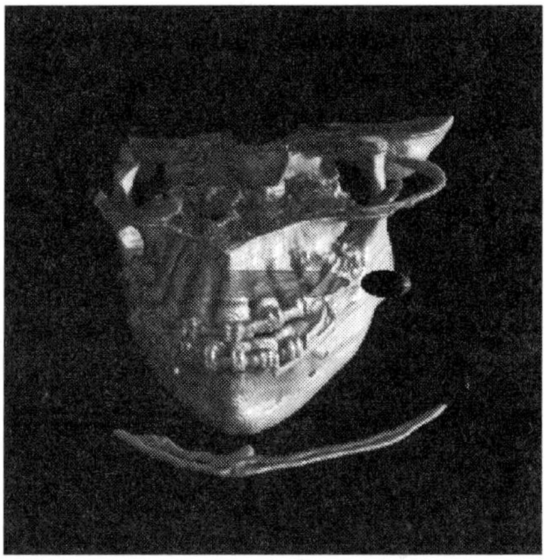

Figure 28.7: The picture shows a jaw and an ellipsoid. With the shadow the relative distance of the ellipsoid to the bone can be estimated.

28.4.2 Shadowing approaches

The ray-casting approach can be further improved by shadowing techniques. Shadows play an important role if the relative depth of two objects is to be determined visibly. As an example, see Fig. 28.7. For brevity we will call this algorithm volume ray-casting.

One of the earliest approaches to shadowing algorithms is the two-phase approach from Kajiya and Von Herzen [19]. In the first phase, the incident light absorption is calculated. The intensity that reaches each

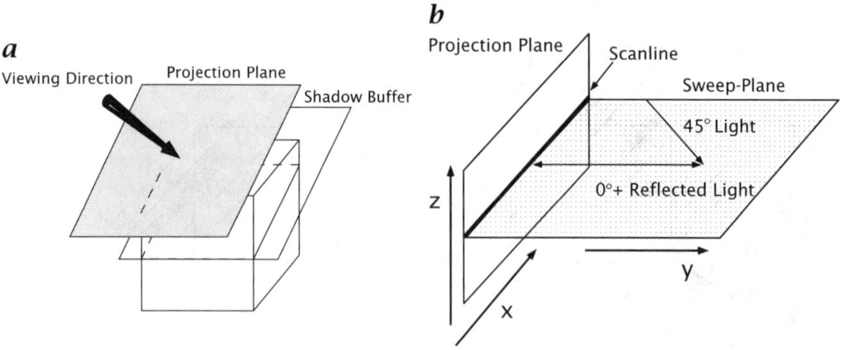

***Figure 28.8:** **a** Grant's approach for shadowing in volume rendering. **b** Sketch of a sweep plane for illustration.*

voxel is stored in a shadow buffer. In the second phase a standard ray-casting is performed whereby during shading the amount of reflected light is multiplied by the locally stored intensity.

The approach developed by Kajiya has two severe limitations. First, it requires a shadow buffer array as large as the original data set. Second, it needs two phases or two sweeps over the data set, which limits the performance if the data read out is time critical.

By restricting the position of the light sources Grant found a more efficient solution [20]. In his solution light sources are either positioned in the viewer half plane in front of the data set or opposite to it, that is, behind the data set (see also Fig. 28.8).

To understand the algorithm, let us assume that the light sources are in the viewer half plane[4]. Assume further that the shadow buffer is a plane (2-D array) that initially coincides with the compositing plane. The latter is located in front of the data set (seen from the viewer position). As the light falls onto this shadow buffer without absorption, each sample point on this plane obtains the same intensity.

Let us now consider the first sample points of all rays cast into the virtual scene from the compositing plane (phase 1). These points lie again on a plane due to the constant sample distance. For simplicity, we call it first resampling plane. The initial intensity at the compositing plane (the start position of each ray) is given by the shadow buffer. For the next sampling plane the shadow buffer is updated by placing it at the first resampling plane position. Given the light intensity of the previous shadow buffer calculation is made as to how much of this light reaches the current shadow buffer. This operation requires a second

[4]This is the most interesting case because, otherwise, the viewer looks into the light sources or the light is reflected in the direction opposite to the viewer. Nevertheless, this second case can be similarly described.

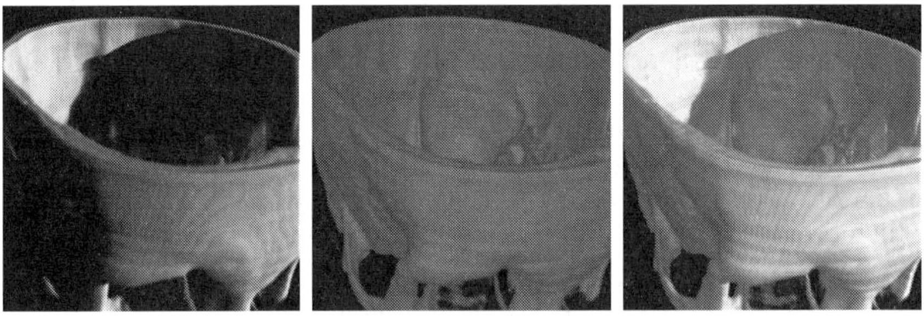

Figure 28.9: *Rendering of a skull imaged by CT:* ***a*** *Using only one light source, for example, at 45°, produces totally black shadow areas that hide information.* ***b*** *Using only one light source, for example, at 0° generates no shadows so that visible information about surface orientation is poor.* ***c*** *With two light sources a combination of depth and structure information is obtained.*

resampling of the data set because the light direction is normally not along either the data set or the resampling grid.

Meinzer's Heidelberg raytracer approach. The disadvantages of Grant's approach are the large buffer size corresponding to the size of the resulting image, in general, and two resampling steps (for one light source). Meinzer overcame these problems by further restricting the light source position [21] to 0° and 45° relative to the viewing direction. He assumes that incident and reflected rays are sweep plane parallel. Sweep planes are planes that are spanned by rays cast from pixels of the scanline. In Meinzer's approach, the 45° light rays are in this plane as well (see also Fig. 28.8). As consequence the scanlines can be generated independently of each other because all operations remain in this plane. Thus the full shadow buffer plane is not necessary (as was the case for Grant's approach) but only one line, the intersection of Grant's shadow buffer with the sweep plane, is required.

Furthermore, due to the restriction of the light rays within sweep planes and their fixation to 0° and 45° relative to the viewer direction they traverse the resampled data set along one main coordinate and along one diagonal direction. This allows a second resampling to be omitted and thus reduces the computational demand of this algorithm.

Number of light sources. For the realization of volume ray-tracing the effects of shadowing have to be considered. For example, without any precautions the volume ray-tracer produces hard shadows without penumbra. A typical result is shown in Fig. 28.9. Areas lying in the shadow are totally black and no information can be gathered about them.

Another example is the use of only a 0° light source (see Fig. 28.9). In this example the depth information can hardly be guessed as shadows do not occur and the direction of the light source does not reveal additional details.

In order to overcome these problems two light sources are necessary. These are sufficient to generate images that exhibit both an illumination of all surfaces directly visible by the viewer and shadowing, which provides additional information about depth.

28.4.3 Methods for accelerating volume visualization

Rendering volume data sets with the forementioned volume rendering algorithms requires minutes per image on a conventional PC. However, transparent regions exhibit no interactions with the light rays. Thus their contribution can be omitted. An algorithmic technique that makes use of exactly this information is space-leaping. Similarly, if the light intensity that reaches a certain sampling point in the volume is below a threshold (e.g., a few percent), further, deeper lying sample points can be neglected because their contribution to the final image is negligible. Both techniques, in combination, cut rendering cost by at least a factor of 10 assuming that the data set exhibits hard surfaces and empty space between them. A good example of what can be reached by these methods can be found in Lacroute [8].

When interactivity or even real-time operation can be supported, progressive refinement (also called dynamic resolution) can be used. It generates a coarse view as long as the user moves the object and gives a detailed view when no interaction occurs [22, 23, 24]. For a survey of these and other approaches see Yagel [25] and for recent implementations see Lacroute [8], Brady et al. [26], Freund and Sloan [27].

28.5 The graphics library VGL

The *VGL* is a set of libraries for volume and polygon rendering, which has been developed by *Volume Graphics GmbH*[5]. The *VGL* combines volume rendering and surface rendering[6] with shadowing techniques. Thus one can, for example, render a scene where volume and surface objects are combined, transparencies of both objects are handled correctly and each object (either surface or volume) can cast a shadow on other objects (again either surface or volume). This flexibility is unique

[5]http://www.volumegraphics.com

[6]The actual version of *VGL* uses the Mesa library, which is not a licensed OpenGL implementation, but nearly 100 % OpenGL compatible. Mesa is copyrighted (C) by Brian Paul, see http://www.ssec.wisc.edu/ brianp/Mesa.html

insofar as this is the only commercially available platform independent application programming interface (API) that combines these features. The *VGL* uses volume rendering algorithms based on algorithmic optimization like space-leaping and early ray-termination. The *VGL* is available for most UNIX flavors (Solaris, IRIX, DEC OSF/1, Linux) as well as for Windows 95 and Windows NT.

Besides the functional features, the *VGL* uses threads for the distribution of the rendering load to several processors. This way, speed-up of a factor of 3.5 could be achieved for rendering a normal image of 256^2 pixel on a 4-processor PentiumPro200 system.

The *VGL* is a C++ class library with classes for the representation of volume data, surface (polygon) data, and even a complete scene. The major programming concept of *VGL* is to define a scene built up of primitives. From *VGL*'s point of view a primitive is either an object defined by volume (voxel) data or an object defined by a set of OpenGL calls. The scene collects all primitives in conjunction with additional specifications concerning the rendering and a render class delivers the rendered image.

The basic *VGL* classes are the image and volume classes, the volume and polygon primitive classes, and the scene class. All classes of the *VGL* are designed to be simple and easy to use. The complexity of *VGL* scenes is not achieved by using complex classes, but by combining simple classes in a very flexible way. The volume and image classes are template-based with the data type for each voxel being the template parameter. The user of *VGL* can render volumes with 8-, 16-, or 32-bit integer, 32-bit floating-point or 32-bit RGBA data per voxel—all in one scene without restrictions concerning the number of volumes and polygon objects in the scene.

28.5.1 VGL image and volume classes

Images and Volumes in the *VGL* are containers for 2- or 3-D data, which are located on a rectilinear grid. The *VGL* contains a base class for images and a base class for volumes with different implementations for either images or volumes. The implementations include images and volumes with their own memory for data, images, and volumes. They can reference parts of other images or volumes, and images and volumes. In addition, they can represent scaled duplicates of other images or volumes. The gap between images and volumes is filled with the "slice" class, which is set up onto a volume and represents a normal image. The slice class gives access to slices of volume data as if they were normal images.

Figure 28.10: *Example scene rendered with* VGL. *The included volume data sets are among other things: magnetic lock scanned with neutrons (top left), courtesy B. Schillinger, Department for Physics, TU Munich; part of an engine block (top right); "Chapel Hill" data set (bottom right), courtesy North Carolina Memorial Hospital; Volume Graphics Logo (bottom middle); Visible Human (bottom left), courtesy US National Library of Medicine; MRT scan of human heart preparation (middle left). All other objects are polygon data distributed with the "Geomview" software package.*

28.5.2 Volume primitives

The volume classes are only a container for 3-D voxel data without any additional information. To render these data, two further information items are missing: the so-called *classification* (leading to opacity and color) and the geometric information (position in the scene and the clipping specifications).

The mapping from voxel data to opacity and color is added by the "render volume" class derived from the volume class. The render volume class takes any volume (even parts of other volumes or zoomed representations of volumes) as source of voxel data and adds an internal look-up table (LUT), which assigns voxel values to opacity and color values. The LUT operation is done before any further processing occurs; in particular the LUT is assigned before the interpolation is accomplished. The consequences of this behavior are discussed in more detail in Section 28.5.

The geometric information is added with the so-called "volume primitive" class. This class takes a "render volume" as source of voxel data in conjunction with classification information and adds the geometry of the volume: rotation, translation, scaling, and clipping.

28.5.3 Polygon primitives

The "polygon (surface) primitives" are defined in the *VGL* by a set of OpenGL function calls. The polygon primitive class represents the interface and container for the OpenGL function calls. In *VGL* point of view OpenGL calls are used to define the shape and aspect of an object; it is not the final method to render surface objects. After building a polygon primitive by creating a polygon primitive object and filling it with appropriate OpenGL code, the polygon primitive is inserted into the scene and handled as any other primitive. The unified handling of primitives includes the geometric operations such as rotation, scaling, and translation; and the clipping definitions. Every primitive, regardless of whether it is a polygon or volume primitive, will be handled in exactly the same way.

28.5.4 The VGL scene

The scene is the master object for all rendering in the *VGL*. The scene is built up by adding primitives, either volume or polygon primitives. Additional information like scene-wide clipping planes, the light sources, the specification of the used rendering algorithm, and the viewer position and viewing direction completes the scene definition. After the scene has been defined in all details, the render call creates the rendered image, which can either be displayed on the screen or processed further inside the *VGL*.

28.5.5 VGL rendering pipeline

The basic principle of volume rendering is to cast rays from the viewer position into the scene and to calculate a resulting color value for each ray, as described in Section 28.4.

The differences between the various implementations of volume rendering reside in how the resulting color for each ray is calculated. Differences can occur in the ray geometry, that is, if parallel or perspective projection is used, or in the algorithm, which generates a resulting color from samples along the ray. The *VGL* in its actual version is based on the ray geometry model introduced by the Heidelberger Raytracer Model [21], but with modifications, for example, to introduce perspective projection [28]. Because of the usage of this ray geometry model, the *VGL* is restricted to two light sources with fixed positions. The long-term development of *VGL* will aim at real ray-tracing approaches without any restrictions in light sources.

The main difference between *VGL* and other commonly used volume rendering packages is located in the rendering pipeline. Nearly all volume rendering methods place the classification of voxels into opacity and color after the interpolation step. By contrast, the *VGL* does the assignment of opacity and color before the interpolation, and interpolates the opacity and color channels separately.

Unlike other volume rendering approaches the *VGL* assumes that there are four independent channels of information available about the space covered by the volume data, the opacity and red, green, and blue colors. Voxel data is typically only monochromatic and represents one (sampled) value in the 3-D space. If the voxel data is sampled according to Shannon's theorem one can think of the voxel data to represent a continuous function $f(\boldsymbol{p})$ with $\boldsymbol{p}$ being a 3-D coordinate. Starting from this function $f(\boldsymbol{p})$ the rendering pipeline with the classification after interpolation proceeds as in an 8-neighborhood $f(N(\boldsymbol{p}))$ of voxels around $\boldsymbol{p}$:

$$\begin{array}{ll} \text{interpolation:} & f'(\boldsymbol{p}) \\ \text{gradients:} & \nabla f'(\boldsymbol{p}) \\ \text{classification:} & \alpha(\boldsymbol{p}), R(\boldsymbol{p}), G(\boldsymbol{p}), B(\boldsymbol{p}) \\ \text{rendering equation} & \end{array} \tag{28.14}$$

The function $f'(\boldsymbol{p})$ describes the resampled function value, $\alpha(\boldsymbol{p})$ gives the opacity and $R(\boldsymbol{p})$, $G(\boldsymbol{p})$, $B(\boldsymbol{p})$ are the red, green, and blue color components at the resampled position $\boldsymbol{p}$, respectively.

The *VGL* rendering pipeline with the "classification before interpolation" corresponds to:

$$\begin{array}{ll} \text{classification:} & \alpha(N(\boldsymbol{p})), R(N(\boldsymbol{p})), G(N(\boldsymbol{p})), B(N(\boldsymbol{p})) \\ \text{interpolation:} & \alpha'(\boldsymbol{p}), R'(\boldsymbol{p}), G'(\boldsymbol{p}), B'(\boldsymbol{p}) \\ \text{gradients:} & \nabla \alpha'(\boldsymbol{p}) \\ \text{rendering equation} & \end{array} \tag{28.15}$$

Hereby $\alpha(N(\boldsymbol{p}))$, $R(N(\boldsymbol{p}))$, $G(N(\boldsymbol{p}))$, $B(N(\boldsymbol{p}))$ describe the 8-neighborhood of voxels around $\boldsymbol{p}$ as having been classified before the resampled values $\alpha'(\boldsymbol{p})$, $R'(\boldsymbol{p})$, $G'(\boldsymbol{p})$, $B'(\boldsymbol{p})$ are generated.

Both approaches have advantages and disadvantages. The standard rendering pipeline does not modify the volume data $f(\boldsymbol{p})$ until the resampling has occurred. The gradients are calculated on the original volume data. Then the assignment of opacity and color occurs, which can in principle take the resampled volume data at $\boldsymbol{p}$ and the gradient $\nabla f'(\boldsymbol{p})$ into account. The flexibility in the classification step is paid with the inflexibility of manipulating the original volume data $f(\boldsymbol{p})$ in the rendering process. One can, in principle, map the resampled volume data $f'(\boldsymbol{p})$ to a totally arbitrary opacity function $\alpha(\boldsymbol{p})$, but the gradients will not coincide with the seen opacity distribution.

The rendering kernel of the *VGL* assumes that the input data is already given as opacity $\alpha(\boldsymbol{p})$ and color distribution ($R(\boldsymbol{p})$, $G(\boldsymbol{p})$, and

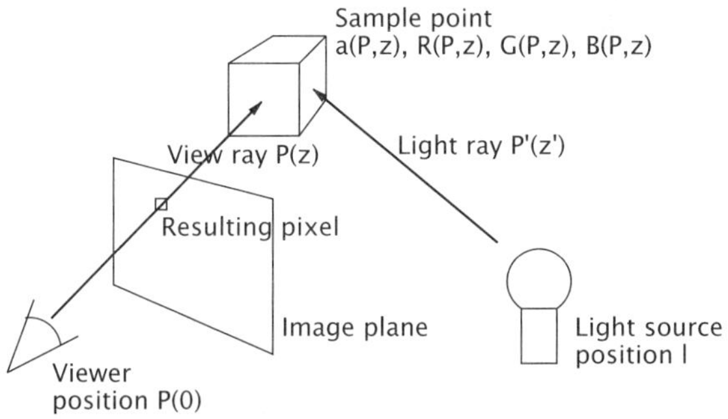

***Figure 28.11:** The geometry of* VGL *rendering.*

$B(\boldsymbol{p})$). After this information has been given—either by assigning opacity and color to $f(\boldsymbol{p})$ or by using RGBA data as volume data source—the following rendering process has a better motivation from physics: The gradients used to estimate surfaces in the volume data are calculated on the opacity $\alpha(\boldsymbol{p})$ and each of the physical features of the volume (opacity and color) is interpolated and processed independently.

Another difference between standard volume rendering and the *VGL* is the different "rendering equation." While standard volume rendering use relies on the over-operator Eq. (28.13) to combine the sampled values along a ray, the *VGL* uses an integration according to the following formula:

$$C_R(P) = \int_0^\infty \exp\left(-\int_0^z \alpha'(P, z')\, \mathrm{d}z'\right) R'(P, z) C_R(P, z)\, \mathrm{d}z \qquad (28.16)$$

and equivalently for C_G and C_B. The resulting color $C_{R,G,B}(P)$, which will be displayed on the screen at pixel position (P_x, P_y), is calculated using an integration along the ray being sent from the viewer position into the scene. The ray is described by $P(z) = P(0) + z \cdot v(p_x, p_y)$ with $P(0)$ being the viewer position and $v(P_x, P_y)$ as the unit direction vector for the ray. The result is then projected onto the screen coordinates (P_x, P_y). The integration is evaluated for each color channel. At every ray position $P(z)$ the emitted color intensity is the product of the "color emitting factor" $R(P, z)$, $G(P, z)$, or $B(P, z)$, and the lighting factor $C_{R,G,B}$. The emitted color intensity at position $P(z)$ will be absorbed on the way to the viewer by the material present between the viewer at $P(0)$ and the point $P(z)$. This is considered with the exponential term $\exp(-\int_0^z \alpha(P, z')\, \mathrm{d}z')$.

The *lighting factor* $C_{R,G,B}$ itself is defined as

$$C_{R,G,B}(P,z) = \sum_{i=0}^{\text{Lights}} I^i_{R,G,B}(P,z) RKF(\alpha'(P,z), \nabla\alpha'(P,z), v(P_x,P_y), l_i) \tag{28.17}$$

The lighting factor at position $P(z)$ is in principle the product of the light intensity $I^i_{R,G,B}$ of light source i at position $P(z)$, with the *rendering kernel function* $RKF(\alpha'(P,z), \nabla\alpha'(P,z), v(P_x,P_y), l_i)$, summed over all light sources. The rendering kernel function describes the relative amount of light that will be reflected into the viewer direction. To calculate this fraction, the rendering kernel has to know the actual position $P(z)$, the opacity and the gradient at position $P(z)$, as well as the viewer position $P(0)$ and the light position l_i.

The light intensity at position $P(z)$ is calculated using an exponential absorption term such as:

$$I^i_{R,G,B}(P,z) = I^i_{R,G,B}(0) \exp\left(-\int_0^d \mathrm{d}t'\ \alpha'(P',z')\right) \tag{28.18}$$

This time the integration runs along a ray from the light source position l_i to the point $P(z)$, described by

$$P'(z') = l_i + z' \frac{P(z) - l_i}{|P(z) - l_i|} \tag{28.19}$$

The parameter d is the distance between the light position l_i and the viewer point in space $P(z)$. The light absorption mentioned here introduces shadows in the rendering process in a very natural way.

These integrals cannot be evaluated analytically, but have to be approximated by numerical integration. The accuracy of the numerical integration result depends strongly on the distance between the discrete steps for the integration. As a rule of thumb, these distances should be chosen to be smaller than the grid distance of the discrete voxel values, but the correct sampling distance also depends on the rendering kernel function.

The *VGL* implements three different rendering algorithms that differs only in the rendering kernel function. These are the so-called *Scatter*, *ScatterHQ* and *MRT* algorithms.

Scatter. The Scatter algorithm has the most trivial rendering kernel function:

$$R(\alpha'(P,z), \nabla\alpha'(P,z), v(P_x,P_y), l_i) \equiv 1 \tag{28.20}$$

In fact only the usage of two light sources with the light absorption term (shadows) gives the contrast of the resulting image.

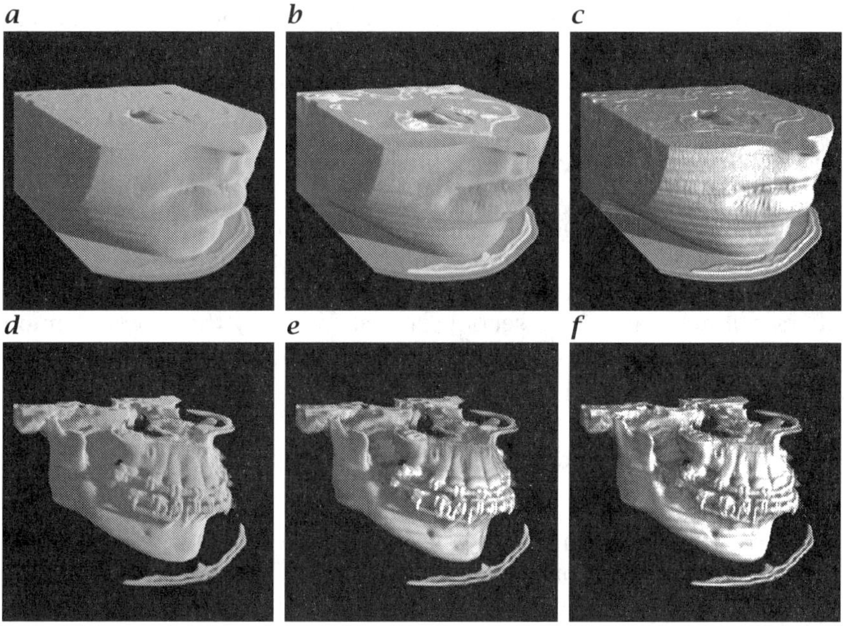

Figure 28.12: *Rendering of a CT scan of a human jaw with* ***a, d*** Scatter, ***b, e*** ScatterHQ, *and* ***c, f*** MRT *algorithms. The top line shows the CT scan including the soft tissue, the bottom line the bone structures only.*

Scatter HQ. The ScatterHQ algorithm inherits the *Scatter* algorithm terms and adds a second rendering kernel term with:

$$R(\alpha'(P,z), \nabla\alpha'(P,z), v(P_x, P_y), l_i) = \alpha'(P,z) \qquad (28.21)$$

These terms give image contrast even without shadowing, but must be evaluated with a very low sampling distance to achieve a numerical integration without inaccuracy, which would introduce image artifacts.

MRT. The *MRT* algorithm inherits the *Scatter* algorithm terms and adds a second gradient-dependent rendering kernel term with:

$$R(\alpha'(P,z), \nabla\alpha'(P,z), v(P_x, P_y), l_i) = \frac{P(z) - l_i}{|P(z) - l_i|}\frac{\nabla\alpha'(P,z)}{|\nabla\alpha'(P,z)|} \qquad (28.22)$$

In addition the *VGL* supports other, so-called projective rendering algorithms, like *maximum intensity projection* (MIP), *XRay* projection and a summation algorithm. These algorithms have in common the fact that they do not inherit the rendering model introduced before, but only traverse the scene along rays and deliver simple results: the sample with the highest opacity value (MIP), the exponentially absorbed light intensity along the ray at the end of the ray (XRay), or the sum of all sample values found along the ray (sum algorithm).

28.6 How to use volume rendering

A volume rendering should consist not only of rendering algorithms for a given voxel data set, but it should also support interactive modifications of rendering parameters to obtain the best possible impression of the volume data. This section describes briefly the most common manipulation possibilities like viewer navigation, clipping, and classification.

28.6.1 Viewer navigation

The navigation model of the *VGL* is similar to that of OpenGL. The position of the viewer inside the scene is described with the so-called "modelview" matrix (concerning transformations see also Section 9.3). The modelview matrix maps the scene coordinates to "eye" coordinates. The viewer has the defined position $(0|0|0)$ in eye coordinates and looks along the negative z-axis.

The image plane, and the projection of the scene onto the image plane are defined with the so-called "projection" matrix. This matrix defines, in particular, if perspective projection or parallel projection is used, where the near and far clipping planes are, and which portion of the scene will be seen in the rendered image.

Because the *VGL* can arrange any number of primitives into one scene, the location of the primitives in the scene is determined by an additional per-primitive matrix, the so-called "object" matrix. The object matrix maps the object coordinates (either voxel coordinates for volume primitives or OpenGL vertex coordinates for polygon primitives) to scene coordinates.

28.6.2 Clipping

Clipping is a valuable tool for volume data examination because it can be used to remove undesired parts of the volume data for the rendering process. In the *VGL*, every primitive can have an arbitrary number of clipping planes[7].

Clipping planes are introduced by defining a plane equation in primitive coordinates, consisting of four parameters. If x_o, y_o, and z_o define

[7]The used OpenGL implementation for rendering OpenGL primitives may introduce a maximum limit of clipping planes.

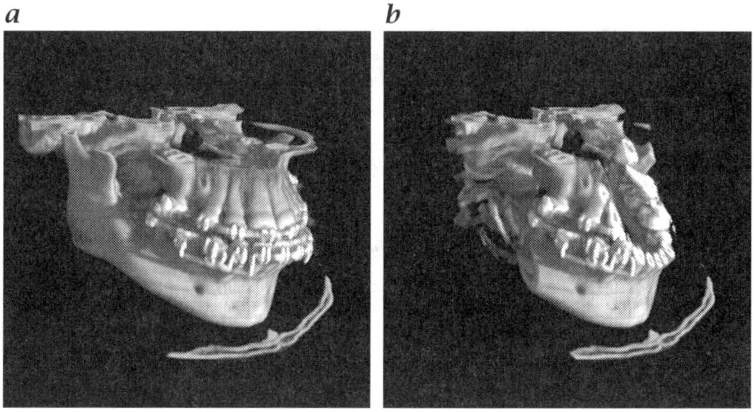

Figure 28.13: Rendering of a CT scan of a human jaw ***a*** *without and* ***b*** *with additional clipping. Clipping can remove undesired parts of the object.*

a point in primitive coordinate system, and a, b, c, and d are the clipping parameters, then the point $(x_o, y_o, z_o)^T$ will be clipped, if

$$x_o \cdot a + y_o \cdot b + z_o \cdot c + d < 0 \tag{28.23}$$

28.6.3 Classification

While surface rendering requires a good preprocessing step to extract the object's shape (either by more or less complex segmentation or by iso-surfacing as described here) volume rendering offers online manipulation of material properties like opacity and color in the classification step. The classification step in the *VGL* uses a LUT approach to map voxel values into opacities and colors. Hereby, the voxel values can be arbitrary. This freedom in the voxel values to opacity and color mapping supports many classification scenarios without any additional effort:

- Global gray-value mapping: depending on the object's gray value the LUT defines its opacity. One can, for example, use a global thresholding to render interesting objects opaque whereas the remaining objects are transparent.
- Combined index and gray-value mapping: another option is to select a coding where the upper bits of the voxel values are the labels for objects and the lower bits are their gray values. This way the upper bits define the voxels of certain objects and the object properties can be manipulated separately, just by loading the correct LUT values for each separated object.

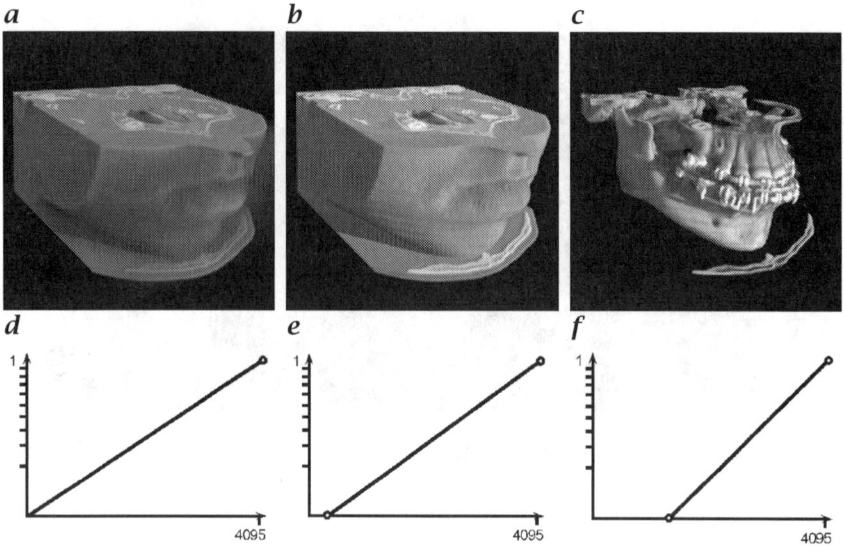

Figure 28.14: *Rendering of a CT scan of a human jaw with* ***a*** *an opacity directly proportional to the CT gray values;* ***b*** *with "noise" removed; and* ***c*** *with "noise" and "soft tissue" removed. The graphs below show the used gray value to opacity setting.*

- Index-based mapping: The voxel gray values need not represent any physical value, but can represent only index values. This approach is very useful for artificial data, which contains information about voxel groups (voxels which belong to one group get the same index value). Each voxel group can be assigned its opacity and color independently from all other voxel groups. One possible field of application is the support of interactive segmentation in a two-phase approach: In this case the original data set is presegmented in the first phase into several thousand elementary regions. Voxels belonging to one region obtain a unique region number. Each such region is assigned the average gray value of its voxels for visualization. In the second phase a merging algorithm operates on these preclassified regions to create real objects out of the elementary regions. As the number of regions is much smaller than the number of voxels in the data set this operation requires only a fraction of a second on a normal PC. By setting the LUT so, that merged regions are visible with their average gray values, while nonmerged regions are invisible (opacity is set to zero), the visualization of the segmentation result is possible in interactive time, and the "merge—LUT setting—visualization" cycle can be repeated very fast. This inter-

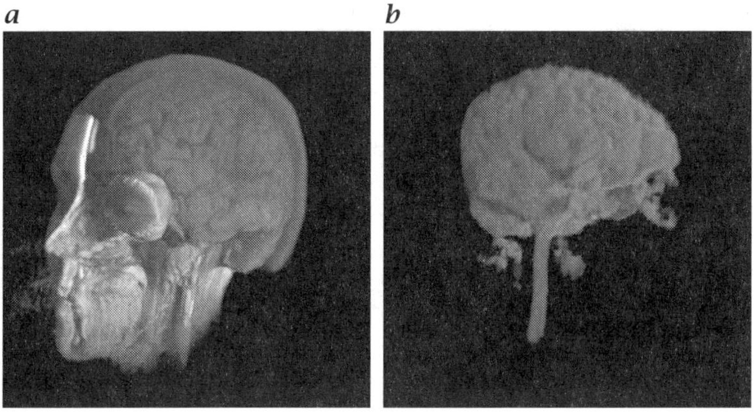

Figure 28.15: ***a*** *Rendering of a presegmented MRI data set ("Chapel Hill" data set, courtesy North Carolina Memorial Hospital): the segments are marked with index bits and contain 256 gray values each.* ***b*** *Rendered segmentation result using the index-based mapping method.*

active segmentation approach has been described by Kühne et al. [29].

- Other combinations with classifiers: Another approach is the integration of classifiers in the visualization process. For example, the voxel can be a feature vector. A classifier can operate on such feature vectors and assign them opacities. Features can, for example, be local mean and spread of gray values, local textures etc. and the classifier can, for example, be a statistical one. The advantage of this approach is that the classification result can be checked immediately and the classifier can be optimized accordingly.

Often, one wants to emphasize the boundary of objects. This gives a more accurate view of the object's shape. A typical approach to solving this problem is to multiply the reflected intensity with the gradient magnitude. A similar result can be achieved with the LUT by combining an indicator for a surface (like the gradient magnitude) along with gray values in the voxel value. High opacities are then assigned to voxels with large surface indicator values.

28.7 Problems, limitations and advantages of volume rendering

Problems that may occur during visualization are discussed herein. The limitations of this rendering approach are also presented.

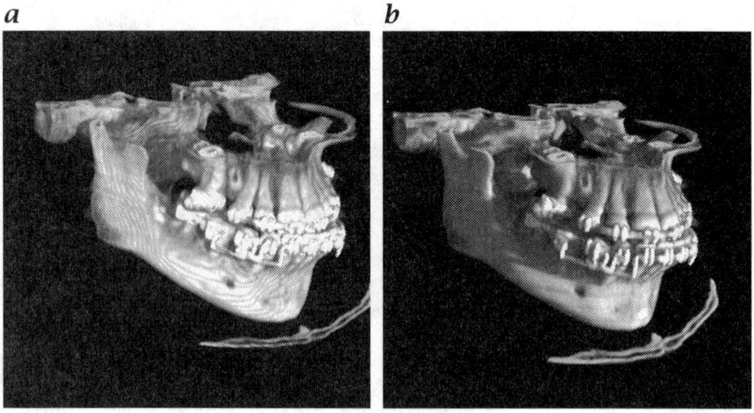

Figure 28.16: ***a*** *Rendering of the human jaw CT scan with too little sampling distance; the render result shows typical artifacts.* ***b*** *The same image rendered with correct sampling distance.*

28.7.1 Aliasing

One of the most striking problems for visualization is aliasing. The source of this problem comes from the resampling step, that is, phase 1 of volume rendering. The resampling determines the accuracy of the numerical integration of the rendering equations. It is recommended to use a resampling distance between successive sampling points of a ray that is smaller than the grid distance between successive voxels. Let us use the term "factor" as the ratio of grid distance to resampling distance. While a factor 1 gives mostly good results, an oversampling by a factor of 2 is often the best trade off between image quality and rendering speed. The latter is inversely proportional to this oversampling factor. Good solutions can also be achieved by using a higher order integration formula for the rendering equation Eq. (28.12) or Eq. (28.16). An elegant solution to this problem without changing the rendering algorithms has been found by de Boer [30].

28.7.2 Classification

Another problem is connected with the classification before interpolation. If, for example, an abrupt change of the opacity as a function of the gray value is chosen, the rendered object appears to have been built up by bricks. It is clear that resampling cannot change this situation very much, because the opacity function presented in the *VGL* rendering kernel represents indeed "bricks." The usage of an arbitrary function as voxel value to opacity mapping will lead to an opacity function $o(x)$, which may no longer comply with Shannon's theorem. A

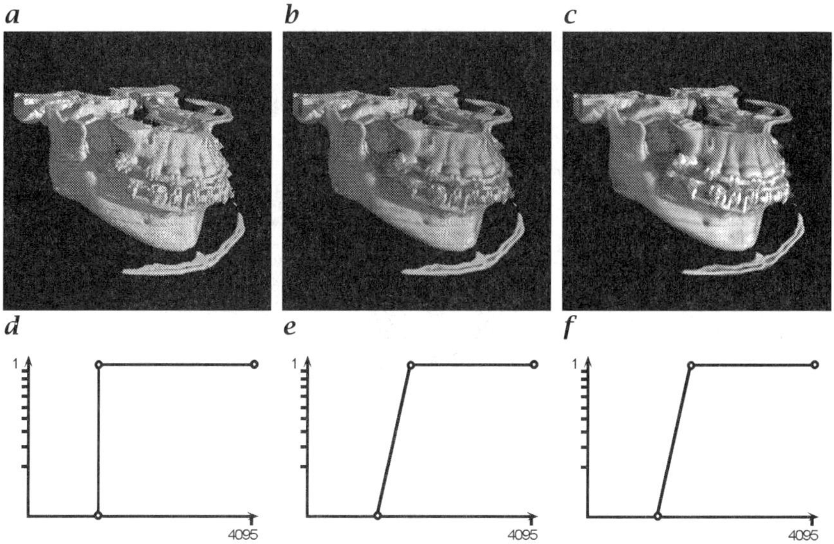

Figure 28.17: Effect of different gray value to opacity mappings: ***a, d*** *threshold LUT;* ***b, e*** *LUT with small transition area;* ***c, f*** *LUT with wide transition area. The lower row shows the selected LUT settings while the upper row shows the rendering results. See text for details.*

suggested remedy uses a gradual change of the opacity with the gray values so as to avoid the introduction of unwanted frequencies in the spectrum of the opacity function $\alpha(\boldsymbol{p})$. In this way the rendering kernel can access data that satisfy Shannon's theorem and give a much better impression of the true shape of an object.

28.7.3 Shadows

Shadows can play an important role during visualization. One example has already been shown (see Section 28.4.2). On the other hand, shadowing is a time-consuming operation that—if omitted—can speed up rendering considerably. The main reason is not that there are fewer computations needed but that several algorithmic optimization methods are more efficient and others can only be used without shadowing. The rendering time savings by omitting shadows in the actual version of *VGL* can be up to a factor of two.

28.7.4 Irregular grids

Currently, only rectilinear grids are supported because they allow efficient implementations. Most data sets can be converted into a rectilinear grid. In some cases, for example, for finite element simulations

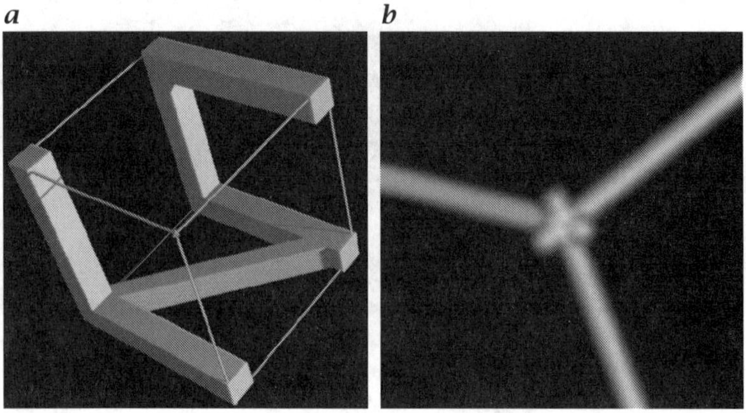

Figure 28.18: ***a*** *Rendering of an artificial data set. The lines of the "bounding box" are only one voxel wide.* ***b*** *Zoomed image of the one-voxel lines. The image resolution achieved by volume rendering is as good as the resolution of the volume data itself.*

where the grid sizes vary by several orders of magnitude a specialized volume rendering algorithm is required. This will be supported by VGL in a later phase.

28.7.5 Noise

Noise is a basic problem for all rendering techniques. Due to its construction volume rendering is not very sensible to it if it is possible to display the noise as semitransparent objects. If not, it is clear that there is a problem: if one cannot at least gradually separate an object from its noise, one cannot visualize it.

28.7.6 Resolution

The resolution that can be achieved by volume rendering is as good as the extent of the smallest information container, the voxel. In order to make the full resolution visible it is recommended to expand the data set by a factor of 2 and render it again. The result is that by this expansion one can use an expensive resampling method whereas interactive volume rendering requires the most simple reconstruction filters like trilinear interpolation to achieve this high speed.

28.7.7 Volume data sources

The modalities of data sets are according to our experience not very critical. We have tested the software tool with MR; and CT images, ultrasound and confocal microscope images have also been used, and even neuron tomographic data sets led to crisp images if the data has been prepared accordingly (i. e., the noise must be partially separable from the information).

28.8 Acknowledgments

Images were kindly provided by Volume Graphics GmbH, Heidelberg, Germany.

28.9 References

[1] Challinger, J., (1993). Scalable parallel volume rendering for nonrectilinear computational grids. In *Visualization'93*, S. Cunningham, ed., Parallel Rendering Symposium, pp. 81–110, IEEE Comp. Soc. San Jose, CA: ACM.

[2] Westermann, R. and Ertl, T., (1997). The VSBUFFER: Visibility ordering of unstructured volume primitives by polygon drawing. In *Proc. IEEE Visualization*, R. Yagel and H. Hagen, eds., pp. 35–42, IEEE. Los Alamitos, CA: IEEE Computer Society.

[3] Wilhelms, J., Gelder, A. V., Tarantino, P., and Gibbs, J., (1996). Hierarchical and parallelizable direct volume rendering for irregular and multiple grids. In *Visualization'96*, R. Yagel and G. Nielson, eds., pp. 57–64, IEEE Comp. Soc. San Francisco, CA: ACM.

[4] Kajiya, J., (1986). The rendering equation. In *Computer Graphics, Proc. of SIGGRAPH'94*, pp. 143–150. New York: ACM Press.

[5] Krüger, W., (1990). Volume rendering and data feature enhancement. *Computer Graphics*, **24**(5):21–26.

[6] Cercignani, C., (1988). *The Boltzmann Equation and Its Applications.* Berlin: Springer.

[7] Duderstadt, J. and Martin, W., (1979). *Transport Theory.* New York: J. Wiley & Son.

[8] Lacroute, P., (1995). *Fast Volume Rendering Using a Shear-Warp Factorization of the Viewing Transform.* PhD thesis, Stanford University, Computer Systems Laboratory, Departments of Electrical Engineering and Computer Science, Stanford, CA 94305–4055.

[9] Barth, R., Beier, E., and Pahnke, B., (1996). *Graphikprogrammierung mit OpenGL.* Bonn: Addision Wesley.

[10] Rogelberg, D. and Fullagar, J. (eds.), (1993). *OpenGL reference manual: the official reference document for OpenGL, release 1/OpenGL Architecture Review Board.* Reading, MA: Addison Wesley.

[11] Akeley, K., (1993). Realityngine graphics. In *Computer Graphics, Proc. of SIGGRAPH'93*, pp. 109–116. New York: ACM Press.

[12] Voorhies, D., (1993). Damn the torpedos. *Byte*, pp. 224–228.

[13] Essex, D., (1997). 3-D price breakthrough. *Byte*, p. 42.

[14] Hummel, R., (1996). Affordable 3-D workstations. *Byte*, pp. 145–148.

[15] Hummel, R., (1997). 3-D mighty mite. *Byte*, p. 47.

[16] Lorensen, W. and Cline, H., (1987). Marching-cubes: A high resolution 3D surface construction algorithm. In *Computer Graphics, Proc. of SIGGRAPH'87*, pp. 163–169. New York: ACM Press.

[17] Schroeder, W., (1997). A topology modifying progressive decimation algorithm. In *Visualization'97*, R. Yagel and H. Hagen, eds., pp. 205–212, IEEE Comp. Soc. Phoenix, AZ: ACM.

[18] Schroeder, W., Martin, K., and Lorensen, B., (1996). *The Visualization Toolkit: An Object Oriented Approach To 3D Graphics*, 2nd edition. Englewood Cliffs, NJ: Prentice Hall.

[19] Kajiya, J. and Von Herzen, B., (1984). Ray tracing volume densities. In *Computer Graphics, Proc. of SIGGRAPH'84*, pp. 164–174. New York: ACM Press.

[20] Grant, C., (1992). *Visibility Algorithms in Image Synthesis.* PhD thesis, University of California, Davis.

[21] Meinzer, H.-P., Meetz, K., Scheppelmann, D., and Engelmann, U., (1991). The Heidelberg ray tracing model. *IEEE Computer Graphics & Applications*, p. 34.

[22] Laur, D., Hanrahan, P., Grant, E., and Spach, S., (1986). Image rendering by adaptive refinement. *IEEE Computer Graphics & Applications*, **20**(4): 29–37.

[23] Levoy, M., (1990). Volume rendering by adaptive refinement. *The Visual Computer*, **6**(1):2–7.

[24] Levoy, M. and Whitaker, E., (1990). Gaze-directed volume rendering. *Computer Graphics & Applications*, **24**(2):217–223.

[25] Yagel, R., (1994). Volume viewing: State of the art survey. In *Volume Visualization Algorithms and Applications*, A. E. Kaufmann, W. Lorensen, and R. Yagel, eds., pp. 74–94.

[26] Brady, M., Jung, K., Nguyen, H., and Nguyen, T., (1997). Two-phase perspective ray casting for interactive volume navigation. In *Visualization'97*, R. Yagel and H. Hagen, eds., IEEE Comp. Soc. Phoenix, AZ: ACM.

[27] Freund, J. and Sloan, K., (1997). Accelerated volume rendering using homogenous region Encoding. In *Visualization'97*, R. Yagel and H. Hagen, eds., pp. 191–196, IEEE Comp. Soc. Phoenix, AZ: ACM.

[28] Günther, T., Poliwoda, C., Reinhart, C., Hesser, J., Männer, R., Meinzer, H.-P., and Baur, H.-J., (1994). VIRIM: A massively parallel processor for real-time volume visualization in medicine. In *Proceedings of the 9th Eurographics Hardware Workshop*, pp. 103–108. Oslo, Norway.

[29] Kühne, G., Poliwoda, C., Hesser, J., and Männer, R., (1997). Interactive segmentation and visualization of volume data sets. In *Visualization'97*, R. Yagel and H. Hagen, eds., Late Breaking Hot Topics, pp. 9–12, IEEE Comp. Soc. Phoenix, AZ: ACM.

[30] de Boer, M., Gröpl, A., Hessser, J., and Männer, R., (1997). Reducing artifacts in volume rendering by higher order integration. In *Visualization'97*, R. Yagel and H. Hagen, eds., Late Breaking Hot Topics, pp. 1–4, IEEE Comp. Soc. Phoenix, AZ: ACM.

29 Databases for Microscopes and Microscopical Images

Nicholas J. Salmon, Steffen Lindek, and Ernst H. K. Stelzer

Light Microscopy Group
European Molecular Biology Laboratory (EMBL), Heidelberg, Germany

Handbook of Computer Vision and Applications
Volume 2
Signal Processing and Pattern Recognition

Copyright © 1999 by Academic Press
All rights of reproduction in any form reserved.
ISBN 0-12-379772-1/$30.00

29.1 Introduction

Modern *microscope* technology as described in Inoue and Spring [1], Shotton [2], enables researchers, technicians and quality assurance personnel to collect large numbers of high-quality images. However, despite the relatively recent addition of digital storage and networking, machines are still generally used in a stand-alone manner insofar as the output is quite simply a huge number of images, with little attempt at proper cataloging, and little beyond the filename to identify the contents of each image.

For years, most light microscopes have restricted data output to storing only pixel data and a small number of associated parameters in standard *image formats*, for example, pixel spacing values. A good example is the TIFF format specification [3], that lists all data tags that can be stored in a TIFF file. Traditionally, developers have not offered the possibility of storing extra information because they could see only limited opportunities for its later use.

Although standard *database* technology has been available for many years, as described in Date [4], England and Stanley [5], Ullman and Widom [6], it was only recently that commercial *relational database* management systems (RDBMS) have really ventured down from large-scale mainframe and workstation systems to inexpensive systems on the desktop. The improvement in quality of such desktop systems, and the more accessible range of interfaces to integrated development environments, now offer the developer of smaller turnover products (such as microscopes) the chance to store data in personalized databases. Moreover, these changes have increased the number of data processing programs that are able to access such database stores—for example, image processing programs such as AVS Express [7].

Commercially available *Laboratory Information Management Systems* (LIMS) [8] demonstrate that relatively slow data acquisition can be combined with data storage and analysis, typically using an RDBMS to store information. Increased usage of LIMS demonstrates how the continual improvement of data collection and processing operations is vital for running many types of laboratories. And as legal demands increase, LIMS becomes mandatory for demonstrating conformance to stringent quality requirements, for example, ISO9000. Potential benefits for LIMS users include better access to information, improved quality of results, better control of costs, and increased processing speed.

In the field of microscopy, information about the operational state of the instrument can be stored automatically. Further information concerning the specimen and experiment being performed can be gathered from the user in a nonintrusive manner by fully integrating the data collection process into the microscope control program. Such a system offers many benefits to any user, as well as scientific collaborators, reviewers, and researchers in associated fields. For example, fast and simple (automatic) instrument configuration, configuration of different instruments to the same state, improved analysis and presentation of results, semiautomatic submissions to other databases, better quality of submissions to other databases, remote monitoring and maintenance, and perhaps, experimental repetition.

In this paper we describe more fully the potential benefits of integrating an RDBMS into a *confocal microscope system* [9] and thus of storing increased amounts of information. We outline the basic design and features of such a system, and finally, consider the future of such techniques.

29.2 Towards a better system for information management

29.2.1 Benefits

Development of an integrated microscope and database system can provide the following benefits to users, scientific collaborators, reviewers, and researchers in associated fields:

Fast, simple, automatic machine configuration. This can be achieved by associating a complete set of configuration parameters with each scan window. Machine adjustment and optimization can then be made by repeatedly changing instrument parameters, rescanning the same sample area into a new scan window, and observing the effect of these changes on the resultant image. The best image can then be quickly selected and the associated parameters "reused" to configure the machine. This is like an advanced "undo" function insofar as users can always return to a preferred machine state. Moreover, functions to reuse subsets of parameters can also be created. Thus, preselected areas can be quickly scanned with the same illumination and detector sensitivity parameters, or the same area can be scanned with different detector sensitivity parameters.

Configuration of different machines to the same state. This is basically an extension of the first point and possible if the microscope configuration interface uses physical parameters, that is, stored image data and associated parameters are in physical units. In particular, stored data must be "real" values, not "data-sheet" values. The microscope magnification should be calibrated and not rely merely on the magnification value stamped on the side of an objective lens. With parameters properly handled as physical values, users are no longer tied to finishing an experiment within a single session, or even using a particular machine, and collaborating scientists can better compare images acquired with identical parameters.

Improved analysis of results. Many properties of a light microscope are not described by a straight-line relationship. Indeed, many variable properties are often assumed to be constant. For example, resolution is not constant over the entire field of view. Thus, storing more information about the machine allows better calibration, using more sophisticated models of machine behavior. Even if a particular variable is not modeled within the database, storing more information about the factors affecting it may enable subsequent development of algorithms to cater to this variance.

For example, image signal intensity is reduced the deeper the focus is in the sample. This is a result of aberrations induced by mismatches in *refractive index* [10]. Image processing programs such as AVS [7] can improve image data using information about the immersion medium, microscope optical system, and position of data samples relative to optical boundaries (such as the sample coverslip). Corrected image data has a more uniform contrast, making images easier to view, and also giving immense improvements in the results of 3-D rendering techniques such as ray tracing.

Improved access to data. Better access to data via *querying* is quickly possible when more information is stored in a modern RDBMS. Such programs are not only optimized to perform fast queries on the data they contain, but typically also offer an array of tools and interfaces which serve both novice and expert programmer in the task of data processing. The RDBMS also offer presentation interfaces to many commonly used office programs, as well as dynamically generated HTML files. Users can perform sort, select, retrieve, and compare operations on image archives, querying not only the filenames, but also the entire spectrum of information associated with the image. Searches can even be performed over a number of database files.

Semiautomatic submissions to other databases. The possibilities of exporting data to other databases are also improved when more data are stored in a RDBMS. In the past, users were satisfied when they could import data into image processing programs. However, storing increased amounts of information with the source microscope images means that more useful, semiautomatic submissions can be made to data warehouses. For example, for biological applications it is highly valuable to export data to a database that also stores biology-related information, such as the *BioImage database* [11], which will contain images from a variety of microscopes, using a large spectrum of microscopical techniques. This allows the comparison of similar samples observed with different techniques that provide different resolution and visualize different types of interaction. This aids the dissemination of data within the research community. In the medical field, the *DICOM* standard, described by Bennett [12], is becoming more widely used for the storage and transfer of data, with a resulting demand for machines able to save using this format.

Remote monitoring and maintenance. If the actual state of the instrument is stored and made available over a computer network, then this information can be examined on-line by a system administrator. Users can thus benefit from fast fault diagnosis and rectification as well as from advice on how to better configure the microscope. An RDBMS is a convenient storage system because it is inherently *multiuser*.

Automatic experimental repetition. For experimental scientific results to be useful, they must be unquestionably repeatable. The greater the amount of information recorded about both machine and sample, the more precisely an experiment can be repeated. By storing data in a database and constructing systems that process this information to automatically repeat large amounts of experimental procedure, the potential for errors is reduced. Scientists can thus independently verify experimental results more easily and quickly, the point from which new progress can be made.

29.3 From flat files to database systems

In early confocal microscope systems, information about the machine configuration was contained within a single text file that could be read and written at any time during program execution. Such a "flat file" format avoided the need for recompilation of the entire microscope program but rapidly became unsuitable for human viewing as content expanded.

Image intensity data was saved to hard disk as a stream of bytes, and information about a particular image was mostly limited to saving pixel spacing information in an adjacent text file. Thus, reading such data into image processing programs required a certain amount of programming effort or manual intervention.

On-line configuration of a number of system parameters was possible, often by calling up a "setup" file, containing a subset of information required to obtain an image. However, the information was intended as an aid simply to obtain an image, rather than to adjust every one of the large number of machine variables perfectly. Indeed, storage of some component settings was impossible because these were mechanical. Moreover, if a hardware component were replaced, then apparently identical machine settings would result in different image data, the reason for which would be untraceable, for example, filter selection by reference to filter wheel positions, rather than to actual filters.

Standard file systems permitted restricted search facilities. That is, laboriously constructed string searches on filenames and parameters contained within the associated text files. Results were returned in a similar user-unfriendly manner.

More recently, it has become standard practice to store image data in more sophisticated, generic file formats that may also hold a number of parameters. A good example is the *LSM410 confocal microscope* (Carl Zeiss Jena GmbH), which stores files in an expanded TIFF format [3]. Real world pixel sizes are stored along with the image data. This offers the advantage of being automatically readable by a large number of image-processing programs, with the additional possibility of performing simple measurement operations, provided that the program can also decode the extra size tags.

Most recently, microscopes with integrated RDBMS have been developed. Examples are the commercially available *LSM510* (Carl Zeiss Jena GmbH) and the instrument used for research at the European Molecular Biology Laboratory (EMBL), the *Compact Confocal Camera* (CCC). These machines use RDBMS to describe their hardware configurations to an unprecedented level of accuracy. Parts can be changed without affecting performance and the machine is automatically configured. Image data and associated parameters are also managed via databases. Each image is associated with its own set of parameters, thereby perfectly defining the state of the machine at the instant the image was recorded. As a vast amount of data can be referenced for quantification of image data, the RDBMS opens up enormous possibilities for data processing.

29.4 Database structure and content

A well-defined *database structure* enables not only faster runtime performance, but also simplifies programming and program structure, speeding up development time of the overall machine control program.

The database must contain sufficient information to enable the microscope control program to achieve automatic machine configuration. This information can be contained by groups of tables termed "component specifications," "part descriptions," and "image acquisition parameters." Additional information, describing the specimen, is required to meet the most fundamental goal of experimental repetition. The following sections describe these groups in more detail[1].

[1]A full example database is available on the CD accompanying this book.

Microsoft Access - [Potential Objective Lenses : Table]

File Edit View Insert Tools Window Help

Field Name	Data Type	Description
ID Potential	Text	Unique, unambiguous name used to select lenses of this type. e.g. Carl Zeiss Apochromat 1.4/63
Magnification	Number	[#] - Nominal magnification as specified by manufacturer. Actual value may differ slightly.
Numerical Aperture Maximum	Number	[#] - Nominal numerical aperture as specified by manufacturer. Actual value may differ slightly.
Numerical Aperture Minimum	Number	[#] - Only required if NA can be varied.
Colour Code	Text	Colour code on the collar.
Immersion Medium	Text	Name of the medium for which the lens was designed. e.g. Oil, Air, Water
Immersion Medium Refractive	Number	[#] - Absolute refractive index for which the lens has been designed.
Free Working Distance	Number	[mm] - Distance from tip of lens to focus minus the coverglass thickness.
Length	Number	[mm] - Distance from tip of lens to top of revolver.
Diameter	Number	[mm] - Distance accross tip of lens.
Travel	Number	[mm] - Maximum distance to which lens tip can be depressed against restraining spring.
Coverglass Thickness Maximu	Number	[mm] - Coverglass thickness with which lens was designed to operate.
Coverglass Thickness Minimur	Number	[mm] - Only required if collar for adjustment is available.
Coverglass Refractive Index	Number	[#] - Absolute coverglass refractive index for which lens was designed to operate.
Pupil Position	Number	[mm] - Distance from top of revolver at which the pupil (entrance aperture, back focal plane...) sits.
Pupil Diameter	Number	[mm] - Diameter of the pupil (entrance aperture, back focal plane...).
Absorption	Yes/No	Is the lens suitable for use in absorption mode ?
Transmission	Yes/No	Is the lens suitable for use in transmission mode ?
Reflection	Yes/No	Is the lens suitable for use in reflection mode ?
Fluorescence	Yes/No	Is the lens suitable for use in fluorescence mode ?
Deep UV	Yes/No	Is the lens suitable for use with wavelengths below 280 nm ?
UV	Yes/No	Is the lens suitable for use with wavelengths below 400 nm ?
Visible	Yes/No	Is the lens suitable for use with wavelengths between 400 and 750 nm ?
NIR	Yes/No	Is the lens suitable for use with wavelengths above 750-3000 nm ?
MIR	Yes/No	Is the lens suitable for use with wavelengths above 3000 nm ?
Phase Contrast	Yes/No	Is the lens suitable for use in Phase Contrast ?
Nomarski DIC	Yes/No	Is the lens suitable for use in Contrast Nomarski Differential Interference Contrast (DIC) ?
Dark Field	Yes/No	Is the lens suitable for use in Dark Field Contrast ?
Hoffmann	Yes/No	Is the lens suitable for use in Hoffmann Contrast ?
Varel	Yes/No	Is the lens suitable for use in Vrenei Contrast ?
Calibration Interval	Number	[days] - Proposed interval between calibrations.
Diagram	OLE Object	See CCC\Database\res\ObjectiveLens.Doc
Summary	Text	Short description of important features.
Description	OLE Object	Document presenting more detailed description.

Figure 29.1: *Database table design showing entries for the specification of a particular type of objective lens. This is a typical spread of entries for any of the "potential" components within the system. Field names with data type "Number" are of type long integer or double. Data type "OLE Object" represents a link to another file or program object. For example, the entry "Diagram" may be a bitmap image. In other "potential" objects, OLE Object entries could be links to spreadsheet files, containing calibration data, for example, filter absorption against wavelength. Many entries are described as nominal, indicating that an entry in another calibration table is required to hold the actual value for a specific component. In contrast, parameters such as "Length" and "Diameter" are not expected to vary significantly between individual components.*

29.4.1 Component specifications

Component specifications are essentially datasheet-like descriptions of items that could *potentially* be used within a complete system. The information is general and, therefore, valid for any machine, so that a single database of such tables could serve a number of machines. The collection of tables describing all possible components is like a library used for machine construction. In our examples, such tables have names with the prefix "Potential." Typically, entries give information on how to control a part, how to incorporate it into the system, and give an indication of the expected performance.

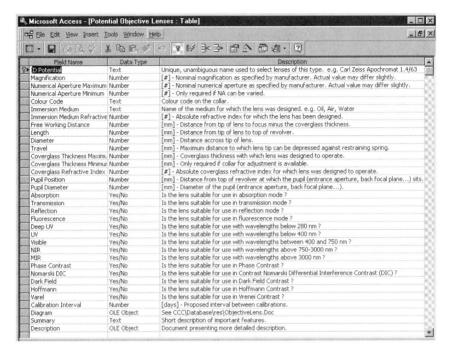

Figure 29.1 shows the structure of the table "Potential Objective Lenses." Many of the entries are described as "nominal." That is, the actual performance may not match the expected performance as specified by the manufacturer. Information about length, diameter, and travel is provided for controlling a revolver containing a number of objective lenses. When automatically changing objective lenses, the current lens must be moved slightly away from the sample. Then, the revolver must be turned so that the new lens is moved to the correct position. Finally, the new lens must be moved so that its focus position is at the same point within the sample as was that of the old objective lens.

Note that only a subset of entries is necessary for the machine to function. However, by offering as many discrete database fields as possible we are helping database users to create a more precise description of the microscope and its components, thereby increasing the possibilities for later searching the database and reducing errors. The alternative to this, offering a general field called "description," allows inconsistent, incomplete entries, thus reducing the efficiency of subsequent queries and data processing (see Chapter 25).

29.4.2 Part descriptions

Each particular machine contains many components. Each component requires a unique entry through which it can be referenced and controlled. In our examples, such tables are prefixed "Available." Because many parts require calibration, separate "Calibration" tables have also been included. A database of "Available" and "Calibration" tables is required for each microscope.

Figure 29.2 shows the tables and relationships required for control of a revolver containing objective lenses. The group of three objective lens tables shows the general relationships used between "Available," "Potential," and "Calibration" tables. Thus, "Calibration Objective Lenses" contains a full record over time of repeated calibrations of the part. "Available Objective Lenses" contains measured values (numerical aperture, magnification etc.) for the part, and also a reference to the part through which it is controlled—a revolver. Likewise, the "Revolver" tables are controlled via a computer interface described in the "Interface" tables. Describing parts in this way ensures that the system delivers constant performance, even if parts are exchanged. This hierarchy of tables essentially describes how real world values are set via the various machine control-interfaces.

29.4.3 Image acquisition parameters

Every time a sample is scanned and data is collected, "Available" parts are set to values that may be different to those used for other scans. To

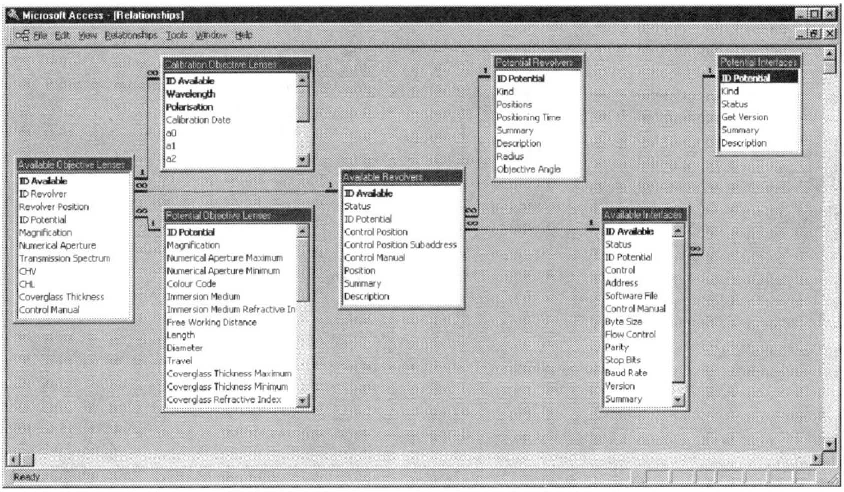

***Figure 29.2:** Tables and relationships required for selection of an objective lens during microscope runtime. If an image is to be acquired with an objective lens of magnification 100, the microscope control program receives a request for this magnification. A search is performed over the "Available Objective Lenses" for "Magnification" 100. If an objective lens matching this criteria is found, the entries "Available Objective Lenses: ID Revolver" and "Available Objective Lenses: Revolver Position" are used to access "Available Revolvers" table to find the particular revolver containing the required objective lens. This in turn is used to check which "Available Interface" must be addressed, and how to move the revolver to the required position.*

record these temporally changing values, another hierarchy of tables is required (Fig. 29.3). These tables can exist in a database file separate from the Part Description and Component Specification tables, as they do not relate to a particular machine. Most conveniently, all information associated with the image data can be stored in a database owned by an individual user. At the topmost level, each set of image and parameter data has been termed a "Recording." A recording may consist of a number of "Tracks," where a track is defined as a path from light source to detector. Thus, at the lowest level, each track refers to tables containing settings for individual system components in that path. All the values are "real world" (laser power in Watts, and not the voltage that must be applied to the laser input to achieve this power).

Any recording can be reloaded into the machine and its parameters reused for automatic reconfiguration. Moreover, because a recording contains absolute values, this information can be used to configure another machine equipped with similar parts.

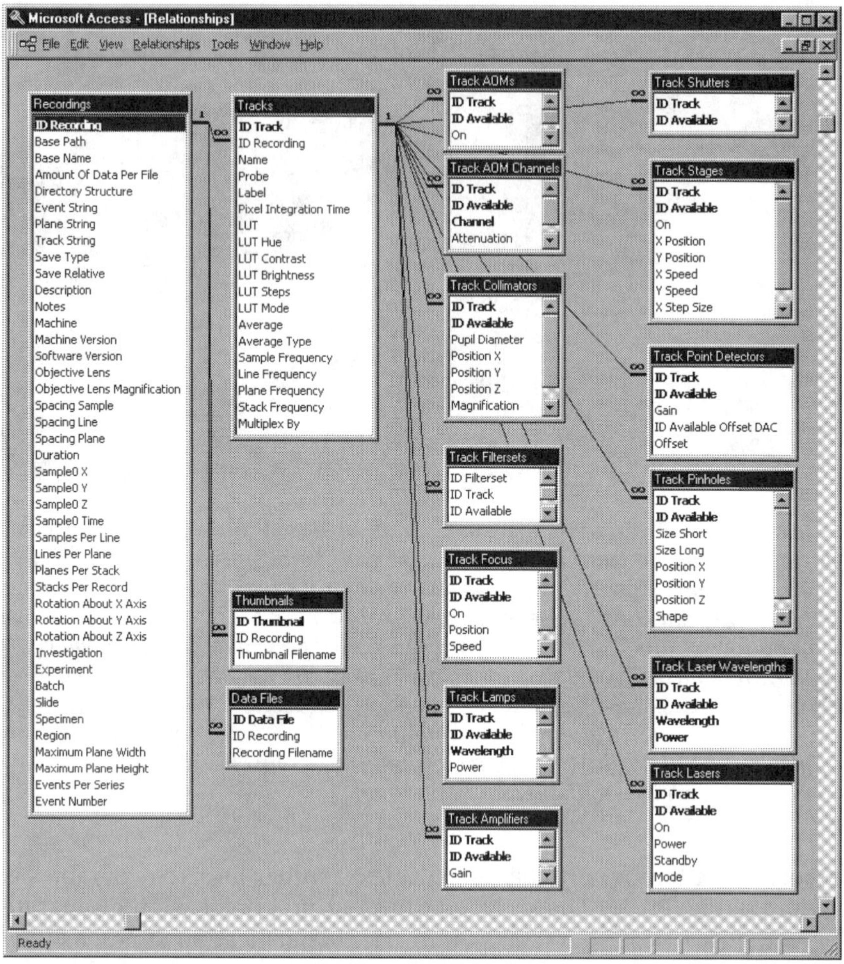

Figure 29.3: *Tables and relationships required for "User database" of image parameter data.*

29.4.4 Workflow and specimen parameters

Any specimen being examined under the microscope has been subject to processing steps prior to observation. If a specimen is observed a number of times, it may also be subject to processing steps between observations, for example, the addition of chemicals. Also, different features or areas of interest might be imaged. Finally, information obtained by the microscope may be subject to post-processing. As the microscope system we are describing is not yet integrated into a complete LIMS, it is sufficient to store a reference to other logbook or database records describing sample preparation. Similarly, postprocessing can refer back to a number of recordings in our microscope database. To reference the sample, a number of text fields are included in the "Recordings" table. Description of the experimental procedure is achieved with the text field "Experimental Step."

29.5 Database system requirements

Whilst an RDBMS market overview is unnecessary and beyond the scope of this report, there are nevertheless a number of points important in the selection of a database program, and the subsequent implementation of programs which access it. For further information concerning selection of a database technology, see Stonebraker [13]. From the following set of requirements it was clear that in the case of the CCC a "desktop" system best covered these needs, and, thus, *Microsoft Access* was selected.

29.5.1 "Fast" standard programming interface

In a *confocal microscope* system, images are generally saved either singly, as one might occasionally save documents from within a word processing application, or automatically as part of a timed sequence of scans. In biological applications using fluorescent probes to mark areas of interest in biological specimens, scan speed is limited. Saving of image sequences must, therefore, be performed as quickly as possible to allow maximum time for data acquisition. Intervals between saving image and parameter data are typically greater than 0.1 s. (This is not the same as video, where only image data is saved quickly, and not parameter data.) A standard interface solution of using embedded *SQL* code within a compiled C++ program, coupled with current computer and software performance[2] can perform a save operation at least one order of magnitude faster than this.

29.5.2 High-level programming environment

Once data has been stored in a database, there are many desirable functions that do not have to be executed if time is critical. For example, searching through an array of thumbnail images to retrieve a particular

---

[2]Saving recording and track information to a test database took 35 ms per image (Computer running Windows NT 4.0, using a 200-MHz Pentium, 128 MB RAM, Matrox MGA Millenium graphics card with 4MB RAM). This was achieved by opening the database, performing all queries and opening all the required tables *at the start* of the time series, so that for each image only "AddNew" and "Update" database operations were required. At the end of the time series, all recordsets were closed. Typical scan times on a confocal fluorescent microscope for a 0.25 MB image are between 0.25 s and 10 s, and the time to save the actual image data to hard disk is less than 20 ms. Thus, the time consumed by the database functionality is acceptably small.

image. Fast implementation of such features is possible using visual query builders (thus removing the need for detailed knowledge of SQL), and high-level programming languages, which allow novice programmers to customize their applications.

29.5.3 Relatively small database content and number of tables

The complete description of a confocal microscope contains about ninety tables, a small number for any RDBMS. Component specifications and part descriptions do not grow or shrink during the lifetime of the microscope, and take up only a few megabytes of space on disk. Again, this is a relatively small amount of data for most database programs. The "User's database" only increases in size by a few kilobytes every time a "Save" operation is performed. So, even with thousands of save operations the amount of data stored in the recordings tables will remain relatively small.

29.5.4 Small number of users

Database files containing Component specifications and Part descriptions will only ever be operated on simultaneously by a single user and a single administrator. User database files are intended to be "single user," although the database is often accessed by a small number of concurrently running processes.

29.5.5 Minimal licensing and installation effort, maximum transportability

Users should be able to backup their archives to transportable media, then view these archives on any computer they choose. Thus, the database program should be separate from the archive files, easy to install and, preferably, available on a number of different computing platforms.

29.6 Data flow—how it looks in practice

Having implemented a table and database structure, a microscope control program must be developed which fully uses this fundamental to achieve our goals of experimental repetition, automatic configuration and so on. Typically, this might be modeled and explained as a number of data flow diagrams. However, for simplicity the following section gives an overview of the tasks to be performed, indicating when, from where, and by whom data is entered into the database. Figure 29.4 is a screenshot of the CCC *microscope user interface*, showing the main information presented to a user working with the machine.

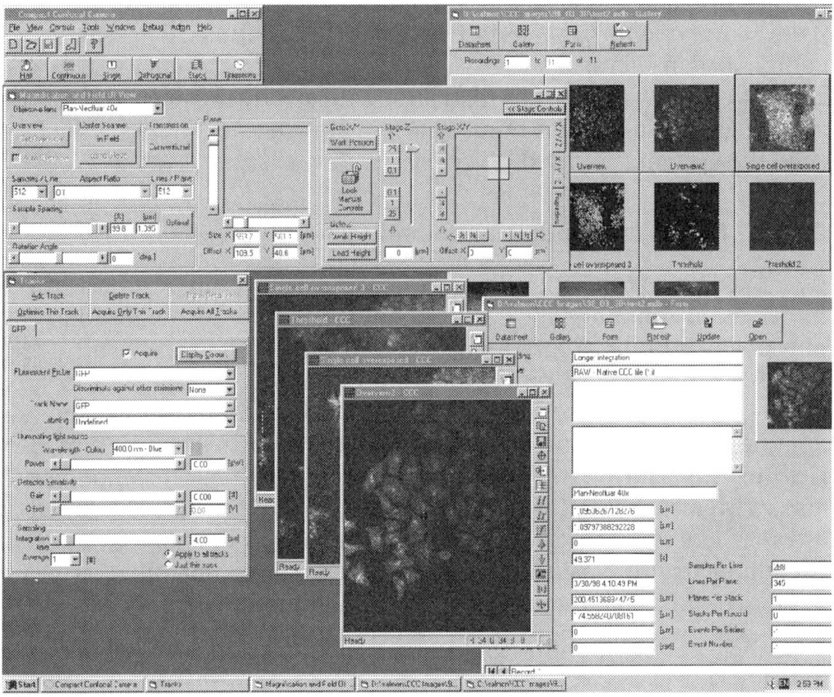

Figure 29.4: *Screenshot of the Compact Confocal Camera (CCC) user interface, showing the main forms required for operation of the machine. The CCC is an example of a microscope that stores machine configuration and image information in an RDBMS. The form in the top left corner contains the main menus, by which all other forms are called up. The two forms on the right represent views onto a database of user images. The top right form shows a gallery of thumbnail images. The bottom right form shows a thumbnail image and associated parameters from a single image. Images and data can be reloaded directly from either of these forms. The cascade of 4 image windows in the middle of the screen show images either just scanned, or images reloaded from a user database. The menu bar on the right-hand side of each window contains the "reuse" buttons—marked "!!" and "!T". The "!!" button automatically overwrites all parameters in the main recording object with parameters from the window in which the "!!" button was pressed. The parameters in the main recording object (in effect, the current state of the machine) are displayed in the two forms on the left-hand side of the screen: "Magnification and Field of View", and "Tracks". The "!T" button automatically overwrites just the tracks information in the main recording object, with parameters from the window in which the "!T" button was pressed, leaving the top-level parameters such as scan window size, samples per line untouched.*

29.6.1 Preconfiguration

Before the microscope can be started, the system administrator completes component specifications and part descriptions. This can be accomplished in Microsoft Access via semiautomatically generated forms. Default calibration data is added automatically by the microscope control program if no data is found. Each component is calibrated the first time the system is started.

29.6.2 Hardware configuration and test

When the user starts the microscope control program, a subset of the information contained in "Potential," "Available," and "Calibration" tables is loaded into program objects. This gives fast access to control values. Complete hardware configuration and test takes a few seconds, during which time a progress bar is displayed. Thus, the bulk of queries are undertaken when time is not critical, that is, not during a timed series of scans. During this startup phase, the state of each component is also written back into the hardware database and the user is notified of errors where system performance is degraded or assistance is required. An administrator, sitting at a remote machine, can open the hardware database and check the status of any or all system components.

Finally, a central "Recording" object is created whose parameters are identical to the user's default startup recording (user preference data can also be stored in a database). This "Recording" object mirrors the "Recordings" tables, thus containing a collection of "Tracks," which in turn contains collections of "Track components."

29.6.3 Scanning and saving

When the user presses the "Scan" button, the central "Recording" object is used as the specification for the required scan. If required, a new window is created, then the microscope scan process is started and sample data displayed. Upon scan completion, the central recording object is copied into the recording object associated with the scan window.

To save the contents of a scan window, the user has merely to select the image database file into which it should be saved and specify a name. The associated recording object is written to the database, and image data is saved to disk in whatever standard format the user selects. If the data consists of a number of tracks or image planes, then these can even be automatically saved as separate gray-scale images or composite color images in a new directory. This vastly simplifies the process of analyzing data in third-party image processing packages.

29.6.4 On-line reuse of saved information

The image databases are fully integrated into the system: the user can browse any database as a gallery of thumbnail images, a tabular list of recording properties, and a single form showing all the parameters from a single recording. Query functions are of course readily available.

At any time, a recording can be selected from one of the database forms and can be opened by the microscope program. Upon opening, a new scan window is created containing a new recording object, which is filled with parameters from the relevant tables. The microscope can be automatically configured to produce an image identical to the one just loaded by copying the recording information from the loaded scan window into the central recording object and updating the user interface to show the new values. Thus, the next scan will use this information for configuring the hardware. Another nice feature is the ability to reuse a subset of the scan window's information, such as "Reuse Tracks."

29.6.5 Sample referencing and experimental procedure

At any time while working with the microscope control program, the user can enter sample details, or describe an experimental step being performed. An example form for entering such data is shown in Fig. 29.5. This information is automatically added to the "recording" information every time a save operation is stored.

29.7 Future prospects

29.7.1 BioImage: a database for multidimensional biological microscope images

The *BioImage database* project [11] [http://www.bioimage.org/], funded by the European Union (EU), is a collaborative project between six European research groups and two industrial partners[3]. Its aim is to develop a new database for scientific use, organizing complex information associated with multidimensional biological data sets. It will provide access to image data acquired by different techniques, such as

[3]The partnership comprises of (1) Centro Nacional de Biotecnología — CSIC, Madrid, Spain, and (2) European Molecular Biology Laboratory, Heidelberg, Germany, who host and run the database servers and who are, respectively, responsible for macromolecular and cellular image data; (3) Biozentrum, University of Basel, Switzerland, who provide electron and scanning probe microscopy expertise; (4) Centro de Investigación y Desarrollo - CSIC, Barcelona, Spain, who are responsible for crystallographic data and links with other databases; (5) Silicon Graphics, Cortaillod, Switzerland, as hardware provider and developer of visualization tools; (6) The European BioInformatics Institute, Cambridge, U.K., as database consultant; (7) Department of Zoology, University of Oxford, U.K., who provide video data expertise; and (8) Informix Software, U.K., as the database technology provider and consultant.

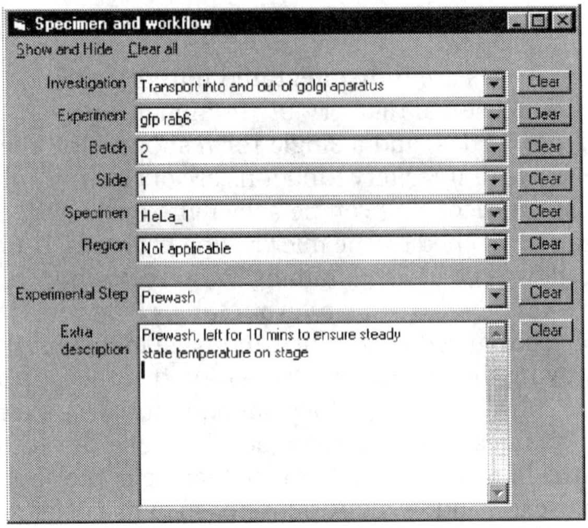

Figure 29.5: *Example form showing user entries for referencing specimen and experiment. In the database, experimental step is a text field. By using a combo-box, a selection of predefined experimental steps can be offered to the user to encourage consistent and useful entries in the database.*

light microscopy and atomic force microscopy, thus emphasizing different, complementary physical aspects of similar objects, and facilitating hitherto unprecedented levels of comparison and data access. To meet these objectives, specific volume image visualization and handling tools will have to be developed, enabling users to compare, overlay, correlate, and combine different images and the associated information. This will enhance the understanding of living processes at the cellular, molecular and, ultimately, atomic level.

The BioImage database will have a structure consisting of five parts.

1. Organizational information, such people, institutes, manufacturers etc.
2. Links to data sets and related meta-data, such as that stored in the "Recordings" tables of the CCC database.
3. Information about the biological specimen, such as sample taxonomy (general), and age (specific).
4. Sample preparation information, such as preparation steps and their physical, chemical and biological parameters, extending to post-processing steps.
5. Instrumentation information, such as microscopes, their components, and their settings during data acquisition as stored in the CCC database.

Technical details about individual microscopes and their components cannot be stored in such great detail as would be the case in an individual microscope such as the CCC because first, the emphasis of the BioImage database is on biological *content of the images* it contains. Second, images from a large spectrum of microscope techniques (electron, light and video, scanning probe microscopy etc.) are to be documented. Component parameters have to be restricted to those which are characteristic for a large set of instrument types and that are necessary for the accurate documentation of the image acquisition process and for subsequent evaluation of the data.

The BioImage database will store considerably more information than the microscopes about the specimen, preparation techniques, and the features visible in individual images. Biological specimens ranging from macromolecules to entire cells and organisms will be documented. Controlled vocabularies either provided by the BioImage database itself or through links to other biological databases like NCBI will allow consistent nomenclature and referencing. The sample preparation will be saved step by step with the possibility to either document the parameters explicitly or to provide links to other on-line databases with a description of the sample preparation (like the Materials-&-Methods part of a publication). For this, the BioImage database must provide links to other key databases such as the Protein Data Bank (PDB) and bibliographic ones.

The possibility of reusing previously saved instrument configuration and sample preparation information at submission time is important to reduce the amount of information required for a single submission. To further aid the submission process, programs that make automatic submissions from other databases will be developed. Therefore, a smart submission interface has to be built that allows checking for and selecting data already existing in the database.

29.7.2 Object relational database management systems (ORDBMS)

Stonebraker [13] describes a simple classification scheme for DBMS applications, defining which type of DBMS is most suitable for a particular project. This indicates that the microscope data acquisition and processing system described in this report would gain certain benefits from being based around an *object relational database.* (A most comprehensive description of features for such an ORDBMS is given by Atkinson et al. [14].) Our experience in developing microscope data acquisition systems has proved that a good database structure greatly simplifies the subsequent task of constructing the microscope control program. All the main program objects mirror the structure of the underlying database, and add functionality that operates on the data these objects contain. It therefore seems like an obvious step to more fully integrate functionality into the database, using a system that can cope with more complex, user-defined data. An ORDBMS typically offers more extensive querying possibilities, which makes it more suited to querying image and scientific data (as opposed to business data). A tighter binding of data to the database would mean that the main bulk of program data would always be within the database process, thus increasing system speed. Fast hardware control could still be accomplished with C++ modules called from within the database. This could also mean greater security in the event of a system crash, as information would already be in the database. Many ORDBMS are oriented towards image storage, fueled by requirements of many web developers.

29.7.3 Feature matching

Algorithms such as described by Faloutsos et al. [15] show how feature information can be extracted from images, which can then be added as entries to an existing database. Such feature information can then be queried. An example of such a "search by image content" is given in Pentland et al. [16].

The precise feature matching algorithm required is heavily dependent upon the type of images (and thus features) in which a user might be interested. A journalist searching a photographic archive for, say, images of fruit, will require different algorithms than a doctor searching for images of tumors in MRI scans.

29.7.4 Conclusions: application to other fields?

In this paper we have set out the benefits of integrating databases into an example image acquisition system (a confocal microscope) and the basic information required for achieving this integration. Similar benefits could clearly be gained by applying the same principles to other image acquisition systems, and, indeed, the coverage of the prototype confocal system at EMBL has already been extended to include a wider range of microscopical techniques. The main consideration before commencing upon such an implementation is the list of potential benefits. Systems with a large number of control parameters would clearly benefit, as many of the advantages for the confocal system involve gaining better on-line control of the machine. Such machines would probably also benefit from the greater amount of analysis that could be performed upon the data acquired. The next considerations concern the data itself. What data is required to enable useful machine control functions such as automatic configuration? What data needs to be stored to really increase the amount of useful off-line analysis, and how should this data be structured? Although data entries would almost certainly be very different for machines in other fields, most implementations could successfully use the top-level structure of the confocal microscope database. That is, groups of tables containing data sheet information, parts information, and time-dependent part information. Finally, feasibility issues need to be addressed. Can the required amounts of data be ordered, stored and accessed fast enough? Are there speed penalties as a result of data security requirements? What are the financial costs of implementing and distributing such a system?

Acknowledgments

The authors wish to thank Janet Salmon for her comments on the manuscript.

29.8 References

[1] Inoue, S. and Spring, K. R., (1997). *Video Microscopy: The Fundamentals,* 2nd edition. New York: Plenum Press.

[2] Shotton, D. (ed.), (1993). *Electronic Light Microscopy: The Principles and Practice of Video Enhanced Contrast, Digital Intensified Fluorescence, and Confocal Scanning Light Microscopy. An Introduction to the Electronic Acquisition of Light Microscope Images.* New York: Wiley-Liss Inc.

[3] Aldus, (1992). *TIFF revision 6.0, final.* Mountain View, CA: Aldus Corporation, Adobe Systems.

[4] Date, C., (1981). *An Introduction to Database Systems.* Reading, MA: Addison-Wesley.

[5] England, K. and Stanley, N., (1995). *The SQL Server Handbook—A Guide to Microsoft Database Computing.* Woburn, MA: Butterworth Heinemann.

[6] Ullman, J. and Widom, J., (1997). *A First Course in Database Systems.* Englewood Cliffs, NJ: Prentice-Hall Engineering.

[7] AVS, (1997). *Gaining Insight Through Data Vizualization. Technology White Paper.* Waltham, MA: Advanced Visual Systems Inc.

[8] Nakagaw, A., (1994). *LIMS: Implementation and Management.* Washington, DC: The Royal Chemistry Society.

[9] Stelzer, E., (1995). The intermediate optical system of laser scanning confocal microscopes. In *Handbook of Biological Confocal Microscopy, 2nd edition,* J. B. Pawley, ed. New York: Plenum Press.

[10] Hell, S., Reiner, G., Cremer, C., and Stelzer, E., (1993). Aberrations in confocal fluorescence microscopy induced by mismatches in refractive index. *Jour. Microscopy,* **169(Pt3)**:391–405.

[11] Shotton, D., (1995). Electronic light microscopy: present capabilities and future prospects. *Histochem. Cell. Biol.,* **104**:97–137.

[12] Bennett, M., (1993). *A Technical Guide To DICOM; Health Imaging.* Dallas, TX: Eastman Kodak Company.

[13] Stonebraker, M., (1986). Object management in a relational data base system. In *COMPCON Spring 86. Thirty-First IEEE Computer Society Inter-*

national Conference, San Francisco, CA, USA, 3-6 March 1986, A. Bell, ed., pp. 336–341. Washington, DC: IEEE Comput. Soc. Press.

[14] Atkinson, M., Bancilhon, F., DeWitt, D., Dittrich, K., Maier, D., and Zdonik, S., (1989). The object-oriented database system manifesto. In *Proceedings of the First International Conference on Deductive and Object-Oriented Databases, Kyoto, Japan, December 1989*, pp. 223–240.

[15] Faloutsos, C., Flickner, M., Niblack, W., Petkovic, F., Equitz, W., and Barber, R., (1993). Efficient and effective querying by image content; IBM Research Report RJ 9453.

[16] Pentland, A., Picard, R., and Sclaroff, S., (1994). Photobook: Tools for content-based manipulation of image databases. In *Storage and Retrieval of Image and Video Databases II, San Jose, CA. February 6-10, 1994*, pp. 2185–2205. San Jose, CA: SPIE.

Index

G

90868
9 780123 797728
ISBN 0-12-379772-1

DATE DUE